CONNECT FEATURES

Simple Assignment Management

Create and deliver homework, quizzes, and tests easily with selectable end-of-chapter problems and test bank questions. Algorithmic versions of select end-of-chapter problems are available to offer additional variety. Assignments can be scored automatically, giving students immediate feedback on their work and side-by-side comparisons with correct answers --all of which can be controlled. Access and review each response; manually grade essay questions or change grades and leave comments for students to review.

Graphing Tool

The graphing tool within Connect Economics provides opportunities for students to draw, interact with, manipulate, and analyze graphs in their online auto-graded assignments as they would with paper and pencil. The Connect graphs are identical in presentation to the graphs in the book, so students can easily relate their assignments to their reading material.

eBook

Connect Plus includes a media-rich eBook that allows you to share your notes with your students. Your students can insert and review their own notes, highlight the text, search for specific information, and interact with media resources. Using an eBook with Connect Plus gives your students a complete digital solution that allows them to access their materials from any computer.

Tegrity

Make your classes available anytime, anywhere. With simple, one-click recording, students can search for a word or phrase and be taken to the exact place in your lecture that they need to review.

EASY TO USE

Learning Management System Integration

McGraw-Hill Campus is a one-stop teaching and learning experience available to use with any learning management system. McGraw-Hill Campus provides single sign-on to faculty and students for all McGraw-Hill material and technology from within the school website. McGraw-Hill Campus also allows instructors instant access to all supplements and teaching materials for all McGraw-Hill products.

Blackboard users also benefit from McGraw-Hill's industry-leading integration, providing single sign-on to access all Connect assignments and automatic feeding of assignment results to the Blackboard grade book.

The **Best** of **Both Worlds**

POWERFUL REPORTING

Connect generates comprehensive reports and graphs that provide instructors with an instant view of the performance of individual students, a specific section, or multiple sections. Since all content is mapped to learning objectives, Connect reporting is ideal for accreditation or other administrative documentation.

Money, Banking, and Financial Markets

Fourth Edition

Stephen G. Cecchetti

Brandeis International Business School

Kermit L. Schoenholtz

New York University
Leonard N. Stern School of Business

Mc
Graw
Hill
Education

2 3 4 5 6 7 8 9 0 DOW/DOW 1 0 9 8 7 6 5 4

ISBN 978-0-07-802174-9
MHID 0-07-802174-X

Senior Vice President, Products & Markets: *Kurt L. Strand*
Vice President, Content Production & Technology Services: *Kimberly Meriwether David*
Managing Director: *Douglas Reiner*
Executive Brand Manager: *Michele Janicek*
Executive Director of Development: *Ann Torbert*
Managing Development Editor: *Christina Kouvelis*
Director of Digital Content: *Doug Ruby*
Digital Development Editor: *Kevin Shanahan*
Marketing Manager: *Katie Hoenicke*
Marketing Specialist: *Jennifer M. Jelinski*
Director, Content Production: *Terri Schiesl*
Content Project Manager: *Brian Nacik*
Media Project Manager: *Susan Lombardi*
Senior Buyer: *Debra R. Sylvester*
Design: *Srdjan Savanovic*
Senior Content Licensing Specialist: *Jeremy Cheshareck*
Photo Researcher: *Sarah Evertson*
Typeface: *10.5/12 Times LT Std*
Compositor: *MPS Limited*
Printer: *R. R. Donnelley*

FRED® is a registered trademark and the FRED® Logo and ST. LOUIS FED are trademarks of the Federal Reserve Bank of St. Louis. http://research.stlouisfed.org/fred2

All credits appearing on page or at the end of the book are considered to be an extension of the copyright page.

Library of Congress Cataloging-in-Publication Data

Cecchetti, Stephen G. (Stephen Giovanni)
  Money, banking, and financial markets / Stephen G. Cecchetti, Brandeis International Business School, Kermit L. Schoenholtz, New York University, Leonard N. Stern School of Business. -- 4th Edition.
    pages cm
  Includes indexes.
  ISBN 978-0-07-802174-9 (alk. paper) -- ISBN 0-07-802174-X (alk. paper)
  1. Money. 2. Banks and banking. 3. Finance. 4. Capital market. I. Schoenholtz, Kermit L. II. Title.
HG221.C386 2015
332--dc23
                                                                    2013037393

The Internet addresses listed in the text were accurate at the time of publication. The inclusion of a website does not indicate an endorsement by the authors or McGraw-Hill Education, and McGraw-Hill Education does not guarantee the accuracy of the information presented at these sites.

www.mhhe.com

Dedication

To my father, Giovanni Cecchetti, who argued tirelessly that financial markets are not efficient; and to my grandfather Albert Schwabacher, who patiently explained why inflation is destructive.

Stephen G. Cecchetti

To my parents, Evelyn and Harold Schoenholtz, and my wife, Elvira Pratsch, who continue to teach me what is true, good, and beautiful.

Kermit L. Schoenholtz

About the Authors

Stephen G. Cecchetti is Professor of International Economics at the Brandeis International Business School. He previously taught at Brandeis from 2003 to 2008. Before rejoining Brandeis in 2014, Cecchetti completed a five-year term as Economic Adviser and Head of the Monetary and Economic Department at the Bank for International Settlements in Basel, Switzerland. He has also taught at the New York University Leonard N. Stern School of Business and, for 15 years, was a member of the Department of Economics at The Ohio State University.

In addition to his other appointments, Cecchetti served as Executive Vice President and Director of Research, Federal Reserve Bank of New York (1997–1999); Editor, *Journal of Money, Credit, and Banking* (1992–2001); Research Associate, National Bureau of Economic Research (1989–2011); and Research Fellow, Centre for Economic Policy Research (2008–present), among others.

Cecchetti's research interests include inflation and price measurement, monetary policy, macroeconomic theory, economics of the Great Depression, and the economics of financial regulation. He has published more than 75 articles in academic and policy journals and has been a regular contributor to the *Financial Times*.

During his time at the Bank for International Settlements, Cecchetti participated in the numerous postcrisis global regulatory reform initiatives. This work included involvement with both the Basel Committee on Banking Supervision and the Financial Stability Board in establishing new international standards.

Cecchetti received an SB in Economics from the Massachusetts Institute of Technology in 1977 and a PhD in Economics from the University of California at Berkeley in 1982.

Kermit L. Schoenholtz is Professor of Management Practice in the Department of Economics of New York University's Leonard N. Stern School of Business, where he teaches courses on financial crises, money and banking, and macroeconomics (http://pages.stern.nyu.edu/~kschoenh). He also directs NYU Stern's Center for Global Economy and Business (www.stern.nyu.edu/cgeb). Schoenholtz was Citigroup's global chief economist from 1997 until 2005. After a year's leave, he served until 2008 as senior advisor and managing director in the Economic and Market Analysis (EMA) department at Citigroup.

Schoenholtz joined Salomon Brothers in 1986, working in their New York, Tokyo, and London offices. In 1997, he became chief economist at Salomon, after which he became chief economist at Salomon Smith Barney and later at Citigroup.

Schoenholtz has published extensively for the professional investment community about financial, economic, and policy developments; more recently, he has contributed to policy-focused scholarly research in economics. He has served as a member of the Executive Committee of the London-based Centre for Economic Policy Research and is a panel member of the U.S. Monetary Policy Forum.

From 1983 to 1985, Schoenholtz was a Visiting Scholar at the Bank of Japan's Institute for Monetary and Economic Studies. He received an MPhil in economics from Yale University in 1982 and an AB from Brown University in 1977.

Preface

The worldwide financial crisis of 2007–2009 was the most severe since that of the 1930s, and the recession it triggered was by far the most widespread and costly since the Great Depression. Around the world, it cost tens of millions of workers their jobs. In the United States, millions of families lost their homes and their wealth. In Europe, a subsequent crisis threatened a breakup of the European Monetary Union, home of the world's second most important currency. To stem these crises, governments and central banks took aggressive and, in many ways, unprecedented actions.

As a result, change will continue to sweep through the world of banking and financial markets for years to come. Some of the ways in which people borrowed—to buy a home or a car or to pay for college—have become difficult or unavailable. Some of the largest financial firms have failed, while others—even larger—have risen. In Europe, two governments defaulted, while others required support from neighboring countries to roll over their debt and that of their banks. Some financial markets have disappeared, but new institutions are surfacing that aim to make markets less vulnerable in the future. And governments everywhere are working on new rules to make future crises both less likely and less damaging.

Just as these crises are re-shaping the global financial system and government policy, they also are transforming the study of money and banking. Some old questions are surfacing with new intensity: Why do such costly crises occur? How can they be prevented? How can we limit their impact? How will these changes affect the financial opportunities and risks that people face?

Against this background, students who memorize the operational details of today's financial system are investing in a short-lived asset. Our purpose in writing this book is to focus on the basic functions served by the financial system while deemphasizing its current structure and rules. Learning the economic rationale behind current financial tools, rules, and structures is much more valuable than concentrating on the tools, rules, and structures themselves. It is an approach designed to give students the lifelong ability to understand and evaluate whatever financial innovations and developments they may one day confront.

The Core Principles Approach

Toward that end, the entire content of this book is based on five *core principles*. Knowledge of these principles is the basis for learning what the financial system does, how it is organized, and how it is linked to the real economy.

1. Time has value.
2. Risk requires compensation.
3. Information is the basis for decisions.
4. Markets determine prices and allocate resources.
5. Stability improves welfare.

These five core principles serve as a framework through which to view the history, current status, and future development of money and banking. They are discussed in detail in Chapter 1; throughout the rest of the text, marginal icons remind students of the principles that underlie particular discussions.

Focusing on core principles has created a book that is both concise and logically organized. This approach does require some adjustments to the traditional methodology used to teach money and banking, but for the most part they are changes in emphasis only. That said, some of these changes have greatly improved both the ease of teaching and the value students draw from the course. Among them are the emphasis on risk and on the lessons from the financial crisis; use of the term *financial instrument;* parallel presentation of the Federal Reserve and the European Central Bank; a streamlined, updated section on monetary economics; and the adoption of an integrated global perspective.

Innovations in This Text

In addition to the focus on core principles, this book introduces a series of innovations designed to foster coherence and relevance in the study of money and banking, in both today's financial world and tomorrow's.

Scan here for quick access to the resources for these problems. Need a barcode reader? Try ScanLife, available in your app store.

Scan here for quick access to the hints for these problems. Need a barcode reader? Try ScanLife, available in your app store.

Federal Reserve Economic Data (FRED)

The Fourth Edition of *Money, Banking, and Financial Markets* systematically integrates the use of economic and financial data from FRED, the online database provided free of charge to the public by the Federal Reserve Bank of St. Louis. As of this writing, FRED offers nearly 150,000 data series from 50-plus sources, including indicators for about 200 countries. Information on using FRED appears in Appendix B to Chapter 1 and on the book's supplementary website (go to www.mhhe.com/moneyandbanking4e and click on Student Edition, then FRED Resources or scan the accompanying QR code, as shown in the margin).

Through frequent use of FRED, students will gain up-to-date knowledge of the U.S. and other economies and an understanding of the real-world challenges of economic measurement; they will also gain skills in analysis and data manipulation that will serve them well for years to come. Many of the graphs in the new edition were produced (and can be easily updated) using FRED. In addition, new end-of-chapter Data Exploration problems call on students to use FRED to analyze key economic and financial indicators highlighted in that chapter. (For detailed instructions for using FRED online to answer the Data Exploration Problems in Chapters 1 to 10, visit www.mhhe.com/moneyandbanking4e and click on Student Edition, then Data Exploration Hints, or scan the accompanying QR code, as shown in the margin). Students can even do some assignments using the FRED app for their mobile devices.

Impact of the Crises

The effects of the global financial crisis of 2007–2009 and the euro-area crisis that began in 2010 are transforming money, banking, and financial markets. Accordingly, from beginning to end, the book integrates the issues raised by these crises and by the responses of policymakers.

The concept of a liquidity crisis surfaces in Chapter 2, and the risks associated with leverage and the rise of shadow banking are introduced in Chapter 3. Issues specific to the 2007–2009 crisis—including securitization, rating agencies, subprime mortgages, over-the-counter trading, and complex financial instruments like credit-default swaps—are included in the appropriate intermediate chapters of the text. Chapter 16 explores the role of the European Central Bank in managing the euro-area crisis. More broadly, the sources of threats to the financial system as a whole are identified throughout the book, and there is a focused discussion on regulatory initiatives to limit such systemic threats. Finally, we present—in a logical and organized manner—the unconventional monetary policy tools that became so prominent in the policy response to the crises and to the weak postcrisis recoveries.

Early Introduction of Risk

It is impossible to appreciate how the financial system works without understanding risk. In the modern financial world, virtually all transactions transfer some degree of risk between two or more parties. These risk trades can be extremely beneficial, as they are in the case of insurance markets. But there is still potential for disaster. In 2008, risk-trading activity at some of the world's largest financial firms threatened the stability of the international financial system.

Even though risk is absolutely central to an understanding of the financial system, most money and banking books give very little space to the topic. In contrast, this book devotes an entire chapter to defining and measuring risk. Chapter 5 introduces the concept of a risk premium as compensation for risk and shows how diversification can reduce risk. Because risk is central to explaining the valuation of financial instruments, the role of financial intermediaries, and the job of central bankers, the book returns to this concept throughout the chapters.

Emphasis on Financial Instruments

Financial instruments are introduced early in the book, where they are defined based on their economic function. This perspective leads naturally to a discussion of the uses of various instruments and the determinants of their value. Bonds, stocks, and derivatives all fit neatly into this framework, so they are all discussed together.

This approach solves one of the problems with existing texts, use of the term *financial market* to refer to bonds, interest rates, and foreign exchange. In its conventional microeconomic sense, the term *market* signifies a place where trade occurs, not the instruments that are traded. This book follows standard usage of the term *market* to mean a place for trade. It uses the term *financial instruments* to describe virtually all financial arrangements, including loans, bonds, stocks, futures, options, and insurance contracts. Doing so clears up the confusion that can arise when students arrive in a money and banking class fresh from a course in the principles of economics.

Parallel Presentation of the Federal Reserve and the European Central Bank

To foster a deeper understanding of central banking and monetary policy, the presentation of this material begins with a discussion of the central bank's role and objectives. Descriptions of the Federal Reserve and the European Central Bank follow. By starting on a theoretical plane, students gain the tools they need to understand how all central banks work. This avoids focusing on institutional details that may quickly become obsolete. Armed with a basic understanding of what central banks do and how they do it, students will be prepared to grasp the meaning of future changes in institutional structure.

Another important innovation is the parallel discussion of the two most important central banks in the world, the Federal Reserve and the European Central Bank (ECB). Students of the 21st century are ill-served by books that focus entirely on the U.S. financial system. They need a global perspective on central banking, the starting point for which is a detailed knowledge of the ECB.

Modern Treatment of Monetary Economics

The discussion of central banking is followed by a simple framework for understanding the impact of monetary policy on the real economy. Modern central bankers think and talk about changing the interest rate when inflation deviates from its target and output deviates from its normal level. Yet traditional treatments of monetary economics employ aggregate demand and aggregate supply diagrams, which relate output to the *price level*. Our approach directly links output to *inflation*, simplifying the exposition and highlighting the role of monetary policy. Because this book also skips the IS-LM framework, its presentation of monetary economics is several chapters shorter. Only those topics that are most important in a monetary economics course are covered: long-run money growth and inflation and short-run monetary policy and business cycles. This streamlined treatment of monetary theory is not only concise but more modern and more relevant than the traditional approach. It helps students to see monetary policy changes as part of a strategy rather than as one-off events, and it gives them a complete understanding of business-cycle fluctuations.

Integrated Global Perspective

Technological advances have dramatically reduced the importance of a bank's physical location, producing a truly global financial system. Twenty years ago money and banking books could afford to focus primarily on the U.S. financial system, relegating international topics to a separate chapter that could be considered optional. But in today's financial world, even a huge country like the United States cannot be treated in isolation. The global financial system is truly an integrated one, rendering separate discussion of a single country's institutions, markets, or policies impossible. This book incorporates the discussion of international issues throughout the text, emphasizing when national borders are important to bankers and when they are not.

Organization

This book is organized to help students understand both the financial system and its economic effects on their lives. That means surveying a broad series of topics, including what money is and how it is used; what a financial instrument is and how it is valued; what a financial market is and how it works; what a financial institution is and why we need it; and what a central bank is and how it operates. More important, it means showing students how to apply the five core principles of money and banking to the evolving financial and economic arrangements that they inevitably will confront during their lifetimes.

Part I: Money and the Financial System.

Chapter 1 introduces the core principles of money and banking, which serve as touchstones throughout the book. It also presents FRED, the free online database of the Federal Reserve Bank of St. Louis. The book often uses FRED data for figures and tables, and every chapter calls on students to use FRED to solve end-of-chapter problems. Chapter 2 examines money both in theory and in practice. Chapter 3 follows with a bird's-eye view of financial instruments, financial markets, and financial institutions. (Instructors who prefer to discuss the financial system first can cover Chapters 2 and 3 in reverse order.)

Part II: Interest Rates, Financial Instruments, and Financial Markets.

Part II contains a detailed description of financial instruments and the financial theory required to understand them. It begins with an explanation of present value and risk, followed by specific discussions of bonds, stocks, derivatives, and foreign exchange. Students benefit from concrete examples of these concepts. In Chapter 7 (The Risk and Term Structure of Interest Rates), for example, students learn how the information contained in the risk and term structure of interest rates can be useful in forecasting. In Chapter 8 (Stocks, Stock Markets, and Market Efficiency), they learn about stock bubbles and how those anomalies influence the economy. And in Chapter 10 (Foreign Exchange), they study the Big Mac index to understand the concept of purchasing power parity. Throughout this section, two ideas are emphasized: that financial instruments transfer resources from savers to investors, and that in doing so, they transfer risk to those best equipped to bear it.

Part III: Financial Institutions.

In the next section, the focus shifts to financial institutions. Chapter 11 introduces the economic theory that is the basis for our understanding of the role of financial intermediaries. Through a series of examples, students see the problems created by asymmetric information as well as how financial intermediaries can mitigate those problems. The remaining chapters in Part III put theory into practice. Chapter 12 presents a detailed discussion of banking, the bank balance sheet, and the risks that banks must manage. Chapter 13 provides a brief overview of the financial industry's structure, and Chapter 14 explains financial regulation, including a discussion of regulation to limit threats to the financial system as a whole.

Part IV: Central Banks, Monetary Policy, and Financial Stability.

Chapters 15 through 19 survey what central banks do and how they do it. This part of the book begins with a discussion of the role and objectives of central banks, which leads naturally to the principles that guide central bank design. Chapter 16 applies those principles to the Federal Reserve and the European Central Bank, highlighting the strategic importance of their numerical inflation objectives and their communications. Chapter 17 presents the central bank balance sheet, the process of multiple deposit creation, and the money supply. Chapters 18 and 19 cover operational policy, based on control of both the interest rate and the exchange rate. Chapter 18 also introduces the monetary transmission mechanism and presents a variety of unconventional monetary policy tools that gained prominence during the financial crisis of 2007–2009 and the weak economic expansion that followed. The goal of Part IV is to give students the knowledge they will need to cope with the inevitable changes that will occur in central bank structure.

Part V: Modern Monetary Economics.   The last part of the book covers modern monetary economics. While most books cover this topic in six or more chapters, this one does it in four. This streamlined approach concentrates on what is important, presenting only the essential lessons that students truly need. Chapter 20 sets the stage by exploring the relationship between inflation and money growth. Starting with inflation keeps the presentation simple and powerful, and emphasizes the way monetary policymakers think about what they do. A discussion of aggregate demand, aggregate supply, and the determinants of inflation and output follows. Chapter 21 presents a complete macroeconomic model with a dynamic aggregate demand curve that integrates monetary policy directly into the presentation, along with short- and long-run aggregate supply curves. In Chapter 22 the model is used to help understand the sources of business cycles, as well as a number of important applications that face monetary policymakers in the world today. Each application stands on its own and the applications are ordered in increasing difficulty to allow maximum flexibility in their use. Finally, Chapter 23 explores the monetary transmission mechanism in some detail and addresses key challenges facing central banks, such as asset price bubbles, the zero bound for nominal rates, and the evolving structure of the financial system.

For those instructors who have the time, we recommend closing the course with a rereading of the first chapter and a review of the core principles. What is the future likely to hold for the six parts of the financial system: money, financial instruments, financial markets, financial institutions, regulatory agencies, and central banks? How do students envision each of these parts of the system 20 or even 50 years from now?

Organizational Alternatives

While this book greatly streamlines the traditional approach to money and banking, it remains flexible enough to be used in a broad variety of courses; up to 19 of the book's 23 chapters can be assigned in the following courses:

General Money and Banking Course. Chapters 1–8, 11, 12, 15, 16, the first section of 17 (through page 462), 18, and 20–22
This course covers the primary material needed to appreciate the connections between the financial system and the economy.

General Money and Banking Course with International Emphasis. Chapters 1–8, 10–12, 15–19, and 20
This alternative to the general money and banking course substitutes chapters on foreign exchange and exchange-rate policy for the macroeconomic model included in courses with less international emphasis.

Financial Markets and Institutions. Chapters 1–9, 11–18
The traditional financial markets and institutions course covers money, financial instruments and markets, financial institutions, and central banking. The focus is on Parts II and III of the book.

Monetary Economics and Monetary Policy. Chapters 1–7, 10–12, 15–23
A course called monetary economics and monetary policy uses the material in Parts II and III as a foundation for understanding the material in Parts IV and V.

A half-semester course for students with a background in financial instruments and institutions might cover only Chapters 1–3 and 15–23.

What's New in the Fourth Edition?

Many things have happened since the last edition. For that reason, all of the figures and data have been updated to reflect the most recent available information. In addition, the authors have made numerous, vital changes to enhance the Fourth Edition of *Money, Banking, and Financial Markets* as outlined here.

New Topics in the Integrated Global Perspective

The Fourth Edition has been revised extensively in light of the regulatory and monetary policy developments in the aftermath of the global financial crisis, and as a result of the euro-area crisis that began in 2010. Throughout the Fourth Edition, the authors have integrated key developments and relevant insights from these experiences. New topics introduced or discussed in much greater detail include:

- Shadow banking
- Systemic risk
- Too big to fail
- Unconventional monetary policy tools
- The euro-area crisis
- The Dodd-Frank financial reform legislation
- Basel III regulatory changes
- Central bank communications

The most extensive changes are in Chapter 14, which now includes a treatment of the Dodd-Frank and Basel III reforms; in Chapter 16, which discusses the Federal Reserve's introduction of a numerical inflation objective and explores the European Central Bank's role in managing the euro-area crisis; and in Chapter 18, which has been updated with coverage of the unconventional monetary policy approaches adopted in the aftermath of the financial crisis.

Data Exploration Problems

Each chapter now includes a set of Data Exploration problems that call on students to use FRED, the online database provided free of charge by the Federal Reserve Bank of St. Louis, to analyze relevant financial and economic data.

Changes at the Federal Reserve

The discussion of the Federal Reserve now highlights the introduction of a numerical inflation objective and the evolving communications strategy (Chapter 16), the use of unconventional policy tools in addressing the financial crisis (Chapter 18), and the impairment of the monetary transmission process during the crisis (Chapter 23). It also reflects the challenge to Fed independence in the aftermath of the crisis (Chapter 15).

Updated Coverage of Current Events

Through new and updated Learning Tools inserts, the authors have captured developments since the Third Edition in the key areas of the financial crisis and monetary policy. Here is a complete list of the new features (including those with major updates):

Lessons from the Crisis
Interbank Lending (Chapter 3)
The ECB and the Crisis of the Euro Area (Chapter 16)
Oasis of Stability (Chapter 19)

In the News
Airtime is Money: The Other Type of Mobile Money (Chapter 2)
High-Frequency Trading: Wait a Second (Chapter 3)
Risk-on, Risk-off May Be Ending (Chapter 5)
Gross's Burning Bond Market Fails to Frighten Investors (Chapter 6)
Bubble Spotting (Chapter 8)
No Insurance Pay-Out on Greek Debt (Chapter 9)
Foreign Exchange: Neighbors Show Little Appetite for Brazil's "War" (Chapter 10)
China Shadow Bankers Go Online as Peer-to-Peer Sites Boom (Chapter 11)
Lessons from the London Whale (Chapter 12)
Fed's Tarullo Says Reviving Glass-Steagall May Be Costly (Chapter 13)
How to Shrink the "Too-Big-to-Fail" Banks (Chapter 14)
The Politicization (or Not) of Central Banks (Chapter 15)
Should the Fed Change Its Target? An Interview with Michael Woodford (Chapter 16)
The Monetary Base Is Exploding. So What? (Chapter 17)
How Jawboning Works (Chapter 18)
Phony Currency Wars (Chapter 19)
Will Fed's "Easy Money" Push Up Prices? (Chapter 20)
Yellen Says Higher Rates Not Assured After Thresholds Hit (Chapter 21)
Potential Output: Rising Permanent Damage (Chapter 22)
Should the Fed Pop Bubbles by Raising Interest Rates? (Chapter 23)

Applying the Concept
The Tri-Party Repo Market (Chapter 12)
The LIBOR Scandal (Chapter 13)

Tools of the Trade
The Basel Accords: I, II, III, and Counting . . . (Chapter 14)

Learning Tools

In a sense, this book is a guide to the principles students will need to critically evaluate and use what they read in the financial press. Reading a newspaper or a blog and applying the information it contains require some basic knowledge. Supplying that knowledge is the purpose of the five types of inserts that complement the chapters, providing a break from the more technical material in the body of the text:

- Applying the Concept
- In the News
- Lessons from the Crisis

- **Tools of the Trade**
- **Your Financial World**.

For a complete listing of the boxed features and their page references, refer to the information found on the inside back cover of this text. At the start of each chapter, the Fourth Edition of the book also introduces *learning objectives,* to which the end-of-chapter problems are linked.

The end-of-chapter material is divided into five sections: *Key Terms, Chapter Lessons, FRED Data Codes, Conceptual and Analytical Problems,* and *Data Exploration.* Key Terms lists all the technical terms introduced and defined in the chapter. The key terms are defined in full in the glossary at the end of the book. To aid student comprehension and retention, Chapter Lessons lists key lessons in an outline that matches the chapter's headings.

For a detailed description of the FRED Data Codes, Data Exploration material, and Conceptual and Analytical Problems, as well as the aforementioned boxed features, please refer to the walkthrough on the pages that follow.

Supplements for Instructors

The following ancillaries are available for quick download and convenient access via the book website at www.mhhe.com/moneyandbanking4e and are password protected for security.

Instructor's Manual

Tori Knight (Carson-Newman College) has collected a broad array of materials for instructors. This manual includes chapter overviews, outlines, and a discussion of how the core principles apply to each chapter. It also addresses concepts students often find difficult, including suggestions for alleviating confusion.

Solutions Manual

Detailed solutions to the end-of-chapter problems are provided in a separate manual by James Fackler (University of Kentucky). Tori Knight (Carson-Newman College) and Matthew Alford (Southeastern Louisiana University) verified the accuracy of the solutions.

Test Bank

Kenneth Slaysman (York College of Pennsylvania) has revised the test bank of 2,500 multiple-choice and 600 short-answer and essay questions. The test bank can be used both as a study guide and as a source for exam questions. It has been computerized to allow for both selective and random generation of test questions.

PowerPoint Slides

PowerPoint slides for classroom use, updated by Marie Reymore (Marian University), are available with the Fourth Edition. The slides outline the main points in each chapter and reproduce major graphs and charts. This handy, colorful supplement will help to maintain students' interest during lecture sessions.

Learning Tools Walkthrough

Learning Objectives

The learning objectives (LOs) introduced at the start of each chapter highlight the material and concepts to be mastered. Every end-of-chapter problem cross-references one LO.

Learning Objectives

Understand . . .

LO1 Money and its functions

LO2 The payments system today and tomorrow

LO3 Money links: inflation and economic growth

YOUR FINANCIAL WORLD
Pay Off Your Credit Card Debt as Fast as You Can

Credit cards are extremely useful. They make buying things easy—sometimes too easy. While we all plan to pay off our credit card balances every month, sometimes we just don't have the resources. So we take advantage of the loans the card issuers offer and pay off only part of what we owe. Suddenly we find ourselves deeply in debt.

How fast should you pay off your credit card balance? All the bank or finance company that issued the card will tell you is the minimum you have to pay. You get to decide whether to pay more, and your decision makes a big difference. We can use the present-value concept to figure out your alternatives.

Let's take a typical example. You have a balance of $2,000 and can afford to pay at least $50 per month. How many monthly payments will you need to make to pay off the full debt? What if you paid $60 or $75 per month? To find the answer, use equation (8) for the present value of a fixed series of payments. In this case, the present value is the loan amount, $2,000; the fixed monthly payment is $50, $60, or $75; and the interest rate is whatever your credit card company charges per month—10 to 20 percent a year. (The average rate is around 13 percent.) We need to figure out the number of payments, or *n* in equation (8).*

Table 4.4 shows the number of months needed to pay off your $2,000 balance at various interest rates and payment amounts. The first entry tells you that if your credit card com-

How fast should you pay off your credit card balance?

Looking more closely, you can see that making large payments is much more important than getting a low interest rate. The lesson is: Pay off your debts as fast as you possibly can. Procrastination is expensive.

Your Financial World

These boxes show students that the concepts taught in the text are relevant to their everyday lives. Among the topics covered are the importance of saving for retirement, the risk in taking on a variable rate mortgage, the desirability of owning stocks, and techniques for getting the most out of the financial news.

Core Principle Marginal Icons

The entire text discussion is organized around the following five core principles: *Time* has value; *risk* requires compensation; *information* is the basis for decisions; *markets* set prices and allocate resources; and *stability* improves welfare. Exploring these principles is the basis for learning what the financial system does, how it is organized, and how it is linked to the real economy. They are discussed in detail in Chapter 1; throughout the rest of the text, marginal icons remind students of the principles that underlie particular discussions.

any way that one might want.[5] When you encounter a financial inst time, try to figure out whether it is used primarily for storing value risk. Then try to identify which characteristics determine its value.

MARKETS

Financial Markets

Financial markets are the places where financial instruments ar They are the economy's central nervous system, relaying and reac quickly, allocating resources, and determining prices. In doing so

Lessons from the Crisis

These boxes explain concepts or issues that are both integral to the chapter and central to understanding how the financial crisis of 2007–2009 and the subsequent crisis in the euro area transformed the world of money, banking, and financial markets. The topics range from specific aspects of the crises such as shadow banks and central bank policy responses to broad concepts like liquidity, leverage, sovereign default, and systemic risk.

LESSONS FROM THE CRISIS
LEVERAGE

Households and firms often borrow to make investments. Obtaining a mortgage for a new home or selling a corporate bond to build a new plant are common examples. The use of borrowing to finance part of an investment is called *leverage.* Leverage played a key role in the financial crisis of 2007–2009, so it is worth understanding how leverage relates to risk and how it can make the financial system vulnerable.

Modern economies rely heavily on borrowing to make investments. They are all leveraged. Yet, the more leverage, the greater the risk that an adverse surprise will lead to bankruptcy. If two households own houses of the same value, the one that has borrowed more—the one that is more highly leveraged and has less net worth—is the more likely to default during a temporary slump in income. This example could apply equally well to firms, financial institutions, or even countries.

Financial institutions are much more highly leveraged than households or firms, typically owning assets of about 10 times their net worth. During the crisis, some important fi-

a drop as small as 3 percent in asset prices could eliminate the cushion created by the net worth and lead to bankruptcy.

When highly leveraged financial institutions experience a loss, they usually try to reduce their leverage—that is, to *deleverage*—by selling assets and issuing securities that raise their net worth (see accompanying figure). However, everyone in the financial system cannot deleverage at once. When too many institutions try to sell assets simultaneously, their efforts will almost surely prove counterproductive: falling prices will mean more losses, diminishing their net worth further, raising leverage, and making the assets they hold seem riskier, thereby compelling further sales.

This "paradox of leverage" reinforces the destabilizing liquidity spiral discussed in Chapter 2 (see Lessons from the Crisis: Market Liquidity, Funding Liquidity, and Making Markets). Both spirals feed a vicious cycle of falling prices and widespread deleveraging that was a hallmark of the financial crisis of 2007–2009. The financial system steadied only after a plunge of many asset prices and massive government interventions.

*For a technical definition of leverage, see the Tools of the Trade box in Chapter 5. For the evolution of U.S. commercial bank

In the News

One article per chapter is featured from major media such as *The New York Times, The Economist, The Financial Times, The Wall Street Journal,* and *Project Syndicate.* These readings show how concepts introduced in the chapter are applied in the financial press. A brief analysis of the article, called "Lessons," reinforces key concepts.

Applying the Concept

These sections showcase history and examine issues relevant to the public policy debate to illustrate how ideas introduced in the chapter can be applied to the world around us. Subjects include the LIBOR scandal; why Long-Term Capital Management caused a near collapse of the world financial system; and what monetary policymakers learned from the Great Depression of the 1930s.

Tools of the Trade

These boxes teach useful skills, including how to read bond and stock tables, how to read charts, and how to do some simple algebraic calculations. Some provide brief reviews of material from the principles of economics course, such as the relationship between the current account and the capital account in the balance of payments.

End-of-Chapter Features

Using FRED: Codes for Data in This Chapter

Data Series	FRED Data Code
Price of gold (U.S. dollars)	GOLDAMGBD228NLBM
Consumer price index	CPIAUCSL
M1	M1SL
M2	M2SL
Currency in circulation	CURRSL
Traveler's checks	TVCKSSL
Demand deposits	DEMDEPSL
Other checkable deposits	OCDSL
Small-denomination time deposits	STDCBSL
Savings deposits and MMDAs*	SAVINGSL
Retail MMMFs**	RMFSL
Nominal GDP	GDP

*Money market deposit accounts
**Money market mutual funds

FRED Data Codes

The FRED table lists key economic and financial indicators relevant to the chapter and the codes by which they are accessed in FRED, the free online database provided by the Federal Reserve Bank of St. Louis. With the data codes, students can use FRED to analyze key economic patterns and illuminate the ideas in the chapter. See Appendix B to Chapter 1 for help using FRED.

Data Exploration

New, detailed end-of-chapter questions ask students to use FRED to analyze economic and financial data relevant to the chapter. Appendix B to Chapter 1 provides information on using FRED and sets the stage for its use thereafter. QR codes in the margin directly link students to the FRED-related web resources available for each chapter.

FRED ECONOMIC DATA | ST. LOUIS FED

Scan here for quick access to the hints for these problems. Need a barcode reader? Try ScanLife, available in your app store.

Data Exploration

For detailed instructions on using Federal Reserve Economic Data (FRED) online to answer each of the following problems, visit www.mhhe.com/moneyandbanking4e and click on Student Edition, then Data Exploration Hints.

1. Find the most recent level of M2 (FRED code: M2SL) and of the U.S. population (FRED code: POP). Compute the quantity of money divided by the population. Do you think your answer is large? Why? *(LO1)*
2. Reproduce Figure 2.3 from 1960 to the present, showing the percent change from a year ago of M1 (FRED code: M1SL) and M2 (FRED code: M2SL). Comment on the pattern over the last five years. Would it matter which of the two monetary aggregates you looked at? *(LO3)*
3. Which usually grows faster: M1 or M2? Produce a graph showing M2 divided by M1. When this ratio rises, M2 outpaces M1 and vice versa. What is the long-run pattern? Is the pattern stable? *(LO3)*
4. Traveler's checks are a component of M1 and M2. Produce a graph of this component of the monetary aggregates (FRED code: TVCKSSL). Explain the pattern you see. *(LO1)*

Conceptual and Analytical Problems

1. Describe at least three ways you could pay for your morning cup of coffee. What are the advantages and disadvantages of each? *(LO2)*
2. You are the owner of a small sandwich shop. A buyer may offer one of several payment methods: cash, a check drawn on a bank, a credit card, or a debit card. Which of these is the least costly for you? Explain why the others are more expensive. *(LO2)*
3. Explain how money encourages specialization, and how specialization improves everyone's standard of living. *(LO3)*
4.* Could the dollar still function as the unit of account in a totally cashless society? *(LO2)*
5. Give four examples of ACH transactions you might make. *(LO2)*
6. As of July 2013, 17 of the 28 countries of the European Union have adopted the euro. The remaining 11 countries, including Great Britain, Denmark, and Sweden, have retained their own currencies. What are the advantages of a common currency for someone who is traveling through Europe? *(LO1)*
7. Why might each of the following commodities not serve well as money? *(LO2)*
   a. Tomatoes
   b. Bricks
   c. Cattle
8. Despite the efforts of the U.S. Treasury and the Secret Service, someone discov-

Conceptual and Analytical Problems

Each chapter contains at least 18 conceptual and analytic problems at varying levels of difficulty, which reinforce the lessons in the chapter. All of the problems are available as assignable content within Connect, McGraw-Hill's homework management platform, organized around learning objectives to make it easier to plan, track, and analyze student performance across different learning outcomes.

Supplements for Students

Online Learning Center

The book's website, www.mhhe.com/moneyandbanking4e, includes a variety of free content for students, including multiple-choice chapter quizzes, PowerPoint slides, and interactive graphs with related exercises. Instructors may access all the book's major supplements using a special password.

McGraw-Hill *Connect®* Economics

Less Managing. More Teaching. Greater Learning.

McGraw-Hill *Connect Economics* is an online assignment and assessment solution that connects students with the tools and resources they'll need to achieve success.

McGraw-Hill *Connect Economics* helps prepare students for their future by enabling faster learning, more efficient studying, and higher retention of knowledge.

McGraw-Hill *Connect Economics* Features

Connect Economics offers a number of powerful tools and features to make managing assignments easier, so faculty can spend more time teaching. With *Connect Economics,* students can engage with their coursework anytime and anywhere, making the learning process more accessible and efficient. *Connect Economics* offers you the features described below.

Simple Assignment Management With *Connect Economics,* creating assignments is easier than ever, so you can spend more time teaching and less time managing. The assignment management function enables you to:

- Create and deliver assignments easily with selectable end-of-chapter questions and test bank items.
- Streamline lesson planning, student progress reporting, and assignment grading to make classroom management more efficient than ever.
- Go paperless with the eBook and online submission and grading of student assignments.

Smart Grading When it comes to studying, time is precious. *Connect Economics* helps students learn more efficiently by providing feedback and practice material when they need it, where they need it. When it comes to teaching, your time also is precious. The grading function enables you to:

- Have assignments scored automatically, giving students immediate feedback on their work and side-by-side comparisons with correct answers.
- Access and review each response; manually change grades or leave comments for students to review.
- Reinforce classroom concepts with practice tests and instant quizzes.

Instructor Library   The *Connect Economics* Instructor Library is your repository for instructor ancillaries and additional resources to improve student engagement in and out of class. You can select and use any asset that enhances your lecture.

Student Study Center   The *Connect Economics* Student Study Center is the place for students to access additional resources. The Student Study Center:

- Offers students quick access to lectures, practice materials, eBooks, and more.
- Provides instant practice material and study questions, easily accessible on the go.
- Gives students access to LearnSmart and SmartBook as described next.

Diagnostic and Adaptive Learning of Concepts: LearnSmart   Learn-Smart is one of the most effective and successful adaptive learning resources in the market today, proven to strengthen memory recall, keep students in class, and boost grades. Distinguishing what students know from what they don't and homing in on concepts they are most likely to forget, LearnSmart continuously adapts to each student's needs by building an individual learning path so students study smarter and retain more knowledge. Reports provide valuable insight to instructors, so precious class time can be spent on higher-level concepts and discussion. LearnSmart:

- Applies an intelligent concept engine to identify the relationships between concepts and to serve new concepts to each student only when he or she is ready.
- Adapts automatically to each student, so students spend less time on the topics they understand and practice more those they have yet to master.
- Provides continual reinforcement and remediation, but gives only as much guidance as students need.
- Integrates diagnostics as part of the learning experience.
- Enables instructors to assess which concepts students have efficiently learned on their own, thus freeing class time for more applications and discussion.

SmartBook   SmartBook is the first and only adaptive reading experience available today. SmartBook changes reading from a passive and linear experience to an engaging and dynamic one in which students are more likely to master and retain important concepts, coming to class better prepared. Valuable reports provide instructors insight as to how students are progressing through textbook content and are useful for shaping in-class time or assessment.

Student Progress Tracking   *Connect Economics* keeps instructors informed about how each student, section, and class is performing, allowing for more productive use of lecture and office hours. The progress-tracking function enables you to:

- View scored work immediately and track individual or group performance with assignment and grade reports.
- Access an instant view of student or class performance relative to section headings.
- Collect data and generate reports required by many accreditation organizations, such as AACSB.

Lecture Capture   Increase the attention paid to lecture discussion by decreasing the attention paid to note taking. For an additional charge Lecture Capture offers new ways for students to focus on the in-class discussion, knowing they can revisit important topics later. Lecture Capture enables you to:

- Record and distribute your lecture with a click of button.
- Record and index PowerPoint presentations and anything shown on your computer so it is easily searchable, frame by frame.
- Offer access to lectures anytime and anywhere by computer, iPod, or mobile device.
- Increase intent listening and class participation by easing students' concerns about note taking. Lecture Capture will make it more likely you will see students' faces, not the tops of their heads.

McGraw-Hill *Connect Plus Economics*   McGraw-Hill reinvents the textbook learning experience for the modern student with *Connect Plus Economics*. A seamless integration of an eBook and *Connect Economics, Connect Plus Economics* provides all of the *Connect Economics* features plus the following:

- An integrated eBook, allowing for anytime, anywhere access to the textbook.
- Dynamic links between the problems or questions you assign to your students and the location in the eBook where that problem or question is covered.
- A powerful search function to pinpoint and connect key concepts in a snap.

In short, *Connect Economics* and *Connect Plus Economics* offer you and your students powerful tools and features that optimize your time and energies, enabling you to focus on course content, teaching, and student learning. *Connect Economics* also offers a wealth of content resources for both instructors and students. This state-of-the-art, thoroughly tested system supports you in preparing students for the world that awaits.

For more information about Connect, go to **www.mcgrawhillconnect.com**, or contact your local McGraw-Hill sales representative.

Tegrity Campus: Lectures 24/7

Tegrity Campus is a service that makes class time available 24/7 by automatically capturing every lecture in a searchable format for students to review when they study and complete assignments. With a simple one-click 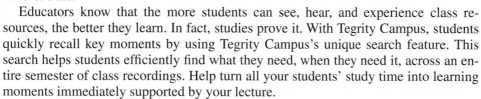 start-and-stop process, you capture all computer screens and corresponding audio. Students can replay any part of any class with easy-to-use browser-based viewing on a PC or Mac.

Educators know that the more students can see, hear, and experience class resources, the better they learn. In fact, studies prove it. With Tegrity Campus, students quickly recall key moments by using Tegrity Campus's unique search feature. This search helps students efficiently find what they need, when they need it, across an entire semester of class recordings. Help turn all your students' study time into learning moments immediately supported by your lecture.

To learn more about Tegrity watch a 2-minute Flash demo at **http://tegritycampus. mhhe.com**.

Assurance of Learning Ready

Many educational institutions today are focused on the notion of *assurance of learning,* an important element of some accreditation standards. *Money, Banking, and Financial Markets* is designed specifically to support your assurance of learning initiatives with a simple, yet powerful solution.

Each test bank question for *Money, Banking, and Financial Markets* maps to a specific chapter heading listed in the text. You can use our test bank software, EZ Test and EZ Test Online, or in *Connect Economics* to easily query for chapter headings and topic tags that directly relate to your course. You can then use the reporting features of EZ Test to aggregate student results in similar fashion, making the collection and presentation of assurance of learning data simple and easy.

AACSB Statement

The McGraw-Hill Companies is a proud corporate member of AACSB International. Understanding the importance and value of AACSB accreditation, *Money, Banking, and Financial Markets,* 4/e recognizes the curricula guidelines detailed in the AACSB standards for business accreditation by connecting selected questions in the text and test bank to the six general knowledge and skill guidelines in the AACSB standards.

The statements contained in *Money, Banking, and Financial Markets,* 4/e are provided only as a guide for the users of this textbook. The AACSB leaves content coverage and assessment within the purview of individual schools, the mission of the school, and the faculty. While *Money, Banking, and Financial Markets,* 4/e and the teaching package make no claim of any specific AACSB qualification or evaluation, we have within the *Money, Banking, and Financial Markets,* 4/e Solutions Manual and Test Bank labeled selected questions according to the six general knowledge and skills areas.

McGraw-Hill Customer Care Contact Information

At McGraw-Hill, we understand that getting the most from new technology can be challenging. That's why our services don't stop after you purchase our products. You can e-mail our Product Specialists 24 hours a day to get product-training online. Or you can search our knowledge bank of Frequently Asked Questions on our support website. For Customer Support, call **800-331-5094**, or visit www.mhhe.com/support. One of our Technical Support Analysts will be able to assist you in a timely fashion.

Acknowledgments

I owe thanks to many more people than I can possibly list, including a large number of academics, central bankers, and financial market participants around the world. A few of these deserve special mention. I would like to thank Robert M. Solow, who set me on the path doing economics as a 20-year-old undergraduate; George A. Akerlof, whose inspiration still guides me, even more than 25 years after he signed my dissertation; William J. McDonough, who gave me the opportunity to watch and ask questions from inside the Federal Reserve; Peter R. Fisher, who was my day-to-day guide to what I was seeing during my time at the Fed; and Jaime Caruana and Hervé Hannoun, whose patience and understanding helped me appreciate the global central bank community.

Of my numerous collaborators and colleagues over the years, Nelson Mark (now at the University of Notre Dame) is the most important. His encouragement, counsel, and friendship have guided me for more than 15 years. In addition, Michael Bryan of the Federal Reserve Bank of Atlanta has been a constant source of help and encouragement, as have numerous friends throughout the central banking world.

Among all of the professional colleagues who took the time to read early versions of the manuscript, I would like to single out Jim Fackler for his insight and patience. This book is much better for the time he generously devoted to correcting my logical mistakes and helping ensure that the exercises would reinforce the lessons in each chapter.

Without all the people at McGraw-Hill/Irwin this book would never have been written. Gary Burke and Paul Shensa first convinced me that I could write this book, and then taught me how. Erin Strathmann worked tirelessly (and daily) to improve the book. Betty Morgan made my sentences and paragraphs readable. And all of the people in production and design turned the words and charts into a beautiful, readable book. Gregg Forte made a notable contribution to the Third and Fourth Editions through his skilled editing of the manuscript.

Without students, universities would not exist. And without a class in money and banking to teach, I would not have written this book. I owe a debt to every student who has sat in a classroom with me. Several deserve special mention for the time and effort they put in to helping with the manuscript: Margaret Mary McConnell of the Federal Reserve Bank of New York, Roisin O'Sullivan of Smith College, Stefan Krause of the Banque de France, Lianfa Li of Peking University, Craig Evers of Brevan Howard, and Georgios Karras of the University of Illinois at Chicago.

And finally, there is my family; my wife Ruth and our sons Daniel and Ethan. For years they put up with my daily routine of writing, rewriting, and rewriting again and again. To them I owe the biggest thanks.

Stephen G. Cecchetti
Brandeis International Business School

There is not enough space here to thank the many people who taught me about financial markets and institutions during my more than two decades of work as a market economist, but a few deserve special mention. Hugh Patrick was an inspiration in graduate school and remains a friend and guide. In the financial markets, I benefited especially from the wisdom of Henry Kaufman and the economists he gathered at Salomon Brothers in the 1980s—Richard Berner, Robert DiClemente, John Lipsky, and Nicholas Sargen. The members of the economics team that I was privileged to lead at Salomon (and later at Citi) continued my education, including (among many others) Lewis Alexander, Robert DiClemente, Don Hanna, Michael Saunders, Christopher Wiegand, and Jeffrey Young.

I also owe an extraordinary debt to my colleagues at the New York University Leonard N. Stern School of Business, who welcomed me, gave me the privilege of teaching excellent students, and entrusted me with the honor of directing Stern's Center for Global Economy and Business (www.stern.nyu.edu/cgeb). For their sustained support and guidance, I thank former Dean Thomas Cooley, current Dean Peter Henry, former Vice Dean Ingo Walter, and the distinguished current and former chairmen of the Department of Economics—David Backus, Paul Wachtel, Lawrence White, and Stanley Zin. David Backus, Kim Ruhl, and Michael Waugh gave me the tools to teach MBA students. Jennifer Carpenter has been my partner as Associate Director of the Center for Global Economy and Business, while John Asker, Thomas Philippon, Laura Veldkamp, and Paul Wachtel have all served as Center research group coordinators and my advisors. Jonathan Robidoux keeps the Center operating efficiently and with a smile each day. Many others deserve thanks for making Stern the thriving research and teaching environment that it is today, but I am especially grateful for the support of Viral Acharya, Gian Luca Clementi, Matthew Richardson, and Stijn van Nieuwerburgh. I also thank A. Michael Cristofi for his research assistance in the preparation of this Fourth Edition.

Of course, my greatest debt is to my wife, Elvira Pratsch. I also thank my parents, Harold and Evelyn, as well as my sister and brother, Sharon and Andy.

Kermit L. Schoenholtz
New York University Leonard N. Stern School of Business

Reviewers

Thank you to the following contributing reviewers for this and previous editions.

Burton Abrams
University of Delaware

Douglas Agbetsiafa
Indiana University at South Bend

Pedro Albuquerque
University of Minnesota at Duluth

Abdiweli Ali
Niagara University

Thomas Martin Allen
Texas A&M University

Brad Altmeyer
South Texas College

Harjit Arora
Lemoyne College

Foued Ayari
Bernard M. Baruch College

Raymond Batina
Washington State University

Clare Battista
California Polytechnic State University

Larry Belcher
Stetson University

Robert Boatler
Texas Christian University

Christa Bouwman
Case Western Reserve University

Latanya Brown
Bowie State University

James Butkiewicz
University of Delaware

Anne Bynoe
Pace University

Douglas Campbell
University of Memphis

Giorgio Canarella
California State University at Los Angeles

Bolong Cao
Ohio University, Athens

Tina Carter
Florida State University at Tallahassee

Matthew S. Chambers
Towson University

Dong Cho
Wichita State University

Nan-Ting Chou
University of Louisville

Isabelle Delalex
Pace University

Mamit Deme
Middle Tennessee State University

Seija Doolittle
Delaware Technical Community College at Wilmington

David Doorn
University of Minnesota at Duluth

Demissew Ejara
William Patterson University

Paul Emberton
Texas State University

Robert Eyler
Sonoma State University

Gregory Fallon
College of Saint Joseph

Richard Froyen
University of North Carolina at Chapel Hill

Craig Furfine
University of Chicago

William Gavin
Washington University

Ronald Gilbert
Texas Tech University

Gregory Gilpin
Montana State University

Lance Girton
University of Utah

Stuart Glosser
University of Wisconsin at Whitewater

William L. Goffe
Oswego State University of New York

Stephan F. Gohmann
University of Louisville

Elias Grivoyannis
Yeshiva University

Joanne Guo
Pace University

David Hammes
University of Hawaii at Hilo

Scott Hein
Texas Tech University

Ying Huang
Manhattan College

Julio Huato
Saint Francis College

Owen Irvine
Michigan State University at East Lansing

Aaron Jackson
Bentley College

Yongbok Jeon
University of Utah at Salt Lake City

George Jouganatos
California State University at Sacramento

Chulhee Jun
Texas Technical University

Chris Kauffman
University of Tennessee at Knoxville

Andrew Kayanga
Dillard University

Kathy Kelly
University of Texas, Arlington

Kent Kimbrough
Duke University

Paul Kubik
DePaul University

Pamela Labadie
George Washington University

Larry Landrum
Virginia Western Community College

Tom Lee
California State University at Northridge

Serpil Leveen
Montclair State University

Melissa Lind
University of Texas, Arlington

Mark Longbrake
Ohio State University at Columbus

Fiona Maclachlan
Manhattan College

Michael Madaris
William Carey University

Ellie Mafi-Kreft
Indiana University

Vincent Marra
University of Delaware

Ralph May
Southwestern Oklahoma State University

Robert McAuliffe
Babson College

Chris McHugh
Tufts University

Alice Melkumian
Western Illinois University

Alla Melkumian
Western Illinois University

Jianjun Miao
Boston University

Peter Mikek
Wabash College

Ossama Mikhail
University of Central Florida

Kyoko Mona
Bernard M. Baruch College

Ray Nelson
Brigham Young University

James Nguyen
Southeastern Louisiana University

David O'Dell
McPherson College

Roisin O'Sullivan
Smith College

Dennis O'Toole
Virginia Commonwealth University

Daniel Owens
University of North Dakota

Hilde Patron-Boenheim
University of West Georgia

Robert Pennington
University of Central Florida

Dennis Placone
Clemson University

Hamideh Ramjerdi
William Patterson University

Ronald Ratti
University of Western Sydney, Australia

Rupert Rhodd
*Florida Atlantic University
at Davie*

Kevin Salyer
University of California, Davis

Julia Sampson
Malone College

Drew Saunders
Purdue University

Timothy J. Schibik
University of Southern Indiana

Sherrill Shaffer
University of Wyoming

Eugene Sherman
Baruch College

Anna Shostya
Bernard M. Baruch College

Harindar Singh
Grand Valley State University

Robert Sonora
Fort Lewis College

Souren Soumbatiants
Franklin University

Richard Stahl
*Louisiana State University at Baton
Rouge*

Herman Stekler
George Washington University

Mark Strazicich
Appalachian State University

William Stronge
Florida Atlantic University

Scott Sumner
Bentely College

Philip Tew
University of Mississippi

Sven N. Thommesen
Auburn University

Mark Toma
University of Kentucky at Lexington

Kudret Topyan
Manhattan College

Brian Trinque
University of Texas at Austin

Rubina Vohra
New Jersey City University

William Walsh
University of St. Thomas

Dale Warmingham
Rutgers University at New Brunswick

Chao Wei
George Washington University

Mark Weinstock
Pace University

Niklas Westelius
Hunter College

Eugene White
Rutgers University at New Brunswick

Ruhai Wu
Florida Atlantic University

King-Yuen Yik
University of Michigan at Ann Arbor

Derek Yonai
Campbell University

Brief Contents

Contents

Part *III* Financial Institutions 267

Part *IV* Central Banks, Monetary Policy, and Financial Stability 393

Part *V*   Modern Monetary Economics   552

Part *I*

Money and the Financial System

Chapter 1

An Introduction to Money and the Financial System

Learning Objectives

Understand . . .

LO1* The parts of the financial system

LO2 The core principles of money and banking

LO3 Special features and organization of the book

This morning, a typical American college student bought coffee at the local café, paying for it with an ATM card. Then she jumped into her insured car and drove to the university, which she attends thanks to her student loan. She may have left her parents' home, which is mortgaged, a few minutes early to avoid construction work on a new dormitory, financed by bonds issued by the university. Or perhaps she needed to purchase this book online, using her credit card, before her first money and banking class began.

Beneath the surface, the financial transactions embedded in this story—even the seemingly simple ones—are quite complicated. If the café owner and the student use different banks, paying for the coffee will require an interbank funds transfer. The company that insures the student's car has to invest the premiums she pays until they are needed to pay off claims. The student's parents almost surely obtained their home mortgage through a mortgage broker, whose job was to find the cheapest mortgage available. And the bonds the university issued to finance construction of the new dormitory were created with the aid of an investment bank.

This brief example hints at the complex web of interdependent institutions and markets that is the foundation for our daily financial transactions. The system is so efficient that most of us rarely take note of it. But a financial system is like air to an economy: If it disappeared suddenly, everything would grind to a halt.

In the autumn of 2008, we came closer to such a financial meltdown than at any time since the 1930s. In the earlier episode, the collapse of the banking system led to the Great Depression. In the recent crisis, some of the world's largest financial institutions failed. Key markets stopped functioning. Credit dried up, even for sound borrowers. As a result, vibrant companies that relied on short-term loans to pay their employees and buy materials faced potential ruin. Even some fundamental ways that we make payments for goods and services were threatened.

Gasping for air in this financial crisis, the global economy during 2008 and 2009 sank into the deepest, broadest, and longest downturn since the 1930s. Around the

*LO Learning Objective

world, tens of millions of people lost their jobs. In the United States, millions lost their homes and their life's savings. Others became unable to borrow to buy a home or go to college. And the weakness added to financial fragility elsewhere, especially in Europe, where the viability of the euro, the world's leading currency after the U.S. dollar, was threatened. The chances are good that you know someone—in your neighborhood, your school, or your family—whose life was changed for the worse by the crisis.

So, what happens in the financial system—whether for good or for bad—matters greatly for all of us. To understand the system—both its strengths and its vulnerabilities—let's take a closer look.

The Six Parts of the Financial System

The **financial system**[1] has six parts, each of which plays a fundamental role in our economy. Those parts are money, financial instruments, financial markets, financial institutions, government regulatory agencies, and central banks.

We use the first part of the system, **money**, to pay for our purchases and to store our wealth. We use the second part, **financial instruments**, to transfer resources from savers to investors and to transfer risk to those who are best equipped to bear it. Stocks, mortgages, and insurance policies are examples of financial instruments. The third part of our financial system, **financial markets**, allows us to buy and sell financial instruments quickly and cheaply. The New York Stock Exchange is an example of a financial market. **Financial institutions**, the fourth part of the financial system, provide a myriad of services, including access to the financial markets and collection of information about prospective borrowers to ensure they are creditworthy. Banks, securities firms, and insurance companies are examples of financial institutions. Government **regulatory agencies** form the fifth part of the financial system. They are responsible for making sure that the elements of the financial system—including its instruments, markets, and institutions—operate in a safe and reliable manner. Finally, **central banks**, the sixth part of the system, monitor and stabilize the economy. The **Federal Reserve System** is the central bank of the United States.

While the essential functions that define these six categories endure, their form is constantly evolving. *Money* once consisted of gold and silver coins. These were eventually replaced by paper currency, which today is being eclipsed by electronic funds transfers. Methods of accessing means of payment have changed dramatically as well. As recently as 1970, people customarily obtained currency from bank tellers when they cashed their paychecks or withdrew their savings from the local bank. Today, they can get cash from practically any ATM anywhere in the world. To pay their bills, people once wrote checks and put them in the mail, then waited for their monthly bank statements to make sure the transactions had been processed correctly. Today, payments can be made automatically, and account holders can check the transactions at any time on their bank's website or on their smartphone.

Financial instruments (or securities, as they are often called) have evolved just as much as currency. In the last few centuries, investors could buy individual stocks through stockbrokers, but the transactions were costly. Furthermore, putting together a portfolio of even a small number of stocks and bonds was extremely time consuming; just collecting the information necessary to evaluate a potential investment was a daunting task. As a result, investing was an activity reserved for the wealthy. Today, financial institutions offer people with as little as $1,000 to invest the ability to purchase

---

[1]Throughout the book, terms in bold red are "key terms" listed at the end of each chapter and defined in the glossary.

"This is Fluffy, my pet money."

shares in *mutual funds,* which pool the savings of a large number of investors. Because of their size, mutual funds can construct portfolios of hundreds or even thousands of different stocks and/or bonds.

The markets where stocks and bonds are sold have undergone a similar transformation. Originally, *financial markets* were located in coffeehouses and taverns where individuals met to exchange financial instruments. The next step was to create organized markets, like the New York Stock Exchange—trading places specifically dedicated to the buying and selling of stocks and bonds. Today, much of the activity that once occurred at these big-city financial exchanges is handled by electronic networks. Buyers and sellers obtain price information and initiate transactions from their desktop computers or from handheld devices. Because electronic networks have reduced the cost of processing financial transactions, even small investors can afford to participate in them. Just as important, today's financial markets offer a much broader array of financial instruments than those available even 50 years ago.

Financial institutions have changed, as well. Banks began as vaults where people could store their valuables. Gradually, they developed into institutions that accepted deposits and made loans. For hundreds of years, in fact, that was what bankers did. Today, a bank is more like a financial supermarket. Walk in and you will discover a huge assortment of financial products and services for sale, from access to the financial markets to insurance policies, mortgages, consumer credit, and even investment advice.

The activities of government regulatory agencies and the design of **regulation** have been evolving and have entered a period of more rapid change, too. In the aftermath of the financial crisis of 1929–1933, when the failure of thousands of banks led to the Great Depression, the U.S. government introduced regulatory agencies to provide wide-ranging financial regulation—rules for the operation of financial institutions and markets—and **supervision**—oversight through examination and enforcement. The U.S. agencies established in the 1930s to issue and enforce these financial rules still operate.

Yet, the evolution of financial instruments, institutions, and markets has led to many changes in the ways that regulatory agencies work. A bank examiner used to count the money in the cash drawers and call borrowers to see if the loans on a bank's books were real. They might even visit workplaces to see if the loans were used as designed to buy equipment or build a factory. Today, banks engage in millions of transactions, many of which are far more complex and difficult to understand than a loan or a mortgage. So, a government examiner also looks at the systems that a bank uses to manage its various risks. In doing so, regulators try to encourage best practices throughout the financial industry.

However, the failure of regulators in the United States and elsewhere around the world to anticipate or prevent the financial crisis of 2007–2009 has led many governments to undertake far-reaching changes to financial regulation and the regulatory agencies. The Dodd-Frank Wall Street Reform and Consumer Protection Act, adopted in 2010 and known as the **Dodd-Frank Act**, is the largest U.S. regulatory change since the 1930s. Also in 2010, regulators of many nations agreed on a third, major update of standards for internationally active banks—known as **Basel III** after the Swiss city where the policymakers meet. Both reforms will take years to implement, and their influence will shape the financial system for decades.

Finally, *central banks* have changed a great deal. They began as large private banks founded by monarchs to finance wars. For instance, King William of Orange created the Bank of England in 1694 for the express purpose of raising taxes and borrowing to finance a war between Austria, England, and the Netherlands on one side and Louis XIV's France on the other. Eventually, these government treasuries grew into the modern central banks we know today. While only a few central banks existed in 1900, now nearly every country in the world has one, and they have become one of the most important institutions in government. Central banks control the availability of money and credit to promote low inflation, high growth, and the stability of the financial system. Because their current mission is to serve the public at large rather than land-hungry monarchs, their operating methods have changed as well. A central bank's decisions used to be shrouded in mystery, but today's policymakers strive for transparency in their operations. Officials at the **European Central Bank** and the U.S. Federal Reserve—two of the most important central banks in the world—go out of their way to explain the rationale for their decisions.

Though the changing nature of our financial system is a fascinating topic, it poses challenges for both students and instructors. How can we teach and learn about money and banking in a way that will stand the test of time, so that the knowledge we gain won't become outmoded? The answer is that we must develop a way to understand and adapt to the evolutionary structure of the financial system. That means discussing money and banking within a framework of core principles that do not change over time. The next section introduces the five core principles that will guide our studies throughout this book.

The Five Core Principles of Money and Banking

Five core principles will inform our analysis of the financial system and its interaction with the real economy. Once you have grasped these principles, you will have a better understanding not only of what is happening in the financial world today but of changes that will undoubtedly occur in the future. The five principles are based on **Time, Risk, Information, Markets,** and **Stability.**

Core Principle 1: Time Has Value

TIME

The first principle of money and banking is that *time has value.* At some very basic level, everyone knows this. If you take a job at the local supermarket, you will almost surely be paid by the hour. An hour's worth of work equals a certain number of dollars. Literally, your time has a price.

On a more sophisticated level, **time** affects the value of financial transactions. Most loan contracts allow the borrower to spread out the payments over time. If you take out an auto loan, for example, the lender will allow you to make a series of monthly payments over three, four, or even five years. If you add up the payments, you'll discover that the total exceeds the amount of the loan. At an interest rate of 4 percent, a four-year, $10,000 car loan will require 48 monthly payments of $226 each. That means you will repay a total of $10,848 (48 times $226). The reason your repayments total more than the loan amount is that you are paying interest to compensate the lender for the time during which you use the funds. That is, the resources you borrowed have an opportunity cost to the lender so you have to pay rent on them.

Interest payments are fundamental to a market economy. In Chapter 4, we will develop an understanding of interest rates and how to use them. Then, throughout the remainder of Part II, we will apply the principle that time has value in our discussion of the valuation of bonds, stocks, and other financial instruments involving future payments. How much should you be willing to pay for a particular stock or bond? Figuring out what alternative investments are worth, and comparing them, means valuing payments made on different future dates. The same principle applies to the question of how much you must invest today to achieve a particular financial objective in the future. How much of your salary, for example, do you need to save each month to meet your goal of buying a house? The length of time your savings will be earning interest is a key to answering this question.

Core Principle 2: Risk Requires Compensation

The world is filled with uncertainty. More events, both good and bad, *can* happen than *will* happen. Some of the possibilities, such as the likelihood of your home doubling in value after you buy it, are welcome. Other possibilities, such as the chance that you might lose your job and not be able to make your car payments, are distinctly unwelcome. Dealing effectively with **risk** requires that you consider the full range of possibilities in order to eliminate some risks, reduce others, pay someone to assume particularly onerous risks, and just live with what's left. Needless to say, no one will assume your risks for free, which brings us to the second core principle of money and banking: *Risk requires compensation.* In the financial world, compensation is made in the form of explicit payments. That is, investors must be paid to assume risk; the higher the risk, the bigger the required payment.

Car insurance is a common example of paying someone else to shoulder a risk you don't want to take. If your car is wrecked in an accident, you will want to be able to repair it. But beyond that, auto insurance shelters drivers from the possibility of losing all their wealth in the event that they cause an accident in which someone is seriously injured. Although the chances of causing such an accident are quite small, the results can be so serious that, even if the government didn't require it, most of us would voluntarily purchase auto insurance. Driving without it just isn't worth the risk. The insurance company pools the premiums that policyholders pay and invests them. Even though some of the premiums will be spent to settle claims when cars are stolen or damaged by collisions, the chance to make a profit is good. So both the insurance company and the drivers who buy policies are ultimately better off.

Bearing in mind that time has value and risk requires compensation, we can begin to see the rationale behind the valuation of a broad set of financial instruments. For example, a lender will charge a higher interest rate on a loan if there is a chance that the borrower will not repay. In Chapters 6 and 7, we will use this principle when we examine the interest rates on bonds. As we will see, a company or a government that is on the verge of being unable to pay its bills may still be able to issue bonds (called *junk bonds*), but it will have to pay an extremely high interest rate to do so. The reason is that the lender must be compensated for the substantial risk that the company will not repay the loan. Risk requires compensation.

Core Principle 3: Information Is the Basis for Decisions

Most of us collect **information** before making decisions. The more important the decision, the more information we gather. Think of the difference between buying a $5 sandwich and a $10,000 used car. You will surely spend more time comparing cars than comparing sandwiches.

What's true for sandwiches and cars is true for finance as well. That is, *information is the basis for decisions.* In fact, the collection and processing of information is the foundation of the financial system. In Chapter 11, we will learn how financial institutions like banks funnel resources from savers to investors. Before a bank makes a loan, a loan officer will investigate the financial condition of the individual or firm seeking it. Banks want to provide loans only to the highest-quality borrowers. Thus, they spend a great deal of time gathering the information needed to evaluate the creditworthiness of loan applicants.

To understand the problem faced by the two parties to any financial transaction, think about a home mortgage. Before making the loan, the mortgage broker examines the applicant's finances and researches the home's value to make sure the applicant can afford the monthly payments and the property is more valuable than the loan.

And before the broker transfers the funds to the seller, the new homeowner must purchase fire insurance. All these requirements arise from the fact that the lender doesn't know much about the borrower and wants to make sure the loan will be repaid. When lenders fail to assess creditworthiness properly, they end up with more borrowers who are unable to repay their loans in the future. Large mistakes like these were a key factor in the wave of U.S. mortgage delinquencies and defaults that preceded the financial crisis of 2007–2009. Even five years later, nearly one-fifth of residential mortgages still exceeded the underlying property value.

Information plays a key role in other parts of the financial system as well. In Chapters 2 and 3, we'll see that many types of transactions are arranged so that the buyer doesn't need to know anything about the seller. When merchants accept cash, they don't need to worry about the customer's identity. When stocks change hands, the buyer doesn't need to know anything about the seller, or vice versa. Stock exchanges are organized to eliminate the need for costly information gathering, facilitating the exchange of securities. In one way or another, information is the key to the financial system.

Core Principle 4: Markets Determine Prices and Allocate Resources

Markets are the core of the economic system. They are the place, physical or virtual, where buyers and sellers meet, where firms go to issue stocks and bonds, and where individuals go to trade assets. Financial markets are essential to the economy, channeling its resources and minimizing the cost of gathering information and making transactions. In fact, well-developed financial markets are a necessary precondition for healthy economic growth. For the most part, the better developed a country's financial markets, the faster the country will grow.

The reason for this connection between markets and growth is that *markets determine prices and allocate resources.* Financial markets gather information from a large number of individual participants and aggregate it into a set of prices that signals what is valuable and what is not. Thus, markets are sources of information. By attaching prices to different stocks or bonds, they provide a basis for the allocation of capital.

To see how prices in the financial markets allocate capital, think about a large firm wishing to finance the construction of a new factory costing several hundred million dollars. To raise the funds, the firm can go directly into the financial markets and issue stocks or bonds. The higher the price investors are willing to pay in the market, the more appealing the idea will be, and the more likely it is that the firm will issue securities to raise the capital for the investment.

We will refer to the financial markets throughout much of this book. While our primary focus in Part II will be the nature of financial instruments, we will also study the markets in which those instruments are traded. Chapters 6 through 10 describe the markets for bonds, stocks, derivatives, and foreign currencies.

Importantly, financial markets do not arise by themselves—at least, not the large, well-oiled ones we see operating today. Markets like the New York Stock Exchange, where billions of shares of stock change hands every day, require rules in order to work properly, as well as authorities to police them. Otherwise, they will not function. For people to be willing to participate in a market, they must perceive it as fair. As we will see, this creates an important role for the government. Regulators and supervisors of the financial system make and enforce the rules, punishing people who violate them. When the government protects investors, financial markets work well and help promote economic growth; otherwise they don't.

Finally, even well-developed markets can break down. When they do—as some did during the financial crisis of 2007–2009—the financial system as a whole can be at risk. So today, governments must also play a role in promoting the healthy operation of markets.

Core Principle 5: Stability Improves Welfare

Most of us prefer stable to variable incomes. We like getting raises, but the prospect of a salary cut is not a pleasant one. This brings us to the fifth core principle of money and banking: *Stability improves welfare*. **Stability** is a desirable quality, not just in our personal lives but in the financial system as a whole. As we saw at the start of this chapter, financial instability in the autumn of 2008 brought us closer to a collapse of the system than at any time since the 1930s, triggering the worst global downturn since the Great Depression. And the banking and government debt crisis in the euro area partly reversed Europe's financial integration, a cornerstone of its successful economic and political framework in recent decades.

If you are wondering whether this principle is related to Core Principle 2 (risk requires compensation), you are right. Because volatility creates risk, reducing volatility reduces risk. But while individuals can eliminate many risks on their own (we'll see how when we study financial instruments in Part II), some risks can only be reduced by government policymakers. Business cycle fluctuations are an example of the sort of instability individuals can't eliminate on their own. And though "automatic stabilizers" like unemployment insurance and the income tax system reduce the burden of recessions on individuals, they cannot eliminate an economic slowdown. Monetary policymakers can moderate these downswings by carefully adjusting interest rates. Central banks also have powerful tools to steady fragile financial systems and to repair or support dysfunctional markets. In stabilizing the economy as a whole, they eliminate risks that individuals can't, improving everyone's welfare in the process.

As we will learn in Part IV of this book, stabilizing the economy is a primary function of central banks like the Federal Reserve and the European Central Bank. Officials of these institutions are charged with controlling inflation and reducing business cycle fluctuations. That is, they work to keep inflation low and stable and to keep growth high and stable. They also have key roles in securing financial stability. When they are successful, they reduce both the risk that individuals will lose their jobs and the uncertainty that firms face in making investment decisions. Not surprisingly, a stable economy grows faster than an unstable economy. Stability improves welfare.

Throughout the book you will notice icons like this in the margin at various points. These will guide you to the core principle that provides the foundation for what is being discussed at that point in the text.

Special Features of This Book

The very first special feature of every chapter in this book is its introduction—each one presents a real-world example that leads to the big questions the chapter is designed to answer, such as: What is money? What do banks do? How does the bond market work? What does the Federal Reserve do to prevent or limit financial crises?

After that real-world setup, the text of each chapter presents the economic and financial theory you need to understand the topics covered. Learning objectives listed at the beginning of the chapter outline the core concepts that are discussed and should be mastered. Each chapter also contains a series of inserts that apply the theory. There are five types of inserts: Your Financial World, Applying the Concept, Lessons from the Crisis, In the News, and Tools of the Trade. Finally, the end of each chapter is divided into four sections: Key Terms, Using FRED, Chapter Lessons, and Problems. Here are some guidelines for using the inserts and end-of-chapter materials.

Your Financial World

When most people decide to make a major purchase, they begin by collecting information. If they are considering buying a car, they will first try to decide which model is best for them and then work hard to pay the lowest price possible. Even for smaller purchases, like clothes or groceries, people first gather information and then buy.

Financial transactions should be no different from consumer purchases. Become informed first, and then buy. If you're thinking, "That's easier said than done," you're right. The problem is that most people have very little knowledge of the financial system, so they don't know how to start or what kind of information to collect.

That's where Your Financial World comes in. These inserts provide basic guidelines for applying economic theory to the bread-and-butter financial decisions you make nearly every day. Your Financial World answers questions about:

- Banking and Payments
  - What's the difference between credit and debit cards?
  - How should you pick a bank?
- Investments
  - Should you own stocks or bonds or gold?
  - Should you invest in the company you work for?
- Credit, Loans, and Mortgages
  - What do you need to know when you shop for a mortgage?
  - What is your credit score and why is it important?
- Insurance
  - How much life insurance do you need?
  - How much car insurance do you need?

YOUR FINANCIAL WORLD
Guard Your Identity

There is a television commercial in which a middle-aged man is sitting in his living room drinking a beer. Out of the man's mouth comes the voice of a woman describing some very expensive clothing she just bought. She didn't care how much the clothes cost because she wasn't paying—she used a credit card that was in the man's name. The ad catches viewers' attention because it is funny. But its primary purpose is to serve as a warning about identity theft, in which one person takes on the identity of another to do things like make credit card purchases.

It is important to realize that someone who has a few pieces of key information about you can get a credit card in your name. To prevent this, you need to protect personal information. Do your best to never tell anyone your birth date and birthplace, your address, or your mother's maiden name. Most importantly, guard your Social Security number. Because it is unique, it is the key to identity theft. Give out your Social Security number only when absolutely

necessary—on tax forms, for employment records, and to open bank accounts. If your driver's license has your Social Security number on it, ask that it be removed. If a business requests it, ask if some alternative number can be used. Importantly, if you get a telephone call or an e-mail from someone you don't know asking for personal data, don't provide it.

Beyond protecting access to personal information, you need to monitor your financial statements closely, looking for things that shouldn't be there. Be on the lookout for unauthorized charges. This means maintaining careful records so that you know what should be on your bank and credit card statements.

Identity theft is a crime, and governments work hard to find and prosecute the offenders. Even so, millions of people are victims each year. Don't be one of them. For more information about identity theft and how to avoid being a victim, see the U.S. Department of Justice's website: *www.justice. gov/criminal/fraud/websites/idtheft.html.*

- Saving and Retirement
  - How big an emergency saving reserve should you have?
  - Is your retirement savings insured?

Applying the Concept

Applying the Concept inserts show how to put theory into practice. They provide real-world examples of the ideas introduced in the chapter, drawn primarily from history or from relevant public policy debates. Here are some of the questions examined in Applying the Concept:

- Why do interest rates rise when inflation goes up?
- Why does a country's exchange rate suddenly plummet?
- Why do large-scale frauds that damage investors occur repeatedly?
- Why is it important for central banks to be free of political influence?
- Can monetary policy be used to stabilize the economy?
- What determines inflation?
- What are the implications of China's exchange rate policy?

Lessons from the Crisis

These inserts cover episodes from the financial crisis of 2007–2009 and from the European banking and government debt crisis that began shortly thereafter. One goal is to give you a framework for understanding these crises and how they are transforming the world of finance. Another goal is to highlight the relevance and power of the ideas in the book more generally. Along the way, the various Lessons from the Crisis offer you insight into the sources and effects of financial instability. They also address the means that governments—including regulators and central bankers—use to counter financial instability. Most chapters contain one such insert.

The topics range from specific aspects of the crises to key issues that have wide application. Here are some of the questions examined in Lessons from the Crisis:

- What factors led to the financial crisis of 2007–2009?
- What made financial institutions especially vulnerable in this period?
- Why do financial markets sometimes stop functioning?
- How do threats to the financial system differ from threats to specific financial institutions?
- When a crisis erupts, what can central banks do to prevent another Great Depression?
- What factors link banks and governments in the euro-area crisis?

In the News

One of the primary purposes of this textbook is to help you understand the business and financial news. Critically evaluating what you read, hear, and see means developing a clear understanding of how the financial system works, as well as reading the news regularly. Like many other skills, critical reading of newspapers and magazines takes practice. You can't just pick up a newspaper and skim through it quickly and efficiently; you need to learn how. Your instructor will make suggestions about what you should read. See Table 1.1 on page 12 for a list of reliable sources of information on the economy and the financial system.

Given your need to become a skilled consumer of financial information, each chapter in this book closes with an article drawn from the financial press. These stories from *The Wall Street Journal,* the *Financial Times, The Economist, Bloomberg Businessweek,* and other sources are reproduced under the heading In the News. Each provides an example of how the concepts introduced in the chapter are discussed in the real world, and each is followed by a brief summary.

Tools of the Trade

Many chapters in this book include an insert called Tools of the Trade that concentrates on practical knowledge relevant to the chapter. Some of these inserts cover basic skills, including how to read bond and stock tables, how to read charts, and how to do some simple algebraic calculations. Others provide brief reviews of material from principles of economics classes, such as the relationship between the current account and the capital account in the balance of payments. Still other Tools of the Trade inserts address questions such as:

- What is leverage, and how does it affect risk?
- What are hedge funds?
- What tools did the Fed use to address the financial crisis?
- How is a recession defined?

End-of-Chapter Sections

Key Terms   A listing of all the technical terms introduced (in bold red) and defined in the chapter. The key terms are defined in full in the glossary at the end of the book.

Table 1.1 Sources of Economic and Financial News and Data

Sources of Daily News

The Wall Street Journal and www.wsj.com

Published six days a week, and available both in print and on the Internet, *The Wall Street Journal* provides news, as well as comprehensive coverage of business and finance. Some content on the website is free.

Financial Times and www.ft.com

The *Financial Times* offers reporting, analysis, and commentary on major business, political, financial, and economic events. The *FT* is written from a distinctly European perspective and includes detailed coverage of non-U.S. business and financial news. Free registration gives access to some of the *FT* web content.

Bloomberg (www.bloomberg.com**)**

Bloomberg offers a wide range of financial market services, including news. A wide variety of news and data can be found on the free portion of its website.

Yahoo! Finance (http://finance.yahoo.com**)**

Yahoo! Finance provides free quotes on stocks, bonds, currencies, and commodities. It also presents news from various sources about business finance and portfolio management.

Sources of Weekly News

The Economist and www.economist.com

The *Economist* covers global politics, economics, business, finance, and science. It not only reports the facts but also analyzes them and draws policy conclusions. The Finance and Economics section, located roughly three-quarters of the way into each print issue, is of particular interest.

Bloomberg Businessweek and www.businessweek.com

Bloomberg Businessweek is a U.S.-based publication that offers balanced reporting and analysis of top economic, financial, business, and technological issues.

Economic and Financial Data

The Federal Reserve Bank of St. Louis maintains a comprehensive database called FRED (**F**ederal **R**eserve **E**conomic **D**ata) that you can access by going to http://research.stlouisfed.org/fred2. This website includes tutorials for using FRED that will help you answer the end-of-chapter problems.

The Bureau of Labor Statistics supplies data on prices, employment, and unemployment at www.bls.gov.

The Bureau of Economic Analysis provides information on gross domestic product, consumption, investment, and other macroeconomic data at www.bea.gov.

The Federal Reserve Board website www.federalreserve.gov provides a variety of banking, monetary, interest rate, and exchange rate data.

Personal Finance Information

Many financial websites offer a variety of personal finance resources, including financial calculators to help you with mortgages, auto loans, and insurance. They are:

- www.choosetosave.org
- www.dinkytown.net
- www.wsj.com (under the "markets" tab, go to "personal finance" then the "family finance" section and look for "tools")

Using FRED: Codes for Data in This Chapter   A table identifying economic and financial data highlighted in the chapter together with the data code (identifier) that is used to retrieve the data from the Federal Reserve's online database, FRED.

Chapter Lessons   A list of the key lessons in the chapter summarized in the form of an outline that matches the chapter headings—a format designed to aid comprehension and retention.

Problems   Each chapter contains two types of problems at varying levels of difficulty: (1) conceptual and analytical problems and (2) data exploration problems using FRED. The problems are designed to reinforce the lessons in the chapter. The data exploration problems ask you to manipulate economic and financial data from FRED (Federal Reserve Economic Data), the extensive online resource maintained and provided free of charge by the Federal Reserve Bank of St. Louis at http://research. stlouisfed.org/fred2. Many of the graphs in this book are based on data in FRED. See Appendix B of this chapter for further information on FRED and how to use it.

The Organization of This Book

This book is organized into five sections. Each one employs core principles to illuminate a particular part of the financial system and applies economic theory to the world around us. The next two chapters will continue our overview of the financial system. First, we'll study money—what it is and how it is used. We'll see that currency allows transactions to be made anonymously, which reduces the need to gather information. This advantage of currency is related to Core Principle 3: Information is the basis for decisions. In Chapter 3, we'll take a bird's-eye view of financial instruments, financial markets, and financial institutions. At various points in that chapter, we'll refer to the first four core principles.

Part II includes detailed descriptions of financial instruments. We'll study bonds, stocks, and derivatives, as well as exchange rates for foreign currency. The valuation of financial instruments requires a comparison of payments made on different dates as well as an estimate of the risk involved in each instrument. Thus, these chapters focus on Core Principles 1 and 2: Time has value and Risk requires compensation.

Throughout Part II and continuing in Part III, we'll discuss financial markets, whose purpose is to facilitate the buying and selling of financial instruments. No one would buy stocks or bonds if they could not be easily resold at little cost. Financial markets also provide the information necessary to understand the value and risk that are associated with particular financial instruments. Core Principles 3 and 4 (Information is the basis for decisions and Markets determine prices and allocate resources) are both relevant to our discussion of markets.

Part III covers financial institutions, especially banks and their regulation. Earlier in this chapter (page 7), we emphasized that financial institutions spend a great deal of time collecting and processing information. Without that information, many financial transactions could not take place. This dependence of banks on information is an example of Core Principle 3: Information is the basis for decisions. Financial regulation is driven by Core Principle 5: Stability improves welfare.

Part IV describes central banks, especially the Federal Reserve and the European Central Bank. These institutions exist to stabilize the real economy as well as the financial system. Thus, like financial regulators in Part III of the book, they embody

Core Principle 5: Stability improves welfare. We'll see how central banks manipulate interest rates and other less conventional policy tools to stabilize the economy.

Finally, Part V brings together material covered in the first four sections to explain how the financial system influences the real economy. We'll use a macroeconomic model to analyze the mechanism through which central banks influence the economy, paying particular attention to the role of the financial system in determining inflation and growth.

Learning money and banking is going to be hard work. Reading and working through the remaining 22 chapters of this book will take lots of time and energy. But when you are done, you will be armed with the tools you need to understand how the financial system works and why it changes as it does. You will be an informed reader of the financial and economic news and know how to put the financial system to use for you. You will understand the various ways that you can pay for your morning coffee and how each one of them works. You will understand the usefulness of bonds and stocks as well as what financial institutions do and how central banks work. You will know how to make sound financial decisions for the rest of your life. You will understand how financial crises arise, how they threaten economic stability, and what can be done to prevent and contain them. Regardless of the career you choose to follow, a solid background in money, banking, and financial markets will help you make sound financial decisions for the rest of your life.

Terms

Basel III, 5	information, 7
central bank, 3	markets, 7
Dodd-Frank Act, 5	money, 3
European Central Bank, 5	regulation, 4
Federal Reserve System, 3	regulatory agencies, 3
financial institution, 3	risk, 6
financial instrument, 3	stability, 8
financial market, 3	supervision, 4
financial system, 3	time, 5

Using FRED: Codes for Data in This Chapter

Data Series	FRED Data Code
Nominal GDP	GDP
Real GDP	GDPC1
GDP deflator	GDPDEF

www.mhhe.com/moneyandbanking4e

Chapter Lessons

1. A healthy and constantly evolving financial system is the foundation for economic efficiency and economic growth. It has six parts:
   a. Money is used to pay for purchases and to store wealth.
   b. Financial instruments are used to transfer resources and risk.
   c. Financial markets allow people to buy and sell financial instruments.
   d. Financial institutions provide access to the financial markets, collect information, and provide a variety of other services.
   e. Government regulatory agencies aim to make the financial system operate safely and reliably.
   f. Central banks stabilize the economy.

2. The core principles of money and banking are useful in understanding all six parts of the financial system.
   a. Core Principle 1: Time has value.
   b. Core Principle 2: Risk requires compensation.
   c. Core Principle 3: Information is the basis for decisions.
   d. Core Principle 4: Markets determine prices and allocate resources.
   e. Core Principle 5: Stability improves welfare.

Conceptual and Analytical Problems

1. List the financial transactions you have engaged in over the past week. How might each one have been carried out 50 years ago? *(LO1)*

2. How were you, or your family or friends, affected by the failure of the financial system to function normally during the financial crisis of 2007–2009? *(LO1)*

3. List three items you formerly bought with cash but now purchase with a debit card. *(LO1)*

4. Various financial instruments usually serve one of two distinct purposes: to store value or to transfer risk. Name a financial instrument used for each purpose. *(LO1)*

5. Financial innovation has reduced individuals' need to carry cash. Explain how. *(LO1)*

6.* Many people believe that, despite ongoing financial innovations, cash will always be with us to some degree as a form of money. What Core Principle could justify this view? *(LO2)*

7. When you apply for a loan, you are required to answer lots of questions. Why? Why is the set of questions you must answer standardized? *(LO2)*

8. Name two distinct financial markets and describe the kind of asset traded in each. *(LO1)*

9.* Why do you think the global financial system has become more globally integrated over time? Can you think of any downside to this increased integration? *(LO1)*

10. The government is heavily involved in the financial system. Explain why. *(LO1)*

*Indicates more difficult problems

11. If offered the choice of receiving $1,000 today or $1,000 in one year's time, which option would you choose, and why? *(LO2)*

12. If time has value, why are financial institutions often willing to extend you a 30-year mortgage at a lower annual interest rate than they would charge for a one-year loan? *(LO2)*

13. Using Core Principle 2, under what circumstances would you expect a job applicant to accept an offer of a low base salary and an opportunity to earn commission over one with a higher base salary and no commission potential? *(LO2)*

14. Suppose medical research confirms earlier speculation that red wine is good for you. Why would banks be willing to lend to vineyards that produce red wine at a lower interest rate than before? *(LO2)*

15.* If the U.S. Securities and Exchange Commission eliminated its requirement for public companies to disclose information about their finances, what would you expect to happen to the stock prices for these companies? *(LO2)*

16. If 2 percent growth is your break-even point for an investment project, under which outlook for the economy would you be more inclined to go ahead with the investment: (1) A forecast for economic growth that ranges from 0 to 4 percent, or (2) a forecast of 2 percent growth for sure, assuming the forecasts are equally reliable? What Core Principle does this illustrate? *(LO2)*

17.* Why are large, publicly listed companies much more likely than small businesses to sell financial instruments such as bonds directly to the market, while small businesses get their financing from financial institutions such as banks? *(LO2)*

18.* During the financial crisis of 2007–2009, some financial instruments that received high ratings in terms of their safety turned out to be much riskier than those ratings indicated. Explain why markets for other financial instruments might have been adversely affected by that development. *(LO2)*

19. Suppose financial institutions didn't exist but you urgently needed a loan. Where would you most likely get this loan? Using Core Principles, identify an advantage and a disadvantage this arrangement might have over borrowing from a financial institution. *(LO2)*

ECONOMIC DATA | ST. LOUIS FED

Scan here for quick access to the hints for these problems. Need a barcode reader? Try ScanLife, available in your app store.

Data Exploration

For detailed instructions on using Federal Reserve Economic Data (FRED) online to answer each of the following problems, visit www.mhhe.com/moneyandbanking4e and click on Student Edition, then Data Exploration Hints.

1. Go to the FRED website (http://research.stlouisfed.org/fred2). Register to set up your own account. Doing so will allow you to save and update graphs, alter them for submitting assignments and making presentations, and receive a notice whenever the data is updated.

2. To begin using FRED, plot the consumer price index (FRED code: CPIAUCSL) and find the date and level of the latest observation. Then, plot the inflation rate measured as the percent change from a year ago of this index.

3. Plot the level of real GDP (FRED code: GDPC1). Then, plot the rate of economic growth as the percent change from a year ago of this index. Describe how real GDP

behaves in recessions, which are denoted in the FRED graph by vertical shaded bars. If you registered on FRED (as in Data Exploration problem 1 on the previous page), save the graph so that you can recall and update it easily when new observations become available.

4. Examine nominal GDP (FRED code: GDP) by repeating the steps in Data Exploration Problem 3. Based on the figure showing percent change from a year ago, what was special about the behavior of nominal GDP during the financial crisis of 2007–2009 compared to previous decades?

5. Plot on one figure the percent change from a year ago of both the GDP deflator (FRED code: GDPDEF) and real GDP (FRED code: GDPC1). How does the GDP deflator link nominal and real GDP? Since the mid-1980s, does it fluctuate more or less than real GDP?

Appendix A to Chapter 1

Measuring Economic Activity, Prices, and the Inflation Rate

Measuring Economic Activity

Gross Domestic Product (GDP) is the most commonly used measure of economic activity. In order to see if the economy is improving, you can look at whether GDP is growing (or shrinking) and the rate of that growth. And to compare well-being in two countries, you can look at the GDP per person in each country—*per capita GDP.*

The definition of GDP is *the market value of final goods and services produced in a country during a year.* Let's look at the pieces of this definition:

- **Market value:** In order to add together production of cars, corn flakes, and computers, we take the market price of each and multiply it times the quantity of each that is produced, and sum the products together. That is, add up (market price of cars × quantity of cars produced) plus (market price of corn flakes × quantity of corn flakes produced), and so on.

- **Final goods and services:** We take only the price of the final product purchased by the person who uses it. For example, when a consumer buys a car, the car is considered a final good so it's included. But when the automobile manufacturer buys steel from a steel company in order to build the car, the steel is an intermediate product so it is not included.

- **In a country:** Only production within the country counts. This means that if a U.S. company owns a factory in China, the production of the factory is included in China's GDP.

- **During a year:** To measure production we need to specify a time period, and the time period is usually one year.

So, to compute U.S. GDP in 2015, for example, we sum the quantity of goods and services produced in the United States in 2015 times their 2015 prices. In an economy with only cars and corn flakes, the calculation would look like this:

GDP in 2015 = (2015 price of cars × quantity of cars produced in 2015)
          + (2015 price of corn flakes × quantity of corn flakes produced in 2015)

Note that we could always measure incomes rather than production. That is, instead of measuring total production, we can measure the total payments made to factors used to produce the output—the payments to labor, capital, and land. Because the revenue from selling all of the goods and services produced must always go to the people responsible for making them—the workers and the owners—total income equals GDP as well.

Real versus Nominal GDP

It is essential when measuring the level of economic activity to distinguish changes in prices from changes in quantities. As defined so far, GDP confuses the two changes. For example, U.S. GDP rose from $15.534 trillion in 2011 to $16.245 trillion in 2012. Computing the annual growth rate, the percentage change from one year to the next, means that the U.S. economy grew by 4.58 percent.

$$\text{GDP growth rate from 2011 to 2012} = \frac{\$16.245\,trillion - \$15.534\,trillion}{\$15.534\,trillion} \times 100$$
$$= 4.58\%$$

This number alone only tells us the sum of the growth in the quantity of output produced (something that is beneficial) and the change in prices (which is not so good). To see the point, look back at the computation for the car and corn flakes economy and note that GDP can rise either because quantities rise or because prices go up.

Separating changes in the quantities from changes in the prices requires computing *real* GDP. To do this, government statisticians fix the prices at a base-year level and then calculate the sum of the quantities times these base-year prices. Currently, real GDP in the United States is reported in year-2009 dollars. That is, statisticians sum up the value of all production in the United States during a year measured at the prices at which the goods and services were sold in the year 2009. This procedure isolates the part of change in GDP that is due to growth in the quantity produced from the part that came from changes in prices.

For the car and corn flakes economy, the formula looks like this:

Real GDP in 2015 = (2009 price of cars × quantity of cars produced in 2015)
    + (2009 price of corn flakes × quantity of corn flakes produced in 2015)

To see what this means for the United States as a whole, we can look at www. bea.gov and find that, in 2011, real GDP (in year-2009 dollars) was $15.052 trillion. In 2012, real GDP (again in year-2009 dollars) had increased to $15.471 trillion. That's an increase of 2.78 percent.

$$\text{Real GDP growth rate from 2011 to 2012} = \frac{\$15.471\,trillion - \$15.052\,trillion}{\$15.052\,trillion} \times 100$$
$$= 2.78\%$$

The GDP Deflator and the Inflation Rate

It should come as no surprise that from nominal and real GDP we get a measure of prices on average in the economy as a whole. We can start by thinking about nominal GDP as the product of real GDP times a measure of prices in the economy as a whole. That is:

$$\textit{Nominal GDP} = \textit{Prices} \times \textit{Real GDP}$$

Looking at this expression, you can see that by taking the ratio of nominal GDP to real GDP we get a measure of prices. This is what's called the GDP *deflator,* and using the data from 2011, we get:

$$\text{GDP deflator in 2011} = \frac{\text{Nominal GDP in 2011}}{\text{Real GDP in 2011}} = \frac{\$15.534\,trillion}{\$15.052\,trillion} = 1.032$$

The same computation for 2012 tells us that the GDP deflator in 2012 is 1.050.

www.mhhe.com/moneyandbanking4e

No one spends much time worrying about the level of the GDP deflator. Instead, we are concerned with the rate at which the index is changing. The inflation rate is defined as the rate of growth in the price level. Using the GDP deflator from 2011 to 2012, we get an inflation rate of 1.74 percent.

$$\text{Inflation rate} = \frac{(1.050 - 1.032)}{1.032} \times 100 = 1.74\%$$

This result makes sense. Because real GDP is designed to strip out the effect of price changes, the inflation rate (1.74 percent) should equal the growth rate of nominal GDP minus the growth rate of real GDP ($4.58\% - 2.78\% = 1.80\%$). Approximation error accounts for the small difference between these two rates (1.74 percent versus 1.80 percent).

While it is the easiest to explain and compute, the GDP deflator is unfortunately not the most commonly used price index. The Consumer Price Index, or CPI, designed to measure the changes in the cost of living, lays claim to that title. We will learn more about the CPI throughout this book, starting with the Tools of the Trade in Chapter 2.

Appendix B to Chapter 1

Using FRED

Scan here for quick access to the hints for these problems. Need a barcode reader? Try ScanLife, available in your app store.

Throughout this book, you will find economic data that highlight the role of money and finance in modern economies. A key new feature of the book is the use of data provided by FRED, the free, highly accessible online database created and maintained by the Federal Reserve Bank of St. Louis. Captions of figures that use data from FRED include FRED codes (identifiers) for finding and updating the data. And the end-of-chapter problem sets now include a group of data exploration problems requiring you to use FRED.

To learn how to use FRED, visit the Data Exploration Hints at www.mhhe.com/moneyandbanking4e. The hints include detailed instructions on using FRED to answer each of the Data Exploration problems in Chapters 1 through 10. Beginning with Chapter 11, the online hints provide instructions only for FRED techniques that were not used in the first 10 chapters.

Also included on the book website, are FRED Resources, where you will find up-to-date links to the tutorials on the FRED website (http://research.stlouisfed.org/fred2). The tutorials show you how to make and alter graphs using the FRED interface through your computer or cell phone. FRED allows you to change the graph type, add data series, change the observation period or frequency of a data series, and transform the data (e.g., percent change, percent change from a year ago, percent change at an annual rate). You can also alter the graph's appearance (e.g., size, background, color, font, line style).

The data in FRED cover many countries, and the information is widely used by students and professional economists alike. As of September 2013, FRED contained more than 140,000 economic time series from more than 50 data producers. FRED is updated daily.

Understanding money and banking requires understanding the data that describe an economy and its financial system. There are many producers of these data, including private associations and universities, government agencies such as central banks and commerce departments, and public international organizations such as the International Monetary Fund. Until recently, however, it was difficult for the general public, including students, to gain direct exposure to such a wide range of data; only businesses and professionals who could afford the services of private data gatherers enjoyed rapid access to broad data sets.

FRED now provides access to a wide set of data through a single interface. By using FRED, this textbook makes acquiring and manipulating the relevant data simple. A close look at data will help you understand key issues such as the nature and causes of business cycles and the tools of monetary policy. When reading news stories about money and finance, you can also use FRED to check their accuracy or get updates.

At the end of each chapter, the data series that are highlighted in the chapter appear in a table along with the data code (identifier) used in FRED. FRED makes it easy to display and examine the data online in graphic form. From the FRED interface, you can also download the data into an Excel spreadsheet for further analysis; or, if you prefer, install an Excel "add-in" from the FRED website that will allow you to more quickly access and manipulate FRED data. Finally, FRED mobile apps allow you to use it directly on iOS and Android devices.

Getting acquainted with FRED as you start reading this book will prepare you to answer the FRED-linked end-of-chapter problems. When you have finished using the book, the ability you have gained to find, manipulate, and understand economic and financial data will be an enduring benefit of your studies.

Chapter 2

Money and the Payments System

Learning Objectives

Understand . . .

LO1   Money and its functions

LO2   The payments system today and tomorrow

LO3   Money links: inflation and economic growth

Parker Brothers' bestselling board game.

The makers of the board game Monopoly print on average about $50 billion of Monopoly money every year—coincidentally about the same as the amount of new U.S. currency (excluding $100 bills) issued in 2010. Every new game has bills totaling 20,580 Monopoly dollars. At a cost of about 15 U.S. dollars per set, this "money" would be a good deal if you could buy things other than Boardwalk and Park Place with it. Unfortunately, attempts to pay for groceries, books, or rent with this particular form of money have been unsuccessful. And that's probably a good thing. Since the mid-1930s, Parker Brothers has sold more than 200 million Monopoly games, containing more than 3 trillion Monopoly dollars.[1]

When we pay for our purchases in the real world, we have lots of choices: crisp new $20 bills, credit cards, debit cards, checks, or more complicated electronic methods. Regardless of the choice we make, we are using *money* to buy our food and clothes and pay our bills. To make sure we can do it, thousands of people work through every night, for the payments system really never sleeps. And the volume of payments is astounding. The Federal Reserve reports that in 2009 there were 109 billion noncash payments made in the United States, 22 percent of which were paper checks. That means something like 95 million paper checks and 340 million electronic payments were processed on an average business day. And, regardless of how you choose to pay, the path that the payment follows is pretty complicated.

To understand why money is so important to the smooth functioning of the economy and how it improves everyone's well-being, we need to understand exactly what

[1]For more fun facts about Monopoly, see *www.monopoly.com*.

money is. Just why is a $20 bill issued by the U.S. government much more useful than $20 in Monopoly money? Furthermore, to quantify the impact of money on the economy, we need to be able to measure it. Those are the goals of this chapter: to understand what money is, how we use it, and how we measure it.

Money and How We Use It

When people use the word *money* in conversation, they mean many different things. Someone who "makes lots of money" has a high income; a person who "has lots of money" is wealthy. We will use the word *money* in a narrower, specialized sense to mean anything that can readily be used to make economic transactions. Formally defined, **money** is *an asset that is generally accepted as payment for goods and services or repayment of debt.* Income, in contrast, is a flow of earnings over time. **Wealth** is the value of assets minus liabilities. Money is one of those assets, albeit a very minor one.

Money, in the sense we are talking about, has three characteristics. It is (1) a means of payment, (2) a unit of account, and (3) a store of value. The first of these characteristics is the most important. Anything that is used as a means of payment must be a store of value and thus is very likely to become a unit of account. Let's see why this is so.

Means of Payment

INFORMATION

The primary use of money is as a **means of payment**. Most people insist on payment in money at the time a good or service is supplied because the alternatives just don't work very well. Barter, in which a good or service is exchanged directly for another good or service, requires that a plumber who needs food find a grocer who needs a plumbing repair. Relying on this "double coincidence of wants" surely causes the economy to run less smoothly. The plumber could pay for his breakfast cereal with a "promise" of plumbing services, which the grocer could then transfer to someone else. But while it would be possible to certify the plumber's trustworthiness, taking payment in money is easier. Money finalizes payments so that buyers and sellers have no further claim on each other. That is money's special role. In fact, so long as a buyer has money, there is nothing more the seller needs to know.

As economies have become more complex and physically dispersed, reducing the likelihood that a seller will have good information about a buyer, the need for money has grown. The increase in both the number of transactions and the number of potential buyers and sellers (the vast majority of whom may never see one another) argues for something that makes payment final and whose value is easily verified. That something is money.

Unit of Account

Just as we measure length using feet and inches, we measure value using dollars and cents. Money is the **unit of account** that we use to quote prices and record debts. We could also refer to it as a standard of value.

"*I suppose mere promises would not suffice.*"

SOURCE: 1987 © Stan Hunt/The New Yorker Collection/www.cartoonbank.com.

YOUR FINANCIAL WORLD
Debit Cards versus Credit Cards

When you go shopping, should you pay with a credit card or a debit card? To decide, you need to understand the difference between the two. First make sure you know which one of your cards is which. Usually an ATM card (the one that you got from the bank when you opened your checking account) is a debit card. But check to make sure.

What's the real difference, from the shopper's point of view? A debit card works just like a check, only faster. When you write a paper check, it usually takes a day or two to go through the system. A debit card transaction goes through right away. The electronic message gets to your bank on the same day, and your account is debited immediately. So, if you want to use your debit card, your account balance has to be higher than the payment you want to make. During and after the financial crisis that began in 2007, debit card use sharply outpaced credit card activity, as lenders and borrowers sought to slow the expansion (or even reduce the outstanding level) of household debt.

A credit card creates a deferred payment. The issuer agrees to make the payment for you, and you repay the debt later. That sounds good, but there's a catch. If you're late paying, there's a late fee. And if you don't pay the entire debt every month, you pay interest on the balance—at what is usually a very high interest rate. If you do pay your entire credit card debt every month, however, there is no late fee and no interest charge. Hence, you get an interest-free loan from the time you make the purchase to the time you pay the balance. If you can pay off your credit cards in full and on time, it's to your advantage to use them.

Credit cards have another advantage over debit cards. They help you to build a credit history, which you'll need when the time comes to buy a car or a house. Because debit cards are just extensions of your bank account, they don't show potential lenders that you are creditworthy. In fact, some businesses, like car rental companies, require their customers to use credit cards for this reason.

Having a unit of account is an incredible convenience. Remember from microeconomics that prices provide the information consumers and producers use to ensure that resources are allocated to their best uses. What matters are the *relative* prices of goods and services. When the price of one product is higher than the price of another, that product is worth more to both producers and consumers. Using dollars makes these comparisons easy. Imagine what would happen if we needed to compute relative prices for each pair of goods. With two goods, we would need only one price. With three goods, we would need three prices. But with 100 goods, we would need 4,950 prices, and with 10,000 goods (substantially less than the 40,000 products in a typical supermarket), we would need nearly 50 million prices.[2] Using money as a yardstick and quoting all prices in dollars certainly is easier.

Store of Value

For money to function as a means of payment, it has to be a **store of value**, too. That is, if we are going to use money to pay for goods and services, then it must retain its worth from day to day. Sellers are much less likely to accept things that are perishable, like milk or lettuce. So the means of payment has to be durable and capable of transferring purchasing power from one day to the next. Paper **currency** does degrade with use ($1 bills have an estimated life span of 71 months in circulation), but regardless of its physical condition, it is usually accepted at face value in transactions.

Of course, money is not the only store of value. We hold our wealth in lots of other forms—stocks, bonds, houses, even cars. Many of these are actually preferable to money as stores of value. Some, like bonds, pay higher interest rates than money.

[2]The general formula is that for *n* goods we need $n(n - 1)/2$ prices, so for 10,000 goods, the number would be 10,000 (9,999)/2 = 49,995,000.

Others, like stocks, offer the potential for appreciation in nominal value, which money does not. Still others, like houses, deliver other services over time. Yet we all hold money because money is liquid. **Liquidity** *is a measure of the ease with which an asset can be turned into a means of payment,* namely money. For example, a bond is much more liquid than a house because it is so much easier and cheaper to sell. The more costly it is to convert an asset into money, the less liquid it is. Because constantly transforming assets into money every time we wished to make a purchase would be extremely costly, we keep some money around.

Financial institutions often use a more specific term—**market liquidity**—for their ability to sell assets for money. A second, related concept—**funding liquidity**—refers to their ability to borrow money to buy securities or make loans. For financial institutions, liquidity in both those senses is critical to their daily operations: A shortfall of either type can lead to their outright failure (see Lessons from the Crisis: Market Liquidity, Funding Liquidity, and Making Markets on page 32).

The Functions of Money

1. Means of payment: Used in exchange for goods and services.
2. Unit of account: Used to quote prices.
3. Store of value: Used to transfer purchasing power into the future.

The Payments System

The **payments system** is the web of arrangements that allow for the exchange of goods and services, as well as assets, among different people. Because the efficient operation of our economy depends on the payments system, a critical public policy concern is that it function well. As we will see in Part IV, that is why central banks are directly involved.

Money is at the heart of the payments system. Whether we realize it or not, virtually every transaction we engage in involves the use of money at some point. Let's go through all the possible methods of payment to see how the system works.

Commodity and Fiat Monies

The first means of payment were things with intrinsic value. These **commodity monies** included everything from silk in China to butter in Norway, whale teeth in Fiji, and salt in Venice. All these things had value even if they were not used as money. The worth of a block of salt, for instance, came from its value as a preservative. But successful commodity monies had other characteristics: They were usable in some form by most people; they could be made into standardized quantities; they were durable; they had high value relative to their weight and size so that they were easily transportable; and they were divisible into small units so that they were easy to trade. For most of human history, gold has been the most common commodity money. It is widely accepted as payment; can be purified and made into standard weight units like coins; and is extremely durable because it does not corrode or tarnish. Moreover, gold is rare (there is only enough in existence to fill about one-third of the Washington

A Revolutionary War "continental" issued by the Continental Congress in 1775. The new government of the United States eventually printed $200 million worth, and by 1781 they no longer had any value.

An assignat issued by the French Revolutionary Government in 1793. Faced with the need to finance wars and food shortages, the government eventually printed 40 billion of them and by the late 1790s they were worthless.

Monument with solid gold), so it has high value relative to weight. And it can be cut into smaller pieces without losing its value.

In 1656, a Swede named Johan Palmstruck founded the Stockholm Banco. Five years later he issued Europe's first paper money.[3] At the time, the Swedish currency was copper ingots, which works poorly as money because of its low value per unit of weight. (Today, copper is worth only about 20 cents per ounce, or roughly 1/100 the value of silver and 1/7,000 the value of gold.) Thus, easy-to-handle paper was welcomed, at least at first.

After a few years of printing paper currency, Palmstruck and his sponsor, the King of Sweden, became overly enamored of the new money. The king needed to finance some wars he was fighting, so he convinced Palmstruck to print more and more notes. Because the bills were redeemable on demand for metal, the system worked only as long as people believed there was enough metal sitting in Palmstruck's vaults. As the number of notes increased, Swedes lost confidence in them and started to redeem them for the metal they supposedly stood for. But Palmstruck had issued too many notes, and his bank failed.

Other people tried issuing paper money during the early 1700s. Eventually governments got into the act. In 1775, the newly formed Continental Congress of the United States of America issued "continentals" to finance the Revolutionary War. Twenty years later, revolutionary France issued the "assignat." Lacking any other source of funding for their wars, both governments issued huge quantities of the currencies, and both currencies eventually became worthless.

The reaction was predictable: People became suspicious of government-issued paper money. But governments need funds and will use all available means to get them. In the United States, the Civil War put pressure on government finances and the two warring parties had little choice but to issue paper money to pay for salaries and supplies. Beginning in 1862, both the Confederate and the Union governments printed and used paper money with no explicit backing. The North's "greenbacks" are still legal tender in the United States, but collectors are the only people who value the Confederate currency.

After the Civil War, the United States reverted to the use of gold as money. Both gold coins and notes backed by gold circulated well into the 20th century. Today, though, we

---

[3]The Chinese were the real monetary pioneers, issuing their first paper currency in the 7th century, 1,000 years before the Europeans.

use paper money—high-quality paper, nicely engraved, with lots of special security features. This type of currency is called **fiat money**, because its value comes from government decree, or *fiat*. Some countries print notes that are durable and attractive, bearing famous works of art in multiple colors. The Australians pioneered making notes out of plastic. But in all cases the money has very little intrinsic worth, and the cost of production is only a small fraction of the face value. The U.S. Treasury's Bureau of Engraving and Printing pays about 9 cents to print a note, regardless of whether it's a $1 or a $100 bill.

Why are we willing to accept these bills as payment for goods or in settlement of debts? There are two reasons. First, we take them because we believe we can use them in the future; someone else will take them from us. Second, the law says we must accept them. That is, the U.S. government stands behind its paper money. Since the first greenbacks were issued in 1862, all U.S. currency has borne the short and simple phrase "This note is legal tender for all debts, public and private." In practice, this means that private businesses accept dollar bills as payment. More important, the U.S. government is committed to accepting the currency it has issued in settlement of debts. We will always be able to pay our taxes in dollars.

Today, some critics of fiat money advocate a return to the gold standard.[4] Their fear is that governments will issue too much paper money, threatening its value and use. Even if a government promises today to limit fiat money, it can renege on that commitment in the future, casting doubt today on the money's value. This credibility problem exemplifies the challenge of making policy **time consistent**.[5] Policy lacks time consistency whenever policymakers have a strong incentive to give up in the future on their current promises or plans.

Supporters of a gold standard argue that removing future policy discretion will ensure a reliable store of value, resulting in greater economic and price stability (Core Principle 5). They view the government's ability to tinker with the volume of fiat money as an unnecessary source of risk. Yet, a gold standard also may not be time consistent. For example, in a crisis, governments can renege on their commitment to use gold as a unit of account. Indeed, many countries, including the United States, exited the gold standard during the Great Depression to restore economic stability (see Chapter 19, Applying the Concept: The Gold Standard: An Exchange-Rate Regime Whose Time Has Passed).[6]

Ultimately, if a fiat currency is to outperform a commodity currency, policymakers must be credibly committed—by law or custom—to limiting the volume in circulation. As long as the government stands behind its paper money and doesn't issue too much of it, we will use it. In the end, money is about trust.

Checks

Checks are another way of paying for things. Unlike currency, the checks you use to pay your rent and electric bill are not legal tender. In fact, they aren't money at all. A **check** is just an instruction to the bank to take funds from your account and transfer them to the person or firm whose name you have written in the "Pay to the order of" line. Thus, when you give someone a check in exchange for a good or service, it is

---

[4]See, for example, Ron Paul, *End the Fed* (New York: Grand Central Publishing, 2009).

[5]Acting in a time-consistent fashion is a big challenge in many settings, from parenting to military strategy. In the world of finance, where expectations about the future (including future policy) are critical, time consistency plays a major role in government oversight of the financial system (Chapter 14) and in monetary policy (Part IV).

[6]For a policymaker's assessment of the gold standard, see the first in the series of online lectures by Federal Reserve Chairman Ben Bernanke at *www.federalreserve.gov/newsevents/lectures/origins-and-mission.htm*.

not a final payment—at least, not in the same sense as currency. Instead, your check sets in motion a series of transactions that eventually lead to the final payment.

Here are the usual steps. You hand the check over to a merchant, who then takes it to the bank. Depending on the arrangement, the bank will credit the amount of the check to the merchant's account either immediately or with a short lag. At the end of the day, the bank sends an electronic image of the check through the check-clearing system along with the other millions of images of checks to be processed that night by a check-processing center run by the Federal Reserve or a private check clearing-house. (The first check clearinghouses were pubs where bank employees met to have a drink and exchange checks.) At the center, the check is transferred from the bank that sent it in to the bank on which it is written—your bank. The account of the bank presenting the check is credited, and the account of the bank on which the check is written is debited (see Figure 2.1). This is the step that uses *money*.

Finally, on receipt of the check, your bank debits your account. (If the balance in your account is insufficient to cover the check, your bank has a few days to return it to

Figure 2.1   The Path of a Paper Check

YOUR FINANCIAL WORLD

Paper Checks Become Digital Images

For at least 30 years, there have been predictions that paper checks would disappear. Credit cards, ATM machines, debit cards, automatic bill payment, and Internet banking were all supposed to get rid of them. Instead, Check 21—the Check Clearing for the 21st Century Act—went into effect in 2004, lowering the cost of making payments by check.

Banks are thrilled. Until the fall of 2004, the check verification and payment process required commercial banks to transport all paper checks to and from a Federal Reserve Bank, and eventually back to the people who wrote them. Paper checks were legal proof of payment, so customers wanted them back. But transporting tons and tons of checks around the country was an expensive headache for banks.

Check 21 gives banks the leeway to process checks electronically. Instead of shipping paper across the country, banks transmit digital images of each check that was written. These images create "substitute checks," and have the same legal standing as the original checks.

Processing checks electronically is definitely cheaper. With the volume of paper checks dwindling and most checks now clearing electronically, the Federal Reserve has reduced the number of its processing centers to 1—down from 45 before Check 21. By 2011, more than 97 percent of checks processed through Federal Reserve Banks were in the form of an electronic image. And experts estimate that Check 21 directly reduced the annual cost of payments by

$1.2 billion, with additional indirect benefits to businesses and consumers of $2 billion.

Reducing the risks of physically transporting checks was one of the big reasons for the passage of Check 21. For several days following the September 11, 2001, terrorist attacks, only military planes were allowed to fly in U.S. airspace and that disrupted the check transportation system eventually grounding $47 billion worth of paper checks.

Speeding up paper check processing does have one downside: People can't write checks with the expectation that they will have a day or two to make a deposit to cover it. There is no more float. The new rules shrink the time between when a check is written and when the account is debited, especially for out-of-town checks.*

For more details on Check 21, payments system development and policies, see the Federal Reserve Board's payment system website www.federalreserve.gov/paymentsys.htm.

*Just because banks are able to move checks through the clearing system more quickly doesn't mean that they are going to offer the depositor more timely access to the funds. In an attempt to reduce fraud, banks restrict access to funds from so-called high-risk checks, such as those for more than $5,000 that are deposited into newly opened accounts, for as long as 9 business days. If you have to shift large quantities of funds and use them quickly, it is important to find out the policies of the financial intermediaries involved before you do it.

Front of Substitute Check

Back of Substitute Check

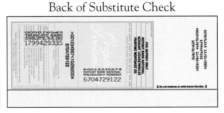

The front of the substitute check includes the following: "This is a legal copy of your check. You can use it the same way you would use the original check."

the sending bank, so the transaction isn't actually final until that period has passed.) In the past all paper checks were returned to the people who originally wrote them. Today, they are scanned and customers can view electronic images on their bank's websites. (See Your Financial World: Paper Checks Become Digital Images.)

Since 2000, the share of checks in the value of noncash transactions has fallen from 58 percent to 23 percent, but paper checks are still with us for several reasons. A canceled check is legal proof of payment and, in many states, laws require banks to return checks to customers. Then there is force of habit. Over time, people may get used to receiving bank statements without their checks, but so far many people still like to receive the processed checks (which can now be copies of check images, as explained in Your Financial World, page 30). Finally, the new electronic mechanisms for clearing checks have lowered costs and kept checks as an important, if dwindling, means of payment.

Electronic Payments

The third and final method of payment is electronic. We are all familiar with credit cards and debit cards. A less well-known form of payment is electronic funds transfers. While there are a large number of credit and debit card transactions, electronic funds transfers account for the bulk of the $40 trillion worth of noncash, noncheck payments made each year in the United States.

What is the difference between debit cards and credit cards? A **debit card** works the same way as a check in that it provides the bank with instructions to transfer funds from the cardholder's account directly to a merchant's account. There is usually a charge for this; the processor of the payment takes a fee based on the size of the transaction.

A **credit card** is a promise by a bank to lend the cardholder money with which to make purchases. When a shopper buys a pair of shoes with a credit card, the shoe store's bank account receives payment immediately, but the money that is used for payment does not belong to the buyer. Instead, the bank that issued the credit card makes the payment, creating a loan the cardholder must repay. For this reason, credit cards do not represent money; rather, they represent access to someone else's money.

With relatively rapid growth in the use of debit cards since 2007, the number of debit card transactions is now about 75 percent greater than the number of credit card payments. But in terms of dollar amount, the typical credit card transaction is more than twice as large as that of the typical debit card; as a result, the total value of credit card payments is still larger, by about 35 percent. And while checks are used less than half as often as credit and debit cards, the average check size is far larger, so the total value of payments by check is still nearly 10 times greater than that for the two card types combined.

Electronic funds transfers are movements of funds directly from one account to another. These transactions are used extensively by banks and are becoming increasingly popular for individuals as well. For individuals, the most common form is the **automated clearinghouse transaction (ACH)**, which is generally used for recurring payments such as paychecks and utility bills. Some merchants use them for one-time transactions as well. ACH transactions are just like checks except that they are entirely electronic. Your bank account is debited or credited automatically, and you receive periodic notifications of the activity in your account. Having surpassed the value of checks in recent years, the value of ACH payments now accounts for more than one-half of the value of all noncash payments.

Banks use electronic transfers to handle transactions among themselves. The most common method is to send money through a system maintained by the Federal Reserve, called Fedwire. The volume and value of payments made through this system are substantial. On a typical day in 2012, the system completed 524,000 transactions with a total value of about $2.4 trillion.

Retail businesses, together with their banks, are experimenting with a variety of new methods of electronic payment. One is the **stored-value card**, which looks like a credit or debit card except that it doesn't bear your name. To use one, you go to the bank or ATM machine and put the card into an electronic device that transfers funds from your checking account to your card. Then you take the card to a merchant who

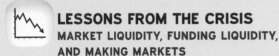

LESSONS FROM THE CRISIS
MARKET LIQUIDITY, FUNDING LIQUIDITY, AND MAKING MARKETS

A "market maker" in stocks, bonds, or other securities is usually a financial institution that buys and sells securities on behalf of clients. If buy orders exceed sell orders for a particular security, the market maker must be able to act as the seller to clear the market. Therefore, market makers usually hold inventories of the specific financial instruments in which they trade, and they borrow to maintain inventories at adequate levels.

Market liquidity—the ability to sell assets—and *funding liquidity*—the ability to borrow money—are both needed to make financial markets function smoothly. If a loss of funding liquidity prevents market makers from holding adequate inventories, trading and market liquidity suffer. Conversely, if market liquidity for some financial instruments declines, the prices of those instruments will fall as they become less attractive to investors; resulting concerns about the safety of the market makers that hold the assets with falling prices may reduce their ability to borrow.

A sudden loss of liquidity was central to the 2007–2009 financial crisis. Before the crisis, many financial institutions relied on short-term borrowing to hold long-term financial instruments because their managers believed that funding liquidity would remain readily available. They also believed that markets would always be liquid—that is, they would always be able to sell the securities and loans that they held. They were wrong on both counts.

In the summer of 2007, investors began to doubt the value of a wide class of securities. As a result, market liquidity for those instruments disappeared, and financial institutions that held them faced large potential losses. In turn, funding liquidity for these institutions evaporated as the potential losses caused their lenders to worry about their safety.

This double "liquidity shock" led many financial institutions to increase cash holdings that they might otherwise have lent to others. Reduced loan supply intensified the vicious spiral of dwindling liquidity and falling securities prices. The private financial system as a whole could not provide sufficient market liquidity or funding liquidity to satisfy heightened demands.

One lesson from the financial crisis is clear: Liquidity is a highly valuable resource that can disappear when it is most needed, so it should not be taken for granted. Even large and seemingly wealthy financial firms can fail if liquidity evaporates.

Liquidity Spiral

Price Decline of a Security

Funding Liquidity Decline

Market Liquidity Decline

In the accompanying figure, a decline of the price of a security makes it more costly for a financial institution to make a market in that security, resulting in a decline of market liquidity. That decline makes the security less attractive to investors, further reducing its price. If the price falls sufficiently, concern about the well-being of market makers diminishes their funding liquidity, advancing a vicious cycle.

has a reader that is capable of deducting funds from the card and depositing them directly into the store's account. The stuff on the card is in fact money, and the system can be set up so that if you lose your card, its current value can be canceled.

Recently, the use of such prepaid cards has grown rapidly, but they still have limited usefulness. The New York City Metropolitan Transit Authority and other city transit systems sell stored-value cards, but it's hard to buy anything with them other than subway and bus rides. The same is true of long-distance phone cards and gift cards sold by chain stores like Barnes & Noble. Attempts to implement the stored-value card more broadly haven't worked very well because most merchants lack the hardware to read the cards.

E-money is another method of payment. It can be used instead of a credit or debit card to pay for purchases on the Internet or via mobile phone. You open an account by transferring funds to the issuer of the e-money. Then, when you are shopping online, you instruct the issuer to send your e-money to the merchant, or in the case of the mobile phone set-up, you can transfer funds at any time to other users of the service, including merchants.

E-money is really a form of private money. It is not issued or guaranteed by the government, so you can't use it to pay your taxes. It's hard to even define what the term *e-money* means. One definition that seems helpful is "monetary value, as represented by a claim on the issuer, which is (a) stored on an electronic device, (b) issued on receipt of funds, and (c) accepted as a means of payment by persons other than the issuer."[7]

The most successful example of e-money today is the M-Pesa in Kenya (see In the News: Airtime is Money). In 2007, a mobile phone company began allowing Kenyans to deposit, withdraw, and transfer funds using their phones. Just five years later, mobile money transfer subscriptions reached 19 million, covering about 70 percent of all mobile phones, an extraordinarily rapid adoption that highlights the value of the service.

The M-Pesa has greatly improved access to the financial system, allowing Kenya to technologically leapfrog the more traditional payments mechanisms of far wealthier countries. For many Kenyans, their cell phone substitutes for a conventional bank account. That may be a sign of the future: According to the World Bank, as of 2012, more than 50 percent of the world's adults—2.5 billion people—do not have a bank account. Even in the wealthy United States, about 12 percent of adults (or about 30 million people), do not have a bank account.[8]

So far, however, e-money has made few inroads in the United States, and its prospects remain questionable. Will individuals develop enough trust in e-money to be willing to use it? Will merchants install the equipment to handle it? Who will be allowed to issue e-money? Still, the day may come when you can park your car and pay the parking meter by simply punching a series of numbers into your cell phone that transfers e-money issued by your phone provider to the city government that owns the parking meter.

The Future of Money

Let's speculate about what might happen to money and each of its three functions in the future. As a *means of payment,* it has already undergone big changes. The time is rapidly approaching when safe and secure systems for payment will use virtually no money at all.

We will always need money as a *unit of account* in which to quote values and prices; the efficiency of quoting prices in commonly understood terms isn't going to change. But the question is, how many units of account will we need? Today, many countries have their own currencies, which give rise to their own units of account. In the future, though, there will be little reason to maintain different units of account across different countries. Price systems will be more like systems of weights and measures. Today, there are two commonly used systems of weights and measures: English (ounces and yards) and metric (grams and meters). We will likely see a similar sort of standardization of money and a dramatic reduction in the number of units of account.

Finally, money as a *store of value* is clearly on the way out. With the advances in financial markets, many financial instruments have become highly liquid. They are easily bought and sold and can be converted into a means of payment quickly and cheaply,

[7]This definition comes from Directive 2000/46 of the European Parliament and the Council of 18 September 2000, "On the Taking Up, Pursuit and Prudential Supervision of the Business of Electronic Money Institutions," *Official Journal of the European Communities,* 275/39, 27 October 2000.

[8]For details on worldwide financial access, see the World Bank's *The Little Data Book on Financial Inclusion 2012.*

IN THE NEWS
Airtime Is Money: The Other Type of Mobile Money

The Economist

The Use of Pre-Paid Mobile-Phone Minutes as a Currency

January 19, 2013

Mobile money in Africa comes in different flavours. The sophisticated sort, exemplified by services such as M-Pesa in Kenya, allows account-holders to transfer legal tender electronically to fellow account-holders by entering commands on a mobile phone. Popular though such services are, they have not stopped an older form of mobile money flourishing. This sort uses pre-paid mobile-airtime minutes as a de facto currency that can be transferred between phones, exchanged for cash with dealers who rent out phones, or bartered for goods and services.

Pre-paid minutes can be swapped for cash or spent in shops most easily in Côte d'Ivoire, Egypt, Ghana and Uganda, says Chris Chan of Tranglo, a Malaysian firm that facilitates "airtime remittances" to mobile phones. Airtime

Can airtime minutes be used as a form of currency?

while providing a better store of value than money. These instruments and the financial markets in which they trade are the subject of the next chapter. For now, though, we can conclude that in the future, there will almost surely be less and less money.

One caution is in order. As we look into the future and try to discern what will happen to money, we should remember that 150 years ago there was virtually no paper currency in circulation. The first credit card was issued in the early 1950s; the first ATM was installed around 1970. Not until the mid-1990s could we shop via the Internet. Forecasting most of these developments, as well as any other trend in technology, is nearly impossible. After all, who could have predicted even 20 years ago that today we would be able to check our bank balances, buy and sell stocks, and pay our utility bills 24 hours a day, seven days a week from the comfort of our homes?

is commonly used as money in Nigeria, too. Hannes Van Rensburg, Visa's boss for sub-Saharan Africa, says this is partly because regulators there have made it difficult for banks to offer the newer form of mobile money.

But even in places like Kenya, airtime minutes are still being used as currency. Unlike mobile money, airtime's value does not rely directly on a government's stability or ability to hold down inflation by, say, showing restraint printing money. Opening a mobile-money account typically requires waiting for days after showing your ID. In contrast, airtime can often be purchased and sent immediately and anonymously. Because many telecoms firms in Africa and elsewhere transfer minutes nationwide free of charge, airtime is especially useful for settling small debts.

In Zimbabwe, for example, American banknotes have largely replaced the hyperinflation-ravaged Zimbabwean dollar. American coins are scarce, however, so pretty much everybody in Zimbabwe transfers airtime in their place at least occasionally, says Oswell Binha, president of the Zimbabwe National Chamber of Commerce in Harare. Zimbabwean shoppers are tired of being given sweets in lieu of change, so shopkeepers who give airtime rather than yet another "$0.63-worth of chocolates" have a competitive advantage, Mr Binha says. Yo! Time, a Harare-based start-up that simplifies these retailer-to-shopper airtime payouts, processes more than 9,000 payouts a day for clients; six months ago the figure was 2,000.

The use of airtime as currency is fuelled by the growing ease of sending minutes abroad. A Dublin firm called ezetop, for example, sells airtime for 238 telecoms firms via the web, text messaging and about 450,000 shops in 20 countries. The value of international airtime transfers has doubled from $350m in 2011 to $700m in 2012, estimates Berg Insight, a consultancy.

Some authorities are concerned about airtime's use as money. As one industry executive puts it, network operators are, in effect, "issuing their own currency" and setting its exchange rate; central banks tend to dislike such things. Others worry that airtime could be used by criminal or extremist groups to move money covertly. According to a senior official at the Financial Action Task Force (FATF), an intergovernmental body in Paris, it appears that some groups buy top-up scratch cards in one country and sell the airtime in another.

The FATF is studying over 50 instances of "suspicious" dealing in airtime from the past two years and plans to issue new guidelines early this year. It is likely that countries and firms will be asked to set rules to obtain more data on buyers and sellers. Transfer caps may also end up lower. But such rules must be set against the good that tradable airtime still does.

SOURCE: © The Economist Newspaper Limited, London (January 19, 2013).

LESSONS OF THE ARTICLE

Almost anything can be a currency, but people prefer currencies that provide a reasonable store of value. And they prefer payments mechanisms that are efficient, anonymous, and allow for big and small transfers. If there is a better currency or payments technology, people can switch. In the story, mobile minutes are attractive for both reasons, beating currencies with uncertain storage value and replacing both cash and coin.

Measuring Money

Changes in the amount of money in the economy are related to changes in interest rates, economic growth, and most important, **inflation**. Inflation is the pace at which prices in general are increasing over time—and the **inflation rate** is a measure of that process.[9] With inflation, you need more units of money to buy the same basket of goods you bought a month or a year ago. Put another way, inflation makes money less valuable. And the primary cause of inflation is the issuance of too much money. When the

[9]The terms "inflation" and "inflation rate" are often used interchangeably. We will refer to inflation as the process of prices rising, and inflation rate as the measurement of the process. The relationship between these terms is analogous to that between "heat" and "temperature." The second is the measure of the first.

Figure 2.2 The Liquidity Spectrum

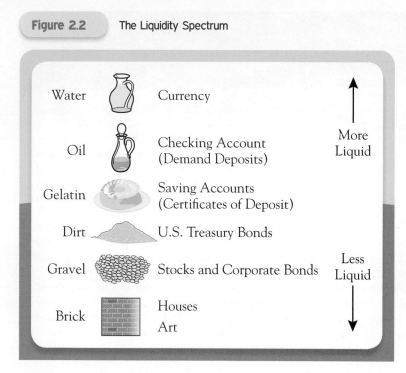

Water	Currency	
Oil	Checking Account (Demand Deposits)	More Liquid ↑
Gelatin	Saving Accounts (Certificates of Deposit)	
Dirt	U.S. Treasury Bonds	
Gravel	Stocks and Corporate Bonds	Less Liquid
Brick	Houses Art	↓

Liquidity is the ease with which you can turn an asset into a means of payment without loss of value.

Continental Congress issued too much currency to finance the Revolutionary War, the number of continentals people needed to purchase food and shelter rose dramatically. Continentals became less valuable. So the value of the means of payment depends on how much of it is circulating.

To use the insight that money growth is somehow related to inflation, we must be able to measure how much money is circulating. This is no easy task. Let's start with money's primary function, as a means of payment. If that were the definition of money, we would measure the quantity of money as the quantity of currency in circulation—an unrealistically limited measure, because there are many ways to complete transactions (effect final payment) without using currency.

A reasonable alternative would be to consider a broad category of financial assets and sort them by their degree of liquidity. That is, we could rank them by the ease with which they can be converted into a means of payment, arranging them along a spectrum from the most liquid (currency) to the least liquid (art, antique cars, and the like). Figure 2.2 shows what our liquidity spectrum would look like.

Once we have our list, we could draw a line and include everything on one side of the line in our measure of money. Over the years, figuring out just where to draw the line has proven very difficult, especially since the introduction of new types of checking accounts. There really is no perfect solution. Instead, we have drawn the line in a number of different places and computed several measures of money, called the **monetary aggregates**: M1 and M2.[10]

Table 2.1 shows the components of the two monetary aggregates as defined by the Federal Reserve, along with the size of each as of March 2013. Let's go through each one to understand how it is constructed. **M1**, the narrowest definition of money, includes only currency and various deposit accounts on which people can write checks. These are the most liquid assets in the financial system. The components of M1 include *currency in the hands of the public,* which is the quantity of dollar bills outstanding excluding the ones in the vaults of banks; *travelers' checks* issued by travel companies, banks, and credit card companies, which are guaranteed by the issuer and usually work just like cash; **demand deposits** at commercial banks, which are standard checking accounts that pay no interest; and other checkable deposits, which are deposits in checking accounts that pay interest.

M2 equals all of M1 plus assets that cannot be used directly as a means of payment and are difficult to turn into currency quickly. These assets in M2 include small-denomination **time deposits** (less than $100,000) that cannot be withdrawn without

---

[10]On March 23, 2006, the Federal Reserve Board ceased collection and publication of a third monetary aggregate, M3. In announcing their decision, officials wrote: "M3 does not appear to convey any additional information about economic activity that is not already embodied in M2 and has not played a role in the monetary policy process for many years."

Table 2.1	The Monetary Aggregates

Monetary Aggregates			Value as of March 2013 (US$ billions)
M1	=	Currency in the hands of the public	1102.5
	+	Traveler's Checks	3.8
	+	Demand Deposits	906.5
	+	Other Checkable Deposits	450.4
		Total M1	**2463.2**
M2	=	M1	
	+	Small-denomination time deposits	600.2
	+	Savings Deposits and Money Market Deposit Accounts	6762.9
	+	Retail Money Market Mutual Fund Shares	634.0
		Total M2	**10460.3**

SOURCE: *Board of Governors of the Federal Reserve.*

advance notice; *savings deposits,* including *money-market deposit accounts,* which pay interest and offer limited check-writing privileges; *retail money-market mutual fund shares,* or shares in funds that collect relatively small sums from individuals, pool them together, and invest them in short-term marketable debt issued by large corporations. Money-market mutual fund shares can be issued by nonbank financial intermediaries, such as brokerage firms. They do carry check-writing privileges. M2 is the most commonly quoted monetary aggregate in the United States, because its movements are most closely related to interest rates and economic growth.

To clarify what the monetary aggregates mean, let's compare their size to the size of the economy. In the first quarter of 2013, nominal U.S. **gross domestic product (GDP)** was $16.5 trillion. Putting that number into the same units as those in Table 2.1, that's $16,500 billion. So GDP is more than six times larger than M1 and nearly 60 percent larger than M2.

Which one of the Ms should we use to understand inflation? That's a difficult question whose answer has changed over time. Until the early 1980s, economists and policymakers looked at M1. But with the introduction of substitutes for standard checking accounts, especially money-market mutual fund shares, M1 became less useful than M2. These innovations enabled people to shift their balances out of the noninterest-bearing accounts in M1 and into accounts that paid interest. As Table 2.1 shows, demand deposits and other checkable deposits in M1 total about $1.4 trillion, which represents about 8 percent of GDP. By comparison, the savings deposits, money-market deposit accounts, and retail money-market mutual fund shares in M2 total $7.4 trillion, representing nearly 45 percent of GDP. M1 is no longer a useful measure of money.

Looking at Figure 2.3 on page 39, you can see that from 1960 to 1980 the growth rates of the two measures of money moved together. After 1980, however, M1 behaved very differently from M2. Here's what happened. In the late 1970s and early 1980s, inflation climbed to over 10 percent for a few years. Needless to say, people who had money in zero-interest checking accounts were upset. Their money was losing value at a rapid rate. They went looking for ways to get checking services along with interest. Soon

TOOLS OF THE TRADE

The Consumer Price Index

Understanding how to measure inflation is central to understanding economics and finance. Most of us keep a close eye on measures like the Consumer Price Index (CPI) to help gauge the value of our salary increases or the purchasing power of the money we hold. And adjusting interest rates for inflation is critical for making investment decisions. (See Chapter 4.)

The CPI is designed to answer the following question: How much more would it cost for people to purchase today the same basket of goods and services that they actually bought at some fixed time in the past?

To calculate the CPI, every few years statisticians at the Bureau of Labor Statistics (BLS) survey people to find out what they bought. This gives us the basket of goods and services bought by the typical consumer. Next, every month the BLS collects information on the prices of thousands of goods and services—everything from breakfast cereal to gasoline to washing machines to the cost of cable television. Combining the expenditure and price surveys allows statisticians to compute the current cost of the basket. Finally, this current cost is compared to a benchmark to yield an index. And the percentage change in this index is a measure of inflation.

To see how this works, let's look at an example. Assume people spend 25 percent of their income on food, 50 percent on housing and 25 percent on transportation. That's the survey information. Examples of the prices are in Table 2.2. Importantly, these are the prices of exactly the same bundle of food, the same size and quality of housing, and the same transportation for each year.

Using the numbers in Table 2.2 we can compute the cost of the basket of goods in each year:

Cost of the basket in 2014

= 0.25 × **Price of food** + 0.5 × **Price of housing**

+ 0.25 × **Price of transportation**

= 0.25 × $100 + 0.5 × $200 + 0.25 × $100

= $150

And for 2015, we get $165. Choosing 2014 as the base year, the index level in each year equals

$$CPI = \frac{\text{Cost of the basket in current year}}{\text{Cost of the basket in base year}} \times 100$$

The result of this computation is the fifth column of the table.

Finally, we can use the index number to compute the inflation rate from the previous year. From 2014 to 2015, this means that

$$\textbf{Inflation Rate 2015} = \frac{\textbf{CPI in 2015} - \textbf{CPI in 2014}}{\textbf{CPI in 2014}} \times 100$$

Using the numbers from Table 2.2 to compute the inflation rate in 2015, we get that

$$\frac{110 - 100}{100} \times 100 = 10\%$$

and for 2016 the result is

$$\frac{120 - 110}{110} \times 100 = 9.1\%$$

(These numbers are just for illustration. The U.S. inflation rate is closer to 2 percent.)

Inflation measured using the CPI tells us how much more money we need to give someone to restore the purchasing power they had in the earlier period when the survey was done. But adjustments in wages based on fixed-expenditure-weight inflation indices like the CPI are known to overcompensate people in an unintended way. This overstatement of inflation comes from what is known as *substitution bias.* Because inflation is not uniform, the prices of some products will increase by more than the prices of others. People can escape some of the inflation by *substituting* goods and services that have sustained less inflation for those that have sustained more. By assuming that any substitution makes people worse off, the index *overstates* the impact of price changes. To address this problem, and take into account changes in spending patterns, the Bureau of Labor Statistics in 2002 began changing the weights every two years. As a result, today's CPI is a more accurate measure of inflation than it used to be.

| Table 2.2 | Computing the Consumer Price Index |

Year	Price of Food	Price of Housing	Price of Transportation	Cost of the Basket	Consumer Price Index
2014	$100	$200	$100	$150	100
2015	110	205	140	165	110
2016	120	210	180	180	120

APPLYING THE CONCEPT
WHERE ARE ALL THOSE $100 BILLS?

A quick look at the Federal Reserve's website, www. federalreserve.gov, tells us that during the winter of 2013, the public held nearly $1.2 trillion in the form of currency. That's a huge amount. To get some sense of the size of this number, you can divide it by the U.S. population at that time, 315 million, to get roughly $3,700 per person. For a household of four, that's an average of nearly $15,000 in cash. What's even more absurd is that more than three-fourths of the $1.2 trillion was held in the form of $100 bills, meaning that there must be twenty-eight $100 bills for each United States resident. Clearly, we do not hold all this cash in our wallets or our homes, nor does it fill the cash registers of local businesses. Where are all those $100 bills?

Not in the United States. In many countries, people do not trust their governments to protect the value of the currency they print. They fear the authorities will print too much, creating inflation. And because money is all about trust, if you don't have confidence in your government, you don't want to hold your wealth in the form of the government's money. In many cases, the lack of faith has been warranted. When the Soviet Union collapsed in the early 1990s, the currency issued by the old regime became nearly worthless. The same thing happened in Argentina in the 1980s.

When people stop trusting the local currency, they look for substitutes. The most sought-after is the U.S. dollar. With the constant addition of new security features, and the stability of the government, everyone seems to have faith in it.* The U.S. Treasury estimates that between one-half and two-thirds of U.S. currency is held outside the United States. That's up to $800 billion—and most of it is in hundreds!

*For a guide to the security features in U.S. currency, go to *www. moneyfactory.gov.* This constant redesign has been successful in thwarting counterfeiting. Estimates are that the proportion of counterfeit bills is about 1 in 10,000. This is definitely not something that anyone should worry about.

Figure 2.3   Growth Rates of Monetary Aggregates, 1960–2013

SOURCE: *Board of Governors of the Federal Reserve System, Release H.6. (FRED data codes: M1SL and M2SL).*

---

financial firms began to offer "money market" accounts that compensated depositors at least in part for inflation. These accounts are part of M2. The movement of funds into the non-M1 portion of M2 meant that the two measures no longer moved together. At the same time, the new money market accounts made M2 accounts more liquid. Analysts interested in the economy's prospects stopped looking at M1 and began to look at M2.

How useful is M2 in tracking inflation? We already know that when the quantity of money grows quickly, it produces very high inflation. A cross-country analysis of

Figure 2.4 Money Growth and Inflation, Monthly 1960–2013

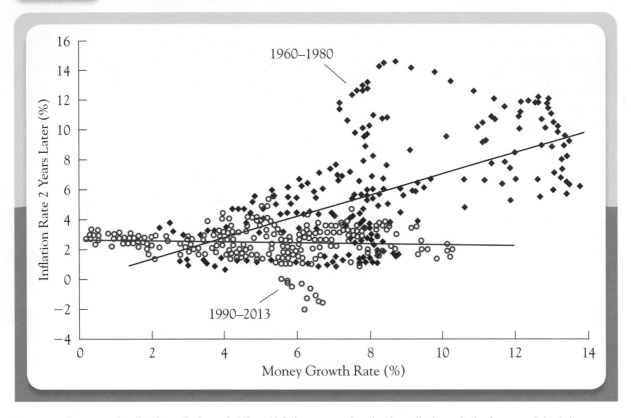

Money growth measured as the 12-month change in M2, and inflation measured as the 12-month change in the Consumer Price Index (FRED data codes: M2SL and CPIAUCSL).

SOURCE: *Board of Governors of the Federal Reserve System and Bureau of Labor Statistics.*

money growth supports this conclusion. In Turkey, Venezuela, and Ukraine, where in the last half of the 1990s the inflation rate ranged from 30 to 75 percent per year, the money supply grew at comparable rates.[11] By contrast, in the United States, Canada, and Europe, the inflation rate averaged only about 2 percent, and the money growth rate stayed in the range of 6 to 7 percent. Because high money growth means high inflation, controlling inflation means controlling the money supply. Imagine how much inflation there would be if people could spend the $3 trillion in Monopoly dollars Parker Brothers has printed over the past eight decades!

How useful is money growth in helping us to control moderate inflation? We will address this question in detail in Chapter 20 of this book. For now, though, let's look at whether money growth helps to forecast inflation.

Figure 2.4 shows M2 growth on the horizontal axis and the inflation rate *two years later* on the vertical axis, both for the United States. The solid red diamonds represent

[11]From 1995 to 2000, inflation averaged 74 percent in Turkey, 42 percent in Venezuela, and 30 percent in Ukraine. At the same time, a measure of money that is close to U.S. M2 grew in those three countries at 86, 33, and 36 percent per year respectively. Data for these comparisons come from the International Monetary Fund's *International Financial Statistics.*

data from 1960 to 1980. Note that, while the relationship is far from perfect in those years, higher money growth was clearly associated with higher inflation two years later. In fact, the correlation was over 0.5.[12] But look at what has happened to the relationship more recently. The hollow blue circles represent data from 1990 to 2013, when there was virtually no relationship at all between the two measures. (The correlation was slightly negative.) Growth in M2 stopped being a useful tool for forecasting inflation.

There are two possible explanations for the fact that M2 no longer predicts inflation. One is that the relationship between the two applies only at high levels of inflation. Figure 2.4 shows that during the period 1960–1980, the inflation rate often rose higher than 5 percent, but from 1990 to 2013, it rarely did. Maybe the relationship between money growth and inflation doesn't exist at low levels of inflation, or it shows up only over longer periods of time. All we really know is that at low levels of money growth, inflation is likely to stay low.

An alternative explanation is that we need a new measure of money that takes into account recent changes in the way we make payments and use money. Once economists have identified the right measure, perhaps we'll be able to predict inflation again.

---

[12]Correlation is a measure of how closely two quantities are related, or change together. The numerical value ranges from +1 to −1. A positive correlation signifies that the two variables move up and down together, while a negative correlation means that they move in opposite directions.

Terms

automated clearinghouse transaction (ACH), 31

check, 28

credit card, 31

currency, 25

debit card, 31

demand deposits, 36

electronic funds transfer, 31

e-money, 32

fiat money, 28

funding liquidity, 26

gross domestic product (GDP), 37

inflation, 35

inflation rate, 35

liquidity, 26

market liquidity, 26

M1, 36

M2, 36

means of payment, 24

monetary aggregates, 36

money, 24

payments system, 26

store of value, 25

stored-value card, 31

time consistent, 28

time deposits, 36

unit of account, 24

wealth, 24

Using FRED: Codes for Data in This Chapter

Data Series	FRED Data Code
Price of gold (U.S. dollars)	GOLDAMGBD228NLBM
Consumer price index	CPIAUCSL
M1	M1SL
M2	M2SL
Currency in circulation	CURRSL
Traveler's checks	TVCKSSL
Demand deposits	DEMDEPSL
Other checkable deposits	OCDSL
Small-denomination time deposits	STDCBSL
Savings deposits and MMDAs*	SAVINGSL
Retail MMMFs**	RMFSL
Nominal GDP	GDP

*Money market deposit accounts

**Money market mutual funds

Chapter Lessons

1. Money is an asset that is generally accepted in payment for goods and services or repayment of debts.
   a. Money has three basic uses:
      i. Means of payment
      ii. Unit of account
      iii. Store of value
   b. Money is liquid. Liquidity is the ease with which an asset can be turned into a means of payment.
   c. For financial institutions, market liquidity is the ease with which they can sell a security or loan for money. Funding liquidity is the ease with which they can borrow to acquire a security or loan.

2. Money makes the payments system work. The payments system is the web of arrangements that allows people to exchange goods and services. There are three broad categories of payments, all of which use money at some stage.
   a. Cash
   b. Checks
   c. Electronic payments

3. In the future, money will be used less and less as a means of payment.

4. To understand the links between money and inflation, we need to measure the quantity of money in the economy. There are two basic measures of money: M1 and M2. M1, the narrowest measure, includes only the most liquid assets. M2, a broader measure, includes assets not usable as a means of payment.
   a. Countries with high money growth have high inflation.
   b. In countries with low inflation, money growth is a poor forecaster of inflation.

Conceptual and Analytical Problems

1. Describe at least three ways you could pay for your morning cup of coffee. What are the advantages and disadvantages of each? *(LO2)*

2. You are the owner of a small sandwich shop. A buyer may offer one of several payment methods: cash, a check drawn on a bank, a credit card, or a debit card. Which of these is the least costly for you? Explain why the others are more expensive. *(LO2)*

3. Explain how money encourages specialization, and how specialization improves everyone's standard of living. *(LO3)*

4.* Could the dollar still function as the unit of account in a totally cashless society? *(LO2)*

5. Give four examples of ACH transactions you might make. *(LO2)*

6. As of July 2013, 17 of the 28 countries of the European Union have adopted the euro. The remaining 11 countries, including Great Britain, Denmark, and Sweden, have retained their own currencies. What are the advantages of a common currency for someone who is traveling through Europe? *(LO1)*

7. Why might each of the following commodities not serve well as money? *(LO2)*
   a. Tomatoes
   b. Bricks
   c. Cattle

8. Despite the efforts of the U.S. Treasury and the Secret Service, someone discovers a cheap way to counterfeit $100 bills. What will be the impact of this discovery on the economy? *(LO3)*

9. You receive a check drawn on another bank and deposit it into your checking account. Even though this is a "demand deposit," the funds are not immediately available for your use. Why? Would your answer change if the check is drawn on the account of another customer of your own bank? *(LO2)*

10. Over a nine-year period in the 16th century, King Henry VIII reduced the silver content of the British pound to one-sixth its initial value. Why do you think he did so? What do you think happened to the use of pounds as a means of payment? If you held both the old and new pounds, which would you use first, and why? *(LO1)*

11. Under what circumstances might you expect barter to reemerge in an economy that has fiat money as a means of payment? Can you think of an example of a country where this has happened recently? *(LO3)*

12. You visit a tropical island that has only four goods in its economy—oranges, pineapples, coconuts, and bananas. There is no money in this economy. *(LO1)*
   a. Draw a grid showing all the prices for this economy. (You should check your answer using the $n(n-1)/2$ formula where n is the number of goods.)
   b. An islander suggests designating oranges as the means of payment and unit of account for the economy. How many prices would there be if her suggestion was followed?
   c. Do you think the change suggested in part b is worth implementing? Why or why not?

13. Consider again the tropical island described in Problem 12. Under what circumstances would you recommend the issue of a paper currency by the government of the island? What advantages might this strategy have over the use of oranges as money? *(LO1)*

*Indicates more difficult problems

14. What factors should you take into account when considering using the following assets as stores of value? *(LO1)*
    a. Gold
    b. Real estate
    c. Stocks
    d. Government bonds

15.* Under what circumstances might money in the form of currency be the best option as a store of value? *(LO3)*

16. Suppose a significant fall in the price of certain stocks caused the market makers in those stocks to experience difficulties with their funding liquidity. Under what circumstances might that development lead to liquidity problems in markets for other assets? *(LO1)*

17.* Consider an economy that only produces and consumes two goods—food and apparel. Suppose the inflation rate based on the consumer price index is higher during the year than that based on the GDP deflator. Assuming underlying tastes and preferences in the economy stay the same, what can you say about food and apparel price movements during the year? *(LO3)*

18. Assuming no interest is paid on checking accounts, what would you expect to see happen to the relative growth rates of M1 and M2 if interest rates rose significantly? *(LO3)*

19. If money growth is related to inflation, what would you expect to happen to the inflation rates of countries that join a monetary union and adopt a common currency such as the euro? *(LO3)*

FRED.
ECONOMIC DATA | ST. LOUIS FED

Scan here for quick access to the hints for these problems. Need a barcode reader? Try ScanLife, available in your app store.

Data Exploration

For detailed instructions on using Federal Reserve Economic Data (FRED) online to answer each of the following problems, visit www.mhhe.com/moneyandbanking4e and click on Student Edition, then Data Exploration Hints.

1. Find the most recent level of M2 (FRED code: M2SL) and of the U.S. population (FRED code: POP). Compute the quantity of money divided by the population. Do you think your answer is large? Why? *(LO1)*

2. Reproduce Figure 2.3 from 1960 to the present, showing the percent change from a year ago of M1 (FRED code: M1SL) and M2 (FRED code: M2SL). Comment on the pattern over the last five years. Would it matter which of the two monetary aggregates you looked at? *(LO3)*

3. Which usually grows faster: M1 or M2? Produce a graph showing M2 divided by M1. When this ratio rises, M2 outpaces M1 and vice versa. What is the long-run pattern? Is the pattern stable? *(LO3)*

4. Traveler's checks are a component of M1 and M2. Produce a graph of this component of the monetary aggregates (FRED code: TVCKSSL). Explain the pattern you see. *(LO1)*

5. Plot the annual inflation rate based on the percent change from a year ago of the consumer price index (FRED code: CPIAUCSL). Comment on the average and variability of inflation in the 1960s, the 1970s, and the most recent decade. *(LO3)*

Chapter 3

Financial Instruments, Financial Markets, and Financial Institutions

Learning Objectives

Understand . . .

LO1   Financial instruments

LO2   Financial markets

LO3   Financial institutions

Long before formal financial institutions and instruments became common, there were times when people lacked the resources to meet their immediate needs. In the terminology of introductory economics, people's incomes were exceeded by their necessary consumption. When a harvest was poor, they would dip into the reserves stored from previous years or exchange assets like land and livestock for food. But often those measures were insufficient, so communities developed informal financial arrangements that allowed people to borrow or lend among themselves. After a poor harvest, those people with relatively good yields would help those with relatively poor ones. When the tables were turned, help would flow the other way. In some societies, families spread out geographically to facilitate these arrangements. For example, in rural Indian communities, households deliberately married off their daughters to families in different regions to increase the chance that their in-laws would be able to respond in a time of crisis.[1] These informal insurance arrangements ensured that everyone had enough to eat.

While family members and friends still make loans among themselves, the informal arrangements that were the mainstay of the financial system centuries ago have given way to the formal financial instruments of the modern world. Today, the international financial system exists to facilitate the design, sale, and exchange of a broad set of contracts with a very specific set of characteristics.

In recent decades, finance has evolved at an unprecedented pace, and our understanding of it has changed, too. Formerly, economists distinguished sharply between **direct finance** (in which a borrower sells a security directly to a lender) and **indirect finance** (in which an institution like a bank stands between the lender and the borrower). If we need a loan to buy a car, we usually get it from a bank or finance company—that's a classic example of indirect finance. Once we get the loan, the car

---

[1]See M. R. Rosenzweig, "Risk, Implicit Contracts, and the Family in Rural Areas of Low-Income Countries," *Economic Journal* 98 (December 1988).

becomes one of our **assets**, and the loan becomes our **liability**. We all have assets and liabilities. Your assets probably include things of value like a bank account and a computer. If you have a student loan or credit card debt, those are among your liabilities. In contrast, if you borrowed directly from your parents or a friend, that would be an instance of direct finance: They own the asset (the loan), and you are obliged to pay them (rather than a bank) directly.

As finance grows increasingly sophisticated and complex, virtually all transactions take on some indirect flavor. Today, even direct finance usually involves a **financial institution** or **intermediary** in some fashion. When a lender purchases a security issued by a specific firm or government, the transaction typically takes place through a securities broker or an investment bank that helps the issuer distribute new stock or bonds. These securities become assets for the lenders who buy them and liabilities to the government or corporation that created them to obtain funds. Frequently, the lenders are themselves intermediaries, such as mutual funds, that gather and hold such securities for their investors.

Reflecting this trend toward *institutionalization,* the only lingering distinction between direct and indirect finance is who owns the underlying asset. Under direct finance, the asset holder has a direct claim on the borrower. In the case of indirect finance, the asset holder owns a claim on a financial institution (like a bank or mutual fund) that, in turn, owns a claim on the borrower.

Put differently, the historical gap between the two forms of finance has narrowed sharply over decades: Whether a modern financial transaction is direct or indirect, intermediaries are usually heavily involved (see Figure 3.1). As we will see later in this chapter (and especially in Chapters 11 through 14), the job of intermediaries is to produce and use the information that makes modern finance effective. As

Figure 3.1   Funds Flowing through the Financial System

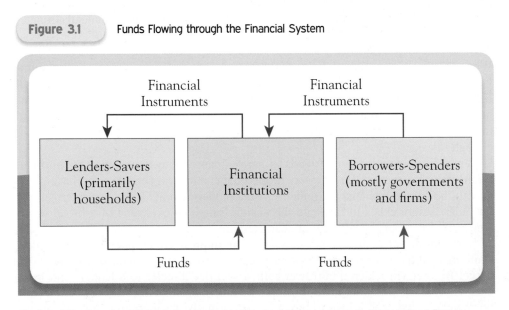

The financial system channels funds from lenders to borrowers through intermediaries. In **indirect finance**, a financial institution like a bank takes the resources from the lender in the form of a deposit (or something like it) and then provides them to the borrower in the form of a loan (or the equivalent). Even in the case of **direct finance**, where the saver acquires a direct claim on the user of the funds, a financial institution like a stockbroker or an investment bank is usually involved in the transaction.

a result, users and providers of funds can better satisfy their needs, and economies can expand.

Indeed, such financial development is inextricably linked to economic growth. A country's financial system has to expand as its level of economic activity rises, or the country will stagnate. The role of the financial system is to facilitate production, employment, and consumption. In a prosperous economy, people have the means to pay for things, and resources flow to their most efficient uses. Savings are funneled through the system so that they can finance investment and allow the economy to grow. The decisions made by the people who do the saving direct the investment.

In this chapter, we will survey the financial system in three steps. First, we'll study *financial instruments,* or *securities,* as they are often called. Stocks, bonds, and loans of all types are financial instruments, as are more exotic agreements like options and insurance. Exactly what are these financial instruments, and what is their role in our economy? Second, we'll look at *financial markets,* such as the New York Stock Exchange and the Nasdaq (National Association of Securities Dealers Automatic Quotations), where investors can buy and sell stocks, bonds, and various other instruments. And finally, we'll look at *financial institutions*—what they are and what they do.

Financial Instruments

A **financial instrument** is the *written legal obligation of one party to transfer something of value, usually money, to another party at some future date, under specified conditions.* Let's dissect this definition to understand it better. First, a financial instrument is a *written legal obligation* that is subject to government enforcement. That is, a person can be compelled to take the action specified in the agreement. The enforceability of the obligation is an important feature of a financial instrument. Without enforcement of the specified terms, financial instruments would not exist.[2]

Second, a financial instrument obligates *one party to transfer something of value, usually money, to another party.* By *party,* we mean a person, company, or government. Usually the financial instrument specifies that payments will be made. For example, if you get a car loan, you are obligated to make monthly payments of a particular amount to the lender. And if you have an accident, your insurance company is obligated to fix your car, though the cost of the repair is left unspecified.

Third, a financial instrument specifies that payment will be made *at some future date.* In some cases, such as a car loan that requires payments,

SOURCE: *2001 © Wayne Bressler/The New Yorker Collection/www.cartoonbank.com.*

---

[2]A myriad of financial arrangements that exist outside the legal system, like loan sharking, are also enforced. But those sorts of obligations are not part of the formal financial system.

Table 3.1 Uses of Financial Instruments

> **Means of Payment:** Purchase of goods or services.
>
> **Store of Value:** Transfer of purchasing power into the future.
>
> **Transfer of Risk:** Transfer of risk from one person or company to another.

the dates may be very specific. In others, such as car insurance, the payment is triggered when something specific happens, like an accident.

Finally, a financial instrument *specifies conditions* under which a payment will be made. Some agreements specify payments only when certain events happen. That is clearly the case with car insurance and with stocks as well. The holder of a stock owns a small part of a firm and so can expect to receive occasional cash payments, called *dividends,* when the company is profitable. There is no way to know in advance, however, exactly when such payments will be made. In general, financial instruments specify a number of possible contingencies under which one party is required to make a payment to another.

Uses of Financial Instruments

Stocks, loans, and insurance are all examples of financial instruments. Taking them as a group, we can see that they have three functions (see Table 3.1). Financial instruments can act as a means of payment, and they can also be stores of value. Thus, they offer two of the three uses of money. (Remember from Chapter 2 that money is a means of payment, a unit of account, and a store of value.) But financial instruments have a third function that can make them very different from money: They allow for the transfer of risk.

Recall that a means of payment is something that is generally accepted as payment for goods and services or repayment of a debt. It is possible to pay for purchases with financial instruments, even if they don't look much like money. An example is the willingness of employees to accept a company's stock as payment for working. (This means of payment was very popular in the late 1990s, when the stock market was booming.) While we cannot yet pay for groceries with shares of stock, the time may come when we can. For now, although some financial instruments may function as means of payment, they aren't terribly good ones.

Having a store of value means that your consumption doesn't need to exactly match your income. For days, months, and years, if necessary, you can spend more than you make, repaying the difference later. Even though most of us are paid weekly or monthly, we eat every day. As stores of value, financial instruments like stocks and bonds are thought to be better than money. Over time, they generate increases in wealth that are bigger than those we can obtain from holding money in most of its forms. These higher payoffs are compensation for higher levels of risk, because the payoffs from holding most financial instruments are generally more uncertain than those that arise from holding money. Nevertheless, many financial instruments can be used to transfer purchasing power into the future.

RISK

The third use of a financial instrument lies in its ability to *transfer risk* between the buyer and the seller. Most financial instruments involve some sort of risk transfer. For example, think of wheat farmers. If only one farm has a huge harvest, that farmer does very well. But if everyone's harvest is huge, then prices can plummet and individual farms can lose money. The risk that the harvest will be too good, resulting in low grain prices, is a risk that most individual farmers do not want to take. A *wheat futures contract* allows the farmer to transfer that risk to someone else. A wheat futures contract is a financial instrument in which two parties agree to exchange a fixed quantity of wheat on a prearranged future date at a specified price. By fixing the price at which the crop will be sold well in advance of the harvest, the farmer can forget about what happens in the wheat market because the risk has been transferred to someone else.

Insurance contracts are another example of a financial instrument that transfers risk—in this case, from individuals to an insurance company. Because a car accident can be financially catastrophic, we buy car insurance and transfer the risk to an insurance company. Because insurance companies make similar guarantees to a large group of people, they have the capacity to shoulder the risk. While the timing of an individual automobile accident is impossible to forecast, a predictable percentage of a large group of drivers will experience accidents over a given period.

Characteristics of Financial Instruments: Standardization and Information

As is obvious from the definition of a financial instrument, these sorts of contracts can be very complex. If you don't believe it, take a look at the fine print in a car insurance policy, a student loan, or even a credit card agreement. Complexity is costly. The more complicated something is, the more it costs to create and the more difficult it is to understand. As a rule, people do not want to bear these costs. Yes, the owner of an oil tanker may be willing to go to the expense of negotiating a specific insurance contract for each voyage a ship makes. The same owner may agree to make premium payments based on the load carried, the distance traveled, the route taken, and the weather expected. But for most of us, the cost of such custom contracts is simply too high.

In fact, people on both sides of financial contracts shy away from specialized agreements. Instead, they use standardized financial instruments to overcome the potential costs of complexity. Because of *standardization,* most of the financial instruments that we encounter on a day-to-day basis are very homogeneous. For example, most mortgages feature a standard application process and offer standardized terms. Automobile insurance contracts generally offer only certain standard options.

Standardization of terms makes sense. If all financial instruments differed in critical ways, most of us would not be able to understand them. Their usefulness would be severely limited. If the shares of Microsoft stock sold to one person differed in a crucial way from the shares sold to someone else, for instance, potential investors might not understand what they were buying. Even more important, the resale and trading of the shares would become virtually impossible, which would certainly discourage anyone from purchasing them in the first place. From this, we conclude that arrangements that obligate people to make payments to one another cannot all be one-of-a-kind arrangements.

Another characteristic of financial instruments is that they communicate *information,* summarizing certain essential details about the issuer. How much do you really want to learn about the original issuer of a financial instrument? Or if you are purchasing an existing instrument, how much do you have to know about the person who is selling it to you? Surely, the less you feel you need to know to feel secure about the transaction, the better. Regardless of whether the instrument is a stock, a bond, a futures contract, or an insurance contract, the holder does not want to have to watch the issuer too closely; continuous monitoring is costly and difficult. Thus, financial instruments are designed to eliminate the expensive and time-consuming process of collecting such information.

INFORMATION

LESSONS FROM THE CRISIS
LEVERAGE

Households and firms often borrow to make investments. Obtaining a mortgage for a new home or selling a corporate bond to build a new plant are common examples. The use of borrowing to finance part of an investment is called *leverage*.* Leverage played a key role in the financial crisis of 2007–2009, so it is worth understanding how leverage relates to risk and how it can make the financial system vulnerable.

Modern economies rely heavily on borrowing to make investments. They are all leveraged. Yet, the more leverage, the greater the risk that an adverse surprise will lead to bankruptcy. If two households own houses of the same value, the one that has borrowed more—the one that is more highly leveraged and has less net worth—is the more likely to default during a temporary slump in income. This example could apply equally well to firms, financial institutions, or even countries.

Financial institutions are much more highly leveraged than households or firms, typically owning assets of about 10 times their net worth. During the crisis, some important financial firms leveraged more than 30 times their net worth.[†] Such high leverage meant that these firms would be vulnerable even to a minor decline in the value of their assets. For example, when a borrower is leveraged more than 30 times,

a drop as small as 3 percent in asset prices could eliminate the cushion created by the net worth and lead to bankruptcy.

When highly leveraged financial institutions experience a loss, they usually try to reduce their leverage—that is, to *deleverage*—by selling assets and issuing securities that raise their net worth (see accompanying figure). However, everyone in the financial system cannot deleverage at once. When too many institutions try to sell assets simultaneously, their efforts will almost surely prove counterproductive: falling prices will mean more losses, diminishing their net worth further, raising leverage, and making the assets they hold seem riskier, thereby compelling further sales.

This "paradox of leverage" reinforces the destabilizing liquidity spiral discussed in Chapter 2 (see Lessons from the Crisis: Market Liquidity, Funding Liquidity, and Making Markets). Both spirals feed a vicious cycle of falling prices and widespread deleveraging that was a hallmark of the financial crisis of 2007–2009. The financial system steadied only after a plunge of many asset prices and massive government interventions.

*For a technical definition of leverage, see the Tools of the Trade box in Chapter 5. For the evolution of U.S. commercial bank leverage, look at the FRED data series "EQTA."

[†]A bank's net worth—its assets minus liabilities—is commonly known as *bank capital*. We will discuss this in more detail in Chapter 12.

Deleveraging Spiral

Bank Wishes to Deleverage

Some Assets Are Sold

Asset Prices Decline

Net Worth Declines and Assets Become Riskier

A number of mechanisms exist to reduce the cost of monitoring the behavior of the counterparties to a financial arrangement. A **counterparty** is the person or institution on the other side of a contract. If you obtain a car loan from your local bank, then you are the bank's counterparty and the bank is yours. In the case of a stock or bond, the issuing firm and the investors who hold the instrument are counterparties.

The solution to the high cost of obtaining information on the parties to a financial instrument is to standardize both the instrument and the information provided about the issuer. We can also hire a specialist whom we all trust to do the monitoring. The institutions that have arisen over the years to support the existence of financial instruments provide an environment in which everyone can feel secure about the behavior of the counterparties to an agreement.

In addition to simply summarizing information, financial instruments are designed to handle the problem of *asymmetric information,* which comes from the fact that borrowers have some information they don't disclose to lenders. Instead of buying new ovens, will a bread baker use a $50,000 loan to take an extended vacation in Tahiti? The lender wants to make sure the borrower is not misrepresenting what he or she will do with borrowed funds. Thus, the financial system is set up to gather information on borrowers before giving them resources and to monitor their use of the resources afterwards. These specialized mechanisms were developed to handle the problem of asymmetric information.

Underlying versus Derivative Instruments

There are two fundamental classes of financial instruments. The first, **underlying instruments** (sometimes called *primitive securities*), are used by savers/lenders to transfer resources directly to investors/borrowers. Through these instruments, the financial system improves the efficient allocation of resources in the real economy.

The primary examples of underlying securities or instruments are stocks and bonds that offer payments based solely on the issuer's status. Bonds, for example, make payments depending on the solvency of the firm that issued them. Stocks sometimes pay dividends when the issuing corporation's profits are sufficient.

The second class of financial instruments is known as **derivative instruments**. Their value and payoffs are "derived" from the behavior of the underlying instruments. The most common examples of derivatives are futures, options, and swaps. In general, derivatives specify a payment to be made between the person who sells the instrument and the person who buys it. The amount of the payment depends on various factors associated with the price of the underlying asset. The primary use of derivatives is to shift risk among investors. We will see some examples in a moment; Chapter 9 discusses derivatives in detail.

A Primer for Valuing Financial Instruments

Why are some financial instruments more valuable than others? If you look at the websites of Yahoo! Finance or Bloomberg, you'll see the prices of many bonds and stocks. These securities are quite different from each other. Not only that, but from day to day, the prices of an individual bond or stock can vary quite a bit. What characteristics affect the price someone will pay to buy or sell a financial instrument?

Four fundamental characteristics influence the value of a financial instrument (see Table 3.2): (1) the *size* of the payment that is promised, (2) *when* the promised payment is to be made, (3) the *likelihood* that the payment will be made, and (4) the *circumstances* under which the payment is to be made. Let's look at each one of these traits.

Table 3.2	What Makes a Financial Instrument Valuable?

Size: Payments that are larger are more valuable.
Timing: Payments that are made sooner are more valuable.
Likelihood: Payments that are more likely to be made are more valuable.
Circumstances: Payments that are made when we need them most are more valuable.

First, people will pay more for an instrument that obligates the issuer to pay the holder $1,000 than for one that offers a payment of $100. Regardless of any other conditions, this simply must be true: *The bigger the promised payment, the more valuable the financial instrument.*

Second, if you are promised a payment of $100 sometime in the future, you will want to know when you will receive it. Receiving $100 tomorrow is different from receiving $100 next year. This simple example illustrates a very general proposition: *The sooner the payment is made, the more valuable is the promise to make it.* Time has value because of opportunity cost. If you receive a payment immediately, you have an opportunity to invest or consume it right away. If you don't receive the payment until later, you lose that opportunity.

The third factor that affects the value of a financial instrument is the odds that the issuer will meet the obligation to make the payment. Regardless of how conscientious and diligent the party who made the promise is, there remains some possibility that the payment will not be made. Because risk requires compensation, the impact of this uncertainty on the value of a financial instrument is clear: *The more likely it is that the payment will be made, the more valuable the financial instrument.*

Finally, the value of a financial instrument is affected by the conditions under which a promised payment is to be made. Insurance is the best example. We buy car insurance to receive a payment if we have an accident, so we can repair the car. No one buys insurance that pays off when good things happen. *Payments that are made when we need them most are more valuable than other payments.*[3]

Examples of Financial Instruments

We'll have quite a bit to say about financial instruments in Part II of the book. For now, let's take a look at some of the most common varieties. The best way to organize them is by whether they are used primarily as stores of value or for trading risk.

Financial Instruments Used Primarily as Stores of Value

1. **Bank loans.** A borrower obtains resources from a lender immediately in exchange for a promised set of payments in the future. The borrower, who can be

[3]This conclusion is related to the principle of declining marginal utility, which you may recall from your study of microeconomics. The idea is that the satisfaction obtained from consumption declines as the level of consumption increases. Each succeeding candy bar brings less pleasure than the last one. Thus, a financial instrument that pays off when marginal utility is high is worth more than one that pays off when marginal utility is low. This means that payoffs that are made when income and wealth are low are more valuable than payoffs that are made when income and wealth are high.

YOUR FINANCIAL WORLD
Disability Income Insurance

People insure their houses so they can rebuild them if they burn down. They insure their cars so they can repair them if they have an accident. And they insure their lives so their families will be financially secure if they die prematurely. But few people insure their most important asset: their ability to produce an income. The biggest risk all of us face is that we will become disabled and lose our earning capacity. Insuring it should be one of our highest priorities.

If you think this advice is alarmist, just look at a few numbers. About one in four 20-year-olds will become disabled for 90 days or longer during their working lives. In fact, the chance you'll become disabled is far higher than the chance of your house suffering a serious fire—which over 40 years is less than 1 in 40.*

Fortunately, you may already have some disability insurance. The government provides some through Social

Security; your employer may insure you; and if you're injured on the job and can't work, there is always workers' compensation insurance. But is that enough? You should evaluate what your needs are likely to be. If the disability insurance you already have is not enough, you should buy more. While it isn't very pleasant to think about what would happen if you became disabled, you need to do it. Surely this is one risk you should transfer to someone else.

*Official statistics indicate that a serious fire occurs in roughly 1 of 1,650 houses each year. So there is a 1,649 chance in 1,650 of a house *not* suffering a big fire in any given year. Over a 40-year period, the probability that a serious fire will *not* occur is $(1,649/1,650)^{40} = 0.976$. That means the chance of a serious fire is 2.4 percent, or fewer than 1 in 40 houses.

---

either an individual or a firm, needs funds to make an investment or purchase, while the lender is looking for a way to store value into the future.

2. **Bonds.** Bonds are a form of loan. In exchange for obtaining funds today, a corporation or government promises to make payments in the future. While bond payments are often stated in fixed dollars, they need not be. Unlike most bank loans, most bonds can be bought and sold in financial markets. Like bank loans, bonds are used by the borrower to finance current operations and by the lender to store value.

3. **Home mortgages.** Most people who wish to purchase a home need to borrow some portion of the funds. A mortgage is a loan that is used to purchase real estate. In exchange for the funds, the borrower promises to make a series of payments. The house is collateral for the loan. **Collateral** is the term used to describe specific assets a borrower pledges to protect the lender's interests in the event of nonpayment. If the payments aren't made, the lender can take the house, a process called *foreclosure.*

4. **Stocks.** The holder of a share of a company's stock owns a small piece of the firm and is entitled to part of its profits. The owner of a firm sells stock as a way of raising funds to enlarge operations as well as a way of transferring the risk of ownership to someone else. Buyers of stocks use them primarily as stores of wealth.

5. **Asset-backed securities.** **Asset-backed securities** are shares in the returns or payments arising from specific assets, such as home mortgages, student loans, credit card debt, or even movie box-office receipts. Investors purchase shares in the revenue that comes from these underlying assets. The most prominent of these instruments are **mortgage-backed securities**, which bundle a large number of mortgages together into a pool in which shares are then sold. Securities backed by *subprime* mortgages—loans to borrowers who are less likely to repay than borrowers of conventional mortgages—played an important role in

the financial crisis of 2007–2009 (see Chapter 7, Lessons from the Crisis: Subprime Mortgages). The owners of these securities receive a share of the payments made by the homeowners who borrowed the funds. Asset-backed securities are an innovation that allows funds in one part of the country to find productive uses elsewhere. Thus, the availability of some sorts of financing no longer depends on local credit conditions.[4]

Financial Instruments Used Primarily to Transfer Risk

1. **Insurance contracts.** The primary purpose of insurance policies is to assure that payments will be made under particular, and often rare, circumstances. These instruments exist expressly to transfer risk from one party to another.

2. **Futures contracts.** A futures contract is an agreement between two parties to exchange a fixed quantity of a commodity (such as wheat or corn) or an asset (such as a bond) at a fixed price on a set future date. A futures contract always specifies the *price* at which the transaction will take place. A futures contract is a type of derivative instrument, since its value is based on the price of some other asset. It is used to transfer the risk of price fluctuations from one party to another.

3. **Options.** Like futures contracts, options are derivative instruments whose prices are based on the value of some underlying asset. Options give the holder the right, but not the obligation, to buy or sell a fixed quantity of the underlying asset at a predetermined price either on a specified date or at any time during a specified period.

4. **Swaps.** Swap contracts are agreements to exchange two specific cash flows at certain times in the future (as discussed in Chapter 9). For example, an interest-rate swap might involve the exchange of payments based on a fixed rate of interest for payments based on a rate of interest that fluctuates (or "floats") with the market. Swaps come in many varieties, reflecting differences in maturity, payment frequency, and underlying cash flows. The cash flows and other contractual arrangements usually are designed so that there is no upfront fee for the swap.

These are just a few examples of the most prominent financial instruments. Together, they allow people to buy and sell almost any sort of payment on any date under any circumstances. Thus, they offer the opportunity to store value and trade risk in almost any way that one might want.[5] When you encounter a financial instrument for the first time, try to figure out whether it is used primarily for storing value or for transferring risk. Then try to identify which characteristics determine its value.

MARKETS

Financial Markets

Financial markets are the places where financial instruments are bought and sold. They are the economy's central nervous system, relaying and reacting to information quickly, allocating resources, and determining prices. In doing so, financial markets

---

[4]For an introduction to how asset-backed securities work, see Andreas Jobst, "What is Securitization?" *Finance and Development*, International Monetary Fund, September 2008.

[5]An important exception is the common desire to borrow using future income as collateral. While young people with good career prospects might wish to spend their future earnings now, lenders worry that such loans will diminish the borrower's incentive to work and repay.

enable both firms and individuals to find financing for their activities. When they are working well, new firms can start up and existing firms can grow; individuals who don't have sufficient savings can borrow to purchase cars and houses. By ensuring that resources are available to those who can put them to the best use, and by keeping the costs of transactions as low as possible, these markets promote economic efficiency. When financial markets cease to function properly, resources are no longer channeled to their best possible use, and we all suffer.[6]

Table 3.3	The Role of Financial Markets

Market Liquidity: Ensure that owners of financial instruments can buy and sell them cheaply and easily.

Information: Pool and communicate information about the issuer of a financial instrument.

Risk Sharing: Provide individuals with a place to buy and sell risks, sharing them with others.

In this section, we will look at the role of financial markets and the economic justification for their existence. Next, we will examine the structure of the markets and how they are organized. Finally, we will look at the characteristics that are essential for the markets to work smoothly.

The Role of Financial Markets

Financial markets serve three roles in our economic system (see Table 3.3). They offer savers and borrowers *liquidity;* they pool and communicate *information;* and they allow *risk sharing.* We encountered the concept of market liquidity in our discussion of money, where we defined it as the ease with which an asset can be turned into money without loss of value. Without financial markets and the institutional structure that supports them, selling the assets we own would be extremely difficult. Thus, we cannot overstate the importance of liquidity for the smooth operation of an economy. Just think what would happen if the stock market were open only one day a month. Stocks would surely become less attractive investments. If you had an emergency and needed money immediately, you probably would not be able to sell your stocks in time. Liquidity is a crucial characteristic of financial markets.

Related to liquidity is the fact that financial markets need to be designed in a way that keeps transactions costs—the cost of buying and selling—low. If you want to buy or sell a stock, you must pay a licensed professional to complete the purchase or sale on your behalf: A **broker** can find you a counterparty, a **dealer** can act as the counterparty, and a broker-dealer can do either or both. While this service can't be free, it is important to keep its cost relatively low. The very high trading volumes that we see in the stock market—several billion shares per day in the United States—is evidence that U.S. stock markets have low transactions costs and are usually very liquid. (One U.S. market in which transactions costs are high is the market for housing. Once you add together everything you pay agents, bankers, and lawyers, you have spent almost 10 percent of the sale price of the house to complete the transaction. The housing market is not very liquid.)

Financial markets pool and communicate information about the issuers of financial instruments, summarizing it in the form of a price. Does a company have good prospects for future growth and profits? If so, its stock price will be high; if not, its stock

---

[6]An example demonstrates the point. Following the September 11, 2001, terrorist attacks, the New York Stock Exchange became inaccessible, and other markets were not functioning properly. Alarmed government officials took measures to ensure that markets would open as soon as possible so that trading could proceed. Without these efforts to get the financial markets up and running, the financial system might quickly have come to a standstill.

TOOLS OF THE TRADE
Trading in Financial Markets

Trading is what makes financial markets work. No one would ever buy a stock or bond if he or she couldn't sell it. Let's take a brief look at how trading works. For this example, we will focus on the stock market.

Placing an order in a stock market is a bit like going to a fast-food restaurant or a coffee shop. You have to enter your order and wait to be served. Not only that, but the order can be very complicated, and how long you wait depends on both what you ordered and on how many other people are waiting to be served.

If you place an order, it will have a number of important characteristics.

- The stock you wish to trade.
- Whether you wish to buy or sell.
- The size of the order—how many shares you wish to trade.
- The price at which you would like to trade.

You can place either a *market order*, in which case your order is executed at the most favorable price currently available on the other side, or a *limit order*, which places a maximum on the price you wish to pay to buy or a minimum on the price you will accept to sell. Placing a market order means you value speed over price; you want the trade to occur as soon as possible and are willing to pay for the privilege. By contrast, you can specify a time at which the limit order is canceled if it hasn't been filled.

Executing the trade requires finding someone to take the other side. To do this, you can seek the help of a broker, who might place your order on an exchange, or find a counterparty through a trading system known as an automated electronic communication network (ECN).

ECNs operate in a very simple way. If you want to buy, you enter a bid. If your bid is better than everyone else's, and there is someone willing to sell at or below the price you bid, then you trade immediately. Otherwise, your bid goes into an order book to wait for a seller. Customer orders interact automatically following a set of priority rules established by the network, but with no one acting as an intermediary in the transaction. The liquidity in the market is provided by the customers.

For a stock like IBM or GE, the New York Stock Exchange is an alternative place to send the order. On the NYSE, liquidity provided by customer orders may be supplemented by designated market makers* (DMMs). A DMM is the person on the floor of the Stock Exchange charged with making a market, ensuring that it is liquid so that people can both buy and sell and that prices aren't overly volatile. For the most part, electronic mechanisms simply match the orders as they come in, keeping track of orders that are outstanding.

On the next page is a portion of the screen from the trading book of the BATS Trading exchanges, which originated as ECNs. BATS operates two exchanges that execute trades electronically. The screen shows outstanding bids and offers for the common stock of Microsoft (MSFT) at 2:15 pm on August 16, 2012. The system shows more than 40,000 limit orders on each side of the market (bids in green; asks in blue) within a few cents of the most recent execution price ($30.87). The system combines the sell (buy) orders of different customers at each price, so we see the aggregate supply (demand) for the stock at that price. If a market sell order for 100 shares were to arrive, the system would match that order with the highest bid ($30.86). If a market buy order for 100 shares were to arrive, the system would match that order with the lowest offer ($30.87). More than 3,000,000 Microsoft shares already had traded that day on the BATS exchanges, while nearly 23,000,000 shares had changed hands on the Nasdaq exchange, where Microsoft shares most frequently trade.

price will be low. Is a borrower likely to repay a bond? The more likely repayment is, the higher the price of the bond. Obtaining the answers to these questions is time consuming and costly. Most of us just don't have the resources or know-how to do it. Instead, we turn to the financial markets to summarize the information for us so that we can look it up on a website.

Finally, while financial instruments are the means for transferring risk, financial markets are the place where we can do it. The markets allow us to buy and sell risks, holding the ones we want and getting rid of the ones we don't want. As we will see in Chapter 5, a prudent investor holds a collection of assets called a **portfolio**, which includes a number of stocks and bonds as well as various forms of money. A well-designed portfolio has a lower overall risk than any individual stock or bond. An investor constructs it by buying and selling financial instruments in the marketplace. Without the market, we wouldn't be able to share risk.

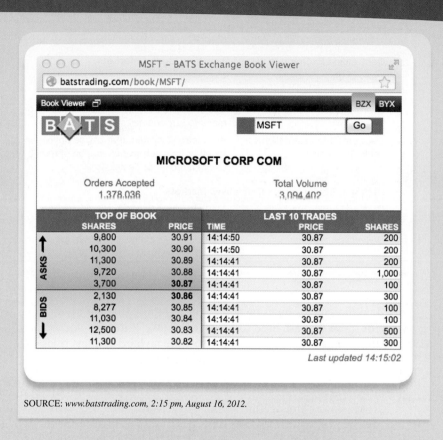

SOURCE: *www.batstrading.com, 2:15 pm, August 16, 2012.*

*For a description of designated market makers, see *www.nyse.com/pdfs/fact_sheet_dmm.pdf.*

The Structure of Financial Markets

There are lots of financial markets and many ways to categorize them. Just take a look at any source of business news. You will see charts and tables for domestic stocks, global stocks, bonds and interest rates, the dollar exchange rate, commodities, and more. Keep going and you will find references to stock markets, bond markets, credit markets, currency trading, options, futures, new securities, and on and on. Grasping the overall structure of all of these financial markets requires grouping them in some sort of meaningful way—but how?

There are three possibilities (see Table 3.4 on page 58). First, we can distinguish between markets where new financial instruments are sold and those where they are re-sold, or traded. Second, we can categorize the markets by the way they trade financial instruments—whether on a centralized exchange or not. And third, we can group them

Table 3.4	The Structure of Financial Markets

Primary versus Secondary Markets

Primary markets:	Markets where newly issued securities are sold.
Secondary markets:	Markets where existing securities are traded.

Centralized Exchanges versus Over-the-Counter Markets

Centralized exchanges:	Secondary markets where dealers meet in a central, physical location.
Over-the-counter markets:	Decentralized secondary markets where dealers stand ready to buy and sell securities electronically.
Electronic communication networks (ECNs):	An electronic system that brings buyers and sellers together for electronic execution of trades without the use of a broker or dealer.

Debt and Equity versus Derivatives Markets

Debt and equity markets:	Markets where financial claims are bought and sold for immediate cash payment.
Derivatives markets:	Markets where claims based on an underlying asset are traded for payment at a later date.

based on the type of instrument they trade—those that are used primarily as a store of value or those that are used to transfer risk. We'll use the vocabulary that is common as of this writing. Bear in mind that there are no hard and fast rules for the terminology used to describe these markets, so it may change.

Primary versus Secondary Markets

A **primary financial market** is one in which a borrower obtains funds from a lender by selling newly issued securities. Businesses use primary markets to raise the resources they need to grow. Governments use them to finance ongoing operations. Most of the action in primary markets occurs out of public view. While a few companies that want to raise funds go directly to the financial markets themselves, most use an investment bank. The bank examines the company's financial health to determine whether the proposed issue is sound. Assuming that it is, the bank will determine a price and then purchase the securities in preparation for resale to clients. This activity, called *underwriting,* is usually very profitable, both for the underwriters and the share purchasers. In a few notable instances, however, such as the 2012 offering of Facebook (FB) shares, many investors lost heavily as the value of the new shares quickly plunged. Because small investors are not customers of large investment banks, most of us do not have direct access to these new securities.

Everyone knows about **secondary financial markets**. Those are the markets where people can buy and sell existing securities. If you want to buy a share of stock in ExxonMobil or Microsoft, you won't get it from the company itself. Instead, you'll buy it in a secondary market from another investor. The prices in the secondary markets are the ones we hear about in the news.

Secondary Market Trading in Stocks

Buying a stock is not like buying a pair of shoes. You can't just go into a store, ask for the stock you want, pay for it with your credit card, and walk out with it in a bag. Instead, you typically ask a broker-dealer to buy the stock for you. Whether the broker dealer obtains it by purchasing it from others or sells it to you from the broker-dealer's own account, your acquisition of the stock is a secondary-market transaction.

The organization of secondary markets for stocks and other securities is changing rapidly. Historically, there have been two types of financial market: **centralized exchanges** and **over-the-counter (OTC) markets**. Some organizations, like the New York Stock Exchange (NYSE) and the large exchanges in London and Tokyo, originated as centralized exchanges, where dealers gathered in person to trade stocks, usually through a system of "open outcry"—shouting bids and offers or using hand signals to make agreements. Others, like the Nasdaq, developed as OTC markets, which are collections of dealers who trade with one another via computer (or, formerly, via phone) from wherever they sit. More recently, **electronic communication networks (ECNs)** have enabled traders (or their brokers) to find counterparties who wish to trade in specific stocks, including those listed on an exchange.

The pace of structural change has accelerated dramatically in the past few years, driven by (1) ongoing technological advances in computing and communications and (2) increasing globalization. The former dramatically lowered the importance of a physical location of an exchange—as new technology allowed the rapid low-cost transmission of orders across long distances—while the latter encouraged unprecedented cross-border mergers of exchanges, integrating larger pools of providers and users of funds.

As part of this process, electronic OTC markets like the Nasdaq and some ECNs have gained the official status of regulated exchanges without establishing a central place of operation. Shifting in the opposite direction, NYSE acquired the largest ECN (Arca) and merged with Euronext, which operates exchanges in London, Paris, and other European cities. The resulting NYSE Euronext group claimed to account for fully one-third of world trading in equities and nearly 8,000 listed issues (including 70 of the largest 100 global corporations). Yet, much of that trading now takes place away from the NYSE floor. Even there, the old system of open outcry has been replaced (as on most exchanges) by computers that record orders, execute transactions, and report trades.[7]

Trading on decentralized electronic exchanges—rather than a physically central one—has advantages and disadvantages. On the plus side, customers can see the orders (look at the Tools of the Trade: Trading in Financial Markets on page 56), the orders are executed quickly, trading occurs 24 hours a day, and costs are low. In addition, decentralization reduces a menacing operational risk that became evident on September 11, 2001, a time before computers dominated the floor of the NYSE and people still depended on gathering there to trade. The NYSE building stood only a few blocks from the World Trade Center. Although the NYSE building was not damaged when the Twin Towers fell, the floor of the exchange became inaccessible. Because trading on the NYSE depended on people meeting there, trading stopped; it did not resume until Monday, September 17. Yet, while New York dealers were shut down, dealers elsewhere in the country could trade via the Nasdaq.

But no system of trading is free of problems. On the minus side, electronic operations have proven prone to errors that threaten the existence of brokers. In addition, amid the complex system of multiple, imperfectly linked exchanges, new trading patterns have arisen that render the entire system fragile, raising serious worries among investors about the liquidity and value of their stocks. For example, consider the following events:

- On December 8, 2005, a "fat-finger incident" cost a Japanese broker more than $300 million when an employee mistyped a sell order.

---

[7]NYSE still assigns "designated market makers" to provide liquidity in selected stocks, but their importance is declining amid the high volume of rapid electronic trade executions.

- On May 6, 2010, a rush of electronic sell orders from one mutual fund's **trading algorithm** (a rule-based program for automatically executing hundreds or thousands of trades) immediately preceded the "flash crash," in which the stock prices of leading U.S. corporations plunged to as low as a penny only to recover all or most of their losses within minutes. The willingness of market makers to provide liquidity (by temporarily purchasing the equities offered for sale) may have been overwhelmed by additional sales from risk-sensitive, **high-frequency traders** (**HFTs**), who can purchase and sell thousands of stocks in a matter of seconds.[8]

- On August 1, 2012, a problem with one U.S. broker's trading algorithm triggered large price swings in many stocks, cost the firm an estimated $440 million, and wiped out about three-fourths of its market value in a day. (see In the News: "High-frequency trading: Wait a second")

In addition to concerns about fragility of the trading system as a whole, efforts to speed up electronic trading drain resources from more efficient uses. To see this point, imagine that an HFT firm relocates its computing facilities closer to an exchange so that it can cut the transmission time for orders by a few microseconds (millionths of a second). The goal of the move is to profit by trading an instant faster than competitors when new information becomes available, such as a stock issuer's quarterly profit statement or the nation's monthly employment report. Yet microsecond gains in trading speed likely diminish the willingness of market makers to provide liquidity because they don't wish to be "picked off" by well-equipped HFTs.[9]

Over time, market makers also may be forced to invest heavily to keep up with the faster turnover of stocks, with little gain to the broader economy. To understand the

An exchange trading floor now is mostly filled by computers, rather than brokers.

[8]For more information on the 2010 flash crash, see the staff report of the CFTC and SEC, *Findings Regarding the Market Events of May 6, 2010, www.sec.gov/news/studies/2010/marketevents-report.pdf.*

[9]Imagine that the TV quiz show *Jeopardy!* allowed a contestant to install her own faster buzzer. Other contestants might hesitate to play or be compelled to invest in similar (or better) equipment.

IN THE NEWS
High-Frequency Trading

The Economist

August 11, 2012

Wait a second

The latest cock-up on Wall Street shows that more safeguards are needed.

Every computer-user knows the feeling of dread when a brand new piece of software causes the entire system to crash. Shareholders in Knight Capital, an American equity broker, now realize how expensive such glitches can be. On August 1st Knight Capital started to use a new software program to execute its trades. Within an hour the program had caused turmoil in the market, sending errant buy-and-sell orders that cost Knight $440m. Shares in the company plunged on the day and, by August 6th, shareholders were forced to accept a rescue that heavily diluted their stakes.

Most trades these days are conducted by computer and are completed without fuss. As in other fields, technology has reduced costs, in particular the spread between the bid and offer prices. If lower trading costs encourage more investors to own shares, then the cost of capital for companies will fall, which is good news for the whole economy.

But there are drawbacks. The Knight glitch was just the latest in a series of cock-ups that have been linked to computerized trading. The most serious of these was the "flash crash" of May 2010, when the Dow Jones Industrial Average plunged 1,000 points within minutes and shares in Accenture, a consultancy, were briefly marked down to a preposterous one cent. Such events make investors fearful of trusting their nest-eggs to the stock market; Knight was the biggest handler of trades by small investors. The cost of capital could go up, not down.

Then there is the systemic risk. This time round, it was only Knight Capital that failed; what if it had been a much larger firm? The crisis of 2008 casts a long shadow. Not only did it show that financial companies can quickly implode, but the subsequent government rescues were highly unpopular with voters. Politicians might hesitate before bailing out another big financial firm, especially if the cause was reckless trading.

This newspaper seldom finds itself on the side of restraining either technology or markets. But in this case there is a doubt whether the returns justify the risk. Society needs a stock market to allocate capital efficiently, rewarding the best companies with higher share prices. But high-frequency traders are not making decisions based on a company's future prospects; they are seeking to profit from tiny changes in price. They might as well be trading baseball cards. The liquidity benefits of such trading are all very well, but that liquidity can evaporate at times of stress. And although high-frequency trading may make markets less volatile in normal times, it may add to the turbulence at the worst possible moment.

Trade in Haste, Repent at Leisure

So what is to be done? The world is not going back to the days of face-to-face trading with prices written on whiteboards by hand (a system that was controlled by a cozy cartel of dealers). But the Securities and Exchange Commission is right to suggest that automated programs should be fully tested before they are used in live trading, and that voluntary guidelines on automated trading should be mandatory.

The regulators could go further. In October 1987 Wall Street suffered Black Monday, when the Dow Jones Industrial Average fell 23% in a day. An early form of programmed trading, called portfolio insurance, was to blame. In the aftermath "circuit breakers" were introduced, allowing trading to be halted when the market suffered a big fall. The same rules could be applied when the market seems excessively volatile, or when volume spikes exponentially. The most successful investor in history, Warren Buffett, says his ideal holding period for shares is for ever. So it surely will not do much harm to investors if, on occasion, they have to wait a second or two before dealing.

SOURCE: © The Economist Newspaper Limited, London (August 11, 2012).

LESSONS OF THE ARTICLE

Information technology lowers the costs of financial transactions, making securities more liquid and the financial system more efficient. But securities trading is now so rapid that further speed gains have diminishing benefits for the economy, while the introduction of untested technologies can undermine trading and cause intermediaries to fail. The article highlights the potential conflict between the incentives of firms that seek a competitive edge through faster trading of stocks and the economy's need for a robust system of exchange.

LESSONS FROM THE CRISIS
INTERBANK LENDING

Interbank lending is a critical foundation of modern financial markets. In normal times, banks lend to each other in large volumes at low cost without collateral for periods ranging from overnight to a few months. These liquid, interbank loans are the marginal source of funds for many banks, and their cost guides other lending rates.

Interbank lending helps smooth the function of markets because it allows banks to satisfy temporary, localized excess demand for funding liquidity (see Chapter 2, Lessons from the Crisis: Market Liquidity, Funding Liquidity, and Making Markets). If a bank could not reliably borrow and lend each day to offset the random ebbs and flows of its deposits and loans, it would need to hold a larger volume of cash to insure itself against unanticipated payment outflows or loan demand. For the banking system as a whole, such extra cash holdings waste resources that could be lent profitably elsewhere.

Events occasionally strain the interbank market. For example, on September 11, 2001, physical disruptions and communication obstacles boosted banks' demand for funds. The Federal Reserve supplied extraordinary amounts of liquidity for a few days until efficient interbank lending was restored.

The financial crisis of 2007–2009 triggered much greater, and more prolonged, strains in interbank lending. Rather than lend out additional liquid assets, anxious banks preferred to hold them in case their own needs might rise. Banks also grew concerned about the safety of their trading partners as the

level of trust and confidence plunged. The rising cost and reduced availability of interbank loans created a vicious circle of increased caution, greater demand for liquid assets, reduced willingness to lend, and higher loan rates.

The waves of the financial crisis may be seen in the accompanying figure that shows the extra cost (or *spread*) of an interbank loan over the expected federal funds rate (the interest rate that the U.S. Federal Reserve chooses to control as its primary policy tool—see Chapter 16). Beginning in August 2007, this spread jumped and remained elevated. When Lehman Brothers failed on September 15, 2008, the spread leapt above 350 basis points as panic dried up interbank lending.

Unprecedented actions by governments to add liquidity and guarantee bank debt eventually eased the record interbank lending strains in 2009, but these actions did not prevent extensive disruptions in the financial system and the global economy. The financial crisis made painfully clear to surviving financial institutions that they cannot always count on being able to borrow at a low cost when needed.

Finally, however severe, the 2007–2009 crisis was hardly an isolated incident. In Chapter 14 we will see that banking crises are quite common. For example, the fragility of banks in the euro area is a key aspect of the broader financial crisis that began there in 2009. In 2012, many banks in Greece, Ireland, Italy, Portugal, and Spain became unable to borrow from banks elsewhere. Had the European Central Bank not conducted extraordinary lending operations, the liquidity crisis probably would have shuttered the banking systems of those five countries, with potentially catastrophic worldwide spillover effects.

problem from the perspective of the economy as a whole, think of an arms race in which all sides acquire more powerful and expensive weapons to hold their opponents at bay: in the end, everyone loses through the waste of resources even if the weapons aren't used.

Finally, the advent of multiple electronic exchanges and ECNs has not resulted in a single, integrated, and transparent U.S. stock market. In such an ideal market, the best bid from any customer would instantly and costlessly be matched against the best offer, and all parties could see the entire schedule of bids and offers prior to trading. Currently, a government rule known as the National Best Bid and Offer (NBBO) mechanism requires brokers to provide the best prevailing prices to customers. Other government rules make all trades visible *after* they occur.

However, not all bids and offers are visible *prior* to a trade. For example, if an ECN is carrying a bid or offer that differs from the latest trade price, it need not be reported to the broader market.[10] In effect, the limit-order books of ECNs are not fully integrated with the limit-order books on regulated exchanges or with each other. The existence of multiple, disconnected order books means that a customer's order may not

[10]The lack of transparency results in a segmentation of market liquidity between an ECN on the one hand and exchanges and other ECNs on the other. Referring to this opacity, observers sometimes use the term "dark pool" to describe the market liquidity in ECNs.

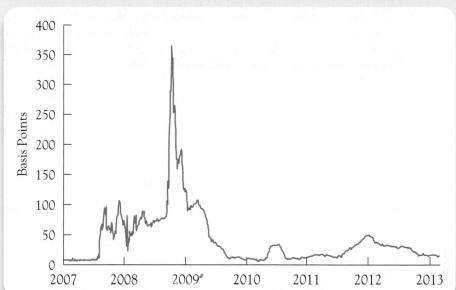

Strains in the Interbank Market: Interbank Lending Rate *Minus* Expected Federal Reserve Policy Interest Rate, 2007–2013

SOURCE: *Bloomberg, www.bloomberg.com*
Note: The vertical scale is in basis points (a basis point is 0.01 percent). The figure shows the gap between two measures: (1) the cost of an interbank loan, represented by the three-month London Interbank Offered Rate (LIBOR, see Chapter 13) and (2) the expected federal funds rate (the Federal Reserve's policy interest rate), represented by a financial instrument called the overnight indexed swap (OIS). One party in an OIS pays a fixed interest rate in return for a payment from the other party equal to the average federal funds rate over the life of the swap. The OIS rate should closely reflect the expected federal funds rate.

be executed at the best possible price. So despite all the costly and sophisticated electronic technology, better integration of the U.S. equity market remains an important subject for investors and regulators alike.

Debt and Equity versus Derivative Markets   A useful way to think of the structure of financial markets is to distinguish between markets where *debt and equity* are traded and those where *derivative instruments* are traded. **Debt markets** are the markets for loans, mortgages, and bonds—the instruments that allow for the transfer of resources from lenders to borrowers and at the same time give investors a store of value for their wealth. **Equity markets** are the markets for stocks. For the most part, stocks are traded in the countries where the companies are based. U.S. companies' stocks are traded in the United States, Japanese stocks in Japan, Chinese stocks in China, and so on. In the United States, in the first quarter of 2013, the market value of corporate equities was $28 trillion, while debt securities (including government debt) outstanding totaled $37 trillion. Derivative markets are the markets where investors trade instruments like futures, options, and swaps, which are designed primarily to transfer risk. To put it another way, in debt and equity markets, actual claims are bought and sold for immediate cash payment; in derivative markets, investors make agreements that are settled later.

Looking at debt instruments in more detail, we can place them in one of two categories, depending on the length of time until the final payment, called the loan's maturity. Debt instruments that are completely repaid in less than a year (from their original issue date) are traded in **money markets**, while those with a maturity of more than a year are traded in **bond markets**. *Money market instruments* have different names and are treated somewhat differently from *bond market instruments*. For example, the United States Treasury issues Treasury bills, which have a maturity of less than one year when they are issued and are traded in the money market. U.S. Treasury notes, which are repaid at the end of 2 to 10 years, trade in the bond markets, as do U.S. Treasury bonds, which are repaid at the end of 20 to 30 years. The same distinction can be made for large private corporations, which issue commercial paper when borrowing for short periods and corporate bonds when borrowing for long periods.

Characteristics of a Well-Run Financial Market

Well-run financial markets exhibit a few essential characteristics that are related to the role we ask them to play in our economies. First, these markets must be designed to keep transaction costs low. Second, the information the market pools and communicates must be both accurate and widely available. If analysts do not communicate accurate assessments of the firms they follow, the markets will not generate the correct prices for the firms' stocks. The prices of financial instruments reflect all the information that is available to market participants. Those prices are the link between the financial markets and the real economy, ensuring that resources are allocated to their most efficient uses. If the information that goes into the market is wrong, then the prices will be wrong, and the economy will not operate as effectively as it could.

Finally, investors need protection. For the financial system to work at all, borrowers' promises to pay lenders must be credible. Individuals must be assured that their investments will not simply be stolen. Lenders must be able to enforce their right to receive repayment (or to seize the collateral) quickly and at low cost. In countries that have weak investor protections, firms can behave deceptively, borrowing when they have no intention of repaying the funds and going unpunished. The lack of proper safeguards dampens people's willingness to invest. Thus, governments are an essential part of financial markets, because they set and enforce the rules of the game. While informal lending networks do develop and flourish spontaneously, they can accommodate only simple, small-scale transactions. Because modern financial markets require a legal structure that is designed and enforced by the government, countries with better investor protections have bigger and deeper financial markets than other countries.

Financial Institutions

Financial institutions are the firms that provide access to the financial markets, both to savers who wish to purchase financial instruments directly and to borrowers who want to issue them. Because financial institutions sit between savers and borrowers, they are also known as *financial intermediaries*, and what they do is known as intermediation. Banks, insurance companies, securities firms, and pension funds are all financial intermediaries. These institutions are essential; any disturbance to the services they provide will have severe adverse effects on the economy.

To understand the importance of financial institutions, think what the world would be like if they didn't exist. Without an intermediary, individuals and households

LESSONS FROM THE CRISIS
SHADOW BANKS

Over the past few decades, financial intermediation and leverage in the United States has shifted away from traditional banks* and toward other financial institutions that are less subject to government rules. These other intermediaries include brokerages, consumer and mortgage finance firms, insurers, investment organizations (such as hedge funds and private equity firms†), money-market mutual funds (MMMFs), and even bank-created asset-management firms, such as special investment vehicles (SIVs).

These other intermediaries have come to be known as *shadow banks* because they provide services that compete with or substitute for those supplied by traditional banks. Unlike banks, however, shadow banks do not accept deposits. In addition, the leverage and risk taking of shadow banks can be greater than that of traditional banks while being less transparent.

Beginning in the 1970s, financial innovation sped the shift of intermediation to the shadow banks and was, in turn, stimulated by it. Broader markets, plunging information costs, new profit opportunities, and government practices all encouraged the development of new financial instruments and institutions to meet customer needs at lower cost.

Over time, the rise of highly leveraged shadow banks—combined with government relaxation of rules for traditional banks—permitted a rise of leverage in the financial system as a whole, making it more vulnerable to shocks (see Lessons from the Crisis: Leverage earlier in this chapter).

Rapid growth in some new financial instruments made it easier to conceal leverage and risk-taking. Derivatives—options, futures, and the like—allow investors to transfer risks at low cost (see Chapter 9). After 2000, the use of customized derivatives that do not trade in open markets (so-called over-the-counter, or OTC, derivatives) rose dramatically. Those derivatives permitted some large financial institutions to take risks that were unknown to their investors and trading partners and to the public officials who were supposed to monitor them. The spillover from the failure of these firms during the financial crisis nearly sank the entire system.

The financial crisis of 2007–2009 transformed shadow banking. During the fateful week that began with the failure of Lehman Brothers on Monday, September 15, 2008, the largest U.S. brokerages failed, merged, or converted themselves into traditional banks in order to secure access to funding. In the same month, the loss of confidence in MMMFs required a U.S. government guarantee to halt withdrawals. During the crisis, many SIVs failed or were reabsorbed by the banks that created them. Many hedge funds chose to shrink or close as investors fled.

The future of shadow banking remains highly uncertain. The crisis has encouraged governments to scrutinize any financial institution that could, by its risk taking, pose a threat to the financial system. Partly as a result, the scope for leverage and risk taking is lower for now, but incentives to take risk—at others' expense—still can fuel future disruptions.

*One traditional form of bank is a commercial bank, which is defined in Chapter 12 as accepting deposits from and making loans to businesses and individuals.

†Hedge funds (defined in Chapter 13) are private, largely unregulated investment partnerships that bring together small groups of wealthy people who meet certain financial requirements. Private equity funds are investment pools that typically invest directly in private companies to gain management control.

wishing to save would either have to hold their wealth in cash or figure out some way to funnel it directly to companies or households that could put it to use. The assets of these household savers would be some combination of government liabilities and the equity and debt issued by corporations and other households. All finance would be direct, with borrowers obtaining funds straight from the lenders.

Such a system would be unlikely to work very well, for a number of reasons. First, individual transactions between saver-lenders and spender-borrowers would likely be extremely expensive. Not only would the two sides have difficulty finding each other, but even if they did, writing the contract to effect the transaction would be very costly. Second, lenders need to evaluate the creditworthiness of borrowers and then monitor them to ensure that they don't abscond with the funds. Individuals are not specialists in monitoring. Third, most borrowers want to borrow for the long term, while lenders favor more liquid short-term loans. Lenders would surely require compensation for the illiquidity of long-term loans, driving the price of borrowing up.

A financial market could be created in which the loans and other securities could be resold, but that would create the risk of price fluctuations. All these problems would restrict the flow of resources through the economy. Healthy financial institutions open up the flow, directing it to the most productive investments and increasing the system's efficiency.

The Role of Financial Institutions

Financial institutions reduce transactions costs by specializing in the issuance of standardized securities. They reduce the information costs of screening and monitoring borrowers to make sure they are creditworthy and they use the proceeds of a loan or security issue properly. In other words, financial institutions curb information asymmetries and the problems that go along with them, helping resources flow to their most productive uses.

At the same time that they make long-term loans, financial institutions also give savers ready access to their funds. That is, they issue short-term liabilities to lenders while making long-term loans to borrowers. By making loans to many different borrowers at once, financial institutions can provide savers with financial instruments that are both more liquid and less risky than the individual stocks and bonds they would purchase directly in financial markets.

Figure 3.2 is a schematic overview of the financial system. It shows that there are two types of financial institutions: those that provide brokerage services (top) and those that transform assets (bottom). Broker institutions give households and corporations access to financial markets and direct finance. Institutions that transform assets take deposits or investments or issue insurance contracts to households. They use the proceeds to make loans and purchase stocks, bonds, and real estate. That is their transformation function. Figure 3.3 shows what the balance sheet for such an institution would include.

The Structure of the Financial Industry

In analyzing the structure of the financial industry, we can start by dividing intermediaries into two broad categories called depository and nondepository institutions. *Depository institutions* take deposits and make loans; they are what most people think of as banks, whether they are commercial banks, savings banks, or credit unions. *Nondepository institutions* include insurance companies, securities firms, mutual fund companies, hedge funds, private equity or venture capital firms, finance companies, and pension funds. Each of these serves a very different function from a bank. Some screen and monitor borrowers; others transfer and reduce risk. Still others are primarily brokers. Here is a list of the major groups of financial institutions, together with a brief description of what they do.

1. **Depository institutions** (commercial banks, savings banks, and credit unions) take deposits and make loans.
2. **Insurance companies** accept premiums, which they invest in securities and real estate (their assets) in return for promising compensation to policyholders should certain events occur (their liabilities). Life insurers protect against the risk of untimely death. Property and casualty insurers protect against personal injury loss and losses from theft, accidents, and fire.
3. **Pension funds** invest individual and company contributions in stocks, bonds, and real estate (their assets) in order to provide payments to retired workers (their liabilities).

Figure 3.2   Flow of Funds through Financial Institutions

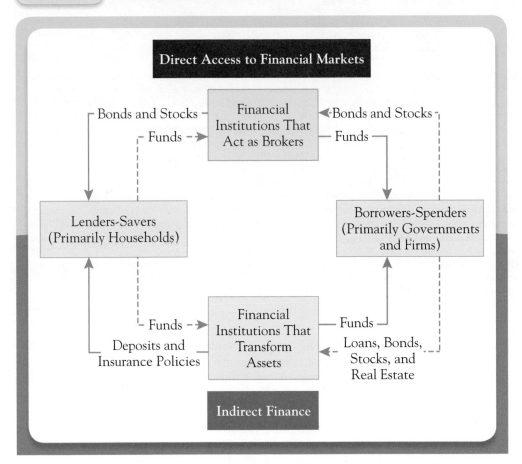

Financial institutions perform both brokerage and asset transformation services. As brokers, they provide access to financial markets, allowing households and firms to buy and sell direct claims on other firms and on governments. Institutions transform assets by taking deposits or investments or issuing insurance contracts to households at the same time that they make loans and purchase stocks, bonds, and real estate.

4. **Securities firms** include brokers, investment banks, underwriters, mutual-fund companies, private equity firms, and venture capital firms. Brokers and investment banks issue stocks and bonds for corporate customers, trade them, and advise customers. All these activities give customers access to the financial markets. Mutual-fund companies pool the resources of individuals and companies and invest them in portfolios of bonds, stocks, and real estate. Hedge funds do the same for small groups of wealthy investors. Customers own shares of the portfolios, so they face the risk that the assets will change in value. But portfolios are less risky than individual securities, and individual savers can purchase smaller units than they could if they went directly to

Figure 3.3   The Simplified Balance Sheet of a Financial Institution

Assets	Liabilities
Bonds	Deposits
Stocks	Shares
Loans	Insurance policies
Real estate	

YOUR FINANCIAL WORLD

Shop for a Mortgage

Everyone loves a bargain. There are people who will spend hours making sure they pay the lowest price they can for virtually anything they buy. Borrowing shouldn't be any different. When the time comes to buy a house, most of us need to borrow. That is, we need to get a mortgage. Because the mortgage payment will almost surely be your biggest monthly expense, getting the cheapest mortgage you can will save you more than a year's worth of bargain hunting in stores.

There are a number of ways to shop for a mortgage. Any real estate agent can hand you a list of mortgage providers in your area. You can also find websites that publish quotes for mortgages. As you look through these lists, you'll notice that many of the firms on them are not banks. Instead, they are *mortgage brokers,* firms that have access to pools of funds earmarked for use as mortgages.

Say, for instance, that a financial firm raises a large amount of financing to be used to make mortgages. A pool of $100 million can finance a thousand $100,000 mortgages. Shares in these pools are sold to investors. If you get a mortgage from one of these firms, it will go into the pool. In the first quarter of 2013, nearly half of the $13 trillion in mortgages in the United States was in these mortgage pools.

Should you care whether you get your mortgage from a traditional bank or a mortgage broker? Should you care if your mortgage is pooled and sold off? The answer is no; it should make no difference to you. In fact, chances are that regardless of which option you choose—bank or mortgage broker—you'll make your payments to a company that does nothing but collect them and monitor your compliance. From your point of view, a mortgage is a mortgage. Get the one that suits you best. But shop before you sign on the dotted line. And if you let the various brokers know that you are shopping around, they may start competing for your business and give you a better deal.

the financial markets. Private equity and venture capital firms also serve wealthy investors: They acquire controlling stakes in a few firms and manage them actively to boost the return on investment before reselling them. In contrast, most mutual funds consist of passive investors, who do not seek to influence management.

5. **Finance companies** raise funds directly in the financial markets in order to make loans to individuals and firms. Finance companies tend to specialize in particular types of loans, such as mortgage, automobile, or certain types of business equipment. While their assets are similar to a bank's, their liabilities are debt instruments that are traded in financial markets, not deposits.

6. **Government-sponsored enterprises (GSEs)** are federal credit agencies that provide loans directly for farmers and home mortgagors. They also guarantee programs that insure loans made by private lenders. Aside from GSEs, the government also provides retirement income and medical care to the elderly through Social Security and Medicare. Pension funds and insurance companies perform these functions privately.

As we continue our study of the relationship between the financial system and the real economy, we will return to the importance of financial institutions, the conduits that channel resources from savers to investors. These intermediaries are absolutely essential to the operation of any economy. When they cease to function, so does everything else. Recall from Chapter 2 that the measures of money (M1 and M2) include checking deposits, savings deposits, and certificates of deposit, among other things. These are all important liabilities of banks. Because they are very liquid, they are accepted as a means of payment. Clearly, the financial structure is tied to the availability of money and credit. But we are getting ahead of ourselves. Before we study financial institutions, we need to look more closely at financial instruments and financial markets, the subjects of Part II of this book.

Terms

asset, 46

asset-backed security, 53

bond market, 64

broker, 55

centralized exchange, 59

collateral, 53

counterparty, 51

dealer, 55

debt market, 63

derivative instrument, 51

direct finance, 45

electronic communications networks
  (ECNs), 59

equity market, 63

financial institutions, 46

financial instrument, 47

financial markets, 54

high-frequency trader (HFTs), 60

indirect finance, 45

intermediary, 46

liability, 46

money market, 64

mortgage-backed security, 53

over-the-counter (OTC)
  market, 59

portfolio, 56

primary financial market, 58

secondary financial market, 58

trading algorithm, 60

underlying instrument, 51

Using FRED: Codes for Data in This Chapter

Data Series	FRED Data Code
U.S. household net worth	TNWBSHNO
Household financial assets	TFAABSHNO
Household deposits	DABSHNO
Market value of equities of nonfarm nonfinancial corporations	MVEONWMVBSNNCB
Credit from U.S. domestic financial sector	TCMAHDFS
Credit from U.S. commercial banks	LOANINV
Residential mortgages	HMLBSHNO
3-month U.S. dollar LIBOR	USD3MTD156N
Number of commercial banks	USNUM
Dow Jones Industrial Average	DJIA
Commercial bank equity/assets ratio (inverse of leverage)	EQTA

www.mhhe.com/moneyandbanking4e

Chapter Lessons

1. Financial instruments are crucial to the operation of the economy.
    a. Financial arrangements can be either formal or informal. Industrial economies are dominated by formal arrangements.
    b. A financial instrument is the written legal obligation of one party to transfer something of value, usually money, to another party at some future date, under certain conditions.
    c. Financial instruments are used primarily as stores of value and means of trading risk. They are less likely to be used as means of payment, although many of them can be.
    d. Financial instruments are most useful when they are simple and standardized.
    e. There are two basic classes of financial instruments: underlying and derivative.
        i. Underlying instruments are used to transfer resources directly from one party to another.
        ii. Derivative instruments derive their value from the behavior of an underlying instrument.
    f. The payments promised by a financial instrument are more valuable
        i. The larger they are.
        ii. The sooner they are made.
        iii. The more likely they are to be made.
        iv. If they are made when they are needed most.
    g. Common examples of financial instruments include
        i. Those that serve primarily as stores of value, including bank loans, bonds, mortgages, stocks, and asset-backed securities.
        ii. Those that are used primarily to transfer risk, including futures and options.

2. Financial markets are essential to the operation of our economic system.
    a. Financial markets
        i. Offer savers and borrowers liquidity so that they can buy and sell financial instruments easily.
        ii. Pool and communicate information through prices.
        iii. Allow for the sharing of risk.
    b. There are several ways to categorize financial markets.
        i. Primary markets that issue new securities versus secondary markets, where existing securities are bought and sold.
        ii. Physically centralized exchanges, dealer-based electronic systems (over-the-counter markets), or electronic networks.
        iii. Debt and equity markets (where instruments that are used primarily for financing are traded) versus derivative markets (where instruments that are used to transfer risk are traded).
    c. A well-functioning financial market is characterized by
        i. Low transactions costs and sufficient liquidity.
        ii. Accurate and widely available information.
        iii. Legal protection of investors against the arbitrary seizure of their property.
        iv. Ability to enforce contracts quickly at low cost.

3. Financial institutions perform brokerage and asset transformation functions.
    a. In their role as brokers or dealers, they provide access to financial markets.
    b. In transforming assets, they provide loans and other forms of indirect finance.
    c. Intermediation reduces transaction and information costs.
    d. Financial institutions, also known as financial intermediaries, help individuals and firms to transfer and reduce risk.

Conceptual and Analytical Problems

1. As the end of the month approaches, you realize that you probably will not be able to pay the next month's rent. Describe both an informal and a formal financial instrument that you might use to solve your dilemma. *(LO1)*

2.* While we often associate informal financial arrangements with poorer countries where financial systems are less developed, informal arrangements often coexist with even the most developed financial systems. What advantages might there be to engaging in informal arrangements rather than utilizing the formal financial sector? *(LO1)*

3. If higher leverage is associated with greater risk, explain why the process of de-leveraging (reducing leverage) can be destabilizing. *(LO2)*

4. The Chicago Mercantile Exchange has announced the introduction of a financial instrument that is based on rainfall in the state of Illinois. The standard agreement states that for each inch of rain over and above the average rainfall for a particular month, the seller will pay the buyer $1,000. Who could benefit from buying such a contract? Who could benefit from selling it? *(LO1)*

5. If you wish to buy an annuity that makes monthly payments for as long as you live, describe what happens to the purchase price of the annuity if (1) your age at the time of purchase goes up, (2) the size of the monthly payment rises, and (3) your health improves. *(LO1)*

6. Which of the following would be more valuable to you: a portfolio of stocks that rises in value when your income rises or a portfolio of stocks that rises in value when your income falls? Why? *(LO1)*

7. *The Wall Street Journal* has a daily listing of what are called "Money Rates" or interest rates on short-term securities. Locate it either in a recent issue of the newspaper by looking at the index on page 1 of the Money and Investing section, or in the Market Data Center of www.wsj.com. The most important money rates are the prime rate, the federal funds rate, and the Treasury bill rate. Describe each of these and report the current rate quoted in the paper. *(LO1)*

8. Designated market makers, who historically have provided liquidity (i.e., have stood by ready to buy and sell) in markets for specific stocks, have declined in importance. Explain this decline in terms of technology and global economic integration. *(LO2)*

9. The design and function of financial instruments, markets, and institutions are tied to the importance of information. Describe the role played by information in each of these three pieces of the financial system. *(LO2)*

10. Suppose you need to take out a personal loan with a bank. Explain how you could be affected by problems in the interbank lending market such as those seen during the 2007–2009 financial crisis. *(LO2)*

11.* Advances in technology have facilitated the widespread use of credit scoring by financial institutions in making their lending decisions. Credit scoring can be defined broadly as the use of historical data and statistical techniques to rank the attractiveness of potential borrowers and guide lending decisions. In what ways might this practice enhance the efficiency of the financial system? *(LO3)*

*Indicates more difficult problems

12. Commercial banks, insurance companies, investment banks, and pension funds are all examples of financial intermediaries. For each, give an example of a source of their funds and an example of their use of funds. *(LO3)*

13. Life insurance companies tend to invest in *long-term* assets such as loans to manufacturing firms to build factories or to real estate developers to build shopping malls and skyscrapers. Automobile insurers tend to invest in *short-term* assets such as Treasury bills. What accounts for these differences? *(LO3)*

14. For each pair of instruments below, use the criteria for valuing a financial instrument to choose the one with the highest value. *(LO1)*
    a. A U.S. Treasury bill that pays $1,000 in six months or a U.S. Treasury bill that pays $1,000 in three months.
    b. A U.S. Treasury bill that pays $1,000 in three months or commercial paper issued by a private corporation that pays $1,000 in three months.
    c. An insurance policy that pays out in the event of serious illness or one that pays out when you are healthy, assuming you are equally likely to be ill or healthy.

    Explain each of your choices briefly.

15. Joe and Mike purchase identical houses for $200,000. Joe makes a down payment of $40,000, while Mike only puts down $10,000; for each individual, the down payment is the total of his net worth. Assuming everything else is equal, who is more highly leveraged? If house prices in the neighborhood immediately fall by 10 percent (before any mortgage payments are made), what would happen to Joe's and Mike's net worth? *(LO2)*

16.* Everything else being equal, which would be more valuable to you—a derivative instrument whose value is derived from an underlying instrument with a very volatile price history or one derived from an underlying instrument with a very stable price history? Explain your choice. *(LO2)*

17. You decide to start a business selling covers for smartphones in a mall kiosk. To buy inventory, you need to borrow some funds. Why are you more likely to take out a bank loan than to issue bonds? *(LO3)*

18. Splitland is a developing economy with two distinct regions. The northern region has great investment opportunities, but the people who live there need to consume all of their income to survive. Those living in the south are better off than their northern counterparts and save a significant portion of their income. The southern region, however, has few profitable investment opportunities and so most of the savings remain in shoeboxes and under mattresses. Explain how the development of the financial sector could benefit both regions and promote economic growth in Splitland. *(LO2)*

19. What would you expect to happen to investment and growth in the economy if the U.S. government decided to abolish the Securities and Exchange Commission? *(LO2)*

20. Use Core Principle 3 from Chapter 1 to suggest some ways in which the problems associated with the shadow banking sector during the 2007–2009 financial crisis could be mitigated in the future. *(LO3)*

21. What risks might financial institutions face by funding long-run loans such as mortgages to borrowers (often at fixed interest rates) with short-term deposits from savers? *(LO3)*

22.* As the manager of a financial institution, what steps could you take to reduce the risks referred to in Problem 21? *(LO3)*

Data Exploration

Scan here for quick access to the hints for these problems. Need a barcode reader? Try ScanLife, available in your app store.

For detailed instructions on using Federal Reserve Economic Data (FRED) online to answer each of the following problems, visit www.mhhe.com/moneyandbanking4e and click on Student Edition, then Data Exploration Hints.

1. Probably the most famous stock index is the Dow Jones Industrial Average. Plot this index (FRED code: DJIA) over the period from 1960 to the present. *(LO2)*

2. Plot the percent change from a year ago of the Dow Jones Industrial Average (FRED code: DJIA). Discuss the behavior of changes in the index before, during, and after recession periods, which are indicated by the vertical, shaded bars in the graph. *(LO2)*

3. Do changes in stock values affect the wealth of households? Beginning in 1960, plot on a quarterly basis the percent change from a year ago of the Dow Jones Industrial Average (FRED code: DJIA) and the percent change from a year ago of household net worth (FRED code: TNWBSHNO). Compare the two lines. *(LO2)*

4. The Dow Jones Industrial Average is an index of the prices of only 30 stocks. Consider a much broader measure of the stock market—the market value of equities (FRED code: MVEONWMVBSNNCB)—which sums the price of each stock times the number of outstanding shares. After plotting it, comment on its pattern since the mid-1990s. *(LO2)*

5. In Data Exploration Problem 3, you looked at changes in household net worth. In Data Exploration Problem 4 you examined stock market wealth. Aside from stock market wealth, what other assets contribute to household net worth? *(LO1)*

Part *II*

Interest Rates, Financial Instruments, and Financial Markets

Chapter 4

Future Value, Present Value, and Interest Rates

Learning Objectives

Understand . . .

LO1 Time and the value of payments

LO2 Present value versus future value

LO3 Nominal versus real interest rates

Lenders have been despised for most of history. The borrowers must pay for their loans, while the lenders just sit around doing nothing. No wonder people have been vilified for charging interest. No wonder that, for centuries, clerics pointed to biblical passages damning interest. Even philosophers weighed in against the practice, including Aristotle, who called the "breeding of money from money" unnatural.

After scorning lenders for millennia, we now recognize their service as a fundamental building block of civilization. Credit is one of the critical mechanisms we have for allocating resources. Without it, our market-based economy would grind to a halt. Even the simplest financial transaction, like saving some of your paycheck each month to buy a car, would be difficult, if not impossible. And corporations, most of which survive from day to day by borrowing to finance their activities, would not be able to function. Credit is so basic that we can find records of people lending grain and metal from 5,000 years ago. Credit probably existed before common measures of value, and it predates coinage by 2,000 years.

Despite its early existence and its central role in economic transactions, credit was hard to come by until the Protestant Reformation. By the 16th century, views had changed, and interest payments were tolerated if not encouraged, so long as the rate charged was thought to be reasonable. Some historians even point to this shift as a key to the development of capitalism and its institutions. Protestant European countries did develop faster than Catholic ones, at least at first.[1] Since then, credit has exploded, facilitating extraordinary increases in general economic well-being. Yet even so, most people still take a dim view of the fact that lenders charge interest. Why?

The main reason for the enduring unpopularity of interest comes from the failure to appreciate the fact that lending has an opportunity cost. Think of it from the point of view of the lender. People who offer credit don't need to make loans. They have alternatives, and extending a loan means giving them up. While lenders can eventually

---

[1]Max Weber makes this argument in his classic work *The Protestant Ethic and the Spirit of Capitalism,* first published in 1905.

recoup the sum they lend, neither the time that the loan was outstanding nor the opportunities missed during that time can be gotten back. So interest isn't really "the breeding of money from money," as Aristotle put it; it's more like a rental fee that borrowers must pay lenders to compensate them for lost opportunities.

It's no surprise that in today's world, interest rates are of enormous importance to virtually everyone—individuals, businesses, and governments. Quoted as a percentage of the amount borrowed, interest rates link the present to the future, allowing us to compare payments made on different dates. Interest rates also tell us the future reward for lending today, as well as the cost of borrowing now and repaying later. To make sound financial decisions, we must learn how to calculate and compare different rates on various financial instruments. In this chapter, we'll explore interest rates using the concepts of future value and present value and then apply those concepts to the valuation of bonds. Finally, we'll look at the relationship between interest rates and inflation.

Valuing Monetary Payments Now and in the Future

To compare the value of payments made on different dates, we need a set of tools called *future value* and *present value*. We'll use them to see how and why the promise to make a payment on one date is more or less valuable than the promise to make a payment on a different date. For example, we already know that if you want to borrow $100 today, your repayment needs to be bigger if you promise to make it in a year than if you promise to make it in a month. But how much more will you have to pay? The answer depends on both the date of payment and the interest rate. For the time being, we're going to assume that we know for sure that you will repay the loan. We'll get to the possibility of default when we study risk in the next chapter.

Future Value and Compound Interest

TIME

What is the future value of one dollar deposited in an interest-bearing account today? To answer this question, let's start with a definition: **Future value** *is the value on some future date of an investment made today.* Say that today you invest $100 in a savings account that guarantees 5 percent interest per year. After one year, you'll have $105 (the investment at its present value of $100 plus $5 in interest). So the future value of $100 one year from now at an interest rate of 5 percent is $105. We could also say that the $100 investment yields $5, which explains why an interest rate is sometimes called a **yield**. Notice that the same calculation works for a simple loan in which you borrow $100 for one year at 5 percent interest. The amount you will need to repay is $105. Remember Core Principle 1: Time has value.

To generalize this concept so that we can handle different interest rates and initial investments of any size, we can express it mathematically. First we need to convert the percentage interest rate into a decimal, so that 5 percent becomes 0.05. *Note that in this expression, as in all mathematical manipulations in this chapter, the interest rate is expressed in decimal terms.* Now we can express future value as an equation. If the present value of your initial investment is $100 and the interest rate is 5 percent, then the *future value* one year from now is:

$$\$100 + \$100 \times (0.05) = \$105$$

Present value of the investment + Interest = Future value in one year

It is essential to convert all interest rates to decimals before doing any computation. This is consistent with the fact that we quote interest rates as "parts per 100," so 5 percent means 5 parts per 100, or 0.05.

This expression shows us immediately that the higher the interest rate, the higher the future value. If the interest rate were to rise to 6 percent, then the future value of $100 would be

$$\$100 + \$100\,(0.06) = \$106$$

In general, the future value, *FV*, of an investment with a present value, *PV*, invested at an interest rate *i* is:

$$FV = PV + PV \times i$$
$$= PV \times (1 + i) \tag{1}$$

Future value in one year

$$= \text{Present value of the investment today} \times (\text{one plus the interest rate})$$

We can see right away that the higher the interest rate or the amount invested, the higher the future value.

But this example is too simple. Most financial instruments don't make single payments in exactly one year, so we need to figure out what happens when the time to repayment varies. Computing the future value of an investment to be repaid two years from now is straightforward, so let's do that first. But because we quote interest rates on a yearly basis, we need to be careful. Using one-year interest rates to compute the value of an investment that will be repaid more than one year from now requires applying the concept of **compound interest**, *which is interest on the interest.* If you leave an investment in an interest-bearing account for two years, during the second year you will receive interest not only on your initial investment but also on the interest you earned for the first year (because they both have an opportunity cost).

Getting back to our example, let's say that you leave your $100 deposit in the bank for two years at 5 percent interest per year. The future value of this investment has four parts. The first three are straightforward. They are the initial investment of $100, the interest on that investment in the first year, and the interest on it in the second year. But because you left the interest from the first year in the bank during the second year, it is as if you made a new deposit at the beginning of the second year, and that earns interest too. So the fourth part of the future value is the interest you receive during the second year on the interest you received in the first year. That's compounding. With an initial deposit of $100 and an interest rate of 5 percent, we can add up these four parts to compute your investment's future value in two years.

$$\$100 + \$100(0.05) + \$100(0.05) + \$5(0.05) = \$110.25$$

Present value of the initial investment

+ Interest on the initial investment in first year

+ Interest on the initial investment in second year

+ Interest on the interest from first year in second year

= Future value in two years

We can use a small amount of algebra[2] to show that this equals

$$\$100(1.05)(1.05) = \$100(1.05)^2$$

---

[2]The algebra is as follows: $\$100 + \$100(0.05) + \$100(0.05) + \$5(0.05) = \$100(1 + 0.05 + 0.05 + 0.05^2) = \$100(1 + 0.05)(1 + 0.05) = \$100(1 + 0.05)^2 = \$100(1.05)^2$. This result relies on algebraic factoring: namely, $(1 + i + i + i^2) = (1 + 2i + i^2) = (1 + i)^2$.

Table 4.1   Computing the Future Value of $100 at 5 Percent Annual Interest

Years into Future	Computation	Future Value
1	$100(1.05)	$105.00
2	$100(1.05)^2	$110.25
3	$100(1.05)^3	$115.76
4	$100(1.05)^4	$121.55
5	$100(1.05)^5	$127.63
10	$100(1.05)^{10}	$162.89

Extending it to three years, four years, or more just means multiplying by (1.05) over and over again. The multiplication takes care of the compounding. Table 4.1 shows the calculations. The final line shows that after 10 years, a deposit with a present value of $100 becomes $162.89. That is, it earns $62.89 in interest. If we had ignored compounding and just multiplied 5 percent by 10 years to get 50 percent, the answer would have been $150. Compounding produced an additional $12.89 in interest over 10 years. To put it as clearly as possible, multiplying the number of years times the annual interest rate gives the *wrong* answer!

Using the computations in Table 4.1, we can derive a general formula for future value.

$$FV_n = PV \times (1 + i)^n \qquad (2)$$

Future value in *n* years = Present value of the investment

$\times$ (One plus the interest rate) raised to *n*

So to compute future value, all we need to do is calculate one plus the interest rate (measured as a decimal) raised to the n*th power and multiply it by the present value.*

Before we go any further, we should stop to consider an important problem. What if you want to put your $100 into a bank for six months, or 2½ years, or any amount of time that is not a round number of years? The answer is that the formula still works. You can compute the future value using equation (2) regardless of whether *n* is a whole number. There is one pitfall, however. *In computing future value, both the interest rate and* n *must be measured in the same time units.* We have been measuring interest rates as the percentage per year, so we were careful to measure *n* in years as well. So, if we want the future value in half of one year, *n* would be ½; if we wanted it in one month, *n* would be 1/12; and if we wanted the future value in one day, *n* would be 1/365.

As you can see, taking advantage of the future-value formula requires an understanding of the transformations needed to convert time from years to months or vice versa. Converting *n* from years to months is easy—everyone knows there are 12 months in a year—but converting the interest rate is harder. If the annual interest rate is 5 percent, what is the interest rate for one month? To figure out the answer, we'll start with the future-value formula, but in months. Remember that compounding means you *cannot* just multiply the monthly interest rate by 12 to get the annual interest rate. Instead, if i^m is the one-month interest rate and *n* is the number of months, then a deposit made for one year will have a future value of $100(1 + i^m)^{12}$. We know that this amount equals

YOUR FINANCIAL WORLD
How Long Does Your Investment Take to Double?

You invest $100 at 5 percent interest. How long will you need to wait until you have $200? That may seem like a simple question, but compounding makes it difficult. The straightforward (some people would call it "brute force") way to find the answer is to take out your calculator and multiply $100 times 1.05 over and over again counting how many times it takes to get to an answer that is close to $200. If you did that, you would find that after the 14th time, you had reached $197.99. And multiplying once more, you would have $207.89. You would conclude that, at 5 percent interest, your investment takes between 14 and 15 years to double.

While the brute force technique works—you can multiply over and over again—it's clumsy. Fortunately, there is a simpler way called the **rule of 72**. If you want to compute the number of years it takes an investment to double, divide the annual interest rate measured as an integer into 72.* So at an interest rate of 5 percent, we would expect an investment to double in 72/5 = 14.4 years (we can check and see that $1.05^{14.4} = 2.02$). If the interest rate were 8 percent, we would estimate 9 years ($1.08^9 = 2.00$).

The rule of 72 shows the power of compounding. It shows that when the interest rate doubles, the time a $100

investment takes to become $200 is cut in half. That is, while it takes 14.4 years to double at 5 percent interest, it takes only 7.2 years at 10 percent (72/10 = 7.2 and $1.10^{7.2} = 1.99$). This rule works for anything that is growing at a constant rate. So, if you want to estimate how long it will take a country's population or company's sales to double, just divide the annual growth rate measured as a percentage per year into 72.

*The rule of 72 is an approximation of the solution to an algebraic problem that requires the use of logarithms. Consider the formula for compound interest, in which the future value after n years is equal to $FV = PV (1 + i)^n$. Setting the present value PV *equal to 1* and the future value FV *equal to 2* and taking logarithms, we get $n = ln(2)/ln(1 + i)$. This formula is exact. Next, we use the approximation that $ln(1 + i) \approx i$ for small i. Substituting this into the equation gives us $n = ln(2)/i$. The $ln(2) = 0.693$, so it might seem that we should be using the rule of 69.3. For very low interest rates, such as we observed after the 2007–2009 financial crisis in Japan, the United States, and parts of Europe, indeed we should. But in the range of interest rates that we often see (4 to 12 percent), 72 works better.

$100(1.05)$, so figuring out the answer means equating the two amounts,

$$(1 + i^m)^{12} = (1.05)$$

and raising each side to the one-twelfth power:

$$(1 + i^m) = (1.05)^{1/12} = 1.0041$$

Converting from decimals to a percentage, the one-month interest rate is 0.41 percent. We can handle any mismatch between the time units of i and n in a similar way (see Tools of the Trade: Computing Compound Annual Rates on page 84).

These fractions of percentage points, like 0.41 percent, are so important in discussing interest rates that they have their own name, basis points. A **basis point** is one one-hundredth of a percentage point. That is, one basis point equals 0.01 percent.

You're probably wondering how useful all this discussion of future value really is. To see, consider the following question: If you put $1,000 per year into the bank at 4 percent interest, how much would you have saved after 40 years? The answer is $98,826—more than twice the $40,000 you deposited. Figuring out the exact answer is complicated because we need to add up the future values of forty $1,000 deposits, each made in a different year, but doing so uses the concept of future value. The first $1,000 is deposited for 40 years, so its future value is

$$\$1,000(1.04)^{40} - \$4,801.02$$

the second $1,000 is deposited for 39 years, so its future value is

$$\$1,000(1.04)^{39} = \$4,616.37$$

and so on. The practical implication of this calculation is that buying one less soda or candy bar per day isn't just good for your physical health; it's good for your financial health, too.

Present Value

It's easy to see why future value is important. We often want to know what savings and investments will be worth in the future. But that isn't the only thing we need to know. There is another, somewhat different task that we face with some regularity. We need to be able to figure out how much a payment promised in the future is worth today. Say you agree to make a $225 loan, and the borrower offers to repay you either $100 a year for three years or $125 a year for two years. Which offer should you take? Answering this question means figuring out the current value of the promised payments on the dates when they will be made. To do that, we'll use the concept of present value, sometimes referred to as *present discounted value.*

TIME

The Definition In our discussion of future value, we used the term *present value* to mean the initial amount invested or deposited. The way we used the term suggests its technical definition: **Present value** *is the value today (in the present) of a payment that is promised to be made in the future.* Put another way, present value is the amount that must be invested today in order to realize a specific amount on a given future date. Financial instruments promise future cash payments, so we need to know how to value those payments. Present value is an integral component of the computation of the price of all financial instruments.

To understand the calculation of present value, go back to future value. Remember that at a 5 percent interest rate, the future value one year from now of a $100 investment today is $105. It follows that at this same 5 percent interest rate, the present value of $105 one year from now is $100. *All we did was invert the future value calculation.*

Reversing the calculation in general terms is just as easy. Start with the fact that the future value of a payment equals the current investment times one plus the interest rate: $FV = PV \times (1 + i)$ [equation 1]. Divide both sides of this expression by $(1 + i)$ to get an expression for how much we need to invest today to realize the future value one year from today. The result is

$$PV = \frac{FV}{(1 + i)} \tag{3}$$

Present value = Future value of the payment divided by (One plus the interest rate)

In our example, we see that

$$\frac{FV}{(1 + i)} = \frac{\$105}{(1.05)} = \$100$$

so the present value of $105 one year from now, at a 5 percent interest rate, is indeed $100.

While future value tells us what today's investment will be worth in the future, present value tells us what promised future payments are worth today. This means that the properties of present value mirror those of future value. In the same way that future value *rises* as the interest rate rises, present value *falls* as the interest rate rises. To see this, first look at the calculation of the present value of $105 in one year at an interest rate of 6 percent. The answer is

$$\frac{\$105}{1.06} = \$99.06$$

LESSONS FROM THE CRISIS
RISK TAKING AND THE SEARCH FOR YIELD

Core Principle 2 teaches us that risk requires compensation. But to secure proper compensation, investors must understand the risks of what they buy.

The present-value analysis of this chapter helps us understand the risk of bonds with different maturities. If interest rates rise, the losses on a long-term bond will exceed the losses on a short-term bond. The reason is that the further in the future the promised payment, the more the present value falls when interest rates rise. As a result, long-term bonds are more sensitive to the risk that interest rates will change. Unsurprisingly, buyers of long-term bonds usually insist on an extra reward as compensation for such *interest-rate risk* (see discussion of the yield curve in Chapter 7).

In some circumstances, many investors underestimate the risks of particular assets. For example, investors lacking sufficient regard for risk typically seek higher-yield bonds even if those bonds are riskier (due to longer maturities or higher default probabilities).

What can prompt the underestimation of risk? Experience suggests that some investors extrapolate from recent patterns and pay less attention to the more distant past. If interest rates have been low and stable for some time,

investors may expect this pattern to persist even if rates tended to be higher and more volatile in earlier periods.

Extrapolation of recent experience also can lead investors to misjudge default risk. For example, business defaults are relatively infrequent during economic expansions. Because such booms are long and recessions are short, investors can become accustomed to unsustainably low levels of corporate default. Again, naively projecting recent experience underestimates the default risks for which investors should be compensated when buying corporate securities.

Investors also may underestimate risk if their professional investment managers take risks that are not evident or are purposely concealed. As a result, when market interest rates are low, some investment managers may try to generate high interest payments to clients by taking greater risks—a so-called search for yield. Until events compel the manager to reduce payments, the investor may think that the manager is unusually skillful rather than lucky and prone to risk.

The search for yield can bid up the prices of risky securities and depress the market compensation for risk below a sustainable level. Eventually, when the risk comes to fruition (say, defaults increase), the prices of riskier securities fall disproportionately, potentially triggering large financial losses. During the financial crisis of 2007–2009, the plunge of corporate and mortgage security prices highlighted how forcefully markets can reprice risk when the search for yield has gone too far. In the euro-area crisis that began in 2009, something similar occurred in the markets for bank and government debt.

less than the $100 needed when the interest rate is only 5 percent. *Present value falls as the interest rate rises.*

What happens if the payment is going to be made in two years instead of one? What is the present value of $105 in two years at an interest rate of 5 percent? Again, we can compute the answer using the future-value formula by asking what present value has a future value of $105 in two years at an interest rate of 5 percent. This is the solution to

$$\$105 = PV(1.05)^2$$

The answer is

$$PV = \frac{\$105}{1.05^2} = \$95.24$$

We can generalize this process by looking at the future value in n years of an investment today: $FV_n = PV(1 + i)^n$. Dividing both sides of this expression by $(1 + i)^n$, we get the general formula for present value:

$$\boxed{PV = \frac{FV_n}{(1 + i)^n}} \qquad (4)$$

Present value = Future value of a payment made in n years divided by (One plus the interest rate) raised to n

From this simple expression, we can deduce three important properties of present value. Present value is higher

1. The higher the future value of the payment, FV_n.
2. The shorter the time until the payment, n.
3. The lower the interest rate, i.

We're going to use equation (4) over and over again. *It is the single most important relationship in our study of financial instruments*, so we have highlighted it in a red rectangle. Once we can figure out the present value of any future payment, then we understand the fundamentals of mortgages, credit cards, car loans, and even stocks.

We will spend the rest of this chapter looking at how present value changes when we change the various components of the formula, and how to use it more generally. But before we do, it is important to note one final similarity between present value and future value. Recall that to calculate future value, n need not be measured in years. We can do the computation even when n is the number of months, so long as the interest rate is measured in months as well. The same is true of present value. So long as we measure n and i in the same time unit, and the interest rate is expressed as a decimal, the formula works.

How Present Value Changes   It is useful to go through each of the three properties of present value, looking at the impact of changing each one: the size of the future payment (FV_n), the time until the payment is made (n), and the interest rate (i). Starting with FV_n, we see that *doubling the future value of the payment, without changing the time of the payment or the interest rate, doubles the present value.* For example, at a 5 percent interest rate, a \$100 payment made in two years has a present value of \$90.70. Doubling the payment to \$200 doubles the present value to \$181.40. In fact, increasing or decreasing FV_n by any percentage will change PV by the same percentage, in the same direction.

We have already seen that *the sooner a payment is to be made, the more it is worth.* How much more? To see, let's return to the example of a \$100 payment at 5 percent interest. How sensitive is the present value of this payment to the time until it is made? Plugging some numbers into the general present-value formula [equation (4)], and allowing the time to go from 0 to 30 years, we can construct Figure 4.1, which shows that the present value of the payment is worth \$100 if it is made immediately but declines gradually to \$23 for a payment made in 30 years.

The rate of decline in the present value is related to the same phenomenon that gives us the rule of 72 (described in Your Financial World: How Long Does Your Investment Take to Double? on page 79). Consider this question: At a 5 percent interest rate, how long into the future must a payment of \$100 be made for it to be worth the same as \$50 received today? The answer is 14.4 years. That is, at 5 percent interest, the present value of \$100 paid in 14.4 years is \$50. Note that 14.4 equals 72 divided by 5, so it is also the number of years an investment takes to double in value when the return is 5 percent per year. We can repeat

"I'm just glad we got out before interest rates went up again."

the computation to see that the investment takes 28.8 years to double twice, which tells us that the present value of $100 paid 28.8 years from now is $25. These two points are highlighted in Figure 4.1.

The interest rate is the third important determinant of the present value of a future payment. To see how important it is, let's look at the present value of a $100 payment made 1, 5, 10, and 20 years from now at various interest rates. The general formula [equation (4)] allows us to do this series of computations. Table 4.2 shows the numerical results. Note what happens as the interest rate increases—that is, as you read down a column in the table or move to the right in the figure. You can see immediately that *higher interest rates are associated with lower present values, no matter what the size or timing of the payment.* Conversely, lower interest rates are associated with higher present values.

Note, too, that *at any fixed interest rate, an increase in the time until a payment is made reduces its present value.* Read across any row of the table and you will see that as the time increases from 1 to 5 to 10 to 20 years, the present value goes down.

The final lesson to take away from these calculations has to do with how present value changes with both time and the interest rate. Table 4.2 shows what happens to the present value of a payment as the interest rate increases. You can see that if the payment is to be made in one year (column 2), as the interest rate increases from 1 percent to 5 percent, the present value falls from $99.01 to $95.24. This is a drop of $3.77, or just under 4 percent. In fact, for the single payment made in one year, the percentage change in the present value is approximately equal to the percentage point change in the interest rate: A rise of 4 percentage points in the interest rate has caused a decline in present value of 4 percent.

Figure 4.1   Present Value of $100 at 5 Percent Interest

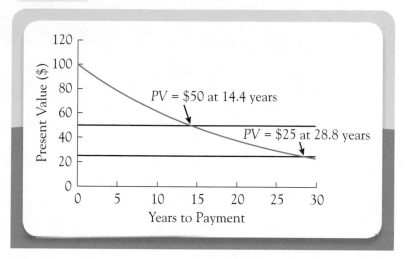

Table 4.2   Present Value of a $100 Payment

Interest Rate	Payment due in			
	1 Year	5 Years	10 Years	20 Years
1%	$99.01	$95.15	$90.53	$81.95
2%	$98.04	$90.57	$82.03	$67.30
3%	$97.09	$86.26	$74.41	$55.37
4%	$96.15	$82.19	$67.56	$45.64
5%	$95.24	$78.35	$61.39	$37.69
6%	$94.34	$74.73	$55.84	$31.18
7%	$93.46	$71.30	$50.83	$25.84
8%	$92.59	$68.06	$46.32	$21.45
9%	$91.74	$64.99	$42.24	$17.84
10%	$90.91	$62.09	$38.55	$14.86
11%	$90.09	$59.35	$35.22	$12.40
12%	$89.29	$56.74	$32.20	$10.37
13%	$88.50	$54.28	$29.46	$ 8.68
14%	$87.72	$51.94	$26.97	$ 7.28
15%	$86.96	$49.72	$24.72	$ 6.11

TOOLS OF THE TRADE
Computing Compound Annual Rates

Comparing changes over days, months, years, and decades can be very difficult. If someone tells you that an investment grew at a rate of 1/2 percent last month, what should you think? You're used to thinking about growth in terms of years, not months. The way to deal with such problems is to turn the monthly growth rate into a *compound-annual rate.* Here's how you do it.

An investment whose value grows 1/2 percent per month goes from 100 at the beginning of the month to 100.5 at the end of the month. Remembering to multiply by 100 to convert the decimal into a percentage, we can verify this:

$$100\left(\frac{100.5 - 100}{100}\right) = 100\left[\left(\frac{100.5}{100}\right) - 1\right] = 0.5\%$$

To convert this monthly rate to an annual rate, we need to figure out what would happen if the investment's value continued to grow at a rate of 1/2 percent per month for the next 12 months. We can't just multiply 0.5 times 12. Instead, we need to compute a 12-month compound rate by raising the one-month rate to the 12th power. Assuming that our index starts at 100 and increases by 1/2 percent per month, we can use the expression for a compound future value to compute the index level 12 months later. Remembering to convert percentages to their decimal form, so that 0.5 percent is 0.005, we find the result is

$$FV_n = PV(1 + i)^n = 100\,(1.005)^{12} = 106.17$$

an increase of 6.17 percent. That's the compound annual rate, and it's obviously bigger than the 6 percent result we

get from just multiplying 0.5 by 12. The difference between the two answers—the one you get by multiplying by 12 and the one you get by compounding—grows as the interest rate grows. At a 1 percent monthly rate, the compounded annual rate is 12.68 percent.

Another use for compounding is to compute the percentage change per year when we know how much an investment has grown over a number of years. This rate is sometimes referred to as the *average annual rate.* Say that over five years an investment has increased 20 percent, from 100 to 120. What annual increase will give us a 20 percent increase over five years? Dividing by 5 gives the wrong answer because it ignores compounding; the increase in the second year must be calculated as a percentage of the index level at the end of the first year. What is the growth rate that after five years will give us an increase of 20 percent? Using the future-value formula,

$$FV_n = PV(1 + i)^n$$
$$120 = 100(1 + i)^5$$

Solving this equation means computing the following:

$$i = \left[\left(\frac{120}{100}\right)^{1/5} - 1\right] = 0.0371$$

This tells us that five consecutive annual increases of 3.71 percent will result in an overall increase of 20 percent. (Just to check, we can compute $(1.0371)^5 = 1.20 = 120/100$.)

Now look at the present value of a payment that will be made in 10 years (column 4 of Table 4.2). As the interest rate goes from 1 to 5 percent, the present value of a $100 payment 10 years from now falls from $90.53 to $61.39. This is a decline of $29.14, or more than 30 percent. *Not only does the present value of a future payment fall with the interest rate; the further in the future the promised payment is to be made, the more the present value falls.* As a result, a change in interest rates has a much greater impact on the present value of a payment made far in the future than it has on one to be made soon. Remember this principle because it will be extremely important when we discuss bonds in the next section.

Applying Present Value

All of our examples thus far have focused on computing the present value of a single payment on a given future date. Thinking of present value in this way gives us enormous flexibility. It means that we can compute the present value not just of a single payment but also of any group of payments made on any number of dates. As we saw

YOUR FINANCIAL WORLD
Should You Buy a New Car Now or Wait?

For a long time you've wanted to buy a new car and you know you'll need a loan to do it. You have $4,000 in savings and figure you can afford a monthly payment of $300. A quick check on the Internet tells you that you can get a four-year loan at 2¾ percent interest. Payments are $220 a month for each $10,000 you borrow. That is, $10,000 is the present value of $220 per month for 48 months at a monthly interest rate of 0.22633 percent (the monthly rate compounded that equals 2¾ percent per year). Because you can afford a $300 payment, you can get a loan of up to $13,636, or (300/220) × $10,000. With a $4,000 down payment, you can afford a car that costs $17,636.

You don't have to buy the car right away, however. You could wait and drive your old car a while longer. What if you wait a year to buy the car? Waiting means you should put $300 per month into the bank along with the $4,000 you already have. At 1 percent interest, at the end of a year you will have $7,659—the future value of the $4,000 plus 12 monthly contributions of $300 each.

For the sake of comparison, let's keep the out-of-pocket cost at $300 per month for 4 years, so that at the end of the year you look for a three-year loan with a $300 payment. At 2¾ percent interest, you can now afford to borrow $10,355. Adding this amount to your savings, you can spend a total of $7,659 + $10,355, or $18,014. So by waiting a year, you'll be able to afford a car that costs about $378 more. (That's approximately the 1 percent interest you earned on your $4,000 down payment plus the 2¾ percent interest you didn't pay on a $13,636 loan: $40 + $375 = $415.)

Should you buy the new car now or wait? It depends on how you feel about the extra $378 you will have available to spend if you wait and how much you'll have to pay to repair your old car in the meantime.*

---

*In addition, there is always the possibility that the price of the car will change. It could go up because of general inflation or down as a result of increases in the efficiency of production. If you have reason to believe that the price may change in a particular direction, factor that into your computation.

---

earlier, to use present value in practice, we need to look at sequences, or streams of payments. And valuing a stream of payments means summing their present values. That is, the value of the whole is the sum of the value of its parts. *Present value is additive.* To see how present value is applied to a stream of payments, we will look at two applications: internal rate of return and the valuation of bonds.

Internal Rate of Return

Imagine that you run a sports equipment factory. As part of your strategic planning, you are considering buying a new machine that makes tennis rackets. The machine costs $1 million and can produce 3,000 rackets a year. If you can sell the rackets for $50 apiece (wholesale), the machine will generate $150,000 in revenue each year. To simplify the analysis, we will assume that the machine is the only necessary input in the production of tennis rackets; that we know the exact amount of revenue it will produce (in reality, that has to be estimated); and that the machine will last for exactly 10 years, during which time it will work perfectly, without requiring any maintenance. At the end of the 10 years, the machine will abruptly cease to operate and will have no resale value. Should you buy the machine?

The answer is: It depends. If you borrow the $1 million to pay for the machine, will the revenue from the machine, $150,000 per year, be enough to cover the payments on the loan? If so and you have something left over, then buying the machine may be a good idea. But if you can't make the payments, then buying the machine is a losing proposition. So you need to figure out whether the machine's revenue will be high enough to cover the payments on the loan you would need to buy it. We'll do this in two steps: First, we'll compute the internal rate of return on your investment in the machine, and second, we'll compare that return to the cost of buying the machine. If the cost is less than the return, then you should buy the machine.

The **internal rate of return** *is the interest rate that equates the present value of an investment with its cost.* For the tennis racket machine, it is the interest rate at which the present value of the revenue from the tennis rackets, $150,000 per year for 10 years, equals the $1 million cost of the machine. To find the internal rate of return, we take the sum of the present value of each of the yearly revenues (we can't take the present value of the total revenue) and equate it with the machine's cost. Then we solve for the interest rate, *i:*

$$\$1,000,000 = \frac{\$150,000}{(1 + i)^1} + \frac{\$150,000}{(1 + i)^2} + \ldots + \frac{\$150,000}{(1 + i)^{10}} \qquad (5)$$

You can solve this equation using a financial calculator or spreadsheet. The answer, 8.14 percent, is the internal rate of return on your investment. That is, the annual rate of return for investing $1 million in the machine is 8.14 percent. But is that rate of return high enough to justify your investment? That depends on the cost of the $1 million you need to buy the machine.

There are two ways you can come up with the $1 million. You can use your company's retained earnings—the funds you've saved from your past profits. Or you can borrow. In the first case, you need to figure out if the machine is more profitable than other ways you might use the funds, just as you might compare interest-bearing investments. The other main use for the retained earnings is to lend it to someone at the same rate at which you could borrow. That is the opportunity cost of your investment. If you borrow the money to buy the machine, you need to know whether you will have a profit left after paying off the loan. Let's assume you're considering borrowing.

Table 4.3 shows the payments you will have to make if you borrow $1 million at various interest rates. To keep the example fairly simple, we'll assume that the loan requires 10 equal payments, one for each year. This type of loan is called a **fixed-payment loan**, and it is exactly the same as a car loan or a mortgage. Using the present-value formula [equation 4], we know that the amount of the loan must equal the present value of the 10 payments. If the interest rate is *i*, then

| Table 4.3 | Fixed Annual Payments on a 10-Year, $1 Million Loan |

Interest Rate	Payment
5%	$129,505
6%	$135,868
7%	$142,378
8%	$149,030
9%	$155,820
10%	$162,745

$$\$1,000,000 = \frac{Fixed\ payment}{(1 + i)} + \frac{Fixed\ payment}{(1 + i)^2} + \ldots + \frac{Fixed\ payment}{(1 + i)^{10}} \qquad (6)$$

$1,000,000 = Present value of 10 equal annual payments at interest rate *i*.

Using this relationship (and the methods described in the appendix to this chapter), we can compute your loan payment at various interest rates, as shown in Table 4.3. As we would expect, when the interest rate rises, the payments rise too.

At what interest rate can you afford a loan to buy the tennis racket machine? Recall that you have $150,000 a year in revenue, and your internal rate of return is 8.14 percent. So as long as the interest rate is 8 percent or less, you know you can cover the

APPLYING THE CONCEPT
EARLY RETIREMENT

Many people want to retire early. They would love to quit work when they turn 40 (that's less than 20 years of work after college) and spend the next 40 years doing whatever they want. In the late 1990s, it looked as if lots of dot-com millionaires had managed to pull it off—at least for a while. But when the Internet bubble burst in 2000, some early re-tirees discovered that they really couldn't afford retirement. Some had to go back to work.

How expensive is early retirement anyway? The answer is, very expensive. Here's the problem. Assume that you're going to live to be exactly 85 years old. Though you're rich, you are willing to live modestly (for a rich person) and spend only $100,000 a year. Remember that you're going to be on vacation 365 days a year and you'll want to put your kids through college, buy new cars, and so on. And you'll still need to pay income taxes, so you won't see all of your income. Assuming you have no other retirement plan, and no Social Security payments (you can't get those for at least 20 years anyway), you'll need $100,000 a year for 45 years.

To figure out how much you need to save by age 40, you can use the present value concept. Think of the amount you need to invest today to have $100,000 in five years. That is:

$$\$100{,}000 = PV(1 + i)^5$$

Assuming a 3 percent interest rate on your investment (that may seem conservative, but long-term Treasury yields fell below that level in 2012), the answer is

$$PV = \frac{\$100{,}000}{(1.03)^5} = \$86{,}261$$

To retire at 40, you need to do this for *each* of the 45 years of your retirement. That is, you need a sequence of $100,000 payments:

$$\frac{\$100{,}000}{(1.03)^1} + \frac{\$100{,}000}{(1.03)^2} + \cdots + \frac{\$100{,}000}{(1.03)^{44}} + \frac{\$100{,}000}{(1.03)^{45}} = \$2{,}451{,}871$$

Retiring at 40 with an income of $100,000 a year means accumulating about $2.5 million in assets (not counting your house). You can see how someone who retired at age 40 with a few million dollars worth of Internet stocks might have had to go back to work when the bubble burst, reducing his or her wealth by 75 percent or more.

The point of this discussion is that retirement, especially early retirement, is expensive. Even if you are willing to work until you are 65, and live on only $50,000 a year (plus Social Security), you'll need to amass more than $700,000. As a rule of thumb, people in their mid-20s should be put-ting away 10 percent of their income toward retirement in order to retire at the same preretirement standard of liv-ing by age 65. It takes significant savings to live without a paycheck.

payments. But we can answer this question with more precision. To see why, notice that the internal rate of return equation (5) is virtually identical to the loan equa-tion (6). In fact, the internal rate of return is the interest rate at which $150,000 a year for 10 years will exactly cover the loan. So we really needed to do this computation only once to answer the question. You should buy the tennis racket machine if its internal rate of return exceeds the interest rate on the loan you would need to finance it. In general, *an investment will be profitable if its internal rate of return exceeds the cost of borrowing.*

Before we go on, we can use the concept of internal rate of return to answer the question at the beginning of the present-value section on page 80: If you agree to make a $225 loan, and the borrower offers to repay either $100 a year for three years or $125 a year for two years, which should you take? The first step in figuring out what to do is to compute the internal rate of return of the two payment streams. For the series of three $100 payments, we need to find the interest rate i that solves

$$\$225 = \frac{\$100}{(1 + i)} + \frac{\$100}{(1 + i)^2} + \frac{\$100}{(1 + i)^3}$$

The answer is $i = 0.159$, or 15.9 percent.

Turning to the alternative, we need to calculate the interest rate that solves

$$\$225 = \frac{\$125}{(1 + i)} + \frac{\$125}{(1 + i)^2}$$

The answer here is $i = 0.073$, or 7.3 percent.

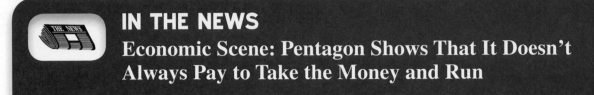

IN THE NEWS
Economic Scene: Pentagon Shows That It Doesn't Always Pay to Take the Money and Run

The New York Times

by Alan B. Krueger

May 24, 2001

Suppose your employer hands you a pink slip and offers you a choice: an annual payment of $8,000 a year for 30 years or a lump sum of $50,000 today. Which would you choose?

This is not just a hypothetical exercise. When it down-sized in the early 1990s, the Defense Department offered many military personnel a similar choice. The military also provided pamphlets and counseling to explain how to make the choice wisely. To the surprise of most economists, the affected personnel rarely followed the military's sound advice.

The decision should depend, of course, on how much one values money received today versus tomorrow. A bird in the hand is worth more today than tomorrow, but how much more? The difference between the value an individual places on a dollar received today as opposed to a year from now is called the discount rate.*

Standard economic theory says that if capital markets work perfectly, people will borrow or lend until their discount rate equals the market rate for borrowing or lending. Someone with a low discount rate will save and accumulate interest; someone with a high discount rate will borrow and accumulate debt. This should continue to the point where their personal discount rates equal the market rate.

Thus, with some justification, the military's pamphlet provided calculations of the present value of the annuity payment using a 7 percent discount rate, the interest rate on money-market funds at the time. If the annuity's present value exceeds the value of the lump sum, the annual payment is a better deal.

Mounting evidence indicates that most people put excessive weight on a bird in the hand. That $8,000 annual payment is worth more than $106,000 if future income is discounted at 7 percent a year—more than double the value of the lump sum. If the discount rate is 10 percent, as high as the interest rate on 30-year fixed-rate mortgages has been the last decade, the promised $8,000 payment is still worth $83,000. The annual payment is a better deal for anyone who can borrow from a bank.

Yet when the military offered essentially this package, three-quarters of enlisted personnel selected the lump sum, according to an article by John Warner of Clemson University and Saul Pleeter of the Defense Department in *The American Economic Review*. The authors also examined a number

This means that if you choose the three $100 payments, you will earn 15.9 percent interest on the loan, while if you accept the two $125 payments, the interest rate will be 7.3 percent. Clearly, the three payments are better for you as the lender, but we had to do quite a bit of work to figure it out.

Bonds: The Basics

One of the most common uses of the concept of present value is in the valuation of bonds. A **bond** is a promise to make a series of payments on specific future dates. It is issued as part of an arrangement to borrow. In essence, the borrower, or seller, gives an IOU to the lender, or buyer, in return for some amount of money. Both governments and corporations need to borrow, so both issue bonds. Because bonds create obligations, they are best thought of as legal contracts that (1) require the borrower to make payments to the lender and (2) specify what happens if the borrower fails to do so.

of other separation packages. The break-even discount rate—or rate that makes the lump sum and annuity payment equivalent—varied from 17 to 20 percent, depending on years of service and salary. Over all, 92 percent of enlisted personnel and 51 percent of officers chose the lump sum.

Because the government could borrow at 7 percent at the time, Mr. Warner and Mr. Pleeter calculate that the Treasury saved $1.7 billion by offering the lump-sum option.

Using a sample of 65,000 departing members of the armed forces, they estimate that the average personal discount rate, taking taxes into account, exceeded 25 percent. Discount rates were higher for the less educated, the young, minorities, and those with dependents; they were lower for officers.

Recognition of this fact helps to explain a number of other phenomena. For instance, the public's penchant for holding high credit card debt—more than $6,000 per household with a credit card—at interest rates near 15 percent a year is also consistent with high discount rates, as are low savings rates. (Indeed, one wonders why the government, which borrows at 5 percent, doesn't offer a credit card to every man, woman, and child at an interest rate of, say, 10 percent. This would help reduce the debt and quench individuals' thirst for fast cash.)

SOURCE: Copyright © 2001 by *The New York Times Co.* Reprinted with permission.

LESSONS OF THE ARTICLE

This article examines a common problem faced by people who are retiring. Should they take a single lump-sum payment or a series of annual payments? Answering this question requires using the concept of present value. The article also describes how most people are extremely impatient, behaving as if their own personal discount rate is extraordinarily high, and how that explains the willingness to borrow at very high interest rates.

*The author is using the term *discount rate* in the same way that we use the term *interest rate* in the present-value calculation. Computing present value requires that we reduce the future payments to their equivalent value today—that is, we need to *discount* them. We all have our own personal discount rate, or interest rate, that is a measure of how patient or impatient we are.

Because there are many different kinds of bonds, to focus our discussion, we'll look at the most common type, a **coupon bond**. Say a borrower who needs $100 "issues" or sells a $100 coupon bond to a lender. The bond issuer is required to make annual payments, called **coupon payments**. The annual amount of those payments (expressed as a percentage of the amount borrowed) is called the **coupon rate**. If the coupon rate is 5 percent, then the borrower/issuer pays the lender/bondholder $5 per year per $100 borrowed. The yearly coupon payment equals the coupon rate times the amount borrowed. The bond also specifies when the issuer is going to repay the initial $100 and the payments will stop, called the **maturity date** or *term to maturity*. The final payment, a repayment of the initial $100 loan, is often referred to as the **principal, face value**, or **par value** of the bond.

Before the advent of computers, an investor buying a bond would receive a certificate with a number of dated coupons attached. To claim the coupon payments, the investor would cut off the coupons and mail them to the bond issuer. At maturity, the

TIME

A coupon bond issued by the Reading Railroad Company on May 1, 1945. Some of the coupons are still attached to the bond.

investor would redeem the certificate for the final payment. The Reading Railroad Company bond pictured here still has some coupons attached.[3]

You can see that the borrower who issues a bond is promising to make a series of regular interest payments over the life of the bond, plus a final payment on the maturity date. How much should someone be willing to pay for such a contract? The answer comes directly from present value: *The price of a bond is the present value of its payments.* To see how to value a bond, we'll start with repayment of the principal; then we'll add the coupon payments.

Valuing the Principal Payment Valuing the bond's principal, or final payment, is a straightforward application of present value. Let's look at a bond that promises a principal payment of $100 on its maturity date n years in the future. The present value of this payment is

---

[3]The bond in the picture is a $1,000 face value 50-year 3½ percent coupon bond issued on May 1, 1945. It promised 100 payments of $17.35, to be made every six months beginning on November 1, 1945, plus a $1,000 final payment on May 1, 1995. The vast majority of bonds pay interest biannually.

$$P_{BP} = \frac{F}{(1+i)^n} = \frac{\$100}{(1+i)^n} \qquad (7)$$

Present value of bond principal (P_{BP}) =

   Principal payment (F) divided by (One plus the interest rate) raised to n.

We can see immediately that the value of the principal payment varies with both the time to maturity and the interest rate. The longer the time until the payment is made—the higher the n—the lower the value of the payment. And the higher the interest rate, i, the lower the value of the payment.

   To see how this works, let's start with an interest rate of 6 percent and a final payment of \$1,000 to be made in 30 years. If the interest rate is 6 percent, the present value of the final payment is

$$P_{BP} = \frac{\$1000}{(1.06)^{30}} = \$174.11$$

Not surprisingly, this promise to make a payment that far in the future is worth only a fraction of the \$1,000 principal. Lowering the interest rate, say to 4 percent, would increase the present value of the principal payment to \$308.32, but it would still be much less than half of the payment itself.

Valuing the Coupon Payments   What about the coupon payments? This series of equal payments resembles the loan payments we examined in our discussion of internal rate of return. There we computed the sum of a series of equal payments by adding up the present value of each payment. Let's look at this process in more detail, starting with two \$10 payments made in consecutive years. Assuming an interest rate of 6 percent, the value of these two payments is

$$\frac{\$10}{1.06} + \frac{\$10}{1.06^2} = \$9.43 + \$8.90 = \$18.33$$

Adding additional payments simply means adding more terms. So for five \$10 payments made over five consecutive years, the present value is

$$\frac{\$10}{1.06} + \frac{\$10}{1.06^2} + \frac{\$10}{1.06^3} + \frac{\$10}{1.06^4} + \frac{\$10}{1.06^5} = \$9.43 + \$8.90 + \$8.40 + \$7.92 + \$7.47 = \$42.12$$

   This example highlights two important properties of periodic fixed payments. First, the longer the payments go on—the more of them there are—the higher their total value. Even though the additional payments fall further into the future, the overall present value still grows. Because a long-term bond (one that lasts for 30 years, for instance) has more payments than a short-term maturity bond (one whose final payment is made, say, in five years), the coupon payments on the long-term bond will be worth more than the coupon payments on the short-term bond.

   Second, as is always the case in present-value calculations, the higher the interest rate, the lower the present value. Raising the interest rate from 6 to 7 percent, for example, lowers the total value of the five future payments on our short-term bond from \$42.12 to \$41.00.

   We can use the present-value expression to write a general formula for a string of yearly coupon payments made over n years. It is simply the sum of the present value of the payments for each year from one to n years:

$$P_{CP} = \frac{C}{(1+i)^1} + \frac{C}{(1+i)^2} + \frac{C}{(1+i)^3} + \ldots + \frac{C}{(1+i)^n} \qquad (8)$$

Present value of a series of bond coupon payments (P_{CP}) = Sum of yearly coupon payments (C) divided by (one plus the interest rate) raised to the power equal to the number of years from now. This formula is messy, but that's why we have calculators and spreadsheets. (For a derivation of a simpler version of this formula, see the appendix to this chapter.)

Valuing the Coupon Payments Plus Principal To value the yearly coupon payments plus the principal, we can combine equations (7) and (8) as follows:

$$P_{CB} = P_{CP} + P_{BP} = \left[\frac{C}{(1+i)^1} + \frac{C}{(1+i)^2} + \frac{C}{(1+i)^3} + \cdots + \frac{C}{(1+i)^n} \right] + \frac{F}{(1+i)^n} \quad (9)$$

Present value of coupon bond (P_{CB})

= Present value of yearly coupon payments (P_{CP})

+ Present value of principal payment (P_{BP})

This formula looks complicated because it is. But we can learn two simple facts just by looking at its parts. The value of the coupon bond, P_{CB}, rises when (1) the yearly coupon payments, C, rise and (2) the interest rate, i, falls. The first of these conclusions follows from the fact that a higher coupon rate means larger payments, and the present value of a larger payment is larger. The second follows directly from the present-value relationship: the lower the interest rate, the higher the present value of any and all future payments.

The fact that lower interest rates mean higher bond prices—and higher interest rates mean lower bond prices—is extremely important. Because bonds promise fixed payments on future dates, the higher the interest rate, the lower their present value. It follows that the *value of a bond varies inversely with the interest rate used to calculate the present value of the promised payment.*

Real and Nominal Interest Rates

In calculating present value, our goal has been to assess the number of dollars you would pay today for fixed dollar payments in the future. To do this, we used the **nominal interest rate**, which is the interest rate expressed in current-dollar terms. We did not worry about the possibility that inflation might change the purchasing power of the dollars. Because borrowers and lenders care about the purchasing power of the money they pay out and receive, they care about inflation. So we need to adjust the return on a loan, looking not just at the nominal interest rate but at the inflation-adjusted interest rate, called the **real interest rate**.

Think about a $100 loan made at 5 percent interest rate for one year. The borrower receives $100 at the beginning of the year and repays $105 at the end of the year. If prices go up 5 percent during the year—that is, if the inflation rate is 5 percent—then the $105 returned to the lender at the end of the year will buy exactly what $100 did at the beginning of the year. The lender's inflation-adjusted return is zero. No lender would be happy with a zero return, so no lender is likely to make a loan at a 5 percent nominal interest rate if expected inflation is 5 percent. (Because the inflation rate can exceed the nominal interest rate, the real interest rate can be negative.)

YOUR FINANCIAL WORLD
Pay Off Your Credit Card Debt as Fast as You Can

Credit cards are extremely useful. They make buying things easy—sometimes too easy. While we all plan to pay off our credit card balances every month, sometimes we just don't have the resources. So we take advantage of the loans the card issuers offer and pay off only part of what we owe. Suddenly we find ourselves deeply in debt.

How fast should you pay off your credit card balance? All the bank or finance company that issued the card will tell you is the minimum you have to pay. You get to decide whether to pay more, and your decision makes a big difference. We can use the present-value concept to figure out your alternatives.

Let's take a typical example. You have a balance of $2,000 and can afford to pay at least $50 per month. How many monthly payments will you need to make to pay off the full debt? What if you paid $60 or $75 per month? To find the answer, use equation (8) for the present value of a fixed series of payments. In this case, the present value is the loan amount, $2,000; the fixed monthly payment is $50, $60, or $75; and the interest rate is whatever your credit card company charges per month—10 to 20 percent a year. (The average rate is around 13 percent.) We need to figure out the number of payments, or n in equation (8).*

Table 4.4 shows the number of months needed to pay off your $2,000 balance at various interest rates and payment amounts. The first entry tells you that if your credit card company is charging a 10 percent annual interest rate (which is comparatively low), and you pay $50 per month, then you will need to make payments for 48.4 months—just over four years.

Looking at the entire table, you can see the advantage of making big payments. Assume you're paying 15 percent, which is realistic. The table shows that increasing your payment from $50 to $60 will allow you to finish paying off your debt in 42.5 months rather than 54.3 months. In other words, paying $10 more a month will allow you to finish paying off the loan one full year sooner. And if you can manage to pay $75 a month, you'll be finished 10 months before that.

*The most straightforward way to do this is to use a spreadsheet to add up the payments until their present value equals the credit card balance. You can also use equation (A5) in the appendix of this chapter, which can be solved using logarithms.

How fast should you pay off your credit card balance?

Looking more closely, you can see that making large payments is much more important than getting a low interest rate. The lesson is: Pay off your debts as fast as you possibly can. Procrastination is expensive.

Table 4.4	Number of Months to Pay Off a $2,000 Credit Card Debt		
Annual Interest Rate	**Monthly Payment**		
	$50	**$60**	**$75**
10%	48.4	38.9	30.1
12%	50.5	40.3	30.9
15%	54.3	42.5	32.2
20%	62.4	47.0	34.5

The point of this example is that borrowers look at the inflation-adjusted cost of borrowing, while lenders focus on the inflation-adjusted return. *No one cares only about the number of dollars. People also care about what those dollars can buy. In other words, everyone cares about real interest rates.* This is why economists think of the nominal interest rate as having two parts, the real interest rate and expected inflation.

Figure 4.2   The Nominal Interest Rate, the Inflation Rate, and the Real Interest Rate

SOURCE: *Three-month Treasury bill rates from the Federal Reserve Board and 12-month inflation rates computed from the Bureau of Labor Statistics Consumer Price Index Research Series. The real interest rate is calculated as the nominal rate minus the inflation rate. This computation assumes that the expected inflation rate over the next 3 months is equal to the actual inflation rate over the previous 12 months (FRED data codes: TB3MS and CPIAUCSL).*

Say that you want to borrow $100 for one year. You find a lender who is willing to give you a loan, but the two of you need to agree on the interest rate. Both of you care about the inflation rate over the coming year, which will affect the purchasing power of the dollars you will use to repay the loan. But neither of you knows what that rate is going to be, so you need to forecast it to conclude your agreement. That is, the nominal interest rate you agree on must be based on *expected inflation* over the term of the loan, plus the real interest rate you agree on.

Writing this statement down in the form of an equation is helpful. The nominal interest rate, *i*, equals the real interest rate, *r*, plus expected inflation, π^e:[4]

$$i = r + \pi^e \tag{10}$$

This is called the *Fisher equation* after the early 20th-century economist Irving Fisher. It shows that in general, the nominal interest rate is positively related to expected inflation. The higher expected inflation, the higher the nominal interest rate. As we can see in Figure 4.2, the data bear this out. While the relationship is not a tight one, higher nominal interest rates are usually associated with higher inflation rates. In 1980 and 1981,

[4]This equation is an approximation that works well only when expected inflation and the real interest rate are low. The exact relationship among the nominal interest rate, the real interest rate, and the expected inflation rate is $(1 + i) = (1 + r)(1 + \pi^e)$, which translates to $(1 + i) = 1 + r + \pi^e + r\pi^e$; after subtracting 1 from each side, the nominal rate, *i*, equals $r + \pi^e + r\,\pi^e$. The approximation, $i = r + \pi^e$, ignores the cross-term $r\pi^e$, the product of the real interest rate and expected inflation, which will not be important when its value is very low (say, $0.05 \times 0.02 = 0.001$). But if, for example, expected inflation is very high, the cross-term can become very important. To illustrate, if the real interest rate is 0.05, or 5 percent, and the expected rate of inflation is 1.00, or 100 percent, the *abbreviated equation* yields a nominal interest rate of $0.05 + 1.00 = 1.05$, or 105 percent. The result implies that, at an inflation rate of 100 percent, an investor would have earned 5 percent after inflation (the real rate) at the end of one year if the nominal interest rate on an investment had been set to 105 percent. But the *full equation* includes the cross-term, $r\pi^e$, which in this case is $(0.05)(1.00) = 0.05$, or 5 percent, meaning that the nominal interest rate would have to be set to 110 percent, not 105 percent, for an investment to earn a real return of 5 percent after one year. In dollar terms, the abbreviated equation produces a one-year real (after inflation) return on an investment of $100 that is $5 below the true real return calculated with the full equation.

APPLYING THE CONCEPT
HIGH INTEREST RATES,
LOW INTEREST RATES

Once we realize that the nominal interest rate moves with expected inflation, big swings in interest rates become less of a mystery. And the fact that the Japanese interest rate is close to zero while the Indian interest rate is about 8 percent also becomes easier to understand. All we need to do to understand these differences is look at differences in inflation. In 2013, for example, Japanese prices were edging slightly lower from year-ago levels, while the Indian inflation rate was an uncomfortable 11 percent per year. This 11-percentage-point difference in inflation rates accounts for more than the 8-percentage-point difference in the nominal interest rates.

Figure 4.3 shows the nominal interest rate and the inflation rate in more than 50 countries and the euro area in early 2013. Note first that higher inflation is associated with higher nominal interest rates. Second, more than half of the points are above the 45-degree line, meaning that in these countries, the nominal interest rate is higher than the inflation rate. Yet, on average, the ex post real interest rate was close to zero—a low level that reflects the weakness of the global economy following the financial crisis of 2007–2009 and the euro-area crisis that began in 2009. Note that, for the majority of countries, the distance of these points from the 45-degree line, which represents the zero real interest rate, does not vary as much as their distance from the horizontal axis, which represents the zero nominal interest rate.

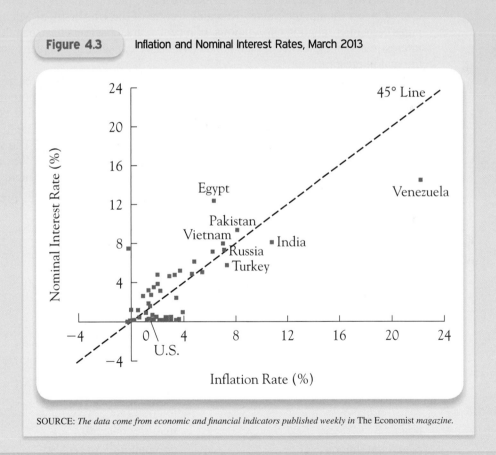

Figure 4.3 Inflation and Nominal Interest Rates, March 2013

SOURCE: *The data come from economic and financial indicators published weekly in* The Economist *magazine.*

for example, U.S. interest rates were sky high; the U.S. Treasury had to pay more than 15 percent for its short-term borrowing. By 1986, interest rates had dropped to more reasonable levels, close to 5 percent. That's a 10-percentage point move in just five years! The figure shows that as inflation fell, nominal interest rates also fell. In fact, the declines were almost identical. Real interest rates didn't change much during this period.

The term *real interest rate* can cause confusion. The financial markets quote nominal interest rates, the ones that appear in the newspaper and on bank statements.[5] They are "real" in the sense that they are real-life interest rates. When people use the term *interest rate* without qualification, they are referring to the *nominal* interest rate, the one they see every day. We will follow this convention, using the term *interest rate* to mean the nominal rate and the term *real interest rate* to refer to the nominal rate less expected inflation.

Unlike the nominal rates, we cannot directly observe the real interest rate; we have to estimate it. The easiest way to do that is to turn the Fisher equation around, rewriting it as

$$r = i - \pi^e \tag{11}$$

Because we know the nominal interest rate, *i,* measuring the real interest rate means subtracting forecasted inflation. There are a number of sources for these forecasts. Twice a year the Federal Reserve Bank of Philadelphia publishes professional forecasts. Once a month, the Survey Research Center of the University of Michigan computes consumer inflation expectations. In recent years, observers have begun to use the interest rates on *inflation-indexed* bonds (which we consider in Chapter 6) to estimate the real interest rate.

But because forecasts are often wrong, our estimate will usually differ from the real interest rate that occurs. Someone who is making an economically important decision will do so based on the expected real interest rate. Some time later, that person will look back and compute the real interest rate actually paid or received. The first of these is known as the *ex ante* real interest rate, meaning "before the fact." The second, or realized rate, is the *ex post* real interest rate, meaning "after the fact." We can always compute the ex post real interest rate, because we know the nominal interest rate and the inflation rate there actually was. But it is the ex ante real interest rate that we really want to know.

[5]One exception is certain bonds whose interest rates are quoted in real, inflation-adjusted terms. We will examine these *inflation-indexed* bonds in detail in Chapter 6.

Terms

basis point, 79
bond, 88
compound interest, 77
coupon bond, 89
coupon payment, 89
coupon rate, 89
face value, 89
fixed-payment loan, 86
future value, 76

internal rate of return, 86
maturity date, 89
nominal interest rate, 92
par value, 89
present value, 80
principal, 89
real interest rate, 92
rule of 72, 79
yield, 76

Using FRED: Codes for Data in This Chapter

Data Series	FRED Data Code
1-year Treasury bill rate	TB1YR
3-month Treasury bill rate	TB3MS
Consumer price index	CPIAUCSL
1-year inflation expectations (Michigan survey)	MICH
Brazil Treasury bill rate	INTGSTBRM193N
Brazil consumer price index	BRACPIALLMINMEI
China discount rate	INTDSRCNM193N
China consumer price index	CHNCPIALLMINMEI
10-year Treasury constant maturity rate	GS10
10-year Treasury inflation-indexed yield	FII10
5-year Treasury constant maturity rate	GS5
5-year Treasury inflation-indexed yield	FII5

Chapter Lessons

1. The value of a payment depends on when it is made.
   a. Future value is the present value of an initial investment times one plus the interest rate for each year you hold it. The higher the interest rate, the higher the future value.
   b. Present value is equal to the value today of a payment made on a future date.
      i. The higher the payment, the higher the present value at a given interest rate.
      ii. The higher the interest rate, the lower the present value of a given payment.
      iii. The longer the time until the payment is made, the lower the present value of a given payment at a given interest rate.
      iv. For a given increase in the interest rate, the present value of a promised payment falls more the farther into the future the payment is to be made.
      v. When computing present value, the interest rate and the time until the payment is to be made must be measured in the same time units.

2. Present value can be used to value any stream of future payments.
   a. The internal rate of return is the interest rate that equates the present value of the future payments or profits from an investment with its current cost.
   b. A coupon bond is a promise to make periodic interest payments and a final principal payment on specific future dates.
      i. The present value of a bond depends on its coupon rate, date of maturity, and the current interest rate.
      ii. The higher the coupon rate, given the maturity and the interest rate, the higher the present value of the bond.
      iii. The price of a bond is inversely related to the interest rate. The higher the price, the lower the interest rate that equates the price with the present value of the promised payments.

www.mhhe.com/moneyandbanking4e

3. The real interest rate is the nominal interest rate minus expected inflation. It expresses the interest rate in terms of purchasing power rather than current dollars.

Conceptual and Analytical Problems

1. Compute the future value of $100 at an 8 percent interest rate 5, 10, and 15 years into the future. What would the future value be over these time horizons if the interest rate were 5 percent? *(LO2)*

2. Compute the present value of a $100 investment made 6 months, 5 years, and 10 years from now at 4 percent interest. *(LO2)*

3. Assuming that the current interest rate is 3 percent, compute the present value of a five-year, 5 percent coupon bond with a face value of $1,000. What happens when the interest rate goes to 4 percent? What happens when the interest rate goes to 2 percent? *(LO2)*

4.* Given a choice of two investments, would you choose one that pays a total return of 30 percent over five years or one that pays 0.5 percent per month for five years? *(LO1)*

5. A financial institution offers you a one-year certificate of deposit with an interest rate of 5 percent. You expect the inflation rate to be 3 percent. What is the real return on your deposit? *(LO3)*

6. Consider two scenarios. In the first, the nominal interest rate is 6 percent, and the expected rate of inflation is 4 percent. In the second, the nominal interest rate is 5 percent, and the expected rate of inflation is 2 percent. In which scenario would you rather be a lender? In which would you rather be a borrower? *(LO3)*

7. You decide you would like to retire at age 65, and expect to live until you are 85 (assume there is no chance you will die younger or live longer). You figure that you can live nicely on $50,000 per year. *(LO3)*
   a. Describe the calculation you need to make to determine how much you must save to purchase an annuity paying $50,000 per year for the rest of your life. Assume the interest rate is 7 percent.
   b. If you wish to keep your purchasing power constant, how would your calculation change if you expected inflation to average 2 percent for the rest of your life?

8. Most businesses replace their computers every two to three years. Assume that a computer costs $2,000 and that it fully depreciates in 3 years, at which point it has no resale value whatsoever and is thrown away. *(LO1)*
   a. If the interest rate for financing the equipment is equal to i, show how to compute the minimum annual cash flow that a computer must generate to be worth the purchase. Your answer will depend on i.
   b. Suppose the computer did not fully depreciate, but still had a $250 value at the time it was replaced. Show how you would adjust the calculation given in your answer to part *a*.
   c. What if financing can only be had at a 10 percent interest rate? Calculate the minimum cash flow the computer must generate to be worth the purchase using your answer to part *a*.

*Indicates more difficult problems

9. Some friends of yours have just had a child. Thinking ahead, and realizing the power of compound interest, they are considering investing for their child's college education, which will begin in 18 years. Assume that the cost of a college education today is $125,000. Also assume that there is no inflation and there are no taxes on interest income that is used to pay college tuition and expenses. *(LO2)*
   a. If the interest rate is 5 percent, how much money will your friends need to put into their savings account today to have $125,000 in 18 years?
   b. What if the interest rate were 10 percent?
   c. The chance that the price of a college education will be the same 18 years from now as it is today seems remote. Assuming that the price will rise 3 percent per year, and that today's interest rate is 8 percent, what will your friends' investment need to be?
   d. Return to part *a,* the case with a 5 percent interest rate and no inflation. Assume that your friends don't have enough financial resources to make the entire investment at the beginning. Instead, they think they will be able to split their investment into two equal parts, one invested immediately and the second invested in five years. Describe how you would compute the required size of the two equal investments, made five years apart.

10. You are considering buying a new house, and have found that a $100,000, 30-year fixed-rate mortgage is available with an interest rate of 7 percent. This mortgage requires 360 monthly payments of approximately $651 each. If the interest rate rises to 8 percent, what will happen to your monthly payment? Compare the percentage change in the monthly payment with the percentage change in the interest rate. *(LO1)*

11.* Use the Fisher equation to explain in detail what a borrower is compensating a lender for when he pays her a nominal rate of interest. *(LO3)*

12. If the current interest rate increases, what would you expect to happen to bond prices? Explain. *(LO2)*

13. Which would be most affected in the event of an interest rate increase—the price of a five-year coupon bond that paid coupons only in years 3, 4, and 5 or the price of a five-year coupon bond that paid coupons only in years 1, 2, and 3, everything else being equal? Explain. *(LO2)*

14. Under what circumstances might you be willing to pay more than $1,000 for a coupon bond that matures in three years, has a coupon rate of 10 percent and a face value of $1,000? *(LO2)*

15.* Approximately how long would it take for an investment of $100 to reach $800 if you earned 5 percent? What if the interest rate were 10 percent? How long would it take an investment of $200 to reach $800 at an interest rate of 5 percent? Why is there a difference between doubling the interest rate and doubling the initial investment? *(LO1)*

16. Rather than spending $100 on paint today, you decide to save the money until next year, at which point you will use it to paint your room. If a can of paint costs $10 today, how many cans will you be able to buy next year if the nominal interest rate is 21 percent and the expected inflation rate is 10 percent? *(LO3)*

17. Recently, some lucky person won the lottery. The lottery winnings were reported to be $85.5 million. In reality, the winner got a choice of $2.85 million per year for 30 years or $46 million today. *(LO2)*
   a. Explain briefly why winning $2.85 million per year for 30 years is not equivalent to winning $85.5 million.
   b. The evening news interviewed a group of people the day after the winner was announced. When asked, most of them responded that, if they were the lucky winner, they would take the $46 million up-front payment. Suppose (just for a moment) that you were that lucky winner. How would you decide between the annual installments or the up-front payment?

18. You are considering going to graduate school for a one-year master's program. You have done some research and believe that the master's degree will add $5,000 per year to your salary for the next 10 years of your working life, starting at the end of this year. From then on, after the next 10 years, it makes no difference. Completing the master's program will cost you $35,000, which you would have to borrow at an interest rate of 6 percent. How would you decide if this investment in your education were profitable? *(LO2)*

19. Assuming the chances of being paid back are the same, would a nominal interest rate of 10 percent always be more attractive to a lender than a nominal rate of 5 percent? Explain. *(LO3)*

20.* Your firm has the opportunity to buy a perpetual motion machine to use in your business. The machine costs $1,000,000 and will increase your profits by $75,000 per year. What is the internal rate of return? *(LO2)*

21.* Suppose two parties agree that the expected inflation rate for the next year is 3 percent. Based on this, they enter into a loan agreement where the nominal interest rate to be charged is 7 percent. If the inflation rate for the year turns out to be 2 percent, who gains and who loses? *(LO3)*

Scan here for quick access to the hints for these problems. Need a barcode reader? Try ScanLife, available in your app store.

Data Exploration

For detailed instructions on using Federal Reserve Economic Data (FRED) online to answer each of the following problems, visit www.mhhe.com/moneyandbanking4e and click on Student Edition, then Data Exploration Hints.

1. How does inflation affect nominal interest rates? *(LO3)*
   a. Plot the three-month U.S. Treasury bill rate (FRED code: TB3MS) from 1960 to the present. What long-run pattern do you observe? What may have caused this pattern?
   b. Plot the inflation rate based on the percent change from a year ago of the U.S. consumer price index (FRED code: CPIAUCSL) from 1960 to the present. How does U.S. inflation history reflect your explanation in part (a)?

2. In Data Exploration Problem 1, you saw the impact of U.S. inflation on short-term U.S. Treasury bill rates. Now examine similar data for Brazil. *(LO3)*
   a. Plot the Brazilian Treasury bill rate (FRED code: INTGSTBRM193N). Notice the range of values and compare them with the range in the U.S. Treasury bill plot from Data Exploration Problem 1.
   b. Plot the inflation rate based on the percent change from a year ago of the Brazilian consumer price index (FRED code: BRACPIALLMINMEI). Comment on the

inflation rate in Brazil. Download the data to a spreadsheet. (You may need to widen the spreadsheet column to see the data.) What happens to the index in the 1990–1994 period?

3. The *expected* real interest rate is the rate that people use in making decisions about the future. It is the difference between the nominal interest rate and the *expected* inflation rate, not the *actual* inflation rate. How does expected inflation over the coming year compare with actual inflation over the past year? Plot the inflation rate since 1978 based on the percent change from a year ago of the U.S. consumer price index (FRED code: CPIAUCSL). Add to this figure as a second line the expected inflation rate from the University of Michigan survey (FRED code: MICH). Is expected inflation always in line with actual inflation? Which is more stable? *(LO3)*

4. Plot the ex ante or *expected* real interest rate since 1978 by subtracting the Michigan survey inflation measure (FRED code: MICH) from the three-month Treasury bill rate (FRED code: TB3MS). Plot as a second line the ex post or *realized* real interest rate by subtracting from the three-month Treasury bill rate (FRED code: TB3MS) the actual inflation rate based on the percent change from a year ago of the consumer price index (FRED code: CPIAUCSL). What does it mean when these two measures are different? *(LO3)*

Appendix to Chapter 4

The Algebra of Present-Value Formulas

In this short appendix, we will derive a formula for computing present value. To do so we need to use some algebra, but the result is worth the trouble. The formula is useful in computing the present value of any series of payments, such as a car loan, a mortgage, or a coupon bond, and the internal rate of return on an investment.

Imagine that you are going to buy a house. You would like to borrow PV dollars at interest rate i and agree to make n equal mortgage payments. How large will your payment be? It will be just big enough so that the present value of all your payments, discounted at interest rate i, equals the amount of the loan.

To compute the payment, we will use the present-value formula. If we call the size of the monthly payments C, then we need to solve the following formula:

$$PV = \frac{C}{(1+i)^1} + \frac{C}{(1+i)^2} + \frac{C}{(1+i)^3} + \ldots + \frac{C}{(1+i)^n} \tag{A1}$$

Each term in expression (A1) is the present value of a payment C made on a future date. To simplify (A1), we multiply it by $[1/(1+i)]$ to get

$$\frac{1}{(1+i)}PV = \frac{1}{(1+i)}\left[\frac{C}{(1+i)^1} + \frac{C}{(1+i)^2} + \frac{C}{(1+i)^3} + \ldots + \frac{C}{(1+i)^n}\right]$$
$$= \frac{C}{(1+i)^2} + \frac{C}{(1+i)^3} + \frac{C}{(1+i)^4} + \ldots + \frac{C}{(1+i)^n} + \frac{C}{(1+i)^{n+1}} \tag{A2}$$

Now subtract (A2) from (A1):

$$PV - \frac{1}{(1+i)}PV = \frac{C}{(1+i)^1} + \frac{C}{(1+i)^2} + \frac{C}{(1+i)^3} + \ldots + \frac{C}{(1+i)^n}$$
$$- \frac{C}{(1+i)^2} - \frac{C}{(1+i)^3} - \ldots - \frac{C}{(1+i)^n} - \frac{C}{(1+i)^{n+1}} \tag{A3}$$

to get

$$\frac{i}{(1+i)}PV = \frac{C}{(1+i)^1} - \frac{C}{(1+i)^{n+1}} \tag{A4}$$

Simplifying this result yields the following formula:

$$PV = \left(\frac{C}{i}\right)\left[1 - \frac{1}{(1+i)^n}\right] \tag{A5}$$

To see how to use this formula, suppose you're taking out a $100,000 mortgage that you agree to repay over 30 years at an interest rate of 8 percent. Remember that the interest rate must be quoted in decimal form and at the same frequency as the payments. For example, if you are going to make monthly payments, then i must be a monthly interest rate. To figure out your annual payment (in reality you would make 360 *monthly* payments), just solve the following formula for C:

$$\$100,000 = \left(\frac{C}{0.08}\right)\left[1 - \frac{1}{(1.08)^{30}}\right] \qquad \text{(A6)}$$

Simplifying the right-hand side gives us

$$\$100,000 = 11.258C \qquad \text{(A7)}$$

So your annual payment will be $8,882.57. We can do the same calculation for 360 monthly payments using a monthly interest rate of 0.6434 percent, which annualizes to 8 percent.

Formula (A5) is very useful in computing the fixed payments due on a loan, the coupon payments on a bond, or the internal rate of return on an investment. Notice that as the number of payments increases (as *n* gets bigger), the term $[1/(1 + i)^n]$ grows smaller. If the payments never end, so that *n* represents infinity, then $[1/(1 + i)^n]$ shrinks to zero. Thus, the present value of a stream of fixed payments that never ends is $[C/i]$.

Chapter 5

Understanding Risk

Learning Objectives

Understand . . .

LO1   Risk as a measure of uncertainty about payoffs

LO2   Statistical measures of risk

LO3   Systematic versus idiosyncratic risk

LO4   Risk reduction: hedging and diversification

Risk may be a four-letter word, but it's one we can't avoid. Every day we make decisions that involve financial and economic risk. How much car insurance should we buy? Should we refinance the mortgage now or a year from now? Should we save more for retirement, or spend the extra money on a new car? Making any decision that has more than one possible outcome is similar to gambling: We put the money on the roulette table and take our chances.

Interestingly enough, the tools we use today to measure and analyze risk were first developed to help players analyze games of chance like roulette and blackjack. For thousands of years, people have played games based on a throw of the dice, but they had little understanding of how those games actually worked. In ancient times, dice of various sorts were used to consult the gods, so any effort to analyze the odds was thought improper. But even those who ignored religious concerns could not correctly analyze a single throw of a die because they did not understand the concept of zero. That meant that the complex computations necessary to develop a theory of probability were impossible.[1]

By the mid-17th century, the power of religion had waned and mathematical tools had developed to the point that people could begin to make sense out of cards, dice, and other games. Since the invention of probability theory, we have come to realize that many everyday events, including those in economics, finance, and even weather forecasting, are best thought of as analogous to the flip of a coin or the throw of a die. For better or worse, we no longer treat these random events as if they were divinely ordained.

Still, while experts can make educated guesses about the future path of interest rates, inflation, or the stock market, their predictions are really only that—guesses. And while meteorologists are fairly good at forecasting the weather a day or two ahead, economists, financial advisors, and business gurus have dismal records. So understanding the possibility of various occurrences should allow everyone to make better choices. While risk cannot be eliminated, it can often be managed effectively.

---

[1]For further details of this history, see Peter L. Bernstein, *Against the Gods: The Remarkable Story of Risk* (Hoboken, NJ: John Wiley & Sons, 1998).

Finally, while most people view risk as a curse to be avoided whenever possible, risk also creates opportunities. The payoff from a winning bet on one hand of cards can often erase the losses on a losing hand. Thus, the importance of probability theory to the development of modern financial markets is hard to overemphasize. People require compensation for taking risks. Without the capacity to measure risk, we could not calculate a fair price for transferring risk from one person to another, nor could we price stocks and bonds, much less sell insurance. The market for options didn't exist until economists learned how to compute the price of an option using probability theory.

In this chapter, we will learn how to measure risk and assess whether it will increase or decrease. We will also come to understand why changes in risk lead to changes in the demand for particular financial instruments and to corresponding changes in the price of those instruments.

Defining Risk

The dictionary definition of *risk,* the "possibility of loss or injury," highlights the perils of putting oneself in a situation in which the outcome is unknown. But this common use of the word doesn't quite fit our purposes because we care about gains as well as losses. We need a definition of risk that focuses on the fact that the outcomes of financial and economic decisions are almost always unknown at the time the decisions are made. Here is the definition we will use:

Risk *is a measure of uncertainty about the future payoff to an investment,* assessed over some *time horizon* and *relative to a benchmark.*

This definition has several important elements. First, risk is a *measure* that can be quantified. In comparing two potential investments, we want to know which one is riskier and by how much. All other things held equal, we expect a riskier investment to be less desirable than others and to command a lower price. Uncertainties that are not quantifiable cannot be priced.

Second, risk arises from *uncertainty about the future.* We know that the future will follow one and only one of many possible courses, but we don't know which one. This statement is true of even the simplest random event—more things can happen than will happen. If you flip a coin, it can come up either heads or tails. It cannot come up both heads and tails or neither heads nor tails; only one of two possibilities will occur.

Third, risk has to do with the *future payoff* of an investment, which is unknown. Though we do not know for certain what is going to happen to our investment, we must be able to list all the possibilities. Imagining all the possible payoffs and the likelihood of each one is a difficult but indispensable part of computing risk.

Fourth, our definition of risk refers to an *investment* or group of investments. We can use the term *investment* very broadly here to include everything from the balance in a bank account to shares of a mutual fund to lottery tickets and real estate.

Fifth, risk must be assessed over some *time horizon.* Every investment has a time horizon. We hold some investments for a day or two and others for many years. In most cases, the risk of holding an investment over a short period is smaller than the risk of holding it over a long one, but there are important exceptions to the rule that we will discuss later.[2]

Finally, risk must be assessed *relative to a benchmark* rather than in isolation. If someone tells you that an investment is risky, you should immediately ask: "Relative to what?" The simplest answer is "Relative to an investment with no risk at all," called

---

[2]In Chapter 8, we will consider evidence that holding stock for one year is riskier than holding it for 20 years.

a *risk-free investment*. But there are other possibilities, often more appropriate. For example, in considering the performance of a particular investment advisor or money manager, a good **benchmark** is the performance of a group of experienced investment advisors or money managers. If you want to know the risk associated with a specific investment strategy, the most appropriate benchmark would be the risk associated with other strategies.

Now that we know what risk is, how do we measure it? We use some rudimentary tools of probability theory, as we will see in the next section.

Measuring Risk

Armed with our definition of risk, we are now ready to quantify and measure it. In this section we will become familiar with the mathematical concepts useful in thinking about random events. We have already used some of these concepts. Recall from the last chapter that the *real* interest rate equals the *nominal* interest rate minus *expected* inflation. Without the proper tools, we weren't able to be explicit about what the term *expected inflation* means. The same is true of the term *expected return*. We see now that the best way to think about expected inflation and expected return is as the average or best guess—the *expected value*—of inflation, or the investment's return out of all the possible values.

Possibilities, Probabilities, and Expected Value

Probability theory tells us that in considering any uncertainty, the first thing we must do is to *list all the possible outcomes* and then *figure out the chance of each one occurring*. When you toss a coin, what are all the *possible* outcomes? There are two and only two. The coin can come down either heads or tails. What is the *chance* of each one of these two outcomes occurring? If the coin is fair, it will come down heads half the time and tails the other half; that's what we mean by *fair*. If we tossed a fair coin over and over again, thousands of times, it would come down heads half the time and tails the other half. But for any individual toss, the coin has an equal chance of coming down heads or tails. To quantify this statement, we can say that the *probability* that the coin will come up heads is one-half.

Probability is a measure of the likelihood that an event will occur. It is always expressed as a number between zero and one. The closer the probability is to zero, the *less* likely it is that an event will occur. If the probability is exactly zero, we are sure that the event will *not* happen. The closer the probability is to one, the *more* likely it is that an event will occur. If the probability is exactly one, the event *will* definitely occur.

Some people prefer to think of random outcomes in terms of frequencies rather than probabilities. Instead of saying that the probability of a coin coming down heads is one-half, we could say that the coin will come down heads once every two tosses on average. Probabilities can always be converted into frequencies in this way.

To grasp these concepts, it is helpful to construct a table. The table lists everything that can happen (all the possibilities) together with their chances of occurring (their probabilities). Let's start with a single coin toss. Table 5.1 lists the possibilities—heads or tails—and the probabilities, both equal to one-half.

Table 5.1 A Simple Example: All Possible Outcomes of a Single Coin Toss

Possibilities	Probability	Outcome
#1	$\frac{1}{2}$	Heads
#2	$\frac{1}{2}$	Tails

APPLYING THE CONCEPT
IT'S NOT JUST EXPECTED
RETURN THAT MATTERS

Your life seems to be going well. You enjoy your job, and it pays enough that you can put a little aside each month. You can't resist the dollar-for-dollar match your employer is offering on contributions to your retirement account, so you're slowly building up some long-term savings. But every so often, you wonder if you're saving enough. One day you go home and fire up the financial planning program on your computer, just to check.

Going through the retirement planner, you enter all the standard information: your age now and when you hope to retire; your salary and the value of all your assets; the monthly contribution to your retirement account and the monthly income you want at retirement. When you finish, the program asks what rate of return to assume. That is, how fast do you expect your savings to grow from now until your retirement? Following the suggestion on the screen and adjusting for inflation, you enter 6 percent, which is modestly below the average *real* return on the stock market over the past 75 years.* The light flashes green, signaling that you're on track to meet your financial goals. But are you?

Maybe. The program did a series of future- and present-value calculations like the ones described in Applying the Concept: Early Retirement in Chapter 4. The green light means that if the assumptions you entered are valid, your saving rate is sufficient. That is, *if* your savings grow at 6 percent

(adjusted for inflation), you'll be okay. So you need to decide whether you think 6 percent is a reasonable number. While it might be your best guess for the return (that's the *expected return*) over the next few decades, it is surely not the only possibility. You have very little sense of what the average return will be between now and the time that you retire.

To get a 6 percent expected return, you will have to take risk. And risk means that you could end up with less. What if your investment return is only 3 percent per year? Over 40 years that's an enormous difference. At 6 percent annual growth, $1 today is worth more than $10 in 40 years, and if you can save $1,000 per year you'll have more than $160,000 saved up. Reducing the growth rate to 3 percent means that the future value of $1 today 40 years from now falls to about $3.25. The lower return means that with the same $1,000 per year savings, you're left with less than $80,000 after 40 years.† You'll have to save more than twice as much to meet the same goal. Now that's risk!

You need to know what the possibilities are and how likely each one is. Only then can you assess whether your retirement savings plan is risky or not.

*Inflation complicates computations over very long time periods. Price increases of 2 or 3 percent per year may not seem like much, but over 40 years they add up. At 2 percent inflation, prices double every 36 years. The simplest approach is to ignore inflation and measure income, wealth, and savings in current dollars. Then use a real rate of interest to compute future and present value.

†These numbers are based on future-value calculations. If you save $1,000 per year, after 40 years you will have $1,000 \times (1.06)^{40} + $1,000 \times (1.06)^{39} + \ldots + $1,000 \times (1.06)^2 + $1,000 \times (1.06) = $164,048.

In constructing a table like this one, we must be careful to list *all* possible outcomes. In the case of a coin toss, we know that the coin can come down only two ways, heads or tails. We know that one of these outcomes *must* occur. We just don't know which one.

One important property of probabilities is that we can compute the chance that one *or* the other event will happen by adding the probabilities together. In the case of the coin flip there are only two possibilities; the probability that the coin will come up either heads or tails must be one. If the table is constructed correctly, then, *the values in the probabilities column will sum to one.*

Let's move from a coin toss to something a bit more complicated: an investment that can rise or fall in value. Assume that for $1,000 you can purchase a stock whose value is equally likely to fall to $700 or rise to $1,400. We'll refer to the amount you could get back as the investment's **payoff**. Following the procedure we used to analyze the coin toss, we can construct Table 5.2. Again we list the possibilities and the probability that each will occur, but we add their payoffs (column 3).[3]

We can now go a step further and compute what is called the **expected value** of the investment. We are familiar with the idea of expected value as the **average** or most likely outcome. The expected value is also known as the **mean**. After listing all

[3]As you go through the examples in the chapter, be aware that it is often very difficult to estimate the probabilities needed to do the risk computations. The best way to do it is often to look at history. Investment analysts usually estimate the possibilities and probabilities from what happened in the past.

| Table 5.2 | Investing $1,000: Case 1 | | |

Possibilities	Probability	Payoff	Payoff × Probability
#1	$\frac{1}{2}$	$ 700	$350
#2	$\frac{1}{2}$	$1,400	$700

Expected value = Sum of (Probability times Payoff) = $1,050

of the possible outcomes and the probabilities that they will occur, we compute the expected value as the sum of their probabilities times their payoffs. (Another way to say this is that the expected value is the probability-weighted sum of the possible outcomes.)

Computing the expected value of the investment is straightforward. In Table 5.2, the first step is to take the probabilities in the second column and multiply them by their associated payoffs in the third column. The results are in the fourth column. Summing them, we get

$$\text{Expected value} = \tfrac{1}{2}(\$700) + \tfrac{1}{2}(\$1,400) = \$1,050$$

which appears at the bottom of the table.

The expected value of an investment is a very useful concept, but it can be difficult at first. The problem is that if we make this investment only once, we will obtain either $700 or $1,400, not $1,050. In fact, regardless of the number of times we make this particular investment, the payoff will *never* be $1,050. But what would happen if we were to make this investment 1 million times? About 500,000 of those times the investment would pay off $1,400 and the other 500,000 times it would pay off $700. (Notice that we just converted the probabilities into frequencies.) So the *average* payoff from the 1 million investments would be

$$\frac{500,000}{1,000,000}(\$700) + \frac{500,000}{1,000,000}(\$1,400) = \$1,050 \text{ (the expected value)}$$

While the world of casino gambling may offer simple bets with just two outcomes, the financial world rarely does. To make the example more realistic, let's double the number of possibilities and look at a case in which the $1,000 investment might pay off $100 or $2,000 in addition to $700 or $1,400. Table 5.3 shows the possibilities, probabilities, and payoffs. We'll assume that the two original possibilities are the most likely; the two new possibilities are much less likely to occur. Note that the probabilities sum to one: 0.1 + 0.4 + 0.4 + 0.1 = 1. Again, we could convert the probabilities to frequencies, so that 0.4 means 4 out of 10. And again, we can compute the expected value by multiplying each probability times its associated payoff and then summing them. So $100 would be the payoff one out of every 10 times, $700 the payoff four out of every 10 times, and so on. To compute the expected value, we would find the average of these 10 investments:

$100 + $700 + $700 + $700 + $700

$+ $1,400 + $1,400 + $1,400 + $1,400 + $2,000 = $10,500$

Table 5.3		Investing $1,000: Case 2	

Possibilities	Probability	Payoff	Payoff × Probability
#1	0.1	$ 100	$ 10
#2	0.4	$ 700	$280
#3	0.4	$1,400	$560
#4	0.1	$2,000	$200

Expected value = Sum of (Probability times Payoff) = $1,050

and

$$\frac{\$10,500}{10} = \$1,050$$

Once again the expected value is $1,050.

Because the expected value of this $1,000 investment is $1,050, the expected gain is $50. But most people don't discuss investment payoffs in terms of dollars; instead, they talk about the percentage return. Expressing the return as a percentage allows investors to compute the gain or loss on the investment regardless of the size of the initial investment. In this case, the **expected return** is $50 on a $1,000 investment, or 5 percent. Note that the two $1,000 investments we just discussed are not distinguishable by their expected return, which is 5 percent in both cases. Does that mean an investor would be indifferent between them? Even a casual glance suggests that the answer is no because the second investment has a wider range of payoffs than the first. The highest payoff is higher and the lowest payoff lower than for the first investment. So the two investments carry different levels of risk. The next section discusses measures of risk.

One last word on expected values. Recall from the last chapter that to compute the real interest rate, we need a measure of *expected inflation*. One way to calculate expected inflation is to use the technique we just learned. That is, list all the possibilities for inflation, assign each one a probability, and then calculate the expected value of inflation.

Measures of Risk

Most of us have an intuitive sense of risk and its measurement. For example, we know that walking on a sidewalk is usually a safe activity. But imagine that one day as you are strolling along, you come upon a three-foot hole in the sidewalk. The only way across is to jump over it. If the hole is just a few inches deep, it won't stop you. But the deeper it is, the greater the risk of jumping across because the greater the range of injuries you could sustain. We all have an intuitive sense that the wider the range of outcomes, the greater the risk. That's why the investment that has four possible payoffs (Table 5.3) seems riskier than the one with two possible payoffs (Table 5.2).

"Come <u>on</u>, Louis. No risk, no reward."

Thinking about risk in terms of the range of possible outcomes is straightforward. The best way to do it is to start with something that has no risk at all—a sidewalk without a hole in it or an investment with only one possible payoff. We will refer to a financial instrument with no risk at all as a risk-free investment or risk-free asset. A **risk-free asset** *is an investment whose future value is known with certainty and whose return is the* **risk-free rate of return**.[4] The payoff that you will receive from such an investment is guaranteed and cannot vary. For instance, if the risk-free return is 5 percent, a $1,000 risk-free investment will pay $1,050, its expected value, with certainty. If there is a chance that the payoff will be either more or less than $1,050, the investment is risky.

Let's compare this risk-free investment with the first investment we looked at, the one in which $1,000 had an equal chance of turning into $1,400 or $700 (see Table 5.2). That investment had the same expected return as the risk-free investment, 5 percent. The difference is that the payoff wasn't certain, so risk was involved. What caused the risk was the increase in the spread of the potential payoffs. The larger the spread, the higher the risk.

These examples suggest that we can measure risk by quantifying the spread among an investment's possible outcomes. We will look at two such measures. The first is based on a statistical concept called the *standard deviation* and is strictly a measure of spread. The second, called *value at risk,* is a measure of the riskiness of the worst case. When the hole in the sidewalk gets deep enough, you risk being killed if you fall in.

Variance and Standard Deviation   The **variance** is defined as the average of the squared deviations of the possible outcomes from their expected value, weighted by their probabilities. We square the differences from the expected value so that high and low payoffs don't cancel each other out and we get a measure of how spread out they are.

It takes several steps to compute the variance of an investment. First, compute the expected value and then subtract it from each of the possible payoffs. Then square each one of the results, multiply it by its probability, and, finally, add up the results. In the example of the $1,000 investment that pays either $700 or $1,400, the steps are:

1. Compute the expected value: $\frac{1}{2}(\$1,400) + \frac{1}{2}(\$700) = \$1,050$
2. Subtract the expected value from each of the possible payoffs:
   $\$1,400 - \$1,050 = +\$350$
   $\$700 - \$1,050 = -\$350$
3. Square each of the results: $\$350^2 = 122,500(\text{dollars}^2)$ and $(-\$350)^2 = 122,500(\text{dollars}^2)$
4. Multiply each result times its probability and add up the results:
   $\frac{1}{2}[122,500(\text{dollars}^2)] + \frac{1}{2}[122,500(\text{dollars}^2)] = 122,500(\text{dollars}^2)$

---

[4]In most financial markets, no truly risk-free asset exists, so the risk-free rate of return is not directly observable. Regardless of our inability to measure it exactly, the risk-free rate of return remains a useful concept.

YOUR FINANCIAL WORLD
Choosing the Right Amount of Car Insurance

Car insurance is expensive, especially for young drivers. That should be no surprise, because the younger you are, the more likely you are to have an accident. Only about one in seven drivers is under 25 years old, but more than one-quarter of the 10 million accidents that happen each year involve a driver between 16 and 24. Men are worse risks than women. It's hard to fault insurance companies for charging higher premiums to drivers who are more likely than others to file claims.

While you must have some insurance—most states require that you have *liability insurance,* to pay for damage and injuries to others if you cause an accident—you do have some choices. The most important choice is whether or not to buy collision insurance, which pays for damage to your car when the accident is your fault. If you go without it, you'll have to pay for the repairs if you cause a crash.

There is no easy way to figure out how much collision insurance to buy, but there are a few things to think about when you make your decision. First, how much is your car worth? If you do have an accident, the insurance company doesn't promise to fix your car regardless of the costs. Instead, the company will pay you what it is worth.

So if your car is old and you crash, the odds are you'll get a check, not a repaired car. Buying collision insurance on old cars is rarely worth it.

What should you do if you have a new car? Here the question is not whether to buy collision insurance but how much. The choice is in something called a *deductible,* the amount you pay for the repair after a crash. If you have a $250 deductible, you'll pay the first $250 and the insurance company will pay the rest. The higher your deductible is, the lower your insurance premium will be.

To see how much your premium can vary, let's look at an example: a 19-year-old male college student living away from home with a good driving record and a good-student discount. On a sedan that cost around $13,000 in 2012, and with a $500 collision deductible, his insurance might cost almost $3,400 per year. Raising the deductible to $1,000 could lower the premium by around $300 per year, to less than $3,100. Can $500 worth of extra insurance possibly be worth paying an extra $300 a year? Only if the driver expects to have an accident once every 20 months. Ideally he won't, so the extra insurance isn't worth paying for.

Writing this procedure more compactly, we get

$$\text{Variance} = \tfrac{1}{2}(\$1,400 - \$1,050)^2 + \tfrac{1}{2}(\$700 - \$1,050)^2 = 122,500(\text{dollars}^2)$$

The **standard deviation** is the (positive) square root of the variance, or:

$$\text{Standard deviation} = \sqrt{Variance} = \sqrt{122,500(\text{dollars}^2)} = \$350$$

The standard deviation is more useful than the variance because it is measured in the same unit as the payoffs: dollars. (Variance is measured in dollars squared.) That means that we can convert the standard deviation into a percentage of the initial investment of $1,000, or 35 percent. This calculation provides a baseline against which we can measure the risk of alternative investments. Given a choice between two investments with the same expected payoff, most people would choose the one with the lower standard deviation. A higher-risk investment would be less desirable.

Let's compare this two-payoff investment with the one that has four possible payoffs. We already concluded that the second investment is riskier, because the payoffs are more spread out. But how much riskier is it? To answer this question, we can compute the standard deviation. That means following the four steps to calculate the variance, and then taking the square root. From the detailed computation in Table 5.4 you can see the standard deviation is $528. This is one and one-half times the $350 standard deviation of the first investment, with only two possible payoffs. Because the two investments have the same expected value, the vast majority of people would prefer the first. The greater the standard deviation, the higher the risk.

Table 5.4 Expected Value, Variance, and Standard Deviation

To compute the expected value, variance, and standard deviation of the four-payoff investment in Table 5.3, follow the steps described in the text nearby:

1. Compute the expected value.
   - List the possible payoffs and their probabilities.
   - Compute the expected value as the sum of the payoff times the probabilities.
2. Compute the variance.
   - From each payoff subtract the expected value.
   - Square the deviation of the payoff from the expected value.
   - Sum the squared deviations times the probabilities.
3. Compute the standard deviation as the positive square root of the variance.

Here's the information we need:

(1) Probability	(2) Payoff	(3) Payoff − Expected Value	(4) (Payoff − Expected Value)^2
0.1	$ 100	($ 100 − $1,050) = −$950	902,500(dollars^2)
0.4	$ 700	($ 700 − $1,050) = −$350	122,500(dollars^2)
0.4	$1,400	($1,400 − $1,050) = +$350	122,500(dollars^2)
0.1	$2,000	($2,000 − $1,050) = +$950	902,500(dollars^2)

1. Using columns (1) and (2), we can compute the expected value:

   Expected value = Sum of (Probability times Payoff)

   $$= 0.1 \times \$100 + 0.4 \times \$700 + 0.4 \times \$1,400 + 0.1 \times \$2,000$$
   $$= \$10 + \$280 + \$560 + \$200$$
   $$= \$1,050$$

2. Using column (4), we can compute the variance:

   Variance = Sum of (Probability × Squared deviation of payoff from expected value)

   $$= 0.1 \times 902,500 + 0.4 \times 122,500 + 0.4 \times 122,500 + 0.1 \times 902,500$$
   $$= 278,500(\text{dollars}^2)$$

3. Finally, using this result, we can compute the standard deviation:

   Standard deviation $= \sqrt{\text{Variance}}$
   $$= \sqrt{278,500(\text{dollars}^2)}$$
   $$= \$528$$

To see this conclusion graphically, start with Case 1 from Table 5.2 where a $1,000 investment is equally likely to rise in value to $1,400 or fall in value to $700. That is, there are two possibilities, each with probability ½: $700 and $1,400. We can plot this on a bar graph, where the horizontal axis has the payoffs $700 or $1,400 and the height of each bar is the probability (in this case 0.5 for both). The result is in the left panel of Figure 5.1. Recall from Table 5.2, that the expected value of this investment is $1,050, the vertical line in the figure.

Figure 5.1   Investing $1,000

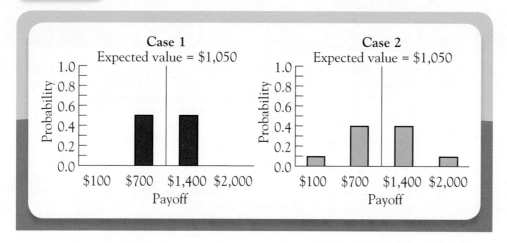

The figure plots the distribution of possible outcomes from a $1,000 investment from Tables 5.2 and 5.3 on pages 108 and 109. In each case, the payoff is on the horizontal axis and the height of each bar equals the probability that outcome will occur.

Compare this to Case 2 from Table 5.3. Recall that in this case, the $1,000 investment has four possible payoffs, $100, $700, $1,400 and $2,000; and these occur with probability 0.1, 0.4, 0.4, and 0.1. As in Case 1, the expected value continues to be $1,050. Using the same method as before, where the height of each bar represents the probability of each outcome, we can plot the right-hand panel of Figure 5.1. Comparing the two figures, we can see that in Case 2, where the investment has four possible payoffs, the distribution is more spread out. This matches the result from computing the standard deviation. *The more spread out the distribution of possible payoffs from an investment, the higher the standard deviation and the bigger the risk.*

Value at Risk   Standard deviation is the most common measure of financial risk, and for most purposes it is adequate. But in some circumstances we need to take a different approach to the measurement of risk. Sometimes we are less concerned with the spread of possible outcomes than with the value of the worst outcome. For example, no one wants the local bank to close its doors. Nor is anyone interested in a discount price for a life insurance policy from an insurance company that is in poor financial condition. Neither the customers nor the government regulators care how well or how badly a financial institution's shareholders fare, so long as they do well enough to keep the doors open. The concept used to assess this sort of catastrophic risk is called **value at risk (VaR)**.

To understand how value at risk works, let's look at an example. Assume you are considering buying a house. In going through your finances, you conclude that you can afford a monthly mortgage payment of $650 and no more. You find a nice house and a mortgage lender who will lend you $100,000 to buy it. But you need to decide on the type of mortgage to get. Should it have a fixed- or adjustable-rate? The answer is different for different people. But let's see if we can organize our thinking.

Assume that the current interest rate on a 30-year fixed-rate mortgage (the most popular kind) is 4 percent, so it has monthly payments around $475, which is within

TOOLS OF THE TRADE

The Impact of Leverage on Risk

In Chapter 3, we saw that leverage added to risks in the financial system (see Lessons from the Crisis: Leverage). Recall that **leverage** is the practice of borrowing to finance part of an investment. Common examples of leverage are borrowing to buy stock (through what is called *margin loans*), corporate borrowing (using bonds), and borrowing to acquire a house (by obtaining a mortgage). In the case of a margin loan, an investor borrows from a brokerage firm to increase the quantity of stock purchased.

How does leverage affect risk and return? To understand the effects of leverage, let's look at an investment of $1,000 with an expected return of 5 percent (a gain of $50) and a standard deviation of 35 percent ($350). That's the example in Table 5.2. What if in addition to investing $1,000 of your own, you borrow $1,000 and invest a total of $2,000? This investment strategy changes the risk involved. The reason is that the lender wants to be repaid the $1,000 loan regardless of how much your investment returns. If the investment's payoff is high, your $2,000 investment will increase in value to $2,800. After repaying the $1,000 loan, you will be left with $1,800—an increase of $800 over your initial investment of $1,000. If your investment falls in value, the $2,000 will become $1,400. After repaying the $1,000 loan, you will be left with $400—a loss of $600.

Because these two results are equally likely, the expected value of your leveraged investment is $\frac{1}{2}($1,800$) + \frac{1}{2}($400$) =$ $1,100. Your expected gain—the difference between your investment of $1,000 and its expected value of $1,100—is now $100 and your expected return is 10 percent. That's double the expected return from your investment of $1,000 without any borrowing—double what it would be without leverage. So we have part of the answer to our question: *Leverage increases the expected return.*

But what about risk? To figure it out, let's calculate the standard deviation of your leveraged investment.

$$\text{St. dev.} = \sqrt{\tfrac{1}{2}(1,800 - 1,100)^2 + \tfrac{1}{2}(400 - 1,100)^2} = \$700$$

The standard deviation has doubled: *twice the expected return at twice the risk!*

We can repeat these calculations for any amount of leverage we want. For example, homebuyers commonly pay 20 percent of the price of a house with their savings and borrow the remaining 80 percent. Because mortgage lenders expect to be repaid, changes in the price of the house become gains or losses to the owner. Say you buy a $100,000 house by borrowing $80,000 and paying $20,000 from your savings, often called your *equity.* A 10 percent increase in your home's value would raise the price to $110,000. Subtracting the $80,000 you borrowed, your $20,000 down payment would become $30,000, a 50 percent increase. On the other hand, if your home's value fell by 10 percent, you would *lose* half your $20,000 down payment. *Leverage magnifies the effect of price changes* (see Figure 5.2).

Figure 5.2	The Effect of Leverage on Risk and Return

To understand leverage, picture a set of two gears, one large and one small. The movement in the price of the leveraged investment is measured by the number of revolutions in the big gear. This explains why some people refer to leverage as "gearing." The investor's risk and return are measured by the number of revolutions in the small gear. The bigger the big gear, the more times the small gear goes around with each revolution of the big gear. That's leverage.

---

your budget.[5] One alternative is a mortgage with the same 30-year term that adjusts once a year, starting at 3 percent. The adjustable-rate mortgage has payments that start at about $420 per month.

This looks great. But remember Core Principle 2: Risk requires compensation. By taking the adjustable-rate mortgage you can save more than $50 per month. But

---

[5]All of the numbers in this example are approximate. To compare payments on fixed- and adjustable-rate mortgages, you can use the calculators at *www.wsj.com* or *www.choosetosave.org*.

The Impact of Leverage

	No Leverage	Leverage Ratio = 2
Your investment	$1,000	$1,000
+ Amount borrowed	0	$1,000
= Total invested	$1,000	$2,000
Possible payoffs	$1,400 or $700	$2,800 or $1,400
Net of repayment	$1,400 or $700	$1,800 or $400
Expected value (net of repayment)	$1,050 (5%)	$1,100 (10%)
Standard deviation	$350 (35%)	$700 (70%)

The example uses the information from Table 5.2, where a $1,000 investment has an equal probability of a $1,400 and a $700 payoff. In the example with leverage on the right, the investor borrows $1,000, invests a total of $2,000, obtains a payoff of either $2,800 or $1,400, and must repay the $1,000 loan for a net payoff of $1,800 or $400.

We can use these examples to develop a formula for the impact of leverage on the expected return and standard deviation of an investment. If you borrow to purchase an asset, you increase both the expected return and the standard deviation by a leverage ratio of

$$\text{Leverage ratio} = \frac{\text{Cost of investment}}{\text{Owner's contribution to the purchase}}$$

where the "Owner's contribution to the purchase" in the denominator is just the cost of investment minus the amount borrowed. If the expected return and standard deviation of the unleveraged investment are 5 percent and 35 percent (as in our first example), then borrowing half and contributing half means that for each dollar invested, the buyer is contributing 50 cents. The formula tells us that the leverage ratio is 1/0.5, which equals 2. Thus the investment's expected return is 2 × 5 percent = 10 percent, and its standard deviation is 2 × 35 percent = 70 percent. (See the accompanying table.) And if the homeowner borrows 80 percent of the purchase price of the house, his or her contribution is 20 percent, so the leverage ratio is 1/(1 − 80/100) = 1/0.2 = 5 times what it would be for someone who could buy the house outright, with no mortgage.

We have focused on the impact of leverage on risk, but leverage has at least as big an impact on value at risk. Note that for the $1,000 investment without leverage in Table 5.2, the worst case was a loss of $300, or 30 percent, half the time. If an investor borrowed 90 percent of the funds needed to make the investment, half the time the investor would lose not only the entire $100 invested but an additional $200 of borrowed funds as well. *Leverage compounds the worst possible outcome.*

adjustable rates can adjust, meaning they can go up and down. That's a risk. Looking closer, you realize that the mortgage contract specifies that the adjustments can be as much as 2 percentage points per year, and can go as high as 11 percent. Which mortgage should you sign up for?

The lower initial monthly payments do seem to come with higher risk. Without doing any computations, we know that the standard deviation of monthly payments for a 4 percent fixed-rate mortgage is zero, and that the standard deviation of the payment for the adjustable-rate mortgage is greater than zero. Let's just say that interest

LESSONS FROM THE CRISIS
SYSTEMIC RISK*

The financial system consists of all the institutions and markets that perform intermediation—matching savers with users of funds. Threats to the system as a whole—known as *systemic risks*—differ from the threats to specific households, firms, or markets. Naturally, governments are more concerned about systemic threats because they can be catastrophic for an economy. Their policy goal is a robust financial system that cannot be brought down by the failure of specific parts.

Cell biology provides a useful analogy for understanding a financial system. Complex organisms are composed of many cells with specialized purposes. Every day, a large number of these cells die (and new ones are created) without threatening the organism as a whole. In financial systems, too, many intermediaries fail and new ones emerge without posing a systemic threat. Yet, in both biology and finance, some disturbances can undermine both the parts and the whole.

This biological analogy can be taken a step further. Think of financial institutions as the cells of the financial system, and think of markets as the central nervous system that coordinates their actions. Cells operating alone cannot make a complex organism function. Their actions are coordinated by the messages that travel along diverse electrical and chemical pathways. In the same way, an effective financial system requires markets that collect and transmit information necessary to coordinate the behavior of financial institutions and others.

How does the biological analogy help us understand systemic risk? It provides hints about what might threaten the system as a whole, not just its parts.

In the world of finance, systemic risk arises when a set of vulnerabilities in markets and financial institutions threatens to disrupt the general function of intermediation. *Common exposure* to a risk can threaten many intermediaries at the same time. Connections among financial institutions and markets, even when unseen, may transmit and amplify a shock across the system. Obstacles to the flow of information make a system more vulnerable, because information is needed to coordinate the system's parts.

A financial system also may contain critical parts (comparable to a heart or a brain) without which it cannot function. Key markets and exchanges may play such a role. Similarly, the largest, most interconnected financial firms are sometimes called *too big to fail* if their failure threatens a cascade of bankruptcies among other firms.

As one possible source of systemic risk, consider the role of liquidity, which is often called the lifeblood of a financial system (see Chapter 2, Lessons from the Crisis: Market Liquidity, Funding Liquidity, and Making Markets). Usually, the smooth circulation of liquid assets around the financial system makes it possible for financial institutions to convert their holdings easily into cash and to trade in markets. But what happens if that circulation is interrupted or if the overall supply of liquidity is inadequate?

Like a heart attack, obstacles to the flow of liquidity pose a catastrophic threat to the financial system. Some financial institutions may become unable to trade or make payments, while markets for a range of assets may dry up. If these shocks weaken other firms, the result can be a wave of bankruptcies.

*Note that *systemic* risk—which refers to the financial system—differs from *systematic* risk, which is defined in this chapter as an economywide risk that alters the size of the economic pie.

---

rates are not expected to change, so the expected value of the monthly payments in the second circumstance is just $420. But what does that tell us?

The computation of the expected value and standard deviation does not seem to get at the heart of the problem. The reason is that it doesn't take proper account of the worst case. The interest rate could rise 2 percent per year for the next four years. That means that your monthly payments could rise to around $535 in the second year after one adjustment, about $665 in the third year, and go up over $800 in the fourth year. While you can readily make the $535 payments, more than $650 per month is out of the question. If interest rates were to rise by 4 percentage points over the next two years, you would no longer be able to afford the mortgage payments. That's the risk.

This mortgage example highlights the fact that sometimes risk should be measured by the value of the worst case rather than be measured by expected value and standard deviation. Value at risk, which measures risk as the maximum potential loss, is more appropriate in the example we just studied. VaR is the answer to the question: How much will I lose if the worst possible scenario occurs? In the example of the $1,000 investment, summarized in Table 5.2, the worst case was a loss of $300. In the more complex $1,000 investment, summarized in Table 5.3, the value at risk was $900—the most you could possibly lose. In the mortgage example the value at risk is the house: If the payment increases beyond $650 a month, you can't make the payments on your loan and you will be forced to sell the house. There are surely cases where the lower payments of an adjustable-rate mortgage are worth the risk, but this may not be one of them.

A more sophisticated value-at-risk analysis would include a time horizon and probabilities. In fact, the formal definition of *Value at Risk* is *the worst possible loss over a specific time horizon, at a given probability.* VaR is a measure of risk that we will find very useful in discussing the management and regulation of financial institutions. By restricting the sorts of financial instruments banks can hold, bank managers and financial regulators try to limit the chances of a financial collapse. Such a collapse is an example of infrequent but potentially catastrophic events sometimes called *tail risks* or *black swans* (like the enormous 2011 earthquake that produced a tsunami and nuclear disaster in Japan). To address the dangers associated with financial tail risks, banks and regulators employ the concept of value at risk.

Risk Aversion, the Risk Premium, and the Risk-Return Tradeoff

The implication of our discussion so far is that most people don't like risk and will pay to avoid it. While some people enjoy risky activities like skydiving and car racing, most of us are more careful. And while some people gamble large sums, most of us don't because we can't sustain large losses comfortably. In fact, the reason we buy insurance is that we want someone else to take the risk. Insurance is an interesting case; remember, for an insurance company to make a profit, it must charge more than it expects to pay out. Thus, insurance premiums are higher than the expected value of the policyholder's losses. We pay to avoid risks because most of us are *risk averse.*

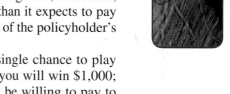

To understand risk aversion, imagine that you are offered a single chance to play a game in which a fair coin will be tossed. If it comes up heads you will win $1,000; if it comes up tails, you will get nothing. How much would you be willing to pay to play the game just once? The expected value of the game is $500—that is, on average, the game yields $500—but you may play only one time. Would you pay $500 to play the game? If so, you are *risk neutral.* Most people would not play the game at $500, though they would at less than that amount. These people are *risk averse.*

Because the coin toss is similar to an investment, we can apply the same logic to investor behavior and conclude that *a risk-averse investor will always prefer an investment with a certain return to one with the same expected return but any amount of uncertainty.* (A risk-neutral person wouldn't care as long as the expected return is the same.) A risk-free investment with a guaranteed return is clearly preferable to a risky investment with the same expected return but an uncertain outcome. In the case of the coin toss, most people would take $500 with certainty rather than risk tossing the coin and getting double or nothing.

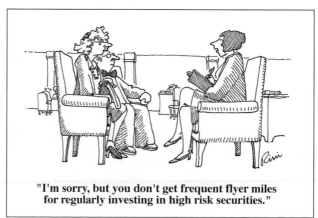

"I'm sorry, but you don't get frequent flyer miles for regularly investing in high risk securities."

Figure 5.3 The Tradeoff between Risk and Expected Return

The higher the risk, the higher the expected return. The risk premium equals the expected return on the risky investment minus the risk-free return.

One result of this desire to avoid risk is that investors require compensation for taking risk. That's the flip side of buying insurance. When we buy insurance, we pay someone else to take our risks, so it makes sense that if someone wants us to take on a risk, we need to be paid to do it. A risky investment, then, must have an expected return that is higher than the return on a risk-free asset. In economic terms, it must offer a **risk premium**. In general, *the riskier an investment, the higher the risk premium (the higher the compensation investors require for holding it)* (see Figure 5.3).

By extension, if riskier investments have higher risk premiums, they must have higher expected returns. Thus, there is a tradeoff between risk and expected return; you can't get a high return without taking considerable risk. So if someone tells you he or she made a big return on an investment, you should suspect that it was a very risky investment. No risk, no reward!

To see how the idea of a risk premium works, take the case of a bond. We will study this in much more detail in Chapters 6 and 7, but for now let's compare bonds issued by Johnson & Johnson (JNJ) with those of Sprint. As of the third quarter of 2012, JNJ was in top-notch financial condition, while Sprint was not. That leads us to expect that the return for holding Sprint's bonds would contain a higher risk premium than would the return for holding JNJ bonds. And it did. In the summer of 2012, the two companies had bonds with a maturity range of about five years. Those from Sprint paid 9.54 percent, while those from JNJ paid 1.40 percent. Meanwhile, a five-year U.S. Treasury note paid a meager 0.71 percent. Because the U.S. Treasury is highly likely to pay, we'll use 0.71 percent as our estimate of the risk-free rate. So, to get an estimate of the risk premium for the JNJ and Sprint bonds, we subtract 0.71 from the rate for each: For Sprint, the result is 9.54 − 0.71 = 8.83 percent; for JNJ, we get 1.40 − 0.71 = 0.69 percent. Not surprisingly, the risk premium on the relatively risky company is much bigger—in this case, nearly 13 times bigger!

Sources of Risk: Idiosyncratic and Systematic Risk

Risk is everywhere. It comes in many forms and from almost every imaginable place. In most circumstances the sources of risk are obvious. For drivers, it's the risk of an accident; for farmers, the risk of bad weather; for investors, the risk of fluctuating stock prices. Regardless of the source, however, we can classify all risks into one of two groups: (1) those affecting a small number of people but no one else and (2) those affecting everyone. We'll call the first of these **idiosyncratic risks**, or *unique* risks, and the second **systematic risks**, or *economywide* risks.[6]

To understand the difference between idiosyncratic and systematic risk, think about the risks facing Ford Motor Company stockholders. Why should the value of Ford's stock go up or down? There are two main reasons. First, there is the risk

[6]These are also sometimes referred to as *specific* and *common risks*.

YOUR FINANCIAL WORLD
Your Risk Tolerance

How much risk should you tolerate? Figuring that out isn't easy, but there are a few ways to get some sense of the right level of risk for you. First, there are risk quizzes, short sets of questions financial advisers give their clients to determine the level of risk they can live with. For instance, "What would you do if a month after you invest in the stock market, the value of your stocks suddenly falls by 20 percent?" Answers might include "Sell right away," "Nothing," and "Buy more." Taking such a quiz is a useful first step, so you might want to try the one in Appendix A of this chapter.

But don't stop there. Even if you are willing to take risks, that doesn't mean you should. You may not have time to make back the losses you might suffer. Think about the difference between a 25-year-old and a 60-year-old both saving for their retirement. Which one of these people can afford to suddenly lose a quarter of her savings? Obviously, it is the 25-year-old. If a 60-year-old loses a quarter of her retirement savings, it's a disaster! Likewise, if you're saving to buy a car or a home, the sooner you are planning to make the purchase, the less you can afford to lose what you have. Always ask yourself: How much can I stand to lose? The longer your time horizon (and the wealthier you are), the more risk you can tolerate.

that Ford will lose sales to other car makers. If Ford fares poorly compared with its competition, its market share (and thus its share of all economic activity) may shrink (see Figure 5.4). This risk is unique to Ford, because if Ford does relatively poorly, someone else must be doing relatively better. Idiosyncratic risk affects specific firms, not everyone.

The second risk Ford's stockholders face is that the U.S. industry as a whole will do poorly (see Figure 5.4). This is systematic, economywide risk. If we think of *idiosyncratic risk* as a change in the *share* of the *auto-market* pie, *systematic risk* is a change in the *size* of the pie of the *entire economy*, of which the auto market is a part. In other words, systematic risk is the risk that everyone will do poorly at the same time. The entire economy could slow for reasons that are completely unrelated to any individual company's performance.

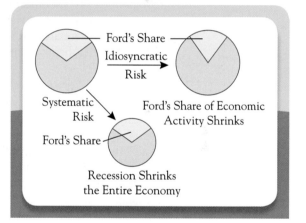

Figure 5.4   Idiosyncratic and Systematic Risk

Macroeconomic factors, such as swings in consumer and business confidence brought on by global economic conditions or changes in the political climate, are the source of systematic risks that affect *all* firms and individuals in the entire economy.

Idiosyncratic risks come in two types. In the first, one set of firms is affected in one way and other firms in another way. An example would be a change in the price of oil. History tells us that when oil prices rise, auto sales fall, and the automobile industry suffers. But higher oil prices improve the profits of firms that supply energy, such as ExxonMobil, Shell, and Texaco. An oil price change that is bad for Ford is good for the oil companies. Looking at the economy as a whole, this is an idiosyncratic risk.

Not all idiosyncratic risks are balanced by opposing risks to other firms or industries. Some unique risks are specific to one person or company and no one else. The risk that two people have an automobile accident is unrelated to whether anyone else has one. We will include these completely independent risks in the category of idiosyncratic risks.

Reducing Risk through Diversification

When George T. Shaheen left his $4 million-a-year job overseeing 65,000 employees of a large management consulting firm to become chief executive of the Webvan Group, he may not have realized how much of a risk he was taking. He thought Webvan would change the way people bought their groceries. Consumers would order their cereal, milk, apples, and ice cream over the Internet, and Webvan would deliver to their door. In November 1999, just a few months after Mr. Shaheen joined the company, his stock in Webvan was worth more than $280 million. But by April 2001, his shares were worth a paltry $150,000 and Mr. Shaheen had left the company. On July 10, 2001, Webvan collapsed and stockholders were left with nothing.

What happened to Webvan and its plan to change the way people shop? Maybe people actually like getting out of the house and going to the grocery store. But this story is about more than shopping; it's also about risk. Shaheen took on so much risk that a single big loss wiped him out. Traders in the financial markets call this experience "blowing up." Surely Shaheen could have done something to protect at least a portion of his phenomenal wealth from the risk that it would suddenly disappear. But what?

Cervantes answered this question in *Don Quixote* in 1605: "It is the part of a wise man to keep himself today for tomorrow, and *not to venture all his eggs in one basket* [emphasis added]." In today's terminology, risk can be reduced through **diversification**, the principle of holding more than one risk at a time. Though it may seem counterintuitive, holding several different investments can reduce the idiosyncratic risk an investor bears. A combination of risky investments is often less risky than any one individual investment. There are two ways to diversify your investments. You can *hedge* risks or you can *spread* them among the many investments. Let's discuss hedging first.

Hedging Risk

Hedging is the strategy of reducing idiosyncratic risk by making two investments with opposing risks. When one does poorly, the other does well, and vice versa. So while the payoff from each investment is volatile, together their payoffs are stable.

Consider the risk an investor faces from a potential change in the price of oil. Increases in the price of oil are bad for most of the economy, but they are good for oil companies. So an investor might buy stock in both General Electric (GE), maker of everything from lightbulbs to dishwashers and jet engines, and Texaco, a large oil company. For the sake of our example, let's assume that oil prices have an equal chance of rising or falling. When they rise, owners of Texaco stock receive a payoff of $120 for each $100 they invested. When oil prices fall, Texaco's shareholders just get their $100 investment back. The reverse is true for GE. When oil prices fall, owners of GE stock get $120 for each $100 they invested; when oil prices rise, they get $100.

Table 5.5 summarizes these relationships.

Let's compare three strategies for investing $100, given the relationships shown in the table:

1. Invest $100 in GE.
2. Invest $100 in Texaco.
3. Invest half in each company: $50 in GE and $50 in Texaco.

Table 5.5 Payoffs on Two Separate Investments of $100

Possibility	Payoff from Owning Only		Probability
	GE	Texaco	
Oil prices rise	$100	$120	$\frac{1}{2}$
Oil prices fall	$120	$100	$\frac{1}{2}$

Regardless of whether you invest $100 in GE or Texaco, the expected payoff is ½($120) + ½($100) = $110; and the

$$\text{Standard deviation of the payoff} = \sqrt{\tfrac{1}{2}(\$120 - \$110)^2 + \tfrac{1}{2}(\$100 - \$110)^2} = \$10$$

But what about the third option? What if you split your $100 and put half in GE and half in Texaco? Because $50 is half the size of your initial investment, the payoff is half as big as well—a $50 investment in either stock pays off either $60 or $50. But the important point about this strategy is that it reduces your risk (see Table 5.6). When oil prices go up, Texaco does well but GE does badly. When oil prices fall, the reverse happens. Regardless of whether oil prices go up or down, you will get back $110 on your $100 investment. Investing $50 in each stock ensures your payoff. Hedging—splitting your investment between two stocks with different payoff patterns—has eliminated your risk entirely.

Table 5.6   Results of Possible Investment Strategies: Hedging Risk

Initial Investment = $100

Investment Strategy	Expected Payoff	Standard Deviation
GE only	$110	$10
Texaco only	$110	$10
$\tfrac{1}{2}$ and $\tfrac{1}{2}$	$110	$ 0

Could George Shaheen have hedged the risk of owning so much Webvan stock? To do it, he would have had to find a company whose stock price would rise when Webvan's fell. That would have been difficult, because Webvan's business concept was new and untested. But Shaheen did have another option.

Spreading Risk

Because investments don't always move predictably in opposite directions, you can't always reduce risk through hedging. Fortunately, there is another way. You can simply **spread risk** around—and that's what George Shaheen should have done. To spread your risk, all you need to do is find investments whose payoffs are unrelated. Let's replace Texaco with Microsoft and assume that GE and Microsoft's payoffs are independent of each other.[7] So we toss a coin once to see if GE does well or badly, and then we toss it a second time to see how Microsoft does. As before, a $100 investment in either company pays off either $120 or $100 with equal probability.

Again, we'll consider three investment strategies: (1) GE only, (2) Microsoft only, and (3) half in GE and half in Microsoft. The expected payoff on each of these strategies is the same: $110. For the first two strategies, $100 in either company, the standard deviation is still $10, just as it was before. But for the third strategy, $50 in GE and $50 in Microsoft, the analysis is more complicated. There are four possible outcomes, two for each stock.

To solve the problem, we need to create a table showing all the possibilities, their probabilities, and the associated payoffs (see Table 5.7). We're familiar with possibilities 2 and 3, in which one stock pays off but the other one doesn't, just as in the GE/Texaco example.

Remember that the standard deviation is the square root of the average of the squared deviations from the expected value, weighted by the probabilities. In this case,

[7]The assumption of independence makes the calculations easier but is not essential. All that we need to know is that the two payoffs, GE and Microsoft, are not perfectly correlated so they do not move in lock-step.

IN THE NEWS
Risk-On, Risk-Off May Be Ending

By James Saft

January 29, 2013

The after-effects of the Great Crisis may still be with us, but the great correlation in global financial markets may be coming to an end. After years of seemingly disparate markets all going up or down in concert, recent weeks have shown signs of assets actually trading on their own merits. If sustained, this would be an important sign not just of a return to normality in financial markets, but that investors see a more stable world.

Then again, it might be a giant head-fake.

Sometimes called "risk-on, risk-off," or Ro-Ro, this has been the dominant trade since the financial crisis broke, with commodities, stocks and especially currencies moving very tightly together in predictable ways, mostly driven by major economic news and global events.

When investors felt things were good, everything "risky," like equities or commodities tied to economic growth, rallied together, sometimes almost without reference to regional or individual differences. At the same time, good news was bad for the dollar, which would rally instead on disappointing or negative developments.

Now there are signs this is ending, especially in the currency markets, which, as the biggest, most liquid and frenetic market often leads the way in setting trends.

Correlation in currency markets is as low as it has been in five years by some measures, according to JP Morgan currency strategist John Normand. Instead, trading is being driven by local issues, from radical new economic and monetary policy in Japan to the prospect of a triple-dip recession in Britain.

Similarly stock markets are no longer trading in lockstep, with Japan, notably, rallying sharply. A key measure of global stock market correlation is down more than 30 percent since June, according to Societe Generale, and is as low as it has been since 2007. . . .

Since Lehman [failed in 2008] we've been in a world in which the signal issue for all markets and assets has been whether or not things, well, are going down the tubes. That central issue has been in various guises, first the banking crisis and then the euro zone crisis, but all of the issues have

---

Table 5.7	Payoffs from Investing $50 in Each of Two Stocks
	Initial Investment = $100

Possibilities	GE	Microsoft	Total Payoff	Probability
#1	$60	$60	$120	$\frac{1}{4}$
#2	$60	$50	$110	$\frac{1}{4}$
#3	$50	$60	$110	$\frac{1}{4}$
#4	$50	$50	$100	$\frac{1}{4}$

that turns out to be the square root of the sum of ¼($120 − $110)² plus ¼($100 − $110)², which is $\sqrt{50(\text{dollars}^2)} = \$7.1$.[8]

Figure 5.5 shows the distribution of outcomes from the possible investment strategies. The left-hand panel plots the payoffs from investing the entire $100 in one stock,

---

[8]Following the steps in Table 5.4, we can compute the standard deviation of investing $50 each in

GE and Microsoft as $\sqrt{\frac{1}{4}(\$120 - \$110)^2 + \frac{1}{4}(\$110 - \$110)^2 + \frac{1}{4}(\$110 - \$110)^2 + \frac{1}{4}(\$100 - \$110)^2}$

$= \sqrt{\frac{1}{4}(\$10)^2 + \frac{1}{4}(\$0)^2 + \frac{1}{4}(\$0)^2 + \frac{1}{4}(\$10)^2} = \sqrt{50(\text{dollars}^2)} = \$7.1.$

been big enough and ugly enough to deeply impact the prospect of almost any asset you care to name.

In that kind of scenario the two key questions are how bad a given piece of news is, and what will be the reaction of governments, particularly central banks. That makes sense because governments and central banks are the only entities big enough to respond forcefully to a huge crisis, and frankly it was going to matter very little if a particular Italian company was well managed or if its products were in demand if Italy exited the euro zone. . . .

High correlations, markets in which everything goes up and goes down, are ones in which many investment techniques simply don't work. The benefit from diversification, long believed to be the market equivalent of a free lunch, has been scant or absent entirely. . . . The fall in global correlations may also be a sign that we are entering a period where globalization is on the defensive, making local politics, economics and other factors much more important.

Japan, from that perspective, is a good example of this. Japan's stock market has rallied and the yen has fallen because of a political development—the rise again of Shinzo Abe to the office of prime minister. That in turn has driven

new radical monetary policy which is likely to be out of proportion to what is being done elsewhere. . . .

It is genuinely too early to know, but if it lasts, a world in which investment has more than two speeds, risk-on or risk-off, would likely be a healthier one.

LESSONS OF THE ARTICLE

Don't put all your eggs in one basket: diversify. The less related the payoffs from different investments, the greater the benefits of diversification. When the payoffs from different assets move together—that is, their correlation is high—the benefits of diversification erode. The article highlights the limits of diversification when market developments are dominated by enormous systematic shocks like the financial crisis of 2007–2009 and the euro-area crisis. The ebb and flow of each crisis resulted in high asset correlations. Yet, even if diversification doesn't always help, it's still the best portfolio strategy.

Figure 5.5   Spreading Risk Payoffs from Two Investment Strategies

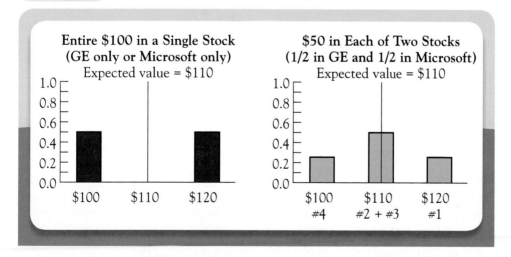

Left panel bar plot is the distribution of payoffs from investing all $100 in either GE or Microsoft, where each pays off either $100 or $110 with probability 1/2. Right panel is the bar plot of the distribution of payoffs from investing $50 each in GM and Microsoft, where each pays off either $50 or $60 with probability 1/2 and are independent (see Table 5.7).

either GE or Microsoft. The right-hand panel has the distribution of the payoffs from investing $50 in each of two stocks (from Table 5.7). The figure makes clear that by spreading your investment among independently risky investments you lower the spread of the outcomes, and lower the risk.

Measures of risk other than standard deviation will give us the same result. When you split your investment between the two stocks, 75 percent of the time the payoff is $110 or higher; only 25 percent of the time is the payoff $100. For most people, that prospect is more appealing than a 50 percent probability of getting $100 and a 50 percent probability of getting $120, the odds an investor faces in holding only one stock.

In the real world, there is no reason for an investor to stop diversifying at two stocks. The more independent sources of risk you hold in your portfolio, the lower your overall risk. Using the same numbers in this example—a payoff of either $100 or $120 per $100 investment, with equal probability—we can increase the number of stocks from two to three to four, and the standard deviation of a $100 investment will fall from $7.1 to $5.8 to $5.0. As we add more and more independent sources of risk, the standard deviation becomes negligible. (Appendix B of this chapter explains the algebra behind this statement.)

In summary, spreading the risk is a fundamental investment strategy. As Cervantes put it (and George Shaheen learned), never put all your eggs in one basket. If Shaheen had sold his Webvan stock and invested the proceeds in a portfolio composed of many stocks representative of the stock market as a whole, he would probably still have most of his $280 million. Diversification really works.

Diversification through the spreading of risk is the basis for the insurance business. A large automobile insurer writes millions of policies. It counts on the fact that not everyone will have accidents at the same time, for the risk of any one policyholder crashing is independent of the risk of another policyholder crashing. If it writes enough policies, the company can expect a predictable number of accident claims each year. When you toss a coin a million times, it will turn up heads around 500,000 times; likewise, assembling a large enough pool of independent risks isn't risky.

Now that we understand both what risk is and how to measure it, we can move on to study the impact of risk on the value of bonds, stocks, and other financial instruments. Using the tools from this chapter we will see how risk affects decisions by individual investors, managers of financial institutions, and officials who make public policy decisions. As we do, always remember Core Principle 2: Risk requires compensation.

Terms

Using FRED: Codes for Data in This Chapter

Data Series	FRED Data Code
S&P 500 stock price index	SP500
30-year conventional mortgage rate	MORTG
1-year adjustable rate mortgage	MORTGAGE1US
Moody's Aaa corporate bond yield	AAA
Moody's Baa corporate bond yield	BAA
BofA Merrill US CCC or below effective yield	BAMLH0A3HYCEY
CBOE Volatility Index: VIX	VIXCLS
CBOE Volatility Index: DJIA	VXDCLS

Chapter Lessons

1. Risk is a measure of uncertainty about the possible future payoffs of an investment. It is measured over some time horizon, relative to a benchmark.

2. Measuring risk is crucial to understanding the financial system.
   a. To study random future events, start by listing all the possibilities and assign a probability to each. Be sure the probabilities add to one.
   b. The expected value is the probability-weighted sum of all possible future outcomes.
   c. A risk-free asset is an investment whose future value, or payoff, is known with certainty.
   d. Risk increases when the spread (or range) of possible outcomes widens but the expected value stays the same.
   e. One measure of risk is the standard deviation of the possible payoffs.
   f. A second measure of risk is value at risk, the worst possible loss over a specific time horizon, at a given probability.

3. A risk-averse investor
   a. Always prefers a certain return to an uncertain one with the same expected return.
   b. Requires compensation in the form of a risk premium in order to take risk.
   c. Trades off between risk and expected return: the higher the risk, the higher the expected return risk-averse investors will require for holding an investment.

4. Risk can be divided into idiosyncratic risk, which is specific to a particular business or circumstance, and systematic risk, which is common to everyone.

5. There are two types of diversification:
   a. Hedging, in which investors reduce idiosyncratic risk by making investments with offsetting payoff patterns.
   b. Spreading, in which investors reduce idiosyncratic risk by making investments with payoff patterns that are not perfectly correlated.

Conceptual and Analytical Problems

1. Consider a game in which a coin will be flipped three times. For each heads you will be paid $100. Assume that the coin comes up heads with probability 2/3. *(LO1)*
   a. Construct a table of the possibilities and probabilities in this game.
   b. Compute the expected value of the game.
   c. How much would you be willing to pay to play this game?
   d. Consider the effect of a change in the game so that if tails comes up two times in a row, you get nothing. How would your answers to parts *a–c* change?

2.* Why is it important to be able to quantify risk? *(LO2)*

3. You are the founder of IGRO, an Internet firm that delivers groceries. *(LO4)*
   a. Give an example of an idiosyncratic risk and a systematic risk your company faces.
   b. As founder of the company, you own a significant portion of the firm, and your personal wealth is highly concentrated in IGRO shares. What are the risks that you face, and how should you try to reduce them?

4. Assume that the economy can experience high growth, normal growth, or recession. Under these conditions you expect the following stock market returns for the coming year: *(LO1)*

State of the Economy	Probability	Return
High Growth	0.2	+30%
Normal Growth	0.7	+12%
Recession	0.1	−15%

   a. Compute the expected value of a $1,000 investment over the coming year. If you invest $1,000 today, how much money do you expect to have next year? What is the percentage expected rate of return?
   b. Compute the standard deviation of the percentage return over the coming year.
   c. If the risk-free return is 7 percent, what is the risk premium for a stock market investment?

5. Using the information from the table in Problem 4, calculate in dollar terms the value at risk associated with the $1,000 investment. *(LO2)*

6. Car insurance companies sell a large number of policies. Explain how this practice minimizes their risk. *(LO4)*

7. Mortgages increase the risk faced by homeowners. *(LO2)*
   a. Explain how.
   b. What happens to the homeowner's risk as the down payment on the house rises from 10 percent to 50 percent?

8. Banks pay substantial amounts to monitor the risks that they take. One of the primary concerns of a bank's "risk managers" is to compute the value at risk. Why is value at risk so important for a bank (or any financial institution)? *(LO2)*

*Indicates more difficult problems

9. Explain how liquidity problems can be an important source of systemic risk in the financial system. *(LO3)*

10.* Give an example of systematic risk for the U.S. economy and how you might reduce your exposure to such a risk. *(LO3)*

11. For each of the following events, explain whether it represents systematic risk or idiosyncratic risk and why. *(LO3)*
   a. Your favorite restaurant is closed by the county health department.
   b. The government of Spain defaults on its bonds, causing the breakup of the euro area.
   c. Freezing weather in Florida destroys the orange crop.
   d. Solar flares destroy earth-orbiting communications satellites, knocking out cell phone service worldwide.

12. You are planning for retirement and must decide whether to purchase only your employer's stock for your 401(k) or, instead, to buy a mutual fund that holds shares in the 500 largest companies in the world. From the perspective of both idiosyncratic and systematic risk, explain how you would make your decision. *(LO3)*

13. For each of the following actions, identify whether the method of risk assessment motivating your action is due to the value at risk or the standard deviation of an underlying probability distribution. *(LO2)*
   a. You buy life insurance.
   b. You hire an investment advisor who specializes in international diversification in stock portfolios.
   c. In your role as a central banker, you provide emergency loans to illiquid intermediaries.
   d. You open a kiosk at the mall selling ice cream and hot chocolate.

14. Which of the investments in the following table would be most attractive to a risk-averse investor? How would your answer differ if the investor was described as risk-neutral? *(LO1)*

Investment	Expected Value	Standard Deviation
A	75	10
B	100	10
C	100	20

15. Consider an investment that pays off $800 or $1,400 per $1,000 invested with equal probability. Suppose you have $1,000 but are willing to borrow to increase your expected return. What would happen to the expected value and standard deviation of the investment if you borrowed an additional $1,000 and invested a total of $2,000? What if you borrowed $2,000 to invest a total of $3,000? *(LO1)*

16. Looking again at the investment described in Problem 15, what is the maximum leverage ratio you could have and still have enough to repay the loan in the event the bad outcome occurred? *(LO1)*

17. Consider two possible investments whose payoffs are completely independent of one another. Both investments have the same expected value and standard

deviation. If you have $1,000 to invest, could you benefit from dividing your funds between these investments? Explain your answer. *(LO4)*

18.* For the situation in Problem 17, suppose that there were 10 independent investments available rather than just two. Would it matter if you spread your $1,000 across these 10 investments rather than two? *(LO4)*

19. You are considering three investments, each with the same expected value and each with two possible payoffs. The investments are sold only in increments of $500. You have $1,000 to invest so you have the option of either splitting your money equally between two of the investments or placing all $1,000 in one of the investments. If the payoffs from investment A are independent of the payoffs from investments B and C and the payoffs from B and C are perfectly negatively correlated with each other (meaning when B pays off, C doesn't and vice versa), which investment strategy will minimize your risk? *(LO4)*

20. In which of the following cases would you be more likely to decide whether to take on the risk involved by looking at a measure of the value at risk? *(LO2)*
    a. You are unemployed and are considering investing your life savings of $10,000 to start up a new business.
    b. You have a full-time job paying $100,000 a year and are considering making a $1,000 investment in the stock of a well-established, stable company.
    Explain your reasoning.

21. You have the option to invest in either Country A or Country B but not both. You carry out some research and conclude that the two countries are similar in every way except that the returns on assets of different classes tend to move together much more in Country A—that is, they are more highly correlated in Country A than in Country B. Which country would you choose to invest in and why? *(LO4)*

Scan here for quick access to the hints for these problems. Need a barcode reader? Try ScanLife, available in your app store.

Data Exploration

For detailed instructions on using Federal Reserve Economic Data (FRED) online to answer each of the following problems, visit www.mhhe.com/moneyandbanking4e and click on Student Edition, then Data Exploration Hints.

1. Plot the percent change from a year ago of the S&P 500 stock index (FRED code: SP500). Visually, has the risk of the S&P 500 index changed over time? *(LO2)*

2. Another way to understand stock market risk is to examine how investors *expect* risk to evolve in the near future. The DJIA volatility index (FRED code: VXDCLS) is one such measure. Plot the level of this volatility index since October 1997 and, as a second line, the percent change from a year ago of the S&P 500 index (FRED code: SP500). Compare their patterns. *(LO2)*

3. For the period since 1986, plot on one graph the 30-year conventional mortgage rate (FRED code: MORTG) and the one-year adjustable mortgage rate (FRED code: MORTGAGE1US). Explain their systematic relationship using Core Principle 2. *(LO2)*

4. Plot the difference since 1979 between the Moody's Baa bond index (FRED code: BAA) and the U.S. Treasury 10-year bond yield (FRED code: GS10). Comment on the trend and variability of this "credit risk premium" (see Chapter 7) before and after the 2007–2009 financial crisis. *(LO1)*

Appendix A to Chapter 5

A Quick Test to Measure Investment Risk Tolerance*

The following quiz, adapted from one prepared by the T. Rowe Price group of mutual funds, can help you discover how comfortable you are with varying degrees of risk. Other things being equal, your risk tolerance score is a useful guide for deciding how heavily you should weight your portfolio toward safe investments versus more risk-oriented, speculative investments.

1. You're the winner of a TV game show. Which prize would you choose?
   ♦ $2,000 in cash (1 point).
   ♦ A 50 percent chance to win $4,000 (3 points).
   ♦ A 20 percent chance to win $10,000 (5 points).
   ♦ A 2 percent chance to win $100,000 (9 points).

2. You're down $500 in a poker game. How much more would you be willing to put up to win the $500 back?
   ♦ More than $500 (8 points).
   ♦ $500 (6 points).
   ♦ $250 (4 points).
   ♦ $100 (2 points).
   ♦ Nothing—you'll cut your losses now (1 point).

3. A month after you invest in a stock, it suddenly goes up 15 percent. With no further information, what would you do?
   ♦ Hold it, hoping for further gains (3 points).
   ♦ Sell it and take your gains (1 point).
   ♦ Buy more—it will probably go higher (4 points).

4. Your investment suddenly goes down 15 percent one month after you invest. Its fundamentals still look good. What would you do?
   ♦ Buy more. If it looked good at the original price, it looks even better now (4 points).
   ♦ Hold on and wait for it to come back (3 points).
   ♦ Sell it to avoid losing even more (1 point).

5. You are a key employee in a start-up company. You can choose one of two ways to take your year-end bonus. Which would you pick?
   ♦ $1,500 in cash (1 point).
   ♦ Company stock options that could bring you $15,000 next year if the company succeeds, but will be worthless if it fails (5 points).

Your total score: _____

*From Jack Kapoor, Les Dlabay, Robert J. Hughes, *Personal Finance* (New York: McGraw-Hill, 2012).

www.mhhe.com/moneyandbanking4e

SCORING

5–18 Points: You are a more conservative investor. You prefer to minimize financial risks. The lower your score, the more cautious you are. When you choose investments, look for high credit ratings, well-established records, and an orientation toward stability. In stocks, bonds, and real estate, look for a focus on income.

19–30 Points: You are a less conservative investor. You are willing to take more chances in pursuit of greater rewards. The higher your score, the bolder you are. When you invest, look for high overall returns. You may want to consider bonds with higher yields and lower credit ratings, the stocks of newer companies, and real estate investments that use mortgage debt.

Appendix B to Chapter 5

The Mathematics of Diversification

With a small amount of mathematics, we can show how diversification reduces risk. Let's begin with two investments in GE and Texaco. We'll label the payoffs to these investments x and y. If x is the payoff to buying GE stock, then it must equal either $120 or $100, each with a probability of one-half (see Table 5.5). Then y is the payoff to buying Texaco stock.

Hedging Risk

In the chapter, we considered splitting our investment between GE and Texaco. If x and y are the payoff from holding GE and Texaco, respectively, then the payoff on the investment is

$$\text{Investment payoff} = \tfrac{1}{2}x + \tfrac{1}{2}y \tag{A1}$$

What is the variance of this payoff? (Because the standard deviation is the square root of the variance, the two must move together—a lower variance means a lower standard deviation—so we can skip the standard deviations.) In general, the variance of any weighted sum $ax + by$ is

$$\text{Var}(ax + by) = a^2\text{Var}(x) + b^2\text{Var}(y) + 2ab\,\text{Cov}(x,y) \tag{A2}$$

where *Var* is the variance and *Cov* is the covariance. While the variance measures the extent to which each payoff moves on its own, the covariance measures the extent to which two risky assets move together. If the two payoffs rise and fall together, then the covariance will be positive. If one payoff rises while the other falls, then the covariance will be negative.

It is useful to express these quantities symbolically. Assume that p_i is the probability associated with a particular outcome x_i. Then the expected value of x is the probability-weighted sum of the possible outcomes.

$$\text{Expected value of } x = E(x) = \bar{x} = \sum_i p_i x_i \tag{A3}$$

As described in the chapter (page 110), the variance of x is the probability-weighted sum of the squared deviations of x from the expected value.

$$\text{Variance of } x = \text{Var}(x) = \sigma_x^2 = \sum_i p_i(x_i - \bar{x})^2 \tag{A4}$$

The covariance of x and y is defined analogously as

$$\text{Covariance of } x \text{ and } y = \text{Cov}(x,y) = \sigma_{x,y} = \sum_i p_i(x_i - \bar{x})(y_i - \bar{y}) \tag{A5}$$

In our GE/Texaco examples, $a = b = \tfrac{1}{2}$, so

$$\text{Var(Investment payoff)} = \tfrac{1}{4}\text{Var}(x) + \tfrac{1}{4}\text{Var}(y) + \tfrac{1}{2}\text{Cov}(x,y) \tag{A6}$$

We know from Table 5.6 that the expected payoff to GE and Texaco is $110 each and the standard deviation is $10 as well. The variance is the standard deviation squared, so it is 100. What about the covariance? We can compute it easily from Table 5.5:

$$\text{Cov(Payoff on GE and Texaco)}$$
$$= \tfrac{1}{2}(100 - 110)(120 - 110) + \tfrac{1}{2}(120 - 110)(100 - 110) = -100 \qquad (A7)$$

Substituting this value into the formula for the variance of the investment payoff, we get

$$\text{Var(Investment payoff)} = \tfrac{1}{4}(100) + \tfrac{1}{4}(100) - \tfrac{1}{2}(100) = 0 \qquad (A8)$$

The fact that the covariance is negative means that the variance, or risk, in a portfolio containing both GE and Texaco stock is lower than the risk in a portfolio containing one or the other. The stocks act as hedges for each other.

Spreading Risk

Showing how spreading reduces risk is a bit more complex. Let's consider spreading our investment between GE and Microsoft. Again, the variance of the investment payoff depends on the variances of the individual stock payoffs and on their covariance. But here we must assume that the covariance between the GE and Microsoft payoffs is zero. That is, they are independent of each other. As before, each stock has a variance of 100, so the variance of a portfolio that is split half and half is

$$\text{Var(Investment payoff)} = \tfrac{1}{4}(100) + \tfrac{1}{4}(100) = 50 \qquad (A9)$$

and the standard deviation is 7.1 (see footnote 8 on page 122).

This result suggests that individual stocks or groups of stocks with independent payoffs are potentially valuable, as they will reduce risk. Let's consider an arbitrary number of independent investments, each with the same individual variance. What is the variance of an equally weighted portfolio of these investments? Assume that the number of investments is n, each with the same expected payoff, $\bar{x}$, and the same variance, σ_x^2. We hold $1/n$ of our portfolio in each stock, so the expected payoff is

$$\text{Expected payoff} = \frac{1}{n}\sum_{i=1}^{n}x_i = \bar{x} \qquad (A10)$$

Because the payoff on each stock is independent of all the rest, the covariances are all zero. So the variance is

$$\text{Variance of payoff} = \left(\frac{1}{n}\right)^2\sum_{i=1}^{n}\sigma_x^2 = \frac{\sigma_x^2}{n} \qquad (A11)$$

That is, the variance of the payoff on a portfolio of n independent stocks is the variance divided by n. Most important, as n increases, the variance declines, so when the value of n is very large, the variance is essentially zero.

In summary, spreading exposure to risk among a wide range of independent risks reduces the overall risk of a portfolio. As we saw in this chapter, this is the strategy that insurance companies use. While the payoff to an individual policyholder is highly uncertain, the payoffs to a large group of policyholders are almost unrelated. By selling millions of insurance policies, the company simply pays the expected value, and the variance will be nearly zero if the payoffs are truly independent.

Chapter 6

Bonds, Bond Prices, and the Determination of Interest Rates

Learning Objectives

Understand . . .

LO1   Present value and bond pricing

LO2   Relationship of prices, yields, and returns

LO3   Key drivers of bond prices

LO4   Risks of default, inflation, and interest rate changes

Virtually any financial arrangement involving the current transfer of resources from a lender to a borrower, with a transfer back at some time in the future, is a form of bond. Car loans, home mortgages, even credit card balances all create a loan from a financial intermediary to an individual making a purchase—just like the bonds governments and large corporations sell when they need to borrow.

When companies like Ford, General Electric, or Walmart need to finance their operations, they sell bonds. When the U.S. Treasury or a state government needs to borrow, it sells bonds. And they do it billions of dollars at a time. Following the financial crisis of 2007–2009, U.S. corporations tried to reduce their debt, but their bonds outstanding remained above \$10 trillion as of 2012. Federal, state, and local American governments have nearly \$15 trillion in outstanding debt as well.[1] The ease with which individuals, corporations, and governments borrow is essential to the functioning of our economic system. Without this free flow of resources through the bond markets, the economy would freeze up.

Historically, we can trace the concept of using bonds to borrow to monarchs' almost insatiable appetite for resources. To maintain lavish lifestyles, fight wars, and explore the globe, kings, princes, and other rulers drew on every available source of financing. Even with these incentives, after thousands of years of civilization only a few possibilities had been developed: outright confiscation; taxation, which is a mild form of confiscation; debasement of currency, in which people are required to exchange their coins for ones that weigh less—in effect, a tax on currency; and borrowing. Monarchs who borrowed directly from international bankers frequently defaulted or failed to make the loan payments they had promised.[2]

[1]These numbers come from the *Flow of Funds Accounts of the United States,* published quarterly by the Federal Reserve Board.

[2]For a detailed analysis of such sovereign defaults, see Carmen M. Reinhart and Kenneth S. Rogoff, *This Time Is Different: Eight Centuries of Financial Folly* (Princeton, NJ: Princeton University Press, 2011).

"*The name's Bond. Duane Bond.*"

SOURCE: *2000 © Michael Crawford/The New Yorker Collection/www.cartoonbank.com.*

Between 1557 and 1696, the various kings of Spain defaulted 14 times. With that track record, it's no wonder they had to pay interest rates close to 40 percent.

The Dutch invented modern bonds to finance their lengthy war of independence against those same Spanish kings who defaulted on loans in the 16th and 17th centuries. Over the next two centuries, the British refined the use of bonds to finance government activities. The practice then spread to other countries. Alexander Hamilton, the first Secretary of the U.S. Treasury and the man whose face appears on the $10 bill, brought bonds to the United States. One of Hamilton's first acts after the formation of the U.S. Treasury in 1789 was to consolidate all the debt remaining from the Revolutionary War. This resulted in the first U.S. government bonds. While the depth and complexity of bond markets have increased in modern times, many of their original features remain.

If we want to understand the financial system, particularly the bond market, we must understand three things. The first is the relationship between bond prices and interest rates (yet another application of present value). The second is that supply and demand in the bond market determine bond prices. The third is why bonds are risky. Let's get started.

Bond Prices

A standard bond specifies the fixed amounts to be paid and the exact dates of the payments. *How much should you be willing to pay for a bond?* The answer depends on the bond's characteristics. We will look at four basic types:

1. *Zero-coupon bonds,* which promise a single future payment, such as a U.S. Treasury bill.
2. *Fixed-payment loans,* such as conventional mortgages.
3. *Coupon bonds,* which make periodic interest payments and repay the principal at maturity. U.S. Treasury bonds and most corporate bonds are coupon bonds.
4. *Consols,* which make periodic interest payments forever, never repaying the principal that was borrowed. (There aren't many examples of these.)

Let's see how each of these bonds is priced. To keep the analysis simple, we'll ignore risk for now.

Zero-Coupon Bonds

U.S. Treasury bills (commonly known as **T-bills**) are the most straightforward type of bond. Each T-bill represents a promise by the U.S. government to pay $100 on a fixed future date. There are no coupon payments, which is why T-bills are known as **zero-coupon bonds**. They are also called *pure discount bonds* (or just discount bonds), because the price is less than their face value—they sell at a discount. This isn't a discount in the sense of a markdown at a clothing store, however. If a $100 face value T-bill sells for $96, the $4 difference is the interest, the payment to the lender for making the loan.

Because a Treasury bill makes a single payment on a future date, its price is just the present value of that payment:

$$\text{Price of \$100 face value zero-coupon bond} = \frac{\$100}{(1 + i)^n} \qquad (1)$$

where i is the interest rate expressed in decimal form and n is the time until the payment is made, measured in the same time units as the interest rate. Suppose the annual interest rate is 5 percent. What is the price of a one-year T-bill? To figure out the answer, take the present value formula, set i at 0.05 and n at 1, and then compute the price:

$$\text{Price of one-year Treasury bill} = \frac{\$100}{(1 + 0.05)} = \$95.24$$

The U.S. Treasury doesn't issue T-bills with a maturity of more than one year; six-month T-bills are much more common. At an annual interest rate of 5 percent, what is the price of such a zero-coupon bond? We can use the present-value formula, again, but this time we have to be careful. Recall that we need to measure i and n in the same time units. Because i is the interest rate for one year, we need to measure n in years, and because six months is half a year,

$$\text{Price of a six-month Treasury bill} = \frac{\$100}{(1 + 0.05)^{1/2}} = \$97.59$$

As you can see, the price of a six-month Treasury bill is higher than that of a one-year T-bill. The shorter the time until the payment is made, the more we are willing to pay for it now. If we go on to compute the price of a three-month T-bill, setting n at 0.25 (one-fourth of a year), we find the answer is $99.02.

Equation (1) shows that for a zero-coupon bond, the relationship between the price and the interest rate is the same as the one we saw in our discussion of present value. When the price moves, the interest rate moves in the *opposite* direction. Thus, we can compute the interest rate from the price using the present-value formula. For example, if the price of a one-year T-bill is $95, then the interest rate is $i = (\$100/\$95) - 1 = 0.0526$, or 5.26 percent.

Fixed-Payment Loans

Conventional home mortgages and car loans are called *fixed-payment loans* because they promise a fixed number of equal payments at regular intervals. These loans are *amortized,* meaning that the borrower pays off the principal along with the interest over the life of the loan. Each payment includes both interest and a portion of the principal. Pricing these sorts of loans is straightforward using the present-value formula: The value of the loan today is the present value of all the payments. If we assume that the annual interest rate is i (measured as a decimal) and that the loan specifies n payments, then

$$\text{Value of a fixed-payment loan} = \frac{\text{Fixed payment}}{(1 + i)} + \frac{\text{Fixed payment}}{(1 + i)^2} + \cdots + \frac{\text{Fixed payment}}{(1 + i)^n} \qquad (2)$$

Using this formula is complicated, so we won't go any further. But when lenders figure out your monthly payment for a car loan or home mortgage, this is how they do it.

YOUR FINANCIAL WORLD
Know Your Mortgage

Survey evidence tells us that a large number of people with adjustable-rate mortgages underestimate how much their monthly payments can change.* Don't be one of these people! When you buy a home and get a mortgage, know what can happen.

There are two basic types of mortgages: conventional fixed-rate and adjustable-rate, also known as ARMs. Fixed-rate mortgages are the easiest to understand because the payments, like the interest rate, are fixed. That means you make the same monthly payment for the entire term of the mortgage. For most people, that term is 30 years. (You can also get 10, 15, and 20 year fixed-rate mortgages.) Because the payments don't change, fixed-rate borrowers are not exposed to the risks of interest rate increases.

ARMs are more complicated, because the interest rate changes. This means that the payments change, too. Getting an adjustable-rate mortgage means knowing about things like interest-rate indexes, margins, discounts, caps, negative amortization, and convertibility:†

- On what interest-rate index is the mortgage rate based? How much does that index move around?
- How big is the mortgage rate margin above the interest-rate index on which it is based?
- How frequently is the rate adjusted?

- Does the ARM have an initial "teaser" interest rate that will almost surely rise? If so, when and by how much?
- What is the maximum change in the interest rate for a single adjustment and what is the highest the interest rate can ever go (the mortgage rate cap)?
- Does the ARM include a payment cap? If you hit the payment cap, will the principal of the loan start to increase? (That's negative amortization.)
- Can you convert the ARM into a fixed-rate mortgage?

This list may seem long, but it is really only the beginning. Getting the right mortgage may be the most important financial decision you ever make, so it is worth spending some time figuring it out. And once you have it, don't forget how your mortgage works.

*In "Do Homeowners Know Their House Values and Mortgage Terms?", Federal Reserve Board Finance and Economics Discussion Paper 2006–3, January 2006, Brian Bucks and Karen Pence estimate that nearly half of people with adjustable-rate mortgages don't know how much the interest rate can move at one time, the maximum rate, or the index to which the mortgage rate is tied.

†The Federal Reserve Board's *Consumer Handbook on Adjustable Rate Mortgages* is a great place to start learning about mortgages.

Coupon Bonds

Recall from Chapter 4 that the issuer of a coupon bond promises to make a series of periodic interest payments called coupon payments, plus a principal payment at maturity. So we can value a coupon bond using (you guessed it) the present-value formula. The price of the coupon bond is

$$P_{CB} = \left[\frac{\text{Coupon payment}}{(1 + i)^1} + \frac{\text{Coupon payment}}{(1 + i)^2} + \ldots + \frac{\text{Coupon payment}}{(1 + i)^n} \right] + \frac{\text{Face value}}{(1 + i)^n} \quad (3)$$

The right side of this equation has two parts. The first part, in brackets, looks just like the fixed-payment loan—and it is, with the important exception that it represents only the interest. The second part, on the far right, looks just like a zero-coupon bond, and it is. It represents the value of the promise to repay the principal at maturity.

Consols

Another type of bond offers only periodic payments. That is, the borrower pays only interest, never repaying the principal. These loans, called **consols** or **perpetuities**, are like coupon bonds whose payments last forever. Because governments are really the only borrowers that can credibly promise to make payments forever, there are no privately issued consols (although a few corporations have issued 100-year coupon bonds). The

British government has a number of consols currently outstanding, the oldest of which was issued in 1853. The U.S. government sold consols once in 1900. The bonds had a special provision allowing the Treasury to buy them back starting in 1930. The Treasury bought back all the consols so you would not be able to find one today.

You won't be surprised to learn that the price of a consol is the present value of all the future interest payments. The fact that the number of payments is infinite complicates things. But we can derive a formula for the price of a consol that makes a coupon payment every year forever.[3] At interest rate i,

$$P_{Consol} = \frac{\text{Yearly coupon payment}}{i} \qquad (4)$$

The price of a consol equals the annual coupon payment divided by the interest rate. So at an interest rate of 5 percent, a consol that promises \$1 per year forever would sell for \$20. If the interest rate changes to 4 percent, the price rises to \$25. Again, the interest rate and the price move in opposite directions.

Bond Yields

Now that we know how to calculate a bond price given the interest rate, we need to move in the other direction and calculate the interest rate, or the return to an investor, implicit in the bond's price. Doing so means combining information about the promised payments with the price to obtain what is called the *yield*—a measure of the cost of borrowing and the reward for lending. When people talk about bonds they use the terms *yield* and *interest rate* interchangeably, so we will too.

Yield to Maturity

The most useful measure of the return on holding a bond is called the **yield to maturity**, or the yield bondholders receive if they hold the bond to its maturity when the final principal payment is made. Take a \$100 face value 5 percent coupon bond with one year to maturity. At maturity, the owner of this bond receives a coupon payment of \$5 plus a principal payment of \$100.[4] Using the formula from equation (3), we know that the price of the bond is

$$\text{Price of one-year 5 percent coupon bond} = \frac{\$5}{(1 + i)} + \frac{\$100}{(1 + i)} \qquad (5)$$

The value of i that solves this equation is the *yield to maturity*. Remembering that present value and interest rates move in opposite directions, we can conclude the following:

1. If the price of the bond is \$100, then the yield to maturity equals the coupon rate. (Recall from Chapter 4 that the coupon rate is the ratio of the annual coupon payments to the face value of the bond.)

---

[3]You may find it troubling that you can add up an infinite number of payments and get a finite number. To see why this works, notice that as the number of years at which the terminal payment occurs increases, $1/(1 + i)^n$ grows very small. After 100 years, at an interest rate of 5 percent, it is 0.008. So the present value of \$1 promised in 100 years is less than one cent. We could just ignore the payments that come after this and get virtually the same answer. To derive the expression for the price of a consol, use the techniques from the Appendix to Chapter 4. Start by calling C the coupon payment and writing the price as the sum of the present value of the (infinite) number of payments $P_{Consol} = \frac{C}{(1 + i)} + \frac{C}{(1 + i)^2} + \frac{C}{(1 + i)^3} + \ldots$. Next, multiply this expression by $[1/(1 + i)]$ to get $\frac{1}{(1 + i)} P_{Consol} = \frac{C}{(1 + i)^2} + \frac{C}{(1 + i)^3} + \frac{C}{(1 + i)^4} + \ldots$. Then subtract this expression from the original, which gives $P_{Consol} - \frac{1}{(1 + i)} P_{Consol} = \frac{C}{(1 + i)}$. Solving for the price yields equation (4).

[4]Most bonds offer two semiannual payments, each equal to half the annual coupon. We will ignore this complication.

2. Because the price rises as the yield falls, when the price is *above* $100, the yield to maturity must be *below* the coupon rate.
3. Because the price falls as the yield rises, when the price is *below* $100, the yield to maturity must be *above* the coupon rate.

Looking at the one-year 5 percent coupon bond, we can see right away that if the yield to maturity is 5 percent, then

$$\frac{\$5}{(1 + 0.05)} + \frac{\$100}{(1 + 0.05)} = \frac{\$105}{1.05} = \$100$$

That's the first point. Now look at what happens when yield to maturity falls to 4 percent. The price becomes

$$\frac{\$5}{(1 + 0.04)} + \frac{\$100}{(1 + 0.04)} = \frac{\$105}{1.04} = \$100.96$$

That's the second point. If the yield to maturity rises to 6 percent, then the price falls to

$$\frac{\$5}{(1 + 0.06)} + \frac{\$100}{(1 + 0.06)} = \$99.06$$

That's the third point. You can try this process with a more complicated bond—say, one with 10 years to maturity that makes more than just one coupon payment—and get exactly the same results.

The fact that the return on a bond depends on the price you pay for it really isn't that mysterious. If you pay $95 for a $100 face value bond, for example, you will receive both the interest payments and the increase in value from $95 to $100. This rise in value, referred to as a **capital gain**, is part of the return on your investment. So when the price of the bond is below the face value, the return is above the coupon rate. When the price is above the face value, the bondholder incurs a **capital loss** and the bond's yield to maturity falls below its coupon rate.

Current Yield

Current yield is a commonly used, easy-to-compute measure of the proceeds the bondholder receives for making a loan. It is the yearly coupon payment divided by the price:

$$\text{Current yield} = \frac{\text{Yearly coupon payment}}{\text{Price paid}} \quad (6)$$

Looking at this expression, we can see that the current yield measures that part of the return from buying the bond that arises solely from the coupon payments. It ignores the capital gain or loss that arises when the price at which the bond is purchased differs from its face value. So if the price is below par, the current yield will be below the yield to maturity.

Let's return to the one-year 5 percent coupon bond and assume that it is selling for $99. The current yield is easy to calculate as

$$\frac{5}{99} = 0.0505$$

or 5.05 percent. The yield to maturity for this bond is the solution to

$$\frac{\$5}{(1 + i)} + \frac{\$100}{(1 + i)} = \$99$$

which is 6.06 percent. The yield to maturity is higher because, if you buy the bond for $99, one year later you get not only the $5 coupon payment but also a guaranteed $1 capital gain for a total of $6.

We can repeat these calculations for a case in which the bond is selling for $101. Then the current yield is

$$\frac{5}{101} = 0.0495$$

or 4.95 percent, and the yield to maturity is

$$\frac{\$5}{(1 + i)} + \frac{\$100}{(1 + i)} = \$101$$

or 3.96 percent.

Putting all this together, we see the relationship between the current yield and the coupon rate. Again, it comes from the fact that current yield moves in the opposite direction from the price: it falls when the bond's price goes up and rises when the price goes down. So when the price equals the face value of the bond, the current yield and coupon rate are equal. When the price rises above the face value, the current yield falls below the coupon rate. And when the price falls below the face value, the current yield rises above the coupon rate.

Table 6.1 summarizes the relationships among the price, coupon rate, current yield, and yield to maturity. We know that when the bond price is less than face value, the current yield and the yield to maturity are both higher than the coupon rate. But because the yield to maturity takes account of the capital gain the bondholder receives, while the current yield does not, the yield to maturity must be even higher than the current yield. When the price is above the face value, the yield to maturity is lower than the current yield, which is lower than the coupon rate.

Holding Period Returns

We have emphasized that if you buy a bond whose yield to maturity deviates from the coupon rate, the price will not be the face value. Similarly, the return from holding a bond need not be the coupon rate. For example, if you pay $95 for a one-year 6 percent coupon bond, one year later you will get both the $6 coupon payment and the $5 difference between the purchase price and the $100 face value at maturity. But this

Table 6.1   Relationship among a Bond's Price and Its Coupon Rate, Current Yield, and Yield to Maturity

Bond price < Face value: Coupon rate < Current yield < Yield to maturity

Bond price = Face value: Coupon rate = Current yield = Yield to maturity

Bond price > Face value: Coupon rate > Current yield > Yield to maturity example is really too simple, because it assumes that the investor holds the bond to maturity. Most holders of long-term bonds plan to sell them well before they mature. And because the price of the bond may change between the time of the purchase and the time of the sale, the return to buying a bond and selling it before it matures—the **holding period return**—can differ from the yield to maturity.

Take an example in which you pay $100 for a 10-year, 6 percent coupon bond with a face value of $100. You intend to hold the bond for one year. That is, you are going to buy a 10-year bond and then a year later, you'll sell a 9-year bond. What is your return from holding this bond? If the interest rate doesn't change (that is, it stays at 6 percent) your return will be $6/$100 = 0.06, or 6 percent. But if the interest rate changes, calculating your return becomes more complicated. Say that over the year you hold the bond, the interest rate falls from 6 to 5 percent. That is, the yield to maturity falls to 5 percent. Using equation (3), we can figure out that you have bought a 10-year bond for $100 and sold a 9-year bond for $107.11. What is your one-year holding period return on the initial $100 investment? It has two parts: the $6 coupon payment and the $7.11 capital gain (the difference between the price at which you bought the bond and the price at which you sold it). So the holding period return is

$$\text{One-year holding period return} = \frac{\$6}{\$100} + \frac{\$107.11 - \$100}{\$100} = \frac{\$13.11}{\$100} = 0.1311$$

$$= 13.11 \text{ percent}$$

Obviously, bond prices can go down as well as up. Consider what happens if the yield to maturity rises to 7 percent so that the price falls to $93.48. Now the one-year holding period return is

$$\text{One-year holding period return} = \frac{\$6}{100} + \frac{\$93.48 - \$100}{\$100} = \frac{-\$.52}{\$100} = -0.0052$$

$$= -0.52 \text{ percent}$$

The coupon payment still represents a 6 percent return, but the capital loss from the price movement is 6.52 percent. The one-year holding period return is negative, as overall there is a small loss.[5]

To generalize these examples, notice that the one-year holding period return is the sum of the yearly coupon payment divided by the price paid for the bond, and the change in the price (price sold minus price paid) divided by the price paid:

$$\text{Holding period return} = \frac{\text{Yearly coupon payment}}{\text{Price paid}} + \frac{\text{Change in price of bond}}{\text{Price paid}} \quad (7)$$

The first part on the right-hand side of this equation is the current yield (equation 6). The second part is the capital gain. So the holding period return is

$$\text{Holding period return} = \text{Current yield} + \text{Capital gain} \quad (8)$$

---

[5]The multiyear case is somewhat more complex. Say that an investor purchased the same 10-year 6 percent coupon bond at par, and then held it for *two* years. If the interest rate were to rise from 7 percent, the price of the now 8-year bond would fall to $94.03 per $100 of face value. This means that the investor would receive $12 in coupon payments plus a capital loss of $5.97, for a total payoff of $106.03. To simplify, let us assume that the first-year coupon cannot be reinvested. Then, using the methods described in the Tools of the Trade on page 84 of Chapter 4, we can compute the annual-rate return as $\left[\left(\frac{106.03}{100}\right)^{1/2} - 1\right] = 0.0297$, or 2.97%. If instead the interest rate were to fall to 4 percent, the price of the bond would rise to $106.46, the total payoff would be $118.46, and the annual-rate return would be 8.84 percent.

Whenever the price of a bond changes, there is a capital gain or loss. The greater the price change, the more important a part of the holding period return the capital gain or loss becomes. The potential for interest-rate movements and changes in bond prices creates risk. The longer the term of the bond, the greater those price movements and the associated risk can be, as we'll see in more detail in the last section of this chapter.

The Bond Market and the Determination of Interest Rates

Now that we understand the relationship between bond prices and various measures of interest rates, we need to figure out how bond prices are determined and why they change. The best way to do that is to look at bond supply, bond demand, and equilibrium prices in the bond market. Once we understand how the bond market determines bond prices, we can figure out why the prices change.

To keep the analysis simple, we need to make a few choices about how to proceed. First, we'll restrict the discussion to the quantity of bonds outstanding, called the *stock of bonds*. (We could look at what causes the changes in the quantity of bonds outstanding—the *flow*—but that would complicate matters.) Second, we are going to talk about *bond prices* rather than interest rates. Because a bond's price, together with its various characteristics, determines its yield, it really doesn't matter whether we talk about yields (interest rates) or bond prices. Once we know the price, we know the yield. Finally, we're going to consider the *market for a one-year zero-coupon bond* (one that makes no coupon payments) with a face value of $100.

If we assume the investor is planning to purchase a one-year bond and hold it to maturity—they have a one-year **investment horizon**—then the holding period return equals the bond's yield to maturity, and both are determined directly from the price. The present-value formula shows that the relationship between the price and the yield on such a bond is simply $P = \$100/(1 + i)$, so $i = [(\$100 - P)/P]$.

For example, if a bond sells for $95, then the yield is $i = \$5/\$95 = 0.0526$, or 5.26 percent.

"Your pot o' gold is doing nothing for you sitting at the end of the rainbow. At the very least, you should put it in a no-risk interest-bearing account."

Bond Supply, Bond Demand, and Equilibrium in the Bond Market

How are bond prices (and bond yields) determined? Not surprisingly, by supply and demand. Some investors are supplying bonds, while others are demanding them. The *bond supply curve* is the relationship between the price and the quantity of bonds people

TOOLS OF THE TRADE
Reading the Bond Page

Every day *The Wall Street Journal* lists the previous day's closing yields for a wide variety of bonds that serve as standards—or benchmarks—for comparison with other financial instruments. Table 6.2 shows some representative data on global government bonds published on February 12, 2013, while Table 6.3 presents some data on corporate bonds. Let's see what we can learn from reading these tables.

Global Government Bonds

Governments issue hundreds of bonds. As of mid-2013, the U.S. Treasury alone had nearly 275 different coupon-bearing instruments outstanding. But investors often focus on the most liquid bonds at key maturities to summarize the evolution of the entire bond market. Table 6.2 uses a two-year bond yield to represent relatively short-term issues and a 10-year bond yield to represent the longer term. In Chapter 7, we'll see how the *term structure of interest rates* relates the level of bond yields to the maturity of the bonds.

The table highlights several points. First, the yields on government bonds vary over time. For example, on February 12, 2013, the "latest" 10-year German government bond was 1.628 percent. The table also shows that the latest yield exceeded the day-earlier (February 11, or "previous") level of 1.609 percent and was markedly lower than the "year-ago" level of 1.976 percent. Assuming that the representative bond had exactly 10 years to maturity on each date, then, as the yield fell, its price in euros rose from €97.92 on February 12, 2012, to €101.10 on February 12, 2013. In contrast, the 10-year U.S. Treasury yield edged only slightly lower over the year, from 1.989 percent to 1.985 percent, raising the U.S. dollar price of the bond by only $0.03, to $100.13.

The second point illustrated by the table is that the yields on government bonds differ substantially across countries. The "latest" yield on the 10-year U.S. Treasury bond was much lower than the yield on Spain's 10-year bond but higher than the yield on Germany's. The difference across countries is also portrayed

---

Table 6.2 Government Bonds

Yields and spreads over or under U.S. Treasurys on benchmark two-year and 10-year government bonds in selected other countries; arrows indicate whether the yield rose (△) or fell (▼) in the latest session

Coupon (%)	Country/Maturity, in years		YIELD (%)				SPREAD UNDER/OVER U.S. TREASURYS, in basis points		
		Latest (•)	Previous	Month ago	Year ago	Latest	Chg from prev	Year ago
0.250	U.S. 2	0.274 △	0.258	0.256	0.282	...	...	...
2.000	10	1.985 △	1.951	1.902	1.989	...	...	...
2.500	France 2	0.291 △	0.282	0.162	0.560	1.7	−0.7	27.8
3.250	10	2.267 △	2.241	2.152	2.911	28.2	−0.8	92.2
0.250	Germany 2	0.189 △	0.179	0.139	0.278	−8.5	−0.6	−0.4
1.750	10	1.628 △	1.609	1.579	1.976	−35.7	−1.5	−1.3
3.000	Italy 2	1.636 ▼	1.709	1.353	3.049	136.2	−8.9	276.7
5.000	10	4.452 ▼	4.557	4.083	5.502	246.7	−13.9	351.3
5.450	Portugal* 2	3.332 ▼	3.366	3.227	13.576	305.8	−5.0	1329.4
3.850	10	6.452 ▼	6.533	6.076	11.937	446.7	−11.5	994.8
6.750	Spain 2	2.656 ▼	2.757	2.090	2.529	238.2	−11.7	224.7
3.500	10	5.310 ▼	5.414	4.870	5.050	332.5	−13.8	306.1
2.250	U.K. 2	0.331 △	0.319	0.405	0.380	5.7	−0.4	9.8
4.000	10	2.104 ▼	2.110	2.083	2.111	11.9	−4.0	12.2

Source: Tullett Prebon, except * marked countries from ICAP plc; historical data prior to 6/8/11; Thomson Reuters.

Table 6.3	Corporate Bonds

Investment-grade spreads that tightened the most . . .

Issuer	Symbol	Coupon (%)	Maturity	SPREAD*, IN BASIS POINTS			STOCK PERFORMANCE	
				Current	Change	Last week	Close	% Chg
Conagra Foods	CAG	3.200	Jan. 25, '23	99	–32	123	$33.30	–0.21
Jefferies	JEF	5.125	Jan. 20, '23	259	–18	261	21.01	1.06
American Express Credit	AXP	2.800	Sept. 19, '16	59	–16	79	...	...
Hewlett-Packard	HPQ	3.000	Sept. 15, '16	194	–16	205	17.10	1.60

. . . And spreads that widened the most

Issuer	Symbol	Coupon (%)	Maturity	Current	Change	Last week	Close	% Chg
Telecom Italia Capital S.A.	TITIM	5.250	Oct. 1, '15	281	44	224	$n.a.	n.a.
Darden Restaurants	DRI	6.000	Aug. 15, '35	265	35	n.a.	46.81	–0.57
Nasdaq OMX	NDAQ	5.550	Jan. 15, '20	230	21	n.a.	30.55	0.56
XL	XL	6.500	April 15, '17	634	20	672	28.41	0.35

*Estimated spread over 2-year, 3-year, 5-year, 10-year or 30-year hot-run Treasury; 100 basis points = one percentage pt.; change in spread shown is for Z-spread.

Note: Data are for the most active issue of bonds with maturities of two years or more.

Source: MarketAxess Corporate BondTicker; WSJ Market Data Group.

SOURCE: *The Wall Street Journal*, 2010. Used with permission of Dow Jones & Company, Inc. via Copyright Clearance Center.

by the bars in the third column from the right, which show the latest *yield spread* versus 10-year Treasuries. The spread for Spain's bond—that is, the yield on Spain's bond minus the yield on the U.S. bond—was 332.5 basis points (a basis point is one hundredth of a percentage point); for Germany's bond, the spread was −35.7 basis points—that is, the yield on Germany's bond was lower than the U.S. bond yield. Recall from Figure 4.3 that the difference between interest rates partly reflects differences in expected inflation. However, in the case of Spain, the difference also reflected risks associated with the euro-area financial crisis (which will be discussed in Chapter 16).

Third, the latest 10-year yield exceeded the latest two-year yield in every country shown in the table. When we study the term structure of interest rates in Chapter 7, we'll learn why this pattern of higher long-term yields is common but does not always hold.

Finally, the yield on each bond differs from its coupon rate (shown in the first column). As noted elsewhere in this chapter, when the yield is higher (lower) than the coupon, the price of the bond is below (above) the par value of 100.

Corporate Debt

Thousands of corporations in the United States issue bonds, and the bonds vary significantly in default risk (see the discussion of default risk on pages 152–154). In line with Core

Principle 2, investors expect to be compensated for those risks. Table 6.3 captures a measure of that compensation—the yield spread over Treasury securities.

The table shows the levels and one-day changes of yield spreads on actively traded corporate bond yields compared to a similar-maturity U.S. Treasury yield. For the Conagra Foods bond, which matures on January 25, 2023, the "current" spread of 99 basis points is the amount by which its previous-day yield exceeded that on the most recent 10-year Treasury issue.

Narrower corporate bond spreads over U.S. Treasuries are associated with lower default risk. Hence, spreads are as diverse as corporate default risks. The narrowest spread shown in the table is 59 basis points, for American Express Credit; the widest is 634, for XL. Spreads can change significantly day-to-day: The table shows that the largest swings in spreads on February 12 were the 32-basis-point tightening for Conagra Foods and the 44-basis-point widening for Telecom Italia Capital S.A. Presumably, these day-to-day changes reflect changing perceptions of each company's default risk.

The last two columns of the table show the stock price level and change for those bond issuers that also issue shares. Note that a gain (loss) in the price of a company's stock, which normally indicates greater (lesser) confidence in the prospects for a company, is not always accompanied by similar change in the yield spread of that company's bond.

are willing to sell, all other things being equal. The higher the price of a bond, the larger the quantity supplied will be for two reasons. From investors' point of view, the higher the price, the more tempting it is to sell a bond they currently hold. From the point of view of companies seeking finance for new projects, the higher the price at which they can sell bonds, the better. Taking our example of a $100 one-year zero-coupon bond, the quantity supplied will be higher at $95 per bond than it will be at $90 per bond, all other things being equal. This means that *the bond supply curve slopes upward.*

The *bond demand curve* is the relationship between the price and quantity of bonds that investors demand, all other things being equal. As the price falls, the reward for holding the bond rises, so the demand goes up. That is, the lower the price potential bondholders must pay for a fixed-dollar payment on a future date, the more likely they are to buy a bond. Again, think of the zero-coupon bond promising to pay $100 in one year. That bond will attract more demand at $90 than it will at $95 per bond, all other things being equal. Thus, *the bond demand curve slopes downward.* Because the price of bonds is inversely related to the yield, the demand curve implies that the higher the demand for bonds, the higher the yield.

MARKETS

Equilibrium in the bond market is the point at which supply equals demand—point E in Figure 6.1. As is always the case with supply and demand analysis, we need to explain how the market adjusts when the price deviates from the price that equates supply and demand—point P_0 in Figure 6.1. Let's look briefly at the two possibilities: either the price is too high or the price is too low. If bond prices start out above the equilibrium point, somewhere greater than P_0, quantity supplied will exceed quantity demanded. That is, excess supply means that suppliers cannot sell the bonds they want to at the current price. To make the sale, they will start cutting the price. The excess supply will put downward pressure on the price until supply equals demand.

When the price is below the equilibrium point, quantity demanded will exceed quantity supplied. Those people who wish to buy bonds cannot get all they want at the prevailing price. Their reaction is to start bidding up the price. Excess demand continues to put upward pressure on the price until the market reaches equilibrium.

So far, so good. But to really understand how bond prices (and bond yields) change over time, we need to learn what determines the location of the supply and demand curves. Over time they shift around, leading to changes in the equilibrium prices. As we discuss the causes of such shifts in the following section, make sure you remember the distinction between moving *along* a supply or demand curve and *shifting* a curve. When the quantity demanded or quantity supplied changes because of a change in the price, it produces a movement along the curve. But when the quantity demanded or supplied at a given price changes, it shifts the entire curve. More important, in the bond market, a shift in either the supply or the demand curve changes the price of bonds, so it changes the yield as well.

Figure 6.1 Supply, Demand, and Equilibrium in the Bond Market

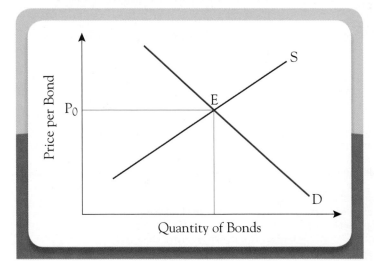

The supply of bonds from borrowers slopes up and the demand for bonds from lenders slopes down. Equilibrium in the bond market is determined by the intersection of supply and demand.

Factors That Shift Bond Supply

What changes the quantity of bonds *supplied* at a given price, shifting the supply curve? We can identify three factors: changes in government borrowing, in general business conditions, and in expected inflation. Let's look at these one at a time.

Changes in Government Borrowing   The government's need to issue bonds affects the supply of bonds out there. Both changes in tax policy and adjustments in spending can affect a government's need to borrow. Regardless of the reason, *any increase in the government's borrowing needs increases the quantity of bonds outstanding, shifting the bond supply curve to the right.* The result is an increase in quantity of the bonds supplied at every price (see Figure 6.2). Because the demand curve stays where it is (remember, we're holding everything else constant), the increase in supply drives the price down. The added supply of U.S. government bonds has reduced prices, raising interest rates.

Changes in General Business Conditions   During business-cycle expansions, when general business conditions are good, investment opportunities abound, prompting firms to increase their borrowing. As the amount of debt in the economy rises, the quantity of bonds outstanding with a given risk goes up. So *as business conditions improve, the bond supply curve shifts to the right,* forcing bond prices down and interest rates up. Again, Figure 6.2 shows what happens. This connection between general business conditions and the supply of bonds also helps explain how weak economic growth can lead to rising bond prices and lower interest rates for bonds with unchanged risk.

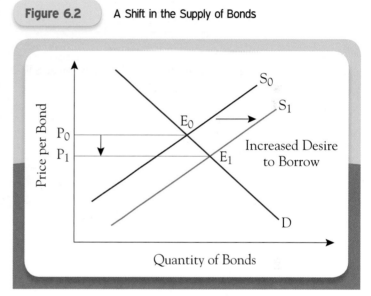

Figure 6.2   A Shift in the Supply of Bonds

When borrowers' desire for funds increases, the bond supply curve shifts to the right, lowering bond prices and raising interest rates.

Changes in Expected Inflation   Bond issuers care about the *real* cost of borrowing—the cost of the loan taking inflation into account. At a given *nominal* interest rate, higher expected inflation means a lower *real* interest rate. And at a lower real interest rate, fewer real resources are required to make the payments promised by a bond. So when expected inflation rises, the cost of borrowing falls and the desire to borrow at every nominal interest rate rises. Figure 6.2 shows that *an increase in expected inflation shifts the bond supply curve to the right.* Higher expected inflation increases the bond supply, reducing bond prices and raising the nominal interest rate.

Table 6.4 summarizes the factors that increase the quantity of bonds supplied at every price, shifting the bond supply curve to the right. Before moving on to shifts in the demand for bonds, we should mention that there is one other factor that shifts the bond supply: changes in corporate taxation. Because such changes in the tax code require government legislation, they don't occur very often. But when they do, they can affect the economywide supply of bonds. Corporations pay taxes on their profits, just as individuals pay taxes on their income, so they are concerned with after-tax profits.

Table 6.4	Factors That Shift Bond Supply to the Right, Lower Bond Prices, and Raise Interest Rates

Change	Effect on Bond Supply, Bond Prices, and Interest Rates	Shift in Bond Supply
An increase in the government's desired expenditure relative to its revenue	Bond supply shifts to the right, bond prices $\downarrow$, and interest rates $\uparrow$	
An improvement in general business conditions	Bond supply shifts to the right, bond prices $\downarrow$, and interest rates $\uparrow$	
An increase in expected inflation, reducing the real cost of repayment	Bond supply shifts to the right, bond prices $\downarrow$, and interest rates $\uparrow$	

Governments often create special tax subsidies that make corporate investments less costly. These tax incentives increase the supply of bonds because they raise the after-tax profitability of investing in new equipment purchased with funds raised from selling bonds. Like the other three factors we have considered, government tax incentives increase bond supply, shift the supply curve to the right, and lower the price of bonds.

Factors That Shift Bond Demand

Now we move on to bond demand. Six factors shift the *demand* for bonds at a given price: wealth, expected inflation, the expected return on stocks and other assets, expected interest rates, risk, and the liquidity of bonds (see Table 6.5).

Wealth The more rapidly the economy grows, the wealthier individuals become. As their wealth increases, they increase their investment in stocks, bonds, real estate, and art. Thus, *increases in wealth shift the demand for bonds to the right*, raising bond

| Table 6.5 | Factors That Shift Bond Demand to the Right, Raise Bond Prices, and Lower Interest Rates |

Change	Effect on Bond Demand	Shift in Bond Demand
An increase in wealth increases demand for all assets including bonds.	Bond demand shifts to the right, bond prices ↑, and interest rates ↓	*(graph: S, D0→D1, E0, E1, P0, P1, Quantity of Bonds)*
A reduction in expected inflation makes bonds with fixed nominal payments more desirable.	Bond demand shifts to the right, bond prices ↑, and interest rates ↓	*(graph: S, D0→D1, E0, E1, P0, P1, Quantity of Bonds)*
A decrease in the expected future interest rate makes bonds more attractive.	Bond demand shifts to the right, bond prices ↑, and interest rates ↓	*(graph: S, D0→D1, E0, E1, P0, P1, Quantity of Bonds)*
An increase in the expected return on the bond relative to the expected return on alternatives makes bonds more attractive.	Bond demand shifts to the right, bond prices ↑, and interest rates ↓	*(graph: S, D0→D1, E0, E1, P0, P1, Quantity of Bonds)*
A fall in the riskiness of the bond relative to the riskiness of alternatives makes bonds more attractive.	Bond demand shifts to the right, bond prices ↑, and interest rates ↓	*(graph: S, D0→D1, E0, E1, P0, P1, Quantity of Bonds)*
An increase in the liquidity of the bond relative to the liquidity of alternatives makes bonds more attractive.	Bond demand shifts to the right, bond prices ↑, and interest rates ↓	*(graph: S, D0→D1, E0, E1, P0, P1, Quantity of Bonds)*

YOUR FINANCIAL WORLD
Understanding the Ads in the Newspaper

You're drinking your coffee and as you read the business news, something catches your eye. An investment company is advertising that their bond mutual funds returned 13½ percent over the last year. But you remember that interest rates have been pretty low—7 percent at most. And a quick check of the numbers in the business section you're holding tells you that your recollection is correct. How could the ad be right?

The answer is that the advertisement is about last year's holding period return, when interest rates were falling. When interest rates fall, bond prices rise and the holding period return is higher than the interest rate. And the longer the term of the bond, the bigger the price movements for a given interest rate change. To see what can happen, take

an example of a 20-year, 7 percent coupon bond with a face value of $100. If the interest rate is initially 7 percent, this bond sells for $100. But if the interest rate falls by even one-half of one percentage point to 6½ percent, the price will rise to about $106.50 giving the owner a 6½ percent capital gain. Adding this to the 7 percent coupon payments, we get a one-year holding period return of 13½ percent.

So the ad isn't really much of a mystery once you think about it. But the implication of the ad, that these are great investments, is something you ought to think about. Remember, if interest rates go back up, things won't be so pretty. When it says at the bottom of the ad that "Past Performance is No Indication of Future Returns" you should take the statement very seriously.

prices and lowering yields (see Figure 6.3). This is what happens in a business-cycle expansion. In a recession, as wealth falls, the demand for bonds falls with it, lowering bond prices and raising interest rates.

Expected Inflation Changes in expected inflation alter investors' willingness to purchase bonds promising fixed-dollar payments. A decline in expected inflation means that the payments promised by the bond's issuer have a higher value than borrowers originally thought, so the bond will become more attractive. *This fall in expected inflation shifts the bond demand curve to the right,* increasing demand at each price and lowering the yield, as shown in Figure 6.3. In short, the higher real return on the bond increases the willingness of would-be lenders to buy it at any given price. Note that the decline in expected inflation has reduced the nominal interest rate that investors require in order to make a loan.

Expected Returns and Expected Interest Rates An investor's desire to hold any particular financial instrument depends on how its return compares to those of alternative instruments. Bonds are no different. *If the expected return on bonds rises relative to the return on alternative investments, the quantity of bonds demanded at every price will rise, shifting the bond demand curve to the right.* This leads us to conclude that bond prices are connected to the stock market. Investors see bonds as an alternative to stocks, so when the stock market

Figure 6.3 A Shift in the Demand for Bonds

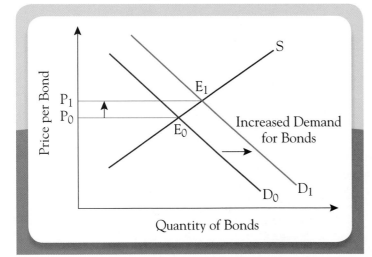

When there is an increase in investors' willingness to hold bonds, the bond demand curve shifts to the right, increasing bond prices and reducing interest rates.

outlook worsens, they shift their portfolios into bonds, increasing demand, driving bond prices up and interest rates down.

Similarly, when interest rates are expected to change in the future, bond prices adjust immediately. Recall that the holding period return on a bond depends on the coupon payment plus the capital gain or loss. When interest rates fall, bond prices rise, creating a capital gain. Whenever interest rates are expected to fall, then bond prices are expected to rise, creating an expectation of a capital gain. This makes bonds more attractive. Knowing that bonds are a good investment, investors increase their demand immediately, driving bond prices up. So *an increase in the expected return on a bond, relative to the return on alternatives, shifts bond demand to the right.*

Risk Relative to Alternatives   On May 13, 2002, a headline in *The Wall Street Journal* read "Japan Gets Irate at Having Its Risk Compared to Botswana." What's going on here? Japan is the third largest economy in the world, with a population of more than 125 million and a GDP in excess of $5 trillion. Botswana is a landlocked country in Southern Africa with a population of 2 million people and a GDP of $18 billion.

The problem was that investors had two reasons to question Japan's budget outlook. First, the fiscal deficit was a very high 7 percent of GDP. Second, over the next few decades, the Japanese government would have to find a way to meet its promises to make pension payments to the growing number of retirees. Together these created the perception that Japan's bonds were risky, which meant that investors would be less interested in holding them.

Remember that investors require compensation for risk, which means that when a bond becomes more or less risky, the demand for the bond changes. The less risky the bond, the higher the price investors are willing to pay for it, all other things being equal. From this we can conclude that *if a bond becomes less risky relative to alternative investments, the demand for the bond shifts to the right.* The reason Japan was irate was because the price of its bonds would be lower, so its borrowing costs would be higher.

Liquidity Relative to Alternatives   As we learned in Chapter 2, market liquidity measures how easily and cheaply investors can convert a financial instrument into cash (the means of payment). A liquid asset is something investors can sell without a large loss in value. Investors like liquidity; the more liquid a bond, the higher the demand for it, all other things being equal. So if a bond's liquidity changes, demand for it changes, too.

During the financial crisis in the fall of 1998, for example, the bonds issued by emerging-market governments in Latin America and Eastern Europe became virtually impossible to sell. The same thing happened to some U.S. mortgage-related bonds during the crisis of 2007–2009 and to the bonds of some euro-area countries beginning in 2010. For all practical purposes, the market for them disappeared. When a buyer could be found, prices were severely depressed. Who wants to buy a bond that is difficult to sell? Liquidity matters. The less liquid a bond is, the lower the demand for it, and the lower the price. So *when a bond becomes more liquid relative to alternatives, the demand curve shifts to the right.*

Understanding Changes in Equilibrium Bond Prices and Interest Rates

Before we continue, let's look again at how bond prices and interest rates move in response to changes in expected inflation and a change in general business conditions.

Figure 6.4 Equilibrium in the Bond Market: The Effect of an Increase in Expected Inflation

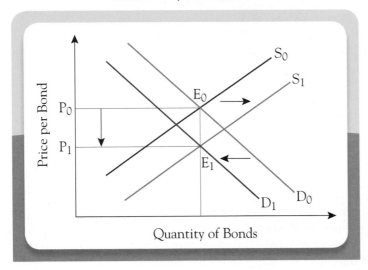

An increase in expected inflation increases bond supply from S_0 to S_1 by lowering the real cost of borrowing. At the same time, it reduces bond demand from D_0 to D_1 by reducing the real interest rate bondholders receive. These two effects reinforce each other, lowering the bond's price from P_0 to P_1 and increasing the interest rate.

Figure 6.5 Equilibrium in the Bond Market: The Effect of a Business-Cycle Downturn

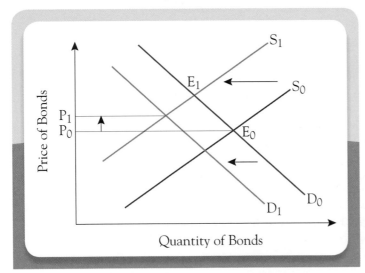

For bonds with unchanged risk, interest rates tend to fall during business-cycle downturns. The combination of reduced investment opportunities for businesses, which shifts the bond supply curve to the left from S_0 to S_1, and a decline in household wealth, which shifts the bond demand curve to the left from D_0 to D_1, causes an increase in bond prices and a drop in the interest rate.

Recall that expected inflation affects both bond supply and bond demand. An increase in expected inflation reduces the real cost of borrowing, shifting bond *supply* to the *right*. But at the same time, this increase in expected inflation lowers the real return on lending, shifting bond *demand* to the *left*. These two effects reinforce each other, lowering the price of the bond and raising the interest rate (see Figure 6.4).

We also saw that changes in business conditions affect both the supply and the demand for bonds. A business-cycle downturn reduces business investment opportunities, shifting the bond *supply* to the left, and reduces wealth, shifting bond *demand* in the same direction. When both curves shift in the same direction, the price can rise or fall. The theory does not give us an unambiguous prediction. In cases like this, we can look for regular movements in the data to help resolve the question. In this case we know that in recessions, interest rates tend to fall, so (for bonds with unchanged risk) prices should increase (see Figure 6.5).

Why Bonds Are Risky

"Bonds Look Attractive Now but They Come with Risks"

—*The Wall Street Journal,* July 26, 2002

How can bonds be risky? They are promises to make fixed payments on future dates. Where is the risk in that? The fact is that the return an investor receives for holding a bond is far from riskless. Bondholders face three major risks (see Table 6.6). **Default risk** is the chance that the bond's issuer may fail to make the promised payment. **Inflation risk** means an investor can't be sure of what the real value of the payments will be, even if they are made. And **interest-rate risk** arises from a bondholder's investment horizon, which may be shorter than the maturity of the bond. If, for example, the interest rate were to rise

APPLYING THE CONCEPT
WHEN RUSSIA DEFAULTED

The idea that risk matters to bond investors is not just a text-book theory. On numerous occasions, investors' concerns about increased risk in certain areas of the globe have led to a significant shift in demand for U.S. Treasury bonds. A notewor-thy example occurred in August 1998, when the Russian gov-ernment failed to make the payments on some bonds held by foreign investors. That is, the Russian government defaulted. Suddenly, no one wanted to hold Russian debt. More impor-tant, people lost confidence in the debt issued by all emerg-ing market countries, including Brazil, Argentina, Turkey, and Thailand. After dumping anything that they thought at all risky, investors went looking for a safe place to put the proceeds.

Because the safest assets around are U.S. Treasury bonds, that is what they bought. The perception during this episode was that the riskiness of U.S. Treasury bonds had fallen relative to the riskiness of virtually everything else. The result was an increase in the price of U.S. Treasury bonds and a decline in their yield. At the same time, the prices of the more risky alternatives fell and their yields rose.

The data in Figure 6.6 show what happened. After the default (at the vertical line in the figure), the price of U.S. Treasury bonds rose by roughly 10 percent while the price of Brazilian bonds fell by more than one-third. Even though it was a half a world away from Russia, investors' demand for Brazilian bonds plummeted. Meanwhile, demand for the safe U.S. Treasury debt went up.

| **Figure 6.6** | Prices of Brazilian Government Debt and U.S. Treasury Bonds, July 1998 to October 1998 |

One bond index is for five- to seven-year U.S. Treasury bonds and the other is for Brazilian government bonds. The indexes, which show the movement in the prices of the bonds, were constructed by Lehman Brothers and supplied by Datastream.

SOURCE: *Data compiled from Thompson Datastream.*

Table 6.6   What Makes Bonds Risky?

1. *Default risk:*	The issuer may not make the promised payments on time.
2. *Inflation risk:*	Inflation may turn out to be higher than expected, reducing the real return on holding the bond.
3. *Interest-rate risk:*	Interest rates may rise between the time a bond is purchased and the time it is sold reducing the bond's price.

between the time the bond is purchased and the time it is sold, the investor would suf-fer a capital loss.[6]

We'll look at each of these sources of risk separately, using the tools for under-standing risk introduced in Chapter 5. Remember that risk arises from the fact that an investment has many possible payoffs during the horizon for which it is held. So in looking at the risk a bondholder faces, we need to ask what the possible payoffs are

[6]Beyond these three primary sources of risk, the buyer of a bond faces a number of more subtle risks. For example, liquidity risk is the possibility that the investor will experience difficulty selling a bond before it matures. An investor who buys a bond denominated in a foreign currency also faces the risk of changes in the exchange rate. A bond may promise payments in euros, say, which must be converted into dollars before they can be used or reinvested.

and how likely each one is to occur. As we do, we will be looking at the impact of risk on the bond's return relative to the risk-free rate. That is, we will try to figure out how certain risks affect the premium investors require over the risk-free return. Once again, *risk requires compensation.*

Default Risk

There is no guarantee that a bond issuer will make the promised payments. While we usually ignore default risk in thinking about U.S. Treasury bonds, we cannot do so when discussing bonds issued by many other governments or by private corporations. When corporations or governments fail to meet their payments, what happens to the price of their bonds?

To figure out the answer, let's list all the possibilities and payoffs that might occur, along with their probabilities. We can then calculate the expected value of the promised payments, from which we can compute the bond's price and yield. Suppose, for example, that the one-year risk-free interest rate is 5 percent. Flim.com, an Internet firm hoping to market its own brand of e-cash called "Flam,"[7] has issued one-year, 5 percent coupon bonds with a face value of $100. This represents a promise to pay $105 in one year. What is the price of this bond?

If Flim.com were risk free, and lenders were certain they would be paid back, the price of the bond would be computed as the present value of the $105 payment, calculated using the 5 percent risk-free interest rate.

$$\text{Price of Flim.com bond if it is risk free} = \frac{\$100 + \$5}{1.05} = \$100$$

But unlike the U.S. Treasury, Flim.com may not make the payments. People might be unwilling to use Flam, so Flim.com could default. Suppose there is a 0.10 probability (1 chance in 10) that Flim.com will go bankrupt before paying bondholders their $105. To simplify the example, we will assume that in the case of default, the bondholders get nothing. This means that there are two possible payoffs, $105 and $0 (see Table 6.7).

Table 6.7 shows that the expected value of the payment on this bond is $94.50. But even if the payment is made, it will be made one year from now, which means that the price we would be willing to pay for the bond today must be the present value of the future payment. Using the risk-free interest rate for this computation, we find that

$$\text{Expected present value of Flim.com bond payment} = \frac{\$94.50}{1.05} = \$90$$

Table 6.7   Expected Value of Flim.com Bond Payment

Possibilities	Payoff	Probability	Payoff × Probabilities
Full payment	$105	0.90	$94.50
Default	$ 0	0.10	$ 0
Expected value = Sum of payoffs times probabilities = $94.50			

[7]This example is not farfetched. In the 1990s a company called flooz.com tried to issue e-money called "flooz."

APPLYING THE CONCEPT
SECURITIZATION

Securitization is the process by which financial institutions pool various assets (such as residential mortgages) that generate a stream of payments and transform them into a bond that gives the bondholder a claim on those payments (instead of a fixed coupon). The resulting bond trades in open markets.

Securitization has grown sharply over the past 30 years and now encompasses more than half of U.S. mortgages (see Table 6.8). *Mortgage-backed securities* (MBS) are just one form of securitized debt. Other commonly securitized debts are student loans, auto loans, and credit card debt. However, any stream of payments can be used to create a bond, even movie box-office receipts or sales of music recordings.

What are the benefits of securitization? Securitization uses the efficiency of markets to lower the cost of borrowing. It does so by (1) facilitating diversification of risks, (2) making assets liquid, (3) allowing greater specialization in the business of finance, (4) broadening markets, and (5) fostering innovation.

- *Diversification* or *risk-spreading*. Owning a security that provides a claim on a tiny portion of the payments from several thousand mortgages is less risky than owning a few mortgages in their entirety. By spreading the total risk of thousands of mortgages among many investors, diversification lowers the cost of funding to home buyers.*

- *Liquidity.* Securitization makes the underlying assets liquid by creating a market for them in the form of a bond. Borrowers thus face lower costs because lenders can sell the assets more easily.

- *Specialization.* Some financial institutions are effective in *originating* (creating) the underlying assets (such as a residential mortgage), while others are more proficient at collecting these assets and issuing and *distributing* the securities. By allowing these institutions to specialize, securitization lowers the cost of funds to borrowers. Because origination and distribution are often separated, this pattern of financial activity is called the *originate-to-distribute* model of securitization.

- *Broadening markets.* Home buyers in a small town need not depend on the ability of a small, local bank to bear the entire risk of holding their long-term mortgages. Instead, securitization gives that small group of home buyers access to investors across the globe who can afford to buy a tiny portion of those mortgages in the form of a marketable security.

- *Innovation.* Financial firms seeking to lower the cost of funds to borrowers can broaden the range of assets that are transformed into securities. They can also develop securities that better fit the preferences of the ultimate buyers.

Table 6.8	U.S. Mortgages Outstanding (Trillions of Dollars), 1980–2012			
	2012	2000	1990	1980
Mortgages	13.2	6.8	3.8	1.5
of which:				
Pools and ABS	7.0	3.1	1.1	0.1

Note: 2012 pools and ABS (asset-backed securities) include securitized mortgages consolidated in 2010 on the balance sheets of the government-sponsored enterprises.

Source: *Federal Reserve Board,* Flow of Funds Accounts of the United States.

*Chapter 11 makes a similar argument with regard to risk-pooling by banks: each depositor owns a very small stake in the thousands of loans made by bank.

So the bond will sell for $90. What yield to maturity does this price imply? If the promised payment is $105, the promised yield to maturity is

$$\text{Promised yield on Flim.com bond} = \frac{\$105}{\$90} - 1 = 0.1667$$

Converting the decimal to a percentage, we get an interest rate of 16.67 percent.[8] Because the default-risk premium is the promised yield to maturity minus the risk-free rate, it is 16.67 percent − 5 percent = 11.67 percent.

[8]This set of calculations could have been done in reverse. Given the yield of 16.67 percent and the characteristics of the bond, it is straightforward to compute the probability of default as 10 percent.

YOUR FINANCIAL WORLD
Bonds Indexed to Inflation

Inflation creates risk that the nominal return you receive on a bond won't be worth as much as you expected. If a bond pays a 6 percent yield but the inflation rate is also 6 percent, then the real return is zero! What can you do? You could accept the inflation risk, buy a regular bond, and hope for the best. But that's not always appealing.

Fortunately, there are alternatives. One is to buy a type of U.S. Treasury bond that compensates you for inflation. This **inflation-indexed bond** is structured so that the government promises to pay you a fixed interest rate plus the change in the Consumer Price Index (the CPI). For instance, if you buy a $1,000 bond with an interest rate of 3 percent plus inflation, and the CPI rises 2 percent, you will get 3 + 2 = 5 percent. If the inflation rate jumps to 5 percent, then you'll get 3 + 5 = 8 percent. Regardless of what inflation turns out to be, you get 3 percent more, so there is no inflation risk. And because the U.S. Treasury issues these bonds, there is little default risk.

The U.S. Treasury sells two types of bonds that are adjusted for inflation, Series I savings bonds and Treasury Inflation-Protected Securities (*TIPS*). Series I savings bonds have a long list of rules about how many can be purchased and how long they need to be held. You can learn about these bonds on the website of the Bureau of Public Debt at www.publicdebt.treas. gov. You can buy and sell TIPS in financial markets, or you can buy them directly from the U.S. Treasury through Treasury Direct (see Your Financial World in Chapter 16).

TIPS, which have been issued regularly since 2003, usually guarantee investors a way to beat inflation. Beginning in late 2011, however, anxieties about future inflation boosted the price of 10-year TIPS so high that the yield fell *below* the annual inflation rate. As of early 2013, that yield dropped to −57 basis points (or 0.57 percentage point below the inflation rate), as TIPS buyers paid a near-record premium for insurance against future inflation risk.

TreasuryDirect

SOURCE: *Courtesy of the Bureau of the Public Debt, U.S. Department of Treasury.*

In calculating the default-risk premium on Flim.com's bond, we computed the expected value of holding the bond—the yield at which the bond is a fair bet. But we know that risk-averse investors require some compensation for bearing risk. The more risk, the greater the compensation they demand. Only a risk-neutral investor would be willing to pay $90 for this bond. Any risk premium will drive the price down below $90 and push the yield to maturity above 16.67 percent.

This example shows that the higher the default risk, the higher the probability that the bondholders will not receive the promised payments. Risk reduces the expected value of a given promise, lowering the price an investor is willing to pay and raising the yield. The higher the default risk, the higher the yield.

Inflation Risk

With few exceptions, bonds promise to make fixed-dollar payments. That is, a $100 face value, one-year bond at 5 percent is a promise to make a $105 payment in one year. If this promise is free of default risk, the bondholder can be sure of receiving the $105 payment. Still, there is a risk of inflation. Remember that what you care about is the purchasing power of the money, not the number of dollars. In other words, bondholders are interested in the *real interest rate,* not just the nominal interest rate. And they don't know what the inflation rate will be.

Let's look at an example that shows how inflation risk affects the interest rate. To begin with, think about the interest rate as having three components: the real interest

Table 6.9	Inflation Risk

	Probabilities		
Inflation Rate	**Case I**	**Case II**	**Case III**
1 percent	0.50	0.25	0.10
2 percent	—	0.50	0.80
3 percent	0.50	0.25	0.10
Expected inflation	2 percent	2 percent	2 percent
Standard deviation	1.0 percent	0.71 percent	0.45 percent

rate, expected inflation, and a compensation for inflation risk. Suppose the real interest rate is 3 percent but we are unsure what the inflation rate will be. It could be either 1 percent or 3 percent with equal probability (see Case I in Table 6.9). Expected inflation is 2 percent, with a standard deviation of 1.0 percent. This means the nominal interest rate should equal the 3 percent real interest rate plus the 2 percent expected inflation plus the compensation for inflation risk. The greater the inflation risk, the larger the compensation for it will be.

In Cases II and III, expected inflation is the same (2 percent) but the standard deviation is lower because we are more certain that the inflation rate will be close to its expected value. That is, Case III is less risky than Case II, which is less risky than Case I. Because risk requires compensation, we would expect the interest rate to be highest in Case I and lowest in Case III. While we may not see this distinction much in the United States or Europe, where inflation is stable, emerging-market countries can go through periods when increases in inflation risk substantially drive up nominal interest rates.

Interest-Rate Risk

To explain interest-rate risk, we'll focus on a U.S. Treasury bond and assume that it is free of default risk and that we know how much inflation there will be, so there also is no inflation risk. Interest-rate risk arises from the fact that investors don't know the holding period return of a long-term bond. Remember that when interest rates change, bond prices move; the longer the term of the bond, the larger the price change for a given change in the interest rate. Now think about what happens if you have a short investment horizon. If you buy a long-term bond, you will need to sell the bond before it matures, so you have to worry about what will happen if the interest rate changes.

Whenever there is a mismatch between your investment horizon and a bond's maturity, there is interest-rate risk. Because the prices of long-term bonds can change dramatically, this can be an important source of risk. For example, on June 14, 2013, the 8.75 percent coupon Treasury bond that matures on August 15, 2020, traded at a price of $149.49 (per $100 face value). When it was originally issued as a 30-year bond in August 1990, its price was $98.747.[9] An investor who bought the bond when

[9]The U.S. Treasury auctions its bonds, so the original selling price is not the exact par value of the bond. To see the original auction prices, go to the website of the Bureau of the Public Debt at *www.publicdebt.treas.gov*.

Gross's Burning Bond Market Fails to Frighten Investors

Bloomberg

By Saumya Vaishampayan and Margaret Collins

October 9, 2012

Paul Smith, a retired attorney in Oakton, Virginia, lost 30 percent of his 401(k) retirement savings during the financial crisis.

He shifted to bond funds from stocks and now holds at least 60 percent of his retirement savings in fixed income. While payouts from some of the bond funds barely keep up with inflation, Smith said, he's worried that stocks could see another decline.

"Both my wife and I are very risk averse," the 64-year-old said in an interview. "Frankly, the volatility in the market is very much a concern to us."

Investors like Smith have poured $982 billion into U.S. bond funds from January 2008 through August [2012] while pulling $439 billion out of equity funds, sacrificing a 115 percent rally in stocks from their lows for the perceived safety of bonds. Money managers and fund executives such as Pimco's Bill Gross and BlackRock Inc. (BLK)'s Laurence D. Fink are warning that the flight to bonds leaves savers exposed to a new round of losses once interest rates rise, a risk many retail clients aren't aware of.

While investors who hold bonds until they mature don't lose money unless the issuer defaults, mutual funds and other holders who trade the securities to maximize yields can suffer losses if interest rates rise. Long-term Treasuries had almost as many losing years as stocks in the past 85 years, and fared worse than equities by that measure when adjusting for inflation, according to Chicago-based Morningstar Inc. (MORN). . . .

From 1926 through 2011, U.S. long-term Treasury bonds had losses in 22 years, compared with 24 years for stocks. When adjusting for the impact of inflation, long-term Treasuries lost money for investors in 33 years, more than the 28 years for stocks. And while losses in stocks tend to be bigger—they declined an inflation-adjusted 37 percent in 1931 and 2008—the record-low interest rates of the past year have increased the potential for large, abrupt declines in bonds. . . .

"If interest rates were to rise rapidly there would be significant losses in bond funds," said Mercer Bullard, associate professor of law at the University of Mississippi and founder of investor advocacy group Fund Democracy. "That can catch a lot of people and hit them with losses they weren't expecting."

Ryan Melvey, 21, holds half of his investments in bonds, a $19,000 portfolio that he started at age 16 with about $4,000 he made from busing tables. He was fully invested in equities in 2008 and has since built a portfolio that he believes will perform, regardless of the economy. . . .

Melvey, a finance major, said he isn't "too worried" about interest-rate risk, pointing to Japan, which has been in a deflationary phase for more than a decade.

"I'd make the argument that interest rates can remain low for a lot longer than people think," Melvey said.

The Federal Reserve has supported the bond market by keeping its target rate for overnight loans among banks between zero and 0.25 percent since December 2008 and embarking on three rounds of unprecedented asset purchases. The Fed said on Sept. 13 it will probably keep the federal funds target rate near zero until at least mid-2015. . . .

Managers of some of the largest bond funds have warned rates can't stay low forever, and investors in bonds may be poised for losses. Gross, manager of the world's biggest bond fund at Pacific Investment Management Co., said the U.S. must begin to close the gap between spending and debt or inflation will result.

"Bonds would be burned to a crisp," Gross, whose Pimco Total Return Fund has $278 billion in assets, wrote in his Oct. 2 investment outlook. . . .

Gross has been buying Treasury Inflation Protected Securities, or TIPS, as a way to profit from a likely inflationary situation in the next few years. . . .

Losses from bond funds going forward may be worse than at other points in history when interest rates rose, such as in 1994 or the late 1970s, said Ken Volpert, principal and head of taxable bonds for Valley Forge, Pennsylvania-based Vanguard Group Inc. . . . Yields in bond funds are so low today that rates don't have to increase much before investors would see negative returns, he said.

LESSONS OF THE ARTICLE

Some investors view long-term bonds as much safer than stocks, but losses on such bonds are similarly frequent, and their inflation-adjusted returns are lower on average. With bond yields near record lows in 2012 and the Federal Reserve pursuing an accommodative monetary policy, worries about bonds encouraged some professional investors to favor equities or to purchase TIPS despite their subzero inflation-adjusted yields.

it was originally issued and sold it 23 years later on June 14, 2013, earned a capital gain of 51 percent. By comparison, an investor who purchased the 1.75 percent coupon 10-year Treasury note when it was issued on May 15, 2013, at $99.45 and sold it 1 month later at its market price of $96.63 on June 14, 2013, suffered a capital loss of nearly 3 percent.

The lesson is that any move in interest rates changes the price of a bond. For investors with holding periods shorter than the maturity of the bond, the potential for a change in interest rates creates risk. The more likely interest rates are to change during the bondholder's investment horizon, the larger the risk of holding a bond.

Terms

capital gain, 138
capital loss, 138
consol or perpetuity, 136
current yield, 138
default risk, 150
holding period return, 140
inflation-indexed bonds, 154

inflation risk, 150
interest-rate risk, 150
investment horizon, 141
U.S. Treasury bill (T-bill), 134
yield to maturity, 137
zero-coupon bond, 134

Using FRED: Codes for Data in This Chapter

Data Series	FRED Data Code
3-month Treasury bill rate	TB3MS
1-year Treasury bill rate	TB1YR
2-year Treasury constant maturity rate	GS2
10-year Treasury constant maturity rate	GS10
30-year Treasury constant maturity rate	GS30
5-year Treasury inflation-indexed yield	FII5
10-year Treasury inflation-indexed yield	FII10
30-year Treasury inflation-indexed yield	FII30
Consumer price index	CPIAUCSL
1-year inflation expectations (Michigan survey)	MICH
Japan Treasury bill rate	INTGSTJPM193N
Brazil Treasury bill rate	INTGSTBRM193N

Chapter Lessons

1. Valuing bonds is an application of present value.
   a. Pure discount or zero-coupon bonds promise to make a single payment on a predetermined future date.
   b. Fixed-payment loans promise to make a fixed number of equal payments at regular intervals.
   c. Coupon bonds promise to make periodic interest payments and repay the principal at maturity.
   d. Consols (perpetuities) promise to make periodic coupon payments forever.

2. Yields are measures of the return on holding a bond.
   a. The yield to maturity is a measure of the interest rate on a bond. To compute it, set the price of the bond equal to the present value of the payments.
   b. The current yield on a bond is equal to the coupon rate divided by the price.
   c. When the price of a bond is above its face value, the coupon rate is greater than the current yield, which is higher than the yield to maturity.
   d. One-year holding period returns are equal to the sum of the current yield and any capital gain or loss arising from a change in a bond's price.

3. Bond prices (and bond yields) are determined by supply and demand in the bond market.
   a. The higher the price, the larger the quantity of bonds supplied.
   b. The higher the price, the smaller the quantity of bonds demanded.
   c. The supply of bonds rises when
      i. Governments need to borrow more.
      ii. General business conditions improve.
      iii. Expected inflation rises.
   d. The demand for bonds rises when
      i. Wealth increases.
      ii. Expected inflation falls.
      iii. The expected return, relative to other investments, rises.
      iv. The expected future interest rate falls.
      v. Bonds become less risky relative to other investments.
      vi. Bonds become more liquid relative to other investments.

4. Bonds are risky because of
   a. Default risk: the risk that the issuer may fail to pay.
   b. Inflation risk: the risk that the inflation rate may be more or less than expected, affecting the real value of the promised nominal payments.
   c. Interest-rate risk: the risk that the interest rate may change, causing the bond's price to change.

Conceptual and Analytical Problems

1. Consider a U.S. Treasury bill with 270 days to maturity. If the annual yield is 3.8 percent, what is the price? *(LO1)*

2.* You are an officer of a commercial bank and wish to sell one of the bank's assets—a car loan—to another bank. Using equation (A5) in the Appendix to Chapter 4, compute the price you expect to receive for the loan if the annual interest rate is 6 percent, the car payment is $430 per month, and the loan term is five years. *(LO1)*

3.* Your financial advisor recommends buying a 10-year bond with a face value of $1,000 and an annual coupon of $80. The current interest rate is 7 percent. What might you expect to pay for the bond (aside from brokerage fees)? *(LO1)*

4.* Consider a coupon bond with a $1,000 face value and a coupon payment equal to 5 percent of the face value per year. *(LO1)*

   a. If there is one year to maturity, find the yield to maturity if the price of the bond is $990.

   b. Explain why finding the yield to maturity is difficult if there are two years to maturity and you do not have a financial calculator.

5. Which of these $100 face value one-year bonds will have the highest yield to maturity and why? *(LO2)*
   a. A 6 percent coupon bond selling for $85.
   b. A 7 percent coupon bond selling for $100.
   c. An 8 percent coupon bond selling for $115.

6. You are considering purchasing a consol that promises annual payments of $4. *(LO2)*
   a. If the current interest rate is 5 percent, what is the price of the consol?
   b. You are concerned that the interest rate may rise to 6 percent. Compute the percentage change in the price of the consol and the percentage change in the interest rate. Compare them.
   c. Your investment horizon is one year. You purchase the consol when the interest rate is 5 percent and sell it a year later, following a rise in the interest rate to 6 percent. What is your holding period return?

7.* Suppose you purchase a 3-year, 5 percent coupon bond at par and hold it for two years. During that time, the interest rate falls to 4 percent. Calculate your annual holding period return. *(LO2)*

8. In a recent issue of *The Wall Street Journal* (or on www.wsj.com or an equivalent financial website), locate the prices and yields on U.S. Treasury issues. For one bond selling above par and one selling below par (assuming they both exist), compute the current yield and compare it to the coupon rate and the ask yield printed in the paper. *(LO2)*

9. In a recent issue of *The Wall Street Journal* (or on www.wsj.com), locate the yields on government bonds for various countries. Find a country whose 10-year government bond yield was above that on the U.S. 10-year Treasury bond and one whose 10-year yield was below the Treasury yield. What might account for these differences in yields? *(LO4)*

10. A 10-year zero-coupon bond has a yield of 6 percent. Through a series of unfortunate circumstances, expected inflation rises from 2 percent to 3 percent. *(LO4)*
   a. Assuming the nominal yield rises by an amount equal to the rise in expected inflation, compute the change in the price of the bond.
   b. Suppose that expected inflation is still 2 percent, but the probability that it will move to 3 percent has risen. Describe the consequences for the price of the bond.

*Indicates more difficult problems

11. As you read the business news, you come across an advertisement for a bond mutual fund—a fund that pools the investments from a large number of people and then purchases bonds, giving the individuals "shares" in the fund. The company claims their fund has had a return of 13½ percent over the last year. But you remember that interest rates have been pretty low—5 percent at most. A quick check of the numbers in the business section you're holding tells you that your recollection is correct. Explain the logic behind the mutual fund's claim in the advertisement. *(LO2)*

12. You are sitting at the dinner table and your father is extolling the benefits of investing in bonds. He insists that as a conservative investor he will only make investments that are safe, and what could be safer than a bond, especially a U.S. Treasury bond? What accounts for his view of bonds? Explain why you think it is right or wrong. *(LO4)*

13.* Consider a one-year, 10 percent coupon bond with a face value of $1,000 issued by a private corporation. The one-year risk-free rate is 10 percent. The corporation has hit on hard times, and the consensus is that there is a 20 percent probability that it will default on its bonds. If an investor were willing to pay at most $775 for the bond, is that investor risk neutral or risk averse? *(LO4)*

14. If, after one year, the yield to maturity on a multiyear coupon bond that was issued at par is higher than the coupon rate, what happened to the price of the bond during that first year? *(LO2)*

15. Use your knowledge of bond pricing to explain under what circumstances you would be willing to pay the same price for a consol that pays $5 a year forever and a 5 percent, 10-year coupon bond with a face value of $100 that only makes annual coupon payments for 10 years. *(LO1)*

16.* You are about to purchase your first home and receive an advertisement regarding adjustable-rate mortgages (ARMs). The interest rate on the ARM is lower than that on a fixed-rate mortgage. The advertisement mentions that there would be a payment cap on your monthly payments and you would have the option to convert to a fixed-rate mortgage. You are tempted. Interest rates are currently low by historical standards and you are anxious to buy a house and stay in it for the long term. Why might an ARM not be the right mortgage for you? *(LO4)*

17. Use the model of supply and demand for bonds to illustrate and explain the impact of each of the following on the equilibrium quantity of bonds outstanding and on equilibrium bond prices and yields: *(LO3)*
    a. A new website is launched facilitating the trading of corporate bonds with much more ease than before.
    b. Inflationary expectations in the economy fall evoking a much stronger response from issuers of bonds than investors in bonds.
    c. The government removes tax incentives for investment and spends additional funds on a new education program. Overall, the changes have no effect on the government's financing requirements.
    d. All leading indicators point to stronger economic growth in the near future. The response of bond issuers dominates that of bond purchasers.

18. Suppose that a sustainable peace is reached around the world, reducing military spending by the U.S. government. How would you expect this development to affect the U.S. bond market? *(LO3)*

19. Use the model of supply and demand for bonds to determine the impact on bond prices and yields of expectations that the real estate market is going to weaken. *(LO3)*

20.* Suppose there is an increase in investors' willingness to hold bonds at a given price. Use the model of the demand for and supply of bonds to show that the impact on the equilibrium bond price depends on how sensitive the quantity supplied of bonds is to the bond price. *(LO3)*

21. Under what circumstances would the purchase of a Treasury Inflation-Protected Security (TIPS) from the U.S. government be virtually risk free? *(LO4)*

22. In the wake of the financial crisis of 2007–2009, negative connotations often surrounded the term "mortgage-backed security." What arguments could you make to convince someone that she may have benefited from the growth in securitization over the past 30 years? *(LO3)*

Data Exploration

ECONOMIC DATA | ST. LOUIS FED

For detailed instructions on using Federal Reserve Economic Data (FRED) online to answer each of the following problems, visit www.mhhe.com/moneyandbanking4e and click on Student Edition, then Data Exploration Hints.

1. Graph investors' long-term expected inflation rate since 2003 by subtracting from the 10-year U.S. Treasury bond yield (FRED code: GS10) the yield on 10-year Treasury Inflation-Protected Securities (FRED code: FII10). Do these market-based inflation expectations appear stable? Did the financial crisis of 2007–2009 affect these expectations? *(LO4)*

Scan here for quick access to the hints for these problems. Need a barcode reader? Try ScanLife, available in your app store.

2. Compare long-run market expectations of inflation with a consumer survey measure of one-year-ahead inflation expectations. Starting with the graph from Data Exploration Problem 1, add as a second line the University of Michigan survey measure of inflation expectations (FRED code: MICH). Why might these measures differ systematically? *(LO4)*

3. How does the variability of annual inflation—an indicator of inflation risk—change over time? Graph the percent change from a year ago of the consumer price index (FRED code: CPIAUCSL) since 1990 and visually compare the decades of the 1990s, the 2000s, and the period that began in 2010. *(LO4)*

4. Download the data from the graph that you produced in Data Exploration Problem 3. Calculate the standard deviation of the annual inflation rate for the three time periods and compare these results against your visual assessment from Data Exploration Problem 3. *(LO4)*

5. Economists sometimes exclude food and energy prices from the "headline" consumer price index and use the resulting "core" price measure to assess inflation prospects. For the period since 1990, plot on one graph the percent change from a year ago of the consumer price index (FRED code: CPIAUCSL) and the percent change from a year ago of the consumer price index excluding food and energy (FRED code: CPILFESL). Visually compare the variability of these two measures of inflation. Why might inflation excluding food and energy be a better predictor of future inflation than headline inflation? *(LO4)*

Chapter 7

The Risk and Term Structure of Interest Rates

Learning Objectives

Understand . . .

LO1   Credit risk and bond ratings

LO2   The yield curve relating bond maturities to yields

LO3   How yields anticipate and signal the future

On October 5, 1998, William McDonough, president of the Federal Reserve Bank of New York, declared "I believe that we are in the most serious financial crisis since World War II."[1] Since August 17, when the Russian government had defaulted on some of its bonds, deteriorating investor confidence had increased volatility in the financial markets. Bond markets were the hardest hit; as lenders re-evaluated the relative risk of holding different bonds, some prices plummeted while others soared. This simultaneous increase in some interest rates and decline in others—a rise in what are called **interest-rate spreads**—was a clear sign to Mr. McDonough that the substantial stress the financial markets were experiencing could easily spread to the wider economy, affecting everyone.

Changes in bond prices, and the associated changes in interest rates, can have a pronounced effect on borrowing costs corporations face. The experience of Ford and General Motors (GM), the American automobile manufacturers, provides an instructive example. Like virtually every large company, the two car makers borrow to maintain and expand their businesses. And the amounts are very large. By 2005, Ford's borrowing exceeded $150 billion while GM's was nearly twice that. The two companies produce about one-third of the cars and trucks Americans buy. And they buy quite a few—nearly 15 million in 2012. But for years before the financial crisis that began in 2007, the fortunes of U.S. automakers were declining. Plummeting sales in the recession of 2007–2009 triggered massive losses that eventually led to the bankruptcy of GM. Even before GM's failure, the perceived riskiness of Ford and GM's bonds led to a decline in the price investors were willing to pay for them. A fall in bond prices means an increase in interest rates and a corresponding rise in the cost the auto companies have to pay to borrow.

---

[1]Mr. McDonough's job was to monitor financial market developments for the Federal Reserve System, to devise government reaction to such financial crises, and to formulate policies that prevented crises. As we will see in our discussion of the structure of the Federal Reserve System in Chapter 16, the Federal Reserve Bank of New York is the largest of the 12 district banks in the Federal Reserve System. The president of that bank plays a special role as the eyes and ears of the government in world financial markets.

These examples highlight the need to understand the differences among the many types of bonds that are sold and traded in financial markets. What was it about the movement in the prices of different bonds that Mr. McDonough found so informative? How did information about profitability affect investors' willingness to lend to GM and Ford? To answer these questions, we will study the differences among the multitude of bonds issued by governments and private corporations. As we will see, these bonds differ in two crucial respects: the identity of the issuer and the time to maturity. The purpose of this chapter is to examine how each of these affects the price of a bond, and then to use our knowledge to interpret fluctuations in a broad variety of bond prices.

Ratings and the Risk Structure of Interest Rates

Default is one of the most important risks a bondholder faces. Not surprisingly, the risk that an issuer will fail to make a bond's promised payments varies substantially from one borrower to another. The risk of default is so important to potential investors that independent companies have come into existence to evaluate the creditworthiness of potential borrowers. These firms, sometimes called rating agencies, estimate the likelihood that a corporate or government borrower will make a bond's promised payments. The first such ratings began in the United States more than 100 years ago. Since 1975, the U.S. government has acknowledged a few firms as "nationally recognized statistical rating organizations" (NRSROs), a designation that has encouraged investors and governments worldwide to rely on their ratings. In 2010, sweeping financial reform legislation (called the Dodd-Frank Wall Street Reform and Consumer Protection Act) included provisions to reduce reliance on ratings agencies. Let's look at these companies and the information that they produce.

Bond Ratings

SOURCE: *Courtesy of Standard & Poor's.*

The best-known bond rating services are Moody's and Standard & Poor's.[2] These companies monitor the status of individual bond issuers and assess the likelihood that a lender/bondholder will be repaid by a borrower/bond issuer. Companies with good credit—those with low levels of debt, high profitability, and sizable amounts of cash assets—earn high bond **ratings**. A high rating suggests that a bond issuer will have little problem meeting a bond's payment obligations.

Table 7.1 reports the rating systems of Moody's and Standard & Poor's. As you can see, they are very similar. Both systems are based on letters and bear a broad similarity to the rankings in minor-league baseball. Firms or governments with an exceptionally strong financial position carry the highest ratings and are able to issue the highest-rated bonds, Triple A. ExxonMobil, Microsoft, and the government of Canada are all examples of entities with Aaa bond ratings.[3]

---

[2]Fitch is a third, less well-known bond rating company. In addition to the big three, seven small agencies also now enjoy the U.S. government's NRSRO designation.

[3]U.S. government debt is a standard of comparison for other dollar-denominated debt because it is widely perceived as among the world's safest financial instruments. In August 2011, however, reacting to the rising debt burden and what it called "political risks," Standard and Poor's downgraded long-term U.S. Treasury debt to AA+. In September 2012, Moody's warned that it may downgrade U.S. debt from Aaa to Aa1 (the highest Aa category) if U.S. budget negotiations in 2013 failed to put the ratio of federal debt to GDP on a declining path in the medium term.

Table 7.1   A Guide to Bond Ratings

	Moody's	Standard & Poor's	Description	Examples of Issuers with Bonds Outstanding in 2012
Investment Grade	Aaa	AAA	Bonds of the best quality with the smallest risk of default. Issuers are exceptionally stable and dependable.	ExxonMobil Microsoft Canada
	Aa	AA	Highest quality with slightly higher degree of long-term risk.	General Electric Procter & Gamble China
	A	A	High-medium quality, with many strong attributes but somewhat vulnerable to changing economic conditions.	JPMorgan Chase Oracle Israel
	Baa	BBB	Medium quality, currently adequate but perhaps unreliable over the long term.	General Mills Time Warner Brazil Italy
Noninvestment, Speculative Grade	Ba	BB	Some speculative element, with moderate security but not well safeguarded.	Goodyear Tire General Motors Turkey
	B	B	Able to pay now but at risk of default in the future.	Hertz Office Depot Venezuela
Highly Speculative	Caa	CCC	Poor quality, clear danger of default.	Cuba* Pakistan*
	Ca	CC	Highly speculative quality, often in default.	
	C	C	Lowest-rated, poor prospects of repayment though may still be paying.	Greece**
	D	D	In default.	

*S&P rated Pakistan B and did not rate Cuba.
**S&P rated Greece CCC.
For a more detailed definition of ratings see Moody's website, *www.moodys.com,* or Standard and Poor's website, *www.standardandpoors.com.*

The top four categories, Aaa down to Baa in the Moody's scheme, are considered **investment-grade bonds**, meaning they have a very low risk of default. These ratings are reserved for most government issuers as well as corporations that are among the most financially sound.[4] Famously, these top ratings also were awarded to many risky mortgage-backed securities (see Lessons from the Crisis: Subprime Mortgages on page 165) that later plunged in value, triggering the financial crisis of 2007–2009 (see Lessons from the Crisis: Rating Agencies on page 166). Table 7.1 gives examples of governments and firms in selected rating levels above default in the autumn of 2012.

The distinction between investment-grade and speculative, noninvestment-grade bonds is an important one. A number of regulated institutional investors, among them some insurance companies, pension funds, and commercial banks, are not allowed to

[4]Government debt ratings are important, as they generally create a ceiling on the ratings for private companies in that country.

LESSONS FROM THE CRISIS
SUBPRIME MORTGAGES

The financial crisis of 2007–2009 initially was known as the *subprime crisis* because of the mortgage-backed securities (MBS, see page 53) that helped trigger the crisis in the United States. What is a subprime mortgage? What role does it play in the mortgage market? And how did it contribute to the financial crisis?

A residential mortgage is called *subprime* when it does not meet key standards of creditworthiness that apply to a conventional *prime* mortgage.* Conventional prime mortgages are those that satisfy the rules for inclusion in a collection or *pool of mortgages* to be guaranteed by a U.S. government agency. For this reason, conventional prime mortgages also are called *qualifying* or *conforming* mortgages.† Prime mortgages in which the loan amount exceeds a government-specified limit are called jumbo prime and do not qualify for the government guarantee.

The purpose of the creditworthiness standards is to increase the likelihood that the borrower will be able to repay the loan. Reducing borrower defaults lowers the cost to the government agency of its guarantee for the mortgage pools that back the MBS. The lending standards for qualifying mortgages typically include rules about the borrower's income, wealth, and credit score (see Your Financial World: Your Credit Rating on page 169). The standards also cover the size of mortgage, the price of the home, and the ratio between those two amounts—known as the *loan-to-value ratio,* or LTV ratio.

Subprime loans may fail to meet some or all of these standards for a qualifying mortgage. Typically, a loan is subprime if it is made to someone with a low credit score or whose income may be low relative to the price of the home; or if the LTV is high; or if the borrower does not provide sufficient documentation of their ability to pay. All of these factors make the loan more risky. Put differently, a subprime loan has a higher probability of default than qualifying loans.

Like conventional mortgages, the subprime type comes in two forms: fixed-rate and adjustable-rate mortgages (the latter are called ARMs—Chapter 6). And like conventional ARMs, subprime ARMs typically provide a low interest rate—known as a *teaser* rate—for the first two or three years. But once this initial period ends, the interest rate *resets* to a higher level—often, a much higher level—for the remaining term of the loan. This structure gives borrowers an incentive to replace their mortgage after the early years to obtain a new, low teaser rate or a fixed-rate loan. This process is called *refinancing*. Rising house prices make it possible to refinance even when a borrower's ability to pay is low because the lender can sell the house to recover the loan if the borrower fails to make timely payments.

During the housing bubble, starting in 2002, the volume of subprime loans surged as mortgage lenders relaxed their lending standards. Borrowers could obtain loans with lower down payments (high LTVs) and ever-poorer documentation. A complacent belief that the rise in nationwide house prices that had continued since the 1930s would persist indefinitely encouraged lending to borrowers with progressively lower ability to pay. When house prices started to fall in 2006, home values began to sink "below water"—that is, the home price fell to less than the amount of the mortgage—and lenders became unwilling to refinance many subprime loans. A wave of defaults followed. And further house price declines meant that lenders would not be able to recover the loan amounts in the increasingly likely event that borrowers would not be able to pay.

Even at their peak, outstanding subprime mortgages probably accounted for less than 15 percent of overall residential mortgages (which were $11 trillion in 2007)—and only a fraction of these were of really terrible quality. So why did subprime mortgage defaults trigger the financial disruptions of 2007–2009? The key reason is that some large, highly leveraged financial institutions held a sizable volume of MBS backed by subprime mortgages. Buying the MBS had allowed the institutions to increase their leverage and risk-taking (see Chapter 5) at the same time that they earned fees for new MBS issuance. In effect, some financial institutions "bet the house" on subprime mortgage securities, and the price collapse of those securities threatened their existence.

*There is another category of nonprime mortgages called alt-A that fall between prime and subprime in their default probability.

†The guarantee on a conforming mortgage pool lowers the default risk on a security backed by the pool. As a result, investors will pay more for the security and borrowers can obtain a cheaper mortgage.

invest in bonds that are rated below investment grade, that is, below Baa on Moody's scale or BBB on Standard & Poor's scale.[5]

Bonds issued by Goodyear, Hertz, and the governments of Turkey and Venezuela are in the noninvestment, speculative grade. These companies and countries may have difficulty meeting their bond payments but are not at risk of immediate default. The final category in Table 7.1, highly speculative bonds, consists of debts that are in serious risk of default.

[5]Restrictions on the investments of financial intermediaries, such as insurance companies, are a matter for government regulators. There is no comprehensive reference for all of the legal restrictions that force financial firms to sell bonds whose ratings fall below Baa. In many cases, such as those of bond mutual funds, the restrictions are self-imposed.

LESSONS FROM THE CRISIS
RATING AGENCIES

Rating mistakes contributed significantly to the financial crisis of 2007–2009. So, as governments sought to reform the financial system in the wake of the crisis, the role of rating agencies naturally attracted great attention.

Investors and regulators around the world relied on the high ratings that agencies had awarded to a large group of mortgage-backed securities (MBS, see page 53, and discussed in Chapter 6). When U.S. housing prices began to fall and MBS prices started to decline, rating agencies began a series of sharp downgrades, sometimes lowering ratings by four notches or more from the highest level (such as Moody's Aaa) directly to speculative grade (below Baa). Such downgrades reinforced the plunge in MBS prices. Losses on the highly rated assets, which were widely held by banks, diminished resources in the financial system sufficiently to help trigger (and later to intensify) the crisis.

What caused the rating errors? Agencies evaluating mortgage debt typically estimate default risks using mathematical models that rely on information about the borrowers, the houses they purchase, and historical patterns of default. However, the data used did not include a period in which U.S. housing prices fell significantly *nationwide,* because such a thing had not happened since the 1930s, during the Great Depression. As a result, the models severely underpredicted the likelihood of default on individual mortgages originated during the housing bubble. When defaults began to surge beyond what their models anticipated, the rating agencies were compelled to reassess their ratings.

Other factors may have also contributed to rating errors. For example, in developing some MBS, issuers typically consulted rating agencies to determine which bond structure would lead to the highest rating (and, presumably, the highest price). Payments for such consultation have the potential to create a conflict of interest when agencies are later called on to give the issue a rating in an objective, independent fashion. Some smaller rating agencies did not offer such consultations, and governments have already moved to prevent such potential conflicts from arising in the future.

Conflicts also can arise from the way rating agencies are compensated. Since the 1970s, the largest U.S. rating agencies have obtained their compensation from issuers (the *issuer pays* model). Some observers argue that such compensation produces an incentive for a favorable rating (*ratings inflation*). Accordingly, one proposed legislative reform would require issuers to pay an independent authority that selects ratings firms to do their work free of influence from the issuer.

Another concern was that the agencies used a single rating scale to represent default probabilities regardless of the liquidity, transparency, and degree of standardization of an issue—a practice that may have led investors to underestimate other important risks.

Bonds with ratings below investment grade are often referred to as **junk bonds** or sometimes more politely as *high-yield bonds* (a reminder that to obtain a high yield, investors must take a large risk).[6] There are two types of junk bonds. The first type, called **fallen angels**, were once investment-grade bonds, but their issuers fell on hard times. The second are cases in which little is known about the risk of the issuer.

MCI WorldCom, the telecommunications giant purchased by Verizon in early 2006, was one company whose bond rating fluctuated between investment grade and junk. When it began issuing bonds in 1997, the firm was below investment grade (Moody's Ba). MCI WorldCom saw its rating rise for several years, until it peaked as a Moody's A from mid-1999 to the end of 2001. Taking advantage of this investment-grade rating, MCI WorldCom issued $11.8 billion worth of bonds in May 2001. Just one year later, MCI WorldCom's rating dropped back to where it started, Ba, and its 10-year bonds were trading for 44 cents on the dollar, less than half of their initial prices. By mid-2002, as the company filed for bankruptcy, its bonds had fallen one more notch to B.

Sovereigns can be "fallen angels," too. For example, bonds issued by Greece were rated A (investment grade) as recently as the spring of 2010. As the financial crisis in the euro area intensified, the rating agencies repeatedly lowered Greece's credit rating (eventually to the lowest grade, C) in the run-up to its March 2012 default. Frequent, sharp downgrades during such periods of market stress raise doubts about the usefulness of the ratings in anticipating default (see also Lessons from the Crisis: Rating Agencies above).

[6]*Junk bond* is an informal term used to mean a highly speculative security that has a low rating; it has no exact or formal definition.

Indeed, for investment-grade sovereign debt, Moody's puts the five-year default rate, weighted by issuer, at nearly 3 percent. The one-year-ahead record is better: 12 months before their default, no sovereign issuer was still rated as investment grade, but more than 1 percent of corporate defaults were.[7]

Material changes in a firm's or government's financial conditions precipitate changes in its debt ratings. The rating services are constantly monitoring events and announcing modifications to their views on the creditworthiness of borrowers. If a particular business or country encounters problems (as occurs with some frequency), Moody's and Standard & Poor's will lower that issuer's bond rating in what is called a **ratings downgrade**. Typically, an average of nearly 2 percent of bonds that begin a year in an investment-grade category—Aaa to Baa—have their ratings downgraded to one of the noninvestment grades. The MCI WorldCom downgrade in May 2002 reflected the agencies' view that the company had too much debt and (given the dismal state of the telecommunications industry at the time) little opportunity to reduce it. **Ratings upgrades** occur as well. Roughly 3 percent of Aa-rated bonds are upgraded to Aaa each year.[8]

Commercial Paper Ratings

Commercial paper is a short-term version of a bond. Both corporations and governments issue commercial paper. Because the borrower offers no collateral, this form of debt is *unsecured.* So only the most creditworthy companies can issue it.[9] Moreover, the amount of commercial paper outstanding plunged during the financial crisis of 2007–2009: After peaking in mid-2007 at $2.1 trillion, it dropped below $1 trillion by 2011. Nevertheless, financial companies, such as Bank of America and Goldman Sachs, still issued the vast majority of it.

Like a U.S. Treasury bill, commercial paper is issued on a discount basis, as a zero-coupon bond that specifies a single future payment with no associated coupon payments. For legal reasons, commercial paper usually has a maturity of less than 270 days.[10] More than one-third of all commercial paper is held by money-market mutual funds (MMMFs), which require very short-term assets with immediate liquidity. Most commercial paper is issued with a maturity of 5 to 45 days and is used exclusively for short-term financing.

The rating agencies rate the creditworthiness of commercial paper issuers in the same way as bond issuers. Again, Moody's and Standard & Poor's have parallel rating schemes that differ solely in their labeling (see Table 7.2). By some estimates, 90 percent of issuers carry Moody's P-1 rating and another 9 percent are rated P-2— the P stands for **prime-grade commercial paper**. Speculative-grade commercial paper does exist, but not because it was originally issued as such.

[7]For an in-depth assessment of sovereign credit ratings, see International Monetary Fund, *Global Financial Stability Report*, "The Uses and Abuses of Sovereign Credit Ratings" (October 2010, Chapter 3). Moody's issuer-weighted cumulative default rate estimates appear in Exhibit 10 of its report "Sovereign Default and Recovery Rates, 1983-2012," June 12, 2013.

[8]Based on authors' estimates for the period 1983 to 2012 using Moody's *Annual Default Study: Corporate Default and Recovery Rates, 1920–2012*, February 28, 2013, Exhibits 29 and 41.

[9]Recall that collateral is something of value pledged by the borrower that the lender could sell if the loan is not repaid. See also Lessons from the Crisis: Asset-Backed Commercial Paper on page 171.

[10]As described in detail by Thomas K. Hahn, "Commercial Paper," *Instruments of the Money Market* (Federal Reserve Bank of Richmond, 1998, Chapter 9), the Securities Act of 1933 generally requires registration of securities, a time-consuming and expensive process. But Section 3(a) (3) of the act exempts securities with less than 270 days to maturity as long as they meet certain requirements.

Table 7.2 Commercial Paper Ratings

	Moody's	Standard & Poor's	Description	Examples of Issuers with Commercial Paper Outstanding in 2012
Investment or Prime Grade	P-1	A-1+, A-1	Strong likelihood of timely repayment.	Coca-Cola General Electric Procter & Gamble
	P-2	A-2	Satisfactory degree of safety for timely repayment.	General Mills Time Warner
	P-3	A-3	Adequate degree of safety for timely repayment.	Alcoa
Speculative, below Prime Grade		B, C	Capacity for repayment is small relative to higher-rated issuers.	
Defaulted		D		

SOURCE: *Thomas K. Hahn, "Commercial Paper,"* Instruments of the Money Market, *Chapter 9, Federal Reserve Bank of Richmond, 1998; www.moodys.com; and www.standardandpoors.com.*

The Impact of Ratings on Yields

RISK

Bond ratings are designed to reflect default risk: The lower the rating, the higher the risk of default. We know investors require compensation for risk, so everything else held equal, the lower a bond's rating, the lower its price and the higher its yield. From Chapter 6 we know that we can think about changes in risk as shifts in the demand for bonds. Increases in risk will reduce investor demand for bonds at every price, shifting the demand curve to the left, decreasing the equilibrium price and increasing the yield (see Figure 7.1).

The easiest way to understand the quantitative impact of ratings on bond yields is to compare different bonds that are identical in every way except for the issuer's credit rating. U.S. Treasury issues have long served as a standard for comparison because they are viewed as having little default risk. This is why they are commonly referred to as **benchmark bonds**, and the yields on other bonds are measured in terms of the **spread over Treasuries**. (Remember from the definition in Chapter 5: Risk is measured relative to a benchmark. For bonds, the most common benchmark is U.S. Treasury bonds.)

We can think of any bond yield as the sum of two parts: the yield on the benchmark U.S. Treasury bond plus a default-risk premium, sometimes called a **risk spread**.

$$\text{Bond yield} = \text{U.S. Treasury yield} + \text{Default risk premium} \qquad (1)$$

If bond ratings properly reflect the probability of default, then the lower the rating of the issuer, the higher the default-risk premium in equation (1). This way of thinking about bond yields provides us with a second insight: When Treasury yields move, all other yields move with them.

These two predictions—that interest rates on a variety of bonds will move together and that lower-rated bonds will have higher yields—are both borne out by the data. To see this, let's look at a plot of the **risk structure of interest rates**. Panel A of Figure 7.2 (on page 170) shows the yield to maturity for long-term bonds with three different

YOUR FINANCIAL WORLD
Your Credit Rating

Companies aren't the only ones with credit ratings; you have one, too. Have you ever wondered how someone decides whether to give you a loan or a credit card? The answer is that there are companies keeping track of your financial information. They rate your creditworthiness, and they know more about you than you might think. Credit-rating companies know all about your credit cards, your car loan or mortgage (if you have one), and whether you pay your bills on time. All of this information is combined in something called a *credit score*. If you have low levels of debt and pay your bills on time, you have a high credit score.

You care about your credit score; here's why. Lenders use credit scores to calculate the interest rate they charge on a loan. With a top credit score, a four-year, $10,000 car loan might have an interest rate of 5 percent and monthly payments of $230. But if your credit score was low, because you missed a payment on a credit card or paid your utility bill late, then the interest rate could be as high as 15 percent, which would mean monthly payments as much as $50 higher. The same principle applies to home mortgages; the better your credit score, the lower the interest rate. It pays to pay all your bills on time.*

*Ironically, someone who has never had a credit card and never owed anyone any money has no credit history at all and so will have a low credit score. You cannot start too soon in creating a record as a good credit risk. And you are entitled to a free annual credit report from each of the credit-rating companies. To find out how to get it, go to www.annualcreditreport.com.

ratings: 10-year U.S. Treasury, Moody's Aaa rated, and Moody's Baa long-term bonds. As you can see from the figure, all of these yields move together. When the U.S. Treasury yield goes up or down, the Aaa and Baa yields do too. While the default-risk premiums do fluctuate—rising particularly in periods of financial stress—changes in the U.S. Treasury yield account for most of the movement in the Aaa and Baa bond yields. Furthermore, the yield on the higher-rated U.S. Treasury bond is consistently the lowest. In fact, over the years from 1971 to 2012, the 10-year U.S. Treasury bond yield averaged more than a full percentage point below the yield on Aaa bonds and two percentage points below the yield on Baa bonds.

How important is one or two percentage points in yield? To see, we can do a simple computation. At an interest rate of 5 percent, the present value of a $100 payment made 10 years from now is $61.39. If the interest rate rose to 7 percent, the value of this same promise would decline to $50.83. So a two-percentage point increase in the yield, from 5 percent to 7 percent, lowers the value of the promise of $100 in 10 years by $10.56, or 17 percent!

From the viewpoint of the borrower, an increase in the interest rate from 5 percent to 7 percent means paying $7 rather than $5 per year for each $100 borrowed. That is a 40 percent difference. Clearly, ratings are crucial to corporations' ability to raise financing. Whenever a company's bond rating declines, the cost of funds goes up, impairing the company's ability to finance new ventures.[11]

Figure 7.1 The Effect of an Increase in Risk on Equilibrium in the Bond Market

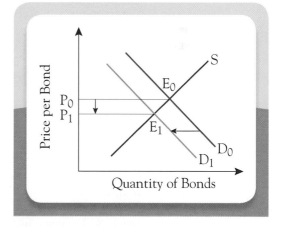

Increased risk reduces the demand for the bond at every price, shifting the demand curve to the left from D_0 to D_1. The result is a decline in the equilibrium price and quantity in the market. Importantly, the price falls from P_0 to P_1, so the yield on the bond must rise.

[11]The same is true for individuals. Consider the impact on the monthly payments required to service a thirty-year, $100,000 mortgage. At an interest rate of 5 percent, payments would be approximately $530 per month. If the interest rate were to increase to 7 percent, the required monthly payments would rise to more than $650. You can compute these amounts using the formulas in the Appendix to Chapter 4.

Figure 7.2 The Risk Structure of Interest Rates

A. Comparing Long-Term Interest Rates

— 10-Year Treasury — Moody's Aaa — Moody's Baa

B. Comparing Short-Term Interest Rates

— Treasury Bills — Commercial Paper

SOURCE: *Board of Governors of the Federal Reserve System. (FRED data codes: GS10, AAA, BAA, CPN3M [since 1997], and TB3MS).*

What is true for long-term bond yields is true for short-term bond yields; they move together, and lower ratings imply higher yields. Compare the yields on three-month U.S. Treasury bills with those on A-1/P-1 commercial paper of the same maturity (see Panel B of Figure 7.2). The two yields clearly move together, and the U.S. Treasury bill yield is always lower than the yield on commercial paper. From 1971 to 2012, the spread of commercial paper over U.S. Treasury bills averaged nearly six-tenths of one percentage point, or roughly 60 *basis points*. (Recall from Chapter 6 that a basis point is one hundredth of a percentage point, or 0.01 percent.)

The lesson is clear; investors must be compensated for assuming risk. The less creditworthy the borrower, the higher the risk of default, the lower the borrower's rating, and the higher the cost of borrowing. And the lower the rating of the bond or commercial paper, the higher the yield.

LESSONS FROM THE CRISIS
ASSET-BACKED COMMERCIAL PAPER

Asset-backed commercial paper (ABCP) is a short-term liability with a maturity of up to 270 days. Unlike most commercial paper, which is unsecured, ABCP is collateralized by assets that financial institutions place in a special portfolio. As we saw in Chapter 3, collateral is something of value that is pledged to pay a loan (in this case, CP) in the event that the borrower does not make the required payments. ABCP has existed for decades, but it played a special role in the housing boom that preceded the financial crisis of 2007–2009.

To lower their costs and limit their own asset holding, some large banks created firms (a form of *shadow bank*) that issued ABCP and used the money to buy mortgages and other loans (see Chapter 3, Lessons from the Crisis: Shadow Banks). The payment stream generated by the loans was used to compensate the holders of the ABCP. This off-balance-sheet financing also allowed banks to boost leverage and take more risk. When mortgage volume surged in the housing bubble, these shadow banks issued more ABCP to finance their rapid expansion.

The mismatch between the long-term maturity of the assets (mortgages) and the short-term maturity of the liabilities (ABCP) posed an underappreciated threat to the ABCP issuers. When the ABCP matures, the issuers have to borrow (or to sell the underlying assets) to be able to return the principal to the ABCP holders. The risk was that the issuers would be unable to borrow—that is, they faced *rollover* risk. If they were also unable to sell the long-term assets easily, these shadow banks would face failure.

ABCP rollover risk played an early role in the financial crisis of 2007–2009. When the value of some mortgages became highly uncertain in 2007, purchasers of ABCP grew anxious that the assets backing their commercial paper might plunge in value. Because they had erroneously viewed ABCP as a very low risk security, the sudden awareness of risk caused a virtual halt to ABCP purchases. Outstanding commercial paper from ABCP issuers began to plunge in the third quarter of 2007, sinking from a peak of more than $900 billion to less than $100 billion by 2012.

Firms that had issued ABCP faced an immediate threat to their survival. Unable to sell their assets or to obtain other funding, some failed. In other cases, banks chose to rescue their shadow banks to limit legal risks and reputational damage. As a result, those banks faced heightened liquidity needs and pressures to sell assets precisely when the cost of funds had surged and asset prices were plunging. The risk that they had sought to shift off balance sheet returned at the worst possible time—in the midst of a crisis.

Differences in Tax Status and Municipal Bonds

Default risk is not the only factor that affects the return on a bond. The second important factor is taxes. Bondholders must pay income tax on the interest income they receive from owning privately issued bonds. These are **taxable bonds**. In contrast, the coupon payments on bonds issued by state and local governments, called **municipal** or **tax-exempt bonds**, are specifically exempt from taxation.[12]

The general rule in the United States is that the interest income from bonds issued by one government is not taxed by another government, although the issuing government may tax it. The interest income from U.S. Treasury securities is taxed by the federal government, which issued them, but not by state or local governments. In the same way, the federal government is precluded from taxing interest on municipal bonds. In an effort to make their bonds even more attractive to investors, however, state and local governments usually choose not to tax the interest on their own bonds, exempting it from all income taxes.

How does a tax exemption affect a bond's yield? Bondholders care about the return they actually receive, after tax authorities have taken their cut. If investors expect to receive a payment of $6 for holding a bond but know they will lose $1.80 of it in taxes, they will act as if the return on the investment is only $4.20. That is, investors base their decisions on the *after-tax yield*.

[12]Municipal bonds come in two varieties. Some are general-obligation bonds backed by the taxing power of the governmental issuer. Others are revenue bonds issued to fund specific projects; these are backed by revenues from the project or operator.

Calculating the tax implications for bond yields is straightforward. Consider a one-year $100 face value taxable bond with a coupon rate of 6 percent. This is a promise to pay $106 in one year. If the bond is selling at par, at a price of $100, then the yield to maturity is 6 percent. From the point of view of the government issuers, the bondholder receives $6 in taxable income at maturity. If the tax rate is 30 percent, the tax on that income is $1.80, so the $100 bond yields $104.20 after taxes. In other words, at a 30 percent tax rate, a 6 percent taxable bond yields the equivalent of 4.2 percent.

This same calculation works for any interest rate and any bond, which allows us to derive a relationship between the yields on taxable and tax-exempt bonds. The rule is that the yield on a tax-exempt bond equals the taxable bond yield times one minus the tax rate:

$$\text{Tax-exempt bond yield} = (\text{Taxable bond yield}) \times (1 - \text{Tax rate}) \quad (2)$$

For an investor with a 30 percent tax rate, then, we can compute the tax-exempt yield on a 10 percent bond by multiplying 10 percent times $(1 - 0.3)$, or 7 percent. Overall, the higher the tax rate, the wider the gap between the yields on taxable and tax-exempt bonds.

The Term Structure of Interest Rates

TIME

A bond's tax status and rating aren't the only factors that affect its yield. In fact, bonds with the same default rate and tax status but different maturity dates usually have different yields. Why? The answer is that long-term bonds are like a composite of a series of short-term bonds, so their yield depends on what people expect to happen in years to come. In this section, we will develop a framework for thinking about *future interest rates.*

The relationship among bonds with the same risk characteristics but different maturities is called the **term structure of interest rates**.

In studying the term structure of interest rates, we will focus our attention on Treasury yields; see Figure 7.3. Comparing information on 3-month (the blue line) and 10-year (the green line) Treasury issues, we can draw three conclusions:

1. *Interest rates of different maturities tend to move together.* The bulk of the variation in short- and long-term interest rates is in the same direction. That is, the blue and green lines clearly move together.
2. *Yields on short-term bonds are more volatile than yields on long-term bonds.* The blue line moves over a broader range than the green line.
3. *Long-term yields tend to be higher than short-term yields.* The green line usually, *but not always,* lies above the blue line.

Default risk and tax differences cannot explain these relationships. What can? We will examine two explanations, the expectations hypothesis and the liquidity premium theory.

The Expectations Hypothesis

Over the years, economists have proposed and discarded numerous theories to explain the term structure of interest rates. We can benefit from their hard work and ignore all the ones they found wanting. The first one we will focus on, called the **expectations hypothesis of the term structure**, is straightforward and intuitive. If we think about yields as the sum of a risk-free interest rate and a risk premium, the expectations hypothesis focuses on the first of those elements. It begins with the observation that the risk-free interest rate can be computed, assuming there is no uncertainty about the

Figure 7.3   The Term Structure of Treasury Interest Rates

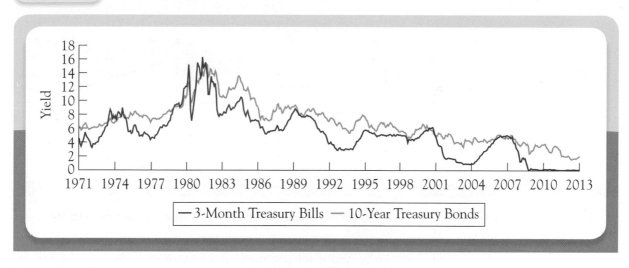

SOURCE: *Board of Governors of the Federal Reserve System. (FRED data codes: TB3MS and GS10).*

future. That is, we know not just the yield on bonds available today but the yields that will be available on bonds next year, the year after that, and so on.

To understand the implications of this statement, think about an investor who wishes to purchase a bond and hold it for two years. Because there is no uncertainty, the investor knows the yield today on a bond with two years to maturity, as well as the yields on a one-year bond purchased today and on a second one-year bond purchased one year from now. Being sure about all of these, the investor will be indifferent between holding the two-year bond and holding a series of two one-year bonds. *Certainty means that bonds of different maturities are perfect substitutes for each other.* This is the essence of the expectations hypothesis.

To see how this works, assume that the current one-year interest rate is 5 percent. The expectations hypothesis implies that the current two-year interest rate should equal the average of 5 percent and the one-year interest rate one year in the future. If that future interest rate is 7 percent, then the current two-year interest rate will be $(5 + 7)/2 = 6\%$.

According to the expectations hypothesis, then, when interest rates are expected to rise in the future, long-term interest rates will be higher than short-term interest rates. This means that the **yield curve**, which plots the yield to maturity on the vertical axis and the time to maturity on the horizontal axis, will slope up. (*The Wall Street Journal*'s Credit Market column often includes a plot of a yield curve for U.S. Treasury issues like the one shown in Figure 7.4.) Analogously, the expectations hypothesis implies that if interest rates are expected to fall, the yield

Figure 7.4   The U.S. Treasury Yield Curve

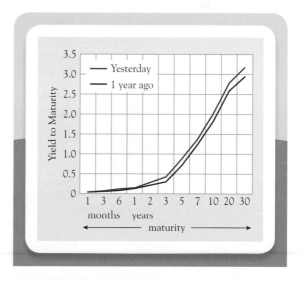

The figure plots the yields on Treasury bills and bonds for January 31, 2013.

SOURCE: *Board of Governors of the Federal Reserve System.*

Figure 7.5   The Expectations Hypothesis and Expectations of Future Short-term Interest Rates

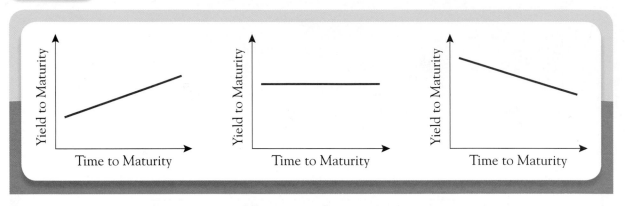

Interest rates are expected to **rise**.   Interest rates are expected to **remain unchanged**.   Interest rates are expected to **fall**.

curve will slope down. And if interest rates are expected to remain unchanged, the yield curve will be flat. (See Figure 7.5.)

If bonds of different maturities are perfect substitutes for each other, then we can construct investment strategies that must have the same yields. Let's look at the investor with a two-year horizon. Two possible strategies are available to this investor:

A. Invest in a two-year bond and hold it to maturity. We will call the interest rate associated with this investment i_{2t} ("i" stands for the interest rate, "2" for two years, and "t" for the time period, which is today). Investing one dollar in this bond will yield $(1 + i_{2t})(1 + i_{2t})$ two years later.

B. Invest in two one-year bonds, one today and a second when the first one matures. The one-year bond purchased today has an interest rate of i_{1t} ("1" stands for one year). The one-year bond purchased one year from now has an interest rate of i_{1t+1}^e, where the "$t+1$" stands for one time period past period t, or next year. The "e," which stands for *expected*, indicates that this is the one-year interest rate investors *expect* to obtain one year ahead. Because we are assuming that the future is known, this expectation is certain to be correct. A dollar invested using this strategy will return $(1 + i_{1t})(1 + i_{1t+1}^e)$ in two years.

The expectations hypothesis tells us that investors will be indifferent between these two strategies. (Remember, the bonds are perfect substitutes for each other.) Indifference between strategies A and B means that they must have the same return, so

$$(1 + i_{2t})(1 + i_{2t}) = (1 + i_{1t})(1 + i_{1t+1}^e) \qquad (3)$$

Expanding equation (3) and taking an approximation that is very accurate, we can write the two-year interest rate as the average of the current and future expected one-year interest rates:[13]

$$i_{2t} = \frac{i_{1t} + i_{1t+1}^e}{2} \qquad (4)$$

---

[13]Expanding (3) gives us $2i_{2t} + i_{2t}^2 = i_{1t} + i_{1t+1}^e + (i_{1t})(i_{1t+1}^e)$. The squared term on the left-hand side and the product term on the right-hand side of this equation are small, and their difference is even smaller. Using the example of 5 percent and 7 percent for the one-year interest rates, we can see that ignoring the two product terms means ignoring $((.06)^2 - (.05^*.07))/2 = (0.0036 - 0.0035)/2 = 0.00005$, an error of 0.005 percentage points.

The Expectations Hypothesis of the Term Structure:

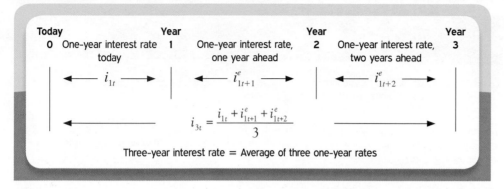

If the one-year interest rate today is i_{1t} = 5%, one-year interest rate, one year ahead is i^e_{1t+1} = 6%, and the one-year interest rate two years ahead, i^e_{1t+2} = 7%, then the expectation hypothesis tells us that the three-year interest rate will be i_{3t} = (5% + 6% + 7%)/3 = 6%.

For a comparison between a three-year bond and three one-year bonds, we get

$$i_{3t} = \frac{i_{1t} + i^e_{1t+1} + i^e_{1t+2}}{3} \tag{5}$$

where the notation i_{3t} stands for a three-year interest rate and i^e_{1t+2} for the expected one-year interest rate two years from now.

The general statement of the expectations hypothesis is that the interest rate on a bond with *n* years to maturity is the average of *n* expected future one-year interest rates:

$$i_{nt} = \frac{i_{1t} + i^e_{1t+1} + i^e_{1t+2} + \ldots + i^e_{1t+n-1}}{n} \tag{6}$$

What are the implications of this mathematical expression? Does the *expectations hypothesis of the term structure of interest rates* explain the three observations we started with? Let's look at each one.

1. The expectations hypothesis tells us that long-term bond yields are all averages of expected future short-term yields—the same set of short-term interest rates—so *interest rates of different maturities will move together.* From equation (6) we see that if the current one-year interest rate, i_{1t}, changes, all the yields at higher maturities will change with it.

2. The expectations hypothesis implies that *yields on short-term bonds will be more volatile than yields on long-term bonds.* Because long-term interest rates are averages of a sequence of expected future short-term rates, if the current 3-month interest rate moves, it will have only a small impact on the 10-year interest rate. Again, look at equation (6).[14]

---

[14]Take a simple example in which the one-year and two-year interest rates, i_{1t} and i_{2t}, are both 5 percent. If the one-year interest rate increases to 7 percent, then the two-year interest rate will rise to 6 percent. The two move together, and the short-term rate is more volatile than the long-term rate.

TOOLS OF THE TRADE
Reading Charts

A picture can be worth a thousand words, but only if you know what it represents. To decode charts and graphs, use these strategies:

1. *Read the title of the chart.* This point may seem trivial, but titles are often very descriptive and can give you a good start in understanding a chart.

2. *Read the label on the horizontal axis.* Does the chart show the movements in a stock price or in the interest rate over minutes, hours, days, weeks, months, or years? Are the numbers spaced evenly?

Look at Figure 7.6, a sample of the Treasury yield curve that appears in *The Wall Street Journal* every day. The horizontal axis extends from three months to 30 years, but the increments are not evenly spaced. In fact, a distance that starts out as three months on the left-hand corner becomes over 10 years at the far right. The axis is drawn in this way for two reasons. First, it focuses the reader's eye on the shorter end of the yield curve. Second, the telescoped axis narrows so that it takes up less space.

Interestingly, this particular yield curve shows a slight downward slope from three months to one year, followed by a steep upward slope. This pattern suggests that investors expected interest rates to decline sharply for the next year and then rise after that, which is exactly what happened.

3. *Read the label on the vertical axis.* What is the range of the data? This is a crucial piece of information because most charts are made to fill the space available. As a result, small movements can appear to be very large. Compare Panel A and Panel B of Figure 7.7 on page 177 on inflation. The first shows the percentage change in the consumer price index from 1960 to 2012; the

second shows the same data starting 25 years later, in 1985.

In Panel A, the vertical axis ranges from −4 percent to 16 percent; in Panel B, it covers only −3 to 7 percent. To fill the second panel visually, the artist changed the vertical scale.

Figure 7.6   Treasury Yield Curve

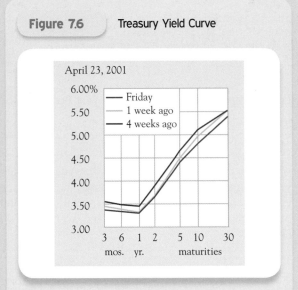

SOURCE: *The Wall Street Journal,* April 23, 2001. Used with permission of Dow Jones & Company, Inc. via Copyright Clearance Center.

3. The expectations hypothesis *cannot* explain why *long-term yields are normally higher than short-term yields* because it implies that the yield curve slopes upward only when interest rates are expected to rise. To explain why the yield curve normally slopes upward, the expectations hypothesis would suggest that interest rates are normally expected to rise. But as the data in Figure 7.3 show, interest rates have been trending downward for nearly 30 years, so anyone constantly forecasting interest-rate increases would have been sorely disappointed.

The expectations hypothesis has gotten us two-thirds of the way toward understanding the term structure of interest rates. By ignoring risk and assuming that investors view short- and long-term bonds as perfect substitutes, we have explained why yields at different maturities move together and why short-term interest rates are more volatile than long-term rates. But we have failed to explain why the yield curve normally slopes upward. To understand this, we need to extend the expectations hypothesis to include risk. After all, we all know that long-term bonds are riskier than short-term

Taking only a superficial look at these two charts can be misleading. Without noticing the difference in their vertical scales, we could conclude that the decline of inflation from 2008 to 2009 was as dramatic as the decline of inflation from 1980 to 1983. But, on closer inspection, inflation fell from 5.4 percent to −2.0 percent in the recent episode, while in the 1980–1983 period, it dropped from 14.6 percent to 2.5 percent. A proper reading of the charts leads to the correct conclusion that the earlier decline was nearly twice as large as the recent one.

| **Figure 7.7** | U.S. Consumer Price Inflation |

SOURCE: *Bureau of Labor Statistics (FRED data code: CPIAUCSL).*

bonds. Integrating this observation into our analysis will give us the *liquidity premium theory* of the term structure of interest rates.

The Liquidity Premium Theory

Throughout our discussion of bonds, we emphasized that even default-free bonds are risky because of uncertainty about inflation and future interest rates. What are the implications of these risks for our understanding of the term structure of interest rates? The answer is that risk is the key to understanding the usual upward *slope* of the yield curve. Long-term interest rates are typically higher than short-term interest rates because long-term bonds are riskier than short-term bonds. Bondholders face both inflation and interest-rate risk. The longer the term of the bond, the greater both types of risk.

The reason for the increase in inflation risk over time is clear-cut. Remember that bondholders care about the purchasing power of the return—the *real* return—they receive from a bond, not just the nominal dollar value of the coupon payments. Computing the real return from the nominal return requires a forecast of future inflation, or *expected* future inflation. For a three-month bond, an investor need only be concerned with inflation over the next three months. For a 10-year bond, however, computation of the real return requires a forecast of inflation over the next decade.

RISK

In summary, uncertainty about inflation creates uncertainty about a bond's real return, making the bond a risky investment. The further we look into the future, the greater the uncertainty about inflation. We are more uncertain about the level of inflation several years from now than about the level of inflation a few months from now, which implies that *a bond's inflation risk increases with its time to maturity.*

What about interest-rate risk? Interest-rate risk arises from a mismatch between the investor's investment horizon and a bond's time to maturity. Remember that if a bondholder plans to sell a bond prior to maturity, changes in the interest rate (which cause bond prices to move) generate capital gains or losses. The longer the term of the bond, the greater the price changes for a given change in interest rates and the larger the potential for capital losses.

Because some holders of long-term bonds will want to sell their bonds before they mature, interest-rate risk concerns them. These investors require compensation for the risk they take in buying long-term bonds. As in the case of inflation, the risk increases with the term to maturity, so the compensation must increase with it.

What are the implications of including risk in our model of the term structure of interest rates? To answer this question, we can think about a bond yield as having two parts, one that is risk free and another that is a risk premium. The expectations hypothesis explains the risk-free part, and inflation and interest-rate risk explain the risk premium. Together they form the **liquidity premium theory of the term structure** of interest rates. Adding the risk premium to equation (6), we can express this theory mathematically as

$$i_{nt} = rp_n + \frac{i_{1t} + i^e_{1t+1} + i^e_{1t+2} + \ldots + i^e_{1t+n-1}}{n} \tag{7}$$

where rp_n is the risk premium associated with an *n*-year bond. The larger the risk, the higher the risk premium, rp_n, is. Because risk rises with maturity, rp_n increases with *n*, the yield on a long-term bond includes a larger risk premium than the yield on a short-term bond.

To get some idea of the size of the risk premium rp_n, we can look at the average slope of the term structure over a long period. From 1985 to mid-2013, the difference between the interest rate on a 10-year Treasury bond and that on a 3-month Treasury bill averaged nearly two percentage points. It is important to keep in mind that this risk premium will vary over time. For example, if inflation is very stable or the variability of the real interest rate were to fall, then the 10-year bond risk premium could easily fall below one percentage point.

Can the liquidity premium theory explain all three of our conclusions about the term structure of interest rates? The answer is yes. Like the expectations hypothesis, the liquidity premium theory predicts that *interest rates of different maturities will move together* and that *yields on short-term bonds will be more volatile than yields on long-term bonds.* And by adding a risk premium that grows with time to maturity, it explains why *long-term yields are higher than short-term yields.* Because the risk premium increases with time to maturity, the liquidity premium theory tells us that the yield curve will normally slope upward; only rarely will it lie flat or slope downward. (A flat yield curve means that interest rates are expected to fall; a downward-sloping yield curve suggests that the financial markets are expecting a significant decline in interest rates.)

APPLYING THE CONCEPT
THE FLIGHT TO QUALITY

Standing in the middle of an open field during a thunderstorm is a good way to get hurt, so few people do it. Instead, they take shelter. Investors do exactly the same thing during financial storms; they look for a safe place to put their investments until the storm blows over. In practical terms, that means selling risky investments and buying the safest instruments they can: U.S. Treasury bills, notes, and bonds. An increase in the demand for government bonds coupled with a decrease in the demand for virtually everything else is called a **flight to quality**. When it happens, there is a dramatic increase in the difference between the yields on safe and risky bonds—the *risk spread* rises.

When the government of Russia defaulted on its bonds in August 1998, the shock set off an almost unprecedented flight to quality. Yields on U.S. Treasuries plummeted, while those on corporate bonds rose. Risk spreads widened quickly; the difference between U.S. Treasury bills and commercial paper rates more than doubled, from its normal level of half a percentage point to over one percentage point. The debt of countries with emerging markets was particularly hard hit.

This flight to quality was what William McDonough called "the most serious financial crisis since World War II" (see the opening of this chapter). Because people wanted to hold only U.S. Treasury securities, the financial markets had ceased to function properly. Mr. McDonough worried that the problems in the financial markets would spread to the economy as a whole. They didn't in the 1998 episode, but they did in the much larger financial crisis of 2007–2009.

The Information Content of Interest Rates

The risk and term structure of interest rates contain useful information about overall economic conditions. These indicators are helpful in evaluating both the present health of the economy and its likely future course. Risk spreads provide one type of information, the term structure another. In the following sections we will apply what we have just learned about interest rates to recent U.S. economic history and show how forecasters use these tools.

Information in the Risk Structure of Interest Rates

When the overall growth rate of the economy slows or turns negative, it strains private businesses, increasing the risk that corporations will be unable to meet their financial obligations. The immediate impact of an impending recession, then, is to raise the risk premium on privately issued bonds. Importantly, though, an economic slowdown or recession does not affect the risk of holding government bonds.

The increased risk of default is not the same for all firms. The impact of a recession on companies with high bond ratings is usually small, so the spread between U.S. Treasuries and Aaa-rated bonds of the same maturity is not likely to move by much. But for issuers whose finances were precarious prior to the downturn, the effect is quite different. Those borrowers who were least likely to meet their payment obligations when times were good are even less likely to meet them when times turn bad. There is a real chance that they will fail to make interest payments. Of course, firms for whom even the slightest negative development might mean disaster are the ones that issue low-grade bonds. The lower the initial grade of the bond, the more the default-risk premium rises as general economic conditions deteriorate. The spread between U.S. Treasury bonds and junk bonds widens the most.

Panel A of Figure 7.8 shows annual GDP growth over four decades superimposed on shading that shows the dates of recessions. (We'll learn more about recession dating in Chapter 22.) Notice that during the shaded periods, growth is usually negative. In Panel B of Figure 7.8, GDP growth is drawn as the red line and the green line is the spread between yields on Baa-rated bonds and U.S. Treasury bonds. Note that the two lines move in opposite directions. (The correlation between the two series is −0.56.) That is, when the risk spread rises, output falls. The risk spread provides a

Figure 7.8 The Risk Spread and GDP Growth

SOURCE: *Bureau of Economic Analysis and Board of Governors of the Federal Reserve System. GDP growth is the percentage change from the same quarter of the previous year, while the yield spread is the difference between the average yield on Baa and 10-year U.S. Treasury bonds during the quarter. Shaded periods denote recessions. (FRED data codes: GDPC1, BAA, GS10, and USREC.)*

useful indicator of general economic activity, and because financial markets operate every day, this information is available well before GDP data, which is published only once every three months. During the financial crisis of 2007–2009, the spread reached its widest level (5.6 percentage points) since the Great Depression of the 1930s.

Information in the Term Structure of Interest Rates

Like information on the risk structure of interest rates, information on the term structure—particularly the slope of the yield curve—helps us to forecast general economic conditions. Recall that according to the expectations hypothesis, long-term interest rates contain information about expected future short-term interest rates. And according to the liquidity premium theory, the yield curve usually slopes upward. The key term in this statement is *usually.* On rare occasions, short-term interest rates exceed long-term yields. When they do, the term structure is said to be *inverted,* and the yield curve slopes downward.

| Figure 7.9 | The Term Spread and GDP Growth |

SOURCE: *Bureau of Economic Analysis and Board of Governors of the Federal Reserve System. GDP growth is the percentage change from the same quarter of the previous year, while the term spread is the difference between the average yield on 10-year U.S. Treasury bond and a 3-month U.S. Treasury bill during the quarter. In Panel B, the spread is lagged one year. Shaded periods denote recessions. (FRED data codes: GDPC1, GS10, TB3MS, and USREC).*

An **inverted yield curve** is a valuable forecasting tool because it predicts a general economic slowdown. Because the yield curve slopes upward even when short-term yields are expected to remain constant—it's the average of expected future short-term interest rates plus a risk premium—an inverted yield curve signals an expected fall in short-term interest rates. If interest rates are comparatively high, they serve as a brake on real economic activity. As we will see in Part IV, monetary policymakers adjust short-term interest rates in order to influence real economic growth and inflation. When the yield curve slopes downward, it indicates that policy is *tight* because policymakers are attempting to slow economic growth and inflation.

Careful statistical analysis confirms the value of the yield curve as a forecasting tool.[15] Figure 7.9 shows GDP growth and the slope of the yield curve, measured as the

[15]See Arturo Estrella and Frederic S. Mishkin, "The Yield Curve as a Predictor of U.S. Recessions," Federal Reserve Bank of New York, *Current Issues in Economics and Finance* 2, no. 7 (June 1996). To learn what the current yield curve tells about the U.S. economic outlook, see the latest monthly analysis of economists at the Federal Reserve Bank of Cleveland: *www.cleveland.fed.org/research/data/yield_curve.*

IN THE NEWS
Banks Decline Yield Curve Invitation to Party On

By Caroline Baum

January 7, 2010

If you were to stop the average person on the street and ask him about the Treasury yield curve, he'd probably look at you with a blank stare.

"What's a yield curve and why should I care about it?" our passer-by might say.

I'm sure lots of people are wondering the same thing, now that the yield curve is garnering headlines.

The yield curve, or the "term structure of interest rates" in economists' parlance, is the pictorial representation of two points connected by a line.

Not any two points, mind you. One point is a short-term interest rate that is either pegged by the central bank (the federal funds rate) or influenced by it (the yield on the three-month Treasury bill). The other point is some long-term interest rate, the yield on the 10- or 30-year Treasury, whose price is determined by the marketplace.

What's so important about these two particular points?

Simple. These two points, in relationship to one another, succinctly describe the stance of monetary policy….

When short-term rates are below long-term rates, banks have an incentive to go out and lend. "Borrow short, lend long" is the first rule of banking. That's why a steep yield curve is expansionary. It's a means to an end, the end being money and credit creation. The central bank provides the raw material in the form of bank reserves. Depository institutions do—or don't do, in the present situation—the rest.

When the yield curve is inverted, with short rates higher than long rates, bank lending screeches to a halt.

The current ultra-steep yield curve is reminiscent of the early 1990s. Back then, banks were saddled with—what else?—bad real estate loans. History repeats itself with increased frequency.

Courtesy of what was at the time an unheard-of low level for the funds rate (3 percent) and a vertical yield curve, banks bought boatloads of U.S. government securities, which carry a zero risk-based capital weighting. The profit went right to the bottom line. Banks healed themselves, then got back to the business of allocating capital to the private sector.

People who are up in arms about the banks getting free money from the Fed and buying Treasuries should relax. That's how it always works. Banks lend to Uncle Sam so they can lend to you. During recessions, there's never much private-sector credit demand, so the Treasury's appetite satisfies the banks' need for high-quality assets.

As a devout believer in the predictive powers of the spread, I have always challenged those who try to deconstruct it, to mold its meaning to fit the current fashion. History shows the "what" matters more than the "why."

An inverted yield curve is one of the most reliable harbingers of recession. Yet when the curve inverted in 2006 and stayed that way through 2007, the protests went out: This time is different! An influx of foreign capital—the

difference between the 10-year and 3-month yields—what is called a **term spread**. Panel A of Figure 7.9 shows GDP growth (as in Figure 7.8) together with the contemporaneous term spread (the growth and the term spread at the same time). Notice that when the term spread falls, GDP growth tends to fall somewhat later. In fact, when the yield curve becomes inverted, the economy tends to go into a recession roughly a year later. Panel B of Figure 7.9 makes this clear. At each point, GDP growth in the current year (e.g., 1990) is plotted against the slope of the yield curve *one year earlier* (e.g., 1989). The two lines clearly move together; their correlation is +0.42. What the data show is that when the term spread falls, GDP growth tends to fall one year later. The yield curve is a valuable forecasting tool.

An example illustrates the usefulness of this information. In the left-hand panel of Figure 7.10, we can see that on January 23, 2001, the yield curve sloped downward from "savings glut"—is depressing long-term rates. The inverted yield doesn't mean what it usually means.

It wasn't different. It just took longer.

So what is the spread telling us now? All systems are go. With the funds rate close to zero and 10-year Treasuries yielding about 3.8 percent, there's a lot of carry in the curve.

Yet money and credit aren't growing. The M2 money supply, which includes savings and time deposits and money market mutual funds in addition to M1's currency and demand deposits, rose an annualized 1.2 percent from May to November, according to the Fed. The three month annualized increase of 4.2 percent is encouraging if it continues.

On the other side of the balance sheet, bank credit fell an annualized 5 percent in the same six-month period. Loans and leases plunged 9.2 percent at an annual rate.

"Banks aren't lending," says Paul Kasriel, chief economist at the Northern Trust Corp. in Chicago.

At least not to non-government entities. Bank purchases of U.S. Treasury and agency securities rose an annualized 21 percent from May to November. The next step is a return to private lending.

. . .

For all its allure, the yield curve isn't acting as a transmission mechanism just yet. That doesn't mean that it won't. When the financial system is impaired, it takes a steeper curve for a longer period of time to produce an expansion in money and credit—just as it did in the early 90s. The invitation to party stands. Banks have yet to RSVP.

With time, the spread will translate into more borrowing and lending. It's the Fed's job to prevent a trickle from becoming a cascade, fanning what would be the third bubble in two decades.

LESSONS OF THE ARTICLE

The slope of the yield curve can help predict the direction and speed of economic growth. At the beginning of 2010, the yield curve was unusually steep, pointing to a strong economic expansion (see Figure 7.9B, where the steep slope in 2010 is shown as a high value for the term spread). However, in the aftermath of the financial crisis of 2007–2009, lenders were especially cautious about extending credit to risky borrowers, even though risk spreads had narrowed sharply from crisis peaks (see Figure 7.8B). The author argues that it is only a matter of time until the steep yield curve encourages lenders to start lending again. However, the willingness to lend depends on how quickly intermediaries gain confidence that borrowers will repay. Even in 2013, many potential borrowers were still repairing their balance sheets, which had been damaged by the record plunge of U.S. housing prices.

3 months to 5 years, then upward for maturities to 30 years. This pattern indicated that interest rates were expected to fall over the next few years. Eight months later, after monetary policy had eased and the U.S. economy had slowed substantially, the Treasury yield curve sloped upward again (see the right-hand panel of Figure 7.10). At that point, growth was at a virtual standstill, and policymakers were doing everything they could to get the economy moving again. They had reduced interest rates by more than 3 percentage points over a period of less than nine months. Thus, investors expected little in the way of short-term interest-rate reductions. This prediction turned out to be wrong, however; interest rates kept falling after the terrorist attacks of September 11, 2001. They continued to fall through the remainder of 2001 as the economy went into a mild recession.

The yield curve did *not* predict the depth or duration of the recession of 2007–2009. One- and two-year market rates did not anticipate the persistent plunge of overnight

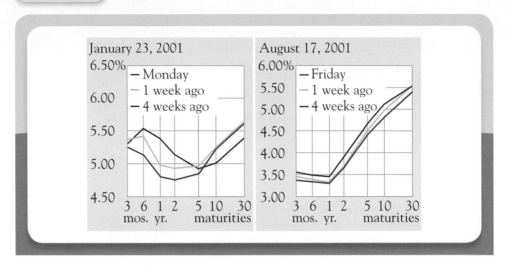

Figure 7.10   The U. S. Treasury Yield Curve in 2001

SOURCE: *Board of Governors of the Federal Reserve System.*

rates. As financial institutions weakened in the crisis, the widening risk spread signaled a severe economic downturn, providing a more useful predictor in this episode.

We started this chapter by asking why different types of bonds have different yields and what it is we can learn from those differences. After a bit of work, we can now see that differences in both risk and time to maturity affect bond yields. The less likely the issuer is to repay or the longer the time to maturity, the riskier a bond and the higher its yield. Even more importantly, both increases in the risk spread and an inverted yield curve suggest troubled economic times ahead.

Terms

Using FRED: Codes for Data in This Chapter

Data Series	FRED Data Code
Moody's Aaa corporate bond yield	AAA
Moody's Baa corporate bond yield	BAA
BofA Merrill Lynch US corporate BBB effective yield	BAMLC0A4CBBBEY
BofA Merrill Lynch US high-yield BB effective yield	BAMLH0A1HYBBEY
BofA Merrill Lynch US high-yield B effective yield	BAMLH0A2HYBEY
BofA Merrill Lynch US high-yield CCC or below effective yield	BAMLH0A3HYCEY
10-year Treasury constant maturity rate	GS10
3-month Treasury bill rate	TB3MS
3-month AA nonfinancial commercial paper rate	CPN3M
Consumer price index	CPIAUCSL
Real GDP	GDPC1
Brazil Treasury bill rate	INTGSTBRM193N

www.mhhe.com/moneyandbanking4e

Chapter Lessons

1. Bond ratings summarize the likelihood that a bond issuer will meet its payment obligations.
    a. Highly rated investment-grade bonds are those with the lowest risk of default.
    b. If a firm encounters financial difficulties, its bond rating may be downgraded.
    c. Commercial paper is the short-term version of a privately issued bond.
    d. Junk bonds are high-risk bonds with very low ratings. Firms that have a high probability of default issue these bonds.
    e. Investors demand compensation for default risk in the form of a risk premium. The higher the risk of default, the lower a bond's rating, the higher its risk premium, and the higher its yield.

2. Municipal bonds are usually exempt from income taxes. Because investors care about the after-tax returns on their investments, these bonds have lower yields than bonds whose interest payments are taxable.

3. The term structure of interest rates is the relationship between yield to maturity and time to maturity. A graph with the yield to maturity on the vertical axis and the time to maturity on the horizontal axis is called the yield curve.
    a. Any theory of the term structure of interest rates must explain three facts:
        i. Interest rates of different maturities move together.
        ii. The yields on short-term bonds are more volatile than the yields on long-term bonds.
        iii. Long-term yields are usually higher than short-term yields.
    b. The expectations hypothesis of the term structure of interest rates states that long-term interest rates are the average of expected future short-term interest rates. This hypothesis explains only the first two facts about the term structure of interest rates.

c. The liquidity premium theory of the term structure of interest rates, which is based on the fact that long-term bonds are riskier than short-term bonds, explains all three facts in part *a*.

4. The risk structure and the term structure of interest rates both signal financial markets' expectations of future economic activity. Specifically, the likelihood of a recession will be higher when
   a. The risk spread, or the range between low- and high-grade bond yields, is wide.
   b. The yield curve slopes downward, or is inverted, so that short-term interest rates are higher than long-term interest rates.

Conceptual and Analytical Problems

1. Consider a firm that issued a large quantity of commercial paper in the period leading to a financial crisis. *(LO1)*
   a. How would you expect the credit rating of the commercial paper to evolve as the crisis unfolds?
   b. Would you alter your prediction if, rather than commercial paper, the firm was instead issuing asset-backed commercial paper?

2. Suppose that a major foreign government defaults on its debt. What, if anything, will happen to the position and slope of the U.S. Treasury yield curve? *(LO2)*

3. What was the connection between house price movements, the growth in subprime mortgages, and securities backed by these mortgages—on the one hand—and—on the other hand—the difficulties encountered by some financial institutions during the 2007–2009 financial crisis? *(LO1)*

4. Suppose that the interest rate on one-year bonds is 4 percent and is expected to be 5 percent in one year and 6 percent in two years. Using the expectations hypothesis, compute the yield curve for the next three years. *(LO2)*

5.* According to the liquidity premium theory, if the yield on both one- and two-year bonds are the same, would you expect the one-year yield in one year's time to be higher, lower, or the same? Explain your answer. *(LO2)*

6. You have $1,000 to invest over an investment horizon of three years. The bond market offers various options. You can buy (i) a sequence of three one-year bonds; (ii) a three-year bond; or (iii) a two-year bond followed by a one-year bond. The current yield curve tells you that the one-year, two-year, and three-year yields to maturity are 3.5 percent, 4.0 percent, and 4.5 percent, respectively. You expect that one-year interest rates will be 4 percent next year and 5 percent the year after that. Assuming annual compounding, compute the return on each of the three investments, and discuss which one you would choose. *(LO2)*

7.* Suppose that the yield curve shows that the one-year bond yield is 3 percent, the two-year yield is 4 percent, and the three-year yield is 5 percent. Assume that the risk premium on the one-year bond is zero, the risk premium on the two-year bond is 1 percent, and the risk premium on the three-year bond is 2 percent. *(LO2)*
   a. What are the expected one-year interest rates next year and the following year?
   b. If the risk premiums were all zero, as in the expectations hypothesis, what would the slope of the yield curve be?

*Indicates more difficult problems

8.* If inflation and interest rates become more volatile, what would you expect to see happen to the slope of the yield curve? *(LO2)*

9. As economic conditions improve in countries with emerging markets, the cost of borrowing funds there tends to fall. Explain why. *(LO3)*

10. Suppose your local government, threatened with bankruptcy, decided to tax the interest income on its own bonds as part of an effort to rectify serious budgetary woes. What would you expect to see happen to the yields on these bonds? *(LO1)*

11.* If, before the change in tax status, the yields on the bonds described in Problem 10 were below the Treasury yield of the same maturity, would you expect this spread to narrow, to disappear, or to change sign after the policy change? Explain your answer. *(LO1)*

12. Suppose the risk premium on U.S. corporate bonds increases. How would the change affect your forecast of future economic activity, and why? *(LO3)*

13. If regulations restricting institutional investors to investment-grade bonds were lifted, what do you think would happen to the spreads between yields on investment-grade and speculative-grade bonds? *(LO1)*

14. Suppose a country with a struggling economy suddenly discovered vast quantities of valuable minerals under government-owned land. How might the government's bond rating be affected? Using the model of demand and supply for bonds, what would you expect to happen to the bond yields of that country's government bonds? *(LO3)*

15. The misrating of mortgage-backed securities by rating agencies contributed to the financial crisis of 2007–2009. List some recommendations you would make to avoid such mistakes in the future. *(LO1)*

16. How do you think the abolition of investor protection laws would affect the risk spread between corporate and government bonds? *(LO1)*

17. You and a friend are reading *The Wall Street Journal* and notice that the Treasury yield curve is slightly upward sloping. Your friend comments that all looks well for the economy but you are concerned that the economy is heading for trouble. Assuming you are both believers in the liquidity premium theory, what might account for your difference of opinion? *(LO3)*

18. Do you think the term spread was an effective predictor of the recession that started in December 2007? Why or why not? *(LO3)*

19.* Given the data in the accompanying table, would you say that this economy is heading for a boom or for a recession? Explain your choice. *(LO3)*

	3-month Treasury-bill	10-year Treasury bond	Baa corporate 10-year bond
January	1.00%	3.0%	7.0%
February	1.05	3.5	7.2
March	1.10	4.0	7.5
April	1.20	4.3	7.7
May	1.25	4.5	7.8

www.mhhe.com/moneyandbanking4e

Scan here for quick access to the hints for these problems. Need a barcode reader? Try ScanLife, available in your app store.

Data Exploration

For detailed instructions on using Federal Reserve Economic Data (FRED) online to answer each of the following problems, visit www.mhhe.com/moneyandbanking4e and click on Student Edition, then Data Exploration Hints.

1. Did the financial crisis of 2007–2009 affect financial and nonfinancial firms to the same extent? For the period beginning in 2006, plot the spread between the interest rates on three-month nonfinancial commercial paper (FRED code: CPN3M) and three-month Treasury bills (FRED code: TB3MS). Plot a similar spread using the interest rates on three-month financial commercial paper (FRED code: CPF3M) and Treasury bills (FRED code: TB3MS). Compare the evolution of these two spreads. *(LO1)*

2. The Federal Reserve Bank of St. Louis publishes a weekly index of financial stress (FRED code: STLFSI) that summarizes strains in financial markets, including liquidity problems. For the period beginning in 1994 plot this index and, as a second line, the difference between the Baa corporate bond yield (FRED code: WBAA) and the 10-year U.S. Treasury bond yield (FRED code: WGS10YR). Does the index STLFSI provide an early warning of stress? *(LO3)*

3. How did the Great Depression (1929–1933) and the Great Recession of 2007–2009 affect expectations of corporate default? To investigate, construct for each of those periods a separate plot of the corporate bond yield spread. For the Depression period, plot from 1930 to 1933 the difference between the Baa corporate bond yield (FRED code: BAA) and the long-term government bond yield (FRED code: LTGOVTBD). For the Great Recession, plot from 2007 to 2009 the difference between the Baa yield (FRED code: BAA) and the 10-year Treasury bond yield (FRED code: GS10). Compare the plots. *(LO1)*

4. How reliably does an inverted yield curve anticipate a recession? How far in advance? Plot from 1970 (as in Figure 7.9A) the difference between the 10-year Treasury yield (FRED code: GS10) and the three-month Treasury bill rate (FRED code: TB3MS). Discuss the variability of the time between an inversion of the yield curve and the subsequent recession. *(LO3)*

5. Download the data from the graph produced in Data Exploration Problem 4 and (a) find the most recent period for which the yield curve was (approximately) flat and (b) the longest time period for which yield curve was inverted. *(LO2)*

Chapter 8

Stocks, Stock Markets, and Market Efficiency

Learning Objectives

Understand . . .

LO1   The characteristics of common stock

LO2   Measures of the level of the stock market

LO3   The valuation of stocks

LO4   Investing in stocks for the long run

LO5   The stock market's role in the economy

Stocks play a prominent role in our financial and economic lives. For individuals, they provide a key instrument for holding personal wealth as well as a way to diversify, spreading and reducing the risks that we face. Importantly, diversifiable risks are risks that are more likely to be taken. By giving individuals a way to transfer risk, stocks supply a type of insurance enhancing our ability to take risk.[1]

For companies, they are one of several ways to obtain financing. Beyond that, though, stocks and **stock markets** are a central link between the financial world and the real economy. Stock prices are fundamental to the functioning of a market-based economy. They tell us the value of the companies that issued the stocks and, like all other prices, they allocate scarce investment resources. The firms deemed most valuable in the marketplace for stocks are the ones that will be able to obtain financing for growth. When resources flow to their most valued uses, the economy operates more efficiently.

Mention of the stock market provokes an emotional reaction in many people. They see it as a place where fortunes are easily made or lost, and they recoil at its unfathomable booms and busts. During one infamous week in October 1929, the New York Stock Exchange lost more than 25 percent of its value—an event that marked the beginning of the Great Depression. In October 1987, prices fell nearly 30 percent in one week, including a record decline of 20 percent in a single day. Crashes of this magnitude have become part of the stock market's folklore, creating the popular impression that stocks are very risky.

In the 1990s, stock prices increased nearly fivefold and Americans forgot about the "black Octobers." By the end of the decade, many people had come to see stocks as

[1]This point was central to our discussions of risk in Chapter 5. Our ability to diversify risk either through the explicit purchase of insurance or through investment strategies means that we are able to do risky things that we otherwise would not do.

almost a sure thing; you could not afford not to own them. In 1998, nearly half of all U.S. households owned some stock, either directly or indirectly through mutual funds and managed retirement accounts.

When the market's inexorable rise finally ended, the ensuing decline seemed more like a slowly deflating balloon than a crash. From early 2000 to the week following the terrorist attacks of September 11, 2001, the stock prices of the United States' biggest companies, as measured by the Dow Jones Industrial Average, fell more than 30 percent. While many stocks recovered much of their loss fairly quickly, a large number did not. During the same period, the Nasdaq Composite index fell 70 percent, from 5,000 to 1,500; it has remained well below its March 2000 peak ever since. Because the Nasdaq tracks smaller, newer, more technologically oriented companies, many observers dubbed this episode the "Internet bubble."

The plunge of the U.S. stock market in the recent financial crisis was much broader and greater, roughly halving the market value by early 2009 from its 2007 peak of about $26 trillion. And, although the stock market surpassed this peak in the first quarter of 2013, it fared less well after accounting for inflation.

Yet, contrary to popular mythology, stock prices do tend to rise—even after adjusting for inflation—over the long term, collapsing only on those infrequent occasions when normal market mechanisms are out of alignment. For most people, the experience of losing or gaining wealth suddenly is more memorable than the experience of making it gradually. By being preoccupied with the potential short-term losses associated with crashes, we lose sight of the gains we could realize if we took a longer-term view. The goal of this chapter is to try to make sense of the stock market—to show what fluctuations in stock value mean for individuals and for the economy as a whole and look at a critical connection between the financial system and the real economy. We will also explain how it is that things sometimes go awry, resulting in bubbles and crashes. First, however, we need to define the basics: what stocks are, how they originated, and how they are valued.

The Essential Characteristics of Common Stock

Stocks, also known as **common stock** or **equity**, are shares in a firm's ownership. A firm that issues stock sells part of itself, so that the buyer becomes a part owner. Stocks as we know them first appeared in the 16th century. They were created to raise funds for global exploration. Means had to be found to finance the dangerous voyages of explorers such as Sir Francis Drake, Henry Hudson, and Vasco de Gama. Aside from kings and queens, no one was wealthy enough to finance these risky ventures alone. The solution was to spread the risk through *joint-stock companies,* organizations that issued stock and used the proceeds to finance several expeditions at once. In exchange for investing, stockholders received a share of the company's profits.

These early stocks had two important characteristics that we take for granted today. First, the shares were issued in *small denominations,* allowing investors to buy as little or as much of the company as they wanted; and second, the shares were *transferable,* meaning that an owner could sell them to someone else. Today, the vast majority of large companies issue stock that investors buy and sell regularly. The shares normally are quite numerous, each one representing only a small fraction of a company's total value. The large number and small size of individual shares—prices are usually below $100 per share—make the purchase and sale of stocks relatively easy.

Figure 8.1	Examples of Stock Certificates

Until recently, all stockowners received a certificate from the issuing company. Figure 8.1, on the left, shows the first stock certificate issued by the Ford Motor Company in 1903, to Henry Ford. The right-hand side of the figure shows a more recent stock certificate issued by the World Wrestling Federation (WWF), renamed World Wrestling Enterprises (WWE). The WWE is the media and entertainment company that produces the wrestling events involving characters like The Rock and Hulk Hogan. The former governor of Minnesota, Jesse Ventura, worked for the WWF before entering politics.

Today, most stockholders no longer receive certificates; the odds are that you will never see one. Instead, the information they bear is computerized, and the shares are registered in the names of brokerage firms that hold them on investors' behalf. This procedure is safer because computerized certificates can't be stolen. It also makes the process of selling the shares much easier.

The ownership of common stock conveys a number of rights. First and most importantly, a stockholder is entitled to participate in the profits of the enterprise. Importantly, however, the stockholder is merely a **residual claimant**. If the company runs into financial trouble, only after all other creditors have been paid what they are owed will the stockholders receive what is left, if anything. Stockholders get the leftovers!

To understand what being the residual claimant means, let's look at the case of a software manufacturer. The company needs a number of things to make it run. The list might include rented office space, computers, programmers, and some cash balances for day-to-day operations. These are the *inputs* into the production of the company's software *output*. If we took a snapshot of the company's finances on any given day, we would see that the firm owes payments to a large number of people, including the owner of the office space it rents, the programmers that work for it, the supplier of its computers, and the bondholders and bankers who have lent the firm resources. The company uses the revenue from selling its software to pay these people. After everyone has been paid, the stockholders get the rest of the revenue. In some years, the company does well and there are funds left over, so the stockholders do well. But when the firm does poorly, the stockholders may get nothing. If the firm performs really poorly, failing to sell enough software to cover its obligations, it can go bankrupt and cease operating entirely. In that case, the stockholders lose their entire investment.

The possibility of bankruptcy brings up an interesting question. What happens if a company's revenue is insufficient to cover its obligations to nonstockholders? What if its revenue is too small to pay the landlord, the programmers, the supplier of the computers,

YOUR FINANCIAL WORLD

A Home Is a Place to Live

A home is a place to live; it is very different from a stock or a bond. When you own a stock, the issuing firm either pays you dividends or reinvests its profits to make the business grow. Bonds pay interest, that's how you are compensated for lending. In either case, you receive an explicit financial return on your investment.

When you buy a house and move in, what you get is a roof over your head. And you do it without paying rent to someone else. That means that you are consuming the dividend or interest payments in the form of what economists call *housing services*. So, if you buy a house, live in it for a while, and then sell it, you should expect to get back the original purchase price, adjusted for inflation. It is as if you bought an inflation-indexed bond and used the coupon payments to live on. What's left at the end is the principal amount, no more.

Data on the long-run real (inflation-adjusted) change in the price of housing are consistent with this. Over the 122 years from 1890 to 2012, the average annual real increase in the value of housing in the United States was only 0.17 percent. That means that if you were to purchase a house for $100,000 and live in it for 30 years (the time it takes to completely pay off a conventional fixed-rate mortgage), you could expect to sell it for around $105,000 plus any adjustment for inflation.

An observer in 2006 might be forgiven for thinking that the long-run rules for housing prices had changed with the millennium. In the first six years of the decade, real house prices surged by 60 percent. By 2009, however, these gains had vanished with the financial crisis, leaving the former long-run pattern intact.

To see the contrast with a financial investment, compare the purchase of the home to the purchase of $100,000 worth of stock. If stocks have an annual average real return of 6 percent, then after 30 years you will have accumulated nearly $575,000. But, unlike the house, this financial investment does not provide you with a place to live. So, when you think about the return to owning a house, remember that you get a place to live—that's the return on your investment.

and the bondholders and other lenders? It would appear that the stockholders' promised participation in the firm's profits would yield a liability rather than a payment. If the company does very poorly, will the stockholders have to pay the firm's creditors?

An arrangement in which the stockholders are held liable for the firm's losses is very unappealing and would surely discourage people from buying stock. Stockholders bore that risk until the early 19th century. It ended with the introduction of the legal concept of limited liability.[2] **Limited liability** means that, even if a company fails completely, the maximum amount that shareholders can lose is their initial investment. *Liability* for the company's losses is *limited* at zero, meaning that investors can never lose more than they have invested. Clearly, buying stock is much more attractive if you know that your maximum potential loss is the price you pay for the stock in the first place.

Beyond participating in the firm's profits, owners of common stock are entitled to vote at the firm's annual meeting. Though managers supervise a firm's day-to-day activities, the shareholders elect the board of directors, which meets several times per year to oversee management. Ultimately, the shareholders' ability to dislodge directors and managers who are performing poorly is crucial to their willingness to purchase shares.[3] This ability to elect and remove directors and managers varies with a country's legal structure. In places where shareholders' legal rights are weak, stock ownership is less appealing, and equities are a less important form of corporate financing.

Today, stock ownership is immensely popular. Investors want to own stocks and companies want to issue them. Over the past century, markets have developed in which

[2]The United States passed the first general law granting limited liability to manufacturing companies in 1811.

[3]Managers and directors may have different priorities and objectives from shareholders. While the firm's owners would like to see the value of their investment increase, managers may be more interested in ensuring that they retain their jobs.

people buy and sell billions of shares every day. This thriving financial trade is possible because

- An individual share represents only a small fraction of the value of the company that issued it.
- A large number of shares are outstanding.
- Prices of individual shares are low, allowing individuals to make relatively small investments.
- As residual claimants, stockholders receive the proceeds of a firm's activities only after all other creditors have been paid.
- Because of limited liability, investors' losses cannot exceed the price they paid for the stock.
- Shareholders can replace managers who are doing a bad job.

Measuring the Level of the Stock Market

MARKETS

Stocks are one way in which we choose to hold our wealth. When stock values rise, we get richer; when they fall, we get poorer. These changes affect our consumption and saving patterns, causing general economic activity to fluctuate. We need to understand the dynamics of the stock market, both to manage our personal finances and to see the connections between stock values and economic conditions. From a macroeconomic point of view, we need to be able to measure the level of fluctuation in all stock values. We will refer to this concept as the *value* of the stock market and to its measures as **stock-market indexes**.

You are probably familiar with price indexes, like the consumer price index, and output indexes, like industrial production and real gross domestic product. The purpose of an index number is to give a measure of scale so that we can compute percentage changes. The consumer price index, for example, is not measured in dollars. Instead, it is a pure number. In June 2013, the value of the Consumer Price Index for All Urban Consumers was 232.94, which isn't very interesting on its own. If, however, you know that 12 months earlier, in June 2012, the same index was 228.92, then you can figure out that prices rose by 1.8 percent over a 12-month period—that's the percentage change in the index.

Stock-market indexes are the same. They are designed to give us a sense of the extent to which things are going up or down. Saying that the Dow Jones Industrial Average is at 10,000 doesn't mean anything on its own. But if you know that the Dow index rose from 10,000 to 11,000, that tells you that stock prices (by this measure) went up 10 percent. As we will see, stock indexes can tell us both how much the value of an average stock has changed and how much total wealth has gone up or down. Beyond that, stock indexes provide benchmarks for performance of money managers, allowing us to measure whether a particular manager has done better or worse than "the market" as a whole.

A quick look at the financial news reveals a number of stock-market indexes, covering both domestic stocks and stocks issued by firms in foreign countries. Our goal in this section is to learn what these are and, more important, what question each is designed to answer. We will start with a detailed discussion of the two most well-known U.S. indexes, the *Dow Jones Industrial Average* and the *Standard & Poor's 500 Index*. A brief description of other indexes and a short history of the performance of the U.S. stock market will follow.

The Dow Jones Industrial Average

The first, and still the best known, stock-market index is the **Dow Jones Industrial Average (DJIA)**. Created by Charles Dow in 1884, the DJIA began as an average of the prices of 11 stocks. Today, the index is based on the stock prices of 30 of the largest companies in the United States. The DJIA measures the value of purchasing a single share of each of the stocks in the index. That is, adding up the per-share prices of all 30 stocks and dividing by 30 yields the index. The percentage change in the DJIA over time is the percentage change in the sum of the 30 prices. Thus, the DJIA measures the return to holding a portfolio of a single share of each stock included in the average.

The Dow Jones Industrial Average is a **price-weighted average**. Price-weighted averages give greater weight to shares with higher prices. To see how this works, take the example of an index composed of just two companies, one with an initial price of $50 and the other with an initial price of $100. The purchase of two shares of stock, one from each company, would cost $150. Now consider the effect of a 15 percent increase in the price of the first stock. It raises the value of the two-stock portfolio by $7.50, or 5 percent, to $157.50. Yet a 15 percent increase in the value of the second stock raises the value of the portfolio by $15, or 10 percent, to $165. The behavior of higher-priced stocks, then, dominates the movement of a price-weighted index like the DJIA.[4]

Since Charles Dow first created his index of 11 stocks, nine of which were railroad stocks, the structure of the U.S. economy has changed markedly. At various times, steel, chemical, and automobile stocks have dominated the DJIA. The index now includes the stocks of information technology firms, such as Microsoft and Intel, as well as of retailing firms, such as Walmart and Home Depot. General Electric is the only one of the original 11 stocks that remains in the index.[5] The DJIA is a large-company index, but as of mid-2013, it did not include the firms with the second and third largest market values: Apple and Google.

The Standard & Poor's 500 Index

The **Standard & Poor's 500 Index** differs from the Dow Jones Industrial Average in two major respects. First, it is constructed from the prices of many more stocks. Second, it uses a different weighting scheme. As the name suggests, the S&P 500 Index is based on the value of 500 firms, the largest firms in the U.S. economy. And unlike the DJIA, the S&P 500 tracks the total value of owning the entirety of those firms. In the index's calculation, each firm's stock price receives a weight equal to its total market value. Thus, the S&P 500 is a **value-weighted index**. Unlike the DJIA, in which higher-priced stocks carry more weight, larger firms are more important in the S&P 500.

To see this, we can return to the two companies in our last example. If the firm whose stock is priced at $100 has 10 million shares outstanding, all its shares together—its total market value, or **market capitalization**—are worth $1 billion. If the second firm—the one whose shares are valued at $50 apiece—has 100 million shares

---

[4]You may wonder how the DJIA has climbed to over 10,000 if it is the average of 30 stock prices, all less than $200 per share. The answer is that the averaging process takes stock splits into account and that the companies included in the index change periodically. There is a simple way to compute the change in the index level: (1) Take the list of 30 stocks in the DJIA and add up the changes from the previous day's close, so if each stock rose by $1, that's $30. (2) Using an online search engine, locate something called the DJIA "divisor." It's a number like 0.130216081 (that's the value for July 29, 2013). (3) Divide the sum of changes in the prices of the DJIA stocks by the divisor and add that to the previous day's close. The result is the current level of the DJIA.

[5]A detailed description of the history and current composition of the DJIA is on the website *www.djindexes.com*.

TOOLS OF THE TRADE

Reading Stock Indexes in the Business News

Each morning, the business news brings reports of the prior day's changes in all the major stock-market indexes. Table 8.1, reproduced from *The Wall Street Journal* of February 13, 2013, is an example of this sort of summary. It includes a number of indexes besides the DJIA, the S&P 500, and the Nasdaq Composite. Some of them cover firms of a particular size. For example, Standard & Poor's MidCap index covers 400 medium-size firms; its SmallCap index covers 600 small firms. And the Russell 2000 tracks the value of the smallest two-thirds of the 3,000 largest U.S. companies. Other indexes cover a particular sector or industry. Note that Dow Jones publishes indexes for transportation and utilities; others provide special indexes for biotechnology, pharmaceuticals, banks, and semiconductors. Many more indexes are published, all of them designed for specific functions. When you encounter a new index, make sure you understand both how it is constructed and what it is designed to measure.

Table 8.1 Major U.S. Stock-Market Indexes

February 12, 2013

| | LATEST | | | | | 52-WEEK RANGE | | | % CHG | |
	High	Low	Close	Net chg	% chg	High	Low	% chg	YTD	3-yr. ann.
Dow Jones										
Industrial Average	14038.97	13968.94	14018.70	47.46	0.34	14018.70	12101.46	8.9	7.0	11.6
Transportation Avg	5921.83	5893.20	5906.86	−2.29	−0.04	5911.33	4847.73	11.8	11.3	14.7
Utility Average	476.74	473.89	476.67	1.84	0.39	496.56	438.05	5.9	5.2	9.4
Total Stock Market	16035.23	15967.40	16008.75	29.42	0.18	16008.75	13329.32	12.7	7.0	12.8
Barron's 400	395.99	395.16	395.62	0.46	0.12	395.83	321.50	9.8	8.1	15.5
Nasdaq Stock Market										
Nasdaq Composite	3196.92	3184.84	3186.49	−5.51	−0.17	3193.87	2747.48	8.7	5.5	13.4
Nasdaq 100	2776.71	2761.41	2762.62	−12.02	−0.43	2864.03	2458.83	7.3	3.8	15.8
Standard & Poor's										
500 Index	1522.29	1515.61	1519.43	2.42	0.16	1519.43	1278.04	12.5	6.5	12.2
MidCap 400	1112.41	1107.01	1111.72	4.67	0.42	1111.72	891.32	14.2	8.9	15.8
SmallCap 600	514.43	511.69	513.94	2.25	0.44	513.94	414.87	12.5	7.8	16.6
Other Indexes										
Russell 2000	918.17	913.73	917.52	4.49	0.49	917.52	737.24	11.8	8.0	14.5
NYSE Composite	8970.90	8918.73	8957.61	38.59	0.43	8965.12	7285.53	11.6	6.1	9.2
Value Line	398.12	396.04	397.76	1.71	0.43	397.76	323.50	9.0	8.1	9.5
NYSE Arca Biotech	1680.80	1663.33	1665.82	−12.30	−0.73	1690.11	1280.90	21.3	7.7	18.9
NYSE Arca Pharma	393.85	391.89	393.03	1.26	0.32	397.24	322.03	17.8	6.3	9.2
KBW Bank	55.79	55.03	55.71	0.58	1.05	55.71	41.00	25.7	8.6	7.6
PHLX§ Gold/Silver	151.07	148.12	150.62	1.30	0.87	202.36	141.60	−21.1	−9.0	−1.9
PHLX§ Oil Service	246.78	245.45	246.49	0.80	0.32	260.81	186.27	−0.9	12.0	8.0
PHLX§ Semiconductor	426.94	423.76	426.28	1.04	0.24	441.88	351.45	0.7	11.0	8.6
CBOE Volatility	13.13	12.63	12.64	−0.30	−2.32	26.66	12.43	−35.3	−29.9	−17.8

§Philadelphia Stock Exchange

Sources: SIX Financial Information; WSJ Market Data Group

outstanding, its market capitalization is $5 billion. Together, the two companies are worth $6 billion.

Now look at the effect of changes in the two stocks' prices. If the first firm's per-share price rises by 15 percent, its total value goes up to $1.15 billion, and the value of the two companies together rises to $6.15 billion—an increase of 2½ percent. (Remember that in the last example, the price-weighted DJIA rose by 10 percent.) Contrast that with the effect of a 15 percent increase in the price of the second stock, which raises the total value of that firm to $5.75 billion. In this case, the value of the two firms together goes from $6 billion to $6.75 billion—an increase of 12½ percent. (In the last example, the price-weighted DJIA rose only 5 percent.)

Clearly, price-weighted and value-weighted indexes are very different. A price-weighted index gives more importance to stocks that have high prices, while a value-weighted index gives more importance to companies with a high market value. Price per se is irrelevant.

Neither price weighting nor value weighting is necessarily the best approach to constructing a stock price index. The S&P 500 is neither better nor worse than the DJIA. Rather, the two types of index simply answer different questions. Changes in a price-weighted index like the DJIA tell us the change in the value of a portfolio composed of a single share of each of the stocks in the index. This tells us the change in the price of a typical stock. Changes in a value-weighted index tell us the return to holding a portfolio of stocks weighted in proportion to the size of the firms. Thus, they accurately mirror changes in the economy's overall wealth.

Other U.S. Stock Market Indexes

Besides the S&P 500 and the DJIA, the most prominent indexes in the United States are the **Nasdaq Composite Index**, or Nasdaq for short, and the **Wilshire 5000**. The Nasdaq is a value-weighted index of nearly 3,000 securities traded on the over-the-counter (OTC) market through the National Association of Securities Dealers Automatic Quotations (Nasdaq) service. The Nasdaq Composite is composed mainly of smaller, newer firms and in recent years has been dominated by technology and Internet companies. The Wilshire 5000 is the most broadly based index in use. It covers all publicly traded stocks in the United States with readily available prices, including all the stocks on national stock exchanges, which together total fewer than 4,000 (contrary to the index's name) as of mid-2013. Like the Nasdaq and the S&P 500, the Wilshire 5000 is value-weighted. Because of its great breadth, this index is a useful measure of overall market wealth. You can find both the latest value of this index and its history at the Wilshire website: web.wilshire.com/Indexes/Broad/Wilshire5000/.

World Stock Indexes

Roughly one-third of the countries in the world have stock markets, and each of these markets has an index. Most are value-weighted indexes like the S&P 500. Listings of other countries' stock indexes are in newspapers such as *The Wall Street Journal* or the *Financial Times,* as well as online at websites such as www.bloomberg.com (see Table 8.2).

Table 8.2 gives some sense of the behavior of stock markets during early 2013. The index levels (in column 3) don't mean much because the indexes themselves aren't comparable. No one would think that the Brazilian stock exchange was bigger than the New York Stock Exchange, even though the Bovespa index stood at 58,497 when

Table 8.2   World Stock Markets

February 12, 2013 Close

Region/Country	Index Name	Close	YTD % Chg	52-Week % Chg	3-Yr Annualized % Chg
World	**DJ Global Index**	273.36	5.1	9.7	8.3
Argentina	Merval	3279.96	14.9	20.5	14.5
Australia	All Ordinaries	4981.50	6.8	15.3	2.8
Brazil	Sao Paulo Bovespa	58497.83	−4.0	−8.6	−2.5
Canada	S&P/TSX Comp	12789.02	2.9	3.5	3.7
China	DJ CBN China 600	22861.92	9.9	9.1	−5.2
France	CAC 40	3686.58	1.2	9.2	0.8
Germany	DAX	7660.19	0.6	13.9	11.7
Hong Kong	Hang Seng	23215.10	2.5	11.7	5.9
Italy	FTSE MIB	16644.45	2.3	1.2	−7.5
Japan	Nikkei Stock Avg	11369.12	9.4	25.6	4.1
Mexico	IPC All-Share	44873.44	2.7	18.6	13.1
Singapore	Straits Times	3270.30	3.3	10.5	6.7
United Kingdom	FTSE 100	6338.38	7.5	7.4	7.2
United States	S&P 500	1519.43	6.5	12.5	12.2

SOURCE: *The Wall Street Journal*, February 12, 2013. Used with permission of Dow Jones & Company, Inc. via Copyright Clearance Center.

the S&P 500 was just 1,519. Instead, we need to focus on the percentage changes in these indexes (in columns 5 and 6). A 100-point move in the Singapore Straits Times index, with a level of 3,270, would be much more significant than a 100-point move in the Japanese Nikkei, with a level of 11,369. But percentage change isn't everything (see Your Financial World: Beware Percentage Changes, on page 201).

Table 8.2 also shows that from February 2012 to February 2013, stock markets rose solidly in many, but not all, countries. The increase in the U.S. S&P 500 index in the 52 weeks ending February 12, 2013 (12.5 percent), was similar to that of the German DAX (13.9 percent) and the French CAC 40 (9.2 percent). The real star of 2012 was Japan's Nikkei Stock Average, which jumped 25.6 percent. At the other end of the spectrum, Brazil's Bovespa index dropped 8.6 percent.

Finally, Table 8.2 shows that the 52-week gains for many countries were larger than the annualized gains over three years. Indeed, in Australia, France, Italy, and Japan, the stock market indexes actually declined over the first two years of that three-year interval.

Investors view global stock markets as a means to diversify risk away from domestic investments. While that remains correct, the benefits from such diversification have tended to decline over time. Stock markets have become increasingly linked by the choices of investors whose changing preferences are rapidly transmitted from one market to the next. The result has been an increased correlation of global markets, especially in periods of financial distress.

Valuing Stocks

People differ on how stocks should be valued. Some believe they can predict changes in a stock's price by looking at patterns in its past price movements. Because these people study charts of stock prices, they are called *chartists*. Other investors, known as *behavioralists*, estimate the value of stocks based on their perceptions of investor psychology and behavior. Still others estimate stock values based on a detailed study of companies' financial statements. In their view, the value of a firm's stock depends both on its current assets and on estimates of its future profitability—what they call the *fundamentals*. Thus, the **fundamental value** of a stock is based on the timing and uncertainty of the returns it brings.

We can use our toolbox for valuing financial instruments to compute the fundamental value of stocks. Based on the size and timing of the promised payments, we can use the present-value formula to assess how much a stock is worth in the absence of any risk. Then, realizing that the payments are uncertain in both their size and timing, we can adjust our estimate of the stock's value to accommodate those risks. Together, these two steps give us the fundamental value.

The chartists and behavioralists question the usefulness of fundamentals in understanding the level and movement of stock prices. They focus instead on estimates of the deviation of stock prices from those fundamental values. These deviations can create short-term bubbles and crashes, which we'll take up later in the chapter. First, though, let's use some familiar techniques to develop an understanding of basic stock valuation.

Fundamental Value and the Dividend-Discount Model

Like all financial instruments, a stock represents a promise to make monetary payments on future dates, under certain circumstances. With stocks, the payments are usually in the form of **dividends**, or distributions made to the owners of a company when the company makes a profit.[6] If the firm is sold, the stockholders receive a final distribution that represents their share of the purchase price.

Let's begin with an investor who plans to buy a stock today and sell it in one year. The principle of present value tells us that the price of the stock today should equal the present value of the payments the investor will receive from holding the stock. This is equal to the selling price of the stock in one year's time plus the dividend payments received in the interim. Thus, the current price is the present value of next year's price plus the dividend. If P_{today} is the purchase price of the stock, $P_{next\ year}$ is the sale price one year later, and $D_{next\ year}$ is the size of the dividend payment, we can write this expression as

$$P_{today} = \frac{D_{next\ year}}{(1 + i)} + \frac{P_{next\ year}}{(1 + i)} \tag{1}$$

where i is the interest rate used to compute the present value (measured as a decimal).

What if the investor plans to hold the stock for two years? To figure out the answer, start by using present value to calculate that the price next year equals the value next

---

[6]To be precise, not all profits are distributed to shareholders. Some of these "earnings" are retained by the firm and used to increase its size. A firm may also use profits to buy back its own stock, thereby increasing the value of the remaining shares. We will ignore these complications.

year of the price in two years plus next year's dividend payment. Using the logic and notation from equation (1), this is

$$P_{next\ year} = \frac{D_{in\ two\ years}}{(1 + i)} + \frac{P_{in\ two\ years}}{(1 + i)} \qquad (2)$$

Substituting equation (2) into equation (1), we get that the current price is the present value of the price in two years plus two dividend payments, one each year, or

$$P_{today} = \frac{D_{next\ year}}{(1 + i)} + \frac{D_{in\ two\ years}}{(1 + i)^2} + \frac{P_{in\ two\ years}}{(1 + i)^2} \qquad (3)$$

Extending this formula over an investment horizon of n years, the result is

$$P_{today} = \frac{D_{next\ year}}{(1 + i)} + \frac{D_{in\ two\ years}}{(1 + i)^2} + \ldots + \frac{D_{n\ years\ from\ now}}{(1 + i)^n} + \frac{P_{n\ years\ from\ now}}{(1 + i)^n} \qquad (4)$$

That is, the price today is the present value of the sum of the dividends plus the present value of the price at the time the stock is sold n years from now. (Notice that this equation is the same as the expression for the price of a coupon bond on page 136 of Chapter 6.)

At this point, you may be asking: What about companies that do not pay dividends? How do we figure out their stock price? The answer is that we estimate when they will start paying dividends and then use the present-value framework. From equation (4) you can see that there is no reason all of the dividends need to be positive. Some of them can be zero, and we can still do the calculation. So if we figure that the company will start paying dividends in 10 years, we just set the first 9 years' worth of dividends equal to zero, and compute the present discounted value of dividend payments starting in year 10.

Returning to our baseline case, looking at the messy equation (4) we can see that unless we know something more about the annual dividend payments, we are stuck. To proceed, we will assume that dividends grow at a constant rate of g per year. That is, the dividend next year will equal the dividend today multiplied by one plus the growth rate:

$$D_{next\ year} = D_{today}(1 + g) \qquad (5)$$

As long as the growth rate remains constant, all we need to do is multiply by $(1 + g)$ to compute future dividends. Following the procedure for computing present value in n years, we can see that the dividend n years from now will be

$$D_{n\ years\ from\ now} = D_{today}(1 + g)^n \qquad (6)$$

Using equation (6), we can rewrite the price equation (4) as

$$P_{today} = \frac{D_{today}(1 + g)}{(1 + i)} + \frac{D_{today}(1 + g)^2}{(1 + i)^2} + \ldots + \frac{D_{today}(1 + g)^n}{(1 + i)^n} + \frac{P_{n\ years\ from\ now}}{(1 + i)^n} \qquad (7)$$

Even if we know the dividend today, D_{today}, and the interest rate, i, as well as an estimate of the dividend growth rate, g, we still can't compute the current price, P_{today}, unless we know the future price, $P_{n\ years\ from\ now}$. We can solve this problem by assuming the firm pays dividends forever and noting that as n gets big $[1/(1 + i)^n]$ approaches zero until it finally disappears. This assumption turns the stock into something like a consol—the strange bond that makes fixed coupon payments forever and never repays the principal.[7] It allows us to convert equation (6) into the following simple formula:[8]

$$P_{today} = \frac{D_{today}(1 + g)}{i - g} \qquad (8)$$

This relationship is the **dividend-discount model**. Using the concept of present value, together with the simplification that the firm's dividends will grow at a constant rate g, we have discovered that the "fundamental" price of a stock is simply the current dividend divided by the interest rate, minus the dividend growth rate. The model tells us that stock prices should be high when dividends (D_{today}) are high, when dividend growth (g) is rapid (that is, when g is large), or when the interest rate (i) is low. (In using the dividend-discount model, we will need to remember to write both i and g as decimals—numbers like 0.03 and 0.05.)

The dividend-discount model is simple and elegant, but we have ignored risk in deriving it. Stock prices change constantly, making investors' returns uncertain. Where does this risk come from, and how does it affect a stock's valuation? We turn now to an analysis of risk.

Why Stocks Are Risky

Recall that stockholders are the firm's owners, so they receive the firm's profits. But their profits come only after the firm has paid everyone else, including bondholders. It is as if the stockholders bought the firm by putting up some of their own wealth and borrowing the rest. This borrowing creates *leverage,* and leverage creates risk. (See the Tools of the Trade box in Chapter 5.)

A simple example will show what happens. Imagine a software business that needs only one computer. Say the computer costs $1,000 and the purchase can be financed by any combination of stock (equity) and bonds (debt). If the interest rate on bonds is 10 percent, for each $100 borrowed the firm must pay $10 in interest. Finally, assume that the company, which produces software, earns $160 in good years and $80 in bad years, with equal probability.

Table 8.3 shows what happens to the company's equity returns as its level of debt changes. The more debt, the more leverage and the greater the owners' risk (as measured by the standard deviation of the equity return). As the proportion of the firm financed by equity falls from 100 percent to 20 percent, the expected return to the equity holders rises from 12 percent to 20 percent, but the associated risk rises substantially as well.

If the firm were only 10 percent equity financed, the stockholders' limited liability could come into play. Issuing $900 worth of bonds would mean incurring an obligation to make $90 in interest payments. If business turned out to be bad, the firm's revenue

---

[7]Because neither the consol nor the stock has a maturity date, it makes sense that they would be formally the same.

[8]To compute equation (8), begin by noticing that if we change notation slightly so that P_j and D_j are the price and dividend in year j, then the original pricing equation (4) can be rewritten as an infinite sum, so that

$P_0 = \sum_{j=1}^{\infty} \frac{D_j}{(1 + i)_j}$. Substituting in the expression for the dividend growth rate, $D_j = (1 + g)^j$, this gives us

$P_0 = \sum_{t=1}^{\infty} \frac{D_0(1 + g)^t}{(1 + i)^t}$. This expression looks exactly like the one for a consol, with the current dividend in place

of the coupon payment and an interest rate equivalent to $(1 + i^*) = (1 + i)/(1 + g)$. That is, we can write

it as $P_0 = \sum_{t=1}^{\infty} \frac{D_0}{(1 + i^*)^t}$. Using the techniques in Appendix to Chapter 4, we can simplify this to $\frac{D_0}{i^*}$. Rewriting

$i^* = \frac{i - g}{1 + g}$ and substituting, we get equation (8).

YOUR FINANCIAL WORLD
Beware Percentage Changes

From the beginning of 2007 until March 2009, the stock price of Bank of America (BAC) fell 94 percent amid the deepest financial crisis since the Great Depression. Only six months later, however, it had jumped up almost 500 percent! Reading these numbers, you might think that BAC stock had recouped its losses and went on to accumulate massive gains.

Not exactly. The stock price plunged from $53.33 in January 2007 to a low of $3.14 in March 2009, before climbing back to $18.59 in September 2009, so even with a 500 percent gain, it still had lost nearly two-thirds of its pre-crisis value.

Sometimes investment reports imply that it is possible to evaluate an asset's overall performance simply by adding the percentage loss over one period to a subsequent percentage gain. But, as this example suggests, nothing could be further from the truth.

What percentage increase will bring an investment in BAC stock back to its original level following the loss of 94 percent? The easiest way to answer this question is to compute a general formula for percentage increase required to bring a losing investment back to its original value. If d

is the initial *decline* in the value of a $100 investment, then $(100 - d)$ is left. What percentage increase in $(100 - d)$ will return the investment to a value of 100? Recall that the percentage change is just the end value, which is $100 minus the initial value $(100 - d)$, divided by the initial value, and multiplied by 100 (so that the answer is a percentage). Putting this all together, we get the formula we are looking for:

Percentage increase required
to return to original value =

$$100 \times \frac{100 - (100 - d)}{(100 - d)} = 100 \times \frac{d}{(100 - d)}$$

What happens to this formula as d increases? For very small losses, such as 1 percent to 5 percent, the percentage increase needed is nearly the same as the loss. But as d increases, the required percentage increase climbs rapidly. While a 10 percent decline requires an 11.1 percent increase to return to the initial level, a 94 percent decline requires a 1,567 percent increase. Beware percentage change!

would be only $80—not enough to pay the interest. Without their limited liability, the common stockholders, who are the firm's legal owners, would be liable for the $10 shortfall. Instead, the stockholders would lose only their initial $100 investment, and no more, and the firm goes bankrupt.

Stocks are risky, then, because the shareholders are residual claimants. Because they are paid last, they never know for sure how much their return will be. Any variation in the firm's revenue flows through to them dollar for dollar, making their returns highly volatile. In contrast, bondholders receive fixed nominal payments and are paid before the stockholders in the event of a bankruptcy.

Table 8.3   Returns Distributed to Debt and Equity Holders under Different Financing Assumptions

Percent Equity (%)	Percent Debt (%)	Required Payments on 10% Bonds ($)	Payment to Equity Holders ($)	Equity Return (%)	Expected Equity Return (%)	Standard Deviation of Equity Return
100%	0	0	$80–$160	8–16%	12%	4%
50%	50%	$50	$30–$110	6–22%	14%	8%
30%	70%	$70	$10–$ 90	3⅓–30%	16⅔%	13⅓%
20%	80%	$80	$ 0–$ 80	0–40%	20%	20%

Firm requires a $1,000 capital investment that can be financed by either stock (equity) or 10% bonds (debt). Revenue is either $80 or $160, with equal probability.

Risk and the Value of Stocks

RISK

Stockholders require compensation for the risk they face; the higher the risk, the greater the compensation. To integrate risk into stock valuation, we will return to the simple question we asked earlier: How will investors with a one-year investment horizon value a stock? Our initial answer was that the stock price equals the present value of the price of the stock in one year's time plus the dividend payments received in the interim. From this statement, we derived the dividend-discount model. But once we recognize the risk involved in buying stock, the answer to our question must change. The new answer is that an investor will buy a stock with the idea of obtaining a certain return, which includes compensation for the stock's risk.

Here is how the process works. Buying the stock for an initial price P_{today} entitles the investor to a dividend $D_{next\ year}$ plus the proceeds from the sale of the stock one year later, at price $P_{next\ year}$. The return from the purchase and subsequent sale of the stock equals the dividend plus the difference in the price, both divided by the initial price:

$$\text{Return to holding stock for one year} = \frac{D_{next\ year}}{P_{today}} + \frac{P_{next\ year} - P_{today}}{P_{today}} \quad (9)$$

Because the ultimate future sale price is unknown, the stock is risky and the investor will require compensation in the form of a risk premium. We will think of the required return as the sum of the risk-free interest rate and the risk premium (sometimes called the *equity risk premium*). We can approximate the risk-free rate as the interest rate on a U.S. Treasury security with a maturity of several months. Such an instrument has virtually no default risk, because the government isn't going to collapse, and it has almost no inflation risk, because U.S. inflation is highly persistent and so is unlikely to change sharply over a few months. In addition, there is very little price risk because interest rates normally don't move quickly and suddenly either.[9] Dividing the required stock return into its two components, we can write

$$\text{Required stock return}\,(i) = \text{Risk-free return}\,(rf) + \text{Risk premium}\,(rp) \quad (10)$$

Combining this equation with our earlier analysis is straightforward. All we need to do is recognize that the interest rate used for the present-value calculation in the dividend-discount model, equation (8), is the sum of the risk-free return and a risk premium. Using this insight, we can rewrite equation (8) as

$$P_{today} = \frac{D_{today}(1 + g)}{rf + rp - g} \quad (11)$$

Table 8.4 Implications of the Dividend-Discount Model with Risk

Stock Prices Are High When
1. Current dividends are high (D_{today} is high).
2. Dividends are expected to grow quickly (g is high).
3. The risk-free rate is low (rf is low).
4. The risk premium on equity is low (rp is low).

Looking at equation (11), we can see that the higher the risk premium investors demand to hold a stock, the lower its price. Similarly, the higher the risk-free return, the lower the stock's price. (See Table 8.4 for a summary.)

We can use equation (11) to see if current stock prices are warranted by fundamentals. Start by finding the current level of the S&P 500 index. At the end of 2012, it was about 1,430. Next, we need to

[9]TIPS (Treasury Inflation-Protected Securities), mentioned in Chapter 6, are a ready source of a nearly risk-free interest rate that is adjusted for inflation. TIPS let us measure the risk-free real interest rate directly in financial markets.

APPLYING THE CONCEPT
THE CHINESE STOCK MARKET

After being closed for more than half a century, China re-opened its stock market in the early 1990s. Since then the market has grown rapidly, so that today there are nearly 2,500 Chinese companies with market capitalization of more than $3.5 trillion—that's nearly one-half of Chinese GDP.

There are two stock exchanges in China, one in Shanghai (on the east coast) and one in Shenzhen (near Hong Kong). When they were started, the idea was to transfer the ownership of state-owned enterprises into private hands. For ideological reasons at the time, government officials wanted to retain control of these companies, so they created a system of restricted share ownership. Two types of shares were issued—A-shares, priced in Chinese *yuan* (China's currency unit), and B-shares, denominated in either U.S. or Hong Kong dollars. To maintain control, the state retained two-thirds of the A-shares.

Until 2001, domestic Chinese investors could hold only A-shares while foreigners could purchase only B-shares.

Despite the fact that the two classes of shares gave owners the same rights, A-shares prices were on average more than four times that of the otherwise identical B-shares. This is strange. Two things that are the same should sell for the same price.

Some observers suggested that the premium resulted from a combination of the lack of Chinese investor sophistication, a shortage of information, and euphoria at being able to purchase common stock. But a critical piece of evidence suggests prices were high because there weren't enough shares to go around. A few years ago, as the Chinese government loosened its grip on the economy, officials decided to reduce their stock holdings and announced a plan to sell the government's A-shares into the market. Prices collapsed, falling by more than 50 percent from their peak. Elementary supply and demand analysis teaches us that when supply is low, prices are likely to be high; and that when supply increases, prices fall.

The lesson is that price differences can be a consequence of institutional constraints. And if they are, when institutional constraints are relaxed prices change.

get estimates for the various numbers in the formula. Historically, the (long-term) risk-free real interest rate has averaged around 2 percent, so $rf = 0.02$. Historical information also suggests that the risk premium is around 4 percent, so $rp = 0.04$. The dividend growth rate is about 2 percent, so $g = 0.02$. And the owner of a $1,430 portfolio of the S&P 500 stocks might expect to receive $69.64 in dividends during 2013.[10] Putting this all into equation (11) gives us $P_{today} = \$1,776$:

$$P_{today} = \frac{D_{today}(1 + g)}{rf + rp - g} = \frac{\$69.64(1.02)}{0.02 + 0.04 - 0.02} = \$1,776$$

This is 24 percent above the actual level of 1,430. There are several plausible explanations for the disparity. One is that the risk premium rp is actually higher; 5 percent would do it. Alternatively, we can justify an S&P 500 level of 1,430 by assuming that the dividend growth rate is really 1.1 percent rather than 2 percent. The conclusion is that this simple dividend-discount model works reasonably well, but is sensitive to assumptions about the risk-free interest rate, the risk premium, and the dividend growth rate.

The Theory of Efficient Markets

Stock prices change nearly continuously. Why? One explanation starts in the same place as the dividend-discount model and is based on the concept of fundamental value. When fundamentals change, prices must change with them.

[10]This amount is adjusted for the fact that companies commonly buy back some of their shares as a complement to paying dividends. Thus, the figure of $69.64 represents a shareholder return (combining dividends *and* stock buybacks) of 4.87 percent, which was the average over the decade to 2012 (see, for example, Aswath Damodaran, "Equity Risk Premiums: Determinants, Estimation and Implications—The 2013 Edition," March 2013, at *http://papers.ssrn.com/sol3/papers.cfm?abstract_id=2238064*).

This line of reasoning gives rise to what is commonly called the theory of efficient markets. The basis for the **theory of efficient markets** is the notion that the prices of all financial instruments, including stocks, reflect all available information.[11] As a result, markets adjust immediately and continuously to changes in fundamental values. If the theory of efficient markets is correct, the chartists are doomed to failure.

The theory of efficient markets implies that stock price movements are unpredictable. If they weren't—if you could accurately forecast that the price of a stock was going to rise tomorrow—you would immediately buy as many shares of the stock as possible. Your action would increase demand for the stock, driving its price up today. In other words, the fact that you think a stock's price will rise tomorrow makes it rise today.[12] When markets are efficient, the prices at which stocks currently trade reflect all available information, so future price movements are unpredictable.

If no one can predict stock price movements, then what good is investment advice? Not much! If the theory of efficient markets is correct, no one can consistently beat the market average. This means that active portfolio management—buying and selling stocks based on someone's advice—will not yield a higher return than that of a broad stock-market index—the market average—year after year.

There is quite a bit of evidence to support the view that stock price changes are unpredictable and that professional money managers cannot beat an index like the S&P 500 with regularity. On average, the return on managed portfolios is about 2 percent *less* than average stock-market returns. But we do see managers who at least claim to exceed the market average year after year.[13] How can this be? There are four possibilities: (1) They are taking advantage of insider information, which is illegal; (2) they are taking on risk, which brings added compensation but means that at times, returns will be extremely poor; (3) they are lucky; or (4) markets are not efficient.

It is intriguing to think that high (or low) investment returns could simply be the result of chance. To understand why this is so, consider the following parable, which appears in Peter Bernstein's book *Capital Ideas*.[14] Suppose that 300 million people all join in a coin-tossing contest. On the first day, each person finds a partner and they each bet a dollar on the coin toss. The winner gets $2 and the loser leaves the game. Each day the coin toss is repeated, with the losers turning their dollars over to the winners, who then stake their winnings on the next day's toss. The laws of chance tell us that, after 10 flips on 10 consecutive mornings, only 220,000 people will still be in the contest, and each will have won a little more than $1,000. Then the game heats up. Ten days later, after 20 tosses, only 286 people will still be playing, and each will have nearly $1,050,000. These winners had no special knowledge. No skill was involved in their accumulation of high returns, just pure chance.

You may be asking what this has to do with investment and efficient markets. The answer is that when there are lots of people placing bets—and there surely are a large

[11]A failure by financial markets to use all information efficiently need not imply the existence of arbitrage profits, that is, of a risk-free opportunity to profit from trading securities. On the contrary, in the absence of transaction costs, two financial instruments with the same risk and expected future payments should trade at the same price. This "no arbitrage" assumption, which is weaker than the efficient markets hypothesis, is widely used in financial research today. Chapter 9 defines arbitrage and explains the pricing of futures contracts using the no-arbitrage approach.

[12]If you felt sure that a stock's price was going to fall, you could take advantage of your forecast by using a strategy called *short selling*. You would borrow shares and sell them with the idea of buying them back at a lower price in the future. This tactic increases the supply of shares for sale, driving the stock's price down.

[13]Remember that someone owns every share in the stock market, so above-average returns to one person must be matched by below-average returns to someone else.

[14]Peter Bernstein, *Capital Ideas: The Improbable Origins of Modern Wall Street* (New York: Free Press, 1993).

number of investors trying to gain advantages in the stock market—there will be a fair number of people who do well just by pure chance. And the problem with the stock market is that the number of people who "win" is about the same as the number we would expect to be lucky.

Investing in Stocks for the Long Run

Stocks appear to be risky, yet many people hold a substantial proportion of their wealth in the form of stock. We can reconcile our perception of risk with observed behavior in two ways. Either stocks are not that risky, or people are not that averse to the risk and so do not require a large risk premium to hold stocks. Which of these explanations is more plausible?

To get a sense of the risk in holding stock, we can look at the one-year return on the S&P 500 Index for each of the past 142 years. The orange line in Figure 8.2 plots the one-year real return to holding this portfolio (including dividend payments and adjusted for inflation using the consumer price index). The one-year real returns shown in Figure 8.2 averaged about 8 percent per year. From a different perspective, the annualized real return on one dollar invested in stocks in 1871 and held until 2013 was somewhat lower, almost 6½ percent.

In looking at the figure, remember to check the axis labels. Start by noting that the scale on the vertical axis goes from −40 percent to +60 percent, a huge range. The minimum return was nearly −40 percent (in 1932), and the maximum was more than 50 percent (in 1936). Over the past 50 years the range has narrowed somewhat, to a maximum annual return of 31 percent (in 1996) and a minimum of −35 percent (in 2008). Nearly half the time, the return on holding stocks has been either less than zero (negative) or above 25 percent (substantially positive). The graph certainly gives the impression that prices fluctuate wildly and that holding stocks is extremely risky.

Figure 8.2 S&P 1-Year and 25-Year Stock Returns, 1872 to 2013

(Returns are Real, Adjusted for Inflation Using the CPI)

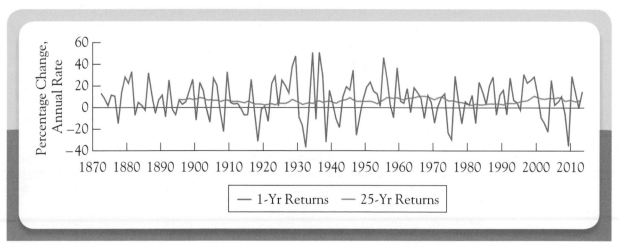

SOURCE: From *Irrational Exuberance,* 2/e. Princeton, 2005. Reprinted with permission by Robert J. Shiller. Estimated after 2004 using source data from the following website: *www.irrationalexuberance.com/index.htm*

YOUR FINANCIAL WORLD
Should You Own Stocks?

Should you own stocks? The answer is yes, especially if you are young! Many people shy away from stocks and invest in bonds (or other interest-bearing assets). But remember that bonds are risky, too—even U.S. Treasury bonds carry interest-rate risk and inflation risk. Though stocks may look risky, history suggests that a well-diversified portfolio of stocks held over the long term is not. The real question is *how* to buy stock.

There are five issues to think about when buying stock: affordability, liquidity, diversification, management, and cost. Prepackaged portfolios called **mutual funds** address all these issues in one way or another. The problem is that there are literally thousands of mutual funds. So, how do we choose? Here are some points to keep in mind:

1. *Affordability.* Most mutual funds allow a small initial investment. You can start with as little as $1,000.

2. *Liquidity.* In an emergency, you may need to withdraw resources quickly. Make sure you can withdraw your investment easily if you need to.

3. *Diversification.* The vast majority of mutual funds are much more diversified than any individual portfolio of stocks. Even so, it is important to check before you buy.

4. *Management.* Mutual funds offer the advantage of professional management. You do need to be careful, as funds in which people make the decisions, so-called managed funds, tend to perform worse than index funds, which are designed to mimic stock market indexes like the S&P 500.

5. *Cost.* Mutual fund managers charge fees for their services. The fees for managed funds run about 1½ percent per year, compared to ½ percent or less for index funds. This is a significant difference. Over 20 years, an investment of $10,000 with an average annual return of 8 percent will amount to $46,610. If you pay a 1 percent fee, so that the return averages only 7 percent, the value of the investment drops to $38,697, or $7,913 less.

Taken together, these considerations persuade many people to invest in index funds. Index funds are affordable and liquid, they offer excellent diversification, and they tend to be cheap. Don't take our word for it; always ask before you invest.

In 1994 though, Professor Jeremy Siegel of the University of Pennsylvania's Wharton School published a book titled *Stocks for the Long Run,*[15] in which he suggested that investing in stocks is risky only if you hold them for a short time. If you buy stocks and hold them for long enough, they really are not very risky.

To see Professor Siegel's point, we can again look at Figure 8.2, this time to see the return to holding stocks for 25 years instead of one. The green line shows the average annual return from investing in the S&P 500 for a 25-year period (versus the one-year return shown by the orange line). We can see immediately that the green line is much smoother and fluctuates over a much smaller range—and it never dips below zero. In fact, the *minimum average* annual inflation-adjusted return over 25 years was 2.5 percent, while the maximum was 11.2 percent. Siegel's point is that if you buy stocks and hold them for the long run—25 years or so—past patterns indicate that your investment is not very risky.

That was not the end of Professor Siegel's analysis. His next step was to compare the returns from holding bonds with those from holding stock. The results were startling. Siegel reported that, between 1871 and 1992, there was no 30-year period when bonds outperformed stocks. In other words, when held for the long term, *stocks are less risky than bonds!*

---

[15]Jeremy J. Siegel. *Stocks for the Long Run: A Guide to Selecting Markets for Long-Term Growth,* 5th ed. (New York: McGraw-Hill, 2014).

IN THE NEWS
Bubble Spotting

By Robert J. Shiller

March 22, 2011

People frequently ask me, as someone who has written on market speculation, where the next big speculative bubble is likely to be. Will it be in housing again? Will it be in the stock market?

I don't know, though I have some hunches. It is impossible for anyone to predict bubbles accurately. In my view, bubbles are social epidemics, fostered by a sort of interpersonal contagion. A bubble forms when the contagion rate goes up for ideas that support a bubble. But contagion rates depend on patterns of thinking, which are difficult to judge.

Big speculative bubbles are rare events.... And, because big bubbles last for many years, predicting them means predicting many years in the future, which is a bit like predicting who will be running the government two elections from now.

But some places appear a little more likely than others to give rise to bubbles. The stock market is the first logical place to look, as it is a highly leveraged investment—and has a history of bubbles. There have been three colossal stock-market bubbles in the last century: the 1920's, the 1960's, and the 1990's. In contrast, there has been only one such bubble in the United States' housing market in the last hundred years, that of the 2000's.

We have had a huge rebound from the bottom of the world's stock markets in 2009. The S&P 500 is up 87% in real terms since March 9 of that year. But, while the history of stock-market prediction is littered with too much failure to try to decide whether the bounceback will continue much longer, it doesn't look like a bubble, but more like the end of a depression scare. The rise in equity prices has not come with a contagious "new era" story, but rather a "sigh of relief" story.

Likewise, home prices have been booming over the past year or two in several places, notably China, Brazil, and Canada, and prices could still be driven up in many other places. But another housing bubble is not imminent in countries where one just burst. Conservative government policies will probably reduce subsidies to housing, and the current mood in these markets does not seem conducive to a bubble.

A continuation of today's commodity-price boom seems more likely, for it has more of a "new era" story attached to it. Increasing worries about global warming, and its effects on food prices, or about the cold and snowy winter in the northern hemisphere and its effects on heating fuel prices, are contagious stories....

But my favorite dark-horse bubble candidate for the next decade or so is farmland—and not just because there have been stories in recent months of booming farmland prices in the US and the United Kingdom.

Of course, farmland is much less important than other speculative assets....But, farmland, at least in certain places, seems to have the most contagious "new era" story right now. It was recently booming.... And the highly contagious global-warming story paints a scenario of food shortages and shifts in land values in different parts of the world, which might boost investor interest further.

Moreover, people nowadays easily imagine that the housing and farmland markets always move together, because prices in both boomed in recent memory, in the early 2000's. But... the latest data on farm prices have not shown anything like the decline in home prices....

The housing-price boom of the 2000's was little more than a construction-supply bottleneck, an inability to satisfy investment demand fast enough, and was (or in some places will be) eliminated with massive increases in supply. By contrast, there has been no increase in the supply of farmland, and the stories that would support a contagion of enthusiasm for it are in place, just as they were in the 1970's in the US, when a similar food-price scare generated the century's only farmland bubble.

SOURCE: Robert J. Shiller, "Bubble Spotting," *www.project-syndicate.org*, March 22, 2011. Used with permission of Project Syndicate.

LESSONS OF THE ARTICLE

Distinguishing *fads* from *fundamentals* makes forecasting bubbles difficult if not impossible. Debate about its causes may persist even after a bubble bursts. The article highlights "contagious" ideas or fads that lead to speculation, especially for assets in limited supply. But not every price jump is due to a fad: If the drivers of the price gains are fundamentals—such as profit prospects, the discount rate, or demographics—the price rise is not a bubble.

For many people, investing in stock is a way of saving for retirement, so their investment horizon is very long. Professor Siegel's calculations tell us that our retirement savings should be invested in stock and that we shouldn't worry about year-to-year fluctuations in their value.[16]

The Stock Market's Role in the Economy

MARKETS

The stock market plays a crucial role in every modern capitalist economy. The prices determined there tell us the market value of companies, which guides the allocation of resources. Firms with a high stock-market value are the ones investors prize, so they have an easier time garnering the resources they need to grow. In contrast, firms whose stock value is low have difficulty financing their operations.

So long as stock prices accurately reflect fundamental values, this resource allocation mechanism works well. The signals are accurate, and investment resources flow to their most socially beneficial uses. But at times, stock prices deviate significantly from the fundamentals and move in ways that are difficult to attribute to changes in the real interest rate, the risk premium, or the growth rate of future dividends.

While many economists believe that markets are reasonably efficient and that prices reflect fundamental values, it is worth entertaining the possibility that shifts in investor psychology may distort prices. The fact is, both euphoria and depression are contagious, so when investors become unjustifiably exuberant about the market's future prospects, prices rise regardless of the fundamentals. Such mass enthusiasm creates **bubbles**, persistent and expanding gaps between actual stock prices and those warranted by the fundamentals. These bubbles inevitably burst, creating crashes. This phenomenon is one explanation for the very jagged pattern in annual stock returns—the large gains followed by equally large losses—shown in Figure 8.2.[17]

Investors surely care about the large gains and losses they see when stock prices rise or fall serendipitously. But they are not the only ones who should be concerned. Bubbles affect all of us because they distort the economic decisions companies and consumers make. Here is what happens to companies. When their stock prices rise, financing becomes easier to obtain. They can sell shares and use the proceeds to fund new business opportunities. In the feeding frenzy of a bubble, companies can sell shares for prices that are too high, so financing new investments becomes too easy. It is not much of a challenge to identify high-technology companies that raised staggering sums in the equity markets in the late 1990s, only to crash and burn several years later. They spent the funds they raised on investments in equipment and buildings that turned out later to be worth nothing to them or anyone else.[18]

The consequences of such a bubble are not innocuous. The companies whose stock prices rise the most can raise financing the most easily. The result is that they invest too much. Meanwhile, firms in businesses that are not the objects of investor euphoria have a more difficult time raising financing, so they invest too little. The distortions can be large, and recovery can be slow, especially because companies find it almost impossible to obtain financing for new projects after the bubble bursts.

---

[16]For a more sobering view of the stock market rise of the late 1990s and the housing bubble of the subsequent decade, see Robert J. Shiller, *Irrational Exuberance,* 2nd ed. (Princeton, NJ: Princeton University Press, 2005).

[17]The fact that large declines tend to be followed by equally large increases is what makes stocks less risky when held over a long period, as Professor Siegel noticed.

[18]Stories about the Internet boom of the late 1990s, together with data on stock prices and market values of firms, are collected in John Cassidy's *Dot.con: How America Lost Its Mind and Money in the Internet Era* (New York: HarperCollins, 2002).

APPLYING THE CONCEPT
WHAT WAS THE INTERNET BUBBLE ALL ABOUT?

During the late 1990s, the stock prices of many new high-technology companies, commonly referred to as *dot-coms*, rose rapidly and then crashed. VA Linux was a representative example. The company's claim to fame was its Unix-based operating system for Web and database servers, which it gave away for free. On the first day of public trading in December 1999, the stock opened at $300 per share. A little over a year later, it was trading at just $5 a share. Other examples are easy to find. In fact, the Nasdaq Composite Index, which is composed of numerous small start-ups as well as large information technology (IT) firms, doubled in value from September 1999 to March 2000, then fell by 70 percent over the next year.

Good things did come from the Internet bubble. One was a change in the way new companies obtain financing. Before 1995, the only funding new companies could get was from people called *venture capitalists,* who specialized in the high-risk business of financing new companies—that is, new ventures. But venture capitalists parted with their resources reluctantly, and only when they were promised extremely high rates of return. By the late 1990s, start-up companies could bypass the venture capitalists and go directly to the capital markets to raise funds. Individual investors could diversify their portfolios in a way that had not been possible a few years before.

The drawbacks of the Internet bubble outweighed the advantages, however. Not only did people who bought these stocks at their peaks incur substantial losses, but the artificially inflated prices also created the mistaken impression that the investments were worthwhile. The boom in stock prices was mirrored by overinvestment in the companies. By 2001, warehouses were piled high with practically new computers left behind by bankrupt dot-com companies. The distortions caused by unjustifiably high stock prices had warped investors' decisions, leaving many worthwhile projects unfunded—an outcome that was bad for everyone.

The impact of stock price bubbles on consumer behavior is equally damaging. Rising equity prices increase individual wealth. The richer we become the more income we spend and the less we save. Unjustifiably high stock prices lead us to buy luxury cars, large houses, and extravagant vacations, which fuels a boom in economic activity. People begin to think they will not need to work as long before they retire. After all, the stock market has made them wealthy, and rich people don't need to work.

The euphoria can't last. When the bubble eventually bursts, individuals are forced to reevaluate their wealth. People discover that their houses and mortgages are too large for their paychecks and their investment accounts are only a shadow of what they once were. Now they need to work harder than ever just to keep up, and their plans for an early retirement are a distant memory. That's not all. Firms that geared up to produce luxury goods for rich shoppers are in trouble. Their wealthy customers disappeared when the bubble burst, and now they are stuck with products people can't afford to buy.

If bubbles result in real investment that is both excessive and inefficiently distributed, crashes do the opposite. The shift from overoptimism to excessive pessimism causes a collapse in investment and economic growth. Normally, the stock market works well and investment funds flow to their most beneficial uses. Occasionally the process goes awry and stock prices move far from any reasonable notion of fundamental value. When these bubbles grow large enough, especially when they lead to crashes, the stock market can destabilize the real economy.

Bubbles have arisen numerous times in stock markets, but housing bubbles appear to be more pernicious because their collapse frequently impairs other important institutions and markets that are critical for economic growth. As we saw in Chapter 3, financial intermediation and the supply of credit suffered when (shadow) banks took large losses on their mortgage-related portfolios in the financial crisis of 2007–2009. And workers whose homes were "under water"—with market values below the outstanding balances on their mortgages—sometimes could not move to better jobs in new locations because they could neither sell nor refinance their homes. Even at the end of March 2013—nearly four years after the economic recovery began—one out of five borrowers still owed more on their mortgages than the market value of their homes.

Finally, large stock market swings alter economic prospects even when they are grounded in fundamentals. In the recent financial crisis, the disruption of liquidity and credit undermined profit prospects for many companies. As their stocks plunged, the incentive to pull back on investment intensified, helping to amplify the recession of 2007–2009.

Terms

bubble, 208

common stock, 190

dividend-discount model, 200

dividends, 198

Dow Jones Industrial Average (DJIA), 194

equity, 190

fundamental value, 198

limited liability, 192

market capitalization, 194

mutual fund, 206

Nasdaq Composite Index, 196

price-weighted average, 194

residual claimant, 191

Standard & Poor's 500 Index, 194

stock market, 189

stock-market indexes, 193

theory of efficient markets, 204

value-weighted index, 194

Wilshire 5000, 196

Using FRED: Codes for Data in This Chapter

Data Series	FRED Data Code
S&P 500 Stock Price Index	SP500
Dow Jones Industrial Average	DJIA
Wilshire 5000 Total Market Index	WILL5000IND
CBOE Volatility Index: VIX	VIXCLS
Market value of equities of nonfarm nonfinancial corporations	MVEONWMVBSNNCB
Total net worth (market value) of nonfarm nonfinancial corporations	TNWMVBSNNCB
Total net worth (historical cost) of nonfarm nonfinancial corporations	TNWHCBSNNCB
Corporate equities held by households	CEABSHNO

Chapter Lessons

1. Stockholders own the firms in which they hold shares.
   a. They are residual claimants, which means they are last in line after all other creditors.
   b. They have limited liability, so their losses cannot exceed their initial investments.

2. There are two basic types of stock-market index.
   a. The Dow Jones Industrial Average is a price-weighted index.
   b. The S&P 500 is a value-weighted index.
   c. For every stock market in the world, there is a comprehensive index that is used to measure overall performance.

3. There are several ways to value stocks.
   a. Some analysts examine patterns of past performance; others follow investor psychology.
   b. The fundamental value of a stock depends on expectations for a firm's future profitability.
   c. To compensate for the fact that stocks are risky investments, investors in stock require a risk premium.
   d. The dividend-discount model is a simple way to assess fundamental value. According to this model, stock prices depend on the current level of dividends, the growth rate of dividends, the risk-free interest rate, and the equity risk premium.
   e. According to the theory of efficient markets, stock prices reflect all available information.
   f. If markets are efficient, then stock price movements are unpredictable, and investors cannot systematically outperform a comprehensive stock-market index like the S&P 500.

4. Stock investments are much less risky when they are held for long periods than when they are held for short periods.

5. Stock prices are a central element in a market economy, because they ensure that investment resources flow to their most profitable uses. When occasional bubbles and crashes distort stock prices, they can destabilize the economy.

Conceptual and Analytical Problems

1. Explain why being a residual claimant makes stock ownership risky. *(LO1)*

2. Do individual shareholders have an effective say in corporate governance matters? *(LO1)*

3. Consider the following information on the stock market in a small economy. *(LO2)*

Company	Shares Outstanding	Price, Beginning of Year	Price, End of Year
1	100	$100	$94
2	1,000	$ 20	$25
3	10,000	$ 3	$ 6

   a. Compute a price-weighted stock price index for the beginning of the year and the end of the year. What is the percentage change?

   b. Compute a value-weighted stock price index for the beginning of the year and the end of the year. What is the percentage change?

www.mhhe.com/moneyandbanking4e

4. To raise wealth and stimulate private spending, suppose the central bank lowers interest rates, making stock market investment relatively attractive. Which stock market index would you monitor to judge the effectiveness of the policy: the Dow Jones Industrial Average or the S&P 500? Why? *(LO2)*

5. Suppose you see evidence that the stock market is efficient. Would that make you more or less likely to invest in stocks for your 401(k) retirement plan when you get your first job? *(LO4)*

6. Professor Siegel argues that investing in stocks for retirement may be less risky than investing in bonds. Would you recommend this approach to an individual in his or her early 60s? *(LO4)*

7. How do venture capital firms, which specialize in identifying and financing promising but high-risk businesses, help the economy grow? *(LO5)*

8.* What are the advantages of holding stock in a company versus holding bonds issued by the same company? *(LO1)*

9. If Professor Siegel is correct that stocks are less risky than bonds, then the risk premium on stock should be zero. Assuming that the risk-free interest rate is 2½ percent, the growth rate of dividends is 1 percent, and the current level of dividends is $70, use the dividend-discount model to compute the level of the S&P 500 that is warranted by the fundamentals. Compare the result to the current S&P 500 level, and comment on it. *(LO4)*

10.* Why is a booming stock market not always a good thing for the economy? *(LO5)*

11. The financial press tends to become excited when the Dow Jones Industrial Average rises or falls sharply. After a particularly steep rise or fall, newspapers may publish tables ranking the day's results with other large advances or declines. What do you think of such reporting? If you were asked to construct a table of the best and worst days in stock market history, how would you do it, and why? *(LO2)*

12. You are thinking about investing in stock in a company that paid a dividend of $10 this year and whose dividends you expect will grow at 4 percent a year. The risk-free rate is 3 percent and you require a risk premium of 5 percent. If the price of the stock in the market is $200 a share, should you buy it? *(LO3)*

13.* Consider again the stock described in Problem 12. What might account for the difference in the market price of the stock and the price you are willing to pay for the stock? *(LO3)*

14. You are trying to decide whether to buy stock in Company X or Company Y. Both companies need $1,000 capital investment and will earn $200 in good years (with probability 0.5) and $60 in bad years. The only difference between the companies is that Company X is planning to raise all of the $1,000 needed by issuing equity, while Company Y plans to finance $500 through equity and $500 through bonds on which 10 percent interest must be paid.

   Construct a table showing the expected value and standard deviation of the equity return for each of the companies. (You could use Table 8.3 as a guide.) Based on this table, in which company would you buy stock? Explain your choice. *(LO3)*

15. Your brother has $1,000 and a one-year investment horizon and asks your advice about whether he should invest in a particular company's stock. What information would you suggest he analyze when making his decision? Is there an alternative

*Indicates more difficult problems

investment strategy to gain exposure to the stock market you might suggest he consider? *(LO4)*

16. Given that many stock-market indexes across the world fell and rose together during the financial crisis of 2007–2009, do you think investing in global stock markets is an effective way to reduce risk? Why or why not? *(LO2)*

17. Do you think a proposal to abolish limited liability for stockholders would be supported by companies issuing stock? *(LO1)*

18. You peruse the available records of some public figures in your area and notice that they persistently gain higher returns on their stock portfolios than the market average. As a believer in efficient markets, what explanation for these rates of returns seems most likely to you? *(LO5)*

19. Do you think that widespread belief in the efficient markets theory was a significant contributor to the 2007–2009 financial crisis? Why or why not? *(LO5)*

20. Based on the dividend-discount model, what do you think would happen to stock prices if there were an increase in the perceived riskiness of bonds? *(LO3)*

21.* Use the dividend-discount model to explain why an increase in stock prices is often a good indication that the economy is expected to do well. *(LO3)*

Data Exploration

For detailed instructions on using Federal Reserve Economic Data (FRED) online to answer each of the following problems, visit www.mhhe.com/moneyandbanking4e and click on Student Edition, then Data Exploration Hints.

Scan here for quick access to the hints for these problems. Need a barcode reader? Try ScanLife, available in your app store.

1. How well does the stock market anticipate the behavior of the economy? Plot since 1950 the percent change from a year ago of the Dow Jones Industrial Average (FRED code: DJIA). Is the index a reliable predictor of business cycle downturns (depicted in the graph by vertical, shaded bars)? *(LO5)*

2. Why might the stocks of small firms outperform large firms over long periods of time? Will this hold over short periods of time, too? Plot since 1979 the stock indexes for small firms (FRED code: WILLSMLCAP) and large firms (FRED code: WILLLRGCAP) using annual data scaled to a common base year of 1979=100. *(LO3)*

3. Compare and contrast the evolution of two leading stock indexes. Plot since 1960 on a quarterly basis the Dow Jones Industrial Average (FRED code: DJIA) and the S&P 500 (FRED code: SP500) scaled to a common base quarter of 1960 Q1=100. *(LO2)*

4. The Dow Jones Industrial Average (FRED code: DJIA) is a price-weighted index of 30 stocks and the S&P 500 (FRED code: SP500) index is a value-weighted average of 500 stocks. Find out which is more volatile. Plot on a quarterly basis since 1970 the percent change from a year ago of each index. Download the data to a spreadsheet and compute the standard deviation for each series over the period. *(LO3)*

5. Have stock dividends become a more important source of income to U.S. households? Plot since 1959 the share of dividend income (FRED code: B703RC-1Q027SBEA) in personal disposable income (FRED code: DSPI). Can you explain the 50-year trend? *(LO5)*

Chapter 9

Derivatives: Futures, Options, and Swaps

Learning Objectives

Understand . . .

LO1 How derivatives transfer risk

LO2 Forward versus futures contracts

LO3 Options and their pricing

LO4 The use and abuse of swaps

Derivatives played a central role in the financial crisis of 2007–2009. One of the key events during the crisis was the fall of AIG, the world's largest insurance company. Through the use of derivatives contracts, AIG had taken enormous risks that it was able to conceal from the view both of government officials and its trading partners. Each contract was arranged over the counter (OTC)—that is, directly between AIG and a single counterparty—rather than through an organized exchange. In the crisis, these hidden risks threatened the entire financial system.

Leading up to the crisis, the tight but largely unseen links that OTC derivatives created among the largest, most important global financial institutions made the entire system vulnerable to the weakest of those institutions. Partly as a result of the *systemic vulnerabilities* posed by OTC derivatives, phrases like "too interconnected to fail" and "too big to fail" filled newspapers and the media (see Chapter 5, Lessons from the Crisis: Systemic Risk). Warren Buffett, the famed investor, called derivatives "weapons of financial mass destruction."

Even in the years before the financial crisis, stories detailing the abuse of derivatives filled the pages of the business press. Derivatives were at the bottom of the scandal that engulfed Enron immediately after it declared bankruptcy in November 2001. As we have learned since then, Enron engaged in a variety of financial transactions whose express purpose was to give the appearance of low debt, low risk, and high profitability. This sleight of hand kept the stock price high and made shareholders happy, so no one complained. In fact, no one even looked. But eventually the day of reckoning came, and the company collapsed.

Financial derivatives were also linked to the collapse of Long-Term Capital Management (LTCM), a Connecticut-based hedge fund, in fall 1998. On a single day in August 1998, LTCM lost an astounding $553 million. By late September, the fund had lost another $2 billion. That left LTCM with more than $99 billion in debt and $100 billion in assets. With loans accounting for 99 percent of total assets, repayment was nearly impossible. LTCM also had significant derivatives positions that did not show up on the balance sheet as assets or liabilities. These off-balance-sheet arrangements, which carried even more risk, were the primary cause of the fund's stunningly swift losses.

Derivatives also played a role in the euro-area crisis that began in earnest in 2010. Many banks that owned Greek government debt had hedged by purchasing derivatives that would compensate them if Greece defaulted (see Credit-Default Swaps on page 234). But policymakers in the euro area sought to reduce Greece's debt burden without triggering an outright default in legal terms. In the end, Greece defaulted, and the derivatives paid off. Yet, had the policymakers succeeded, financial firms that thought they were protected would have faced large, unanticipated losses. Fears of such exposure, along with doubts about the insurance provided by derivatives, likely accelerated deleveraging and aggravated financial instability.

If derivatives are open to abuse, why do they exist? The answer is that when used properly, derivatives are extremely helpful financial instruments. They can be used to reduce risk, allowing firms and individuals to enter into agreements that they otherwise wouldn't be willing to accept. Derivatives can also be used as insurance. For example, in winter 1998, a snowmobile manufacturer named Bombardier offered a $1,000 rebate to buyers should snowfall in 44 cities total less than half what it had averaged over the preceding three years. Sales rose 38 percent. The existence of "weather derivatives" enabled Bombardier to undertake this risky marketing strategy. Paying the rebates would have bankrupted the company, but Bombardier purchased derivatives that would pay off if snowfall were low. By using this unorthodox form of insurance, Bombardier transferred the risk to someone else.

What exactly are derivatives, and why are they so important? Though they play a critical role in our financial well-being, most people barely know what they are. This chapter will provide an introduction to the uses and abuses of derivatives.

The Basics: Defining Derivatives

To understand what derivatives are, let's begin with the basics. A **derivative** is a financial instrument whose value depends on—is *derived* from—the value of some other financial instrument, called the *underlying asset.* Some common examples of underlying assets are stocks, bonds, wheat, snowfall, and orange juice.

A simple example of a derivative is a contractual agreement between two investors that obligates one to make a payment to the other, depending on the movement in interest rates over the next year. This type of derivative is called an interest-rate *futures contract.* Such an arrangement is quite different from the outright purchase of a bond for two reasons. First, derivatives provide an easy way for investors to profit from price declines. The purchase of a bond, in contrast, is a bet that its price will rise.[1] Second, and more important, in a derivatives transaction, one person's loss is always another person's gain. Buyer and seller are like two people playing poker. How much each player wins or loses depends on how the game progresses, but the total amount on the table doesn't change.

While derivatives can be used to *speculate,* or gamble on future price movements, the fact that they allow investors to manage and reduce risk makes them indispensable to a modern economy. Bombardier used a derivative to hedge the risk of having to pay rebates in the event of low snowfall (we discussed hedging in Chapter 5). As we will see, farmers use derivatives regularly, to insure themselves against fluctuations in the market prices of their crops. Risk can be bought and sold using derivatives. Thus, *the purpose of derivatives is to transfer risk from one person or firm to another.*

---

[1]Investors can bet that prices will fall using a technique called *short selling.* The investor borrows an asset from its owner for a fee, sells it at the current market price, and then repurchases it later. The short seller is betting that the price of the asset will fall between the time it is sold and the time it is repurchased.

"At the Hawescroft School we've de-emphasized singing and drawing and emphasized stocks and derivatives."

SOURCE: *2004 © Peter Steiner/The New Yorker Collection/www.cartoonbank.com.*

When people have the ability to transfer risks, they will do things that they wouldn't do otherwise. Think of a wheat farmer and a bread baker. If he or she cannot insure against a decline in the price of wheat, the farmer will plant fewer acres of wheat. And without a guarantee that the price of flour will not rise, the baker will build a smaller bakery. Those are prudent responses to the risks created by price fluctuations. Now introduce a mechanism through which the farmer and the baker can guarantee the price of wheat. As a result the farmer will plant more and the baker will build a bigger bakery. Insurance is what allows them to do it! Derivatives provide that insurance. In fact, by shifting risk to those willing and able to bear it, derivatives increase the risk-carrying capacity of the economy as a whole, improving the allocation of resources and increasing the level of output.

While derivatives allow individuals and firms to manage risk, they also allow them to conceal the true nature of certain financial transactions. In the same way that stripping a coupon bond separates the coupons from the principal payment, buying and selling derivatives can unbundle virtually any group of future payments and risks. A company that hesitates to issue a coupon bond for fear analysts will frown on the extra debt can instead issue the coupon payments and the principal payment as individual zero-coupon bonds, using derivative transactions to label them something other than borrowing. Thus, if stock-market analysts penalize companies for obtaining funding in certain ways, derivatives (as we will see) allow the companies to get exactly the same resources at the same risk but under a different name.

Derivatives may be divided into three major categories: forwards and futures, options, and swaps. Let's look at each one.

Forwards and Futures

Of all derivative financial instruments, forwards and futures are the simplest to understand and the easiest to use. *A* **forward***, or* **forward contract***, is an agreement between a buyer and a seller to exchange a commodity or financial instrument for a specified amount of cash on a prearranged future date.* Forward contracts are private agreements between two parties. Because they are customized, forward contracts are very difficult to resell to someone else.

Trading pit at the New York Mercantile Exchange in New York City that appeared in the movie *Trading Places* with Eddie Murphy and Dan Aykroyd.

To see why forward contracts are difficult to resell, consider the example of a yearlong apartment lease, in which the renter agrees to make a series of monthly payments to the landlord in exchange for the right to live in the apartment. Such a lease is a sequence of 12 forward contracts. Rent is paid in predetermined amounts on prearranged future dates in exchange for housing. While there is some standardization of leases, a contract between a specific renter and a specific landlord is unlike any other rental contract. Thus, there is no market for the resale or reassignment of apartment rental contracts.

In contrast, a **future***, or* **futures contract***, is a forward contract that has been standardized and sold through an organized exchange.*

Table 9.1	Interest-Rate Futures

(1)	(2)	(3)	(4)	(5)	(6)	(7)
	Open	High	Low	Settle	Chg	Open Interest
Interest Rate Futures						
Treasury Bonds (cbt)-$100,000; pts 32nds of 100%						
March	131–190	131–225	131–120	131–140	−8.0	1,904,882
June	130–125	130–170	130–075	130–090	−8.5	110,774

This table reports information on a contract for delivery of $100,000 face value worth of 10-year 6 percent coupon U.S. Treasury bonds.

Column 1 reports the month when the contract requires delivery of the bonds from the short position/seller to the long position/buyer.

Column 2. "Open" is the price quoted when the exchange opened on the morning of February 12, 2013. This need not be the same as the price at the preceding afternoon's close. The price in the first row, 131-190, is quoted in 32nds and represents the cost of $100 face value worth of the 10-year 6 percent coupon U.S. Treasury bonds. In this case, the open price is 131 plus 19.0 32nds. The open price in the second row, 130-125, means 130 plus 12.5 32nds.

Columns 3 and 4. "High" and "Low" are the highest and lowest prices posted during the trading day.

Column 5. "Settle" is the closing or settlement price at the end of the trading day. This is the price used for *marking to market.*

Column 6. "Change" is the change in the closing price, measured in 32nds, from the preceding day's closing price.

Column 7. "Open Interest" is the number of contracts outstanding, or open. For contracts near expiration, this number is often quite large. Most of the time, contract sellers repurchase their positions rather than delivering the bonds, a procedure called *settlement by offset.*

SOURCE: *The Wall Street Journal,* November 23, 2012. Used with permission of Dow Jones & Company, Inc. via Copyright Clearance Center.

A futures contract specifies that the seller—who has the *short position*—will deliver some quantity of a commodity or financial instrument to the buyer—who has the *long position*—on a specific date, called the *settlement* or *delivery* date, for a predetermined price. No payments are made initially when the contract is agreed to. The seller/short position benefits from declines in the price of the underlying asset, while the buyer/long position benefits from increases.[2]

Take the U.S. Treasury bond futures contract that trades on the Chicago Board of Trade (CBOT, which is a part of the CME Group). The contract specifies the delivery of $100,000 face value worth of 10-year, 6 percent coupon U.S. Treasury bonds at any time during a given month, called the *delivery* month.[3] Table 9.1 shows the prices and

[2]The term *short* refers to the fact that one party to the agreement is obligated to deliver something, whether or not he or she currently owns it. The term *long* signifies that the other party is obligated to buy something at a future date.

[3]A bond issued by the U.S. Treasury with an original maturity of 10 years or less is officially called a "Treasury note," but we use the term "Treasury bond" in this chapter for simplicity. The seller of a U.S. Treasury bond futures contract need not deliver the exact bond specified in the contract. The Chicago Board of Trade, a part of the CME Group, maintains a spreadsheet of conversion factors to use in adjusting the quantity (face value) when delivery of some other bond is made. While these particular futures allow for delivery at any time during the delivery month, other futures may require delivery on a specific day. Specifications of the contract are available at: *www.cmegroup.com/trading/interest-rates/us-treasury/10-year-us-treasury-note_contract_specifications.html*

trading activity for this contract on February 12, 2013. The fact that the contract is so specific means there is no need for negotiation. And the existence of the exchange creates a natural place for people who are interested in a particular futures contract to meet and trade. Historically, exchanges have been physical locations, but with the Internet came online trading of futures. In recent years, firms have created virtual futures markets for a wide variety of products, including energy, bandwidth, and plastics.

One more thing is needed before anyone will actually buy or sell futures contracts: assurance that the buyer and seller will meet their obligations. In the case of the U.S. Treasury futures contract, the buyer must be sure that the seller will deliver the bond, and the seller must believe that the buyer will pay for it. Market participants have found an ingenious solution to this problem. Instead of making a bilateral arrangement, the two parties to a futures contract each make an agreement with a *clearing corporation*. The clearing corporation, which operates like a large insurance company, is the counterparty to both sides of a transaction, guaranteeing that they will meet their obligations. This arrangement reduces the risk buyers and sellers face. The clearing corporation has the ability to monitor traders and the incentive to limit their risk taking (see Lessons from the Crisis: Central Counterparties and Systemic Risk).

Margin Accounts and Marking to Market

To reduce the risk it faces, the clearing corporation requires both parties to a futures contract to place a deposit with the corporation itself. This practice is called posting **margin** in a *margin account.* The margin deposits guarantee that when the contract comes due, the parties will be able to meet their obligations. But the clearing corporation does more than collect the *initial margin* when a contract is signed. It also posts daily gains and losses on the contract to the margin accounts of the parties involved.[4] This process is called *marking to market,* and it is done daily.

Marking to market is analogous to what happens during a poker game. At the end of each hand, the amount wagered is transferred from the losers to the winner. In financial parlance, the account of each player is marked to market. Alternative methods of accounting are too complicated, making it difficult to identify players who should be excused from the game because they have run out of resources. For similar reasons, the clearing corporation marks futures accounts to market every day. Doing so ensures that sellers always have the resources to make delivery and that buyers always can pay. As in poker, if someone's margin account falls below the minimum, the clearing corporation will sell the contracts, ending the person's participation in the market.

An example will help you understand how marking to market works. Take the case of a futures contract for the purchase of 1,000 ounces of silver at $20 per ounce. The contract specifies that the buyer of the contract, the long position, will pay $20,000 in exchange for 1,000 ounces of silver. The seller of the contract, the short position, receives the $20,000 and delivers the 1,000 ounces of silver. We can think about this contract as guaranteeing the long position the ability to buy 1,000 ounces of silver for $20,000 and guaranteeing the short position the ability to sell 1,000 ounces of silver for $20,000. Now consider what happens when the price of silver changes. If the price rises to $21 per ounce, the seller needs to give the buyer $1,000 so that the buyer pays only $20,000 for the 1,000 ounces of silver. By contrast, if the price falls to $19 an ounce, the buyer of the futures contract needs to pay $1,000 to the seller to make sure that the seller receives

---

[4]On February 12, 2013, the March U.S. Treasury bond futures contract in Table 9.1 declined 8/32 per $100 face value worth of bonds. A single contract covers 1,000 times that amount, so the value of each contract fell by ($8/32)(1000) = $250.00. Marking to market means that, at the end of the day for each outstanding contract, the clearing corporation debited the long position/buyer and credited the short position/seller $250.00.

$20,000 for selling the 1,000 ounces of silver. Marking to market is the transfer of funds at the end of each day that ensures the buyers and sellers get what the contract promises.

Hedging and Speculating with Futures

Futures contracts allow the transfer of risk between buyer and seller. This transfer can be accomplished through hedging or speculation. Let's look at *hedging* first. Say a government securities dealer wishes to insure against declines in the value of an inventory of bonds. Recall from Chapter 5 that this type of risk can be reduced by finding another financial instrument that delivers a high payoff when bond prices fall. That is exactly what happens with the sale of a U.S. Treasury bond futures contract: the seller/short position benefits from price declines. Put differently, the seller of a futures contract—the securities dealer, in this case—can guarantee the price at which the bonds are sold. The other party to this transaction might be a pension fund manager who is planning to purchase bonds in the future and wishes to insure against possible price increases.[5] Buying a futures contract fixes the price that the fund will need to pay. In this example, *both sides use the futures contract as a hedge. They are both hedgers.*[6]

Producers and users of commodities employ futures markets to hedge their risks as well. Farmers, mining companies, oil drillers, and the like are sellers of futures, taking short positions. After all, they own the commodities outright, so they want to stabilize the revenue they receive when they sell. In contrast, millers, jewelers, and oil distributors want to buy futures to take long positions. They require the commodity to do business, so they buy the futures contract to reduce risk arising from fluctuations in the cost of essential inputs.

What about *speculators*? Their objective is simple: They are trying to make a profit. To do so, they bet on price movements. Sellers of futures are betting that prices will fall, while buyers are betting that prices will rise. Futures contracts are popular tools for speculation because they are cheap. An investor needs only a relatively small amount of investment—the margin—to purchase a futures contract that is worth a great deal. Margin requirements of 10 percent or less are common. In the case of a futures contract for the delivery of $100,000 face value worth of 10-year, 6 percent coupon U.S. Treasury bonds, the Chicago Board of Trade (the clearing corporation that guarantees the contract) requires an initial margin of only $1,210 per contract. That is, an investment of only $1,210 gives the investor the same returns as the purchase of $100,000 worth of bonds. It is as if the investor borrowed the remaining $98,790 without having to pay any interest.[7]

To see the impact of this kind of leverage on the return to the buyer and seller of a futures contract, recall from footnote 4 that a decline of 8/32nds in the price of the Treasury bond futures contract meant that the long position/buyer lost $250.00, while the short position/seller gained $250.00. With a minimum initial investment of $1,210 for each contract, this represents a 20.7 percent loss to the futures contract buyer and a 20.7 percent gain to the futures contract seller. In contrast, the owner of the bond itself would have lost $250.00 on an approximately $100,000 investment, which is a loss of just 0.25 percent! *Speculators, then, can use futures to obtain very large amounts of leverage at a very low cost.*

Arbitrage and the Determinants of Futures Prices

To understand how the price of a futures contract is determined, let's start at the settlement date and work backward. On the settlement or delivery date, we know that the price

---

[5]Recall from Chapters 4 and 6 that bond prices and interest rates move in opposite directions. That means the bond dealer who sells the futures contract is insuring against interest rate increases.

[6]Hedgers who buy futures are called *long hedgers* and hedgers who sell futures are called *short hedgers*.

[7]It is even possible to arrange a margin account so that the balance earns interest.

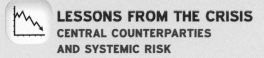

LESSONS FROM THE CRISIS
CENTRAL COUNTERPARTIES AND SYSTEMIC RISK

We know that a loss of liquidity and transparency can threaten the financial system as a whole (see Chapter 5, Lessons from the Crisis: Systemic Risk). Lack of liquidity can make trading impossible, while lack of transparency can make traders unwilling to trust one another. Both can cause markets to seize up and trigger a cascade of failures. Transparent, liquid financial markets are less prone to such systemic disruptions.

How can we make markets more robust? One way is to shift trading from over-the-counter (OTC) markets, where products tend to be customized, to transactions with a **central counterparty (CCP)** in standardized financial instruments.*

OTC trading is bilateral, that is, directly between buyer and seller, rather than through an intermediary. By contrast, a CCP is an entity that interposes itself between the two sides of a transaction, becoming the buyer to every seller and the seller to every buyer. Trading on most stock, futures, and options exchanges goes through CCPs. As a result, when you buy or sell a stock, you neither know nor care who the ultimate seller or buyer is because you are trading with the CCP of the exchange.

When trading OTC with many partners, a firm can build up excessively large positions without other parties being aware of the risk it is acquiring. In contrast, a CCP has the *ability*, as well as the *incentive*, to monitor the riskiness of its counterparties. Because all trades occur with the CCP, it can see whether a trader is taking a large position on one side of a trade. Standardization of contracts also facilitates CCP monitoring. If it finds itself trading with a risky counterparty, a CCP can insist on a risk premium to protect itself. A CCP also can refuse to trade with a counterparty that may not be able to pay. And it can insist on frequent marking of prices to market to measure and control risks effectively.

A CCP also limits its own risk through economies of scale. Most of the trades that a CCP conducts can be offset against one another. Therefore, the volume of net payments that must occur on any given day are only a small fraction of the gross value of the trades, sharply lowering the risk of nonpayment.

The history of CCPs reveals their practical benefits. Since 1925, when all U.S. futures contracts began trading through a CCP, no contract has failed despite many subsequent financial disruptions, including the Great Depression. CCPs have helped markets function well even when traders cannot pay. For example, when one large energy futures trader (Amaranth) failed in 2006, the futures market adjusted smoothly because the CCP could use the trader's collateral to satisfy its contracts with other firms. Futures markets also absorbed the losses from the spectacular 2011 collapse of a large commodities brokerage (MF Global) that misused customer money.

In contrast, systemic threats and disruptions have arisen repeatedly with OTC contracts: in 1998, when the possible demise of the hedge fund LTCM threatened numerous counterparties of its OTC interest-rate swaps; and again, during the financial crisis of 2007–2009, with a number of firms active in OTC derivatives, including Bear Stearns, Lehman Brothers, and AIG.

*For more details on CCPs, see Stephen G. Cecchetti, Jacob Gyntelberg, and Marc Hollanders, "Central Counterparties for Over-the-Counter Derivatives," *BIS Quarterly Review*, September 2009, pp. 45–58.

---

of the futures contract must equal the price of the underlying asset the seller is obligated to deliver. The reason is simple: If, at expiration, the futures price were to deviate from the asset's price, then it would be possible to make a risk-free profit by engaging in offsetting cash and futures transactions. If the current market price of a bond were below the futures contract price, someone could buy a bond at the low price and simultaneously sell a futures contract (take a short position and promise to deliver the bond on a future date). Immediate exercise of the futures contract and delivery of the bond would yield a profit equal to the difference between the market price and the futures price. Thinking about this example carefully, we can see that the investor who engages in these transactions has been able to make a profit without taking on any risk or making any investment.

The practice of simultaneously buying and selling financial instruments in order to benefit from temporary price differences is called **arbitrage**, and the people who engage in it are called *arbitrageurs*. Arbitrage means that two financial instruments with the same risk and promised future payments will sell for the same price. If, for example, the price of a specific bond is higher in one market than in another, an arbitrageur can buy at the low price and sell at the high price. The increase in demand in the market where the price is low drives the price up there, while the increase in supply in the market where the price is high drives the price down there, and the process continues until prices are equal in the two markets. As long as there are arbitrageurs, on the day when a futures contract is settled, the price of a bond futures contract will be the same as the market price—what is called the *spot price*—of the bond.

So we know that on the settlement date, the price of a futures contract must equal the spot price of the underlying asset. But what happens before the settlement date? The principle of arbitrage still applies. The price of the futures contract depends on the fact that someone can buy a bond and sell a futures contract simultaneously. Here's how it's done. First, the arbitrageur borrows at the current market interest rate. With the funds, the arbitrageur buys a bond and sells a bond futures contract. Now the arbitrageur has a loan on which interest must be paid, a bond that pays interest, and a promise to deliver the bond for a fixed price at the expiration of the futures contract. Because the interest owed on the loan and received from the bond will cancel out, this position costs nothing to initiate.[8] As before, if the market price of the bond is below the futures contract price, this strategy will yield a profit. *Thus, the futures price must move in lockstep with the market price of the bond.*

To see how arbitrage works, consider an example in which the spot price of a 4 percent coupon 10-year bond is $100, the current interest rate on a 3-month loan is also 4 percent (quoted at an annual rate), and the futures market price for delivery of a 4 percent, 10-year bond is $101. An investor could borrow $100, purchase the 10-year bond, and sell a bond future for $101 promising delivery of the bond in three months. The investor could use the interest payment from the bond to pay the interest on the loan and deliver the bond to the buyer of the futures contract on the delivery date. This transaction is completely riskless and nets the investor a profit of $1—without even putting up any funds. A riskless profit is extremely tempting, so the investor will continue to engage in the transactions needed to generate it. Here that means continuing to buy bonds (driving the price up) and sell futures (forcing the price down) until the prices converge and no further profits are available.[9]

Table 9.2 summarizes the positions of buyers and sellers in the futures market.

Table 9.2   Who's Who in Futures

	Buyer of a Futures Contract	Seller of a Futures Contract
This is called the	*Long* position	*Short* position
Obligation of the party	Buy the commodity or asset on the settlement date	Deliver the commodity or asset on the settlement date
What happens to this person's margin account after a *rise* in the market price of the commodity or asset?	*Credited*	*Debited*
Who takes this position to *hedge*?	The *user* of the commodity or *buyer* of the asset who needs to insure against the price *rising*	The *producer* of the commodity or owner of the asset who needs to insure against the price *falling*
Who takes this position to *speculate*?	Someone who believes that the market price of the commodity or asset will *rise*	Someone who believes that the market price of the commodity or asset will *fall*

[8]Unlike you and me, the arbitrageur can borrow at an interest rate that is close to the one received from the bond. There are two reasons for this. First, the arbitrageur is likely to be a large financial intermediary with a very high credit rating; second, the loan is collateralized by the bond itself.

[9]In a commodity futures contract, the futures price will equal the present value of the expected spot price on the delivery date, discounted at the risk-free interest rate.

Options

Everyone likes to have options. Having the option to go on vacation or buy a new car is nice. The alternative to having options, having our decisions made for us, is surely worse. Because options are valuable, people are willing to pay for them when they can. Financial options are no different; because they are worth having, we can put a price on them.

Calculating the price of an option is incredibly complicated. In fact, no one knew how before Fischer Black and Myron Scholes figured it out in 1973. Traders immediately programmed their famous Black-Scholes formula into the computers available at the time, and the options markets took off. By June 2000, the market value of outstanding options was in the neighborhood of $500 billion. Today, hundreds of millions of options contracts are outstanding, and millions of them change hands every day.

Before we learn how to price options, we'll need to master the vocabulary used to describe them. Once we have the language, the next step is to move on to how to use options and how to value them.

Calls, Puts, and All That: Definitions

Like futures, options are agreements between two parties. There is a seller, called an *option writer,* and a buyer, called an *option holder.* As we will see, option writers incur obligations, while option holders obtain rights. There are two basic options, *puts* and *calls.*

A **call option** is the right to buy—"call away"—a given quantity of an underlying asset at a predetermined price, called the **strike price** (or *exercise price*), on or before a specific date. For example, a January 2014 call option on 100 shares of IBM stock at a strike price of 200 gives the option holder the right to buy 100 shares of IBM for $200 apiece prior to the third Friday of January 2014. The writer of the call option *must* sell the shares if and when the holder chooses to use the call option. The holder of the call is *not required* to buy the shares; rather, the holder has the option to buy and will do so only if buying is beneficial. When the price of IBM stock exceeds the option strike price of 200, the option holder can either call away the 100 shares from the option writer by *exercising* the option or sell the option to someone else at a profit. If the market price rose to $205, for example, then exercising the call would allow the holder to buy the stock from the option writer for $200 and reap a $5 per share profit. Whenever the price of the stock is above the strike price of the call option, exercising the option is profitable for the holder, and the option is said to be *in the money* (as in "I'm in the money!"). If the price of the stock exactly equals the strike price, the option is said to be *at the money*. If the strike price exceeds the market price of the underlying asset, it is termed *out of the money*.

A **put option** gives the holder the right but not the obligation to sell the underlying asset at a predetermined price on or before a fixed date. The holder can "put" the asset in the hands of the option writer. Again, the writer of the option is obliged to buy the shares should the holder choose to exercise the option. Returning to the example of IBM stock, consider a put option with a strike price of 200. This is the right to sell 100 shares at $200 per share, which is valuable when the market price of IBM stock falls below $200. If the price of a share of IBM stock were $190, then exercising the put option would yield a profit of $10 per share.

The same terminology that is used to describe calls—in the money, at the money, and out of the money—applies to puts as well, but the circumstances in which it is used are reversed. Because the buyer of a put obtains the right to sell a stock, the put is *in the money* when the option's strike price is *above* the market price of the stock. It is *out of the money* when the strike price is *below* the market price.

While it is possible to customize options in the same way as forward contracts, many are standardized and traded on exchanges, just like futures contracts. The mechanics of trading are the same. A clearing corporation guarantees the obligations embodied in the option—those of the option writer. And the option writer is required to post margin. Because option holders incur no obligation, they are not required to post margin.

There are two types of calls and puts: American and European. **American options** can be exercised on any date from the time they are written until the day they expire. As a result, prior to the expiration date, the holder of an American option has three choices: (1) continue to hold the option, (2) sell the option to someone else, or (3) exercise the option immediately. **European options** can be exercised only on the day that they expire. Thus, the holder of a European option has two choices on a date prior to expiration: hold or sell. The vast majority of options traded in the United States are American.

Using Options

Who buys and sells options, and why? To answer this question, we need to understand how options are used. *Options transfer risk* from the buyer to the seller, so they can be used for both hedging and speculation. Let's take hedging first. Remember that a hedger is buying insurance. For someone who wants to purchase an asset such as a bond or a stock in the future, a call option ensures that the cost of buying the asset will not rise. For someone who plans to sell the asset in the future, a put option ensures that the price at which the asset can be sold will not go down.

To understand the close correspondence between options and insurance, think of the arrangement that automobile owners have with their insurance company. The owner pays an insurance premium and obtains the right to file a claim in the event of an accident. If the terms of the policy are met, the insurance company is obligated to pay the claim. If no accident occurs, then there is no claim and the insurance company makes no payment; the insurance premium is lost. In effect, the insurance company has sold an American call option to the car's owner where the underlying asset is a working car and the strike price is zero. This call option can be exercised if and only if the car is damaged in an accident on any day before the policy expires.

Options can be used for speculation as well. Say that you believe that interest rates are going to fall over the next few months. There are three ways to bet on this possibility. The first is to purchase a bond outright, hoping that its price will rise as interest rates fall. This is expensive, because you will need to come up with the resources to buy the bond. A second strategy is to buy a futures contract, taking the long position. If the market price of the bond rises, you will make a profit. As we saw in the last section, this is an attractive approach, because it requires only a small investment. But it is also very risky, because the investment is highly leveraged. Both the bond purchase and the futures contract carry the risk that you will take a loss, and if interest rates rise substantially, your loss will be large.

The third strategy for betting that interest rates will fall is to buy a call option on a U.S. Treasury bond. If you are right and interest rates fall, the value of the call option will rise. But if you are wrong and interest rates rise, the call will expire worthless and

YOUR FINANCIAL WORLD
Should You Believe Corporate Financial Statements?

Corporations work hard to appear as profitable as possible. They employ squadrons of accountants and financial wizards to dress up their financial statements so that reported profits are as high and stable as possible. While financial statements must meet exacting accounting standards, that does not mean they accurately reflect a company's true financial position. The problem is that the standards are so specific they provide a road map for the creation of misleading statements. Remember that derivatives render the names attached to particular risks and payoffs arbitrary and irrelevant. But accounting regulations are all about names. That is the way the system works, and there is nothing illegal about it.

So what are investors supposed to do? First, never trust an accounting statement that doesn't meet the standards set forth by financial regulators. For example, during the Internet boom of the late 1990s, many firms published so-called pro forma financial statements based on their own definitions of revenue and costs. To look profitable, these companies had to make their own accounting rules. Such tinkering implies that a firm has something to hide.

Second, the more open a company is in its financial accounting, the more likely that it is honest. One of the lasting effects of the credit rating failures associated with the financial crisis of 2007–2009 is that investors now punish companies that publish opaque financial statements. Honesty really is the best policy; the more information a firm makes public, the more credible it will be with investors.

Finally, remember that diversification reduces risk. If you own shares in many different companies, you are better protected against the possibility that some of them will be less than honest in their disclosures.

your losses will be limited to the price you paid for it. This bet is both highly leveraged and limited in its potential losses.

In the same way that purchasing a call option allows an investor to bet that the price of the underlying asset will rise, purchasing a put option allows the investor to bet that the price will fall. Again, if the investor is wrong, all that is lost is the price paid for the option. In the meantime, the option provides a cheap way to bet on the movement in the price of the underlying asset. The bet is highly leveraged, because a small initial investment creates the opportunity for a large gain. But unlike a futures contract, a put option has a limited potential loss.

So far we have discussed only the purchase of options. For every buyer there must be a seller. Who is it? After all, an option writer can take a large loss. Nevertheless, for a fee, some people are willing to take the risk and bet that prices will not move against them. These people are simply speculators. A second group of people who are willing to write options are insured against any losses that may arise. They are primarily dealers who engage in the regular purchase and sale of the underlying asset. These people are called *market makers* because they are always there to make the market. Because they are in the business of buying and selling, market makers both own the underlying asset so that they can deliver it and are willing to buy the underlying asset so that they have it ready to sell to someone else. If you own the underlying asset, writing a call option that obligates you to sell it at a fixed price is not that risky. These people write options to obtain the fee paid by the buyer.

Writing options can also generate clear benefits. To see how, think about the case of an electricity producer who has a plant that is worth operating only when electricity prices exceed a relatively high minimum level. Such peak-load plants are relatively common. They sit idle most of the time and are fired up only when demand is so high that prices spike. The problem is that when they are not operating—which is the normal state of affairs—the owner must pay maintenance charges. To cover these charges, the producer might choose to write a call option on electricity. Here's how the strategy works. For a fee, the plant owner sells a call option with a strike price that is higher than the price at which the plant will be brought on line. The buyer of the call might be someone who uses electricity and wants insurance against a spike in prices. The option fee will cover the producer's maintenance cost while the plant is shut down. And, because the producer as option writer owns the underlying asset here—electricity—he or she is hedged against the possibility that the call option will pay off. As the price of electricity rises, the plant's revenue goes up with it.

Options are very versatile and can be bought and sold in many combinations. They allow investors to get rid of the risks they do not want and keep the ones they do want. In fact, options can be used to construct synthetic instruments that mimic the payoffs of virtually any other financial instrument. For example, the purchase of an at-the-money call and simultaneous sale of an at-the-money put gives the exact same payoff pattern as the purchase of a futures contract. If the price of the underlying asset rises, the call's value increases just as a futures contract does, while the put remains worthless. If the price falls, the put seller loses, just as a futures contract does, while the call is out of the money. Finally, options allow investors to bet that prices will be volatile. Buy a put and a call at the same strike price, and you have a bet that pays off only if the underlying asset price moves up or down significantly.

In summary, options are extremely useful. Remember the example at the beginning of the chapter, in which the snowmobile manufacturer Bombardier purchased insurance so it could offer its customers a rebate? What it bought were put options with a payoff tied to the amount of snow that fell. The puts promised payments in the event of low snowfall. This hedged the risk the company incurred when it offered rebates to the purchasers of its snowmobiles. The providers of this insurance, the sellers of the snowfall options, may have been betting that snowfall would not be low. That is, they may have been speculating—but not necessarily. After all, there are many companies whose sales and profits rise during warm weather and who are well positioned to take such a risk. Insurance companies, for instance, have lower claims during warm winters, because there are fewer accidents when there is less snow. If there is little snow, the insurance company has the funds to make the payments, while if there is lots of snow they can use the price they were paid to write the put to help pay the cost of the claims they face.[10]

Table 9.3 provides a summary of what options are, who buys and sells them, and why they do it.

Pricing Options: Intrinsic Value and the Time Value of the Option

An option price has two parts. The first is the value of the option if it is exercised immediately, and the second is the fee paid for the option's potential benefits. We will refer to the first of these, the value of the option if it is exercised immediately, as the *intrinsic value*. The second, the fee paid for the potential benefit from buying the option, we will call the **time value of the option** to emphasize its relationship to the time of the option's expiration. This means that

$$Option\ price = Intrinsic\ value + Time\ value\ of\ the\ option$$

[10]Bombardier purchased its snowfall insurance from Enron (prior to that company's bankruptcy). As it turned out, there was sufficient snowfall, so no payments were made either from Bombardier to the buyers of the snowmobiles or from Enron to Bombardier.

| Table 9.3 | A Guide to Options |

	Calls	**Puts**
Buyer	*Right* to *buy* the underlying asset at the strike price prior to or on the expiration date. "Hey, send it over!"	*Right* to *sell* the underlying asset at a fixed price prior to or on the expiration date. "Here it is; it's yours now!"
Seller (Writer)	*Obligation* to *sell* the underlying asset at the strike price prior to or on the expiration date.	*Obligation* to *buy* the underlying asset at the strike price prior to or on the expiration date.
Option is *in the money* when	Price of underlying asset is *above* the strike price of the call.	Price of underlying asset is *below* the strike price of the put.
Who *buys* one	Someone who • Wants to *buy* an asset in the future and insure the price paid will not *rise.* • Wants to bet that the price of the underlying asset will rise.	Someone who • Wants to *sell* an asset in the future and insure the price paid will not fall. • Wants to bet that the price of the underlying asset will fall.
Who *sells (writes)* one	Someone who • Wants to bet that the market price of the underlying asset will *not* rise. • A broker who is always willing to sell the underlying asset and is paid to take the risk.	Someone who • Wants to bet that the market price of the underlying asset will *not* fall. • A broker who is always willing to buy the underlying asset and is paid to take the risk.

As an example, before we launch into a discussion of option valuation in general, let's apply what we know about present value and risk analysis. Consider the example of an at-the-money European call option on the stock of XYZ Corporation that expires in one month. Recall that a European option can be exercised only at expiration and that an at-the-money option is one for which the current price equals the strike price. In this case, both equal $100. So, the intrinsic value of this call option is zero. To the extent that it has any value at all, that value resides entirely in the option's time value. Assume that, over the next month, the price of XYZ Corporation's stock will either rise or fall by $10 with equal probability. That is, there is a probability of ½ the price will go up to $110, and there is a probability of ½ it will fall to $90. What is the value of this call option?

To find the answer, we can compute the expected present value of the payoff. Let's assume that the interest rate is so low that we can ignore it. (If the payoff were postponed sufficiently far into the future or the interest rate were high enough, we could not ignore the present-value calculation but would have to divide by one plus the interest rate.) Now notice that the option is worth something only if the price goes up. In the event that XYZ's stock price falls to $90, you will allow the option to expire without exercising it. For a call option, then, we need to concern ourselves with the upside, and the expected value of that payoff is the probability, ½, times the payoff, $10, which is $5. This is the time value of the option.

Now think about what happens if, instead of rising or falling by $10, XYZ's stock will rise or fall by $20. This change increases the standard deviation of the stock price. In the terminology used in options trading, the stock price *volatility* has increased. Doing the same calculation, we see that the expected payoff is now $10. As the volatility of the stock price rises, the option's time value rises with it.

General Considerations   In general, calculating the price of an option and how it might change means developing some rules for figuring out its intrinsic value and time value. We can do that using the framework from Chapter 3. Recall that the value of any financial instrument depends on four attributes: the size of the promised payment, the timing of the payment, the likelihood that the payment will be made, and the circumstances under which the payment will be made.[11] As we consider each of these, remember that the most important thing about an option is that the buyer is not obligated to exercise it. An option gives the buyer a choice! What this means is that someone holding an option will never make any additional payment to exercise it, so its value cannot be less than zero.

Because the options can either be exercised or expire worthless, we can conclude that the intrinsic value depends only on what the holder receives if the option is exercised. The intrinsic value is the difference between the price of the underlying asset and the strike price of the option. This is the *size of the payment* that the option represents, and it must be greater than or equal to zero—the intrinsic value cannot be negative. For an in-the-money call, or the option to buy, the intrinsic value to the holder (the long position) is the market price of the underlying asset minus the strike price. If the call is at the money or out of the money, it has no intrinsic value. Analogously, the intrinsic value of a put, or the option to sell, equals the strike price minus the market price of the underlying asset, or zero, whichever is greater.

At expiration, the value of an option equals its intrinsic value. But what about prior to expiration? To think about this question, consider an at-the-money option—one whose intrinsic value is zero. Prior to expiration, there is always the chance that the price of the underlying asset will move so as to make the option valuable. This potential benefit is represented by the option's time value. *The longer the time to expiration,* the bigger the likely payoff when the option does expire and, thus, the more valuable it is. Remember that the option payoff is asymmetric, so what is important is the chance of making profit. In the last example, think about what will happen if the option expires in three months instead of one and the stock price has an equal probability of rising or falling $10 each month. The expected payoff rises from $5.00 (for the one-month call option) to $7.50 (for the three-month call option). (Over three months, the stock can either rise by $30 with probability ⅛, rise by $10 with probability ⅜, fall by $10 with probability ⅜ or fall by $30 with probability ⅛. When the price falls, the call option is not exercised, so the expected value of the three-month call is ⅛ × $30 + ⅜ × $10 = $7.50.)

The likelihood that an option will pay off depends on the volatility, or standard deviation, of the price of the underlying asset. To see this, consider an option on IBM stock that is currently at the money—one with a strike price that equals the current price of the stock. The chance of this option being in the money by the time it expires

---

[11]Because the pricing of European options is easier to understand, we will talk about options as if they can be exercised only at the expiration date. The principles for pricing American options are the same, however.

YOUR FINANCIAL WORLD
Should You Accept Options as Part of Your Pay?

What if someone offers you a job in return for a salary and stock options? Should you take it? Before you do, ask questions! Let's look at what you need to know. Many firms that offer options on their own stock to employees view the options as a substitute for wages. Employees receive call options that give them the right to purchase the company's stock at a fixed price. The strike price is usually set at the current market price of the stock, so that when employees receive the options, they are at the money. Normally, the expiration date is from one to 10 years in the future. Because the options are long-term, they will have substantial value, as measured by the option's time value. But there is a catch. Employees generally are not allowed to sell them and may need to remain with the firm to exercise them.

Nevertheless, the price of the company's stock could skyrocket, so the options may bring a substantial payoff. To take an extreme example, from January 1991 to January 2000, Microsoft's stock price rose from $2 to $116 per share. An employee with 1,000 options to purchase the stock at $2 would have made $114,000 by exercising them. Though Microsoft employees were winners, there are many losers in the options game. Employees holding options to purchase stock in General Motors or Lehman, both of which went bankrupt in 2008, got nothing.

So what should you do? If taking the options means accepting a lower salary, then you are paying for them, and you should think hard before you take the offer. Stock options are almost like lottery tickets, but with a drawing that may not occur for years. They give you a small chance to make a large profit. But investing in the same company that pays your salary is a risky business. If the company goes broke or you lose your job, the options will be worthless to you. So think hard before you trade a high-paying job for a lower-paying job with options.

increases with the volatility of IBM's stock price. Think about an option on an asset whose price is simply fixed—that is, whose standard deviation is zero. This option will never pay off, so no one would be willing to pay for it. Add some variability to the price, however, and there is a chance that the price will rise, moving the option into the money. That is something people will pay for. Thus, the option's time value increases with the volatility of the price of the underlying asset. Taking this analysis one step further, we know that regardless of how far the price of the underlying asset falls, the holder of a call option cannot lose more. In contrast, whenever the price rises higher, the call option increases in value. Increased volatility has no cost to the option holder, only benefits.

We have emphasized that options provide insurance, allowing investors to hedge particular risks. The bigger the risk being insured, the more valuable the insurance, and the higher the price investors will pay. Thus, *the circumstances under which the payment is made* have an important impact on the option's time value. Table 9.4 summarizes the factors that affect the value of options.

The Value of Options: Some Examples

To see how options are valued, we can examine a simple example. The daily news reports the prices of options that are traded on organized exchanges. Table 9.5 shows the prices of IBM puts and calls on November 23, 2012, as reported on the website of *The Wall Street Journal*. Panel A shows the prices of options with different strike prices but the same expiration date, January 2013. Panel B shows the prices of options with different expiration dates but the same strike price. From the top of the table we can see that the price of IBM stock, the underlying asset on which these options were written, was $193.49 per share at the close of that day.

Table 9.4   Factors Affecting the Value of Options

Option value = Intrinsic value + Time value

Increase in one factor, holding all others fixed	Call (the right to buy)	Put (the right to sell)
Increase in the strike price	Decrease (intrinsic value falls)	Increase (intrinsic value rises)
Increase in the market price of the underlying asset	Increase (intrinsic value rises)	Decrease (intrinsic value falls)
Increase in the time to expiration	Increase (time value rises)	Increase (time value rises)
Increase in the volatility of the underlying asset price	Increase (time value rises)	Increase (time value rises)

Table 9.5   Prices of IBM Puts and Calls

At the close on Friday, November 23, 2012
IBM stock price at close = $193.49

A. January Expiration

	Calls			Puts		
Strike Price	Call Price	Intrinsic Value	Time Value of Call	Put Price	Intrinsic Value	Time Value of Put
$180	$14.72	$13.49	$1.23	$ 1.29	$ 0.00	$1.29
185	10.36	8.49	1.87	2.17	0.00	2.17
190	6.70	3.49	3.21	3.59	0.00	3.59
195	4.00	0.00	4.00	5.77	1.51	4.26
200	2.00	0.00	2.00	9.00	6.51	2.49
210	0.40	0.00	0.40	17.40	16.51	0.89

B. Strike Price of 190

	Calls			Puts		
Expiration Month	Call Price	Intrinsic Value	Time Value of Call	Put Price	Intrinsic Value	Time Value of Put
Dec	5.22	3.49	1.73	1.79	0.00	1.79
Jan	6.70	3.49	3.21	3.59	0.00	3.59
Apr	9.77	3.49	6.28	7.54	0.00	7.54

Intrinsic value of a call = Stock price − Strike price, or zero, whichever is larger.
Intrinsic value of a put = Strike price − Stock price, or zero, whichever is larger.
Time value of the option = Option price − Intrinsic value.

SOURCE: *The Wall Street Journal*, November 23, 2012. Used with permission of Dow Jones & Company, Inc. via Copyright Clearance Center.

By examining the table, we can discover the following:

- At a given price of the underlying asset and time to expiration, the higher the strike price of a call option, the lower its intrinsic value and the less expensive the option. That is, as you read down the column labeled "Strike Price" in Panel A, the intrinsic value under "Calls" (IBM stock price minus the strike price) falls. For example, as the strike price goes from $185 to $190, the intrinsic value falls from $8.49 to $3.49.

- At a given price of the underlying asset and time to expiration, the higher the strike price of a put option, the higher the intrinsic value and the more expensive the option. (See the "Intrinsic Value" column for Puts in Panel A.) As the strike price rises from $195 to $200, the intrinsic value of the IBM put (the strike price minus the IBM stock price) rises from $1.51 to $6.51.

- The closer the strike price is to the current price of the underlying asset, the larger the option's time value. (See the two columns in Panel A labeled "Time Value of Call" and "Time Value of Put.") For a call option with a strike price of $190 and an intrinsic value of $3.49, the time value is $3.21. As the strike price goes down to $185, the time value falls to $1.87.

- Deep in-the-money options have lower time value (see the time value of the calls in Panel A). Because a deep in-the-money call option is very likely to expire in the money, buying one is much like buying the stock itself. Note that the call with a strike price of $180 and an intrinsic value of $13.49 has a time value of only $1.23, much less than the $3.21 time value of a call with an intrinsic value of $3.49.

- The longer the time to expiration at a given strike price, the higher the option price. Looking at the prices of both puts and calls in Panel B of Table 9.5, you can see that as you read down those columns and the time to expiration rises, the price goes up with it. That is because the option's time value is going up. A $190 IBM call that expires in January sells for $6.70, while the price of one that expires three months later sells for $9.77. The same rule applies to puts.

Swaps

Like other derivatives, swaps are contracts that allow traders to transfer risks. Swaps come in numerous varieties. We will study two types: *Interest-rate swaps* allow one swap party—for a fee—to alter the stream of payments it makes or receives. Interest-rate swaps have been used widely for decades to synchronize receipts and payments. *Credit-default swaps* (CDS) are more recent. CDS are a form of insurance that allow a buyer to own a bond or mortgage without bearing its default risk. We will see that CDS played an important role in the financial crisis of 2007–2009 and were also a factor in the euro-area crisis that began in 2010.

Interest-Rate Swaps

Government debt managers—the people at the U.S. Treasury who decide when and how to issue U.S. Treasury bonds, notes, and bills—do their best to keep public borrowing costs as low as possible. That means (a) selling bonds at the lowest interest rates possible and (b) ensuring that government revenues will be available when payments must be made. Because of the structure of financial markets, keeping interest costs low usually is not a problem. Demand for long-term government bonds is high.

APPLYING THE CONCEPT
WHAT WAS LONG-TERM CAPITAL MANAGEMENT DOING?

From mid-August to late September 1998, Long-Term Capital Management (LTCM), a *hedge fund* based in Greenwich, Connecticut, lost more than $2.5 billion, placing itself in danger of default. (For a detailed description of hedge funds, see the Tools of the Trade box in Chapter 13.) The prospect of LTCM's failure struck fear into world financial markets, prompting the Federal Reserve Bank of New York to form a group of 14 banks and investment companies to purchase the company. How did so much wealth disappear so fast, and why did so many people care? Until the crisis of 2007–2009, there was no comparable case in which the financial community was so desperate to avoid a bankruptcy.

The answer is that LTCM had engaged in a large number of complex speculative transactions, including interest-rate swaps and options writing, which all failed simultaneously. One of the bets LTCM had made was based on the belief that interest-rate spreads would shrink. Following the Russian government bond default on August 17, 1998, financial market participants' willingness to take on risk declined dramatically, so the risk premium exploded. (Recall the discussion of this episode in Chapter 6.) As a result, the spread between corporate bonds and U.S. Treasury bonds grew in a way that had never before occurred. By relying on historical data, LTCM lost billions. While the interest-rate spread did

eventually shrink, so that the bets LTCM had made paid off in the long run, marking to market drove the fund bankrupt.

The really scary part of this episode was that many of the transactions LTCM had engaged in involved instruments that could not easily be resold. The most amazing discovery was the $1 ¼ trillion (yes, trillion) in interest-rate swaps. Granted, this was a notional principal of all the transactions added together, but the problem is that swaps are individualized, bilateral transactions. The fact that LTCM was willing to make a swap agreement with a particular counterparty was no guarantee that some other party would. Thus, a normal bankruptcy settlement, in which assets are sold off in the marketplace and the proceeds given to the failed company's creditors, was not an option. LTCM's failure would mean it could not honor its side of the agreements, which would mean the counterparties would not be able to honor their own agreements, creating a cascade of failure. Its collapse would jeopardize the entire financial system. Large banks, insurance companies, pension funds, and mutual-fund companies with whom LTCM did business were at risk of being bankrupted themselves.

In short, while one person's derivatives loss is another's gain, the system works only if the winners can collect. In this case, the Federal Reserve had no choice but to step in and ensure that the financial system remained sound. LTCM was essentially sold to its creditors—the banks from which it had borrowed—and then closed down about a year later.*

*For a detailed history of the rise and fall of Long-Term Capital Management, see Roger Lowenstein, *When Genius Failed* (New York: Random House, 2000).

(They are used as collateral in many financial transactions.) Thus, government debt managers can sell them at relatively high prices. Selling long-term debt also limits rollover risk if future investors come to doubt the government's willingness or ability to repay.

Managing government revenues is more of a challenge. Revenues tend to rise during economic booms and fall during recessions. Even if tax revenues fall, the government must still make its bond payments. Short-term interest rates, like tax revenues, tend to move with the business cycle, rising during booms and falling during recessions (see Chapter 21). Ensuring that future interest expenses match future tax revenues might be easier if government borrowers issued short-term bonds.

This difficulty leaves the public debt manager in a quandary. Which is more important, keeping interest costs and rollover risk down by issuing long-term debt or matching costs with tax revenues by issuing short-term debt? Fortunately, derivatives allow government debt managers to meet both these goals using a tool called an interest-rate swap.

Understanding Interest-Rate Swaps
Interest-rate swaps are agreements between two counterparties to exchange periodic interest-rate payments over some future period, based on an agreed-upon amount of principal—what's called the **notional principal**. The term *notional* is used here because the principal of a **swap** is not borrowed, lent, or exchanged; it just serves as the basis for calculation of the periodic cash flows between the counterparties to the swap. In the simplest type of interest-rate swap,

RISK

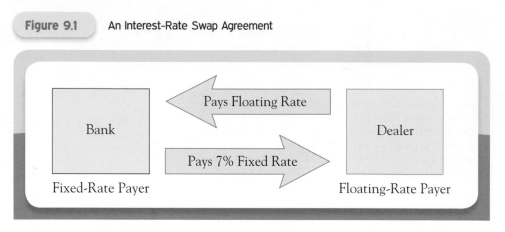

Figure 9.1 An Interest-Rate Swap Agreement

The bank agrees to pay a fixed rate to the swap dealer in exchange for payments based on a floating rate. The fixed-rate payments match the bank's loan income, while the floating-rate payments match the payments promised to the bank's deposit holders.

one party agrees to make payments based on a fixed interest rate, and in exchange the counterparty agrees to make payments based on a floating interest rate. The effect of this agreement is to transform fixed-rate payments into floating-rate payments and vice versa. For example, the five-year swap rate available online in the FRED database (FRED code: MSWP5) is the rate paid for five years by the fixed-rate payer in return for receiving floating payments of three-month LIBOR.[12]

Figure 9.1 shows a typical interest-rate swap. A bank agrees to make payments to a swap dealer at a fixed interest rate, say, 7 percent, in exchange for payments based on a floating rate determined in the market. Both payments are based on the same agreed-upon principal, say $100 million. That is, the notional principal on the swap is $100 million. The bank is the **fixed-rate payer** and the swap dealer is the **floating-rate payer**. Put slightly differently, the two parties enter into a series of forward agreements in which they agree today to exchange interest payments on a series of future dates for the life of the swap. As in a futures contract, no payment is made at the outset.

Now let's return to the government debt manager's problem. Remember that the government can issue long-term debt cheaply but its revenues tend to fluctuate with the short-term interest rate, going up when short-term interest rates rise and down when they fall. The solution is to sell long-term bonds and then enter into an interest-rate swap. The government becomes the floating-rate payer for the term of the bonds.

Pricing and Using Interest-Rate Swaps Pricing interest-rate swaps means figuring out the fixed interest rate to be paid. To do so, financial firms begin by noting the market interest rate on a U.S. Treasury bond of the same maturity as the swap, called the *benchmark*. The rate to be paid by the fixed-rate payer, called the *swap rate*, will be the benchmark rate plus a premium. The difference between the benchmark rate and the swap rate, called the **swap spread**, is a measure of risk: For example, the spread of the 10-year swap rate over the 10-year Treasury bond yield averaged about ⅓ percentage point during the 10 years to mid-2013. In recent years, the swap spread has attracted

---

[12]The London Interbank Offered Rate (LIBOR), the rate at which banks in London make short-term loans to each other, often serves as the floating rate.

IN THE NEWS
No Insurance Pay-Out on Greek Debt

FINANCIAL
TIMES

By Richard Milne and David Oakley

March 1, 2012

Billions of dollars in credit default insurance on Greek sovereign bonds will not yet be paid out despite next week's restructuring of €186bn of the country's debt, an industry body has ruled in a move that raised complaints from some investors.

The International Swaps and Derivatives Association (ISDA) decided that the bonds had not suffered a so-called credit event, industry jargon for a default on debt or a significant negative change in its terms.

Under Greece's planned restructuring, some £186bn of bonds will next week be swapped for new, longer-maturing debt with lower coupon payments. A further €20bn is expected to be swapped next month as part of a second round of restructuring.

The body's determinations committee rejected two requests to declare a credit event. One was based on grounds that the European Central Bank was being given de facto seniority in a controversial debt swap and the other cited the introduction by Greece of legislation that would require any recalcitrant bondholders to take part in the swap should support for the deal pass a certain level.

Many traders and investors expect a credit event still to be declared as soon as next week. However, the effectiveness of credit default swaps has still been called into question following the ISDA ruling.

Bill Gross, who runs the world's biggest private bond fund at Pimco, said on CNBC television that the decision not to declare a credit event on the writedown of Greek sovereign debt set a dangerous precedent.

He said ISDA's decision should be seen as a disappointment to buyers of CDS. However, Pimco is one of the

voting members of the ISDA determinations committee that decided against a pay-out.

Paul Griffiths, global head of fixed income at Aberdeen Asset Managers, said: "This may be bad news for the CDS market. In the longer-term, there is an almost metaphysical question. Why is CDS there? Why does it exist?"

Michael Hampden-Turner, credit strategist at Citi, said: "The credit derivative market could be undermined by a failure of the CDS settlement process, because it would mean that prudent bond holders who used CDS to hedge their exposure might not be able to able to satisfy the requirements for settlement and end up getting back less money."

However, one senior risk manager at a US bank said: "I don't think this decision makes any difference. We all know that CDS is not perfect. It is still a useful instrument."

The complicated nature of Greece's debt swap has sparked an intense debate over whether sovereign CDS, used by many banks and other investors to reduce their exposure to countries such as Italy, are worth less than had previously been thought.

ISDA itself has left the door open to future claims if bond holders are forced to take losses as part of next week's bond swap. . . .

LESSONS OF THE ARTICLE

Derivatives allow investors to transfer risk to those who can best bear it. But a financial contract, like a sovereign CDS, whose execution and settlement are uncertain and subject to unpredictable interpretation, may provide no hedge at all. When investors cannot reliably hedge unwanted risks, they accept less risk overall. In this instance, that means holding less debt of risky sovereigns like the government of Greece.

substantial attention as a measure of systematic risk, or overall risk in the economy (see Chapter 5). When it widens, it signals that general economic conditions are deteriorating.

Interest-rate swaps are just one example of the exchange of future payoffs. Investors engage in a wide variety of swaps involving foreign exchange and equities, though interest-rate swaps are the most important. By one estimate, at the end of 2012, the notional value of interest-rate swaps worldwide was $370 trillion—about 15 times the total of foreign currency swaps at the time.[13]

Who uses all these interest-rate swaps? Two groups have a comparative advantage in issuing bonds of a particular maturity. The first group is government debt managers, who find long-term fixed-rate bonds cheaper to issue but prefer short-term variable-rate obligations for matching revenues with expenses. The second group uses interest-rate swaps to reduce the risk generated by commercial activities. The prime example is a bank that obtains funds by offering interest-bearing checking accounts but makes mortgage loans at a fixed rate. In essence, the bank is issuing short-term variable-rate bonds (the checking accounts) and buying long-term fixed-rate bonds (the mortgages) with the borrowed funds. The problem is, changes in the slope of the yield curve create risk. That is, the revenue from the mortgages may fall short of the payments due on the checking accounts. Swaps insure the bank against such a shortfall.

In thinking about the size and importance of particular interest-rate swaps, we need to keep several points in mind. The first is that the primary risk in a swap is the risk that one of the parties will default. Aside from a major financial crisis, that risk is not very high because the other side can enter into another agreement to replace the one that failed. (The case of Long-Term Capital Management, described in Applying the Concept on page 231, is a notable exception when widespread default became a real possibility.) Second, unlike futures and options, swaps are not traded on organized exchanges; they are bilateral agreements between two financial intermediaries. For various reasons, a bank that enters into a swap agreement with another bank may not want to make the same kind of arrangement with a pension fund. Thus, swaps are very difficult to resell.

Credit-Default Swaps

On September 16, 2008, the Federal Reserve Bank of New York, part of the U.S. central bank, made an extraordinary $85 billion loan to American International Group (AIG). AIG, the largest insurance company in the world, was on the verge of collapse because it had sold several hundred billion dollars worth of **credit-default swaps (CDS)**.

A CDS is a *credit derivative* that allows lenders to insure themselves against the risk that a borrower will default. The buyer of a CDS makes payments—like insurance premiums—to the seller, and the seller agrees to pay the buyer *if* an underlying loan or security defaults. The CDS buyer pays a fee to transfer the risk of default—the credit risk—to the CDS seller.

Using CDS, a lender can make a loan without facing the possibility of default. By combining a loan with a CDS to insure against default, a lender who is good at identifying attractive loan opportunities and collecting the loan payments can function efficiently, while letting someone else worry about the default risk. This division of labor can improve resource allocation.

A CDS agreement often lasts several years and requires that collateral be posted to protect against the inability to pay of either the seller or the buyer of the insurance. For example, the seller provides collateral to ensure that the buyer will be paid in the event that the underlying loan or security defaults and the seller is unable to pay. The collateral for a CDS varies with the credit rating of the seller and buyer.

The market for CDS expanded astronomically in the years before the financial crisis of 2007–2009 but then shrank rapidly. The volume of CDS (based on the initial value of the underlying assets), which was about $6 trillion at the end of 2004, soared to

---

[13]Data on interest-rate swaps are collected and regularly published by the Bank for International Settlements in Basel, Switzerland. For recent information, see its website, *www.bis.org*.

$58 trillion at the end of 2007 before plunging to $33 trillion two years later. By the end of 2012, it had fallen to $25 trillion.

CDS contributed to the financial crisis in three important ways: (1) fostering uncertainty about who bears the credit risk on a given loan or security, (2) making the leading CDS sellers mutually vulnerable, and (3) making it easier for sellers of insurance to assume and conceal risk.

Financial institutions do not report the amount of their CDS purchases and sales, so their depositors or investors do not know how much risk they bear. This loss of transparency makes the financial system more vulnerable to a shock that threatens trust in counterparties.

Because CDS contracts are traded over the counter (OTC), even traders cannot identify others who take on concentrated positions on one side of a trade. As a result, CDS dealers—typically the largest financial institutions—are collectively exposed to a failure by any weak dealer, much like a train can go off the tracks when one flimsy car derails. When you read the phrase "too interconnected to fail" in the financial news, think of the mutual—but hidden—vulnerabilities of the large CDS vendors. So long as CDS trading lacks transparency, the lingering worry is that a failure of one institution could bring down the financial system as a whole (see Lessons from the Crisis: Central Counterparties and Systemic Risk on page 220).

As noted earlier, derivatives used properly can improve the allocation of risk and foster healthy risk taking. It follows that undermining the credibility of derivative contracts can have a damaging impact. The euro-area crisis that began in September 2010 presents a notable example. Having observed the U.S. crisis, euro-area policymakers feared that a chaotic default on Greek sovereign debt would lead to a catastrophic financial disruption. Consequently, they hoped to restructure Greek debt without a legal "event of default" that would trigger large CDS payouts (see In the News on page 233).

As an unintended consequence, however, their actions encouraged doubt about the value of CDS as insurance, making banks and others even less willing to hold the debt of other weak euro-area sovereigns (e.g., Ireland, Italy, Portugal, and Spain), not just Greece. Uncertainty encouraged banks to shrink their balance sheets, adding to downward pressure on credit supply and the economy at a delicate stage of the crisis. Eventually, Greece's default prompted a CDS payout without augmenting the crisis, but doubts about CDS and other means of hedging (such as short selling) probably had already added to the turmoil.

Terms

American option, 223
arbitrage, 220
call option, 222
central counterparty (CCP), 220
credit-default swap (CDS), 234
derivatives, 215
European option, 223
fixed-rate payer, 232
floating-rate payer, 232
forward contract, 216

futures contract, 216
interest-rate swap, 231
margin, 218
notional principal, 231
put option, 222
strike price, 222
swap, 231
swap spread, 232
time value of an option, 225

Using FRED: Codes for Data in This Chapter

Data Series	FRED Data Code
1-year swap rate	MSWP1
2-year swap rate	MSWP2
5-year swap rate	MSWP5
10-year swap rate	MSWP10
10-year U.S. Treasury yield	GS10
Central bank liquidity swaps held by Federal Reserve	SWPT
CBOE Volatility Index: VIX	VIXCLS

Chapter Lessons

1. Derivatives transfer risk from one person or firm to another. They can be used in any combination to unbundle risks and resell them.

2. Futures contracts are standardized contracts for the delivery of a specified quantity of a commodity or financial instrument on a prearranged future date, at an agreed-upon price. They are a bet on the movement in the price of the underlying asset on which they are written, whether it is a commodity or a financial instrument.
   a. Futures contracts are used both to decrease risk, which is called hedging, and to increase risk, which is called speculating.
   b. The futures clearing corporation, as the counterparty to all futures contracts, guarantees the performance of both the buyer and the seller.
   c. Participants in the futures market must establish a margin account with the clearing corporation and make a deposit that ensures they will meet their obligations.
   d. Futures prices are marked to market daily, as if the contracts were sold and repurchased every day.
   e. Because no payment is made when a futures contract is initiated, the transaction allows an investor to create a large amount of leverage at a very low cost.
   f. The prices of futures contracts are determined by arbitrage within the market for immediate delivery of the underlying asset.

3. Options give the buyer (option holder) a right and the seller (option writer) an obligation to buy or sell an underlying asset at a predetermined price on or before a fixed future date.
   a. A call option gives the holder the right to buy the underlying asset.
   b. A put option gives the holder the right to sell the underlying asset.
   c. Options can be used both to reduce risk through hedging and to speculate.
   d. The option price equals the sum of its intrinsic value, which is the value if the option is exercised, plus the time value of the option.
   e. The intrinsic value depends on the strike price of the option and the price of the underlying asset on which the option is written.
   f. The time value of the option depends on the time to expiration and the volatility in the price of the underlying asset.

4. Interest-rate swaps are agreements between two parties to exchange a fixed for a variable interest-rate payment over a future period.

a. The fixed-rate payer in a swap typically pays the U.S. Treasury bond rate plus a risk premium.

b. The flexible-rate payer in a swap normally pays the London Interbank Offered Rate (LIBOR).

c. Interest-rate swaps are useful when a government, firm, or investment company can borrow more cheaply at one maturity but would prefer to borrow at a different maturity.

d. Swaps can be based on an agreed-upon exchange of any two future sequences of payments.

5. Credit-default swaps (CDS) are a form of insurance in which the buyer of the insurance makes payments (like insurance premiums) to the seller, who in turn agrees to pay the buyer if an underlying loan or security defaults.

a. A CDS agreement often lasts several years and requires that collateral be posted to protect against the inability to pay of the seller or the buyer of insurance.

b. If financial institutions do not report CDS sales and purchases, it is not clear who bears credit risk on a given loan or security.

c. When CDS are traded over the counter, even traders cannot identify others who take on concentrated risks on one side of a trade.

6. Derivatives allow firms to arbitrarily divide up and rename risks and future payments, rendering their actual names irrelevant.

Conceptual and Analytical Problems

1. An agreement to lease a car can be thought of as a set of derivative contracts. Describe them. *(LO2)*

2. How is entering into a forward contract similar to barter? Can you think of costs associated with forward contracts that are minimized or eliminated with futures contracts? *(LO2)*

3. In spring 2002, an electronically traded futures contract on the stock index, called an E-mini future, was introduced. The contract was one-fifth the size of the standard futures contract, and could be traded on the 24-hour CME Globex electronic trading system. Why might someone introduce a futures contract with these properties? *(LO1)*

4. A hedger buys a futures contract, taking a long position in the wheat futures market. What are the hedger's obligations under this contract? Describe the risk that is hedged in this transaction, and give an example of someone who might enter into such an arrangement. *(LO1)*

5. A futures contract on a payment of $250 times the Standard & Poors' 500 Index is traded on the Chicago Mercantile Exchange. At an index level of $1,000 or more, the contract calls for a payment of over $250,000. It is settled by a cash payment between the buyer and the seller. Who are the hedgers and who are the speculators in the S&P 500 futures market? *(LO1)*

6. Explain why trading derivatives on centralized exchanges rather than in over-the-counter markets helps reduce systemic risk. *(LO1)*

7. What are the risks and rewards of writing and buying options? Are there any circumstances under which you would get involved? Why or why not? *(Hint:* Think of a case in which you own shares of the stock on which you are considering writing a call.) *(LO3)*

8. Suppose XYZ Corporation's stock price rises or falls with equal probability by $20 each month, starting where it ended the previous month. What is the value of a three-month at-the-money European call option on XYZ's stock if the stock is priced at $100 when the option is purchased? *(LO3)*

9.* Why might a borrower who wishes to make fixed interest rate payments and who has access to both fixed- and floating-rate loans still benefit from becoming a party to a fixed-for-floating interest-rate swap? *(LO4)*

10. Concerned about possible disruptions of the supply of oil from the Middle East, the chief financial officer (CFO) of American Airlines would like to hedge the risk of an increase in the price of jet fuel. What tools could the CFO use to hedge this risk? *(LO3)*

11.* How does the existence of derivatives markets enhance an economy's ability to grow? *(LO1)*

12. Credit-default swaps provide a means to insure against default risk and require the posting of collateral by buyers and sellers. Explain how these "safe-sounding" derivative products contributed to the 2007–2009 financial crisis. *(LO4)*

13. Of the following options, which would you expect to have the highest option price? *(LO3)*
   a. A European three-month put option on a stock whose market price is $90 where the strike price is $100. The standard deviation of the stock price over the past five years has been 15 percent.
   b. A European three-month put option on a stock whose market price is $110 where the strike price is $100. The standard deviation of the stock price over the past five years has been 15 percent.
   c. A European one-month put option on a stock whose market price is $90 where the strike price is $100. The standard deviation of the stock price over the past five years has been 15 percent.

14. What kind of an option should you purchase if you anticipate selling $1 million of Treasury bonds in one year's time and wish to hedge against the risk of interest rates rising? *(LO3)*

15. You sell a bond futures contract and, one day later, the clearinghouse informs you that it had credited funds to your margin account. What happened to interest rates over that day? *(LO2)*

16. You are completely convinced that the price of copper is going to rise significantly over the next year and want to take as large a position as you can in the market but have limited funds. How could you use the futures market to leverage your position? *(LO2)*

17. Suppose you have $8,000 to invest and you follow the strategy you devise in Problem 16 to leverage your exposure to the copper market. Copper is selling at $3 a pound and the margin requirement for a futures contract for 25,000 pounds of copper is $8,000. *(LO2)*
   a. Calculate your return if copper prices rise to $3.10 a pound.
   b. How does this compare with the return you would have made if you had simply purchased $8,000 worth of copper and sold it a year later?
   c. Compare the risk involved in each of these strategies.

18.* The following table shows the yields on the fixed and floating borrowing choices available to three firms. Firms A and B want to be exposed to a floating interest

*Indicates more difficult problems

rate while Firm C would prefer to pay a fixed interest rate. Which pair(s) of firms (if any) should borrow in the market they do not want and then enter into a fixed-for-floating interest-rate swap? *(LO4)*

	Fixed Rate	Floating Rate
Firm A	7%	LIBOR + 50 bps
Firm B	12%	LIBOR + 150 bps
Firm C	10%	LIBOR + 150 bps

Note: LIBOR, which stands for London Interbank Offered Rate, is a floating interest rate.

19. Suppose you were the manager of a bank that raised most of its funds from shortterm variable-rate deposits and used these funds to make fixed-rate mortgage loans. Should you be more concerned about rises or falls in short-term interest rates? How could you use interest-rate swaps to hedge against the interest-rate risk you face? *(LO4)*

20.* Basis swaps are swaps where, instead of one payment stream being based on a fixed interest rate, both payment streams are based on floating interest rates. Why might anyone be interested in entering a floating-for-floating interest-rate swap? (You should assume that both payment flows are denominated in the same currency.) *(LO4)*

Data Exploration

For detailed instructions on using Federal Reserve Economic Data (FRED) online to answer each of the following problems, visit www.mhhe.com/moneyandbanking4e and click on Student Edition, then Data Exploration Hints.

Scan here for quick access to the hints for these problems. Need a barcode reader? Try ScanLife, available in your app store.

1. Central banks occasionally engage in "liquidity swaps" with each other. Plot and interpret the Fed's provision of dollar liquidity swaps (FRED code: SWPT) to other central banks since 2007. To facilitate your interpretation, view the FRED "Notes" about this data series. *(LO4)*

2. Define the swap rate and then plot the five-year swap rate (FRED code: MSWP5). Describe a transaction involving the swap rate and the actions of the participating parties. *(LO4)*

3. The swap spread is the difference between the swap rate and the yield on the equivalent-maturity Treasury bond. Explain why a widening swap spread may be a signal of deteriorating economic conditions. Plot since 2000 the difference between the five-year swap rate (FRED code: MSWP5) and the five-year Treasury yield (FRED code: GS5). Interpret the evolution of this five-year swap spread since July 2007. *(LO4)*

4. Risk-averse investors care greatly about asset price volatility. Using the FRED "Notes" about the data series, briefly define the VIX Volatility Index (FRED code: VIXCLS) of the Chicago Board Options Exchange (CBOE). Plot since 2004 the VIX and the percent change from a year ago of the S&P500 stock market index (FRED code: SP500). Interpret the graph. *(LO3)*

5. Commercial banks trade *trillions* of dollars of derivative contracts, but what is their *net* exposure in derivatives markets? Plot the difference between what commercial banks are owed (FRED code: DFVACBW027SBOG) and what they owe (FRED code: DNVACBW027SBOG) on their derivative positions. *(LO1)*

Chapter 10

Foreign Exchange

Learning Objectives

Understand . . .

LO1 Nominal and real exchange rates

LO2 The relationship of exchange rates, the price level, and inflation

LO3 Currency supply and demand

LO4 Government intervention in foreign exchange

Every year, moving goods and services around the globe becomes easier. Currently, the volume of international transactions (summing exports and imports of goods and services) amounts to more than one-half of world GDP. Today, Americans buy cell phones and clothing made in China, computers assembled in Singapore, and fruit grown in Chile. But global business deals aren't limited to goods and services. Individuals, companies, and governments also invest abroad, buying and selling stocks and bonds in financial markets around the globe. The magnitude of the international flow of goods, services, and assets is impossible to ignore. To understand the nature of these transactions, we must become familiar with a key tool that makes this trade possible: *exchange rates.*

Whenever you buy something that has been made abroad, whether it is an article of clothing, a car, a stock, or a bond, someone somewhere has exchanged dollars for the currency used where the item was made. The reason is simple: You want to use dollars to pay for an imported shirt that you buy in a local store, but the Malaysian producer wants to be paid in *ringgit*. All cross-border transactions are like this; the buyer and seller both want to use their own currency. The exchange rate, at its most basic level, is the tool we use to measure the price of one currency in terms of another.

Exchange rates have broad implications both for countries and for individuals. Take the case of South Korea in the winter of 1998. As economic and financial turmoil spread through Asia starting in the summer of 1997, output and employment plunged. In Korea, large industrial companies and financial institutions approached bankruptcy. From October 1997 to January 1998, the number of South Korean *won* needed to purchase one dollar more than doubled, rising from 900 to 1,900 (see Figure 10.1). The consequences were dramatic, both inside and outside the country. When the cost of buying the won plummeted, South Korean products became much cheaper for foreigners to buy. As the value of the won dropped, the U.S. prices of Hyundai cars and

Figure 10.1   South Korean Won–Dollar Exchange Rate, 1997–1999

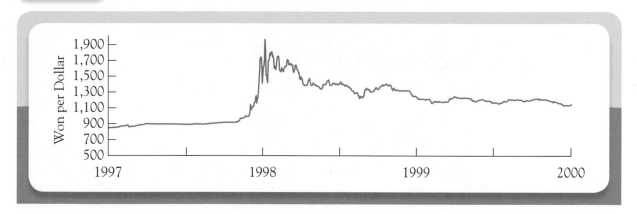

FRED data code: EXKOUS.

Samsung televisions fell with it. At the same time, U.S.-made products became extremely expensive for South Koreans to buy. In fact, the crisis became so severe that many Korean students at U.S. colleges and universities had to go home. The price of a U.S. education, measured in won, had doubled, and many Korean students just couldn't afford to continue.

Exchange rates go through long swings as well as sudden spikes. In 1973, the currency used in the United Kingdom, the **British pound** or "pound sterling," was worth $2.50. Over the next 36 years, its value declined by more than 35 percent, so that by late 2012 one pound was worth $1.60 (see Figure 10.2). Nevertheless, Americans visiting Great Britain during the summer of 2012 did not return thinking that their vacations had been inexpensive. At an exchange rate of $1.60, a hotel room in London cost about the same as in New York, and even a trip to McDonald's was nearly as expensive as in the United States.

Figure 10.2   Dollar–Pound Exchange Rate, 1971–2013

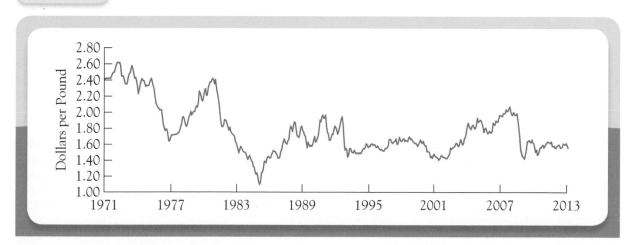

FRED data code: EXUSUK.

How are foreign exchange rates determined, and what accounts for their fluctuation over days, months, years, and decades? This chapter provides an introduction to foreign exchange rates and exchange markets.

Foreign Exchange Basics

After graduation, you are planning to travel to Europe. You would like to see the Eiffel Tower in Paris, the Colosseum in Rome, and the Parthenon in Athens. As you pack, you worry a little about paying your hotel bills and the tab for all that great food you expect to eat. The waiters in French, Italian, and Greek restaurants aren't interested in your dollar bills; they want to be paid in their own currency. But you are fortunate, for while the French, Italians, and Greeks speak different languages, they all use the same coins and bills. In fact, buying anything in Europe—at least in the countries that are members of the European Monetary Union—means exchanging your dollars for **euros**. So when you get to Europe, you will care about the rate of exchange between the dollar and the euro. The price of one euro in dollars is called the dollar–euro exchange rate.

The Nominal Exchange Rate

Exchanging dollars for euros is like any other economic transaction: you are using your money to buy something—in this case, money to spend in another country. The price you pay for this currency is called the nominal exchange rate, or simply the *exchange rate*. Formally defined, the **nominal exchange rate** *is the rate at which one can exchange the currency of one country for the currency of another country.* The dollar–euro exchange rate is the number of dollars you can get for each euro. In June 2013, one euro (the symbol for the euro is €) would buy $1.30. So an American who went to Europe in June 2013 paid $130 for €100.

Exchange rates change every day. Figure 10.3 shows the dollar–euro exchange rate since the inception of the euro in January 1999 to January 2013. The figure plots the number of dollars per euro, which is the conventional way to quote the dollar–euro exchange rate. When the euro was introduced, it was worth $1.17. But by October 2000, less than two years later, it could be exchanged for only 83 cents. Such a decline in the value of one currency relative to another is called a **depreciation** of the currency that is falling in value. During the first 22 months of the euro's existence, it depreciated nearly 30 percent relative to the dollar. Later in this chapter, we will consider the reasons for large movements in exchange rates.

At the same time that the euro was falling in value, the dollar was rising. After all, if you can buy fewer dollars with one

"When did your dad first explain foreign-currency exchange rates to you?"

Figure 10.3   Dollar–Euro Exchange Rate, 1999–2013

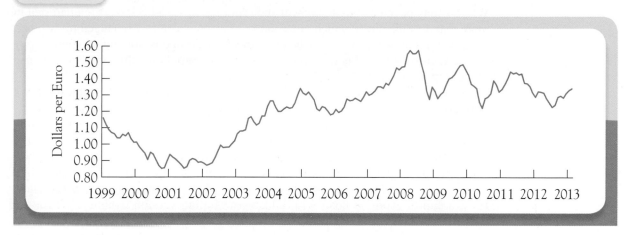

FRED data code: EXUSEU.

euro, you can get more euros for one dollar. The rise in the value of one currency relative to another is called an **appreciation** of the currency that is rising in value. During 1999 and 2000, the euro's depreciation was matched by the dollar's appreciation; they are really one and the same. When one currency goes up in value *relative to another,* the other currency must go down.

Note that, theoretically, exchange rates can be quoted in units of either currency—for example, as the number of dollars needed to buy one euro or as the number of euros needed to buy one dollar. The two prices are equivalent; one is simply the reciprocal of the other. In practice, however, each currency has its convention. The price of the British pound is quoted in the same way as the euro, so that people talk about the number of dollars that can be exchanged for one pound (£). The price of the Japanese **yen** (¥) is quoted as the number of yen that can be purchased with one dollar.

Unfortunately, there is no simple rule for determining which way a particular exchange rate should be quoted. Most rates tend to be quoted in the way that yields a number larger than one. The fact that €1 equaled $1.17 when the euro was created on January 1, 1999, is the likely explanation for why we talk about the number of dollars needed to purchase one euro. Ever since, people have quoted dollars per euro, even though there have been significant periods of time when the number was less than one. If you need to guess which way to quote an exchange rate, the best guess is that it is the way that yields a number larger than one. But the real solution is always to state the units explicitly, to avoid confusion.

A 20-euro note used in the countries that participate in the European Monetary Union.

The Real Exchange Rate

While it may be interesting to know that one euro is worth $1.30, you are interested in more than just the rate at which one country's currency can be exchanged for another. What you really want to know when you travel to Europe is how much you can buy with that euro. When all is said and done, will you return home thinking that your trip was cheap or expensive?

Because nominal exchange rates do not provide an answer to this question, we now turn to the concept of a **real exchange rate**, *the rate at which one can exchange the goods and services from one country for the goods and services from another country.* It is the cost of a basket of goods in one country *relative* to the cost of the same basket of goods in another country. To grasp this concept, we will start with the real exchange rate between two cups of espresso, one American and the other Italian. The local Starbucks charges $1.95 for an espresso; in Florence, Italy, a cup of espresso costs €1.00. (Yes, the Italian version is better, but for the sake of the example, let's pretend they're the same.) Using the nominal dollar–euro exchange rate as of June 2013, $1.30 per euro, this means that to buy an espresso in Florence, you need to spend $1.30. More important, you can exchange one cup of Starbucks espresso for 1.5 cups of Italian espresso. This is the *real* exchange rate. You will return from your European vacation thinking that espresso was very cheap in Italy.

There is a simple relationship between the real exchange rate and the nominal exchange rate, which we can infer from our espresso calculation. To compute the real exchange rate, we took the euro price of an espresso in Italy and multiplied it by the nominal exchange rate, the number of dollars per euro. Then we divided it into the dollar price of a cup of espresso in the United States:

Real coffee exchange rate

$$= \frac{\text{Dollar price of espresso in the U.S. (\$1.95)}}{\text{Euro price of espresso in Italy (€1.00)} \times \text{Dollars per euro (\$1.30/€)}} \quad (1)$$

$$= \frac{\text{Dollar price of espresso in the U.S. (\$1.95)}}{\text{Dollar price of espresso in Italy (€1.00)} \times (\$1.30/€)}$$

$$= \frac{\$1.95}{\$1.30}$$

$$= 1.50$$

At these prices and exchange rate, one cup of Starbucks espresso buys 1.5 cups of Italian espresso. Note in equation (1) that the units of measurement cancel out. In the denominator, we multiplied the price in euros times the nominal exchange rate (measured as dollars per euro) to get an amount stated in dollars. Then we divided that number into the numerator, also expressed in dollars. The real exchange rate has no units of measurement.

In summary, to figure out the real coffee exchange rate in equation (1), we divided the dollar price of coffee in the United States by the dollar price of coffee in Italy. We can use the same procedure to compute the real exchange rate more broadly by comparing the prices of a set of goods and services that are commonly purchased in any country. If we can transform a basket of goods and services produced in the United States into more than one basket produced in Europe, as in the coffee example, then we are likely to return from a trip to Paris, Rome, and Athens thinking that the cost of living there is relatively cheap. Using this idea, we can write the real exchange rate as

$$\text{Real exchange rate} = \frac{\text{Dollar price of domestic goods}}{\text{Dollar price of foreign goods}} \qquad (2)$$

From this definition of the real exchange rate, we can see that whenever the ratio in equation (2) is more than one, foreign products will seem cheap.

The real exchange rate, then, is much more important than the nominal exchange rate. It is the rate that measures the relative price of goods and services across countries, telling us where things are cheap and where they are expensive. The real exchange rate is the guiding force behind international transactions. When foreign goods are less expensive than domestic goods, their prices create an incentive for people to buy imports. Competing with foreign imports becomes more difficult for local producers. Think about what would happen if you could ship cups of espresso to the United States from Italy and sell them in an import shop. Starbucks would lose business. Obviously, you can't do that with freshly brewed coffee, but you can do it with clothing, electronics, cars, airplanes, and a wide variety of other goods and services. As a result, the competitiveness of U.S. exports depends on the real exchange rate. *Appreciation* of the real exchange rate makes U.S. exports more expensive to foreigners, reducing their competitiveness, while *depreciation* of the real exchange rate makes U.S. exports seem cheaper to foreigners, improving their competitiveness.

Foreign Exchange Markets

The volume of foreign exchange transactions is enormous. On an average day in 2010, $4.0 trillion in foreign currency was traded in a market that operates 24 hours every business day.[1] Given 260 business days in a normal year, the annual volume of foreign exchange transactions is about $1,035 trillion. To get a sense of how huge this number is, compare it to world output and trade. The World Bank estimates that in 2010, world GDP (at market prices) was $63 trillion, and international trade transactions (measured as exports plus imports) accounted for about $33 trillion of that amount. Hence, the volume of foreign exchange transactions is about 16 times world GDP and more than 30 times the value of world trade.

Because of its liquidity, the U.S. dollar is one side of roughly 85 percent of these currency transactions.[2] That means that someone who wishes to exchange Thai baht for Japanese yen is likely to make two transactions, the first to convert the baht to dollars and the second to convert the dollars to yen. Most likely these transactions will take place in London, because the United Kingdom is home to more than one-third of foreign exchange trades—about twice the volume in New York. Other significant foreign exchange trading takes place in Hong Kong, Singapore, Sydney, Tokyo, and Zurich (each about 4 to 6 percent).

---

[1]This estimate, the latest available, comes from a triennial survey by the Bank for International Settlements in Basel, Switzerland. The complete survey is available at *www.bis.org*.

[2]The liquidity of the market for dollars creates a premium, driving up the dollar's value in the same way that liquidity increases the price of a bond.

TOOLS OF THE TRADE
Following Exchange Rates in the News

Exchange rates are reported in the business news. *The Wall Street Journal* carries a daily Foreign Exchange column that describes events in the markets, as well as a table reporting the most recent nominal exchange rates between the U.S. dollar and various foreign currencies. (Because the rates quoted are generally for transactions of $1 million or more, they normally are not available to tourists.) The column and the table, one of which is reprinted here, appear in both the print and online versions of the paper. Let's run through Table 10.1 to see how to read it.

Column 1: The name of the country together with the name of its currency.

Column 2: The number of dollars that could be purchased per unit of foreign currency at the close of business on Friday, November 23, 2012. Looking at the entry for "**UK pound**" we can see that on that date, one British pound purchased $1.6029.

Column 3: The numbers of units of foreign currency needed to purchase one dollar at the close of business on Friday, November 23, 2012. Looking at the entry for "**Japan** yen" we can see that on that date, you could exchange 82.40 Japanese yen for one dollar.*

Column 4: The year to date change in the U.S. dollar equivalent. That is, the percent change since January 1, 2012, in the units of foreign currency that could be purchased per dollar, so positive values mean that the dollar has appreciated relative to a particular currency, while negative

values imply a depreciation of the dollar. In some cases, the exchange rate hasn't moved, so the entry reads "unch" for "unchanged." To see how it works, notice that the "**Euro area** euro" in this column is −0.1 percent. This means that during the first 11 months of 2012 the dollar depreciated slightly against the euro, declining by 0.1 percent from roughly €0.7715 per dollar to €0.7707 per dollar.

For a few large foreign currency markets, like Britain's and Japan's, the table quotes the forward as well as the spot rates. *Spot rates* are the rates for an immediate exchange (subject to a two-day settlement period). *Forward rates* are the rates at which foreign currency dealers are willing to commit to buying or selling a currency in the future, so they give some indication of whether market participants expect currencies to appreciate or depreciate over time.

In thinking about foreign exchange rates, be sure to keep track of whether you are quoting the number of U.S. dollars that can be exchanged for one unit of foreign currency, as in column 2 of the table, or the number of units of foreign currency that can be purchased with one dollar. They are easy to confuse. If you went to Europe and confused $1.2975 per euro with €0.7707 per dollar, you would think everything was less expensive than it really is, and you end up buying something for more than you originally planned to pay.

*Note the reciprocal nature of the rates in columns 2 and 3. For any entry, the value in column 2 times the value in column 3 equals 1, so either value divided into 1 equals the other value.

Exchange Rates in the Long Run

How are exchange rates determined? To answer this question, we will divide our discussion into two parts. This section will look at the determination of the long-run exchange rate and the forces that drive its movement over long periods, such as decades. The next section will consider what causes exchange rates to vary over the short term—a few days or months, or even years.

The Law of One Price

The starting point for understanding how long-run exchange rates are determined is *the law of one price*. The **law of one price** is based on the concept of *arbitrage*—the idea that identical products should sell for the same price. Recall from our discussion in Chapter 9 that two financial instruments with the same risk and promised future payments will sell for the same price. We might refer to this phenomenon as financial arbitrage. If we extend the concept of arbitrage from financial instruments to goods and services, we can conclude that identical goods and services should sell for the

Table 10.1   Currencies

U.S.–dollar foreign-exchange rates in late New York trading, November 23, 2012

	(1) Country/currency	(2) Fri in US$	(3) Fri per US$	(4) US$ vs, YTD chg (%)		(1) Country/currency	(2) Fri in US$	(3) Fri per US$	(4) US$ vs, YTD chg (%)
Americas					**Europe**				
	Argentina peso	0.2074	4.8211	11.9		Czech Rep. koruna	0.0512	19.53	−1.1
	Brazil real	0.4803	2.0819	11.6		Denmark krone	0.174	5.7486	0.2
	Canada dollar	1.0074	0.9926	−2.8		Euro area euro	1.2975	0.7707	−0.1
	Chile peso	0.002091	478.16	−8		Hungary forint	0.004594	217.68	−10.5
	Colombia peso	0.0005484	1823.5	−6		Norway krone	0.1767	5.6601	-5.3
	Ecuador US dollar	1	1	unch		Poland zloty	0.3156	3.1688	−8.1
	Mexico peso	0.0771	12.965	−7		Romania leu	0.2862	3.4945	4.8
	Peru new sol	0.3866	2.5865	−4.1		Russia ruble	0.03222	31.037	−3.5
	Uruguay peso†	0.05113	19.558	−1.3		Sweden krona	0.151	6.6238	−3.7
	Venezuela b. fuerte	0.22988506	4.35	unch		Switzerland franc	1.0775	0.9281	−1
Asia-Pacific					1-mos forward	1.0779	0.9277	−1
					3-mos forward	1.0791	0.9267	−0.9
	Australian dollar	1.0461	0.956	−2.4		6-mos forward	1.0809	0.9252	−0.8
	China yuan	0.1604	6.2328	−1.4		Turkey lira	0.5575	1.7938	−6.4
	Hong Kong dollar	0.129	7.7504	−0.2		UK pound	1.6029	0.6239	−3
	India rupee	0.01803	55.45045	4.6		1-mos forward	1.6027	0.6239	−3.2
	Indonesia rupiah	0.000104	9613	6.4		3-mos forward	1.6026	0.624	−3.2
	Japan yen	0.01214	82.4	7.1		6-mos forward	1.602	0.6242	−3.3
	1-mos forward	0.01214	82.38	6.7	**Middle East/Africa**				
	3-mos forward	0.01215	82.31	6.7					
	6-mos forward	0.01216	82.23	6.8		Bahrain dinar	2.652	0.3771	unch
	Malaysia ringgit§	0.3268	3.0597	−3.7		Eqypt pound	0.1642	6.0891	0.6
	New Zealand dollar	0.8236	1.2142	−5.6		Israel shekel	0.259	3.8605	1.3
	Pakistan rupee	0.01041	96.045	6.9		Jordan dinar	1.4127	0.7079	−0.2
	Philippines peso	0.0243	41.068	−6.3		Kenya shilling	0.01164	85.882	1
	Singapore dollar	0.8179	1.2227	−5.7		Kuwait dinar	3.5404	0.2825	1.5
	South Korea won	0.0009213	1085.45	−6.5		Lebanon pound	0.0006649	1503.95	−0.1
	Taiwan dollar	0.03434	29.12	−3.8		Saudi Arabia riyal	0.2666	3.7505	unch
	Thailand baht	0.03256	30.711	−2.8		South Africa rand	0.1126	8.8771	9.8
	Vietnam dong	0.00005	20838	−1		UAE dirham	0.2722	3.6732	unch

Source: ICAP plc.

*Floating rate   †Financial   §Government rate   ‡Russian Central Bank rate   **Commercial rate

SOURCE: *The Wall Street Journal.* Copyright 2012 by Dow Jones Company, Inc. Reproduced with permission of Dow Jones and Company, Inc.

same price regardless of *where* they are sold. Identical televisions or cars should cost the same whether they are sold in St. Louis or Philadelphia. When they don't, someone can make a profit.

For instance, if a specific model television were cheaper in St. Louis than in Philadelphia, someone could buy it in St. Louis, drive to Philadelphia, and sell it at a profit. This opportunity to profit from arbitrage would increase demand for televisions in St. Louis, where the price is low, and increase the supply of televisions in Philadelphia, where the price is high. Higher demand drives prices up, while a larger

MARKETS

YOUR FINANCIAL WORLD
Investing Abroad

More diversification is always better. Increasing the number of independent risks in a portfolio by spreading investments across a broader set of stocks and bonds can reduce risk without decreasing the expected return. That is the rationale behind investing in mutual funds and the reason for investing abroad as well. In the same way that someone living in Kansas would not hesitate to invest in an Ohio company, there is no reason why someone who lives in the United States should hesitate to invest outside the United States.

For many years, some financial advisors have been telling their clients in the United States to hold a portion of their equity portfolios in foreign stocks. But you don't need an investment advisor to heed this advice. As soon as you begin to save for your retirement—which should be as soon

as you get a steady job—you should diversify your investments internationally. So long as the returns on stocks in other countries do not move in lockstep with the U.S. stock market, holding them will reduce the risk in your investment portfolio. Experience indicates that the returns on other countries' stock markets move somewhat independently of the U.S. stock market. And the benefits of diversification are not counteracted by exposure to the risk of exchange rate fluctuations. True, buying British stock means trading dollars for pounds and then changing back to dollars at a later date. In the meantime, the exchange rate could move. But the evidence shows us that holding foreign stocks reduces risk without sacrificing returns, despite the risk of exchange rate fluctuations.

supply forces them down. The process will continue until the television sells for the same price in both cities. Of course, complete price equalization occurs only in the absence of transportation costs. If it costs $10 to transport the television 900 miles from the Mississippi River to the East Coast, then arbitrage will continue until the price in St. Louis is within $10 of the price in Philadelphia.

We can extend the law of one price from cities in the same country to cities in different countries. Instead of St. Louis and Philadelphia, think of Detroit, Michigan, and Windsor, Ontario—two cities separated by the Detroit River and the Canadian border. The river can be crossed by bridge or tunnel in roughly one minute. Ignoring transportation costs, then, once we have converted a price from U.S. to Canadian dollars, the cost of a television should be the same in both cities. If a TV costs $500 in the United States, at a nominal exchange rate of 0.99 Canadian dollar per U.S. dollar (see Table 10.1), the Canadian price should be $(500 \times 0.99) = 495$ Canadian dollars. That is, the law of one price tells us that

$$\text{Canadian dollar price of a TV in Windsor, Ontario} = \frac{(\text{U.S. dollar price of a TV in Detroit})}{\times (\text{Canadian dollars per U.S. dollar})} \quad (3)$$

This example shows once again the importance of using the correct units when working with exchange rates. In converting the U.S. dollar price to Canadian dollars, we multiply by the number of Canadian dollars needed to buy one U.S. dollar. That is, we compute (U.S. dollars) times (Canadian dollars/U.S. dollar) equals Canadian dollars. This is the same calculation we did earlier to figure out the U.S. dollar price of an Italian cup of coffee. There, we multiplied (euros) times (U.S. dollars/euro) to get U.S. dollars.

Returning to the law of one price, we can see immediately that it fails almost all the time. The fact is that the same commodity or service sells for vastly different prices in different countries. Why? Transportation costs can be significant, especially for heavy items like marble or slate. Tariffs—the taxes countries charge at their borders—are high sometimes, especially if a country is trying to protect a domestic industry. And technical specifications can differ. A television bought in Paris will not work in

St. Louis because it requires a different input signal. A car sold in Great Britain cannot be used in the United States or continental Europe because its steering wheel is on the right. Moreover, tastes differ across countries, leading to different pricing. Finally, some things simply cannot be traded. A haircut may be cheaper in New Delhi than in Philadelphia, but most Americans simply can't take advantage of that price difference.

Purchasing Power Parity

Since the law of one price fails so often, why do we bother with it? Because even with its obvious flaws, the law of one price is extremely useful in explaining the behavior of exchange rates over long periods, like 10 or 20 years. To see why, we need to extend the law from a single commodity to a basket of goods and services. The result is the theory of **purchasing power parity (PPP)**, which means that one unit of U.S. domestic currency will buy the same basket of goods and services anywhere in the world. This idea may sound absurd, but let's look at its implications.

According to the theory of purchasing power parity, the dollar price of a basket of goods and services in the United States should be the same as the dollar price of a basket of goods and services in Mexico, Japan, or the United Kingdom. In the case of the United Kingdom, this statement means that

$$\text{Dollar price of basket of goods in U.S.} = \text{Dollar price of basket of goods in U.K.} \qquad (4)$$

Rearranging this expression gives us

$$\frac{\text{Dollar price of basket of goods in U.S.}}{\text{Dollar price of basket of goods in U.K.}} = 1 \qquad (5)$$

The left-hand side of equation (5) is familiar: It is the real exchange rate [see equation (2) on page 245]. Thus, *purchasing power parity implies that the real exchange rate is always equal to one.* The implication of this conclusion is straightforward. It is that the purchasing power of a dollar is always the same, regardless of where in the world you go.

This idea must seem doubly absurd. If a dollar doesn't even buy the same number of cups of coffee in Italy and the United States, how can it have the same purchasing power all the time, everywhere in the world? On any given day, it doesn't. But over the long term, exchange rates do tend to move, so this concept helps us to understand changes that happen over years or decades. To see how, remember that the dollar price of a foreign basket of goods is just the foreign currency price of the basket of goods times the number of dollars per unit of foreign currency. This means that if we quote the price of a basket of goods in the United Kingdom in pounds instead of dollars, then

$$\frac{\text{Dollar price of basket of goods in U.S.}}{(\text{Pound price of basket of goods in U.K.}) \times (\text{Dollars per pound})} = 1 \qquad (6)$$

so

$$\frac{\text{Dollar price of basket of goods in U.S.}}{\text{Pound price of basket of goods in U.K.}} = (\text{Dollars per pound}) \qquad (7)$$

That is, purchasing power parity implies that when prices change in one country but not in another, the exchange rate should change as well. When prices rise within a country, the effect is called inflation. If inflation occurs in one country but not in another, the change in prices creates an international inflation differential. So purchasing power parity tells us that changes in exchange rates are tied to differences in inflation from one country to another. Specifically, the currency of a country with high inflation will depreciate.

To see this point, think about what would happen if there were no inflation in the United Kingdom, but prices in the United States doubled. We would not expect the dollar–pound exchange rate to stay the same. Instead, we would predict that one dollar would now buy half as many British pounds as it did before (that is, twice as many dollars would be needed to purchase one pound).[3] There is strong evidence to support this conclusion, but the data must be drawn over fairly long periods, and the relationship is not perfect.

Take, for instance, the U.S. dollar–British pound exchange rate plotted in Figure 10.2 (page 241). Recall that in 1973, one pound was worth around $2.50. By the end of 2012, a pound was worth $1.60—a decline of 36 percent, or 1.1 percent per year for 40 years. Over the same period, U.S. prices increased an average of 4.26 percent per year, while British prices increased an average of 5.57 percent per year—a difference of 1.31 percent per year. While the relationship between the inflation and exchange rates is not perfect, it surely explains much of the movement in the dollar–pound exchange rate over the 40-year period.

What is true for the United Kingdom is true for the rest of the world. To confirm it, we can look at a plot of (a) the historical difference between inflation in other countries and inflation in the United States against (b) the percentage change in the number of units of other countries' currencies required to purchase one dollar—that is, the average annual depreciation of the exchange rate.

Figure 10.4 presents data for 62 countries drawn from files maintained by the International Monetary Fund. Each point represents a country. The difference between its average annual inflation and that of the U.S. is on the horizontal axis, and the average annual percentage change in the exchange rate between the country's currency and the U.S. dollar is on the vertical axis. Points further to the right represent countries with higher levels of inflation, and points higher up are countries whose dollar-exchange rate experienced more depreciation over the 30-year period of the sample. The solid line is a 45-degree line that is consistent with the theoretical prediction of purchasing power parity. On the 45-degree line, exchange rate movements exactly equal differences in inflation. Granted, the points don't all lie exactly on the line, but the pattern is clearly there. The higher a country's inflation, the greater the depreciation in its exchange rate.

Take the example of Bolivia. From 1980 to 2010, Bolivia's inflation minus U.S. inflation averaged 40 percent per year, and the Bolivian currency (originally the bolivar, now the boliviano) depreciated at an average annual rate of 42 percent. Putting that into perspective, the 2010 Bolivian price level was more than 465,000 times the 1980 Bolivian price level, and the exchange rate depreciated by an enormous multiple. That means purchasing one dollar in the foreign exchange market required 286,000 times as many bolivianos in 2010 as in 1980. Importantly, Figure 10.4 shows that there are no countries with high inflation differentials and small exchange rate changes or big exchange rate changes and low inflation differentials. All of the points lie close to the 45-degree line.

---

[3]It is possible to show this mathematically. If P represents the domestic (U.S.) currency price of a basket of goods, P^f the foreign currency price of the foreign (British) basket of goods, and e the nominal exchange rate, expressed as the domestic currency price of foreign currency (dollars per pound), then purchasing power parity tells us that $(P/eP^f) = 1$ (eq. 5), so $e = (P/P^f)$ (eq. 7). When converted from levels to rates of change, this expression implies that the percent change in the exchange rate equals the difference between domestic and foreign inflation.

Figure 10.4   Exchange Rate Movements and Inflation Differentials, 1980–2010

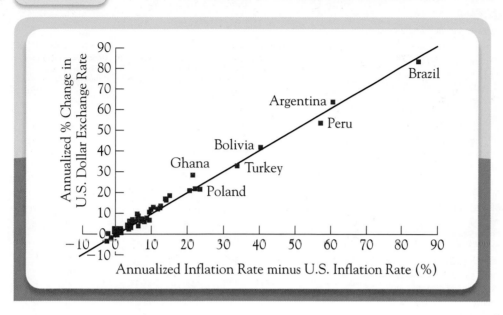

SOURCE: *The International Monetary Fund*

The data in Figure 10.4 tell us that purchasing power parity held true over a 30-year period. Even if we look at an interval as short as a decade, the connection between movements in the exchange rate and differences in inflation across countries usually holds up to scrutiny. But the same exercise applied to periods of a few weeks, months, or even years would be a total failure. We know that from examining the plots of the Korean won–U.S. dollar exchange rate in Figure 10.1 and the dollar–euro exchange rate in Figure 10.3. Recall that the Korean won went through a sudden, steep depreciation, falling from 900 to 1,900 won to the dollar in just a few months, at the end of 1997. The pattern of Korean inflation at the time, a relatively steady 7½ percent versus 1½ percent in the United States, simply cannot explain this sudden change.

Similarly, from the euro's inception in January 1999, the dollar–euro rate fell steadily for two years, dropping more than 25 percent (see Figure 10.3). At the same time, inflation in the euro area ran a full percentage point *below* U.S. inflation. Examples like these are the norm, not the exception. Over weeks, months, and even years, nominal exchange rates can deviate substantially from the levels implied by purchasing power parity. So, while the theory can help us to understand long swings in exchange rates, it provides no explanation for the short-term movements we see all the time. Fortunately, we do have some equipment in our tool kit that we can use to explain short-term movements in exchange rates.

Before continuing, we should note the meaning of two additional terms. We often hear currencies described as **undervalued** or **overvalued**. When people use these terms, they often have in mind a current market rate that deviates from what they consider to be purchasing power parity. For example, a person who thinks that one dollar should purchase one euro—that is, that one to one is somehow the "correct" long-run exchange rate—would say that if one dollar purchases only €0.90, it is *undervalued* relative to the euro, or the euro is *overvalued* relative to the dollar.

APPLYING THE CONCEPT
THE BIG MAC INDEX

By the close of the 20th century, the Big Mac was available to consumers in 121 countries. Regardless of where it was sold, a Big Mac was defined as "two all-beef patties, special sauce, lettuce, cheese, pickles, onions on a sesame seed bun." Needless to say, every McDonald's restaurant requires payment in the local currency. In 1986, the staff of *The Economist* magazine realized that this presented an opportunity. Together, the market exchange rate and the price of a Big Mac would allow them to estimate the extent to which a country's currency deviates from the level implied by purchasing power parity.

Twice a year, under headlines like "Big Mac-Currencies" and "Burgernomics," *The Economist* publishes a table showing Big Mac prices in more than 40 countries. Table 10.2 is based on Big Mac prices from *The Economist* edition of July 25, 2012. Using Big Mac prices as a basis for comparison, it shows the extent to which each country's currency was undervalued or overvalued relative to the U.S. dollar. As you look at the table, you will realize that with the exception of the pound and the euro, all exchange rates are quoted as the number of units of local currency required to purchase one dollar. The pound and the euro are exceptions—they are quoted as the number of dollars required to purchase one pound or one euro.

To see how the **Big Mac index** works, take the case of Denmark. The Danish currency is called the *krone* (which means "crown") and in mid-2012, a Big Mac cost DKr28.5 in Copenhagen. At an exchange rate of 6.14, that's equivalent to $4.65 (adjusted for rounding error). To figure out the purchasing power parity value of one dollar in krone, we can use the relationship in equation (7), which tells us to divide the price of a Big Mac in krone by the dollar price: 28.5 krone per Big Mac/$4.33 per Big Mac = 6.59 krone per dollar (adjusted for rounding error). If the theory of purchasing power parity holds, then 6.59 krone should buy one dollar. But instead, the price of one dollar in the currency markets was 6.14 krone, which means that the Danish krone was *overvalued* by 7 percent. For the Chinese *yuan*, the same calculation implies an *undervaluation* of roughly −43 percent.

The Big Mac index is a clever idea, and it works surprisingly well considering that it is based on a single commodity that is not tradeable, and whose local price surely depends on costs like wages, rent, and taxes.

Table 10.2 — A Feast of Burgernomics
The Big Mac Index

Country	Big Mac prices In local currency	In U.S. dollars*	Implied PPP† of the dollar	Actual dollar exchange rate July 25	Under(−)/over(+) valuation against the dollar, %†
United States‡	$4.33	4.33	—	—	—
Argentina	Peso 19	4.16	4.39	4.57	−4
Australia	A$4.56	4.68	1.05	0.97	8
Brazil	Real 10.08	4.94	2.33	2.04	14
Britain	£2.69	4.16	1.61§	1.55§	−4
Canada	C$3.89	3.82	0.90	1.02	−12
Chile	Peso 2050	4.16	473.71	493.05	−4
China**	Yuan 15.65	2.45	3.62	6.39	−43
Colombia	Peso 8600	4.77	1987.29	1804.48	10
Costa Rica	Colones 1200	2.40	277.30	501.02	−45
Czech Republic	Koruna 70.33	3.34	16.25	21.05	−23
Denmark	DK 28.5	4.65	6.59	6.14	7
Egypt	Pound 16	2.64	3.70	6.07	−39
Euro area††	€3.58	4.34	1.21§§	1.21§§	0
Hong Kong	HK$16.50	2.13	3.81	7.76	−51
Hungary	Forint 830	3.48	191.80	238.22	−19
India***	Rupee 89	1.58	20.57	56.17	−63
Indonesia	Rupiah 24200	2.55	5592	9482.50	−41
Israel	Shekel 11.9	2.92	2.75	4.08	−33
Japan	Yen 320	4.09	73.95	78.22	−5
Latvia	Lats 1.69	2.94	0.39	0.57	−32
Lithuania	Litas 7.8	2.74	1.80	2.85	−37
Malaysia	Ringgit 7.4	2.33	1.71	3.17	−46
Mexico	Peso 37	2.70	8.55	13.69	−38
New Zealand	NZ$5.1	4.00	1.18	1.27	−7
Norway	Kroner 43	7.06	9.94	6.09	63
Pakistan	Rupee 285	3.01	65.86	94.61	−30
Philippines	Peso 118	2.80	27.27	42.20	−35
Poland	Zloty 9.1	2.63	2.10	3.46	−39
Russia	Rouble 75	2.29	17.33	32.77	−47
Saudi Arabia	Riyal 10	2.67	2.31	3.75	−38
Singapore	S$4.40	3.50	1.02	1.26	−19
South Africa	Rand 19.95	2.36	4.61	8.47	−46
South Korea	Won 3700	3.21	855.00	1151.00	−26
Sri Lanka	Rupee 290	2.21	67.01	131.00	−49
Sweden	SKr 48.4	6.94	11.18	6.98	60
Switzerland	SFr 6.5	6.56	1.50	0.99	52
Taiwan	NT$75	2.48	17.33	30.20	−43
Thailand	Baht 82	2.59	18.95	31.70	−40
Turkey	Lira 8.25	4.52	1.91	1.83	4
UAE	Dirhams 12	3.27	2.77	3.67	−25
Ukraine	Hryvnia 15	1.86	3.47	8.09	−57
Uruguay	Peso 99	4.53	22.88	21.87	5
Venezuela	Bolivar 34	7.92	7.86	4.29	83

*At market exchange rate (July 25, 2012)
†Purchasing-price parity; local price divided by price in United States
‡Average of four cities
§Dollars per pound
**Average of five cities
††Weighted average of prices in euro area
§§Dollars per euro
***Maharaja Mac

Exchange Rates in the Short Run

While purchasing power parity helps us to understand movements in nominal exchange rates over decades, it cannot explain the weekly, monthly, or even yearly movements we see. What can? What sorts of phenomena are responsible for the nearly constant movement in exchange rates? To explain short-run changes in nominal exchange rates, we turn to an analysis of the supply of and demand for currencies. Because, in the short run, prices don't move much, these nominal exchange rate movements represent changes in the real exchange rate. That is, a 1 or 2 percent change in the *nominal* dollar–euro exchange rate over a day or week creates a roughly equivalent change in the *real* dollar–euro exchange rate.

The Supply of Dollars

As is always the case in discussing foreign exchange, we need to pick a home country and stick to it. The most natural choice for us is the United States, so we'll use the U.S. dollar as the domestic currency. Consistent with this, we will discuss the number of units of foreign currency that it takes to purchase one dollar. For example, we will talk about the number of euros per dollar.

Who supplies dollars to the foreign exchange markets? People who have them, of course—primarily people in the United States. There are two reasons why someone who is holding dollars would want to exchange them for euros or yen: (1) to purchase goods and services produced abroad, like a Japanese television set, dinner in Paris, or tuition at a foreign university; and (2) to invest in foreign assets, such as bonds issued by the German telecommunications company Deutsche Telekom, or shares in Honda, the Japanese manufacturer of cars and motorcycles.

Figure 10.5 shows the **supply of dollars** in the dollar–euro market. Just like any other supply curve, it slopes upward. The higher the price a dollar commands in the market, the more dollars are supplied. And the more valuable the dollar, the cheaper are foreign-produced goods and foreign assets *relative to domestic ones* in U.S. markets.

Figure 10.5   The Dollar–Euro Market

To see why, suppose you are planning to buy a car. You have narrowed your options to a German-made Volkswagen Jetta and an American-made Ford Focus. Price is important to you. Because the Volkswagen is manufactured abroad, a change in the value of the dollar will affect your decision. As the dollar increases in value, the price of the Jetta falls and you become more likely to buy the Jetta. If you do, you will be supplying dollars to the foreign exchange market. What is true for your car purchase is true for everything else. The more valuable the dollar, the cheaper foreign goods, services, and assets will be and the higher the supply of dollars in the dollar–euro market. Thus, *the supply curve for dollars slopes upward,* as shown in Figure 10.5.

The Demand for Dollars

Foreigners who want to purchase American-made goods, assets, or services need dollars to do so. Suppose a European student would like to attend college in the United

YOUR FINANCIAL WORLD
Don't Bet on Exchange Rates

Lots of people have an opinion about the likely course of exchange rates. Should you listen to them to try to turn a profit on changes in the exchange rate? Probably not. To see why, let's look at a recent episode in economic history. In 2008, U.S. imports exceeded exports by nearly 5 percent of GDP (that's a really big current account deficit); the economy was faltering; the stock market was declining; but still the dollar was strong. Moreover, the Japanese yen remained strong after more than a decade of stagnation and record low interest rates. Anyone who followed such matters would tell you that both the dollar and the yen should have depreciated. But having a good sense of what will happen over the long run doesn't help much in the short run. What the experts can't tell you is when the dollar will depreciate.

So how can you get a forecast of the future exchange rate? You can look at the *forward markets* for the major currencies. In these markets, foreign currency dealers agree today to a price at which they will sell euros (or yen or other major currencies) three months from now. Because they

don't want to incur losses, the dealers will use all the information available to them (including interest rates) to make the most accurate forecast they can for the exchange rate on the day they agree to make the transaction. But if you look at the newspaper, you will discover that forward rates of major currencies are virtually always within 1 or 2 percent of the current spot rate. In other words, the best forecast is that the exchange rate won't change much. (Take a look at the "Exchange Rates" column in the business section of a newspaper like *The Wall Street Journal* to confirm this claim.) This tendency holds true even if the Big Mac index or more sophisticated calculations based on purchasing power parity tell us that the exchange rate should move significantly in one direction or another.

The problem is that, in the short run, exchange rates are inherently unpredictable. No one has any idea what is going to happen over the next week, month, or even year. In short, the best forecast of the future exchange rate is usually today's exchange rate. Because you really can't do any better than that, betting on exchange rates is a bad idea.

States. The school will accept payment only in dollars, so paying the tuition bill means exchanging euros for dollars. The lower the dollar–euro exchange rate—the fewer euros needed to buy one dollar—the cheaper the tuition bill will be from the viewpoint of a European student. At a given dollar price, the fewer euros needed to purchase one dollar, the cheaper are American-made goods and services. And the cheaper a good or service, the higher the demand for it. The same is true of investments. The cheaper the dollar—the lower the dollar–euro exchange rate—the more attractive are U.S. investments and the higher is the **demand for dollars** with which to buy them. Thus, *the demand curve for dollars slopes downward* (see Figure 10.5).

MARKETS

Equilibrium in the Market for Dollars

The equilibrium exchange rate, labeled *E* in Figure 10.5, equates the supply of and demand for dollars. Because the values of all the major currencies of the world (including the dollar, the euro, the yen, and the pound) float freely, they are determined by market forces. As a result, fluctuations in their value are the consequence of shifts in supply or demand.

Shifts in the Supply of and Demand for Dollars

Shifts in either the supply of or the demand for dollars will change the *equilibrium exchange rate*. Let's begin with *shifts in the supply of dollars*. Remember that Americans wanting to purchase products from abroad or to buy foreign assets will supply dollars to the foreign exchange market. Anything that increases their desire to import goods and services from abroad, or their preference for foreign stocks and bonds, will increase the supply of dollars, leading to a depreciation of the dollar. Figure 10.6 shows the mechanics of this process.

What causes Americans' preferences for foreign goods, services, and assets to increase, prompting them to supply more dollars to the foreign exchange market shifting the supply of dollars to the right? This question has many answers. The list includes the following possibilities:

A rise in the supply of dollars Americans use to purchase foreign goods and services can be caused by

- *An increase in Americans' preference for foreign goods.* For instance, a successful advertising campaign might convince American consumers to buy more imported olive oil. To fill the new orders, U.S. importers would exchange dollars for euros, shifting the dollar supply curve to the right.

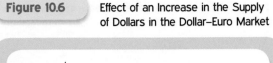

Figure 10.6   Effect of an Increase in the Supply of Dollars in the Dollar–Euro Market

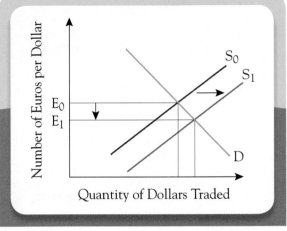

A rise in the supply of dollars Americans use to purchase foreign assets can be caused by

- *An increase in the real interest rate on foreign bonds (relative to U.S. bonds).* With U.S. real interest rates holding steady, an increase in the return on foreign bonds would make them a more appealing investment. Because buying German bonds means exchanging dollars for euros, a rise in the desire to purchase foreign bonds shifts the supply curve for dollars to the right. (Remember that the real interest rate is the nominal interest rate minus expected inflation, so real interest rates increase either when the nominal interest rate rises and expected inflation holds steady or when expected inflation falls and the nominal interest rate remains the same.)

TIME

- *An increase in American wealth.* Just as an increase in income raises consumption of everything, an increase in wealth raises investment in everything. The wealthier we are, the more foreign investments we will make, and the more dollars we will exchange for euros, shifting the supply of dollars to the right.

- *A decrease in the riskiness of foreign investments relative to U.S. investments.* Lower-risk bonds are always more desirable than others, regardless of their country of origin. If the risk associated with foreign investments falls, Americans will want more of them. To get them, they will increase the supply of dollars in the foreign exchange market.

RISK

- *An expected depreciation of the dollar.* If people think the dollar is going to lose value, possibly because of inflation, they will want to exchange it for foreign currency. To see why, assume that the euro is currently worth €0.77 per dollar and that you expect it to move to €0.70 per dollar over the next year. If you exchange $100 for euros today, you will get €77. Reversing the transaction a year later, you will be left with $110: a 10 percent return. The point is simple: If investors think the dollar will decline in value—it will depreciate—they will sell dollars, increasing the supply of dollars in the foreign exchange market.

Figure 10.7

Effect of an Increase in the Demand for Dollars in the Dollar–Euro Market

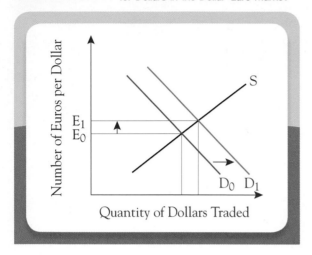

To understand *shifts in the demand for dollars*, all we need to do is review the list just presented, this time from the point of view of a foreigner. Anything that increases the desire of foreigners to buy American-made goods and services, or to invest in U.S. assets, will increase the demand for dollars and shift the demand curve to the right. Increases in demand come about when foreigners prefer more American-made goods, when the real yield on U.S. bonds rises (relative to the yield on foreign bonds), when foreign wealth increases, when the riskiness of American investments falls, and when the dollar is expected to appreciate. All these events increase demand, shifting the demand curve to the right and causing the dollar to appreciate (see Figure 10.7). Table 10.3 summarizes all the events that increase the supply of and demand for dollars in the foreign exchange market.

Explaining Exchange Rate Movements

The supply and demand model of the determination of exchange rates helps to explain short-run movements in currency values. Let's return to the 30 percent appreciation of the dollar relative to the euro that occurred between January 1999 and October 2000 (see Figure 10.3 on page 243). Over this period, the number of euros required to purchase one dollar increased. Our model allows us to conclude that the cause was either a decrease in the dollars supplied by Americans or an increase in the dollars demanded by foreigners. The first would shift the supply curve to the left and the second would shift the demand curve to the right, increasing the equilibrium exchange rate and making dollars more valuable. To figure out which of these is right, we need to look for other evidence.

Table 10.3

Causes of an Increase in the Supply of and Demand for Dollars

Increased Supply Shifts Supply Curve to the Right (Leads to a fall in the value of the dollar)	**Increased Demand Shifts Demand Curve to the Right** (Leads to a rise in the value of the dollar)
Increase in American preference for foreign goods	Increase in foreign preference for American goods
Increase in real interest rate on foreign bonds (relative to U.S. bonds)	Increase in real interest rate on U.S. bonds (relative to foreign bonds)
Increase in American wealth	Increase in foreign wealth
Reduction in riskiness of foreign investment (relative to U.S. investment)	Reduction in riskiness of U.S. investment (relative to foreign investment)
Expected depreciation of the dollar	Expected future dollar appreciation

LESSONS FROM THE CRISIS
CURRENCY RISK AND ROLLOVER RISK

During the crisis of 2007–2009, some non-U.S. banks faced a sudden threat to their survival: When the interbank market dried up, they found it difficult to borrow the U.S. dollars needed to fund their dollar loans and securities (see Chapter 3, Lessons from the Crisis: Interbank Lending).*

When a bank lends in a foreign currency, it typically borrows in that currency, too. Banks face *currency risk* if they borrow in one currency and lend in another. If the currency in which they lent appreciates relative to the currency in which they borrowed, they benefit. If the opposite occurs, so the currency in which they borrowed rises in value relative to the currency in which they lent, they lose. The larger the mismatch between lending and borrowing in a currency, the greater the currency risk.

But simply matching the currencies of assets and liabilities does not eliminate all the risks the bank faces. Because loans usually have a longer maturity than borrowings, banks still face a danger that funding liquidity in the foreign currency will dry up. This danger is called *rollover risk*. If a bank is unable to "roll over" its short-term foreign currency borrowing (that is, renew at maturity), it must either sell the foreign-currency assets it has purchased or accept increased currency risk by borrowing in domestic currency. A crisis may eliminate even these options and thus threaten the bank's survival.

To see the relationship between currency risk and rollover risk, consider the balance sheet of a hypothetical Japanese bank (Table 10.4). The bank has borrowed short term and made long-term loans in both U.S. dollars and Japanese yen. But because of the way it did this, it has a currency mismatch of $100 million. This is the gap between its lending and borrowing in the foreign currency. At an initial exchange rate of ¥100/US$, in yen this gap equals ¥10 billion. What is the bank's currency risk? If the yen appreciates to ¥99/US$—so instead of taking 100 yen to purchase 1 dollar, it now only takes 99—the bank loses ¥100 million. If the yen depreciates to ¥101/US$, the bank gains ¥100 million. The bank also has rollover risk in dollars. If it cannot roll over its $100 million liability, the bank must repay it by selling dollar loans or by borrowing in yen. The latter adds to its currency risk.

In the financial crisis of 2007–2009, the rollover risk facing internationally active banks became acute and posed a threat to the financial system as a whole. From a policy perspective, the goal was not just to create an adequate supply of dollars, but to deliver it to the banks that needed it. Only the central bank of the United States (the Federal Reserve) can create dollars, but the Fed is not in a position to know all about non-U.S. private banks in need of dollar funding.

So, to limit its credit exposure, the U.S. central bank arranged a series of extraordinary dollar swaps with 10 other central banks, who accepted the currency and credit risks of lending these newly created dollars to their domestic banks. Unprecedented cooperation among central banks allowed for an aggressive and successful policy response to the threat of a currency-driven meltdown.

Table 10.4	Simple Balance Sheet of a Hypothetical Japanese Bank	
Assets **Long Term**		**Liabilities** **Short Term**
¥10 billion		¥20 billion
US$200 million		US$100 million

*We defined funding liquidity in Chapter 2 as the ease with which a financial institution can borrow to buy securities or make loans.

Looking at the statistics on the supply of dollars, we see that the U.S. current account deficit—exports minus imports—increased from $200 billion at the end of 1998 to $450 billion by the close of 2000. That is, Americans increased their net purchases of foreign goods during this period, *raising* the supply of dollars shifting the supply curve to the right. But at the same time, investment funds were pouring into the United States from abroad. Fall 1998 was a time of financial stress, and during times of crisis, investors tend to shift into the safest place, which they view as the United States. Moreover, 1999 was the peak of the U.S. stock-market bubble. Foreign capital streamed toward the dot-com companies, especially those on the Nasdaq (see the discussion at the end of Chapter 8). As a result, foreigners' demand for dollars skyrocketed, outstripping the increased supply of dollars and driving up the "price"—the exchange rate. That is, the demand for dollars shifted to the right by more than the supply for dollars did. In the long run, however, such a move was unsustainable, so the dollar eventually depreciated, returning to a level more consistent with the theory of purchasing power parity.

Government Policy and Foreign Exchange Intervention

The more a country relies on exports and imports, the more important its exchange rate. Currency appreciation drives up the price foreigners pay for a country's exports as it reduces the price residents of the country pay for imports. This shift in foreign versus domestic prices hurts domestic businesses. Companies with big export businesses suffer the most, along with businesses whose products compete with imported goods. They often respond by pressuring elected officials to reduce the value of the currency. After all, government policymakers may influence the prices of lots of goods and services. Milk, rent, and electric power are just a few possibilities. Why not exchange rates too?

Government officials can intervene in foreign exchange markets in several ways. Some countries adopt a fixed exchange rate and act to maintain it at a level of their choosing. We will discuss the implications of this approach in Chapter 19. For now, all we need to know is that exchange rates can be controlled if policymakers have the resources available and are willing to take the necessary actions.

Large industrialized countries and common currency zones like the United States, Europe, and Japan generally allow currency markets to determine their exchange rate. Even so, there are occasions when officials in these countries try to influence the currency values. Sometimes they make public statements in the hope of influencing currency traders. But talk is cheap, and such statements rarely have an impact on their own. At other times, policymakers will buy or sell currency in an attempt to affect demand or supply. This approach is called *foreign exchange intervention*.

Some countries hardly ever attempt to influence their exchange rates in this way, while others intervene in the markets frequently. Between 1997 and mid-2013, the United States intervened only twice; both times it was pressured to do so by other allies. Among the major industrialized countries, the Japanese are the most frequent participants in foreign exchange markets. The spring of 2002 provides a good example of their approach.

In the latter half of the 1990s, the Japanese economy was stagnant; real GDP grew at a rate of about 1 percent. In 2001, the economic situation worsened and output fell 2 percent. After trying almost every other approach imaginable to resuscitate the economy, Japanese officials decided to see if depreciating the yen would help. The idea was to help Japanese exporters increase their foreign sales by reducing the prices foreigners paid for Japanese products. In late May 2002, Japan's Ministry of Finance sold yen in exchange for dollars, hoping to drive down the price by increasing the supply of yen. While the yen did depreciate very modestly as a result of intervention, by the end of the month its price was higher than it had been before the intervention.

Why did the Japanese government's policy fail? Shouldn't an increase in the supply of yen, regardless of where it comes from, lead to a depreciation? The primary reason the intervention didn't work was that, while the Japanese Ministry of Finance was selling yen, the Bank of Japan was buying them. We'll study the details when we get to Chapter 19, but here is a quick version of the story. The Bank of Japan is in charge of monetary policy in Japan, which means controlling a particular short-term interest rate. Operationally, the result was that, within a few days, the Bank of Japan reversed the Ministry's foreign exchange intervention. If it hadn't, the interest rate it wished to control would have changed. Thus, foreign exchange interventions will be ineffective unless they are accompanied by a change in the policy interest rate. That is the reason countries like the United States rarely intervene in the foreign exchange markets.

IN THE NEWS
Foreign Exchange: Neighbors Show Little Appetite for Brazil's "War"

FINANCIAL TIMES

By Jonathan Wheatley

November 13, 2012

Has Brazil won the currency war? Ministers certainly seem happy with the real's current level of about R$2 to the US dollar, back from about R$1.50 last year. They say they will defend the currency at its present level and admit that, after years of arguing for a freely floating exchange rate, they are now operating a "dirty float" of R$2.00 to R$2.10 to the dollar.

That is a significant change of stance for Brazil. But it is not alone in re-examining its exchange rate policy. Elsewhere in the region—notably in Colombia, Chile and Peru—governments have watched in alarm as their currencies have been carried up on a tide of global liquidity unleashed by . . . loose monetary policy across the developed world.

Their responses, however, have varied, as have the results. By the time Brazil's currency reached its peak of R$1.50 to the dollar, the real had strengthened by about 40 per cent over the preceding two years, eating away at the competitiveness of Brazilian exports. Guido Mantega, finance minister, coined the term "currency war" in September 2010 after [U.S. monetary policy] led to what he called aggressive, protectionist devaluations of the US dollar and other currencies.

How to respond? Brazil did not want to shut out all foreign inflows. The government's priority is to generate jobs and growth. Foreign direct investment—running at about $60bn a year—is a crucial element in that, so could not be targeted. For the same reason, ministers did not want to deter foreigners from investing in Brazilian equities. But speculative "hot money", attracted to Brazilian bonds by the country's very high interest rates, was an obvious target.

Within weeks of declaring the currency war open, Mr Mantega had announced a 6 per cent tax on foreign investment in Brazilian domestic fixed income. . . . The fixed income tax was followed in March last year by higher taxes on overseas borrowing by Brazilian companies and from August last year by a steady reduction in Brazil's policy interest rate, from 12.5 per cent to 7.25 per cent today . . . .

Brazil only made explicit its attempts to manage its exchange rate as recently as last month. "For us, the ideal is a floating currency, without manipulation," Mr Mantega told a local newspaper. "But if the whole world is going to manipulate their exchange rates, we will too."

Other countries have balked at that kind of heterodoxy. In Chile, currency appreciation has contributed to steadily weakening exports to the extent that the country's trade balance has turned negative over the past few months. Yet authorities have so far resisted pressure for greater intervention in foreign exchange markets. . . .

Colombia has ruled out Brazilian-style currency warfare . . . [but] the government has stepped up its dollar purchases in foreign exchange markets, helping the peso to relax a little since midyear.

Peru, too, has turned to increased foreign exchange intervention as well as higher reserve requirements for local banks in an effort to slow currency appreciation and lessen the potentially destabilizing effects of rising foreign inflows.

Yet none of these countries has joined Brazil in its crusade. Indeed, Brazil's success in stemming the rise of the real may have less to do with the currency war than with its economy's sluggish performance. . . .

Other countries with a more orthodox approach to economic policy have fared much better. Chile is growing at an annual rate of about 5.5 per cent. Colombia is growing at about 5 per cent and Peru at about 7 per cent. . . .

While [Brazil] continues to use targeted tax breaks to pick winners among industrial sectors, it has also turned recently to measures designed to promote competitiveness across the economy, such as lower payroll taxes to encourage hiring.

Like its faster-growing neighbours, it may be realising such long-term, structural measures are more effective than fighting a currency war.

SOURCE: Jonathan Wheatley, "Foreign Exchange: Neighbors show little appetite for Brazil's 'war,'" *Financial Times, www.ft.com,* November 13, 2012 © The Financial Times Ltd. 2012. All rights reserved.

LESSONS OF THE ARTICLE

Large flows of capital into a small economy can trigger a big currency appreciation, which threatens its exports and makes it vulnerable to a sudden reversal of the flows. After 2008, many emerging market economies complained about capital inflows from advanced economies with low interest rates. As the article notes, Brazil tried to manage its exchange rate through market interventions such as taxing capital inflows, but few countries see that as an effective long-term strategy.

Terms

appreciation (of a currency), 243	nominal exchange rate, 242
Big Mac index, 252	overvalued currency, 251
British pound, 241	purchasing power parity (PPP), 249
demand for dollars, 254	real exchange rate, 244
depreciation (of a currency), 242	supply of dollars, 253
euro, 242	undervalued currency, 251
law of one price, 246	yen, 243

Using FRED: Codes for Data in This Chapter

Data Series	FRED Data Code
U.S. dollar/euro exchange rate	EXUSEU
Japanese yen/U.S. dollar exchange rate	EXJPUS
U.S. dollar/U.K. pound exchange rate	EXUSUK
Brazilian real/U.S. dollar exchange rate	EXBZUS
Chinese yuan/U.S. dollar exchange rate	EXCHUS
Mexican peso/U.S. dollar exchange rate	EXMXUS
South Korean won/U.S. dollar exchange rate	EXKOUS
Swiss franc/U.S. dollar exchange rate	EXSZUS
Trade-weighted U.S. dollar index: broad	TWEXBMTH
Trade-weighted U.S. dollar index: major currencies	TWEXMMTH
Real trade-weighted U.S. dollar index: broad	TWEXBPA
Real trade-weighted U.S. dollar index: major currencies	TWEXMPA

Chapter Lessons

1. Different areas and countries of the world use different currencies in their transactions.
    a. The nominal exchange rate is the rate at which the currency of one country can be exchanged for the currency of another.
    b. A decline in the value of one currency relative to another is called depreciation.
    c. An increase in the value of one currency relative to another is called appreciation.
    d. When the dollar appreciates relative to the euro, the euro depreciates relative to the dollar.
    e. The real exchange rate is the rate at which the goods and services of one country can be exchanged for the goods and services of another.
    f. About $4 trillion worth of currency is traded every day in markets run by brokers and foreign exchange dealers.

2. In the long run, the value of a country's currency is tied to the price of goods and services in that country.
   a. The law of one price states that two identical goods should sell for the same price, regardless of location.
   b. The law of one price fails because of transportation costs, differences in taxation and technical specifications, and the fact that some goods cannot be moved.
   c. The theory of purchasing power parity applies the law of one price to international transactions; it states that the real exchange rate always equals one.
   d. Purchasing power parity implies that countries with higher inflation than other countries will experience exchange rate depreciation.
   e. Over decades, exchange rate changes are approximately equal to differences in inflation, implying that purchasing power parity holds.

3. In the short run, the value of a country's currency depends on supply of and demand for the currency in foreign exchange markets.
   a. When people in the United States wish to purchase foreign goods and services or invest in foreign assets, they must supply dollars to the foreign exchange market.
   b. The more foreign currency that can be exchanged for one dollar, the greater will be the supply of dollars. That is, the supply curve for dollars slopes upward.
   c. Foreigners who wish to purchase American-made goods and services or invest in U.S. assets will demand dollars in the foreign exchange market.
   d. The fewer units of foreign currency needed to buy one dollar, the higher the demand for dollars. That is, the demand curve for dollars slopes downward.
   e. Anything that increases the desire of Americans to buy foreign-made goods and services or invest in foreign assets will increase the supply of dollars (shift the supply curve for dollars to the right), causing the dollar to depreciate.
   f. Anything that increases the desire of foreigners to buy American-made goods and services or invest in U.S. assets will increase the demand for dollars (shift the demand curve for dollars to the right), causing the dollar to appreciate.

4. Some governments buy and sell their own currency in an effort to affect the exchange rate. Such foreign exchange interventions are usually ineffective.

Conceptual and Analytical Problems

1. If the U.S. dollar–British pound exchange rate is $1.50 per pound, and the U.S. dollar–euro rate is $0.90 per euro: *(LO1)*
   a. What is the pound per euro rate?
   b. How could you profit if the pound per euro rate were above the rate you calculated in part *a*? What if it were lower?

2. If a computer game costs $30 in the United States and £26 in the United Kingdom, what is the real "computer game" exchange rate? Look up the current dollar–pound exchange rate in a newspaper or an online source, and compare the two prices. What do you conclude? *(LO1)*

3. Suppose the euro–dollar exchange rate moves from $0.90 per euro to $0.92 per euro. At the same time, the prices of European-made goods and services rise 1 percent, while prices of American-made goods and services rise 3 percent. What has happened to the real exchange rate between the dollar and the euro?

Assuming the same change in the nominal exchange rate, what if inflation were 3 percent in Europe and 1 percent in the United States? *(LO2)*

4.   The same television set costs $500 in the United States, €450 in France, £300 in the United Kingdom, and ¥100,000 in Japan. If the law of one price holds, what are the euro–dollar, pound–dollar, and yen–dollar exchange rates? Why might the law of one price fail? *(LO1)*

5.* What does the theory of purchasing power parity predict in the long run regarding the inflation rate of a country that fixes its exchange rate to the U.S. dollar? *(LO2)*

6.* Can purchasing power parity help predict short-term movements in exchange rates? *(LO2)*

7.   You need to purchase Japanese yen and have called two brokers to get quotes. The first broker offered you a rate of 125 yen per dollar. The second broker, ignoring market convention, quoted a price of 0.0084 dollars per yen. To which broker should you give your business? Why? *(LO1)*

8.   During the 1990s, the U.S. Secretary of the Treasury often stated, "a strong dollar is in the interest of the United States." *(LO4)*
  a. Is this statement true? Explain your answer.
  b. What can the Secretary of the Treasury actually do about the value of the dollar relative to other currencies?

9.   The following table gives selective data on nominal exchange rates, price levels, and real exchange rates for Country A and three other countries. Country A uses the dollar (A$) as its currency. Fill in the blanks in the table. *(LO1)*

	Nominal Exchange Rate (A$ per unit of other currency)	Price Level in Country A	Price Level in Other Country	Real Exchange Rate
Country B	A$1.25 per unit of currency B	114.5	88.3	
Country C		114.5	95.6	1.23
Country D	A$0.55 per unit of currency D	114.5		0.80

10.   If the price (measured in a common currency) of a particular basket of goods is 10 percent higher in the United Kingdom than it is in the United States, which country's currency is undervalued, according to the theory of purchasing power parity? *(LO2)*

11.* You hear an interview with a well-known economist who states that she expects the U.S. dollar to strengthen against the British pound over the next five to ten years. This economist is known for her support of the theory of purchasing power parity. Using an equation to summarize the relationship predicted by purchasing power parity between exchange-rate movements and the inflation rates in the two countries, explain whether you expect inflation in the United States to be higher or lower on average compared with that in the U.K. over the period in question. *(LO2)*

*Indicates more difficult problems

12. Using the model of demand and supply for U.S. dollars, what would you expect to happen to the U.S. dollar exchange rate if, in light of a worsening geopolitical situation, Americans viewed foreign bonds as more risky than before? (You should quote the exchange rate as number of units of foreign currency per U.S. dollar.) *(LO3)*

13. Suppose that the Chinese central bank has been intervening in the foreign exchange market, buying U.S. dollars in an effort to keep its own currency, the yuan, weak. Use the model of demand and supply for dollars to show what the immediate effect would be on the yuan–dollar exchange rate of a decision by China to allow its currency to float freely. *(LO3)*

14. Consider again the situation described in Problem 13, where China decided to allow the yuan to float. What would you expect to happen to
    a. U.S. exports to China?
    b. U.S. imports from China?
    c. The U.S. trade deficit with China?
    Explain your answers. *(LO4)*

15. Use the model of demand for and supply of foreign currency to analyze the following scenarios. *(LO3)*
    a. Impressed with the magnificent scenery from Vancouver during the coverage of the Winter Olympics, French and German tourists flock to the west coast of Canada. Explain the impact on the euro–Canadian dollar exchange rate in the short run.
    b. Driven by waves of national pride, consumers across the world (including in the United States) decide to buy home-produced products where possible. Explain how the demand for and supply of U.S. dollars would be affected. What can you say about the impact on the equilibrium dollar exchange rate?

16. Suppose an Italian bank has short-term borrowings of 400 million euros and 100 million U.S. dollars and made long-term loans of 300 million euros and 250 million U.S. dollars. The euro–dollar exchange rate is initially $1.50 per euro.
    a. Ignoring other assets and liabilities, place each item on the appropriate side of the bank's balance sheet.
    b. List the risks that this bank faces.
    c. If the euro–dollar exchange rate moved to $1.60 per euro, would the bank gain or lose? Provide calculations to support your answer. *(LO3)*

17.* Suppose government officials in a small open economy decided they wanted their currency to weaken in order to boost exports. What kind of foreign exchange market intervention would they have to make to cause their currency to depreciate? What would happen to domestic interest rates in that country if its central bank doesn't take any action to offset the impact on interest rates of the foreign exchange intervention? *(LO4)*

18. Suppose the interest rate on a one-year U.S. bond is 10 percent and the interest rate on an equivalent Canadian bond is 8 percent. If the interest-rate parity condition holds (see Appendix to Chapter 10), is the U.S. dollar expected to appreciate or depreciate relative to the Canadian dollar over the next year? Explain your choice. *(LO3)*

19. Most countries do not attempt to manage their exchange rates with intervention in the foreign currency markets, but some do. Under which circumstances is such an intervention likely to be ineffective? *(LO4)*

20. Suppose you see the following newspaper headline: "Japan's Finance Ministry Sells Yen for U.S. Dollars." What is the objective of this policy? If the policy goal is achieved, what will happen to the prices of Japanese imports to the United States? What will happen to the prices of U.S. goods purchased by residents of Japan? *(LO4)*

Data Exploration

For detailed instructions on using Federal Reserve Economic Data (FRED) online to answer each of the following problems, visit www.mhhe.com/moneyandbanking4e and click on Student Edition, then Data Exploration Hints.

1. Exchange rates can exhibit sudden changes as well as long-run patterns. *(LO1)*
   a. Plot the U.S. dollar–Australian dollar exchange rate (FRED code: EXUSAL) without recession bars and identify long-run swings and short-term spikes. Which currency is appreciating when the plotted exchange rate falls?
   b. Repeat the exercise for the Japanese yen–U.S. dollar exchange rate (FRED code: EXJPUS).

2. Plot since 1999 without recession bars the real exchange rate between U.S. goods and euro-area goods according to equation (2) in the text. Use the consumer price index (divided by 1.95 to set a common base year of 2005 = 100 for the U.S. and euro-area indexes) for the price of U.S. goods (FRED code: CPIAUCSL), use the harmonized index of consumer prices for the price of euro-area goods (FRED code: CP0000EZ17M086NEST), and use the U.S. dollar–euro exchange rate (FRED code: EXUSEU). Why might this measure of the real exchange rate be persistently below unity since 2003? *(LO1)*

3. Write in algebraic form a calculation of U.K. pounds per euro that uses U.S. dollars per U.K pound (FRED code: EXUSUK) and U.S. dollars per euro (FRED code: EXUSEU). Then plot since 1999 the exchange rate of U.K. pounds per euro using these two U.S. dollar exchange rates. *(LO1)*

4. Examine an episode of large-scale intervention by the Bank of Japan (BoJ) in the yen–dollar foreign exchange market. Plot between January 2003 and January 2005 a measure of BoJ intervention (FRED code: JPINTDUSDJPY). Do positive values of this intervention indicator reflect purchases or sales of yen by the BoJ? What was the BoJ's policy objective? To investigate whether the intervention of 2003–2004 was effective, add the Japanese yen–U.S. dollar exchange rate (FRED code: EXJPUS) to the chart, but scaled on the right axis. *(LO5)*

Appendix to Chapter 10

Interest-Rate Parity and Short-Run Exchange Rate Determination

There is another way to think about the determinants of exchange rates in the short run. Rather than focus on the supply of and demand for currency, we can look at exchange rates from an investor's point of view. If the bonds issued in different countries are perfect substitutes for one another, then arbitrage will equalize the returns on domestic and foreign bonds. And because investing abroad means exchanging currencies, the result is a relationship among domestic interest rates, foreign interest rates, and the exchange rate. From this intuition, we can develop an understanding of the short-run movements in exchange rates.

Let's take the example of an American investor with a one-year investment horizon and $1,000 to invest in either a one-year U.S. Treasury bond or a one-year German government bond. Because the investor is from the United States, we will assume that at the end of the year when the bonds mature, she wants to receive dollars. The question is: Which investment is more attractive? To find the answer, we need to compute the dollar return on buying a one-year $1,000 U.S. Treasury bond and compare it to the dollar return on converting $1,000 to euros, buying a German government bond, and converting the proceeds back to dollars after one year. The value of the first investment is easy to find. If the one-year U.S. Treasury interest rate is i, then one year later an initial investment of $1,000 is worth $1,000 \times (1 + i)$. But the currency conversion complicates the calculation of the return to the foreign investment.

Computing the return to investing $1,000 in a one-year German bond requires a series of steps. First, the investor needs to take the $1,000 and convert it to euros. If E is the dollar–euro exchange rate measured as the number of euros per dollar, then $1,000 purchases $E \times 1,000$ euros. Next, the investor purchases the German bond. If the one-year German bond rate is i^f, a $1,000 investment yields $E \times 1,000 \times (1 + i^f)$ euros in one year. Finally, at the end of the year, the investor must exchange the euros for dollars. If we call E^e the expected future exchange rate—the number of euros per dollar expected in a year's time—then the dollar return to a $1,000 investment in foreign bonds is

$$\text{Value of \$1,000 invested in foreign bonds after one year} = \frac{\$1,000E(1 + i^f)}{E^e} \quad \text{(A1)}$$

Looking at this equation, we can see that for the U.S. investor, the return to holding the German bond has two parts: (1) the interest income and (2) the expected change in the exchange rate. By doing a little algebra and using an approximation, we can rewrite equation (A1) to divide the return into these two parts. The result is

$$\text{Value of \$1,000 invested in foreign bonds after one year} = \$1,000E(1 + i^f)\left(1 - \frac{\Delta E^e}{E}\right) \quad \text{(A2)}$$

where ΔE^e is the expected change in the exchange rate.

www.mhhe.com/moneyandbanking4e

This expression tells us that the return on the foreign bond is the foreign interest rate minus the expected percentage change in the dollar–euro exchange rate.

To see why the return depends on the change in the exchange rate, take an example in which the dollar–euro rate is €1/$1 at the start of the year and €1.05/$1 at the end of the year. That is, at the start of the year, you exchange one dollar for one euro, but at the end of the year the dollar is worth 1.05 euros—an appreciation of 5 percent in the value of the dollar. If the German interest rate is 6 percent, then a $1,000 investment will yield $1,000 × (1.06/1.05) = $1,010. Because the dollar has appreciated by 5 percent, the return on a 6 percent German bond is only 6 percent − 5 percent = 1 percent.

Returning to our comparison of a domestic and a foreign bond, we know that if the investor is indifferent between the two, their returns must be the same. That must be the case for the two bonds to be perfect substitutes. The implication is that

Value of $1,000 invested in U.S. Treasury bonds for one year

$$= \text{Value of \$1,000 invested in foreign bonds after one year} \qquad (A3)$$

This means that

$$\$1,000(1 + i) = \$1,000(1 + i^f)\left(1 - \frac{\Delta E^e}{E}\right) \qquad (A4)$$

or using an approximation

$$i = i^f - \frac{\Delta E^e}{E}$$

This equation, called the *interest parity condition,* tells us that the U.S. interest rate equals the German interest rate minus the dollar's expected appreciation. (These calculations ignore the risk of exchange rates moving in an unexpected way.)

If the interest parity condition did not hold, people would have an incentive to shift their investments until it did. For instance, if the U.S. interest rate exceeded the German interest rate minus the expected depreciation in the dollar, then foreign and domestic investors would sell German bonds and buy U.S. Treasury bonds. Their action would drive down the price of German bonds and drive up the price of U.S. bonds, raising the foreign interest rate and lowering the domestic rate until the relationship held.

Because we know the current U.S. and German interest rates, the interest parity condition tells us what the current dollar–euro exchange rate should be for a given expected future dollar–euro exchange rate. The interest rate parity condition tells us that the current value of the dollar will be higher

1. the higher U.S. interest rates,
2. the lower German interest rates, and
3. the higher the expected future value of the dollar.

These are the same conclusions we arrived at using supply and demand theory.

www.mhhe.com/moneyandbanking4e

Part *III*

Financial Institutions

Chapter 11

The Economics of Financial Intermediation

Learning Objectives

Understand . . .

LO1   How intermediaries promote efficiency

LO2   The central role of information costs

LO3   Incentive problems in finance

The financial crisis of 2007–2009 alerted everyone that general economic well-being is closely tied to the health of the financial institutions that make up the financial system. The financial system is a lot like plumbing. When it's working well, we pay little attention. But its failure almost inevitably leads to a costly economic mess. The breadth, depth, and persistence of financial disruptions in the crisis brought us closer to a second Great Depression than at any time since the first one, in the 1930s.

As described in Chapter 1, our financial system is made up of six components: money, financial instruments, financial markets, financial institutions, government regulatory agencies, and the central bank. In Parts I and II we covered the first three of these components. In Part III we focus on the fourth, financial institutions, and the fifth, government regulatory agencies. In this chapter, we examine financial institutions' purpose, which is known as *financial intermediation*. As we learned in Chapter 3, financial institutions intermediate between savers and borrowers, and so their assets and liabilities are primarily financial instruments. Various sorts of banks, brokerage firms, investment companies, insurance companies, and pension funds all fall into this category. These are the institutions that pool funds from people and firms who save and lend them to people and firms who need to borrow, transforming assets and providing access to financial markets. They funnel savers' surplus resources into home mortgages, business loans, and investments.

As we discussed briefly at the end of Chapter 3, financial intermediaries are involved in both direct finance—in which borrowers sell securities directly to lenders in the financial markets—and indirect finance, in which a third party issues claims to those who provide funds and acquires claims from those who use them. Intermediaries investigate the financial condition of the individuals and firms who want financing to figure out which have the best investment opportunities. As providers of indirect finance, banks want to make loans only to the highest-quality borrowers. When they do their job correctly, financial intermediaries increase investment and economic growth at the same time that they reduce investment risk and economic volatility.

Ensuring that the best investment opportunities and highest-quality borrowers are funded is extremely important. Any country that wants to grow must ensure that its financial system works. When a country's financial system crumbles, its economy fails with it. That is what happened in the United States in the Great Depression of the 1930s, when a series of bank closings was followed by an increase in the unemployment rate to more than 25 percent and a fall of nearly one-third in the level of economic activity (measured by GDP). The Asian crisis of 1997, in which the banking systems of Thailand and Indonesia collapsed, is a more recent example. The deep, prolonged economic plunge of 2008–2009 highlights how a financial crisis, once started, can spread devastation across the global economy, triggering a spiral of economic and financial decline that is difficult to halt. And the subsequent turmoil in the euro area depressed some economies in the region enough to rival the traumatic 1930s experience. Without a stable, smoothly functioning financial system, no country can prosper.

The strong relationship between financial development and economic development is clearly apparent from the data. Figure 11.1 plots a commonly used measure of financial activity—the ratio of credit extended to the private sector (both through financial intermediaries and markets) to gross domestic product (GDP)—against real GDP per capita. The resulting strong correlation, roughly 0.7, is no surprise. There aren't any rich countries that have very low levels of financial development.

In theory, the market system may seem neat and simple, but the reality is that economic growth is a messy, chaotic thing. The flow of information among parties in a market system is particularly rife with problems—problems that can derail real growth

Figure 11.1   Financial and Economic Development

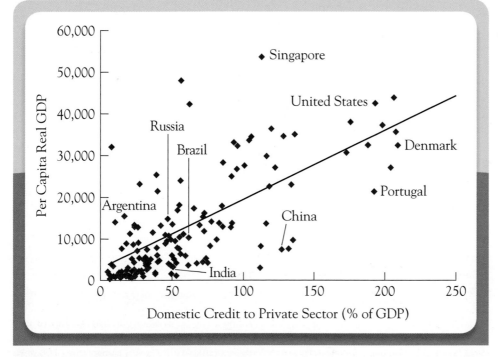

SOURCE: *Financial development is measured as total financial system credit extended to the private sector. World Development Indicators, the World Bank. All data are for 2011. www.worldbank.org.*

unless they are addressed properly. In this chapter, we will discuss some of these information problems—including several that contributed to the financial crisis of 2007–2009—and learn how financial intermediaries attempt to solve them.

The Role of Financial Intermediaries

Markets are remarkably effective at coordinating the behavior of millions of firms and households in an economy. And financial markets are among the most important markets of all; they price economic resources and allocate them to their most productive uses. In many countries over the past 20 years, the value of stock and bond markets has come to rival or even surpass the value of outstanding loans through financial intermediaries. But as we will see, intermediaries, including banks and securities firms, continue to play a key role in both these types of finance.

Table 11.1 illustrates the importance of different channels of finance. As you look at the table, note two things. First, to make comparisons across countries of vastly

Table 11.1 The Relative Importance of Financing Channels

(Averages for 1990–2010)

| Country | Securities Markets | | Loans | |
	Stock Market Capitalization as Percent of GDP (A)	Outstanding Domestic Debt Securities as Percent of GDP (B)	Credit Extended by Banks and Other Financial Institutions as Percent of GDP (C)	Ratio of Loans to Securities C/(A+B) (D)
Industrialized Countries				
France	62.4	44.6	91.9	0.86
Germany	40.7	45.4	107.4	1.25
Italy	32.2	34.7	73.9	1.10
Japan	77.0	43.1	194.3	1.62
United Kingdom	125.6	15.2	136.0	0.97
United States	111.6	92.6	160.0	0.78
Emerging Market Countries				
Argentina	26.6	4.3	16.2	0.52
Brazil	32.7	11.6	35.6	0.80
China	40.6	8.1	98.0	2.01
India	42.6	1.3	29.6	0.67
Russia	35.1	NA	20.1	0.57

The items in columns A, B, and C are expressed as a percentage of GDP. But because the items are not components of GDP, there is no reason that the percentages should add to 100. Data are missing in some years for some countries. NA = not available.

(Stock Market Cap: GFDD.DM.01); (Domestic Private Debt Securities: GFDD.DM.03); (Credit by Intermediaries: GFDD.DI.12)

SOURCE: *Global Financial Development Database, World Bank. http://data.worldbank.org/data-catalog/global-financial-development. Updates are also available through FRED.*

different size, we measure everything relative to GDP. Second, there is no reason that the value of a country's stock market, bonds outstanding, or bank loans cannot be bigger than its GDP. In fact, we would expect it to be much larger, because the value of a company to its owners is often several times the level of one year's sales. This means that when you add up all the types of financing, direct and indirect, as a percentage of GDP, the numbers will generally sum to more than 100 in an advanced economy.

To see the lessons from the table, take the example of France, in the first row. The value of the French stock market (the value of the shares of all companies listed on the exchanges) is equivalent to 62.4 percent of that country's GDP (column A); the value of French debt securities is 44.6 percent of GDP (column B). Adding columns A and B tells us that, in France, securities finance equals 107 percent of GDP. That exceeds the amount of credit extended by French banks and other intermediaries—91.9 percent of GDP (column C). The final column, D, reports the ratio of loans to securities. For France, the result is 0.86, which means that financing via securities markets was somewhat larger than loans. For the industrialized countries in the table, the range of that ratio is between 0.78 and 1.62, so the French case is not unusual. In many emerging markets, the ratio is somewhat lower because in recent decades their stock markets have expanded notably. However, domestic private debt securities play only a small role in most emerging market economies, which underscores the costs and challenges of developing this alternative to loan and stock finance.

These data highlight the importance of intermediaries. Banks are still critical providers of financing around the world, although bank lending may not be the dominant source of financing that it once was. And intermediation is not limited to bank lending. Intermediaries determine which firms can access the stock and bond markets. Just as banks decide the size of a loan and the interest rate to be charged, securities firms set the volume and price of new stock and bond issues when they purchase them for sale to investors. And other intermediaries, like mutual funds, help individual investors sort among the thousands of stocks and bonds that are issued to develop a diversified portfolio with the desired risk characteristics.

Why are financial intermediaries so important? The answer has to do with information. To understand the importance of information in the role financial intermediaries play in the economy, consider the online company eBay. This virtual auction house may seem an unlikely place to start, but while eBay deals primarily with physical objects, it faces some of the same information problems as financial firms. As an online intermediary, eBay provides a mechanism through which almost anyone can auction off almost anything. At any time, upwards of 100 million items are for sale at www.ebay.com—everything from $5 dinner plates to a $140 million "giga-yacht." And people buy them! For just the single year 2012, eBay reported total transactions valued at more than $75 billion, entered into by more than 100 million active users.

While millions of items are for sale on eBay, if you look carefully you'll notice an absence of financial products. You can purchase collectible coins and paper currency on eBay, but you can't borrow. There are no listings for Samantha's student loan, Chad's car loan, Chloe's credit card balance, or Mort's mortgage—at least, not yet. And though you can buy defaulted bond certificates, like the Reading Railroad bond shown in Chapter 4 (which was purchased on eBay), you can't buy or sell bonds on which the issuer is still making payments. People are selling cars and even real estate on eBay, but no one is auctioning off checking account services. (There are hints that this may be changing. See the In the News story near the end of this chapter.)

Think for a moment about why eBay doesn't auction off mortgages. First, Mort might need a $100,000 mortgage, and not many people can finance a mortgage of that size. The people who run eBay could try to establish a system in which 100 people sign up to lend Mort $1,000, but it would be extremely complex and cumbersome. Imagine collecting the payments, figuring out how to repay the lenders, and writing all the legal contracts that go with the transaction. Just as important, before offering to finance Mort's mortgage, lenders would want to know something about Mort and the house he's proposing to buy. Is Mort accurately representing his ability to repay the loan? Does he really intend to buy a house with the loan? The questions are nearly endless, and answering them is both difficult and time consuming.

Financial intermediaries exist so that individual lenders don't have to worry about getting answers to all of these questions. Most people take for granted the ability of the financial system to shift resources from savers to investors, but when you look closely at the details, you're struck by how complicated the task is. It's amazing the enterprise works at all. Lending and borrowing involve both *transactions costs,* like the cost of writing a loan contract, and *information costs,* like the cost of figuring out whether a borrower is trustworthy. Financial institutions exist to reduce these costs.

In their role as financial intermediaries, financial institutions perform five functions (see Table 11.2): (1) pooling the resources of small savers; (2) providing safekeeping and accounting services, as well as access to the payments system; (3) supplying liquidity by converting savers' balances directly into a means of payment whenever needed; (4) providing ways to diversify risk; and (5) collecting and processing information in ways that reduce information costs. As we go through these, you'll see that the first four have to do with lowering transactions costs. That is, by specializing and providing these services to large numbers of customers, a financial firm can reduce the cost of providing them to individual customers. As in other fields, experts can do a better job than others, and more cheaply at that. The fifth function on the list, collecting and processing information, is a category all by itself, so we'll consider it in more detail.

While we will not discuss international banks in any depth, it is worth mentioning that they provide an additional set of services that complements those offered by your neighborhood bank. International banks handle transactions that cross national borders. That may mean taking deposits from savers in one country and providing them to investors in another country. It may also mean converting currencies in order to facilitate transactions for customers who do business or travel abroad.

Table 11.2 A Summary of the Role of Financial Intermediaries

1. *Pooling savings*	Accepting resources from a large number of small savers/lenders in order to provide large loans to borrowers.
2. *Safekeeping and accounting*	Keeping depositors' savings safe, giving them access to the payments system, and providing them with accounting statements that help them to track their income and expenditures.
3. *Providing liquidity*	Allowing depositors to transform their financial assets into money quickly, easily, and at low cost.
4. *Diversifying risk*	Providing investors with the ability to diversify even small investments.
5. *Collecting and processing information services*	Generating large amounts of standardized financial information.

Pooling Savings

The most straightforward economic function of a financial intermediary is to pool the resources of many small savers. By accepting many small deposits, banks empower themselves to make large loans. So, for example, Mort might get his $100,000 mortgage from a bank or finance company with access to a large group of savers, 100 of whom have $1,000 to invest (see Figure 11.2). Similarly, a government or large company that wishes to borrow billions of dollars by issuing bonds will rely on a financial intermediary to find buyers for the bonds.

To succeed in this endeavor—pooling people's savings in order to make large loans—the intermediary must attract substantial numbers of savers. This means convincing potential depositors of the institution's soundness. Banks are adept at making sure customers feel that their funds will be safe. In the past, they did so by installing large safes in imposing bank buildings. Today, they rely on their reputations, as well as on government guarantees like deposit insurance. We'll return to this topic in Chapter 14.

Figure 11.2   Financial Intermediaries Pool Savings

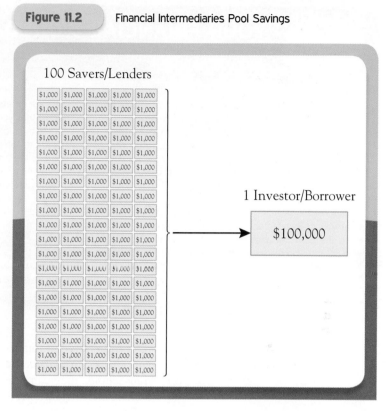

Financial intermediaries pool the funds of many small savers and lend them to one large borrower.

Safekeeping, Payments System Access, and Accounting

Goldsmiths were the original bankers. To keep their gold and jewelry safe, they had to construct vaults. Soon people began asking the goldsmiths to store gold for them in return for a receipt to prove it was there. It didn't take long for someone to realize that trading the goldsmith's receipts was easier than trading the gold itself. The next step came when the goldsmith noticed that there was quite a bit of gold left in the vault at the end of the day, so that some of it could safely be lent to others. The goldsmiths took the resources of those with gold to spare—the savers of the day—and channeled them to individuals who were short—the borrowers. Today, banks are the places where we put things for safekeeping—not just gold and jewelry, but our financial wealth as well. We deposit our paychecks and entrust our savings to a bank or other financial institution because we believe it will keep our resources safe until we need them.

When we think of banks, safekeeping is only one of several services that immediately come to mind. The others are Internet and mobile access, automated teller machines, credit and debit cards, checkbooks, and monthly bank statements. In providing depositors with these physical and electronic services, a bank gives them access to the payments system—the network that transfers funds from the account of one person or business to the account of another. The bank provides depositors a way to get cash into

YOUR FINANCIAL WORLD
Your First Credit Card

Credit card interest rates are outrageous, running to more than 30 percent in some cases (really)! In Chapter 4, Your Financial World: Pay Off Your Credit Card discussed how expensive borrowing can be and demonstrated why you should pay off your credit card debt as quickly as possible. The odds are, when you get your first credit card, the interest rate will be extremely high. Why?

Unless your parent signed your credit card papers (or you worked a steady job before starting college), as a student you have no credit history, and the company that issued the card will assume the worst. So you're lumped in with people who have very poor credit, who would rather get lower-interest loans elsewhere but can't. This is adverse selection at its worst (see page 278 for a definition of adverse selection). When you get your first credit card, the assumption is that you are in a group of people who will have a high default rate. No wonder the issuers charge high interest rates. It is compensation for the risk they are taking. And just to prove the point, this is not a very profitable business.*

You need a credit card to build up a credit history, to establish yourself as a person who repays loans promptly. After a while, you'll be able to get a new card at a lower interest rate. But in the meantime, remember that your interest rate is extremely high, so borrowing is very expensive.

*There are a number of studies of the credit card industry. Paul S. Calem and Loretta J. Mester's study "Consumer Behavior and the Stickiness of Credit-Card Interest Rates," *American Economic Review* 85, no. 5 (December 1995), pp. 1327–1336, examines the nature of the credit card industry.

The door to the largest gold vault in the world at the Federal Reserve Bank of New York. The only entry is through a 10-foot passageway cut into a 9-foot high, 90-ton steel cylinder that rotates 90 degrees to open and close the vault. Many governments keep their gold here.

MARKETS

their wallets and to finalize payments using credit cards, debit cards, and checks. And because banks specialize in handling payments transactions, they can offer all these services relatively cheaply. Financial intermediaries reduce the costs of financial transactions.

This is not a trivial matter. It would be a disaster if we didn't have a convenient way to pay for things. By giving us one, financial intermediaries facilitate the exchange of goods and services, promoting specialization. Remember that in efficient economies—those that manage to get the most output from a given set of inputs—people and companies concentrate on the activities at which they are best and for which their opportunity cost is lowest. This principle of *comparative advantage* leads to specialization so that each of us ends up doing just one job and being paid in some form of money. But as specialization increases, more and more trading must take place to ensure that most of us end up with the goods and services we need and want. The more trading, the more financial transactions; and the more financial transactions, the more important it is that those transactions be cheap. If getting hold of money and using it to make payments were costly, that would put a damper on people's willingness to specialize. Financial intermediaries, by providing us with a reliable and inexpensive payments system, help our economy to function more efficiently.

Beyond safekeeping and access to the payments system, financial intermediaries provide bookkeeping and accounting services. They help us to manage our finances. Just think about your financial transactions over the past few months. If you work, you were paid, probably more than once. If you rent an apartment or own a home, you paid the rent or mortgage and probably the electric and gas bills. You paid your phone bill. Then there's transportation. If you have a car, you may have made a loan payment. You surely paid for gasoline and possibly for a repair. You purchased food, too, both at the grocery store and in various restaurants. And don't forget the movies and books you bought, perhaps through your mobile phone or tablet. As you get older, you may shoulder the expense of having children, along with saving for their education and your retirement. The point is, our financial lives are extraordinarily complex, and we need help keeping track of them. Financial intermediaries do the job: They provide us with bookkeeping and accounting services, noting all our transactions for us and making our lives more tolerable in the process.

Before we continue, we should note that providing safekeeping and accounting services, as well as access to the payments system, forces financial intermediaries to write legal contracts. Writing individualized contracts to ensure that each customer will maintain a checking account balance as required, or repay a loan as promised, would be extremely costly. But a financial intermediary can hire a lawyer to write one very high-quality contract that can be used over and over again, thus reducing the cost of each use. In fact, much of what financial intermediaries do takes advantage of what are known as *economies of scale*, in which the average cost of producing a good or service falls as the quantity produced increases. As we will see later, information is subject to economies of scale just as other goods and services are.

Providing Liquidity

One function that is related to access to the payments system is the provision of liquidity. Recall from Chapter 2 that *liquidity* is a measure of the ease and cost with which an asset can be turned into a means of payment. When a financial asset can be transformed into money quickly, easily, and at low cost, it is said to be very liquid. Financial intermediaries offer us the ability to transform assets into money at relatively low cost. That's what ATMs are all about—converting deposit balances into money on demand.

Financial intermediaries provide liquidity in a way that is both efficient and beneficial to all of us. To understand the process, think about your bank. Two kinds of customers visit the bank: those with funds, who want to make deposits, and those in need of funds, who want to make withdrawals or take out loans. Depositors want easy access to their funds—not just the currency they withdraw every week or so but the larger amounts they may need in an emergency. Borrowers don't want to pay the funds back for awhile, and they certainly can't be expected to repay the entire amount on short notice.

In the same way that an insurance company knows that not all its policyholders will have automobile accidents on the same day, a bank knows that not all its depositors will experience an emergency and need to withdraw funds at the same time. The bank can structure its assets accordingly, keeping enough funds in short-term, liquid financial instruments to satisfy the few people who will need them and lending out the rest. And because long-term loans usually have higher interest rates than short-term money-market instruments—for instance, commercial paper and U.S. Treasury bills—the bank can offer depositors a higher interest rate than they would get otherwise.

Even the bank's short-term investments will do better than an individual depositor's could, because the bank can take advantage of economies of scale to lower its transactions costs. It isn't much more expensive to buy a $1 million U.S. Treasury bill than it is to buy one worth only $1,000. By collecting funds from a large number of small investors, the bank can reduce the cost of their combined investment, offering each individual investor both liquidity and high rates of return. Pooling large numbers of small accounts in this way is very efficient. By doing so, an intermediary offers depositors something they can't get from the financial markets on their own.

The liquidity services financial intermediaries provide go beyond fast and easy access to account balances. Intermediaries offer both individuals and businesses lines of credit, which are similar to overdraft protection for checking accounts. A line of credit is essentially a preapproved loan that can be drawn on whenever a customer needs funds. Home equity lines of credit, credit-card cash advances, and business lines of credit are examples. Like a deposit account, the line of credit provides a customer with access to liquidity, except that in this case withdrawals may exceed deposit balances. To offer this service profitably, a financial intermediary must specialize in liquidity management. That is, it must design its balance sheet so that it can sustain sudden withdrawals.

Diversifying Risk

If you had $1,000 or $10,000 or even $100,000 to invest, would you want to keep it all in one place? Would you be willing to lend it all to a single person or firm? By now you have read Chapter 5, so you know the answer to this question: Don't put all your eggs in one basket, it's unnecessarily risky. But even without knowing much about diversifying through hedging and spreading risk, you would sense intuitively that lending $1 to each of 1,000 borrowers is less risky than lending $1,000 to just one borrower, and putting $1 in each of 1,000 different stocks is safer than putting $1,000 in one stock. Financial institutions enable us to diversify our investments and reduce risk.

Banks mitigate risk in a straightforward way: They take deposits from thousands or even millions of individuals and make thousands of loans with them. Thus, each depositor has a very small stake in each one of the loans. For example, a bank might collect $1,000 from each of one million depositors and then use the resulting $1 billion to make 10,000 loans of $100,000 each. So each depositor has a 1/1,000,000 share in each of the 10,000 loans.

To picture this, look back at Figure 11.2 (page 273) and imagine that it shows 10,000 times as many deposits and 10,000 times as many mortgages. Next, picture each of those deposits cut up into 10,000 pieces, each assigned to a different loan. That is, each deposit contributes 10 cents to each loan. That's diversification! And because the bank specializes in taking deposits and making loans, it can minimize the cost of setting up all the necessary legal contracts to do this.

All financial intermediaries provide a low-cost way for individuals to diversify their investments. Mutual fund companies offer small investors a low-cost way to purchase a diversified portfolio of stocks and eliminate the idiosyncratic risk associated with any single investment. Many of the mutual funds based on the Standard & Poor's 500 index (described in Chapter 8) require a minimum investment of as little as a few thousand dollars. Because the average price of each stock in the index usually runs between $40 and $60, a small investor would need more than $20,000 to buy even a single share of stock in each of the 500 companies in the index (not to mention the fees the investor would need to pay to a broker to do it). Thus, the mutual fund company lets a small investor buy a fraction of a share in each of the 500 companies in the fund. And because mutual fund companies specialize in this activity, the cost remains low.

Collecting and Processing Information

One of the biggest problems individual savers face is figuring out which potential borrowers are trustworthy and which are not. Most of us do not have the time or skill to collect and process information on a wide array of potential borrowers. And we are understandably reluctant to invest in activities about which we have little reliable information. The fact that the borrower knows whether he or she is trustworthy, while the lender faces substantial costs to obtain the same information, results in an *information asymmetry*. Very simply, borrowers have information that lenders don't.

By collecting and processing standardized information, financial intermediaries reduce the problems information asymmetries create. They screen loan applicants to guarantee that they are creditworthy. They monitor loan recipients to ensure that they use the funds as they have claimed they will. To understand how this process works, and the implications it has for the financial system, we need to study information asymmetries in more detail.

Information Asymmetries and Information Costs

Information plays a central role in the structure of financial markets and financial institutions. Markets require sophisticated information to work well; when the cost of obtaining that information is too high, markets cease to function. Information costs make the financial markets, as important as they are, among the worst functioning of all markets. The fact is, the issuers of financial instruments—borrowers who want to issue bonds and firms that want to issue stock—know much more about their business prospects and their willingness to work than potential lenders or investors—those who would buy their bonds and stocks. This **asymmetric information** is a serious hindrance to the operation of financial markets. Solving this problem is one key to making our financial system work as well as it does.

To understand the nature of the problem and the possible solutions, let's go back to eBay. Why are the people who win online auctions willing to send payments totaling $75 billion a year to the sellers? An amazing amount of trust is involved in these transactions. To bid at all, buyers must believe that an item has been described accurately. And winners must be sure that the seller will send the item in exchange for their payments, because the normal arrangement is for the seller to be paid first.

eBay's feedback rating system awards +1 point for each positive comment, 0 points for each neutral comment, and –1 point for each negative comment

How can buyers be sure they won't be disappointed by their purchases when they arrive, assuming they arrive at all? The fact that sellers have much more information about the items they are selling and their own reliability creates an information asymmetry. Aware of this problem, the people who started eBay took two steps. First, they offered insurance to protect buyers who don't receive their purchases. Second, they devised a feedback forum to collect and store information about both bidders and sellers. Anyone can read the comments posted in the forum or check an overall rating that summarizes their content. Sellers who develop good reputations in the feedback forum command higher prices than others; buyers who develop bad reputations can be banned from bidding. Without this means of gathering information, eBay probably could not have been successful. Together, the buyers' insurance and the feedback forum make eBay run smoothly.[1]

---

[1]A low-cost, reliable payments system helps, too. The easier it is for buyers to pay sellers, the more likely both are to use the auction site. Realizing the need for a payments system, eBay users created *PayPal,* which allows buyers and sellers to set up electronic accounts through which to make and receive payments for their eBay transactions. Because many sellers are too small to take credit cards, this innovation greatly facilitated the online exchanges. Initially an independent concern, PayPal became so central to eBay's success that the auction site's owners bought it.

APPLYING THE CONCEPT
THE MADOFF SCANDAL

Fraud is the most extreme version of moral hazard. Even so, the fraud perpetrated by Bernard Madoff stands out. Thousands of investors lost billions of dollars, making it among the largest scams in history.* The swindle went undetected for decades and affected wealthy individuals and financial firms from around the world with extensive experience in finance.

Yet, Madoff's fraud was nothing more than a classic *Ponzi scheme*. Named after Charles Ponzi, who conducted a similar sting in the United States just after World War I, a Ponzi scheme is a fraud in which an intermediary collects funds from new investors, but instead of investing them, uses the funds to pay off earlier investors. Money has to flow in at least as fast as it flows out. When that flow reverses, the fraud unravels and the final investors become big losers.

How do such frauds succeed at different times in different places? How can they last so long and become so damaging?

The answer is that investors fail to screen and monitor the managers who receive their funds (such as Madoff or Ponzi). Screening and monitoring are costly. The appearance of satisfied early investors discourages new investors from paying such costs. Many investors assume that others have already done the monitoring needed.

A facade of public respectability contributes to the success of a Ponzi scheme, and Madoff was a master at burnishing his reputation in the public eye. He had been the chairman of a major stock exchange (Nasdaq; see Chapter 8) and of the organization of U.S. securities dealers (NASD). He also was a philanthropist.

The U.S. government agency responsible for overseeing Madoff's firm, the Securities and Exchange Commission (SEC), also failed to detect the scheme. One whistleblower warned the oversight agency about possible fraud as early as 2000. Yet, the swindle ended in 2008 only because the financial crisis had prompted withdrawals from many firms, including Madoff's. Otherwise, the scam might still be going on.

With the benefit of hindsight, there were red flags that warned of a problem. Yet, everyone acted as if someone else was monitoring, so they could enjoy the *free ride* (see page 282 for a definition of a free rider). The Madoff scam is a painful reminder that there is no such free ride.

*As of May 2011, the government-appointed trustee responsible for returning investors' stolen money estimated the losses net of funds recovered at about $10 billion.

The two problems eBay faced arise in financial markets, too. In fact, information problems are the key to understanding the structure of our financial system and the central role of financial intermediaries. Asymmetric information poses two important obstacles to the smooth flow of funds from savers to investors. The first, called **adverse selection**, arises before the transaction occurs. Just as buyers on eBay need to know the relative trustworthiness of sellers, lenders need to know how to distinguish good credit risks from bad. The second problem, called **moral hazard**, occurs after the transaction. In the same way that buyers on eBay need reassurance that sellers will deliver their purchases after receiving payment, lenders need to find a way to tell whether borrowers will use the proceeds of a loan as they claim they will. The following sections will look at both these problems in detail to see how they affect the structure of the financial system.

Adverse Selection

Used Cars and the Market for Lemons The 2001 Nobel Prize in Economics was awarded to George A. Akerlof, A. Michael Spence, and Joseph E. Stiglitz "for their analyses of markets with asymmetric information." Professor Akerlof's contribution came first, in a paper published in 1970 titled "The Market for Lemons."[2] Akerlof's paper explained why the market for used cars—some of which may be "lemons"— doesn't function very well. Here's the logic.

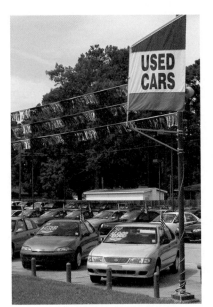

Used Cars: clean, reliable, and priced just right!

[2]See "The Market for 'Lemons': Quality Uncertainty and the Market Mechanism," *Quarterly Journal of Economics* (August 1970). This paper contains very little mathematics and is quite readable. You can find it through your university library using an electronic storage system called JSTOR.

Suppose the used-car market has only two cars for sale, both 2010 model Honda Accords. One is immaculate, having been driven and maintained by a careful elderly woman who didn't travel much. The second car belonged to a young man who got it from his parents, loved to drive fast, and did not worry about the damage he might cause if he hit a pothole. The owners of these two cars know whether their own cars are in good repair, but used-car shoppers do not.

Let's say that potential buyers are willing to pay $15,000 for a well-maintained car, but only $7,500 for a "lemon"—a car with lots of mechanical problems. The elderly woman knows her car is a "peach." It's in good condition and she won't part with it for less than $12,500. The young man, knowing the poor condition of his car, will take $6,000 for it. But if buyers can't tell the difference between the two cars, without more information they will pay only the average price of $11,250. (A risk-averse buyer wouldn't even pay that much.) That is less than the owner of the good car will accept, so she won't sell her car and it disappears from the market. The problem is that if buyers are willing to pay only the average value of all the cars on the market, sellers with cars in above-average condition won't put their cars up for sale. Only the worst cars, the lemons, will be left on the market.

Information asymmetries aside, people like to buy new cars, and when they do, they sell their old cars. People who can't afford new cars, or who would rather not pay for them, are looking to buy good used cars. Together, these potential buyers and sellers of used cars provide a substantial incentive for creative people to solve the problem of adverse selection in the used-car market. Some companies try to help buyers separate the peaches from the lemons. For instance, *Consumer Reports* has long provided information about the reliability and safety of particular makes and models. More recent is the CARFAX service, which provides potential car buyers the detailed history, including reported accidents and airbag deployments, of a specific used vehicle. Car dealers may try to maintain their reputations by refusing to pass off a clunker as a well-maintained car. For a fee, a mechanic will check out a used car for a potential buyer. Finally, many car manufacturers offer warranties on the used cars they have certified. We have found ways to overcome the information problems pointed out by Professor Akerlof, and as a result both good and bad used cars sell at prices much closer to their true value.

Adverse Selection in Financial Markets   When it comes to information costs, financial markets are not that different from the used-car market. In the same way that the seller of a used car knows more about the car than the buyer, potential borrowers know more about the projects they wish to finance than prospective lenders. And in the same way that information asymmetries can drive good cars out of the used-car market, they can drive good stocks and bonds out of the financial market. To see why, let's start with stocks.

RISK

Think about a simple case in which there are two firms, one with good prospects and one with bad prospects. If you can't tell the difference between the two firms, you will be willing to pay a price based only on their average quality. The stock of the good company will be undervalued. Because the managers know their stock is worth more than the average price, they won't issue it in the first place. That leaves only the firm with bad prospects in the market. And because most investors aren't interested in companies with poor prospects, the market is very unlikely to get started at all.

The same thing happens in the bond market. Remember that risk requires compensation. The higher the risk, the greater the risk premium. In the bond market, this relationship between risk and return affects the cost of borrowing. The more risky the borrower, the higher the cost of borrowing. If a lender can't tell whether a borrower

YOUR FINANCIAL WORLD

Private Mortgage Insurance

If you try to buy a house with a down payment of less than 20 percent of the purchase price, the lender may require you to buy private mortgage insurance (PMI). PMI insures the lender in the event that the borrower defaults on the mortgage. This type of insurance can be expensive. For example, if you make a down payment of $10,000, or 10 percent, on a $100,000 home and finance the rest of the purchase price with a 30-year, 4 percent, fixed-rate mortgage, the required private mortgage insurance will raise your monthly payment from $430 to $470. But if you want to buy a house and you don't have savings that meet the 20 percent down payment requirement, you will have no choice but to purchase PMI.

Fortunately, you can cancel the insurance when the amount you owe on your mortgage falls to less than 80 percent of the value of your home. This can happen in two ways. The first is that you make your payments, gradually reducing the principal on the loan. (Recall from Chapter 6 that each loan payment is part interest and part repayment of principal.) But paying off the first $10,000 of a $90,000 30-year mortgage will take you at least 10 years. The second way you can cancel your PMI is if the value of your house rises, in which case you can contact the insurance provider and ask to drop the insurance. The law is on your side. So long as you have been making your mortgage payments on time, you have the right to cancel your PMI when your stake in the house—your net worth—rises above 20 percent of its value.

is a good or bad credit risk, the lender will demand a risk premium based on the average risk. Borrowers who know they are good credit risks won't want to borrow at this elevated interest rate, so they will withdraw from the market, leaving only the bad credit risks. The result is the same as for used cars and stocks: Because lenders are not eager to buy bonds issued by bad credit risks, the market will disappear.

Solving the Adverse Selection Problem

From a social perspective, the fact that managers might avoid issuing stock or bonds because they know the market will not value their company correctly is not good. It means that the company will pass up some good investments. And because some of the best investments will not be undertaken, the economy won't grow as rapidly as it could. Thus, it is extremely important to find ways for investors and lenders to distinguish well-run firms from poorly run firms. Well-run firms need to highlight their quality so they can obtain financing more cheaply. Investors need to distinguish between high- and low-risk investments so they can seek compensation corresponding to the level of risk they are taking on. The question is how to do it.

Recall how buyers and sellers in the used-car market developed ways to address the problem of distinguishing good from bad cars? The answer here is similar. First, because the problem is caused by a lack of information, we can create more information for investors. Second, we can provide guarantees in the form of financial contracts that can be written so a firm's owners suffer together with the people who invested in the company if the firm does poorly. This type of arrangement helps to persuade investors that a firm's stocks and bonds are of high quality. And as we will see later, financial intermediaries can do a great deal to reduce the information costs associated with stock and bond investments.

Disclosure of Information   One obvious way to solve the problem created by asymmetric information is to generate more information. This can be done in one of two ways: government-required disclosure, and the private collection and production

APPLYING THE CONCEPT
DEFLATION, NET WORTH, AND INFORMATION COSTS

A casual reader of the business press might get the impression that **deflation**, when prices are declining on average, is a fate we would rather not contemplate. Deflation is associated with the Great Depression of the 1930s, when consumer prices and output both fell about 30 percent. It is also associated with Japan's economic underperformance since the early 1990s, when the price level peaked and began to decline.

Deflation is the opposite of the more familiar inflation. Inflation is when prices are going up, on average. Deflation is when they are going down. A primary reason deflation is so bad is that it aggravates information problems in ways that inflation does not. It does so by reducing a company's net worth. To see why, think about a typical firm's balance sheet. Its assets are buildings, machines, and product inventories. Its liabilities include various kinds of debt, much of it fixed in nominal terms. That is, companies borrow fixed numbers of

dollars. Now think about the consequences of a decline in the price level. When prices fall, the dollar value of the firm's liabilities remains the same. The value of the firm's assets, however, tends to fall with the price level. Deflation drives down a firm's net worth, making it less trustworthy as a borrower. Remember, net worth solves the problems of adverse selection and moral hazard, allowing firms to obtain loans. With a low net worth, firms can no longer obtain financing because lenders cannot overcome the difficulty of asymmetric information. The same problems also afflict households, whose key assets (especially houses and stocks) usually decline in value in a deflation, reducing the capacity of households to borrow against collateral.

The connection among net worth, information, and the availability of credit to borrowers helps to explain the dynamics of the business cycle. Think about what happens at the start of a recession. The value of a firm (as measured by the present value of its expected future sales) falls, compounding lenders' information problems. Lenders, suddenly more concerned about a borrower's creditworthiness, become more reluctant to make loans. The availability of investment funds falls, pushing the economy further into recession.

---

of information (like CARFAX for used cars). In most industrialized countries, *public companies*—those that issue stocks and bonds that are bought and sold in public financial markets—are required to disclose voluminous amounts of information. For example, in the United States the Securities and Exchange Commission requires firms to produce public financial statements that are prepared according to standard accounting practices. Corporations are also required to disclose, on an ongoing basis, information that could have a bearing on the value of their firms. And since August 2000, U.S. companies have been required to release to the public any information they provide to professional stock analysts.[3]

As we learned in 2001 and 2002, however, these requirements can go only so far in assuring that investors are well informed. Despite government regulations designed to protect investors, Enron, WorldCom, Global Crossing, and numerous other companies managed to distort the profits and debt levels published in their financial statements. With the help of some unethical accountants, company executives found a broad range of ways to manipulate the statements to disguise their firms' true financial condition. While accounting practices have changed since then and financial statements may now convey more information than they once did, everyone remains on guard. Information problems persist.

What about the private collection and sale of information? You might think that this would provide investors with what they need to solve the adverse selection problem, but unfortunately it doesn't work. While it is in everyone's interest to produce credible proof of the quality of a company's activities, such information doesn't really exist. In a limited sense there is private information collected and sold to investors. Various

---

[3]Some people were concerned that Regulation FD, for "fair disclosure," might have the perverse effect of causing firms to make less information public. Fortunately, evidence shows that public corporations are now providing more information to both professional stock analysts and individual investors. Today, virtually all company conference calls—the mechanism used to disseminate information about a firm's financial performance—are open to individual investors.

research services like Moody's, Value Line, and Dun and Bradstreet collect information directly from firms and produce evaluations.

These reports are not cheap. For example, Value Line charges nearly $600 a year for its weekly publication. To be credible, the companies examined can't pay directly for the research themselves, so investors have to. And while some individuals might be willing to pay, in the end they don't have to and so they won't. Private information services face what is called a free-rider problem. A **free rider** is someone who doesn't pay the cost to get the benefit of a good or service, and free riding on stock-market analysis is easy to do. Even though these publications are expensive, public libraries subscribe to some of them. Reporters for *The Wall Street Journal* and other periodicals read them and write stories publicizing crucial information. And individual investors can simply follow the lead of people they know who subscribe to the publications. Of course, all these practices reduce the ability of the producers of private information to actually profit from their hard work.

Collateral and Net Worth While government-required disclosure and private information collection are crucial, they haven't solved all the information problems that plague investors and the firms they invest in. Fortunately, other solutions exist. One is to make sure that lenders are compensated even if borrowers default. If a loan is insured in some way, then the borrower isn't a bad credit risk.

There are two mechanisms for ensuring that a borrower is likely to repay a lender: collateral and net worth. Recall from Chapter 3 that **collateral** is something of value pledged by a borrower to the lender in the event of the borrower's default. Collateral is said to *back* or *secure* a loan. Houses serve as collateral for mortgages; cars, as collateral for car loans. If the borrower fails to keep up with the mortgage or car payments, the lender will take possession of the house or car and sell it to recover the borrowed funds. In circumstances like these, adverse selection is less of a concern; that's why collateral is so prevalent in loan agreements. When banks make loans without collateral—**unsecured loans**, like credit card debt—they typically charge very high interest rates. Adverse selection is the reason. (See Your Financial World: Your First Credit Card on page 274.)

Net worth is the owner's stake in a firm, the value of the firm's assets minus the value of its liabilities. Under many circumstances, net worth serves the same purpose as collateral. If a firm defaults on a loan, the lender can make a claim against the firm's net worth. Consider what would happen if a firm with a high net worth borrowed to undertake a project that turned out to be unsuccessful. If the firm had no net worth, the lender would be out of luck. Instead, the firm's owners can use their net worth to repay the lender.

The same is true of a home mortgage. A mortgage is much easier and cheaper to get when a homebuyer makes a substantial down payment. For the lender, the risk is that the price of the home will fall, in which case its value will not be sufficient to fully compensate the lender in the event of a default. But with a large down payment, the homeowner has a substantial stake in the house, so even if the price falls, the mortgage can likely be repaid even if the borrower defaults. From the perspective of the mortgage lender, the homeowner's equity serves exactly the same function as net worth in a business loan.

The importance of net worth in reducing adverse selection is the reason owners of new businesses have so much difficulty borrowing money. If you want to start a bakery, for example, you will need financing to buy equipment and cover the rent and payroll for the first few months. Such seed money is very hard to get. Most small business owners must put up their homes and other property as collateral for their business loans. Only after they have managed to establish a successful business, and have built up some net worth in it can they borrow without pledging their personal property.

Moral Hazard: Problem and Solutions

The phrase *moral hazard* originated when economists who were studying insurance noted that an insurance policy changes the behavior of the person who is insured. Examples are everywhere. A fire insurance policy written for more than the value of the property might induce the owner to arson; a generous automobile insurance policy might encourage reckless driving. Employment arrangements suffer from moral hazard, too. How can your boss be sure you are working as hard as you can if you'll get your paycheck at the end of the week whether you do or not? Moral hazard arises when we cannot observe people's actions and so cannot judge whether a poor outcome was intentional or just a result of bad luck.

"It's been moved and seconded that we fly the company plane to Zurich, split the bank accounts, and go our merry ways."

SOURCE: 1994 © Henry Martin/The New Yorker Collection/www.cartoonbank.com.

Thus, a lender's or investor's information problems do not end with adverse selection. A second information asymmetry arises because the borrower knows more than the lender about the way borrowed funds will be used and the effort that will go into a project. Moral hazard plagues both equity and bond financing, making it difficult for all but the biggest, best known companies to issue either stocks or bonds successfully. Let's look at each type of financing and examine the ways people have tried to solve the problem of moral hazard.

Moral Hazard in Equity Financing   If you buy a stock, how do you know the company that issued it will use the funds you have invested in the way that is best for you? The answer is that it almost surely will not. You have given your funds to managers, who will tend to run the company in the way most advantageous to them. The separation of your ownership from their control creates what is called a *principal–agent problem,* which can be more than a little costly to stockholders. Witness the luxurious offices, corporate jets, limousines, and artwork that executives surround themselves with, not to mention the millions of dollars in compensation they pay themselves. Managers gain all these personal benefits at the expense of stockholders.

A simple example will illustrate this point. Let's say that your cousin Ina, who is a whiz at writing software, has an idea for a program to speed up wireless Internet access. Together, the two of you estimate she needs $10,000 to write the program and sell it to an interested buyer. But Ina has only $1,000 in savings, so you will have to contribute $9,000. Family etiquette dictates that once you've made the investment, you won't be able to monitor Ina's progress—to tell whether she is working hard or even if she is working at all. If everything goes well, you think you can sell the program to Microsoft for $100,000, which is ten times the initial investment. But Ina had better work quickly or someone else may make it to market first and Ina's program won't be worth nearly as much.

The difficulty in this arrangement is immediately apparent. If Ina works hard and all goes according to plan, she will get 10 percent of the $100,000 (that's $10,000) and you will get the rest, a whopping $90,000. But if Ina runs into programming problems or spends part of the time surfing instead of working, someone else may bring the product to market first, reducing the value of Ina's software to $10,000. The problem is, Ina's decision to go surfing would cost her only $9,000, but it would cost you $81,000! And because you wouldn't be able to tell why the venture failed, you're unlikely to part with your $9,000 in the first place.

Moral hazard: How can you be sure that your investment isn't being used to buy one of these vacation homes in Tahiti?

Solving the Moral Hazard Problem in Equity Financing Solutions to the moral hazard problem in equity finance are hard to come by. Information on the quality of management can be useful, but only if owners have the power to fire managers—and that can be extremely difficult. Requiring managers to own a significant stake in their own firm is another possibility. If Ina comes up with the entire $10,000, then there is no separation between ownership and control and no question whether Ina will behave in the owner's interest—she is the owner. But people who have good ideas don't always have the resources to pursue them. Ina doesn't have the $10,000 she needs.

During the 1990s, a concerted attempt was made to align managers' interests with those of stockholders. Executives were given stock options that provided lucrative payoffs if a firm's stock price rose above a certain level. This approach worked until managers found ways to misrepresent their companies' profitability, driving up stock prices temporarily so they could cash in their options. Accounting methods have been reformed in an attempt to reduce such abuses, but at this writing, no one has devised a foolproof way of ensuring that managers will behave in the owners' interest instead of their own.

Moral Hazard in Debt Finance When the managers of a company are the owners, the problem of moral hazard in equity financing disappears. This suggests that investors should prefer debt financing to equity financing. But debt financing has its problems, too. Imagine that instead of buying a 90 percent share in your cousin Ina's software venture, you lend her $9,000 at an 11 percent annual interest rate. The debt contract specifies that she will repay you $9,990 in one year's time. This arrangement dramatically changes Ina's incentives. Now, if she works hard, she gets $90,010, but if she goes surfing, she still has to repay the $9,990, leaving her nothing at the end of the year. Surely this solves your problem.

Debt does go a long way toward eliminating the moral hazard problem inherent in equity finance, but it doesn't finish the job. Because debt contracts allow owners to keep all the profits in excess of the loan payments, they encourage risk taking. Suppose Ina decides to use some or all of the $10,000 to buy lottery tickets. That's an extremely risky thing to do. The problem is, if her lottery number comes up, she gets the winnings, but if she loses, you pay the cost. That's not a very desirable outcome for you, the lender. While in the real world the danger isn't quite that extreme, the problem still exists. Lenders need to find ways to make sure borrowers don't take too many risks. Unfortunately, borrowers' limited liability has the same effect that an insurance policy has on the insured. People with risky projects are attracted to debt finance because they get the full benefit of the upside, while the downside is limited to their collateral, if any.

Solving the Moral Hazard Problem in Debt Finance To some degree, a good legal contract can solve the moral hazard problem that is inherent in debt finance. Bonds and loans often carry *restrictive covenants* that limit the amount of risk a borrower can assume. For example, a covenant may restrict the nature of the goods or services the borrower can purchase. It may require the firm to maintain a certain level of net worth, a minimum balance in a bank account, or a minimum credit rating. Home mortgages often come with restrictive covenants requiring the homeowners to

LESSONS FROM THE CRISIS
INFORMATION ASYMMETRY AND SECURITIZATION

This chapter highlights the importance of *screening* credit risks to limit adverse selection and of *monitoring* the recipients of funds to limit moral hazard. It also warns that *free riding* can diminish screening and monitoring. A key source of the financial crisis of 2007–2009 was insufficient screening and monitoring in the securitization of mortgages (see Chapter 6, Applying the Concept: Securitization).

Mortgage securitization problems started with the initial mortgage lenders—the *originators*—who eased standards and reduced screening to increase the volume of lending and the short-term profitability of their businesses. The result was many risky mortgages: When housing prices began to fall in 2006, defaults soared.

At the next stage of securitization, the firms that assembled these mortgages into securities for sale—the *distributors*—did little to forestall the decline of lending standards by originators. Had they wished to, they could have required that the originators demonstrate a high level of net worth and invest it in the mortgages that they sold.

When lending standards decline, securitization becomes like a game of "hot potato." Players in the game try to pass risky loans—the hot potato—along to the next player as quickly as they can, while it's still possible. The game ends when defaults soar, leaving someone with the loss.

Rating agencies might have halted the game early. Instead, they awarded their top ratings to a large share of mortgage-backed securities, severely underestimating the riskiness of the loans. In retrospect, we can now see that the agencies had little incentive to expend the resources necessary to adequately screen the underlying loans or the lenders.

Finally, many investors (and government officials responsible for overseeing intermediaries) assumed they could rely on other people—they were free riders. Rather than undertake their own costly screening efforts, they assumed the assessment of the rating agencies was accurate.

Implicitly, the participants in the process acted as if the ultimate collateral—the value of houses—would always be adequate to contain the damage from adverse selection. Had housing prices risen indefinitely, as many appeared to assume they would, the collateral would have protected investors against any damage. But, when housing prices and the value of the collateral started to plunge, the effects of adverse selection threatened the financial system as a whole.

purchase fire insurance or to make monthly deposits toward payment of their property taxes. (Failure to pay property taxes can lead the government to seize the borrower's house, complicating the mortgage company's attempt to recover its principal.)

Table 11.3 summarizes this section's discussion of how financial relationships are affected by information problems, together with a list of the various solutions used to address the problems information costs create.

Table 11.3	The Negative Consequences of Information Costs

1. Adverse selection. Lenders can't distinguish good from bad credit risks, which discourages transactions from taking place.

   Solutions include

   Government-required information disclosure

   Private collection of information

   Pledging of collateral to insure lenders against the borrower's default

   Requiring borrowers to invest substantial resources of their own

2. Moral hazard. Lenders can't tell whether borrowers will do what they claim they will do with the borrowed resources; borrowers may take too many risks.

   Solutions include

   Requiring managers to report to owners

   Requiring managers to invest substantial resources of their own

   Covenants that restrict what borrowers can do with borrowed funds

Financial Intermediaries and Information Costs

The problems of adverse selection and moral hazard make securities finance expensive and difficult to get. These drawbacks lead us immediately to loans and the role of financial institutions. Much of the information that financial intermediaries collect is used to reduce information costs and minimize the effects of adverse selection and moral hazard. To reduce the potential costs of adverse selection, intermediaries screen loan applicants. To minimize moral hazard, they monitor borrowers. And when borrowers fail to live up to their contracts with lenders, financial intermediaries penalize them by enforcing the contracts. Let's look more closely at how financial firms screen and monitor borrowers to reduce information costs. And then we will conclude with a quick look at how firms finance growth and investment.

Screening and Certifying to Reduce Adverse Selection

To get a loan, whether from a bank, a mortgage company, or a finance company, you must fill out an application. As part of the process, you will be asked to supply your Social Security number. The lender uses the number to identify you to a company that collects and analyzes credit information, summarizing it for potential lenders in a credit score.

Your personal credit score (described in Chapter 7 in Your Financial World: Your Credit Rating) tells a lender how likely you are to repay a loan. It is analogous to eBay's feedback forum rating or to an expert appraiser's certification of the authenticity and condition of an original painting. The credit rating company *screens* you and then *certifies* your credit rating. If you are a good credit risk with a high credit score, you are more likely than others to get a loan at a relatively low interest rate. Note that the company that collects your credit information and produces your credit score charges a fee each time someone wants to see it. This overcomes the free-rider problem.

Banks can collect information on a borrower that goes beyond what a loan application or credit report contains. By noting the pattern of deposits and withdrawals from your account, as well as your use of your debit card if you have one, they can learn more about you than you might like. Banks monitor both their individual and their business customers in this way. Again, the information they collect is easy to protect and use. The special information banks have puts them in an almost unique position to *screen* customers and reduce the costs of adverse selection. This expertise helps to explain another phenomenon, the fact that most small and medium-size businesses depend on banks for their financing.

Financial intermediaries' superior ability to screen and certify borrowers extends beyond loan making to the issuance of bonds and equity. Underwriters—large financial institutions, like Goldman Sachs, JPMorgan Chase, and Morgan Stanley—screen and certify firms seeking to raise funds directly in the financial markets. Without certification by one of these firms, companies would find it difficult to raise funds.

In the financial world, Goldman Sachs, JPMorgan Chase, and Morgan Stanley have as much brand recognition as Coke does in the soft drink world.

Large intermediaries go to great lengths to market their expertise as underwriters; they want people to recognize their names the world over, just as everyone recognizes Coca-Cola. A can of Coke, the best-selling soft drink in the world, is instantly recognizable, whether the fine print is in English, Chinese, Arabic, or Swedish. Financial institutions have applied this concept, which marketing people call branding, to their certification of financial products. If JPMorgan Chase, a well-known bank and securities firm, is willing to sell a bond or stock, the brand name suggests that it is a high-quality investment.

Monitoring to Reduce Moral Hazard

If someone weren't watching over your shoulder, you might take the money you borrowed for a business project and fly off to Tahiti. To address the risk that sellers might take the money and run, eBay developed buyers' insurance. In the financial world, intermediaries insure against this type of moral hazard by monitoring both the firms that issue bonds and those that issue stocks.

Car dealers provide an interesting example of how this process works. Dealers have to finance all those shiny new cars that sit on the lot, waiting for buyers to show up. One way to do this is with a bank loan that is collateralized by the cars themselves. But the bank doesn't completely trust the dealer to use the loan proceeds properly. Every so often, the bank manager will send an associate to count the number of cars on the lot. The count tells the manager whether the dealer is using the borrowed funds properly. In monitoring the dealer this way, the bank is enforcing the restrictive covenants contained in the loan contract. Because banks specialize in this type of monitoring, they can do it more cheaply than individual borrowers and lenders.

Many financial intermediaries (other than banks) hold significant numbers of shares in individual firms. When they do, they find ways to monitor the companies' activities. For example, the California Public Employee Retirement System (CalPERS) manages more than $250 billion in assets, the income from which is used to pay retired employees' pensions. About 1.1 million "members" of CalPERS depend on the fund's managers to carefully monitor its investments. Before buying a company's stock, CalPERS' managers do a significant amount of research on the firm; once they have purchased the shares, they monitor the firm's activities very closely. In some cases, they place a representative on the company's board of directors to monitor and protect CalPERS' investment firsthand.

In the case of some new companies, a financial intermediary called a *venture capital firm* does the monitoring. Venture capital firms (like Kleiner Perkins or Draper Fisher) specialize in investing in risky new *ventures* in return for a stake in the ownership and a share of the profits. To guard against moral hazard and ensure that the new company has the best possible chance of success, the venture capitalist keeps a close watch on the managers' actions.

Finally, the threat of a takeover helps to persuade managers to act in the interest of the stock- and bondholders. If managers don't do a good job of watching out for shareholders' interests, another company can buy the firm and replace them. In the 1980s, some firms specialized in such tactics. Today, this approach has become the business model of *private equity firms,* a few of which (like Bain Capital and Kohlberg Kravis Roberts) have become very large themselves. When the new owners put their own people in charge of the firm, they eliminate the moral hazard problem.

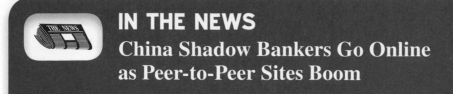
Bloomberg

By Luo Jun

July 24, 2012

Jack Qiu, spending evenings in front of his laptop in the southern Chinese city of Guangzhou, is earning the best returns of his life: 14.2 percent on an annualized basis in just two months.

He's doing it by lending money to strangers online. An accountant by day, Qiu has turned out to be a better loan manager by night than most banks. Only two investments out of his 80,000 yuan ($12,525) total, each worth 100 yuan, have gone unpaid. Nonperforming loans at a Chinese lender, on average, would be almost four times as much. . . .

Peer-to-peer lending is taking off in China as traditional methods of private lending among family and acquaintances, part of the country's unregulated $2.4 trillion shadow-banking system, move online. More than 2,000 websites have been set up nationwide since 2007, China National Radio reported in May. . . .

Akin to LendingClub.com or Prosper.com in the U.S., China's peer-to-peer lenders let individuals invest a minimum of 50 yuan in projects ranging from small-business expansion to funding newlyweds' honeymoons for as much as 23 percent interest, the highest rate allowed under Chinese law. While the returns are higher than parking the money in bank accounts earning 3 percent, they're dwarfed by some underground shadow-banking investment yields that can go as high as 100 percent. . . .

Existing outside of regulators' jurisdiction, online lending sites aren't without risks. The China Banking Regulatory Commission in September issued a warning about web-based brokers, cautioning that their bad-loan ratio is "significantly higher" than that of banks—without specifying the figure—and that they can cross the line into illegality such as fraud, funding illegitimate businesses or money laundering. . . .

Online peer-to-peer lending started in the U.K. in 2005 and spread to the U.S., Germany and elsewhere. Prosper Marketplace Inc., the first such U.S. lender, reported a 179 percent increase in volume in 2011 and has almost 1.4 million members funding $369 million in loans.

Lending online became popular in China after a tightening of bank credit in 2010 following two years of stimulus spending to fight the global financial crisis. With total loan volume less than $1 billion, it's still a tiny part of the country's shadow-banking universe—along with underground lending, off-balance-sheet financing by banks and investments by trust firms—that policy makers . . . are trying to bring under government oversight. . . .

The Ppdai site, which calls itself China's first and largest, was founded by former Microsoft Corp. engineer Zhang Jun. . . . Like San Francisco-based Prosper, Ppdai requires borrowers to list basic personal information and details of their financing needs. Investors review the requests and make investments that meet their criteria. About 80 percent of the total 400 million yuan of lending brokered by Ppdai since 2007 has gone to small businesses. . . . Only 3 percent of China's 42 million small and medium-sized firms are able to get loans from banks, according to an estimate by Citic Securities Co., while 36.7 trillion yuan of household savings are parked in banks. . . .

About 3.5 percent of Ppdai's loans aren't paid off on time, Zhang said, while 1.2 percent have been overdue for at least 90 days, the definition of nonperforming at Chinese banks. That compares with the 0.9 percent bad-loan ratio of the nation's commercial banks as of the end of March, according to data from the banking regulator. . . .

China's lack of a credit-scoring system makes risk management difficult for peer-to-peer lending, giving potential lenders no way to gauge borrowers' creditworthiness. . . . "Coming from a technology background, it took us a while to realize that risk management is key to the business," Zhang said. "But we can do just enough to reduce default and prevent fraud, so we urge investors again and again not to put all their eggs in one basket." . . .

LESSONS OF THE ARTICLE

Will peer-to-peer lending sites grow enough to offer serious competition to banks and other financial intermediaries? Not unless they can likewise expand lenders' ability to screen and monitor borrowers to minimize the problems of adverse selection and moral hazard. With only rudimentary screening by peer-to-peer lenders, only the borrowers know the risks of the loans.

How Companies Finance Growth and Investment

Before concluding, let's pause and take stock. We began this chapter by noting two things: (1) Wealthy countries all have high levels of financial development, and (2) intermediaries play key roles both in lending and securities finance. The first is explained by the fact that the financial system improves the efficient operation of the economy, helping to channel resources to their most productive uses. Our discussion suggests that information problems are the primary explanation for the second.

But a corporation that wants to undertake an investment project can obtain financing not only directly from financial markets, through the issuance of stocks or bonds; or indirectly from a financial intermediary, in the form of a loan; it can also use its own profits. That is, instead of distributing profits to shareholders in the form of dividends, the firm can retain the earnings and use them as a source of investment financing.

You may be surprised to learn that the vast majority of investment financing comes from internal sources. Looking at Figure 11.3, notice that in both the United States and the United Kingdom, for example, more than 80 percent of business investment comes from internal sources. The only possible explanation for this fact is that information problems make external financing—obtained either by issuing into markets or by borrowing from financial institutions—prohibitively expensive and difficult to get. It's not just individuals that have to finance their activities without any help—businesses do, too. The fact that managers have superior information about the way in which their firms are and should be run makes internal finance the rational choice.

Figure 11.3   Sources of Business Finance

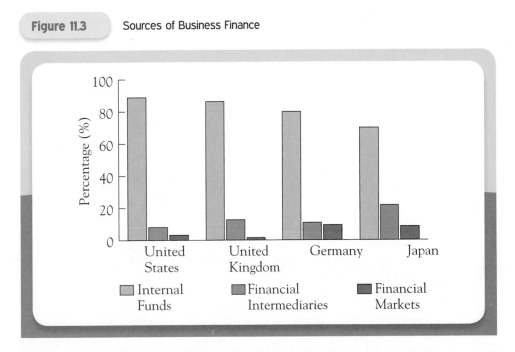

SOURCE: Data are averages for 1970 to 1994, computed from Table 1 of Jenny Corbett and Tim Jenkinson, "How is Investment Financed?" *The Manchester School Supplement,* 1997, pp. 69–93. Used with permission.

Terms

adverse selection, 278

asymmetric information, 277

collateral, 282

deflation, 281

free rider, 282

moral hazard, 278

net worth, 282

unsecured loan, 282

Using FRED: Codes for Data in This Chapter

Data Series	FRED Data Code
Total credit market debt owed	TCMDO
Total credit market debt owed by households	HSTCMDODNS
Total credit market debt owed by nonfinancial corporations	NCBTCMDODNS
Total credit market debt owed by domestic financial sector	TCMDODFS
Market value of equities (of nonfinancial corporations)	MVEONWMVBSNNCB
Population	POP
Bank loans and leases	TOTLL
Gross value added of financial corporations	A454RC1Q027SBEA
Nominal GDP	GDP
Total debt to equity ratio (United States)	TOTDTEUSQ163N
Total debt to equity ratio (Germany)	TOTDTEDEQ163N

Chapter Lessons

1. Financial intermediaries specialize in reducing costs by
   a. Pooling the resources of small savers and lending them to large borrowers.
   b. Providing safekeeping, accounting services, and access to the payments system.
   c. Providing liquidity services.
   d. Providing the ability to diversify small investments.
   e. Providing information services.

2. For potential lenders, investigating borrowers' trustworthiness is costly. This problem, known as asymmetric information, occurs both before and after a transaction.
   a. Before a transaction, the least creditworthy borrowers are the ones most likely to apply for funds. This problem is known as adverse selection.
   b. Lenders and investors can reduce adverse selection by
      i. Collecting and disclosing information on borrowers.
      ii. Requiring borrowers to post collateral and show sufficient net worth.
   c. After a transaction, a borrower may not use the borrowed funds as productively as possible. This problem is known as moral hazard.
      i. In equity markets, moral hazard exists when the managers' interests diverge from the owners' interests.

ii. Finding solutions to the moral hazard problem in equity financing is difficult.

iii. In debt markets, moral hazard exists because borrowers have limited liability. They get the benefits when a risky bet pays off, but they don't suffer a loss when it doesn't.

iv. The fact that debt financing gives managers/borrowers an incentive to take too many risks gives rise to restrictive covenants, which require borrowers to use funds in specific ways.

3. Financial intermediaries can manage the problems of adverse selection and moral hazard.
   a. They can reduce adverse selection by collecting information on borrowers and screening them to check their creditworthiness.
   b. They can reduce moral hazard by monitoring what borrowers are doing with borrowed funds.
   c. In the end, the vast majority of firms' finance comes from internal sources, suggesting that information problems are too big for even financial intermediaries to solve.

Conceptual and Analytical Problems

1. Describe the problem of asymmetric information that an employer faces in hiring a new employee. What solutions can you think of? Does the problem persist after the person has been hired? If so, how and what can be done about it? Is the problem more or less severe for employees on a fixed salary? Why or why not? *(LO2)*

2. In some cities, newspapers publish a weekly list of restaurants that have been cited for health code violations by local health inspectors. What information problem is this feature designed to solve, and how? *(LO2)*

3. What problem associated with asymmetric information was central to Bernard Madoff's success in cheating so many investors for so long? *(LO2)*

4. Financial intermediation is not confined to bank lending but is also carried out by nonbank firms such as mutual fund companies. How do mutual funds help overcome information problems in financial markets? *(LO1)*

5. In some countries it is very difficult for shareholders to fire managers when they do a poor job. What type of financing would you expect to find in those countries? *(LO3)*

6. Define the term *economies of scale* and explain how a financial intermediary can take advantage of such economies. *(LO1)*

7. The Internet can have a significant influence on asymmetric information problems. *(LO2)*
   a. How can the Internet help to solve information problems?
   b. Can the Internet compound some information problems?
   c. On which problem would the Internet have a greater impact, adverse selection or moral hazard?

8. The financial sector is heavily regulated. Explain how government regulations help to solve information problems, increasing the effectiveness of financial markets and institutions. *(LO1)*

9. One of the solutions to the adverse selection problem associated with asymmetric information is the pledging of collateral. However, the collateral may be riskier than initially thought. As an example, explain why the collateral did not work adequately to mitigate the mortgage securitization problems associated with the financial crisis of 2007–2009. *(LO3)*

10.* Deflation causes the value of a borrower's collateral to drop. Define deflation and explain how it reduces the value of a borrower's collateral. How might a lender who anticipates deflation alter the terms of a loan? *(LO3)*

11. In 2002 the trustworthiness of corporate financial reporting was called into question when a number of companies corrected their financial statements for past years. What impact did their action have on the financial markets? *(LO3)*

12. You are in charge of setting policies for implementing construction loans at a bank once the loan officer has approved the borrowers' applications. (Construction loans finance the development of a structure during the building process and are later converted to mortgages.) How would you protect your bank's interests? *(LO3)*

13.* Your parents give you $2,000 as a graduation gift and you decide to invest the money in the stock market. If you are risk averse, should you purchase some stock in a few different companies through a website with low transaction fees or put the entire $2,000 into a mutual fund? Explain your answer. *(LO1)*

14. Suppose a new website was launched providing up-to-date, credible information on all firms wishing to issue bonds. What would you expect to happen to the overall level of interest rates in the bond market? *(LO1)*

15. Suppose two types of firms wish to borrow in the bond market. Firms of type A are in good financial health and are relatively low risk. The appropriate premium over the risk-free rate of lending to these firms is 2 percent. Firms of type B are in poor financial health and are relatively high risk. The appropriate premium over the risk-free rate of lending to these firms is 6 percent. As an investor, you have no other information about these firms except that type A and type B firms exist in equal numbers. *(LO2)*
    a. At what interest rate would you be willing to lend if the risk-free rate were 5 percent?
    b. Would this market function well? What type of asymmetric information problem does this example illustrate?

16. Consider again the low-risk type A firm described in Problem 15. If you were the financial advisor to such a firm, what suggestions would you make to the firm's management about obtaining borrowed funds? *(LO3)*

17. Consider a small company run by a manager who is also the owner. If this company borrows funds, why might a moral hazard problem still exist? *(LO3)*

18.* The island of Utopia has a very unusual economy. Everyone on Utopia knows everyone else and knows all about the firms they own and operate. The financial system is well developed on Utopia. Everything else being equal, how would you expect the mix on Utopia between internal finance (where companies use their own funds such as retained earnings) and external funding (where companies obtain funds through financial markets) to compare with other countries? What role would financial intermediaries play in this economy? *(LO1)*

*Indicates more difficult problems

19. You and a friend visit the headquarters of a company and are awestruck by the expensive artwork and designer furniture that grace every office. Your friend is very impressed and encourages you to consider buying stock in the company, arguing that it must be really successful to afford such elegant surroundings. Would you agree with your friend's assessment? What further information (other than the usual financial data) would you obtain before making an investment decision? *(LO3)*

20. Under what circumstances, if any, would you be willing to participate as a lender in a peer-to-peer lending arrangement? *(LO1)*

Data Exploration

For general information on using Federal Reserve Economic Data (FRED) online, visit www.mhhe.com/moneyandbanking4e and click on Student Edition, then FRED Resources.

Scan here for quick access to the resources for these problems. Need a barcode reader? Try ScanLife, available in your app store.

1. Financial intermediaries connect savers and borrowers. Examine growth in intermediation from the following perspectives. *(LO1)*
   a. Plot the ratio of total credit market debt owed (FRED code: TCMDO) to population (FRED code: POP). (*Hint:* Because credit market debt is expressed in billions and population in thousands, multiply TCMDO by 1 million to correct for the difference in units.) Interpret the plot.
   b. Plot the ratio of total credit market debt to nominal GDP. Interpret the plot.
   c. Plot the ratio to nominal GDP of the value added by financial corporate business (FRED code: A454RC1Q027SBEA). Interpret the plot since 2005.

2. How has the use of credit evolved in key sectors of the economy? Plot as ratios to total credit market debt outstanding (FRED code: TCMDO) the debt of (a) households (FRED code: HSTCMDODNS), (b) nonfinancial corporate businesses (FRED code: NCBTCMDODNS), and (c) the domestic financial sector (FRED code: TCMDODFS). Compared with the prior two decades, account for the pattern of debt in the household sector since 2000. What do the downturns during the financial crisis in the household and financial sector ratios mean in terms of leverage? What important sector is omitted from this plot? *(LO1)*

3. Financial crisis is often associated with rising, and then persistently high, unemployment rates. Plot the U.S. unemployment rate during the Great Depression until the end of the 1930s (FRED code: M0892AUSM156SNBR). Compare the U.S. experience then with unemployment rates in Spain (FRED code: ESPURHARMQDSMEI), Greece (FRED code: GRCURHARMQDSMEI), Italy (FRED code: ITAURHARMMDSMEI), and Portugal (FRED code: PRTURHARMMDSMEI) since the beginning of the financial crisis in 2007. (Turn off the recession bars for the European data plot.) *(LO3)*

4. The rise of securities markets and the expansion of intermediation by nonbanks has come partly at the expense of commercial banks. Plot the ratio of bank credit (FRED code: TOTLL) to total credit market debt outstanding (FRED code: TCMDO), and comment on the trend. *(LO1)*

5. Deflation raises the real burden of repaying fixed-rate debt. Japan has recently experienced a long deflation. *(LO3)*

   a. Plot the percent change from a year ago of consumer prices in Japan (FRED code: JPNCPIALLQINMEI), and discuss the long-term patterns of inflation and deflation. (Turn off the recession bars.)

   b. Plot on a new graph the percent change from a year ago of the GDP deflator in Japan (FRED code: JPNGDPDEFQISMEI). How does it compare with the post-1994 evolution of consumer prices? (Turn off the recession bars.) *(Hint: The GDP deflator is a price index for* all *final goods and services produced domestically. It is a broader measure than the price index for goods and services consumed by households in part a.)*

   c. Why might deflation become self-perpetuating?

Further Data Exploration. If you wish to learn more about how the channels of financing vary across countries, take a look at the World Bank's Global Financial Development Database (GFDD) (http://data.worldbank.org/data-catalog/global-financial-development). The GFDD can be used online or downloaded in an Excel spreadsheet. It includes annual data from 1960 for more than 200 countries. Relevant data for Chapter 11 include private credit from intermediaries (GFDD.DI.12), stock market capitalization (GFDD.DM.01), and private debt securities (GFDD.DM.03), all measured as a share of nominal GDP. These data are displayed for a few countries in Table 11.1. The GFDD includes many other indicators of financial depth, access, efficiency, and stability. All GFDD indicators are also available through FRED.

Chapter 12

Depository Institutions: Banks and Bank Management

Banks are the most visible financial intermediaries in the economy. Most of us use the word *bank* to describe what people in the financial world call **depository institutions**. These are the financial institutions that accept deposits from savers and make loans to borrowers. What distinguishes depository institutions from **nondepository institutions** is their primary source of funds—that is, the liability side of their balance sheets. Depository institutions include commercial banks, savings and loans, and credit unions—the financial intermediaries most of us encounter in the course of our day-to-day lives.

Banking is a business. Actually, it's a combination of businesses designed to deliver the services discussed in Chapter 11. One business provides the accounting and record-keeping services that track the balances in your accounts. Another grants you access to the payments system, allowing you to convert your account balances into cash or transfer them to someone else. Yet a third business pools the savings of many small depositors and uses them to make large loans to trustworthy borrowers. A fourth business offers customers diversification services, buying and selling financial instruments in the financial markets in an effort to make a profit. Banks trade in the financial markets not just as a service to their customers but in an effort to earn a profit for their owners as well.

The intent of banks, of course, is to profit from each of these lines of business. Our objective in this chapter is to see how they do it. Not all banks make a profit. While some banks are extremely large, with hundreds of billions of dollars in loans and securities on their balance sheets, their access to funds is no guarantee of profitability. The risk that banks may fail is a problem not just for their owners and managers but for the rest of us, too. In the four years from 2009 to 2012, more than 400 U.S. banks failed outright, and others were pushed into mergers, reflecting the most severe financial crisis since the 1930s.

We have emphasized repeatedly that financial and economic development go hand in hand. An economy that lacks the financial institutions to effectively channel resources from savers to investors is much less likely to thrive. This statement applies regardless of whether a country is rich or poor. The United States and Japan provide a striking example. By virtually any standard, both countries are well off. Yet during the 1990s, U.S. banks made substantial profits, while Japanese banks suffered prodigious losses. At the same time, Japan's economy grew at a rate of just over 1 percent, while the U.S. economy grew at a rate well over 3 percent. The financial problems of Japanese banks played an important role in Japan's poor economic performance. Banks are important; when they are poorly managed, we all suffer. Similarly, the damage to U.S. banks in the crisis of 2007–2009 helped make the U.S. recovery that began in 2009 the weakest since the Great Depression.

In this chapter, we will examine the business of banking. We will see where depository institutions get their funds and what they do with them. That is, we will study the sources of banks' liabilities and learn how they manage their assets. And because banking is a risky business, we will examine the sources of risk that bankers face, as well as how those risks can be managed.

The Balance Sheet of Commercial Banks

To focus our discussion of depository institutions, we will concentrate on what are called *commercial banks.* These institutions were established to provide banking services to businesses, allowing them to deposit funds safely and borrow them when necessary. Today, many commercial banks offer accounts and loans to individuals as well. To understand the business of commercial banking, we'll start by examining the commercial bank's balance sheet. Recall that a balance sheet is a list of a household or firm's assets and liabilities: the sources of its funds (liabilities) and the uses to which those funds are put (assets). A bank's balance sheet says that

$$\text{Total bank assets} = \text{Total bank liabilities} + \text{Bank capital} \qquad (1)$$

Banks obtain their funds from individual depositors and businesses, as well as by borrowing from other financial institutions and through the financial markets. They use these funds to make loans, purchase marketable securities, and hold cash. The difference between a bank's assets and liabilities is the bank's capital, or *net worth*—the value of the bank to its owners. The bank's profits come both from service fees and from the difference between what the bank pays for its liabilities and the return it receives on its assets (a topic we'll return to later).

Table 12.1 shows a consolidated balance sheet for all the commercial banks in the United States in January 2013. It reports the sum of all the items on all the balance sheets of the 6,100 or so commercial banks that existed in the United States at the time. The government collects these statistics in the course of supervising and regulating the financial system, to ensure bank safety and soundness. The numbers in the table are also related to the measures of money discussed in Chapter 2. Recall that the monetary aggregate M2 includes deposits, which are liabilities of the banking system.

Assets: Uses of Funds

Let's start with the asset side of the balance sheet—what banks do with the funds they raise. Table 12.1 shows that assets are divided into four broad categories: cash, securities, loans, and all other assets. Roughly 21 percent of assets, or $2.7 trillion, is held in the form of securities; 55 percent ($7.2 trillion), in the form of loans; and the remaining 24 percent in the form of cash and *"other assets."* The last category includes mostly buildings and equipment, as well as collateral repossessed from borrowers who

Table 12.1   Balance Sheet of U.S. Commercial Banks, January 2013

Assets in billions of dollars (numbers with % sign are percentages of total assets)

Cash items			1714.3	13.1%
Securities*			2740.2	20.9%
U.S. government and agency	1869.8	14.3%		
Other securities	870.3	6.6%		
Loans			7199.4	55.0%
Commercial and industrial	1517.1	11.6%		
Real estate (including mortgage)	3554.2	27.1%		
Consumer	1111.9	8.5%		
Interbank	127.1	1.0%		
Other (including loss allowance)	889.1	6.8%		
Other assets (including trading allowance)			1447.7	11.0%
Total Commercial Bank Assets			**13101.6**	

Liabilities in billions of dollars (numbers with % sign are percentages of total liabilities)

Deposits			9262.0	79.5%
Large time deposits	1542.1	13.2%		
Borrowings			1565.0	13.4%
From banks in the U.S.	148.6	1.3%		
From others	1416.3	12.2%		
Other liabilities			822.4	7.1%
Total Commercial Bank Liabilities			**11649.4**	
Bank Assets − Bank Liabilities = Bank Capital			**1452.2**	

*Securities include mortgage-backed securities worth $1,343.9 billion, equivalent to 10.3% of assets.

SOURCE: *Data are for the week ending January 23, 2013, seasonally adjusted, from Board of Governors of the Federal Reserve System statistical release H.8. "Assets and Liabilities of Commercial Banks in the United States," available at www.federalreserve.gov/releases/h8/current.*

defaulted. In looking at consolidated figures like the ones in Table 12.1, we can get some sense of their scale by comparing them to *nominal GDP.* In the first quarter of 2013, U.S. nominal GDP was roughly $16.5 trillion, so total bank assets were equivalent to nearly 80 percent of one year's GDP.

Cash Items   Cash assets are of three types. The first and most important is **reserves**. Banks hold reserves because regulations require it and because prudent business practice dictates it. Reserves include the cash in the bank's vault (and the currency in its ATM machines), called **vault cash**, as well as the bank's deposits at the Federal Reserve System. Cash is the most liquid of the bank's assets; the bank holds it to meet customers' withdrawal requests.

Cash items also include what are called *cash items in process of collection.* When you deposit your paycheck into your checking account, several days may pass before your

Figure 12.1 U.S. Commercial Bank Assets, 1973–2012

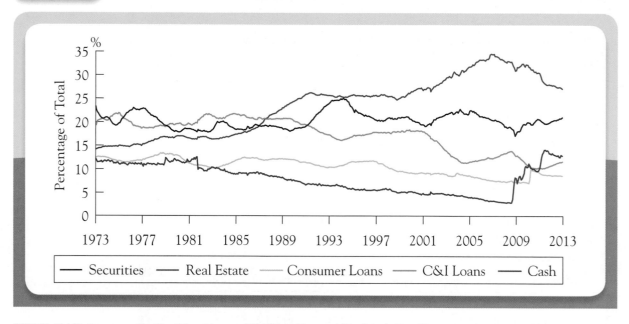

SOURCE: *Monthly data, seasonally adjusted from "Assets and Liabilities of Commercial Banks in the United States," Board of Governors of the Federal Reserve System Statistical Release H.8.* (FRED data codes: INVEST, REALLN, CONSUMER, BUSLOANS, CASACBM027SBOG, and TLAACBM027SBOG).

bank can collect the funds from your employer's bank. In the meantime, the uncollected funds are considered your bank's asset because the bank is expecting to receive them.

Finally, cash includes the balances of the accounts that banks hold at other banks. In the same way that individuals have checking accounts at the local bank, small banks have deposit accounts at large banks, and those accounts are classified as cash. Over the years, the practice of holding such accounts has declined, so the total quantity of these *correspondent bank* deposits has shrunk.

In January 2013, banks held more than 13 percent of their assets in cash (see Table 12.1). Up to the financial crisis of 2007–2009, that share was much smaller (in early 2007, it was about 3 percent; see Figure 12.1). Banks usually try to minimize their cash holdings because they typically earn less interest than loans or securities. However, the crisis forced them to change their strategy: A heightened possibility of bank runs, credit line takedowns, and borrower defaults prompted them to scramble for liquidity, and as market interest rates fell and the Federal Reserve began to pay interest on reserves, the opportunity cost of holding cash plummeted.

Securities The second largest component of bank assets is marketable securities. While banks in many countries can hold stock, U.S. banks cannot, so this category of assets includes only bonds. Banks' bond holdings are split between U.S. government and agency securities, which account for 14.3 percent of their assets, and other securities (including state and local government bonds), which account for an additional 6.6 percent.[1]

[1]While there is nothing to prevent banks from holding corporate bonds, regulatory rules make the practice expensive. In Chapter 14, we will learn that banks are required to hold capital based on the composition of their balance sheets. The amount of capital required to extend a loan to a corporation is the same as the amount required to purchase a corporate bond. But because interest rates banks can charge on loans are generally higher than interest rates on corporate bonds, there is no price incentive to purchase a bond.

Note that about half of all the securities are mortgage-backed (10.3 percent of assets). Nevertheless, a sizable proportion of the securities held by banks are very liquid. They can be sold quickly if the bank needs cash, which makes them a good backup for the bank's cash balances. For this reason securities are sometimes referred to as *secondary reserves.*

Figure 12.1 shows the trends in the composition of bank assets over the past four decades. Focusing on the line representing securities, we can see that the share of securities in bank assets has varied around 20 percent throughout the period.

Loans   Loans are the primary asset of modern commercial banks, accounting for well over one-half of assets. We can divide loans into five broad categories: business loans, called commercial and industrial (C&I) loans; real estate loans, including both home and commercial mortgages as well as home equity loans; consumer loans, like auto loans and credit card loans; interbank loans (loans made from one bank to another); and other types, including loans for the purchase of other securities. These types of loans vary considerably in their liquidity. Some, like home mortgages and auto loans, usually can be securitized and resold. (We discussed this process in Chapter 3, in connection with asset-backed securities.) Others, like small business loans, may be very difficult to resell.

The primary difference among various kinds of depository institutions is in the composition of their loan portfolios. Commercial banks make loans primarily to businesses; savings and loans provide mortgages to individuals; credit unions specialize in consumer loans. See the Tools of the Trade box on page 304 for a more detailed description of the various types of depository institutions.

Figure 12.1 shows that, prior to the crisis of 2007–2009, commercial banks became more and more involved in the real estate business. Their involvement grew for a number of reasons. First, the rise of the commercial paper market made securities market debt finance more convenient for large firms, which reduced the quantity of commercial and industrial loans demanded. (Commercial paper is described in Chapter 7.) Second, the creation of mortgage-backed securities meant that banks could sell the mortgage loans they had made. This innovation reduced the risk associated with an illiquid asset, encouraging banks to move into the business of home lending. So, on top of making more real estate loans, banks also acquired mortgage-backed securities (MBS), which recently accounted for about one-half of securities held (see Table 12.1). Since the crisis, however, banks appear to have reduced their overall real estate exposure, underscoring the critical role that housing prices and MBS played in the 2007–2009 episode (see Lessons from the Crisis: Information Asymmetry and Securitization in Chapter 11).

Liabilities: Sources of Funds

To finance their operations, banks need funds. They get them from savers and from borrowing in the financial markets. To entice individuals and businesses to place their funds in the bank, institutions offer a range of deposit accounts that provide safekeeping and accounting services, access to the payments system, liquidity, and diversification of risk (see Chapter 11), as well as interest payments on the balance. There are two types of deposit accounts, transaction and nontransaction accounts. Transaction accounts are known as checkable deposits. As of January 2013, checkable deposits totaled $1.36 trillion, or nearly 15 percent of total deposits in the commercial banking system.

Checkable Deposits   "Demand deposits," which allow a customer to withdraw funds without notice on a first-come, first-served basis, make up the largest component

YOUR FINANCIAL WORLD
Choosing the Right Bank for You

Choosing the right bank takes some work. First, you should decide exactly why you need a bank and whether a particular bank will serve your needs conveniently and cheaply. Shop around for the best deal. Make sure the bank will pay a competitive interest rate on your deposit balance and you won't be paying for services you don't use. You may want to make sure the bank will give you immediate access to your deposits. The ability to reach someone either in person or on the phone during hours that are convenient for you is also important. And be sure the bank has a reputation for courteous, efficient service. Because service isn't cheap, ask what it will cost you. Will you have to pay a fee to see a teller in person? Will you have to pay a fee to cash a check? If you have friends with needs similar to yours, find out where they bank and ask whether they're happy with the cost and service.

The Internet has revolutionized banking. Traditional "bricks and mortar" banks now provide many of their services on the Internet. Using your smartphone or computer,

you can access your account, review and pay your bills, or transfer funds. In fact, when you decide to open a bank account, you may be tempted to give your business to an Internet bank—one without any local branches. If you do, be careful. Looking at your computer screen, you may not be able to tell where the website you are viewing is physically located. While many people think the irrelevance of physical location is a real benefit of the Internet, in making financial transactions, it presents a challenge. Unfortunately, U.S. laws and regulations may not protect transactions with institutions located outside the United States. Instead, the laws and regulations of a foreign bank's home country may apply. So if you choose an Internet bank, make sure that its operations are located in the United States. The easiest way to find out is to verify that the bank is a member of the *Federal Deposit Insurance Corporation (FDIC)*. You can check by going to http://research.fdic.gov/bankfind. If a bank is listed there, it is a legitimate U.S. bank, and your deposits will be insured.

of checkable deposits. Banks also offer customers a variety of similar options that fall into the category of checking accounts, such as insured market rate accounts. A typical bank will offer half a dozen or more of these, each with slightly different characteristics. In addition to the names created by banks' marketing departments, economists use various other terms in speaking of checkable deposits. For example, some economists call them "sight deposits" because a depositor can show up to withdraw them when the bank is in sight.

Over the years, financial innovation has reduced the importance of checkable deposits in the day-to-day business of banking. As a share of total liabilities, checkable deposits plummeted from 40 percent in the 1970s to less than 15 percent in early 2013. The reason for their decline is that checking accounts pay little or no interest; they are a low-cost source of funds for banks but a low-return investment for depositors. As interest rates rose through the 1970s and remained high into the 1990s, individuals and businesses realized the benefits of reducing the balances in their checking accounts and began to look for ways to earn higher interest rates. Banks obliged by offering innovative accounts whose balances could be shifted automatically when the customers' checking accounts ran low.[2] Thus, traditional checking accounts are no longer the principal source of bank funds.

Nontransaction Deposits
In January 2013, nontransaction deposits, including savings and time deposits, accounted for more than half of all commercial bank

---

[2]This is also related to a practice called *deposit sweeping,* in which banks take checking account balances and put them into savings deposits, thereby reducing the level of reserves they are required to hold. Over recent decades, deposit sweeping has lowered required reserves even as the monetary aggregates have risen markedly.

liabilities. Savings deposits, commonly known as *passbook savings* accounts, were popular for many decades, though they are less so today. Time deposits are *certificates of deposit* (CDs) with a fixed maturity. When you place your savings in a CD at your local bank, it is as if you are buying a bond issued by that bank. But unlike government or corporate bonds, there isn't much of a resale market for your small CD. So if you want to withdraw your funds before the CD matures, you must get them back from the bank. To discourage early withdrawals, banks charge a significant penalty.

Certificates of deposit come in two varieties: small and large. Small CDs are issued for $100,000 or less; *large certificates of deposit* exceed $100,000 in face value. Large CDs are negotiable, which means that they can be bought and sold in the financial markets, just like bonds and commercial paper. Investors in this *wholesale money market* include corporate treasurers and others with large cash balances to manage. Because large CDs can be resold, they have become an important source of bank financing. When a bank needs funds, it can issue large CDs, in addition to commercial paper and more conventional bonds.

Borrowings   Borrowing is the second most important source of bank funds. Figure 12.2 shows that borrowing grew increasingly important over the past four decades, until the financial crisis of 2007–2009 triggered greater bank caution. Today, borrowings account for somewhat less than 15 percent of bank liabilities. Banks borrow in a number of ways. First, they can borrow from the Federal Reserve. We'll have much more to say about such **discount loans** in Part IV. For now, think of this source of funds as borrowing from the government.

Figure 12.2   U.S. Commercial Bank Liabilities, 1979–2012

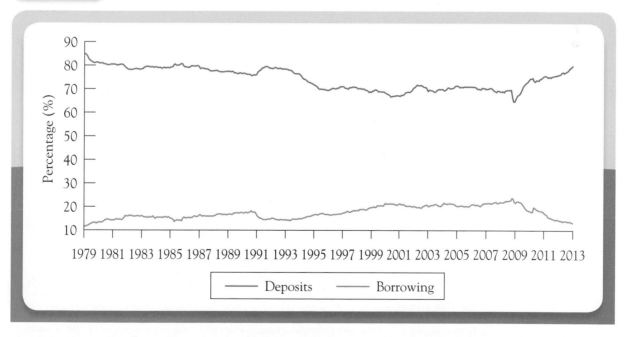

SOURCE: *Monthly data, seasonally adjusted from "Assets and Liabilities of Commercial Banks in the United States," Board of Governors of the Federal Reserve System Statistical Release H.8.* (FRED data codes: DPSACBM027SBOG, BOWACBM027SBOG, and TLBACBM027SBOG).

More often, banks borrow from other banks. That is, banks with **excess reserves** will lend their surplus funds to banks that need them through an interbank market called the **federal funds market**. Loans made in the federal funds market are unsecured—they lack collateral—so the lending bank must trust the borrowing bank. Look back at the balance sheet in Table 12.1; you will see interbank loans listed as an asset and borrowings from banks in the United States listed as a liability.[3] Besides borrowing from U.S. banks in the federal funds market, commercial banks also borrow from foreign banks.

Finally, banks borrow using an instrument called a **repurchase agreement**, or **repo**, a short-term collateralized loan in which a security is exchanged for cash, with the agreement that the parties will reverse the transaction on a specific future date, typically the next day. For example, a bank that has a U.S. Treasury bill might need cash, while a pension fund might have cash that it doesn't need overnight. Through a repo, the bank would give the T-bill to the pension fund in exchange for cash, agreeing to buy it back—repurchase it—with interest the next day. In short, the bank gets an overnight loan and the pension fund gets some extra interest, along with the protection provided by collateral. The details are shown in Figure 12.3.

Figure 12.3   Mechanics of an Overnight Repurchase Agreement

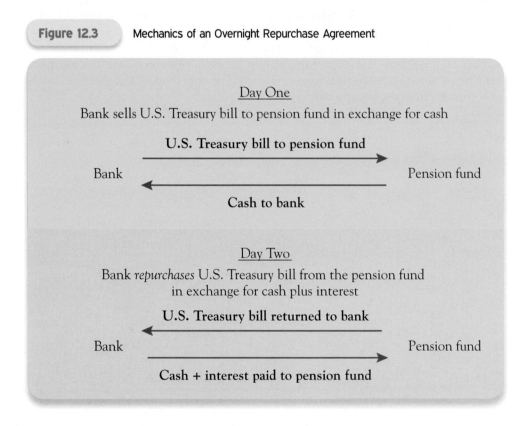

[3]An astute reader will notice that the amount of "Interbank loans" on the asset side of the balance sheet does not match the amount for "Borrowings from Banks in the U.S." on the liability side of the balance sheet. In fact, the two amounts differ by more than $20 billion. If the data in the table cover the entire banking system, shouldn't loans to banks (assets) equal borrowings from banks (liabilities)? There are two reasons why the amounts do not match. First, the data in the table are constructed from a survey that covers all large banks but only a minority of small banks. Large banks tend to be borrowers, while small banks tend to be lenders. The way in which the data are collected, then, distorts the comparison. Second, small banks may report their lending to large banks as deposits rather than as interbank loans. For both these reasons, the entry on the liability side of Table 12.1 is larger than the corresponding entry on the asset side.

Bank Capital and Profitability

Net worth equals assets minus liabilities, whether we are talking about an individual's net worth or a bank's. In the case of banks, however, net worth is referred to as **bank capital**, or *equity capital*. (Important tip: Do not confuse bank capital and cash reserves. Capital appears on the liability side of the balance sheet, whereas reserves are an asset.) If the bank's owners sold all its assets (without taking a loss) and used the proceeds to repay all the liabilities, capital is what would be left. We can think of capital as the owners' stake in the bank.

Capital is the cushion banks have against a sudden drop in the value of their assets or an unexpected withdrawal of liabilities. It provides some insurance against insolvency (the inability to repay debts when a firm's liabilities exceed its assets). An important component of bank capital is **loan loss reserves**, an amount the bank sets aside to cover potential losses from defaulted loans. At some point a bank gives up hope that a loan will be repaid and the loan is *written off*, or erased from the bank's balance sheet. At that point the loan loss reserve is reduced by the amount of the loan that has defaulted.

Looking once again at the balance sheet in Table 12.1 (page 297), we can see that in January of 2013, bank capital in the U.S. commercial banking system totaled nearly $1.5 trillion. That nearly $1.5 trillion of capital was combined with $11.6 trillion worth of liabilities to purchase $13.1 trillion in assets. So the ratio of debt to equity in the U.S. banking system was about 8 to 1. That's a substantial amount of leverage, but it is nearly 25 percent below the average commercial bank debt-to-equity ratio that prevailed prior to the financial crisis of 2007–2009. As we saw in Chapter 3, Lessons from the Crisis: Leverage, the crisis compelled banks to reduce their leverage sharply. (Recall that the term *leverage* refers to the portion of an asset that is purchased using borrowed funds.)

To put this ratio of 8 to 1 into perspective, we can compare it to the debt-to-equity ratio for nonfinancial businesses in the United States, which is less than 1 to 1. Household leverage is much lower, roughly ⅓ to 1.[4] Recall from Tools of the Trade in Chapter 5 that leverage increases both risk and expected return. If you contribute half the purchase price of a house and borrow the other half, both your risk and your expected return double. If you contribute one-fifth of the purchase price and borrow the other four-fifths, your risk and expected return go up by a factor of 5 (see the Tools of the Trade box in Chapter 5). So if a bank borrows $8 for each $1 in capital, its risk and expected return increase a whopping 9 times! Banking, it seems, is a very risky business. As we will see in Chapter 14, one of the explanations for the relatively high degree of leverage in banking is the existence of government guarantees like deposit insurance, which allow banks to capture the benefits of risk taking without subjecting depositors to potential losses.

There are several basic measures of bank profitability. The first is called **return on assets (ROA)**. Return on assets equals a bank's net profit after taxes divided by the bank's total assets:

$$ROA = \frac{\text{Net profit after taxes}}{\text{Total bank assets}} \qquad (2)$$

---

[4]You can arrive at these figures yourself by looking at the *Flow of Funds Accounts of the United States,* which is computed by the Board of Governors of the Federal Reserve (see its website). The appropriate tables are L.100 for households and L.102 for nonfarm nonfinancial corporate business; both include assets, liabilities, and net worth for their parts of the U.S. economy.

TOOLS OF THE TRADE
A Catalog of Depository Institutions

While the financial landscape is constantly shifting, it is safe to assume that depository institutions will be with us for some time. These are the financial intermediaries for whom deposits are the primary source of funds. There are three basic types of depository institution: commercial banks, savings institutions, and credit unions.

Commercial Banks

A commercial bank is an institution that accepts deposits and uses the proceeds to make consumer, commercial, and real estate loans. Originally established to meet the needs of businesses, many of these banks now serve individual customers as well. Commercial banks tend to specialize as community, regional and super-regional, or money center banks. As a result of mergers during the crisis of 2007–2009, roughly 40 percent of U.S. commercial bank deposits are in four institutions (ranked in order of deposits): Bank of America, Wells Fargo, JPMorgan Chase, and Citigroup.

Community Banks

Community banks are small banks—those with assets of less than $1 billion—that concentrate on serving consumers and small businesses. These are the banks that take deposits from people in the local area and lend them back to local businesses and consumers. Of the 7,100 banks and savings institutions in the United States at the end of 2012, more than 90 percent were community banks.

Regional and Super-Regional Banks

Regional and super-regional banks are larger than community banks and much less local. Besides consumer and residential loans, these banks also make commercial and industrial loans. Regional banks obtain their funds through borrowing as well as from deposits. These banks can be very large. When the largest regional bank, Wachovia, faced a bank run in 2008, it was taken over by Wells Fargo.

Money Center Banks

A few large banks—only five or six—do not rely primarily on deposit financing. These banks rely instead on borrowing for their funding. They stand at the center of the *wholesale money market*, the market for short-term debt. Citigroup and JPMorgan Chase are two examples. (Recall from Chapter 3 that money-market instruments are bonds with a maturity of less than 12 months.)

Savings Institutions

Savings institutions are financial intermediaries that were established to serve households and individuals. They provide both mortgage and lending services and a place for households to deposit their savings. There are two types of savings institutions, S&Ls and savings banks.

Savings and Loan Institutions

Savings and loan institutions (S&Ls) were established in the 1800s to help factory workers become homeowners. They accepted workers' savings deposits and used the funds to make loans to homebuyers, most of whom were not served by traditional banks. These institutions traditionally specialized in taking short-term deposits and turning them into residential mortgages. The S&Ls that still exist today engage in a much broader range of financial activities.

Savings Banks

Most savings banks are mutually owned. That is, the depositors are also the legal owners. These institutions specialize in residential mortgages that are funded by deposits. They are permitted to exist only in certain states. When the largest savings bank, Washington Mutual, failed during the crisis of 2007–2009, JPMorgan Chase acquired its deposits.

Credit Unions

Credit unions are nonprofit depository institutions that are owned by people with a common bond—members of police associations, union members, and university students and employees. Credit unions specialize in making small consumer loans. They originated in the 19th century to meet the needs of people who could not borrow from traditional lenders. Before credit unions existed, many ordinary people had nowhere to turn when they faced unexpected home repairs or medical emergencies.

Not all these depository institutions are likely to survive the financial innovations and economic upheaval of the coming decades. Commercial banks will likely remain with us, but savings institutions have already declined in importance and are at risk of disappearing altogether due to changes in the mortgage business. Whether credit unions remain viable will depend on their continuing ability to exploit their advantage in verifying members' creditworthiness.

ROA is an important measure of how efficiently a particular bank uses its assets. By looking at the different units' ROAs, for example, the manager of a large bank can also compare the performance of the bank's various lines of business. But for the bank's owners, return on assets is less important than the return on their own investment, which is leveraged at an average ratio of 9 to 1. (The leverage ratio equals total assets divided by bank capital. It also equals the debt-to-equity ratio plus 1.) The bank's return to its owners is measured by the **return on equity (ROE)**, which equals the bank's net profit after taxes divided by the bank's capital:

$$ROE = \frac{\text{Net profit after taxes}}{\text{Bank capital}} \tag{3}$$

Not surprisingly, ROA and ROE are related to leverage. One measure of leverage is the ratio of bank assets to bank capital. Multiplying ROA by this ratio yields ROE:

$$ROA \times \frac{\text{Bank assets}}{\text{Bank capital}} = \frac{\text{Net profit after taxes}}{\text{Total bank assets}} \times \frac{\text{Bank assets}}{\text{Bank capital}} \tag{4}$$

$$= \frac{\text{Net profit after taxes}}{\text{Bank capital}} = ROE$$

For a typical U.S. bank, prior to the financial crisis of 2007–2009, the return on assets was about 1.3 percent, while the return on equity was 10 to 12 times that high. For large banks, the return on equity tends to be higher than for small banks, which suggests greater leverage, a riskier mix of assets, or the existence of significant economies of scale in banking. The poor performance of many large banks in the crisis, combined with moderate returns in its aftermath, suggests that their pre-crisis higher returns (compared to small banks) at least partly reflected more leverage or a riskier asset mix. Nevertheless, recent research also points to sizable economies of scale for banks with assets exceeding $100 billion.[5]

Before continuing, it is important to introduce one more measure of bank profitability: net interest income. This measure is related to the fact that banks pay interest on their liabilities, creating interest expenses, and receive interest on their assets, creating interest income. Deposits and bank borrowing create interest expenses; securities and loans generate interest income. The difference between the two is the bank's *net interest income*.

Net interest income can also be expressed as a percentage of total assets to yield a quantity called **net interest margin**. This is the bank's **interest-rate spread**, which is the (weighted) average difference between the interest rate received on assets and the interest rate paid for liabilities. A bank's net interest margin is closely related to its return on assets. Just take the bank's fee income minus its operating costs, divide by total assets, add the result to the net interest margin, and you get its ROA. Roughly equivalent to a manufacturer or retailer's gross profits and gross profit margin, net interest income and net interest margin reveal a great deal about a bank's business.

Well-run banks have high net interest income and a high net interest margin. And because we would expect most of a bank's loans to be repaid, net interest margin tells us not just current profitability but future profitability as well; it is a forward-looking measure. If a bank's net interest margin is currently improving, its profitability is likely to improve in the future.

[5]See John P. Hughes and Loretta Mester, "Who Said Large Banks Don't Experience Scale Economies? Evidence from a Risk-Return-Driven Cost Function," Federal Reserve Bank of Philadelphia Working Paper No. 11-27, 2011.

APPLYING THE CONCEPT
GROWTH AND BANKING IN CHINA AND INDIA

China and India are experiencing phenomenal economic growth rates of 7 to 11 percent per year. As high as that is, some people think growth could be even higher if the banks in the two countries worked properly. Let's look to see why.

While the Chinese financial system is large overall, banks account for a disproportionate share of intermediation there. In 2004, 75 percent of all China's capital—190 percent of GDP—was channeled through banks.* That's twice the amount in South Korea, relative to its GDP, and three times what goes through Chile's banking system. This heavy reliance on banks for financing is a sign of inadequate financial development. The solution is to encourage the development of debt and equity markets, with broad participation by small savers.

In addition to accounting for too large a proportion of China's financial system, Chinese banks are directing resources inefficiently. State-owned enterprises that account for around 35 percent of China's GDP receive a much larger share of the credit. That is, banks are directing funds to government-favored firms. This fact should not be all that surprising given that the government implicitly backs loans made to the companies it owns. Improvement will require both that the government stop providing the guarantees

(probably by selling the companies) and that banks learn to evaluate the creditworthiness of borrowers.

Turning to India, instead of attracting too many deposits, there banks attract too few. Overall, the Indian financial system is 1.4 times the country's GDP, half that in China, and banks attract deposits equal to only 60 percent of GDP. The problem is that the Indian people mistrust banks, holding more than half of their wealth in physical assets such as land, houses, cattle, and especially gold. Solving this problem requires finding a way to lure savers to make deposits in banks.

While private Indian firms have more access to bank financing than their Chinese counterparts, it could be better. First, Indian banks need to stop holding so many Indian government bonds—they are holding an amount equal to 46 percent of deposits. And second, the government has to stop directing banks to make at least 40 percent of loans to small borrowers in favored sectors. Reforms are needed to free banks to lend where the resources can be best used.

If Chinese and Indian banks are given the proper incentives to direct financial resources to their most economically efficient uses, it will enhance living standards in those two countries. Without a well-functioning financial system, growth will not be as high as it could be.

*These estimates, along with the information that follows, are from the McKinsey Global Institute, "Putting China's Capital to Work: The Value of Financial System Reform," May 2006; and Diana Farrell and Susan Lund, "Reforming India's Financial System," *The McKinsey Quarterly Report*, June 5, 2006.

Off-Balance-Sheet Activities

A financial firm's balance sheet provides only so much information. To generate fees, banks engage in numerous **off-balance-sheet activities**. Recall that banks exist to reduce transactions costs and information costs as well as to transfer risks. When they perform these services, bankers expect to be compensated. Yet many of these activities do not appear as either assets or liabilities on the bank's balance sheet, even though they may represent an important part of a bank's profits.

For example, banks often provide trusted customers with lines of credit, which are similar to the credit limits on credit cards. The firm pays the bank a fee in return for the ability to borrow whenever necessary. When the agreement is signed, the bank receives the payment and the firm receives a *loan commitment*. However, not until a loan has actually been made—until the firm has *drawn down* the credit line—does the transaction appear on the bank's balance sheet.

In the meantime, the bank is compensated for reducing both transactions and information costs. Without the loan commitment, the firm would find credit difficult and potentially expensive to obtain on short notice (a transactions cost). And because the bank usually knows the firms to which it grants lines of credit, the cost of establishing their creditworthiness (an information cost) is negligible.

INFORMATION

Letters of credit are another important off-balance-sheet item for banks. These letters guarantee that a customer of the bank will be able to make a promised payment. For example, a U.S. importer of television sets may need to reassure a Chinese

YOUR FINANCIAL WORLD

The Cost of Payday Loans

If you drive through the streets of most U.S. cities, you will eventually pass a store with a sign saying "Checks Cashed." These financial intermediaries provide loans to people who cannot borrow from mainstream financial institutions such as banks. In addition to their check-cashing business—they charge about 3 percent to cash a payroll or government check, more if the bearer can't produce acceptable identification—these firms offer small loans.

The most common type of loan these stores offer is a *payday loan.* To get one, you just walk into the store with an ID card, a utility or phone bill, a checkbook, and some pay stubs; you come out with cash. Why do you need all these documents? The utility bill proves where you live; the pay stubs establish that you are employed, how much you make, and when you are paid. You need the checkbook so you can write a check that the store will hold until your next payday, when it will send your check to the bank. With just these few requirements, the store will lend you up to $500 for the week or two weeks until you are paid.

The catch is that there is a fee, and it's huge. Payday lenders charge a fee equal to 15 percent of the loan's principal. So if you borrow $500, you will have to repay a minimum of $575. That's the size of the check you will need to

write to get the loan. To understand what this arrangement can mean, suppose that you need to renew the loan on your next payday, so you don't want the lender to cash the check you gave him or her initially. To do this, you will have to pay the fee again. So you keep the loan for a year, paying $75 every two weeks to stay current. At the end of the year you will have paid $1,950 in "interest" (the lender calls it "fees") on a $500 loan. And you'll still owe the original $500!

Not surprisingly, at these interest rates, payday loans appeal only to people who can't get credit anywhere else. While data are hard to come by, it appears that well over half of payday borrowers fail to repay their loans, which explains the high fees.

Laws are changing in states and at the federal level to rein in payday lending practices. In 2010, for example, the Dodd-Frank Act (discussed in Chapter 14) created the Consumer Financial Protection Bureau (CFPB) and explicitly included payday lending within its supervisory mandate. The CFPB now monitors payday lending to prevent consumer harm. Its challenge will be to do so without blocking the flow of credit to those able to manage it. For further information, visit the CFPB website at www.consumerfinance.gov.

---

exporter that the firm will be able to pay for the imported goods when they arrive. This customer might request that the bank send a *commercial letter of credit* to the Chinese exporter guaranteeing payment for the goods on receipt. By issuing the letter of credit, the bank substitutes its own guarantee for the U.S. importer's credit risk, enabling the transaction to go forward. In return for taking this risk, the bank receives a fee.

A related form of the letter of credit is called a *standby letter of credit.* These letters, which are issued to firms and governments that wish to borrow in the financial markets, are a form of insurance. Commercial paper, even when it is issued by a large, well-known firm, must be backed by a standby letter of credit that promises the bank will repay the lender should the issuer default. What is true for large corporations is true for state and local governments as well: in most cases, they need a bank guarantee to issue debt. As with loan commitments, letters of credit expose the bank to risk in a way that is not readily apparent on the bank's balance sheet.

"What I'd like, basically, is a temporary line of credit just to tide me over the rest of my life."

SOURCE: 1985 © J.B. Handelsman/The New Yorker Collection/www.cartoonbank.com.

Because off-balance-sheet activities create risk for financial institutions, they have come under increasing scrutiny in recent years. Recall the case of Long-Term Capital Management (LTCM), which we discussed in Chapter 9. While LTCM's balance sheet carried assets worth over $100 billion when the firm got into trouble, the risky instruments that did *not* appear on its balance sheet—the $1.25 trillion in interest-rate swaps—were what scared everyone. A similar problem arose in the financial crisis of 2007–2009, when the invisible, off-balance-sheet risks taken by some of the largest banks added to doubts about their solvency (see Chapter 3, Lessons from the Crisis: Shadow Banks). By allowing for the transfer of risk, modern financial instruments enable individual institutions to concentrate risk in ways that are very difficult for outsiders to discern.

Bank Risk: Where It Comes from and What to Do about It

Banking is risky both because depository institutions are highly leveraged and because of what they do. The bank's goal is to make a profit in each of its lines of business. Some of these are simply fee-for-service activities. For example, a financial institution might act as a broker, buying and selling stocks and bonds on a customer's behalf and charging a fee in return. Banks also transform deposit liabilities into assets such as loans and securities. In the process, they pool savings, provide liquidity services, allow for diversification of risk, and capitalize on the advantages they have in producing information. All along, the goal is to pay less for the deposits the bank receives than for the loans it makes and the securities it buys. That is, the interest rate the bank pays to attract liabilities must be lower than the return it receives on assets.

In the process of all these activities, the bank is exposed to a host of risks. They include the chance that depositors will suddenly withdraw their balances, that borrowers will not repay their loans, that interest rates will change, and that the bank's securities trading operation will do poorly. Each of these risks has a name: *liquidity risk, credit risk, interest-rate risk,* and *trading risk.* To understand how these risks arise and what can be done about them, we will look at each in detail.

Liquidity Risk

All financial institutions face the risk that their liabilities holders (depositors) will seek to cash in their claims. The holder of a checking account can always take cash out at an ATM or make a transfer to someone else via mobile phone or over the Internet. This risk of a sudden demand for liquid funds is called **liquidity risk**. Banks face liquidity risk on both sides of their balance sheets. Deposit withdrawal is a liability-side risk, but there is an asset-side risk as well. Recall from our discussion of off-balance-sheet activities that banks provide households and firms with lines of credit—promises to make loans on demand. When this type of loan commitment is claimed, or *taken down,* the bank must find the liquidity to cover it.

If the bank cannot meet customers' requests for immediate funds, it runs the risk of failure. Even if a bank has a positive net worth, illiquidity can still drive it out of business. Who would put their funds in a bank that can't always provide cash on demand? For this reason, bankers must manage liquidity risk with great care. Failure to do so in the crisis of 2007–2009 led to bank runs—such as the run on Wachovia in September 2008—and to the failures of numerous bank and nonbank intermediaries.

Figure 12.4	Balance Sheet of a Bank Holding $5 Million in Excess Reserves

Assets		Liabilities	
Reserves	$ 15 million	Deposits	$100 million
Loans	$100 million	Borrowed funds	$ 30 million
Securities	$ 35 million	Bank capital	$ 20 million

To fully understand liquidity risk and how banks manage it, let's look at a simpli-fied balance sheet. Figure 12.4 shows a stripped-down version of the balance sheet of a hypothetical bank. Keep in mind that the two sides of a balance sheet must always balance. Any change in the level of assets must be mirrored by an equal change in the level of liabilities.

In Figure 12.4, bank liabilities are composed primarily of deposits, along with some borrowing and $20 million of bank capital. Liabilities total $150 million. The bank's assets include $15 million in reserves. Banking regulations require that banks hold a portion of their assets either as vault cash or as deposits at the Fed. That portion is stated as a specific percentage of the bank's deposits. If we assume that **required reserves** are 10 percent of deposits, then the $100 million in deposits shown on the balance sheet means that the bank is required to hold $10 million in reserves. The fact that the bank is holding $15 million in reserves means that it has $5 million in *excess reserves.*

TIME

To assess liquidity risk, we need to ask how the bank will handle a customer's de-mand for funds. What happens if a corporate customer arrives at the bank and requests a withdrawal of $5 million? Because the bank has $5 million in excess reserves, it can honor the customer's request immediately, without difficulty. Similarly, if the bank were forced suddenly to honor a $5 million loan commitment, it could do so by draw-ing down its reserves. In the past, this was a common way to manage liquidity risk; banks would simply hold sufficient excess reserves to accommodate customers' with-drawals. This is a passive way to manage liquidity risk.

The problem is, holding excess reserves is expensive, because it means forgoing the higher rate of interest that typically can be earned on loans or securities. Banks work hard to find other ways to manage the risk of sudden withdrawals and drawdowns of loan commitments. There are two other ways to manage the risk that customers will require cash: The bank can adjust its assets or its liabilities. To see how it's done, let's look at Figure 12.5. This bank has $10 million in reserves to back its $100 million in deposits, so it has no excess reserves. If a customer makes a $5 million withdrawal, the bank can't simply deduct it from reserves. Instead, the bank will need to adjust another part of its balance sheet.[6]

This bank has two choices in responding to the shortfall created by the $5 million withdrawal: It can adjust either its assets or its liabilities. On the asset side, the bank has several options. The quickest and easiest one is to sell a portion of its securities portfolio. Because some of them are almost surely U.S. Treasury securities, they can be sold quickly and easily at relatively low cost. The result of this action is shown in

[6]If you're thinking that the bank can finance part of the withdrawal from reserves, because the $5 million withdrawal will reduce required reserves by $500,000, you're right. But that still leaves the bank $4.5 million short.

Figure 12.5   Balance Sheet of a Bank Holding No Excess Reserves

Assets		Liabilities	
Reserves	$ 10 million	Deposits	$100 million
Loans	$100 million	Borrowed funds	$ 30 million
Securities	$ 40 million	Bank capital	$ 20 million

the top panel of Figure 12.6. Note that assets and liabilities are both $5 million lower than they were prior to the withdrawal (compare Figure 12.5). Banks that are particularly concerned about liquidity risk can structure their securities holdings to facilitate such sales.

A second possibility is for the bank to sell some of its loans to another bank. This option is shown in the bottom panel of Figure 12.6. While not all loans can be sold, some can. Banks generally make sure that a portion of the loans they hold are marketable for just such purposes.

Yet another way to handle the bank's need for liquidity is to refuse to renew a customer loan that has come due. Corporate customers have short-term loans that are periodically renewed, so the bank always has the option of refusing to extend the loan again for another week, month, or year. But this course of action is not very appealing. Failing to renew a loan is guaranteed to alienate the customer and could well drive the customer to another bank. Recall from Chapter 11 that banks specialize in solving information problems by screening to find customers who are creditworthy and then monitoring them to ensure they repay their loans. The idea is to separate good customers from bad ones and develop long-term relationships with the good ones. The last

Figure 12.6   Balance Sheet of a Bank Following a $5 Million Withdrawal and Asset Adjustment

Withdrawal Is Met by Selling Securities

Assets		Liabilities	
Reserves	$ 10 million	Deposits	$95 million
Loans	$100 million	Borrowed funds	$30 million
Securities	$ 35 million	Bank capital	$20 million

Withdrawal Is Met by Reducing Loans

Assets		Liabilities	
Reserves	$10 million	Deposits	$95 million
Loans	$95 million	Borrowed funds	$30 million
Securities	$40 million	Bank capital	$20 million

Figure 12.7	Balance Sheet of a Bank Following a $5 Million Withdrawal and Liability Adjustment

Withdrawal Is Met by Borrowing

Assets		Liabilities	
Reserves	$ 10 million	Deposits	$95 million
Loans	$100 million	Borrowed funds	$35 million
Securities	$ 40 million	Bank capital	$20 million

Withdrawal Is Met by Attracting Deposits

Assets		Liabilities	
Reserves	$ 10 million	Deposits	$100 million
Loans	$100 million	Borrowed funds	$ 30 million
Securities	$ 40 million	Bank capital	$ 20 million

thing a bank wants to do is to refuse a loan to a creditworthy customer it has gone to some trouble and expense to find.

Moreover, bankers do not like to meet their deposit outflows by contracting the asset side of the balance sheet because doing so shrinks the size of the bank. And because banks make a profit by turning liabilities into assets, the smaller their balance sheets, the lower their profits. For this reason alone, today's bankers prefer to use liability management to address liquidity risk. That is, instead of selling assets in response to a deposit withdrawal, they find other sources of funds.

There are two ways for banks to obtain additional funds. First, they can borrow to meet the shortfall, either from the Federal Reserve or from another bank. The result of such an action is shown in the top panel of Figure 12.7. As you can see, while deposits have fallen by $5 million, borrowing has made up the difference.

A second way to adjust liabilities in response to a deposit outflow is to attract additional deposits. The most common way to do so is to issue large-denomination CDs (with a value over $100,000), effectively borrowing in the wholesale money market.[7] In the bottom panel of Figure 12.7, these nontransaction deposits are combined with checking accounts. As we saw earlier, large certificates of deposit have become an increasingly important source of funds for banks. Now we know why: It is because they allow banks to manage their liquidity risk without changing the asset side of their balance sheets.

In the crisis of 2007–2009, many of the usual mechanisms for managing liquidity risk failed. Banks could neither sell their illiquid assets nor obtain at a reasonable cost the funding needed to hold those assets. When the interbank lending and wholesale money markets dried up, many banks faced a threat to their survival (see Chapter 3, Lessons from the Crisis: Interbank Lending).

---

[7]Unlike transactions deposits such as checking accounts, CDs are not subject to a reserve requirement. Thus, a change in the composition of a bank's deposits affects the level of reserves it is required to hold and hence its balance sheet.

Credit Risk

Banks profit from the difference between the interest rate they pay to depositors and the interest rate they receive from borrowers. That is, the return on their assets exceeds the cost of their liabilities. At least, that's the idea. But to ensure that this profit-making process works, for the bank to make a profit, borrowers must repay their loans. There is always some risk that they won't. The risk that a bank's loans will not be repaid is called **credit risk**. To manage their credit risk, banks use a variety of tools. The most basic are diversification, in which the bank makes a variety of different loans to spread the risk, and credit risk analysis, in which the bank examines the borrower's credit history to determine the appropriate interest rate to charge.

Diversification means spreading risk, which can be difficult for banks, especially those that focus on certain kinds of lending. Because banks specialize in information gathering, it is tempting to try to gain a competitive advantage in a narrow line of business. The problem is, if a bank lends in only one geographic area or only one industry, it exposes itself to economic downturns that are local or industry-specific. It is important that banks find a way to hedge such risks.

Credit risk analysis produces information that is very similar to the bond rating systems discussed in Chapter 7. There we saw that rating agencies like Moody's and Standard & Poor's produce letter ratings for large corporations wishing to issue bonds. Banks do the same for small firms wishing to borrow, and credit rating agencies perform the service for individual borrowers (see Your Financial World: Your Credit Rating in Chapter 7). Credit risk analysis uses a combination of statistical models and information that is specific to the loan applicant. The result is an assessment of the likelihood that a particular borrower will default. When the bank's loan officers decide to make a loan, they use the customer's credit rating to determine how high an interest rate to charge. To the interest rate they must pay on their liabilities, they add a markup that will allow them to make a profit. The poorer a borrower's credit rating, the higher the interest rate they will charge.[8]

In the crisis of 2007–2009, many banks seriously underestimated the risks associated with mortgage and other household credit. They had not anticipated the first decline of nationwide housing prices since the Great Depression or the surge of unemployment to double-digit rates. As a consequence, they overestimated the value of the collateral. Rising defaults prompted large losses and impaired their capital, although not as much as crisis-driven trading losses on mortgage-backed and related securities (see page 317).

Interest-Rate Risk

Because banks are in the business of turning deposit liabilities into loan assets, the two sides of their balance sheet do not match up. One important difference is that a bank's liabilities tend to be short term, while its assets tend to be long term. This mismatch between the maturities of the two sides of the balance sheet creates **interest-rate risk**.

To understand the problem, think of both the bank's assets and its liabilities as bonds. That is, the bank's deposit liabilities are just like bonds, as are its loan assets. (The bank must have some capital as well.) We know that a change in interest rates will affect the value of a bond; when interest rates rise, the price of a bond falls. More

---

[8]Banks can also manage their credit risk by purchasing *credit default swaps* (CDS), a type of derivative that allows lenders to insure themselves against the chance that a borrower will default. For a discussion of CDS, see pages 234–235 of Chapter 9.

important, the longer the term of the bond is, the greater the change in the bond's price at any given change in the interest rate. (Refer back to Chapter 4 to refresh your memory.) Thus, when interest rates rise, banks face the risk that the value of their assets will fall more than the value of their liabilities (reducing the bank's capital). Put another way, if a bank makes long-term loans, it receives payments from borrowers that do not vary with the interest rate. But its short-term liabilities—those with variable interest rates—require the bank to make larger payments when interest rates rise. So rising interest rates reduce revenues relative to expenses, directly lowering the bank's profits.

The best way to see this point is to focus on a bank's revenue and expenses. Let's start by dividing the bank's assets and liabilities into two categories, those that are interest-rate sensitive and those that are not. The term *interest-rate sensitive* means that a change in interest rates will change the revenue produced by an asset. Because newly purchased short-term bonds always reflect a change in interest rates, short-term bonds that are constantly maturing and being replaced with new ones produce interest-rate-sensitive revenue. In contrast, when the bank purchases long-term bonds, it receives a fixed stream of revenue. Purchasing a 5 percent, 10-year bond means getting $5 per $100 of face value for 10 years, regardless of what happens to interest rates in the meantime. So the revenue stream from a long-term bond is not interest-rate sensitive.

Suppose that 20 percent of a bank's assets fall into the first category, those that are sensitive to changes in the interest rate. Another 80 percent fall into the second category, those that are not sensitive to changes in the interest rate. If the interest rate has been stable at 5 percent for some time, then for each $100 in assets, the bank receives $5 in interest.

The bank's liabilities tend to have a different structure. Let's assume that half the bank's deposits are interest-rate sensitive and half are not. In other words, half the bank's liabilities are deposits that earn variable interest rates, so the costs associated with them move with the market rate. Interest-bearing checking accounts fall into this category. The remainder of the bank's liabilities are time deposits such as certificates of deposit, which have fixed interest rates. The payment a bank makes to the holder of an existing CD does not change with the interest rate.

For the bank to make a profit, the interest rate on its liabilities must be lower than the interest rate on its assets. The difference between the two rates is the bank's net interest margin. Assuming that the interest rate on its liabilities has been 3 percent, the bank has been paying out $3 per $100 in liabilities. Because the bank is receiving 5 percent interest on its assets, its net interest margin is 2 percent (5 minus 3). This margin is the bank's profit.

Now look at what happens if interest rates rise 1 percent for interest-sensitive assets and liabilities. For each $100 in assets, the bank's revenue goes up from $(0.05 \times \$100) = \$5$ to $[(0.05 \times \$80) + (0.06 \times \$20)] = \$5.20$. But the cost of its liabilities goes up too, from $(0.03 \times \$100) = \$3$ to $[(0.03 \times \$50) + (0.04 \times \$50)] = \$3.50$. So a one-percentage point rise in the interest rate reduces the bank's profit from $(\$5 - \$3) = \$2$ per $100 in assets to $(\$5.20 - \$3.50) = \$1.70$, a decline of $0.30, or 15 percent. This example illustrates a general principle: When a bank's liabilities are more interest-rate-sensitive than its assets are, an increase in interest rates will cut into the bank's profits.

The first step in managing interest-rate risk is to determine how sensitive the bank's balance sheet is to a change in interest rates. Managers must compute an estimate of the change in the bank's profit for each one-percentage-point change in the interest rate. This procedure is called *gap analysis,* because it highlights the gap, or difference, between the yield on interest-rate-sensitive assets and the yield on interest-rate-sensitive

LESSONS FROM THE CRISIS
INSUFFICIENT BANK CAPITAL

The financial crisis of 2007–2009 and the recession that it triggered led to projected losses on U.S. bank assets of nearly $1 trillion.* For comparison, the total capital of U.S. depositories before the crisis began was about $1.3 trillion. Had the U.S. government not provided massive support to the banking system, many banks probably would have become *insolvent*—unable to repay their debts because their liabilities would have exceeded their assets.

What is bank capital? Why do banks hold it? Through what mechanism did the crisis erode capital?

A bank's capital is its net worth—the difference between the value of its assets and the value of its liabilities. The capital a bank holds cushions it against many risks, including declines in the market value of assets—so-called *market risk*. The larger a bank's capital cushion, the less likely that it will be made insolvent by an adverse surprise.

In the financial crisis, U.S. bank capital was insufficient to cushion against the market risks that surfaced. Put another way, banks were too leveraged: They had too many assets for each unit of capital, making them vulnerable to market risk.

How did declines in the market value of assets arise in the crisis? The process began in 2007 when surging mortgage defaults depressed the value of many mortgage-backed securities. U.S. banks were sensitive to such declines because they held more than $4 trillion in mortgages.

Even when borrowers make timely interest payments, mortgages and the securities backed by them can pose market risk. *Mark-to-market* accounting rules require banks to adjust the recorded value of the assets on their balance sheets when the market value of those assets changes. When the market price rises, the value of the assets is "written up." When the price falls, the value is "written down." Because bank capital is the difference between assets and liabilities, *writedowns* reduce a bank's capital.

Why didn't banks hold a larger capital cushion against market and other risks? The answer is that capital is costly. Financial institutions must pay for capital, compensating the investors that provide it with dividends and the like.

To boost profits, intermediaries try to reduce costs, including the amount of capital they require. They also may take more risk by increasing leverage. The more leverage, the greater the possible reward for each unit of costly capital—and the greater the risk. Highly leveraged firms are vulnerable even to modest declines in market prices. When a financial institution is leveraged 30 times—as some were before the crisis—a drop in asset prices of as little as 3 percent can wipe out the capital cushion and lead to bankruptcy. Yet, even some top-rated mortgage securities plunged in price by one-third, threatening widespread insolvency among the institutions that held them.

*See the projection in the IMF *Global Financial Stability Report*, April 2009, Table 1.15.

liabilities. In our example, the asset-liability gap is (20 percent − 50 percent) = −30. Multiplying this gap times the projected change in the interest rate yields the change in the bank's profit. A gap of −30 tells us that a one-percentage-point increase in the interest rate will reduce the bank's profit by 30 cents per $100 in assets, which is the same answer we got in the last paragraph. Gap analysis can be refined to take account of differences in the maturity of assets and liabilities, but the analysis quickly becomes complicated.[9] Table 12.2 summarizes all of these calculations.

Bank managers can use a number of tools to manage interest-rate risk. The simplest approach is to match the interest-rate sensitivity of assets with the interest-rate sensitivity of liabilities. For instance, if the bank accepts a variable-rate deposit, it then uses the funds to purchase short-term securities. A similar strategy is to make long-term loans at a floating interest rate—as in adjustable-rate mortgages (ARMs)—instead of at the fixed interest rate characteristic of a conventional mortgage. But while this approach reduces interest-rate risk, it increases credit risk. Rising interest rates put additional strain on floating-rate borrowers, increasing the likelihood that they will default on their payments.

[9]A more sophisticated examination of interest-rate risk, called *duration analysis,* includes a measure of the interest-rate sensitivity of bond prices. A bond's duration is related to its maturity. The percentage change in the market value = −(duration of the bond) × (percentage-point change in the interest rate). Bankers compute the weighted-average duration of their liabilities and subtract it from the weighted-average duration of their assets to get a duration gap, which can be used to guide the bank's risk management strategy. For a complete treatment, see Chapter 9 in Anthony Saunders and Marcia Millon Cornett, *Financial Institutions Management: A Modern Perspective,* 8th ed. (New York: McGraw-Hill/Irwin, 2014).

Table 12.2	An Example of Interest-Rate Risk

The impact of an interest-rate increase on bank profits (per $100 of assets)

	Assets	Liabilities
Interest-rate sensitive	$20	$50
Not interest-rate sensitive	$80	$50
Initial interest rate	5%	3%
New interest rate on interest-rate-sensitive assets and liabilities	6%	4%

	Revenue from Assets	Cost of Liabilities
At initial interest rate	$(0.05 \times \$20) + (0.05 \times \$80) = \$5.00$	$(0.03 \times \$50) + (0.03 \times \$50) = \$3.00$
After interest-rate change	$(0.06 \times \$20) + (0.05 \times \$80) = \$5.20$	$(0.04 \times \$50) + (0.03 \times \$50) = \$3.50$

Profits at initial interest rate: ($5.00) − ($3.00) = $2.00 per $100 in assets

Profits after interest-rate change: ($5.20) − ($3.50) = $1.70 per $100 in assets

Gap Analysis

Gap between interest-rate-sensitive assets and interest-rate-sensitive liabilities:

(Interest-rate-sensitive assets of $20) − (Interest-rate-sensitive liabilities of $50) = (Gap of −$30)

While restructuring assets to better match those of liabilities can reduce risk, the fact that it also reduces potential profitability has led bankers to look for other ways to control interest-rate risk. Alternatives include the use of derivatives, specifically interest-rate swaps, to manage interest-rate risk. Recall from Chapter 9 that an interest-rate swap is an agreement in which one party promises to make fixed-interest-rate payments in exchange for floating-interest-rate payments. For a bank that is holding long-term assets and short-term liabilities, an interest-rate swap is exactly the sort of financial instrument that will transfer the risk of rising interest rates to another party.

Trading Risk

There was a time when banks merely took deposits and made loans, holding them until they were completely paid off. Today, banks not only engage in sophisticated asset and liability management but they hire traders to actively buy and sell securities, loans, and derivatives using a portion of the bank's capital, in the hope of making additional profits for the bank's owners. But trading financial instruments is risky. If the price at which an instrument is purchased differs from the price at which it is sold, the risk is that the instrument may go down in value rather than up. This type of risk is called **trading risk**, or sometimes *market risk*.[10]

---

[10]Because regulators in the United States won't allow banks to hold stock (equity), the traders employed by the bank can't, either. But because the traders buy and sell derivatives that are based on bonds, commodities, and foreign exchange, the rule against stock ownership doesn't restrict their ability to take risks.

IN THE NEWS
Lessons from the London Whale

The New York Times

Editorial

January 20, 2013

A detailed report put out by JPMorgan Chase last week on how it lost $6 billion from ill-fated trading in 2012 should be required reading for policy makers and financial executives. The 129-page document serves as a case study of how excessive complexity and poor oversight still threaten many parts of the financial system more than four years after the failure of Lehman Brothers.

The subject of the report is the bank's trading of complex derivatives known as credit default swaps that are similar to the instruments that forced the government to bail out the American International Group in 2008. At JPMorgan, the nation's largest bank and one of many that received government aid during the crisis, these investments did not threaten the institution's survival as they did with A.I.G. But they caused losses large enough to dent the bank's reputation for managing risk well, and cost its top executive, Jamie Dimon, a 50 percent reduction in his 2012 pay.

The report, which was prepared by JPMorgan executives, is not exhaustive: it does not explain, for instance, how an early loss estimate of $2 billion eventually grew to $6 billion. But it provides important insights into why the losses took the bank and regulators by surprise. The main reason is that they were not paying attention to a small group of traders working for the bank's chief investment unit, which was supposed to be hedging, or protecting against future losses.

In fact, far from mitigating the bank's risk, the London-based traders amassed a large, complex financial portfolio in the misguided hope that doing so would help the bank avoid a relatively modest loss of about $100 million, according to the report. As they dug themselves into a deeper and deeper hole, the risks they were taking were either kept from or ignored by senior managers and bank supervisors.

But not everybody was oblivious. Investors at other banks and hedge funds who were trading with JPMorgan noticed and took advantage of the situation. They even dubbed the group's principal trader the "London Whale" because he took a very large position in the market.

The report's findings suggest that some of the riskiest trading would have been either prohibited or at least better monitored had regulators finished drafting regulations about derivatives and short-term trading by banks that are required under the Dodd-Frank financial reform law.

But the far bigger lesson from this report is that senior bank officials and regulators need to be more vigilant than they have been in overseeing potentially risky activity wherever it may be taking place. The report found that even as the London group, which makes trades for JPMorgan itself, engaged in more complex transactions and took on more risk, its activities were more lightly monitored than the trading by other divisions, like JPMorgan's investment bank, which provides financial services and advice to corporations and others.

The board of JPMorgan did the right thing in making this report public so that investors, depositors and the general public can better understand what happened. Last week, federal banking regulators ordered JPMorgan to improve its risk management systems and told its board to report on its progress. Given the nature of risk, we will probably not know how well these measures are working until the next crisis.

LESSONS OF THE ARTICLE

Whatever their purpose, trading operations are notoriously difficult to monitor, and they can go dramatically wrong. Traders gamble with someone else's money and are prone to taking too much risk. In big, global intermediaries, where the firm's top leaders have no direct control over traders who transact in complex instruments, oversight is particularly challenging. If management and compensation systems don't keep up with risk taking, or a trader's superiors lack proper training and incentives, trading failures can bring down the entire financial institution.

Managing trading risk is a major concern for today's banks. Some of the largest banks in the world have sustained billions of dollars in losses as a result of unsupervised risk taking by employees in their trading operations. The problem is that traders normally share in the profits from good investments, but the bank pays for the losses. Heads, the trader wins; tails, the bank loses. This arrangement creates moral hazard: Traders have an incentive to take more risk than bank managers would like.

The solution to the moral hazard problem in trading is to compute the risk the portfolios traders generate using measures like standard deviation and value at risk (see Chapter 5). The bank's risk manager then limits the amount of risk any individual trader is allowed to assume and monitors each trader's holdings closely, at least once a day. Yet, large banks find it difficult to monitor their traders (and the managers who are supposed to be the monitors). As a result, multi-billion-dollar losses due to trading risk are surprisingly frequent at large banks—even those that are well managed (see In the News: Lessons from the London Whale). The higher the risk inherent in the bank's portfolio, the more capital the bank will need to hold to make sure the institution remains solvent.

In the crisis of 2007–2009, some banks, especially large ones, sharply underestimated the risks associated with mortgage-backed securities and related derivatives. As market prices on these financial instruments plunged, losses on their large holdings of these instruments seriously depleted their bank capital and threatened insolvency (see Lessons from the Crisis: Insufficient Bank Capital on page 314).

Other Risks

Beyond liquidity, credit, interest-rate, and trading risk, banks face an assortment of other risks. A bank that operates internationally will face foreign exchange risk and sovereign risk. *Foreign exchange risk* comes from holding assets denominated in one currency and liabilities denominated in another. For example, a U.S. bank that holds dollar-denominated liabilities might purchase bonds issued by Sony Corporation or make a loan to a Japanese business. Both those assets would be denominated in yen. Thus, when the dollar–yen exchange rate moves, the dollar value of the bank's assets will change. Banks manage their foreign exchange risk in two ways. They work to attract deposits that are denominated in the same currency as their loans, thereby matching their assets with their liabilities, and they use foreign exchange futures and swaps to hedge the risk. But both approaches can introduce other risks that need to be managed (see Chapter 10, Lessons from the Crisis: Currency Risk and Rollover Risk).

Sovereign risk arises from the fact that some foreign borrowers may not repay their loans, not because they are unwilling to, but because their government prohibits them from doing so. When a foreign country is experiencing a financial crisis, the government may decide to restrict dollar-denominated payments, in which case a U.S. bank would have difficulty collecting payments on its loans in the country. Such circumstances have arisen on numerous occasions. Examples include Asia in 1997, Russia in 1998, and Argentina in 2002. In all these cases governments and corporations alike had difficulty raising enough dollars to repay their dollar-denominated debts. In such crises, a bank has very little recourse in the courts and little hope of recovering the loans. In 2011–2012, Europe's sovereign debt crisis prompted sufficient fear that some countries would give up the euro (and re-create their own currencies) that many banks moved assets out of countries on the geographic periphery of the euro area to avoid so-called *redenomination risk*. The result was a capital flight that threatened the euro itself.

Managing sovereign risk is difficult. Banks have three options. The first is diversification, which means distributing the bank's loans and securities holdings throughout the world, carefully avoiding too much exposure in any country where a crisis might arise. Second, the bank can simply refuse to do business in a particular country or set of countries. And third, the bank can use derivatives to hedge sovereign risk.

It should go without saying that bank managers need accurate and timely information to control all these "other risks," in addition to the risks related to liquidity, credit, interest rates, and trading. Yet, one of the lessons of the 2007–2009 financial crisis is that many banks lacked real-time information that would allow them to assess their various risk exposures at the bankwide level. Most important, some large banks with many business lines and legal entities operating across national borders lacked facilities to quickly aggregate and report the information that management needed for effective risk control. The resulting uncertainties deepened anxieties about counterparty risks among intermediaries and contributed to the crisis. Unsurprisingly, governments now keep closer tabs on large banks' risk management efforts, including the quality of their analysis and reporting systems.

The final risk that banks face is the risk that their computer systems may fail or their buildings burn down (or blow up); what's called **operational risk**. When terrorists destroyed the World Trade Center towers on September 11, 2001, power and communications were disrupted in a large and important part of lower Manhattan. Many financial firms located in or near the World Trade Center quickly switched to backup sites, but others couldn't. The Bank of New York, a large commercial bank, was one of those that fell victim to operational risk. The Bank of New York (now The Bank of New York Mellon) plays an important role in the U.S. financial system, handling hundreds of billions of dollars worth of transactions each day in the U.S. Treasury securities market and serving as one of only two major repo clearing banks (see Applying the Concept: The Tri-Party Repo Market). Prior to September 11, the bank maintained both its primary and backup operations within blocks of the World Trade Center (see Figure 12.8).

Figure 12.8   The Bank of New York and September 11, 2001

SOURCE: *Copyright American Map Corporation, Lic. No. AMC033007.*

The two red stars show the location of the Bank of New York's primary operations and the backup site. They are both within half a mile of the center of the World Trade Center complex that was destroyed by terrorists on September 11, 2001. Because these buildings became inaccessible, the Bank of New York ceased operation for several days.

APPLYING THE CONCEPT
THE TRI-PARTY REPO MARKET*

Repurchase agreements (repos) are a key form of short-term finance for many intermediaries. For lenders, like the treasurers of corporations or municipalities, repo is a close substitute for cash, making it a virtual component of the payments system. On the borrowing side, securities dealers use the repo market to fund their inventories of stocks and bonds, giving it a critical role in the capital markets.

Economists at the Bank for International Settlements (BIS) estimate that the volume of outstanding repos approached $5 trillion at the end of 2007, or nearly half the overall liabilities of the commercial banking system.** But in 2008, anxious repo lenders sought to avoid receiving illiquid or questionable collateral (such as mortgage-backed securities) as protection if repo borrowers failed to repay, so the repo lenders stopped lending and the repo market shriveled, aggravating the financial crisis.

Since the crisis, policymakers have focused on lingering sources of fragility in the repo market. The peculiar mechanism for clearing repo trades remains a key concern. A large share of repo transactions occur in the "tri-party" market, in which a borrower and a lender each contract with a third party (a bank) to transfer the collateral first from the borrower to the lender and then back to the borrower when the repo unwinds.

In the United States, two banks—Bank of New York Mellon and JPMorgan Chase—provide these repo safekeeping and transfer (also called clearing) services using a process that creates operational and liquidity risks for the financial system as a whole. In the interval between the usual late-afternoon implementation of a new repo agreement and the early-morning expiration of a previous one, these two banks become large creditors to the repo borrowers. This intraday exposure to individual borrowers makes them vulnerable to counterparty and collateral risks. In a crisis, such concentrated exposures can lead to fire sales and the paradox of leverage, in which collateral sales depress asset prices and aggravate the loss of capital in the financial system (see Chapter 3, Lessons from the Crisis: Leverage).

Policymakers concerned about systemic fragilities have promoted reforms in the tri-party repo market to synchronize the creation of new repo loans and the settlement of expiring loans. Making these transactions simultaneous would reduce the intraday lending exposure of the two clearing banks and the overall fragility of the market. However, the reform process remained ongoing in 2013, partly because of the technical challenges of allocating various types of collateral across multiple repo contracts and counterparties in a speedy, cost-effective manner. As a result, the repo market remains an important source of vulnerability in the U.S. financial system.

*This article is based largely on Copeland et al., "Key Mechanics of the Tri-Party Repo Market," *FRBNY Economic Policy Review* 18, no. 3 (November 2012).

**Peter Hördahl and Michael King, "Developments in Repo Markets during the Financial Turmoil," *BIS Quarterly Review,* December 2008.

Not only were power and communications to these buildings knocked out by the terrorist attack, but no one could even get to them. The bank practically shut down for several days and recovered only slowly, losing an estimated $140 million in the process. In placing the backup site so close to the bank's primary operations, managers had made an enormous mistake: They had failed to take account of a significant operational risk.[11]

These risks are serious business. One study estimates that over the 10 years ending in 2002, there were more than 100 events in which U.S. financial institutions lost a total of $100 million.[12] More recently, responding to a 2008 survey from the Bank for International Settlements, a sample of 81 banks in Europe and North America reported losses of €50 billion, including 140,000 events each costing more than €20,000.

In principle, managing operational risk is straightforward, but in practice it can be difficult. The bank must make sure that its computer systems and buildings are

[11]For a discussion of the problems that occurred in the U.S. financial system following the destruction of the World Trade Center towers, see the Federal Reserve Bank of New York's *Economic Policy Review,* November 2002, special issue on the economic effects of September 11. Of particular note are Michael J. Fleming and Kenneth D. Garbade, "When the Back Office Moved to the Front Burner: Settlement Fails in the Treasury Market after September 11," and James J. McAndrews and Simon Potter, "Liquidity Effects of the Event of September 11, 2001."

[12]See Patrick de Fountnouville, Virginia DeJesus-Rueff, John Jordan, and Eric Rosengren, "Capital and Risk: New Evidence on Implications of Large Operational Losses," *Journal of Money, Credit, and Banking* 38, no. 7 (October 2006), pp. 1819–1846.

Table 12.3	Risks Banks Face and How They Manage Them

Type of Risk	Source of Risk	Recommended Responses
Liquidity Risk	Sudden withdrawals by depositors or takedowns of credit lines	1. Hold sufficient cash reserves to meet customer demand. 2. Manage assets—sell securities or loans (contracts the size of the balance sheet) 3. Manage liabilities—attract more deposits (maintains the size of the balance sheet)
Credit Risk	Default by borrowers on their loans	1. Diversify to spread risk. 2. Use statistical models to screen for creditworthy borrowers. 3. Monitor to reduce moral hazard.
Interest-Rate Risk	Mismatch in maturity of assets and liabilities coupled with a change in interest rates	1. Closely match the maturity of both sides of the balance sheet. 2. Use derivatives such as interest-rate swaps.
Trading (Market) Risk	Trading losses in the bank's own account	Closely monitor traders using risk management tools, including value at risk.

sufficiently robust to withstand potential disasters. That means both anticipating what might happen and testing to ensure the system's readiness. Forecasting the possibilities can be daunting. Who could have predicted what happened on September 11?

Table 12.3 summarizes the four major risks banks face and the recommended risk-management strategies.

Terms

Using FRED: Codes for Data in This Chapter

Data Series	FRED Data Code
Number of commercial banks	USNUM
Bank failures	BKFTTLA641N
Net interest margin	USNIM
Return on equity	USROE
Net loan losses/Average total loans	USLSTL
Loan loss reserve/Total loans	USLLRTL
Commercial bank assets	TLAACBM027SBOG
Cash assets	CASACBM027SBOG
Securities	INVEST
Loans	LOANS
Commercial bank liabilities	TLBACBM027SBOG
Deposits	DPSACBM027SBOG
Borrowings	BOWACBM027SBOG
Bank capital or net worth (assets less liabilities)	RALACBM027SBOG

Chapter Lessons

1. Bank assets equal bank liabilities plus bank capital.
   a. Bank assets are the uses for bank funds.
      i. They include reserves, securities, and loans.
      ii. Over the years, commercial and industrial loans have become less important and mortgages more important as a use for bank funds.
   b. Bank liabilities are the sources of bank funds.
      i. They include transaction and nontransaction deposits as well as borrowings.
      ii. Over the years, transaction deposits have become less important as a source of bank funds.
   c. Bank capital is the contribution of the bank's owners; it acts as a cushion against a fall in the value of the bank's assets or a withdrawal of its liabilities.
   d. Banks make a profit for their owners. Measures of a bank's profitability include return on assets (ROA), return on equity (ROE), net interest income, and net interest margin.
   e. Banks' off-balance-sheet activities have become increasingly important in recent years. They include
      i. Loan commitments, which are lines of credit firms and households can use whenever necessary.
      ii. Letters of credit, which are guarantees that a customer will make a promised payment.
2. Banks face several types of risk in day-to-day business. They include
   a. Liquidity risk—the risk that customers will demand cash immediately.
      i. Liability-side liquidity risk arises from deposit withdrawals.
      ii. Asset-side liquidity risk arises from the use of loan commitments to borrow.

    iii. Banks can manage liquidity risk by adjusting either their assets or their liabilities.

  b. Credit risk—the risk that customers will not repay their loans. Banks can manage credit risk by

    i. Diversifying their loan portfolios.

    ii. Using statistical models to analyze borrowers' creditworthiness.

    iii. Monitoring borrowers to ensure that they use borrowed funds properly.

    iv. Purchasing credit default swaps (CDS) to insure against borrower default.

  c. Interest-rate risk—the risk that a movement in interest rates will change the value of the bank's assets more than the value of its liabilities.

    i. When a bank lends long and borrows short, increases in interest rates will drive down the bank's profits.

    ii. Banks use a variety of tools, such as gap analysis, to assess the sensitivity of their balance sheets to a change in interest rates.

    iii. Banks manage interest-rate risk by matching the maturity of their assets and liabilities and using derivatives like interest-rate swaps.

  d. Trading risk—the risk that traders who work for the bank will create losses on the bank's own account. Banks can manage this risk using complex statistical models and closely monitoring traders.

  e. Other risks banks face include foreign exchange risk, sovereign risk, and operational risk.

Conceptual and Analytical Problems

1. Explain how a bank manager uses Core Principles 1, 2, and 3 (time has value, risk requires compensation, and information is the basis for decisions) to select assets and issue liabilities consistent with shareholder preferences. *(LO1)*

2. Consider a bank with the following balance sheet. You read in the local newspaper that the bank's return on assets (ROA) was 1 percent. What were the bank's after-tax profits? *(LO2)*

Bank Balance Sheet (in millions)			
Assets		**Liabilities**	
Reserves	$100	Deposits	$1,000
Loans	$500	Borrowing	$ 0
Securities	$500	Bank capital	$ 100

3. Based on the following information about banks A and B, compute for each bank its return on assets (ROA), return on equity (ROE), and leverage ratio. *(LO2)*

   a. Bank A has net profit after taxes of $1.8 million and the following balance sheet:

Bank A (in millions)			
Assets		**Liabilities**	
Reserves	$ 5	Deposits	$100
Loans	$70	Borrowing	$ 10
Securities	$45	Bank capital	$ 10

   b. Bank B has net profit after taxes of $0.9 million and the following balance sheet:

Bank B (in millions)			
Assets		**Liabilities**	
Reserves	$ 7.5	Deposits	$75.0
Loans	$55.0	Borrowing	$ 3.0
Securities	$23.5	Bank capital	$ 8.0

4. Banks hold more liquid assets than do most businesses. Explain why. *(LO1)*

5. Explain why banks' holdings of cash have increased significantly as a portion of their balance sheets in recent times. *(LO1)*

6. Why are checking accounts no longer the primary source of funds for commercial banks in the United States? *(LO2)*

7. The volume of commercial and industrial loans made by banks has declined over the past few decades, while the volume of real estate loans has risen. Explain why this trend occurred and how it contributed to banks' difficulties during the financial crisis of 2007–2009. *(LO2)*

8.* Why do you think that U.S. banks are prohibited from holding equity as part of their own portfolios? *(LO3)*

9. Explain how a bank uses liability management to respond to a deposit outflow. Why do banks prefer liability management to asset management? *(LO1)*

*Indicates more difficult problems

www.mhhe.com/moneyandbanking4e

10. A bank with a two-year investment horizon has issued a one-year certificate of deposit for $50 million at an interest rate of 2 percent. With the proceeds, the bank has purchased a two-year Treasury note that pays 4 percent interest. What risk does the bank face in entering into these transactions? What would happen if all interest rates were to rise by 1 percent? *(LO3)*

11.* In response to changes in banking legislation, the past two decades have seen a significant increase in interstate branching by banks in the United States. How do you think a development of this type would affect the level of risk in the banking business? *(LO3)*

12. Consider the balance sheets of Bank A and Bank B. If reserve requirements were 10 percent of transaction deposits and both banks had equal access to the inter-bank market and funds from the Federal Reserve, which bank do you think faces the greatest liquidity risk? Explain your answer. *(LO3)*

Bank A
(in millions)

Assets		Liabilities	
Reserves	$ 50	Transaction Deposits	$200
Loans	$920	Nontransaction Deposits	$600
Securities	$250	Borrowings	$100

Bank B
(in millions)

Assets		Liabilities	
Reserves	$ 30	Transaction Deposits	$200
Loans	$920	Nontransaction Deposits	$600
Securities	$ 50	Borrowings	$100

13. Looking again at the information available on Bank A and Bank B in Problem 12, which bank do you think is at the greatest risk of insolvency? What other information might you use to assess the risk of insolvency of these banks? *(LO3)*

14. Bank Y and Bank Z both have assets of $1 billion. The return on assets for both banks is the same. Bank Y has liabilities of $800 million while Bank Z's liabilities are $900 million. In which bank would you prefer to hold an equity stake? Explain your choice. *(LO2)*

15.* You are a bank manager and have been approached by a swap dealer about participating in fixed for floating interest-rate swaps. If your bank has the typical maturity structure, which side of the swap might you be interested in paying and which side would you want to receive? *(LO3)*

16. If lines of credit and other off-balance-sheet activities do not, by definition, appear on the bank's balance sheet, how can they influence the level of liquidity risk to which the bank is exposed? *(LO3)*

17. Suppose a bank faces a gap of −20 between its interest-sensitive assets and its interest-sensitive liabilities. What would happen to bank profits if interest rates were to fall by 1 percentage point? You should report your answer in terms of the change in profit per $100 in assets. *(LO2)*

18.* Duration analysis is an alternative to gap analysis for measuring interest-rate risk. (See footnote 9 on page 314.) The duration of an asset or liability measures how sensitive its market value is to a change in the interest rate: the more sensitive, the longer the duration. In Chapter 6, you saw that the longer the term of a bond, the larger the price change for a given change in the interest rate.

Using this information and the knowledge that interest-rate increases tend to hurt banks, would you say that the average duration of a bank's assets is longer or shorter than that of its liabilities? *(LO1)*

19. Suppose you were the manager of a bank with the following balance sheet.

Bank Balance Sheet (in millions)			
Assets		**Liabilities**	
Reserves	$ 30	Checkable Deposits	$200
Securities	$150	Time Deposits	$600
Loans	$820	Borrowings	$100

You are required to hold 10 percent of checkable deposits as reserves. If you were faced with unexpected withdrawals of $30 million from time deposits, would you rather:

a. Draw down $10 million of excess reserves and borrow $20 million from other banks?

b. Draw down $10 million of excess reserves and sell securities of $20 million?

Explain your choice. *(LO1)*

20. Suppose you are advising a bank on the management of its balance sheet. In light of the financial crisis of 2007–2009, what arguments might you make to convince the bank to hold additional capital? *(LO2)*

Data Exploration

For general information on using Federal Reserve Economic Data (FRED) online, visit www.mhhe.com/moneyandbanking4e and click on Student Edition, then FRED Resources.

1. Are U.S. banks increasing in size? Plot since 1984 on a quarterly basis the number of U.S. commercial banks (FRED code: USNUM) and, on the right scale, the volume of their deposits (FRED code: DPSACBM027SBOG). Download the data and compute the average deposit size of banks in the first quarters of 1984 and 2013. Do these sizes accurately portray a *typical* commercial bank? *(LO1)*

Scan here for quick access to the resources for these problems. Need a barcode reader? Try ScanLife, available in your app store.

2. Commercial banks have become increasingly involved in real estate market. Plot the percent change from a year ago of real estate loans made by commercial banks (FRED code: REALLN), and discuss the relationship between the booms and busts in real estate lending and the expansions and recessions of the U.S. economy. *(LO3)*

3. Plot since 1990 the return on equity of small banks (banks with assets of less than $1 billion; FRED code: US1ROE) and of large banks (banks with assets greater than $15 billion; FRED code: USG15ROE). How do you explain the long-run pattern? *(LO2)*

www.mhhe.com/moneyandbanking4e

4. Banks sometimes manage liquidity risk by issuing large, marketable certificates of deposits when other deposits decline. How important is this practice? Plot the share of large time deposits (FRED code: LTDACBM027SBOG) in total deposits (FRED code: DPSACBM027SBOG). Explain how this share evolved over the long run and after 2004. *(LO3)*

5. What share of U.S. banks fail? Plot since 2000 the fraction (in percent) of bank failures (FRED code: BKFTTLA641N) relative to the number of banks (FRED code: USNUM). Comment on the timing and the proportion of failures. Were most of the failing banks large or small? *(LO3)*

Chapter 13

Financial Industry Structure

Learning Objectives

Understand . . .

LO1 Banking industry structure

LO2 Nondepository institutions

Canada, a nation of 35 million people, has 24 domestic banks. If the United States had the same ratio of banks to population, it would have something like 215 banks. In fact, as of the first quarter of 2013, about 6,000 commercial banks exist within U.S. borders, all vying to serve some 315 million Americans. While the United States and Canada are extremes, most countries' banking systems more closely resemble the Canadian structure. In Japan, for example, 127 million people depend on 120 banks; in the United Kingdom, 63 million people are served by 155 domestically incorporated banks; and in China, there are fewer than 200 banks for 1.35 billion people!

Amazingly, the United States once had even more banks than it does today. As Figure 13.1 shows, the number of commercial banks peaked at nearly 15,000 in 1984 and has been falling ever since. The figure also shows an odd pattern in the structure of banks. For decades, most U.S. banks were **unit banks**, or banks without branches. Throughout the 1950s and 1960s, more than two-thirds of banks were unit banks. Over the last quarter of the 20th century, however, the pattern changed. Today, less than one-fourth of banks in the United States are unit banks. What explains this change in structure?

The decline in the total number of banks and the increase in the number of banks with branches are not the only changes the U.S. banking industry has seen in recent years. In April 1998, the Traveler's Insurance Company, together with its investment banking and brokerage subsidiary Salomon Smith Barney, merged with Citibank, then the second largest commercial bank in the country, to become Citigroup. At the time of its creation, Citigroup had $700 billion in assets and more than 100 million customers in 100 countries. It was also illegal. But by the end of 1999, the law that forbade such combinations had been repealed, and Citigroup began buying up even more financial firms. Today, Citigroup and a few other megabanks provide a broad assortment of products offered by almost all other financial institutions. These may include the functions of an insurance company, a pension fund, a securities broker, a collection of mutual funds, a finance company and—of course—a commercial bank, all rolled into one.

Figure 13.1 Number of Insured Commercial Banks in the United States, 1935–2012

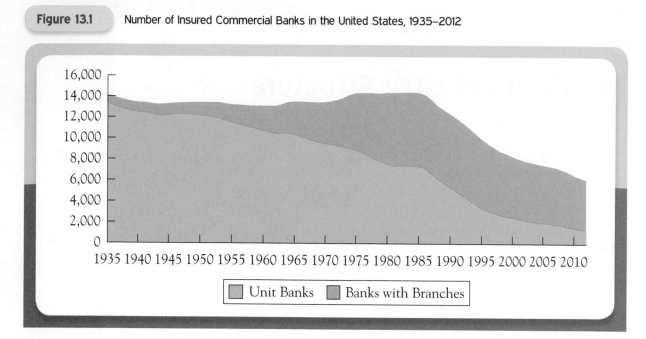

SOURCE: *FDIC Historical Statistics on Banking, www2.fdic.gov/hsob/hsobRpt.asp.* (FRED data code: USNUM).

The crisis of 2007–2009 has transformed the U.S. financial industry. The failure or forced merger of several large banks and other depository institutions accelerated concentration, boosting the deposit share of the top four commercial banks by about 7 percentage points, to around 40 percent of the total. In July 2008, the U.S. government placed the two massive government-sponsored enterprises (GSEs, page 68) for housing finance in conservatorship (wiping out their private shareholders, but allowing them to operate while insolvent). In September 2008, the investment banking era that had prevailed since the 1930s came to an abrupt end as the four largest independent investment banks failed, merged, or became bank holding companies. The ensuing run on money-market mutual funds (MMMFs) was stopped only by a government guarantee of MMMF liabilities. And the federal government invested several hundred billion dollars to restore the capital of the largest U.S. financial institutions, bailing out their creditors to stabilize the financial system. Aside from the GSEs, these institutions have repaid the government, but, as recently as 2012, a few "private" intermediaries still had the U.S. government as their largest shareholder.

To understand the changing structure of the financial industry, we will discuss the services offered by both depository and nondepository financial institutions. Together, they provide a broad menu of services: buying and selling securities; offering loans, insurance, and pensions; and providing checking accounts, credit cards, and debit cards. Most financial institutions perform at least a few of these functions. Visit the website of any large bank, for instance, and you will discover that you can get not only checking and savings accounts, loans and credit cards, but insurance and stockbrokerage services. The first half of this chapter will consider current trends in the banking industry, including the tendency toward consolidation with nondepository institutions. The second half of the chapter will study the functions and characteristics of nondepository institutions.

Banking Industry Structure

Today's banking system bears little resemblance to the one Americans knew in 1960 or 1970. Then people used their neighborhood banks. Not only did customers walk into the bank to conduct their business, but they knew the tellers and bank managers they saw there. Today most of us don't go beyond the ATM in the lobby, and if we do, we probably don't recognize the employees inside. Some of us do our banking via mobile phone or over the Internet and never see the bank's "bricks and mortar." Banks have been transformed so that location doesn't matter the way it once did. This change has occurred on both the national and the international level.

The best way to understand the structure of today's banking industry is to trace it back to its roots. That means looking at the legal history of banking. In this section we'll learn that banking legislation is the reason we have so many banks in the United States. We'll look at the trend toward consolidation that has been steadily reducing the number of banks since the mid-1980s. And we'll briefly consider the effects of globalization.

A Short History of U.S. Banking

If you want to start a bank, you can't just rent a space, put up a sign, and open the door. You need permission in the form of a **bank charter**. Until the Civil War, all bank charters were issued by state banking authorities. Because the authors of the U.S. Constitution feared a strong central government, in the early years of the Republic the federal government was weak and sometimes ineffectual. State governments were often more powerful. Until 1863, in fact, there was no national currency. Instead, state banks issued banknotes that circulated in much the way dollar bills do today. But while the state-chartered banks usually promised to redeem their banknotes in gold, they did so only if the bearer presented them at the bank. As the bearer traveled farther and farther from the bank, the value of the notes fell. So a note issued by a New York bank was worth less in Philadelphia than it was in New York.

A $10 banknote issued by the Central Bank of Tennessee in 1853.

Besides currency that did not hold its value from one place to another, the early American financial system was plagued by insufficient capital and fraud. Banks regularly failed, and when they did, their banknotes became worthless. As we saw in Chapter 2, given the license to print money, most people will print too much. With so many different banknotes circulating, telling the sound money from the unsound became inordinately confusing and inefficient. The whole point of printing money is to reduce information costs and facilitate trade. Still, reasonable people hesitated to accept banknotes issued by banks they weren't familiar with, so money was not widely accepted. In the end, the system just didn't work.

Radical change came during the Civil War, when Congress passed the National Banking Act of 1863, initiating a gradual shift in power away from the states. Although the new law didn't eliminate state-chartered banks, it did impose a 10 percent tax on their issue of banknotes. At the same time, the act created a system of federally chartered banks, or *national banks,* which would be supervised by the Office of the Comptroller of the Currency, inside the U.S. Department of the Treasury. These new national banks could issue banknotes tax-free. Congress's intent was to put the state banks out of business by taking away their source of funds.

While the act did get rid of state-issued banknotes, state banks devised another way to raise funds, by creating demand deposits. This explains the origin of the **dual banking system** we have today, in which banks can choose whether to get their charters from the Comptroller of the Currency at the U.S. Treasury or from state officials. Roughly three-quarters of U.S. banks now have a state charter and the rest have a federal charter. The decision is related to a bank's profitability. State banking authorities have been more permissive than federal authorities in the types of operations they allow. Because greater flexibility in a bank's operations means a better chance of making a profit, state charters have been the overwhelming choice.

Furthermore, if the Comptroller of the Currency won't allow a bank to engage in a particular practice, the bank can always change its charter. This ability to switch back and forth between state and federal charters created what amounts to regulatory competition, which has hastened innovation in the financial industry. In the 1990s, changes in banking law required federal and state agencies to coordinate their oversight of financial intermediaries. But the globalization of the financial system, together with banks' ability to move funds easily across international boundaries, means that today regulatory competition exists not so much between state and federal government regulators but between regulators of different countries.

The first national banknote issued in 1863.

Following the Banking Act of 1863, the next major event in U.S. banking history occurred in 1933, in the midst of the Great Depression. From 1929 to 1933, more than a third of all U.S. banks failed; individual depositors lost $1.5 billion, or about 3 percent of total bank deposits. Millions of small savers lost their life savings.

To protect depositors and make banks safer, Congress enacted the Glass-Steagall Act of 1933, which created the Federal Deposit Insurance Corporation (FDIC) and severely limited the activities of commercial banks. The FDIC provided insurance to individual depositors, so they would not lose their savings in the event that a bank failed. The act also restricted bank assets to certain approved forms of debt and forbade banks from dealing in securities, providing insurance, or engaging in any of the other activities undertaken by nondepository institutions.

By separating commercial banks from investment banking, the law limited the ability of financial institutions to take advantage of economies of scale and scope that might exist in various lines of business. Nevertheless, this restriction on banks' activities remained in place until 1999, when the Gramm-Leach-Bliley Financial Services Modernization Act repealed the Glass-Steagall Act. We will return to this topic shortly. The repeal of the Glass-Steagall Act in 1999 eliminated the restrictions on banks' activities, but it renewed concerns about potential mismanagement of large financial holding companies.

The financial crisis of 2007–2009 underscored these concerns and led to the biggest financial reform since the Great Depression, the Dodd-Frank Wall Street Reform and Consumer Protection Act of 2010. Dodd-Frank aims to prevent financial crises and new government bailouts of financial intermediaries. In more than 800 pages of complex legislation, it sets out new rules for financial institutions and markets; requires closer government oversight over key establishments, called **systemically important financial institutions (SIFIs)** regardless of their legal form; and sharply alters the authorities of the government agencies that govern the financial system. Like Glass-Steagall, the Volcker rule—a part of Dodd-Frank named after the former Federal Reserve chairman who advocated it—also forbids insured depositories from proprietary trading, segmenting this and other business activities so that deposit insurance cannot subsidize bank risk-taking.

We will explore the Dodd-Frank Act and its implications in some depth in Chapter 14. But it is already clear that Dodd-Frank—and the hundreds of rules and procedures that the government is still developing to implement it—will continue to change the financial landscape significantly in coming years, much like the reforms of the 1930s did in their time. What remains unclear is how successful it will be in preventing another financial crisis.

Competition and Consolidation

None of the historical events we have discussed explains why there are roughly 6,000 commercial banks in the United States as of early 2013 or why that number has been shrinking since the mid-1980s. To unravel the mystery, let's return to Figure 13.1. Notice the division between banks with branches and banks that don't have branches. As we mentioned in the introduction, banks that do not have branches are called *unit banks*. The alternative, which is familiar to most of us today, is a bank with many branches spread out over a wide geographic area. Large banks like the Big Four—Bank of America, Citibank, JPMorgan Chase, and Wells Fargo—maintain branches in many cities across many states and foreign countries. We'll return to these banks in a moment. For now, notice from the figure that in 1935, the vast majority of banks had no branches; today, nearly three-quarters of them do. In fact, if we look at the numbers, we see that in 1935 there were 14,125 commercial banks in the United States, with a total of 17,237 offices; as of the first quarter of 2013, there were roughly 6,000 banks, but they had a whopping 90,000 offices! Today's banks not only have branches, they have lots of them.

The number of banks and bank branches in the United States tells only part of the story; we also need to look at bank size. Table 13.1 shows that the U.S. banking system is composed of a large number of very small banks and a small number of very large ones. Roughly 1 percent of the banks hold more than 75 percent of all bank assets. In fact, the Big Four alone account for around 40 percent of assets and deposits in the U.S. commercial banking system.

Table 13.1   Number and Assets of Commercial Banks in the United States

Size of Institution (Assets)	Number	Percent of Total Assets
Less than $100 million	1,915	0.8%
$100 million to $1 billion	3,596	7.9%
$1 billion to $10 billion	447	8.6%
$10 billion or more	90	82.6%
Total	6,048	100% ($13.4 trillion)

SOURCE: *FDIC Quarterly Banking Profile, First Quarter 2013, Table III-A. Percentages do not sum to 100% due to rounding.*

"*Of course, you could try another bank, if there were any other banks.*"

SOURCE: *1998 © Robert Mankoff/The New Yorker Collection/www.cartoonbank.com.*

The primary reason for this structure is the McFadden Act of 1927, which required that nationally chartered banks meet the branching restrictions of the states in which they were located.[1] Because some states had laws that forbade branch banking, the result was a large number of very small banks.[2] Advocates of legal limits on branching argued that they prevented concentration and monopoly in banking in the same way that antitrust laws prevented concentration in manufacturing.

The McFadden Act produced a fragmented banking system nearly devoid of large institutions. The result was a network of small, geographically dispersed banks that faced virtually no competition. In many states, more efficient and modern banks were legally precluded from opening branches to compete with the small, inefficient ones that were already there. In these states, the result was a network of small community banks that faced no competitive pressures to innovate.

Not only that, but the system was prone to failure. Because the only loan applications these local banks received were from residents of their own communities, their loan portfolios were insufficiently diversified. In a farming town, the bank's fortunes depended on the weather, because its loan portfolio was composed almost entirely of agricultural loans. Aware of the problem, the bank manager would eventually stop making loans because the risk was simply too great. When credit ceased to flow into the community, farmers curtailed their operations. In the end, the bank's owners made a healthy profit because the bank was protected from competition—but everyone else in town suffered.

Some banks reacted to branching restrictions by creating **bank holding companies**. A holding company is a corporation that owns a group of other firms. In some contexts, it may be thought of as the *parent firm* for a group of subsidiaries. Bank holding companies have been around since the early 1900s. Initially, they were created not just as a way to evade branching restrictions but as a way to provide nonbank financial services in more than one state. In 1956, the U.S. Congress passed the Bank Holding Company Act, which broadened the scope of what bank holding companies could do, allowing them to provide various nonbank financial services. Over the years, changes in laws and regulations have added asset management, investment advice, insurance, leasing, collections, and real estate services to the list of allowable activities.

Beginning in the early 1970s, technology enabled banks to borrow and lend at a distance. The combination of the U.S. mail, telephone service, and finally the

---

[1]The 1956 Douglas Amendment applied the same restrictions to bank holding companies, requiring that any out-of-state expansion be expressly approved by the host state.

[2]In the nation's early years, the states were starved for revenue; they could neither issue their own currency nor tax interstate trade. The fees the states earned for granting bank charters and the taxes they levied on bank profits became important sources of revenue for state government. The fees gave the state governments an incentive to create many small banks, while the taxes gave them an interest in protecting banks and ensuring they would be profitable. The result was a fragmented banking system with little competition. See R. Kroszner and P. Strahan, "What Drives Deregulation? Economics and Politics of the Relaxation of Bank Branching Restrictions," *Quarterly Journal of Economics* 114 (November 1999), pp. 1437–1467.

YOUR FINANCIAL WORLD
Pawnshops

Contrary to their portrayal in the movies and on TV, pawnshops are not disreputable establishments frequented by criminals who are selling stolen goods. They are legitimate businesses that provide a useful service. Think of a pawnshop as a neighborhood nondepository institution that makes collateralized loans and sells a wide variety of merchandise on the side. The pawnshop's main business is to provide very small loans—smaller than a bank would consider—to people who lack access to the conventional financial system.

Say you have something valuable, like a piece of jewelry, a bicycle, or a camera. You need cash, so you take the valuable item to a pawnshop. The pawnbroker will offer you a loan on the condition that you leave the item there as collateral. When you repay the loan along with interest and fees, the pawnbroker will return your collateral. But if you don't repay the loan on time, the pawnbroker takes the collateral and sells it. The merchandise that's for sale in the pawnshop was collateral for defaulted loans.

Needless to say, the terms of the loan are favorable to the pawnbroker, not to you. The loan amount is usually less than half the value of the collateral, and the interest rate is high: 3 to 5 percent *per month* is standard. There is also a fee that can drive up the interest rate to several hundred percent per year. While such an arrangement may seem outrageous, it is better than the payday loan described in Chapter 12. Because pawnbrokers' loans are collateralized, the interest rates charged are more reasonable than the ones on payday loans. So if you ever find yourself in dire straits, with no other source of credit, you can go to a pawnshop.

Internet dramatically reduced the importance of physical location in banking. Without the need to personally visit the bank to conduct their business, people ceased to care whether a bank was chartered in the state where they lived. Today, ATMs, laptop computers, cell phones, and debit and credit cards allow depositors access to means of payment even when they are far from home. Credit companies can evaluate any individual or firm's creditworthiness, so a bank can make a loan regardless of the borrower's location.

In changing the way people use the financial system, technology has eroded the value of the local banking monopoly. In the 1970s and 1980s, states responded by loosening their branching restrictions.[3] Then in 1994, Congress passed the Riegle-Neal Interstate Banking and Branching Efficiency Act. This legislation reversed the restrictions put in place almost 70 years earlier by the McFadden Act. Since 1997, banks have been able to acquire an unlimited number of branches nationwide. While some banks couldn't handle the new competition and went out of business, the vast majority that ceased independent operations disappeared through mergers with other banks. The number of commercial banks has thus fallen by about one-half over the past

---

[3]A number of other changes took place as well. For example, until 1980, federal law restricted the interest rate banks could pay on deposits. Under Regulation Q, they were prohibited from paying interest on checking accounts, and were limited to a maximum rate of just over 5 percent on savings deposits. As inflation and interest rates rose in the late 1970s, these restrictions became prohibitive. Many depositors withdrew their funds from banks and placed them in money-market mutual funds, whose interest rates were not restricted by law.

Table 13.2 Key Legislation Affecting the U.S. Banking Industry

1927 McFadden Act	Outlawed interstate branching and required national banks to abide by the laws of the states in which they operated.
1933 Glass-Steagall Act	Established federal deposit insurance and prohibited commercial banks from engaging in the insurance and securities businesses.
1994 Riegle-Neal Act	Repealed the McFadden Act's prohibition of interstate branching.
1999 Gramm-Leach-Bliley Act	Repealed the Glass-Steagall Act's prohibition of mergers between commercial banks and insurance companies or securities firms.
2010 Dodd-Frank Act	Aims to prevent financial crises and government bailouts of intermediaries, partly through government oversight of systemically important financial institutions (SIFIs).

two decades, and the number of savings institutions—savings and loans plus savings banks—has fallen even more.

The Riegle-Neal Act allowed banks to diversify geographically. Today a bank that wants to establish operations in a new state can purchase a bank already located in that state. In doing so, it acquires the bank's customers, as well as its employees and their knowledge of the state's business and legal environment. The results have been dramatic. Banks became more profitable: their operating costs and loan losses fell; the interest rates paid to depositors rose while the interest rates charged to borrowers fell. The only people who suffered were the employees of inefficient banks, who had to work harder and were paid less as a result of the new competition. So, the deregulation of banks provided sizable benefits for the economy.[4]

Table 13.2 summarizes the key events in the evolution of the U.S. banking industry over the last century.

The financial crisis of 2007–2009 has focused attention on the costs of deregulation. Did the poor management of some megabanks reveal the limits to expanding institutional scale and scope? Have the biggest banks already outrun those economies? Has deregulation encouraged banks to take on too much risk? Has deregulation motivated some banks to become "too big to fail" in order to secure a government bailout in the event of distress?

Addressing these complex questions is mostly an issue for government supervision, which is the subject of Chapter 14. However, scholars and policymakers also are reviewing whether the benefits of deregulation noted earlier warrant the extra risks associated with those large intermediaries that became a burden on taxpayers and the economy during the financial crisis. Some analysts argue that the crisis-induced increase in banking concentration raises both the likelihood and expected cost of a future financial crisis.[5]

---

[4]One way to tell that deregulation improved growth is to look at what happened in different states. Separating the impact of deregulation from that of a variety of other effects on growth can be tricky. The fact that states deregulated at different times allows economists to disentangle the effects. See J. Jayaranthe and P. Strahan, "The Finance-Growth Nexus: Evidence from Bank Branch Deregulation," *Quarterly Journal of Economics* 111 (1996), pp. 639–670.

[5]See, for example, Chapter 7 of the *Annual Report* of the Bank for International Settlements, 2009.

The Globalization of Banking

Toward the end of the 20th century, U.S. banking underwent not just a national but an international transformation. An explosion in international trade had increased the need for international financial services. Very simply, every time a Japanese company purchased software produced in the United States or an American bought a television set manufactured in China, payments had to be made across national boundaries. Today, the international banking system has adjusted to the needs of an interdependent, globalized world. Large U.S. banks like JPMorgan Chase and Citibank have stationed ATMs on the streets of Frankfurt, Buenos Aires, and other major capitals. In New York, keen observers can spot the foreign offices of Barclays, Deutsche Bank, and Tokyo-Mitsubishi. By 2012, U.S. banks' claims on their own foreign offices were nearly $2 trillion, plus they had another $1 trillion of direct claims on foreigners. And more than 300 foreign banks with assets totaling more than $3 trillion had established a presence in the United States.

There are a number of ways banks can operate in foreign countries, depending on such factors as the legal environment. The most straightforward approach is to open a foreign branch that offers the same services as those in the home country. Certain legal structures also allow U.S. banks to engage in operations outside of the country, opening what looks to the casual observer like a branch (but may have a different legal status). For example, a bank can create an international banking facility (IBF), which allows it to accept deposits from and make loans to foreigners outside the country. Or the bank can create a subsidiary called an Edge Act corporation, which is established specifically to engage in international banking transactions. Alternatively, a bank holding company can purchase a controlling interest in a foreign bank. From our point of view, the classification of the particular enterprise is less important than the fact that U.S. banks take advantage of various methods to operate outside the country.

Foreign banks, of course, can take advantage of similar options. They can purchase an interest in a U.S. bank, open branches on U.S. soil, create a U.S. subsidiary, or open what is called an *agency office*. These alternatives differ in the spectrum of financial services they can provide.

MARKETS

The growth of international banking has had an economic impact similar to that of deregulation in the United States. Today, a borrower in France, Brazil, or Singapore can shop for a loan virtually anywhere in the world, and a depositor seeking the highest return can do the same. All this competition has made banking a tougher business. Profits are harder for bankers to come by today than they were in 1970, when depositors and borrowers were captive to small local banks. But while bankers' lives may be more difficult, on balance the improved efficiency of the financial system has enhanced growth everywhere.

One of the most important aspects of international banking is the eurodollar market. **Eurodollars** are dollar-denominated deposits in foreign banks. For reasons we will explain shortly, a bank in London, Zurich, or the Cayman Islands might offer its best customers the ability to make their deposits in dollars. In response, Ford Motor Corporation might convert a $1 million deposit in its New York bank to a eurodollar deposit in the bank's Cayman Islands subsidiary. After the $1 million has been deposited in Ford's Cayman Islands account, it is lent back to the New York bank. So, the account continues to provide Ford with all the same functions of the deposit at the same time that the New York bank now has a loan liability from its off-shore subsidiary.

Both Ford and the New York bank have an incentive to do this. For the bank, the Cayman Islands deposit is cheaper. It is not subject to U.S. reserve requirements, nor is the bank required to pay a deposit insurance premium on the balance. Moreover, regulatory supervision is more lax in the middle of the Gulf of Mexico than it is in the United States, which reduces the cost of compliance. Finally, profits from the offshore bank may be subject to a lower corporate income tax rate than profits originating inside the United States. These advantages allow the bank to pay Ford a higher interest rate on the deposit, and they increase the bank's net interest margin.

A number of forces conspired to create the eurodollar market. Originally, it was a response to restrictions on the movement of international capital that were instituted at the end of World War II with the creation of the Bretton Woods system of exchange rate management. (We will learn more about the international monetary system and capital controls in Chapter 19.) To ensure that the pound would retain its value, the British government imposed restrictions on the ability of British banks to finance international transactions. In an attempt to evade these restrictions, London banks began to offer dollar deposits and dollar-denominated loans to foreigners. The result was what we know today as the eurodollar market. The Cold War accelerated the market's development when the Soviet government, fearful that the U.S. government might freeze or confiscate them, shifted its dollar deposits from New York to London. In the United States, a combination of factors propelled the eurodollar market forward. In the 1960s, U.S. authorities tried to prevent dollars from leaving the country and made it costly for foreigners to borrow dollars in the United States for use elsewhere in the world. Then in the early 1970s, a combination of domestic interest-rate controls and high inflation rates made domestic deposits much less attractive than eurodollar deposits, which paid comparatively high interest rates.

Today, the eurodollar market in London is one of the biggest and most important financial markets in the world. And the interest rate at which banks lend each other eurodollars, called the **London Interbank Offered Rate (LIBOR)**, serves as the benchmark for more than $300 trillion (notional principal) of interest-rate derivatives, making it the leading global interest-rate indicator. It also is the standard against which many private loan rates are measured. For example, some adjustable-rate home mortgages in the United States carry an interest rate that is pegged to LIBOR. LIBOR figured prominently in the financial crisis of 2007–2009 when the interbank lending market dried up: the gap between LIBOR and the expected Federal Reserve policy interest rate provided a key measure of the intensity and persistence of the liquidity crisis (see Chapter 3, Lessons from the Crisis: Interbank Lending). However, revelations in 2012 that LIBOR had been widely manipulated by global banks raised serious doubts about its future as an interest-rate benchmark and led to government intervention to reform the way LIBOR is determined (see Applying the Concept: The LIBOR Scandal).

The Future of Banks

Today's banks are bigger, fewer in number, and more international in reach than the banks of yesteryear; they also have more to offer in the way of services. A typical large commercial bank now offers investment and insurance products as well as the more conventional deposit accounts and loans. This trend began in 1998 with Citigroup's creation (see the chapter introduction).

In November 1999, the Gramm-Leach-Bliley Financial Services Modernization Act effectively repealed the Glass-Steagall Act of 1933, allowing a commercial bank, investment bank, and insurance company to merge and form a **financial holding company**. Citigroup, which already included all three, became legal. Since then, investment firms like J.P. Morgan, which once dealt only in securities, were acquired by

APPLYING THE CONCEPT
THE LIBOR SCANDAL

For decades, LIBOR—the London Interbank Offered Rate—served as the premier global benchmark for private interest rates. The British Bankers' Association (BBA), a group of the largest London banks, published daily LIBOR rates for 15 maturities, ranging from overnight to 10 years, for the U.S. dollar and for nine other currencies. Ideally, these 150 benchmarks represented the rates at which banks of impeccable credit status lent to each other each day.

However, unlike other interest-rate benchmarks, such as U.S. Treasury bill rates or the federal funds rate, LIBOR rates were *not* based on actual transactions but rather on a daily survey of a panel of banks (18 London banks for dollar LIBOR, fewer banks for other currencies). Each panel bank voluntarily submitted to the BBA its estimate of the rate at which it "could borrow funds, were it to do so by asking for and then accepting interbank offers in reasonable market size, just prior to 11.00am London time."*

From one perspective, this survey approach is a feature rather than a flaw. At some maturities and for some currencies, there is little activity on which to base a transactions measure of interest rates. Even for the dollar, euro, and yen, activity is concentrated in the shortest maturities out to six months at most. Consequently, for illiquid instruments, a survey might provide more information than the market itself.

As LIBOR—and its sister rates in Frankfurt (EURIBOR) and Tokyo (TIBOR)—became benchmarks for trillions of dollars (or euros or yen) of derivative contracts, even a tiny one-basis-point (0.01 percent) change in these rates could result in millions in profits and losses on interest-rate derivatives. Hence, LIBOR's extraordinary success, combined with its reliance on good-faith reporting, also boosted incentives for BBA panel banks to manipulate it—both for profit and for their credit reputation—by submitting misleading rates to the BBA.

Beginning in 2012, the U.K. and U.S. governments revealed the extent of the LIBOR scandal, announcing record fines for two panel banks ($450 million and $1.5 billion, respectively) for multiyear manipulations of LIBOR. Meanwhile, as investigations of other banks continued, prosecutors began to charge bank employees with criminal fraud, and huge private lawsuits against LIBOR panel banks sought to recover the losses from the manipulation.

According to government reports, even before the financial crisis of 2007–2009, derivatives traders had encouraged their banks to submit misleading rates to benefit their derivatives holdings. And when the financial crisis began, some banks lowballed their LIBOR submissions to avoid standing out from the crowd and to appear more sound than in fact they were. Panel banks feared that reporting their true (higher-than-average) cost of funds might worry their depositors and prompt a run (see Chapter 14 for more on bank runs).

To restore the credibility of LIBOR and shift it to a transactions-based measure, U.K. regulators arranged for the transfer of ownership and administration of LIBOR as of 2014 from the BBA to an exchange (NYSE Euronext). But fixing "survey LIBOR" will not be easy. A transactions-based LIBOR would reduce the ease of manipulation, but only for the few maturities and currencies that are truly liquid (and even these can become illiquid in a crisis). At the same time, the potential legal exposure for the banks is causing some to withdraw from LIBOR-like surveys. Yet, with hundreds of trillions of dollars of derivatives and other contracts still based on LIBOR, governments fear that the disappearance of LIBOR—even temporarily—would spark another financial crisis. So, any transition to a better LIBOR will have to be carefully managed.**

*For more details on LIBOR, see *www.bbalibor.com/bbalibor-explained/faqs*.

**For the British government's proposed reforms, see "The Wheatley Review of LIBOR: final report" at *www.gov.uk/government/publications/the-wheatley-review*.

commercial banks (in this case, Chase Manhattan), while commercial banks like Bank of America have purchased large securities dealers and retail brokers (Merrill Lynch). To serve all their customers' financial needs, bank holding companies are converting to financial holding companies.

Financial holding companies are a limited form of **universal bank**, a type of firm that engages in a wide range of financial (and possibly nonfinancial) activities. Depending on the country, such an arrangement provides more or less separation among the banking, insurance, and securities industries. The most extreme example is Germany, where universal banks do everything under one roof, including direct investment in the shares of nonfinancial firms. In the United States, different financial activities must be undertaken in separate subsidiaries, and financial holding companies are still prohibited from making equity investments in nonfinancial companies.

The owners and managers of these large financial firms cite three reasons to create them. First, their range of activities, properly managed, permits them to be well diversified, so their profitability does not rely on one particular line of business. This reduced risk should increase the value of the firm.[6] Second, these firms are large enough to take advantage of **economies of scale**. A financial holding company needs only one CEO and one board of directors regardless of its size. Only one accounting system is required to run the company. Third, these companies hope to benefit from **economies of scope**. In the same way that a supermarket offers all sorts of food and nonfood items under one roof, financial holding companies offer customers a wide variety of services, all under the same brand name. This, too, should reduce costs—or maybe the people who run these firms are just trying to build empires.

While Citigroup was creating the first of these full-service financial firms in the United States, the rest of the financial world was not standing still. Individual firms were working to provide customers with the same services they could obtain from more traditional financial intermediaries. Money-market mutual funds competed with banks in providing liquidity services to customers. Mortgage brokers gave consumers a choice in how to borrow for the purchase of a home and then sold the mortgages in the financial marketplace. Today, people who need an auto loan or any kind of insurance can get dozens of price quotes in a few hours just by logging onto the Internet. The screening of loan applicants, which was once the job of the neighborhood banker, has been standardized and now can be done by virtually anyone. Then there are discount brokerage firms like Charles Schwab and E-Trade, which provide low-cost access to the financial markets. Unlike the banks of the past, these alternative financial intermediaries don't have balance sheets of their own. Instead, for a fee they provide their customers with access to financial markets.

In fact, thanks to recent technological advances, almost every service traditionally provided by financial intermediaries can now be produced independently, without the help of a large organization. Loan brokers can give large borrowers access to the pooled funds of many small savers. A variety of financial firms, including brokerage firms and mutual-fund companies, provides connections to the payments system, as well as the ability to transform assets into money quickly and at low cost. One of these days, even the electric company may get into the act. Or, as we have seen in Kenya's M-Pesa system, perhaps the cell phone provider will do so (see Chapter 2). And many intermediaries, including mutual-fund companies and pension funds, help customers to spread, share, and transfer risk. Finally, the production of information to mitigate the problems of adverse selection and moral hazard has become a business in and of itself.

As we survey the financial industry, then, we see two trends running in opposite directions. On the one hand, large firms are working hard to provide one-stop shopping for financial services. On the other hand, as we will see in Chapter 14, pressures are growing on governments to restrain or even break up the largest, most complex intermediaries that might need government support in a crisis. In addition, the industry is splintering into a host of small firms, each of which serves a very specific purpose. Will the future be one of generalists, specialists, or both? We will have to wait and see. In the meantime, let's look more closely at the role of nondepository financial institutions. And as we do, let's think about whether their products can be provided more easily and cheaply alone or together with other financial services.

---

[6]Financial economists disagree on whether the reduced risk would actually increase the firm's value. Some people argue that firms should not diversify themselves but leave the choice to their stockholders. An investor can always purchase shares in two companies that would otherwise merge, in proportion to whatever risk exposure the investor desires. There also is concern that a firm with many different lines of business may not be as well managed as specialized firms.

Nondepository Institutions

A survey of the financial industry reveals a broad array of intermediaries. Besides depository institutions, there are five major categories of nondepository institution: insurance companies; pension funds; securities firms, including brokers, mutual-fund companies, and investment banks; finance companies; and government-sponsored enterprises. This classification is neither exhaustive nor meant to imply that an institution's activities are restricted to a particular category. Nondepository institutions also include an assortment of alternative intermediaries, such as pawnshops (see Your Financial World, page 333), payday loan centers (see Your Financial World, page 307), rent-to-own centers, peer-to-peer lending firms (see In the News, page 288), and even loan sharks.

Table 13.3 shows that depository institutions accounted for less than one-third of the $54.6 trillion in assets held by financial intermediaries in 2012. In the decades after 1970, the share of intermediation handled by banks fell steadily until the crisis of 2007–2009 temporarily depressed the assets of many nonbanks, but the relative decline of depositories subsequently resumed. Insurance companies suffered a similar fate as their share of intermediation fell from 18.5 percent in 1970 to 12.8 percent in 2012. Meanwhile, mutual funds have been the big winners, growing from a 3.5 percent share in 1970 to nearly 25 percent in 2012. Pension funds increased in importance as

Table 13.3   Relative Size of U.S. Financial Intermediaries, 1970–2012

	Assets ($ billions) 2012	Percent of all Intermediary Assets		
		1970	1990	2012
Depository Institutions				
Commercial banks	$13,070	37.2%	29.3%	24.0%
Savings institutions	1,153	18.8	12.1	2.1
Credit unions	898	1.3	1.9	1.6
Insurance Companies				
Life insurance	5,562	14.8	12.1	10.2
Property and casualty	1,436	3.7	4.7	2.6
Pension Funds				
Private pension funds	6,599	8.1	14.4	12.1
Government pension funds	4,639	4.4	6.5	8.5
Mutual Funds				
Money market funds	2,507	0.0	4.4	4.6
Stock and bond funds	10,783	3.5	5.7	19.8
Finance Companies	1,600	4.7	5.4	2.9
Government-Sponsored Enterprises	6,305	3.4	3.7	11.6
Total Assets of All U.S. Financial Institutions in 2012 = $54.6 trillion				

NOTE: As of 2012, mutual funds include closed-end and exchange-traded funds.

SOURCE: *Board of Governors of the Federal Reserve System,* Flow of Funds of the United States, *December 6, 2012, Tables L.109 to L.128; and FDIC, Statistics on Depository Institutions.*

well, rising from 12.5 percent of all assets in 1970 to more than 20 percent over the 42-year period.

Our goal in this section is to understand the role of each of these types of nondepository institution in our financial system. We will do so by focusing on the functions of each. Recall from Chapter 11 that the functions of financial institutions can be divided into five categories: (1) pooling the resources of small savers; (2) providing safekeeping and accounting services, which allow people to make payments and track their assets; (3) supplying liquidity by converting resources into means of payment whenever needed; (4) providing diversification services; and (5) collecting and processing information in order to reduce information costs. We will use the same system to classify nondepository institutions.

Insurance Companies

Insurance companies began with long sea voyages. Centuries ago, distant trade and exploration were fraught with risk, and that risk generated a demand for insurance. Modern forms of insurance can be traced back to around 1400, when wool merchants insured their overland shipments from London to Italy for 12 to 15 percent of their value. (Overseas shipments were even more expensive to insure.) The first insurance codes were developed in Florence in 1523. They specified the standard provisions for a general insurance policy, such as the beginning and end of the coverage period and the time frame for receipt of payment following a loss. They also stipulated procedures for handling fraudulent claims in an attempt to reduce the moral hazard problem.

In 1688, Lloyd's of London was established. Today, Lloyd's is famous for insuring singers' voices, dancers' legs, even food critics' taste buds, as well as more traditional assets like airplanes and ships. The best-known insurance company in the world, Lloyd's began in a small London coffeehouse whose proprietor, Edward Lloyd, catered to retired sea captains who had prospered in the East Indies spice trade. Having sailed many of the trade routes themselves, these captains possessed special knowledge of the hazards of sea voyages. They used their knowledge to assess the risks associated with particular routes and to dabble in marine insurance. The risks were not inconsequential. In the 17th century, a typical voyage to the Spice Islands (part of Indonesia) and back lasted three years. Only one in three ships returned with their cargo, and as few as one in eight sailors lived to tell of the adventure. The rewards of a successful voyage were coveted spices like nutmeg, a single sack of which could make a sea captain wealthy for the rest of his life.

To obtain insurance, a ship's owner would write the details of the proposed voyage on a piece of paper, together with the amount he was willing to pay for the service, and then circulate the paper among the patrons at Edward Lloyd's coffeehouse. Interested individuals would decide how much of the risk to accept and then sign their names under the description of the voyage. This customary way of doing business became the source of the term *underwriter.* Underwriting was open to anyone who wished to assume the risk associated with sea voyages. Because Lloyd's predated by several centuries the concept of limited liability, in which investors' losses were confined to the amount of their investment, underwriting implied unlimited liability. The saying was that an underwriter was liable down to his last cufflink.

Today Lloyd's provides insurance through the more conventional structure of a limited liability company. The losses of individual investors in a syndicate are limited to the amount of their initial investment, and no person is exposed to the possibility of financial ruin.

Two Types of Insurance   At their most basic level, all insurance companies operate like Lloyd's of London. They accept premiums from policyholders in exchange for the promise of compensation if certain events occur. A homeowner pays a premium in return for the promise that if the house burns down, the insurance company will pay to rebuild it. For the individual policyholder, then, insurance is a way to transfer risk. In terms of the financial system as a whole, insurance companies specialize in three of the five functions performed by intermediaries: They pool small premiums and make large investments with them; they diversify risks across a large population; and they screen and monitor policyholders to mitigate the problem of asymmetric information.

Insurance companies offer two types of insurance: life insurance and **property and casualty insurance**. Life insurers—companies like Prudential of America, Metropolitan Life, and John Hancock Mutual Life—sell policies that protect the insured against the loss of earnings from disability, retirement, or death. Property and casualty companies sell policies that protect households and businesses from losses arising from accident, fire, and natural disaster. Both types of intermediary allow individuals to transfer their risk to a group. While a single company may provide both kinds of insurance, the two businesses operate very differently.

Life insurance comes in two basic forms, called term and whole life insurance, as well as a variety of hybrids. **Term life insurance** provides a payment to the policyholder's beneficiaries in the event of the insured's death at any time during the policy's term. The premium depends on the very predictable proportion of people (of a given age) who will die. Term policies are generally renewable every year so long as the policyholder is less than 65 years old. Many people obtain term life insurance through their employers, an arrangement called group life insurance.

Whole life insurance is a combination of term life insurance and a savings account. The policyholder pays a fixed premium over his or her lifetime in return for a fixed benefit when the policyholder dies. Should the policyholder decide to discontinue the policy, its cash value will be refunded. As time passes and the policyholder ages, the emphasis of the whole life policy shifts from insurance to savings. Someone who lives to a ripe old age will have accumulated substantial savings in a whole life policy, which can be cashed in if the policyholder chooses. Whole life insurance tends to be an expensive way to save, though, so its use as a savings vehicle has declined markedly as people have discovered cheaper alternatives.

Most adults have experience with property and casualty insurance because driving a car without it is illegal. Auto insurance is a combination of property insurance on the car itself and casualty insurance on the driver, who is protected against liability for harm or injury to other people or their property. Holders of property and casualty insurance pay premiums in exchange for protection during the term of the policy.

On the balance sheets of insurance companies, these promises to policyholders show up as liabilities. While some claims may already be in process, most of them are future claims. On the asset side, insurance companies hold a combination of stocks, bonds, and other assets. Property and casualty companies profit from the fees they charge for administering the policies they write; the claims are covered by the premiums. Because the assets are essentially reserves against sudden claims, they have to be liquid. A look at the balance sheet of a property and casualty insurer will show a preponderance of government and other liquid securities and money-market instruments.

Life insurance companies hold assets of longer maturity than property and casualty insurers. Because most life insurance payments will be made well into the future, this better matches the maturity of the companies' assets and liabilities. Furthermore, while stocks may carry a relatively low degree of risk when held for periods of 25 years or

YOUR FINANCIAL WORLD
How Much Life Insurance Do You Need?

We discussed disability insurance in Chapter 3 and automobile insurance in Chapter 5. What about life insurance? How much should you buy? The first question is whether you should buy any at all. The purpose of life insurance is to take care of the people you are supporting should something unpleasant happen to you. Think of it as replacement income that will be there when you're not. People with young children are the ones who need life insurance the most. If a parent dies, someone will have to raise those children and put them through school, and a life insurance policy will pay the bills. Life insurance is *not* for a single college student with no obligations, so don't let anyone sell it to you if you don't need it.

If you think you need life insurance, the next step is to decide what kind. The best approach is to buy *term life insurance,* which will pay off only if you die. Because other kinds of life insurance include investment components, they are more costly. And because the people who need life insurance most are young families with limited incomes and big expenses, the more affordable the policy, the better. Making your insurance and investment decisions separately is also easier than trying to achieve all your goals with a single vehicle.*

Finally, how much life insurance should you buy? If you are married with two small children, most advisors recommend that you buy a term policy worth six to eight times your annual income. While that might cover your family's living expenses until the children are grown, consider carefully whether it will be enough to send them to college. If you and your spouse each earn $35,000 a year, each of you might need $400,000 worth of life insurance. For someone who is between 30 and 40 years old, a $400,000 policy might cost about $500 a year, so out of your joint annual income of $70,000, you and your spouse would be spending $1,000 on term life insurance. That's expensive, so don't buy more than you need.

*Your parents and grandparents may have purchased whole life insurance policies for two reasons. First, in the past, individuals did not have access to all the investment choices that are available today. Second, tax laws were different; for some people, saving through a whole life insurance policy had tax advantages. But with the creation of tax-deferred savings vehicles like individual retirement accounts (IRAs), those benefits disappeared. Today, you would likely pay a life insurance company much more than the value of any tax benefits to you to administer a whole life insurance policy.

more (recall the discussion in Chapter 8), insurance companies cannot risk the possibility that they may be forced to sell stocks when prices are low in order to pay policyholders' claims. As a result, life insurance companies hold mostly bonds.

The Role of Insurance Companies Like life insurers, property and casualty insurers pool risks to generate predictable payouts. That is, they reduce risk by spreading it across many policies. Recall from Chapter 5 that a group of investments with uncorrelated returns is less risky than any individual investment. The same is true of insurance contracts. While there is no way to know exactly which policies will require payment—who will have an automobile accident, lose a house to fire, or die—the insurance company can accurately estimate the percentage of policyholders who will file claims. Doing so allows managers to compute, with little uncertainty, how much the firm will need to pay out in any given year. From the point of view of policyholders, property and casualty insurance allows them to spread the risk of accident and damage across a large group of individuals.

In Chapter 11, we discussed the problem of asymmetric information in stock and bond finance. Recall that when a lender or investor cannot tell a good borrower or investment from a bad one, the tendency is for only the worst opportunities to present themselves. This phenomenon is called adverse selection. Furthermore, once borrowers or entrepreneurs have received financing, they have less incentive to avoid risk than the lender or investor. That problem is called moral hazard.

While adverse selection and moral hazard create significant problems in the stock and bond markets, they create worse problems in the insurance market. A person who has terminal cancer surely has an incentive to buy life insurance for the largest amount possible—that's adverse selection. And without fire insurance, people would have more fire extinguishers in their houses. Fire insurance creates moral hazard, encouraging homeowners to be less careful in protecting their homes than they would otherwise. Insurance companies work hard to reduce both these problems. By screening applicants, they can reduce adverse selection. A person who wants to buy a life insurance policy often must undergo a physical evaluation: weight, blood pressure, blood tests, and health history. Only those who pass the exam are allowed to purchase policies. And people who want automobile insurance must provide their driving records, including traffic citations and accident histories. While bad drivers may be allowed to buy car insurance, they will need to pay more for it. By screening drivers and adjusting their premiums accordingly, then, insurance companies can reduce their losses due to adverse selection.

Insurance companies have ways to reduce moral hazard as well. Policies usually include restrictive covenants that require the insured to engage or not to engage in certain activities. To qualify for fire insurance, a restaurant owner might be required to have the sprinkler system examined periodically; to obtain insurance against physical injury, a baseball or basketball player might be precluded from riding a motorcycle. Beyond such covenants, insurance policies often include *deductibles,* which require the insured to pay the initial cost of repairing accidental damage, up to some maximum amount. Or they may require *coinsurance,* in which the insurance company shoulders a percentage of the claim, perhaps 80 or 90 percent, and the insured assumes the rest of the cost.

"We cannot write a life policy for your husband, Mrs. Blaine, because he is already dead. In insurance terms, that is considered a preexisting condition."

It is interesting to speculate about the future of insurance in an age in which firms can collect more and more information at lower and lower cost. Remember that insurance is meant to shift risk from individuals to groups, not to shift the responsibility for events that are certain to happen. For example, no one expects an insurance company to sell life insurance to a person with a terminal disease.

Herein lies a potential problem. If, with the decoding of the human genome, tests become available whereby a person can determine their probability of developing a terminal disease, then they may be able to use this information to get a fairly good idea of their life expectancy and relative cost of health care. If applicants for health insurance were to withhold this information from insurance companies, the adverse selection problem could become severe enough to cause the industry to collapse. By contrast, if applicants chose to reveal this information, they might not be able to obtain insurance. Someone who has a high probability of getting heart disease at a young age will still be able to get automobile insurance, but getting life or health insurance will

APPLYING THE CONCEPT
REINSURANCE AND "CAT BONDS"

To get a mortgage on a home, you'll need insurance. Regardless of where you live, your lender will require you to have fire insurance, and in some places you may also need insurance against natural disasters like floods, earthquakes, or hurricanes. Without such insurance you won't get a mortgage, and without a mortgage you won't buy a house. Clearly, it's in everyone's interest for insurance companies to provide such insurance and spread the risk. But sometimes this kind of insurance isn't easy to obtain.

Imagine that an insurer is thinking of offering earthquake insurance in California. Unlike automobile accidents, when an earthquake hits, a large number of policyholders will all file claims at the same time. The result for the insurance company is a large, undiversified risk. To offer earthquake insurance and stay in business, a property and casualty insurance company must find some way to insure itself against catastrophic risks—large natural disasters that generate a significant number of payouts simultaneously.

Reinsurance companies offer a solution to this problem by providing insurance to insurance companies. Say the California insurer estimates that an earthquake would generate payments of $15 billion (the approximate loss in the 1994 earthquake in Northridge, Los Angeles). The company may have the resources to cover only the first $1 billion of policyholders' claims. To write the full $15 billion worth of insurance, the company will need to buy $14 billion of reinsurance.

Reinsurance companies are enormous; they operate all over the world. Their geographic spread allows them to diversify their risk, because earthquakes don't happen at the same time in both California and Japan. The fact that reinsurance companies can spread their risk globally gives them the ability to withstand individual losses, even if they are catastrophic. For this to work, reinsurers have to be big.

So big, in fact, that they have become near monopolies, driving up the price of reinsurance in the process.

The rising cost of reinsurance has spurred the creation of a second solution to the problem of insuring catastrophic risk. Financial experts have designed catastrophic bonds, or *cat bonds,* which allow individual investors to share a very small portion of the reinsurance risk. It works like this. Through an investment bank, an insurance company will sell a quantity of cat bonds, immediately investing proceeds in low-risk financial instruments like U.S. Treasury bonds. If a catastrophe occurs, the U.S. Treasury bonds are sold and the resulting funds used to pay the claims the insurance company faces. But if no earthquake, fire, or hurricane hits during the policy period, the cat bond owners receive a substantial return that can be as high as 10 percentage points above the yield on U.S. Treasury bonds of equal maturity.* This high level of compensation, coupled with a very low correlation with the return on most other investments, means that cat bonds can both improve the expected return and lower the risk of a typical investor's portfolio. Nevertheless, the demand for cat bonds remains limited, with issuance of less than $7 billion in 2012, just below the 2007 peak.

The existence of reinsurance and cat bonds has clear benefits. These mechanisms for transferring and spreading the risk of catastrophic disaster improve the risk–return tradeoff for individual investors, enable insurance companies to offer more insurance than they could otherwise, and allow prospective homeowners to get the insurance they need—and the mortgage financing they want—to purchase a home.

---

*One of the first cat bonds to be issued was a $400 million offering in 1997 by the United Services Automobile Association (USAA), an insurer of current and past military personnel and their families. The bond agreement provided that if USAA's losses from a hurricane rated category 3, 4, or 5 exceeded $1 billion over the next year, bondholders would pay 80 percent of the next $500 million in claims.

be very difficult. Providing affordable insurance for such "preexisting conditions" was one of the leading motivations for the U.S. health care reforms that began to take effect in 2014.

Pension Funds

Like an insurance company, a pension fund offers people the ability to make premium payments today in exchange for promised payments under certain future circumstances. Also like an insurance company, pension funds do not accept deposits. They do help people to develop the discipline of saving regularly, getting them started early and helping them to stick with it. As we saw in Chapter 4, the earlier a person begins saving and the more disciplined he or she is, the better off that person will be later in life. Saving from an early age means enjoying a higher income at retirement. Pension plans not only provide an easy way to make sure that a worker saves and has sufficient resources in old age; they help savers to diversify their risk. By pooling the savings of many small investors, pension funds spread the risk, ensuring that funds will be available to investors in their old age.

People can use a variety of methods to save for retirement, including employer-sponsored plans and individual savings plans, both of which allow workers to defer income tax on their savings until they retire. Nearly everyone who works for a large corporation in the United States has an employer-administered pension plan. There are two basic types: defined-benefit (DB) pension plans and defined-contribution (DC) pension plans. Regardless of the type, many employer-sponsored plans require a person to work for a certain number of years before qualifying for benefits. This qualifying process is called **vesting**. Think of vesting as the point at which the contributions your employer has made to the pension plan on your behalf belong to you. Changing jobs before your pension contributions have been vested can be very costly.

Let's take a look at how the two types of pension plan work. **Defined-benefit plans** were once more common than they are today. Participants in DB plans receive a lifetime retirement income based on the number of years they worked at the company and their final salary. For example, someone who worked for the same company for 30 years and retired at a salary of $100,000 might receive 2 percent of that salary for each year of service, or $60,000 per year. That may seem good, but to reap such benefits, most people would need to work a very long time for the same firm.

Defined-contribution plans are replacing defined-benefit plans, and they are very different. These plans are sometimes referred to by names like "401(k)" after their designations in the Internal Revenue Service code. In a defined-contribution plan, the employee and employer both make contributions into an investment account that belongs to the employee. Unlike a defined-benefit plan, in a DC plan the employer takes no responsibility for the size of the employee's retirement income. Instead, at retirement the employee receives the accumulated funds in the account and must decide what to do with them. The options include accepting a lump sum, removing small amounts at a time, or converting the balance to a fixed monthly payment for life by purchasing an annuity (see Your Financial World: Annuities).

You can think of a pension plan as the opposite of life insurance. One pays off if you live, the other if you don't. The two vehicles are similar enough that the same institution often offers both. And not surprisingly, the balance sheets of pension funds look a lot like those of life insurance companies; both hold long-term assets like corporate bonds and stocks. The only difference is that life insurance companies hold only half the equities that pension funds do.[7]

Finally, it is worth noting that the U.S. government does provide insurance for private, defined-benefit pension systems. If a company goes bankrupt, the Pension Benefit Guaranty Corporation (PBGC) will take over the fund's liabilities. The PBGC currently guarantees more than 25,000 pension funds covering 43 million workers and retirees. While the PBGC's insurance is capped, so that highly paid employees like airline pilots are not fully protected, it still increases the incentive for a firm's managers to engage in risky behavior. To guard against this possibility, regulators monitor pension funds closely. Even so, some experts believe that PBGC could end up owing hundreds of billions of dollars in the not-too-distant future. Indeed, the spate of pension plan failures and investment setbacks in the financial crisis of 2007–2009 doubled the PBGC's deficit to $22 billion in fiscal 2009 compared with the prior year; by fiscal 2012, it was $34 billion.

[7]The heavier emphasis on equities makes pension funds more risky. This is a risk that is potentially borne by the plans' participants. But as mentioned later in this section, defined-benefit pension plans are insured by the U.S. government, so in reality this is a risk borne broadly by everyone.

APPLYING THE CONCEPT
PUBLIC PENSIONS AND THE SOCIAL SECURITY SYSTEM

Providing for the elderly is a tremendous challenge for any society. Traditionally, children cared for their parents when they became old. But with the advent of modern industrial societies and an associated increase in geographic mobility, many elderly parents no longer live with their children. Today the expectation is that people will save enough while they are working to pay their own way when they retire. If they don't, the general view is that in a civilized society, government should care for the poor.

During the 20th century, the governments of many countries created pension systems that provided a guaranteed income to the elderly. These programs were financed by tax revenues paid by the young. As long as workers' incomes were growing quickly enough and the population itself was growing, the arrangement worked well. Around 1970, however, both economic growth and population growth began to slow in industrialized countries. At the same time, medical care was improving, raising the prospect of a longer life for everyone. Gradually the ratio of workers to retirees began to fall, so fewer and fewer working people were supporting more and more retirees.

Today, to remain financially viable, these systems must change. One solution—to raise the age at which full retirement benefits are received to 70 instead of 67—has so far been politically unpalatable. Failure to deal with the problem has set the stage for a crisis. In the United States, the Social Security system will eventually be unable to meet the obligations currently on its books.

Social Security is not a pension system in the traditional sense of the term. All U.S. workers pay Social Security tax (see the line labeled "FICA" on your pay stub); in return, the government promises to make payments to them when they retire. But with the Social Security taxes it collects from workers, the government can do only one of two things: it can give it to current retirees or spend it on general programs. As such, Social Security is a "pay-as-you-go" system that transfers revenues directly from current workers to current retirees.

This is a very different arrangement from a private pension fund, in which contributions accumulate and are invested for the long term and only after many years are paid out to retirees. Not only is the source of funds different but the allocation of risk differs too. In the current Social Security system, the responsibility to pay retirees belongs to younger generations. They foot the bill; they face the risk. If the economy does poorly, for example, wages of the young who are working will fall, making it more burdensome to pay the taxes required to honor promises to retirees. In contrast, in a private pension system, individuals' own savings provide their retirement incomes and they themselves face the risk that the return on their investments may be low.

The Social Security system's finances are in bad shape. According to the government's 2012 estimates, by 2033 tax income will be sufficient to finance only 75 percent of promised benefits. There are only a few ways the problem can be repaired. The government can reduce the benefits promised to future retirees, raise the tax rate that future workers pay, or convert the system into one that mirrors a private pension plan, with individual accounts. Most proposals to fix the system involve some combination of all three of these approaches. For example, suggestions to *privatize* the system involve reducing benefits to those who are currently working, raising their Social Security taxes, and placing new revenues into individual accounts similar to defined-contribution pension funds. In such a system, the government would continue to guarantee that the poor do not starve, but those who are well enough off to take care of themselves would have to do so.

At this point, all anyone knows is that the Social Security system will have to change and the faster the better. In evaluating the proposals to fix it, keep in mind two key questions: Who will pay the bills and who will shoulder the risks?

Securities Firms: Brokers, Mutual Funds, and Investment Banks

The broad class of securities firms includes brokerages, investment banks, and mutual fund companies. In one way or another, these are all financial intermediaries. The primary services of brokerage firms are accounting (to keep track of customers' investment balances), custody services (to make sure valuable records such as stock certificates are safe), and access to secondary markets (in which customers can buy and sell financial instruments). Brokers also provide loans to customers who wish to purchase stock on margin. And they provide liquidity, both by offering check-writing privileges with their investment accounts and by allowing investors to sell assets quickly. Mutual-fund companies like Vanguard, Fidelity, and Dreyfus offer liquidity services as well; their money-market mutual funds are a key example. But the primary function of mutual funds is to pool the small savings of individuals in diversified portfolios that are composed of a wide variety of financial instruments.

All securities firms are very much in the business of producing information. But while brokers and mutual funds provide some investment advice to their retail customers, information is at the heart of the investment banking business. Investment banks like Goldman Sachs, Morgan Stanley, and JPMorgan Chase—all now divisions of bank holding companies—are the conduits through which firms raise funds in the capital markets. Through their **underwriting** services, these investment banks issue new stocks and a variety of other debt instruments. Most commonly, the underwriter guarantees the price of a new issue and then sells it to investors at a higher price, a practice called *placing the issue*. The underwriter profits from the difference between the price guaranteed to the firm that issues the security and the price at which the bond or stock is sold to investors. But because the price at which the investment bank sells the bonds or stocks in financial markets can turn out to be lower than the price guaranteed to the issuing company, there is some risk to underwriting. For most large issues, a group of investment banks will band together and spread the risk among themselves rather than one of them taking the risk alone.

Information and reputation are central to the underwriting business. Underwriters collect information to determine the price of the new securities and then put their reputations on the line when they go out to sell the issues. A large, well-established investment bank will not underwrite issues indiscriminately. To do so would reduce the value of the bank's brand, along with the fees the bank can charge.

In addition to underwriting, investment banks provide advice to firms that want to merge with or acquire other firms. Investment bankers do the research to identify potential *mergers and acquisitions* and estimate the value of the new, combined company. The information they collect and the advice they give must be valuable because they are paid handsomely for them. In facilitating these combinations, investment banks perform a service to the economy. Mergers and acquisitions help to ensure that the people who manage firms do the best job possible. Managers who don't get the most out of the resources entrusted to them risk having their company purchased by executives who can do a better job. This threat of a takeover—sometimes described as the *market for corporate control*—provides discipline in the management of individual companies and improves the allocation of resources across the economy.

Finance Companies

Finance companies are in the lending business. They raise funds directly in the financial markets by issuing commercial paper and securities and then use them to make loans to individuals and corporations. Because these companies specialize in making loans, they are concerned largely with reducing the transactions and information costs that are associated with intermediated finance. And because of their narrow focus, finance companies are particularly good at screening potential borrowers' creditworthiness, monitoring their performance during the term of the loan, and seizing collateral in the event of a default.

TOOLS OF THE TRADE
Hedge Funds

Hedge funds are strictly for millionaires. These investment partnerships (sometimes referred to as *nontraditional investment funds*) bring together small groups of people who meet certain wealth requirements. To avoid various legal regulations, hedge funds come in two basic sizes: they can have a maximum of either 99 investors, each of whom has at least $1 million in net worth, or 499 investors, each of whom has at least $5 million in net worth. The larger hedge funds can also accept funds from institutional investors like pension funds, mutual funds, and insurance companies so long as their net worth is at least $25 million. The minimum investment in a hedge fund is usually $100,000. These really are millionaires' investment clubs.

Hedge funds are run by a general partner, or manager, who is in charge of day-to-day decisions. Managers are very well paid, receiving an annual fee of at least 2 percent of assets plus 20 percent of profits. In a year in which the fund's return on investment is 10 percent, the manager of an average-size fund of $500 million will receive $20 million in fees.

Because these funds are unregulated, finding out what their portfolios contain can be a challenge even for the fund's investors: the manager need not tell anyone. This secrecy creates the very real possibility of moral hazard. If a fund starts to incur losses, determining the reason for the fall in value is often impossible. To ensure that the manager's incentives match those of the investors, the manager is required to keep a large fraction of his or her own wealth in the fund. By and large, this requirement solves the problem of moral hazard; fraudulent behavior is extremely rare.

The name *hedge fund* may suggest that these funds employ the diversification techniques discussed in Chapter 5, but they do not. Hedging reduces risk by grouping together individual investments whose returns tend to move in opposite directions, but hedge funds are not low-risk enterprises. Because they are organized as private partnerships, hedge funds are not constrained in their investment strategies; they can trade in derivatives and borrow to create leverage.

A.W. Jones founded the first hedge fund in 1949. His fund combined leverage with short selling (the practice of borrowing a stock or bond whose price you believe will fall, selling it, and then buying it back at a lower price before repaying the lender). Jones divided the fund's equities into two groups: companies whose stock prices he thought would fall and companies whose stock prices he thought would rise. He sold the first group short and used the proceeds to buy shares in the second group. The term *hedge* in the name *hedge fund* comes from the fact that when the market in general went up or down, moving all stocks in the same direction, the fund would take losses on one group of stock but turn a profit on the second. It was hedged against movements in the market as a whole. Jones turned a profit when the stocks he sold short went down relative to the stocks he purchased. And those profits were substantial.

Today we would refer to Jones's fund as a "long-short hedge fund" because he was long on some stocks and short on others. In 2012, according to research firm Pertrac, more than 12,000 hedge funds managed more than $2.3 trillion. The long-short approach is only one of the strategies their managers follow. *Macro fund* managers take unhedged positions in the hope of benefiting from shifts in interest rates or national market conditions. *Global fund* managers engage in international stock picking. And the managers of *relative value funds* try to exploit small, transitory differences in the prices of related securities, such as U.S. Treasury bills and bonds. Long-Term Capital Management, the hedge fund that collapsed in September 1998 (see Chapter 9), was following this last strategy, trying to take advantage of price differences between U.S. Treasury bonds of slightly different maturities. Playing games with interest rates is what led the firm to amass $1.25 trillion in interest-rate swaps.*

Regardless of the strategies they use, hedge fund managers typically strive to create returns that roughly equal those of the stock market (as measured by a comprehensive index like the S&P 500) but are uncorrelated with it. So while individual hedge funds are very risky—something like 10 percent of them close down every year—a portfolio that invests in a large number of these funds can expect returns equal to the stock market average with less risk. That is why people like hedge funds and why successful hedge fund managers are so well paid.

*For an insightful history and analysis of hedge funds, see Sebastian Mallaby, *More Money than God: Hedge Funds and the Making of a New Elite* (New York: Penguin Press, 2011).

Most finance companies specialize in one of three loan types: consumer loans, business loans, and what are called sales loans. Some also provide commercial and home mortgages. *Consumer finance* firms provide small installment loans to individual consumers. If you visit an appliance store to purchase a new refrigerator, you may be offered a deal that includes "no money down and no payments for six months." If you accept this loan offer, you'll be asked to fill out an application and to wait a few minutes while someone checks your credit. The credit is usually supplied not by the store but by a finance company like Wells Fargo. This kind of consumer credit allows people without sufficient savings to purchase appliances such as television sets, washing machines, and microwave ovens.

Business finance companies provide loans to businesses. If you want to start your own airline, for example, you will need to acquire some airplanes. That isn't as difficult as it may sound, because you don't need to shell out the entire $100 million price of a new plane. Airplanes, like automobiles, can be leased. That is, a business finance company buys the plane and then leases it back to you, an approach that significantly reduces the cost of starting your new enterprise. While this example is extreme, finance companies will purchase many types of equipment and lease them back to firms.

In addition to equipment leasing, business finance companies provide both inventory loans and accounts receivable loans. Inventory loans enable firms to keep their shelves stocked so that when a customer asks for a product, the firm can fill the order. Accounts receivable loans provide firms with immediate resources in anticipation of receipt of customers' payments. The purpose of both these loan types is to provide short-term liquidity to firms.

Sales finance companies specialize in larger loans for major purchases, such as automobiles. Car dealers customarily offer financing to people who are shopping for a new car. When you purchase a car, at a certain point in the negotiations the salesperson will ask how you intend to pay for it. Unless you have sizable savings or are buying a very cheap car, you will need to borrow. The car business is organized so that you don't need to leave the dealership to get your loan; someone there will take care of it for you. The financing is arranged through a finance company, possibly a finance division of the manufacturer, that specializes in making car loans.

Government-Sponsored Enterprises

You will not be surprised to learn that the U.S. government is directly involved in the financial intermediation system and that the risk taking of government-related intermediaries contributed importantly to the financial crisis of 2007–2009. You might be surprised that intermediation by a variety of government agencies grew markedly after the crisis and accounted for most new home mortgages.

In some cases, the government provides loan guarantees; in others, it charters financial institutions to provide specific types of financing, such as home, farm, and student loans. In 1968, when Congress wanted to expand its support for mortgage lending to low- and moderate-income families, it privatized the Depression-era Federal National Mortgage Association (**Fannie Mae**) and, in 1970, issued a similar charter for a competing entity, the Federal Home Loan Mortgage Corporation (*Freddie Mac*). Each was thus chartered by the government as a corporation with a public purpose, a hybrid corporate form known as a government-sponsored enterprise (GSE). While the debt issued by Fannie and Freddie was not guaranteed by the government, market participants generally assumed that it would be in a crisis.

In 1968, Congress also established the Government National Mortgage Corporation (*Ginnie Mae*) as a GSE that is wholly owned by the federal government. The U.S. government explicitly guarantees Ginnie Mae debt. (To provide student loans, Congress in 1974 chartered the Student Loan Marketing Association—Sallie Mae—as a GSE but by 2004 had terminated the charter, making Sallie Mae a wholly private-sector firm).

IN THE NEWS
Fed's Tarullo Says Reviving Glass-Steagall May Be Costly

Bloomberg

By Craig Torres and Joshua Zumbrun

December 4, 2012

Federal Reserve Governor Daniel Tarullo said enacting a law similar to the Glass-Steagall Act that separates investment and commercial banking could impose "substantial costs" by curtailing the range of services offered by individual banks.

Two other proposals, to place a cap on banks' non-deposit financing or to require firms to maintain certain levels of long-term debt, may better reduce the risks that led to the 2008 financial crisis and brought down firms such as Bear Stearns Cos., Lehman Brothers Holdings Inc., and American International Group Inc.

"The reinstatement of Glass-Steagall would mean that bank clients could no longer retain one financial firm that would have the capacity to offer the whole range of financing options," Tarullo said today . . . . Another cost to such a rule could be damage caused to the many small banks that provide some capital market services to small businesses, he said.

Tarullo, 60, has overseen the implementation of the Dodd-Frank Act, the most sweeping overhaul of financial regulation since the 1930s, and a reorganization of the Fed's approach to inspecting banks and ensuring financial stability. He was Obama's first appointee to the Fed and is the lead governor in charge of bank supervision and regulation.

Government Support

The Fed and lawmakers in recent years have mitigated some of the "too big to fail problem," in which the collapse of a firm threatens the broader financial system and would require government support, Tarullo said in response to audience questions.

"I would certainly not say it's been eliminated," Tarullo said of the risk posed by too-big-to-fail firms.

In expressing skepticism about Glass-Steagall, Tarullo said many firms at the center of the financial crisis in 2008 and 2009 were either stand-alone banks or investment banks, such as Lehman Brothers and Washington Mutual Inc.

Such firms wouldn't necessarily be subject to a break-up under Glass-Steagall.

Capping a bank's non-deposit liabilities as a fraction of U.S. GDP has "considerable conceptual appeal," Tarullo said. Such an approach "allows relative flexibility to the firm in meeting that constraint" since the firm could shrink its balance sheet through selling any assets it wished.

At their founding, the GSEs had similar financial characteristics. They issued short-term bonds and used the proceeds to provide loans or guarantees of one form or another. Because of their explicit or implicit relationship to the government, they paid less than private borrowers for their liabilities and passed on some of these benefits in the form of subsidized mortgages and loans.

As the crisis of 2007–2009 highlighted, housing intermediation is by far the largest of these government-sponsored activities. In 2012, mortgage loans and mortgage guarantees issued by GSEs and other federal agencies exceeded $6 trillion, or more than half of the residential mortgage market of nearly $11 trillion. For comparison, outstanding Treasury securities—including bills, notes, and bonds—totaled $11 trillion.

In the years preceding the 2007–2009 crisis, Fannie and Freddie had taken advantage of their implicit government backstop by operating on a slim capital cushion. Each had a leverage ratio (assets divided by capital) that was around three times higher than that of the average U.S. bank (recall the discussion in Chapter 12). In 2005, for

Certain Size

If research showed economies of scale and scope in banking were unlikely to be realized beyond a certain size, then policy makers would "have a point of reference for setting the cap," he said.

Further analysis of the proposal would be needed, Tarullo said, and may "suggest alternative means to the same policy goals."

A proposal to require banks to increase the use of long-term debt "would not seem to carry significant hurdles," he said. . . .

The central bank has used annual stress tests of banks' capital strength to boost tier one common capital to $803 billion for the 19 largest banks from $420 billion in the first quarter of 2009. The ratio of capital to assets weighted for risk has about doubled to 10.9 percent from 5.4 percent. . . .

In the past two months, Tarullo has introduced two new ideas for bank regulation. He said in an Oct. 10 speech that it would be "appropriate" for Congress to legislate an upper boundary for the largest banks that are able to preserve a "too-big-to-fail" quality.

The Fed governor said on Nov. 28 at the Yale School of Management in New Haven, Connecticut, that the central bank is planning tougher capital and leverage rules for U.S. units of foreign banks.

"We need to adjust the regulatory requirements for foreign banks in response to changes in the nature of their activities in the United States, the risks attendant to those changes, and instructions from Congress," Tarullo said.

LESSONS OF THE ARTICLE

In 2010, Congress enacted the Dodd-Frank financial reforms to prevent future crises but left many specifics to be decided by regulators like the Fed. Their challenge is to reduce systemic risk without rendering the financial system inefficient. To limit the "too big to fail" problem, policymakers are trying a number of remedies, including capping the size and leverage of the largest financial firms and prohibiting certain risky activities. The article notes that segmenting the activities of intermediaries today (as did the Glass-Steagall Act in 1933) would increase costs without eliminating systemic risk (see Chapter 5, Lessons from the Crisis: Systemic Risk).

example, their financial statements showed a leverage ratio of about 30 to 1. With such low levels of capital, these two massive GSEs could not withstand the surge of defaults when home prices began to decline nationwide in 2006.

Despite numerous public efforts to save them, a run on GSE debt in the summer of 2008 compelled the U.S. Treasury to place Fannie and Freddie into conservatorship—a bankruptcy procedure that allows them to operate despite insolvency. A year later, the Congressional Budget Office estimated that the government's commitments to those GSEs would add nearly $300 billion to the federal deficit in 2009, most of which reflected the value of their assets and liabilities when conservatorship began.[8]

In the crisis, Fannie and Freddie proved to be too big to fail—their demise probably would have toppled the entire financial system. This did *not* come as a surprise.

[8]See Congressional Budget Office, "An Overview of Federal Support for Housing," *Economic and Budget Issue Brief,* November 3, 2009.

YOUR FINANCIAL WORLD
Annuities

Most college students don't have to worry about annuities, at least not yet. But it is very likely that when you retire, you will turn your retirement savings into an annuity. And, in the meantime, someone may try to sell you one. Here's what annuities are and how they work.

An annuity is a financial instrument in which a person (called the "annuitant") makes a payment in exchange for the promise of a series of future payments. Similar to a bond, annuities are typically sold by insurance companies, and they come in many forms and have many names. There are fixed-period versus lifetime annuities. A fixed-period annuity makes fixed monthly or annual payments for a specified period like 10 or 15 years. By contrast, a lifetime annuity guarantees periodic payments for the remainder of the annuitant's life (and possibly, that of the person's spouse as well). An annuity is the reverse of life insurance. A life insurance policyholder pays the insurance company each year or month, with the beneficiaries receiving a lump sum when he or she dies. An annuitant makes a lump-sum payment and then receives a stream of payments until death.

Then there are deferred versus immediate annuities. An immediate annuity starts right away, while with a deferred annuity, contributions are made and investment returns accrue for payment at a later date.

Once you realize that annuities are a type of investment, things get even more complicated. Insurance companies offer fixed versus variable annuities. Fixed annuities guarantee the principal value plus a minimum interest rate, like a bond. Variable annuities can be invested in a variety of mutual funds offered by the insurance company, and the growth depends on the performance of the funds. Variable annuities are complicated, and insurance companies will combine them with life insurance products.

Getting the right portfolio of insurance and annuities is particularly difficult. Unlike the case for stocks and bonds, no simple risk measures currently exist to help investors assess specific insurance and annuity products. Economists have proposed that insurers disclose a standardized index that quantifies the benefits of each product to someone whose health is poor (compared with someone who is healthy), and a separate "mortality" indicator for the benefits to their beneficiaries if they die. These two numbers would go a long way to help customers (or their financial advisors) find the most appropriate products.*

Where does this leave us today? Annuities are useful, but you should probably hold off buying one until you are ready to retire. Invest your retirement savings in index mutual funds with low expense ratios, and buy term life insurance. When the time comes to retire, then call an insurance company and buy an annuity. That's going to be the cheapest, easiest, and simplest way to go.

For more information on annuities, what they are and how they work, go to www.iii.org/individuals/annuities.

* For details on these indexes, see "Better Guidance on Matters of Life and Death," *The Region*, Federal Reserve Bank of Minneapolis, June 2012.

In earlier years, many economists and policymakers had warned about the threat to the financial system posed by Fannie and Freddie.[9]

In 2011, a Treasury report proposed to reduce the role of the GSEs by compelling them to (1) raise the fees for their guarantees, (2) require down payments of at least 10 percent, (3) reduce the size of individual mortgages eligible for GSE guarantees, and (4) wind down their investment portfolios at a pace of at least 10 percent annually. The report also identified three potential long-run options for GSE reform: (1) privatizing, (2) privatizing but with a government mechanism to provide credit during a crisis, and (3) privatizing with government reinsurance for crisis episodes. The two latter options still would pose a long-run risk to taxpayers. In the summer of 2013, President Obama endorsed legislative efforts to wind down the GSEs over time, while maintaining a "limited" government role in housing finance over the long term. Yet, as of mid-2013, the GSEs, together with agencies such as the Federal Housing Administration

---

[9]To understand the vulnerability of the GSEs that economists highlighted, see Viral Acharya et al., *Guaranteed to Fail* (Princeton, NJ: Princeton University Press, 2011).

and the Department of Veterans Affairs, still finance the overwhelming share of new residential mortgages. Concerned about supporting the recovery of the housing market, the government has been reluctant to throttle the GSEs. You'll have to watch the financial news to see how government involvement in housing finance evolves.

Table 13.4 summarizes the characteristics and roles of financial intermediaries.

Table 13.4   Summary of Financial Industry Structure

Financial Intermediary	Primary Sources of Funds (Liabilities)	Primary Uses of Funds (Assets)	Services Provided
Depository Institution (Bank)	Checkable deposits Savings and time deposits Borrowing from other banks	Cash Loans Securities	• Pooling of small savings to provide large loans • Diversified, liquid deposit accounts • Access to payments system • Screening and monitoring of borrowers
Insurance Company	Expected claims	Corporate bonds Government bonds Stocks Mortgages	• Pooling of risk • Screening and monitoring of policyholders
Securities Firm	Short-term loans	Commercial paper Bonds Stocks	• Management of asset pools • Clearing and settling trades
Investment Bank			• Immediate sale of assets • Access to spectrum of assets, allowing diversification • Evaluation of firms wishing to issue securities • Research and advice for investors
Mutual-Fund Company (including exchange-traded funds, ETFs)	Shares sold to customers	Commercial paper Bonds Mortgages Stocks Real estate	• Pooling of small savings to provide access to large, diversified portfolios, which can be liquid
Finance Company	Bonds Bank loans Commercial paper	Mortgages Consumer loans Business loans	• Screening and monitoring of borrowers
Pension Fund	Policy benefits to be paid out to future retirees	Stocks Government bonds Corporate bonds Commercial paper	• Pooling of employees' and employers' contributions • Diversification of long-term investments to ensure future income for retirees
Government-Sponsored Enterprise	Bonds Loan guarantees	Mortgages Farm loans Guarantee payments	• Largest share of housing finance • Access to financing for borrowers who cannot obtain it elsewhere

Terms

bank charter, 329

bank holding company, 332

defined-benefit pension plan, 345

defined-contribution pension plan, 345

dual banking system, 330

economies of scale, 338

economies of scope, 338

eurodollars, 335

Fannie Mae, 349

financial holding company, 336

hedge fund, 348

London Interbank Offered Rate (LIBOR), 336

property and casualty insurance, 341

systemically important financial institutions (SIFIs), 330

term life insurance, 341

underwriting, 347

unit bank, 327

universal bank, 337

vesting, 345

whole life insurance, 341

Using FRED: Codes for Data This Chapter

Data Series	FRED Data Code
Commercial banks	USNUM
Banks with total assets over $20 billion	FREQ5
Bank failures	BKFTTLA641N
Return on equity	USROE
Equity to assets ratio	EQTA
Credit market assets held by domestic financial sectors	TCMAHDFS
Held by commercial banks	CBUSCCBTCMAHDFS
Held by private pension funds	PPFTCMAHDFS
Held by brokers and dealers	BDTCMAHDFS
Held by property and casualty insurers	PCICTCMAHDFS
Held by life insurers	LICTCMAHDFS
Held by money market mutual funds	MMMFTCMAHDFS
Held by mutual funds	MFTCMAHDFS
Held by government-sponsored enterprises	GSETCMAHDFS
3-month U.S. dollar LIBOR	USD3MTD156N

Chapter Lessons

1. The United States has a comparatively large but declining number of banks.
    a. The large number of banks in the United States is explained by restrictions on branching, both within and across state lines, that were imposed by the federal government in 1927.

b. The large number of banks in the United States is a sign of an anticompetitive legal environment.

c. Since 1997, banks have been permitted to operate in more than one state. This change has increased competition and driven many small, inefficient banks out of business.

d. Between 1933 and 1999, banks were prohibited from engaging in the securities and insurance businesses.

e. Banking has been expanding not just across state boundaries but across international boundaries.

   i. Many U.S. banks operate abroad, and a large number of foreign banks do business in the United States.

   ii. Eurodollars—dollar deposits in foreign banks—play an important part in the international financial system.

f. The financial industry is constantly evolving. With changes in regulations, financial services can now be provided in two ways:

   i. through a large universal bank, which provides all the services anyone could possibly need.

   ii. through small specialized firms, which supply a limited number of services at a low price.

2. Nondepository institutions are playing an increasingly important role in the financial system. Five types of financial intermediary may be classified as nondepository institutions.

a. Insurance companies.

   i. Life insurance companies insure policyholders against death through term life insurance and provide a vehicle for saving through whole life insurance.

   ii. Property and casualty companies insure individuals and businesses against losses arising from specific events, like accidents and fires.

   iii. The two primary functions of insurance companies are to:
- allow policyholders to transfer risk.
- screen and monitor policyholders to reduce adverse selection and moral hazard.

b. Pension funds perform two basic services.

   i. They allow employees and employers to make payments today so that employees will receive an income after retirement.

   ii. They spread risk by ensuring that those employees who live longer than others will continue to receive an income. For this reason, pension funds may be thought of as the opposite of life insurance.

c. Securities firms include three basic types of financial intermediary: brokers, mutual-fund companies, and investment banks.

   i. Brokers give customers access to the financial markets, allowing them to buy and sell securities.

   ii. Mutual-fund companies provide savers with small-denomination shares in large, diversified investment pools.

   iii. Investment banks screen and monitor firms before issuing their securities.

d. Finance companies specialize in making loans to consumers and businesses for the purchase or lease of specific products, such as cars and business equipment.

e. Government-sponsored enterprises supply direct financing and provide loan guarantees for low-interest mortgages, student loans, and agricultural loans.

Conceptual and Analytical Problems

1. For many years you have used your local, small-town bank. One day you hear that the bank is about to be purchased by Bank of America. From your vantage point as a retail bank customer, what are the costs and benefits of such a merger? *(LO1)*

2. Why have technological advances hindered the enforcement of legal restrictions on bank branching? *(LO1)*

3. How did the financial crisis of 2007–2009 affect the degree of concentration in the U.S. banking industry? *(LO1)*

4. Banks have been losing their advantage over other financial intermediaries in attracting customers' funds. Why? *(LO2)*

5. An industry with a large number of small firms is usually thought to be highly competitive. Is that supposition true of the banking industry? What are the costs and benefits to consumers of the current structure of the U.S. banking industry? *(LO1)*

6.* What was the main rationale behind the separation of commercial and investment banking activities in the Glass-Steagall Act of 1933? Why was the act repealed? *(LO1)*

7. Explain what the phrase "too-big-to-fail" means in reference to financial institutions. How did the policy responses to the financial crisis of 2007–2009 affect the too-big-to-fail problem? *(LO1)*

8. Discuss the problems life insurance companies will face as genetic information becomes more widely available. *(LO2)*

9. When the values of stocks and bonds fluctuate, they have an impact on the balance sheets of insurance companies. Why is that impact more likely to be a problem for life insurance companies than for property and casualty companies? *(LO2)*

10.* Compare and contrast the structures of bank holding companies, financial holding companies, and universal banks. *(LO1)*

11. What are the benefits of collaboration between a large appliance retailer and a finance company? *(LO2)*

12. Why did government-sponsored enterprises (GSEs) such as Freddie Mac and Fannie Mae have substantially higher leverage ratios than the average U.S. bank in the years preceding the financial crisis of 2007–2009? Explain how this made the enterprises more vulnerable to the house-price declines that precipitated the crisis. *(LO2)*

13. Consider two countries with the following characteristics. Country A has no restrictions on bank branching and banks in Country A are permitted to offer investment and insurance products along with traditional banking services. In Country B, there are strict limits on branch banking and on the geographical spread of a bank's business. In addition, banks in Country B are not permitted to offer investment or insurance services. Explain each of your choices for the following. *(LO1)*
    a. In which country do you think the banking system is more concentrated?
    b. In which country do you think the banking system is more competitive?
    c. In which country do you think, everything else being equal, banking products are cheaper?

*Indicates more difficult problems

14. You examine the balance sheet of an insurance company and note that its assets are made up mainly of U.S. Treasury bills and commercial paper. Is this more likely to be the balance sheet of a property and casualty insurance company or a life insurance company? Explain your answer. *(LO2)*

15.* Statistically, teenage drivers are more likely to have an automobile accident than adult drivers. As a result, insurance companies charge higher insurance premiums for teenage drivers. Suppose one insurance company decided to charge teenagers and adults the same premium based on the average risk of an accident for all drivers. Using your knowledge of the problems associated with asymmetric information, explain whether you think this insurance company will be profitable. *(LO2)*

16. Use your knowledge of the problems associated with asymmetric information to explain why insurance companies often include deductibles as part of their policies. *(LO2)*

17. Suppose you have a defined-contribution pension plan. As you go through your working life, in what order would you choose to have the following portfolio allocations: (a) 100 percent bonds and money-market instruments, (b) 100 percent stocks, (c) 50 percent bonds and 50 percent stocks? *(LO2)*

18. As an employee, would you prefer to participate in a defined-benefit pension plan or a defined-contribution pension plan? Explain your answer. *(LO2)*

19. In the aftermath of the financial crisis of 2007–2009, there have been calls to reinstate the separation of commercial and investment banking activities that was removed with the repeal of the Glass-Steagall Act. Do you think this is a good way to reduce systemic risk? *(LO1)*

20. Suppose a well-known financial holding company agreed to be the underwriter for a new stock issue. After guaranteeing the price to the issuing company but before selling the stocks, a scandal surrounding the business practices of the holding company is revealed. How would you expect this scandal to affect (a) the financial holding company and (b) the issuing company? *(LO1)*

Data Exploration

For general information on using Federal Reserve Economic Data (FRED) online, visit www.mhhe.com/moneyandbanking4e and click on Student Edition, then FRED Resources.

Scan here for quick access to the resources for these problems. Need a barcode reader? Try ScanLife, available in your app store.

1. One aspect of the 2007–2009 financial crisis was a run on some money market mutual funds (MMMFs). Plot weekly data for 2008 on institutional MMMF deposits (FRED code: WIMFSL), and identify the timing of the run visually. Next, download the data and report the size of the deposit outflow in the week that the run peaked. Why did this run end? *(LO1)* (*Hint:* Turn off the recession bars.)

2. When did the financial crisis of 2007–2009 peak and why? Plot weekly data for 2006–2010 for 1-week U.S. dollar LIBOR (FRED code: USD1WKD156N) and the effective federal funds rate (FRED code: DFF). Explain the pattern. *(LO1)* (*Hint:* For consistency, plot both series on the same frequency by specifying *"Weekly, ending Wednesday."*)

3. How did competition from money market mutual funds affect traditional savings institutions that provided mortgages at fixed interest rates? Beginning with 1981, plot the ratio of retail money market mutual funds (FRED code: WRMFSL) to the sum of savings and small time deposits at savings institutions (FRED codes: SVGTI and STDTI). What favored money funds in the 1980s and 1990s? Why did the ratio shrink in the first half of the 2000s? *(LO1)*

4. How have the market shares of banks and traditional savings institutions evolved over time? Plot the fraction (in percent) of credit market assets held by the entire domestic financial sector (TCMAHDFS) that is held by commercial banks (FRED code: CBUSCCBTCMAHDFS). Plot a similar market share for the assets held by savings institutions (FRED code: SITCMAHDFS). Explain the long-term trends that you observe. *(LO2)*

Further Data Exploration: The FDIC's website (www.fdic.gov/bank/statistical) provides several databases that allow for further exploration of the U.S. banking system. For example, the summary tables (at the FDIC website, select "Summary of Deposits" and then "Summary Tables.") provide details of bank deposits by class of bank charter, asset size, deposit size, and region. "Statistics on Banking" tables (www2.fdic.gov/SDI/SOB) detail assets and liabilities (and other characteristics) of banks by type and size, both nationally and at the state level. Finally, the "Historical Statistics on Banking" section (www2.fdic.gov/hsob/index.asp) provides data on the evolution of the insured banking system since the FDIC's origin in 1934.

Chapter 14

Regulating the Financial System

The painful effects of the global crisis of 2007–2009 brought home the importance of the financial system in our lives. Millions of people lost their jobs, their homes, and their wealth. Healthy firms needing to borrow temporarily to pay their employees or suppliers faced ruin. As the crisis peaked in the fall of 2008, the global economy suffered its deepest and broadest downturn since the Great Depression, and policymakers took unprecedented action to keep the crisis from precipitating a second Great Depression. In 2010, after financial conditions stabilized, the U.S. government enacted the most ambitious financial reforms since the 1930s. The Dodd-Frank Wall Street Reform and Consumer Protection Act aims to prevent another crisis and to limit the moral hazard from the government's interventions during the global crisis.

Although no financial crisis since the 1930s has matched the severity of the 2007–2009 episode, disruptions to the financial system are surprisingly frequent and widespread. After 2010, millions of people in the euro area faced devastating losses from the combination of a plunge in their sovereigns' creditworthiness, the weakening of banks holding debt from those sovereigns, and rising doubts about the viability of the euro. More broadly, since 1970, 119 countries experienced 146 banking crises. Including other types of financial disruptions, a crisis has occurred in an average of eight countries each year since 1970.[1]

And virtually no part of the world has been spared from banking crises; large, advanced economies have suffered along with smaller, less developed ones. Indeed, banking disruptions appear to cause greater damage and persist longer in advanced economies, perhaps because the financial systems are deeper and more critical for sustaining economic efficiency. Partly as a result, governments in advanced economies also are likely to undertake a wider range of actions to support their banks, including liquidity support, guarantees of bank liabilities, and recapitalizations of weakened banks.

---

[1] In addition to the banking crises, there were 218 currency crises and 66 sovereign debt crises since 1970. Of these, 28 were "twin crises" and 8 were "triple crises" in the same country at the same time, so that the total number of serious financial disturbances was 346. See Luc Laeven and Fabián Valencia, "Systemic Banking Crises: An Update," IMF Working Paper (WP/12/163), June 2012.

When financial crises occur, governments step in and put financial intermediaries back on track. They often do so by assuming responsibility for the banking system's liabilities so that depositors won't lose their savings. But the cleanup can also require the injection of capital into failed institutions. Not only are these crises expensive to clean up, but they also can have a dramatic impact on growth in the countries where they occur.

Table 14.1 shows information on the economic impact and fiscal cost of selected banking crises between 1970 and 2011. The data show what one would expect: Bigger

| Table 14.1 | Banking Crises: Output Losses, Fiscal Costs, and Public Debt Increases (Percent of GDP), 1970–2011 |

Country	Crisis Dates	Output Loss	Fiscal Cost	Public Debt Increase
ADVANCED ECONOMIES				
Ireland	2008–	106.0	40.7	72.8
Finland	1991–1995	69.6	12.8	43.6
Spain	1977–1981	58.5	5.6	3.8
Iceland	2008–	43.0	44.2	72.2
Greece	2008–	43.0	27.3	44.5
Spain	2008–	39.0	3.8	30.7
Portugal	2008–	37.0	0.0	33.6
Sweden	1991–1995	32.9	3.6	36.2
Italy	2008–	32.0	0.3	8.6
United States	2007–2009	31.0	4.5	23.6
Median (full sample)		**32.9**	**3.8**	**21.4**
EMERGING ECONOMIES				
Thailand	1997–2000	109.3	43.8	42.1
Latvia	2008–	106.0	5.6	28.1
Philippines	1983–1986	91.7	3.0	44.8
Panama	1988–1989	85.0	12.9	−2.6
Indonesia	1997–2001	69.0	56.8	67.6
Argentina	1980–1982	58.2	55.1	33.1
Korea	1997–1998	57.6	31.2	9.9
Cote d'Ivoire	1988–1992	45.0	25.0	13.6
Uruguay	1981–1985	38.1	31.2	83.3
Turkey	2000–2001	37.0	32.0	15.3
Median (full sample)		**26.0**	**10.0**	**9.1**

Notes: Output loss is the gap between actual and pre-crisis trend growth. Both output loss and the increase of the public debt ratio cover three years from the crisis start. Fiscal cost covers direct outlays to the financial sector. The specific country episodes are the top 10 (ranked by output loss) for which all three measures are available. The medians are calculated from the full samples of banking crises in each class (23 in advanced economies and 123 in emerging economies).

SOURCE: Luc Laeven and Fabián Valencia, "Systemic Banking Crises: An Update," IMF Working Paper WP/12/163, June 2012. Used with permission.

crises are worse for output. And crises in advanced economies lead to a larger increase in public debt as a percent of GDP.

Some degree of default is normal at every bank, including well-run ones. But in 1998, when 35 percent of all loans made by Korean banks defaulted, it was more than just bad luck. Clearly, the Korean financial system was failing to perform one of its primary functions, the efficient channeling of resources from savers to borrowers so that credit goes to firms based on the merit of their proposed investments. Instead, borrowers who shouldn't have received loans got them, and projects that shouldn't have been funded went ahead. Because resources were wasted, Korea's growth and income were lower than they could have been. To put the output loss shown in Table 14.1 into perspective, Korea has invested an average of nearly 35 percent of GDP annually since 1970, so the country lost one to two years' worth of business investment.

Banking crises are not a recent phenomenon; the history of commercial banking over the last two centuries is replete with periods of turmoil and failure. By their very nature, financial systems are fragile and vulnerable to crisis. Unfortunately, when a country's financial system collapses, its economy goes with it, and with economic crisis comes the risk of violence and revolution. Keeping banks open and operating, then, is as essential to maintaining our way of life as a ready military defense. Because a healthy financial system benefits everyone, governments are deeply involved in the way banks and other intermediaries function. As a result, the financial sector is subject to voluminous rules and regulations, and financial institutions must withstand constant scrutiny by official examiners. The importance of this government oversight in ensuring financial stability is hard to exaggerate. When government oversight fails, as it did in many countries in the years before the crisis of 2007–2009 and in the runup to the euro-area crisis that erupted in 2010, the costs can be enormous.

The purpose of this chapter is fourfold. First, we will look at the sources and consequences of financial fragility. By and large, financial crises are banking crises, so we will focus on that sector. Included in this group are **shadow banks** that, like banks, have liabilities that can be withdrawn at face value virtually without notice but are usually subject to less oversight than banks.[2] Next, we will look at the institutional safeguards—for instance, deposit insurance—the government has built into the system in an attempt to avert financial crises. Third, we'll study the regulatory and supervisory environment of the banking industry. Finally, we'll examine emerging approaches to regulation that focus on the safety of the financial system rather than on individual institutions.

The Sources and Consequences of Runs, Panics, and Crises

In a market-based economy, the opportunity to succeed is also an opportunity to fail. New restaurants open and others go out of business. Only 1 in 10 restaurants survives as long as three years. In principle, banks should be no different from restaurants: new ones should open and unpopular ones close. But few of us would want to live

---

[2]Some types of intermediaries routinely depend on short-term funding that closely substitutes for deposits, completely fulfilling this definition of a shadow bank. These intermediaries typically include money market mutual funds and securities brokers. Other classes of intermediaries—such as hedge funds—include a range of firms that vary more in the extent to which they depend on short-term funding (like the repo and asset-backed commercial paper markets) and leverage.

in a world where banks fail at the same rate as restaurants. Banks serve some essential functions in our economy: They provide access to the payments system, and they screen and monitor borrowers to reduce information problems. If your favorite restaurant closes suddenly, you can still eat, but if your bank closes, you lose your ability to make purchases and pay your rent. So while no one suggests that the government appoint officials to minimize restaurant closings, everyone expects the government to safeguard banks.

Banks' fragility arises from the fact that they provide liquidity to depositors. That is, they allow depositors to withdraw their balances on demand. If you want the entire amount in your checking account converted into cash, all you need to do is go to your bank and ask for it; the teller is obligated to give it to you. If a bank cannot meet this promise of withdrawal on demand because of insufficient liquid assets, it will fail.

Banks not only guarantee their depositors immediate cash on demand; they promise to satisfy depositors' withdrawal requests on a first-come, first-served basis. This commitment has some important implications. Suppose depositors begin to lose confidence in a bank's ability to meet their withdrawal requests. They have heard a rumor that one of the bank's largest loans has defaulted, so that the bank's assets may no longer cover its liabilities. True or not, reports that a bank has become **insolvent** can spread fear that it will run out of cash and close its doors. Mindful of the bank's first-come, first-served policy, frenzied depositors may rush to the bank to convert their balances to cash before other customers arrive. In effect, they hope that getting to the bank early will let them withdraw their "investment" (deposit) at a price above its true value (the value of the banks' assets). Such a **bank run** can cause a bank to fail.

In short, a bank run can be the result of either real or imagined problems. No bank is immune to the loss of depositors' confidence just because it is profitable and sound. In practice, runs often start with shakier banks and then spread to healthier ones as confidence erodes.

The financial crisis of 2007–2009 is replete with examples of runs on banks and on the much less regulated shadow banks, which also provide liquidity to the financial system. The United Kingdom faced its first run on a large bank in more than a century when, in September 2007, depositors rushed to withdraw funds from Northern Rock, a major housing lender (see neighboring photos). Meanwhile, the largest savings bank in the United States, Washington Mutual, failed when depositors fled in September 2008. That same month, withdrawals from Wachovia Bank—at the time the fourth largest U.S. commercial bank— led to its emergency sale.

Quiet, invisible runs on shadow banks were even more dramatic, as they punctuated the peaks of the financial crisis. In March 2008, short-term lenders and other creditors stopped lending to Bear Stearns, the fifth largest U.S. investment bank. The run halted only when the Federal Reserve Bank of New York stepped in to help the then-second largest U.S. commercial bank, JPMorgan Chase, acquire Bear. A similar sudden stop in private lending led the U.S. government to take over Fannie Mae and Freddie Mac (the huge government-sponsored housing finance enterprises described in Chapter 13) in September 2008. The financial crisis peaked later that month when a run

Crowds trying to get into the Northern Rock bank in Kingston upon Thames, United Kingdom, on September 17, 2007.

on Lehman Brothers—the fourth largest U.S. investment bank—precipitated its bankruptcy. Shortly thereafter, losses on Lehman debt compelled a money-market mutual fund (MMMF) to "break the buck"—that is, to lower its share value below $1; that fixed value is traditionally promised by all MMMFs so that their customers can treat their shares as if they were bank deposits. Fearful that other MMMFs would "break the buck," investors in those funds rushed to withdraw their investments at the promised $1 per share, a value they thought might exceed the true market value of the fund's assets. The resulting runs undermined a key component of the U.S. intermediation mechanism.

What matters during a bank run is not whether a bank is solvent, but whether it is liquid. Solvency means that the value of the bank's assets exceeds the value of its liabilities—that is, the bank has a positive net worth. Liquidity means that the bank has sufficient reserves and immediately marketable assets to meet depositors' demand for withdrawals. False rumors that a bank is *insolvent* can lead to a run that renders a bank **illiquid**. If people believe that a bank is in trouble, that belief alone can make it so.

When a bank fails, depositors may lose some or all of their deposits, and information about borrowers' creditworthiness may disappear. For these reasons alone, government officials work to ensure that all banks are operated in a way that minimizes their chance of failure. But that is not their main worry. The primary concern is that a single bank's failure might cause a small-scale bank run that could turn into a system-wide **bank panic**. This phenomenon of spreading panic on the part of depositors in banks (or of creditors to shadow banks like MMMFs) is called **contagion**. Contagion was powerful at the peak of the 2007–2009 financial crisis, as depositors and creditors grew anxious about the well-being of financial intermediaries around the world.

INFORMATION

Information asymmetries are the reason that a run on a single bank can turn into a bank panic that threatens the entire financial system. Recall from Chapter 11 that if there is no way to tell a good used car from a bad one, the only used cars on the market will be lemons. What is true for cars is even truer for banks. Most of us are not in a position to assess the quality of a bank's balance sheet. In fact, because banks often make loans based on sophisticated statistical models, only an expert with knowledge of market conditions and access to all details about a bank's assets can estimate their worth. Depositors, then, are in the same position as uninformed buyers in the used car market: They can't tell the difference between a good bank and a bad bank. And if the cost of withdrawal is tiny, who wants to keep a deposit in a bank if there is even a small chance that it could be insolvent? So when rumors spread that a certain bank is in trouble, depositors and other creditors begin to worry about their own banks' financial condition. Concern about even one bank can create a panic that causes profitable banks throughout the nation to fail, leading to a complete collapse of the banking system.

While banking panics and financial crises can easily result from false rumors, they can also occur for more concrete reasons. Because a bank's assets are a combination of loans and securities, anything that affects borrowers' ability to make their loan payments or drives down the market value of securities has the potential to imperil the bank's finances. The decline of U.S. housing prices and the resulting wave of mortgage defaults that began in 2006 set the stage for the crisis of 2007–2009 by lowering the value of assets on the balance sheets of intermediaries around the world. Recessions—widespread downturns in business activity—have a clear negative impact on a bank's balance sheet. When business slows, firms have a harder time paying their debts. People lose their jobs and suddenly can't make their loan payments. As default rates rise, bank assets lose value, and bank capital drops. With less capital, banks are forced to contract their balance sheets, making fewer loans. This decline in loans, in turn, means less business investment, which amplifies the downturn. Large asset price declines and deep recessions can lead to widespread failure of banks and shadow banks.

The history of banking in the United States shows clear evidence that downturns in the business cycle put pressure on banks, substantially increasing the risk of panics. To see this, we can look at the period from 1871 to 1914, prior to the creation of the Federal Reserve System. Over those four-plus decades, there were 11 business cycles—booms followed by recessions. Bank panics occurred during seven of them, five of which were very severe. They often started near the business cycle peak, when investors began to anticipate a downturn. The next series of severe bank panics occurred during the Great Depression of the 1930s, when output fell by roughly one-third. Bank panics usually start with real economic events or their prospect, not just rumors.[3]

Financial disruptions can also occur whenever borrowers' net worth falls, as it does during a deflation (see Applying the Concept: Deflation, Net Worth, and Information Costs in Chapter 11). Companies borrow a fixed number of dollars to invest in real assets like buildings and machines, whose values fall with deflation. The same applies to households acquiring houses. So a drop in prices reduces companies' and households' net worth (but not their loan payments). This decline in net worth aggravates the adverse selection and moral hazard problems caused by information asymmetries, making loans more difficult to obtain. If borrowers cannot get new financing, business and residential investment will fall, reducing overall economic activity and raising the number of defaults on loans. As more and more borrowers default, banks' balance sheets deteriorate, compounding information problems and creating a full-blown crisis. This **adverse feedback** between financial and economic activity is a key characteristic of deep crises.

The Government Safety Net

There are three reasons for the government to get involved in the financial system:

1. To protect investors.
2. To protect bank customers from monopolistic exploitation.
3. To safeguard the stability of the financial system.

First, the government is obligated to protect small investors, many of whom are unable to judge the soundness of their financial institutions. While competition is supposed to discipline all the institutions in the industry, in practice only the force of law can ensure a bank's integrity. As small investors, we rely on the government to protect us from mismanagement and malfeasance.

Second, the tendency for small firms to merge into large ones reduces competition, ultimately ending in monopolies. In general, monopolies exploit their customers, raising prices to earn unwarranted profits. Because monopolies are inefficient, the government intervenes to prevent the firms in an industry from becoming too large. In the financial system, that means ensuring that even large banks face competition.

Third, the combustible mix of liquidity risk and information asymmetries means that the financial system is inherently unstable. A financial firm can collapse much more quickly than an industrial company. For a steel corporation, an electronics manufacturer,

STABILITY

---

[3]To better understand the role of business cycles in the U.S. bank runs of the 19th and 20th centuries up through the Great Depression, see Gary B. Gorton, *Misunderstanding Financial Crises: Why We Don't See Them Coming* (New York: Oxford University Press, 2012).

or an automobile maker, failure occurs slowly as customers disappear one by one. But a financial institution can create and destroy the value of its assets in an astonishingly short period, and a single firm's failure can bring down the entire system.[4]

Government officials employ a combination of strategies to protect investors and ensure the stability of the financial system. First, they provide the safety net to insure small depositors. Authorities both operate as the *lender of last resort,* making loans to banks that face sudden deposit outflows, and provide *deposit insurance,* guaranteeing that depositors receive the full value of their accounts should an institution fail. But this safety net causes bank managers to take on too much risk, leading to the regulation and supervision that we will discuss later in the chapter.

This section will examine the unique role of depository institutions in our financial system. The point is that we need banks. While they are essential, they are also fragile. This leads to a discussion of the components of the safety net and the problems it creates. The next section will look at the government's responses to these problems.

The Unique Role of Banks and Shadow Banks

As the key providers of liquidity, banks ensure a sufficient supply of the means of payment for the economy to operate smoothly and efficiently. This critical role and the problems associated with it make banks a key focus of attention for government regulators. Shadow banks are also major providers of liquidity, and following their role in the financial crisis of 2007–2009, they also have attracted intense attention from regulators around the world.

We all rely heavily on these intermediaries for access to the payments system. If banks, MMMFs, and securities brokers were to disappear, we would no longer be able to transfer funds—at least not until someone stepped forward to take their place. Other financial institutions—insurance companies, pension funds, and the like—do not have this essential day-to-day function of facilitating payments.

Furthermore, because of their role in liquidity provision, banks and shadow banks are prone to runs. These intermediaries hold illiquid assets to back their liquid liabilities. In the case of banks, their promise of full and constant value to depositors is based on assets of uncertain value. The fixed-value shares of MMMFs are like bank deposits in all but name. The liabilities of other shadow banks are less similar but have important deposit-like characteristics. For example, repurchase agreements are usually overnight contracts, so a repo lender can refuse to roll over the loan to a securities broker at virtually any time, an action similar to a deposit withdrawal. In contrast, pension funds and insurance companies (and even some hedge funds) may hold illiquid assets, but their liability holders cannot withdraw funds whenever they want.

Moreover, banks and shadow banks are linked to one another both on their balance sheets and in their customers' minds. Take a quick look back at Table 12.1 (page 297)

---

[4]One culprit in creating this high degree of risk is derivatives. Like dynamite, when used properly derivatives are extremely beneficial, allowing the transfer of risk to those who can best bear it. But in the wrong hands, derivatives can bring down even the largest, most respected institutions. The failure of Barings Bank in 1995 is an example. One of the oldest and best-known banks in England, Barings collapsed in just two months after a single trader wiped out the bank's capital with losses of more than $1 billion on futures positions worth more than $17 billion. Large, opaque bets like that can be made only using derivatives. And, because they can be made in ways that are extremely difficult for government regulators to detect, these high-risk actions have the potential to put the entire financial system at risk. In the crisis of 2007–2009, the most dramatic example of a system-threatening derivatives exposure was that of American International Group (AIG), the largest U.S. insurer. In September 2008, AIG became unable to meet the obligations arising from hundreds of billions of dollars of credit-default swaps (see pages 234–235).

"Yes, we do have the authority to regulate you."

SOURCE: 1996 © Bruce Eric Kaplan/The New Yorker Collection/ www.cartoonbank.com.

and you will see that in January 2013 interbank loans made up 1.0 percent of U.S. commercial banking system assets—which was less than one-tenth of all bank capital. Prior to the crisis, interbank lending had been substantially greater and represented roughly one-third of all bank capital. If a bank begins to fail, it will default on its loan payments to other banks and thereby transmit its financial distress to them. Similarly, MMMFs hold large volumes of commercial paper, most of which was issued by banks. And (shadow) banks are among the key repo lenders to securities brokers and hedge funds. Banks and shadow banks are so interdependent that they are capable of initiating contagion throughout the financial system.

Other financial institutions also may pose such risks, but these intermediaries typically are very large and few in number (see footnote 4 regarding the derivatives exposure of AIG, the largest U.S. insurer). While the ramifications of a financial crisis outside the system of banks and shadow banks may be more limited, they are still damaging. As a result, the government also protects individuals who do business with finance companies, pension funds, and insurance companies.

For example, government regulations require insurance companies to provide proper information to policyholders and restrict the ways the companies manage their assets. The same is true for securities firms and pension funds, whose assets must be structured to ensure that they will be able to meet their obligations many years into the future.[5]

The Government as Lender of Last Resort

The best way to stop a bank failure from turning into a bank panic is to make sure solvent institutions can meet their depositors' withdrawal demands. In 1873 the British economist Walter Bagehot suggested the need for a **lender of last resort** to perform this function. Such an institution could make loans to prevent the failure of solvent banks and could provide liquidity in sufficient quantities to prevent or end a financial panic. Specifically, Bagehot proposed that Britain's central bank should lend freely on good collateral at a high rate of interest. By lending freely he meant providing liquidity on demand to any intermediary that asked for it. Good collateral would provide assurance of the borrowing institution's solvency, and the high interest rate would penalize the borrower for failing to hold enough reserves or easily salable assets to meet deposit outflows and would promote rapid repayment when funding conditions normalized.

The existence of a lender of last resort significantly reduces, but does not eliminate, contagion. The series of three bank panics that occurred during the Great Depression of the 1930s is one example of the failure of a lender of last resort. While the Federal Reserve had the capacity to operate as a lender of last resort in the 1930s, Figure 14.1 shows that banks did not take advantage of the opportunity to borrow when they needed to. In fact, their borrowing fell during panics, reaching levels well below normal compared to the boom years of the 1920s. So as banks became illiquid, the

[5]All nondepository institutions are subject to some form of regulation. State regulators oversee insurance companies; the Pension Benefits Guaranty Corporation regulates private pension funds. Securities firms are overseen by a combination of the Securities and Exchange Commission, a government agency, and the Financial Industry Regulatory Authority. The Commodity Futures Trading Commission oversees commodity brokers and derivatives exchanges. Finance companies are regulated by state agencies, as well as by the Federal Reserve if they are subsidiaries of bank holding companies.

YOUR FINANCIAL WORLD

The Securities Investor Protection Corporation

Brokerage firms will advertise that they are members of the SIPC—that's the Securities Investor Protection Corporation. The SIPC provides insurance in the event that a brokerage firm fails, owing its customers cash and securities. It is insurance against fraud.

It is important to understand what SIPC insurance is and what it is not. If a bank accepts your deposits and uses the funds to make bad loans, your savings are protected by the FDIC against the bank's failure. By contrast, SIPC insurance replaces missing securities or cash that was supposed to be there—up to a limit of $500,000. It does not compensate individuals for investments that lost value because market prices fell, nor will it cover individuals who were sold worthless securities. The SIPC protects against theft by a broker. One sizable SIPC payout in recent years was to the victims of Bernard Madoff's Ponzi scheme (see Chapter 11, Applying the Concept: The Madoff Scandal).

For more information on the SIPC, go to www.sipc.org For comprehensive information on investor rights, look at the website of the Financial Industry Regulatory Authority (FINRA)—the industry's self-regulatory body—at www.finra.org/investors/ProtectYourself.

Federal Reserve's lending declined. The mere existence of a lender of last resort, then, will not keep the financial system from collapsing.

There is another flaw in the concept of a lender of last resort. For the system to work, central bank officials who approve the loan applications must be able to distinguish an illiquid from an insolvent institution. But during a crisis, computing the market value of a bank's assets is almost impossible, because there are no market prices. (If a bank could sell its marketable assets in the financial markets, it wouldn't need a loan from the central bank.) Because a bank will go to the central bank for a direct loan only after having exhausted all opportunities to sell its assets and borrow from other banks without collateral, its illiquidity and its need to seek a loan from the government raise the question of its solvency. Officials, anxious to keep the crisis from deepening, are likely to be generous in evaluating the bank's assets and to grant a loan even if they suspect the bank may be insolvent. Knowing this, bank managers will tend to take too many risks.

In other words, the central bank's difficulty in distinguishing a bank's insolvency from its illiquidity creates moral hazard for bank managers. It is important for a lender of last resort to operate in a manner that minimizes the tendency for bankers to take too much risk in their operations.

Figure 14.1

Lending by the Federal Reserve to Commercial Banks, 1914–1940

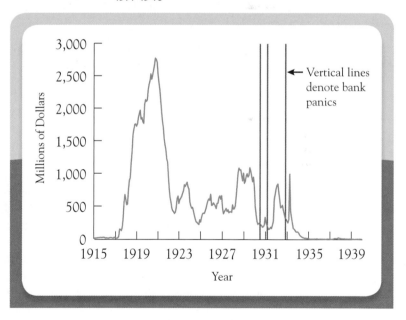

Figure shows discount loans to commercial banks from the Federal Reserve System.

SOURCE: *Bank panic dates are from Milton Friedman and Anna J. Schwartz,* A Monetary History of the United States: 1863 to 1960 *(Princeton, NJ: Princeton University Press, 1963).*

APPLYING THE CONCEPT

THE DAY THE BANK OF NEW YORK BORROWED $23 BILLION

While the existence of a lender of last resort may encourage bank managers to take too many risks, very few people would argue for abolishing the safeguard outright. There have been days when the system worked exactly as it should. November 20, 1985, was one of them. On that day the Bank of New York's computer system went haywire. BONY, as it was known, plays a central role in the U.S. Treasury securities market. The bank (now Bank of New York Mellon) acts as a clearinghouse, buying bonds from sellers and then reselling them to buyers.

On November 20, a software error prevented BONY from keeping track of its Treasury bond trades.* For 90 minutes transactions poured in, and the bank accumulated and paid for U.S. Treasury bonds, notes, and bills. Importantly, BONY promised to make payments without actually having the funds. But when the time came to deliver the securities and collect from the buyers, BONY employees could not tell who the buyers and sellers were or what quantities and prices they had agreed to. The information had been erased. By the end of the day, the Bank of New York had bought and failed to deliver so many securities that it was committed to paying out $23 billion that it did not have, at least until it could correct for the computer error.

Without a way to come up with $23 billion quickly, BONY wasn't able to make payments to sellers who had delivered their securities. These sellers had made additional transactions in the expectation that they would be paid. Unless BONY found a way to make the promised payments, the problem would spread to other institutions. The Federal Reserve, as lender of last resort, stepped in and made a collateralized loan of $23 billion, preventing a computer problem at one very important bank from becoming a full-blown financial crisis.

*BONY's computers could store only 32,000 transactions at a time. When more transactions arrived than the computer could handle, the software's counter restarted at zero. Because the counter number was the key to where the trading information was stored, the information was effectively erased. (Had all the original transactions been processed before the counter restarted, there would have been no problem.)

Finally, as we learned in the crisis of 2007–2009, the U.S. lender-of-last-resort mechanism has not kept pace with the evolution of the financial system. Like many government practices in the financial arena, the conventional rules for Fed discount lending were (and remain) based on the legal *form* of the borrower rather than on its economic *function*. Some intermediaries facing sudden flight by their very short-term creditors were not banks—to whom the Fed usually lends—but shadow banks, which do not normally have access to Fed loans. Only by using its emergency lending authority—something last done in the Great Depression of the 1930s—was the Fed able to lend to such nonbank intermediaries to stem the crisis.[6]

During the turmoil, the Fed utilized this emergency authority repeatedly when it needed to lend to securities brokers, MMMFs, insurers, other nonbank intermediaries, and even to nonfinancial firms. Based on this emergency authority, it developed a variety of new policy tools—including the Primary Dealer Credit Facility through which the authorities lent directly to nonbank securities dealers—to deliver liquidity where and when it was needed. While this ad hoc, reactive approach helped to both stem runs and counter their impact, it had limited value in preventing them in the first place.

Lending to nonbank intermediaries also added massively to the moral hazard usually associated with the lender of last resort. These intermediaries generally are not subject to regulation or supervision by the Federal Reserve, and the level of oversight they received from other agencies was typically less intense and intrusive than that applied to banks. Accordingly, in the absence of new oversight, the access to central bank loans granted by the Fed in the crisis will encourage these borrowers to take greater risks in the future.

---

[6]The Fed's authority to lend to nonbanks during the 2007–2009 crisis was based on Section 13(3) of the Federal Reserve Act. At the time, this rule allowed the Board of Governors "in unusual and exigent circumstances" to lend against collateral to any "individual, partnership, or corporation"—that is, to nonbanks. However, as you will see later in this chapter, the Dodd-Frank Act curtailed this emergency authority. You can view the current Federal Reserve Act at *www.federalreserve.gov/aboutthefed/fract.htm*.

Government Deposit Insurance

Congress's response to the Federal Reserve's inability to stem the bank panics of the 1930s was to create nationwide **deposit insurance**. The Federal Deposit Insurance Corporation guarantees that a depositor will receive the full account balance up to some maximum amount even if a bank fails. Bank failures, in effect, become the problem of the insurer; bank customers need not concern themselves with their bank's risk taking. So long as a bank has deposit insurance, customers' deposits are safe, even in the event of a run or bank failure.

Here's how the system works. When a bank fails, the FDIC resolves the insolvency either by closing the institution or by finding a buyer. The first approach, closing the bank, is called the *payoff method*. The FDIC pays off all the bank's depositors, then sells all the bank's assets in an attempt to recover the amount paid out. Under the payoff method, depositors whose balances exceed the insurance limit, currently $250,000, suffer some losses.

In the second approach, called the *purchase-and-assumption method*, the FDIC finds a firm that is willing to take over the failed bank. Because the failed institution is insolvent—on the balance sheet, its liabilities exceed its assets—no purchaser will do so for free. In fact, the FDIC has to pay banks to purchase failed institutions. That is, the FDIC sells the failed bank at a negative price. Depositors prefer the purchase-and-assumption method to the payoff method because the transition is typically seamless, with the bank closing as usual at the end of the week and reopening on Monday morning under new ownership. In a purchase and assumption, no depositors, even those whose account balances exceed the deposit insurance limit, suffer a loss.

No private or small public-sector insurance fund would be able to withstand a run on all the banks it insures—but the FDIC is. Because the U.S. Treasury backs the FDIC, it can withstand any crisis that does not undermine the nation's sovereign credit standing.

Since its inception, deposit insurance clearly helped to prevent runs on commercial banks. Even so, it did not prevent the crisis of 2007–2009 and the runs associated with it. The prime reason is that deposit insurance covers only depository institutions. But as the financial system developed, shadow banks—money market funds, securities brokers, and the like—gained importance. Those entities are sufficiently like banks that they, too, face the risk of runs by their short-term creditors. However, these nonbanks lack the benefits of deposit insurance, and, until the latter part of the crisis, they had no access to a lender of last resort. Although some traditional banks suffered runs during the crisis—mostly by large depositors with balances in excess of the insurance limit—most of the runs were against shadow banks that bid for funds in the competitive ("wholesale") money markets.

Problems Created by the Government Safety Net

We know that insurance changes people's behavior. Protected depositors have no incentive to monitor their bankers. Knowing this, bankers take on more risk than they would normally, because they get the benefits while the government assumes the costs. In protecting depositors, then, the government creates moral hazard. This is not just a theory. We can find evidence for this assertion by comparing bank balance sheets before and after the implementation of deposit insurance. Recall from Chapter 12 that commercial banks in the United States have significant leverage; their assets are about 9 times the size of their capital. In the 1920s, before the deposit insurance system was created, banks' ratio of assets to capital was about 4 to 1. Most economic and financial historians believe that government insurance led directly to the rise in risk.

LESSONS FROM THE CRISIS
SHOULD THE LENDER OF LAST RESORT ALSO SUPERVISE?

Who supervises the financial industry? How do the supervisors interact with the central bank as the *lender of last resort* (LOLR)? Different countries have answered these questions in different ways. Some have multiple regulators with overlapping jurisdictions. Others have only one regulator or a small number with little overlap. Some countries assign supervision to the central bank, but others do not.

The crisis exposed faults in every system. It also strengthened the case for making the central bank the leading financial supervisor. Let's take a brief but critical look at some examples.

At one end of the regulatory spectrum sits the United States with its large number of overlapping regulators. Table 14.2 (on page 374) lists the regulators of depository institutions as of mid-2013. Additional agencies oversee other financial activities, such as the trading of securities and commodities and the sale of insurance. Although the Federal Reserve—the U.S. LOLR—supervises both bank holding companies, which operate the largest banks, and nonbank systemically important financial institutions (SIFIs), most intermediaries lie outside the Fed's supervisory sphere.

At the opposite end of the spectrum from the United States sits the United Kingdom, which concentrates regulation in only two agencies. As of 2013, the Financial Conduct Authority (FCA) regulates market behavior and product innovation, while the central bank—the Bank of England—performs all other regulation and supervision and serves as the lender of last resort. Inside the central bank, the Prudential Regulatory Authority (PRA) is the micro-prudential regulator, and the Financial Policy Committee (FPC) is the macro-prudential regulator (see pages 382–385).

The approach of countries in continental Europe is closer to that of their British neighbor than to that of the United States. In 2011, the European Union created three European authorities to coordinate national-level supervision of banks, of securities and markets, and of insurance and pensions, respectively. At the national level, most countries have a small number of regulators including, in some cases, the national central banks. Since 2012, the ECB has led the European Systemic Risk Board, which examines macro-prudential risks. The national central banks, rather than the ECB, act as the LOLR in their countries. As of 2014, the European Central Bank (ECB) supervises the largest intermediaries (just as the Fed supervises U.S. SIFIs), and a further expansion of this authority is being discussed.

The financial crisis of 2007–2009 tested regulatory arrangements everywhere. Effective crisis management requires that policymakers act urgently to limit contagion from a weak financial institution, a loss of market function, or a threat to funding liquidity. Which structure was more likely to promptly detect and respond to systemic risks? How well did each arrangement fare in responding to the liquidity shortfall? How reliably were emergency lenders—each country's LOLR—able to distinguish between illiquid and insolvent intermediaries?

Unfortunately, none of the existing structures fared noticeably better than the others. The experience of 2007–2009 did not instill confidence in any of the regulatory approaches that existed before the crisis and continues to drive major changes in Europe and the United States.

Multiple regulators complicated the U.S. response. The Federal Reserve had limited information about the firms that posed the most virulent systemic threats—Bear Stearns, Lehman Brothers, and AIG—because it had no supervisory role over those institutions. The Fed provided emergency liquidity to Bear and AIG but not to Lehman. Would better knowledge have prompted the Fed to address these threats differently or at an earlier stage? We can only speculate.

Looking at the United Kingdom, it is difficult to argue that the streamlined system facilitated rapid analysis and response. If anything, the British experience highlights the problems that arise when the central bank is not the financial supervisor. Ineffective coordination among the Bank of England, the U.K. Treasury, and the supervisory agency during that period has been widely seen as a factor in the run on Northern Rock, the first run on a major U.K. bank in more than a century (see page 362).*

The lack of immediate, direct access to supervisory information also was a handicap for the ECB, which became a supervisor only as of 2014. During the crisis, the ECB may have compensated for its information handicap by acting early to flood the euro-area system with liquidity.

*See Stephen Cecchetti, "Why Central Banks Should Be Supervisors," *VOX*, November 30, 2007, *www.voxeu.org/index.php?q=node/755.*

And that is not the only problem. Government officials are especially worried about the largest institutions because they can pose a threat to the entire financial system. Although the failure of a community bank is unfortunate, the prospect of a large financial conglomerate going under is a regulator's worst nightmare. The financial havoc that could be caused by the collapse of an institution holding more than a trillion dollars in assets is too much for most people even to contemplate.

What this means is that some intermediaries are treated as *too big to fail* or *too interconnected to fail*. Putting such an institution through the usual mechanism for resolving a business failure—bankruptcy court—may force the bankruptcy of many households, firms, and other intermediaries that have contracted with the failed institution. Thus, too big to fail really means too big or too complex to shut down or sell in an orderly fashion without large and painful spillovers. Regulators call such an institution *too big to resolve*, and the Dodd-Frank law gave rise to a special legal designation for such a firm: systemically important financial institution (SIFI).

Experience has led the managers of these too-big-to-fail intermediaries to expect that if their institutions begin to founder, the government will find a way to bail them out. Regulators allowed Lehman Brothers to fail in September 2008, but the painful financial and economic disruptions that ensued served only to reinforce the widespread expectation that government will bail out the largest and most interconnected financial institutions.

A bailout of a failed bank can take many forms. In most cases, the deposit insurer quickly finds a buyer; otherwise, the government, as lender of last resort, usually makes a loan to buy time to fashion a solution. Depositors whose balances do not exceed the insurance limit will be made whole. But in the crisis of 2007–2009, most of the creditors to banks were protected, not just the insured depositors. Following the Lehman failure, governments in Europe and the United States guaranteed all of the liabilities of their largest banks. In particular, they promised that the holders of new bonds issued by the banks would not incur losses. Without these guarantees, the evaporation of funding liquidity probably would have led to a rapid cascade of failures because banks would be unable to fund themselves. In a number of cases, unlike in a normal bankruptcy, the managers of failing banks also kept their jobs.

During the crisis, governments also *recapitalized* some intermediaries—that is, gave them public money in return for partial ownership rights—to prevent a run by their creditors. In effect, governments declared recapitalized intermediaries to be too big to fail while they allowed smaller institutions to go under. In the United States, for example, the FDIC shut down 140 banks in 2009, the largest number since 1992. In these ways, the government, not the market, chose the winners and the losers.

Because it undermines the market discipline that depositors and creditors impose on banks and shadow banks, this **too-big-to-fail policy** is ripe for reform. Given the $250,000 insurance limit, a corporation with millions of dollars to deposit would normally be concerned about the quality and riskiness of the assets a bank holds. If the bank or MMMF were to fail, the corporation would face significant losses. Thus, the threat of withdrawal of these large balances restrains the bank or MMMF from taking on too much risk.[7] But for very large banks, the too-big-to-fail policy renders the deposit insurance ceiling meaningless. In the aftermath of the crisis of 2007–2009, everyone knew which banks were too big to fail and that the authorities would support them. With little threat that depositors will flee, bank managers are inclined to take greater risk than they otherwise would. The too-big-to-fail policy compounds the problem of moral hazard, encouraging managers of large banks to engage in extremely risky behavior (and putting small banks at a competitive disadvantage).

During the financial crisis, many shadow banks also received government bailouts and guarantees that foster moral hazard. Like their bank brethren, some of the largest shadow banks obtained government support because their failure was perceived as too costly in a crisis. And the problem is not limited to the too-big-to-fail class. The U.S. government guaranteed the liabilities of all MMMFs—most of which are small—in

---

[7]Intermediaries can suffer what is known as a *silent run* when repo lenders refuse to roll over their loans to a securities broker or when investors electronically sell their shares in a MMMF rumored to be in trouble. Today, even traditional banks can suffer a silent run. If depositors with balances that exceed the insurance limit fear that their bank is in trouble, they needn't line up at the teller window to get their money. They can simply go online to initiate an electronic withdrawal.

order to halt a run. Whenever the government provides such a safety net without charging an appropriate fee for it in advance of the protection, the government creates an incentive for financial institutions to take risks that can threaten the system as a whole.

Why do government authorities provide this free safety net in a crisis? After all, they know that some quick-fix policies create bad incentives and impose large burdens on taxpayers. In the midst of a crisis, however, they must balance the often-conflicting goals of *crisis mitigation* and *crisis prevention*. Frequently, there are no good choices. Like an emergency room doctor trying to save a dying patient, a government official will occasionally act to rescue the financial system from urgent threats that, if left to play out on their own, would lead to an economic catastrophe. Of course, the taxpayer foots the bill.

Naturally, in the aftermath of a crisis, limiting the unintended consequences of the government safety net is the leading problem facing regulators. Some argue that too-big-to-fail institutions are simply too big to exist and that they need to be broken up, removing certain business activities from them in ways that limit incentives for risk taking. However, that approach does not eliminate the bad incentives arising from deposit insurance and from the government guarantees provided to smaller institutions during the crisis. Later in this chapter, we'll analyze how the Dodd-Frank law addresses these challenges, and we will assess its shortcomings. We'll also discuss how, through a variety of fees and charges, governments could discourage certain kinds of risk taking, thereby limiting systemic threats.

The conflict between crisis prevention and crisis mitigation exemplifies the problem of *time consistency* (see page 28). In good times, governments and central banks typically promise not to bail out financial behemoths and other intermediaries, hoping to limit their risk-taking and thus prevent a crisis. But these intermediaries know that, in bad times, policymakers will have an overwhelming incentive to bail them out to limit a crisis. If these policymakers also have the tools to implement a bailout, their good-times promises will lack credibility. When it is not feasible to make a credible commitment, policy cannot be time consistent.

One approach to this problem is to remove the policy tools entirely—to substitute legal rules for discretionary bailouts. Following the crisis of 2007–2009, bankruptcy lawyers proposed to modify the bankruptcy code to make it safely applicable to the resolution of large financial intermediaries.[8] So far, however, these ideas remain on the drawing board. Another approach—which characterizes the postcrisis regulatory reform in the United States—is to make bailouts more difficult, but not impossible, for policymakers to implement. The more difficult a bailout, the less likely a crisis, but the more dangerous an actual crisis will be. There is no costless way to overcome the time-consistency challenge. As you think about the Dodd-Frank legislation, consider the extent to which it reduces this time-consistency problem, and the cost at which it does so.

Regulation and Supervision of the Financial System

Government officials employ three strategies to ensure that the risks created by the safety net are contained. Government *regulation* establishes a set of specific rules for intermediaries to follow. Government *supervision* provides general oversight of financial institutions. And formal *examination* of an institution's books by specialists provides detailed information on the firm's operation.

---

[8]See, for example, Kenneth E. Scott and John B. Taylor (eds.), *Bankruptcy Not Bailout: A Special Chapter 14* (Stanford, CA: Hoover Institution Press, 2012).

APPLYING THE CONCEPT
DOES DEPOSIT INSURANCE REALLY WORK?

The idea that our savings are protected by a government-backed guarantee is something we all take for granted. Only some crazy economist would ask whether deposit insurance makes sense. Well, does it? Surprisingly, the evidence is that it may not. Deposit insurance, which is supposed to stabilize the financial system, may do more harm than good.

The problem is that insurance changes people's behavior. Protected depositors have no incentive to monitor their bankers' behavior. Knowing this, a bank's managers take on more risk than they would otherwise, because they reap the benefit of risky bets that pay off while the government assumes the cost of the ones that don't. In protecting depositors, then, the government creates moral hazard. In 1980, the deposit insurance limit in the United States was raised to $100,000, four times its earlier level. Over the following ten years, several thousand depository institutions (banks, savings and loans) failed. That was more than four times the number that failed in the nearly half century since deposit insurance was created in 1935. While a vast majority of the institutions that failed in the 1980s were small, the cost of reimbursing depositors exceeded $180 billion.

So, in an attempt to eliminate banking-system panics, deposit insurance created another problem. To limit bankers' incentives to take risk, governments were forced to set up regulatory and supervisory structures. Among other things, there are now constraints on the assets banks can hold, rules governing the minimum levels of capital that banks must maintain, and requirements that banks make public information about their balance sheets.

Does this complex mechanism actually work to stabilize the financial system? The evidence is not encouraging. A summary of research concludes that explicit deposit insurance actually makes financial crises more likely.[*] When countries have either implemented a new scheme or expanded an existing one, the probability of crises has increased. More recent data show that deposit schemes usually exist where bank crises occur.[†]

So, if deposit insurance schemes do more harm than good, what should we do to stabilize the financial system? One possibility is to try to write ever-more-detailed regulations. This is one way to view the Basel process described in the Tools of the Trade in this chapter. But for large sophisticated banks, this seems unlikely to work. Big banks have the resources to hire people who will figure out ways to take risks that the banks' managers want to take regardless of the written regulations.

If detailed rules won't work, what will? The key is to find a way to give bank managers and owners incentives to protect depositors on their own. One suggestion is to require big banks to issue subordinated debt. These are unsecured bonds, with the lender being paid only after all other bondholders are paid. Someone who buys a bank's subordinated debt has a strong incentive to monitor the risk taking behavior of the bank. The price of these publicly traded bonds then provides the market's evaluation of the quality of the bank's balance sheet and serves to discipline its management. Another approach to ensure prudent management is to defer a large part of managers' compensation so that it is received only if the bank remains solvent some years into the future.

[*]A. Demirgüç-Kunt and E. Kane, "Deposit Insurance around the Globe: Where Does It Work?" *Journal of Economic Perspectives* 16, no. 2 (2002), pp. 175–195.

[†]L. Laeven and F. Valencia, "Systemic Banking Crises: An Update," IMF Working Paper WP/12/163, June 2012.

As we look at each of these, keep in mind that the goal of government regulation is not to remove all the risk that investors face. Financial intermediaries themselves facilitate the transfer and allocation of risk, improving economic efficiency in the process. Regulating risk out of existence would eliminate one of the purposes of financial institutions. Consider also that efforts to tighten regulations on banks may push risk-taking somewhere outside of the view of the authorities. The result may not be a safer financial system.

Wary of asking taxpayers to pick up the bill for bank insolvencies, officials created regulatory requirements that are designed to minimize the cost of such failures to the public. The first screen, put in place to make sure the people who own and run banks are not criminals, is for a new bank to obtain a charter. Once a bank has been chartered and has opened for business, a complex web of detailed **regulations** restricts competition, specifies what assets the bank can and cannot hold, requires the bank to hold a minimum level of capital, and makes public information about the bank's balance sheet.

As we all know, rules are one thing; enforcement is another. Posting a speed limit on an interstate highway is just the first step in preventing people from driving too fast. Unless the police patrol the highways and penalize speeding drivers, such laws are worthless. The same is true of banking regulations. The best-designed regulatory structure in the world won't be worth the paper it's written on unless someone monitors banks' compliance. Government supervisors are the highway patrol of the banking

Table 14.2   Regulators of Depository Institutions

Type of Intermediary	Regulators
Commercial Banks	1. Federal Deposit Insurance Corporation 2. Office of the Comptroller of the Currency (Nationally chartered banks) 3. Federal Reserve System (State-chartered banks that are Federal Reserve members) 4. State authorities (All state-chartered banks)
Savings Banks Savings and Loans	1. Office of the Comptroller of the Currency (since 2011) 2. Federal Deposit Insurance Corporation 3. State authorities
Credit Unions	1. National Credit Union Administration 2. State authorities

world. They monitor, inspect, and examine banks and other intermediaries to make sure their business practices conform to regulatory requirements.

Banks are regulated and supervised by a combination of the U.S. Treasury, the Federal Reserve, the FDIC, and state banking authorities (see Table 14.2). The overlapping nature of this regulatory structure means that more than one agency works to safeguard the soundness of each bank. A bank can effectively choose its regulators by choosing whether to be a state or national bank and whether or not to belong to the Federal Reserve System. If one regulator allows an activity that another prohibits, a bank's managers can threaten to switch, or argue that a competitor who answers to a more permissive regulator has an unfair advantage.

The consequences of such **regulatory competition** are twofold. First, regulators force each other to innovate, improving the quality of the regulations they write. But regulatory competition has a less desirable outcome: It allows bank managers to shop for the most lenient regulator—the one whose rules and enforcement are the least stringent. Especially since the repeal of the ban on interstate branching, regulatory agencies have tried to prevent this outcome. Today state authorities usually defer to the Federal Reserve, whose supervisors impose uniform regulations on all state-chartered banks. The Comptroller of the Currency cooperates with the Fed to ensure that national banks receive similar treatment.

However, the financial crisis of 2007–2009 highlighted cases of *"regulator shopping"* that resulted in ineffective oversight. One example was the supervision of AIG— the largest U.S. insurer—by the small U.S. Office of Thrift Supervision (OTS) that also had supervised failed savings banks like Countrywide, IndyMac, and Washington Mutual. OTS naturally had less experience than other supervisors with the insurance business—especially with the complex derivatives that AIG sold. In effect, AIG had chosen its supervisor by purchasing a small savings bank years earlier. In 2010, the Dodd-Frank Act closed the OTS—the only regulatory agency that was shut down following the crisis—and merged it with the Office of the Comptroller of the Currency.

The arbitrary and complex structure of U.S. financial regulators does not stop with the banks. Some shadow banks—such as securities brokers—are subject to regulation

YOUR FINANCIAL WORLD
Are Your Deposits Insured?

The sign says "Each depositor insured to $250,000." But what does it really mean? Are your deposits fully insured? The answer to this question can be complicated. Here are a few things to keep in mind.

First, deposit insurance covers individuals, not accounts. It insures depositors. This means that if you hold your accounts jointly with a spouse, parent, sibling, friend, or business partner, the FDIC will insure each of you up to $250,000, assuming that each person has an equal share in the account. For instance, if you hold a savings account jointly with your spouse or partner, deposit insurance will cover a total balance of $500,000, or $250,000 for each of you.

Second, because deposit insurance covers individuals rather than accounts, if you have more than one account at the same bank, all in your own name, they will be insured together up to the insurance limit. For example, if you have a checking account, a savings account, and a personal business account (an account for what is known legally as a sole proprietorship), they will be added together and insured up to the $250,000 maximum.

Finally, if you have accounts at more than one bank, they will be insured separately, up to a total of $250,000 at each bank. But if the two banks merge, your accounts will be covered as if they had been opened at the same bank.

Most people are unlikely to accumulate $250,000 in even a combination of their checking and savings accounts, so the $250,000 insurance limit is not something to be too concerned about. But the FDIC also insures "self-directed retirement accounts" as well. These retirement savings that you control are in individual retirement accounts (IRAs) and the like. Many people will hit the limit well before they retire. If the interest rate is 4 percent, and you deposit $400 per month in one of these accounts, you will hit the $250,000 insurance limit in less than 30 years. And, as you will recall from Chapter 4, $250,000 in retirement savings is not all that much. So insuring your retirement savings is something you will need to worry about.

Finally, like all government regulations, the rules for government deposit insurance can change. If you really need to know whether you are insured or just want the peace of mind of knowing that your information is current, you can check the FDIC's website, www.fdic.gov.

by both the Securities and Exchange Commission (SEC) and the Commodity Futures Trading Commission (CFTC). The SEC also regulates MMMFs. And hedge funds have not been subject to regulation, aside from the 2010 Dodd-Frank requirement for fund advisers to register with the SEC and to act with care (i.e., as a fiduciary).

Restrictions on Competition

One long-standing goal of financial regulators has been to prevent banks from growing too big and powerful, both because their failure might threaten the financial system and because banks that have no real competition exploit their customers. As we saw in Chapter 13, throughout most of the 20th century banks faced numerous restrictions that kept them small. And until 1999, banks could not own securities firms or insurance companies.

While recent legislation has changed the banking industry, restrictions on bank size remain. Bank mergers still require government approval. Before granting it, officials must be convinced on two points. First, the new bank must not constitute a monopoly in any geographic region. Second, if a small community bank is to be taken over by a large regional bank, the small bank's customers must be well served by the merger.

But government officials also worry that the greater the competition among banks, the more difficulty banks will have making a profit. Competition reduces the prices customers must pay and forces companies to innovate in order to survive. These effects are as true of the market for deposits and loans as they are of the markets for cars and computers. Competition raises the interest rate bankers pay on deposits and lowers the interest rate they receive on loans; it spurs them to improve the quality of the services they provide. Normally we think of these effects of competition as being positive, but there is a negative side as well. Lower interest margins and reduced fee income cause bankers to look for other ways to turn a profit. Some may be tempted to assume more risk—that is, to make loans and purchase securities that are riskier than advisable, to increase leverage, or to rely excessively on short-term funding.

There are two ways to avoid this type of moral hazard. First, government officials can explicitly restrict competition. That is the solution regulators have chosen in a number of countries; it was also one of the purposes of branching restrictions.[9] (Branching restrictions create networks of small, geographically separated independent banks that face very little competition in their regions.) A second way to combat bankers' tendency to take on too much risk is to prohibit them from making certain types of loans and from purchasing particular securities.

The financial crisis of 2007–2009 accelerated the ongoing concentration in the U.S. financial system. When banks and shadow banks weakened or failed during the crisis, regulators encouraged other institutions to buy them. JPMorgan Chase, already the second largest U.S. bank, acquired both Bear Stearns, the fifth largest broker, and Washington Mutual, the largest savings bank. Bank of America, the number one bank in the country, purchased both Merrill Lynch, the largest broker, and Countrywide, the biggest housing lender. And Wells Fargo, the fifth largest commercial bank, took over Wachovia, the fourth largest. Following this consolidation, roughly 40 percent of deposits at U.S. commercial banks were held in only four banks—Bank of America, Citi, JPMorgan Chase, and Wells Fargo.

Thus, in the process of trying to keep the crisis from deepening by merging failing banks with the largest ones, authorities made the too-big-to-fail problem even bigger—in a future crisis, it will be even costlier to allow these swollen intermediaries to fail. Unless their risk taking is restrained, the protected status of these megabanks will encourage their managers to take greater risks, increasing the likelihood of another crisis. Later in this chapter, we'll see how a combination of capital requirements, limits on leverage, regulatory scrutiny, and restrictions on their activities can help to limit such systemic risks.

Asset Holding Restrictions and Minimum Capital Requirements

One way to prevent bankers from exploiting their safety net is to restrict banks' balance sheets. Such regulations take two forms: restrictions on the types of asset banks can hold and requirements that they maintain minimum levels of capital. While banks are allowed to build big office buildings and buy corporate jets for top executives, their financial assets are heavily restricted. U.S. banks cannot hold common stock.[10] Regulations also restrict both the grade and quantity of bonds a bank can hold. For example, banks are generally prohibited from purchasing bonds that are below investment grade, and their holdings from any single private issuer cannot exceed 25 percent of their capital. The size of the loans they can make to particular borrowers is also limited. For example, the Federal Reserve requires that one bank's exposure to another not exceed 25 percent of the bank's capital. While these restrictions on asset holdings are quite detailed, they are really just a matter of common sense and sound risk management. In

[9]In addition, until the early 1970s, regulation restricted the interest rates U.S. banks could pay on deposits. Regulation Q prohibited interest payments on demand deposits and placed a ceiling on interest payments on time and savings deposits. Its purpose was to restrict competition in order to improve banks' profitability.

[10]Common stock holdings were one of the sources of the problems Japanese banks faced in the 1990s. As the Japanese stock market collapsed, the value of Japanese bank assets declined precipitously, to the point where many banks became insolvent.

effect, regulators are telling bankers to do what they should be doing already: holding a well-diversified portfolio of liquid, high-grade bonds and loans.

Minimum capital requirements complement these limitations on bank assets. Recall that bank capital represents the net worth of the bank to its owners. Capital serves as both a cushion against declines in the value of the bank's assets, lowering the likelihood of the bank's failure, and a way to reduce the problem of moral hazard. Capital requirements take two basic forms. The first requires most banks to keep their ratio of capital to assets above some minimum level, regardless of the structure of their balance sheets. This approach is equivalent to capping leverage, which (as we saw in Chapter 3, Lessons from the Crisis: Leverage) is a key means of taking risk.

The second requires banks to hold capital in proportion to the riskiness of their operations. The computation is extremely complicated and the rules change frequently, but basically a bank must first compute the risk-adjusted level of its assets given the likelihood of a loan or bond default. Then a capital charge is assessed against that level. Of course, banks face a multitude of other risks, including trading risk, operational risk, and the risk associated with their off-balance-sheet operations. Regulators require banks to hold capital based on assessments of those risks as well. (See Tools of the Trade for a description of recent changes in capital requirements.)

Unfortunately, over time, banks can learn to evade or "game" any fixed set of rules. For example, in the half dozen years leading up to the 2007–2009 crisis, banks in the United States and Europe purchased large volumes of U.S. mortgage-backed securities precisely because these assets carried (misleadingly) high ratings, which reduced the capital they needed to hold under their national capital rules. Lower capital meant more leverage, which increased both risk and expected return. (See Chapter 5, Tools of the Trade.) As Figure 14.2 shows, overall assets of the largest banks in Europe and

Figure 14.2   Total Assets and Risk-Weighted Assets of the 10 Largest Publicly Listed Banks in Europe and the United States, 2002–2007

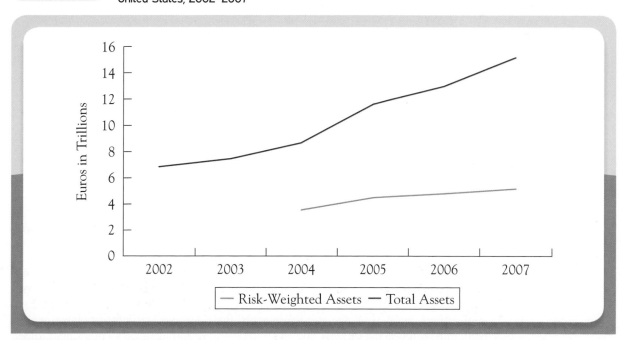

SOURCE: *International Monetary Fund,* Global Financial Stability Report, *Box 1.3, April 2008.*

TOOLS OF THE TRADE
The Basel Accords: I, II, III, and Counting . . .

Global financing took off in the 1980s as bankers realized they could expand their operations across national boundaries and turn a profit internationally. While this was a welcome development for most bank customers, not everyone appreciated the competition from abroad. In some countries, bankers complained that the foreign banks that were invading their turf held an unfair competitive advantage.

Because no one likes competition, we should always be suspicious of this sort of complaint. But in this case, the bankers did have a point. Competing with a foreign bank whose home country allows it to hold a lower level of capital is impossible. Holding extra capital is costly. Banks that hold less capital than others, and therefore take on more leverage, have lower costs and can offer borrowers lower interest rates.

This legitimate complaint led to a movement to create international regulations that would promote financial stability within countries and ensure a competitive balance with banks that operate globally. The result was the 1988 **Basel Accord**, named after the Swiss town where the world's bank regulators meet. The accord established a requirement that internationally active banks must hold capital equal to or greater than 8 percent of their risk-adjusted assets. Assets would be placed in one of four different categories based on their risk of default. The associated risk weights would range from zero to 100 percent (see Table 14.3).

The Basel Accord is not a law but a set of recommendations for banking regulation and supervision. The committee that writes and amends the accord has no direct authority over the banks in any country. Instead, its members work to develop a code of best practice that will help government officials around the world to ensure the safety and soundness of their banking systems.

The Basel Accord had several positive effects. First, by linking minimum capital requirements to the risk a bank takes

Table 14.3	1988 Basel Accord Risk Weights	
Borrower		**Risk Weight**
Sovereign debt issued by industrialized countries*		Zero
Claims on industrialized countries' banks		20%
Residential mortgages		50%
Consumer and corporate loans		100%

*Industrialized countries are defined as members of the Organization for Economic Cooperation and Development (OECD). Currently, 34 countries belong to the OECD, including Mexico, Turkey, and Korea as well the United States, Germany, Japan, and Great Britain.

on, it forced regulators to change the way they thought about bank capital. Second, it created a uniform international system. Finally, the accord provided a framework that less developed countries could use to improve the regulation of their banks.

While the original Basel Accord was constructive, it had—and still has—limitations. In adjusting for asset risk, the accord failed to differentiate between bonds issued by the U.S. government and those issued by emerging-market countries like Turkey: both received a weight of zero. And a corporate bond received a weight of 100 percent regardless of whether it was AAA rated or junk. Not only that, but a bank got no credit for reducing risk through diversification. Making one loan of

the United States rose much faster than their risk-weighted assets. To change bank incentives, regulators of many countries have agreed to impose a cap on leverage and to reform the risk-weighted capital requirements that proved too easy to game (see Tools of the Trade in this chapter).

Disclosure Requirements

Many intermediaries are required to provide information, both to their customers about the cost of their products and to the financial markets about their balance sheets. Regulations regarding disclosures to customers are responsible for the small print on loan applications and deposit account agreements; their purpose is to protect consumers. A bank must tell you the interest rate charged on a loan and must do so in a standardized

$100 million received the same risk weight as making 1,000 loans of $100,000 each. These shortcomings encouraged banks to shift their holdings toward riskier assets in ways that did not increase their required bank capital.

By the mid-1990s, bank regulators and supervisors had concluded that the Basel Accord needed revision. Starting in 1998, the Basel Committee on Banking Supervision, which wrote the original accord, negotiated a revised framework for determining whether banks have sufficient capital. The new Basel Accord is based on three pillars: a revised set of minimum capital requirements; supervisory review of bank balance sheets; and increased reliance on market discipline to encourage sound risk management practices. The first measure refines the estimation of risk-adjusted assets to reflect more accurately the risk banks actually take. For example, bonds issued by highly rated corporations receive a 20 percent weight; junk bonds, a 150 percent weight. However, the low risk weights on mortgage-backed securities helped encourage risky leverage in the runup to the crisis of 2007—2009 (see page 377). The second measure requires supervisors to attest to the soundness of bank managers' risk estimation and control methods. Supervisors now review the way banks assess their risk and decide how much capital they should hold. The third measure requires banks to make public their risk exposure and the level of capital they hold. Banks that can show they are behaving responsibly will be rewarded in the market with better credit ratings and higher stock prices.*

In the aftermath of the financial crisis of 2007–2009, regulators refined and extended the Basel Accord, and in 2010 they agreed on Basel III, which is being implemented in stages through 2018. The new agreement combines micro- and macro-prudential reforms that address both institution-level and system-level risks (see the section on macro-prudential regulation starting on page 382). While the details are quite complex, the basics are not. By expanding the coverage of assets for which banks are required to hold capital, and by tightening the definition of capital itself, Basel III more than doubled the capital cushion a typical bank is required to hold.

Basel III goes beyond these refinements of Basel II by making three important additions. First, it set restrictions on leverage—the ratio of total assets to equity—that supplement capital requirements based on risk-weighting of assets. Because risk-weighting is difficult, subjective, and subject to evasion by banks, a leverage ratio forms a second line of defense in case some assets turn out to be much riskier than anyone thought.

Second, the newest agreement introduces a set of three buffers over and above the minimum capital requirement itself. Should a bank's capital position deteriorate, Basel III's new *capital conservation buffer* restricts the payment of dividends and bonuses. The purpose is to preserve the bank as a going concern. Next, the *countercyclical capital buffer* rises in good times and declines in bad times, helping to reduce the procyclicality of credit supply. Finally, the *systemic capital surcharge* raises the minimum capital requirement on SIFIs.

Third, Basel III adds a *liquidity requirement* that compels banks to hold an amount of high-quality liquid assets (like U.S. Treasury securities) to meet deposit outflows and the exercise of contingent (preexisting) loan commitments that might occur during a crisis. The goal is to ensure that banks can meet their obligations without relying on fire sales of their assets—something that has a negative impact on everyone else—or on borrowing from the lender of last resort, the central bank.

*The Basel Committee on Banking Supervision constantly revises its recommendations to bank regulators. For information about the committee's activities and the Basel Accords in general, see its website at *www.bis.org/bcbs/aboutbcbs.htm.*

way that allows you to compare interest rates at competing banks. (This regulation is similar to the one that requires grocery stores to show the price of cheese, peanut butter, or popcorn per ounce, allowing customers to tell which brand or size is cheapest.) The bank must also tell you the fees it charges to maintain a checking account—the cost of check clearing, the monthly service charge, the fee for overdrafts, and the interest rate paid on the balance, if any.

Disclosure of accounting information to the financial markets protects depositors in a different way. It allows both regulators and the financial markets to assess the quality of a bank's balance sheet. Because the information is published in a standardized format according to clearly specified accounting rules, government officials can tell whether a bank is obeying the regulations, and financial analysts can compare one bank to another. With this information, both regulators and the financial markets can penalize banks that are taking too much risk.[11]

Disclosure also played a critical role in ending the financial crisis of 2007–2009. By late 2008, the solvency of the largest intermediaries was in doubt. That uncertainty made their own managers cautious about taking risk and it made potential lenders wary of doing business with them. The doubts and hesitancy contributed to the extreme fragility in many financial markets. As we saw in Chapter 3 (Lessons from the Crisis: Interbank Lending), even interbank lending dried up after Lehman Brothers failed in September 2008. Part of the remedy was a special disclosure procedure in which the U.S. Treasury conducted an extraordinary set of "stress tests" on banks and, in May 2009, published the results. The tests evaluated, on a common basis, the prospective capital needs of the 19 largest U.S. banks in light of the deep recession that was well under way. While observers questioned whether the tests were stringent enough, the results were sufficient to reassure the government, market participants, and the banks themselves that most or all of the 19 were solvent. Partly as a result, conditions improved in financial markets. And, armed with the stress-test evidence of their well-being, most large banks were able to attract new private capital for the first time since Lehman had failed.

Supervision and Examination

The government enforces banking rules and regulations through an elaborate oversight process called **supervision**, which relies on a combination of monitoring and inspection. Supervision is done both remotely, using the detailed reports banks are required to file, and through on-site **examination**. All chartered banks must file quarterly reports known as *call reports*. (Their official name is the *Consolidated Reports of Condition and Income*.) These reports detail the level and sources of banks' earnings, asset holdings, and liabilities. Supervisors process the reports using a statistical model that allows them to identify institutions whose solvency is deteriorating and to spot industry trends.

Examiners also visit banks in person. Every depository institution that is insured by the FDIC is examined at least once a year. Examiners arrive at a bank unannounced and look into virtually every aspect of its operation. They once counted the cash in each teller's drawer. While they no longer do that, they do call borrowers randomly to confirm that they actually have a loan and that the balance on the bank's books is correct. Examiners also verify that the loan collateral really exists, even visiting farms to make sure the grain that backs a farm loan is actually in the silo. At the largest institutions, examiners are on site all the time. They follow a process known as *continuous examination,* which is a bit like bridge painting—once they get to the end of the process, they go back to the beginning and start over.

The most important part of a bank examination is the evaluation of past-due loans. Bank managers are understandably reluctant to write off a loan, wanting to keep it on the books as long as possible after the borrower has begun to miss payments. Loan officers exercise substantial discretion in deciding when to declare a loan in default. For example, they can choose to increase the size of the loan by the missed interest payments. The examiner's job is to make sure that when borrowers stop making payments, loans are written off and the bank's balance sheet properly reflects the losses.

---

[11]Writing disclosure rules turns out to be extremely difficult, especially for off-balance-sheet activities. For example, regulators need to know whether a bank that buys or sells interest-rate swaps is hedging risk on its balance sheet or taking on more risk. Because positions can change very quickly, sometimes minute by minute, regulators are challenged to figure out exactly what should be reported and when.

Supervisors use what are called the **CAMELS** criteria to evaluate the health of the banks they monitor. This acronym stands for **C**apital adequacy, **A**sset quality, **M**anagement, **E**arnings, **L**iquidity, and **S**ensitivity to risk. Examiners give the bank a rating from one to five in each of these categories, one being the best, and then combine the scores to determine the overall rating. The CAMELS ratings are *not* made public. Instead, they are used to make decisions about whether to take formal action against a bank or even to close it. Current practice is for supervisors to act as consultants, advising banks how to get the highest return possible while keeping risk at an acceptable level that ensures they will stay in business.

Evolving Challenges for Regulators and Supervisors

Thus far, our discussion has focused on the regulation and supervision of depository institutions. But globalization and technological innovation, combined with changes in the law, have challenged the traditional structure of regulation and supervision. Today, we bank in a bazaar where a wide range of intermediaries offers a broad array of financial services. We no longer know or care whether the product or service we buy is supplied by someone in town or on the other side of the country. In fact, when you call the bank, the person who answers the phone may live in India, for all you know. Telecommunications has made the location of financial service providers irrelevant.

Besides the globalization of financial services, other changes have challenged regulators and supervisors. First, today's marketplace offers financial instruments that allow individuals and institutions to price and trade almost any risk imaginable. Moreover, because derivatives allow the transfer of risk without a shift in the ownership of assets, a financial institution's balance sheet need not say much about its health. To understand the meaning of this change, consider the traditional rules for computing the minimum required level of bank capital. Historically, the minimum capital level was based on measures such as the default risk of a bank's assets. But in a world where banks can buy and sell derivatives that promise payment in the event of default—like the *credit-default swaps* discussed in Chapter 9—such measures become almost meaningless. Regulators and supervisors need to adapt. (See Tools of the Trade on pages 378–379 for a discussion of recent attempts at modernizing financial regulations.)

Added to the challenge of globalization and financial innovation is the fact that during the 1990s, Congress removed the functional and geographic barriers that once separated commercial banking from other forms of intermediation and outlawed interstate banking. Institutions like Bank of America and JPMorgan Chase now are not just commercial banks but investment banks, insurance companies, and securities firms all rolled into one. Each part of these large organizations is regulated and supervised by different agencies, both functionally and geographically. Surely it would serve the public interest more to minimize the likelihood that such an institution as a whole might fail rather than examine each business line separately.

Realizing this truth, regulators and supervisors have begun to think about their jobs in a different way. In the future they will have no choice but to combine forces along both geographic and functional lines. State and federal agencies must either cooperate or merge, as must regulators of banks, insurance companies, and securities firms. A compelling case can be made for a super-regulator that would make the entire process more uniform and coherent, avoiding rules and practices that merely shift risk-taking from an intermediary of one legal form to another. Finally, as the international financial system becomes more and more integrated, the need for cooperation across national borders continues to increase. The day may come when the world needs an international agency to formulate the rules for the global financial system.

IN THE NEWS
How to Shrink the "Too-Big-to-Fail" Banks

THE WALL STREET JOURNAL.
WSJ.com

Richard W. Fisher and Harvey Rosenblum

March 11, 2013

A dozen megabanks today control almost 70% of the assets in the U.S. banking industry. . . . Implicit government policy has made these institutions exempt from the normal processes of bankruptcy and creative destruction. Without fear of failure, these banks and their counterparties can take excessive risks.

. . . The megabanks can raise capital more cheaply than can smaller banks. . . . This is patently unfair. It makes for an uneven playing field, tilted to the advantage of Wall Street against Main Street, and it places the financial system and the economy in constant jeopardy. It also undermines citizens' faith in the rule of law and representative democracy.

The 2010 Dodd-Frank Wall Street Reform and Consumer Protection Act was a well-intentioned response to the problem. Its stated promise—to end "too big to fail"—rings hollow. . . . Market discipline is still lacking for the largest dozen

or so institutions, as it was during the last financial crisis. Why should a prospective purchaser of bank debt practice due diligence if in the end, regardless of new layers of regulation and oversight, the issuing institution won't be allowed to fail?

The return of marketplace discipline and effective due diligence of banking behemoths is long overdue. We offer a modest proposal to level the playing field:

First, we would roll back the federal safety net—deposit insurance and the Federal Reserve's discount window—to apply only to traditional commercial banks, and not to the nonbank affiliates of bank holding companies or the parent companies themselves, where the safety net was never intended to be.

Second, customers, creditors and counterparties of all nonbank affiliates and the parent holding companies would sign a simple, legally binding, unambiguous disclosure acknowledging and accepting that there is no government guarantee—ever—backstopping their investment. A similar disclaimer would apply to bank deposits outside the FDIC insurance limit and other unsecured debts.

Third, we recommend that the largest financial holding companies be restructured so that every one of their corporate entities is subject to a speedy bankruptcy process, and in the case of banking entities themselves, that they be of a size that is "too small to save." Addressing institutional size is vital to maintaining a credible threat of failure, thereby

Micro-Prudential Versus Macro-Prudential Regulation

STABILITY

Just as important, regulators must recognize that the goal of financial stability does not mean the stability of individual financial institutions. Too often supervisors have viewed their role as ensuring that no firm fails. The government official's job is not to stabilize the profits of an individual bank or insurance company. To do so would be to defeat the purpose of competition, rendering the entire system less efficient than it could be. Rather, the regulator's goal should be to prevent large-scale catastrophes.

The financial crisis of 2007–2009 has made avoidance of systemic threats a top priority for government (see Chapter 5, Lessons from the Crisis: Systemic Risk). As a result, regulators are broadening their focus beyond **micro-prudential** oversight to encompass **macro-prudential** regulation. Traditional regulation is micro-prudential—it aims at limiting the risks *within* intermediaries in order to reduce (but not eliminate) the possibility of an individual institution's failure. Before the crisis, micro-prudential had been the sole focus of regulators, but it is insufficient to prevent systemic risks. That is the goal of macro-prudential regulation.[12]

[12]Indeed, most failures of intermediaries do not threaten the financial system, so efforts to secure the solvency of individual institutions may do little to make the financial system more secure.

providing a convincing case that policy has truly changed. This step gets both bank incentives and structure right, neither of which is accomplished by Dodd-Frank.

The downsized, formerly too-big-to-fail banks would be just like the other 99.8%, failing with finality when necessary—closed on a Friday and reopened on Monday under new ownership and management in the customary process managed by the Federal Deposit Insurance Corporation.

The aim of our three-step proposal is simple: All banks would be subject to the same regulatory oversight—and most important, they would all be subject to the market discipline exercised by owners and creditors.

Had this plan been in place a decade ago, it would have altered the insidious behaviors that contributed to the crisis, avoiding the bailouts and their aftermath, the cost of which our nation's citizens will bear for years to come. The Government Accountability Office and others estimate the cost of the financial crisis, measured in lost output and jobs, to be between $10 trillion and $20 trillion, roughly one year of U.S. output down the drain.

Most of all, adoption of our proposal would have avoided a crisis that undermined Americans' belief in the fairness and justice of the economic system. The United States was founded on the principle of economic freedom, underpinned by secure property rights and by a strong aversion to special favors and subsidies to the few. Those fundamental virtues were undermined by the recent financial crisis and government's response to it. . . .

SOURCE: Richard W. Fisher and Harvey Rosenblum, "How to Shrink the 'Too-Big-to-Fail' Banks," *The Wall Street Journal,* March 11, 2013. Used with permission of Dow Jones & Company, Inc. via Copyright Clearance Center, Inc.

LESSONS OF THE ARTICLE

Despite the Dodd-Frank Act, megabanks enjoy an implicit subsidy not available to smaller banks: They borrow at lower costs because many creditors believe that they would be bailed out in a crisis. Ending that subsidy requires that if they fail, they can be quickly put under new ownership or liquidated without a bailout and without damaging the financial system or the economy. To make this feasible, the article proposes to shrink them. It also proposes to narrow the federal safety net, but that may not reduce the government's incentive to bail out the largest intermediaries in a crisis.

How does macro-prudential regulation aim to limit systemic risks?[13] It treats systemic risk taking by an intermediary as a kind of *pollution* that spills over to other financial institutions and markets. To limit such costly spillovers, or **externalities**, regulators can use an evolving set of macro-prudential tools that work like the taxes and fees that governments use to limit pollution.

There are two types of externalities that pose systemic risks requiring regulatory intervention. These are known as (1) **common exposure** and (2) **pro-cyclicality**, which refers to the links between the financial sector and the economy that amplify boom and bust cycles.

Common Exposure   When many institutions have an exposure to the same specific risk factor, it can make the system vulnerable to a shock to that factor. The shock may be small, but the institutions with an exposure to it can all be brought down at once. In biology, for example, the animals in an ecosystem may be sensitive to changes in climate or chemistry or to the introduction of a new life form. Imagine the risks posed to the indigenous elk when wolves were returned to Yellowstone National Park.

[13]The following section draws significantly on the discussion of systemic risk in the BIS *Annual Report,* June 2009, pages 128–135.

More dramatically, think of the mass extinctions that punctuate the history of life on earth. Mass extinctions occur only infrequently, but they represent occasions in which many forms of life were similarly vulnerable to a change in their environment.

In finance, common exposures arise directly and indirectly. Intermediaries may be directly exposed to a frail institution through financial contracts. Or they may be exposed unknowingly through their counterparties, who are themselves directly exposed to the frail institution. Institutions might be damaged if a vulnerable intermediary is driven into a *fire sale* of its assets at depressed prices that further undermines market liquidity. Finally, all institutions may be vulnerable to the same underlying risks, such as a wave of mortgage defaults or the inability to roll over short-term debt.

In the crisis of 2007–2009, risky mortgages were embedded in many financial instruments, infecting financial markets such as those for asset-backed commercial paper (see Chapter 7, Lessons from the Crisis: Asset-Backed Commercial Paper) and for repo loans, which are the lifeblood of securities brokers (Chapter 12). The infection damaged financial institutions through their portfolios and through their access to credit. When the contagion spread to the repo market, a biologist might say that the crisis became an "extinction-level event" for the species known as large U.S. investment banks: In the week after the fall of the Lehman Brothers investment bank in September 2008, the three largest of the remaining investment banks merged with a bank or became bank holding companies themselves to qualify for support from the U.S. government.

The problem of common exposure may be related to the size of the institution, but it does not have to be. Large intermediaries usually are more interconnected, so they are typically a greater source of systemic risk. However, even a set of small institutions (like MMMFs) that have identical balance sheets face common risks and in doing so can represent a systemic hazard. Once again, a biological analogy is instructive. To survive, living creatures need water in its liquid form: Their size does not matter. Liquidity is a matter of survival in finance, too.

Pro-cyclicality   How do the cyclical patterns in finance and other economic activity pose systemic risks? As the crisis of 2007–2009 illustrates, financial activity is prone to virtuous and vicious cycles. The interaction between financial and economic activity can be mutually reinforcing—recall the concept of adverse feedback mentioned on page 364—leading to unsustainable booms and busts.

In a boom, investor complacency lowers market risk premia (i.e., investors' optimism causes them to accept compensation that is too low for the risks they are taking). The lower risk premia boost asset prices, spending, and profits and thus reinforce the prevailing optimism. Rising asset prices raise wealth and the value of collateral, making it easier for lenders to overcome the information asymmetries that lead to adverse selection and moral hazard. Both the value of intermediary capital and the willingness to leverage that capital rise, increasing credit supply and spurring new economic activity that encourages further euphoria—even among regulators. Rising asset prices also lower the cost of making markets, adding to liquidity and complacency.

As we saw in the crisis that began in 2007, busts reverse this process. Falling asset prices depress wealth, collateral, bank capital, credit supply, and liquidity. Leveraged intermediaries scramble to deleverage (to reduce risk taking), but the financial system cannot deleverage all at once in a safe fashion. The liquidity and deleveraging spirals highlighted in the Lessons from the Crisis of Chapters 2 and 3 reinforce the vicious cycle both in finance and in economic activity. The depletion of capital makes the financial system vulnerable even to a modest shock. And regulators typically become more cautious, urging banks to limit risky lending (even though the riskiest loans were made during the boom). Only an entity outside the financial system—usually the government—can supply the liquidity to counter a systemic crisis and, if necessary, restore the capital of the damaged intermediaries.

Macro-prudential Policy   To limit the kind of risk taking that can lead to a systemic crisis, macro-prudential regulation aims to make intermediaries bear—or *internalize*—the costs that their behavior imposes on others. In the same way, pollution taxes are designed to make the polluter bear the cost of the pollution.

Macro-prudential policy applies some familiar regulatory tools in unfamiliar ways. For example, regulatory capital requirements might vary with an institution's contribution to systemic risk. That contribution depends on an intermediary's interconnectedness and the riskiness of its balance sheet and is often correlated with its size. To be effective in limiting systemic threats, a *systemic capital surcharge*—think of a tax on pollution—would be disproportionately larger for firms that contribute the most to systemic risk.[14] In this way, intermediaries would have an incentive to limit the systemic risks that they create, just as a pollution tax encourages polluters to clean up their act. Consistent with this approach, in the summer of 2013, the FDIC proposed higher capital requirements (in the form of a supplementary leverage ratio requirement) for the "largest, most systemically important banking institutions."

To counter the systemic risks from boom/bust finance, macro-prudential regulators also could make capital requirements vary with the business cycle. In good times, capital requirements would rise above the long-run average to create a capital buffer against adverse shocks and to discourage euphoria. When leaner times arrive, regulators would allow intermediaries to use their ample capital buffer to meet the credit needs of healthy borrowers. Overall, the effect would be to dampen the cyclical swings of credit supply that can be an important source of economic instability.

Other macro-prudential tools may be new and different.[15] For example, regulators could require banks to buy catastrophe insurance: In the event of a systemic crisis, the payout from the insurance contract would replenish bank capital precisely when the financial system needs it. Another approach would be to have banks issue so-called contingent convertible (CoCo) bonds that convert to equity in the event of a capital shortfall. In these ways, intermediaries would pay in advance for the potential cost of restoring the system's capital in a crisis rather than relying on a future government capital infusion that burdens taxpayers. The price of the insurance (or the cost of issuing the CoCo bond) would also function as a brake on risk taking if it rises with the intermediary's contribution to systemic risk.

Ultimately, addressing systemic risk will require a broad framework of macro-prudential supervision that includes (1) rules and mechanisms that promote better risk management on the part of intermediaries and (2) reforms that reduce the vulnerability of the financial system to the liquidation of any single financial firm. In the final section of this chapter, we will see how the Dodd-Frank reform addresses these needs.

Regulatory Reform: The Dodd-Frank Act of 2010

The Dodd-Frank Wall Street Reform and Consumer Protection Act imposes the most far-reaching changes in U.S. financial regulation since the 1930s, when the Glass-Steagall Act separated the commercial side from the investment side of banking and

[14]See Nikola Tarashev, Claudio Borio, and Kostas Tsatsaronis, "The Systemic Importance of Financial Institutions," *BIS Quarterly Review*, September 2009, pp. 75–87. For one measure of U.S. financial institutions' contributions to systemic risk, see the website of the NYU Stern Volatility Lab: *http://vlab.stern.nyu.edu/analysis/RISK.USFIN-MR.MES.*

[15]See, for example, Samuel Hanson, Anil Kashyap, and Jeremy Stein, "A Macroprudential Approach to Financial Regulation," *Journal of Economic Perspectives* 25, no. 1 (Winter 2011), available at *http://pubs.aeaweb.org/doi/pdfplus/10.1257/jep.25.1.3.*

when many of today's federal financial agencies (including the FDIC and the SEC) were born. Like the 1930s reforms, Dodd-Frank will significantly alter the structure of finance—its institutions, markets, and practices—perhaps for decades.

The act requires government regulators to design and implement hundreds of new rules for a wide range of financial activities, including banking, derivatives, and insurance. This summary of the 800-page act is unavoidably incomplete: As of July 2013, less than 40 percent of the nearly 400 new rules that Dodd-Frank requires federal regulatory agencies to write had been completed; another 30 percent had been proposed; and the final third had not yet been addressed.[16] For that and other reasons, uncertainty about Dodd-Frank's impact will persist for years.[17]

The Act's Goals and Means
Dodd-Frank has four primary goals: (1) to make the financial system robust; (2) to anticipate and prevent financial crises by limiting systemic risk; (3) to end "too big to fail"; and (4) to reduce the moral hazard resulting from policy actions such as those taken in the 2007–2009 crisis, including the risks to U.S. taxpayers from government bailouts. The act addresses each of these goals in multiple ways.

Strengthening the Financial System
Dodd-Frank encourages transparency and simplification throughout the financial system and improves its resilience. Reminiscent of limits imposed on banks before 1999, Dodd-Frank forbids depositories from engaging in a variety of risky activities such as trading securities for their own accounts (see footnote 17). It increases the liability of credit rating agencies for ratings errors while compelling greater disclosure to limit the agencies' conflicts of interest (see Chapter 7, Lessons from the Crisis: Rating Agencies). It requires intermediaries that originate and distribute asset-backed securities to have "skin in the game" through partial ownership of the instruments. And, consistent with the new Basel III international standards (see the Tools of the Trade earlier in this chapter), it also encourages regulators to increase the capital banks hold.

Preventing Crises Through Systemic Risk Management
Led by the Treasury Secretary, Dodd-Frank's new super-committee of top U.S. regulators, the Financial System Oversight Council (FSOC), aims to identify and forestall threats to the system. The new Office of Financial Research (OFR), which expands the regulators' data-gathering and analysis capacity, supports the FSOC's effort to locate and quantify systemic risks. The FSOC has the authority to designate nonbanks and banks as systemically important financial institutions (SIFIs), making them subject to enhanced oversight by the Federal Reserve, including heightened capital requirements consistent with systemic risk.[18] In July 2013, three years after the Dodd-Frank Act became law, the FSOC designated for the first time two *nonbank* intermediaries—American International Group (AIG) and General Electric Capital Corporation (GECC)—as SIFIs. Should a SIFI's weakness

---

[16]See Davis Polk, "Dodd-Frank Progress Report," July 2013, *www.davispolk.com/Dodd-Frank-Rulemaking-Progress-Report.*

[17]One example—Section 619 of the act, also known as the "Volcker rule"—highlights the regulators' challenge. It was not until October 2011, about 15 months after the act was passed, that federal agencies issued a proposal to implement the Volcker rule, which prohibits insured depositories from trading for their own account, investing in private equity funds, and owning hedge funds. The 300-page proposal included hundreds of questions for banks, and it garnered thousands of comments from the public, all of which the agencies must consider. The Dodd-Frank deadline for implementing Section 619 was July 2012, but as of mid-2013 the regulators had not yet agreed on a final rule. The greatest difficulty is that they cannot readily distinguish between bank market-making, which Dodd-Frank permits, and trading for a bank's own account, which it does not.

[18]The act also requires that SIFIs undergo annual stress tests, such as those carried out under the Fed's annual Comprehensive Capital Analysis and Review (see *www.federalreserve.gov/bankinforeg/ccar.htm*).

"gravely threaten" the financial system, the FSOC, together with the Federal Reserve Board and the FDIC, can require it to close down under Dodd-Frank's new resolution procedure (using the FDIC's "Orderly Liquidation Authority"), which aims to avoid a disruptive bankruptcy like the Lehman Brothers fiasco of September 2008.

Ending "Too Big to Fail" and Reducing Moral Hazard   One leading motivation for Dodd-Frank was the desire to eliminate government bailouts of institutions whose failure would be deemed too risky for the financial system. Not only are bailouts unpopular, but even the possibility of them lowers the borrowing costs of the largest banks and gives those banks an incentive to take too much risk. Simply put, bailouts create moral hazard. Among other things, the act makes it much more difficult for the Federal Reserve to make loans to nonbank intermediaries. (We will discuss central bank lending in more detail in Chapter 18.) Dodd-Frank also constrains the FDIC's guarantee powers, which were used extensively in the crisis to sustain banks' funding capacity. Finally, the act requires all SIFIs to have resolution plans ("living wills") and gives the FDIC new powers to take over SIFIs, even if they are not banks.

Where Dodd-Frank Falls Short
Despite its length and complexity, the Dodd-Frank Act fails to address several glaring problems that contributed to the crisis of 2007–2009. It also has created a broad new difficulty.[19]

Here are some of the biggest shortcomings:

1. The act fails to streamline the U.S. regulatory apparatus, which remains complex and unwieldy, with a multiplicity of regulators that have overlapping responsibilities.

2. Many government guarantees still largely come for free. The failure to charge a fee commensurate with the risk sustains moral hazard.

3. As of 2013, five years after Fannie Mae and Freddie Mac were put under direct federal control, Congress is still debating how to restructure these government-sponsored enterprises (GSEs), which contributed to the mortgage bubble preceding the crisis and have cost taxpayers more than $100 billion.

4. The act largely ignores key shadow banks like money market mutual funds (MMMFs), which received a blanket federal guarantee during the crisis. MMMFs generally are too small to be SIFIs, but collectively they create systemic risk through common exposures—namely, their vulnerable short-term funding and their herd-like asset management. Dodd-Frank also does not address potentially systemic financial markets—like the market for repurchase agreements (repo)—that may themselves be vulnerable to a run and a fire sale.

5. Dodd-Frank continues to regulate according to institutional *form* rather than *function*. Supervisors who compel banks and nonbank SIFIs to reduce their risk-taking may find, over time, that as a result of financial innovation and efforts of intermediaries to circumvent regulation, systemic risk has migrated to shadow banks with different legal forms.

6. Perhaps most important, many observers still doubt that Dodd-Frank will end big bailouts. A major reason is the perception that designation as a SIFI implies a government guarantee for some creditors (e.g., uninsured depositors). So long as

---

[19]Many of the ideas in this section are based on Viral Acharya, Thomas F. Cooley, Matthew P. Richardson, and Ingo Walter, *Regulating Wall Street: The Dodd-Frank Act and the New Architecture of Global Finance* (Hoboken, NJ: Wiley, 2010).

private market participants expect bailouts of SIFIs, these institutions will enjoy lower funding costs than other intermediaries, tilting the playing field further in favor of SIFIs and promoting financial concentration. Over time, the greater the concentration, the more that SIFIs will be seen as public utilities that cannot be allowed to fail in a crisis. Breaking this vicious cycle is possible only if intermediaries can fail without systemic repercussions.

And here is the new difficulty: While Dodd-Frank may reduce the chances of a crisis, past experience and the powerful dynamics of financial innovation make it likely that one will eventually occur. And when it does, regulators will find that Dodd-Frank limits policy flexibility (such as the new constraints on action by the Federal Reserve and the FDIC) in ways that could make the crisis more difficult to contain.

Terms

adverse feedback, 364
bank panic, 363
bank run, 362
Basel Accord, 378
CAMELS, 381
common exposure, 383
contagion, 363
deposit insurance, 369
examination, 380
externality, 383
illiquid, 363

insolvent, 362
lender of last resort, 366
macro-prudential, 382
micro-prudential, 382
pro-cyclicality, 383
regulation, 373
regulatory competition, 374
shadow bank, 361
supervision, 380
too-big-to-fail policy, 371

Using FRED: Codes for Data in This Chapter

Data Series	FRED Data Code
Failures of depositories	BKFTTLA641N
FDIC failure and assistance transactions	BKIFDCA641N
Purchase and assumption transactions	BKTTPIA641N
Payout transactions	BKTTPOA641N
Commercial bank equity/assets ratio	EQTA
Retail MMMFs	RMFSL
Institutional MMMFs	IMFSL
Discount window borrowings	DISCBORR
Asset-backed commercial paper outstanding	ABCOMP

Chapter Lessons

1. The collapse of banks and the banking system disrupts both the payments system and the screening and monitoring of borrowers.
   a. Intermediaries are insolvent when their liabilities exceed their assets.
   b. Because banks guarantee their depositors cash on demand on a first-come, first-served basis, they are subject to runs. Shadow banks like MMMFs and securities brokers also face runs because some of their liabilities can be withdrawn at face value without notice.
   c. A bank run can occur simply because depositors have become worried about a bank's soundness. Shadow banks also may face runs due to a loss of confidence.
   d. The inability of depositors to tell a sound from an unsound bank can turn a single bank's failure into a bank panic, causing even sound banks to fail through a process called contagion. Shadow banks face similar risks.
   e. A financial crisis in which the entire system of banks and shadow banks ceases to function can be caused by
      i. False rumors.
      ii. The actual deterioration of balance sheets for economic reasons.

2. The government is involved in every part of the financial system.
   a. Government officials may intervene in the financial system in order to
      i. Protect small depositors.
      ii. Protect bank customers from exploitation.
      iii. Safeguard the stability of the financial system.
   b. Most financial regulations apply to depository institutions, while shadow banks usually face less regulation.
   c. Intermediaries that are less prone to runs, such as pension funds and most insurers, face less intrusive government oversight than the banking industry.
   d. The U.S. government has established a two-part safety net to protect the nation's financial system.
      i. The Federal Reserve acts as the lender of last resort, providing liquidity to solvent institutions in order to prevent the failure of a single intermediary from becoming a systemwide panic.
      ii. The Federal Deposit Insurance Corporation (FDIC) insures individual depositors helping to prevent bank runs by reducing depositors' incentive to flee at the first whiff of trouble.
   e. The government's safety net encourages bank managers to take more risk than they would otherwise, increasing the problem of moral hazard.

3. Through regulation and supervision, government officials reduce the amount of risk banks can take, lowering their chances of failure. Regulators and supervisors
   a. Restrict competition.
   b. Restrict the types of assets banks can hold.
   c. Require banks to hold minimum levels of capital.
   d. Require banks to disclose their fees to customers and their financial indicators to investors.
   e. Monitor banks' compliance with government regulations.

4. Regulators use macro-prudential tools to limit systemic threats to the financial system. Such risks usually arise from externalities—costly spillovers from the behavior of intermediaries. These externalities have two sources: (1) *common exposure* of

intermediaries to frail institutions or to underlying risks and (2) *pro-cyclicality* of the links between financial and economic activity, which amplifies boom and bust cycles.

Conceptual and Analytical Problems

1. Explain how a bank run can turn into a bank panic. *(LO1)*

2. Current technology allows large bank depositors to withdraw their funds electronically at a moment's notice. They can do so all at the same time, without anyone's knowledge, in what is called a silent run. When might a silent run happen, and why? *(LO1)*

3. Explain why financial institutions such as pension funds and insurance companies are not as vulnerable to runs as money-market mutual funds and securities dealers. *(LO1)*

4. Explain the link between falling house prices and bank failures during the financial crisis of 2007–2009. *(LO1)*

5. Discuss the regulations that are designed to reduce the moral hazard created by deposit insurance. *(LO3)*

6. During the financial crisis of 2007–2009, the Federal Reserve used its emergency authority to lend to nonbank intermediaries. Explain how this extension of the lender of last resort function added to moral hazard. *(LO2)*

7.* Why is the banking system much more heavily regulated than other areas of the economy? *(LO3)*

8.* Explain why, in seeking to avoid financial crises, the government's role as regulator of the financial system does not imply it should protect individual institutions from failure. *(LO2)*

9. Explain how macro-prudential regulations work to limit systemic risk in the financial system. *(LO3)*

10. Why were runs during the financial crisis of 2007–2009 not limited to institutions with large exposures to subprime mortgage lending? *(LO1)*

11.* Do you think that the central bank, as lender of last resort, should also supervise the financial industry? Why or why not? *(LO3)*

12. Suppose you have two deposits totaling $280,000 with a bank that has just been declared insolvent. Would you prefer that the FDIC resolve the insolvency under the "payoff method" or the "purchase and assumption" method? Explain your choice. *(LO2)*

13.* How might the existence of the government safety net lead to increased concentration in the banking industry? *(LO2)*

14. One goal of the Dodd-Frank Wall Street reform is to end the too-big-to-fail problem. How does it propose to do so? Why might it fail? *(LO3)*

15. A government can overcome the challenge of time consistency only if it is both *able* and *willing* to make credible commitments. With this in mind, how might the U.S. laws and procedures for bankruptcy affect the too-big-to-fail problem? *(LO2)*

*Indicates more difficult problems

16. If banks' fragility arises from the fact that they provide liquidity to depositors, as a bank manager, how might you reduce the fragility of your institution? *(LO1)*

17.* Why do you think bank managers are not always willing to pursue strategies to reduce the fragility of their institutions? *(LO1)*

18. Regulators have traditionally required banks to maintain capital-asset ratios of a certain level to ensure adequate net worth based on the size and composition of the bank's assets on its balance sheet. Why might such capital adequacy requirements not be effective? *(LO3)*

19. You are the lender of last resort and an institution approaches you for a loan. You assess that the institution has $800 million in assets, mostly in long-term loans, and $600 million in liabilities. The institution is experiencing unusually high withdrawal rates on its demand deposits and is requesting a loan to tide it over. Would you grant the loan? *(LO2)*

20. You are a bank examiner and have concerns that the bank you are examining may have a solvency problem. On examining the bank's assets, you notice that the loan sizes of a significant portion of the bank's loans are increasing in relatively small increments each month. What do you think might be going on and what should you do about it? *(LO3)*

Data Exploration

For general information on using Federal Reserve Economic Data (FRED) online, visit www.mhhe.com/moneyandbanking4e and click on Student Edition, then FRED Resources.

Scan here for quick access to the resources for these problems. Need a barcode reader? Try ScanLife, available in your app store.

1. When banks failed in the 1929–1933 period, the lack of deposit insurance meant that depositors experienced sizable losses. How big were these losses? For September 1929 through February 1933, plot the deposits in suspended banks (FRED code: M09039USM144NNBR). Download the data and sum the deposits lost to bank failures in 1932. Using this total, compute its ratio to 1932 gross domestic product of $58.7 billion. Using that ratio, how large would the losses be compared to first-quarter 2013 nominal GDP of $16.5 trillion. *(LO1)*

2. How frequently are the payoff and the purchase-and-assumption methods used by the FDIC? Plot the total number of institutions receiving such assistance (FRED codes: BKTTPIA641N for purchase and assumption; BKTTPOA641N for the payoff method). On the same graph, plot as a second line the purchase and assumption data separately (so that your graph will show one line with the total and a second line with the purchase and assumption data only). Describe the evolution over the long run. From what you know about the total number of depository institutions, does the total number of resolutions seem high or low? *(LO2)*

3. Examine the capital ratios of large banks (FRED code: EQTA5) and small banks (FRED code: EQTA1). What can you say about the risk-taking propensity of these banks over the long run? How did the financial crisis of 2007–2009 influence the risk-taking of large banks? *(LO3)*

4. How important was the lender-of-last-resort function of the Federal Reserve in the financial crisis of 2007–2009? Beginning in 2000, plot the ratio (in percent) of borrowing from the Fed (FRED code: DISCBORR) to its asset holdings (FRED code: WRESCRT). What happened to the borrowing ratio during the 2007–2009 financial crisis? *(LO2)*

5. Shadow banks typically fund their assets by issuing liabilities of shorter maturity that are close substitutes for bank deposits. The maturity mismatch between their assets and liabilities creates *rollover risk* that can trigger *fire sales* and systemic disruption. Plot the outstanding level of one such liability—asset-backed commercial paper (FRED code: ABCOMP)—from the start of 2002 to the end of 2007. Based on the plot, discuss how the use of asset-backed commercial paper influenced the financial crisis of 2007–2009? *(LO1)*

Part *IV*

Central Banks, Monetary Policy, and Financial Stability

Chapter 15
Central Banks in the World Today

Learning Objectives

Understand . . .

LO1 Functions and objectives of central banks

LO2 Features of an effective central bank

LO3 Fiscal challenges for central banks

Beginning in the summer of 2007, the most severe and persistent financial crisis since the Great Depression shook intermediaries, markets, and economies around the globe. Some of the largest financial institutions failed, and the market disruptions triggered the worst global recession since the Second World War. The panic peaked after the September 2008 run on Lehman Brothers—the fourth largest U.S. investment bank— as investors around the globe sought to hold only the safest, most liquid assets they could find. Investors stopped lending to intermediaries, who stopped lending to each other. As the storm spread, the global financial system bordered on complete collapse for the first time in 75 years.

Central banks neither foresaw nor prevented the crisis of 2007–2009. Even long after the tempest began, they did not see how menacing it would become. Yet, as the expanding storm continuously poked new holes in the financial boat, policymakers developed new tools to plug the holes. When the financial hurricane finally reached its late-2008 crescendo, the world's leading central banks played a key role in bringing the financial system and the economy back to safe harbor. They acted in unprecedented fashion—on their own as well as with other central banks and with government finance ministries—to prevent the financial system from capsizing and, over time, to restore financial and economic stability.

The **central bank** of the United States is the Federal Reserve (widely known as the Fed for short). The people who work there are responsible for making sure that our financial system functions smoothly so that the average citizen can carry on without worrying about it. During the financial crisis, the Fed fell short of this goal. Nevertheless, it managed in 2008 to prevent the looming collapse of the financial system and to foster a vast improvement of financial conditions in 2009 that helped end the long, deep economic slump.

The euro area consists of 18 countries (as of January 2014) that have adopted the euro as their common currency (the euro area is a subset of the European Union, which consists of 28 countries). The central bank of the euro area is the European Central Bank (ECB). After working to safeguard the euro during the global crisis of 2007–2009, the ECB in 2010 began to face a banking and sovereign debt crisis in several euro-area countries. A flight of capital and deposits out of those countries threatened an end to the euro itself, but extraordinary liquidity provision by the ECB purchased time for governments to address the euro area's vulnerabilities.

Earlier caution under similar circumstances on the part of Japan's central bank, the Bank of Japan, had provided a negative lesson to the Fed and the ECB: Beginning in the 1990s, the Bank of Japan allowed the country to sink into deflation following the collapse of huge bubbles in the stock market and real estate market. Over the next two decades, Japan's price deflator for gross domestic product sank by nearly 20 percent from its peak, adding to the real burden of debt.

These watershed events will leave a lasting imprint on global economies, the financial system, and policymaking. Many changes resulting from recent crises are likely to prove permanent rather than temporary. As we saw in Chapters 12 and 13, the crisis of 2007–2009 has already transformed the structure of the financial industry in the United States, with further change on the horizon. Chapter 14 highlighted the new regulatory environment, especially Basel III, Dodd-Frank, and new approaches to managing systemic risk.

In Part IV, we will study the evolving role of central banks. Central banks do not act only during times of crisis. Their work is vital to the day-to-day operation of any modern economy. Today there are about 175 central banks in the world: Virtually every country has one.[1] Yet, despite the vast powers of these institutions and the constant news reports on their activities, most people have only a vague idea of what they are and what they do.

This chapter begins to explain the role of central banks in our economic and financial system. It describes the origins of modern central banking and examines the complexities policymakers now face in meeting their responsibilities. It also highlights a central question that has become politically controversial following the crisis actions of the Fed, the ECB, and other central banks; namely, what is the proper relationship between a central bank and the government?

The Basics: How Central Banks Originated and Their Role Today

The central bank started out as the government's bank and over the years added various other functions. A modern central bank not only manages the government's finances but provides an array of services to commercial banks. It is the bankers' bank. Let's see how this arrangement came about.

The Government's Bank

Governments have financial needs of their own. Some rulers, like King William of Orange, created the central bank to finance wars. Others, like Napoléon Bonaparte, did it in an effort to stabilize their country's economic and financial system.[2]

---

[1] For a list of the world's central banks and their websites, see the website of the Bank for International Settlements: *www.bis.org/cbanks.htm.*

[2] The Bank of England was chartered in 1694 for the express purpose of raising taxes and borrowing to finance a war between Austria, England, and the Netherlands on one side and Louis XIV's France on the other. The Banque de France was created in 1800 in the aftermath of the deep recession and hyperinflation of the French Revolutionary period. For a more detailed discussion, see Glyn Davies' *A History of Money: From Ancient Times to the Present Day* (Cardiff: University of Wales Press, 2002).

While central banks have been around since the late 1600s, these early examples are really the exceptions, as central banking is largely a 20th-century phenomenon. In 1900, only 18 countries had central banks. Even the U.S. Federal Reserve did not begin operating until 1914.[3] As the importance of the government and the financial system grew, the need for a central bank grew along with it. Today it is hard to imagine not having one.

As the government's bank, the central bank occupies a privileged position: It has a monopoly on the issuance of currency. *The central bank creates money.* Historically, central bank money has been seen as more trustworthy than that issued by kings, queens, or emperors. Rulers have had a tendency to default on their debts, rendering their currencies worthless. By contrast, early central banks kept sufficient reserves to redeem their notes in gold. People must have faith in money if they are to use it, and experience tells us that this type of institutional arrangement creates that faith. Today the Federal Reserve has the sole legal authority to issue U.S. dollar bills.[4]

The ability to print currency means that the central bank can control the availability of money and credit in a country's economy. As we'll see in later chapters, most central banks go about this by adjusting short-term interest rates. This activity is what we usually refer to as **monetary policy**. In today's world, central banks use monetary policy to stabilize economic growth and inflation. An expansionary or accommodative policy, through lower interest rates, raises both growth and inflation over the short run, while tighter or restrictive policy reduces them. We will discuss the mechanics of monetary policy in more detail in later chapters.

Understanding why a country would want to have its own monetary policy is important. At its most basic level, printing paper money is a very profitable business. A $100 bill costs only a few cents to print, but it can be exchanged for $100 worth of goods and services. It is logical that governments would want to maintain a monopoly on printing paper money and to use the revenue it generates to benefit the general public. (Although, when we list the objectives of the central bank later in this chapter, profit maximization will not be one of them.)

Government officials also know that losing control of the printing presses means losing control of inflation. A high rate of money growth creates a high inflation rate. Giving the currency-printing monopoly to someone else can be disastrous, resulting in high inflation and damage to the economy's ability to function smoothly. (In fact, attempts to destabilize the value of a country's currency through counterfeiting have been used as a weapon in wars. See Applying the Concept on page 397.) Nevertheless, some countries have done it. The leading example is the euro area, whose member-states ceded the conduct of monetary policy to the ECB as part of a broader move toward economic integration. To limit inflation risks, they enshrined rules for the ECB in a treaty, helping to secure the ECB's credibility even amid crisis. We will see, however, that securing price stability and the viability of the euro over the long run also requires sound management of the euro area's government budgets and debt.

---

[3]For two short periods in the 19th century, the United States did have a national bank that served many of the functions of a central bank. Early American dislike for the centralization of power doomed these institutions, the First Bank of the United States (1791–1811) and the Second Bank of the United States (1816–1836). In the next chapter, we will see how industrial and financial development after the Civil War convinced people that they could not live without a central bank. See Michael F. Bryan and Bruce Champ's "Fear and Loathing of Central Banks in America," *Economic Commentary* of the Federal Reserve Bank of Cleveland, June 2002, for a brief description of this history.

[4]While once upon a time you could redeem dollar bills for gold, today all the Federal Reserve promises is that it will give you a crisp new dollar bill for a worn old one—and that is enough for the average person, given the public's faith in the Federal Reserve.

APPLYING THE CONCEPT
WHY IS STABLE MONEY SUCH A BIG DEAL?

by David E. Altig*

On Wednesday, July 10, 1940, Adolf Hitler's Luftwaffe attacked British air bases along the coasts of Scotland and eastern and southeastern England. Four months later, the Battle of Britain was over, bringing an end to German hopes of direct military conquest of the British Isles.

But the end of the air raids would not end the attack on the United Kingdom. Shortly after their defeat in the Battle of Britain, the Germans began to produce a new weapon that, while less obviously violent than Luftwaffe bombs, was recognized as no less virulent. That weapon was counterfeit British pounds.

Operation Bernhard, as the counterfeiting enterprise would be known, was named for Bernhard Kruger, the SS officer who oversaw the production of the bogus notes by slave labor in the Sachsenhausen concentration camp near Berlin. By contemporary accounts, the plan resulted in the manufacture of about £150,000,000 in counterfeit notes of various denominations—in the neighborhood of $7 billion by today's standards. Kruger's operation enlisted the support of known counterfeiters as well as professionals and skilled tradesmen among the camp's population. It incorporated production techniques that ran the gamut from detailed material analyses to the manual labor of prisoners who "seasoned" the bogus bills by passing them from one another, folding and soiling them to give them a realistic worn appearance.

The objective was simple, devious, and pernicious: To undermine public confidence in the pound and, by so doing, irreparably damage the British economy. In the end, the plot did not succeed in destroying confidence in Britain's currency, and eventually, the counterfeiting program shifted toward financing various clandestine Nazi activities outside the United Kingdom. Ironically, this shift in the operation's focus was made possible precisely because the initial goal of undermining the pound's value was not realized.

Operation Bernhard is a particularly interesting example of the use of counterfeiting as warfare, but it is by no means unique or unprecedented. One of the earliest known instances of counterfeiting as a weapon occurred during the city-state conflicts of Renaissance Italy (the historical period that would inspire Machiavelli's *The Prince*). The instigator in this case was one Galeazzo Sforza, a Milanese duke, who in 1470 (when Machiavelli was an infant) attempted to undermine the economic well-being of his enemies in the rival city-state of Venice by adding counterfeiting Venetian currency to the corpus of general treachery that he regularly practiced. (History records the duke as a particularly odious character, whose cruelty led to a successful assassination plot by Milanese elites in 1476.)

There are many, many more examples, including American counterfeiting of North Vietnamese dong during the Vietnam War and modern terrorist aggressions. The ubiquitous impulse to undermine the value of, and confidence in, the currency of one's enemies is testament to the indispensable role of a stable and reliable monetary standard in modern economies. In fact, so broad and deep is the potential damage of a successful counterfeiting campaign, some reports indicate that professional German military officers initially opposed Operation Bernhard partly on the grounds that it constituted an unacceptable attack on civilian populations. What do attempts to counterfeit an enemy's currency during wartime have in common with decisions to adopt another country's currency during peacetime? Both are inspired by the power of a stable monetary standard and, conversely, the consequences of losing it. Both illustrate why preserving the value of the nation's currency is one of a central bank's most important responsibilities.

*Excerpt from *Why Is Stable Money Such a Big Deal?* Economic Commentary of the Federal Reserve Bank of Cleveland, May 1, 2002.

The Bankers' Bank

The political backing of the government, together with their sizable gold reserves, made early central banks the biggest and most reliable banks around. The notes issued by the central bank were viewed as safer than those of smaller banks, making it easier for holders to convert their deposits into cash. This safety and convenience quickly persuaded most other banks to hold deposits at the central bank as well.

As the bankers' bank, the central bank took on key roles it plays today. The important day-to-day jobs of the central bank are to (1) provide loans during times of financial stress, (2) manage the payments system, and (3) oversee commercial banks and the financial system. The central bank's ability to create money means that it can make loans even when no one else can, including during a crisis. We discussed this "lender of last resort" function in Chapter 14 and will provide more detail in Chapter 18. For now, all we need to say is that by ensuring that sound banks and financial institutions can continue to operate, the central bank makes the whole financial system more stable. Many people believe this is the most important function of any modern central bank.

Second, every country needs a secure and efficient payments system. People require ways to pay each other, and financial institutions need a cheap and reliable way to transfer funds to one another.[5] The fact that all banks have accounts there makes the central bank the natural place for these *interbank* payments to be settled. In today's world, interbank payments are extremely important. Look at the daily volume on the Federal Reserve's *Fedwire* system. In 2012, an average of more than $2.4 trillion per day was transferred over the Fedwire—more than one-seventh of the annual U.S. gross domestic product.

Finally, as we saw in our discussion of banking regulation, someone has to watch over commercial banks and nonbank financial institutions so that savers and investors can be confident they are sound. Those who monitor the financial system must have sensitive information. For example, they need to know the exact methods institutions use to make lending and credit decisions. Needless to say, such knowledge would be very useful to the institutions' competitors. Government examiners and supervisors are the only ones who can handle such information without conflict of interest. In some countries they are housed in the central bank, while in others they work in separate agencies. In the United States, as we saw in Chapter 14, the examiners work in various places, including the Federal Reserve.

As the government's bank and the bankers' bank, central banks are the biggest, most powerful players in a country's financial and economic system. Central bankers are supposed to use this power to stabilize the economy, making us all better off. And for the most part, that is what they do. But any institution with the power to ensure that the economic and financial systems run smoothly also has the power to create problems. By limiting its lending early in the financial crisis of 2007–2009, the Bank of England may have contributed to the first depositor run on a major British bank in more than a century. And following the breakup of the Soviet Union, the failure of the Bank of Russia to exert any control over the expansion of money and credit led to a very high inflation rate, while Russian economic activity in the 1990s was virtually halved.

Before we go on to examine the goals and objectives of central bankers in detail, it is essential that we understand what a modern central bank is *not*. First, a central bank does not control securities markets, though it may monitor and participate in bond and stock markets. Second, the central bank does not control the government's budget. In the United States, the budget is determined by Congress and the president through **fiscal policy**. The U.S. Treasury then administers the government, managing the collection of funds through the tax system and writing checks to pay for the government's expenditures. The Fed acts only as the Treasury's bank, providing a place for money paid to the government to be deposited, making good on the government's checks, and helping to borrow funds when they are needed. Not just in the United States but throughout the world, the common arrangement today is for the central bank to serve

---

[5]Prior to the creation of the Federal Reserve's payment system, banks were not always willing to honor the obligations of other banks at par. Thus, a $100 bank note from a particular Philadelphia bank might be worth only $95 in New York. And the discount would vary depending on the perceived creditworthiness of the Philadelphia bank. This system was very cumbersome and expensive. One of the jobs of the Federal Reserve is to act as an intermediary, ensuring that all banks' commitments are valued at par so that the rest of us don't have to worry. In the same way, the ECB acts today to facilitate payments in euros at par from, say, a bank in Rome to one in Berlin.

Table 15.1	The Functions of a Modern Central Bank

1. *The Government's Bank*
   a. Executes financial transactions for the government.
   b. Through interest rates, controls the availability of money and credit.
2. *The Bankers' Bank*
   a. Guarantees that sound intermediaries can do business by *lending* to them, even during crises.
   b. Operates a *payments system* for interbank payments.
   c. *Oversees* financial institutions to ensure confidence in their soundness.

the government in the same way that a commercial bank serves a business or an individual. The treasury or finance ministry manages fiscal policy, and the central bank offers a set of services that make such management possible.

Table 15.1 lists the functions of a modern central bank.

Stability: The Primary Objective of All Central Banks

The central bank is essentially part of the government.[6] Whenever we see an agency of the government involving itself in the economy, we need to ask why. What makes individuals incapable of doing what we have entrusted to the government? In the case of national defense and pollution regulation, the reasons are obvious. Most people will not voluntarily contribute their resources to the army. Nor will they spontaneously clean up their own air. To put it slightly differently, government involvement is justified by the presence of externalities (the uncompensated impact on one entity from the actions of another; see page 383) or **public goods** (those that the public cannot be excluded from using and whose use does not limit use by others).

The rationale for the existence of a central bank is equally clear. While economic and financial systems may be fairly stable most of the time, when left on their own they are prone to episodes of extreme volatility. Prior to the advent of the Fed, the U.S. financial system was extremely unstable. It was plagued by frequent panics. Even with a central bank, these systems don't necessarily work well.

The historical record is filled with examples of failure, like the Great Depression of the 1930s, when the banking system collapsed, economic activity plunged by one-third, and, at its worst, one-quarter of Americans were unemployed for nearly a decade. Economic historians blame the Federal Reserve for the severity of that episode. The claim is that monetary policymakers failed to provide adequate money and credit, with the result that 10,000 of the country's 25,000 banks, accounting for 13 percent of all

---

[6]Technically, the legal organization of central banks can be quite complex. Some are inside their country's government, some are private banks, and others are a combination. As we will see in Chapter 16, the Federal Reserve is in that last category, part government and part private bank. As a practical matter, because they all have a set of tasks that only they are allowed to perform, we will treat central banks as if they are a part of the government.

deposits, were closed. The Fed also bears considerable responsibility for the crisis of 2007–2009. It was largely passive as intermediaries took on increasing risk amid an unprecedented housing bubble, and it allowed the financial hurricane to intensify for more than a year after the storms began. Unlike the Great Depression, however, the Fed used all its emergency authority in historically unprecedented ways to steady the financial system when the crisis peaked in 2008. The Fed's tenacity and flexibility helped promote a huge recovery of financial conditions in 2009 and avoid a second Great Depression. Similarly, increasingly aggressive liquidity provision by the ECB beginning in 2010 was essential to sustaining euro-area banks in the face of runs on several countries' banking systems.

Central bankers work to reduce the volatility of the economic and financial systems by pursuing five specific objectives:

STABILITY

1. Low and stable inflation.
2. High and stable real growth, together with high employment.
3. Stable financial markets and institutions.
4. Stable interest rates.
5. A stable exchange rate.

The job of the central bank is to improve general economic welfare by managing and reducing systematic risk. As we learned in Chapter 5, through diversification, people can manage idiosyncratic risk—the risk associated with individual persons or organizations—but not systematic risk, which affects everyone (and is distinct from *systemic* risk, which we generally use to refer to the financial sector of the economy). Instability in any of these five objectives poses a systematic or economywide risk. Keep in mind that it is probably impossible to achieve all five of the central bank's objectives simultaneously. Tradeoffs must be made. As we will see, stabilizing inflation may result in less stable growth, and stable interest rates may be inconsistent with all the other objectives.

Low, Stable Inflation

An official of the International Monetary Fund (the closest thing there is to a world central bank) once summarized virtually every economist's view when he said, "Uncontrolled inflation strangles growth, hurting the entire populace, especially the indigent."[7] That is why many central banks take as their primary job the maintenance of **price stability**. As a practical matter, that means keeping inflation low and stable. The consensus is that when inflation rises for any extended period, the central bank is at fault.

The rationale for seeking price stability is straightforward. Standards, everyone agrees, should be standard. A pound should always weigh a pound, a cup should always hold a cup, and a yard should always measure a yard. Similarly, a dollar should always be worth a dollar. What is true for physical weights and measures should be true for the unit of account as well. The purchasing power of one dollar, one yen, or one euro should remain stable over long periods. Maintaining price stability enhances money's usefulness both as a unit of account and as a store of value.

Prices are central to everything that happens in a market-based economy. They provide the information individuals and firms need to ensure that resources are allocated to their most productive uses. When a seller can raise the price of a product, for

[7]Kenneth S. Rogoff, "An Open Letter to Joseph Stiglitz," International Monetary Fund, July 2, 2002.

YOUR FINANCIAL WORLD
Why Inflation Is Bad for You

If you ask most people why inflation is bad, they will say it is responsible for a decline in what they can purchase with their incomes. For them, inflation causes a drop in their standard of living: Prices have gone up, but their incomes, including their wages, haven't. Economists view inflation differently. To them, inflation occurs when everything that is denominated in dollars goes up proportionally—prices, incomes, savings account balances, everything. It is as if everything is suddenly measured in cents instead of dollars. How could this possibly make anyone worse off?

The problem is that high inflation tends to be more volatile than low inflation, so the higher inflation is, the greater the risk. When inflation is averaging 2 percent per year, chances are slim that it will more than double to 5 percent. Such an increase would mean that the central bank had lost control, at least temporarily. But if the rate of inflation is closer to 15 percent, an increase of 3 percentage points to 18 percent, a change of only one-fifth, could easily happen.

To see how this affects virtually everyone, recall from Chapter 6 that unpredictable inflation makes bonds risky.

Higher-than-expected inflation reduces the *real* return a bondholder ultimately receives. This real return is the nominal return minus inflation, so if the nominal interest rate is 5 percent and inflation turns out to be 2 percent, then the real return is 3 percent. If the inflation rate ends up at 5 percent, the real return drops to zero. That's a risk. Because risk requires compensation, inflation risk drives up the interest rate required to entice investors to hold bonds.

Now think about two common financial transactions: getting a home mortgage and saving for retirement. When you buy a house, your goal is to get the lowest mortgage interest rate you can find. Inflation risk drives up mortgage interest rates, increasing your monthly payments and forcing you to purchase a less expensive house. Turning to your retirement savings, inflation risk makes it more difficult to know how much to save, because you are unsure what the purchasing power of your savings will be 40 or 50 years from now. Long-term planning is hard enough without the added burden of inflation risk.

example, that is supposed to signal that demand has increased, so producing more is worthwhile. But volatile inflation degrades the information content of prices. When all prices are rising together, understanding the reasons becomes difficult. Did consumers decide they liked an item, shifting demand? Did the cost of producing the item rise, shifting supply? Or was inflation responsible for the jump in price? If the economy is to run efficiently, we need to be able to tell the difference.

If the inflation rate were predictable—say, 10 percent year in and year out—we might be able to adjust, eventually. But unfortunately, as inflation rises, it becomes less stable. If our best guess is that the rate of inflation will be 2 percent over the coming year, we can be fairly certain that the result will be a price level increase of between 1 and 3 percent. But experience tells us that when we expect the inflation rate to be around 10 percent, we shouldn't be surprised if it ends up anywhere between 8 and 12 percent. The higher inflation is, the less predictable it is, and the more systematic risk it creates.[8]

RISK

Moreover, high inflation is bad for growth. This fact is obvious in extreme cases, such as the one in Zimbabwe, where prices doubled every day in November 2008, resulting in the second largest inflation on record.[9] In such cases of **hyperinflation**, prices contain virtually no information, and people use all their energy just coping with the crisis, so growth plummets. The Zimbabwe economy shrank by nearly 20 percent

---

[8]Inflation is costly for other reasons as well. They include the cost of going to the bank more often, the cost of changing prices more often, and distortions created by the way the tax rules are written.

[9]For a table of hyperinflations ranked by their scale, see Steve Hanke and Nicholas Kruse, "World Hyperinflations," Cato Institute Working Paper No. 8, August 2012 (*www.cato.org/publications/working-paper/world-hyperinflations*). The largest hyperinflation occurred in Austria, where, in July 1946, prices doubled on average every 15 hours.

the year inflation peaked. Only when Zimbabweans gave up using the local currency in favor of the U.S. dollar (a process called "dollarization") did the economy begin to grow again.

Because low inflation is the basis for general economic prosperity, most people agree that it should be the primary objective of monetary policy. But how low should inflation be? Zero is probably too low. There are several reasons for this. First, if the central bank tries to keep the inflation rate at zero, there is a risk of deflation—a drop in prices. Deflation makes debts more difficult to repay, which increases the default rate on loans, affecting the health of banks. Recall from Chapter 11 (Applying the Concept: Deflation, Net Worth, and Information Costs) that deflation lowers the value of collateral and may prevent some borrowers from obtaining loans. Second, if the inflation rate were zero, an employer wishing to cut labor costs would need to cut nominal wages, which is difficult to do. With a small amount of inflation, the employer can simply leave wages as they are, and workers' real wages will fall. So a small amount of inflation makes labor markets work better, at least from the employer's point of view.

High, Stable Real Growth

When Ben S. Bernanke was sworn in as the 14th chairman of the Board of Governors of the Federal Reserve System, he said "Our mission, as set forth by the Congress, is a critical one: to preserve price stability, to foster maximum sustainable growth in output and employment, and to promote a stable and efficient financial system that serves all Americans well and fairly."[10] We just discussed the first of these; preserving price stability requires keeping inflation low and stable. And we will look at financial stability in a moment. For now, let's examine the second item on Chairman Bernanke's list: to foster maximum sustainable growth in output and employment. When central bankers talk like this, what they mean is that they are working to dampen the fluctuations of the business cycle. Booms are popular, but recessions are not. In recessions, people get laid off and businesses fail. Without a steady income, individuals struggle to make their auto, credit card, and mortgage payments. Consumers pull back, hurting businesses that rely on them to buy products. Reduced sales lead to more layoffs, and so on. The longer the downturn goes on, the worse it gets.

By adjusting interest rates, central bankers work to moderate these cycles and stabilize growth and employment. The idea is that there is some long-run *normal* level of production called **potential output** that depends on things like technology, the size of the capital stock, the number of people who can work, and their usual working hours. Growth in these *inputs* leads to growth in *potential output*—**sustainable growth**. In the United States, growth averages 2 to 3 percent per year. Over the short run, output may deviate from its potential level, and growth may deviate from its long-run sustainable rate. In recessions, the economy stalls, incomes stagnate, and unemployment rises. By lowering interest rates, monetary policymakers can moderate such declines.[11]

Similarly, there are times when growth rises above sustainable rates, and the economy overheats. These periods may seem to bring increased prosperity, but because they don't last forever, they are followed by reduced spending, lower business investment,

---

[10]Remarks by Chairman Ben S. Bernanke at the ceremonial swearing-in by President George W. Bush, Board of Governors of the Federal Reserve System, Washington, D.C., February 6, 2006.

[11]Financial crises typically depress economic growth below their prior sustainable path for many years. In the most extreme U.S. example, the Great Depression, the U.S. economy did not regain its pre-1929 trend until 1942, when wartime production was in full swing.

and layoffs. A period of above-average growth has to be followed by a period of below-average growth. The job of the central bank during such periods is to raise interest rates and keep the economy from operating at unsustainable levels.

Importantly, in the long run, stability leads to higher growth. The reason is that unstable growth creates risk for which investors need to be compensated in the form of higher interest rates. With higher interest rates, businesses and households borrow less, which means that they have fewer resources to spend. To understand how this works, think about getting a loan to buy a car. The more certain you are that you will have a good, steady job over the next few years, the larger the loan you will feel comfortable taking on. If you are nervous that you might lose your job, you will be cautious. What is true for you and your car loan is true for every person and every company. The greater the uncertainty about future business conditions, the more cautious people will be in spending. Stability leads to higher growth.[12]

The importance of keeping sustainable growth as high as possible is hard to overstate. The difference between an economy that grows at 4 percent per year and one that grows at 2 percent per year is the difference between an economy that doubles in size over 18 years and one that grows by less than 50 percent in the same period. (This calculation uses the rule of 72 described in Your Financial World: How Long Does Your Investment Take to Double? in Chapter 4.) Keeping employment high is equally important. In the same way that you can never get back the study time you lost when you went to the movies before an exam, it is impossible for the economy to recover what unemployed people would have produced had they been working during a downturn. You can't get the lost time back. Our hope is that policymakers can manage the country's affairs so that we will stay on a high and sustainable growth path.

The levels of growth and employment aren't the only things of importance, though. Stability matters too. Together with financial crises, fluctuations in general business conditions are the primary source of systematic risk. As we have said a number of times, uncertainty about the future makes planning more difficult, so getting rid of uncertainty makes everyone better off.

RISK

Financial System Stability

The Federal Reserve was founded to stop the financial panics that plagued the United States during the late 19th and early 20th centuries. It took a while to work out the kinks in the system. As we have seen, the U.S. financial system collapsed again in the early 1930s, as policymakers at the Federal Reserve watched. Between then and 2007, the Fed's track record in preventing or mitigating crises improved substantially. However, recent experience demonstrates that financial and economic catastrophes are not limited to history books. Accordingly, **financial system stability** is an integral part of every modern central banker's job. It is essential for policymakers to ensure that the markets for stocks, bonds, and the like continue to operate smoothly and efficiently.

If people lose faith in financial institutions and markets, they will rush to low-risk alternatives, and intermediation will stop. Savers will not lend and borrowers will not be able to borrow. Getting a car loan or a home mortgage becomes impossible, as does selling a bond to maintain or expand a business. When the financial system collapses, economic activity does, too.

---

[12]For a discussion on the relationship between the level and volatility of growth, both the evidence and the theory, see Philippe Aghion and Abhijit Banerjee, *Volatility and Growth* (Cambridge, UK: Oxford University Press, 2005).

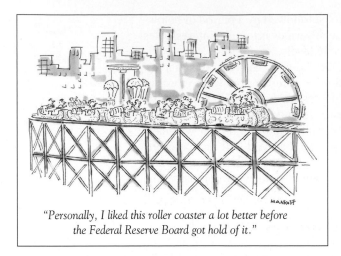

"Personally, I liked this roller coaster a lot better before the Federal Reserve Board got hold of it."

SOURCE: 1997 © Robert Mankoff/The New Yorker Collection/www.cartoonbank.com.

The possibility of a severe disruption in the financial markets is a type of systematic risk. Nothing that a single individual does can eliminate it. Central banks must control this risk, making sure that the financial system remains in good working order. The *value at risk,* not the standard deviation, is the important measure here. Recall from Chapter 5 that value at risk measures the risk of the maximum potential loss of a specific intermediary. Newer measures of risk seek to quantify the impact that losses at an individual intermediary could have on the stability of the *financial system as a whole.*[13] When thinking about financial stability, central bankers want to minimize the risk of a disaster and keep the chance of this maximum loss as small as possible. Their struggles in the crisis of 2007–2009 revealed just how difficult it can be to achieve these goals.

Interest-Rate and Exchange-Rate Stability

If you ask them, most central bankers will tell you that they do their best to keep interest rates and exchange rates from fluctuating too much. They want to eliminate abrupt changes. But if you press them further, they will tell you that these goals are secondary to those of low inflation, stable growth, and financial stability. The reason for this hierarchy is that *interest-rate stability* and *exchange-rate stability* are means for achieving the ultimate goal of stabilizing the economy; they are not ends unto themselves.

It is easy to see why interest-rate volatility is a problem. First, most people respond to low interest rates by borrowing and spending more. Individuals take out loans to purchase cars, new appliances and the like, while corporations issue more bonds and use the proceeds to enlarge their operations. Conversely, when interest rates rise, people borrow and spend less. So, by raising expenditure when interest rates are low and reducing expenditure when interest rates are high, interest-rate volatility makes output unstable. Second, interest-rate volatility means higher risk—and a higher risk premium—on long-term bonds. (Remember from Chapter 7 that the long-term interest rate is the average of expected future short-term interest rates plus a risk premium that compensates for the volatility of short-term interest rates.) Risk makes financial decisions more difficult, lowering productivity and making the economy less efficient. Because central bankers control short-term interest rates, they are in a position to control this risk and stabilize the economy.

Stabilizing exchange rates is the last item on the list of central bank objectives. The value of a country's currency affects the cost of imports to domestic consumers and the cost of exports to foreign buyers. When the exchange rate is stable, the dollar price of a car produced in Germany is predictable, making life easier for the foreign automobile manufacturer, the domestic retailer, and the American car buyer. Planning ahead is easier for everyone.

[13]To view estimated contributions of specific U.S. intermediaries to systemic risk, see *http://vlab.stern.nyu.edu/analysis/RISK.USFIN-MR.MES.*

Table 15.2	The Objectives of a Modern Central Bank

STABILITY

1. *Low, stable inflation* — Inflation creates confusion and makes planning difficult. When inflation is high, growth is low.
2. *High, stable growth* — Stable, predictable growth is higher than unstable, unpredictable growth.
3. *Financial system stability* — Stable financial markets and institutions are a necessity for an economy to operate efficiently.
4. *Stable interest rates* — Interest-rate volatility creates risk for both lenders and borrowers.
5. *Stable exchange rates* — Variable exchange rates make the revenues from foreign sales and the cost of purchasing imported goods hard to predict.

Different countries have different priorities. While the Federal Reserve and the European Central Bank may not care much about exchange-rate stability, the heads of central banks in more trade-oriented countries do. In countries where exports and imports are central to the structure of the economy, officials might reasonably argue that good overall macroeconomic performance follows from a stable exchange rate.

Table 15.2 summarizes the five objectives of a modern central bank.

Meeting the Challenge: Creating a Successful Central Bank

The past several decades were amazing in many ways. The Internet and cell phones came into widespread use. Overall economic conditions improved nearly everywhere, and especially in rapidly growing emerging economies, such as those of Brazil, China, and India. Virtually across the globe, inflation was lower and more stable than in the 1980s. In the United States, the inflation rate fell from an average of 5.6 percent in the 1980s to 2.6 percent in the first decade of the 21st century and continued to edge lower.

Outside of the United States, improvements were even more dramatic. In 1980, nearly two-thirds of the countries in the world were experiencing an inflation rate in excess of 10 percent per year and nearly one in three was experiencing negative growth. Thirty years later, only one country in nine had a two-digit inflation rate, while something like 150 countries were growing at rates in excess of 2 percent per year. And not only was inflation lower and growth higher for many countries, both were more stable, until the global financial crisis struck.

What explains this long period of stability? A prime candidate is that technology sparked a boom just as central banks became better at their jobs. First, monetary policymakers realized that sustainable growth had gone up, so they could keep interest rates low without worrying about inflation. Second, central banks were redesigned. It wasn't just that new central banks were established, like the ECB. The structure of existing central banks changed significantly. The Bank of England is more than three centuries old (its building in London has stood for more than 200 years) but its operating charter was completely rewritten in 1998. The same year brought major changes in the organizational structure of the Bank of Japan. Federal Reserve operations have

LESSONS FROM THE CRISIS
THREATS TO FED INDEPENDENCE

The Federal Reserve and the Treasury cooperated closely during the financial crisis of 2007—2009. At times, in working feverishly to restore financial stability, the Fed appeared to act as if it were an agent of the Treasury—"the government's bank" (see page 395).*

In doing so, did the Federal Reserve sacrifice its monetary policy independence and its objective of low, stable inflation? The crisis has fueled uncertainty about the economic and inflation outlook. However, the return to high and sustained inflation that some observers fear is far from inevitable.

To be sure, many Fed actions in the crisis were radical and precedent-setting. Utilizing its emergency powers for the first time since the 1930s, the Fed lent directly to nonbanks (including Bear Stearns and AIG) and purchased commercial paper from nonfinancial firms. To counter the September 2008 liquidity crisis, the Fed doubled its assets in the space of two months. To lower mortgage costs, it acquired more than a trillion dollars of mortgage securities. And, of course, the Fed cut its policy rate to nearly zero.

Has the crisis made the Fed a slave of U.S. government policy wishes? Hardly. In a financial crisis, the policy goals of financial stability, stable growth, and stable prices may be mutually consistent. As a result, an independent central bank may wish to cooperate with fiscal authorities—which, in the U.S. case, is the Treasury—to promote financial stability and forestall deflation.

However, an independent central bank also must be prepared to reverse course when necessary to keep inflation low. A central bank balance sheet that *stays* bloated over the long term *eventually* leads to inflation (see Chapter 17). The central bank also needs the proper tools to reverse its emergency actions when the time is right (see the Chapter 18 discussion of paying interest on reserves).

If the central bank reverses course in a timely fashion, inflation need not result (see the Chapter 18 discussion of exit strategies from unconventional policy). The difficulty is judging when to exit. Given the uncertainties about the financial system and the economy, the chances of a policy misjudgment are high. Waiting too long to exit will lead to inflation. Exiting prematurely—as the Fed did in 1936 and as the Bank of Japan did in 1999—can undermine economic recovery.

Have Fed actions undermined its anti-inflation credibility? Not yet. As of mid-2013, professional forecasters and participants in the Treasury market seemed confident that the Fed will succeed at keeping inflation low over the long term. Surveys of forecasters point to average inflation of about 2 percent over the next decade, similar to the gap between 10-year nominal and inflation-adjusted Treasury bond yields—called the "inflation break-even rate."

Perhaps the greatest threat to Fed independence is the popular backlash following the crisis bailouts of intermediaries like AIG. If heightened congressional scrutiny leads to political efforts to influence future monetary policy decisions, confidence in the Fed's commitment to low inflation could quickly erode. The risk of legislative interference will be greatest when the Fed wishes to raise the level of interest rates.

*For example, in hurriedly arranging the emergency acquisition of Bear Stearns in March 2008, the Federal Reserve Bank of New York (FRBNY) had to accept collateral with highly uncertain market value. This action put U.S. taxpayers at risk of loss, a move that generally only the Treasury would undertake. The Treasury Secretary endorsed the action in a letter on March 17, 2008 (see *http://finance.senate.gov/press/Bpress/2008press/prb040108a.pdf*). One year later, the Treasury added that it would "seek to remove" these risky assets from the Fed's balance sheet or "to liquidate" them. In effect, the Fed had acted in a temporary, emergency capacity as "the government's bank" to address a systemic crisis until the Treasury gained the flexibility to respond. By 2013, the Fed had earned a profit on these interventions.

---

changed, too, fostering transparency and accountability. The first public announcement of a move in the federal funds rate was made on February 4, 1994. By 2012, the Federal Reserve had announced an official inflation goal and had begun quarterly disclosures of economic growth and inflation forecasts along with policy rate projections.

Many people believe that improvements in economic performance after the 1980s were related at least in part to the policy followed by these restructured central banks. Improving monetary policy is not just a matter of finding the right person for the job. There is an ample supply of highly qualified people. In fact, in many countries there is a long history of central bankers who have tried but failed because they weren't free to pursue effective policies. Successful policymaking is as much a consequence of the institutional structure and context as of the people who work in the institutions. Nowhere is that more true than in central banking.

Today, in the aftermath of the financial crisis, economists are exploring how to improve financial regulation, and reconsidering the role that central banks should play in financial supervision. However, there remains a strong consensus among economists about the best way to design a central bank for making effective monetary policy. To be successful, a central bank must (1) be independent of political pressure, (2) make decisions by committee, (3) be accountable to the public and transparent in communicating its policy actions, and (4) operate within an explicit framework that clearly states its goals and makes clear the tradeoffs among them.

The Need for Independence

The idea of **central bank independence**—that central banks should be independent of political pressure—is a new one. After all, the central bank originated as the government's bank. It did the bidding first of the king or emperor and then of the democratically elected congress or parliament. Politicians rarely give up control over anything, much less something as important as monetary policy. But in the 1990s, nearly every advanced-economy government that hadn't already done so made the central bank independent of the finance ministry. The Banque de France became independent in 1993. Political control of the Bank of England and the Bank of Japan ended in 1998. And the new European Central Bank was independent from the day it opened on July 1, 1998.

Independence has two operational components. First, monetary policymakers must be free to control their own budgets. If politicians can starve the central bank of funding, then they can control the bank's decisions. Second, the bank's policies must not be reversible by people outside the central bank. Prior to 1998, policymakers at the Bank of England merely recommended interest-rate changes to the Chancellor of the Exchequer, a political official. That is, interest rate policy was ultimately decided by the British equivalent of the U.S. Secretary of the Treasury. Since 1998, the Bank of England's Monetary Policy Committee has made those decisions autonomously. The same is true in the United States, where the Federal Open Market Committee's decisions on when to raise or lower interest rates cannot be overridden by the president, Congress, or the Supreme Court.

Successful monetary policy requires a long time horizon. The impact of today's decisions won't be felt for a while—several years, in many instances. Democratically elected politicians are not a particularly patient bunch; their time horizon extends usually to the next election. The political system encourages members of Parliament and members of Congress to do everything they can for their constituents before the next election—including manipulating interest rates to bring short-term prosperity at the expense of long-term stability. The temptation to forsake long-term goals for short-term gains is difficult for most politicians to resist. Given the ability to choose, politicians are likely to select monetary policies that are overly accommodative. They will keep interest rates too low, raising output and employment quickly (before the election), but causing inflation to go up later (after the election). Low interest rates are very popular because there are more borrowers than lenders.

You can think of central bank independence as a means to overcome a classic version of the time-consistency problem: If monetary policy were always made by decision makers with a short horizon, people would expect them to run inflationary policies at some time in the future when it might be expedient to temporarily boost economic growth. As a result, inflation expectations would tend to be high today.

In the same way, societies may be able to reduce inflation and inflation expectations efficiently if they delegate monetary policy to an independent central bank that *strongly* prefers low inflation.[14] The reason is that the central bank's commitment to keep inflation low in the future would be made credible by its prudent inflation preferences,

---

[14]For readers with advanced math skills, see Kenneth Rogoff, "The Optimal Degree of Commitment to an Intermediate Monetary Target," *The Quarterly Journal of Economics* 100, no. 4 (November 1985), pp. 1169–1189.

making policy time consistent. Like many problems involving time consistency, this example illustrates how a constraint on policy discretion (when legislators tie their hands and entrust monetary policy decisions to the inflation-averse central bank) can lead to a more favorable policy outcome (in this case, lower inflation).

In light of these considerations, governments have moved responsibility for monetary policy into a separate, largely apolitical, institution. To insulate policymakers from the daily pressures faced by politicians, governments must give central bankers control of their budgets and authority to make irreversible decisions and must appoint them to long terms of office.

The Fed's extraordinary actions during the crisis of 2007–2009, however successful in stemming a second Great Depression, led to a political backlash in the United States against central bank independence. The consensus among economists is strongly in favor of central bank independence.[15] Yet, the Fed's emergency actions in the crisis—including large bailouts and extraordinary credit provisions—may invite legislative interference in the day-to-day conduct of conventional monetary policy, making it less effective in keeping inflation low and stable. As the popular revulsion for bailouts grew in 2009, proposals to conduct government audits of all monetary policy decisions garnered widespread support in Congress but these plans were eventually watered down in the Dodd-Frank Act of 2010. The lingering political question is whether Congress will choose to sacrifice the hard-won gains on the inflation front by weakening central bank independence. If so, it would be another costly legacy of the financial crisis (see Lessons from the Crisis: Threats to Fed Independence on page 406).

Decision Making by Committee

Should important decisions be made by an individual or by a committee? Military planners know they can't have groups making decisions in the heat of a battle; someone has to be in charge. But monetary policy isn't war. Monetary policy decisions are made deliberately, after significant amounts of information are collected and examined. Occasionally a crisis does occur, and in those times someone does need to be in charge. But in the course of normal operations, it is better to rely on a committee than an individual. Though extraordinary individuals can be trusted to make policy as well as a committee, building an institution on the assumption that someone of exemplary ability will always be available to run it is unwise. And given the difficulty of removing a central bank governor—a feature that is built into the central bank system—the cost of putting the wrong person in charge can be very high (the same reason is often cited for preferring legislatures over monarchs).

The solution, then, is to make policy by committee. Pooling the knowledge, experience, and opinions of a group of people reduces the risk that policy will be dictated by an individual's quirks. Besides, in a democracy, vesting so much power in one individual poses a legitimacy problem. For these reasons, monetary policy decisions are made by committee in all major central banks in the world. As we will discuss in Chapter 16, the Federal Reserve has its Federal Open Market Committee, the European Central Bank its Governing Council, and the Bank of Japan its Policy Board. The number of members varies from 9 in the United Kingdom and Japan to (currently) 24 at the ECB—but, crucially, it is always bigger than one.

---

[15]Naturally, there is some dissent. For the case against central bank independence, see Nobel Prize winner Joseph Stiglitz, "A Revolution in Monetary Policy: Lessons in the Wake of the Global Financial Crisis." C.D. Deshmukh Memorial Lecture, Reserve Bank of India, January 2013, available at *http://rbidocs.rbi.org.in/rdocs/Speeches/PDFs/PSS030113FL.pdf.*

APPLYING THE CONCEPT

INDEPENDENT CENTRAL BANKS DELIVER LOWER INFLATION

What drove politicians to give up control over monetary policy? It was the realization that independent central bankers would deliver lower inflation than they themselves could. Researchers noticed that the degree of control politicians can exert over central banks varies greatly across countries, and is related to inflation outcomes. Figure 15.1 shows an index of central bank independence* on the horizontal axis and average inflation rates from 1973 to 1988 on the vertical axis. Note that Germany and Switzerland, the two countries with the most independent central banks, had the lowest inflation, averaging around 3 percent per year over the 15-year period. Conversely, New Zealand and Spain, the two countries with the least independent central banks, had the highest inflation—between 7 and 9 percent.

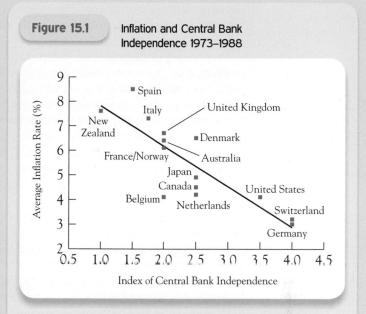

Figure 15.1   Inflation and Central Bank Independence 1973–1988

SOURCE: Alberto Alesina and Lawrence H. Summers, "Central Bank Independence and Macroeconomic Performance: Some Comparative Evidence," *Journal of Money, Credit, and Banking* 25 (May 1993), pp. 151–162. Copyright 1993 The Ohio State University. Reproduced with permission.

Even the politicians were convinced. They knew that the more control they had over the central bank, the more money they were likely to create. While printing more money relieves short-term fiscal problems, it eventually drives inflation higher. Encouraged by voters, politicians tied their own hands, turning over control of monetary policy to an independent central bank. Constraining political discretion reduced the time-consistency challenge (see page 407), helping to lower inflation expectations.

The design of the European Central Bank (ECB) is a clear example of the logic that independence promotes time consistency and leads to lower inflation. Politicians in Spain, Italy, and France, where inflation had been running over 6 percent per year for several decades, wanted their economies to be more like Germany's. In hopes that the new institution would deliver low inflation, they chose the German central bank, the Deutsche Bundesbank, as a model. By most accounts, the treaty that established the ECB gives it greater legal independence than the mandates of any other central bank. And, as one would expect, inflation has been consistently low in the euro area.

*The index of central bank independence measures the ability of the central bank to use its policy tools without political interference. It is constructed using information on things like the length of the central bank governor's term, whether the governor can be fired, whether government representatives participate directly in monetary policy decisions, and whether the central bank is required to finance government deficits. The less the central bank is constrained by the government, the more independent it is.

The Need for Accountability and Transparency

There is a big problem with central bank independence: It is inconsistent with representative democracy. The idea of putting appointed technocrats in charge of one of the most important government functions is inherently undemocratic.[16] Politicians answer to the voters; by design, independent central bankers don't. How can

[16]High courts, such as the U.S. Supreme Court, provide the leading example in democracies of an independent body of unelected experts making key policy decisions. In Germany, where the Bundesbank was unusually powerful, the central bank was widely known as the "fourth branch of government."

we have faith in our financial system if there are no checks on what the central bankers are doing? The economy will not operate efficiently unless we trust our policymakers.

Proponents of central bank independence realized they would need to solve this problem if their proposals were going to be adopted. Their solution was twofold. First, politicians would establish a set of goals; second, the policymakers would publicly report their progress in pursuing those goals. Explicit goals foster **accountability** and disclosure requirements create **transparency**. While central bankers are powerful, our elected representatives tell them what to do and then monitor their progress. Technically speaking, legislatures usually grant central banks **instrument independence**—the authority to use their tools as they see fit to achieve mandated objectives—not **goal independence**. That means requiring plausible explanations for their decisions, along with supporting data.

The institutional means for assuring accountability and transparency differ from one country to the next. In some cases, the government establishes an explicit numerical target for inflation, while in others the central bank defines the target. In the United Kingdom, the government sets a specific target each year; in the European Union, the central bank is asked only to pursue "price stability" as its primary objective; in the United States, the Federal Reserve is asked to deliver price stability as one of a number of objectives. Similar differences exist in the timing and content of information made public by central banks. Today every central bank announces its policy actions almost immediately, but the extent of the statements that accompany the announcement and the willingness to answer questions vary. The Federal Reserve's statements tend to be only a few paragraphs long, while the statements of the ECB president and vice president may be several pages. The Fed holds a long press conference quarterly when forecasts are updated; the ECB every month.

INFORMATION

Over time, these differences in communications strategy have narrowed substantially, and central bank statements are far more informative today than they were in the early 1990s. Until 1994, for example, the Federal Reserve didn't announce its policy decisions publicly. Secrecy, once the hallmark of central banking, is now understood to damage both the policymakers and the economies they are trying to manage. For monetary policy to be a stabilizing force, central bankers need to explain their actions in periodic public statements, like the ones that follow every Federal Open Market Committee (FOMC) meeting. In essence, the economy and financial markets should respond to information that everyone receives, not to speculation about what policymakers are doing. Thus, policymakers need to be as clear as possible about what they are trying to achieve and how they intend to achieve it. There really shouldn't be any surprises.

The crisis of 2007–2009 heightened the importance of transparency, both to make policy effective and to secure popular support for unprecedented actions. As we will see in Chapter 18, some unconventional monetary policies can be implemented *only* by communicating them. And transparency can help counter the uncertainties and anxieties that feed liquidity and deleveraging spirals (see Chapter 3, Lessons from the Crisis: Leverage).

The Policy Framework, Policy Tradeoffs, and Credibility

We've seen that a modern central bank has a long list of objectives—low, stable inflation; high, stable growth; a stable financial system; and stable interest and exchange rates. To meet these objectives, central bankers must be independent, accountable, and good communicators. Together these qualities make up what we will call the **monetary policy framework**. The framework exists to resolve ambiguities that arise in the course of the central bank's work.

Looking at the bank's objectives, we can see the problem. Setting a goal of low inflation is easy, but there are many ways to measure inflation. The central bank needs to decide which measure to use and then stick with it. Thus, the FOMC stated in 2012 that an annual inflation of 2 percent in the price index of personal consumption expenditures is consistent over the long run with its mandate as given in the Federal Reserve Act. In the euro area, the ECB seeks a rise of less than, but close to, 2 percent, in the harmonized index of consumer prices, or HICP. More important than the details, though, is the fact that officials have told us what they are trying to do. Their statement helps people to plan at the same time that it holds officials accountable to the public.

The monetary policy framework also clarifies the likely responses when goals conflict with one another. There is simply no way that policymakers can meet all their objectives at the same time. Aside from crisis episodes, they have only one instrument—the interest rate—with which to work, and it is impossible to use a single instrument to achieve a long list of objectives. To take a recent example, by mid-2004, the U.S. economy had recovered completely from the recession of 2001, and the inflation rate had started to rise. When this happens, the appropriate response is to tighten policy, raising interest rates. So, starting on June 30, 2004, the FOMC did just that. Seventeen times over the next two years policymakers raised the target interest rate—each time by 25 basis points. Obviously, if interest rates are changing every few months, they are not stable. More important, raising the interest rate means reducing the availability of money and credit at the risk of slowing growth. The goal of keeping inflation low and stable, then, can be inconsistent with the goal of avoiding a recession. By the end of 2006, inflation remained low while growth had slowed slightly. The financial crisis that erupted in August 2007 began more than a year after the Fed had stopped raising rates.

Central bankers face the tradeoff between inflation and growth on a daily basis. In March 2008, with inflation soon to rise above 5 percent for the first time since 1991, the Federal Open Market Committee nevertheless cut its policy rate by an outsized 75 basis points to 2.25 percent and highlighted in its statement that "downside risks to growth remain." Although the committee members expressed concern about indications of rising inflation expectations, they judged that it was more important to cut the policy rate in an effort to halt the financial contagion that had resulted from the run on Bear Stearns, the fifth largest U.S. investment bank. As is often the case, policymakers were forced to choose among competing objectives amid great uncertainty. Indeed, two FOMC members dissented, preferring a less aggressive rate cut. As it turned out, when the financial crisis intensified later that year, inflation worries gave way to deflation fears and the prospect of the deepest recession since World War II.

Because policy goals often conflict, central bankers must make their priorities clear. The public needs to know whether policymakers are focusing primarily on price stability or whether they are willing to allow a modest rise in inflation to avoid a slowdown in economic activity. The public also needs to know the roles that interest-rate and exchange-rate stability play in policy deliberations. This important part of the policy framework limits the discretionary authority of the central bankers, ensuring that they will do the job they have been entrusted with. Thus, it is an essential part of the bank's communication responsibilities.

Finally, a well-designed policy framework helps policymakers establish **credibility**. For central bankers to achieve their objectives, everyone must trust them to do what

Table 15.3	The Principles of Central Bank Design

1. *Independence*	To keep inflation low, monetary decisions must be made free of political influence.
2. *Decision making by committee*	Pooling the knowledge of a number of people yields better decisions than decision making by an individual. But effective crisis response requires a clear chain of command.
3. *Accountability and transparency*	Policymakers must be held accountable to the public they serve and clearly communicate their objectives, decisions, and methods.
4. *Policy framework*	Policymakers must clearly state their policy goals and the tradeoffs among them.

they say they are going to do. This is particularly important when it comes to keeping inflation low. The reason is that most economic decisions are based on expectations about future inflation. We saw this relationship when we studied the determination of interest rates: The nominal interest rate equals the real interest rate plus expected inflation. The same is true for wage and price decisions. Firms set prices based partly on what they believe inflation will be in the future. They make wage agreements with workers based on expected future inflation. The higher their expectations for future inflation, the higher prices, wages, and interest rates will be. Expected inflation creates inflation. Successful monetary policy, then, requires that inflation expectations be kept under control. The most straightforward way for the central bank to do so is to announce its objectives, show resolve in meeting them, and explain its actions clearly along the way. By making their preferences clear and their commitments reliable, policymakers can overcome the time-consistency challenge. If, instead, they are seen as likely to renege on a promise—such as the promise to keep inflation low and stable—policy's impact will be diminished.

Table 15.3 summarizes the principles of central bank design and can serve as a check list for evaluating the operation of any central bank we come across.

Fitting Everything Together: Central Banks and Fiscal Policy

Before a European country can join the common currency area and adopt the euro, it is supposed to meet a number of conditions. Two of the most important are that the country's annual budget deficit—the excess of government spending over revenues each year—cannot exceed 3 percent of GDP and the government's total debt—its accumulated level of outstanding bonds and other borrowings—cannot exceed 60 percent of GDP.[17] Once a country gains membership in the monetary union, failure to maintain

[17]In practice, these limits were open to political interpretation, so countries that failed to meet them were allowed to join anyway. For example, in fall of 1998, Belgium's debt was 122 percent of its GDP—more than double the stated limit. But because the debt was forecast to decline in the future, the requirement was waived.

these standards is supposed to lead to pressure from other member countries and (in theory) even to substantial penalties.[18]

Remember that the central bank does not control the government's budget. Fiscal policy, the decisions about taxes and spending, are the responsibility of elected officials. But by specifying a range of "acceptable" levels of borrowing, Europeans sought to restrict the fiscal policies that member countries enact. For the European Central Bank to do its job effectively, all the member countries' governments must behave responsibly.

While fiscal and monetary policymakers share the same ultimate goal—to improve the well-being of the population—conflicts can arise between them. Fiscal policymakers are responsible for providing national defense, educating children, building and maintaining transportation systems, and aiding the sick and poor. They need resources to pay for these services. Thus, funding needs create a natural conflict between monetary and fiscal policymakers. Central bankers, in their effort to stabilize prices and provide the foundation for high sustainable growth, take a long-term view, imposing limits on how fast the quantity of money and credit can grow. In contrast, fiscal policymakers tend to ignore the long-term inflationary effects of their actions and look for ways to spend resources today at the expense of prosperity tomorrow. For better or worse, their time horizon often extends only until the next election. Some fiscal policymakers resort to actions intended to get around restrictions imposed by the central bank, eroding what is otherwise an effective and responsible monetary policy.

In the earliest days of central banks, a government that needed money would simply order the bank to print some. Of course, the result was inflation and occasionally hyperinflation. That is what led to the evolution of the independent central banks. Today the central bank's autonomy leaves fiscal policymakers with two options for financing government spending. They can take a share of income and wealth from the country's citizens through taxes, or they can borrow by issuing bonds in the financial markets.

Because no one likes taxes, and officials fear angering the electorate, politicians often turn to borrowing in order to finance some portion of their spending. But a country can issue only so much debt. Beyond some limit, future tax revenues will not cover the payments that are due to lenders. At that point, the only solution is to turn to the central bank for the means to finance spending. As a technical matter, the government will "sell" new bonds directly to the central bank—bonds that no one else wants to buy. This process, often referred to as "monetizing the debt," eventually leads to inflation. In fact, if officials can't raise taxes and are having trouble borrowing, inflation is the only way out.

While central bankers hate it, inflation is a real temptation to shortsighted fiscal policymakers. It is a way to get resources in their hands. The mechanism is straightforward. The government forces the central bank to buy its bonds and then uses the proceeds to finance spending. But doing so increases the quantity of money in circulation, sparking inflation. While the rise in inflation may ultimately do great damage to the country's well-being, it also benefits fiscal policymakers: It reduces the value of the bonds the government has already sold, making them easier to repay. Inflation is a way for governments to default on a portion of the debt they owe.

[18]The "Stability and Growth Pact of 1997" dictated that "medium-term budgets" must be "close to balance or in surplus." That mechanism first came under significant strain in 2003. The previously agreed upon penalties that would be triggered by budget deficits in excess of 3 percent of GDP were not levied on the offending countries. In the aftermath of the 2007–2009 financial crisis, many countries far surpassed the deficit limit. In 2011, additional rules (called the "sixpack") enhanced mutual surveillance of fiscal policies. As of 2013, a new fiscal compact called for enshrining budget and debt rules in the national constitutions of euro-area states.

IN THE NEWS
The Politicisation (or Not) of Central Banks

FINANCIAL
TIMES

By Gavyn Davies

January 9, 2013

The macroeconomic debate is now buzzing about "political dominance" over the central banks, under which elected politicians force central bankers to take actions they would not choose to take, if left to their own devices. . . . This is clearly what is happening in Japan, where the incoming Shinzo Abe government is not only imposing a new inflation target on the Bank of Japan (which is legitimate), but is changing the leadership of the central bank to ensure that the BoJ adopts policies compliant with the fiscal regime. This is not just political dominance, it is fiscal dominance, where monetary policy is subordinated to the decisions of those who set budgetary policy.

There have also been some early signs of political or fiscal dominance emerging elsewhere, notably in the use of the ECB balance sheet to finance cross-border financial support operations in the Eurozone. . . . Many investors have concluded that there is now an inevitable trend in place that will overthrow central bank independence throughout the developed world, allowing politicians to expand fiscal policy, while simultaneously inflating away the burden of public debt.

It seems to me that this is a very premature conclusion. While there is no denying that this is indeed the objective in Japan, the direct opposite seems to be happening in the rest of the developed world.

Why do many economists believe that much greater political control over the central banks is now inevitable? The reasons for this fall into two main categories.

First, it is argued that the central banks are now operating far outside the realms of traditional monetary policy, and have crossed the border into territory that has always been deemed to be clearly "political" in western democracies. This territory includes the allocation of credit between different sectors, the distribution of income between generations, and the fate of individual private companies in the financial sector. Since this has *de facto* occurred in a major way since the financial crisis, it is argued that the re-imposition of political control over these decisions is inevitable.

. . . [However,] none of the recent actions of the central banks, including the 2008 bank rescues and the subsequent credit easing, have been contrary to the wishes of elected

U.S. fiscal and monetary policies to combat the crisis of 2007–2009 have led many observers to worry both about future inflation risks and about renewed financial instability. On the fiscal side, in 2009, the federal government's deficit neared 10 percent of GDP for the first time since World War II. On the monetary policy side, the Federal Reserve accumulated assets at an unprecedented pace as it sought to prevent a meltdown of the financial system.

At some stage, both these policies must be reversed to prevent a large future inflation. A failure to reverse them also eventually would undermine investor confidence in U.S. Treasuries. As of mid-2013, however, the level of long-term Treasury yields remained consistent with low future inflation.

While many politicians do act in their countries' long-term interests, there are plenty of examples of poor fiscal policymaking. In early 2002, Argentina's economy collapsed when banks refused to honor their depositors' withdrawal requests. Unemployment skyrocketed, output plummeted, and the president was forced to resign. The full story is complicated, but we can understand one aspect of it without much trouble. During 2001, Argentina's provincial governments (the equivalent of the state governments in the United States) began to experience significant budget problems. Their response was to start paying their employees with government bonds. But unlike the bonds we normally see, these were in small denominations—1, 2, 5, 10, 20 pesos, and so on. Not surprisingly, these small-denomination bonds were immediately used as means of officials. . . . As a result, there are very few signs that the political process sees any urgent need to re-assert any control over central bankers in these areas. Obviously, this could change if central bankers were to become more hawkish in ways that could prove politically unpopular, but to date there is little sign of that happening either.

The second reason given for the inevitability of political control over the central banks concerns the relationship between fiscal and monetary policy. . . . The argument runs as follows. [Faced with] . . . rising public debt ratios . . . politicians will "order" the central bank to expand the monetary base to finance [large] budget deficits. This will hold down the public debt ratio, and if it causes inflation to rise, that might be a welcome side effect.

. . . . This has now happened in Japan, but it has taken a full two decades of failing economic activity to get there. . . . [Elsewhere] in the world, the current situation is a long way from fiscal dominance over the central bankers. In the US, for example, the Fed has, entirely voluntarily, announced an open-ended program of bond purchases, which will be continued until unemployment falls substantially. Furthermore, the Fed chairman has hinted that he thinks that, for a while, fiscal policy should be more supportive of economic activity.

Does that not constitute an open invitation to the fiscal authorities to run temporarily higher deficits, financed to a large extent by monetization? Yet, instead, the fiscal authorities have just announced a budgetary tightening . . . in 2013, and the policy mix in the UK and the eurozone is not dissimilar. That does not fit the definition of fiscal dominance. . . . In fact, it seems more like monetary dominance. . . . Fiscal dominance will only become a major issue if and when the central bankers decide to tighten policy.

LESSONS OF THE ARTICLE

When its interest-rate target is at zero, a central bank may welcome fiscal stimulus to promote economic stability. The inflationary danger arises if a central bank acquiesces to government pressure to purchase (*monetize*) its debt. Such pressures usually rise with the cost of issuing securities to the public, but—as of mid-2013—government bond yields remained extremely low in most advanced economies.

payment, becoming money in effect. By mid-2002, this new form of money accounted for roughly 40 percent of the currency circulating in Argentina and the Central Bank of Argentina lost control over the amount of money circulating in the economy.

So, we see that the actions of fiscal policymakers can subvert the best efforts of central bankers. If the government can shut down the banking system and issue its own money, then the central bank's independence is irrelevant. The Federal Reserve, the European Central Bank, the Bank of Japan, and the other central banks around the world are only independent for as long as their governments let them be. When faced with a fiscal crisis, politicians often look for the easiest way out. If that way is inflating the value of the currency today, they will worry about the consequences tomorrow.

This brings us back to the criteria for inclusion in the European Monetary Union. The founders of the system wanted to ensure that participating governments kept their fiscal houses in order so that none of them would be tempted to pressure the European Central Bank to create inflation and bail them out. Monetary policy can meet its objective of price stability only if the government lives within its budget and never forces the central bank to finance a fiscal deficit. In 2010, large fiscal deficits propelled government bond yields sharply higher in several euro-area countries and triggered a financing crisis in Greece, helping to weaken the euro. And, over the next two years, the crisis spread to Ireland, Portugal, Spain, and then Italy. In response, euro-area governments created a facility for lending to member states that face difficulty borrowing in markets. As a condition of borrowing, a government is required to restore fiscal discipline. As of this writing, the credibility and independence of the European Central Bank have kept euro-area inflation expectations low despite the region's fiscal problems.

Stepping back and looking at the problem more broadly, we can say that governments face the challenge of time consistency in setting fiscal policy, just as they do in making monetary and regulatory policy. The value of any debt depends on investors' belief that they will be paid back (see Chapter 6). For a government, the problem is that future fiscal authorities may have an incentive to renege on the promises their predecessors made. If lenders believe that future developments will compel default, the value of the debt will plunge today, regardless of how cautious the current government may be. If, as a result, today's government can no longer borrow, it may turn to the central bank for direct monetary finance.

Laws and other rules that constrain future governments—such as the constitutional commitments of many U.S. states to run balanced budgets or the mutual fiscal surveillance of the member countries of the euro area—address the time-consistency challenge by making today's fiscal promises more credible.

In the absence of fiscal credibility, rapid government debt accumulation can lead to higher inflation expectations even in the face of cautious monetary policy. Indeed, in a famous analysis, 2011 Nobel Prize winner Thomas Sargent and coauthor Neil Wallace show that an otherwise credible, anti-inflationary central bank cannot prevent high inflation if a government issues debt without end.[19] Put differently, to keep inflation low over the long run, (1) institutions must ensure the time consistency of both monetary *and* fiscal policy, and (2) fiscal policy must not dominate monetary policy.

In summary, responsible fiscal policy is essential to the success of monetary policy. Our discussions earlier in the chapter allowed us to conclude that there is no way for a poorly designed central bank to stabilize prices, output, the financial system, and interest and exchange rates, regardless of the government's behavior. To be successful, a central bank must be independent, accountable, and clear about its goals. It must also have a well-articulated communications strategy and a sound decision-making mechanism. We turn in Chapter 16 to a detailed discussion of the structure of major central banks to see what makes them successful.

---

[19]Thomas Sargent and Neil Wallace, "Some Unpleasant Monetarist Arithmetic," Federal Reserve Bank of Minneapolis *Quarterly Review,* Fall 1981.

Terms

accountability, 410

central bank, 394

central bank independence, 407

credibility, 411

financial system stability, 403

fiscal policy, 398

goal independence, 410

hyperinflation, 401

instrument independence, 410

monetary policy, 396

monetary policy framework, 411

potential output, 402

price stability, 400

public goods, 399

sustainable growth, 402

transparency, 410

Using FRED: Codes for Data in This Chapter

Data Series	FRED Data Code
U.S. potential GDP	GDPPOT
U.S. real GDP	GDPC1
U.S. 10-year Treasury constant maturity rate	GS10
U.S. 10-year Treasury inflation-indexed yield	FII10
U.S. consumer price index	CPIAUCSL
U.S. consumer price index (less food and energy)	CPILFESL
Personal consumption expenditures price index	PCEPI
Personal consumption expenditures price index (less food and energy)	PCEPILFE
Euro area harmonized index of consumer prices	CP0000EZ17M086NEST
Euro area harmonized index of consumer prices (less unprocessed food and energy)	00XFUNEZ17M086NEST

Chapter Lessons

1. The functions of a modern central bank are to
   a. Adjust interest rates and other tools to control the quantity of money and credit in the economy.
   b. Operate a payments system.
   c. Lend to sound banks during times of stress.
   d. Oversee the financial system.

2. The objective of a central bank is to reduce systematic risk in the economic and financial system. Specific objectives include
   a. Low and stable inflation.
   b. High and stable growth and employment.
   c. Stable financial markets and institutions.
   d. Stable interest rates.
   e. Stable exchange rates.

   Because these objectives often conflict, policymakers must have clear priorities.

3. The best central banks
   a. Are independent of political pressure.
   b. Make decisions by committee rather than by an individual.
   c. Are accountable to elected representatives and the public.
   d. Communicate their objectives, actions, and policy deliberations clearly to the public.
   e. Articulate clearly how they will act when their goals conflict.
   f. Are credible in their efforts to meet their objectives.

4. Fiscal policy can make the central bank's job impossible because
   a. Politicians tend to take a short-term view, ignoring the inflationary impact of their actions over the long term.

b. Politicians are predisposed toward financing techniques that will create inflation.

c. Inflation provides immediate revenue and reduces the value of the government's outstanding debt.

d. Responsible fiscal policy is a precondition for successful monetary policy.

e. Central banks remain independent at the pleasure of politicians.

Conceptual and Analytical Problems

1. In 1900, there were 18 central banks in the world; today, there are about 175. Why does nearly every country in the world now have a central bank? *(LO1)*

2. The power of a central bank is based on its monopoly over the issuance of currency. Economics teaches us that monopolies are bad and competition is good. Would competition among several central banks be better? Provide arguments both for and against. *(LO1)*

3. Explain the costs of each of the following conditions and explain who bears them. *(LO1)*
   a. Interest-rate instability
   b. Exchange-rate instability
   c. Inflation
   d. Unstable growth

4. Provide arguments for and against the proposition that a central bank should be allowed to set its own objectives. *(LO1)*

5. When countries in a common currency area show persistently rising ratios of public debt to GDP, how does it affect the credibility of an inflation-targeting central bank? *(LO3)*

6. A country in the European Monetary Union that runs very large public deficits or shows a persistently high and rising debt-to-GDP ratio violates a fiscal compact among the member countries of the union. Explain how this fiscal violation poses a challenge for the ECB in the form of moral hazard. *(LO3)*

7. How do long terms of office for central bankers help overcome the problem of time inconsistency in monetary policy? *(LO3)*

8. What problems does a central bank face in a country with inefficient methods of tax collection? *(LO3)*

9. The Maastricht Treaty, which established the European Central Bank, states that the governments of the countries in the European Monetary Union must not seek to influence the members of the central bank's decision-making bodies. Why is freedom from political influence crucial to the ECB's ability to maintain price stability? *(LO2)*

10. Transparency is a key element of the monetary policy framework. *(LO2)*
    a. Explain how transparency helps eliminate the problems that are created by central bank independence.
    b. In what ways did the financial crisis of 2007–2009 emphasize the importance of central bank transparency?
    c. Since 1993, the Bank of England has published a quarterly *Inflation Report.* Find a copy of the report on the bank's website, www.bankofengland.co.uk. Describe its contents and explain why the bank might publish such a document.

11.* While central bank transparency is widely accepted as desirable, too much open-ness may have disadvantages. Discuss what some of these drawbacks might be. *(LO2)*

12. Which do you think would be more harmful to the economy—an inflation rate that averages 5 percent a year and has a high standard deviation or an inflation rate of 7 percent that has a standard deviation close to zero? *(LO1)*

13. Suppose the central bank in your country has price stability as its primary goal. Faced with a choice of having monetary policy decisions made by a well-qualified individual with an extremely strong dislike of inflation or a committee of equally well-qualified people with a wide range of views, which choice would you recommend? *(LO2)*

14. Suppose the president of a newly independent country asks you for advice in designing the country's new central bank. For each of the following design features, choose which one you would recommend and briefly explain your choice: *(LO2)*
    a. Central bank policy decisions that are irreversible or central bank policy decisions that can be overturned by the democratically elected government.
    b. The central bank has to submit a proposal for funding to the government each year or the central bank finances itself from the earnings on its assets and turns the balance over to the government.
    c. The central bank policymakers are appointed for periods of four years to coincide with the electoral cycle for the government or the central bank policymakers are appointed for 14-year terms.

15. "A central bank should remain vague about the relative importance it places on its various objectives. That way, it has the freedom to choose which objective to follow at any point in time." Assess this statement in light of what you know about good central bank design. *(LO2)*

16.* The long list of central bank goals includes the stability of interest rates and exchange rates. You look on the central bank website and note that they have increased interest rates at every one of their meetings over the last year. You read the financial press and see references to how the exchange rate has moved in response to these interest-rate changes. How could you reconcile this behavior with the central bank pursuing its objectives? *(LO1)*

17. Provide arguments for why you think the financial crisis of 2007–2009 did or did not compromise the independence of the Federal Reserve. *(LO2)*

18. Suppose in an election year, the economy started to slow down. At the same time, clear signs of inflationary pressures were apparent. How might the central bank with a primary goal of price stability react? How might members of the incumbent political party who are up for re-election react? *(LO1)*

19. Assuming that they could, which of the following governments do you think would be more likely to pursue policies that would seriously hinder the central bank's pursuit of low and stable inflation? Explain your choice. *(LO3)*
    a. A government that is considered highly creditworthy both at home and abroad in a politically stable country with a well-developed tax system, or
    b. A government of a politically unstable country that is heavily indebted and considered an undesirable borrower in international markets.

*Indicates more difficult problems

20.* Suppose the government is heavily in debt. Why might it be tempting for the fiscal policymakers to sell additional bonds to the central bank in a move that it knows would be inflationary? *(LO3)*

Data Exploration

Scan here for quick access to the resources for these problems. Need a barcode reader? Try ScanLife, available in your app store.

For general information on using Federal Reserve Economic Data (FRED) online, visit www.mhhe.com/moneyandbanking4e and click on Student Edition, then FRED Resources.

1. According to Figure 15.1, New Zealand in the 1970s and 1980s combined high inflation with relatively little central bank independence. In 1989, New Zealand became the first country to adopt an inflation target. How did this policy regime shift affect inflation? Plot the inflation rate based on New Zealand's "core" consumer price index (FRED code: CPGRLE01NZQ659N) beginning in 1970. Was inflation after 1990 lower and more stable than before? Download the data and compute the average and the standard deviation of inflation for: (a) the period through 1989 and (b) the period from 1990 to the present. *(LO1)*

2. Financial stability is a goal of most central banks. Based on a graph showing the evolution of the European Central Bank's assets (FRED code: ECBASSETS), how important was this goal for the ECB (a) before 2007, (b) during the crisis period of 2007–2009, and (c) when the euro-area crisis intensified in 2011–2012? *(LO1)*

3. Interest rate stability is a common goal of central banks. When has the Federal Reserve been relatively successful at keeping interest rates stable? Compare quarterly *changes* since 1965 of the federal funds rate (FRED code: FEDFUNDS) with the *level* of inflation based on the percentage change from year-ago levels of the consumer price index (FRED code: CPIAUCSL). Are stable interest rates associated with high or low inflation? Why? *(LO1)*

4. To what extent has the Federal Reserve "monetized" government debt? Plot since 1970 the change from a year ago (measured in billions of dollars) in gross federal debt (FRED code: FYGFD) and the change from a year ago (measured in billions of dollars) in the federal debt held by the Federal Reserve System (FRED code: FDHBFRBN). *(LO3)*

Chapter 16

The Structure of Central Banks: The Federal Reserve and the European Central Bank

Learning Objectives

Understand . . .

LO1   The structure of the Federal Reserve System

LO2   The effectiveness of the Federal Reserve System

LO3   The structure of the Eurosystem

LO4   The euro-area crisis and the ECB

The instability and chaos that accompany financial panics damage more than just the banks that are directly involved. Fear of losing one's savings is a great disincentive to making deposits in banks, and making fewer deposits means smaller banks and fewer loans. Everyone is slow to regain confidence in the financial system after a panic, making it hard for anyone to get financing. New businesses can't get the resources they need to get started; established companies can't find the financing they need to expand. The more frequent the panics, the worse the situation gets, and the slower the economy grows.

That description sounds like the world after the financial crisis of 2007–2009. But it describes even more aptly the financial flaws of the United States during the late 19th and early 20th centuries. Between 1870 and 1907, the nation experienced 21 financial panics of varying severity. In the mostly agrarian economy of the time, a typical crisis began with either a crop failure that left farmers with nothing to sell or a bumper crop that drove prices down below costs. Either way, farmers defaulted on their loans. The losses damaged the balance sheets of rural banks, leading them to withdraw funds from larger banks in New York or Chicago, where they held deposits. If the rural banks' withdrawals were large enough, the urban banks would be forced to call in their own loans or to refuse renewal of loans that were coming due. As word of the financial difficulties spread, other banks would become concerned and begin to call in their loans as well. Finally, when average people (small depositors) heard of the problem, they would flock to their local banks, demanding to receive their balances in the form of currency or gold.[1]

---

[1]The process could also go the other way, from the big banks to the small ones. A large loan default in New York, for example, would force the large city bank to try to acquire reserves from the small country banks. The small banks would then be forced to start calling in loans, and the process would go on from there.

Unless confidence in the system was restored quickly, such runs left bankers with no choice but to close their doors. During the Panic of 1907, an astonishing two-thirds of banks found themselves temporarily unable to redeem deposits in cash. The situation led one prominent German banker to observe that the U.S. banking system was at the same point in the early 1900s that Europe's had been in the 1400s. In the intervening centuries, Europeans had developed a system of central banks; Americans hadn't.

The prevailing philosophy of many 19th-century Americans was that centralized government of any form should be kept to a minimum. But the punishing effects of frequent financial panics led people to reconsider the merits of a powerful central bank. In 1913, Congress passed the Federal Reserve Act, which created the U.S. Federal Reserve System. As the central bank's knowledge of how policy mechanisms worked grew, its governance improved. By the 1990s, the Fed was widely recognized as a key promoter of low inflation and maximum sustainable growth.

President Barack Obama nominates Janet Yellen to succeed Ben Bernanke as the 15th chair of the Board of Governors of the Federal Reserve System.

While central banking had stabilized European financial systems before 1900, the 20th century was another story. In that century, Europe experienced high inflation rates, low growth, high and volatile interest rates, and unstable exchange rates. After two world wars, governments' free spending led to unrelenting fiscal deficits. When European economies stagnated in the 1970s and 1980s, a consensus built that inflation was the fundamental problem and poor monetary policy was to blame. Leaders came to believe that the only way to ensure both political and economic stability was to forge closer ties among the continent's countries. They decided the best solution was a common currency and a single central bank. The result was the European monetary union, with its common currency, the euro, and its central bank, the *European Central Bank (ECB)*.

Europe's monetary union—born in 1999—was the natural outgrowth of a decades-long process that established the free movement of goods, services, and capital throughout the continent of more than 500 million people. Like the Fed, the ECB is based on principles that support the goal of price stability (principles we learned about in Chapter 15). We turn now to an examination of these two central banks to see how their structure helps them to meet their objectives.

The Structure of the Federal Reserve System

The Federal Reserve Act, passed in 1913 and amended numerous times since then, established what is now known as the **Federal Reserve System**. It is composed of three branches with overlapping responsibilities.[2] There are 12 regional *Federal Reserve Banks,* distributed throughout the country; a central governmental agency, called the *Board of Governors of the Federal Reserve System,* located in Washington D.C.; and the *Federal Open Market Committee.* In addition, a series of advisory committees

---

[2]The Dodd-Frank Act of 2010, discussed in Chapter 14, was the most recent source of extensive changes in the Federal Reserve Act. It curtailed the Fed's authority as a lender of last resort but made it the supervisor of systemically important financial institutions (SIFIs).

make recommendations to the board and the Federal Reserve Banks. Finally, there are the private banks that are members of the system. This complex structure diffuses power in a way that is typical of the U.S. government, creating a system of checks and balances that reduces the tendency for power to concentrate at the center.

All national banks (those chartered by the federal government) are required to belong to the Federal Reserve System. State banks that receive their charters from individual state banking authorities have the option of joining, but most do not. The original reason was cost. Prior to a change in the law in 1980, member banks were required to hold noninterest-bearing reserve deposits at the Fed, while nonmember banks could hold reserves in interest-bearing securities, such as U.S. Treasury bills. Today, members and nonmembers alike must hold reserve deposits at the Fed on which the Fed now pays interest, so there is no real distinction between them.

The Federal Reserve Banks

In the heart of Wall Street, two blocks from the site where the World Trade Center towers once stood, sits a large, fortresslike building that is the home of the Federal Reserve Bank of New York. Deep in the fourth subbasement is the largest gold vault in the world, stocked with many more bars than are in Fort Knox. All of this gold belongs to foreign countries and international organizations like the International Monetary Fund. It is stored there for free. You can take a tour to see the gold vault if you call ahead, but you won't get into the rest of the building without an invitation. When the bank was built, one of the vaults held cash, but today that vault is filled with excess furniture. Cash is stored across the Hudson River in New Jersey, in a three-story vault the size of a football field. People rarely enter the vault, and there are no tours— just thick walls, fences, security cameras, and armed guards. (The cash is stored on pallets of about 160 shrink-wrapped blocks of 4,000 notes each. It is moved around entirely by small robotic forklifts.)

The Federal Reserve Bank of New York is the largest of the 12 **Federal Reserve Banks**, accounting for about one-fifth of all Reserve Bank employment. The Reserve Banks, together with their branches, constitute the operational arm of the Federal Reserve System; and with more than 17,000 employees as of 2013, they account for the bulk of System employment. (All 12 have cash vaults, but only New York has gold.) Figure 16.1 shows the location of the banks and the region or "district" each one serves. From a modern vantage point, this map looks very odd. Why is nearly one-third of the continental United States served by a single bank in San Francisco while the Philadelphia district is so small? And why are two of the 12 banks in Missouri?

The gold vault at the Federal Reserve Bank of New York. It contains about one-fifth of official gold reserves in the world: nearly 200 million troy ounces worth almost $250 billion at mid-2013 prices. A single gold bar in this picture weighs 400 ounces and is worth almost $500,000.

One explanation is that the lines were drawn in 1914, so they represent the population density at the time. Then there was politics. Senator Carter Glass, one of the authors of the Federal Reserve Act, was from Richmond, Virginia, the headquarters of the fifth district; Speaker of the House Champ Clark came from Missouri, the state with two Reserve Banks. But more important, politicians decided that no district should coincide with a single state. The Federal Reserve Bank of New York, for example, serves all of New York State as well as northern New Jersey (where the cash vault is), a small slice of southwestern Connecticut, Puerto Rico, and the Virgin Islands. The purpose of this arrangement is twofold: to ensure that every district contains as broad a mixture

Figure 16.1

The Federal Reserve System

The 12 Federal Reserve Banks and their districts.

STABILITY

of economic interests as possible and that no person or group can obtain preferential treatment from the Reserve Bank.

Reserve Banks are strange creations, part public and part private. They are federally chartered banks and private, nonprofit organizations, owned by the commercial banks in their districts. As such, they are overseen by both their own boards of directors and the Board of Governors, an arm of the federal government. The method for choosing the nine members of each Reserve Bank's board of directors ensures the inclusion of not only bankers but other business leaders and people who represent the public interest. Six directors are elected by the commercial bank members of the Reserve Bank (three directors representing commercial banks and three representing the public), and the remaining three directors (also representing the public) are appointed by the Board of Governors. Though the range of views represented is wide, everyone has an interest in ensuring economic and financial stability.

Each Reserve Bank has a president, one of whose key responsibilities, as we will discuss later, is to sit periodically as a voting member of the Federal Open Market Committee. Subject to the approval of the Board of Governors, the president is selected for a five-year term by the six members of the bank's board of directors who represent the public.[3] (All 12 presidents' terms run concurrently, starting and ending at exactly the same time.) Reserve Bank presidents tend to come from one of three groups. Some have worked their way up inside the Federal Reserve System and are experts on the business of the district banks. Others are academic economists who have

---

[3]All nine directors used to appoint the Reserve Bank president, but the bailouts during the crisis of 2007–2009 fed the perception that the Federal Reserve System was too sympathetic to the financial institutions they regulate. In reaction, the Dodd-Frank Act of 2010 excluded the three commercial bank representatives on the Reserve Bank board from the process of selecting the president.

studied the financial system. Then there are former bankers, people who were once customers of the Federal Reserve. Because the presidents work together, the fact that they come from diverse backgrounds means that collectively they have the experience to manage the wide-ranging responsibilities of the Federal Reserve Banks.

The Reserve Banks conduct the day-to-day business of the central bank, serving as both the government's bank and the bankers' bank. Here is a brief list of the functions they perform:

1. As the bank for the U.S. government, they
   a. Issue new currency (Federal Reserve notes) and destroy old, worn currency.
   b. Maintain the U.S. Treasury's bank account and process electronic payments.
   c. Manage the U.S. Treasury's borrowings. That means issuing, transferring, and redeeming U.S. Treasury bonds, notes, and bills. But like you and your bank, the Treasury decides what it wants, and the Federal Reserve Banks just do it.

2. As the bankers' bank, they
   a. Hold deposits for the banks in their districts.
   b. Operate and ensure the integrity of a payments network for transferring funds.
   c. Make funds available to commercial banks within the district through *discount loans* on which they charge interest at the *discount rate.*
   d. Supervise and regulate financial institutions in the district to ensure their safety and soundness, as well as evaluate proposed bank mergers and new operations.
   e. Collect and make available data on business conditions.

In addition to these duties, the Federal Reserve Bank of New York provides services to foreign central banks and to certain international organizations that hold accounts there. The Federal Reserve Bank of New York is also the system's point of contact with financial markets. It is where Treasury securities are auctioned, foreign currency is bought and sold, and the Federal Reserve's own portfolio is managed through what are called *open market operations.* In the financial crisis of 2007–2009, the Federal Reserve Bank of New York also operated a variety of special new *liquidity and credit facilities* that supplied funds to intermediaries and allowed the Fed to acquire a portfolio of non-Treasury assets, ranging from commercial paper to mortgage-backed securities (see Chapter 18 Tools of the Trade).

Finally, the Reserve Banks play an important part in formulating monetary policy. They do it primarily through their representation on the Federal Open Market Committee (FOMC), which makes interest-rate decisions and determines the size and composition of the Fed's balance sheet, and less importantly through their participation in setting the **discount rate**, the interest rate charged on loans to commercial banks. The Federal Reserve Act specifies that the discount rate is to be set by each of the Reserve Bank's board of directors, with the approval of the Board of Governors, and strictly speaking, it is. But the directors have virtually no say over the discount rate, because it is set automatically at a premium above the overnight interest rate that the FOMC controls. Once the FOMC makes its decision, there is nothing left for anyone else to do.[4] That's why in Figure 16.2 detailing the complex structure of the Federal Reserve System a solid line labeled "controls" runs from the FOMC to the discount rate. (We will learn more about this topic in Chapter 18.)

---

[4]The only exception so far was during the financial crisis of 2007–2009, when the governors reduced the spread of the discount rate above the federal funds rate to encourage borrowing.

Figure 16.2   The Structure and Policy Organization of the Federal Reserve System

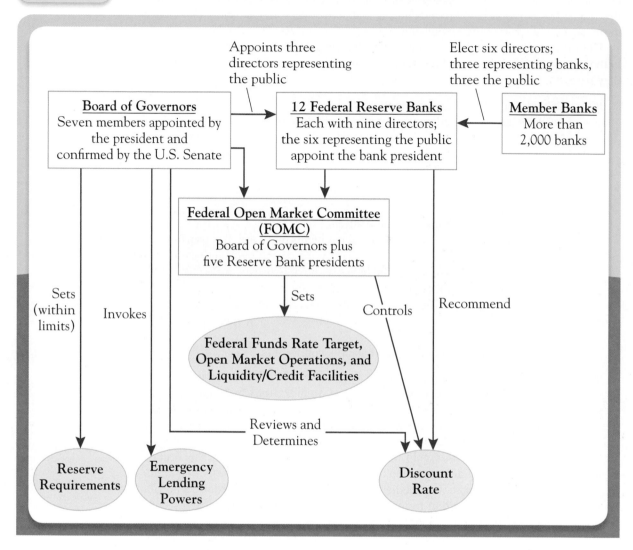

The Board of Governors

The headquarters of the Federal Reserve System sits at the corner of 20th Street and Constitution Avenue in northwest Washington, D.C., a short walk from the White House in one direction and the State Department in the other. The seven members of the board, who are called governors, are appointed by the president and confirmed by the U.S. Senate for 14-year terms. The long terms are intended to protect the board from political pressure. The fact that the terms are staggered—one beginning every two years—limits any individual president's influence over the membership. The board has a chairman and two vice chairmen, appointed by the president from among the seven governors for four-year renewable terms.[5] The board's membership usually

---

[5]To elevate the board's mandate for financial stability, the Dodd-Frank Act of 2010 created the new role of vice chairman for supervision.

YOUR FINANCIAL WORLD
Treasury Direct

The Federal Reserve takes care of the U.S. Treasury's banking needs. It is the government's banker, assisting the government by operating auctions for U.S. Treasury bonds when the government needs to borrow, keeping track of who owns the Treasury bonds, making interest payments on them every six months, and paying the principal when they mature. Although much of the Treasury's debt is bought and held by large financial institutions like banks, pension funds, and insurance companies, you can buy it yourself, without anyone's help, through *Treasury Direct*.

Treasury Direct lets you purchase as little as $1,000 worth of Treasury securities without paying any broker fees. All you need to do is fill out a few forms, write a check, and send them in. Everything you need to get started is available at the Bureau of Public Debt's website.

As a technical matter, buying a government bond means bidding at an auction that is held two or three times a week. How do you know what price to bid? Individuals aren't experts on bond pricing, so if they had to figure out how much to bid, Treasury Direct would never work. The solution is to place what is called a *noncompetitive bid*. This guarantees you will receive the bond you want at the average auction price, which is based on the bids of people who know what they are doing. Individuals send in checks to cover the face value of the bonds they want, and because the auction is normally designed so that the purchase price is less than face value, you get a small refund in the mail a few weeks later. The only complicated part of this is deciding exactly which bonds you want to buy.

Once you have bought the bonds, you will receive a notice of the interest payments, as well as periodic statements listing what you own. If you decide you want to sell the bonds, the Fed will do it for you at the highest market price available. Treasury Direct is by far the cheapest way to buy U.S. Treasury securities, especially in small amounts and for issues like Treasury Inflation Protection Securities (see the discussion of TIPS in *Your Financial World,* Chapter 6), which are difficult to purchase on the open market but easy to buy at auction.

includes academic economists, bank regulators, and bankers. To ensure adequate regional representation on the board, no two governors can come from the same Federal Reserve district. The Federal Reserve Act explicitly requires "a fair representation of the financial, agricultural, industrial, and commercial interests."

Together with a staff of about 2,500, the **Board of Governors of the Federal Reserve System** performs the following duties:

- Sets the reserve requirement, which determines the level of reserves banks are required to hold.
- Approves or disapproves discount rate recommendations made by the Federal Reserve Banks.
- Acts as rule-writing agency for consumer credit protection laws (with enforcement by the Consumer Financial Protection Bureau).
- Approves bank merger applications.
- Supervises and regulates the Reserve Banks, including their budgets and their presidents' salaries.
- Along with the Reserve Banks, regulates and supervises the banking system, examining individual banks, nonbank systemically important financial institutions (SIFIs), and financial market utilities (FMUs) for safety and soundness and for compliance with the law.
- Invokes **emergency powers** to lend to nonbanks when circumstances are deemed "unusual and exigent." These powers provided the authority for much of the Fed's emergency lending in the crisis of 2007–2009 but were curtailed by the Dodd-Frank Act of 2010 (see Chapter 14, page 387).

- Analyzes financial and economic conditions, both domestic and international.
- Collects and publishes detailed statistics about the system's activities and the economy at large. As you have seen throughout this book, the Federal Reserve Economic Database (FRED) provides a wide variety of information about the United States and other economies, including data collected directly by the Fed about the amount of money in the economy (M1 and M2), interest rates, exchange rates, the banking system's assets and liabilities, the level of production in U.S. industry, and the level of household wealth.

The seven governors do not have their own support staff. Instead, they request help and information from the directors of various departments, who assign individuals to specific tasks. The directors answer to the chair of the Board of Governors.

The Federal Open Market Committee

When most people think about the Federal Reserve, what comes to mind is not the payments system or bank supervision but interest-rate setting. And when the business press discusses the Fed, its attention is really on the **Federal Open Market Committee (FOMC)**. This is the group that sets interest rates and adjusts the Fed's balance sheet to control the availability of money and credit to the economy. The FOMC has been around since 1936 and has 12 voting members. These are the seven governors, the president of the Federal Reserve Bank of New York, and a rotating selection of four of the remaining 11 Reserve Bank presidents. The chair of the Board of Governors chairs the FOMC as well, and the committee's vice chair is the president of the Federal Reserve Bank of New York. While only five of the 12 Reserve Bank presidents vote at any one time, all of them participate in the meeting.

The FOMC could control any interest rate, but the rate it chooses to control is the **federal funds rate**, the rate banks charge each other for unsecured overnight loans on their excess deposits at the Fed. We will discuss the details of this arrangement in the next two chapters. For now, keep in mind that the rate the FOMC controls is a nominal interest rate. However, because inflation expectations don't change quickly when a credible central bank aims at price stability, the FOMC in effect controls the *real* interest rate. (Recall that the real interest rate equals the nominal interest rate minus expected inflation.) The real interest rate plays a central role in economic decisions. The higher the real interest rate, the more expensive borrowing is, and the less likely a company is to build a new factory or an individual is to purchase a new car. Furthermore, the lower the level of purchases by firms and households, the lower the level of growth will be. So by controlling the federal funds rate, the FOMC influences real growth. (This mechanism is described in Part V.)

The Board Room at the Federal Reserve in Washington, DC., with its oblong table. This is the meeting place of the Federal Open Market Committee and Board of Governors of the Federal Reserve System.

The FOMC currently meets eight times a year, or roughly once every six weeks, in the Board Room at the Federal Reserve in Washington, D.C. During times of crisis, the committee can confer and change policy over the telephone. Because these "inter-meeting" policy shifts signal the financial markets that the FOMC believes conditions are dire, they are reserved for extraordinary times, like the aftermath of the terrorist attacks on the World Trade Center of September 2001. One measure of the financial crisis of 2007–2009 is that it prompted 12 unscheduled FOMC meetings, surpassing the cumulative total of recent decades!

Since 2009, all scheduled FOMC meetings have taken place over a two-day period, starting around 2 p.m. one afternoon, and finishing the next day at 1:00 p.m. In addition to the seven governors and 12 Reserve Bank presidents, numerous board staff members attend, along with at least one senior staff member from each Reserve Bank. In all, between 50 and 60 people are there. The primary purpose of the meeting is to decide on the target interest rate and, in response to the crisis of 2007–2009, on the scale and mix of assets to acquire. No less important, the FOMC agrees on how to communicate its policies to the public, including any **forward guidance** about likely future policy. The FOMC itself does not engage in the financial market transactions that are required to keep the market federal funds rate near this target or to manage the Fed's portfolio. That job falls to the system open market account (SOMA) manager, who, together with his or her staff, works for the Federal Reserve Bank of New York. The policy directive simply instructs the New York Fed's staff to buy and sell securities so as to maintain the market federal funds rate at the target or to assemble the desired asset mix.

To figure out who really controls these key policy decisions, we need to look closely at how the FOMC works, focusing on the information that is distributed in advance and the mechanics of the meeting. Two important documents are distributed to all attendees prior to each meeting: the *Beige Book* and the *Tealbook*. The Beige Book is a compilation of anecdotal information about current business activity, collected by the staffs of the Reserve Banks and published about two weeks before the meeting. This is the only FOMC document that is released to the public before the meeting. The Tealbook contains two parts: the board staff's economic forecast for the next few years (until 2010, this part was called the *Greenbook*) and a discussion of financial markets and current policy options (formerly called the *Bluebook*). The Tealbook is distributed electronically during the week preceding the meeting. It is a confidential document and is not released to the public until five years after the meeting. On a quarterly basis, the governors and the Reserve Bank presidents also submit in advance of the meeting their own projections for economic growth, unemployment, inflation, and (since 2012) the timing and pace of future changes to the target federal funds rate.

An FOMC meeting is a formal proceeding that can be divided into two parts, each beginning with a staff report followed by a round of discussion that includes all of the meeting's participants (consisting of the 12 voting members and the remaining seven Reserve Bank presidents). Here's the usual order in which people speak:

1. The SOMA desk manager reports on financial market conditions and actions taken to achieve the target interest rate and the desired asset mix since the last meeting.

2. Senior staff of the Board comment on the economic situation and financial developments, and present the staff's forecast (from the Tealbook).

3. One at a time, committee members (including Reserve Bank presidents who are not currently voting) discuss their view of the economic outlook, including specific regional information. During the process, speakers also may comment in response to others' statements. The chair speaks at the end, concluding what is called the *economic go-round*.

4. The director of the Division of Monetary Affairs, who doubles as the secretary of the FOMC, describes the two or three policy options (from the Tealbook). In

recent years, the options often focus on adjustments to the Fed's asset mix and to the forward guidance regarding future policy.

5. Again, one at a time, the committee members comment on the policy options, with the chair speaking last.

6. A vote is taken, with the chair voting first, the vice chair second, and then the committee members in alphabetical order.

The staff may respond to questions following their presentations, and there is some give-and-take among the FOMC members. One advantage of two-day meetings is that members also can engage each other informally—for example, over dinner on the first night. At 2:00 p.m. on the second day, an hour or two after the meeting adjourns, the committee releases a policy statement containing its decisions and a brief explanation of them. At a quarterly frequency, an update to the economic and target federal funds rate projections of the 19 FOMC members is provided to the committee before its meeting; after those meetings, the update is released simultaneously with the policy statement and is followed at about 2:30 p.m. with a press conference by the Fed chair. Finally, three weeks later, detailed minutes summarizing the deliberations are released on the FOMC's public website.

To see where the committee's power lies and who controls interest-rate and asset mix decisions, notice a few things (see Table 16.1). First, and foremost, the chair is the voice of the Federal Reserve System. He or she speaks to Congress and the public on behalf of the FOMC. Second, note that the governors make up a majority of the

Table 16.1   A User's Guide to the Fed

The Federal Reserve System is complicated, so here is a list of the key players:

Chair of the Board of Governors	Most powerful person in the Federal Reserve System. Also chair of the FOMC. Effectively controls FOMC meetings and monetary policy. Appointed by the U.S. president to a four-year term, subject to U.S. Senate confirmation; must be one of the governors.
Other members of the Board of Governors	Supervise and regulate an important portion of the financial industry. All are voting members of the FOMC. Appointed by the president to 14-year terms, subject to U.S. Senate confirmation. The two vice chairs (of which one is designated for supervision) must be members of the Board of Governors.
President of the Federal Reserve Bank of New York	Runs the biggest and most important of the Reserve Banks, where monetary policy operations are carried out and much of the Fed's work for the Treasury is done. Also provides services to commercial banks in the district. As with the presidents of the other Reserve Banks, appointed by the nonbanking members of the bank's board of directors, with the approval of the Board of Governors, for a five-year term. Also vice chair of the FOMC.
Presidents of the 11 other Federal Reserve Banks	Provide services to commercial banks in their districts. All participate in every FOMC meeting and four serve one-year terms as voting members of the FOMC on a rotating basis.

The Board of Governors and each of the Reserve Banks maintain websites that publish data, economic research, speeches, and information about customer services. In addition, the FOMC maintains a list of its meeting times on the Board of Governors website, along with links to the committee's statements, minutes, transcripts, and economic projections, as well as the chair's press conferences. The place to start is www.federalreserve.gov.

TOOLS OF THE TRADE
Decoding the FOMC Statement

As the financial crisis deepened in 2008, the range of FOMC policy actions broadened, and financial stability rose to the top of the Fed's agenda. Accordingly, the form of the **FOMC statement** released at the end of the FOMC's regularly scheduled meetings changed markedly. Nevertheless, some of the statement's familiar components remained:

- A clear statement of the committee's decision at the meeting regarding its target or target range for the federal funds rate (the interest rate that the FOMC controls).

- A summary of the committee's view of economic conditions, especially the inflation outlook.

- A description of how the outlook is expected to influence *future* policy.

- A description of the policy tools, in addition to the federal funds rate, that the Fed will use to achieve its objectives (to understand these, you have to follow current events very closely).

- A report of the voting.

Consider, for example, the following excerpt from the FOMC statement of December 12, 2012, when the committee first specified threshold levels below which unemployment and inflation would have to fall before it would raise the federal funds target rate above the near-zero range.

Consistent with its statutory mandate, the Committee seeks to foster maximum employment and price stability. The Committee remains concerned that, without sufficient policy accommodation, economic growth might not be strong enough . . . [and] . . . anticipates that inflation over the medium term likely will run at or below its 2 percent objective.

. . . If the outlook for the labor market does not improve substantially, the Committee will continue its purchases of Treasury and agency mortgage-backed securities, and employ its other policy tools as appropriate, until

such improvement is achieved in a context of price stability.

. . . the Committee expects that a highly accommodative stance of monetary policy will remain appropriate for a considerable time after the asset purchase program ends and the economic recovery strengthens. In particular, the Committee decided to keep the target range for the federal funds rate at 0 to 1/4 percent and currently anticipates that this exceptionally low range for the federal funds rate will be appropriate at least as long as the unemployment rate remains above 6-1/2 percent, inflation between one and two years ahead is projected to be no more than a half percentage point above the Committee's 2 percent longer-run goal, and longer-term inflation expectations continue to be well anchored. . . .

Voting for the FOMC monetary policy action were: Ben S. Bernanke, Chairman; William C. Dudley, Vice Chairman; Elizabeth A. Duke; Dennis P. Lockhart; Sandra Pianalto; Jerome H. Powell; Sarah Bloom Raskin; Jeremy C. Stein; Daniel K. Tarullo; John C. Williams; and Janet L. Yellen. Voting against the action was Jeffrey M. Lacker . . . .

Interpreting these statements takes some practice, especially as the Fed widens the range of policy tools and provides more complex, outcome-based (or "state-contingent") forward guidance. A summary of the one here might go like this: "The weak recovery is keeping inflation below the Fed's medium-term objective, while unemployment remains high. The Fed will use its various policy tools to stimulate economic activity aggressively, keeping the policy target rate near zero until unemployment or inflation (or inflation expectations) break out of ranges consistent with the inflation objective."

By going to the FOMC's website at www.federalreserve.gov/fomc, you can look at recent statements and see how they have been changing. What do you think the Fed will do next?

committee, and they work together daily at the headquarters of the Federal Reserve in Washington, D.C. Third, aside from the quarterly projections of FOMC members, the most important information distributed to all committee members before a meeting is the Tealbook forecast and policy options. The Tealbook is prepared by the Federal Reserve Board staff, which is controlled by the chair. Fourth, the chair sets the agenda for the FOMC meeting, determines the order in which people speak, and proposes the FOMC policy statement (see Tools of the Trade above). Finally, though the votes are made public immediately after the meeting, committee members observe a blackout period from a week preceding an FOMC meeting to a week following the meeting, during which they do not speak publicly about the economic outlook or current monetary policy. Dissenters, who are identified immediately in the press release that comes the afternoon of the meeting, usually wait a week to explain their views in public. And remember, the Board of Governors controls the Reserve Banks' budgets, as well as the salaries of their presidents.

Press reports, then, do give a good sense of where the FOMC's power lies. The chair of the Fed is the FOMC's most important member. So, if you want to know whether interest rates are likely to go up or down, or whether the Fed will alter the size and composition of its portfolio, that is the person you should listen to most closely. To have an impact on policy, governors or Reserve Bank presidents must build support for their positions through their statements at the meeting and in public speeches. While the chair is very powerful, the committee structure provides an important check on his or her power. Indeed, even two dissents on an FOMC vote are unusual, while three dissents—an outcome that has occurred only once since the 1980s—could raise doubts about the chair's leadership.

Assessing the Federal Reserve System's Structure

In the previous chapter, we developed a checklist for assessing a central bank's structure. We said that an effective central bank is one in which policymakers are largely independent of political influence, make decisions by committee, are accountable and transparent, and state their objectives clearly. Let's evaluate the Federal Reserve System using these criteria.

Independence from Political Influence

We set out three criteria for judging a central bank's independence: budgetary independence, irreversible decisions, and long terms in office. The Fed meets each of these. It controls its own budget. The Fed's substantial revenue is a combination of interest on the government securities it holds and fees charged to banks for payments system services, including check clearing, electronic funds transfers, and the like. In fact, the Fed's income is so large that, in a typical year, 95 percent of it is returned to the U.S. Treasury.[6] Interest-rate changes are implemented immediately and can be changed only by the FOMC—no one else can reverse or change them. The terms of the governors are 14 years; the chair's term runs for four years; and the Reserve Bank presidents serve for five years (and they aren't even appointed by politicians).

Even though the structural elements required to maintain an independent monetary policy are in place, the Fed occasionally comes under political attack. As we have said, raising interest rates is never popular. In 2009, public outrage over the financial crisis and the bailouts of large intermediaries made the Fed a political target, posing the biggest threat to its independence in many years. Many legislators favored greater scrutiny

---

[6]In 2012, interest rates were extraordinarily low, while the Fed's crisis and postcrisis asset purchases had expanded its balance sheet massively. Prior to the crisis, you could usually approximate the Fed's interest income by multiplying the value of its securities holdings—nearly $3 trillion—by the U.S. Treasury's one-year interest rate, roughly 0.17 percent in 2012. You'll get a number around $5 billion. (The same calculation in 2007 resulted in a figure of roughly $40 billion.) However, Fed net income actually hit a record $91 billion in 2012, because the Fed's holdings of long-term Treasury bonds and non-Treasury assets (mostly mortgage-backed securities) provided a higher yield than one-year Treasuries. The Fed returned $89 billion to the Treasury.

APPLYING THE CONCEPT
THE EVOLUTION OF FEDERAL RESERVE INDEPENDENCE

Like most large bureaucracies, the Federal Reserve moves very slowly and deliberately. Nevertheless, there have been some defining moments when the Fed's structure changed suddenly and significantly. The first one came in 1935, after the economywide financial failures that led to the Great Depression of the 1930s. To remove monetary policy from the political arena, the Secretary of the Treasury and the Comptroller of the Currency, two political appointees who served at the pleasure of the president, were kicked off the Federal Reserve Board, and the FOMC was created.

But independence in name is not independence in fact. During World War II, the Federal Reserve became part of the war effort, which meant ensuring a cheap source of funds for the Treasury. The Fed worked to keep interest rates low by making sure that bond prices remained high. Importantly, when the Treasury went to issue securities, to keep prices high the Fed would buy what the public refused to purchase. Early in 1951, the Secretary of the Treasury, who was under pressure to finance the new Korean War, tried to force the Fed to purchase significant quantities of bonds directly from the Treasury. Faced with rising inflation, the FOMC had announced its desire to curtail credit growth by reducing the rate at which it purchased government debt. President Truman was forced to step in and resolve the standoff. On March 4, 1951, the president, the secretary of the Treasury, and the Federal Reserve chair reached an "accord" and issued a joint announcement establishing the FOMC's independence in setting interest rates and controlling the rate of monetary expansion.*

These two events provided the foundation for the Federal Reserve's independence in forming monetary policy. Of course, the FOMC's ability to do its job still depends on the willingness of politicians to refrain from interference. The president and the secretary of the Treasury can make comments criticizing the FOMC's monetary policy decisions, and Congress does have the ability to revoke the Fed's independence. Following the financial crisis of 2007–2009, congressional criticism of the Fed became unusually intense, while proposals to limit Fed independence flourished. In contrast, the U.S. government proposed to expand the Fed's supervisory powers to help prevent another financial crisis.

*For a brief summary of this history, see Carl E. Walsh, "Federal Reserve Independence and the Accord of 1951," *Federal Reserve Bank of San Francisco Weekly Letter,* No. 93-21, May 28, 1993.

of the Fed. And while the U.S. government proposed to enhance the Fed's supervisory powers because of the financial crisis, some in Congress sought to strip it of those powers altogether. Ultimately, the Dodd-Frank Act of 2010 curtailed the Fed's emergency lending powers and required new disclosures of Fed transactions, but it also widened Fed supervisory responsibility (see Chapter 14).

Decision Making by Committee

The Fed clearly makes decisions by committee, because the FOMC *is* a committee. While the chair of the Board of Governors may dominate policy decisions, the fact that there are 12 voting members provides an important safeguard against arbitrary action by a single individual. In the Federal Reserve, no one person can become a dictator.

Accountability and Transparency

The FOMC releases huge amounts of information to the public. Prior to each meeting, the committee publishes the Beige Book and makes it publicly available. Within a couple of hours of the meeting's adjournment, the committee releases and posts on its website a brief policy statement giving its decisions and its reasoning. (At quarterly intervals, committee members' economic and target federal funds rate projections are released at the same time as the policy statement, and about a half-hour later the Fed chair gives a press conference.) Then, three weeks later, the committee publishes a detailed summary of the meeting—the minutes—that also states how each member

INFORMATION

YOUR FINANCIAL WORLD

The Fed Can't Save You from a Stock-Market Crash

Will the Federal Reserve keep the stock market from crashing, helping us all to sleep better at night? We have already said that the central bank's job is to reduce systematic risk by stabilizing prices, output growth, and the financial system. But there is only so much that a central bank can, should, or will do. In the end, no one can save us from all the risks we face.

The history of the stock market in the late 1990s and early 2000s provides a stark illustration of the pressures central bankers face and the limits of their actions. As equity prices rose in 1998 and 1999, many investors came to believe that then Federal Reserve Board chairman Alan Greenspan would not let the stock market decline significantly. He and his colleagues on the FOMC would bail everyone out. Their reasoning went like this: Changes in wealth change consumption patterns. That is, the richer we all become, the more we spend; conversely, the poorer we are, the less we spend. A stock-market crash would reduce spending, sending the economy into a severe recession—something

the "Greenspan Fed" would not allow. For investors, this assumption meant that they could buy stocks without worrying about the downside; they need not fear a crash. While owning stock used to be risky, it wasn't anymore. Or so many people believed in 1999. And the lower the perceived risk, the smaller the risk premium became. This drove prices up even further. (Remember that the lower the risk, the more you will pay for a financial instrument.)

What happened? The answer is that the Fed doesn't control the stock market; it merely sets interest rates and ensures that banks have funds to honor their commitments. As the stock market declined through 2001 and 2002, the FOMC lowered its interest-rate target from 6 percent to 1 percent to avert a recession. Growth was sluggish for a few years, and inflation rose only slightly. But keeping stocks from falling from their unsustainable heights was beyond the Fed's control, even if members had wanted to do it. No one can eliminate the risk that is inherent in an investment—not even the most powerful central bank in the world.

voted and gives the reasons for any dissenting votes. And after a five-year waiting period, the FOMC publishes the word-for-word transcript of the meeting along with the Tealbook and other staff presentations. Added to these documents is the Federal Reserve Board's twice-yearly "Monetary Policy Report to the Congress," which provides great detail about the outlook and the considerations behind policy setting. This report is accompanied by the chair's appearance before Congress to discuss the state of the nation's economy. Members of the FOMC also give frequent public speeches, and occasionally they testify before Congress. In an average year, the chair gives 15 to 20 speeches, and other governors and Reserve Bank presidents speak 5 to 10 times each. All of these communications—the Beige Book, the statement, the press conference, the minutes, the transcripts, the biannual report, the testimony, and the speeches—can be found on various Fed websites.

This avalanche of information seems enough to give everyone a sense of what the FOMC is doing and why. But some things are still missing from the Fed's communications. For example, unlike some central banks, the FOMC does not agree on or publish a *consensus* economic or interest rate projection (the individual members' projections are summarized anonymously in a table). In addition, key inputs into the decision-making process—documents like the staff forecast and the policy options in the Tealbook—and the meeting transcript are not made public until five years after the fact. The Fed also delays the dissemination of information about the recipients of its loans because it does not want to trigger a run on a fragile—or even on a healthy—intermediary. On the other hand, as we will discuss in a moment, the Fed's 2012 shift to an inflation-targeting strategy should facilitate and focus Fed communications, making both the message and the policy more effective (see also Tools of the Trade).

Policy Framework

The Congress of the United States has set the Federal Reserve's objectives: "The Board of Governors of the Federal Reserve System and the Federal Open Market Committee shall maintain long run growth of the monetary and credit aggregates commensurate with the economy's long run potential to increase production, so as to promote effectively the goals of maximum employment, stable prices, and moderate long-term interest rates."

What should we make of this vague statement? Some people see ambiguity as advantageous. Because laws are difficult to change, they argue, we wouldn't want the Fed's objectives to be extremely specific; the imprecision of the language means the Fed has considerable leeway in setting its own goals. For most of its existence, the FOMC was unable or unwilling to tell us exactly how it interprets this broad mandate.

"I've called the family together to announce that, because of inflation, I'm going to have to let two of you go."

SOURCE: 1974 © Joseph Farris/The New Yorker Collection/www.cartoonbank.com.

Today, however, the FOMC's approach is largely transparent, and (although Fed officials resist being labeled inflation-targeters) the strategy is consistent with the **inflation-targeting** framework that Chairman Ben Bernanke had advocated when he was a professor at Princeton University. The strategic shift was enshrined in the FOMC's January 2012 special Statement on Longer-Run Goals and Monetary Policy Strategy, which the committee expects to reaffirm each year.[7] This FOMC consensus on longer-run strategy is likely to prove a key legacy of Bernanke's leadership.

STABILITY

Most important, the FOMC Statement quantifies the inflation goal over the longer term—namely, an annual rise of 2 percent in the price index for personal consumption expenditures. With each monthly release of that price index (which is somewhat different from the Consumer Price Index reported monthly in the news media), observers can judge whether inflation is headed toward that objective. "In setting monetary policy," the statement said, "the Committee seeks to mitigate deviations of inflation from its longer-run goal and deviations of employment from the Committee's assessments of its maximum level."

Importantly, the FOMC does *not* set a specific standing goal for longer-run "normal" economic growth, for maximum employment, or for the "normal" level of unemployment because—unlike the longer-run inflation rate—the Fed does not control these outcomes. The FOMC's quarterly "Summary of Economic Projections" does, however, give the latest anonymous estimates of each of the 19 FOMC participants for longer-run unemployment, inflation, and output growth. Finally, the strategy specifies a "balanced approach" whenever the FOMC faces a tradeoff between its goals of minimizing deviations of inflation from the 2-percent target and deviations of employment from the FOMC's assessment of its maximum sustainable level. Put differently, the speeds at which the FOMC seeks to realize each of these two goals can differ when the goals conflict with each other.

[7]The special January 2012 FOMC Statement is at *www.federalreserve.gov/newsevents/press/monetary/ 20120125c.htm.* The FOMC reaffirmed this Statement with minor changes at its meeting in January 2013.

The European Central Bank

As recently as 1998, Romans shopped with *lire,* Berliners with *deutsche marks,* and Parisians with *francs.* The Banca d'Italia, Italy's central bank, controlled the number of lire that circulated, while the Bundesbank managed the quantity of deutsche marks, and the Banque de France the volume of francs. But on January 1, 1999, the majority of Western European countries adopted a common currency. Today, residents of Rome, Berlin, and Paris all make their purchases in euros, and monetary policy is the job of the **European Central Bank (ECB)**. In the same way that a dollar bill is worth a dollar everywhere in the United States, a euro note is worth a euro everywhere in the **euro area**. By 2014, the euro had become the currency of 18 countries (see the map in Figure 16.3).

Figure 16.3   The European System of Central Banks

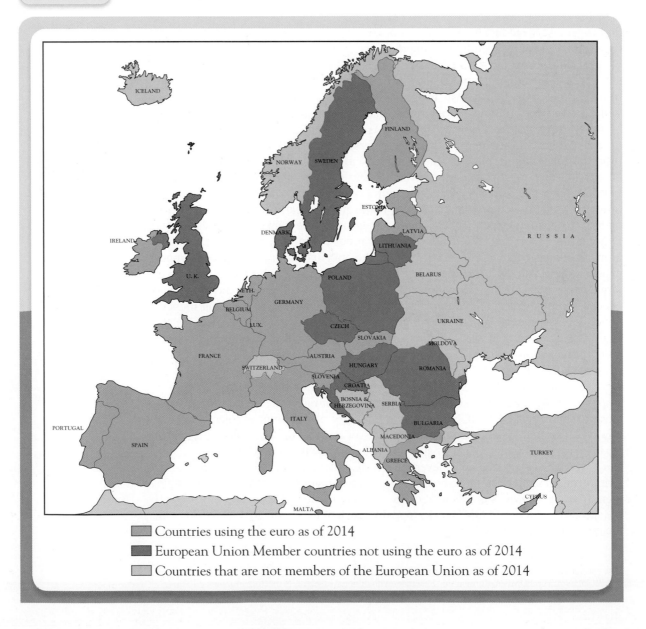

Countries using the euro as of 2014

European Union Member countries not using the euro as of 2014

Countries that are not members of the European Union as of 2014

The agreement to form a European monetary union was formalized in the Treaty of Maastricht, named for the Dutch city in which it was signed in 1992. The treaty initiated a lengthy process that led ultimately to the creation of the **European System of Central Banks (ESCB)**, which is composed of the European Central Bank (ECB) in Frankfurt, Germany, and the National Central Banks (NCBs) in the 28 countries in the European Union. The ECB and the NCBs of the 18 countries that participate in the monetary union make up what is known as the **Eurosystem**, which shares a common currency and common monetary policy. At this writing, Denmark, Sweden, and the United Kingdom, as well as 7 of the 13 countries that joined the European Union since May 1, 2004, remained outside the Eurosystem and retained control over their monetary policy.

A myriad of names and abbreviations are associated with central banking in Europe. To avoid confusion, we will refer to the institution that is responsible for monetary policy in the euro area as the European Central Bank. Our goal is to understand its basic organizational structure.[8] As we examine the ECB, keep in mind that, in economic terms, Europe is larger, and the euro area is only a bit smaller, than the United States.

Organizational Structure

The Eurosystem mirrors the structure of the Federal Reserve System in several ways. There is the six-member **Executive Board of the ECB**, which is similar to the Board of Governors; the **National Central Banks**, which play many of the same roles as the Federal Reserve Banks; and the **Governing Council**, which formulates monetary policy, just as the FOMC does.[9] The Executive Board has a president (Mario Draghi of Italy until October 2019) and a vice president (Vitor Constâncio of Portugal until May 2018), who play the same role as the leaders of the Federal Reserve's Board of Governors. ECB Executive Board members are appointed by a committee composed of the heads of state of the countries that participate in the monetary union (see Table 16.2 on page 438).

The ECB and the NCBs together perform the traditional operational functions of a central bank, which we learned about in the last chapter. In addition to using interest rates to control the availability of money and credit in the economy, they are responsible for the smooth operation of the payments system and the issuance of currency. Together, they also serve as the lender of last resort. And, starting in 2014, the ECB is the euro area's leading bank supervisor. Like the Fed, it directly supervises the large systemic banks. While the details differ from country to country, the National Central Banks continue to serve as bankers to the banks and governments in their countries, just as the Federal Reserve Banks serve the banks in their districts and the U.S. government.

There are several important differences between the Fed and the ECB, however. Some exist by design and others as a result of the way the system came into being

---

[8]Two publications are helpful in understanding European monetary policy. The first chief economist of the ECB, Otmar Issing, who also served on the ECB Executive Board in its first eight years, explains the evolution of ECB policies in *The Birth of the Euro* (Cambridge, UK: Cambridge University Press, 2008). *The Monetary Policy of the ECB,* published by the ECB in 2011, provides a technical description of how things work.

[9]While the ECB may appear to be modeled after the Federal Reserve System, its structure is actually based on that of the Deutsche Bundesbank, the German central bank. Europeans uniformly viewed the Bundesbank as being successful in stabilizing the post-World War II German economy, so it was a natural model, but the real reason for the new structure was politics. The designers of the ECB had to find a way to create a common central bank that incorporated all of the existing national central banks. This meant adding a new central administration while retaining the NCBs, which already existed.

| Table 16.2 | Key Aspects of the European Central Bank |

European Central Bank (ECB)	The central authority in Frankfurt, Germany, that oversees monetary policy in the common currency area. (Established July 1, 1998.)
National Central Banks (NCBs)	The central banks of the countries that belong to the European Union.
European System of Central Banks (ESCB)	The ECB plus the NCBs of all the countries in the European Union, including those that do not participate in the monetary union.
Eurosystem	The ECB plus the NCBs of euro-area countries; together, they carry out the tasks of central banking in the euro area.
ECB Executive Board	The six-member body in Frankfurt that oversees the operation of the ECB and the Eurosystem.
Governing Council	The (currently) 24-member committee that makes monetary policy in the common currency area.
Euro	The currency used in the countries of the European Monetary Union.
Euro area	The countries that use the euro as their currency.

(see Table 16.3). First, the implementation of monetary policy—the ECB's day-to-day interaction with the financial markets—is accomplished at all the national central banks, rather than being centralized as it is in the United States. Second, the ECB's budget is controlled by the National Central Banks, not the other way around. This arrangement means that the NCBs control the finances of the Executive Board and its headquarters in Frankfurt. Third, the ECB supplies reserves primarily through collateralized lending to the banks rather than through sales and purchases of securities.

The focus of the ECB's activity is on the control of money and credit in the Eurosystem—that is, on monetary policy. The Governing Council, the equivalent of the Fed's FOMC, is composed of the six Executive Board members and the governors of the 18 (as of 2014) central banks in the euro area. Meetings to consider monetary policy actions are held monthly in Frankfurt, at the ECB's headquarters. Decisions are often made by consensus rather than by formal votes of the Council. The rationale for this approach is easy to understand. The Governing Council members are charged with setting policy for the euro area as a whole, regardless of economic conditions in the individual countries they come from. For the governor of the Banque de France to vote to raise interest rates at a time when the French economy is on its way into a recession would be difficult, even if it is the right thing to do for the euro area as a whole. Occasionally, however, votes occur and Governing Council members air their dissent in public.[10]

A number of important safeguards were included in the Treaty of Maastricht to ensure the central bank's independence. First, there are the terms of office: Executive Board members serve eight-year terms (without the possibility of reappointment), and member nations must appoint their central bank governors for a minimum of five

---

[10]An important difference between the ECB's Governing Council and the FOMC is that the governors of the Federal Reserve Board always hold the majority of the seats on the FOMC (7 out of 12) while the Executive Board members are always a minority on the Governing Council (6 out of a current 24). In the Eurosystem, power is less centralized than it is at the Fed.

Table 16.3   Comparing the FOMC with the ECB's Governing Council

	FOMC	Governing Council
Independence		
Budgetary control	Controlled by the Board of Governors.	Controlled by the NCBs.
Decisions irreversible	Yes.	Yes.
Terms of appointment	Governors 14 years, Reserve Bank presidents 5 years.	Executive Board members 8 years; heads of NCBs minimum of 5 years.
Threat of legislative change	Requires an act of Congress.	Requires agreement of all signatories to Treaty of Maastricht.
Decision making		
	Committee of 19 members; governors and New York Reserve Bank president always vote; 11 other Reserve Bank presidents rotate 4 voting slots.	Committee of 24 members, all participating equally.
Accountability and transparency		
Policy deliberations	Immediate release of target interest rate with a brief statement including the votes of the committee members; quarterly forecasts and press conference by the chair.	Immediate release of target interest rate with an explanatory statement; the president and vice president answer questions.
	Minutes of the meeting released after three weeks.	Release of minutes under consideration (as of September 2013).
	Transcripts released after 5 years.	No transcripts.
Other information	Twice-yearly reports to Congress.	Quarterly report to the European Parliament.
	Public speeches of members.	Public speeches of members.
	Data collection and dissemination.	Data collection and dissemination.
	Publication of research reports, along with FOMC members' quarterly forecasts of inflation and growth.	Publication of research reports, along with twice-yearly staff forecasts of inflation and growth.
Policy framework		
	Dual mandate of price stability and maximum sustainable employment; "balanced approach" to tradeoffs between goals. Price stability defined numerically.	Price stability is paramount and defined numerically. All other goals are secondary.
Cooperation with fiscal policymakers		
	No explicit mechanism. Not authorized to purchase most state and municipal debt.	Stated requirements for member countries' deficits and debt levels that are frequently violated. Selectively purchases sovereign debt of member-states.

IN THE NEWS
Should the Fed Change Its Target?: Interview with Michael Woodford

Bloomberg

By Mark Whitehouse

January 6, 2013

When Michael Woodford speaks, central bankers listen. The Columbia University economist is widely regarded as one of the world's foremost experts on monetary policy.

In September, . . . he made waves with a paper explicitly advocating a significant change in the way central banks work: Instead of focusing primarily on inflation, he wrote, they should aim for a target level of economic output (expressed in nominal dollar terms).

. . . Since then, the Federal Reserve . . . explicitly stated that it will keep interest rates near zero as long as the unemployment rate remains above 6.5 percent and inflation holds below 2.5 percent. We spoke with Woodford . . . to find out what he thinks about the Fed's latest efforts.

Q: What was the thought process that led you to support nominal GDP targeting?

A: Actually, it's an approach I've been advocating for at least a decade . . . . The idea is to have a target criterion with two qualities: It must focus on the level of a nominal variable rather than its growth rate, and it should involve some combination of prices and economic activity. I settled on nominal GDP—the dollar value of all the goods and services produced in the economy—because it's a measure that a central banker can talk about and be understood by the general public, and it avoids contentious issues such as the correct definition in practice of the "output gap."

I see it more as a refinement than as a move away from inflation targeting. In practice, targeting only means having a definite goal for inflation in the medium to long run, not an exclusive emphasis on inflation in deciding the appropriate nearer-term path for the economy. It is emphasized in . . . the Fed's official statement [in January 2012] that announced its inflation target, that one should also take into account the projected path for real economic activity when making short-run policy decisions. I think the Fed should be more explicit about how exactly it expects to choose among possible short-run paths . . . and I think that a commitment to a nominal GDP target path—one that is chosen so as to yield the desired inflation rate in the medium to long run, while also explaining how to balance the inflation outlook with the outlook for real GDP growth in the short run—would be a good way to do that.

---

years. Second, the ECB's financial interests must remain separate from any political organization. Third, the treaty states explicitly that the Governing Council cannot take instructions from any government, so its policy decisions are irreversible. The fact that the ECB is the product of a treaty agreed to by all of the countries of the European Union makes it extraordinarily difficult to change any of the terms under which it operates. People who study central banks generally agree that these provisions make the ECB's legal mandate the strongest in the world.

Before we move on, it is worth noting that a number of additional European Union countries, particularly those in eastern Europe, may enter the monetary union in the coming years. In anticipation, the Governing Council of the ECB planned a complex system of rotation (to be implemented when euro-area membership reaches 19 countries) that bears a passing resemblance to the system used by the FOMC. If the plan is implemented, the Executive Board members will still have permanent votes on the Governing Council, just as the Board of Governors of the Federal Reserve System does, while the leaders of the NCBs will rotate. Over time, as the ECB gains popular

Q: To what extent have the Fed's latest moves—stating the levels of unemployment and inflation at which it would consider raising rates—brought its policy closer to what you propose?

A: They have moved closer in one important respect: They are now talking about future policy in terms of economic outcomes, rather than a calendar date that will determine when interest rates should begin to rise. And it has some flavor of nominal GDP targeting because it involves both inflation and the real economy. The problem is that it's not clear what the new policy means for the longer term. Will the Fed always push interest rates down to zero when unemployment rises above 6.5 percent, or is this just a temporary thing? I presume it's the latter, but then the temporary policy runs the risk of raising doubts about how policy will be conducted later. A nominal GDP target would explain why they're doing what they're doing now, and also how they would shift to a less accommodative regime in the future, once the "catch up" to the target path has occurred.

Q: What new kinds of risks might a nominal GDP targeting regime introduce?

A: The biggest risk is miscommunication. People might think you've discarded the inflation target, rather than simply choosing an appropriate nearer-term target that is actually intended to guarantee the target inflation rate over the long run. That could lead them to expect higher inflation, a development that would make it harder to avoid higher actual inflation. The risk is particularly great now, because all the Fed's extraordinary measures have created a lot of uncertainty about what its current policy really is.

LESSONS OF THE ARTICLE

Targeting nominal GDP (NGDP) is an alternative to inflation targeting. When NGDP stayed far below its pre-2007 trend in many countries after the financial crisis, advocates argued that NGDP targeting would speed economic recovery by influencing private expectations. However, if the trend rate of real economic growth changes, inflation becomes unpredictable under NGDP targeting. As of mid-2013, no country has adopted NGDP targeting, but the Fed's announced policy thresholds for unemployment and inflation do aim at speeding recovery by influencing future expectations.

legitimacy and council members face less risk of home-country criticism, an enlarged Governing Council may decide that greater reliance on voting will make their decision process more efficient.

Accountability and Transparency

Like the Federal Reserve, the ECB distributes large volumes of information both on paper and on its website, in all of the ECB's official languages. Included are a weekly balance sheet, a monthly statistical bulletin, an analysis of current economic conditions, biannual forecasts of inflation and growth, research reports relevant to current policy, and an annual report. In addition, the president of the ECB appears before the European Parliament every quarter to report on monetary policy and answer questions, and Governing Council members speak regularly in public. But the most important aspect of the ECB's communication strategy concerns statements about the Governing Council's policy deliberations. (Like the FOMC, the Governing Council of the ECB

INFORMATION

LESSONS FROM THE CRISIS
THE EURO-AREA CRISIS AND THE ECB

As we have seen, the Maastricht Treaty provided the European Central Bank (ECB) with a legal foundation that makes it highly independent. Yet, even an independent central bank cannot secure price stability over the long term if fiscal policymakers do not control the rise of public debt, nor can it ensure economic stability in the face of bank runs.

Aside from their prescriptions for the ECB, however, the authors of the Maastricht Treaty designed no equivalently credible institutions to provide for fiscal and financial stability in the euro area. In other words, the treaty mastered the time-consistency problems of monetary policy but not of fiscal and prudential policy.

When the euro-area crisis began in earnest in 2010, policymakers had to scramble to keep the monetary union from breaking up. Triggered by the global crisis of 2007–2009, the emergency was a uniquely self-reinforcing mix of crises in sovereign debt, banking, and governance.

Here's what happened. The financial crisis of 2007–2009 severely damaged euro-area banks, and the economy plunged into a deep recession. Where fiscal deficits already were large, as in Greece, they widened sharply further. Where fiscal deficits were contained but the entire banking sector had overextended itself with risky lending, as in Spain, the national government was forced to borrow heavily to bail out the banks and support economic activity as well. These two problems—weakened banks and overstretched sovereigns—then fed on each other. Insolvent countries could no longer support insolvent banks. Investors ran from the hard-hit sovereigns, refusing to lend more, and depositors ran from hard-hit banks. Everyone sought safety in countries where they felt they could trust the governments.

The runs hit Greece, Portugal, and Ireland first (and worst), before moving on to Spain and Italy. In Figure 16.4, we can see the consequences for bonds issued by these countries. Yield spreads that had been unrealistically (and unwisely) low prior to the crisis exploded, even surpassing pre-euro levels that had compensated investors for currency and inflation risks. As the crisis deepened, depositors and bondholders feared both sovereign default and *redenomination risk*—the re-introduction of a domestic currency that would depreciate versus the euro.

As this story makes clear, the actions of the fiscal policymakers and prudential regulators in some countries of the euro area had spillover effects on other euro-area countries. If one country in a monetary union borrows too much, its default can damage the credit reputations of others. If one country's debt has been purchased by banks throughout the monetary union, default can render the banks elsewhere insolvent. Conversely, if risk taking renders a nation's banks insolvent, the need to insure their deposits and recapitalize them can render the government insolvent, too. As a result, much like bank runs, bad news in one country can lead to contagion in other fragile states.

Because of these spillover effects, a country in a monetary union might believe that it can count on transfers from other states to bail it out (or bail out its banks) in a crisis. This incentive to "free ride" arises from the moral hazard created when governments provide each other a kind of insurance, either explicit or implicit, without a commensurate fee for the insurance or without rules that contain bad behavior on the part of the financial or public sector (like the rules found in private-sector debt covenants).

Controlling this moral hazard is difficult because it requires (1) enforcement across borders and (2) constraining the behavior of a *future* government (the problem of time consistency). In practice, managing these externalities requires market discipline (such as when investors charge borrowers a risk premium) combined with institutions that limit risk taking and share unavoidable costs in bad times.

In the United States, these "common currency area" risks are controlled by a variety of institutional arrangements. First, the federal government, which is much larger than all of the state governments combined, effectively insures states against local shocks by automatic transfers from those doing relatively better to those doing relatively worse. Second, labor market flexibility (including worker mobility across states) cushions U.S. states against region-specific shocks. Third, as we saw in Chapter 14, the cost of protecting the U.S. financial system is shared across state boundaries—most deposits are in banks regulated, supervised, and insured by federal, not state, authorities. (Imagine how bank customers would feel if a small state rather than the FDIC was insuring the deposits of a U.S. megabank.) And finally, to contain moral hazard from risk sharing, the constitutions of most U.S. states limit their accumulation of debt, in most cases by requiring balanced budgets.

What this suggests is that for the euro area to survive, it will have to change. Its financial system must evolve in a way that (1) cuts the ties between banks and sovereigns and controls systemic risk in the financial system and (2) limits fiscal profligacy. This is the only way to keep depositors from running from banks in countries perceived to be weak and to moderate the subsidies that would otherwise go from parsimonious governments with disciplined banks, at one extreme, to spendthrift ones with risky banks, at the other extreme.

targets a short-term interest rate on interbank loans, provides forward guidance, and has developed several liquidity-supplying facilities that alter its asset scale and mix in order to counter widespread financial disruptions.)

Following each of the Governing Council's monthly meetings on monetary policy, the president and vice president of the ECB hold a news conference in Frankfurt.

Figure 16.4   10-Year Yield Spreads of Selected Euro-Area Government Bonds over German Government Bonds (Basis Points), 1990–2013

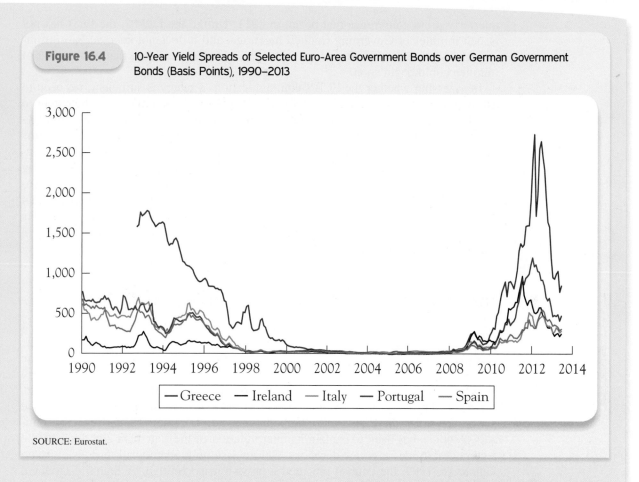

SOURCE: Eurostat.

The first of these means creating a truly pan-European financial system. This requires regulation, supervision, resolution, and deposit insurance at the level of the euro area, not of individual countries. Only then will depositors be indifferent between deposits held in Athens, Berlin, Madrid, or Rome.

Second, new mechanisms must be put in place to control fiscal free-riding. The designers of the monetary union were aware of this problem, but the deficit caps (3 percent of GDP per year) and debt caps (not more than 60 percent of GDP) proved unenforceable.

As of this writing, numerous problems remain largely unresolved. There is no common deposit insurance scheme. Nor is there a reliable means to limit fiscal free-riding. Indeed, policy actions to contain the crisis may have weakened treaty rules aimed at fiscal discipline.

The ECB has been at the center of the management of the crisis. Like the Fed, it offered banks liquidity through new and inventive means to contain the disruptions. These included *longer-term refinancing operations* (LTROs) that for the first time extended credit at three years' maturity; and *outright monetary transactions* (OMT), in which the ECB offered to purchase without limit the secondary-market debt (with maturities of up to three years) of sovereigns that implement a credible, monitored program of fiscal repair.

The ECB's extraordinary policy efforts restored financial market calm after mid-2012 (as you can see in Figure 16.4). But the ECB cannot solve the euro area's structural problems. By helping to stabilize the financial system, it gave the 18 governments of the monetary union a better chance to create a banking union and address fiscal problems; the future of the euro area depends on their progress.

The proceedings begin with the president reading a several-page statement announcing the council's interest-rate decision, together with a brief report on current economic and financial conditions in the euro area. The president and vice president then answer questions. A transcript of all their remarks is posted on the ECB's website (www.ecb.int) soon afterward. This procedure was the model for the Fed chair's quarterly press conference that began in 2011. Unlike the FOMC, the ECB has not issued minutes of Governing Council meetings, and it does not keep verbatim transcripts. However, in the summer of 2013, ECB leaders indicated that publication of minutes could begin soon.

In assessing whether the ECB's communications strategy is sufficient, we need to ask two questions. First, does the information that is released minimize the extent to which people will be surprised by future policy actions? Second, does it hold policymakers accountable for their decisions? On the first issue, the primary problem turns out to be that occasionally a number of conflicting opinions are expressed. While confusion in communication was a problem when the ECB first got started, the Governing Council now knows the importance of providing a unified public front, and its members' public statements are more consistent. On the second issue, indications are that the system is working and that there is accountability. The ECB is forced to justify its actions to the euro-area public, explaining its policies and responding to criticisms in more than a dozen languages.

The Price Stability Objective and Monetary Policy Strategy

STABILITY

The Treaty of Maastricht states, "The primary objective of the European System of Central Banks [ESCB] shall be to maintain price stability. Without prejudice to the objective of price stability, the ESCB shall support the general economic policies in the [European] Community," including the objective of sustainable and noninflationary growth. Like the Fed's legislatively dictated objectives, this statement is quite vague. However, the treaty is widely understood to place priority on price stability as the top objective for the ECB, while the Fed's mandate does not. The Governing Council's response has been to explain its interpretation of the statement and describe the factors that guide its policy decisions. Before assuming operational responsibility on January 1, 1999, the council prepared a press release entitled "A Stability-Oriented Monetary Policy Strategy." The strategy has two parts. First, there is a numerical definition of price stability. Second, the Governing Council announces its intention to focus on a broad-based assessment of the outlook for future prices, with money playing a prominent role.[11]

The ECB's Governing Council defines price stability as an inflation rate of close to, but less than, 2 percent, based on a euro-area-wide measure of consumer prices. The index, called the harmonized index of consumer prices (HICP), is similar to the U.S. consumer price index (CPI). The HICP is an average of retail price inflation in all the countries of the monetary union, weighted by the size of their gross domestic products. So inflation in Germany, where more than one-fourth of the total economic activity in the euro area occurs, is much more important to policy decisions than inflation in Ireland, whose economy is about one-sixteenth the size of Germany's. This arrangement has important implications for monetary policy operations, because there will surely be times when the proper policy for Ireland is to raise interest rates but the proper policy for Germany is to lower them. Given Ireland's relative size, a change in

[11]The ECB refers to this statement as its "two-pillar" strategy. Observers have been critical of the way money is included in the policy framework. If the goal is to stabilize prices, why isn't money growth just one of a wide range of indicators that are factored into policy decisions? Following a 2004 policy review, ECB practice has effectively downgraded the importance of the monetary pillar, blunting this type of criticism.

inflation or growth there has little impact on the euro area as a whole. The same is true for other small countries in the union.

The fact that the economically large countries matter much more than the small ones can affect the dynamics of the Governing Council's interest-rate decisions—remember the Council includes the heads of all the euro-area national central banks, as well as the members of the Executive Board. While the Governing Council's job is to stabilize prices in the euro area as a whole, one wonders whether the smaller countries might have undue influence on its policy decisions. To understand this concern, imagine what would happen if all the Governing Council's members pressed for actions appropriate to their own countries. The result would be a policy appropriate to the median country. And because there are only four large countries in the ECB—Germany, France, Italy, and Spain—the median country is likely to be small: Ranked by nominal GDP, Greece is the median country, accounting for less than 2 percent of 2012 euro-area GDP. The custom of drawing half the Executive Board members from the large countries and half from the small ones is not a foolproof counterweight to this tendency.

These potential shortcomings notwithstanding, evidence strongly suggests that the ECB is doing the job it is supposed to do. Despite an extraordinary crisis since 2010, the long-run inflation projections of professional forecasters remain steady at about 2 percent as of 2013, highlighting the ECB's credibility. Put differently, the Governing Council's policy has been appropriate to the euro area as a whole; it has not been skewed toward smaller countries' concerns. The specificity of the price stability objective set forth in the Treaty of Maastricht holds policymakers accountable, limiting discretion in their decision making.[12]

---

[12] Strong evidence for the effectiveness and credibility of the ECB can be found in Stephen Cecchetti and Kermit Schoenholtz, "How Central Bankers See It: The First Decade of ECB Policy and Beyond," NBER Working Paper 14489, November 2008.

Terms

Using FRED: Codes for Data in This Chapter

Data Series	FRED Data Code
Federal funds rate	FEDFUNDS
Discount rate (primary credit)	DPCREDIT
Personal consumption expenditures price index	PCEPI
Euro area harmonized index of consumer prices	CP0000EZ17M086NEST
France gross sovereign debt (percent of GDP)	GGGDTAFRA188N
Germany gross sovereign debt (percent of GDP)	GGGDTADEA188N
Italy gross sovereign debt (percent of GDP)	GGGDTAITA188N
Japan gross sovereign debt (percent of GDP)	GGGDTAJPA188N
Spain gross sovereign debt (percent of GDP)	GGGDTAESA188N
U.S. gross sovereign debt (percent of GDP)	GGGDTAUSA188N

Chapter Lessons

1. The Federal Reserve System is the central bank of the United States. Its decentralized structure comprises three primary elements:
   a. Twelve Federal Reserve Banks, each with its own board of directors, that
      i. Serve as the government's bank, issuing currency, maintaining the U.S. Treasury's bank account, and handling the Treasury's securities.
      ii. Serve as the bankers' bank, holding deposits, operating a payments system, making loans, and evaluating the safety and soundness of financial institutions in their districts.
   b. The seven-member Board of Governors in Washington, D.C., including the chair
      i. Regulates and supervises the financial system.
      ii. Oversees the Federal Reserve Banks.
      iii. Publishes economic data.
   c. The Federal Open Market Committee
      i. Makes monetary policy by setting interest rates or altering the balance sheet.
      ii. Has 12 voting members, including the seven governors and five of the 12 Reserve Bank presidents.
      iii. Meets eight times a year.
      iv. Is controlled largely by the chair.

2. The FOMC's success in meeting its objectives is enhanced by
   a. Its independence, which comes from its members' long terms, budgetary autonomy, and the irreversibility of its policy decisions.
   b. Clear communication of its policy decisions through an explanatory statement that is distributed immediately, through a quarterly press conference, and through minutes that are published three weeks after each scheduled meeting.
   c. Regular public appearances of the committee's members.

3. The European Central Bank (ECB) is the central bank for the countries that participate in the European Monetary Union—the euro area.
   a. The Eurosystem is composed of three distinct parts:
      i. The National Central Banks (NCBs) provide services to the banks and
      governments in their countries.
      ii. The European Central Bank (ECB) in Frankfurt, with its six-member Execu-
      tive Board, oversees the monetary system.
      iii. The Governing Council makes monetary policy decisions.
   b. The ECB's primary objective is to stabilize prices in the common currency area.
   c. The ECB's success in meeting its policy objectives is aided by the timely announcement of policy decisions, press conferences in which top ECB officials
   respond to questions, and the release of twice-yearly forecasts.

Conceptual and Analytical Problems

1. What are the Federal Reserve's goals, and who established them? How are Fed
   officials held accountable for meeting them? Explain why the chair is the most
   influential Fed official. *(LO1)*

2. Go to the Federal Reserve Board's website and locate the FOMC's most recent
   statement. What did the committee members say at their last meeting regarding
   the Federal funds target and the two goals of price stability and sustainable economic growth? *(LO2)*

3. Some people have argued that the high inflation of the late 1970s was a conse-
   quence of the fact that Federal Reserve Board Chairman Arthur Burns did what
   President Richard Nixon wanted him to do. What policy do you think President
   Nixon might have wanted? *(LO2)*

4. How might the ECB's pursuit of price stability as its primary objective restrict its
   response to the sovereign debt crisis in the euro area? *(LO4)*

5. Evaluate the following statement: "The Treaty of Maastricht helped solve the
   time-consistency problem in monetary policy but not fiscal policy." *(LO4)*

6. How did the response to the financial crisis of 2007–2009 alter the appointment
   process of presidents of the Federal Reserve Banks? *(LO1)*

7. What are the goals of the ECB? How are its officials held accountable for meeting them? *(LO3)*

8. Why did the sovereign debt problem of Greece—a country that accounts for less
   than 2 percent of euro-area GDP—threaten the banking system throughout the
   euro area? *(LO4)*

9. Go to the ECB's website and locate the most recent introductory statement made
   by the president of the ECB at the press conference following a Governing Council meeting. What was the Governing Council's policy decision? How was it
   justified? Is there any reference to financial stability measures? *(LO4)*

10. Do you think the FOMC has an easier or a harder time agreeing on monetary
    policy than the Governing Council of the ECB? Why? *(LO3)*

www.mhhe.com/moneyandbanking4e

11. Why did the "no-bailout" clause of the Maastricht Treaty come under stress during and after the financial crisis of 2007–2009? *(LO4)*

12. Do you think the current procedures for appointing members to the Board of Governors are consistent with the principles of good central bank design? Explain your answer. *(LO1)*

13.* Currently, all the national central banks in the Eurosystem are involved with the implementation of monetary policy. What do you think the advantage would be of centralizing the conduct of these day-to-day interactions with financial markets at the ECB in Frankfurt? Are there any disadvantages you can think of? *(LO3)*

14. If you were charged with redrawing the boundaries of the Federal Reserve districts, what criteria would you use to complete the task? *(LO1)*

15. In 2012, the FOMC stated for the first time that it aims over the longer run at an inflation rate of 2 percent (based on the price index of personal consumption expenditures). How might this announcement help secure price stability? *(LO2)*

16. Do you think the members of the ECB's Governing Council should take formal votes? Why or why not? If they do vote, how do you think the votes should be allocated? *(LO3)*

17. Why do you think the statement released after each Federal Open Market Committee meeting retains the same basic structure? *(LO2)*

18. Do you think, in the interest of transparency, the chair of the Federal Reserve Board should explain in detail the subtleties surrounding policy decisions? Why or why not? *(LO2)*

19.* If you were asked to design a new central bank, what two institutional design features of (a) the Federal Reserve System and (b) the ECB would you adopt? Explain your choices. *(LO1)*

ECONOMIC DATA | ST. LOUIS FED

Scan here for quick access to the resources for these problems. Need a barcode reader? Try ScanLife, available in your app store.

Data Exploration

For general information on using Federal Reserve Economic Data (FRED) online, visit www.mhhe.com/moneyandbanking4e and click on Student Edition, then FRED Resources.

1. How large are the public debt burdens of key euro-area economies? Are they rising or falling? Plot without recession bars the debt-to-GDP ratios of Germany (FRED code: GGGDTADEA188N), Italy (FRED code: GGGDTAITA188N), and the euro area as a whole (FRED code: GGGDTAEZA188N). Extend each line (matching its color) using the projections of the International Monetary Fund (FRED codes: GGGDTPDEA188N, GGGDTPITA188N, and GGGDTPEZA188N, respectively). Are these ratios consistent with the Maastricht Treaty's public debt-to-GDP guideline of 60 percent? *(LO4)*

2. The European Central Bank (ECB) has translated its primary objective of price stability into an explicit, quantitative goal of keeping euro-area annual inflation close to, but below, 2 percent over the medium term. Plot the percent change from a year

*Indicates more difficult problems

ago of the euro-area price level (FRED code: CP0000EZ17M086NEST). Evaluate the performance of the ECB on average since 2000 and over shorter intervals. Download the data and compute the average inflation rate for the full period and for the periods 2008–2009, 2010–2011, and 2012–present. *(LO4)*

3. In 2012, the Federal Reserve announced an inflation objective of 2 percent "over the longer run" for the price index of personal consumption expenditures (FRED code: PCEPI). However, many analysts focus on the "core" price index (FRED code: PCEPILFE), which omits the volatile food and energy components. For the Fed's horizon, does this difference matter? Plot the percent change from a year ago for both price measures since 2000. Download the data and compute the averages and standard deviations over that period. What do you conclude? *(LO2)*

4. The FOMC statement of December 12, 2012, indicated that the target range for the federal funds rate would remain appropriate at least until the rate of unemployment falls below 6½ percent or the projected rate of inflation one to two years ahead exceeds the FOMC's 2 percent objective by one-half percentage point. From January until December 2012, plot the effective federal funds (FRED code: FEDFUNDS), the unemployment rate (FRED code: UNRATE), and the inflation rate based on the percent change from a year ago of the core price index for personal consumption expenditures (FRED code: PCEPILFE). Judging by the data, would you expect FOMC interest-rate policy to change soon? *(LO2)*

5. In August 2007 and in March 2008, the Federal Reserve Board reduced the discount rate to ease liquidity conditions for banks. Plot discount window borrowing (FRED code: DISCBORR) between January 2007 and December 2008. As a second line, plot on the right axis the difference between the discount rate (FRED code: DPCREDIT) and the federal funds rate target (FRED code: DFEDTAR). Did narrowing the spread between the discount rate and the federal funds target rate trigger the borrowing surge in September–October 2008? *(LO2)*

Chapter 17

The Central Bank Balance Sheet and the Money Supply Process

Learning Objectives

Understand . . .

LO1 The central bank's balance sheet

LO2 Changing the size and mix of the balance sheet

LO3 The deposit expansion multiplier

LO4 The monetary base and the money supply

On the morning of September 11, 2001, four hijacked planes crashed: two into the World Trade Center Towers in New York City, one into the Pentagon in Washington, D.C., and one in a field in western Pennsylvania. Thousands of people died, and the world changed. The disruptions were enormous. All nonmilitary aircraft in the United States were immediately grounded and U.S. airspace was closed. In the Wall Street area, power and communications networks were shut down, closing the financial markets. Yet New Yorkers found they could still go to an ATM anywhere outside the immediate neighborhood of the attacks and withdraw cash. Despite the massive disruptions in the Wall Street area, the electronic network that processed the withdrawals continued to work.

Conditions were anything but normal inside the financial community, where the risk of a systemwide collapse was very real. But because of the immediate action of Federal Reserve officials, the financial system held together, and most of us never realized how close we came to catastrophe. At 11:45 a.m., three hours after the attacks began, the Federal Reserve Board issued a terse statement: "The Federal Reserve is open and operating. The discount window is available to meet liquidity needs." Over the next week, people throughout the Federal Reserve System made sure there was enough money circulating to keep the economy going. They bought nearly $100 billion worth of U.S. Treasury securities, extended tens of billions of dollars in loans to U.S. banks, and provided foreign central banks with the billions of dollars they needed to ensure that commercial banks in their countries could meet their obligations. They did it all from backup sites because the Federal Reserve's primary operating site, two blocks from the World Trade Center, was inaccessible.

This was one of the great successes of modern central banking. In extraordinary circumstances, quick action by the Fed kept the financial markets afloat. While some institutions and individuals will never recover from the terrorist attacks, the financial system—one of the terrorists' primary targets—returned to near normal within weeks.

Many observers assign part of the blame for the financial crisis of 2007–2009 to the policies of the Federal Reserve. However, most would agree that the Fed's extraordinary actions in 2008–2009 were critical in preventing a complete meltdown of the U.S. (and global) financial system. As one former Fed chairman put it, the Fed under Chairman Ben Bernanke went to the limits of its powers to secure financial stability in the depths of crisis.

Many of the Fed's actions in the crisis of 2007–2009 were unprecedented or had not been seen since the 1930s. For the first time since the Great Depression, the Fed lent to nonbanks and even to nonfinancial companies. The central bank created new mechanisms to increase the overall supply of liquidity and to deliver it where and when it was needed. Following the failure of Lehman Brothers in September 2008, the Fed became the "intermediary of last resort," allowing its assets to double in a matter of weeks—an unparalleled expansion. To substitute for markets that had stopped functioning normally, the Fed acquired more than $1 trillion of loans and securities that had previously been traded in the market. These extraordinary actions will affect the Fed's balance sheet for years, in contrast to the brief and much smaller policy actions after September 11, 2001.

The stories of the financial crises of September 11, 2001, and of 2007–2009 stand in stark contrast to what happened more than 70 years earlier, when policy failures led to the collapse of the U.S. banking system and precipitated the Great Depression of the 1930s. At the time, Federal Reserve officials didn't fully understand how their actions affected the supply of credit in the economy. They failed to recognize the link between changes in the Fed's balance sheet and the growth rate of money. They thought that so long as they supplied more and more cash to the economy, and so long as commercial bank account balances at the Federal Reserve banks were growing, money and credit were easily available. They were wrong. The financial system collapsed because the Fed officials had failed to provide the liquidity that sound banks needed to stay in business. As a result, virtually no one could borrow; both the amount of credit and the quantity of money in the economy plummeted.

The Fed's policymakers did their best in the 1930s, and their best wasn't very good. But at least they did it in public, which is not always the case. When the economy is suffering, or when central bankers are taking actions they aren't supposed to, they have a tendency to hide what they are doing. At times, central bankers have delayed publication of statistics or distorted the information they did provide. That's what the central bank of Thailand did in 1997. The Bank of Thailand was committed to stabilizing the value of its currency, the Thai *baht,* at an exchange rate of about 26 to one U.S. dollar. To do so, officials had to convince foreign exchange traders that they had enough dollars to buy baht if market participants started to sell. To be convinced, currency traders had to see the numbers. But in summer 1997, officials at the Bank of Thailand refused to tell anyone, even their own Minister of Finance, how many dollars the bank held.[1] When the truth got out, and everyone learned that the cupboard was bare, the baht collapsed, ending 1997 at 50 to one dollar.

To appreciate what went right in the Fed's response to September 2001 and to the crisis of 2007–2009—and what went wrong both in the United States in the 1930s and in Thailand in 1997—we need to understand how the central bank interacts with

[1]The Bank of Thailand hadn't actually sold its dollar reserves on the open market. Officials had engaged in forward transactions that committed them to sell the dollars in the future. Thus, they could claim to have dollars that in reality were committed to others. For a detailed description of this episode, see Paul Blustein, *The Chastening: Inside the Crisis That Rocked the Global Financial System and Humbled the IMF* (New York: PublicAffairs, 2001).

the financial system. What is it that central banks buy and sell? What are the assets and liabilities on their balance sheets? How do they control those assets and liabilities, and why might they want to hide them from the public? More to the point, how is the central bank's balance sheet connected to the money and credit that flow through the economy? Where *do* the trillions of dollars in our bank accounts actually come from? In answering these questions, we will combine our knowledge of how central banks work with our understanding of commercial bank operations. Let's see how the system works.

The Central Bank's Balance Sheet

As the government's banker and the bankers' banker, the central bank engages in numerous financial transactions. It supplies currency, provides deposit accounts to the government and commercial banks, makes loans, and buys and sells securities and foreign currency. All these activities cause changes in the **central bank's balance sheet**. Because the balance sheet is the foundation of any financial institution, understanding the day-to-day operation of a central bank must start with an understanding of its assets and liabilities and how they change. The structure of the balance sheet gives us a window through which we can study how the institution operates.

Central banks publish their balance sheets regularly. The Federal Reserve and the European Central Bank both do so weekly; you can find the information on their websites. (To get a sense of the changing scale and composition of the Fed's balance sheet, see Applying the Concept on page 454.) Publication is a critical part of the transparency that makes monetary policy effective. The actual published data is complicated and includes items we don't need to worry about here. Instead, we'll focus on a stripped-down version of the balance sheet, one that has been reduced to the most important components. Figure 17.1 shows the major assets and liabilities that appear in every central bank's balance sheet in one form or another. Note that the entries are divided not only into columns, with assets on the left and liabilities on the right, but into categories as well. The top row shows the assets and liabilities the central bank holds in its role as the government's bank, and the bottom row shows the assets and liabilities it holds as the bankers' bank. Let's examine each entry, starting with the assets.

Assets

The central bank's balance sheet shows three basic assets: securities, foreign exchange reserves, and loans. The first two are needed so that the central bank can perform its

Figure 17.1   The Central Bank's Balance Sheet

	Assets	Liabilities
Government's Bank	Securities Foreign exchange reserves	Currency Government's account
Bankers' Bank	Loans	Accounts of the commercial banks (reserves)

role as the government's bank; the loans are a service to commercial banks. Let's look at each one in detail.

1. *Securities* are the primary assets of most central banks. Traditionally, the Fed exclusively held Treasury securities, mostly short maturity. However, during the 2007–2009 financial crisis, the central bank chose to acquire a variety of riskier assets, including more than $1 trillion of mortgage-backed securities (MBS, page 53), making MBS the largest component of Federal Reserve assets. The quantity of securities it holds is controlled through purchases and sales known as *open market operations*. It is important to emphasize that independent central banks, not fiscal authorities, determine the quantity and mix of securities they purchase.

2. **Foreign exchange reserves** are the central bank's and government's balances of foreign currency. These are held in the form of bonds issued by foreign governments. For example, the Fed holds euro-denominated bonds issued by the German government as well as yen-denominated bonds issued by the Japanese government. These reserves are used in **foreign exchange interventions**, when officials attempt to change the market values of various currencies.

3. *Loans* are usually extended to commercial banks. But, in 2008 and 2009, as part of its extraordinary response to the financial crisis, the Fed made substantial loans to nonbanks as well. There are several kinds of loans, and their importance varies depending on how the central bank operates. **Discount loans** are the loans the Fed makes when commercial banks need short-term cash. Discount loans usually are in the millions of dollars, but the volume temporarily surged in 2008 to beyond $100 billion as the Fed battled the liquidity crisis (see Chapter 2, Lessons from the Crisis: Market Liquidity, Funding Liquidity, and Making Markets).

Prior to the financial crisis of 2007–2009, U.S. Treasury securities were the biggest, most important asset on the Federal Reserve's balance sheet. Through its liquid securities holdings the Fed controls the federal funds rate and the availability of money and credit. Foreign exchange reserves play only a small role in Fed policy, and (aside from crises) loans are almost always modest. At other central banks, this ranking of assets often differs. For example, the ECB's primary assets are collateralized loans (repos) to the banks, rather than securities.[2] In many trade-dependent economies, the primary focus is often on the level of foreign exchange reserves.

Liabilities

Turning to the liabilities side of the central bank's balance sheet, we see three major entries: currency, the government's deposit account, and the deposit accounts of the commercial banks. Again, these can be divided into two groups based on their purpose. The first two items allow the central bank to perform its role as the government's bank, while the third allows it to fulfill its role as the bankers' bank. Let's look at each in turn, again using the example of the United States to illustrate some important details.

1. *Currency.* Nearly all central banks have a monopoly on the issuance of the currency used in everyday transactions. Take a look at the top of any dollar bill

---

[2]Where the government debt market is neither deep nor liquid—as in many euro-area countries—adjustments in bank lending can be more effective than purchases and sales of securities as a means of central bank control.

APPLYING THE CONCEPT
THE FED'S BALANCE SHEET: IMPACT OF THE CRISIS

The Federal Reserve's response to the crisis of 2007–2009 transformed the size and composition of its assets and liabilities in unprecedented fashion. Table 17.1 contrasts the balance sheet at an early stage of the crisis (December 2007) with that after the worst of the crisis had passed (December 2009).

The massive expansion of the balance sheet stands out. At the end of the two-year period, the amount of assets was 2.5 times larger—$2.2 trillion versus $900 billion. Most of this increase occurred in September and October 2008, following the collapse of Lehman Brothers. Under normal circumstances, such an increase would be expected to drive up prices and nominal GDP. But this time, nominal GDP barely moved. Instead, the Fed's actions helped to prevent a repeat of the plunge of the money supply and nominal GDP that occurred in the Great Depression (see Applying the Concept: Monetary Policy in the 1930s on page 473).

As for the composition of the assets, we can see that the increase was concentrated in securities, which surged by more than $1 trillion to reach 2.3 times the amount held at the beginning of the period. Purchases of mortgage-backed and U.S. agency securities more than accounted for this gain. The Fed also boosted its lending sharply, accepting a wide variety of collateral. Some of the loans from its emergency operations (including those related to the failure of Bear Stearns in March 2008 and the collapse of AIG in September 2008) are likely to remain on the Fed's books for some time. In the discussion of unconventional monetary policy in Chapter 18, we will take a closer look at the changing scale and mix of the Fed's assets during the crisis.

The liability side of the balance sheet also was transformed during the crisis: commercial bank deposits rose nearly 100 times! This surge was triggered by the post-Lehman panic, when the Fed sought to calm banks desperately seeking a liquidity cushion by purchasing more securities and boosting discount lending. Yet, even after the liquidity crisis subsided in 2009, banks showed a clear desire to hold massive excess reserves. Lending their reserves at low interest rates to risky borrowers was unattractive for banks that faced a much higher cost of capital than before the crisis. Beginning in October 2008, banks also received interest on their reserves held at the Fed (the policy tool of paying interest on reserves is discussed in Chapter 18), further diminishing the opportunity cost of holding reserves.

Table 17.1	Balance Sheet of the Federal Reserve: December 2009 and December 2007 (Billions of dollars, month-end)	
	2009	**2007**
Assets		
Securities	$ 1,835	$ 797
Of which:		
Mortgage-backed	901	0
Federal agency debt	158	0
Foreign exchange reserves	25	47
Loans	276	25
Gold	11	11
Other assets	91	14
Total	**2,239**	**894**
Liabilities		
Currency	$ 883	$ 792
Governments' accounts	149	5
Commercial bank deposits	1,073	11
Other liabilities	81	49
Total	**2,187**	**857**
Capital (Assets minus Liabilities)	$ 52	$ 37
Notes (period mean):		
Nominal GDP	$14,454	$14,338
M1	1,696	1,376
M2	8,544	7,501

"Securities" includes all forms of repurchase agreements. "Foreign exchange reserves" does not include the U.S. Treasury Exchange Stabilization fund.

SOURCE: *Federal Reserve release H.4.1 and U.S. Treasury and Federal Reserve Foreign Exchange Operations, Quarterly Report, Table 1.*

and you will see the words "Federal Reserve Note." Currency—that is, currency circulating in the hands of the *nonbank* public—is the principal liability of most central banks.

2. *Government's account.* Governments need a bank account just like the rest of us. They have to have a place to deposit their income and a way to pay for the things they buy. The central bank provides the government with an account into which

the government deposits funds (primarily tax revenues) and from which the government writes checks and makes electronic payments. By shifting funds between its accounts at commercial banks and the Fed, the Treasury usually keeps its account balance at the Fed fairly constant. However, to improve the Fed's ability to purchase assets during the financial crisis, the Treasury temporarily increased its central bank deposits, which peaked at more than $500 billion in November 2008.

3. *Commercial bank accounts* (**reserves**). Commercial bank reserves are the sum of two parts: deposits at the central bank *plus* the cash in the bank's own vault. The first of these functions like the commercial bank's checking account. In the same way that you can take cash out of a commercial bank, the bank can withdraw its deposits at the central bank. And just as you can instruct your bank to transfer some part of your account balance to someone else, a commercial bank can transfer a portion of its deposit account balance to another bank. **Vault cash** is part of reserves; it is not part of item 1, which includes only cash held by the nonbank public. Because a bank's vault cash is available to meet depositors' withdrawal demands, it serves the insurance function for which reserves are designed. Reserves are assets of the commercial banking system and liabilities of the central bank. Reflecting policy actions taken during and after financial crises, reserves constitute the largest liability of both the Fed and the ECB as of 2013.

Of all central bank liabilities, bank reserves are the most important in determining the quantity of money and credit in the economy, and for this reason, they play a central role in monetary policy operations. Increases normally lead to a rise in deposits and to growth in the availability of money and credit; decreases do the opposite. As we saw in Chapter 12, there are two types of reserves: those that banks are required to hold, called **required reserves**, and those they hold voluntarily, called **excess reserves**. Originally, the government required banks to hold a certain level of reserves to ensure banks' safety and soundness. However, as a result of financial innovations that reduce the demand for checkable deposits, required reserves declined well below the level of overall reserves that banks wish to hold. Indeed, today's bankers hold excess reserves both as insurance against unexpected outflows and for use in conducting their day-to-day business.

The Importance of Disclosure

Buried in the mountain of paper that every central bank publishes is a statement of the bank's own financial condition. This balance sheet contains what is probably the most important information that any central bank makes public. Every responsible central bank in the world discloses its financial position regularly, most of them every week. In the same way that shareholders require a periodic accounting of the activities of the companies they own, we are all entitled to the information on our central bank's balance sheet. Without public disclosure of the level and change in the size of foreign exchange reserves and currency holdings, it is impossible for us to tell whether the policymakers are doing their job properly. Publication of the balance sheet is an essential aspect of central bank transparency. Delays, like those during the Mexican debt crisis of 1994–1995, are a clear sign of impending disaster.

Another sign of trouble is misrepresentation of the central bank's financial position. A particularly egregious case of lying by a central bank occurred in the Philippines in 1986, when then-President Ferdinand Marcos was desperate to remain in power. We

INFORMATION

know now that Marcos ordered the central bank to print enormous amounts of currency so that he could try to buy enough individual votes to win the election. And the central bank kept quiet about the elaborate scheme to conceal the monetary expansion.[3]

The Monetary Base

Together, currency in the hands of the public and reserves in the banking system—the privately held liabilities of the central bank—make up the **monetary base**, also called **high-powered money**. As we will see in the next section, the central bank can control the size of the monetary base, the base on which all other forms of money stand. (The term *high-powered* comes from the fact that the quantity of money and credit in the economy is a multiple of currency plus banking system reserves.) As we will see later in this chapter, when the monetary base increases by a dollar, the quantity of money typically rises by several dollars.

To get some sense of the relationship between the monetary base and the quantity of money, we can look at a few numbers. In January 2013, the U.S. monetary base was $2.75 trillion. At the same time, M1 was $2.47 trillion and M2 was $10.45 trillion. So M1 was smaller than the monetary base, while M2 was nearly 4 times as great as the monetary base. Later in the chapter we'll return to these relationships and learn how the financial crisis of 2007–2009 altered them. But first, let's see how the central bank adjusts its balance sheet and changes the size of the monetary base.

Changing the Size and Composition of the Balance Sheet

Unlike you and me, the central bank controls the size of its balance sheet. That is, policymakers can enlarge or reduce their assets and liabilities at will, without asking anyone. We can't do that. To see the point, think about a simple transaction you engage in regularly, like buying $50 worth of groceries. When you arrive at the checkout counter, you have to pay for your purchases. Let's say you do it with a check. When the supermarket deposits your check in the bank, your $50 moves through the payments system. It is credited to the supermarket's account and, eventually, debited from yours. As long as you started with at least $50 in your checking account, the process works smoothly. The grocery store's bank account is $50 larger and yours is $50 smaller.

Now think about a standard transaction in which the central bank buys a $1 million government security. What's the difference between this purchase and yours at the grocery store? First, there is its size. The central bank's transaction is 20,000 times as big as yours. But that's not all. To see another important difference, let's look at the mechanics of the security purchase. To pay for the bond, the central bank writes a $1 million check payable to the bond dealer who sells the bond. (In real life, the transaction is done electronically.) After the check is deposited, the dealer's commercial bank account is credited $1 million. The commercial bank then sends the check back to the central bank. When it gets there, something unusual happens. Remember, at the end of your check's journey, your bank debited your checking account $50. But when the central bank's $1 million check is returned, the central bank credits the reserve account of the bank presenting it $1 million. And that's it. The central bank can simply

---

[3]Newspaper stories at the time documented what happened in the Philippines. See, for example, Chris Sherwell, "Banknotes in Triplicate Add to Filipino's Confusion," *Financial Times,* February 22, 1986.

buy things (the $1 million bond, for instance) and then create liabilities to pay for them (the $1 million increase in reserves in the banking system). It can increase the size of its balance sheet as much as it wants.

Turning to the specifics of this process, we'll look at four types of transaction: (1) an *open market operation,* in which the central bank buys or sells a security; (2) a *foreign exchange intervention,* in which the central bank buys or sells foreign currency reserves; (3) the extension of a *discount loan* to a commercial bank by the central bank; and (4) the decision by an individual to *withdraw cash* from the bank. Each of these has an impact on both the central bank's balance sheet and the banking system's balance sheet. Open market operations, foreign exchange interventions, and discount loans all affect the *size* of the central bank's balance sheet and change the size of the monetary base. Cash withdrawals by the public are different. They shift components of the monetary base, changing the composition of the central bank's balance sheet but leaving its size unaffected.

To figure out the impact of each of these four transactions on the central bank's balance sheet, we need to remember one simple rule: When the value of an asset on the balance sheet increases, either the value of another asset decreases so that the net change is zero or the value of a liability rises by the same amount. What's true for assets is also true for liabilities. An increase in a liability is balanced either by a decrease in another liability or by an increase in an asset. The principle is the same regardless of whose balance sheet we are looking at.

In the following sections, we will discuss these transactions in the context of the Federal Reserve's institutional structure. As we go through the examples, remember that the securities and foreign exchange transactions are managed by the Federal Reserve Bank of New York, while discount loans are extended by all 12 Reserve Banks.

Open Market Operations

When the Federal Reserve buys or sells securities in financial markets, it engages in **open market operations**. These open market purchases and sales have a straightforward impact on the Fed's balance sheet. To see how the process works, take the common case in which the Federal Reserve Bank of New York purchases $1 billion in U.S. Treasury bonds from a commercial bank.[4] To pay for the bonds, the Fed transfers $1 billion into the reserve account of the seller. The exchange is done electronically. Panel A of Figure 17.2 shows the change in the Federal Reserve's balance sheet. This is called a **T-account**. The left side shows the change in assets and the right side gives the change in liabilities. Panel A of Figure 17.2 shows the impact of this **open market purchase** on the Fed's balance sheet: its assets and liabilities both go up $1 billion, increasing the monetary base by the same amount.

What is the impact of the Fed's open market purchase on the banking system's balance sheet? The Fed exchanged $1 billion in securities for $1 billion in reserves, both of which are banking system assets. Panel B of Figure 17.3 shows the balance-sheet effect of the exchange.

Note that there are no changes on the liabilities side of the banking system's balance sheet, and the changes on the asset side sum to zero.

---

[4]The Fed purchases securities from a list of *primary government securities dealers,* which includes a combination of banks and securities dealers. While we could examine the mechanics of the Fed's purchase assuming the other side is either an investment bank or a dealer, it would complicate the analysis without providing additional insight.

| Figure 17.2 | Balance Sheet Changes after the Federal Reserve Purchases a U.S. Treasury Bond |

A. Federal Reserve's Balance Sheet

Assets		Liabilities	
Securities +$1 billion (U.S. Treasury bond)		Reserves +$1 billion	

B. Banking System's Balance Sheet

Assets		Liabilities	
Reserves +$1 billion Securities −$1 billion (U.S. Treasury bond)			

| Figure 17.3 | Balance Sheet Changes after the Federal Reserve Purchases a German Government Bond |

A. Federal Reserve's Balance Sheet

Assets		Liabilities	
Foreign exchange reserves +$1 billion (German government bonds in euros)		Reserves +$1 billion	

B. Banking System's Balance Sheet

Assets		Liabilities	
Reserves +$1 billion Securities −$1 billion (German government bonds)			

Looking at Figure 17.2, you'll notice that reserves are an asset to the banking system but a liability to the Federal Reserve. This may seem confusing, but it shouldn't. It's like your own bank account. The balance in that account is your asset, but it is your bank's liability.

Before we move on, we should note that if the Fed *sells* a U.S. Treasury bond through what is known as an **open market sale**, the impact on everyone's balance sheet is reversed. All the credits in the two figures become debits and vice versa. The Fed's balance sheet shrinks, as does the monetary base; the banking system's reserves decline, while its securities holdings increase.[5]

Foreign Exchange Intervention

What happens if the U.S. Treasury instructs the Federal Reserve to buy $1 billion worth of euros? The answer is that the Federal Reserve Bank of New York buys German government bonds, denominated in euros, from the foreign exchange departments of large commercial banks and pays for them with dollars.[6] Like an open market bond purchase, this transaction is done electronically and the $1 billion payment is credited directly to the reserve account of the bank from which the bonds were bought. The impact on the Fed's balance sheet is almost identical to that of the open market

[5]Prior to the financial crisis of 2007–2009, the Fed virtually never sold securities. It always bought; the only question was how much. The Fed had always intentionally left itself in a position in which it needed to buy securities on a temporary basis through repurchase agreements. During the crisis, however, the Fed sold securities to limit the expansion of its balance sheet. Over time, it will probably reduce its assets further by allowing some assets to mature and selling others.

[6]As a technical matter, the Fed first purchases euro currency with dollars and then uses the proceeds to buy the German government bonds. But because it owns the euro currency for a very short time, only a few hours, we are ignoring that intermediate transaction.

YOUR FINANCIAL WORLD
Why We Still Have Cash

For years experts have been predicting the demise of paper currency—cash. First credit cards were going to take over; now it is electronic forms of money. But still we have cash. In fact, we have more cash than ever. During the 1990s, as more and more people got hold of credit cards and clever people tried to introduce e-money, the volume of dollar bills outstanding rose 8 percent per year. To put it in concrete terms, the amount of U.S. currency in the hands of the public doubled in 10 years. By 2013, currency in circulation amounted to something like $3,700 per U.S. resident. The per capita level of currency in the euro area was similar: more than €2,700 (the equivalent of $3,500). Nothing seems to dissuade people from holding paper notes issued by the central bank.

There are a number of explanations for this phenomenon. First, there is convenience: the easiest way to repay $20 you borrowed from a friend is to use cash. Second, some people use cash to avoid paying taxes. Third,

large-denomination notes of major trusted currencies (like $100 bills and €500 bills) are widely held outside their area of origin (see Applying the Concept: Where Are All Those $100 Bills? in Chapter 2). Finally, there is the fact that cash provides anonymity. When you pay with cash, no one cares who you are and the transaction can't be traced back to you. This arrangement has obvious advantages for people engaged in drug dealing, smuggling, and other black-market activities. But if the demand for cash came solely from people engaged in illegal activities, the proper response would be to outlaw it. The fact is that law-abiding people use cash for legal transactions in which they would prefer to remain nameless. Surely we don't want to lose the ability to hide some of our purchases from public view.

Because cash is almost completely anonymous, there is little chance that electronic products will completely replace paper currency any time soon.

operation, as Panel A of Figure 17.3 shows. The Fed's assets and liabilities both rise by $1 billion, and the monetary base expands with them.

Because the Federal Reserve bought the euros from a commercial bank, the impact on the banking system's balance sheet is straightforward. The result, shown in Panel B of Figure 17.3, is nearly identical to the impact when the Fed bought bonds through an open market purchase (see Figure 17.2). In both cases, the banking system's securities portfolio falls by $1 billion and reserve balances rise by an equal amount. The only difference is the exact assets that decline. In a standard open market operation, the reduction is in bank holdings of U.S. government bonds; here it is in their holdings of euro-denominated assets.

Discount Loans

The Federal Reserve does not force commercial banks to borrow money; the banks ask for loans. To get one, a borrowing bank must provide collateral.[7] While this usually takes the form of U.S. Treasury bonds, the Fed has always been willing to accept a broad range of securities and loans as the collateral for lending to banks. During the crisis, when discount loans surged, this willingness facilitated lending. Not surprisingly, when the Fed makes such a loan, it changes the balance sheet of both institutions. For the borrowing bank, the loan is a liability that is matched by an offsetting increase in the level of its reserve account. For the Fed, the loan is an asset that is created in exchange for a credit to the borrower's reserve account. The impact on the Federal Reserve's balance sheet is shown in Panel A of Figure 17.4.

[7]Remember, *collateral* is the term used to describe specific assets pledged by a borrower that a lender can seize in the event of nonpayment. To obtain a discount loan, a bank must identify specific assets (usually bonds) that the Fed can take if the bank doesn't repay the loan. The ECB, which relies primarily on collateralized lending to implement policy, publishes each day a list of eligible collateral. As of August 2013, that list contained more than 38,000 financial instruments.

Figure 17.4 Balance Sheet Changes after the Federal Reserve Makes a Discount Loan

A. Federal Reserve's Balance Sheet		B. Banking System's Balance Sheet	
Assets	**Liabilities**	**Assets**	**Liabilities**
Discount loans +$100 million	Reserves +$100 million	Reserves +$100 million	Discount loans +$100 million

Note that the increase in loans is an asset to the Fed, while the change in reserves increases its liabilities. Once again, the impact on the Fed's balance sheet is the same as that of an open market purchase or an increase in foreign exchange reserves. The extension of credit to the banking system raises the level of reserves and expands the monetary base.

The impact on the banking system's balance sheet mirrors the impact on the Fed, with reserves and loans both increasing. In this case, however, commercial banks have increased the size of their balance sheet by borrowing from the Fed (see Panel B of Figure 17.4).

In summary, open market purchases, an increase in foreign exchange reserves, and the extension of discount loans all increase the reserves available to the banking system, expanding the monetary base. We turn now to a different type of transaction, one that affects only the composition—not the size—of the monetary base.

Cash Withdrawal

The Federal Reserve can always shift its holdings of various assets, selling U.S. Treasury bonds and using the proceeds to buy Japanese yen, or engaging in an offsetting sale of a U.S. Treasury security after a bank takes out a discount loan. But the same is not true of its liabilities. Because the Fed stands ready to exchange reserves for currency on demand, it does not control the mix between the two. The nonbank public—the people who hold the cash—controls that.

You may be surprised to learn that when you take cash from an ATM, you are changing the Federal Reserve's balance sheet. The reason is that vault cash is part of reserves, while the currency holdings of the nonbank public—your cash and mine—are not. By moving your own assets out of your bank and into currency, you force a shift from reserves to currency on the Fed's balance sheet. The transaction is complicated, involving the nonbank public (you and me), the banking system, and the central bank, so understanding it means looking at three balance sheets.

Consider an example in which you withdraw $100 from your checking account. This transaction changes the composition of the asset side of your balance sheet, as shown in Panel A of Figure 17.5. (Because there is no change in your liabilities, the changes in the asset side of your balance sheet must sum to zero.)

But that isn't all. By taking $100 out of the cash machine, you had an impact on your bank's balance sheet as well. Remember, cash inside the bank—vault cash—counts as reserves, so by withdrawing cash from your bank, you decreased the banking system's reserves. The change in the banking system's T-account is shown in Panel C of Figure 17.5.

It should come as no surprise to you that when you take your money out of the bank, the bank's balance sheet shrinks. Here we see that your cash withdrawal forced the

Figure 17.5   Balance Sheet Changes after a Private Person Withdraws Cash from His or Her Bank Account

A. Nonbank Public's Balance Sheet

Assets		Liabilities
Currency	+$100	
Checkable deposits	−$100	

B. Federal Reserve's Balance Sheet

Assets	Liabilities	
	Currency	+$100
	Reserves	−$100

C. Banking System's Balance Sheet

Assets		Liabilities	
Reserves	−$100	Checkable deposits	−$100

banking system to contract its balance sheet. Note that the change in bank assets equals the change in bank liabilities.

Finally, there is the Federal Reserve. Remember, the Fed controls the size of its own balance sheet, so your transactions can't affect that. But what you can do is change the composition of the Fed's liabilities. By withdrawing cash, you changed the amount of currency outstanding—a change that shows up on the Fed's balance sheet as a shift from reserves to currency. Both are liabilities. Panel B of Figure 17.5 shows what the Fed's balance sheet looks like. Note that the monetary base hasn't changed. Remember that the monetary base equals currency plus reserves, and one went up while the other went down. But the *relative size* of each component of the monetary base has changed.

Table 17.2 summarizes the impact of each of the four transactions we have just studied on the size and composition of the Federal Reserve's balance sheet. Open market operations and foreign exchange interventions are both done at the discretion of

Table 17.2   Changes in the Size and Composition of the Federal Reserve's Balance Sheet and the Monetary Base

Transaction	Initiated by	Typical Action	Impact
Open market operation	Central bank	Purchase of Treasury bond	Increases reserves, the size of the Fed's balance sheet, and the monetary base
Foreign exchange intervention	Central bank	Purchase of German government bond	Increases reserves, the size of the Fed's balance sheet, and the monetary base
Discount loan	Commercial bank	Extension of loan to commercial bank	Increases reserves, the size of the Fed's balance sheet, and the monetary base
Cash withdrawal	Nonbank public	Withdrawal of cash from ATM	Decreases reserves and increases currency, leaving the size of the Fed's balance sheet and the monetary base unchanged

the central bank, while the level of discount borrowing is decided by the commercial banks. The nonbank public decides how much currency to hold.

It is worth noting that there are countries where the process works differently. As we will see in Chapter 19, when a central bank wishes to control its country's exchange rate rather than the domestic interest rate, one way to do so is to stand ready to buy and sell foreign currency. In such cases, foreign exchange intervention is not truly under the central bank's control. Instead, the private sector decides when the purchases and sales are made and how large they are. That is essentially what the Bank of Thailand was doing in 1997, and when it started to run out of foreign currency reserves, the system collapsed.

The Deposit Expansion Multiplier

Central bank liabilities form the base on which the supplies of money and credit are built; that is why they are called the *monetary base*. The central bank controls the monetary base, causing it to expand and contract. But most of us don't focus much attention on the monetary base. Our primary interest is in the broader measures of money, M1 and M2, which are mostly liabilities of private banks. Recall from Chapter 2 that M1 is currency plus demand deposits and M2 adds time deposits to M1. This is the *money* we think of as available for transactions. What is the relationship between the central bank's liabilities and these broader measures of money? How do reserves become bank deposits? The answer is that the banking system makes them, in a process called **multiple deposit creation**.

Deposit Creation in a Single Bank

To see how deposits are created, let's start with an open market purchase in which the Federal Reserve buys $100,000 worth of securities from a bank called *First Bank*. While First Bank may have its own reasons for selling the securities, we are assuming that the Fed initiated the transaction. So if First Bank doesn't sell the securities, some other bank will.

The Fed's purchase leaves the bank's total assets unchanged, but it shifts $100,000 out of securities and into reserves, increasing reserves by the amount of the open market purchase. The impact on First Bank's balance sheet is shown in Panel A of Figure 17.6. (It is similar to Panel B of Figure 17.2.)

What does First Bank do in response to this change in the composition of its assets? The bank's management must do something. After all, it just sold a U.S. Treasury bond to the Fed and received reserves that typically bear a lower interest rate in exchange. If it does nothing, the bank's revenue will fall, and so will its profits. With liabilities unchanged, the increase in First Bank's reserves doesn't affect the quantity of reserves the bank is required to hold, so it counts as an increase in *excess reserves*. Remember that banks hold reserves for two reasons: because regulators require them and because banks need them to conduct their daily business. But when reserves rise in response to the sale of a security, something profitable has to be done with the proceeds.

The most natural thing for a bank to do is to lend out the excess—and no more. To keep the example simple, assume that First Bank has just received a loan application from Office Builders Incorporated (OBI). OBI is seeking $100,000 to finance the continued construction of an office building. First Bank approves the loan and credits OBI's checking account with an additional $100,000. Figure 17.6 Panel B shows First Bank's balance sheet immediately after the loan is made.

APPLYING THE CONCEPT
THE FED'S RESPONSE ON SEPTEMBER 11, 2001

Until the financial crisis of 2007–2009, U.S. banks typically held about $40 billion worth of cash in their vaults and $10 billion in reserve deposits at Federal Reserve Banks. Their discount loan balance was virtually zero. On a typical day, the trading desk of the Federal Reserve Bank of New York purchased $3 billion to $5 billion worth of bonds in temporary open market operations but did not intervene in the foreign exchange markets.

The days following September 11, 2001, were *not* normal. The Wall Street area in lower Manhattan became inaccessible, and some very large banks were forced to temporarily close. Although these banks could receive payments to their accounts at the Fed, they could not make payments. Thus, funds were flowing into a few huge reserve accounts, but nothing was coming out—these banks were sucking up the lifeblood of the financial system, its liquidity.

Fed officials saw the looming crisis and reacted immediately, providing reserves to all banks that needed them. A group of about 20 New York Fed employees slept in the New York Fed's building the night of September 11 so they could carry out open market operations the next morning. Then

they moved to a contingency site across the Hudson River to continue their work. On Thursday, September 13, and Friday, September 14, the Fed increased its security holdings by more than $70 billion, made $8 billion in discount loans, and bought almost $20 billion worth of euros.

Helping to boost reserves was the fact that because civilian planes were grounded, a paper check drawn on a bank very far from the bank where it was deposited could not be flown to the district of the paying bank for collection. The amount of a credited but uncollected check is called *float*, which is an increase in the credited bank's reserves at the Fed unbalanced by a reduction in the paying bank's reserves. By Thursday, September 13, float had exploded, rising from its usual level of about $0.5 billion to a whopping $50 billion.

Thus, we see that over a two-day period, the Fed's transactions and the rise of float increased banking system reserves by almost $150 billion.* This massive injection of reserves was quickly drained over the next week as the system returned to normal. Because the banking system withstood the enormous shock and was able to meet its commitments, people's finances were more or less unaffected.

*The Fed's actions are described in detail in the Federal Reserve Bank of New York's 2001 annual report on open market operations, available at *www.newyorkfed.org/markets/omo/omo2001.pdf*. As we saw in Chapter 2 (Your Financial World), check clearing is now electronic, so float has largely disappeared.

OBI did not take out its $100,000 loan to leave it in First Bank's checking account. The company borrowed to pay suppliers and employees. So OBI's financial officer proceeds to write checks totaling $100,000. As First Bank makes good on OBI's checks, OBI's checking account balance falls, but so does First Bank's reserve account balance. When the entire $100,000 loan has been spent, First Bank's balance sheet looks like Panel C of Figure 17.6.

Figure 17.6   Changes in First Bank's Balance Sheet after the Fed's Purchase of a U.S. Treasury Bond

A. Immediate Impact

Assets		Liabilities
Reserves	+$100,000	
Securities	−$100,000	

B. After the Extension of a Loan

Assets		Liabilities	
Reserves	+$100,000	Checkable deposits	+$100,000
Securities	−$100,000		
Loans	+$100,000		

C. After Withdrawal by the Borrower

Assets		Liabilities	
Reserves	$0	Checkable deposits	$0
Securities	−$100,000		
Loans	+$100,000		

In summary, following a $100,000 open market purchase of securities by the Fed, First Bank makes a loan equal to the amount of newly created excess reserves. That loan replaces the securities as an asset on First Bank's balance sheet.

Deposit Expansion in a System of Banks

First Bank's loan and OBI's expenditures can't be the end of the story because the suppliers and employees paid by OBI took their checks to the bank and deposited them. As the checks made their way through the payments system, First Bank's reserves were transferred to the reserve accounts of the suppliers' and employees' banks. *Only the Fed (the central bank) can create and destroy the monetary base.* The nonbank public determines how much of it ends up as reserves in the banking system and how much is in currency; all the banks can do is move the reserves they have around among themselves. So, assuming cash holdings don't change following an open market purchase, the reserves created by the Fed must end up somewhere. Let's follow them to see where they go.

We'll start by making four assumptions that allow us to focus on the essential parts of the story: (1) banks hold no excess reserves; (2) the reserve requirement is 10 percent of checking account deposits; (3) when the level of checking account deposits and loans changes, the quantity of currency held by the nonbank public does not; and (4) when a borrower writes a check, none of the recipients of the funds deposit them back in the bank that initially made the loan. Now, let's say that OBI uses the $100,000 loan to pay for steel girders from American Steel Co. American Steel deposits the $100,000 in its bank, Second Bank, which credits American's checking account. When OBI's check clears, Second Bank's reserve account at the Federal Reserve Bank is credited with $100,000. That's the transfer of reserves from First Bank. The result is shown in Panel A of Figure 17.7.

The additional $100,000 in American Steel's checking account is costly for Second Bank to service. American Steel will want to receive interest on its idle balance as well as access to it for payments. And the reserves Second Bank just received usually pay

Figure 17.7 Changes in Balance Sheets

Assuming a 10 percent reserve requirement, banks hold no excess reserves, and there are no changes in currency holdings.

less interest than a loan. In the same way that First Bank lent out its new reserves following the Fed's open market purchase, Second Bank will make a loan after American Steel has made its deposit. How large will the loan be? Because the reserve requirement is 10 percent, Second Bank must hold an additional $10,000 in reserves against the new $100,000 deposit. Individual banks can't make loans that exceed their excess reserves, so the largest loan Second Bank can make is $90,000—and that's what it does. (Remember, we're assuming banks hold no excess reserves.) If the borrower immediately uses the $90,000 loan, Second Bank's balance sheet will look like Figure 17.7 Panel B.

This new loan, and the reserves that go with it, must go somewhere, too. Let's say that it is deposited in yet another bank, Third Bank, which makes a loan equal to 90 percent of the new deposit. The change in Third Bank's balance sheet is shown in Panel C of Figure 17.7. (Recall, we're assuming that the owner of the checking account at Third Bank doesn't withdraw any cash.)

At this point, a $100,000 open market purchase has created $100,000 + $90,000 = $190,000 in new checking account deposits at Second Bank and Third Bank and $100,000 + $90,000 + $81,000 = $271,000 in new combined loans at First Bank, Second Bank, and Third Bank. But the process doesn't stop there. The $81,000 loan from Third Bank is deposited into Fourth Bank, where it creates an additional $81,000 in checking account deposits. Fourth Bank then makes a loan that is 90 percent of $81,000, or $72,900, and the $72,900 is deposited. And so on, as shown in Figure 17.8.

Table 17.3 shows the consequences of a $100,000 open market purchase for the banking system as a whole. As the $100,000 in new reserves spreads through the banking system, it generates $1,000,000 in deposits and $1,000,000 in loans. With a 10 percent reserve requirement, each added dollar in reserves expands to $10 in deposits, increasing the quantity of money by a factor of 10.

With a bit of algebra, we can derive a formula for the **deposit expansion multiplier**—the increase in commercial bank deposits following a one-dollar open market purchase, (assuming there are no excess reserves in the banking system and no changes in the amount of currency held by the nonbank public).

There's an easy way and a hard way to figure out the size of the deposit expansion multiplier. Let's start with the easy way. Imagine that the entire banking system is composed of a single bank—call it the Monopoly Bank. When the country's banking system is made up of just one bank, everyone has to use it. That means that any payment made from one person to another is just a transfer between two accounts in the Monopoly Bank. Because the managers of the Monopoly Bank know this, they don't need to worry about losing reserves when they make a loan.

Figure 17.8 Multiple Deposit Creation

Assuming a 10 percent reserve requirement, banks hold no excess reserves, and there are no changes in currency holdings.

| Table 17.3 | Multiple Deposit Expansion following a $100,000 Open Market Purchase Assuming a 10% Reserve Requirement |

Bank	Increase in Deposits	Increase in Loans	Increase in Reserves
First Bank	$ 0	$ 100,000	$ 0
Second Bank	$ 100,000	$ 90,000	$ 10,000
Third Bank	$ 90,000	$ 81,000	$ 9,000
Fourth Bank	$ 81,000	$ 72,900	$ 8,100
Fifth Bank	$ 72,900	$ 65,610	$ 7,290
Sixth Bank	$ 65,610	$ 59,049	$ 6,561
.	.	.	.
.	.	.	.
.	.	.	.
The Banking System	$1,000,000	$1,000,000	$100,000

So here's the question. For each dollar change in reserves arising from a transaction with the Fed, how much can the Monopoly Bank change its deposits? If we continue to assume that the Monopoly Bank holds no excess reserves and that there is no change in currency held by the nonbank public, then its level of reserves is just the **required reserve ratio** r_D times its deposits. If required reserves are RR and deposits are D, the level of reserves can be expressed

$$RR = r_D D \qquad (1)$$

Any change in deposits creates a corresponding change in reserves, expressed as

$$\Delta RR = r_D \Delta D \qquad (2)$$

Now let's go back to the question we started with: What is the change in the level of deposits following a one-dollar change in reserves? From equation (2), we can see that the answer is

$$\Delta D = \frac{1}{r_D} \Delta RR \qquad (3)$$

So for every dollar increase in reserves, deposits increase by $(1/r_D)$. This is the simple deposit expansion multiplier. If the reserve requirement is 10 percent, as it was in our example, then the simple deposit expansion multiplier equals $(1/0.1) = 10$, and a $100,000 open market purchase generates a $1,000,000 = 10 \times \$100,000$ increase in the quantity of money. To see why this makes sense, note that if deposits rose by more than $1,000,000 following the addition of $100,000 in reserves, the banking system would violate the reserve requirement. And if deposits rose by less than 10 times the change in reserves, some banks would be holding excess reserves, which violates one of the assumptions we made at the outset.

The hard way to compute the simple deposit expansion multiplier is to look back at Table 17.3 and add up the entries. Notice that starting with Third Bank, each entry in the column "Increase in Deposits" equals $(1 - r_D)$ times the entry above it, where r_D is the reserve requirement (measured as a decimal). With a reserve requirement of 10 percent, $r_D = 0.10$, $(1 - r_D) = 0.90$, so each entry is 0.90 times the one above it. For example, $90,000 equals 0.90 times $100,000; $81,000 equals 0.90 times $90,000.

Thus, a one-dollar increase in reserves creates an increase in deposits equal to the sum of this series: $[1 + (1 - r_D) + (1 - r_D)^2 + (1 - r_D)^3 + \ldots]$. Using a formula from the Appendix to Chapter 4, we can determine that this expression equals $(1/r_D)$.

Before we continue, it is important to emphasize that there is nothing magical about *increases* in reserves and deposit *expansion*. A *decrease* in reserves will generate a deposit *contraction* in exactly the same way. That is, a $100,000 open market sale, in which the Fed sells a security in exchange for reserves, will reduce the level of deposits. From equation (3), we see that with a 10 percent reserve requirement, the contraction in deposits is $10 \times \$100,000 = \$1,000,000$.

The Monetary Base and the Money Supply

We have made considerable headway in understanding the link between the central bank's balance sheet and the quantity of money in the economy. A change in reserves precipitates a significant change in the level of loans and checkable deposits in the banking system. But the simple deposit expansion multiplier is too simple. In deriving it, we ignored a few important details.

First, we assumed that banks lent out the entirety of the reserves that were not required, leaving no excess reserves in the banking system. In fact, banks do hold some excess reserves, in part to protect against unexpected deposit outflows, but also for other reasons. Demand for excess reserves can change dramatically and unpredictably. For example, during the financial crisis of 2007–2009, excess reserves surged as banks built a safety cushion to insure themselves against the loss of funding liquidity (see Chapter 2, Lessons from the Crisis: Market Liquidity, Funding Liquidity, and Making Markets) and unanticipated drawdowns of credit lines.

Second, we ignored the fact that the nonbank public holds cash. As people's account balances rise, they have a tendency to hold more cash. From our discussion of the central bank's balance sheet, we know that when individuals change their cash holdings, they change the level of reserves in the banking system. Both these considerations affect the relationship among reserves, the monetary base, and the quantity of money in the economy. Let's look at the relationship in more detail.

Deposit Expansion with Excess Reserves and Cash Withdrawals

To see how important excess reserves and cash holdings are, we can go back through the deposit expansion story, this time taking them into account. Assume that banks want to hold excess reserves equal to 5 percent of checking account deposits and that the holder of a checking account withdraws 5 percent of a deposit in cash. Recall that the reserve requirement is 10 percent.

To understand the implication of these changes, let's go back to the example in the last section, in which the Fed purchased $100,000 worth of securities from First Bank (Panel A of Figure 17.6), which proceeded to make a $100,000 loan to Office Builders Incorporated (Panel B of Figure 17.6). OBI then used the $100,000 to purchase steel from American Steel, which withdrew the funds from First Bank and deposited them in a checking account in Second Bank. This brings us to the T-account in Panel A of Figure 17.7. If American Steel takes some of the $100,000 in cash and Second Bank wishes to hold excess reserves, then the next loan cannot be $90,000.

Assuming that American Steel removes 5 percent of its new funds in cash, that leaves $95,000 in the checking account and $95,000 in Second Bank's reserve account.

"God bless you, sir."

(Look back at Panel C of Figure 17.5 to see the impact of a cash withdrawal on the banking system's balance sheet.) Because Second Bank wishes to hold excess reserves equal to 5 percent of deposits, it will want to keep reserves of 15 percent of $95,000, or $14,250. That means making a loan of only $80,750. Instead of Panel B of Figure 17.7, Second Bank's balance sheet looks like Figure 17.9.

We can continue as before, following the proceeds of Second Bank's loan as it is deposited in Third Bank. Assuming that the depositor of the loan's proceeds wishes to hold 5 percent of the deposit in cash and that Third Bank wants to hold excess reserves equal to 5 percent of deposits, the increase in deposits will be $80,750 minus $4,037.50 equals $76,712.50, and Third Bank will make a loan of $65,205.63, keeping reserves of $11,506.87. Compare these numbers with the ones in Table 17.3 and you will see how much smaller the deposit expansion becomes if we take into account excess reserves and cash withdrawals.

In the last section, we derived the result that a one-dollar change in reserves created a change in deposits equal to one over the reserve requirement, or $(1/r_D)$. So, for an r_D of 10 percent, a $1 change in reserves generated a $10 change in deposits. But now the analysis is more complicated and the deposit expansion is smaller. The desire of banks to hold excess reserves and the desire of account holders to withdraw cash both reduce the impact of a given change in reserves on the total deposits in the system. The more excess reserves banks desire to hold, and the more cash the public withdraws, the smaller the impact. In fact, these two factors operate in the same way as an increase in the reserve requirement.

The Arithmetic of the Money Multiplier

To better understand the relationship between deposits and reserves, we can derive the *money multiplier,* which shows how the quantity of money (checking account deposits plus currency) is related to the monetary base (reserves in the banking system plus currency held by the nonbank public). Keep in mind that the monetary base is the quantity that the central bank can control.

Figure 17.9	Change in Second Bank's Balance Sheet following a Deposit and Extension of a Loan

Assets		Liabilities	
Required reserves	+$ 9,500	American Steel's checking account	+$95,000
Excess reserves	+$ 4,750		
Loan	+$80,750		

Assuming excess reserves and cash holdings. Note: American Steel also has $5,000 in cash.

If we label the quantity of money *M* and the monetary base *MB*, the money multiplier *m* is defined by the relationship

$$M = m \times MB \tag{4}$$

To derive the money multiplier, we start with a few simple relationships: money equals currency *(C)* plus checkable deposits *(D)*; the monetary base *(MB)* equals currency plus reserves in the banking system *(R)*; and reserves equal required reserves *(RR)* plus excess reserves *(ER)*. Writing these relationships as simple equations, we have

$$M = C + D, \qquad \text{Money} = \text{Currency} + \text{Checkable deposits} \tag{5}$$

$$MB = C + R, \qquad \text{Monetary base} = \text{Currency} + \text{Reserves} \tag{6}$$

$$R = RR + ER, \qquad \text{Reserves} = \text{Required reserves} + \text{Excess reserves} \tag{7}$$

These are just accounting definitions; the next step is to incorporate the behavior of banks and individuals. Starting with banks, we know that their holdings of required reserves depend on the required reserve ratio r_D. But what about excess reserves? In our earlier discussion, we assumed that banks hold excess reserves as a proportion of their deposits, and that *the amount of excess reserves a bank holds depends on the costs and benefits of holding them.* The cost of excess reserves is the interest on the loans that could be made with them, less the interest received on reserve balances, while the benefits have to do with safety should deposits be withdrawn suddenly. The higher the interest rate on loans, the lower banks' excess reserves will be; the greater banks' concern over the possibility of deposit withdrawals, the higher their excess reserves will be.

Labeling the **excess reserve-to-deposit ratio** {*ER/D*}, we can rewrite the reserve equation (7) as

$$R = RR + ER \quad \text{Reserves} = \text{Required reserves} + \text{Excess reserves}$$
$$= r_D D + \{ER/D\}D \tag{8}$$
$$= (r_D + \{ER/D\})D$$

That is, banks hold reserves as a proportion of their deposits.

Turning to the nonbank public, we need to take account of their currency holdings. Again, as in the preceding example, we assume that people hold currency as a fraction of their deposits. That is,

$$C = \{C/D\}D \tag{9}$$

where {*C/D*} is the **currency-to-deposit ratio**. The *decision of how much currency to hold depends on costs and benefits* in the same way as the decision to hold excess reserves. The cost of currency is the interest it would earn on deposit, while the benefit is its lower risk and greater liquidity. As interest rates rise, cash becomes less desirable. But if the riskiness of alternative holdings rises or liquidity falls, then cash becomes more desirable, and {*C/D*} will rise.

Bringing all these elements together, we can rewrite the expression for the monetary base using the reserve and currency expressions. That gives us

$$MB = C + R \qquad \text{Monetary base} = \text{Currency} + \text{Reserves}$$
$$= \{C/D\}D + (r_D + \{ER/D\})D \tag{10}$$
$$= (\{C/D\} + r_D + \{ER/D\})D$$

We see now that the monetary base has three uses: required reserves, excess reserves, and cash in the hands of the nonbank public. But our interest is in the relationship

YOUR FINANCIAL WORLD
Your Excess Reserves

Banks hold excess reserves to ensure that they have sufficient resources to meet unexpected withdrawals. Your bank guarantees that it will provide you with immediate access to the funds in your checking account, either by giving you cash or by honoring your check when it arrives. Sound business practice means having a little extra on hand, just in case people withdraw more money than usual. That is a cost of operating the bank.

In the same way that a bank holds excess reserves to insure itself against unexpectedly large withdrawals, individuals need to have an emergency fund to pay for unexpected expenses that can't be postponed. The appropriate size of the emergency fund varies from person to person; the exact amount depends on considerations like your tolerance for risk, the number of income earners in your household, the amount of your income, the deductible on your insurance policies, and the stability of your employment. Most financial planners recommend that individuals hold emergency funds equal to a minimum of three, and preferably six to nine, months' income in cash accounts. The accumulation of an emergency fund is the first step in any investment program. Unless you really like risk, make sure you have such a fund before you make any other investments. Like a bank, we all need excess reserves.

between the quantity of money and the monetary base. To find this, we can solve equation (10) for the level of deposits.

$$D = \frac{1}{\{C/D\} + r_D + \{ER/D\}} \times MB \qquad (11)$$

This expression tells us how much deposits change with a change in the monetary base. Notice that if we ignore excess reserves and cash withdrawals, so that {ER/D} and {C/D} both equal zero, we get the same result as in equation (3), that a change in deposits equals ($\frac{1}{r_D}$) times the change in the monetary base. For a reserve requirement of 10 percent, that meant that a one-dollar change in the monetary base increased deposits by $10. Adding the excess reserve-to-deposit and currency-to-deposit ratios that we used in the example after Figure 17.9, 5 percent each, this equation tells us that a one-dollar increase in the monetary base will increase deposits by [1/(0.10 + 0.05 + 0.05)] = 5.

Returning to the derivation of the money multiplier, we can take the expression for money and rewrite it as

$$\begin{aligned} M &= C + D \qquad \text{Money} = \text{Currency} + \text{Checkable deposits} \\ &= \{C/D\}D + D \qquad\qquad\qquad\qquad\qquad\qquad (12) \\ &= (\{C/D\} + 1)D \end{aligned}$$

Substituting D from equation (11) gives us the final answer:

$$\boxed{M = \frac{\{C/D\} + 1}{\{C/D\} + r_D + \{ER/D\}} \times MB} \qquad (13)$$

Money = Money multiplier × Monetary base

This result is somewhat complicated, but it is worth studying. Equation (13), highlighted by the red rectangle, tells us that the quantity of money in the economy depends on four variables:

LESSONS FROM THE CRISIS
THE IMPACT ON MONEY SUPPLY

The central bank supplies the *monetary base*—the sum of bank reserves and currency in circulation—but it is banks and the banking system that supply money. Chapter 17 explains this useful adage: bank behavior determines the *deposit expansion multiplier*—the increase in the quantity of money that comes from an extra dollar of reserves.

The financial crisis of 2007–2009 highlighted the role of bank behavior in the money supply process. When the crisis peaked in September 2008, the deposit expansion multiplier plummeted to a fraction of its normal value. Why?

The standard process of deposit expansion assumes that banks wish to lend out most of an additional dollar of reserves supplied by the Fed. Multiple deposit expansion occurs as the banking system repeatedly lends the extra asset until the Fed's addition to reserves is used up.

However, following the collapse of Lehman Brothers in September 2008, banks panicked. In seeking to hold more excess reserves, they short-circuited the deposit expansion process, and the deposit expansion multiplier collapsed.

What caused the panic? The liquidity crisis threatened the banks' survival (see Chapter 2, Lessons from the Crisis: Market Liquidity, Funding Liquidity, and Making Markets). Excess reserves that banks hold at the Fed are the most liquid assets in the U.S. financial system. They can be used to make a payment or be converted into cash immediately. Amid the crisis, the extra profits that banks might be able to make by lending out their excess reserves were far too small to be worth the risk they faced—failure if they couldn't make a payment or honor a withdrawal request when necessary.

The Fed met the surge in liquidity demand in unprecedented fashion. During the five months following August 2008, officials added more than $800 billion to reserves—an increase of nearly 20 times. And because banks had virtually no interest in lending out these reserves, almost all of the increase flowed into excess reserves.*

The behavior of the monetary aggregates M1 and M2 highlights the impact of bank caution. Over those five months, the absolute increase of M2—$538 billion—was *smaller* than the Fed's addition to reserves! Instead of the normal multiple deposit expansion, the crisis led to only a fractional expansion. Banks were so wary that they accumulated reserves in excess of demand deposits. As a result, the M2 money multiplier plunged by about half, while the M1 multiplier dropped below 1 (see Figure 17.11).

What would have happened if the Federal Reserve had not met the radical increase in the demand for excess reserves? The experience of the Great Depression suggests that banks, desperate for liquid assets, would have cut back loans to healthy borrowers much more aggressively, and the money supply would have collapsed (see Applying the Concept: Monetary Policy in the 1930s on page 473).

The Fed learned a key lesson from its 1930s failure: a panic by banks can undermine the money supply even if bank reserves and currency in circulation are growing. Supporting the money supply may require an explosion of the monetary base until the panic-driven demand for reserves recedes. The lesson paid off: the aggressive liquidity supply by the Federal Reserve in the financial crisis of 2007–2009 was a critical difference between this episode and the Great Depression.

*In October 2008, the Federal Reserve began paying interest on reserves (see the Chapter 18 discussion of this policy tool). This shift helps explain why reserve demand stayed high even as the crisis receded.

---

1. The monetary base, which is controlled by the central bank.
2. The reserve requirement imposed by regulators on banks that accept deposits.
3. The desire on the part of banks to hold excess reserves.
4. The demand for currency by the nonbank public.

To see how the quantity of money in the economy changes, we can look at the impact of each of these four elements. The first is the easiest. We know that if the monetary base increases, holding bank and public behavior constant, the quantity of money increases. Looking at the second and third elements—those factors affecting reserves—we see that an increase in either the reserve requirement or banks' excess reserve holdings decreases the money multiplier. So for a fixed level of the monetary base, an increase in either r_D or $\{ER/D\}$ reduces M.

Finally, there is the currency-to-deposit ratio. What happens when individuals increase their currency holdings at a fixed level of the monetary base? Because $\{C/D\}$ appears in both the numerator and the denominator of the money multiplier in equation (13), we can't immediately tell whether the change creates an expansion

Table 17.4 Factors Affecting the Quantity of Money

Factor	Who Controls It	Change	Impact on M
Monetary base	Central bank	Increase	Increase
Required reserve-to-deposit ratio	Central bank	Increase	Decrease
Excess reserve-to-deposit ratio	Commercial banks	Increase	Decrease
Currency-to-deposit ratio	Nonbank public	Increase	Decrease

or a contraction. Fortunately, logic gives us the answer that is correct whenever, as has usually been the case, deposits exceed total reserves. (Reserves have surpassed checkable deposits since 2008 but remain well below total deposits.) When an individual withdraws cash from the bank, he or she increases currency in the hands of the public and decreases reserves, so the monetary base is unaffected. But the decline in reserves creates a multiple deposit contraction. (Remember, every dollar in reserves creates more than a dollar's worth of deposits, raising the quantity of money more than a dollar.) Because each extra dollar held in currency raises M by only a dollar, when reserves are converted to currency, the money supply contracts. Table 17.4 summarizes the effect of changes in the four components of the money supply.

A short numerical example illustrates the computation of the money multiplier.[8] At the end of 2012, banks held required reserves of \$111.6 billion and excess reserves of \$1,458.7 billion. Currency in the hands of the public was \$1,092.4 billion, while deposit accounts (demand deposits plus other checkable deposits) amounted to \$1,401.6 billion. These amounts imply that the required reserve ratio (r_D) was (111.6/1,401.6) = 0.08; the excess reserve-to-deposit ratio $\{ER/D\}$ was (1,458.7/1,401.6) = 1.04; and the currency-to-deposit ratio $\{C/D\}$ (1,092.4/1,401.6) = 0.78. Substituting these amounts into equation (13), we get the M1 money multiplier:

$$m = \frac{0.78 + 1}{0.78 + 0.08 + 1.04} = \frac{1.78}{1.90} = 0.94 \tag{14}$$

That year-end 2012 value for the M1 multiplier is only about half the value preceding the financial crisis of 2007–2009. The plunge reflected a surge in excess reserves, which boosted the excess reserve-to-deposit ratio $\{ER/D\}$ from only 0.03 at the end of 2006 to 1.04 at the end of 2012. Replacing 1.04 with 0.03 in equation (14) raises the multiplier to 2.00. The enormous level of excess reserves at the end of 2012, when interest rates were close to zero, reflected the low opportunity cost of holding idle reserve balances and the lingering caution among banks in the aftermath of the financial crisis.

---

[8]The example in the following paragraph is based on the Federal Reserve Board's H.3 and H.6 releases that are neither seasonally adjusted nor adjusted for changes in reserve requirements. In addition, the excess reserve number used is not the official one, but includes "surplus vault cash," which serves the same economic purpose as conventionally calculated excess reserves. As of July 2013, the H.3 release no longer reports excess reserves, but these can be estimated by subtracting reserve balances required (FRED code: RESBALREQ) from total reserve balances maintained (FRED code: RESBALNS). Note that these new measures of reserves exclude vault cash.

APPLYING THE CONCEPT
MONETARY POLICY IN THE 1930S

STABILITY

The notion of the money multiplier was originally developed to analyze U.S. monetary history from 1860 to 1960.* The 1930s were among the most turbulent years in that era. While we may never know what really caused the collapse of the U.S. economic and financial system during the Great Depression, we have learned some important lessons about how to run monetary policy. One of them is that central bankers need to look at both the monetary base and the money multiplier to figure out whether their policies are working.

In the early 1930s, Federal Reserve officials saw their balance sheet growing. From the beginning of 1931 to early 1934, currency plus reserves increased 14 percent, from $7 billion to $8 billion. That was more than double the annual growth rate during the 1920s boom. It really seemed as if the monetary base was growing very fast, and that was all that monetary policy could do. But what policymakers failed to understand was that, while their liabilities were growing, the money multiplier was plummeting. Beginning in late 1930, the ratio of M2 to the monetary base fell almost continuously, from 6½ to 3½. The wholesale collapse of banking and the financial system had increased the risk that bank deposits would not remain liquid, driving up both individual currency holdings and banks' excess reserve holdings. The result was that the quantity of money in the economy fell by roughly a quarter at the same time that the monetary base was growing! Figure 17.10 shows the pattern. In the top panel, you can see the monetary base increasing steadily while M2 collapses. The bottom panel displays the dramatic increase in the currency-to-deposit ratio that was largely responsible for the decline in the money multiplier that is also shown there.

The conclusion is that the central bank needs to worry not just about its own balance sheet, but about the ability of the financial system to transform reserves into deposits. Failure of either one is disastrous.

Figure 17.10   Components of Money, 1928–1936

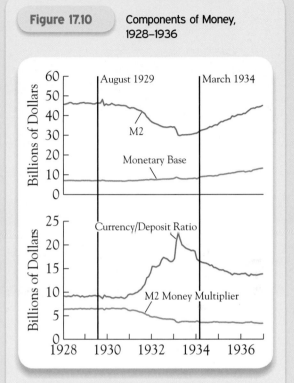

Data show that during the Great Depression, from mid-1929 to early 1934 the monetary base was growing while M2 was collapsing. The reason was that the money multiplier was falling because the currency/deposit ratio rose sharply as a result of bank panics.

SOURCE: Data compiled from Milton Friedman and Anna J. Schwartz. *A Monetary History of the United States* (Princeton, NJ: Princeton University Press, 1963). © 1963 NBER, 1991 renewed. Reprinted by permission of Princeton University Press.

*Almost everything you would ever want to know about this period in U.S. monetary history is contained in Milton Friedman and Anna J. Schwartz, *A Monetary History of the United States, 1867 to 1960* (Princeton, NJ: Princeton University Press, 1963).

The Limits of the Central Bank's Ability to Control the Quantity of Money

At this point, we might discuss why the various factors affecting the quantity of money change over time. For example, market interest rates affect the cost of holding both excess reserves and currency. So as interest rates increase, we would expect to see both $\{ER/D\}$ and $\{C/D\}$ fall, increasing the money multiplier and the quantity of money. If these changes in the money multiplier were predictable, a tight link would exist between the monetary base and the quantity of money—a link the central bank might

Figure 17.11 The M1 and M2 Money Multipliers, 1980–2013

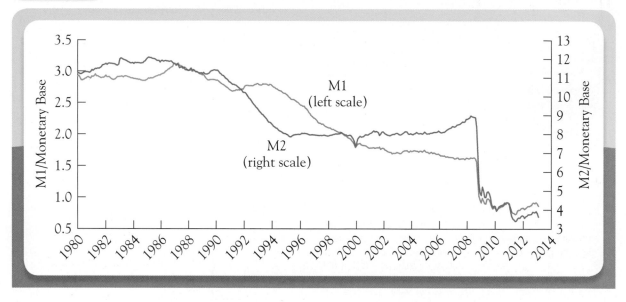

SOURCE: *Board of Governors of the Federal Reserve System (FRED data codes: M1SL, M2SL, and AMBSL).*

choose to exploit in its policymaking. While such a link made sense in a discussion of the U.S. economy in the 1930s (see Applying the Concept on page 473), and might still be important in emerging countries like China and India, for countries with sophisticated financial systems it no longer is. In places like the United States, Europe, and Japan, the link between the central bank's balance sheet and the quantity of money circulating in the economy has become too weak and unpredictable to be exploited for policy purposes.[9]

The problem is that the money multiplier is just too variable; you can see it in the data. Figure 17.11 plots the ratio of the M1 and M2 to the monetary base from 1980 to 2013. The results are striking. Both money multipliers were reasonably stable during the 1980s, but then began to fall steadily over the next decade or so, and then plunged after the failure of Lehman Brothers in 2008 (see Lessons from the Crisis: The Impact on Money Supply on page 471). From 1994 to 2013, the M1 multiplier fell from almost 3 to less than 1.

If the problem were confined to M1, policymakers could turn to controlling M2. But as the data show, the M2 multiplier has followed roughly the same pattern as the M1 multiplier, falling from 12 in the mid-1980s to 8 by the end of the 1990s, and plunging below 4 by 2011.

The conclusion is clear: The relationship between the monetary base and the quantity of money is not something that a central bank can exploit for short-run

[9]For 20 years, the Federal Reserve was required to publish target ranges for the growth rate of the monetary aggregates. Twice a year, in the *Monetary Policy Report to Congress,* we could count on getting a look at the FOMC's targets for money growth. That is, until the July 2000 issue. Buried in a footnote of that report was the following announcement: "At its June meeting, the FOMC did not establish ranges for growth of money and debt in 2000 and 2001. The legal requirement to establish and to announce such ranges had expired, and . . . for many years [they] have not provided useful benchmarks for the conduct of monetary policy." See footnote 2 in Section 1 of the report, available on the Federal Reserve Board's website.

IN THE NEWS
The Monetary Base Is Exploding. So What?

gregmankiw.blogspot.com

By Greg Mankiw

Monday, December 28, 2009

An article in Saturday's *Wall Street Journal* says that some big-league investors are betting that inflation will rise significantly. The reason? "The nation's exploding monetary base is a harbinger of inflation." Is this right? Probably not.

It is true that the monetary base is exploding [see Table 17.1]. Normally, such a surge in the monetary base would be inflationary. The textbook story is that an increase in the monetary base will increase bank lending, which will increase the broad monetary aggregates such as M2, which in the long run leads to inflation.

That is not happening right now, however. The broader monetary aggregates are not surging. Much of the base is instead being held as excess reserves.

But, you might ask, won't the inflationary logic eventually take hold as the economy recovers and banks start lending more freely? Not necessarily. Recall that the Fed now pays interest on reserves. As long as the interest rate on reserves is high enough, banks should be happy to hold onto those excess reserves. That should prevent a surge in the monetary base from being inflationary.

Here is one way to think about it. The standard way of reducing the monetary base is open market operations. The Fed sells Treasury bills, say, and drains reserves from the banking system, reducing the monetary base. But consider what this means in the current monetary regime. An open market operation merely removes interest-paying reserves from a bank's balance sheet and replaces them with interest-paying T-bills. What difference does it make? None at all.

Both reserves and T-bills are interest-paying obligations of the Federal government (including the Federal Reserve). They are essentially perfect substitutes. The monetary base, however, includes one of them but not the other, largely for historical reasons.

The bottom line is that when reserves pay interest, the monetary base is a pretty uninteresting economic statistic.

Does this mean that investors should stop worrying about inflation? No. Yet the worry should stem not from the monetary base but from the political economy and difficult tradeoffs facing monetary policymakers. As the economy recovers, interest rates will likely need to rise. Will the Bernanke Fed, feeling the political heat, get behind the curve and allow inflation to take off? Will it decide that a little bit of inflation is not so bad compared with the alternative of risking an anemic recovery, a double dip recession, or (gasp!) congressional action to reduce Fed independence? Maybe. This is, I think, the right way to argue that higher future inflation is a plausible outcome.

I don't know whether such inflation worries are justified. But I am pretty sure that the exploding monetary base is not, by itself, a reason to fear a coming surge in inflation.

SOURCE: Greg Mankiw, *gregmankiw.blogspot.com,* December 28, 2009. Used with permission.

LESSONS OF THE ARTICLE

The link between rapid money growth and inflation is well established. But rapid growth of the monetary base need *not* lead to rapid money growth. Beginning in 2008, the M1 and M2 money multipliers (the ratios of the monetary aggregates to the monetary base) collapsed as banks hesitated to lend out their reserves (see Figure 17.11). Also, the interest paid on reserves by the Fed tends to raise banks' demand for reserves and lower the money multiplier. Nonetheless, when the U.S. recovery strengthens enough, the Fed will have to raise the target federal funds rate to keep inflation low.

policy purposes. Instead, as we will discuss in detail in Chapter 20, modern central banks keep an eye on trends in money growth because that is what ultimately determines inflation. For short-run policy, however, interest rates have become the monetary policy tool of choice, while, in a financial crisis, other balance-sheet tools help address liquidity needs and market disruptions more directly. That is the subject of the next chapter.

Terms

central bank's balance sheet, 452

currency-to-deposit ratio, 469

deposit expansion multiplier, 465

discount loans, 453

excess reserves, 455

excess reserve-to-deposit ratio, 469

foreign exchange intervention, 453

foreign exchange reserves, 453

high-powered money, 456

monetary base, 456

multiple deposit creation, 462

open market operations, 457

open market purchase, 457

open market sale, 458

required reserve ratio, 466

required reserves, 455

reserves, 455

T-account, 457

vault cash, 455

Using FRED: Codes for Data in This Chapter

Data Series	FRED Data Code
Nominal GDP	GDP
M1	M1SL
M2	M2SL
Monetary base	AMBSL
Monetary base (NSA)	BOGMBASE
Currency in circulation	CURRSL
Checkable deposits	TCDSL
Total reserve balances maintained (NSA)	RESBALNS
Reserve balance requirements (NSA)	RESBALREQ
Discount window borrowings	DISCBORR
Treasury securities held by Fed (NSA)	TREAST
Federal Reserve assets (NSA)	WALCL
MBS held by Fed (NSA)	MBST

NSA: not seasonally adjusted.

Chapter Lessons

1. The central bank uses its balance sheet to control the quantity of money and credit in the economy.
   a. The central bank holds assets and liabilities to meet its responsibilities as the government's bank and the bankers' bank.
   b. Central bank assets include securities, foreign exchange reserves, and loans.

c. Central bank liabilities include currency, the government's account, and reserves.

d. Reserves equal commercial bank account balances at the central bank plus vault cash.

e. The monetary base, also called high-powered money, is the sum of currency and reserves, the two primary liabilities of the central bank.

2. The central bank controls the size of its balance sheet.

a. The central bank can increase the size of its balance sheet, raising reserve liabilities and expanding the monetary base, through
   i. Open market purchases of domestic securities.
   ii. The purchase of foreign exchange reserves (in the form of bonds issued by a foreign government).
   iii. The extension of a loan to a commercial bank.

b. The central bank can decrease the size of its balance sheet, lowering reserve liabilities and reducing the monetary base, through the sale of domestic or foreign securities.

c. The public's cash withdrawals from banks shift the central bank's liabilities from reserves to currency and shrink the size of the banking system balance sheet.

3. Bank reserves are transformed into checkable deposits through multiple deposit creation. In the simplest case, this process is limited by the reserve requirement.

a. When a bank's reserves increase, the bank makes a loan that becomes a deposit at a second bank.

b. The second bank then makes another loan, but the amount of the loan is limited by the reserve requirement.

c. This process continues until deposits have increased by a multiple that is equal to one over the reserve requirement.

4. The money multiplier links the monetary base to the quantity of money in the economy.

a. The size of the money multiplier depends on
   i. The reserve requirement.
   ii. Banks' desire to hold excess reserves.
   iii. The public's desire to hold currency.

b. While the central bank controls the level of the monetary base, it cannot control the money multiplier. Financial crises can trigger dramatic changes in the multiplier.

c. Practices such as deposit sweeping have weakened the connection between the central bank's balance sheet and the quantity of money.

Conceptual and Analytical Problems

1. Follow the impact of a $100 cash withdrawal through the entire banking system, assuming that the reserve requirement is 10 percent and that banks have no desire to hold excess reserves. *(LO3)*

2. Suppose a major bank needs to borrow $20 billion overnight that it cannot obtain from private creditors. The Fed is willing to make a discount loan of $20 billion provided that it will not alter interbank lending rates. How can it do so? *(LO1)*

3. Compute the impact on the money multiplier of an increase in the currency-to-deposit ratio from 10 percent to 15 percent when the reserve requirement is 10 percent of deposits, and banks' desired excess reserves are 3 percent of deposits. *(LO3)*

4. Does the Federal Reserve frequently purchase or sell gold or foreign exchange as part of its efforts to change the money supply? *(LO1)*

5. Consider an open market purchase by the Fed of $3 billion of Treasury bonds. What is the impact of the purchase on the bank from which the Fed bought the securities. Compute the impact on M1 assuming that: (1) the required reserve ratio is 10 percent, (2) the bank does not wish to hold extra reserves, and (3) the public does not wish to hold currency. *(LO3)*

6. When you withdraw cash from your bank's ATM, what happens to the size of the Fed's balance sheet? Is there any reason for the Fed to react to your action? *(LO1)*

7.* Why is currency circulating in the hands of the nonbank public considered a liability of the central bank? *(LO1)*

8. How did the financial crisis of 2007–2009 affect the size and composition of the balance sheet of the Federal Reserve? *(LO1)*

9. Suppose the currency-to-deposit ratio is 0.25, the excess reserve-to-deposit ratio is 0.05. and the required reserve ratio is 0.10. Which will have a larger impact on the money multiplier: a rise of 0.05 in the currency ratio or in the excess reserves ratio? *(LO4)*

10. Is the money multiplier model still useful for policymakers? If not, why not? *(LO4)*

11. Based on Figure 17.11, explain why the multipliers fell sharply with the onset of the financial crisis of 2007–2009. Why did they remain at this lower level after the crisis ended? *(LO3)*

12. The U.S. Treasury maintains accounts at commercial banks. What would be the consequences for the money supply if the Treasury shifted funds from one of those banks to the Fed? *(LO2)*

13.* Explain how an incomplete understanding at the Federal Reserve of the relationship between the central bank's balance sheet and the money supply contributed to the Great Depression. How did the Fed's behavior during the financial crisis of 2007–2009 illustrate that it had learned a valuable lesson from the Great Depression? *(LO4)*

14. Suppose you examine the central bank's balance sheet and observe that since the previous day, reserves had fallen by $100 million. In addition, on the asset side of the central bank's balance sheet, securities had fallen by $100 million. What activity did the central bank carry out earlier in the day to lead to these changes in the balance sheet? *(LO3)*

15. Do you think the central bank was aiming to increase, decrease, or maintain the size of the money supply by carrying out the changes described to its balance sheet in Problem 14? Explain your answer. *(LO4)*

*Indicates more difficult problems

16. Looking again at the situation described in Problem 14, do you think the size of the banking system's balance sheet would be affected immediately by these changes to the central bank's balance sheet? Explain your answer. *(LO2)*

17. Do you think the Federal Reserve successfully carried out its role as lender of last resort in the wake of the terrorist attacks on September 11, 2001? Why or why not? *(LO2)*

18.* In carrying out open market operations, the Federal Reserve usually buys and sells U.S. Treasury securities. Suppose the U.S. government paid off all its debt. Could the Federal Reserve continue to carry out open market operations? *(LO2)*

19. In which of the following cases will the size of the central bank's balance sheet change? *(LO2)*

 a. The Federal Reserve conducts an open market purchase of $100 million U.S. Treasury securities.

 b. A commercial bank borrows $100 million from the Federal Reserve.

 c. The amount of cash in the vaults of commercial banks falls by $100 million due to withdrawals by the public.

20.* You pick up the morning newspaper and note a headline reporting a major scandal about the Federal Deposit Insurance Corporation that is likely to undermine the public's confidence in the banking system. What impact, if any, do you think this scandal might have on the relationship between the monetary base and the money supply? *(LO4)*

Data Exploration

Scan here for quick access to the resources for these problems. Need a barcode reader? Try ScanLife, available in your app store.

For general information on using Federal Reserve Economic Data (FRED) online, visit www.mhhe.com/moneyandbanking4e and click on Student Edition, then FRED Resources.

1. Plot on a weekly basis the ratio of currency (FRED code: CURRENCY) to checkable deposits (FRED code: TCD) from the start of 2000 through 2002. Download the data and identify the week of the downward spike in the graph. Do you think the spike reflects the currency term in the numerator or the deposits term in the denominator? Explain your reasoning. *(LO2)*

2.* Figure 17.11 shows a sharp decline of the M1 money multiplier in 2008. What caused the drop? Using the indicators for currency (FRED code: CURRENCY), total reserve balances maintained (FRED code: RESBALNS), reserve balances required (FRED code: RESBALREQ), and checkable deposits (FRED code: TCDSL), plot since 2000 the currency-to-deposit ratio and the excess reserve-to-deposit ratio. Which one caused the M1 money multiplier to plunge? (*Hint:* To estimate excess reserves, see footnote 8. Divide RESBALREQ by 1000 to convert the units to billions of dollars.) *(LO3)*

3. In the Great Depression, the Fed allowed the money supply to decline. To confirm that the Federal Reserve learned from this lesson, plot since 2000 the M2 multiplier—the ratio of M2 (FRED code: M2SL) to the monetary base (FRED code: AMBSL)—and, on the right axis, the level of M2. Explain how the Fed was conducting policy in order to sustain the expansion of M2. *(LO4)*

4. Prior to the financial crisis of 2007–2009, the Fed seldom reduced its holdings of Treasury securities. Plot for the 2007–2009 period the Fed's Treasury holdings (FRED code: TREAST) and its total assets (FRED code: WALCL) on a weekly basis. Did the Fed's practices change during the crisis? If so, how? (*Hint:* Examine Table 17.1 to help with your response.) *(LO2)*

5. Thousands of the data series on FRED are provided directly by the Board of Governors of the Federal Reserve System, including hundreds of indicators from the Fed's weekly balance sheet report (H.4.1 Factors Affecting Reserve Balances). How does this balance sheet transparency affect the conduct of monetary policy? *(LO1)*

Chapter 18

Monetary Policy: Stabilizing the Domestic Economy

Learning Objectives

Understand . . .

LO1   Fed and ECB conventional policy tools

LO2   How policy tools link to objectives

LO3   Simple guides for policy setting

LO4   Unconventional policy tools

Central bankers have a long list of goals and a short list of tools they can use to achieve them. They are supposed to stabilize prices, output, the financial system, exchange rates, and interest rates, yet the only real power they have comes from their control over their own balance sheet and their monopoly on the supply of currency and reserves. To achieve their goals, policymakers can change the size of the monetary base by buying and selling assets—primarily government securities in the case of the Fed—and by making loans to banks. They can also alter the mix of assets they hold.

Traditionally, central banks choose a target for the market interest rate on overnight interbank loans and adjust the scale of the monetary base to hit that target. In the United States, the rate at which banks make overnight loans to each other is known as the federal funds rate. Through a "channel" or "corridor" system, the Fed limits the deviations of the market federal funds rate from the target by adjusting the rate they charge for discount loans to banks in need of funds (*the discount rate,* which sets a ceiling on the market federal funds rate) and the rate they pay on reserves banks hold at the central bank (*the deposit rate,* which puts a floor under the market federal funds rate). These three interest rates—the federal funds rate, the discount rate, and the deposit rate—are the primary tools of monetary policy during normal times.[1] However, when key markets do not function properly, as in a financial crisis, or when policymakers judge conventional interest rate policy to be inadequate, central banks also may adjust the size and composition of their balance sheet to achieve key policy goals.

Interest rates play a central role in all of our lives. They are the cost of borrowing for those of us who need resources and the reward for lending to those of us with savings. Higher interest rates tend to restrict the growth of credit, making it harder for businesses and households to get financing and for individuals to find or keep jobs. Little

---

[1]As we will see, the Fed has a fourth conventional policy tool, reserve requirements, but that instrument has taken a back seat to the other three in macroeconomic management.

wonder that everyone is preoccupied with interest rates and that the business press is constantly speculating about whether the Federal Open Market Committee will change its target.

Between September 2007 and December 2008, the FOMC lowered its target for the federal funds rate 10 times, including once between normally scheduled meetings, taking it from 5.25 percent to a range of 0 to 0.25 percent. This marked the first time since the 1930s that the Fed hit the **zero bound** on the nominal federal funds rate. Because banks can always hold cash—which pays zero interest—they will not lend their reserves at a negative nominal interest rate. Therefore, the nominal policy rate faces a zero bound—it can never fall below zero.[2]

The Fed's extraordinary reduction of the federal funds rate was a direct consequence of policymakers' belief that real economic activity was plunging amid the worst global financial crisis since the Great Depression. From the start of 2008, real GDP fell in five of the succeeding six quarters. When it hit bottom in the spring of 2009, GDP was about 4 percent lower than a year earlier, the largest drop in more than 60 years. The unemployment rate climbed nearly 6 percentage points—a post–World War II record—from its trough of 4.4 percent to a peak of 10 percent. For a few months in mid-2008 during an oil-related inflation spike, the Fed's rate-cutting briefly paused, but as the deep recession lowered inflation, policy rates resumed their march to the zero bound.

Remarkably, even setting the federal funds rate target at essentially zero wasn't enough to stabilize the economy! The crisis had undermined the willingness and ability of major financial intermediaries to lend. It had disrupted the function of key financial markets, including those for interbank loans, commercial paper, home mortgages, and even municipal bonds. Healthy nonfinancial firms that had always been able to borrow short term in order to pay their employees, purchase materials for production, and the like suddenly couldn't find access to funds and faced ruin. At the same time, fears of deflation (akin to Japan's experience in the 1990s) threatened to keep the real interest rate (the nominal interest rate minus the expected inflation rate) from falling as the Fed eased. As we will see in Chapter 21, it is the real interest rate that drives economic activity.

In this environment, the Federal Reserve moved to substitute itself for dysfunctional intermediaries and markets. To do that, policymakers undertook the most dramatic alteration of the Fed's balance sheet in history (see Figure 18.1). Beginning with the Bear Stearns rescue in March 2008, the Fed lent massively to fragile financial institutions. Then, after the September 2008 failure of Lehman Brothers, the Fed's balance sheet exploded in unprecedented fashion (see Chapter 17, Table 17.1, and Figure 18.1). Authorities created a variety of new programs aimed at supplying funds directly to key financial markets by directly or indirectly purchasing a wide variety of financial instruments. At various points during 2008 and 2009, the Fed lent more than $100 billion through the discount window, offered nearly $500 billion of credit at auction, acquired more than $300 billion of long-term Treasury securities and $1 trillion of mortgage-backed securities, and had net holdings of commercial paper (CP) in excess of $300 billion. Over time, as financial conditions normalized and the economy bottomed, the Fed's discount lending and its interventions in the CP market wound down.

---

[2]In theory, altering the unit of account electronically ("e-dollars") would make it feasible to pay negative interest rates, but no country has tried this. See Miles Kimball, "How Paper Money Is Holding the U.S. Recovery Back," November 2012, *www.qz.com/21797/the-case-for-electric-money-the-end-of-inflation-and-recessions-as-we-know-it.*

| Figure 18.1 | U.S. Federal Reserve Assets (billions of U.S. dollars), July 2007–July 2013 |

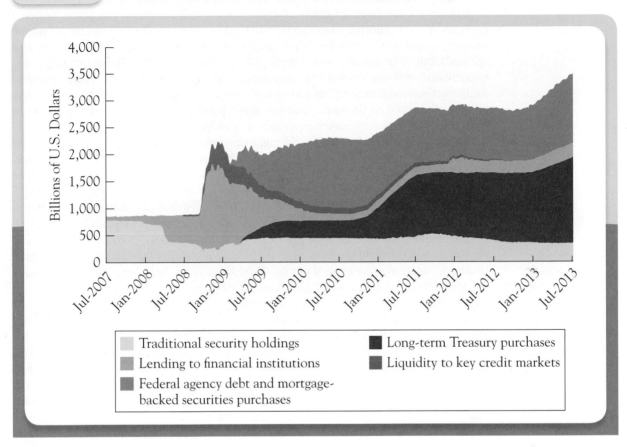

Traditional security holdings
Lending to financial institutions
Federal agency debt and mortgage-backed securities purchases

Long-term Treasury purchases
Liquidity to key credit markets

SOURCE: *Federal Reserve Bank of Cleveland.*

Yet, the Fed's balance sheet continued to expand in unprecedented fashion, climbing above $3.5 trillion in mid-2013, about four times the precrisis level. Despite this rapid expansion of the monetary base and a near-zero federal funds rate, the economic recovery from the Great Contraction of 2007–2009 proceeded at the slowest pace in postwar experience—after four years of anemic growth, the unemployment rate remained well above the peak of the previous recession.

Other major central banks, including the Bank of England, the Bank of Japan, and the ECB, pursued similar policies. In each case, policy interest rates fell to record lows, while the size of the central bank balance sheets expanded in extraordinary fashion.

The Federal Reserve has been widely accused of failing to anticipate the financial crisis and even of contributing to it. And, its aggressive actions to restore financial and economic stability following the crisis have proven controversial, attracting radically different reactions, including praise for effective monetary policy stabilization, criticism for massive market intervention, and warnings about severe inflation risks.

We have emphasized on several occasions that the economy relies on the central bank to ensure the stability of the financial system when it is under stress. In Chapter 17, we saw that the Federal Reserve reacted to the terrorist attacks of September 11, 2001, by temporarily flooding the banking system with reserves through discount window loans. Looking back from the perspective of the Fed's response to the crisis of 2007–2009, the September 11 episode seems remarkably small, brief, and contained.

To sum up, the financial crisis of 2007–2009 and the ensuing recession were the most severe and enduring since the Great Depression, while the subsequent economic recovery was the weakest. To steady the financial system and the economy, the Fed utilized its three principal **conventional policy tools**—the federal funds rate target, the rate for discount window lending, and the deposit rate—to the fullest possible extent to support economic activity, including lowering its federal funds target rate essentially to zero. Policymakers then proceeded to develop and use a variety of **unconventional policy tools**—including massive purchases of risky assets and the communication of its intent to keep interest rates low over an extended period. To be able to lend to a wide range of institutions, the Fed—for the first time since the 1930s—invoked its emergency powers to lend to nonbanks (see Chapter 15, Lessons from the Crisis). These unconventional measures added meaningfully to the conventional actions.

Against this extraordinary background, *Time* magazine called the Fed "the most important and least understood force shaping the American—and global—economy." In this chapter, we will see how the Fed uses its policy tools, both conventional and unconventional, to achieve economic stability. We will see that those tools are quite similar to those of other central banks. We will focus on three links: the link between the central bank's balance sheet and its policy tools; between the policy tools and monetary policy objectives; and between monetary policy and the real economy.

Let's begin with the operational details that define the tools available to central banks. Then we'll turn to a discussion of the link between those tools and the policymakers' objectives. That discussion will explain why—aside from periods of financial crisis or near-zero interest rates—modern monetary policy is equivalent to interest-rate policy. We'll examine how policymakers arrive at a target for the federal funds rate. Finally, we'll turn to a discussion of a number of unconventional policy tools that were used in the crisis of 2007–2009 and in the postcrisis recovery and explain how they augment conventional policy. We'll also look briefly at how central banks can exit from unconventional policy accommodation (just as they exit from conventional policy easing by hiking interest rates).

To keep the discussion manageable, we'll focus on monetary policy in large economies like that of the United States (where trade is a relatively small part of GDP) and of the euro area (a more "open" economy—i.e., where trade is a somewhat larger part of GDP). Chapter 19 will discuss exchange rates and other issues that are important to central banks in more trade-dependent (more open) economies.

The Federal Reserve's Conventional Policy Toolbox

Like all central banks, the Federal Reserve can, if policymakers wish, control the quantity of reserves that commercial banks hold. Reserves are injected into the banking system through an increase in the size of the Fed's balance sheet, either because of a decision by the Fed to buy securities or because of a bank's decision to borrow from the Fed. Besides the quantity of reserves, the central bank can control either the size of the monetary base or the price of its components. Like most modern central banks, the Fed usually sets policy by focusing its attention on prices. The three prices it concentrates on are the interest rate at which banks borrow and lend reserves overnight, the

| Table 18.1 | The Tools of U.S. Monetary Policy |

	What Is It?	How Is It Controlled?	What Is Its Impact?
Target Federal Funds Rate	Interest rate charged on overnight loans between banks.	Supply of reserves adjusted through open market operations to meet expected demand at the target rate.	Changes interest rates throughout the economy.
Discount Rate	Interest rate charged by the Federal Reserve on loans to commercial banks.	Set at a premium over the target federal funds rate.	Ceiling on market federal funds rate. Means to provide liquidity to banks in times of crisis.
Deposit Rate	Interest rate paid by the Federal Reserve on reserves held by banks.	Set at a spread below the target funds rate.	Sets a floor under the market federal funds rate.
Reserve Requirement	Fraction of deposits that banks must keep either on deposit at the Federal Reserve or as cash in their vaults.	Set by the Federal Reserve Board within a legally imposed range.	Stabilizes the demand for reserves. Not used to alter monetary policy.

interest rate at which banks can borrow reserves from the Fed, and the interest rate that the Fed pays on reserves that banks hold at the central bank.[3]

In examining day-to-day monetary policy, understanding the institutional structure of the central bank and financial markets is essential. What is true in one country may or may not be true elsewhere. Because cataloging the structure and tools of monetary policy around the world is too big a task, we will begin with the Federal Reserve and financial markets in the United States. In the next section, we will look at the ECB's operating procedures to see how they differ.

The Federal Reserve has four conventional monetary policy tools, also known as *monetary policy instruments* (see Table 18.1).

1. The **target federal funds rate**, the interest rate at which banks make overnight loans to each other.
2. The **discount rate**, the interest rate the Fed charges on the loans it makes to banks and that forms a ceiling for the market federal funds rate.
3. The **deposit rate**, the interest rate that the Fed pays on reserves that banks hold in their accounts at the central bank and that puts a floor under the market federal funds rate.
4. The **reserve requirement**, the level of balances a bank is required to hold either as vault cash or on deposit or at a Federal Reserve Bank.

We will examine these four tools in detail. As we do, keep in mind that each has multiple purposes. That is, these tools are related to several of the central bank's functions and objectives.

[3]In October 2008, at the peak of the financial crisis, Congress authorized the Fed to pay interest on reserves, and it began to do so immediately. This authority brought the Fed's set of conventional policy tools in line with that of other major central banks like the ECB. Later in this chapter, we will see how important this tool can be.

The Target Federal Funds Rate and Open Market Operations

The target federal funds rate is the Federal Open Market Committee's primary policy instrument. Financial market participants are constantly speculating about movements in this rate. FOMC meetings always end with a decision on the target level, and the statement released after the meeting begins with an announcement of that decision. To a large extent, this is U.S. monetary policy. But because the federal funds rate is the rate at which banks lend reserves to each other overnight, it is determined in the market, not controlled by the Fed. With this qualification in mind, we will distinguish between the *target* federal funds rate set by the FOMC and the **market federal funds rate**, at which transactions between banks take place.[4]

The name *federal funds* comes from the fact that the funds banks trade are their deposit balances at Federal Reserve Banks. On any given day, banks target the level of reserves they would like to hold at the close of business. But as the day goes by, the normal flow of business may leave them with more or less reserves than they want to hold. This discrepancy between actual and desired reserves gives rise to a market for reserves, with some banks lending out their excess and others borrowing to cover a shortfall. Without this market, banks would need to hold substantial quantities of excess reserves as insurance against shortfalls. While transactions are often made through brokers (third parties who bring buyers and sellers together), they are all bilateral agreements between two banks. Because the loans are unsecured—there is no collateral to fall back on in the event of nonpayment—the borrowing bank must be creditworthy in the eyes of the lending bank, or the loan will not be made.

MARKETS

If the Fed wanted to, it could force the market federal funds rate to equal the target rate all the time by participating directly in the market for overnight reserves, both as a borrower and as a lender. However, policymakers believe that the federal funds market provides valuable information about the health of specific banks. When a bank cannot get an overnight loan from any other bank, it's a key sign of trouble. Accordingly, as mentioned earlier in the chapter, the Fed allows the federal funds rate to fluctuate around its target in a channel or corridor defined by the discount rate and the deposit rate.

Operationally, the discount rate is set at a spread above the target federal funds rate, and the deposit rate is set at a spread below the target federal funds rate. When the market federal funds rate climbs to the discount rate, banks may borrow from the Fed at the discount rate. When the market federal funds rate falls to the deposit rate, banks can deposit their excess reserves at the Fed at the deposit rate. Consequently, the discount rate functions as a cap on the market federal funds rate and the deposit rate as a floor beneath the market federal funds rate. The Fed can adjust the width of the so-called channel or corridor around the target federal funds rate when it wishes to allow a wider or narrower range of fluctuations in the market federal funds rate (see Applying the Concept on page 494).

The Fed's approach places it in a somewhat awkward position. It targets an interest rate at the same time that it wants to allow an interbank lending market to flourish. Instead of adopting a strategy that would fix the interest rate at the target directly, the Fed chooses to control the federal funds rate by manipulating the quantity of reserves.

---

[4]The market federal funds rate is often referred to as the "effective" federal funds rate. Published daily by the Fed, it is the average of the interest rates on market transactions in federal funds weighted by the size of the transactions.

Using *open market operations,* the Fed adjusts the supply of reserves, with the goal of keeping the market federal funds rate close to the target rate. That is, the Fed buys or sells securities to add or drain reserves as required to meet the expected demand for reserves at the target rate.

We can use a standard supply-and-demand diagram to analyze the market in which banks borrow and lend reserves. The demand curve for reserves is downward sloping. At higher market interest rates, holding reserves that pay only the Fed's deposit rate is more costly than at lower market rates. However, when the federal funds rate in the market drops to the deposit rate, banks are willing to hold any amount of reserves supplied beyond this level, so the demand curve turns flat. Keeping the market federal funds rate at the target means balancing supply and demand for reserves at that target rate. The staff of the Open Market Trading Desk does this by first estimating the demand for reserves at the target rate each morning, and then supplying that quantity for the day. This means the daily supply for reserves is vertical. That is, it is vertical until the market federal funds rate reaches the discount rate; at that point banks will borrow from the Fed rather than paying a higher interest rate in the market.

All of this is pictured in Figure 18.2: the reserve demand curve slopes down and turns flat at the deposit rate, while the reserve supply curve is vertical until it reaches the discount rate, at which point it becomes horizontal. Within a day, the federal funds rate can fluctuate in a range from the deposit rate to the discount rate. But as the reserve demand curve shifts from day to day, or when the FOMC decides to raise or lower their federal funds rate target, the Fed staff will use open market operations to shift the daily reserve supply curve to accommodate the change, thereby ensuring that the market

Figure 18.2   The Market for Bank Reserves

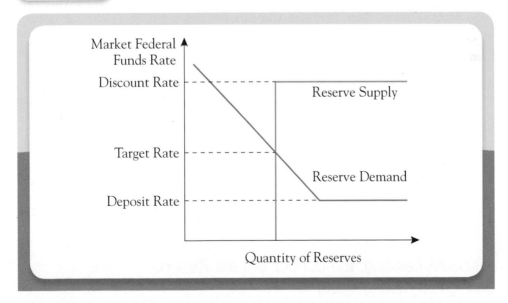

Reserve demand generally slopes down because the higher the market funds rate, the more costly it is to hold reserves paying the deposit rate. Reserve demand turns flat at the deposit rate, because banks face no better alternative to holding reserves at that rate. For levels of the market federal funds rate below the discount rate, reserve supply is vertical at the point that the open market trading desk estimates reserve demand will equal the target funds rate. At the discount rate, reserve supply becomes horizontal.

| Figure 18.3 | The Market for Bank Reserves |

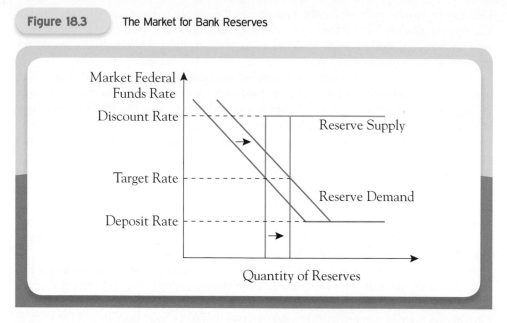

An increase in reserve demand is met by an open market purchase that increases reserve supply, thereby keeping the market federal funds rate at the target.

federal funds rate stays near the target. Figure 18.3 shows a case in which, through open market purchases that increase reserve supply, the Federal Reserve's staff maintains the market federal funds rate at its target following an increase in reserve demand.

Let's take a moment to compare the FOMC's target rate with the market rate over the last two decades, to see how well the Fed's staff has met its objective. Figure 18.4 plots both the target federal funds rate (the dark line that moves stepwise) and the market federal funds rate (the orange line that jumps around) beginning in 1992. As you can see, the market interest rate was close to the target on most days after the year 2000. Changes in the reserve accounting rules in 1998 (described later in the chapter), combined with improvements in information systems both within banks and at the Fed, made it easier for the Open Market Trading Desk to estimate reserve demand. The use of the discount rate as a daily ceiling on the funds rate after 2002 appears to have stabilized the market rate even further.

However, the financial crisis of 2007–2009 introduced new targeting errors. The loss of liquidity in the interbank lending market in September 2008 made it extremely difficult for Fed officials to hit their target. The result is the spikes we see in the graph. At the end of 2008, the FOMC announced a range for the funds rate—shown as a floor and a cap—rather than a specific target. As liquidity conditions normalized, the spikes largely disappeared.

STABILITY

Discount Lending, the Lender of Last Resort, and Crisis Management

When a central bank extends credit to commercial banks, its balance sheet changes. So by controlling the quantity of loans it makes, a central bank can control the size of reserves, the size of the monetary base, and ultimately interest rates. While the Fed could take this approach (and did for the first decade of its existence in the early 20th century),

Figure 18.4   Target Federal Funds Rate and Daily Market Rate, 1992–2013

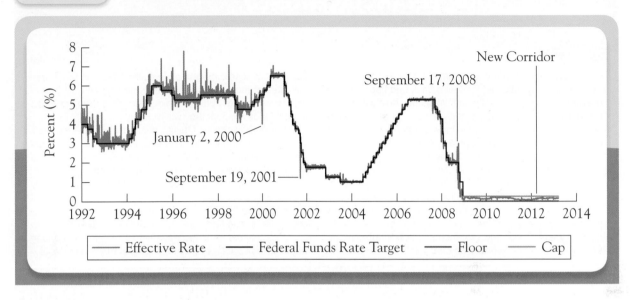

SOURCE: *Board of Governors of the Federal Reserve System.*

today it does not. Lending by Federal Reserve Banks to commercial banks, called **discount lending**, is usually small aside from crisis periods. During a normal week, the entire Federal Reserve System makes only a few hundred million dollars in loans. Yet, discount lending is the Fed's primary tool for ensuring short-term financial stability, eliminating bank panics, and preventing the sudden collapse of institutions that are experiencing financial difficulties. When there is a crisis, discount lending explodes. On Wednesday, September 12, 2001, the first business day after the collapse of the World Trade Center, banks borrowed $45.5 billion from the Fed! In the preceding week, borrowing had averaged just over $100 million per day. Similarly, in the weeks after Lehman failed in September 2008, discount lending surged to $110 billion, while total Fed lending (including credit provided to nonbanks) reached $700 billion!

STABILITY

Recall that crises were the primary impetus for the creation of the Federal Reserve in the first place. The idea was that some central government authority should be capable of providing funds to sound banks to keep them from failing during financial panics. The knowledge that the central bank would not allow solvent banks to become illiquid—that depositors could always get their funds—became one of the important safeguards against bank runs. The central bank, then, is the **lender of last resort**, making loans to banks when no one else will or can. But a bank is supposed to show that it is sound to get a loan in a crisis. This means having assets that the central bank is willing to take as collateral, because the central bank does not make uncollateralized loans. A bank that does not have assets it can use as collateral for a discount loan is a bank that should probably fail. Indeed, this is the principal reason that Fed officials gave when they explained why they could not prevent Lehman's failure in September 2008.

For most of its history, the Federal Reserve loaned reserves to banks at a rate *below* the target federal funds rate. Borrowing from the Fed was cheaper than borrowing from another bank. Even so, no one borrowed, because the Fed required banks to exhaust all other sources of funding before they applied for a loan. Moreover, banks that used

YOUR FINANCIAL WORLD
What the Federal Funds Rate Means to You

On learning that the FOMC controls the federal funds rate, most people's reaction is, "I'm not a bank and I don't borrow overnight, so why should I care?" What they do care about is the interest rate they pay on student loans, or auto loans, or home mortgages. But because interest rates often move together, people who care about long-term interest rates must care about short-term interest rates.

Remember from our discussion of the term structure of interest rates in Chapter 7 that the long-term interest rate is the average of expected future short-term interest rates. Thus, the rate charged on a 30-year, fixed-rate home mortgage is the average of the expected one-year rates for the next 30 years. Those one-year interest rates, in turn, are averages of the expected one-day interest rates for the next

365 days. Unless everyone expects the FOMC to keep interest rates at the same level for a very long time, the interest rates you care about will move—by less than the target federal funds rate, but they will move.

To see how important this is, we can look at the example of a 30-year mortgage. In mid-2006, the federal funds target was 5¼ percent; the interest rate on a 30-year, fixed-rate mortgage was 6¾ percent; and the monthly payment of principal and interest on a 30-year, $100,000 loan was roughly $650. By January 2013, the FOMC had lowered the federal funds target to the zero-to-1/4 percent range, and the mortgage interest rate had sunk below 3½ percent. At the January 2013 interest rate, the payment on the $100,000 loan was less than $450 per month, a drop of more than $200!

discount loans regularly faced the possibility of being denied loans in the future. Needless to say, these practices created quite a disincentive to borrow from the Fed. Almost everyone was willing to pay high rates in the marketplace rather than ask the Fed for a loan; only banks with nowhere else to go went to the Fed. But by severely discouraging banks from borrowing, the Fed destabilized the interbank market for reserves causing some of the upward spikes that you can see in Figure 18.4. Eventually, officials decided to make the process more rational. In 2002, they instituted the discount lending procedures that are in place today.

In addition to providing a mechanism for stabilizing the financial system, the current discount lending procedures also help the Fed meet its interest-rate stability objective. To see how this all works, we need to look at the details of how lending functions. The Federal Reserve makes three types of loans, called *primary credit, secondary credit,* and *seasonal credit.* The Fed controls the interest rate on these loans, not the quantity of credit extended. The banks decide how much to borrow, and the rules are not very complicated. Let's look at each one in turn.

Primary Credit   **Primary credit** is extended on a very short-term basis, usually overnight, to institutions that the Fed's bank supervisors deem to be sound (as measured by the standardized ratings they produce).[5] Banks seeking to borrow must post acceptable collateral to back the loan.[6] The interest rate on primary credit is set at a spread *above* the federal funds target rate. This is called the **primary discount rate**.[7] The term *discount rate* usually refers to this primary discount rate.

As long as a bank qualifies and is willing to pay the penalty interest rate, it can get the loan. The rules allow a borrowing bank to lend the funds again if it wishes. Primary

---

[5]Banks with CAMELS ratings of 1 or 2 qualify for primary credit. The ratings are described in Chapter 14.

[6]The list of acceptable collateral is fairly broad, including not only government securities and investment-grade corporate bonds but consumer loans, commercial and agricultural loans, and some mortgage obligations.

[7]In the case of a financial emergency resulting from an act of war, military or terrorist attack, natural disaster, or other catastrophic event, the primary discount rate can be reduced to the target federal funds rate.

credit is designed to provide additional reserves at times when the open market staff's forecasts are off and so the day's reserve supply falls short of the banking system's demand. In that case, the market federal funds rate will rise above the FOMC's target. Providing a facility through which banks can borrow at a penalty rate above the target puts a cap on the market federal funds rate. Banks will go to the discount window and borrow reserves from the Fed rather than go into the federal funds market and pay a rate above the primary discount rate. So the system is designed both to provide liquidity in times of crisis, ensuring financial stability, and to keep reserve shortages from causing spikes in the market federal funds rate. By restricting the range over which the market federal funds rate can move, this system helps to maintain interest-rate stability.

Secondary Credit   Secondary credit is available to institutions that are not sufficiently sound to qualify for primary credit. Because secondary credit is provided to banks that are in trouble, the **secondary discount rate** is set above the primary discount rate. There are two reasons a bank might seek secondary credit. The first is the standard one: a temporary shortfall in reserves. But short-run secondary borrowing is very unusual. Banks that request secondary credit from the Fed are banks that can't borrow from anyone else. By offering to pay a rate above the primary discount rate, a bank signals other banks that it doesn't qualify for primary credit. By paying the Fed the secondary discount rate for funds, the bank advertises that it is in trouble. It is hard to see any but the most desperate banker doing this. Indeed, even during the crisis of 2007–2009, secondary credit did not exceed $1 billion.

So who is secondary credit for, anyway? It is for banks that are experiencing longer-term problems that they need some time to work out. There are times when banks have serious financial difficulty that they can resolve without failing. A bank that takes a large loss from poor lending decisions will become undercapitalized, but it may be able to raise funds to continue operating if it is given enough time. Such a bank has nothing to lose by requesting secondary credit. Without it, it will fail anyway. But before the Fed makes the loan, it has to believe there is a good chance the bank will be able to survive. You can see why secondary credit is rare.

Seasonal Credit   Seasonal credit is used primarily by small agricultural banks in the Midwest to help in managing the cyclical nature of farmers' loans and deposits.[8] Historically, these banks had poor access to national money markets, so the Fed stepped in to provide credit, charging them a market-based interest rate.[9] In recent years, however, there has been a move to eliminate seasonal credit. While the Fed still extends about $100 million of seasonal credit during the summer months, there seems little justification for the practice any longer. Banks that used seasonal credit in the past now have easy access to longer-term loans from large commercial banks.

Reserve Requirements

Reserve requirements are the fourth tool in the monetary policymaker's toolbox. Since 1935, the Federal Reserve Board has had the authority to set the reserve requirements, the minimum level of reserves banks must hold either as vault cash or on deposit at

[8]During spring and summer, as farmers plant and cultivate their crops, the demand for loans rises and deposits decline, driving down bank reserves. Harvests and crop sales bring repayment of loans and increases in deposits, raising bank reserves.

[9]The interest rate charged on seasonal credit is the average of the market (effective) federal funds rate and market rate on 90-day negotiable certificates of deposit, both averaged over the previous two weeks.

the Fed.[10] Required reserves equal the required reserve ratio times the level of deposits to which the requirement is applied. (In Chapter 17, we wrote this relationship as $RR = r_D D$.) As we saw in the last chapter, changes in the reserve requirement affect the money multiplier and the quantity of money and credit circulating in the economy. Increasing it reduces the deposit expansion potential of the banking system, lowering the level of money supported by a given monetary base. So, by adjusting the reserve requirement, the central bank can influence economic activity. Unfortunately, the reserve requirement turns out not to be very useful. One reason is that small changes in the reserve requirement have a large—really, too large—impact on the level of deposits. But there are other reasons it isn't a good way to control the quantity of money. To see why, we need to look at the details.

The method for computing required reserves is complex. Everything is based on two-week averages. The reserve requirement is applied to two-week average balances in accounts with unlimited checking privileges—*transaction deposits.* This reserve computation period ends every second Monday. The reserves a bank must hold are also averaged over a two-week period, called the *maintenance period,* which begins on the third Thursday after the end of the computation period. That may sound a bit complicated, but really it isn't. What it means is that the banks and the Fed both know exactly what level of reserves every bank is required to hold during a given maintenance period well *before* the period starts. All banks have 16 days to figure out their deposit balances before they even need to start holding reserves. This procedure is called *lagged-reserve accounting,* and it makes the demand for reserves more predictable.

In 1980, the Monetary Control Act changed the rules slightly so that the Fed can now set the reserve requirement ratio between 8 percent and 14 percent of these transactions deposits. Now that interest is paid on reserves, the reserve requirement is not very costly to banks. Yet, to help small banks, the law specifies a graduated reserve requirement that is similar to the graduated income tax. The first few million dollars in deposits are exempt; then the reserve requirement ratio rises to 3 percent for deposits up to $80 million or so. For everything above that level, the rate is 10 percent.[11] The accounting rules allow banks to carry small amounts of excess reserves forward and backward one maintenance period to meet their reserve requirements.

The purpose of the reserve requirement has changed over the years. In the beginning, reserves were required to ensure banks were sound and to reassure depositors that they could withdraw currency on demand. With the advent of deposit insurance, the rationale for requiring reserves changed. Today, the reserve requirement exists primarily to stabilize the demand for reserves and help the Fed to maintain the market federal funds rate close to target. A critical element in the Fed's daily open market operations is an estimate of the reserve demand for the day. The better the forecast, the easier it is to keep the market federal funds rate close to the FOMC's target. Changes in the reserve accounting rules over the years have made the open market operations staff's job of estimating reserve demand easier. Before August 1998, the computation and maintenance periods overlapped. Banks had to manage their deposits and reserves at the same time, and the result was a volatile market federal funds rate. Since summer

[10]Originally, the requirements were specified in the Federal Reserve Act and could not be changed. For a concise history of reserve requirements, see Joshua N. Feinman, "Reserve Requirements: History, Current Practice, and Potential Reform," *Federal Reserve Bulletin* 79, no. 6 (June 1993), pp. 569–589.

[11]The level at which the higher reserve requirement kicks in changes every year, based on the amount of transaction deposits in the banking system. In 2013, the reserve requirement was zero for the first $12.4 million in deposits, 3 percent for deposits up to $79.5 million, and 10 percent above that. For updates, see *www.federalreserve.gov/monetarypolicy/reservereq.htm.*

1998, with the implementation of the lagged-reserve accounting system, things calmed down quite a bit. As you can see from Figure 18.4, except on the occasion of crises, the market federal funds rate now stays much closer to the target.

The case against using the reserve requirement as a direct policy tool is persuasive. An example will help to illustrate the pitfalls of using the reserve requirement as a policy tool. Following the banking crises of the Great Depression, U.S. banks began accumulating excess reserves. By the beginning of 1936, less than half of the $5.6 billion of reserves held in the banking system were required; the rest were excess reserves. The Federal Reserve Board was puzzled and became concerned that the high level of excess reserves could be used to support a rapid expansion of deposits and loans, which would lead to inflation. To head off the possibility, beginning in August 1936 the Fed used its newly acquired powers and in three steps doubled the reserve requirement. Suddenly, $3 billion in excess reserves was reduced to $1 billion. But the Fed had underestimated banks' desire to hold excess reserves to protect against the possibility of renewed bank runs. So, bank executives spent the next year rebuilding their reserve balances until excess reserves were back to the level where they had been before the reserve requirement was raised. The consequences for the economy were grim. While the monetary base remained relatively stable, the money multiplier plummeted, driving M1 and M2 down. As monetary aggregates fell, the economy went along with them. From its peak in spring 1937 to its trough less than a year later, real GDP fell more than 10 percent.

Operational Policy at the European Central Bank

Like the Federal Reserve's, the ECB's monetary policy toolbox contains an overnight interbank rate (equivalent to the federal funds rate), a rate at which the central bank lends to commercial banks (equivalent to the discount rate), a reserve deposit rate, and a reserve requirement. While the conventional toolkit is the same, the details are different, so let's have a look at them.

The ECB's Target Interest Rate and Open Market Operations

While the ECB occasionally engages in outright purchases of securities, it provides reserves to the European banking system primarily through collateralized loans in what are called *refinancing operations*. In normal times, the main refinancing operation is a weekly auction of two-week **repurchase agreements (repo)** in which the ECB, through the National Central Banks (NCBs), provides reserves to banks in exchange for securities and then reverses the transaction two weeks later. The usual policy instrument of the ECB's Governing Council is the minimum interest rate allowed at these refinancing auctions, which is called the main refinancing operations **minimum bid rate**. This is the European equivalent of the Fed's target federal funds rate, so we will refer to it as the *target refinancing rate*.

In normal times, the main refinancing operation provides banks with virtually all of their reserves. But since 2007, in an effort to steady financial markets, the ECB has provided most reserves through longer-term refinancing at maturities of three months and more. And to stabilize bank funding in late 2011 and early 2012—a period of intense financial disruptions in the euro area—the ECB extended the maturities of the loans to three years in longer-term refinancing operations that supplied more than

APPLYING THE CONCEPT
THE CHANNEL SYSTEM AND THE FUTURE OF MONETARY POLICY

It is their monopoly over the supply of currency and reserves—the monetary base—that gives central banks influence over the economic and financial system. As a practical matter, modern policymakers usually choose to use this monopoly power to influence the price of reserves in overnight markets. That's the federal funds rate in the United States. But numerous factors are altering the demand for the monetary base. Innovations in payments systems have reduced our demand for currency and the use of information technology has lowered reserve requirements as banks sweep client funds from checking to savings accounts. In contrast, the 2008 introduction of interest payments on reserves has boosted demand for excess reserves. But suppose for a moment that demand for reserves has shriveled: How could monetary policy operate?

To see, we can look at the cases of Australia, Canada, and New Zealand. Central bankers there have eliminated reserve requirements entirely, but retain monetary policy control. They do it through a "channel" or "corridor" system that involves setting not only a target interest rate, but also a lending and deposit rate—just as the Fed and the ECB do. The lending rate is the rate charged on discount loans, while the deposit rate is the rate paid by the central bank on commercial bank reserve deposits. As reserve demand fluctuates during the day, the overnight interest rate stays between these two bounds.

Figure 18.5 shows the reserve market with a channel system. Recall that reserve demand slopes down because the higher the market interest rate, the more costly it is to hold reserves. In the channel system, reserve demand becomes flat when the interbank market rate falls to the deposit rate, because banks have no better alternative than the deposit rate. Reserve supply is a step function: vertical at the level of reserves the central bank initially chooses to supply and horizontal at the lending rate.

The channel system has important implications for the behavior of overnight market interest rates. At the beginning of the day, central bank staff estimates that reserve demand will be at RD_0, so they supply the quantity of reserves that they believe will yield the target rate. But as the day progresses, reserve demand turns out to be different from what was expected. If demand rises significantly to RD_1 the overnight rate will start to rise. But once it gets to the lending rate, banks can simply borrow from the central bank, capping the rate. If reserve demand falls to RD_2 then banks will deposit reserves in the central bank, putting a floor under the overnight rate.

Now let's go back to the question we started with: What happens as reserve demand goes to zero? The answer is that this system still works. Banks in need of funds will never be willing to pay more than the central bank's lending rate and those that have excess funds will never be willing to lend at a rate below the central bank's deposit rate. Overnight interest rates will always be inside the corridor, giving monetary policymakers a tool to influence the economy.

€1 trillion to banks. The financial turmoil also led the ECB to boost open market purchases of securities, including the debt of euro-area sovereigns that had difficulties borrowing in private markets. As a result, the combination of loans provided through longer-term refinancing operations and securities holdings denominated in euros became the largest component of the ECB's assets, accounting for more than one-half of the total in early 2013.

While the ECB's main refinancing operations are broadly similar to the Fed's daily open market operations, there are some differences. The most important one is that these operations are done at all the National Central Banks simultaneously. As of 2014, there were 18 NCBs (and as the Eurosystem expands to include more countries, the number will grow). The Fed's open market operations are executed from only one location, the Federal Reserve Bank of New York. And while the Fed solicits prices from a short list of 21 securities dealers in the course of its normal operations, literally hundreds of European banks participate in the ECB's weekly auctions. Finally, because of the differences in financial structure in different euro-area countries, the collateral that is accepted in refinancing operations differs from country to country. Under normal circumstances, the Fed takes U.S. government securities (although the range of accepted collateral widened during the crisis of 2007–2009). In contrast, the Eurosystem (composed of the ECB and the NCBs) treats tens of thousands of different marketable assets as eligible collateral, including not only government-issued bonds but also privately issued bonds and bank loans. Even when the rating on government bonds of one euro-area country fell below investment grade in 2010, the ECB continued to accept them as collateral.

Figure 18.5   The Channel System

Central banks using a channel system set not only a target for the overnight interbank interest rate, but also a lending rate that they change for reserve loans and a deposit rate that they pay when banks' reserve accounts contain excess reserves. As a result, as the demand for reserves fluctuates, the overnight interest rate always remains between the two limits.

The Marginal Lending Facility

The **ECB's Marginal Lending Facility** is the analog to the Federal Reserve's primary credit facility. Through this facility, the ECB provides overnight loans to banks at a rate that is normally well *above* the target-refinancing rate. The spread between the marginal lending rate and the target refinancing rate is set by the Governing Council and was 50 basis points in mid-2013. As in the case of discount borrowing from the Fed, commercial banks initiate these borrowing transactions when they face a reserve deficiency that they cannot satisfy more cheaply in the marketplace. Banks do borrow regularly, and on occasion the amounts they borrow are large. The similarity between this procedure and the Federal Reserve's primary credit facility is no accident, because the ECB's system (which is itself based on the German Bundesbank's) was the model for the 2002 redesign of the Fed's discount window.

The Deposit Facility

Banks with excess reserves at the end of the day can deposit them overnight in the **ECB's Deposit Facility** at an interest rate substantially *below* the target-refinancing rate. Again, the spread is determined by the Governing Council and was 50 basis points in mid-2013. While they are usually small, these deposits can be substantial, because they include all the excess reserves in the Eurosystem's banks. Deposits at the ECB averaged €350 *million* from 1999 to 2006 but temporarily surged above €800 *billion* during the euro-area crisis. Like their U.S. counterparts, which chose to boost their reserves after the Lehman failure instead of extending loans, euro-area commercial banks preferred the safety of zero-interest rate excess reserves at the central bank (the ECB) over lending to banks in Greece, Ireland, Italy, Portugal, and Spain. These latter banks, in the geographic periphery of the euro area, depended on the ECB's monetary operations for their funding (and survival).

Keep in mind that the deposit facility places a floor on the interest rate that can be charged on reserves. Because a bank can always deposit its excess reserves in the deposit facility at a rate 50 basis points below the target refinancing rate, it will never make a loan at a lower rate. Once again, the ECB's deposit facility was the model for the Fed's deposit rate that was introduced in October 2008.

Reserve Requirements

The ECB requires that banks hold minimum reserves based on the level of their liabilities. The reserve requirement of 1 percent is applied to checking accounts and other deposits with a maturity of up to two years. Deposit levels are averaged over a month, and reserve levels must be held over the following month. Like the Fed, the ECB pays interest on reserves so the cost of meeting the reserve requirement is relatively low, and banks do not go out of their way to escape it.

The European system is designed to give the ECB tight control over the short-term money market in the euro area. And it usually works well. Figure 18.6 shows the target refinancing rate, which is the minimum bid rate in the weekly auctions, as the red line running through the center of the graph, with the marginal lending rate above and the deposit rate below (both in blue). The **overnight cash rate** is the European analog to the market federal funds rate, the rate banks charge each other for overnight loans. As

---

Figure 18.6   Euro-Area Overnight Cash Rate and ECB Interest Rates, 1999–2013

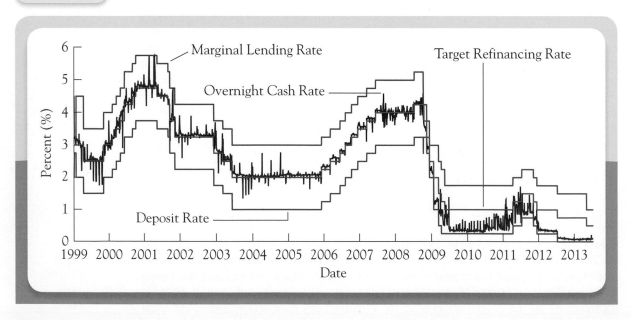

SOURCE: *European Central Bank.*

you can see, this rate fluctuates quite a bit. After the Lehman failure in 2008, it stayed below the target refinancing rate for most of the period, as the ECB flooded the system with liquidity. Yet, even in this period, the overnight cash rate remained within the band formed by the marginal lending rate and the deposit rate.

This pattern contrasts starkly with that of the U.S. market federal funds rate before 2002. Looking back at Figure 18.4, we can see that the market federal funds rate occasionally moved more than 100 basis points above or below the target. In fact, over the first 10 years plotted there, the funds rate was more than 100 basis points away from the target 28 times, or nearly three times a year. The European system is clearly more successful than that in keeping the short-term rate close to target. Indeed, as the Federal Reserve gradually introduced a version of the ECB's conventional policy toolkit, the funds rate was more than 100 basis points away from the target on only three occasions between 2002 and mid-2013, all of which occurred during the crisis of 2007–2009.

Linking Tools to Objectives: Making Choices

Monetary policymakers use the various tools they have to meet the objectives society gives them. Their goals—low and stable inflation, high and stable growth, a stable financial system, stable interest and exchange rates—are (or should be) given to them by their elected officials. But day-to-day policy is left to the technicians, who must then decide which tools are the best for the job.

Over the years, a consensus has developed among monetary policy experts, both inside and outside central banks, that (1) the reserve requirement is not useful as an operational instrument, (2) central bank lending is necessary to ensure financial stability, and (3) short-term interest rates are the tool to use to stabilize short-term fluctuations in prices and output. Later in this chapter, we will see how exceptional conditions—such as dysfunctional financial markets or nominal short-term interest rates at zero—can lead to the use of unconventional policy tools, but even those tools aim to influence some market interest rate. The logic of this conclusion is straightforward. To follow it, let's start by listing the features that distinguish good policy instruments from bad ones.

STABILITY

Desirable Features of a Policy Instrument

A good monetary policy instrument has three features.

1. It is easily *observable* by everyone.
2. It is *controllable* and quickly changed.
3. It is tightly *linked* to the policymakers' objectives.

These features seem obvious. After all, a policy tool wouldn't be very useful if you couldn't observe it, control it, or predict its impact on your objectives. But beyond the obvious, it is important that a policy instrument be easily observable to ensure transparency in policymaking, which enhances accountability. Controllability is important in both the short term and the long term. An instrument that can be adjusted quickly in the face of a sudden change in economic conditions is clearly more useful than one that takes time to adjust. And the more predictable the impact of an instrument, the easier it will be for policymakers to meet their objectives.

Requiring that a monetary policy instrument be observable and controllable leaves us with only a few options to choose from. The reserve requirement won't work. Because banks cannot adjust their balance sheets quickly, changes need to be announced some time in advance. Then there are the components of the central bank's balance sheet—commercial bank reserves, the monetary base, loans, and foreign exchange reserves—as well as their prices—various interest rates and the exchange rate. (Exchange rate policy is discussed in the next chapter.) But how do we choose between controlling quantities and controlling prices? Over the years, central banks have switched from one to the other. For example, from 1979 to 1982, the Fed did try targeting bank reserves, with an eye toward reducing the inflation rate from double-digit levels. Inflation fell quickly, so in a sense the policy was a success. But one side effect of choosing to control reserves was that interest rates became highly variable, rising from 14 percent to over 20 percent and then falling to less than 9 percent, all in a period of less than six months.

The consensus today is that the Fed's strategy of targeting reserves rather than interest rates in the period from 1979 to 1982 was a way of driving interest rates to levels that would not have been politically acceptable had they been announced as targets. Even in an environment of double-digit inflation rates, the FOMC could not explicitly raise the target federal funds rate to 20 percent. By saying they were targeting the quantity of reserves, the committee members escaped responsibility for the high interest rates. When inflation had fallen and interest rates came back down, the FOMC reverted to targeting the federal funds rate. And that is what it has done ever since. (Although the Fed's balance sheet expansion after 2008 did not aim to alter the federal funds rate target, it did aim to reduce longer-term interest rates.)

Appearances and politics aside, there is a very good reason the vast majority of central banks in the world today choose to target an interest rate rather than some quantity on their balance sheet. To understand it, let's look at what would happen if the FOMC chose to target the quantity of reserves in the banking system. Targeting the quantity of reserves requires holding supply constant at the target level. That means supply is vertical not only each day (as in Figure 18.2) but that it is fixed over much longer periods of weeks or possibly even months. The consequences of this are easy to see. With reserve supply fixed, a shift in reserve demand changes the federal funds rate. When reserve demand increases, the market federal funds rate will go up and when reserve demand falls, the market federal funds rate will go down. If the Fed chooses to target the quantity of reserves, it gives up control of the federal funds rate. Figure 18.7 shows what can happen: as reserve demand increases and falls, the market federal funds rate fluctuates over a range that is determined by the intersection of supply and demand.

Figure 18.7 The Market for Bank Reserves when the Fed Targets the Quantity of Reserves

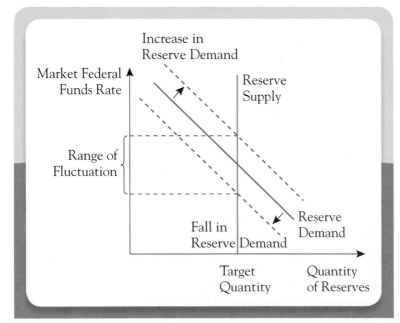

When the Fed targets the quantity of reserves, a shift in reserve demand causes the market federal funds to move. An increase in reserve demand forces the interest rate up, while a fall in reserve demand forces the interest rate down.

APPLYING THE CONCEPT
INFLATION TARGETING

If you can focus central bankers' attention clearly on a well-articulated objective, you will get better policy. The problem is how to do it. During the 1990s, a number of countries adopted a policy framework called **inflation targeting** in an effort to improve monetary policy performance. And it seems to have worked, at least until the financial crisis of 2007–2009. Countries that embraced inflation targeting achieved both lower inflation and (until the crisis) higher real growth.

Inflation targeting bypasses intermediate targets and focuses directly on the objective of low inflation. It is a monetary policy strategy that involves the public announcement of a numerical inflation target, underscoring the central bank's commitment to price stability. When the target is credible, everyone believes policymakers will keep the inflation rate low, so long-term expectations of inflation remain low, anchoring long-term interest rates and promoting growth. As we saw in Chapter 15, one of the keys to any successful central bank policy is for policymakers to convince the public that they will keep inflation low. Inflation targeting is designed to convince people that monetary policy will deliver low inflation.

Often, central banks that employ inflation targeting operate under what has been described as a *hierarchical mandate,* in which price stability comes first and everything else comes second. The United Kingdom, Australia, Chile, and South Africa are among the roughly two dozen countries that target inflation. Most observers put the ECB in the group as well. This hierarchical approach contrasts with the Federal Reserve's *dual mandate,* in which price stability and economic growth are on an equal footing. Nevertheless, consistent with an inflation-targeting strategy, the Fed announced a quantitative inflation objective in 2012 but set no target for economic growth.

To understand how inflation targeting works, let's look at the British example. The Bank of England Act of 1998 both granted the Bank of England independence and dictated its objective: to deliver price stability, as defined by the government's inflation target. A nine-member Monetary Policy Committee meets monthly to determine short-term interest rates in an effort to meet this objective, which has been defined as consumer price inflation of 2.0 percent. Because transparency is a crucial part of inflation targeting, the Bank of England publishes the minutes of its Monetary Policy Committee's meetings, as well as quarterly forecasts of inflation in its *Inflation Report.*

By focusing on a clearly defined and easily observable numerical inflation statistic and requiring frequent communication with the public, inflation targeting increases policymakers' accountability and helps to establish their credibility. Not only do central bankers know what they are supposed to do, but everyone else does, too. The result is not just lower and more stable inflation but—usually—higher and more stable growth as well.

However, as we saw in the global crisis of 2007–2009, inflation targeting is not sufficient to prevent financial disruptions that undermine economic stability.

From the discussion in Chapter 15 we can infer that, in order to meet their objectives, central bankers will tend to adopt operating procedures that keep interest rates from becoming volatile. Interest rates are the primary linkage between the financial system and the real economy, so stabilizing growth means keeping interest rates from being overly volatile. In the context of choosing an operating target, that means keeping unpredictable changes in reserve demand from influencing interest rates and feeding into the real economy. The best way to do this is to target interest rates.[12]

Operating Instruments and Intermediate Targets

Before continuing, we should pause to consider some terms and concepts that often crop up in discussions of central banking. Central bankers sometimes use the terms *operating instrument* and *intermediate target.* Operating instruments refer to actual tools of policy. These are instruments that the central bank controls directly. Every

---

[12]More than 40 years ago, William Poole first observed that the decision to target either interest rates, or an aggregate like reserves or the monetary base, depends on what is less predictable. Is it the money multiplier that links the monetary base to monetary aggregates? Or is it the linkage between money and the real economy? (This is the velocity of money which we will discuss in Chapter 20.) Poole showed that if the money multiplier is less predictable, policymakers should target interest rates, otherwise, it is better to target the monetary base. See William Poole, "Optimal Choice of Monetary Policy Instruments in a Simple Stochastic Macro Model," *Quarterly Journal of Economics* 84, no. 2 (1970), pp. 197–216.

| Figure 18.8 | Instruments, Targets, and Objectives |

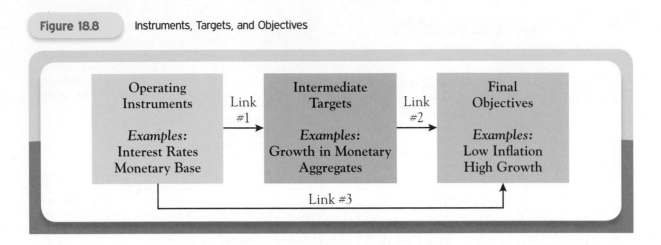

central bank can control the size of its balance sheet, for instance. It can choose to use this power to control the monetary base if it wishes, or to control the interest rate in the market for reserves, as the FOMC does. These are the operating instruments.

Central bankers use the term **intermediate targets** to refer to instruments that are not directly under their control but lie instead somewhere between their policymaking tools and their objectives (see Figure 18.8). The monetary aggregates are a prime example of intermediate targets. The idea behind targeting M2, for example, is that changes in the monetary base, or reserves, affect the monetary aggregates before they influence inflation or output. So in targeting M2, central bankers can more effectively meet their objectives. They don't actually care about money growth itself, in other words; it is just a useful indicator. And announcing targets for money growth that can be monitored by the public increases policymakers' accountability.

Over the last two decades of the 20th century, central bankers largely abandoned intermediate targets, having realized that they didn't make much sense. Link #1, between the operating instruments and the intermediate target, may shift (this is the problem described at the end of Chapter 17) or link #2, between money growth and the final inflation and growth objectives, may change (we will discuss this in Chapter 20). If either of these happened, the central bank would need to explain why it was changing its target and it would look as if policymakers don't know what they are doing. So while people still do discuss intermediate targets, it is hard to justify using them. Instead, policymakers focus on how their actions directly affect their target objectives—link #3. The most prominent example of this is the practice of *inflation targeting,* which has become the most common policy framework among central bankers (see Applying the Concept: Inflation Targeting).

A Guide to Central Bank Interest Rates: The Taylor Rule

Interest-rate setting is about numbers. The members of the FOMC set the target federal funds rate at, say, 0 or 2 or 4 percent; the Governing Council of the ECB chooses a specific level for the main refinancing rate. And these policymakers don't merely pick the number; they also choose the day on which to make the changes. How do they do it? The answer is that they have large staffs—at the Fed and the ECB, hundreds of people—who distill huge amounts of information into manageable sets of policy recommendations. Committee members digest all the information, meet, and reach a decision. We could try to list all the factors they consider and explain how each influences the committee's decision, but that would take another book.

What we can do is study a simple formula that approximates what the FOMC does. Called the **Taylor rule** after the economist who created it, Professor John Taylor of Stanford University, it tracks the actual behavior of the target federal funds rate and relates it to the real interest rate, inflation, and output.[13] The formula is

$$\text{Target fed funds rate} = 2 + \text{Current inflation} + \tfrac{1}{2}(\text{Inflation gap}) + \tfrac{1}{2}(\text{Output gap}) \qquad (1)$$

This expression assumes a long-term real interest rate of 2 percent, which is added to current inflation, the inflation gap, and the output gap. The inflation gap is current inflation minus an inflation target, both measured as percentages; the output gap is the percentage deviation of current output (real GDP) from potential output. (As Chapter 21 discusses in detail, potential output is what the economy is capable of producing when its resources are being used at normal rates.) When inflation exceeds the target level, the inflation gap is positive; when current output is above potential output, the output gap is positive.

The Taylor rule says that the target federal funds rate should be set equal to the current level of inflation plus a 2 percent real interest rate, plus a factor related to the deviations of inflation and output from their target or normal levels. For example, if inflation is currently 3 percent, the inflation target is 2 percent, and real GDP equals its potential level so there is no output gap, then the target federal funds rate should be set at $2 + 3 + \frac{1}{2} = 5\frac{1}{2}$ percent.

This rule functions like a thermostat, tuning the policy interest rate target if the economy (measured as inflation and output) is too hot or cold. It makes intuitive sense: When inflation rises above its target level, the response is to raise interest rates; when output falls below the target level, the response is to lower interest rates. If inflation is currently on target and there is no output gap (current real GDP equals potential GDP), then the target federal funds rate should be set at its neutral rate of target inflation plus 2.

The Taylor rule has some interesting properties. Consider what happens if inflation rises by 1 percentage point, from 2 percent to 3 percent, and the inflation target is 2 percent (assume that everything else remains the same). What happens to the target federal funds rate? The increase in inflation affects two terms in the Taylor rule, current inflation and the inflation gap. Because the inflation target doesn't change, both these terms rise 1 percentage point. The increase in current inflation feeds one for one into the target federal funds rate, but the increase in the inflation gap is halved. *A 1 percentage point increase in the inflation rate raises the target federal funds rate 1½ percentage points.*

Significantly, the Taylor rule tells us that for each percentage point increase in inflation, the real interest rate, which is equal to the nominal interest rate minus expected inflation, goes up half a percentage point (assuming that expected inflation matches actual inflation). Because economic decisions depend on the real interest rate, this means that higher inflation leads policymakers to raise the inflation-adjusted cost of borrowing, thereby slowing the economy and ultimately reducing inflation. If central

---

[13]The Taylor rule first appeared in "Discretion versus Policy Rules in Practice," *Carnegie-Rochester Conference Series on Public Policy* 39 (1993), pp. 195–214. For a retrospective on the rule's influence, see Evan F. Koenig, Robert Leeson, and George A. Kahn, eds., *The Taylor Rule and the Transformation of Monetary Policy* (Stanford, CA: Hoover Institution Press, 2012).

banks failed to do this, if they allowed the real interest rate to fall following an increase in inflation, the result would be further increases in production and further increases in inflation.

The Taylor rule also states that for each percentage point output is above potential—that is, for each percentage point in the output gap—interest rates will go up half a percentage point.

The fractions that precede the terms for the inflation and output gaps—the halves in equation (1)—depend both on how sensitive the economy is to interest-rate changes and on the preferences of central bankers. The more central bankers care about inflation, the bigger the multiplier for the inflation gap and the lower the multiplier for the output gap. It is not unusual for central banks to raise the target interest rate by twice the increase in inflation while virtually ignoring the output gap.

Returning to the United States, we see that implementing the Taylor rule requires four inputs: (1) the constant term, set at 2 in equation (1); (2) a measure of inflation; (3) a measure of the inflation gap; and (4) a measure of the output gap. The constant is a measure of the average risk-free real interest rate over the long run, which can and does change. Since 1980, the inflation-adjusted one-year Treasury yield has averaged nearly 2 percent.

Next we need to add measures of current inflation and the inflation gap. What index should we use? While the CPI is widely known, economists believe that the price index of personal consumption expenditure (PCE) is a more accurate measure of inflation and, in 2012, the Fed set its inflation goal in terms of the annual rise of this measure. The index comes from the national income accounts and is based on the "C" in "Y = C + I + G + X − M." Using the Fed's inflation goal of 2 percent, the neutral target federal funds rate is 4 percent (2 plus 2). For the output gap, the natural choice is the percentage by which GDP deviates from a measure of its trend, or potential.

Figure 18.9 (see page 503) plots the FOMC's actual target federal funds rate, together with the rate predicted by the Taylor rule. The result is striking: The two lines are reasonably close to each other. The FOMC usually changed the target federal funds rate when the Taylor rule predicted it should. While the rule didn't match policy exactly, it did predict what policymakers would do in a general way. And what is really remarkable is that Professor Taylor created his rule around 1992, at the beginning of the period shown in the graph.

Before we get carried away and replace the FOMC with an equation, or begin betting in the financial markets based on the Taylor rule's predictions, we should recognize some caveats. First, at times the target rate does deviate from the Taylor rule, and with good reason. The Taylor rule is too simple to take account of sudden threats to financial stability, such as the terrorist attacks of September 11, 2001.

Indeed, we can learn from the periods in which the policy rate deviates from the Taylor rule. For example, why did the FOMC set the federal funds rate target below the Taylor rule in 1992–1993, 2002–2005, and 2008–2009 (see Figure 18.9)? The answer is that these periods were characterized by at least one of two factors: (1) unusually stringent conditions across an array of financial markets or (2) deflationary worries that arose as nominal interest rates approached their zero bound.

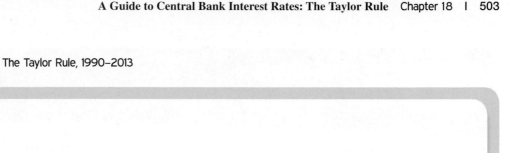

Figure 18.9   The Taylor Rule, 1990–2013

SOURCE: *Board of Governors of the Federal Reserve System and authors' calculations as of June 2013. (FRED data codes: GDPPOT, GDPC1, JCFXE, and FEDFUNDS)*

When financial conditions are much stronger or much weaker than usual, policymakers seeking to stabilize the economy may set an interest rate target that differs substantially from the Taylor rule. We can think of financial conditions as a measure that indicates the state of a broad array of markets, including both the prices of assets and the volume of transactions in these assets. Euphoric conditions are often associated both with high prices and volumes in asset trading and with easy access to credit, while depressed conditions are linked with the opposite states (see Chapter 8 for a discussion of asset bubbles). Although the policy target rate influences financial conditions, the link is a loose one: financial conditions can and do vary substantially, even in the absence of any changes in the policymakers' target interest rate.

Financial conditions affect policy choices because they alter prospects for private spending and for inflation. Lax or easy conditions mean that households and firms are more readily able to borrow, to spend out of wealth, and to invest. Plunging asset prices and the loss of credit work in the opposite direction. Consequently, a tightening or easing in financial conditions is a signal to policymakers about the future path of economic activity and inflation, and this affects their evaluation of appropriate levels of the interest rate and the Taylor rule.

An interesting example of this interaction arose in 2004–2006, when Federal Reserve policymakers chose to raise the target federal funds rate in an effort to moderate economic growth and inflation risks. However, from the perspective of broad financial conditions, policy remained accommodative, and the economy continued to grow vigorously. This pattern suggests that the Fed hiked rates too cautiously, a view reinforced by the subsequent pickup of inflation.

In 2008, even though the Fed cut rates below the Taylor rule, the collapse of financial conditions and the economy suggests that it was too cautious. Just like

IN THE NEWS
How Jawboning Works

THE WALL STREET JOURNAL.
WSJ.com

by David Wessel

January 9, 2013

Central bankers always have had a lot of power, notably the power to print money and move interest rates. The past few years have revealed the power of their words.

The Federal Reserve has been influencing financial markets with pledges to keep rates low for "an extended period" or, recently, until the unemployment rate falls below 6.5%. These days, scholars seeking to understand how monetary policy moves economies are looking more closely at "communications" and "signaling" than at the money supply.

The clearest example comes from Europe. In July, Mario Draghi, president of the European Central Bank, defused an intensifying crisis of confidence in the euro with two sentences scribbled in the margins of an otherwise routine

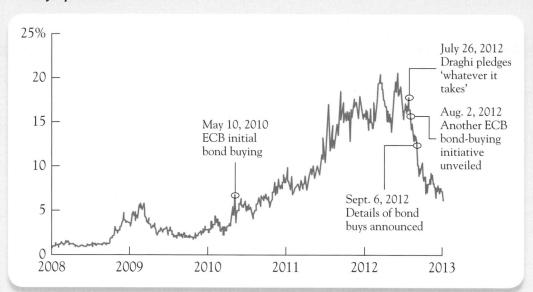

Weighty Words.

May 10, 2010
ECB initial
bond buying

July 26, 2012
Draghi pledges
'whatever it
takes'

Aug. 2, 2012
Another ECB
bond-buying
initiative
unveiled

Sept. 6, 2012
Details of bond
buys announced

Market assessment of risk of two or more euro-zone governments defaulting fell after Mario Draghi's vow to do "whatever it takes" to save the euro.

NOTE: Country-specific risks derived from credit derivative swap trading for Austria, Belgium, Germany, Spain, France, Greece, Ireland, Italy, Netherlands, Portugal.

SOURCE: *ECB, The Wall Street Journal,* January 9, 2013. Used with permission of Dow Jones & Company, Inc. via Copyright Clearance Center, Inc.

Japan in the 1990s, the Fed did not act early enough to prevent the interest rate implied by the Taylor rule from sinking below zero. Indeed, for the first time in at least 50 years, in 2009 the Taylor rule suggested that the appropriate policy rate was negative for the United States as well as for several other major economies. In this environment, even a zero-rate target probably was too high to counter weakness in speech. "Within our mandate, the ECB is ready to do whatever it takes to preserve the euro," he said. "And believe me, it will be enough."

That may prove to be the most successful central-bank verbal intervention in history.

A few weeks later, the ECB pledged to buy bonds of governments shunned by markets if those governments made belt-tightening commitments accepted by fellow euro-zone countries. No government has sought that help so the ECB hasn't spent a single euro. Yet global anxiety about an imminent euro crisis has abated.

Prepared by number-crunching Ph.D.s at the ECB, the chart accompanying this column tracks financial markets' assessment of the risk that two or more euro-zone governments would default in the following 12 months. The gauge rose, was curbed temporarily by the May 2010 creation of a European bailout fund and some ad hoc ECB bond buying, then soared. It remained high until Mr. Draghi spoke in July, then fell sharply.

Europe hasn't solved any fundamental problem. Several economies are burdened by huge debt loads. Austerity has contributed to deep recessions. Southern Europe's wages and productivity make its exports uncompetitive with Germany's. Prospects for growth are lousy. Forging a pan-European banking union and deposit-insurance fund—or a broader political union—remains more talk than action. Yet euro-anxiety has abated. How did Mr. Draghi pull this off?

A bit of background: The creation of the euro made it easy for investors to flee a country's bonds. Worried about Spain? Simply move euros to Germany. If such a run happened in the U.S. or the U.K., the Fed or Bank of England could print money and buy the bonds that investors were abandoning. Spain can't: It surrendered that power to the ECB. If Spain were a typical emerging market, the value of its currency would collapse—and that, in turn, would make its wares attractive to foreigners. But Spain doesn't have its own currency.

. . . In a classic run on a solvent bank, the textbook response is for the central bank to lend the bank cash to pay depositors. But when a country in Europe faces a run, the ECB has been reluctant to be that "lender of last resort." So investors demanded higher interest rates from Spain and Italy, worried either that they wouldn't be paid back or that the euro zone would break up and they might be paid back in a currency other than euros.

Mr. Draghi saw this. . . . The message to markets was that if there were a run on Spain or Italy, the ECB would be there as long as the governments of Europe gave it cover. So Spain doesn't need to go begging to the rest of Europe and the ECB because the rates it is paying to borrow have fallen. But the reason rates have fallen is that markets figure Spain can get help if needed. This convenient stalemate has eased global fears that the euro will implode. The ECB may never buy a single Spanish bond.

But (there's always a "but") a couple of problems: One, this stalemate has left Spain with an unemployment rate of 26.6%, and that isn't a typo. Two, no one is sure how this would work if Spain did pull the emergency lever. Would the ECB set a ceiling on Spanish rates? Would it stop buying Spanish bonds if Spain didn't keep its fiscal promises, as it says it would? Would investors respond by buying more Spanish bonds because prospects for repayment improved—or by dumping their portfolios onto the ECB?

Mr. Draghi undoubtedly is hoping words will suffice.

SOURCE: David Wessel, "How Jawboning Works," *The Wall Street Journal*, January 9, 2013. Used with permission of Dow Jones & Company, Inc. via Copyright Clearance Center, Inc.

LESSONS OF THE ARTICLE

Communication is a powerful tool of a credible central bank. Forward guidance about monetary policy influences market prices and economic behavior today. Similarly, a central bank that pledges to act as lender of last resort can halt a run on a bank or a sovereign debtor. However, any promise about policy may get tested, so a central bank must follow through if it is to remain credible and effective.

the global economy. Yet, as we have seen, a central bank is unable to set its policy rate below zero.

Because of this zero bound, central banks naturally wish to avoid circumstances that would require a negative policy rate. Thus, if the economy is weak and inflation is both low and falling below the central bank's objective, policymakers might set their target rate temporarily below the one implied by the Taylor rule. This approach accepts as a cost the possibility that inflation will rise temporarily above the objective in the future. The benefit is a lower risk of hitting policy's zero bound. Such a *risk management* approach to policy was a key element of the FOMC's thinking when during 2002–2005 it set the target federal funds rate below the level implied by the Taylor rule. Yet, some economists—including the creator of the Taylor rule—now argue that the Fed's low rate target during this period amplified the housing bubble and contributed to the crisis that followed.[14]

Finally, there is another reason to question the practicality of the Taylor rule in making monetary policy: the lack of real-time data. Policy must be made based on the information available at the time. Figure 18.9 was drawn using data available in June 2013—data that were revised many times after their first release (see Your Financial World: Economic History Is Constantly Changing on page 515). So while we might be able to make good monetary policy for 2005 using the Taylor rule and the data available to us today, that ability really isn't of much practical use. Real-world policymakers have no choice but to make decisions based on information that is less than completely accurate. Their good judgment is the key to successful monetary policy.

Unconventional Policy Tools

We have seen that most central banks set a target for the overnight interbank lending rate in an effort to stabilize the economy and keep inflation low. However, there are two circumstances when additional policy tools can play a useful stabilization role: (1) when lowering the target interest-rate to zero is not sufficient to stimulate the economy and (2) when an impaired financial system prevents conventional interest-rate policy from supporting economic growth.[15] In both cases, unconventional monetary policy can add to the stimulus already coming from conventional policy. When these circumstances arose during the financial crisis of 2007–2009 and in the euro-area crisis that followed, central banks used a variety of unconventional policy tools to supplement conventional interest-rate policy. In this section, we'll examine some of those tools.

First, however, let's dismiss a common belief: that monetary policy becomes ineffective when the target rate is at zero and the financial system is impaired. In these circumstances, skeptics often speak of a "liquidity trap," in which monetary expansion has no impact. Central banks are said to be "pushing on a string." In fact, central banks have powerful tools at their disposal, even in such extreme circumstances. But the problem for central bankers is that the impact of these rarely used unconventional tools is far less predictable than that of day-to-day interest-rate policy. And being responsible public officials, policymakers are loath to treat the economy as a laboratory, risking sudden increases in inflation and the like. This means that using unconventional policies is much more complicated than simply changing an interest-rate target. In addition, the exit from unconventional policies can be difficult and destabilizing. For these reasons, central bankers use unconventional tools only in extraordinary situations when interest-rate policy is clearly insufficient for economic stabilization.

What are the key unconventional policy approaches? While various central banks may label them differently, there are three broad categories: (1) **forward guidance**, in which the central bank communicates its intentions regarding the future path of monetary

---

[14]See, for example, John Taylor, "The Financial Crisis and the Policy Responses: An Empirical Analysis of What Went Wrong," November 2008 (*www.stanford.edu/~johntayl/FCPR.pdf*).

[15]In that circumstance we say that the *transmission* of monetary policy to the economy is impaired. In Chapter 23 we will look at how the usual transmission mechanism can be undermined.

TOOLS OF THE TRADE
Some Unconventional Policy Tools

To stabilize the financial system and the economy during the crisis of 2007–2009, the Fed undertook a range of unprecedented policy actions, both in scale and scope. We saw earlier that the target federal funds rate dropped to the zero bound, while the Fed's balance sheet ballooned. We also saw that the authorities purchased a large volume of assets with credit risk, while cutting traditional holdings of short-term Treasuries (Figure 18.1).

These extraordinary (and frequently controversial) policy interventions were made possible by the introduction of a wide variety of new, temporary policy tools. In this chapter, we have discussed four conventional tools: the target federal funds rate, the discount rate, the deposit rate, and reserve requirements. In addition to these, the Federal Reserve officially recognizes several other unconventional tools, or facilities, which are described in Table 18.2.

Several of these facilities involved lending to nonbanks, something the Fed can do only by invoking its emergency powers in "unusual and exigent circumstances." Look for updates of the Fed's toolkit at www.federalreserve.gov/ monetarypolicy.

Note that Table 18.2 leaves out several important mechanisms that the Fed used extensively in the crisis and thereafter. For example, in 2009, it purchased more than $1 trillion of mortgage-backed securities to help lower the cost of mortgages in a thin market. The volume of that "targeted asset purchase" exceeded the entire Fed balance sheet prior to the crisis! The Fed also expressed its intent to keep the federal funds rate low for an extended period in order to influence long-term interest rate expectations. Such "forward guidance" is discussed later in this chapter.

Table 18.2 Some Unconventional Policy Tools

Policy Tool	Description
Term Auction Facility (TAF) (expired 2010)	The Fed auctions a fixed volume of funds at maturities less than three months against collateral to depository institutions.
Primary Dealer Credit Facility (PDCF) (expired 2010)	The Fed lends overnight to primary dealers (including nonbanks) against a broad range of collateral.
Term Securities Lending Facility (TSLF) (expired 2010)	The Fed provides Treasury securities in exchange for a broad range of collateral in order to promote market liquidity.
Asset-backed Commercial Paper (ABCP) Money-Market Mutual Fund (MMMF) Liquidity Facility (expired 2009)	The Fed lends to depositories and bank holding companies to finance purchases of ABCP from MMMFs.
Commercial Paper Funding Facility (CPFF) (expired 2010)	The Federal Reserve Bank (FRB) of New York finances the purchase of commercial paper from eligible issuers via primary dealers.
Money-Market Investor Funding Facility (MMIFF) (expired 2009)	The FRB New York funds investment vehicles that purchase assets from MMMFs.
Term Asset-Backed Securities Loan Facility (TALF) (expired 2010)	The FRB New York lends to holders of high-rated newly issued asset-backed securities (ABS), using the ABS as collateral.

policy; (2) **quantitative easing** (QE), in which the central bank supplies aggregate reserves beyond the quantity needed to lower the policy rate (such as the federal funds rate in the United States) to its target (usually zero); and (3) **targeted asset purchases** (TAP), in which the central bank alters the mix of assets it holds on its balance sheet in order to change their relative prices (interest rates) in a way that stimulates economic activity. When the Fed refers to its unconventional policy of *large-scale asset purchases,* the term covers both targeted asset purchases and, if the purchases are unsterilized, quantitative easing.[16] That is, Fed large-scale asset purchases are TAP, QE, or both.

In the next section we describe how these three unconventional mechanisms work. Finally, we'll look at how one of the four conventional policy tools—paying interest on reserves—helps a central bank to exit smoothly from unconventional policies (like QE and TAP) that expand the central bank's balance sheet or result in the acquisition of illiquid assets.

Forward Guidance

The simplest unconventional approach a central bank can take is to provide "forward guidance"—guidance today about policy target rates in the *future*. For example, if policymakers believe that inflation will stay well below their objective (see Applying the Concept: Inflation Targeting on page 499), they might express the intention to keep the policy target rate low for an extended period. This forward guidance could have a specific termination date, or its duration could be made contingent on a future change in economic conditions (say, an upturn in business activity or a rise of employment).

How does forward guidance influence the economy and inflation? To stimulate activity, central bank forward guidance aims at lowering the long-term interest rates that affect private spending. As Chapter 7 highlights, long-term bond yields depend in part on expectations about future short-term rates, which the central bank has the power to alter. Consequently, what central bankers say about their future plans can be very important. However, to be effective, forward guidance needs to be credible. Otherwise, long-term market interest rates may not respond as the central bank hopes.

In the past, policymakers used several mechanisms to make their commitments about future policy credible. For example, from the late 1930s until 1951, the Fed purchased long-term Treasury bonds with the objective of capping their interest rates at an artificially low level.[17] However, exiting from such intervention can be disruptive because investors face the prospect of immediate capital losses when yields rise. Consequently, if bondholders fear that the central bank will stop intervening, they may sell immediately. In such circumstances, the only way to sustain the cap on long-term interest rates would be for the central bank to buy *all* the bonds.

Today, many central banks engage in inflation targeting, a policy framework that affects the credibility of forward guidance and can be reinforced by it. For example, forward guidance aimed at keeping interest rates low will be most credible for an inflation-targeting central bank precisely when inflation is expected to stay below target for some time. The reason is that the guidance is time consistent: Future policymakers will not wish to renege. For the same reason, forward guidance can be used to counter the risk of deflation when the target interest rate is at zero and cannot be reduced.

---

[16]In a 2009 speech, Fed Chairman Ben Bernanke differentiated between quantitative easing and credit easing, without referring to targeted asset purchases. But, unlike credit easing, the broader category of targeted asset purchases also includes the acquisition of assets that have the same default risk as the assets sold (e.g., selling Treasury bills to purchase Treasury bonds). See *www.federalreserve.gov/newsevents/speech/bernanke20090113a.htm.*

[17]The 10-year Treasury bond yield remained close to 2 percent in this period.

How has the Federal Reserve used forward guidance? The answer is, with increasing frequency and refinement. In 2002–2004, the FOMC believed that inflation would sink undesirably low and worried about the possibility of deflation. Accordingly, the FOMC stated that its target federal funds rate would stay low for the "foreseeable future" or for a "considerable period." When the Fed began to tighten in 2004, it assured markets that the withdrawal of accommodation would occur at a "measured pace" to avoid fears of sharp rate hikes.

In late 2008, having lowered the policy target to zero during the crisis, policymakers announced that "weak economic conditions are likely to warrant exceptionally low levels of the federal funds rate for some time."[18] Finally, in December 2012, the FOMC went further, stating its expectation that "highly accommodative monetary policy will remain appropriate for a considerable time after . . . the economic recovery strengthens."[19] It also introduced specific thresholds (projected inflation above 2½ percent or an unemployment rate of less than 6½ percent) for raising the target rate.

Although forward guidance can be effective, the Fed's experience suggests that it is difficult to anticipate and reach consensus on the desirable policy path and to communicate these policy intentions in a simple yet precise way. Another concern is the potential for disturbing side effects, including asset price bubbles. Consequently, forward guidance is provided most often in extraordinary circumstances—when the conventional policy toolbox is insufficient to manage expectations.

Quantitative Easing

Quantitative easing (QE) is perhaps the most well-known mechanism to relax the monetary stance when the policy target rate is close to zero. QE occurs when the central bank expands the supply of aggregate reserves to the banking system *beyond* the level that would be needed to maintain its policy rate target. The central bank uses the proceeds from this reserve expansion to

| Table 18.3 | How Quantitative Easing Affects the Central Bank Balance Sheet |

Assets	Liabilities
Treasury bonds (+$1 billion)	Reserves (+$1 billion)

buy assets, thereby expanding its overall balance sheet. In the example in Table 18.3, the central bank adds $1 billion to commercial bank reserves held in their accounts at the Fed and acquires $1 billion in Treasury bonds.

Figure 18.10 illustrates the impact of QE on supply and demand in the federal funds market. At a market federal funds rate of zero, an addition to aggregate reserves no longer reduces the funds rate. The reason is that banks will hold cash (which pays zero interest) rather than lend in the federal funds market at a rate below zero. As a result, the Fed can add limitlessly to reserves—and to the assets on its balance sheet—without depressing the market federal funds rate below zero. The amount of QE is the volume of reserves in excess of the level needed to keep the policy rate at its target, in this case zero. In Figure 18.10, it is the gap between points A and B.

A simple thought experiment shows that QE *can* shape the path of economic growth and inflation, even if the financial system is impaired. Imagine that the central bank

[18]Statement of the Federal Open Market Committee, December 16, 2008. See *www.federalreserve.gov/newsevents/press/monetary/20081216b.htm.*

[19]Statement of the Federal Open Market Committee, December 12, 2012. See *www.federalreserve.gov/newsevents/press/monetary/20121212a.htm.*

Figure 18.10 Quantitative Easing

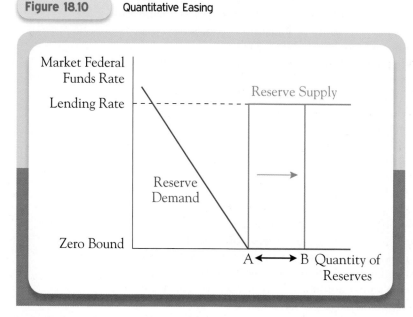

In quantitative easing, the central bank expands the supply of reserves so that the vertical portion of the supply curve lies to the right of the level needed to keep the market funds rate at its target (in this case, zero). The market federal funds rate remains at zero because banks have no better alternative than holding more reserves. The amount of QE is the volume of reserves beyond the level needed to keep the market funds rate at its target (the gap between points A and B).

expands reserves to the point where it purchases *all* of the assets in the economy. For QE to be ineffective, it would imply that the central bank could purchase the entire economy without influencing the level of prices! This nonsensical outcome means that QE, applied with sufficient vigor, can alter economic growth and inflation prospects.

Nonetheless, it is difficult to predict the effects of QE. Fed policymakers argue that their balance sheet expansion helped to lower long-term interest rates, but there is disagreement among experts about the impact—especially in deep, liquid markets—partly because of the lack of experience with QE.[20] Moreover, the mechanism by which QE affects economic prospects is not clear. When interest rates are at zero, banks are indifferent between holding cash, reserve deposits at the central bank, and short-term government debt. All of these assets are riskless, so an increase in the supply of reserves (QE) may simply lead banks to hold more of them rather than provide additional loans to households and firms. This is one version of a "liquidity trap."

Such claims of QE's ineffectiveness were common when the Bank of Japan undertook the practice in the late 1990s. Japanese banks accumulated massive excess reserves, but lending continued to decline. We can see why this happened. After sustaining devastating losses, banks sought to rebuild their financial positions by *deleveraging*—that is, their objective was to lower the ratio of their assets to bank capital (recall Chapter 3, Lessons from the Crisis: Leverage).

How, then, might QE succeed (short of a central bank acquiring a large portion of the assets in an economy to alter the price level)? One mechanism is that it can add credibility to a policymaker's expressed intention to keep interest rates low. Suppose that investors believe that a central bank will keep its policy rate at the zero floor until after it will have exited from QE. Then, announcements of asset purchases that will expand aggregate reserves (QE) could lower bond yields by extending the time horizon over which bondholders expect a zero policy rate. This helps explain why the Fed announces its asset purchase plans well in advance: In doing so, it reinforces the impact of its forward guidance.

A key problem with QE is that central banks do not know how much is needed to be effective. They can only calibrate the appropriate level of reserves by experimentation.

[20]For differing opinions on the impact of QE, see the favorable view of Ben Bernanke ("Opening Remarks," pp. 6–9, *www.federalreserve.gov/newsevents/speech/bernanke20120831a.htm*) and the skeptical view of Michael Woodford ("Accommodation at the Zero Lower Bound," pp. 240–243, *www.kc.frb.org/publicat/sympos/2012/Woodford_final .pdf*) that were presented at the Federal Reserve Bank of Kansas City's August 2012 Economic Policy Symposium.

As the central bank boosts aggregate reserves (and expands its balance sheet), it can observe the impact on financial conditions and the economy. Naturally, this lack of predictability makes policymakers uncomfortable because the experiment might result in an undesirable pickup of inflation. Nevertheless, when conventional policy tools have been exhausted, QE can be an important tool for central bankers to prevent a sustained deflation.

How has the Federal Reserve used QE? Its first and largest application since the Great Depression occurred immediately after the Lehman failure in September 2008, and was subsequently labeled "QE1" (see how the Fed's balance sheet jumped in Figure 18.1). In 2010, and again in 2012, the FOMC judged that inflation was likely to remain below its goal and unemployment would stay far above long-term norms. Consequently, in each of those years, the committee introduced a new round of balance sheet expansion, but perhaps with diminishing marginal impact. Overall, the combination of QE1, QE2, and QE3 boosted the Fed's assets to $3.5 trillion as of mid-2013, up from the pre-QE1 level of less than $900 billion in August 2008. Over the same period, excess reserves in the banking system jumped from less than $2 *billion* to nearly $2 *trillion*. If the FOMC's 2013 pace of asset purchases continues unchanged, the Fed's balance sheet will reach $4 trillion by early 2014. Ultimately, the Fed's experience highlights policymakers' uncertainty about the appropriate dosage of QE. They also lack experience in exiting from QE.

Other major central banks—including the Bank of England, the ECB, and the Bank of Japan—also applied sizable doses of QE beginning in 2008. In each of these instances, central bank balance sheets expanded as policy interest rates sank to record lows. Were the policies effective? These economies showed less resilience than the United States, but their performance might have been even worse without QE.

The newest big QE experiment began in April 2013, when the Bank of Japan announced a round of asset purchases that would double its monetary base in less than two years. Using QE, the Bank aims to end Japan's deflation that began in the 1990s and to achieve its new 2 percent inflation target by 2015. Japan's experience with QE is bound to influence how policymakers in many countries judge the effectiveness of this policy tool.

Targeted Asset Purchases

In contrast to quantitative easing, which increases the *size* of the central bank's balance sheet, targeted asset purchases (TAP) shift the *composition* of the balance sheet toward selected assets in order to boost their relative price and stimulate economic activity.[21]

A simple example of TAP would be for the central bank to sell short-term U.S. Treasury bills and buy mortgage-backed securities (MBS, see page 53) of similar maturity. As seen in Table 18.4, this shift leaves the size of the balance sheet unchanged. Only the mix of assets is altered.

Table 18.4   How Targeted Asset Purchases Affect the Central Bank's Balance Sheet

Assets	Liabilities
3-month Treasury bills (−$1 billion) Mortgage-backed securities (+$1 billion)	

[21]For the theory of targeted asset purchases, see pp. 243–252 in Michael Woodford, "Accommodation at the Zero Lower Bound," Federal Reserve Bank of Kansas City Economic Policy Symposium, August 2012, *www.kc.frb.org/publicat/sympos/2012/Woodford_final.pdf*.

How does TAP alter the outlook for the economy and inflation? The central bank's actions can influence both the *cost* and *availability* of credit. When the central bank acquires an asset, such as MBS, it increases the overall demand for the asset. Increased demand tends to boost its price while driving its yield down. In the absence of private demand for the targeted asset, the central bank's purchase makes credit available where none existed.

The impact of TAP is likely to be greater in thin, illiquid markets. Under such conditions, even small interventions can have a magnified effect on market prices. The impact of TAP is also likely to be larger the bigger the difference between the yield on the asset that the central bank buys and the yield on the asset that the central bank sells. Assets with similar yields and risk characteristics are usually *close substitutes*. Assets with different risk characteristics and yields are less substitutable. By altering the relative supply of such assets to private investors, TAP narrows their interest-rate differences.

The Federal Reserve's use of TAP in the financial crisis was unprecedented. In Figure 18.1, assets with default risk ("Lending to financial institutions" and "Liquidity to key credit markets") temporarily became the largest component of the Fed's balance sheet. Over time, the largest examples of TAP were the Fed's acquisitions of more than $1.3 trillion of MBS and more than $1.6 trillion of long-term Treasury debt. The goal was to lower yields on mortgages and other long-term bonds and support interest-sensitive outlays, especially for housing.

Like the Fed, the ECB used TAP (and other targeted actions) aggressively in seeking to calm the euro-area crisis. To limit the widening yield spreads on the sovereign debt of countries on the periphery of the euro area (namely, Greece, Ireland, Italy, Portugal, and Spain), the ECB acquired more than €200 billion of this debt in its "securities market program." It also offered to purchase without limit the secondary-market debt (up to three years in maturity) of any country that accepted the stringent fiscal conditions for such "outright monetary transactions" (see In the News). Finally, the ECB widened the range of acceptable collateral in order to boost the relative prices of troubled assets and to make funds available to periphery banks lacking better collateral.

Like QE, TAP is significantly more unwieldy for central bankers than conventional interest-rate policy. A central bank cannot reliably anticipate the impact of TAP on the cost of credit. And TAP poses concerns that need not arise with QE. For example, like fiscal policy, TAP favors some users of credit over others. The special access that the Fed provided to issuers of commercial paper during the crisis is one example. In normal times, using conventional policy techniques, a central bank typically avoids such direct allocation of credit, promoting market competition rather than picking winners. TAP purposely deviates from such *asset neutrality* in order to influence relative prices.

Exiting from TAP probably also is more difficult than unwinding QE. TAP assets are generally harder to sell—that is, they are less liquid—than short-term Treasuries, so the central bank may not be able to get rid of them exactly when it wants without a significant price discount. In addition, political influences can become important if powerful users of credit and their government representatives seek to hinder the Fed from selling specific assets for fear of raising the costs of a particular class of borrowers.

Making an Effective Exit

When central banks pursue conventional interest-rate targets, officials think about the policy choices they face every six to eight weeks. Deliberations are continuous, forming a *strategy* that influences expectations about the future path of their instrument and their objective. Decisions are not a series of one-time, unrelated choices. We can think of central bankers setting interest rates as participating in a complicated game—like chess—that requires them to make moves today while keeping in mind moves they may need to make far in the future.

The introduction of and exit from unconventional policies—such as forward guidance, quantitative easing, and targeted asset purchases—also require looking into the future. Without a consistent and credible approach, policymakers may be unable to keep inflation expectations close to their inflation objective. And, if they fail, unstable inflation expectations could lead to broader economic instability.

Compared with conventional policy, exiting from QE and TAP poses additional obstacles that appear technical but have important implications. The key question is whether a central bank that wishes to raise interest rates in order to tighten policy conditions will be able to do so as quickly as desired. With conventional policy, the answer is yes. In the case of QE and TAP, the answer depends on the size and composition of the central bank's balance sheet and on the toolset available to the policymakers.

With conventional policy, a central bank that wishes to hike the policy rate can do so by modestly trimming the aggregate reserves that it supplies to the banking system. A central bank may hold enough short-term risk-free assets (such as Treasury bills) to reduce the supply of reserves merely by allowing some of these assets to mature. If necessary, the authorities also could sell a portion of these assets, which are among the most liquid.

What happens when QE and TAP have vastly expanded the amount of reserves and assets on the central bank's balance sheet? The answer is that the central bank may need to sell a large volume of assets to reduce reserve supply sufficiently to raise the policy rate target. But TAP assets are typically more difficult to sell (less liquid) than Treasury bills. Moreover, the value of any TAP assets that default will plunge. In these circumstances, a central bank may be unable to sell assets and withdraw reserves from the banking system rapidly enough to hike the policy interest rate when it desires. So what can authorities do?

Following the financial crisis of 2007–2009, many people worried that the swollen balance sheets of the Fed and other central banks would lead to runaway inflation. Everybody knows that a timely exit from QE and TAP is necessary to keep inflation low. But will it be possible?

The answer is yes. In fact, central banks like the Fed have several policy options that allow them to tighten without having to sell their assets. The most important one is that policymakers can employ a conventional tool in an unconventional way: namely, they can raise the deposit rate that the central bank pays on reserves. Figure 18.11 on page 514 shows an example in which the Fed raises its deposit rate from zero to a new positive rate X. The deposit rate sets a floor for the market federal funds rate, even if the Fed does not reduce its supply of reserves. The reason is that, once the market funds rate falls to the deposit rate, banks have no better alternative than to hold additional reserves on deposit at the central bank. Their reserve demand shifts from RD_0 to RD_1 in the figure, moving the equilibrium of reserve demand and supply from point A to point B.

So, by hiking the deposit rate, the Fed can raise the target federal funds rate without reducing the level of reserve supply or changing the composition of its balance sheet. Unlike the typical monopolist, who can control either price or quantity, the Fed can control both! Paying interest on reserves allows a central bank to use two powerful policy tools independently of one another: (1) it can adjust the target rate for interbank loans without changing the size or composition of its balance sheet, and (2) it can

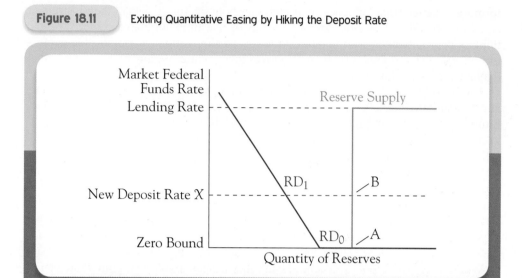

Figure 18.11 Exiting Quantitative Easing by Hiking the Deposit Rate

By hiking the deposit rate from zero to X, the central bank changes reserve demand from RD_0 to RD_1. RD_1 turns flat at the new deposit rate X (dashed red line), because banks have no better alternative to holding reserves when the market funds rate falls to X. By hiking the deposit rate, the central bank raises the floor for the market funds rate without reducing the supply of reserves. The equilibrium in reserve supply and demand moves from point A to point B.

adjust the size and composition of its balance sheet without changing the target rate for interbank loans.

This flexibility means that the central bank can change its balance sheet in a fashion consistent with financial stability while keeping inflation under control. Specifically, if they wish to hike the target interest rate, policymakers holding large quantities of illiquid assets can avoid a fire sale by simply raising the deposit rate that they pay on reserves.[22] Central bankers are unlikely to acquire illiquid assets except in extreme circumstances, but their toolbox allows them to do it without sacrificing inflation credibility—provided, that is, that they can adjust the rate that they pay on reserves (the deposit rate) when necessary. Today, leading central banks like the Fed and the ECB have this authority and use it.

Concluding Remarks

In truth, central bankers have a nearly impossible job. They are supposed to stabilize the economy and financial system at the same time that they provide services to commercial banks and the government. To perform this task, we give them control

---

[22]The Fed's extraordinary holdings of long-term Treasuries and MBS, combined with its obligation to pay interest on reserves, mean that the central bank bears interest-rate risk well in excess of historical norms. As a result, says a 2013 analysis by Federal Reserve Board staff, when interest rates rise, the Fed could face net losses that temporarily halt its remittances to Treasury. However, the analysis also judges that the large asset holdings will have boosted the Fed's cumulative earnings over time. See Seth B. Carpenter, Jane E. Ihrig, Elizabeth C. Klee, Daniel W. Quinn, and Alexander H. Boote, "The Federal Reserve's Balance Sheet and Earnings: A Primer and Projections," Finance and Economics Discussion Series No. 2013-01, Federal Reserve Board, January 2013, *www.federalreserve.gov/pubs/feds/2013/index.html.*

YOUR FINANCIAL WORLD
Economic History Is Constantly Changing

The publication of new economic growth data makes headlines. Every three months, the Department of Commerce's Bureau of Economic Analysis publishes information on GDP for the preceding quarter. So at the end of April, we get the first estimate of growth for January through March, and news reporters trumpet it. Such attention would make sense except for the fact that the data are then revised numerous times. Only the initial estimates come out in April; in May, June, and July, they are revised as government statisticians slowly accumulate more information about what actually happened. And every July for the next three years they are revised again. By July 2013, GDP for the first quarter of 2010 had been revised six times! Every five years or so after that, the data are revised yet again as new surveys of the population and business activity become available and as statisticians advance the base year for decomposing GDP into prices and quantities (see Appendix A to Chapter 1).

These revisions would be irrelevant if they were small, but they are not. An example will show how large the change can be. Figure 18.12 plots the progression of estimates of GDP growth for the third quarter of 1990, the trough of a mild recession.* The initial estimate, published in October 1990, suggested that the economy had grown +1.8 percent. The economy had been doing poorly, so this news was welcome. But as the data were revised, the story changed. Growth estimates dropped to −1.9 percent for a while, finally settling at zero percent in 2004.

What this means is that history is constantly changing. Our view of what really happened in the economy must be adjusted regularly. So when you see a headline announcing the publication of data on recent growth in GDP, remember that today's figure is just a rough estimate. And the uncertainty is high: The standard deviation of revisions from the earliest to the latest estimates of GDP is 1.6 percent, or more than half the 2.6 percent average growth rate since 1980. So, five years or more will pass before economists know what actually happened.

*These data come from a real-time database maintained by the Federal Reserve Bank of Philadelphia. For a description of the data, see Dean Croushore and Tom Stark, "A Funny Thing Happened on the Way to the Data Bank: A Real-Time Data Set for Macroeconomists," *Business Review* of the Federal Reserve Bank of Philadelphia, September/October 2000, pp. 15–27.

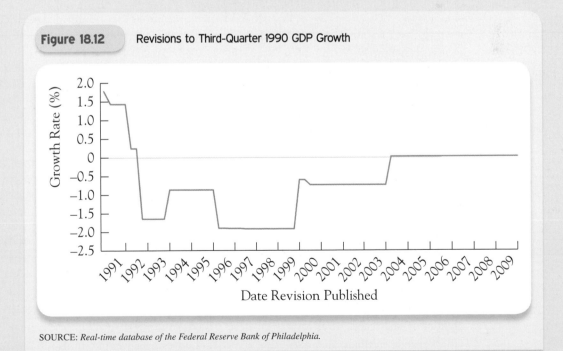

Figure 18.12 Revisions to Third-Quarter 1990 GDP Growth

SOURCE: *Real-time database of the Federal Reserve Bank of Philadelphia.*

over their own balance sheet, allowing them to buy and sell securities in the financial markets and make loans to banks. In normal times, they choose to control the price of reserves, which is an interest rate. Because movements in interest rates affect the entire economic system, control over interest rates usually gives monetary policymakers the leverage they need to stabilize inflation rates, growth rates, and the financial system. As we will see in detail in Part V, higher interest rates slow inflation and growth by reducing the availability of credit; lower interest rates stimulate economic activity by making credit cheaper and easier to get. But monetary policy requires unconventional tools when interest rates sink to the zero lower bound, or when financial institutions or markets become dysfunctional.

Over the years, central bankers have learned from their mistakes. They understand the importance of keeping the financial system running smoothly and have refined their ability to lend quickly in times of crisis. And because everyone understands the importance of keeping inflation low, we have designed our central banks to deliver price stability. The outcome is that the inflation rate is lower now than it was from 1970 to 1995.

Today we have a set of principles that tells us how central banks should be designed and how they should use interest rates to stabilize their economy. But central bankers cannot do the job alone. Sound monetary policy must be combined with responsible fiscal policy to build a healthy economic and financial system. Moreover, with the fading economic importance of national borders, the time has passed when even large central banks could avoid taking international conditions into account. To fill this hole in our analysis, we turn in Chapter 19 to a study of exchange rate management and the international financial system.

Terms

conventional policy tools, 484

deposit rate, 485

discount lending, 489

discount rate, 485

ECB's Deposit Facility, 495

ECB's Marginal Lending Facility, 495

forward guidance, 506

inflation targeting, 499

intermediate targets, 500

lender of last resort, 489

market federal funds rate, 486

minimum bid rate, 493

overnight cash rate, 496

primary credit, 490

primary discount rate, 490

quantitative easing, 508

repurchase agreement (repo), 493

reserve requirement, 485

secondary discount rate, 491

target federal funds rate, 485

targeted asset purchases, 508

Taylor rule, 501

unconventional policy tools, 484

zero bound, 482

Using FRED: Codes for Data in This Chapter

Data Series	FRED Data Code
FRB assets	WALCL
MBS	WSHOMCB
Treasuries	WSHOTS
Agencies	WSHOFDSL
Repos	WARAL
Loans	WALLNL
Federal funds rate	FEDFUNDS
Discount rate	WPCREDIT
Interest paid on excess reserves	INTRESEXCW
Required reserves	REQRESNS
Total reserves	TOTRESNS
Primary credit	WPC
Potential GDP	GDPPOT
Real GDP	GDPC1
Personal consumption expenditures price index	PCEPI
Personal consumption expenditures price index (less food and energy)	JCXFE

Chapter Lessons

1. The Federal Reserve has four conventional monetary policy tools.
   a. The target federal funds rate is the primary instrument of monetary policy.
      i. Open market operations are used to control the federal funds rate.
      ii. The Fed forecasts the demand for reserves each day and then supplies the amount needed to meet the demand at the target rate.
   b. The discount lending rate is used to supply funds to banks, particularly during crises.
      i. The Fed sets the primary lending rate at a spread above the target federal funds rate.
      ii. In setting the primary lending rate above the target federal funds rate, the Fed is attempting to stabilize the market interest rate on overnight interbank lending. The primary lending rate is the ceiling for the market rate on overnight interbank loans.
      iii. The Fed also makes loans to banks in distress and to banks in need of seasonal liquidity.
   c. The deposit rate is the rate that the Fed pays on reserves held by banks at the central bank.
      i. The deposit rate is set at a spread below the target federal funds rate.
      ii. The deposit rate determines the floor for the market rate on overnight interbank loans.
   d. Reserve requirements are used to stabilize the demand for reserves.
      i. Banks are required to hold reserves against certain deposits.

    ii. Banks can hold either deposits at Federal Reserve Banks that earn interest or vault cash.

    iii. Reserves are accounted for in such a way that everyone knows the level of reserves required before banks must hold them.

2. The European Central Bank's primary objective is price stability.
    a. The ECB provides liquidity to the banking system primarily through auctions called refinancing operations.
    b. The minimum bid rate on the main refinancing operations, also known as the target refinancing rate, is the target interest rate controlled by the Governing Council.
    c. The ECB allows banks to borrow from the marginal lending facility at an interest rate that is set above the target refinancing rate.
    d. Banks with excess reserves can deposit them at national central banks and receive interest at a spread below the target refinancing rate.
    e. European banks are required to hold reserves; they receive an interest rate on their balances that is equal to the average of the rate in recent refinancing operations.

3. Monetary policymakers use several tools to meet their objectives.
    a. The best tools are observable, controllable, and tightly linked to objectives.
    b. Short-term interest rates are the primary tools for monetary policymaking.
    c. Modern central banks do not use intermediate targets like money growth.

4. The Taylor rule is a simple equation that describes movements in the federal funds target rate. It suggests that
    a. When inflation rises, the FOMC raises the target interest rate by 1½ times the increase.
    b. When output rises above potential by 1 percent, the FOMC raises the target interest rate half a percentage point.

5. Unconventional monetary policy can supplement conventional policy when a zero policy rate is not low enough to stabilize the economy or when an impaired financial system prevents conventional interest-rate policy from working. The three principal unconventional tools of the central bank are:
    a. Forward guidance: communication regarding expected future policy target rates.
    b. Quantitative easing: supplying aggregate reserves beyond the quantity needed to lower the policy rate to the target (usually zero).
    c. Targeted asset purchases: changing the mix of assets at the central bank to alter their relative prices.

6. Unconventional monetary policy is unpredictable and potentially disruptive, so it is used only in those extraordinary circumstances when the conventional toolkit is insufficient to stabilize the economy. One conventional policy tool—the payment of interest on reserves—can help a central bank exit smoothly from unconventional monetary policy.

Conceptual and Analytical Problems

1. Suppose, one morning, the Open Market Trading Desk drastically underestimates the demand for reserves when deciding the quantity of reserves to supply to the market. Based on analysis of the market for bank reserves, explain why

the market federal funds rate will not exceed the discount rate regardless of how large the gap between estimated and actual reserve demand. *(LO2)*

2. Consider a situation where reserve requirements are binding and the Federal Reserve decides to reduce the requirements. How would the Open Market Trading Desk act to maintain the interest rate target, assuming the demand for excess reserves remains unchanged. *(LO2)*

3. Suppose the Federal Reserve did not pay interest on excess reserves. How would the reserve demand curve differ from that in Figure 18.2? *(LO1)*

4.* In a graph of the market for bank reserves, show how the Federal Reserve limits deviations of the market federal funds rate from its interest rate target under the channel system. Next, show how the Open Market Trading Desk would implement a decision by the FOMC to raise the target federal funds rate. Assume that the Fed alters the discount and deposit rates to maintain fixed spreads between them and the target federal funds rate. *(LO1)*

5. From 1979 to 1982, the FOMC used money growth as an intermediate target. To do so, the committee instructed the Open Market Trading Desk to target the level of reserves in the banking system. What was the justification for doing so? Explain why the result was unstable interest rates. Would you advocate a return to reserve targeting? Why or why not? *(LO2)*

6. Federal Reserve buying of mortgage-backed securities is an example of a targeted asset purchase. Explain how the Fed's actions are intended to work. *(LO2)*

7. The strategy of inflation targeting, which seeks to keep inflation close to a numerical goal over a reasonable horizon, has been referred to as a policy of "constrained discretion." What does this mean? *(LO2)*

8. The charge given by Congress to the Federal Reserve is to "promote effectively the goals of maximum employment, stable prices, and moderate long-term interest rates." Discuss whether the Taylor rule conforms to this mandate. *(LO3)*

9. Discuss the coefficients on the inflation gap and output gap terms in the Taylor rule given in equation (1). If you could change the relative importance of the coefficients, what would you choose? *(LO3)*

10. Use the following Taylor rule to calculate what would happen to the real interest rate if inflation increased by 3 percentage points. *(LO3)*

$$\text{Target federal funds rate} = 2 + \text{Current inflation} + \tfrac{1}{2}(\text{Inflation gap}) + \tfrac{1}{2}(\text{Output gap})$$

11.* The Taylor rule in Problem 10 is thought to be a reasonably good description of policy behavior in the United States in the absence of unusual financial market conditions or deflationary worries. Taking into account what you know about the policy goals of the ECB and that the average growth rate tends to be lower in Europe than in the United States, how would you amend the Taylor rule to better approximate policymaking behavior by the ECB? *(LO3)*

12. Go to the website of the Federal Reserve Board at www.federalreserve.gov and find the section describing monetary policy tools. Which unconventional tools employed during the financial crisis of 2007–2009 has the Fed stopped using? What do you think determined the order in which various facilities were shut down? Which, if any, of the tools still remain in operation? *(LO4)*

*Indicates more difficult problems

13.* Use your knowledge of the problems associated with asymmetric information to explain why, prior to the change in the Federal Reserve's discount lending facility in 2002, banks were extremely unlikely to borrow from the facility despite funds being available at a rate below the target federal funds rate. *(LO1)*

14. The ECB pays a market-based interest rate on required reserves and a lower rate on excess reserves. Explain why the system is structured this way. *(LO1)*

15. Based on the liquidity premium theory of the term structure of interest rates, explain how forward guidance about monetary policy can lower long-term interest rates today. Be sure to account for both future short-term rates and for the risk premium. How does the effectiveness of forward guidance depend on its time consistency? *(LO4)*

16. With the policy interest rate at zero, how might a central bank counter unwanted deflation? *(LO4)*

17.* Outline and compare the ways in which the Federal Reserve and the ECB added to or adjusted their monetary policy tools in response to the financial crisis of 2007–2009 and the subsequent financial crisis in the euro area. *(LO2)*

18. How might the Federal Reserve exit from the unconventional policies it employed during the financial crisis of 2007–2009 without causing inflationary problems? *(LO4)*

19. The central bank of a country facing economic and financial market difficulties asks for your advice. The bank hit the zero bound with its policy interest rate, but it wasn't enough to stabilize the economy. Drawing on the actions taken by the Federal Reserve during the financial crisis of 2007–2009, what might you advise this central bank to do?

20.* Suppose ECB officials ask your opinion about their operational framework for monetary policy. You respond by commenting on their success at keeping short-term interest rates close to target but also express concern about the complexity of their process for managing the supply of reserves. What specific changes would you suggest the ECB make to its system in the future? *(LO3)*

Data Exploration

Scan here for quick access to the resources for these problems. Need a barcode reader? Try ScanLife, available in your app store.

For general information on using Federal Reserve Economic Data (FRED) online, visit www.mhhe.com/moneyandbanking4e and click on Student Edition, then FRED Resources.

1. Plot the Taylor Rule since 1990 on a quarterly basis (similar to Figure 18.9). For the output gap, use the percent deviations of real GDP (FRED code: GDPC1) from potential output (FRED code: GDPPOT). For inflation, use the percent change from a year ago of the price index for personal consumption expenditures (FRED code: PCEPI). Assume that the long-run risk-free rate averages 2 percent and the target inflation rate is 2 percent. When complete, compare the Taylor rule rate against the actual federal funds rate (FRED code: FEDFUNDS) after 2007. *(LO3)*

2. Inflation is expected to rise when the Taylor rule persistently and significantly exceeds the federal funds rate. Conversely, inflation is expected to decline when the federal funds rate exceeds the rule. Using the same indicators as in Data Exploration Problem 1, plot since 1965 on a quarterly basis the *gap* between the Taylor rule and

www.mhhe.com/moneyandbanking4e

the federal funds rate, together with the inflation rate. Over long periods of time, does inflation rise when the Taylor rule exceeds the federal funds rate? Does it fall when the federal funds rate exceeds the Taylor rule? *(LO3)*

3. Assess the impact of targeted asset purchases by plotting since 2003 on a monthly basis the Federal Reserve's holdings of mortgage-backed securities (FRED code: MBST) and (on the right scale) the average yield on 30-year fixed-rate mortgages (FRED code: MORTGAGE30US). Discuss how these purchases might support both the housing market and the banking system. *(LO4)*

4. In 2002, the Federal Reserve began to set the discount rate *above* the federal funds rate, reversing its previous practice of keeping the discount rate below the funds rate. To assess the impact, plot on a monthly basis from 1990 to 2007 the difference between the federal funds rate and the discount rate *before* (FRED codes: FEDFUNDS and MDISCRT) and after the policy shift (FRED codes: FEDFUNDS and WPCREDIT), using the same line color. On the right scale, plot the level of discount window borrowing (FRED code: DISCBORR). Did the new penalty rate for discount loans significantly diminish borrowing? What might account for this result? *(LO1)*

5. With nominal interest rates at zero, expectations of deflation raise the real interest rate. Japan has faced the zero-bound and deflation problems for many years. Plot since 2000 the nominal interest rate on Japanese Treasury bills (FRED code: INTGSTJPM193N), the inflation rate based on the percent change from a year ago of Japan's consumer price index (FRED code: JPNCPIALLMINMEI), and an estimate of the real interest rate based on the difference between these two indicators. Comment on the risks that deflation poses in an economy with a zero nominal interest rate. *(LO1)*

Chapter 19

Exchange-Rate Policy and the Central Bank

Learning Objectives

Understand . . .

LO1   Links between exchange rates and monetary policy

LO2   The mechanics of exchange-rate management

LO3   Costs, benefits, and risks of fixed exchange rates

LO4   Fixed exchange-rate regimes

On the morning of September 22, 2000, the Federal Reserve Bank of New York's foreign exchange desk began buying euros for the first time since the currency came into existence 21 months earlier. Meanwhile, central bank officials in Frankfurt, London, Tokyo, and Ottawa (Canada) did the same. Among them, they bought between €4 and €6 billion. The Fed alone bought €1.5 billion for $1.34 billion. At this writing, the Fed has conducted only one **foreign exchange intervention** since the September 2000 operation.[1]

The whole operation took about two hours; when it was over, the central banks announced what they had done. As the ECB wrote in its press release, they did it because of "shared concern about the potential implications of recent movements in the euro exchange rate for the world economy." Since its inception on January 1, 1999, the euro had fallen steadily from $1.18 to $0.85, a decline of more than 25 percent. Though its low value had made exports cheap, bolstering the foreign sales of European-made products, it had also forced up the prices of imports. ECB officials, charged with maintaining price stability, found the high price of imports particularly troubling because they really did not want to raise interest rates just to bolster the value of their currency (which is what they would have had to do). Experts debated whether the euro should be worth $1.10 or $1, but most agreed that $0.85 was too low.

The coordinated intervention in the foreign exchange market made headlines around the world. The euro appreciated briefly, rising to $0.89 on the day of the intervention,

---

[1]On March 18, 2011, the Fed sold $1 billion of Japanese yen in a coordinated intervention involving the ECB and the central banks of Canada, Japan, and the United Kingdom. The central banks acted jointly to counter the sudden rise in the value of the yen that followed Japan's March 11 earthquake and tsunami. After those natural disasters, currency speculators purchased yen, believing that Japanese holders of foreign assets would sell their investments abroad and repatriate the funds to finance domestic reconstruction. The intervention weakened the yen for a few weeks, but it began to appreciate again and surpassed the March peak by July.

but by mid-October, it had returned to $0.85. The action may have been dramatic, but it wasn't effective. To understand why the intervention didn't work, and why the Fed almost never engages in such foreign currency transactions, we need to examine the mechanics of how a central bank manages its country's exchange rate.

The United States economy is huge and largely self-contained. Exports and imports together account for only about 30 percent of GDP. For the most part, the U.S. economy produces what it consumes and invests, so, on most days, policymakers at the Fed are justified in concentrating on the domestic economy and letting the exchange rate take care of itself. In contrast, highly *open* economies are more exposed to trade developments in the rest of the world, so changes in their exchange rates can have a dramatic impact on them. For example, in small economies, imports and exports together frequently exceed 100 percent of GDP, so their central banks do not have the luxury of ignoring the exchange rate. While large economies typically are less exposed, trade accounts for nearly of half of GDP in the euro area and a bit more than half in China, the world's largest exporter and the second-largest economy.

Argentina provides an interesting example of how external and domestic factors interact in the making of monetary policy. Over the years, Argentina has suffered from severe inflation. During the 1970s, inflation averaged about 100 percent, meaning that prices doubled every year, while the economy grew about 3 percent a year. By 1989, inflation had climbed to more than 2,000 percent per year and the price level was *60 billion* times what it had been 20 years before. Needless to say, growth fell. In 1990, real GDP was below its 1973 level and Argentina's economy was at a standstill.

The cause of such high inflation is often a combination of failed fiscal policy and failed monetary policy. Politicians want to spend too much, so they lean on central bankers to print more money. To discipline policymakers, in 1991 Argentineans implemented a mechanism called a *currency board,* which had two important attributes. First, Argentina's central bank, the Banco Central de la Republica Argentina, guaranteed that it would exchange Argentinean pesos for U.S. dollars on a one-for-one basis; it fixed its exchange rate. Second, the central bank was required to hold dollar assets equal to its domestic currency liabilities, again at a one-to-one exchange rate. For every peso note that was issued and every peso in commercial bank reserves that it created, the Central Bank of Argentina had to hold one U.S. dollar.

The results were almost miraculous. Inflation fell immediately; after a few years, it had completely disappeared. But as we will see later, the victory didn't last. By early January 2002, the currency board had collapsed, GDP had fallen by a quarter, and inflation had risen to more than 30 percent.

The examples of the euro purchases in 2000 and the Argentine exchange-rate actions suggest a connection between domestic monetary policy and exchange-rate policy. To avoid raising domestic interest rates, the ECB organized a coordinated intervention to shore up the value of the euro. To control the inflationary impulses of fiscal and monetary authorities, Argentina fixed its exchange rate to the dollar. If exchange-rate policy is inseparable from interest-rate policy, we have left something essential out of our analysis by ignoring cross-border transactions. To rectify the omission, we turn now to a discussion of exchange-rate regimes. Why is a country's exchange rate linked to its domestic monetary policy? Are there circumstances when exchange-rate stabilization becomes the overriding objective of central bankers? If so, should they try to fix the rate at which their currency can be exchanged for some other currency? Should a country even consider giving up its currency entirely?

Linking Exchange-Rate Policy with Domestic Monetary Policy

Exchange-rate policy is integral to any monetary policy regime. The city of Chicago, for instance, has a fixed exchange rate with the rest of the United States—both use the dollar—so it has no independent monetary policy. Because Chicago's monetary policy is made by the FOMC, interest rates in Chicago are the same as interest rates everywhere else in the United States. Any discrepancy between the price of a bond in Chicago and the price of the same bond in San Francisco is wiped out instantly by arbitrage, as investors buy the bond where it is cheap and sell it where it is expensive (all this is done electronically). What is true for Chicago is true for any country: *when capital flows freely across a country's borders, a fixed exchange rate means giving up domestic monetary policy.*

There are two ways to see the connection between exchange rates and monetary policy. The first comes from thinking about the market for goods and *purchasing power parity;* the second builds on the Chicago/San Francisco bond market arbitrage example. Purchasing power parity tells us about the long-run tendencies of exchange rates, while capital market arbitrage shows us how short-run movements in exchange rates are tied to the supply and demand in the currency markets. Let's look at each of these approaches in more detail.

Inflation and the Long-Run Implications of Purchasing Power Parity

In Chapter 10, we studied the long-run determinants of exchange rates starting with the *law of one price.* Ignoring transportation costs, the law of one price says that identical goods should sell for the same price regardless of where they are sold. That is, the same television set should sell for the same price in Philadelphia and St. Louis. The concept of purchasing power parity extends the logic of the law of one price to a basket of goods and services. As long as goods can move freely across international boundaries, one unit of domestic currency should buy the same basket of goods anywhere in the world.

This apparently simple idea has important implications. It means that when prices change in one country but not in another, the exchange rate will adjust to reflect the change. If Mexican inflation is higher than U.S. inflation, for instance, the Mexican peso should depreciate relative to the dollar. If everything in Mexico costs more pesos, dollars should cost more pesos, too. Figure 10.4 confirmed that this principle works well over periods of several decades. *In the long run, changes in the exchange rate are tied to differences in inflation.*

To understand how this works, recall that purchasing power parity means that

$$\text{Pesos per dollar} = \frac{\text{Peso price of basket of goods in Mexico}}{\text{Dollar price of basket of goods in U.S.}} \tag{1}$$

Taking the percentage change of both sides of this expression, we get[2]

$$\begin{bmatrix} \text{Percentage change} \\ \text{in number of pesos} \\ \text{per dollar} \end{bmatrix} = \begin{bmatrix} \text{Percentage change in} \\ \text{peso price of basket} \\ \text{of goods in Mexico} \end{bmatrix} - \begin{bmatrix} \text{Percentage change in} \\ \text{dollar price of basket} \\ \text{of goods in U.S.} \end{bmatrix} \tag{2}$$

---

[2]In going from equation (1) to equation (2), we are using the approximation that the percentage change in (X/Y) equals the percentage change in X *minus* the percentage change in Y. This approximation works best for small percentage changes.

Because the percentage change in the price of the basket of goods is the same as inflation, we can rewrite this expression as

$$\begin{bmatrix} \text{Percentage change} \\ \text{in number of pesos} \\ \text{per dollar} \end{bmatrix} = [\text{Mexican inflation rate}] - [\text{U.S. inflation rate}] \quad (3)$$

Thus, when the Mexican inflation rate is higher than the U.S. inflation rate, the number of pesos needed to buy a dollar rises. When the U.S. inflation rate is higher than the Mexican inflation rate, the reverse is true. An example can help us to see how this works. Say we need 10 pesos to purchase a dollar (so a peso is worth 10 cents) at the beginning of the year. During the year, the Mexican inflation rate is 5 percent, and the U.S. inflation rate is 2 percent. At the end of the year, we would expect the exchange rate to change so we need 3 percent more pesos to purchase a dollar, or 10.3 pesos per dollar.

Purchasing power parity has immediate implications for monetary policy. If the Banco de México, Mexico's central bank, wants to fix its exchange rate, then Mexican monetary policy must be conducted so that Mexican inflation matches U.S. inflation. Alternatively, if Mexico wants its inflation rate to diverge from the U.S. inflation rate, the peso–dollar exchange rate must be allowed to vary. *The central bank must choose between a fixed exchange rate and an independent inflation policy; it cannot have both.*

We could stop here, except for the fact that purchasing power parity works only over long periods, like decades. That is, even though the exchange rate *eventually* adjusts to differences between prices at home and abroad, deviations from purchasing power parity can last for years. While this time lag in exchange-rate movements might appear to ease restrictions on monetary policy, in fact it does not. To understand why, we need to examine what happens in the capital markets when investors can move their funds freely across international boundaries.

Interest Rates and the Short-Run Implications of Capital Market Arbitrage

In the short run, a country's exchange rate is determined by supply and demand. The exchange value of the dollar depends on factors such as the preferences of Americans for foreign assets and the preferences of foreign investors for U.S. assets. In the short run, investors play a crucial role, because they are the ones who can move large quantities of dollars, euros, pounds, or pesos across international borders. Assuming that governments allow funds to flow into and out of their countries, these movements can occur very quickly.

To understand the implications of international capital mobility, we need to look at how investors decide whether to purchase a foreign or a domestic bond. Given two bonds of equal risk, investors will always buy the one with the higher expected return. And when two otherwise identical bonds differ in yield, investors will bid up the price of the high-return bond and bid down the price of the low-return bond until the two converge. Thus, arbitrage in the capital market ensures that two equally risky bonds have the same expected return.

Like purchasing power parity, capital market arbitrage has immediate implications for monetary policy. Think about two bonds that are identical except that one is issued in Chicago and the other in San Francisco. The two bonds are equally risky, with the same time to maturity and the same coupon rate. Arbitrage ensures that they will sell

YOUR FINANCIAL WORLD
Emerging Market Crises and You

One morning you awaken to news of a severe financial crisis in an emerging market country. As in Asia in 1997 and Latin America in 2002, some part of the developing world appears to be near collapse. The guardians of the financial system—officials from the central bank, the finance ministry, and international organizations like the IMF—are convening to decide what to do. In the meantime, the market value of investments in the emerging world is plummeting as traders flee to safety, moving their money into the United States and Europe. What should you do?

If you followed the advice in Chapter 10, some of your investments are in foreign stocks and bonds, so this crisis looks as if it may have an impact on you. Will it? The answer is it will probably have little sustained effect. Here's why. First, your portfolio should be well diversified, so you will be prepared for the possibility that some of your investments will do poorly. Second, most emerging market countries are small in an economic sense—the fact that they are "emerging" means they are at an early stage of development—so

your investments there will be small. To give some idea of just how small these countries are economically and financially, note that Malaysia's GDP is about one-fiftieth the size of the U.S. GDP, and the Malaysian stock market is one-fortieth the size of the U.S. financial market. In fact, if you diversified your investments internationally, purchasing stocks based on the size of each country's capital market, for each $100 you invested, you would put $35 in the United States, $22 in western Europe, $7 in Japan, and 90 cents in Malaysia! So, even if the Malaysian stock market were to fall by 50 percent, you would only lose 45 cents per $100 you had invested.

Finally, most of your investments are likely to be in a retirement account, which you probably won't need for decades. Over the years that you hold these investments, their value will go up and down; occasional losses are just bumps in the road. As long as you take a long-term perspective and diversify your holdings, these crises will have only a negligible impact on you.

for the same price and so have the same interest rate. Does it matter that both these bonds make payments in dollars?

To answer this question, we can substitute bonds issued in different countries that promise payments in their currencies. What happens if we compare a Chicago bond to an otherwise identical bond issued in London and denominated in pounds? At what interest rates will investors be indifferent between the Chicago bond and the London bond?

Consider a hypothetical case in which the Bank of England decides to fix the exchange rate at $1.50 per pound. If the pound–dollar exchange rate is fixed, and everyone expects that it will remain fixed, we can ignore the fact that the two investments are denominated in different currencies. Say a U.S. investor is considering what to do with $1,500 over the next year. The options are to buy a one-year Chicago bond with an interest rate we will call simply i or a one-year London bond with an interest rate i^f (the superscript f stands for *foreign*). Investing in London requires converting dollars to pounds and buying the bond at the beginning of the year, then taking the proceeds and reconverting them to dollars at the end of the year.

At a fixed exchange rate of $1.50 per pound, $1,500 becomes £1,000 (the "£" is the symbol used for the pound). After a year, this amount becomes £1,000 $(1 + i^f)$. Reconverting to dollars, again at the fixed exchange rate of $1.50 per £, the U.S. investor has $1,500 $(1 + i^f)$. In deciding which bond to buy, then, the investor should compare $1,500 $(1 + i^f)$ to the return from the Chicago bond, which is $1,500 $(1 + i)$. Because arbitrage in the capital market equates these two returns, under a fixed exchange rate:

$$\$1,500(1 + i^f) = \$1,500(1 + i) \qquad (4)$$

and so

$$i^f = i \qquad (5)$$

Thus, investors will be indifferent between investing in a dollar-denominated bond in Chicago or a pound-denominated bond in London only when the interest rates in the two cities are the same. If interest rates differ in Chicago and London, and the dollar–pound exchange rate is fixed, investors will move funds back and forth, wiping out the difference. This example is analogous to the comparison between bonds sold in Chicago and in San Francisco. Because the dollar exchange rate between the two cities is fixed and capital is free to move between them, their interest rates must be the same.[3]

Capital Controls and the Policymakers' Choice

At first glance, it may seem as if policymakers can choose between stabilizing the domestic interest rate and stabilizing the exchange rate. But our discussion of interest rates and arbitrage in the last section depended critically on the ability of investors to move capital across international boundaries. If capital cannot flow freely between London and Chicago, there is no mechanism to equate interest rates in the two countries, and our logic falls apart. Thus, we need to revise our conclusion: so long as capital can flow freely between countries, monetary policymakers must choose between fixing their exchange rate and fixing their interest rate. A country *cannot*

- be open to international capital flows,
- control its domestic interest rate, *and*
- fix its exchange rate.

Policymakers must choose two of these three options.

Looking around the world, we see that different countries have made different choices. The United States, for example, has an open capital market, a controlled domestic interest rate, and a freely floating dollar. During the 1990s, Argentina maintained an open capital market but fixed its exchange rate with the dollar, giving up control of domestic interest rates. But these are not the only alternatives; there is another possibility that is worth exploring. If a country is willing to forgo participation in international capital markets, it can impose **capital controls**, fix its exchange rate, and still use monetary policy to pursue its domestic objectives.

Capital controls go very much against the grain of modern economic thinking. The consensus among economists is that open capital markets benefit everyone. In the same way that international trade allows countries to exploit their comparative advantage, internationally integrated capital markets ensure that capital goes to its most efficient uses. The free flow of capital across borders enhances competition, improves opportunities for diversification, and equalizes rates of return (adjusted for risk). As this view took hold in the late 20th century, countries removed the restrictions on the flow of capital that had been initiated earlier in the century.[4]

---

[3]Taking the analysis one step further, when the exchange rate is free to move, capital market arbitrage ensures that the expected return on bonds of similar maturity and risk will be the same when expressed in the same currency. This is the logic that leads to the interest-rate parity condition discussed in the Appendix to Chapter 10.

[4]Like central banks, controls on international capital flows are a 20th-century innovation. One of the hallmarks of the period between the world wars (the 1920s and 1930s) was the strong movement toward national autonomy. As the world economy collapsed during the Great Depression, countries tried to isolate themselves by instituting restrictions on both the trade in goods and services and the transfer of capital. Restrictions on the ability of foreigners to own domestic assets, and on everyone's ability to transfer currency or gold out of a country, became common. Many of these became part of the international financial system after World War II and were maintained by industrialized countries into the 1970s and beyond. Until 1979, the British government maintained controls on investments made abroad by U.K. residents. Until 1974, the United States imposed a special tax on interest received by Americans on foreign bonds.

APPLYING THE CONCEPT
MALAYSIA IMPOSES CAPITAL CONTROLS

Following the financial crises that enveloped Thailand and Indonesia in 1997, then Korea and Russia in 1998, many emerging markets suffered extreme stress. To reduce risk, foreign investors simply pulled out. They sold those countries' bonds, driving their prices down and their interest rates up, and then converted the proceeds into foreign currencies, driving the value of the domestic currencies down. As in a bank run, no one wanted to be last in line to sell; everyone rushed to leave at once. Plummeting exchange rates and skyrocketing interest rates brought these economies to their knees. Banks and industrial firms that had once been able to borrow easily became desperately short of funds.

The typical response of countries experiencing such a financial crisis is for the government to borrow from other countries and the International Monetary Fund (IMF) and use the borrowed funds to meet its obligations. Eventually, interest rates come down, the exchange rate recovers, foreign investors return, and the government repays the loans. But Malaysia adopted a different course. Believing there was nothing inherently wrong with the nation's economy and that the crisis resembled a bank run more than anything else, officials took the extreme step of implementing strict capital controls. By placing severe limits on investors' ability to remove money from the country, they ensured that foreign investments would remain there. More important, they could fix the value of their currency, the ringgit, and lower domestic interest rates.

At the time, Western economists condemned the policy, claiming that it would destroy the country's economy for years to come. While experts continue to argue about the wisdom of Malaysia's capital controls, their initial response was clearly mistaken. Malaysia's recovery took only two years, compared to five years for Thailand and Indonesia. Would the recovery have been even faster without the capital controls? We will never know for sure. In 2012, the IMF reversed its long-held position, indicating that capital controls can sometimes be useful.* But if countries start instituting capital controls every time there is a whiff of crisis, they will dramatically increase the risk of investing in emerging markets. Investors will become wary of putting money into foreign countries if they aren't sure they will be able to take it out whenever they want.**

*See IMF, "The Liberalization and Management of Capital Flows: An Institutional View," November 14, 2012, *www.imf.org/external/pubs/ft/survey/so/2012/POL120312A.htm.*

**For a detailed description of the Malaysian experience in 1998, see Ethan Kaplan and Dani Rodrik, "Did the Malaysian Capital Controls Work?" National Bureau of Economic Research Working Paper No. 8142, February 2001.

When we look at large industrialized countries, the benefits of open capital markets are easy to see. U.S. workers benefit from the jobs at Honda's assembly plant in Marysville, Ohio, which produced its one millionth automobile for export in 2013. U.S. investors also benefit from their access to Brazilian and Indian stocks (as discussed in Chapter 10, Your Financial World: Investing Overseas). On the downside, disturbances in one country's financial market—such as the U.S. mortgage securities market in 2007—can be quickly transmitted to markets and institutions in other countries through their various interconnections. The global financial crisis of 2007–2009 and the euro-area crisis that followed are prime examples.

For emerging-market countries, greater openness of capital markets poses other risks, too. The problem is that capital that flows into a country can also flow out, and it can do so quickly. That means that countries with open capital markets are vulnerable to sudden changes in investor sentiment. Investors may decide to sell a country's bonds, driving their prices down and their interest rates up. They convert the proceeds of the sale into foreign currency, driving the value of the domestic currency down. If everyone loses confidence in a country at the same time, the result is similar to a bank run: All foreign investors leave at once, precipitating a financial collapse. Thailand in 1997 (discussed in Chapter 17), Korea in 1998 (described in Chapter 10), and the euro-area economies overwhelmed by sovereign debt and banking crises in 2012 are just three examples. (We will examine the mechanics of these crises in the next section of this chapter.)

It is tempting for government officials to try to avert such crises by restricting people's ability to move capital into and out of a country—by imposing controls on the flow of capital. There are two basic types of capital control. *Inflow controls* restrict the

STABILITY

ability of foreigners to invest in a country; *outflow controls* place obstacles in the way of selling investments and taking funds out. China has long operated with extensive capital controls in both directions that are being gradually relaxed. During much of the 1990s, foreigners wishing to invest in Chile were required to make a one-year, zero-interest deposit of 20 percent of the investment at the central bank. This inflow control penalized short-term investments, encouraging investors to invest for a longer period. In 2009, rapid capital inflows and a rising currency led Brazil to impose a tax on foreign purchases of domestic securities.

Outflow controls include restrictions on the ability of domestic residents to purchase foreign assets, and often include prohibitions on removing currency from the country. In the fall of 1998, Malaysian citizens were prohibited from taking more than 1,000 ringgit in cash (worth a bit more than $250 at the time) out of the country, while the most foreigners could take out of the country was the amount they had brought with them when they entered the country. Any nonresident who sold a Malaysian security was required to hold the proceeds in the country for at least 12 months before taking it out. These controls temporarily cut Malaysia off from the world capital market (see Applying the Concept: Maylasia Imposes Capital Controls).

Mechanics of Exchange-Rate Management

Because both the Federal Reserve and the European Central Bank adjust their balance sheets to maintain their overnight interbank interest rates at target level (or to influence longer-term interest rates), they must have given up control of their exchange rates. No wonder their intervention on September 22, 2000, had almost no effect on the value of the euro. Even so, Fed and ECB policies *do* have an impact on the value of the dollar and the euro. And if either central bank chose to, it could give up controlling interest rates and target the exchange rate instead.

How would they do it? What are the mechanics of exchange-rate management and exchange-rate intervention? We have seen that everything the central bank does has something to do with its balance sheet. Foreign exchange intervention is no exception. So to look at the mechanics of exchange-rate management, we'll start with the central bank's balance sheet. Once we understand the balance-sheet effects of foreign currency intervention, we can look more closely at what large central banks like the Fed and the ECB actually do.

The Central Bank's Balance Sheet

If all policymakers want to do is to fix the exchange rate, there is a simple way to do it: They can offer to buy and sell their country's currency at a fixed rate. For example, if officials at the Federal Reserve decided to fix the dollar–euro exchange rate at one to one, they would simply stand ready to exchange dollars for euros whenever anyone asked. Buying euros wouldn't be much of a problem, because the Federal Reserve can print all the dollars it needs. But selling euros in exchange for dollars might pose some difficulty unless the Fed had a substantial euro reserve. We will ignore this complication for now and return to it in the next section, when we discuss the problem of speculative attacks.

In this example, as the Fed works to maintain a fixed dollar–euro exchange rate, its balance sheet shifts. When it buys euros, it increases its dollar liabilities; when it sells euros, it reduces its dollar liabilities (refer back to the section of Chapter 17

Figure 19.1 Change in the Federal Reserve's Balance Sheet Immediately following a Purchase of Euros

Assets	Liabilities
Euro reserves +$1.34 billion (German government bonds)	Commercial bank reserves +$1.34 billion

titled "Foreign Exchange Intervention"). These interventions have an impact on interest rates and, through the deposit expansion multiplier, on the quantity of money in the economy as well. Buying euros or selling dollars increases the supply of reserves to the banking system, putting downward pressure on interest rates and expanding the quantity of money. Remember that in taking these actions, the Fed responds to the market. The decision to buy and sell euros is made by financial market participants, not the Fed. Just by looking at the mechanics of the central bank's balance sheet, we can see that *controlling the exchange rate means giving up control of the size of reserves so that the market determines the interest rate.*

To see how this process works in practice, let's go back to September 2000, when the largest central banks in the world intervened to bolster the value of the euro. We'll focus on the Federal Reserve's decision to purchase €1.5 billion in exchange for $1.34 billion, ignoring the actions of the other central banks on that day as well as the open market operations that followed. When Fed employees bought euros, they did it the same way they buy anything else: They created liabilities to the commercial banks. Then, as soon as they received the €1.5 billion from foreign exchange dealers, they spent it on bonds issued by euro-area governments. We will refer to these bonds as German government bonds, because that is primarily how the Fed holds its euro-denominated reserves.

The balance-sheet implications of this exchange are straightforward. Figure 19.1 shows the results of the intervention. Looking at the asset side, and following the standard convention of reporting the value of the central bank's foreign exchange reserves in domestic currency units, we see that the Fed has increased its euro-denominated foreign exchange reserve assets by $1.34 billion. On the liabilities side of the balance sheet, we see that commercial bank reserves have increased by the same amount.

This T-account should look familiar. If we focus on the liabilities side of the balance sheet, we see that the purchase of German government bonds is identical to a purchase of U.S. Treasury bonds. That is, the purchase of a security has added reserves to the banking system. The only difference is the issuer of the bond. Like any other change in reserves, this one has a direct impact on the quantity of money in the economy. In other words, it is expansionary, so it reduces domestic interest rates. *A foreign exchange intervention has the same impact on reserves as a domestic open market operation.*

Will this intervention change the exchange rate? Figure 19.2 shows what happens. Recall from Chapter 10 that the dollar exchange rate is determined by the supply of and demand for dollars. The Fed did supply dollars to the market through its intervention, but more important, the interest rate has fallen. Remember that whenever investing in the United States becomes less attractive relative to investing somewhere else, the result is a decrease in the demand for dollars that will be used by foreigners to purchase

Figure 19.2   Effect of a Decrease in U.S. Interest Rates Relative to Interest Rates in the Euro Area

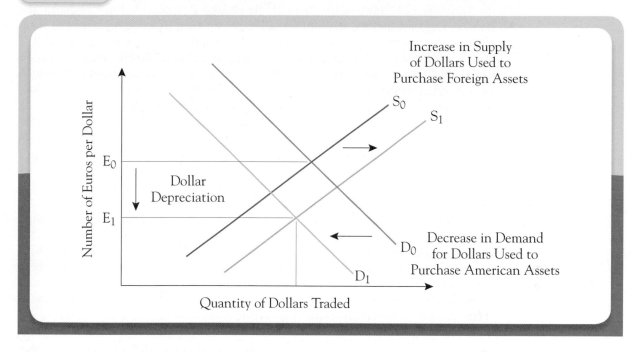

U.S. assets and an increase in the supply of dollars that will be used by Americans to purchase foreign assets. In this example, assuming that the Fed does nothing but purchase German government bonds, the U.S. interest rate will fall while European interest rates remain the same. Foreign investors will want to buy fewer American bonds, and they will need fewer dollars to do it. As a result, the demand for dollars in the foreign exchange market falls. Meanwhile, U.S. investors will want to buy more foreign bonds, and they supply more dollars to do that. The demand and supply shifts shown in Figure 19.2 together drive the value of the dollar down and the value of the euro up. The dollar depreciates and the euro appreciates, reducing the number of euros offered per dollar in the foreign exchange market.

MARKETS

You may think there is something strange about this discussion. We started with a foreign exchange intervention in which the Fed purchased euros and noted its impact on the dollar–euro exchange rate. But the reason the exchange rate moved was that the domestic interest rate changed, shifting the demand for dollars in the foreign exchange market. By making domestic U.S. investment less attractive, the intervention prompted people to purchase fewer dollars, driving the price of dollars down. Our conclusion is that *a foreign exchange intervention affects the value of a country's currency by changing domestic interest rates.*

This conclusion has an important implication. It means that *any central bank policy that influences the domestic interest rate will affect the exchange rate.* The fact that we started with an exchange-rate intervention is irrelevant. An open market purchase or sale works exactly the same way. If the Federal Reserve bought U.S. Treasury bonds instead of euro-denominated bonds, the action would drive down U.S. interest rates, decreasing the demand for dollars in the foreign exchange market and causing a decline in the value of the dollar. There is nothing special about a foreign exchange intervention.

Sterilized Intervention

On September 22, 2000, when the ECB, the Federal Reserve, the Bank of Japan, the Bank of England, and the Bank of Canada all intervened to buy euros, none of them changed their domestic interest-rate targets. No wonder the value of the euro didn't change! But that means their transactions must have been different from the one we just studied. We assumed that when the Fed bought euros, it increased commercial bank reserves, which would reduce interest rates in the absence of any other action. Such a move is an example of an **unsterilized foreign exchange intervention**, one that changes central bank liabilities. But in large countries, central banks don't operate that way. Instead, they engage in **sterilized foreign exchange interventions**, in which a change in foreign exchange reserves alters the asset side of the central bank's balance sheet but the domestic monetary base remains unaffected.

A sterilized intervention is actually a combination of two transactions. First there is the purchase or sale of foreign currency reserves, which by itself changes the central bank's liabilities. But this is immediately followed by an open market operation of exactly the same size, designed to offset the impact of the first transaction on the monetary base. For example, the Fed's purchase of a German government bond, which would increase reserves, is offset by the sale of a U.S. Treasury bond. Together, these two actions leave the level of reserves unchanged. Such an intervention is sterilized with respect to its effect on the monetary base, or the size of the central bank's balance sheet. *An intervention is unsterilized if it changes the monetary base and sterilized if it does not change the monetary base.*

To see what happens in practice, let's go back to September 22, 2000, one last time. Between 7:11 a.m. and 9:20 a.m., the Federal Reserve Bank of New York sold $1.34 billion in exchange for €1.5 billion. We have already seen that the initial impact on the Fed's balance sheet was to increase the level of reserves in the banking system. But the FOMC had not changed the target federal funds rate, so the job of the Open Market Trading Desk was the same as it had been every day since May 17, when the prevailing 6½ percent target rate had been put in place.

To do their job, the Federal Reserve Bank of New York staff entered the intervention numbers into their spreadsheet before estimating the size of the day's temporary operation. In figuring out what to do to keep the federal funds rate on target, they took account of the quantity of reserves their colleagues had already added. By 10:00 a.m., when the open market operations were completed, the impact of the foreign exchange intervention on the Fed's liabilities had disappeared. The foreign exchange desk had purchased bonds issued by a euro-area government, paying for them with reserves, and the Open Market Desk had sold U.S. Treasury bonds to reverse the potential impact.

Figure 19.3 shows the result on the Fed's balance sheet. Notice two things. First, commercial bank reserves remain unchanged following a sterilized intervention, so domestic monetary policy does not change. Second, the intervention changes the *composition* of the asset side of the central bank's balance sheet. The Fed has swapped U.S. Treasury bonds for bonds issued by the German government.

"If this doesn't help you don't worry, it's a placebo."

Figure 19.3   Change in the Federal Reserve's Balance Sheet following a *Sterilized* Purchase of Euro-Denominated Bonds

Assets		Liabilities
Euro reserves	+$1.34 billion	Commercial bank reserves unchanged
(German government bonds)		
Securities	−$1.34 billion	
(U.S. Treasury bonds)		

Could this change in the mix of assets on the central bank's balance sheet alter the exchange rate in a sustained fashion? In normal times, the answer is no: as we observed, the sterilized intervention in support of the euro in 2000 had no sustained effect. In deep, well-functioning markets, small shifts in central bank assets are dwarfed by the actions of private traders. Recall from Chapter 10 that the daily volume of foreign exchange transactions averaged more than $4 trillion in 2010! A change of a few billion dollars in central bank assets is a mere drop in this ocean.

However, as we saw in the discussion of targeted asset purchases (TAPs) in Chapter 18, changes in the composition of a central bank balance sheet can alter the relative prices of assets if (1) markets are thin or functioning poorly and (2) the policy shift is large compared to the level of market transactions. The Fed's 2009 purchase of more than $1 trillion of mortgage-backed securities in crisis-weakened markets is a prime example. Most observers believe that these Fed actions did what they were intended to do: lower mortgage yields at a time when loans were very difficult to get.

Just like the yield on mortgage securities, an exchange rate is an asset price. And during the 2007–2009 crisis, virtually all financial markets, including foreign exchange markets, were thinner and less effective than usual. In that setting, sterilized currency intervention might have had a bigger impact than in normal times, but there was no intervention that would allow us to judge.

The Costs, Benefits, and Risks of Fixed Exchange Rates

Many countries allow their exchange rates to float freely, so that the value of their currencies is determined in the financial markets. But others—especially small, emerging-market countries—fix their exchange rates. That is, officials of the central bank and the finance ministry agree that the best policy is to maintain a predictable value for their currency, so they target the exchange rate. Why do some countries make that decision? Surely fixing the exchange rate has costs as well as benefits. We now turn to a brief discussion of the tradeoffs.

STABILITY

Assessing the Costs and Benefits

The owners of the Blue Jays, Toronto's major league baseball team, probably wouldn't mind if the Bank of Canada decided to fix the exchange rate for the U.S. and Canadian dollars. They face a common problem for companies engaged in international trade:

they pay most of their expenses in one currency and receive the bulk of their revenues in another. Suppose that the Blue Jays receive about 80 percent of their roughly $200 million of annual revenue in Canadian dollars but pay 80 percent of their expenses—including a $108 million annual payroll (in 2012) and the bills for chartered planes and fancy hotel rooms—in U.S. dollars. So if the Canadian dollar depreciates, as it did during 2008, the Blue Jays incur a financial loss. Unless they hedge this exchange-rate risk, for each 10 percent drop in the value of the Canadian dollar they will lose something like $16 million. The more volatile exchange rates become, the worse the problem gets. If the exchange rates were fixed, the Blue Jays' risk would disappear.[5]

Goods and services aren't the only things that cross international borders; capital does, too. Fixed exchange rates not only simplify operations for businesses that trade internationally, they also reduce the risk that investors face when they hold foreign stocks and bonds. Think of what happens if you buy a Korean government bond. Unlike a U.S. Treasury bond, on which the interest rate tells you the return, a Korean bond involves the possibility that the dollar–Korean *won* exchange rate may change. An increase in the number of won needed to purchase one dollar—so that the dollar becomes more valuable—would reduce the return on the Korean bond by the amount of the dollar's appreciation.[6]

So fixed exchange rates seem to be a good idea for both businesses and investors. They also have another potential benefit. A fixed exchange rate ties policymakers' hands. Remember that in the long run, the exchange rate is determined by inflation differentials. In countries that are prone to bouts of high inflation, a fixed exchange rate may be the only way to establish a credible low-inflation policy. It enforces low-inflation discipline on both central bankers and politicians, and an exchange rate target enhances transparency and accountability.

There is one serious drawback to a fixed exchange rate, however. It *imports* monetary policy. Fixing your currency's value to that of another country means adopting the other country's interest-rate policy. When Argentina fixed the exchange rate of the peso to the U.S. dollar, policymakers gave up control of Argentinean interest rates and effectively handed it over to the FOMC. Needless to say, when the FOMC set the target federal funds rate, committee members didn't worry much about what was going on in Argentina. What this means is that a fixed exchange rate makes the most sense when the two countries involved have similar macroeconomic fluctuations. Ideally, their cyclical ups and downs are perfectly synchronized. Otherwise, the country with the flexible exchange rate that is in control of monetary policy (e.g., the United States) might be raising interest rates to combat domestic inflation at the same time that the other country (e.g., Argentina) is going into recession.

In deciding whether to fix their country's exchange rate, policymakers should consider several additional matters. First, when a country fixes its exchange rate, the central bank is offering to buy and sell its own currency at a fixed rate. To honor this commitment to purchase currency, monetary policymakers will need ample currency

---

[5]The Toronto Blue Jays may hedge their foreign exchange risk in the derivatives market. In effect, they can pay someone for insurance against moves in the exchange rate. Doing so makes their expenses and profits more predictable, but it isn't free.

[6]A numerical example helps clarify this point. Assume that a U.S. investor converts $1,000 into Korean won at a rate of 1,000 won per dollar and then buys a one-year, 5 percent Korean government bond. At the end of the year, the bond pays 1,050,000 won. If the exchange rate has not changed, this amount can be exchanged for $1,050. But if the dollar appreciates 5 percent during the year, so that the exchange rate rises to 1,050 won per dollar, then the American investor is left with only $1,000. The total return to holding the Korean bond equals the Korean interest rate minus the dollar's appreciation. The Appendix to Chapter 10 describes this phenomenon in more detail.

reserves. For instance, a country that fixes its exchange rate to the dollar needs to hold dollars in reserve. Living up to this promise in a world of free-flowing capital requires a high level of foreign exchange reserves. For many countries, the billions of dollars required are both difficult to obtain and expensive to keep.

Second, because floating exchange rates act as automatic macroeconomic stabilizers, fixing the exchange rate means reducing the domestic economy's natural ability to respond to macroeconomic shocks. Imagine a country on the verge of recession. If monetary policymakers can, they will react by lowering interest rates in an attempt to keep the economy from slowing. Beyond the direct effect on investment and consumption, lower interest rates make domestic bonds less attractive to foreigners, reducing the demand for the domestic currency and driving down its value. The resulting currency depreciation drives down the price foreigners must pay for domestic exports, increasing the demand for them and amplifying the impact of the initial interest-rate reduction. With a fixed exchange rate, this stabilization mechanism is completely shut down.

Third, if the nominal exchange rate is fixed, a country may need its prices and wages to decline to offset any loss of ability to compete in world markets. If, instead, prices and wages are inflexible, a country that loses *competitiveness* may experience persistently high levels of unemployment, income losses, and government deficits (like the economies on the geographic periphery of the euro area amid that region's crisis).

Fourth, policymakers need to consider the robustness of the banking system. To fix an exchange rate, a central bank may need to accommodate large swings in reserve demand that bring about booms and busts in money, credit, the economy, and the well-being of banks. Yet, the ability of the central bank to serve as lender of last resort may be limited if it must sell assets to defend the exchange rate.

The Danger of Speculative Attacks

While fixed exchange rates may have benefits for a country's economy, they are fragile and prone to a type of crisis called a **speculative attack**. To understand the nature of a speculative attack, imagine that a country is trying to maintain a fixed exchange rate. Now suppose that for some reason, financial market participants come to believe that the government will need to devalue its currency in the near future. The problem is usually one of time consistency: If investors expect policymakers to renege on their promise to defend the exchange rate, they will attack the currency now and force an immediate devaluation.

The mechanics of the attack are straightforward. Take the example of the attack on the Thai *baht* in 1997. Through the mid-1990s, the Bank of Thailand was committed to maintaining a fixed exchange rate of approximately 26 baht to the U.S. dollar. To do so, officials had to make sure foreign currency traders believed that the Bank of Thailand had enough dollars on hand to buy however many baht the traders wanted to sell. In summer 1997, financial market participants began to question whether the reserves at the central bank really were big enough, and they swung into action. Speculators borrowed baht at domestic Thai interest rates, took them to the central bank to convert them to dollars at the rate of 26 to one, and then invested the dollars in short-term, interest-bearing securities in the United States. The immediate impact of these transactions was to drain the Bank of Thailand's dollar reserves. The lower the dollar reserves, the less likely that the Thais would be able to meet further requests to convert baht into dollars. And the more baht speculators borrowed to convert into dollars, the further the reserves fell.

MARKETS

The details are instructive. Imagine that, anticipating a severe depreciation, you borrow 2.6 million baht. You take them to the Bank of Thailand and convert them into $100,000 at the fixed rate of 26 to one. With the proceeds, you buy U.S. Treasury bills. One week later, your expectations are realized and the baht depreciates by 10 percent. Now you need only $90,909 to obtain the 2.6 million baht with which to repay the loan. You've made an almost instant profit of over $9,000.[7] Because international currency speculators have very deep pockets, they can quickly drain billions of dollars from a central bank this way—and make a huge profit in the process.[8]

What causes a speculative attack? There are three possibilities. The first brings us back to fiscal policy: remember that politicians can make the central banker's job impossible. Ensuring that a currency retains its value means keeping domestic inflation at the same level as that of the country to which your exchange rate is pegged. If investors begin to think that at current levels, government spending must ultimately increase inflation, they will stop believing that officials can maintain the exchange rate at its fixed level. This seems to have been an important part of what happened during the Asian crisis of 1997.

A second possibility arises from financial instability. If a country's banking system is insufficiently capitalized or otherwise unsound, a central bank may face pressure to relax monetary policy to avoid or contain a financial crisis. If investors doubt that the central bank will keep interest rates high enough for a sufficient time to defend the currency peg, an attack may follow. This may be one reason territories with successful fixed exchange-rate arrangements, like Hong Kong, favor high bank capital ratios.

Finally, speculative attacks can occur even when policymakers are behaving responsibly and financial institutions are healthy. They can arise spontaneously out of nowhere. If by chance enough currency speculators simply decide that a central bank cannot maintain its exchange rate, they will attack it, mobilizing tens of billions of dollars virtually overnight. To make matters even worse, spontaneous speculative attacks are a bit like bank runs; they can be contagious.

Many observers suspect that in today's world, no central bank has the resources to withstand such an attack in the absence of capital controls. It would take substantial foreign exchange reserves to even think about trying.

"Part of me wants to help you with your crisis, Hargraves, but part of me wants to go to lunch."

[7]This simple example ignores both the interest you would need to pay to borrow the baht and the interest you would receive on the Treasury bills. An exact calculation would take the difference between the two interest rates into account and would likely reduce the profit. But because such transactions are usually done over days or weeks at most, this adjustment would have only a modest impact on the return. The point is that this is a very profitable transaction.

[8]In September 1992, the Bank of England belonged to the European Exchange Rate Mechanism, which linked the exchange rates of many countries. It effectively pegged the pound to the then-independent German currency, the deutsche mark. In an attempt to contain domestic inflation, the Germans raised interest rates dramatically, a policy the British did not want to follow. When speculators realized that the situation was untenable—that the Bank of England could not fix its exchange rate and have a lower interest rate than the Germans—they attacked. Investor George Soros is reputed to have made more than $1 billion betting that the pound would be devalued.

APPLYING THE CONCEPT
THE GOLD STANDARD: AN EXCHANGE-RATE REGIME WHOSE TIME HAS PASSED

If you take a dollar bill to the Federal Reserve, officials will give you a new one. Should they offer to give you gold instead? That would be returning to the time when the dollar was "as good as gold." Today, advocates of a return to the **gold standard** claim that it would eliminate inflation. As evidence, they point to the time before World War I, when the United States was on the gold standard and inflation averaged less than 1 percent per year. What these advocates don't advertise is that, while inflation was low on *average,* it was highly variable, fluctuating between +3¼ percent and −3¼ percent. In fact, for much of the late 19th century, prices fell steadily. Only early in the 20th century did they rise back to a level not far above where they started in 1880.

The focus on past inflation obscures the long list of reasons few economists today advocate a return to the gold standard. To begin with, the gold standard obligates the central bank to fix the price of something we don't really care about. Instead of stabilizing the prices of the goods and services we buy and consume, the central bank fixes the dollar price of gold. In place of fluctuations in the market price of gold, there are fluctuations in the dollar price of goods.

Then there is the fact that, under the gold standard, the amount of money in the economy would depend on the amount of gold available. More gold equals more money. Because, in the long run, inflation is tied to money growth, this means that inflation depends on the rate at which gold is mined. Why should monetary policy be determined by the rate at which South Africa and Russia dig gold from the ground? Moreover, any political disruption in those parts of the world could have dramatic monetary policy effects.

The case for gold grows even less persuasive when we realize that the gold standard is an exchange-rate policy, too. The promise to convert dollars into gold means that international transactions must be settled in gold. So when the value of imports does not exactly match the value of exports, gold is transferred from one country to another. Thus, a country with a current account deficit—whose imports exceed its exports—has to pay the difference by transferring gold to countries with current account surpluses. (See the Appendix to Chapter 19 for a description of balance-of-payments accounting.) With less gold, the country's central bank must contract its balance sheet, raising interest rates, reducing the quantity of money and credit in the economy, and driving domestic prices down. Under a gold standard, countries running current account deficits will be forced into deflation. Meanwhile, countries with current account surpluses can allow their gold inflows to generate inflation, but they need not. Under the gold standard, a central bank can have too little gold, but it can never have too much.

Economic historians believe that gold flows played a central role in spreading the Great Depression of the 1930s throughout the world. After World War I, all the major countries in the world worked to reconstruct the gold standard. By the late 1920s, they had succeeded. At the time, both the United States and France were running current account surpluses, absorbing the world's gold into their vaults. But instead of allowing the gold inflows to expand the quantity of money in their financial systems, authorities in both countries tightened monetary policy in an attempt to cool off their overheated, inflation-prone economies. The result was catastrophic, because it forced countries with current account deficits and gold outflows to tighten their monetary policies even more. The resulting deflation increased the likelihood that people would default on loans, destroying the economic and financial system in the United States and elsewhere.* Economic historians place the blame squarely on the gold standard. What makes their argument truly convincing is the fact that the sooner a country left the gold standard and regained control of its monetary policy, the faster its economy recovered.

From our vantage point in the 21st century, the gold standard is a historical artifact that caused great trouble. Most economic experts do not wish to see it restored.** Doing so would not even be time consistent: In bad times, investors would expect governments to exit the gold standard—as they eventually did in the 1930s—encouraging self-fulfilling speculative attacks.

*In Applying the Concept: Deflation, Net Worth, and Information Costs in Chapter 11, we discussed how deflation increases the adverse selection problems caused by information asymmetries. This is one of the mechanisms people today believe made the Great Depression of the 1930s so deep.

**For a survey of academic economists, see *www.igmchicago. org/igm-economic-experts-panel/poll-results?SurveyID=SV_ cw1nNUYOXSAKwrq.*

Summarizing the Case for a Fixed Exchange Rate

The easiest way to summarize this discussion is to make a list of the conditions under which adopting a fixed exchange rate makes sense for a country. A country will be better off fixing its exchange rate if it has all five of these:

- A poor reputation for controlling inflation on its own.
- An economy that is well integrated with the one to whose currency the rate is fixed, trading significantly with it and sharing similar macroeconomic characteristics, especially a synchronized business cycle.

- A high level of foreign exchange reserves.
- A high degree of price and wage flexibility.
- A robust banking system.

Regardless of how closely a country meets these criteria, fixed exchange rates are still risky to adopt and difficult to maintain.

Fixed Exchange-Rate Regimes

Our final task in this chapter is to study some examples of fixed exchange-rate regimes, to see how they work. We will look at managed exchange-rate pegs, in which policy-makers try to restrict the exchange rate to a certain range; at currency boards, in which the central bank holds foreign currency assets as backing for the domestic monetary base; and at dollarization (or euroization), in which a country eliminates its own currency and begins using one issued by another country.

Exchange-Rate Pegs and the Bretton Woods System

Despite the calamity of the 1930s, the world remained enamored of fixed exchange rates and the gold standard. So in 1944, a group of 44 countries agreed to form the *Bretton Woods system.* Named for the New Hampshire resort where the agreement was signed, it was a system of fixed exchange rates that offered more policy flexibility over the short term than had been possible under the gold standard.

The Bretton Woods system lasted from 1945 to 1971. Though the details of the system were complex, the basic idea is not. Each country maintained an agreed-upon exchange rate with the U.S. dollar—that is, it *pegged* its exchange rate to the dollar. To make the system work, every country had to hold dollar reserves and stand ready to exchange its own currency for dollars at the fixed rate. The dollar was what is known as a *reserve currency,* and it was convertible into gold at a rate of $35 per ounce. The choice of the dollar as the reserve currency was based on several factors. First, the United States was the biggest of the Allies (the victors in World War II), both economically and militarily. Second, dollars were relatively abundant.

Because other countries did not want to adopt U.S. monetary policy, their fixed exchange rates required complex capital controls. Even so, countries had to intervene regularly, buying or selling dollars to maintain their exchange rates at the peg. Adjustments were made to the *exchange-rate pegs,* but only in response to perceived long-term imbalances. What gave the system some flexibility was the *International Monetary Fund* (IMF). The IMF was created to manage the Bretton Woods system by making loans to countries in need of short-term financing to pay for an excess of imports over exports. For a number of years, the system worked reasonably well, but as capital markets started to open up, it came under increasing strain.

With a fixed exchange rate and the free movements of capital across international borders, countries could not have their own discretionary monetary policies. Recall the example of Mexico cited earlier in this chapter. The long-run implications of purchasing power parity meant that, if Mexican inflation deviated from U.S. inflation, the dollar–peso exchange rate had to change. In the late 1960s, the countries in the Bretton Woods system were in the same position as Mexico. Because their exchange rate was fixed to the dollar, participating countries were forced to adopt policies that resulted in the same amount of inflation as in the United States. When U.S. inflation began to

LESSONS OF THE CRISIS
OASIS OF STABILITY

How do you preserve economic, price, and currency stability when the neighborhood is in a crisis?.

In 2010 and 2011, investors who worried about a potential breakup of the euro area viewed the Swiss franc as a safe haven and fled the euro. In the 20 months to August 2011, the Swiss currency appreciated from about CHF 1.50 per euro to a peak of CHF 1.04 per euro. As a small, open economy, Switzerland's cross-border trade accounts for more than 90 percent of its GDP, making its currency an important policy focus. The surging franc rendered many Swiss firms uncompetitive, especially versus the euro area, which accounts for the majority of Swiss trade. The franc's rise also threatened to tilt Switzerland, where prices had been largely stable, into a disruptive deflation.

What to do? Switzerland's central bank—the Swiss National Bank (SNB)—had already lowered interest rates close to zero, so it could no longer employ conventional monetary policy tools to offset the contractionary impact of the strong franc. Instead, on September 6, 2011, the SNB made the following unprecedented announcement:

> **Swiss National Bank sets minimum exchange rate at CHF 1.20 per euro**
>
> *The current massive overvaluation of the Swiss franc poses an acute threat to the Swiss economy and carries the risk of a deflationary development.*
>
> *The Swiss National Bank (SNB) is therefore aiming for a substantial and sustained weakening of the Swiss*

franc. With immediate effect, it will no longer tolerate a EUR/CHF exchange rate below the minimum rate of CHF 1.20. The SNB will enforce this minimum rate with the utmost determination and is prepared to buy foreign currency in unlimited quantities.

The key word in the SNB announcement is "unlimited." To stop the runaway franc, the central bank chose to supply investors with as many Swiss francs as they wished to hold at the price of 1.20 Swiss francs per euro. In the midst of a crisis, anything less than the SNB's commitment to unlimited Swiss franc sales (and unlimited euro purchases) might have stimulated demand for francs, aggravating the crisis.

The SNB's announcement was and remains controversial. Some observers worried about the inflationary risks of letting investors—rather than the central bank—determine the size of its balance sheet. Others worried about the risk of SNB portfolio losses if the euro were to break up. Both groups wondered how the SNB could eventually reduce its balance sheet back to a normal size.

The SNB was resolute. Between July 2011 and December 2012, its massive purchases of euros boosted the Swiss monetary base by more than 350 percent. Despite Switzerland's small economy, its foreign exchange reserves jumped above $500 billion, making it the sixth largest holder globally. As of mid-2013, the SNB's balance sheet remains enormous, but its intervention had thus far achieved the stated goals: capping the franc and heading off the threat of a destabilizing deflation. With consumer prices falling slightly below year-ago levels, Swiss bond yields remained very low in mid-2013, as is consistent with having a credible central bank.

rise in the late 1960s (yet another disastrous side effect of the Vietnam War), many countries balked; they didn't want to match the rise in inflation.

By 1971, the system had completely fallen apart. The response of American officials has been to allow the dollar to float freely ever since. Europeans took a different tack; for much of the time from the collapse of the Bretton Woods system to the adoption of the euro in 1999, they maintained various fixed exchange-rate mechanisms. Because capital flowed freely among these countries, that meant giving up their ability to set interest rates.

Hard Pegs: Currency Boards and Dollarization

The international monetary system took a big hit in 1971 when the Bretton Woods system collapsed. Since then, a consensus has developed that countries whose economies are open to international capital flows must choose between completely flexible, market-determined exchange rates and what have come to be known as **hard pegs**. In a hard-peg system, the central bank implements an institutional mechanism that ensures its ability to convert a domestic currency into the foreign currency to which it is pegged. The danger of a speculative attack means anything less is unworkable. As

STABILITY

APPLYING THE CONCEPT
IMPLICATIONS OF CHINA'S EXCHANGE-RATE REGIME

In June 2013, the amount of foreign exchange reserves held by China's central bank reached $3.5 trillion. This massive stockpile, which accounts for more than one-fourth of all the currency reserves in the world, has risen by more than 20 times since 2000 (see Figure 19.4). What prompted this unprecedented accumulation of reserves in one country? What are the Chinese doing with the reserves? What are the implications for the future?*

The increase of reserves reflects China's sustained current account surpluses—the excess of exports over imports. These surpluses typically are paid for in U.S. dollars—the usual means of payment in international trade. Between 2005

Figure 19.4 China's Foreign Exchange Reserves (billions of U.S. dollars), 1989–2013

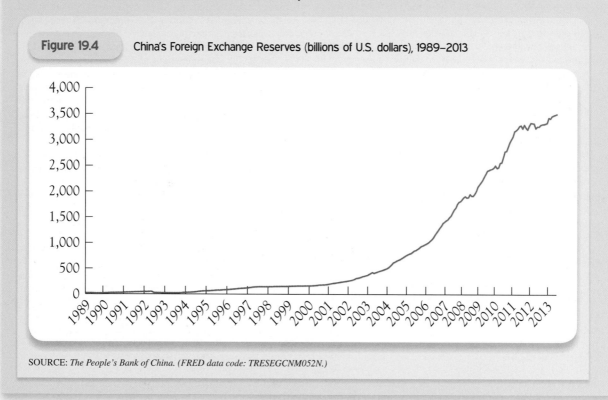

SOURCE: *The People's Bank of China. (FRED data code: TRESEGCNM052N.)*

---

one leading monetary policymaker and scholar put it, "pegs are not sustainable unless they are very hard indeed."[9]

Only two exchange-rate regimes can be considered hard pegs: currency boards and dollarization. With a **currency board**, the central bank commits to holding enough foreign currency assets to back all domestic currency liabilities at a fixed rate. With **dollarization** or euroization, one country formally adopts the currency of another country for use in all its financial transactions. Let's look at examples of both systems.

Currency Boards and the Argentinean Experience Somewhere between 10 and 20 currency boards operate in the world today. The best known is the one in Hong Kong. The Hong Kong Monetary Authority (HKMA) operates a system whose sole objective is to maintain a fixed exchange rate of 7.8 Hong Kong dollars to one U.S.

---

[9]See Stanley Fischer, "Exchange Rate Regimes: Is the Bipolar View Correct?" *Journal of Economic Perspectives* 15, no. 2 (Spring 2001), pp. 3–24.

and 2009, the surpluses averaged $300 billion annually, more than 6 percent of China's GDP. In 2011 and 2012, the surpluses sank below 3 percent of GDP.

China's fixed exchange-rate regime supported large export surpluses. The country's leaders promoted export-led growth by pegging their currency, the **renminbi**, to the U.S. dollar (the unit of account of the renminbi is the **yuan**, and its exchange rate is reported as the number of yuan per unit of foreign currency). Partly as a result, in 2009 China surpassed Germany to become the world's largest exporter. And Chinese exports have not faltered, aside from an interruption during the global recession of 2008–2009.

After July 2005, policymakers in China adjusted the dollar peg repeatedly, allowing the renminbi to appreciate by more than 25 percent versus the dollar, aside from a temporary pause during the global financial crisis. Overall, the appreciation, combined with the rise in Chinese prices, appears to have limited or even halted China's gains in *international competitiveness*—the ability to produce and sell traded products at prices lower than anyone else. But China's role as the world's premier manufacturer has not been threatened by the rising renminbi.

When a country runs a current account surplus, it also runs a capital account deficit (see Appendix to Chapter 19). This means that it is either making loans to foreigners or buying their assets. What assets does China purchase with its surpluses? The answer is mostly U.S. government and agency securities, to the point that China has become the leading financier of the U.S. government: according to the U.S. Treasury, as of June 2012, China owned about $1.3 trillion of Treasury and agency debt. Beyond these bond holdings, investors based in China held more than $200 billion of U.S. corporate equities, while Chinese firms also have increased their direct investment abroad.

It is a paradox that China, with enormous capital needs at home, continues to lend in such large volume to the United States, a mature economy with lower expected returns on investment. China will probably face additional currency losses on its foreign assets when the renminbi eventually rises to reflect the country's trade competitiveness and long-run growth prospects. China's reserve managers seem well aware of this troubling prospect but have little room for maneuver. If China tries to avert these projected losses by lowering its dollar holdings, the risk is that the renminbi will thereby rise sooner against the dollar, undermining the fixed exchange rate and hurting exports.

China's leaders can slow the rate of reserve accumulation by promoting domestic consumption, but this process is likely to take place gradually over many years. China's households save a high portion of their income as a precaution against rainy-day threats (such as unemployment or illness) and to provide for retirement. The savings that cannot be utilized well at home flow out of the country—that's the capital account deficit. Until these excess savings dwindle, China's foreign reserves will probably continue to rise.

A rise of trade protectionism in other countries could change this picture more abruptly. The temptation to impose protectionist measures typically strengthens in periods of high or rising unemployment. For example, in 1971, when the Japanese yen was fixed at a low value and U.S. unemployment was high, the United States imposed a 10 percent tariff on imports coming from Japan, prompting that country's policymakers to allow their currency's value to rise. During the financial crisis of 2007–2009, policymakers in most countries foreswore measures that would threaten global trade. But it remains to be seen whether politicians will be able to sustain that pledge in the midst of high unemployment lingering after the crisis.

*This box draws extensively on Eswar Prasad and Aaron Sorkin, "Sky's the Limit? National and Global Implications of China's Reserve Accumulation," Brookings Institution, July 22, 2009, *www.brookings.edu/articles/2009/0721_chinas_reserve_prasad.aspx.*

dollar. Because (as of May 2013) the HKMA holds roughly $305 billion in foreign currency (dollar) assets, it can issue nearly 2.4 trillion Hong Kong dollars in liabilities. The rules of the currency board provide that the HKMA can increase the size of Hong Kong's monetary base only if it can accumulate additional dollar reserves. Over the year following the collapse of Lehman Brothers in September 2008, inflows from abroad boosted HKMA foreign currency assets by nearly 50 percent, because investors viewed the Hong Kong dollar as a safe haven in the crisis.

As this example suggests, with a currency board, the central bank's only job is to maintain the exchange rate. While that means that policymakers cannot adjust monetary policy in response to domestic economic shocks, the system does have its advantages. Prime among them is the control of inflation. As we noted in the introduction to this chapter, Argentina decided to adopt a currency board in April 1991 to end triple-digit inflation, and the approach worked. After three years, the inflation rate had dropped to 4 percent; by 1998, it was nearly zero. Forgoing the ability to stabilize domestic growth seems like a small price to pay for this sort of inflation performance, especially in an inflation-prone economy.

IN THE NEWS
Phony Currency Wars

The Economist

February 16, 2013

OFFICIALS from the world's biggest economies meet on February 15th–16th in Moscow on a mission to avert war. Not one with bombs and bullets, but a "currency war." Finance ministers and central bankers worry that their peers in the G20 will devalue their currencies to boost exports and grow their economies at their neighbors' expense.

Emerging economies, led by Brazil, first accused America of instigating a currency war in 2010 when the Federal Reserve bought heaps of bonds with newly created money. That "quantitative easing" (QE) made investors flood into emerging markets in search of better returns, lifting their exchange rates. Now those charges are being leveled at Japan. Shinzo Abe, the new prime minister, has promised bold stimulus to restart growth and vanquish deflation. He has also called for a weaker yen to bolster exports; it has duly fallen by 16% against the dollar and 19% against the euro since the end of September (when it was clear that Mr Abe was heading for power).

The complaints, however, are overdone. Rather than condemning the actions of America and Japan, the rest of the world should praise them—and the euro zone would do well to follow their example.

Turning Swords into Printing Presses

The war rhetoric implies that America and Japan are directly suppressing their currencies to boost exports and suppress imports. That would be a zero-sum game which could degenerate into protectionism and a collapse in trade. But this is not what they are doing. When central banks have lowered their short-term interest rate to near zero and thus exhausted their conventional monetary methods, they turn to unconventional means such as QE or convincing people that inflation will rise. Both actions should lower real (inflation-adjusted) interest rates. This may now be happening in Japan.

The principal goal of this policy is to stimulate domestic spending and investment. As a by-product, lower real rates usually weaken the currency as well, and that in turn tends to depress imports. But if the policy is successful in reviving domestic demand, it will eventually lead to higher imports.

Aggressive monetary expansion in a big economy suffering from weak demand and subdued inflation is good for the rest of the world, not bad. The International Monetary Fund concluded that America's first rounds of monetary laxity boosted its trading partners' output by as much as 0.3%. The dollar did weaken, but that became a motivation for Japan's stepped-up assault on deflation. The combined monetary boost on opposite sides of the Pacific has been a powerful elixir for global investor confidence.

European officials, fearful that their countries' exports are caught in the crossfire, have entertained loopy ideas such as directly managing the value of the euro. Instead, the euro zone should stop grumbling and start emulating Japan: the European Central Bank should ease monetary policy, if necessary through QE. This would both blunt the euro's rise and combat recession in the zone's periphery.

That option may not be available to emerging markets, such as Brazil, where inflation remains a problem. In their case, limited capital controls may be a sensible short-term defense against destabilizing inflows of hot money.

Should Japan's attack on the yen move beyond rhetoric to actual intervention in the markets to drive its value down, then the rest of the world would be right to condemn it. Until that happens, other countries should avoid groundless fearmongering about currency wars. Finance ministers and central banks should be fighting stagnation, not each other.

LESSONS OF THE ARTICLE

Global economic weakness puts policymakers on guard against other countries' efforts to gain a competitive edge by devaluing their currencies. In the Great Depression, such "beggar thy neighbor" policies triggered protectionism. Since the financial crisis, however, major central banks emphasize that their stimulative policies aim to restore domestic spending, with currency depreciation a side effect of monetary expansion.

But currency boards do have their problems. First, by giving up the ability to control the size of its balance sheet, the central bank loses its role as the lender of last resort to the domestic banking system. The Banco Central de la Republica Argentina solved this problem by establishing standby letters of credit (described in Chapter 12) from large U.S. banks. When the time came to make emergency loans to local banks, officials borrowed dollars from U.S. banks and then made loans in pesos. But their lending was limited to the amount of dollar credit that foreign banks were willing to extend.

In 2001, the Argentinean currency board collapsed and authorities were forced to allow the peso to float. Within a few months, dollars that had once cost one peso apiece cost three. What caused the collapse? Entire books have been written to answer this question, but several points will take us a long way toward understanding what happened. First, the peso was pegged to the U.S. dollar, despite the fact that Argentina's economy doesn't have much to do with the U.S. economy. When the dollar appreciated in the 1990s, it made the peso more valuable as well. The overvalued peso priced Argentinean exporters out of their markets, which were not in the United States.

A 5-peso note issued by the government of the Province of Buenos Aires in 2001.

Over a period of years, the fact that their exports were too expensive ended up severely damaging Argentina's economy.

But the overvalued exchange rate was only part of the story; fiscal policy was the other part. While the Argentinean economy grew at a healthy rate of nearly 4½ percent per year through much of the 1990s, government spending rose even faster—so fast that the government needed to borrow an average of nearly 4 percent of GDP per year just to pay its bills. The more the government borrowed, the more wary lenders became of continuing to lend. Undeterred, politicians spent until they simply ran out of money.

The problem was worst at the provincial government level (analogous to the state governments in the United States), where borrowing became impossible even to meet the payroll. So provincial government officials began printing a sort of bond and using it to pay their employees. The bonds issued by the provincial government of Buenos Aires, called *patacones,* paid 7 percent annual interest and matured in one to five years (see the photo). What made them special was that they were the same physical size as currency and were issued in small denominations of one to 100 pesos in order to pay employees and retirees. Observers estimated that Argentina's provincial governments eventually issued 40 percent of the currency in circulation. When politicians began printing their own money, the claim that Argentinean inflation would roughly mirror U.S. inflation—a requirement for the long-run viability of the fixed exchange rate—was no longer credible and the currency board collapsed. Always remember, irresponsible politicians can undermine any monetary policy regime.

Dollarization in Ecuador   Some countries just give up and adopt the currency of another country for all their transactions, completely eliminating their own monetary policy. This practice need not be based on the dollar. Monaco, the small country for the rich and famous on the southern coast of France, adopted the French franc in 1865 and uses the euro today.[10]

---

[10]Other small countries that have euroized include Andorra, Kosovo, Montenegro, San Marino, and Vatican City.

Monaco is very small, covering less than 50 square miles (about twice the size of Manhattan), with a population of only 30,000. Ecuador, with a population of 15 million spread over 100,000 square miles, is another story. In 1999, Ecuador experienced a severe financial crisis. Real GDP fell more than 7 percent, the inflation rate rose to 50 percent, the banking system nearly collapsed, and the currency, the *sucre,* went into freefall, losing two-thirds of its value relative to the dollar in a year. In January 2000, Ecuador officially gave up its currency. Within six months, the central bank had bought back all the sucres in circulation. Almost immediately, interest rates dropped, the banking system reestablished itself, inflation fell dramatically, and growth resumed. Ecuador's move to dollarization was successful enough that a year later El Salvador followed suit. Panama has been dollarized since 1904.

Why would a country choose to give up its currency? In the case of a small emerging-market country, there are a host of reasons. First, with no exchange rate, there is no risk of an exchange-rate crisis—no possibility of either a large depreciation or a sudden capital outflow motivated by the fear of depreciation. Second, using dollars or euros or yen can help a country to become integrated into world markets, increasing its trade and investment. Finally, by rejecting the possibility of inflationary finance, a country can reduce the risk premium it must pay on loans and generally strengthen its financial institutions. But it does need to find some way to get the dollars it will need to keep the monetary base growing, which can prove to be a challenge.

The benefits of dollarization are balanced against the loss of revenue that comes from issuing currency—what is called *seignorage.* Remember, printing a $100 bill costs only a few cents. When Ecuador decided to dollarize, it gave those profits to the United States. Second, dollarization effectively eliminates the central bank as the lender of last resort because, again, the Federal Reserve prints dollars, not the Central Bank of Ecuador. If a banking emergency arises in Ecuador, the government will need to find some way to get dollars to provide the needed liquidity. (This is the problem Argentina solved by paying large U.S. banks for standby letters of credit.) Third, there is the loss of autonomous monetary or exchange-rate policy. But because foreign investors' lack of confidence in domestic policymakers was what created Ecuador's crisis, it is hard to see that loss as a serious one. Finally, any country that adopts the dollar as its currency gets U.S. monetary policy, like it or not. Obviously, this drawback is least worrisome for countries whose economies are closely tied to that of the United States. While it might make sense for countries like Mexico or Canada, for Ecuador the decision isn't so clear.

Note that dollarization is not the same as a monetary union. The decision by European countries to adopt a common currency, the euro, was fundamentally different from a country's decision to adopt the dollar. When the FOMC makes its decisions, the affairs of Ecuador and El Salvador carry no weight. And as we have already noted, dollarized countries forgo the revenue from issuing currency and are forced to make special arrangements to provide emergency loans to domestic banks. In contrast, all European countries participating in the monetary union take part in monetary policy decisions, and all share in the revenue that comes from printing euros. Europe's national banks still operate as lenders of last resort in making euro loans. In sum, a monetary union is shared governance; euroization is not.[11] Moreover, with its shared

---

[11]The ECB's decision in May 2010 to continue accepting Greek sovereign debt as collateral—despite its fall below investment grade—exemplifies how shared governance in the European Monetary Union favors many forms of risk sharing. Central banks typically accept only investment-grade debt as collateral.

institutions, a monetary union generally is even harder than a hard peg (see page 539). Yet, because a member country of a monetary union cannot control the money supply by itself, some important characteristics of monetary unions are analogous to those of dollarized or euroized countries. And, because a country may be able to withdraw from a monetary union (and reintroduce its own currency), investors may still require a currency-related risk premium to hold that country's liabilities.

Terms

capital controls, 527
currency board, 540
dollarization, 540
foreign exchange intervention, 522
gold standard, 537
hard peg, 539
renminbi, 541

speculative attack, 535
sterilized foreign exchange intervention, 532
unsterilized foreign exchange intervention, 532
yuan, 541

Using FRED: Codes for Data in This Chapter

Data Series	FRED Data Code
U.S. dollar/euro exchange rate	EXUSEU
Japanese yen/U.S. dollar exchange rate	EXJPUS
Mexican peso/U.S. dollar exchange rate	EXMXUS
Mexico consumer price index	MEXCPIALLMINMEI
U.S. consumer price index	CPIAUCSL
U.S. dollar/U.K. pound exchange rate	EXUSUK
12-month U.S. dollar LIBOR	USD12MD156N
12-month U.K. pound LIBOR	GBP12MD156N
Thai baht/U.S. dollar exchange rate	EXTHUS
Korean won/U.S. dollar exchange rate	EXKOUS
Chinese yuan/U.S. dollar exchange rate	EXCHUS
Malaysian ringgit/U.S. dollar exchange rate	EXMAUS
Canadian dollar/U.S. dollar exchange rate	EXCAUS
Swiss franc/U.S. dollar exchange rate	EXSZUS
Price of gold (U.S. dollars)	GOLDAMGBD228NLBM
China foreign exchange reserves (excluding gold)	TRESEGCNM052N

Chapter Lessons

1. When capital flows freely across a country's borders, fixing the exchange rate means giving up discretionary monetary policy.
   a. Purchasing power parity implies that in the long run exchange rates are tied to inflation differentials across countries.
   b. Capital market arbitrage means that in the short run the exchange rate is tied to differences in interest rates.
   c. Monetary policymakers can have only two of the following three options: open capital markets, control of domestic interest rates, and a fixed exchange rate.
   d. Countries that impose controls on capital flowing in and/or out can fix the exchange rate without giving up discretionary monetary policy.

2. Central banks can intervene in foreign exchange markets.
   a. When they do, it affects their balance sheet in the same way as an open market operation.
   b. Foreign exchange intervention affects the exchange rate by changing domestic interest rates. This is called unsterilized intervention.
   c. A sterilized intervention is a purchase or sale of foreign exchange reserves that leaves the central bank's liabilities unchanged. It has no lasting impact on the exchange rate in a deep, well-functioning currency market.

3. The decision to fix the exchange rate has costs, benefits, and risks.
   a. Both corporations and investors benefit from predictable exchange rates.
   b. Fixed exchange rates can reduce domestic inflation by importing the monetary policy of a country with low inflation.
   c. Fixed exchange-rate regimes are fragile and leave countries open to speculative attacks.
   d. The right conditions for choosing to fix the exchange rate include
      i. A poor reputation for inflation control.
      ii. An economy that is well integrated and cyclically synchronized with the one to whose currency the rate is fixed.
      iii. A high level of foreign exchange reserves.
      iv. A high degree of price and wage flexibility.
      v. A robust banking system.

4. There are a number of examples of exchange-rate systems.
   a. The Bretton Woods system, set up after World War II, pegged exchange rates to the U.S. dollar. It collapsed in 1971 after U.S. inflation began to rise.
   b. Most fixed exchange-rate regimes are no longer thought to be viable in the absence of capital controls.
   c. Two that may work are currency boards and dollarization (or euroization).
   d. With a currency board, the central bank holds enough foreign currency reserves to exchange the entire monetary base at the promised exchange rate.
   e. Argentina's currency board collapsed when the regional governments began printing their own money.
   f. Dollarization is the total conversion of an economy from its own currency to the currency of another country.
   g. Several Latin American countries have adopted the dollar recently, with good results over the short run. Several small European countries have adopted the euro.

Conceptual and Analytical Problems

1. Explain the mechanics of a speculative attack on the currency of a country with a fixed exchange-rate regime. *(LO4)*

2. Country A frequently experiences large business cycle swings. Under what conditions might it be appropriate for country A to dollarize? *(LO1)*

3. In the first half of 1997, the Bank of Thailand maintained a fixed exchange rate of 26 Thai baht to the U.S. dollar, but Thai interest rates were substantially higher than those in the United States and Japan. Thai bankers were borrowing money in Japan and lending it in Thailand. *(LO3)*
   a. Why was this transaction profitable?
   b. What risks were associated with this method of financing?
   c. Describe the impact of a depreciation of the baht on the balance sheets of Thai banks involved in these transactions.

4. During the time of the currency board, Argentinean banks offered accounts in both dollars and pesos, but loans were made largely in pesos. Describe the impact on banks of the collapse of the currency board. *(LO4)*

5. Investors became nervous just before the 2002 Brazilian presidential election. As a result, the risk premium on Brazilian government debt increased dramatically and Brazil's currency depreciated significantly. *(LO1)*
   a. How could concern over an election drive up the risk premium?
   b. How was the risk premium connected to the value of the currency?

6. Explain why a well-capitalized domestic banking system might be important for the successful maintenance of a fixed exchange-rate regime. *(LO4)*

7.* Explain why a central bank is usually more effective at holding the value of its domestic currency at an artificially low level for a sustained period than at an artificially high level. *(LO3)*

8. Why might a sterilized foreign exchange market intervention have a greater impact on the exchange rate in times of financial stress than in times of normal market conditions? *(LO2)*

9. When asked about the value of the dollar, the chair of the Federal Reserve Board answers, "The foreign exchange policy of the United States is the responsibility of the secretary of the Treasury; I have no comment." Discuss this answer. *(LO1)*

10.* Explain why a consensus has developed that countries should either allow their exchange rates to float freely or adopt a hard peg as an exchange-rate regime? *(LO3)*

11. Explain the costs and benefits of dollarization. Could a dollarized regime collapse? *(LO4)*

12. You observe that two countries with a fixed exchange rate have current inflation rates that differ from each other. You check the recent historical data and find that inflation differentials have been present for several months and that they have not remained constant. How would you explain these observations in light of the theory of purchasing power parity? *(LO2)*

*Indicates more difficult problems

13. Assuming the country is open to international capital flows, which of the following combinations of monetary and exchange-rate policies are viable? Explain your reasoning. *(LO1)*
    a. A domestic interest rate as a policy instrument and a floating exchange rate.
    b. A domestic interest rate as a policy instrument and a fixed exchange rate.
    c. The monetary base as a policy instrument and a floating exchange rate.

14. Show the impact on the Federal Reserve's balance sheet of a foreign exchange market intervention where the Fed sells $1,000 worth of foreign exchange reserves. Explain what impact, if any, the intervention will have on the domestic money supply. *(LO2)*

15. If the Federal Reserve decides to sterilize the foreign exchange market intervention described in Problem 14, show the impact on the Fed's balance sheet. What would the overall impact be on the monetary base? What would be the impact, if any, on the exchange rate? You should assume that the intervention took place in a deep, well-functioning foreign exchange market. *(LO2)*

16. Use a supply-and-demand diagram for dollars to show the impact of an increase in U.S. interest rates relative to interest rates in the euro area in the wake of a foreign exchange market intervention by the Federal Reserve. *(LO2)*

17. Do you think the U.S. dollar is more likely to strengthen or weaken over the next few months? Explain your reasoning. *(LO1)*

18. China's stock of foreign exchange reserves has risen more than 20 times since 2000, and reached $3.5 trillion in mid-2013. Do you think that pace of reserve accumulation is likely to continue? Why or why not? *(LO4)*

19.* Consider a small open economy with a wide array of trading partners all operating in different currencies. The economy's business cycles are not well synchronized with any of the world's largest economies and the policymakers in this country have a well-earned reputation for being fiscally prudent and honest. In your view, should this small open economy adopt a fixed exchange-rate regime? *(LO3)*

20. A small Eastern European economy asks your opinion about whether they should pursue the path to joining the European Economic and Monetary Union (EMU) or simply "euroize" (i.e., dollarize by using the euro for all domestic transactions). What advice would you give? *(LO3)*

Data Exploration

For general information on using Federal Reserve Economic Data (FRED) online, visit www.mhhe.com/moneyandbanking4e.com and click on Student Edition, then FRED resources.

Scan here for quick access to the resources for these problems. Need a barcode reader? Try ScanLife, available in your app store.

1. Panama, Ecuador, and El Salvador began using the U.S. dollar as their domestic currency in 1904, 2000, and 2001, respectively. How do you expect their inflation rates to compare with U.S. inflation? Plot since 1960 the percent change from a year ago of consumer prices in Panama (FRED code: DDOE02PAA086NWDB), Ecuador (FRED code: DDOE02ECA086NWDB), El Salvador (FRED code: DDOE01S-VA086NWDB), and the United States (FRED code: PCEPI). Download these data

and (starting with the country's date of dollarization) compare the average inflation rate in each country with U.S. inflation. *(LO4)*

2. Did the September 2000 currency intervention by the United States and other countries influence the dollar–euro exchange rate? Plot for the September–October 2000 period the daily dollar–euro exchange rate (FRED code: DEXUSEU) and, on the right scale, the Fed's sales of dollars for euros (FRED code: USINTDMRKTDM). Was the intervention successful? If not, why not? *(LO2)*

3. Some claim that adoption of a gold standard would contribute to price stability. Was price stability a feature of the U.S. gold standard that prevailed prior to World War I (see Applying the Concept on page 537)? Based on a plot of the general price level (FRED code: M04051USM324NNBR), discuss U.S. price developments from 1880 to 1914. *(LO4)*

4. China is the world's largest exporter and has a fixed *nominal* rate of exchange with the U.S. dollar. However, China's *real* exchange rate, which determines the country's competitiveness, can change even when the nominal rate is fixed. Plot since 1993 the nominal exchange rate of yuan per dollar (FRED code: EXCHUS). When did China begin to allow its currency to appreciate on a sustained basis? Add to the graph the real exchange rate (see equation 2 in Chapter 10) by adjusting the yuan–dollar exchange rate for relative consumer price changes in China (FRED code: CHNCPIALLMINMEI) and the United States (FRED code: CPIAUCSL). (*Hint:* Divide the U.S. price index by 1.95 to set a common base year of 2005 = 100 for both price indexes used in the real exchange-rate formula.) How has China's real exchange rate evolved recently? What impact should these changes have on China's exports?

5. In September 1992, a speculative attack compelled the United Kingdom to devalue the British pound versus the German currency (the deutsche mark). How did monetary policies in both countries influence this outcome? Plot from 1990 to 1992 the discount rates in the United Kingdom (FRED code: INTDSRGBM193N) and Germany (FRED code: INTDSRDEM193N), and (on the right scale) the exchange rate of German marks per British pound (obtained by multiplying the number of U.S. dollars per pound [FRED code: EXUSUK] by the number of deutsche marks per U.S. dollar (FRED code: EXGEUS)]. What do you conclude? *(LO3)*

www.mhhe.com/moneyandbanking4e

Appendix to Chapter 19

What You Really Need to Know about the Balance of Payments

The international financial system exists to sustain the flow of capital and goods among countries. To understand how it works, we need to define three important terms connected with the international balance of payments. They are the current account balance, the capital account balance, and the official settlements balance.

The *current account* tracks the flow of payments across national boundaries. When an American purchases a television set made in Korea, or a Japanese consumer buys a copy of Microsoft Windows, the transaction shows up as part of the U.S. current account. The *current account balance* is simply the difference between a country's exports and imports of goods and services. A full accounting would include unilateral transfers, such as the money foreign workers send home to relatives, as well as investment income, such as the interest payments Americans receive on Mexican bonds. But we will ignore these and stick to the simple version: when a country's exports exceed its imports, its current account balance will be positive—that is, it will have a *current account surplus*.

To grasp the importance of the current account, you need to realize that countries have budgets, just like individuals. If you spend more than your income, you have two options: sell something you own or get a loan. What is true for an individual is also true for a country. Think of the revenue earned from selling exports to foreigners as the country's income, and the cost of imports bought from overseas as its spending. When spending exceeds income, the result is a current account deficit. To pay for its overspending, the country must either sell something it owns or borrow.

Take an example in which there is only one international transaction, your purchase of a new television set made in South Korea. When you buy your new TV, you want to pay in dollars, but the Samsung dealer wants to be paid in Korean won. Because you have sold nothing to anyone in South Korea, you have no won to pay. There are two ways to get the won you need. You can appeal to a South Korean to purchase some asset you own, like a share of IBM stock, or you can try to get a South Korean to give you a loan—in essence, to buy a bond that you issue. Only after you have sold an asset to someone who has Korean won will you be able to pay for and import the television set.

The *capital account* tracks the purchase and sale of assets—stocks, bonds, real estate, and the like—between countries. When a German buys shares in IBM or an American purchases a Brazilian government bond, the transaction appears in the capital account. The *capital account balance* is the difference between a country's capital inflows and capital outflows. When a country's capital account is in surplus, it has a net capital inflow. Its residents are either selling assets to foreigners or borrowing money from abroad.

Finally, the *official settlements balance* is the change in a country's official reserve holdings. During the time of the gold standard, these reserves took the form of gold bars. It shows the change in the central bank's foreign exchange reserves (or gold reserves).

The international balance of payments is an accounting framework that relates these three pieces. Their relationship is simple: They must sum to zero.

$$\text{Current account balance} + \text{Capital account balance}$$

$$+ \text{Official settlements balance} = 0$$

This accounting identity has important implications. If, as is normally the case in developed economies today, official reserve positions are unchanged so the official settlements balance is zero, then the current account balance plus the capital account balance sum to zero. So, a current account deficit must be matched by a capital account surplus, for example. If a country is importing more than it is exporting, it must either borrow from abroad or sell assets to foreigners to finance excess purchases.

When we add the official settlements balance, the analysis changes slightly. Now we see that if a country is running a current account deficit, there are two ways to pay for it. A country can run a capital account surplus or it can draw down its foreign exchange reserves. If capital controls are in place, so that the capital account balance is zero, then drawing down foreign exchange reserves is the only option. Countries with current account deficits will lose reserves, while those with current account surpluses will accumulate reserves. Finally, if foreigners want to sell their investments and take the proceeds home, they will force a country either to run a current account surplus—something it cannot do quickly without a severe economic contraction—or to drain foreign exchange from the central bank's reserves.

Part *V*

Modern Monetary Economics

Chapter 20

Money Growth, Money Demand, and Modern Monetary Policy

Learning Objectives

Understand . . .

LO1 Monetary aggregates

LO2 The quantity theory of money

LO3 The velocity of, and demand for, money

LO4 Monetary targeting

Anyone who listens carefully to what central bankers say, or reads what they write, will form the clear impression that 21st-century monetary policy has very little to do with money, despite its focus on inflation. That impression is reinforced by the technical papers that monetary economists write. Everyone talks about interest rates and exchange rates; no one talks about money.

But digging deeper, you will find that central bankers and monetary economists *do* care about money. After decades of studying the economy, the Nobel Prize–winning economist Milton Friedman wrote, "inflation is always and everywhere a monetary phenomenon." Most economists would agree. We see concern for money, too, in statements made by officials of the European Central Bank (ECB). In Chapter 16, we discussed the stability-oriented strategy that the ECB's Governing Council adopted in the fall of 1998 to achieve the objective of price stability. The council's strategy assigned money a prominent role that was, in its members' words, "signaled by the announcement of a quantitative reference value for the growth rate of a broad monetary aggregate." The idea was that deviations of money growth from the reference value signaled a risk to European price stability. Since then, the ECB's monthly announcements of its target interest rate have regularly mentioned money growth.

Obviously, money plays a significant role in the formulation of European monetary policy. The contrast with the United States could not be more striking. In July 2000, after roughly a quarter century of publishing twice-yearly target ranges for the monetary aggregates, the Federal Open Market Committee (FOMC) stopped doing so, explaining that "these ranges [no longer] provide useful benchmarks for monetary policy."[1] While the Federal Reserve still collects and publishes data on the monetary aggregates, FOMC members now mention them only in passing. They rarely make any reference to money in public announcements of the federal funds target rate. In 2001,

[1]This announcement appeared as a footnote in the biannual *Monetary Policy Report to Congress.*

Federal Reserve Board Governor Laurence H. Meyer even went so far as to say that money "plays virtually no role in the conduct of monetary policy."[2]

What accounts for the distinctly different treatment of money growth in the two largest central banks in the world? Why does the ECB make regular public references to money growth, while the Fed never does? If money growth is tied to inflation, why don't central bankers in the United States pay more attention to it? The goal of this chapter is twofold. First, it examines the link between money growth and inflation in order to clarify the role of money in monetary policy. Second, it explains the logic underlying central bankers' focus on interest rates.

Why We Care about Monetary Aggregates

We start with the single most important fact in monetary economics: the relationship between money growth and inflation rates. Panel A of Figure 20.1 shows the average annual inflation and money growth in 160 countries over the three decades from 1980 to 2009. This graph is striking for two reasons. The first is its scale: Some countries suffered inflation that averaged more than 200 percent *a year* over three decades.

Figure 20.1   Inflation Rates and Money Growth

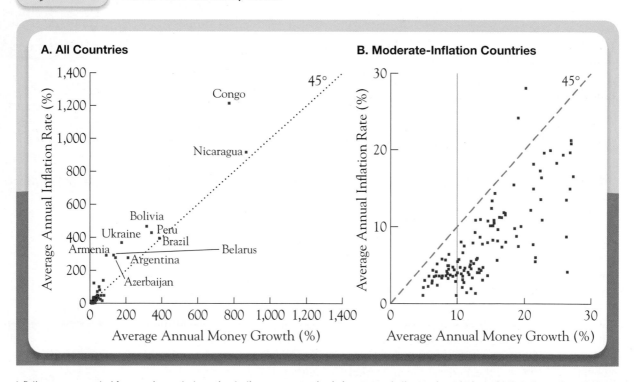

Inflation was computed from each country's analog to the consumer price index; money is the rough equivalent of M2. Data are from 1980 to 2009.

SOURCE: *These figures are based on data from the International Monetary Fund's International Financial Statistics.*

[2]Laurence H. Meyer, "Does Money Matter?" The 2001 Homer Jones Memorial Lecture, Washington University, St. Louis, Missouri, March 28, 2001.

Second, every country with high inflation had high money growth. History provides no examples of countries with high inflation and low money growth or with low inflation and high money growth.

One thing the figure does not show because of its scale is the huge number of points that fall very close to the origin, representing countries with both low inflation and low money growth. Panel B of Figure 20.1 displays the data for the 130 countries that experienced moderate money growth (averaging less than 30 percent) over the three decades from 1980 to 2009. While the relationship between money growth and inflation is less striking it is still clearly there. The higher the rate of money growth is, the higher the inflation rate is likely to be. The two variables move together. This evidence alone tells us that *to avoid sustained episodes of high inflation, a central bank must be concerned with money growth. Avoiding high inflation means avoiding persistent rapid money growth.*

Both panels of Figures 20.1 include a 45-degree line. Note that the points representing countries with very high inflation tend to lie above the line, while the points representing countries with moderate to low inflation tend to fall below it. As the simplified graph in Figure 20.2 shows, points lying above the 45-degree line represent countries where average inflation exceeds average money growth; points lying below the 45-degree line represent countries where money growth exceeds inflation. To understand this relationship, think about what would happen if the inflation rate rose to 900 percent a year, as was the case in Nicaragua (see Panel A of Figure 20.1). That means prices would be rising about 4½ percent a week. When the currency that people are holding loses value that rapidly, they will work to spend what they have as quickly as possible.[3] As we will see shortly, spending money more quickly has the same effect on inflation as an increase in money growth.

Figure 20.2   Money Growth and Inflation

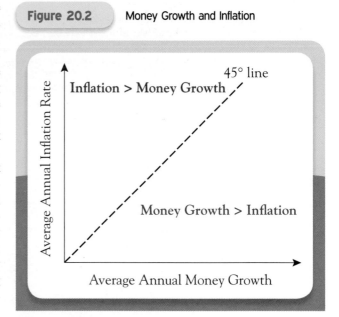

Connecting this relationship to central bank policy is straightforward. Recall from Chapter 17 that the central bank controls the size of its own balance sheet. Policymakers can purchase as many assets as they want, issuing currency and commercial bank reserve liabilities to do so. Those liabilities, in turn, form the monetary base. Through the process of deposit expansion, the banking system turns the monetary base into the monetary aggregates. Thus, the monetary aggregates cannot grow rapidly without at least the tacit consent of the central bank. By limiting the rate at which they purchase securities, policymakers can control the rate at which aggregates like M2 grow. In other words, *it is impossible to have high, sustained inflation without monetary accommodation.*

Not surprisingly, evidence of the link between inflation and money growth is the foundation on which modern monetary policy is built. That is why the ECB pays close attention to growth in the monetary aggregates. But to use the link as a policy

[3]In some countries suffering from hyperinflation, workers may be paid more than once a day because cash loses value so quickly.

APPLYING THE CONCEPT
INFLATION AND THE COLLAPSE OF THE SOVIET UNION

In 1990, the Soviet Union collapsed, leaving in its place 15 independent countries known as the "former Soviet Republics." These new countries had several characteristics in common. One of them was their horrible inflation experience. In Latvia from 1991 to 1994, the inflation rate averaged just below 300 percent per year—the lowest rate of the 15 countries. In Georgia in 1994, prices rose 15,600 percent, or roughly 10 percent per week.

The source of these extraordinary levels of inflation was not hard to find: it was rapid money growth. Because the governments of these countries were the successors to the Soviet Union, a command economy, at first they were responsible for controlling every aspect of their citizens' economic lives. Virtually everyone worked for and was paid by the government. But while these states were committed to extremely high levels of expenditure, they had virtually no sources of revenue. There was no way to collect taxes and no way to borrow. The only available source of revenue was to print money, so that is what government officials did. They printed lots of it, raising money growth rates to well over 100 percent a year. From 1992 to 1993, for example, the Ukrainian equivalent of M2 increased by a factor of 20. Not surprisingly, such high money growth was matched by high inflation. Ukraine's 2,000 percent rate of money growth was accompanied by 4,000 percent inflation.

Officials in these countries realized that inflation had to be brought under control, or people would revolt (again). So they made a number of changes. The most important was to take the authority to print money out of the hands of politicians and turn it over to an independent central bank (see pages 407–408 on the importance of central bank independence). Together with vast economic reforms that shrank the size of most of the governments dramatically, this depoliticizing of monetary policy produced an amazing transformation. By 2001, the rate of inflation had dropped to less than 10 percent in 9 of the 15 countries; only Belarus had an inflation rate of more than 50 percent. As money growth fell, inflation dropped with it.

Former Soviet Republics

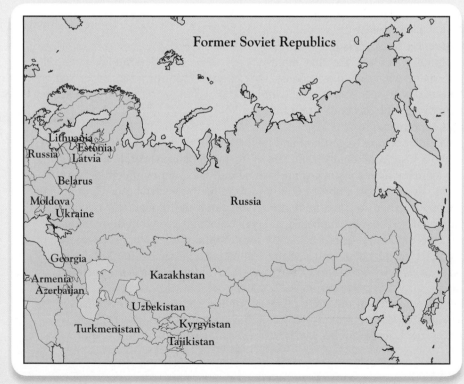

guide, central bankers must understand how it works. Looking back at Figure 20.1, we can see that all money growth is not created equal. Something beyond just differences in money growth accounts for the differences in inflation across countries. To see the point, look at Panel B of Figure 20.1 and note the vertical line drawn at the point where annual money growth averages 10 percent. Points lying on or near the line represent countries that experienced average annual inflation rates of between 1 percent and 8 percent. What accounted for the differences in inflation among those countries?

Still other questions arise. For instance, Figure 20.1 shows average inflation and money growth over a 30-year period. The results suggest that money growth is a useful guide to understanding long-term movements in inflation. But what happens over shorter periods of a few months or years? Answering this question requires moving beyond the simple statistical relationship shown in Figure 20.1. We need to develop a deeper understanding of the link between money growth and inflation, one that is based on economic decisions.

The Quantity Theory and the Velocity of Money

What accounts for the fact that high money growth is accompanied by high inflation? Recall that during times of inflation, the value of money is falling. If we think about the value or purchasing power of money in terms of the goods needed to get money, the impact of inflation becomes clear. Normally, we think of how many dollars we need to buy a cup of coffee or a sandwich; that's the money price of the sandwich. But we can turn the question around and ask how many cups of coffee or sandwiches a person needs to buy one dollar. A fall in the number of cups of coffee it takes to buy one dollar represents a decline in the price, or value, of money.

If someone asked you how the price of a cup of coffee is determined, having learned your microeconomics, you would answer that it depends on the supply of and demand for coffee. When the supply of coffee rises but demand does not, the price falls. Not surprisingly, the same is true of the price of money: it is determined by supply and demand. Given steady demand, an increase in the supply of money drives the price of money down. That's inflation. If the central bank continuously floods the economy with large amounts of money, inflation will reach very high levels.

Velocity and the Equation of Exchange

To understand the relationship between inflation and money growth, we need to focus on money as a means of payment. Imagine a simple economy that is composed of four

This note, issued by the Central Bank of Hungary in 1946, is the highest-denomination currency note ever issued. Its face value is 100 million trillion *pengö* (that's a 1 followed by 20 zeros). The note was produced for use during one of the most extreme hyperinflations in history, which took place in Hungary following World War II. Starting in 1944, the amount of currency in circulation grew from 12 billion pengö (a number with 11 digits) to a 27-digit total in 1946. In two short years, the quantity of money had increased by a factor of about 10,000 trillion, reducing the value of this note to the equivalent of 20 cents.

college students: one has $100 in currency; the second has two tickets to the weekend football game, worth $50 each; the third has a $100 calculator; and the fourth has a set of 25 high-quality drawing pencils that sell for $4 apiece. Each of these students wants something else. The one with the $100 in currency needs a calculator, so she buys it. The student who sold the calculator to her wants to see the football game, so he uses the cash she paid him to buy the two tickets. Finally, the student who sold the football tickets needs some pencils for a drawing class, so the cash changes hands again.

Let's analyze the effect of these transactions. Their total value is $100 × (1 calculator) + $50 × (2 football tickets) + $4 × (25 drawing pencils) = $300. In this four-person economy, the $100 was used three times, resulting in $300 worth of transactions. In general terms, we can write this as

$$\text{(Number of dollars)} \times \text{(Number of times each dollar is used)} \tag{1}$$
$$= \text{Dollar value of transactions}$$

To interpret this expression, note that the number of dollars is the quantity of money in the economy. The number of times each dollar is used (per unit of time) is called the **velocity of money**. The more frequently each dollar is used, the higher the velocity of money.

Applying this same logic to the economy as a whole is straightforward because virtually every transaction uses money at some stage. For our purposes here, we will restrict the analysis to sales and purchases of final goods and services produced in a country during a given period and measured at market prices. That is, we will focus on **nominal gross domestic product**. Every one of the purchases counted in nominal GDP requires the use of money. So,

$$\text{(Quantity of money)} \times \text{(Velocity of money)} = \text{Nominal GDP} \tag{2}$$

Because we have data on both the quantity of money and nominal GDP, we can use equation (2) to compute the velocity of money. Each definition of money—each monetary aggregate—has its own velocity. In the first quarter of 2013, GDP equaled $16.53 trillion and M1 equaled $2.47 trillion, so M1 had a velocity of 6.69. In the same period, M2 equaled $10.44 trillion, so the velocity of M2 was 1.58. We will come back to this topic shortly.

To manipulate the expression for velocity in equation (2), we can rewrite it using algebraic symbols. We'll use the letter M to represent money and V to represent velocity. Nominal GDP can be divided into two parts, the price level and the quantity of real output (or real GDP). Calling these two factors P and Y, we can state that nominal GDP = P times Y. Using this notation, we can rewrite equation (2) as

$$MV = PY \tag{3}$$

This expression, called the **equation of exchange**, tells us that *the quantity of money multiplied by its velocity equals the level of nominal GDP,* written as the price level times the quantity of real output.

With money on the left-hand side and prices on the right, the equation of exchange provides the link between money and prices that we are looking for. But our real concern is with inflation, not the price level, and money growth, not the quantity of money. We need to manipulate equation (3) to allow for the percentage change in each factor.

Noting that the percentage change of a product like MV or PY is the sum of the percentage changes in each factor,[4] we can write

$$\boxed{\begin{array}{ccccc} \%\Delta M & + & \%\Delta V & = & \%\Delta P & + & \%\Delta Y \\ \text{Money growth} & + & \text{Velocity growth} & = & \text{Inflation} & + & \text{Real growth} \end{array}} \qquad (4)$$

where the symbol "$\%\Delta$" stands for percentage change. We know that the percentage change in the quantity of money is money growth; the percentage change in the price level is inflation; and the percentage change in real GDP is real growth. So equation (4) tells us that *money growth plus velocity growth equals inflation plus real growth.*

The Quantity Theory of Money

In the early 20th century, the economist Irving Fisher wrote down the equation of exchange and derived the implication in equation (4). Next, he assumed that no important changes occur in payment methods or the cost of holding money. If the interest rate is fixed and there is no financial innovation, then velocity will be constant. Fisher also assumed that real output is determined solely by economic resources and production technology, so it too is fixed in the short run. In other words, Fisher assumed that $\%\Delta V = 0$ and $\%\Delta Y = 0$. He concluded that money growth translates directly into inflation, an assertion that is termed the **quantity theory of money**. According to Fisher's theory, changes in the aggregate price level are caused solely by changes in the quantity of money. So if the central bank pours more money into the economy, it drives up the prices of existing goods and services. Raising the quantity of money by 10 percent raises prices by 10 percent; doubling the quantity of money doubles the price level. As Milton Friedman said, *inflation is a monetary phenomenon.*

The fact that individuals require money to complete transactions means that we can reinterpret the quantity theory of money to describe the equilibrium between money demand and money supply. Note that in the classroom economy described earlier, the number of dollars needed equaled the total dollar value of the transactions divided by the number of times each dollar was used. That is, money demanded (M^d) equals the total value of transactions divided by the velocity of money. For the economy as a whole, the demand for money equals nominal GDP divided by velocity:

$$M^d = \frac{1}{V}PY \qquad (5)$$

Next, recall that the supply of money (M^s) is determined by the central bank and the behavior of the banking system. Equilibrium in the money market means that supply equals demand ($M^d = M^s$), which equals the quantity of money in the economy (M). Rearranging equation (5) gives us $MV = PY$. Assuming that velocity and real output are both constant, as Irving Fisher did, we can once again conclude that money growth equals inflation.

---

[4]This statement is based on the approximation that the change in the natural log of a variable x is approximately equal to its percentage change. To see how it works, first take the natural log of the product $M_t V_t$: $ln(M_t V_t) = ln(M_t) + ln(V_t)$. Now subtract $ln(M_{t-1}V_{t-1})$ from the left-hand side and $ln(M_{t-1}) + ln(V_{t-1})$ from the right-hand side to get $ln(M_t V_t) - ln(M_{t-1} V_{t-1}) = [ln(M_t) - ln(M_{t-1})] + [ln(V_t) - ln(V_{t-1})]$. This means that the change in the natural log of MV equals the change in the natural log of M plus the change in the natural log of V. Next, use the fact that the difference in the log is the log of the ratio, $[ln(M_t) - ln(M_{t-1})] = ln(M_t/M_{t-1})$. We can rewrite this as $ln[1 + (M_t - M_{t-1})/M_{t-1}]$, and use the fact that the natural log of one plus a small number is approximately equal to the small number, so $ln(M_t/M_{t-1}) \approx (M_t - M_{t-1})/M_{t-1}$, which is the percentage change. Putting all of this together gives us the fact that the percentage change of a product is the sum of the percentage change of the elements: $\%\Delta(MV) = \%\Delta M + \%\Delta V$.

YOUR FINANCIAL WORLD
Understanding Inflation Statistics

When people think about inflation, they usually have the Consumer Price Index (CPI) in mind. The CPI is the most commonly used and closely watched measure of inflation in the United States.* Given its prominence, we should understand its limitations.

The CPI, published monthly by the Bureau of Labor Statistics, is used widely to make adjustments for inflation and to measure changes in the cost of living from month to month and year to year. The index is designed to answer the following question: how much more would it cost today to purchase the same basket of goods and services that was bought on a fixed date in the past? To calculate the CPI, every two years government statisticians ask a representative sample of people what they actually buy. Then they construct a representative "market basket" of goods and services and track how much it costs from month to month. Inflation, as measured by the CPI, is the percentage change in the price of this basket of goods.

The CPI tends to overstate inflation. That is, its estimates of the change in the cost of living are biased upward. There are several sources of bias. The first comes from the fact that consumers' *buying patterns* change all the time, while the Bureau of Labor Statistics' surveys are infrequent. (Figure 20.3 shows the relative weights used to divide the market basket among different types of expenditures in 2012.) Consumers tend to shift their purchases away from goods that have become relatively more expensive and toward those that have become less expensive. Their willingness to make such substitutions lessens the impact of price changes on their standard of living. To the extent that statisticians fail to take such substitutions into account, the measure of consumer price inflation that they compile will overstate changes in the cost of living. (Inflation measured by the new *chained CPI,* which better accounts for the substitution effect, averaged 0.3 percent lower than the conventional CPI between 2000 and 2012.)

A second source of bias arises from the fact that statisticians have tremendous difficulty taking into account improvements in the *quality* of goods and services included in the consumer price index. Suppose, for example, that all cinemas introduce a three-dimensional (3D) projection system that enhances the moviegoing experience, raising ticket prices at the same time. If consumers are willing to pay the higher ticket prices because they value the improved 3D image quality, statisticians may simply record the increase in ticket prices without accounting for the increase in quality. The result is that inflation is overstated.

Government statisticians are aware of all of these problems and are constantly working to minimize the bias they create. As a result, today the inflation overstatement probably has declined from earlier estimates of 1 percent or more annually.† Nevertheless, suppose that the CPI still exaggerates inflation by about ½ percentage point per year. So, when the CPI rises by 2 percent, the real cost of living, correctly measured, rises only about 1½ percent. While a bias of that size doesn't amount to much if prices are rising at 10 or 15 percent a year, it becomes significant to both policymakers and consumers at the low levels of inflation common in recent years. For central bankers who wish to maintain price stability—zero inflation, correctly measured—the CPI's bias means that they need to systematically

The quantity theory of money accounts for some important characteristics of the patterns shown in Figure 20.1. First, it tells us why high inflation and high money growth go together. Second, it explains the tendency for moderate- and low-inflation countries to fall below the 45-degree line in Panel B of Figure 20.1. That is, money growth tends to be higher than inflation in those countries because they are experiencing real growth. Looking at equation (4), we can see that if velocity is constant, then money growth equals the sum of inflation and real growth. At a given level of money growth, the higher the level of real growth is, the lower the level of inflation will be. So in countries that are growing, inflation will be lower than money growth, causing their economies to fall below the 45-degree line in Panel B of Figure 20.1.

The Facts about Velocity

If Irving Fisher was correct in assuming that the velocity of money is constant, his assumption would have important implications for monetary policy. Because the trend in real growth is determined by the structure of the economy and the rate of technological progress, countries could control inflation directly by limiting money growth. This logic led Milton Friedman to conclude that central banks should simply set money growth

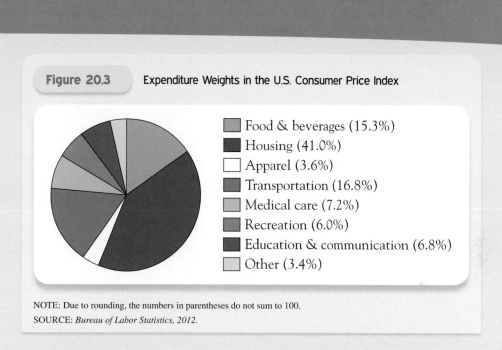

Figure 20.3   Expenditure Weights in the U.S. Consumer Price Index

- ■ Food & beverages (15.3%)
- ■ Housing (41.0%)
- □ Apparel (3.6%)
- ■ Transportation (16.8%)
- ■ Medical care (7.2%)
- ■ Recreation (6.0%)
- ■ Education & communication (6.8%)
- ■ Other (3.4%)

NOTE: Due to rounding, the numbers in parentheses do not sum to 100.
SOURCE: *Bureau of Labor Statistics, 2012.*

adjust their inflation objective: in this case, raising it by about ½ percentage point. That is, rather than setting their objective at zero measured inflation, they must choose some positive rate above that. For the rest of us, a CPI bias of ½ percentage point would mean that if the index goes up 2 percent a year, we need only a 1½ percent raise to maintain our standard of living.

*Tools of the Trade in Chapter 2 gives a brief introduction to the CPI.

†Earlier estimates of the CPI bias are discussed in Robert J. Gordon, "The Boskin Commission Report: A Retrospective One Decade Later," *International Productivity Monitor* 12 (Spring 2006), pp. 7–22.

at a constant rate.[5] That is, policymakers should strive to ensure that the monetary aggregates like M1 and M2 grow at a rate equal to the rate of real growth plus the desired level of inflation. Friedman was aware that the central bank does not control the monetary aggregates precisely and that the link between the monetary base and M1 and M2 fluctuates over time. Policymakers cannot control the money multiplier because it depends both on how much currency individuals decide to hold and how much excess reserves banks decide to maintain. To make the rule viable, he suggested changes in regulations that would limit banks' discretion in creating money and tighten the relationship between the monetary aggregates and the monetary base, reducing fluctuations in the money multiplier. For example, an increase in the reserve requirement or restrictions on the number and types of loans banks could make would have such an effect.

But even if the relationship between the monetary base and the monetary aggregates were constant, Friedman's recommendation that the central bank should keep money growth constant would stabilize inflation only if velocity were constant. In countries with inflation rates above 10 or 20 percent per year, changes in velocity can probably be safely ignored. In those economies, lowering inflation really does require lowering

[5]The original statement of what has come to be known as Friedman's *k percent rule* is in Milton Friedman, *A Program for Monetary Stability* (New York: Fordham University Press, 1960).

money growth. But in countries where the inflation rate is below 10 percent per year, changes in the velocity of money could have a significant impact on the relationship between money growth and inflation.

How much does the velocity of money fluctuate? To find out, we can look at some data. Panel A of Figure 20.4 shows the velocity of M2 from 1959 to 2013. There appear

Figure 20.4   The Velocity of M2, 1959–2013

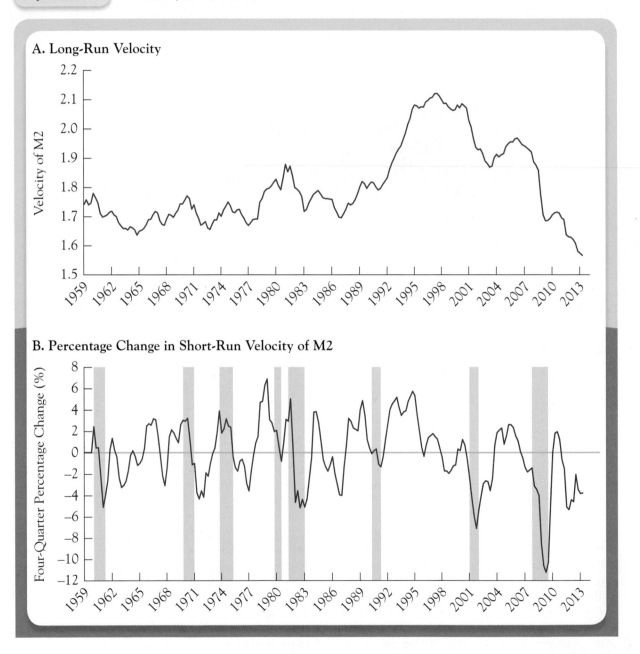

SOURCE: *Panel A is seasonally adjusted quarterly U.S. nominal GDP from the Bureau of Economic Analysis, divided by quarterly averages of monthly seasonally adjusted M2 from the Board of Governors of the Federal Reserve System. Panel B is four-quarter changes in the velocity of M2, plotted in panel A. Shaded areas depict recessions. (FRED data code: M2V.)*

to be two distinct periods. Until 1998, the trend rises; thereafter, it falls. However, over the full 54 years, the net effect is only a modest decline of velocity at an annual rate of 0.2 percent. Taken as a whole, these historical data seem reasonably consistent with Fisher's conclusion that *in the long run, the velocity of money is stable, so that controlling inflation means controlling the growth of the monetary aggregates.*

But central bankers are concerned with inflation rates over quarters or years, not half a century. The monetary aggregates, even broad ones, can be useful guides to short-term policy only to the extent that they signal changes in inflation during the periods monetary policymakers care about. And the long-run view in the top panel of Figure 20.4 masks some important short-run movements. To see them, we can look at the four-quarter (short-run) percentage change in M2 velocity, shown in Panel B of Figure 20.4. The shaded bars in the figure represent recessions. Looking at the figure, we can see that in the short run, velocity fluctuates quite a bit, sometimes by very large amounts. The scale of the figure runs from −12 to +8 percent!

The first step in understanding short-run movements in velocity is to examine what happened in the past. Returning to Figure 20.4, notice the increase in velocity in the late 1970s and early 1980s. This was a period when nominal interest rates peaked at more than 20 percent, triggering significant financial innovations, including the introduction of stock and bond mutual funds that allow investors checking privileges. The first of these developments made holding money very costly; the second allowed individuals to economize on the amount of money they held. Neither currency nor the checking accounts of the time paid interest, so with a 10 percent rate of inflation, the real rate of interest on money was −10 percent. Meanwhile, innovations like mutual funds outside of M2 (which allow for small-denomination withdrawals and provide transactions services similar to those of checking accounts) mean that individuals no longer needed to hold as much money. Together these reduced the amount of money individuals held for a given level of transactions, raising the velocity of money. In contrast, since the late 1990s, falling interest rates, combined with innovations that slashed the cost of holding money, lowered M2 velocity.

These data clearly suggest that fluctuations in the velocity of money are tied to changes in people's desire to hold money. To understand and predict changes in the velocity of money, then, policymakers must understand the demand for money. We turn to that topic next.

The Demand for Money

The best way to understand money demand, the determinants of the velocity of money, and the relationship between money and inflation is to ask why individuals hold money. What do they do with the money that is supplied to them? Recall from Chapter 2 that money can be a means of payment, a unit of account, and a store of value. While the unit-of-account function is crucial to the economy, it provides no justification for holding money, so we will ignore it here and focus on the first and third functions. People hold money in order to pay for the goods and services they consume (the means-of-payment function) and as a way of holding their wealth (the store-of-value function). These two forms of demand are referred to as the **transactions demand for money** and the **portfolio demand for money**, respectively.[6] As we look at each of them, keep

---

[6]This framework for discussing the demand for money was originally developed by John Maynard Keynes and is known as Keynes's liquidity preference theory.

APPLYING THE CONCEPT
THE ECB'S REFERENCE VALUE FOR MONEY GROWTH

At the start of the European Monetary Union in 1999, the monetary policy strategy of the European Central Bank assigned a prominent role to money. Many of the ECB's practices are modeled on those of its predecessor, the German Bundesbank, widely viewed as one of the most successful central banks in the world. In the 1970s, as inflation rose into the double digits in the United States and throughout most of Europe, the Bundesbank kept inflation in Germany at levels that would be acceptable even today. Policymakers there did so by setting annual targets for the monetary aggregates. Several decades later, in the hope that the Bundesbank's reputation for controlling inflation would rub off on them, ECB policymakers decided to set a "quantitative reference value for the growth rate of a broad monetary aggregate."

For the first four years of its existence, the ECB announced what amounted to a target growth rate of 4½ percent for euro-area M3 (the region's equivalent of M2). Officials computed the rate using the percentage-change version of the equation of exchange (equation [4]). That meant they had to make assumptions about real growth, velocity

growth, and the desired level of inflation. They assumed the euro-area economy was growing at a rate of 2 to 2½ percent per year, velocity was declining by ½ to 1 percent per year, and inflation should be 1 to 2 percent annually. Substituting the midpoints of those ranges into equation (4), we get

$$\text{Money growth} - \tfrac{3}{4} = 1\tfrac{1}{2} + 2\tfrac{1}{4},$$

$$\textit{so } \text{Money growth} = 4\tfrac{1}{2} \text{ percent}$$

The ECB was heavily criticized for its use of money growth targets. Observers claimed that the relationship between money growth and inflation was too unpredictable to be useful in the short run. They argued that the velocity of money in the newly created euro area would be difficult to forecast (see Figure 20.7). For a new central bank with no proven record of controlling inflation, they charged, this was a potentially dangerous move that could damage policymakers' credibility. Possibly in response to their critics, in May 2003 ECB policymakers decided to downgrade the role of money growth in their strategy. From then on, money growth would be used as "a crosscheck," not a major part of their strategy. And the Governing Council would no longer review the reference value every year, emphasizing its usefulness only as a long-run benchmark.

in mind that our objective is to understand fluctuations in the velocity of money. The more money individuals want to hold (all other things equal), the lower the velocity of money will be.

The Transactions Demand for Money

The quantity of money people hold for transactions purposes depends on their nominal income, the cost of holding money, and the availability of substitutes. Let's look at each of these briefly, taking income first. The higher people's nominal income, the more they will spend on goods and services. The more they purchase, the more money they will need. This observation is the basis for the conclusion that nominal money demand rises with nominal income, part of the quantity theory of money [look back at equation (5) on page 559]. Thus, *the higher nominal income is, the higher nominal money demand will be.*

Deciding how much money to hold depends on the costs and benefits. The benefits are easy to appreciate: holding money allows people to make payments. The costs are equally easy to understand. Because money can always be used to purchase an interest-bearing bond, the interest that people lose in not buying the bond is the opportunity cost of holding money. The nominal interest rate is the one that matters here. Compare money (which we temporarily assume pays zero interest) to a bond that pays interest. The difference between the two is the rate that matters, and that's the nominal interest rate on the bond (if money paid interest, one would subtract that rate to measure the opportunity cost of holding money). Of course, the bond is not a means of payment; it must be converted into money before it can be used to pay for transactions. So the

TIME

decision to hold money or bonds depends on how high the bond yield is and how costly it is to switch back and forth between the two. For a given cost of switching between bonds and money, as the nominal interest rate rises, then, people reduce their checking account balances, shifting funds into and out of higher-yield investments more frequently. Thus, the fact that the transactions demand for money falls as the interest rate rises has immediate implications for velocity. *The higher the nominal interest rate—that is, the higher the opportunity cost of holding money—the less money individuals will hold for a given level of transactions, and the higher the velocity of money.*[7]

This relationship explains why inflation tends to exceed money growth in the high-inflation countries shown in Panel A of Figure 20.1; that is why the points representing high-inflation countries tend to lie above the 45-degree line. At high levels of inflation, when prices are rising at a rate of 1,000 or 1,500 percent a year, money is losing value very quickly. At those levels, the opportunity cost of holding money is equivalent to the cost of inflation, a real return of $-1,000$ or $-1,500$ percent a year. People respond to the high cost of holding money by keeping as little of it as possible, getting rid of it as quickly as they can. They purchase durable goods that have a zero real return, which is quite a bit better than the real return of $-1,000$ percent they would get from holding money. Their frantic spending drives up the velocity of money. The quantity theory of money tells us that with national income held constant, inflation equals money growth plus growth in velocity. Because high inflation brings an increase in velocity, inflation must be higher than money growth in these countries, placing them above the 45-degree line in Panel A of Figure 20.1.

Besides interest rates, *the transactions demand for money is affected by technology.* Financial innovation allows people to limit the amount of money they hold. The best way to think about this is to imagine that innovation reduces the cost of shifting funds from an interest-bearing bond to a checking account. The lower the transactions cost, the more frequently people will shift money from their bond funds to their checking accounts, and the less money people will choose to hold.

This has direct implications for the impact of financial innovation on the transactions demand for money. To see what they are, think about a case in which your bank offers a new kind of product that features free automatic transfers between an account with interest at the level of a bond and your traditional checking account. You sign up for the account, but continue using your old checks and debit card. This new account has the feature that each time you make a purchase, your bank automatically shifts the amount of the purchase from the bonds you are holding to your checking account, where it remains for one day before being paid to your creditor. As a result your checking account will never have more than one day's worth of purchases in it, so you will hold much less money. Financial innovations that lower the cost of shifting money between bonds (or other investments) and a checking account will lower money holdings at a given level of income. The immediate implication is that financial innovations that economize on the money holding increase the velocity of your money.

Thus, an increase in the liquidity of stocks, bonds, or any other asset reduces the transactions demand for money. The advent of automatic teller machines and financial products that allow customers to make payments directly from their stock or bond mutual funds, often at no extra cost, means that today people don't need to hold as much

---

[7]The fact that higher interest rates raise velocity means that they put upward pressure on inflation. And yet, as we will see in the following chapters, monetary policymakers combat high inflation by raising interest rates. The apparent contradiction is resolved by the fact that, while interest rate increases might drive velocity higher, they reduce real growth by even more—enough to make the overall effect the one that we have come to expect.

YOUR FINANCIAL WORLD
Free Checking Accounts Are Rarely Free

Banks are always trying to attract new customers. To do so, some banks advertise free checking accounts. But are these accounts really free? The answer is almost surely no. In fact, bankers joke that "*free* checking" really means "*fee* checking" because of all the fees customers end up paying. While banks don't normally impose a monthly service charge on such accounts, that doesn't make them free.

Depending on the bank, customers with "free checking" may pay a fee to use the ATM or to visit a teller in person. They pay additional fees for notary public services, certified bank checks, and bounced checks. The insufficient funds charge is especially high for customers with "free checking," who are more likely than other customers to overdraw their accounts.

Overdrafts, in fact, are very profitable for banks. Here's why. If you write a check for $100 more than your account balance, the bank will cover it but will charge you a fee, usually $25 to $35. You will have only a week or so to pay back the overdraft. In other words, the bank is offering you

a $100 loan at a weekly interest rate of 25 percent or more. While banks are normally required to disclose the interest rates they charge on loans, regulators have not designated overdrafts as loans. As a result, banks haven't had to tell people who overdraw their accounts that they are paying a compound annual interest rate of more than 10,000,000 percent! But the 2013 *Study of Overdraft Programs* by the new Consumer Finance Protection Bureau hinted at the need for better disclosure and other reforms.*

There are two lessons here. First, don't be fooled by offers of free checking. Before you open a checking account, figure out what services you are going to need and find the bank that meets your needs most cheaply. Second, don't overdraw your account. There is almost always a cheaper way to borrow money.

*See *http://files.consumerfinance.gov/f/201306_cfpb_whitepaper_overdraft-practices.pdf*.

cash in their wallets and their checking accounts as their parents and grandparents once did.

Finally, *we all hold money to ensure ourselves against unexpected expenses*. We will include this form of demand, sometimes called the **precautionary demand for money**, as a part of transactions demand. The idea is that emergencies may arise that require immediate payments, for which we hold some amount of money in reserve. As we saw in Your Financial World: Your Excess Reserves in Chapter 17, an individual's rainy-day fund is analogous to a bank's excess reserves. The level of precautionary balances we hold in such funds is usually related to our income and our level of expenditures. The higher our normal expenses, the larger our rainy-day funds will be. The precautionary demand for money also rises with risk. While this effect is probably small, the higher the level of uncertainty about the future, the higher the demand for money and the lower the velocity of money will be.

The Portfolio Demand for Money

Money is just one of many financial instruments that we can hold in our investment portfolios. As a store of value, money provides diversification when held along with a wide variety of other assets, including stocks and bonds. To understand the portfolio demand for money, note that a checking account balance or a money-market account is really just a "bond" with zero time to maturity. That means we can use the framework presented in Chapter 6, where we discussed the demand for bonds, to understand the portfolio demand for money.

Recall that the demand for bonds depends on several factors, including wealth, the return relative to alternative investments, expected future interest rates on bonds, risk relative to alternative investments, and liquidity relative to alternative investments. Each of these affects the portfolio demand for money. As wealth increases, individuals increase their holdings of all assets. A prudent person holds a diversified portfolio that includes stocks, bonds, real estate, and money. As wealth rises, the quantity of all these investments, including money, rises with it. So money demand varies directly with wealth. Note that this rule applies even at a fixed level of expenditures: A rich person who has the same expenses as a poor person will still hold more money.

In studying the demand for bonds, we noted that an investor's desire to hold any specific financial instrument depends on how well it compares with alternative investments. The higher the expected return relative to the alternatives, the higher the demand for an asset will be. The same is true for money: The higher its return relative to the alternatives, the higher the demand. Put slightly differently, a decline in bond yields will increase the portfolio demand for money.

Because expectations that interest rates will change in the future are related to the expected return on a bond, they will affect the demand for money as well. To understand why, remember that the price of a bond varies inversely with the interest rate. When interest rates rise, bond prices drop and bondholders suffer a capital loss. So if you think interest rates are likely to rise, bonds will become less attractive than money to you. (Recall that the prices of short-term bonds fluctuate less than the prices of long-term bonds. Money is the ultimate short-term bond because it has zero time to maturity.) As a result, you will sell the bonds in your portfolio and increase your money holdings—at least until interest rates stop rising. When interest rates are expected to rise, then, money demand goes up.

Next there is risk. In our discussion of bonds, we noted that a decline in risk relative to that of alternative investments increases the demand for bonds. While the riskiness of money can decrease, what usually happens is that the riskiness of other assets increases, driving up the demand for money.[8] Looking back at Panel B of Figure 20.4, we can see that during and after the financial crisis of 2007–2009, the velocity of M2 plunged. One cause was an increase in uncertainty (risk), which drove investors to shift their funds into money.

RISK

Finally there is liquidity, a measure of the ease with which an asset can be turned into a means of payment. While some forms of money are more liquid than others, they are all closer to becoming a means of payment than other alternatives. If a sudden decrease in the liquidity of stocks, bonds, or other assets occurred, we would expect to see an increase in the demand for money.

Table 20.1 summarizes all of the factors that influence the demand for money.

Targeting Money Growth in a Low-Inflation Environment

So here is where we stand. In the long run, inflation is tied to money growth. In a high-inflation environment, where money growth and inflation are both running higher than 100 percent, moderate variations in the growth of velocity are a mere annoyance. What

---

[8]To grasp why money can be risky, think of an example in which the nominal interest rate on money is zero (that is literally true for cash and nearly true for many bank deposits). When money pays no interest, its return is minus inflation. That is, money loses value at the rate of inflation. The less certain inflation is, the more uncertain the return on money, and the more risky it is. So inflation uncertainty increases the riskiness of holding money.

Table 20.1	Determinants of Money Demand: Factors That Cause Individuals to Hold More Money
Transactions Demand for Money	
Nominal income	The higher nominal income, the higher the demand for money.
Interest rates	The lower interest rates, the higher the demand for money.
Availability of alternative means of payment	The less available alternative means of payment, the higher the demand for money.
Portfolio Demand for Money	
Wealth	As wealth rises, the demand for money goes up.
Return relative to alternatives	As the return on alternatives falls, the demand for money goes up.
Expected future interest rates	As expected future interest rates rise, the demand for money goes up.
Risk relative to alternatives	As the riskiness of alternatives rises, the demand for money goes up.
Liquidity relative to alternatives	As the liquidity of alternatives falls, the demand for money goes up.

"Forgive the mess. Warren just put everything into cash."

SOURCE: 2001 © Lee Lorenz/The New Yorker Collection/www.cartoonbank.com.

is important is the resolve of central bank officials (and politicians) to bring inflation down. There is no magic to it; the only solution is to reduce money growth.

In a low-inflation environment, controlling inflation is not so simple. The quantity theory of money tells us that our ability to use money growth as a policy guide depends on the stability of the velocity of money. In the United States, the velocity of the broad monetary aggregate M2 appears sufficiently stable for M2 to serve as a benchmark for controlling inflation over the long run—over periods of several decades. But in the short run, the velocity of money varies substantially. Yet the mere fact that velocity fluctuates is not reason enough to dismiss money growth as a policy target.

As we saw in Chapter 18, an intermediate target can be useful when stable links exist between it and the policymakers' operating instrument, on the one hand, and their policy objective on the other. This statement implies two criteria for the use of money growth as a direct monetary policy target: (1) a stable link between the monetary base and the quantity of money and (2) a predictable relationship between the quantity of money and inflation. The first of these allows policymakers to predict the impact of changes in the central bank's balance sheet on the quantity of money. The second allows them to translate changes in money growth into changes in inflation. These criteria cannot be solely qualitative in nature; central bankers need numerical estimates of these relationships. Policymakers must be able to say that a 1 percent change in the monetary base will generate an x percent change in a monetary aggregate like M2, which will then translate into a y percent change in inflation, and over what time period.

The relationship between money demand and its determinants listed in Table 20.1 must be stable and predictable—a problem for U.S. policymakers.

The Instability of U.S. Money Demand

To study the demand for money quantitatively, we will focus on the impact of the two factors that affect the transactions demand for money, nominal income and interest rates. Recalling the logic of the equation of exchange [equation (3) on page 558], we can conclude that the first factor, nominal income, is roughly proportional to money demand. Doubling people's nominal income means doubling the dollar value of the transactions they engage in, which requires double the original amount of money. That means we can focus on nominal income divided by the quantity of money, which equals velocity. This brings us to the second factor, interest rates (or more precisely, the opportunity cost of holding money). Is there a stable relationship between the velocity of money and the opportunity cost of holding it?

The data displayed in Figure 20.5 bear directly on this question. The figure shows the velocity of M2 on the vertical axis and the opportunity cost of holding M2 on the horizontal axis. The opportunity cost of M2 is defined as the yield on a three-month U.S. Treasury bill (an alternative asset) minus the return on holding M2, as computed by the Federal Reserve Bank of St. Louis. Note that this opportunity cost is a measure of the real return that individuals give up when they decide to hold M2 rather than a three-month Treasury bill. Each point on the figure represents a particular quarter.

Figure 20.5   M2 Velocity and Opportunity Cost, 1979–2013

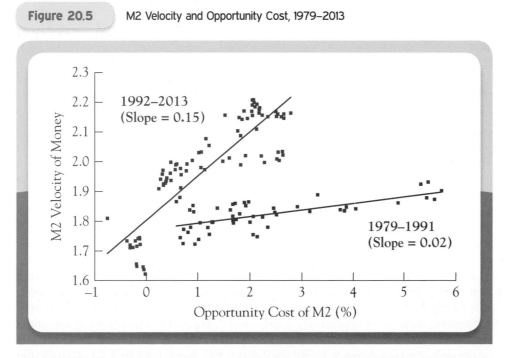

Data are quarterly. Velocity was computed as the ratio of Nominal GDP to M2. The opportunity cost of M2 was computed as the three-month Treasury bill rate less the rate of return on M2. The two solid lines are regression lines fitted to the separate samples.

SOURCE: *Federal Reserve Bank of St. Louis. (FRED data codes: M2V, TB3MS, and M2OWN).*

TOOLS OF THE TRADE

Using Statistical Models in Policy Evaluation

For policymakers to do their jobs, they need to know how changes in policy will affect their objectives. An essential question in any monetary policy decision is how much to adjust interest rates in order to keep prices stable and economic growth high. Unlike theory, policymaking is about numbers; it requires quantitative estimates of the relative impact of alternative policies. These estimates are based on statistical models that summarize the correlations among economic variables. To obtain the necessary information, economists at the central bank collect historical information and analyze it in an attempt to determine how past changes in policy have affected the economy. Their estimates allow policymakers to answer questions such as "If we raise the federal funds rate by one percentage point, how much lower will the rate of inflation be two years from now?"

Such an exercise may seem straightforward, but it has pitfalls. For an economic prediction to be valid, it must be based on data drawn from a historical period in which the same set of policies—sometimes called the policy *framework* or the policy *regime*—was in place. If it isn't, the results can be seriously misleading. A sports analogy will help to make the point. In the United States, a football team has four downs to make 10 yards, but in Canada, a football team gets only three downs before being forced to give up the ball. As a result, Canadian football teams regularly kick the ball away on the third down. Needless to say, no one would think of using data from Canadian football games to predict third-down behavior in a U.S. game.

In the mid-1970s, Nobel Prize–winning economist Robert Lucas observed that what is true in sports is true in economics.* In the same way that altering the rules of a game will change the players' strategies, altering the set of economic policies in place will change people's economic decisions. For example, no one would use data from a fixed-exchange-rate period to model the impact of interest-rate policy in a floating-exchange-rate system. Nor would anyone use information from a period when central bankers targeted money growth, allowing interest rates to vary, to predict the impact of a shift to targeting interest rates. Economic and financial decisions, Lucas noted, are based on expectations about the future, including what policymakers will do. Any change in policymakers' behavior will change people's expectations, altering their behavior and the observed relationships among economic variables.

This observation, known as the **Lucas critique**, has had a profound influence on the way policymakers formulate their recommendations. It implies that in predicting the effects of a change in policy, policymakers must take into account how people's economic behavior will change with it. To understand the impact of policies never before implemented, Lucas emphasized, policymakers must rely heavily on economic theory, modeling people's reactions to changes in their environment.

*The original Lucas critique is described in Robert E. Lucas Jr., "Econometric Policy Evaluation: A Critique," *Carnegie-Rochester Conference Series on Public Policy* 1, 1976, pp. 19–46.

They fall into two distinct groups. The first group, shown as dark blue squares, covers the decade of the 1980s. The second group, shown as red squares, covers the 1990s through 2013. What we want to know is whether an increase in the opportunity cost of holding money can be used to forecast an increase in velocity. (Recall that higher interest rates raise the opportunity cost of holding money, reducing the demand for money at a given level of income and increasing its velocity.)

The answer to our question is yes, there is a relationship between the velocity of money and the opportunity cost of holding money, but that relationship shifted quite a bit between the two decades. To see how much it shifted, consider an increase from 1 to 2 percent in the opportunity cost of holding M2. In the 1980s, the implication of a 1 percent increase in opportunity cost was an increase of almost 1¼ percent in the velocity of M2, from roughly 1.82 to 1.84. Since the early 1990s, the same change in opportunity cost drove velocity up 7½ percent, from 1.97 to 2.12. That is, the sensitivity of money demand to a change in the interest rate rose by a factor greater than six. The relationship between money demand and interest rates that held in the 1980s broke down in the 1990s. Using the relationship from the 1980s as a basis for policymaking in the 1990s and thereafter would not have produced the desired result.

There are several possible explanations for the instability of U.S. money demand over these three decades. The primary one has to do with the introduction of financial instruments that paid higher returns than money but could still be used as means of payment. While officials have tried to account for the new instruments by changing the composition of the monetary aggregates (see Applying the Concept on page 572), money demand continues to appear unstable.

A second explanation for the shift in the relationship between the velocity of M2 and its opportunity cost has to do with changes in mortgage refinancing rates. As long-term interest rates fell throughout the 1990s and into the 21st century, they spurred periods of intense activity in the mortgage market. Because every U.S. mortgage comes with the right to repay early, the holder of a conventional 30-year, fixed-rate mortgage can terminate the loan contract at any time by simply repaying the balance. When mortgage interest rates fall dramatically, large numbers of people pay off their old, high-interest mortgages and replace them with new, low-interest mortgages. The incentive to refinance a mortgage can be significant, even for what might seem a small decline in interest rates.

When a mortgage is refinanced, it creates demand for money in several ways. Many people who are refinancing take the opportunity to remove some of their equity in their home. The proceeds go into liquid deposit accounts, which are part of M2, until they are spent on home renovations or other major purchases. In addition, funds for the new mortgage must be collected from investors and transferred to holders of the old mortgage. Along the way, they flow through an account that is part of M2. So when mortgage interest rates fall, M2 tends to grow rapidly. Once interest rates stabilize and the wave of refinancing subsides, M2 settles down and even shrinks. But in the meantime, velocity fluctuates.

The breakdown in the relationship between money demand and interest rates that occurred in the United States during the early 1990s drove researchers back to their computers to build better, more robust statistical models. The data for the 1992–2013 period shown in Figure 20.5 suggest that they should have been successful, and to some extent they were. Nevertheless, the debate over the stability of money demand in the United States serves as a cautionary note for policymakers.

Targeting Money Growth: The Fed and the ECB

Though today virtually no central bank targets money growth, the practice was common in the 1970s. In the United States, the FOMC first adopted explicit objectives for money growth on January 15, 1970. Five years later, Congress passed a law directing the chair of the Federal Reserve Board to make quarterly appearances to testify to the Fed's money growth targets for the coming year. In addition, the Full Employment and Balanced Growth Act, passed in 1978, required the Fed to publish ranges for money growth in its twice-yearly *Monetary Policy Report to Congress.*

But announcing an objective is one thing; achieving it is something else. The FOMC rarely hit its money growth targets. Finally in July 2000, after the requirements of the 1978 legislation had expired, the committee stopped publishing them. A number of observers, including some inside the Federal Reserve, have argued that policymakers could have hit their money growth targets using procedures that were then in place. But to do so would have meant adjusting the federal funds rate target frequently, and by large amounts—something policymakers were unwilling to do. By the summer of

APPLYING THE CONCEPT

FINANCIAL INNOVATION AND THE SHIFTING VELOCITY OF MONEY

In our discussion of the transactions demand for money, we emphasized the impact of financial innovations on the quantity of money demanded. By changing the amount of money people need to hold at a given level of income, financial innovations influence the velocity of money. While innovations like ATMs and bond mutual funds that offer check-writing privileges make people's lives easier, they create serious difficulties for statisticians who are trying to construct useful definitions of the monetary aggregates.

Recall from Chapter 2 that the different measures of money are defined based on the liquidity of available financial assets. For example, M2 includes all the assets in M1 plus some others that are less liquid. But financial innovations can change the liquidity of the assets we hold. Ideally, the definitions of the monetary aggregates can be adjusted to take new financial instruments into account, but that task isn't easy.

To see the impact of financial innovations on measures of money, we can examine a particular historical episode: the introduction of the interest-bearing deposit account, including money-market mutual fund accounts in the 1970s. As funds shifted from traditional checking accounts to these new instruments, the velocity of money appeared to rise, as the red line in Figure 20.6 shows. That line represents the velocity of money according to the old definition of M2, which excluded money-market deposit accounts and money-market mutual fund accounts. Had the definition of M2 remained the same, velocity would have risen by a factor of two. Instead, with the benefit of hindsight, statisticians redefined M2 to keep velocity fairly constant at 1.5 to 2, as the blue line in Figure 20.6 shows.

The monetary aggregates can always be adjusted after the fact to account for changes in the financial system. For monitoring long-run economic conditions, that is sufficient. The real difficulty is calculating the impact of such changes as they are occurring so that the information can be used for short-run policymaking. Could anyone have known before the fact precisely how the introduction of new interest-bearing deposit accounts would influence money demand? How quickly will velocity rebound after its plunge during the financial crisis of 2007–2009? These are the sorts of questions that advocates of targeted money growth need to answer.

| Figure 20.6 | Velocity of M2, Old and New Definitions, 1959–2013 |

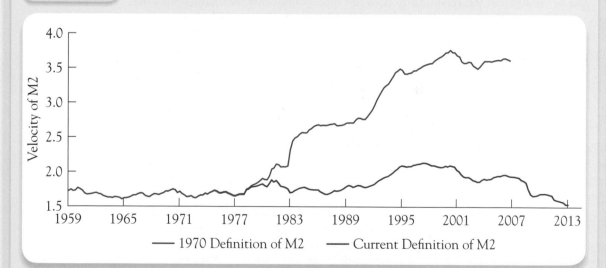

— 1970 Definition of M2   — Current Definition of M2

Old definitions excluded other checkable deposits from M1. The old definition of M2 also excluded money-market deposit accounts and retail money-market mutual fund shares. M2 data using the old definition are available up to 2007.

SOURCE: *Board of Governors of the Federal Reserve Board. (FRED data code: M2V.)*

Figure 20.7   Velocity of Euro-Area M3, 1995–2013

Velocity is measured as nominal GDP divided by M3 for the 17 countries of the euro area as of 2013. The red line is a simple time trend.

SOURCE: *Eurostat and International Monetary Fund. (FRED data codes: EUNGDP and MYAGM3EZQ196N.)*

2003, even Milton Friedman had given up. "The use of the quantity of money as a target has not been a success," he conceded. "I'm not sure I would as of today push it as hard as I once did."[9]

European monetary policymakers view matters differently. As we saw at the beginning of the chapter and in Applying the Concept: The ECB's Reference Value for Money Growth, the ECB's Governing Council periodically announces a money growth rate that is intended to serve as a long-run reference value. Large deviations from this reference value require an explanation. The difference of opinion between the Fed and the ECB on this matter can be traced to their divergent views on the stability of money demand. Researchers who study the demand for money in the euro area have concluded that it is stable, which implies that changes in velocity are predictable. This assumption is the justification for the ECB's emphasis on money in its monetary policy framework.

The ECB's strategy is based on data like those shown in Figure 20.7. From 1995 to 2013, the velocity of euro-area M3 (the equivalent of U.S. M2) declined from 0.37 to 0.24. While short-run fluctuations in velocity were significant, European policymakers point to the tendency of velocity to return to its long-run downward trend over periods of a few years. (Recall that in computing the ECB's reference value for money growth, described in Applying the Concept on page 564, statisticians assumed that velocity would decline between ½ and 1 percent a year.)

Even given this difference in their emphasis on money growth, the ECB and the Fed have both chosen interest rates as their conventional operating target. The reason is that

[9]Simon London, "Lunch with the FT: Milton Friedman," *Financial Times,* June 6, 2003.

IN THE NEWS
Will Fed's "Easy Money" Push Up Prices?

THE WALL STREET JOURNAL.
WSJ.com

David Wessel

January 17, 2013

The Federal Reserve has held short-term interest rates near zero for four years. It expects to keep them there for another couple of years. It has printed money—more than $2 trillion—and pumped that into the economy. . . . Is inflation inevitable from this extraordinarily expansionary monetary policy?

"There are some people who think that's going to be inflationary," Fed Chairman Ben Bernanke acknowledged this week at the University of Michigan. "Personally, I don't see much evidence in that."

Is he right? The short answer, in my view, is yes. But it is worth weighing arguments on the other side.

More Money Means More Inflation
Milton Friedman taught: "Inflation is always and everywhere a monetary phenomenon in the sense that it is and can be produced only by a more rapid increase in the quantity of money than in output."

That is true in the very long run, but the link between the money supply and the inflation rate is hard to discern in data and is largely irrelevant to predicting inflation over the next several years. It would be difficult to spark and sustain inflation with so many unemployed workers, empty stores and offices and underused factories.

The Fed's money-printing has increased the money supply. Banks have parked at the Fed about $1.5 trillion more than their required reserves. Inflation-phobes predict those reserves will someday turn into loans, flooding the economy with credit and triggering inflation.

Mr. Bernanke says that won't happen because, unlike his predecessors, he has the legal authority to boost the interest rate (now 0.25%) the Fed pays banks on those reserves. . . . "We have all the tools we need to undo our monetary-policy stimulus and to take that away before inflation becomes our problem," Mr. Bernanke insists.

That is plausible, though untested.

The Fed Will Get Inflation Because It Wants It
This argument comes in two forms. One relies on the historical fact that debtor governments end up with inflation because it allows them to repay debts with cheapened currency. But the effect of higher inflation on the U.S. budget deficit is limited. . . .

interest rates are the link between the financial system and the real economy. Changes in interest rates are one of the primary tools central bankers have for influencing the economy. By keeping interest rates stable, policymakers can insulate the real economy from disturbances that arise in the financial system. For example, the payments system can change quickly. The introduction of more liquid financial instruments or newly configured electronic systems can have a direct impact on the way money is used and therefore on velocity. If policymakers wanted to, they could keep money growth constant in the face of such innovations. But doing so would create volatility in interest rates, which could destabilize the real economy. This point was made in Chapter 18, which discussed the rationale for choosing the interest rate rather than the quantity of reserves as an operating instrument. There we noted that the best way to keep changes in reserves from influencing interest rates and affecting the real economy is to target interest rates. While inflation is tied to money growth in the long run, interest rates are the tool policymakers use to stabilize inflation in the short run.

The other relies on the argument from some academics that higher inflation would rouse the economy from its torpor. With inflation close to 2%, today's zero interest rates work out to minus 2%, adjusted for inflation. Given the weak economy, the Fed would like inflation-adjusted interest rates to be even lower so more people borrow.

. . . Mr. Bernanke and Fed Vice Chairwoman Janet Yellen, a potential Bernanke successor, reject this. They say it . . . would undermine the Fed's hard-won victory over inflation in the 1980s.

Take the Fed at its word: It doesn't *want* inflation.

The Fed Doesn't Want Inflation, But Will Get It Anyway

This is harder to dismiss.

Today's central banks rely on containing "inflationary expectations." If everyone believes that the Fed will do what is needed to keep inflation to 2% over the next few years, then they will expect inflation of 2% and factor that into wages, prices and interest rates, even if something makes prices jump for a time. . . .

But the Fed has said it would tolerate inflation slightly above the 2% target if unemployment remains high. . . . If something causes consumers, businesses and markets to expect more inflation, it will be tougher for the Fed to avoid it.

There also is the possibility that the Fed will misread the economy and wait too long to raise interest rates. . . .

Finally, it is possible that Fed officials will lack the courage to weather political attacks and will be slow to raise interest rates or sell the bank's huge bond portfolio, perhaps at big losses that are economically insignificant but sure to be controversial. Mr. Bernanke says that isn't so, but he likely will be gone from the Fed when that time comes. . . .

SOURCE: David Wessel, "Will Fed's 'Easy Money' Push-Up Prices?" *The Wall Street Journal*, January 17, 2013. Used with permission of Dow Jones Company, Inc. via Copyright Clearance Center, Inc.

LESSONS OF THE ARTICLE

Both theory and experience confirm that money growth drives inflation in the long run. In the short run, however, the link is loose. Beginning in 2008, the volume of base money in the United States (and in other advanced economies) soared, but inflation didn't follow. The Fed is committed to keeping inflation low and argues that it has the tools to do so. As the U.S. economy recovers, the Fed's claims will be tested.

The idea that targeting money growth destabilizes interest rates is not just a theoretical possibility. For roughly three years from October 1979 to October 1982, as part of the effort to reduce inflation from more than 10 percent the FOMC used reserves to target money growth, allowing the federal funds rate to fluctuate. Figure 20.8 shows the results. The shaded area represents the period when the FOMC targeted the quantity of money. Notice how volatile the interest rate was during that three-year period. In fact, over intervals as short as three to four months, the federal funds rate fluctuated as much as 10 percentage points, rising from 11½ percent in September 1979 to 20 percent in March 1980, then falling to 10 percent in July 1980 before climbing back to 20 percent in December 1980. This sort of volatility, caused by policymakers' inability to forecast shifts in the velocity of money, would surely damage the real economy. Realizing the problem, policymakers have turned to the only viable alternative: targeting and smoothing fluctuations in interest rates. In the next chapter, we will study how they use interest rates to stabilize inflation and growth.

STABILITY

Figure 20.8 The Federal Funds Rate, 1975–2013

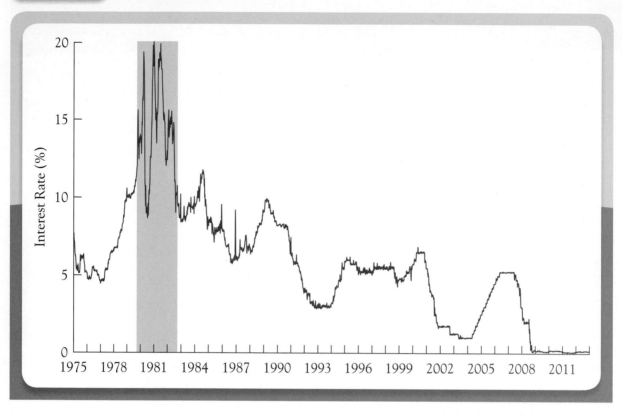

The shaded bar represents the period from October 1979 to October 1982, when the Federal Reserve targeted the quantity of money.

SOURCE: *Data are the effective federal funds rate, weekly, from the Board of Governors of the Federal Reserve System. (FRED data code: FF.)*

Terms

Using FRED: Codes for Data in This Chapter

Data Series	FRED Data Code
M1	M1SL
M2	M2SL
U.S. consumer price index	CPIAUCSL
Brazil consumer price index	BRACPIALLMINMEI
Nominal GDP	GDP
M2 velocity	M2V
M1 velocity	M1V
U.S. chained consumer price index	SUUR0000SA0
GDP deflator	GDPDEF
M2 own rate of return	M2OWN
U.S. 3-month Treasury bill rate	TB3MS
Federal funds rate	FEDFUNDS

Chapter Lessons

1. There is a strong positive correlation between money growth and inflation.
   a. Every country that has had high rates of sustained money growth has experienced high rates of inflation.
   b. At very high levels of inflation, inflation exceeds money growth.
   c. At moderate to low inflation, money growth exceeds inflation.
   d. Ultimately, the central bank controls the rate of money growth.
2. The quantity theory of money explains the link between inflation and money growth.
   a. The equation of exchange tells us that
      i. The quantity of money times the velocity of money equals nominal GDP.
      ii. Money growth plus velocity growth equals inflation plus real growth.
   b. If velocity and real growth were constant, the central bank could control inflation by keeping money growth constant.
   c. In the long run, velocity is stable, so controlling inflation means controlling money growth.
   d. In the short run, the velocity of money is volatile.
3. Shifts in velocity are caused by changes in the demand for money.
   a. The transactions demand for money depends on income, interest rates, and the availability of alternative means of payment.
   b. The portfolio demand for money depends on the same factors that determine the demand for bonds: wealth, expected future interest rates, and the return, risk, and liquidity associated with money relative to alternative investments.
4. The quantity theory of money and theories of money demand have a number of implications for monetary policy.
   a. Countries with high inflation can reduce inflation by controlling money growth.

b. Countries with low inflation can control inflation by targeting money growth only if the demand for money is stable in the short run.

c. In the United States, the relationship between the velocity of M2 and its opportunity cost (the yield on an alternative investment) has proven unstable over time.

d. The instability of money demand in the United States has caused Federal Reserve policymakers to pay less attention to money growth than to interest rates.

e. In the euro area, ECB officials view money demand as relatively stable, so they pay more attention to money growth than the Fed does.

f. Regardless of the stability of money demand, central banks target interest rates to insulate the real economy from disturbances in the financial sector.

Conceptual and Analytical Problems

1. Why is inflation higher than money growth in high-inflation countries and lower than money growth in low-inflation countries? *(LO1)*

2.* Explain why giving an independent central bank control over the quantity of money in the economy should reduce the occurrences of periods of extremely high inflation, especially in developing economies. *(LO1)*

3. If velocity were constant at 2 while M2 rose from $5 trillion to $6 trillion in a single year, what would happen to nominal GDP? If real GDP rose 3 percent, what would be the level of inflation? *(LO2)*

4. According to Irving Fisher, when velocity and output are fixed, the quantity theory of money implies that inflation equals money growth. What does the quantity theory imply for inflation in the long run in an economy with growing output and stable velocity? *(LO2)*

5. If velocity were predictable but not constant, would a monetary policy that fixed the growth rate of money work? *(LO2)*

6. Describe the impact of financial innovations on the demand for money and velocity. *(LO3)*

7. Suppose that expected inflation rises by 3 percent at the same time that the yields on money and on nonmoney assets both rise by 3 percent. What will happen to the demand for money? What if expected inflation rose by only 2 percent? What if the yield on nonmoney assets rose by 4 percent? *(LO3)*

8.* Explain how money growth reduces the purchasing power of money. *(LO2)*

9. Provide arguments both for and against the Federal Reserve's adoption of a target growth rate for M2. What assumptions would be necessary to compute such a target rate? *(LO1)*

10. Explain why we observed a fall in the velocity of M2 during the financial crisis of 2007–2009. *(LO3)*

11. Comment on the role given to money in the monetary policy strategy of the ECB. *(LO1)*

*Indicates more difficult problems

12. Countries A and B both have the same money growth rate and in both countries, real output is constant. In Country A velocity is constant while in Country B velocity has fallen. In which country will inflation be higher? Explain why. *(LO2)*

13. Consider a country where the level of excess reserves fluctuates widely and unpredictably. Would such a country be a good candidate for a money growth rule to guide monetary policy? Explain your answer. *(LO4)*

14. Draw a graph of money demand and money supply with the nominal interest rate on the vertical axis and money balances on the horizontal axis. Assume the central bank is following a money growth rule where it sets the growth rate of money supply to zero. Use the graph to illustrate how fluctuations in velocity imply that targeting money growth results in greater volatility of interest rates. *(LO4)*

15. Using the same graph as that described in Problem 14, show how the central bank could use its control over the quantity of money to target a particular level of interest rate in the face of changes in velocity. *(LO4)*

16. Why might targeting the money supply lead to lower output growth than targeting the rate of interest? Consider your responses to Problems 14 and 15 before you answer. *(LO4)*

17. Which of the following factors would increase the transactions demand for money? Explain your choices. *(LO3)*
    a. Lower nominal interest rates.
    b. Rumors that a computer virus had invaded the ATM network.
    c. A fall in nominal income.

18. Which of the following factors would increase the portfolio demand for money? Explain your choices. *(LO3)*
    a. A new website allows you to liquidate your stock holdings quickly and cheaply.
    b. You expect future interest rates to rise.
    c. A financial crisis is looming.

19.* Suppose a central bank is trying to decide whether to target money growth. Proponents of the move are confident that the new policy would be successful as, under the existing policy regime, they observed a stable statistical relationship between money growth and inflation. What warning might you issue to the central bank when they ask your advice? *(LO1)*

Data Exploration

For general information on using Federal Reserve Economic Data (FRED) online, visit www.mhhe.com/moneyandbanking4e.com and click on Student Edition, then FRED resources.

1. A scatterplot may reveal a relationship between two indicators. Construct a scatterplot of annual data beginning in 1959 for inflation and money growth. Measure these as the percent change from a year ago of consumer prices (FRED code: CPIAUCSL) and M2 (FRED code: M2SL), respectively. Then, display a second scatterplot of annual data beginning in 1959 for inflation (measured as before) and the federal funds rate (FRED code: FEDFUNDS). Which indicator is

Scan here for quick access to the resources for these problems. Need a barcode reader? Try ScanLife, available in your app store.

more closely linked to inflation: money growth or the interest rate? Does that tell us which is the better policy instrument? *(LO2)*

2. Plot the percent change from a year ago of the velocity of money (FRED code: A14187USA163NNBR) between 1922 and 1939. Compare the typical scales of the velocity declines during the recessions of this interwar period and the velocity declines during the recessions shown in Panel B of Figure 20.4. Were the 1929–1933 and 2007–2009 periods special? What role might wealth have played in these two episodes? *(LO3)*

3.* In Chapter 18 Data Exploration Problem 2, you plotted the inflation rate together with the gap between the Taylor rule and the federal funds rate. Visually, when the Taylor rule gap was positive, inflation appeared relatively high; when it was negative, inflation appeared relatively low. Download the two indicators and compute the correlation between the gap and inflation (a) from 1992 to 1999; and (b) from 2000 to the present. What do the results suggest? *(LO4)*

4. In Figure 20.1, which compares money growth and inflation over an extended time period is Mexico above or below the 45-degree line? Plot since 1987 on a quarterly basis the percent change from a year ago of the consumer price index (FRED code: MEXCPIALLQINMEI) and M1 (FRED code: MYAGM-1MXM189N) in Mexico. Then download the data and calculate the averages of these inflation and money growth measures. Where would Mexico appear on Figure 20.1? Were there episodes since 1987 when Mexico was on the other side of the 45-degree line? If so, why? *(LO2)*

5. In theory, the velocity of money should rise with the cost of holding it. To assess the theory, plot the opportunity cost of holding M2—defined as the difference between the three-month Treasury bill rate (FRED code: TB3MS) and the interest rate on M2 components (FRED code: M2OWN)—and (on the right scale) the percent change from a year ago of M2 velocity (FRED code: M2V). What do you conclude?

Chapter 21

Output, Inflation, and Monetary Policy

Learning Objectives

Understand . . .

LO1   Output and inflation in the long run

LO2   Aggregate demand and aggregate supply

LO3   Equilibrium in the short run and the long run

Governments publish economic data constantly. Almost every day we receive new information on some aspect of the economy with news stories quoting experts on what it all means. Is inflation on the way up? Is the economy on the verge of recession? An important part of such analyses is speculation about the impact of the new data on monetary policy. In our discussion of central banking, we noted that conjecture about policymakers' likely reaction fills the financial news. And no wonder, for members of the committees that set interest rates—the FOMC in the United States and the Governing Council in the euro area—always tie their policy actions to current and expected future economic conditions.

Needless to say, everyone is preoccupied with monetary policy. While traders in the financial markets are trying to outguess each other, to make a profit by betting on the next move in interest rates, the rest of us are just hoping the central bank will succeed in keeping inflation low and real growth high. How do policymakers do it? What is the mechanism through which changes in the interest rate influence inflation and output? And what are the limits of policymakers' power to control the economy?

As we just learned in Chapter 20, in the long run, inflation is tied to money growth. Over periods of several decades, high money growth leads to high inflation. Furthermore, long-run growth depends on technology, the size of the capital stock, and the number of people who can work. But over shorter periods of months or years, changes in the rate of money growth tell us little about future movements in the inflation rate. That is especially true when inflation is low, as it has been throughout much of the industrialized world over the past two decades.

The objective of this chapter is to understand fluctuations in inflation and real output and how central banks use conventional interest-rate policy to stabilize them. To do it, we will develop a macroeconomic model of fluctuations in the business cycle in which monetary policy plays a central role. From this, we will see that short-run movements in inflation and output can arise from two sources: shifts in the quantity of aggregate output demanded (i.e., changes in consumption, investment, government spending, or net exports) and shifts in the quantity of aggregate output supplied (that is, changes in the costs of production). Modern monetary policymakers work to reduce the volatility that each of these creates by adjusting the target interest rate.

We will develop our macroeconomic model in three steps, beginning with a description of long-run equilibrium. We then move on to derive the *dynamic aggregate demand curve,* which shows the quantity of real output demanded by those people who use it at each level of inflation, that is, how real output is related to changes in the prices, not just their level. Here we will see the critical role of monetary policy. Then, we introduce aggregate supply, which is the level of real output supplied by firms at each level of inflation. There is both a short-run and a long-run version of the aggregate supply curve. In the short run, equating dynamic aggregate demand with short-run aggregate supply gives us the equilibrium levels of output and inflation. Business cycles are movements in this short-run equilibrium. And because we have built monetary policy into the model, we will see how modern central banks can use their policy tools to stabilize short-run fluctuations in output and inflation.

As we proceed through the chapter, keep in mind that our ultimate objective is to understand how modern central bankers determine the target interest rate. When policymakers change the target rate, what are they reacting to, and what is the impact on the economy?

Output and Inflation in the Long Run

The best way to understand fluctuations in the business cycle is as deviations from some benchmark or long-run equilibrium level. The booms and recessions that make up business cycles are temporary movements away from this long-run equilibrium level. So we begin with the following question: what would the levels of inflation and output be if nothing unexpected happened for a long time? The answer to this question is that in the long run, current output equals **potential output**—the level of output given existing technology and normal use of resources—and the inflation rate equals the level implied by the rate of money growth.

Potential Output

Potential output is what the economy is capable of producing when its resources are used at normal rates. Imagine you are running a company that produces baseball bats for the Milwaukee market. You have estimated the demand for bats based on the information available to you, purchased machines, and hired workers to operate them. If everything goes according to plan, you'll make a nice profit. But suddenly the Milwaukee Brewers, a team that hasn't won a championship for a long time, wins the World Series and the number of kids who play baseball in your area increases dramatically. Your bat sales skyrocket. To meet the increased demand, you begin running your factory around the clock.

What happened? The fact that the Brewers have won the World Series has driven your output above the normal level—that is, above your potential output. Now, what if the local professional basketball team, the Milwaukee Bucks, were suddenly successful? This would create a boom in the sale of basketballs at the expense of baseball equipment, forcing you to cut back on production below normal levels. The reduction in the rate at which you use your resources would drive your output level below the potential level at which you could produce.

YOUR FINANCIAL WORLD

Using the Word Inflation

Everyone talks about *inflation,* but what do they mean? In normal conversation, when people use the word *inflation,* they are referring to price increases. If the price of gasoline or the cost of a basket of groceries rises, that's inflation. When *The Wall Street Journal* reports that the inflation rate was one- or two-tenths of 1 percent over the past month, it means that the average price level went up. But, as it is commonly used, the term *inflation* does not distinguish a one-time change in the price level from a situation in which prices are rising continuously.

Economists use the term more precisely. To them, *inflation* means a *continually rising price level.* That is, inflation refers to a *sustained rise* that continues for a substantial period. In discussing changes in inflation, economists emphasize the distinction between *temporary* and *permanent*

changes. A temporary change is a one-time adjustment in the price level, while a permanent change is a rise or fall in the long-run course of inflation.

To see the difference, consider an example in which the inflation rate is zero. Then, suddenly, gasoline prices rise, driving that month's Consumer Price Index (CPI) up by 1 percent. The next month, however, because energy prices don't change again, the CPI is unchanged as well. At the end of this episode, the inflation rate is where it started, at zero, but the price level as measured by the CPI is 1 percent higher. Temporary changes in inflation lead to adjustments in the price level and can have many causes aside from monetary policy. But only changes in monetary policy can cause permanent increases or decreases in inflation.

Over time, conditions at your baseball bat factory are likely to change. First, if you come to believe that an increase or decrease in the demand for your product is permanent, you will change the scale of your factory, redesigning it to enlarge or reduce its size. And second, technological improvements allow you to increase the factory's production at given levels of capital and labor. In other words, your factory's normal level of output evolves over time—usually going up, but occasionally going down. So, in the short run production can deviate from normal, while in the long run the normal level itself changes.

What is true for the Milwaukee bat manufacturer is true for the economy as a whole. There is a normal level of production that defines potential output. But potential output is not a fixed level. Because the amount of labor and capital in an economy can grow, and improved technology can increase the efficiency of the production process, potential output tends to rise over time. Furthermore, unexpected events can push current output away from potential output, creating what is called an **output gap**. When current output climbs above potential it creates an **expansionary output gap**; when current output falls below potential, it creates a **recessionary output gap**. These output gaps eventually cancel each other out, so that *in the long run, current output equals potential output.*

STABILITY

Long-Run Inflation

The other key to long-run equilibrium is inflation. In the last chapter, we saw that the equation of exchange, $MV = PY$, implies that money growth plus the change in the velocity of money equals inflation plus real growth:

$$\%\Delta M + \%\Delta V = \%\Delta P + \%\Delta Y$$

where M is the quantity of money, V is the velocity of money, P is the price level, Y is real output, and "$\%\Delta$" stands for percentage change. We can restate this equation in terms of potential output, which we will call Y^P. In the long run, because current output equals potential output, real growth must equal growth in potential output ($\%\Delta Y = \%\Delta Y^P$) and changes in velocity are unimportant ($\%\Delta V = 0$). From this we can conclude that, *in the long run, inflation equals money growth minus growth in potential output ($\%\Delta P = \%\Delta M - \%\Delta Y^P$)*.

While central bankers focus primarily on controlling short-term nominal interest rates, they keep an eye on money growth. They know that when they adjust the level of reserves in the banking system to meet their target nominal interest rate, their action affects the rate at which money grows. That is what ultimately determines inflation. So concern for money growth is never far from their minds. But in the short run, over periods even as long as a few years, fluctuations in velocity weaken this link substantially.

We turn now to a discussion of the role of monetary policy in the determination of fluctuations in current output and inflation. To understand that role, we need to develop a simple macroeconomic model—a shorthand description of the economy that helps us to organize our thinking.

Monetary Policy and the Dynamic Aggregate Demand Curve

Policymakers know that money growth is an important benchmark for tracking long-run inflation trends, so they pay close attention to it. In fact, when faced with very high inflation, central bankers will focus almost exclusively on controlling money growth. Reducing the growth of the money supply is the only way to bring down inflation of 50 or 100 percent per year. But with 1 or 2 or even 5 percent inflation, restraining money growth is not a central short-run policy objective. Under such circumstances, modern central bankers concentrate on manipulating interest rates in order to keep inflation low and close the gap between current and potential output. Thus, the Federal Reserve Open Market Committee's policy statements announce and explain interest-rate decisions or planned changes in the scale and composition of Fed assets, but make virtually no mention of money growth. If we want to understand the role of central bankers in stabilizing the economy—and particularly how policymakers themselves think about their role—we need to examine the connection between short-term interest rates and policymakers' inflation and output objectives.

Because our task is somewhat complex, it is useful to have an overview of where we are going. The goal is to understand the relationship between inflation and the quantity of aggregate output demanded by those people that use it. To get there, we will proceed in three steps. First, we examine the relationship between aggregate expenditure and the real interest rate. Next, we study how monetary policymakers adjust their interest-rate instrument in response to changes in inflation. And finally, we put these two together to construct the dynamic aggregate demand curve that relates output and inflation. A short summary, also shown in Figure 21.1, is as follows:

1. **Aggregate expenditure and the real interest rate:** We begin with a description of how *aggregate expenditure*—primarily investment and consumption—depend on the real interest rate. As the real interest rate rises, investment and consumption fall, reducing the level of aggregate expenditure. There is a *downward sloping* relationship between the quantity of aggregate expenditure and the real interest rate.

2. **Inflation, the real interest rate, and the monetary policy reaction curve:** Next, we will see that monetary policymakers respond to increases in inflation

Figure 21.1   Inflation, Monetary Policy, and Aggregate Demand

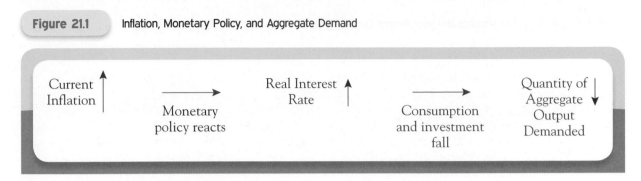

When inflation rises, policymakers react by raising the real interest rate. Higher real interest rates reduce consumption and investment, lowering the quantity of aggregate output demanded.

by raising their policy-controlled interest rate. And, importantly, they raise their nominal policy rate by more than the change in inflation (see, for example, the Taylor rule on pages 500–506). So, because of the way policymakers react, when inflation rises, the real interest rate goes up. There is an *upward sloping* relationship between inflation and the real interest rate that we will call the *monetary policy reaction curve.*

3. **The dynamic aggregate demand curve:** Putting 1 and 2 together—the fact that monetary policymakers react to higher inflation by raising the real interest rate and that a higher real interest rate reduces the level of aggregate expenditure— gives us a relationship between inflation and the quantity of aggregate output demanded that we will call the *dynamic aggregate demand curve.* And like conventional demand curves, this one slopes down, so that's how we will draw it. The dynamic aggregate demand curve is a downward-sloping relationship between inflation and aggregate output.

Before continuing, it is important to keep in mind that economic decisions of households to consume and of firms to invest depend on the *real* interest rate, not the nominal interest rate. So, to alter the course of the economy, central banks must influence the real interest rate. As it turns out, in the short run, when monetary policymakers operating in a credible policy framework change the nominal interest rate, they change the real interest rate. To see why, remember that the nominal interest rate (i) equals the real interest rate (r) plus expected inflation (π^e): $i = r + \pi^e$. Solving this for r, tells us that $r = i - \pi^e$, or the real interest rate equals the nominal interest rate minus expected inflation. Importantly, inflation expectations reflect the credibility of the central bank—its record of matching word and deed (see the discussion of credibility on pages 410–412). For a central bank that is effective at stabilizing inflation and output, inflation expectations adjust slowly in response to changes in economic conditions. This means that when policymakers change i, π^e doesn't change, so changes in the nominal interest rate change the real interest rate.

Data for the past several decades make it clear that movements in the short-term nominal interest rate are also movements in the short-term real interest rate. To see this, look at Figure 21.2, which plots the nominal federal funds rate—the one the FOMC controls—against a measure of the real federal funds rate constructed using survey data on expected inflation. The figure shows that the nominal and real federal funds rates rise and fall together. So, when the Federal Reserve raises the nominal federal

Figure 21.2   The Nominal and Real Federal Funds Rates

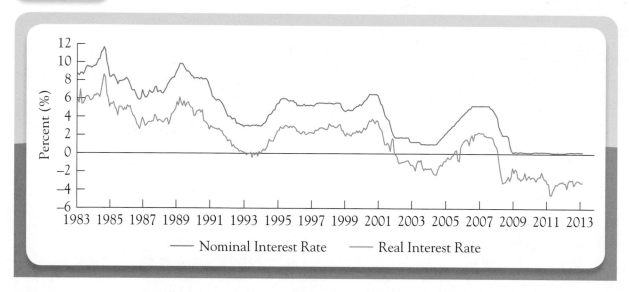

The real federal funds rate is computed as the monthly nominal effective federal funds rate minus expected inflation for the next year from the University of Michigan's Survey of Consumers. The FRED data codes are FEDFUNDS and MICH, respectively.

SOURCE: *Federal funds rate data are from the Federal Reserve; inflation expectations data are drawn from the median expected change in prices during the next 12 months, Table 32 of the Michigan Survey, available at www.sca.isr.umich.edu.*

funds rate, it raises the real federal funds rate as well. Conversely, when the Fed lowers the nominal federal funds rate, it lowers the real federal funds rate with it.

The real interest rate, then, is the lever through which monetary policymakers influence the real economy. In changing real interest rates, they influence consumption, investment, and other components of aggregate expenditure. Let's see how this all works.

Aggregate Expenditure and the Real Interest Rate

The Components of Aggregate Expenditure and the Real Interest Rate

To understand the impact of monetary policy on the economy we need to link the real interest rate to the level of output. This task requires a detailed description of aggregate expenditure and its relationship to the real interest rate. The best way is to start with the national income accounting identity from principles of economics that analyzes the uses of the economy's output. Doing so allows us to divide aggregate expenditure into four parts:

Aggregate expenditure = Consumption + Investment + Government purchases + (Exports − Imports)

$$Y \quad = \quad C \quad + \quad I \quad + \quad G \quad + \quad (X \quad - \quad M)$$

The terms in this expression are defined as follows:

1. **Consumption** (*C*) is spending by individuals for items like food, clothing, housing, transportation, entertainment, and education accounting for around 68 percent of GDP.

2. **Investment** (*I*) is spending by firms for additions to the physical capital they use to produce goods and services.[1] Examples would include new buildings and equipment. The cost of newly constructed residential homes, as well as the change in the level of business inventories, is also included. All together, these expenditures averaged 17 percent of U.S. GDP since 2000.

3. **Government purchases** (*G*) is spending on goods and services by federal, state, and local governments. New military equipment and schools fall into this category, as well as the salaries of public school teachers, police officers, and firefighters; but transfers, like unemployment insurance payments and Social Security are not included. Total federal, state, and local government purchases in the United States averaged around 19 percent of GDP since 2000.

4. **Net exports** equals *exports* minus *imports* (*X* − *M*). Remember that exports are goods and services produced in one country and sold to residents of another country; imports are purchases of foreign-made goods and services. The difference between the two represents the net expenditure for domestically produced goods.[2] Since 2000, U.S. net exports have been negative, averaging −4 percent of GDP.

For our purposes, it is helpful to think of aggregate expenditure as having two parts, one that is sensitive to changes in the real interest rate and one that is not. Three of the four components of aggregate expenditure—consumption, investment, and net exports—are *sensitive* to changes in the real interest rate. Among these, investment is the most important. Deciding whether to replace an existing machine or purchase a new one is a complicated matter, dependent on a comparison of the revenue generated by the investment with the cost of financing it. This decision boils down to a comparison of the return on the investment and the cost of borrowing to finance it.[3] An investment can be profitable only if its internal rate of return exceeds the cost of borrowing. From this, we can conclude that the higher the cost of borrowing, the less likely that an investment will be profitable. Because borrowers and lenders both care about the real return, we see immediately that the higher the real interest rate, the lower the level of investment. Higher interest rates also reduce residential investment—the construction of new homes—as larger mortgage payments make houses less affordable.

While investment may be the most important component of aggregate expenditure that is sensitive to real interest rates, it isn't the only one. Consumption and net exports respond to the real interest rate as well. What is true for a business considering an investment, for example, is true for a family thinking of buying a new car. Higher real interest rates mean higher inflation-adjusted car-loan payments, which make new cars more costly. Furthermore, as the real interest rate rises, the reward to saving goes up. More saving means lower consumption.

The case of net exports is more complicated. Briefly, when the real interest rate in the United States rises, U.S. financial assets become more attractive to foreigners.[4]

TIME

---

[1]Remember that economists use the term *investment* differently from the way it is used in the business press. In the business press, an investment is a financial instrument like a stock or bond that people use as a means of holding their wealth. Importantly, though, people who make such a "financial investment" or who purchase a house from its current owner aren't creating anything new; they are buying something that already exists. To an economist, investment is the creation of new physical capital.

[2]Net exports are often referred to as the *current account surplus:* see the Chapter 19 Appendix, What You Really Need to Know about the Balance of Payments.

[3]See the discussion of internal rate of return in Chapter 4.

[4]There is a more detailed discussion in Chapter 10.

This rise in the desirability of U.S. assets to foreigners increases the foreign demand for dollars, causing the dollar to appreciate (see Chapter 19, pages 529–531, for the impact of the policy interest rate on the exchange rate). The higher the value of the dollar, the more expensive U.S. exports will be, and the cheaper U.S. imports will be. Together, lower exports and higher imports mean lower net exports. Again, the higher real interest rate has reduced a component of aggregate expenditure.

Finally, there is government expenditure. While changes in the real interest rate may have an impact on the government's budget by raising the cost of borrowing, the effect is likely to be small, so we will ignore it.

For three of the four components of aggregate expenditure, then, our conclusion is the same: When the real interest rate *rises*

- Consumption (C) *falls* because the reward to saving and the cost of financing purchases are now higher.
- Investment (I) *falls* because the cost of financing has gone up.
- Net exports $(X - M)$ *fall* because the domestic currency has appreciated, making imports cheaper and exports more expensive.

Figure 21.3   Aggregate Expenditure and the Real Interest Rate

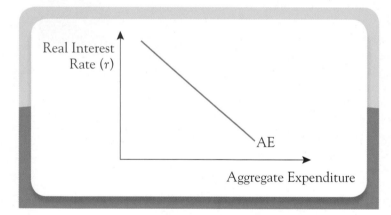

A fall in the real interest rate leads to an increase in aggregate expenditure.

Thus, as shown in Figure 21.3, *a rise in the real interest rate reduces the level of aggregate expenditure.*[5]

Bear in mind, though, that the components of aggregate expenditure can change for reasons unrelated to the real interest rate. Consumption or investment can rise when individuals or businesses become more confident about their future income or sales, or when their net worth increases. Government purchases can increase because of a change in fiscal policy, and net exports can climb because of movement in the exchange rate. Any of these would shift the aggregate expenditure curve in Figure 21.3 to the right, increasing the level of aggregate expenditure at every level of the real interest rate.

Table 21.1 provides a summary of the relationship between aggregate expenditure and the real interest rate.

We can see immediately how the relationship between the real interest rate and the level of aggregate expenditure helps central bankers to achieve one of their objectives: stabilizing current output at a level close to potential output. When economic activity speeds up or slows down and current output moves above or below potential output, policymakers can adjust the real interest rate in an effort to close the expansionary or recessionary gap. But as we have emphasized repeatedly throughout our study of monetary policy, central bankers spend much of their time worrying instead about keeping inflation low.

The Long-Run Real Interest Rate   Before diving into a description of the relationship between monetary policy and inflation, there is one more thing we must do.

[5]If you have studied intermediate macroeconomics, you will recognize this relationship as the "IS" curve.

Table 21.1   The Relationship between Aggregate Expenditure and the Real Interest Rate

What is it?	The downward-sloping relationship between the quantity of aggregate expenditure $(C + I + G + NX)$ and the real interest rate (r).
Why does it slope down?	When the real interest rate rises, the components of aggregate expenditure, especially consumption and investment, fall.
When does it shift?	When aggregate expenditure goes up for reasons unrelated to changes in the real interest rate, the relationship shifts to the right. Examples include: 1. Increases in optimism that drive up consumption or investment. 2. Rising net worth that increases spending. 3. Changes in fiscal policy that raise government expenditure or reduce taxes. 4. Increases in net exports that are unrelated to changes in the real interest rate.

We need to figure out what happens to the real interest rate over the long run. Earlier we discussed the concept of potential output and noted the economy's tendency to move toward that normal level over time. In this section we have examined how various components of aggregate expenditure respond to the real interest rate. We have seen that higher real interest rates, holding constant things like business and consumer confidence as well as government expenditure, are associated with lower levels of aggregate expenditure. Putting these two discussions together, we can conclude that there must be some level of the real interest rate at which aggregate expenditure equals potential output. That is, there is some level of aggregate expenditure that is consistent with the normal level of output toward which the economy moves over the long run. This concept is important enough that we will give it a name, the **long-run real interest rate**. *The long-run real interest rate equates the level of aggregate expenditure to the quantity of potential output.*

To figure out the level of the long-run real interest rate, take the aggregate expenditure curve drawn in Figure 21.3 and find the interest rate that is consistent with the quantity of potential output (Y^P).[6] You can see how to do it in Figure 21.4. This figure helps us to understand the two possible reasons that the long-run real interest rate can change: (1) shifts in the aggregate expenditure curve, and (2) changes in the level of potential output.

First, take the case in which the level of potential output remains fixed, but there is a rise in some of the components of aggregate expenditure that do not respond to the real interest rate. One example of this is a rise in government purchases (all other things held equal). When G goes up, it increases the level of aggregate expenditure at every real interest rate, shifting the aggregate expenditure curve to the right. The result is shown in Panel A of Figure 21.5. For the level of aggregate expenditure to remain equal to the (unchanged) quantity of potential output, the interest-sensitive components of aggregate expenditure must fall. For that to happen, the long-run real interest

---

[6]Computing a numerical estimate for the long-run real interest rate is unfortunately complicated because it is related to the return on capital investment (adjusted for risk) in the economy as a whole, a quantity that is very difficult to calculate. In the United States, estimates typically show an average over time of around 2½ percent. However, like potential output, the long-run real interest rate can change significantly as economic conditions evolve. See John C. Williams, "The Natural Rate of Interest," *Federal Reserve Bank of San Francisco Economic Letter,* 2003–32, October 31, 2003.

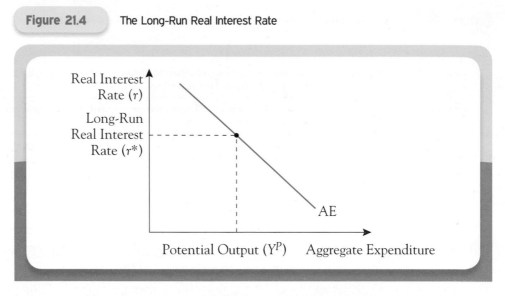

| Figure 21.4 | The Long-Run Real Interest Rate |

The long-run real interest rate (r^*) equates aggregate expenditure with potential output (Y^P).

rate must rise.[7] Besides government purchases, there are portions of consumption, investment, and net exports that are not sensitive to the real interest rate. If any of those components rises, driving aggregate expenditure up at every level of the real interest rate, the long-run real interest rate must go up.

What about the second case in which a change in potential output causes a change in the long-run real interest rate? This has an inverse effect on the real interest rate. When the quantity of potential output rises, the level of aggregate expenditure must rise with it. As we have seen, an increase in the level of aggregate expenditure requires a decline in the real interest rate. (Take a look at Panel B of Figure 21.5.) In addition, when potential output goes up, the long-run real interest rate falls.

In summary, the long-run real interest rate (r^*) is that level at which aggregate expenditure (C + I + G + NX) equals potential output (Y^P). When components of aggregate expenditure that are not sensitive to the real interest rate rise, the long-run real interest rate rises with them. But when potential output rises, the long-run real interest rate falls. Importantly, the level of the long-run real interest rate is a consequence of the structure of the economy; it is not something policymakers can choose.

Inflation, the Real Interest Rate, and the Monetary Policy Reaction Curve

We now move to the *second of the three steps* in our derivation of the relationship between inflation and the level of aggregate output demanded: In response to changes in inflation, policymakers adjust their policy-controlled interest rate.

In autumn 2012, consumer price inflation in the United States was a bit less than 2 percent, while current output was more than 5 percentage points below the Congressional Budget Office's estimate of potential output. That enormous output gap, one of the

[7]This effect is related to what is sometimes called "crowding out." The idea is that government spending can take the place of investment. The more common type of crowding out occurs when the government borrows funds to increase spending, thereby increasing the supply of bonds. An increase in the supply of bonds drives the price of bonds down, increasing the interest rate, and reducing investment. When the economy is operating at its potential and the government borrows, firms can't, so investment is crowded out.

Figure 21.5   Change in the Long-Run Real Interest Rate

A. Shifts in Aggregate Expenditure

Real Interest Rate (r)

r_1^*

r_0^*

AE_1

AE_0

Y^P Aggregate Expenditure

When aggregate expenditure shifts *right* from AE_0 to AE_1, the long-run real interest rate *increases* from r_0^* to r_1^*.

B. Changes in Potential Output

Real Interest Rate (r)

r_0^*

r_1^*

AE

Y_0^P Y_1^P Aggregate Expenditure

When potential output *increases* from Y_0^P to Y_1^P, the long-run real interest rate *falls* from r_0^* to r_1^*.

largest since the Great Depression, reflected the weak recovery following the financial crisis of 2007–2009. At the conclusion of its meeting on January 30, 2013, the Federal Open Market Committee released a statement that included the following sentence: "The Committee decided to keep the target range for the federal funds rate at 0 to ¼ percent and currently anticipates that this exceptionally low range for the federal funds rate will be appropriate at least as long as the unemployment rate remains above 6½ percent, inflation between one and two years ahead is projected to be no more than a half percentage point above the Committee's 2 percent longer-run goal, and longer-term inflation expectations continue to be well anchored."

That is, the FOMC members had concluded that economic conditions justified keeping nominal interest rates low so that they could keep the real interest rate down in an effort to raise aggregate expenditure and close the recessionary output gap. The committee's forward-looking statement was providing *forward guidance* (see Chapter 18 on unconventional monetary policy tools) to keep the policy rate low at least as long as the stated economic thresholds are not breached. The goal was to keep medium-term market rates low, too, by influencing policy expectations.

Statements made by the European Central Bank's Governing Council following its monthly meetings at that time reveal similar thinking. On February 7, 2013, the ECB also left its target interest rate at a then-record low (of 0.75 percent). With inflation modestly above 2 percent, the statement following the meeting read, in part, that "inflation rates have declined further, as anticipated, and are expected to fall below 2% in the coming months. . . . Inflation

"How many times have I asked you not to discuss stubbornly high interest rates in front of the children?"

APPLYING THE CONCEPT

INVESTMENT AND THE BUSINESS CYCLE

Fluctuations in investment are one of the most important sources of changes in aggregate expenditure. Over short periods of a quarter or a year, consumption and government purchases tend to be fairly stable; and net exports are just too small to account for much of the variation in aggregate output. So understanding fluctuations in the business cycle means understanding changes in investment.

To grasp this point, look at Figure 21.6, which plots the ratio of investment to gross domestic product over the past 50 years. The shaded bars designate recessions. Note that from 1960 to 2013, investment fluctuated from less than 13 percent of GDP to nearly 21 percent of GDP. More to the point, during every recession, investment itself falls by

between 2 and 5 percent of GDP, which is roughly the same size as the fall in GDP itself. In other words, when we talk about a recession, what we are really talking about is a drop in investment.

What causes the level of investment to change? The tools we have developed suggest two possibilities: changes in the real interest rate and changes in expectations about future business conditions. Remember, an investment will be profitable when its real internal rate of return exceeds its real cost of financing. Once again, the real interest rate is what matters in economic decisions. The higher the real cost of financing, the less likely that an investment will be profitable. And the lower the expected future revenue from an investment is, the lower the real internal rate of return will be. So the higher the real interest rate and the less optimistic business people are about the future, the fewer investments firms will undertake and the more likely the economy will fall into recession.

Figure 21.6   Investment and the Business Cycle: The Ratio of Investment to GDP

SOURCE: *Ratio of nominal gross private domestic investment (GPDI) to nominal gross domestic product (GDP), seasonally adjusted at annual rates, from the Department of Commerce, Bureau of Economic Analysis. The FRED data codes are in parentheses. Shaded bars denote recessions, dated by the National Bureau of Economic Research.*

expectations for the euro area remain firmly anchored in line with our aim of maintaining inflation rates below, but close to, 2%." While the specifics of the FOMC's and the Governing Council's statements may differ, both clearly indicate that policymakers set their short-run nominal interest rate targets in response to economic conditions in general, and inflation in particular.[8] Low inflation leads to low nominal and real interest rates.

[8]The fact that policy does not have an immediate impact on either inflation or output complicates matters substantially. In fact, interest-rate changes must anticipate changes in inflation and output, so they must be based on forecasts as much as on current levels. That is why, in their public comments, central bankers nearly always refer to inflation expectations and to likely future developments.

These two examples are representative of the sorts of things central bankers commonly say. Looking at the details, we can conclude that when current inflation is high or current output is running above potential output, central bankers will set a relatively high policy interest rate; when current inflation is low or current output is well below potential, they will set a low policy interest rate. Importantly, central bankers envision themselves as reacting to changes in the economic environment. And while they state their policies in terms of nominal interest rates, they do so knowing that changes in the nominal interest rate will translate into changes in the real interest rate. As we have discussed, these changes in the real interest rate influence the economic decisions of firms and households. We can summarize all of this in the form of a **monetary policy reaction curve** that approximates the behavior of central bankers.

Deriving the Monetary Policy Reaction Curve   We introduced a version of the monetary policy reaction curve in Chapter 18 when we looked at a rule of thumb (the Taylor rule) for understanding how the FOMC sets its federal funds rate target. There we saw that in order to ensure that deviations of inflation from the target rate are only temporary, policymakers respond to changes in inflation by changing the real interest rate in the same direction. That is, *higher current inflation requires a policy response that raises the real interest rate*, and *lower current inflation requires a policy response that lowers the real interest rate.* This means that the monetary policy reaction curve slopes upward as shown in Figure 21.7.

Where do we draw the reaction curve? What determines its location? The location depends on where policymakers would like the economy to end up in the long run, which is the equilibrium toward which the economy tends over time. For the real interest rate, the economy moves toward the long-run real interest rate that equates aggregate expenditure with potential output. That interest rate is shown as r^* in Figure 21.7. For inflation, the answer is the central bank's target level (π^T). *The monetary*

Figure 21.7   The Monetary Policy Reaction Curve

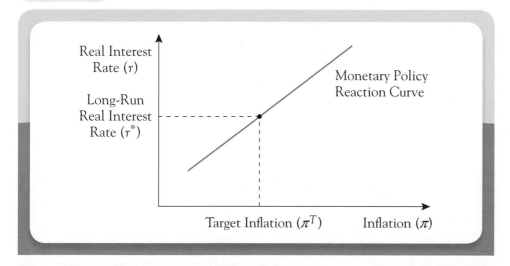

Monetary policymakers react to increases in current inflation by raising the real interest rate, while decreases lead them to lower it. The monetary policy reaction curve is located so that the central bank's target inflation is consistent with the long-run real interest rate, which equates aggregate expenditure with potential output.

policy reaction curve is set so that when current inflation equals target inflation, the real interest rate equals the long-run real interest rate. That is, $r = r^*$ when $\pi = \pi^T$.

While the long-run real interest rate and the inflation target tell us the location of the monetary policy reaction curve, what governs its slope? Is the curve steep or flat? The answer is that the slope depends on policymakers' objectives. When central bankers decide how aggressively to pursue their inflation target, and how willing they are to tolerate temporary changes in inflation, they are determining the slope of the monetary policy reaction curve. They are deciding whether to respond to deviations of current inflation from target inflation with small or large changes in the real interest rate. Policymakers who are aggressive in keeping current inflation near target will have a steep monetary policy reaction curve; while those who are less concerned will have a reaction curve that is relatively flat. We look at the implications of this difference at the end of the next chapter.

Shifting the Monetary Policy Reaction Curve   When policymakers adjust the real interest rate, they are either moving along a fixed monetary policy reaction curve or shifting the curve. A movement along the curve is a reaction to a change in current inflation. A shift in the curve represents a change in the level of the real interest rate at every level of inflation. To see what can shift the monetary policy reaction curve, we need to examine the variables we held constant when we drew the curve in Figure 21.7. In that analysis, we held both target inflation π^T and the long-run real interest rate r^* fixed. If either of these variables changes, the entire curve shifts. Looking at Figure 21.8, we can see that a *decrease* in π^T shifts the curve to the left (Panel A), as does an *increase* in r^* (Panel B). Analogously, a decline in the long-run real interest rate r^*, or an increase in the inflation target π^T, shift the monetary policy reaction curve to the right.

From our earlier discussion, we know that the long-run real interest rate (r^*) is determined by the structure of the economy. Central bank policymakers cannot choose

---

Figure 21.8   Shifting the Monetary Policy Reaction Curve

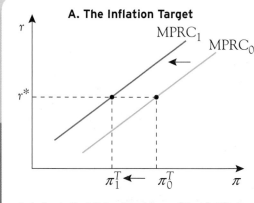

A decline in the inflation target from π_0^T to π_1^T shifts the monetary policy reaction curve to the left from MPRC$_0$ to MPRC$_1$.

An increase in the long-run real interest rate from r_0^* to r_1^* shifts the monetary policy reaction curve to the left from MPRC$_0$ to MPRC$_1$.

Table 21.2	The Monetary Policy Reaction Curve

What is it?	The upward-sloping relationship between inflation (π) and the real interest rate (r) set by monetary policymakers.
Why does it slope upward?	When inflation rises, monetary policymakers raise the real interest rate.
What determines its location?	Drawn so that, when current inflation equals target inflation ($\pi = \pi^T$), policymakers set the real interest rate equal to the long-run real interest rate ($r = r^*$).
When does it shift?	1. When the central bank's inflation target (π^T) changes. A decline shifts the curve to the left. 2. When the long-run real interest rate (r^*) changes. An increase shifts the curve to the left.

it. What if r^* were to rise as a consequence of an increase in government purchases, or some other component of aggregate expenditure that is not sensitive to the real interest rate? The result of such an increase is a shift to the left in the monetary policy reaction curve as shown in Panel B of Figure 21.8. Remember that the curve is drawn so that the real interest rate equals its long-run level at the point where inflation meets the central bank's target. An increase in the long-run real interest rate means that policymakers have set a higher real interest rate at every level of current inflation. Assuming that policymakers have not changed their inflation target, this shift means that the long-run nominal interest rate rises as well.

Table 21.2 summarizes the properties of the monetary policy reaction curve (MPRC).

The Dynamic Aggregate Demand Curve

Deriving the Dynamic Aggregate Demand Curve   We are now ready to move to the *third* and *final step* outlined at the beginning of this section: The construction of the **dynamic aggregate demand curve** that relates inflation and the level of output, accounting for the fact that monetary policymakers respond to changes in current inflation by changing the interest rate. Doing it means answering the following question: What happens to the quantity of aggregate output demanded when current inflation changes? From our earlier discussion, we know that central bankers respond to an increase in current inflation by raising the real interest rate. That is, they move along their monetary policy reaction curve (shown in Figure 21.7). We also know that a higher real interest rate lowers the level of aggregate expenditure by reducing investment, consumption, and net exports. (That's in Figure 21.3.) Putting these two together, we see that when inflation rises, the quantity of aggregate output demanded falls. Inflation and the quantity of aggregate output demanded move in opposite directions, so the *dynamic aggregate demand curve* shown in Figure 21.9 slopes downward.[9]

---

[9]Figuring out the location of the dynamic aggregate demand curve is somewhat complicated. To do it, recall that along the monetary policy reaction curve the real interest rate equals the long-run real interest rate at the point where inflation equals the central bank's target level. And the long-run real interest rate is the level at which aggregate expenditure equals potential output. This all means that the dynamic aggregate demand curve must go through the point where output equals potential output at the same time that inflation equals target inflation. We will come back to this in the next chapter.

Figure 21.9   The Dynamic Aggregate Curve

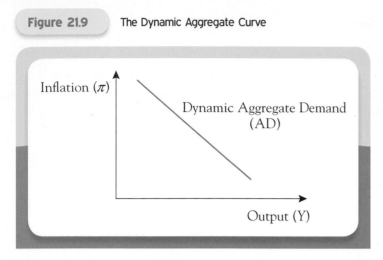

As inflation rises, monetary policymakers increase the real interest rate, lowering interest-rate-sensitive components of aggregate expenditure.

To understand the dynamic aggregate demand curve, think about what happens when current inflation rises. In response, monetary policymakers raise the real interest rate, moving the economy upward along the monetary policy reaction curve. The higher real interest rate reduces the interest-sensitive components of aggregate expenditure (consumption, investment, and net exports), causing a fall in the quantity of aggregate output demanded by the people in the economy who use it. Higher current inflation means less aggregate output demanded. In contrast, in response to lower current inflation, policymakers reduce the real interest rate, moving downward along the monetary policy reaction curve. Their action raises consumption, investment, and net exports, causing the quantity of aggregate output demanded to rise. Thus, *changes in current inflation move the economy along a downward-sloping dynamic aggregate demand curve.* (Take a look back at Figure 21.1 and the summary that goes along with it.)

Why the Dynamic Aggregate Demand Curve Slopes Down   To recap, the dynamic aggregate demand curve slopes down because higher current inflation induces policymakers to raise the real interest rate, depressing various components of aggregate expenditure. But this is only one reason that increases in inflation are associated with falling levels of aggregate output demanded by the people who use it. Economists have suggested a number of others. One is that the higher the rate of inflation for a given rate of money growth, the lower the level of real money balances in the economy. That is, when P grows faster the M, (M/P) falls. And with a lower level of real money balances, people purchase fewer goods. This is the implication of the equation of exchange ($MV = PY$). So, even if the monetary policymakers do not change the real interest rate when inflation goes up—the monetary policy reaction curve is flat—the effect of inflation on real money balances causes the dynamic aggregate demand curve to slope down.

In addition, higher inflation reduces wealth, which lowers consumption. It does this in two ways. First, inflation means that the money everyone holds is gradually declining in value. Second, inflation is bad for the stock market, because as it rises, uncertainty about inflation rises with it, rendering equities a relatively more risky and hence less attractive investment. A drop in the value of stocks reduces wealth.

Yet another reason for the downward slope of the dynamic aggregate demand curve is that inflation can have a greater impact on the poor than it does on the wealthy, redistributing income to those who are better off. For example, minimum wage workers tend to have incomes that are fixed in dollar terms, so inflation erodes their purchasing power. And because the rich consume a smaller portion of their income than others, saving a greater portion than the poor (who can't afford to save at all), this redistribution lowers consumption in the economy as a whole, reducing the quantity of aggregate output demanded.

YOUR FINANCIAL WORLD
It's the Real Interest Rate That Matters

In 2012, the 10-year Treasury yield dropped and stayed below 2 percent for the first time in more than 60 years. And business reporters were writing columns about how near-zero interest rates were hurting savers, especially retirees living off interest income.* With money-market mutual fund accounts yielding less than 10 basis points, the less-well-off elderly were having trouble paying their bills.

Yet, no one should be wishing for a return to the high interest rates of the late 1970s. Those nominal interest rates were high because the inflation rate was high. In fact, in 1979, when the nominal interest rate was around 12 percent, inflation was even higher—nearly 14 percent. This means that the real interest rate was below zero, not unlike 2012! It's the real interest rate that matters.

An example illustrates the importance of focusing on the real interest rate. Consider a retired person who is living off the income from a $500,000 savings account. Say that inflation and the nominal interest rate have both been stable for some time, at 8 percent and 10 percent, respectively. At a 10 percent nominal rate, the annual interest income on half a million dollars would be $50,000. But think about what would happen if the retiree spent the entire $50,000 in annual income. Each year, the purchasing power of the income would fall 8 percent because of inflation. After 9 years, the person's real income would be only half what it was initially (remember the rule of 72).

To avoid such a reduction in purchasing power, it is important not to spend all the interest income. Instead, the person should save a portion of the income, increasing the size of the savings account at the same rate as inflation. In this case, maintaining the inflation-adjusted value of the savings

account at its original level means increasing the balance by 8 percent each year. Of the first year's income of $50,000, then, $40,000 must be returned to the savings account; only $10,000 can be spent. Notice that in this example, the real interest rate is 2 percent, and that $10,000 exactly equals 2 percent of the $500,000 balance. The result would be no different if the interest rate was 4 percent and inflation was 2 percent. The real interest rate would still be 2 percent, which is the maximum that can be spent and keep the purchasing power of the savings account balance from eroding.†

High nominal interest rates can be misleading. They fool people into thinking that their incomes are high. But because high nominal rates almost always result from high inflation, spending all the interest income causes a gradual decline in the purchasing power of one's savings. To maintain the real purchasing power of their interest income, a person can spend only the real return. High interest rates are almost never a good thing; low inflation is.

*Peter Coy, "Interest Rates Near Zero Put Savers in a Bind," *Bloomberg Businessweek*, December 20, 2012.

†Because of the way the income tax system works, the effect of high nominal interest rates is even worse than this example suggests. The problem is that income tax is computed on nominal interest income. Consider the example of a bond with a 10 percent nominal yield in an economy with 8 percent inflation. Someone whose income is taxed at a 25 percent rate would receive a 7½ percent after-tax nominal return on the bond. But because inflation is 8 percent, the after-tax real return on the bond would be −½ percent. In other words, if the nominal interest rate is 10 percent and inflation is 8 percent, a $500,000 investment would deliver an after-tax real purchasing power loss of $2,500.

Then there is the fact that inflation creates risk; the higher the inflation rate, the greater the risk. Most people want to insure themselves against risk, and that means increased saving, just in case. More saving means a lower level of consumption and lower quantity of aggregate output demanded. Finally, there is the fact that rising inflation makes foreign goods cheaper in relation to domestic goods, driving imports up and net exports down. In every case, *higher inflation means a lower level of aggregate output demanded,* causing the dynamic aggregate demand curve to slope downward.

Shifting the Dynamic Aggregate Demand Curve   In deriving the dynamic aggregate demand curve, we saw that increases in inflation bring a monetary policy response that raises the real interest rate. Those movements in the real interest rate, in turn, cause changes in the quantity of aggregate output demanded by those who use it, moving the economy *along* the dynamic aggregate demand curve. In our derivation we held constant the location of both the aggregate expenditure curve and the monetary policy reaction curve. In the first case, we assumed that factors influencing demand other than the real interest rate were fixed; and in the second that the inflation target and the long-run real interest rate were fixed. Shifts in any of these will *shift* the dynamic aggregate demand curve.

Let's start by looking at shifts in the aggregate expenditure curve. In the absence of any change in monetary policy, changes in components of aggregate expenditure not caused by movements in the real interest rate shift the dynamic aggregate demand curve. That is, changes in consumption, investment, government purchases, or net exports that are unrelated to changes in the real interest rate shift the dynamic aggregate demand curve, with declines leading to contractions and increases leading to expansions.

To understand these sources of shifts in the dynamic aggregate demand curve, take the case of an increase in consumer confidence. When people become more optimistic about the future, believing that the risk of being laid off has eased, they are more likely to purchase a new car or go on an expensive vacation. Increases in consumer confidence tend to raise consumption at every level of the real interest rate, increasing the level of aggregate expenditure. Assuming unchanged monetary policy, this shifts the dynamic aggregate demand curve to the right (as shown in the top panel of Figure 21.10).

What is true for consumer confidence is true for all of the components of aggregate expenditure. Increased optimism about future business prospects raises investment at every level of the real interest rate, shifting the dynamic aggregate demand curve to the right. Increases in government spending (or decreases in taxes) increase aggregate expenditure and have the same effect. And increases in net exports that are unrelated

Figure 21.10   Shifting the Dynamic Aggregate Demand Curve

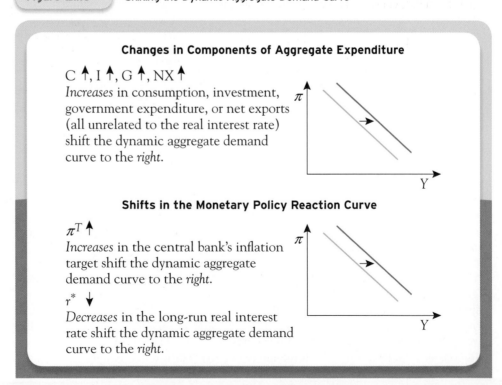

Changes in Components of Aggregate Expenditure

$C \uparrow, I \uparrow, G \uparrow, NX \uparrow$
Increases in consumption, investment, government expenditure, or net exports (all unrelated to the real interest rate) shift the dynamic aggregate demand curve to the *right*.

Shifts in the Monetary Policy Reaction Curve

$\pi^T \uparrow$
Increases in the central bank's inflation target shift the dynamic aggregate demand curve to the *right*.

$r^* \downarrow$
Decreases in the long-run real interest rate shift the dynamic aggregate demand curve to the *right*.

to the real interest rate do the same thing—they are expansionary, shifting the dynamic aggregate demand curve to the right.

Turning to the monetary policy reaction curve, whenever it shifts, the dynamic aggregate demand curve shifts, too. To see why, consider an increase in the central bank's inflation target, what some people might characterize as a permanent easing of monetary policy. The result is the opposite of the decline shown in Panel A of Figure 21.8. The rise in the inflation target shifts the monetary policy reaction curve to the right, lowering the real interest rate that policymakers set at every level of inflation. At the new, higher inflation target, the lower real interest rate increases the quantity of aggregate output demanded at every level of inflation, shifting the dynamic aggregate demand curve to the right.

Changes in the long-run real interest rate shift the dynamic aggregate demand curve as well. To see why, consider a case in which the level of potential output increases. Because the long-run real interest rate equates aggregate expenditure with potential output, when potential output rises, the long-run real interest rate must fall, driving up the interest-rate-sensitive components of aggregate expenditure. This has the same effect on the monetary policy reaction curve as an increase in policymakers' inflation target. A fall in the long-run real interest rate shifts the curve to the right, reducing the real interest rate policymakers set at every level of inflation and shifting the dynamic aggregate demand curve to the right.[10]

Looking at these two changes, we see that any shift in the monetary policy reaction curve shifts the dynamic aggregate demand curve in the same direction. Expansionary monetary policy that lowers the interest rate associated with each level of inflation, increases the quantity of aggregate output demanded at each level of inflation and shifts the dynamic aggregate demand curve to the right (as shown in the bottom panel of Figure 21.10). And contractionary monetary policy that raises the interest rate associated with each level of inflation, decreases the quantity of aggregate output demanded at each level of inflation, shifting the dynamic aggregate demand curve to the left.

Table 21.3 summarizes the properties of the dynamic aggregate demand curve.

Table 21.3   The Dynamic Aggregate Demand Curve

What is it?	The downward-sloping relationship between inflation and the quantity of aggregate output demanded by the people who use it.
Why does it slope down?	1. A rise in inflation leads monetary policymakers to raise the real interest rate (along the monetary policy reaction curve). 2. A higher real interest rate drives down the interest-sensitive components of aggregate expenditure (especially consumption and investment).
When does it shift?	When aggregate demand goes up for reasons unrelated to changes in the real interest rate, the relationship shifts to the right. Examples include: 1. Changes in components of aggregate expenditure not sensitive to the real interest rate (monetary policy unchanged). 2. Shifts in the monetary policy reaction curve.

[10]In the next chapter, we will examine what happens if the central bank observes the change in potential output only with a lag, temporarily delaying the shift of the MPRC curve shown in Panel B of Figure 21.8.

Aggregate Supply

The dynamic aggregate demand curve is downward-sloping. It tells us that higher current inflation is associated with a lower quantity of aggregate output demanded. But this alone doesn't explain how inflation and the quantity of output are determined by those people who use it. To do that, we need to introduce an aggregate supply curve. The aggregate supply curve tells us where along the dynamic aggregate demand curve the economy ends up. So, to complete the analysis, we now move to an examination of aggregate supply and the behavior of the firms that produce the economy's output. Critically, there are short-run and long-run versions of the aggregate supply curve. When combined with the dynamic aggregate demand curve, the short-run aggregate supply curve tells us where the economy settles at any particular time; while the long-run curve, together with dynamic aggregate demand, tells us the levels of inflation and the quantity of output that the economy is moving toward in the long term.

| **Figure 21.11** | Short-Run Aggregate Supply Curve |

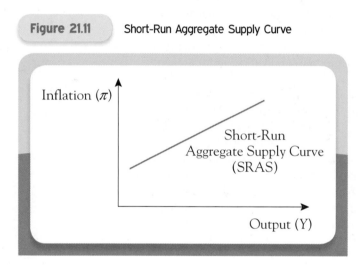

Inflation persistence means the short-run aggregate supply curve slopes up.

Short-Run Aggregate Supply

The **short-run aggregate supply curve (SRAS)** *is the upward-sloping relationship between current inflation and the quantity of output.* It tells us that as inflation rises, producers increase the quantity of output supplied. The reason is that prices of factors used as inputs in production, especially wages paid to workers, are costly to adjust, so they change infrequently. In the short run, they are sticky. For producers, this means that costs of production—wages paid to workers, rents paid for buildings, prices paid for raw material inputs—are fixed in the short run, so increases in prices of the things that firms sell mean higher profits and more supply. Put another way, in the short-term production costs don't change much, so when product (or retail) prices rise firms increase supply in order to take advantage. From this we can conclude that in the short run, higher inflation elicits more aggregate output supplied by the firms that produce it (see Figure 21.11).[11]

Shifts in the Short-Run Aggregate Supply Curve

Changes in product-price inflation create movements *along* a short-run aggregate supply curve. In coming to this conclusion, we assumed that production costs didn't change. What if they do? When production costs change, the short-run aggregate supply curve *shifts*. This can happen for any of three reasons:

1. Deviations of current output from potential output.
2. Changes in expectations of future inflation.
3. Factors that drive production costs up or down.

[11]The short-run aggregate supply curve is a close relative of the Phillips Curve that you may have already seen. The Phillips Curve is the downward-sloping relationship between inflation and unemployment. Because unemployment is related to the level of output—higher output means lower unemployment—there is a clear correspondence.

Let's look at each one of these in some detail.

When current output equals potential output, so that there is no output gap, the short-run aggregate supply curve remains stable. But when current output rises above potential output, inflation rises, and when current output falls below potential output, inflation falls. To understand the relationship between output gaps and inflation, recall that potential output is the level at which firms are using labor and capital at normal rates. But when current output falls below potential output, creating a *recessionary output gap,* part of the economy's capacity is idle. Firms have little trouble hiring new workers under these conditions, and their plants and equipment are underutilized. As a result, firms tend to raise the prices of the products that they sell and wages they pay their workers by less than they did when current output equaled potential output. That is, production costs rise more slowly so inflation falls.

When current output exceeds potential output, creating an *expansionary output gap,* the opposite happens. Firms have difficulty hiring new workers and retaining those already on the payroll. They pay overtime to their employees and use their plants and equipment at levels they can only maintain temporarily. Under these circumstances, firms will increase their product prices and the wages that they pay their workers by more than they would if they were operating at normal levels. So, when there is an expansionary gap, production costs rise more quickly and inflation goes up.

We can conclude that when current output deviates from potential output, inflation adjusts. A recessionary output gap, in which current output falls below potential output, forces inflation down; an expansionary output gap, in which current output rises above potential output, drives inflation up (see the top two panels of Figure 21.12 and Applying the Concept: Inflation Changes and Output Gaps on page 603).

Output gaps are only one of the sources of production cost changes that shift the short-run aggregate supply. A change in expectations about future inflation is another. Workers and firms care about real wages and real product prices—the level of compensation and profits measured in goods and services that they can purchase. As we noted earlier, it is costly to adjust wages and prices, so they change infrequently. More importantly, during months or even years for which they are fixed, inflation erodes the real wages paid to workers and real prices charged by firms. This makes everyone concerned about future inflation, and the higher expected inflation is, the more nominal wages and nominal prices will rise. As a result, changes in inflation expectations are analogous to changes in production costs. An increase in expected inflation increases production costs lowering production at every level of current inflation and shifting the short-run aggregate supply curve to the left as shown in the third panel of Figure 21.12.

Finally, changes in the prices of raw material inputs, as well as other external factors that change production costs, shift the short-run aggregate supply curve. The most common example of an input price change is a movement in the price of energy. When oil prices rise, increasing the cost of production, firms are forced to raise the prices of their products. The sharp increases in oil prices in the 1970s, from $3.50 a barrel in 1973 to $10 a barrel in 1976 and $39 a barrel in 1980, contributed to inflation during that decade.[12] Conversely, when oil prices fall, as they did in 1986 and again in 1999, inflation tends to fall. The same thing happens when labor costs rise, as they do when payroll taxes increase or the cost of employer-provided health insurance rises. *An increase in production costs causes the short-run aggregate supply curve to shift to the left*, as shown in the last panel of Figure 21.12.

---

[12]Compared with this episode, the surge of oil prices in 2007–2008 had far less impact on inflation because long-term inflation expectations were well anchored.

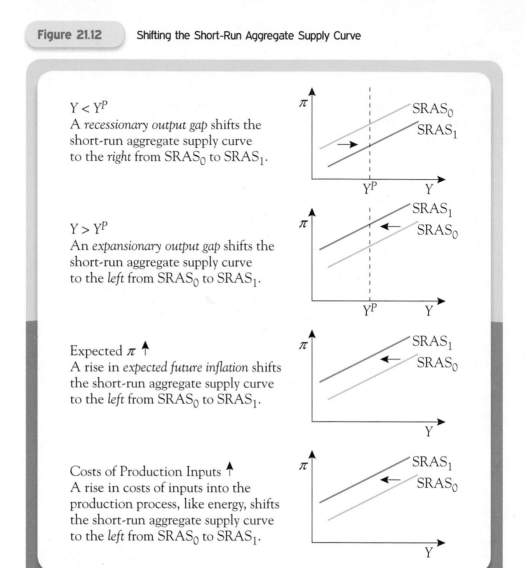

Figure 21.12   Shifting the Short-Run Aggregate Supply Curve

$Y < Y^P$
A *recessionary output gap* shifts the short-run aggregate supply curve to the *right* from $SRAS_0$ to $SRAS_1$.

$Y > Y^P$
An *expansionary output gap* shifts the short-run aggregate supply curve to the *left* from $SRAS_0$ to $SRAS_1$.

Expected π ↑
A rise in *expected future inflation* shifts the short-run aggregate supply curve to the *left* from $SRAS_0$ to $SRAS_1$.

Costs of Production Inputs ↑
A rise in costs of inputs into the production process, like energy, shifts the short-run aggregate supply curve to the *left* from $SRAS_0$ to $SRAS_1$.

The Long-Run Aggregate Supply Curve

The final step in completing our discussion of output and inflation fluctuations is to examine the long run. What happens after prices and wages have had time to make the adjustments that in the long run bring output and inflation back to normal? The answer (from the first part of this chapter) is that the economy moves to the point where current output equals potential output, while inflation is determined by money growth. The implications of this answer are that in the long run, current output must equal potential output, and inflation must be determined by monetary policy. That is, in the long run, output and inflation are unrelated, and that *the **long-run aggregate supply curve (LRAS)** is vertical at the point where current output equals potential output*.

This conclusion makes sense. From our earlier discussion we know that the short-run aggregate supply curve shifts whenever current output rises above or falls below

APPLYING THE CONCEPT
INFLATION CHANGES
AND OUTPUT GAPS

Inflation usually responds to the output gap after a lag. To see, take a look at Figure 21.13, which plots changes in the inflation rate (the red line) against the output gap, lagged six quarters (the yellow line) over the period 1988 to 2013. Inflation generally falls with a lag when there is a recessionary output gap and rises when current output exceeds potential output. Importantly, an output gap has little immediate impact on inflation; its effect takes more than a year to

be felt. By looking closely at the data in the figure, we can estimate that a 1 percent recessionary output gap (current output that is 1 percent below potential) drives the inflation rate down 0.1 percentage point over the following five to six quarters. Note, however, that inflation failed to decline after the financial crisis of 2007–2009 as much as past patterns imply that it would. The Fed's commitment to keep inflation low and stable appears to have anchored both inflation expectations and actual inflation. At the same time, the Congressional Budget Office may have overestimated potential GDP after the crisis, making the output gap overly negative in Figure 21.13. (See Chapter 22, In the News, on page 644.)

Figure 21.13   The Output Gap and Changes in the Inflation Rate, 1988–2013

In this figure the output gap is measured as the percentage deviation of current real gross domestic product (GDPC1) from potential real gross domestic product (GDPPOT). The change in the inflation rate is measured as the two-year change in the annual inflation rate based on the Consumer Price Index excluding food and energy (CPILFESL).

SOURCE: *Real GDP data are from the Bureau of Economic Analysis; potential real GDP data from the Congressional Budget Office; and consumer price data from the Bureau of Labor Statistics. The FRED codes are in parentheses.*

potential output, creating an expansionary or recessionary output gap. When current output equals potential output, the short-run aggregate supply curve does not shift. The fact that the short-run aggregate supply curve is stable when there is no output gap means that the long-run aggregate supply curve is vertical at that point.

In deriving the short-run aggregate supply curve, we noted that inflation depends on inflation expectations. That is, when workers and firms make the wage and price decisions that determine today's inflation, they do it with an eye toward future inflation. And an increase in expected inflation is just like an increase in production costs, shifting the short-run aggregate supply curve to the left (as in the bottom of Figure 21.12).

Figure 21.14 Short- and Long-Run Aggregate Supply Curves

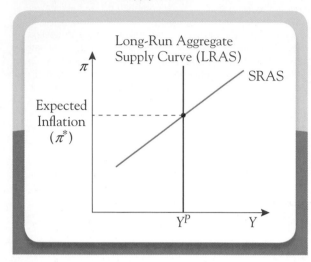

The long-run aggregate supply curve (LRAS) is vertical at the point where current output equals potential output.

To summarize, the short-run aggregate supply curve shifts *both* when current output deviates from potential output *and* when expected inflation deviates from current inflation. For the economy to remain in long-run equilibrium, then, in addition to current output equaling potential output, current inflation must equal expected inflation. So *at any point along the long-run aggregate supply curve, current output equals potential output ($Y = Y^P$) and current inflation equals expected inflation ($\pi = \pi^e$).* This is drawn in Figure 21.14, where the upward-sloping short-run aggregate supply curve (SRAS) intersects the vertical long-run aggregate supply curve (LRAS) at the point where inflation equals expected inflation.

Table 21.4 provides a summary of the properties of the short- and long-run aggregate supply curves.

Table 21.4 Aggregate Supply

	Short-Run Aggregate Supply Curve (SRAS)	Long-Run Aggregate Supply Curve (LRAS)
What is it?	The upward-sloping relationship between inflation (π) and the quantity of aggregate output (Y) supplied by the firms that produce it.	The vertical relationship between inflation (π) and the quantity of aggregate output supplied.
What is its slope?	Because production costs adjust slowly, increases in product prices make it profitable to increase quantity supplied, so the SRAS is upward sloping.	In the long run, all prices and wages adjust and the economy moves to the point where current output equals potential output, so the LRAS is vertical at $Y = Y^P$.
What determines its location?	It intersects the long-run aggregate supply curve (LRAS) where inflation equals expected inflation ($\pi = \pi^e$).	The LRAS is vertical at potential output.
When does it shift?	1. When there is a recessionary output gap ($Y < Y^P$), the SRAS shifts to the right. 2. When there is an expansionary output gap ($Y > Y^P$), the SRAS shifts to the left. 3. When expected inflation increases, the SRAS shifts to the left. 4. When production costs rise, the SRAS shifts to the left.	When potential output (Y^P) changes, the LRAS shifts. An increase in Y^P shifts the LRAS to the right; a decrease shifts it to the left.

TOOLS OF THE TRADE
Output Growth and Output Gaps

In testimony before Congress on February 29, 2012, Federal Reserve Board Chairman Ben Bernanke said, "With output growth in 2012 projected to remain close to its longer-run trend, [FOMC] participants did not anticipate further substantial declines in the unemployment rate over the course of this year." Central bankers say this sort of thing all the time. They talk about whether economic growth will move above or below—or, in this case, remain close to—its longer-run sustainable pace and hence change or maintain current levels of inflation or unemployment. But if you open an economics textbook, or even look at current research on how to best conduct monetary policy, you will see everything written in terms of the *level* of current output, *potential output,* and the *output gap;* not real growth. What's going on? When central bankers mention growth, are they speaking the same language as the macroeconomists who study output gaps?

To reconcile monetary policymakers' words with the models in economics textbooks, we can start with the fortunate fact that the economy is usually growing. Investment increases the size of the capital stock used for production, and new hires raise the number of people working. And then there are technological improvements: Inventions and innovations are continually raising individual productivity. Increases in the available amounts of capital and labor, together with improvements in productivity, are the sources of economic growth. And because economic growth implies an increase in the normal level of production, potential output is constantly rising. These increases in the economy's productive capacity shift the long-run aggregate supply curve (LRAS) to the right.

When monetary policymakers use the term *growth,* they are talking about increases in both actual and potential output. Unless these are equal, an output gap opens up. That is, when Y grows faster than Y^p, it creates an expansionary output gap and when Y grows more slowly than Y^p, it creates a recessionary output gap. Only when Y and Y^p grow at the same rate—that's the maximum sustainable growth rate—will the economy be at its long-run equilibrium with output equal to potential output.

So, while it may appear that policymakers' words about growth don't match their deeds in addressing output gaps, they do. Just remember that the economy is usually growing, and so long as actual and potential output both grow at the same pace, no output gap will develop.

Equilibrium and the Determination of Output and Inflation

Short-Run Equilibrium

We now have the tools we need to understand both the movements in output and inflation in the short run and their determination in the long run. Short-run equilibrium is determined by the intersection of the dynamic aggregate demand curve (AD) with the short-run aggregate supply curve (SRAS). Combining the AD curve from Figure 21.9 and the SRAS curve from Figure 21.11, we get Figure 21.15. Current output and inflation are determined by the intersection at point E in the figure. And, like all supply and demand diagrams, changes in inflation and output arise from shifts in either supply, demand, or both. We'll have a detailed look at the sources and consequences of these shifts in Chapter 22.

Adjustment to Long-Run Equilibrium

What happens when current output deviates from potential output so that there is an output gap? Earlier we saw that output gaps lead to *shifts* in the short-run aggregate supply curve. This means that if there is either an expansionary or a recessionary output gap, the economy cannot be in long-run equilibrium. To see how adjustment to long-run equilibrium works, let's look at two cases: one in which current output is

Figure 21.15   Short-Run Determination of Output and Inflation

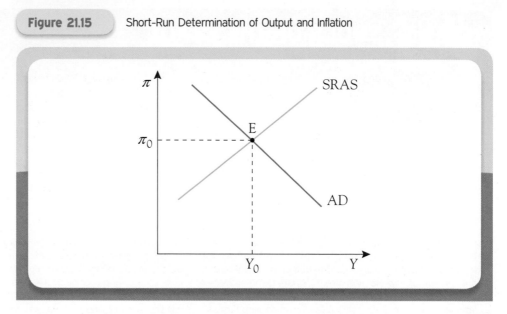

In the short run, inflation and output are determined by the intersection of the short-run aggregate supply curve (SRAS) and the dynamic aggregate demand curve (AD), at point E above.

above potential $(Y > Y^P)$, and one in which it is below potential $(Y < Y^P)$. When current output exceeds potential the resulting expansionary output gap exerts upward pressure on production costs, shifting the short-run aggregate supply curve to the left. This process continues until output returns to potential, as shown in Panel A of Figure 21.16. At first, the quantity of aggregate output demanded equals the quantity supplied in the short run at point 1, where current output Y_0 exceeds potential output Y^P. The resulting expansionary output gap puts upward pressure on production costs, shifting the short-run aggregate supply curve to the left until it reaches point 2, where current output equals potential output and there is no output gap. Only at this point do inflation and output stop changing.

Now consider the second case, in which current output, Y_0, is lower than potential output, Y^P. This recessionary output gap places downward pressure on production costs, shifting the short-run aggregate supply curve to the right. Again, the process continues until current output returns to potential, as shown in Panel B of Figure 21.16. At first, the quantity of aggregate output demanded equals the quantity supplied in the short run at point 1, where current output falls short of potential output. The resulting recessionary output gap causes the short-run aggregate supply curve to shift to the right as shown. As it does, current output increases until it equals potential output and inflation falls, until the economy reaches point 2. At this point, output and inflation are steady.

This example has several important implications. First, it shows that the economy has a self-correcting mechanism. When output moves away from its long-run equilibrium level, inflation moves away from the central bank's target and policymakers respond by changing the real interest rate. This moves the economy along the dynamic aggregate demand curve until it returns to its long-run equilibrium. Second, the fact that inflation changes whenever there is an output gap reinforces our conclusion that in the long run output returns to potential output. This is why we drew the long-run aggregate supply curves as a vertical line in the figures.

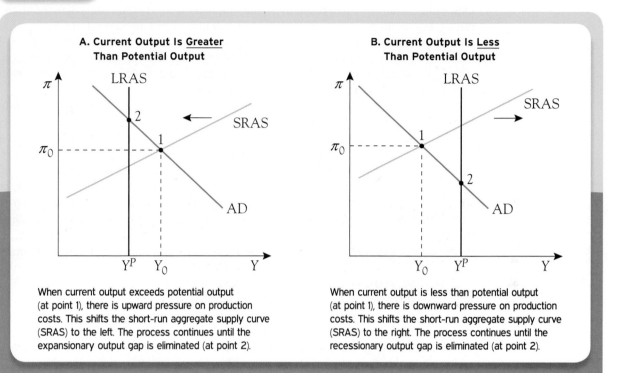

Figure 21.16   Adjustment to Long-Run Equilibrium

A. Current Output Is <u>Greater</u> Than Potential Output

When current output exceeds potential output (at point 1), there is upward pressure on production costs. This shifts the short-run aggregate supply curve (SRAS) to the left. The process continues until the expansionary output gap is eliminated (at point 2).

B. Current Output Is <u>Less</u> Than Potential Output

When current output is less than potential output (at point 1), there is downward pressure on production costs. This shifts the short-run aggregate supply curve (SRAS) to the right. The process continues until the recessionary output gap is eliminated (at point 2).

Long-run equilibrium is the point at which the economy comes to rest. Because we will be using it as a benchmark for understanding fluctuations, it is important to list its properties. As we noted earlier, in the long run, current inflation must equal expected inflation. Furthermore, when current output equals potential output, the real interest rate equals the long-run real interest rate. And going back to the monetary policy reaction curve, we know that policymakers set the real interest rate equal to this long-run level when current inflation equals their inflation target. So there are three conditions for long-run equilibrium:

1. Current output equals potential output ($Y = Y^P$),
2. Current inflation is steady and equal to target inflation ($\pi = \pi^T$), and
3. Current inflation equals expected inflation ($\pi = \pi^e$).

The Sources of Fluctuations in Output and Inflation

The next chapter uses the framework we have just developed to help us understand a series of problems that are of direct interest to policymakers. But before getting to that, let's finish up with a brief discussion of the possible sources of fluctuations in U.S. inflation and real growth and then a quick examination of the data. What might have caused these fluctuations over the past half century?

Looking at the macroeconomic model, we can see that output and inflation movements can arise from either demand or supply shifts. To figure how we might tell them apart, notice that while shifts in either the dynamic aggregate demand curve or the short-run aggregate supply curve can have the same effect on inflation, they have opposite effects on output. So, if the dynamic aggregate demand curve shifts to the right, increasing inflation, it will result in higher output as well. By contrast, when the short-run aggregate supply curve shifts to the left, inflation rises and output falls. That is, the possible sources of fluctuations are: (1) shifts in the dynamic aggregate demand curve that cause output and inflation to rise and fall together, moving in the *same* direction; and (2) shifts in the short-run aggregate supply curve that move output and inflation in *opposite* directions, one rises when the other one falls.

So, what are the likely sources of economic fluctuations? Let's start with inflation. Recall that in long-run equilibrium, inflation equals the central bank's target, which is equal to inflation expectations. So, if we see inflation rise or fall permanently, it must be that policymakers changed their inflation target, consciously or not. By contrast, short-run inflation fluctuations have more than one possible source. Inflation goes up in the short run when either the dynamic aggregate demand curve shifts to the right, or when the short-run aggregate supply curve shifts to the left. The first of these comes from either increases in the components of aggregate expenditure that are not sensitive to the real interest rate (higher government expenditure, business optimism, or consumer confidence) or a permanent easing of monetary policy (when the monetary policy reaction curve shifts to lower the real interest rate at every level of inflation). Each of these shifts dynamic aggregate demand to the right, increasing inflation. The second comes from increases in the costs of production, like a rise in oil prices or higher inflation expectations—each of which shifts the short-run aggregate supply curve to the left, driving inflation up.[13]

Turning to output, there are again two possible sources of fluctuations. Output drops when either the dynamic aggregate demand curve or the short-run aggregate supply curve shift to the left. For demand, either a decline in aggregate expenditure or a shift to the left in the monetary policy reaction curve drives current output below potential output. This brings up the interesting possibility that policymakers could be the sources of recessions. On the supply side, increases in either production costs or inflation expectations drive output down (at the same time that they drive inflation up). Which is it? Let's see if we can figure it out.

What Causes Recessions?

For years, economists have argued over the cause of recessions. Is it (1) shifts in the dynamic aggregate demand curve brought about by changes in consumer confidence, business optimism, or monetary policy; or (2) shifts in the short-run aggregate supply curve caused by increases in oil prices and other production costs? We can make some progress toward figuring out the answer by recalling that with a shift in the dynamic aggregate demand curve output and inflation move in the same direction, while a shift in short-run aggregate supply moves output and inflation in opposite directions. So if demand shifts were the cause of recessions, we should see inflation decline when output falls. And if production cost increases were the source, then we should see inflation rise as the economy weakens.

Table 21.5 lists the dates of recessions since the mid-1950s. The peak (column 1) is the beginning of the recession, when economic activity was at its highest before beginning to slide and the trough (column 2) is the lowest point of the recession, when economic activity began to rise. The third column of the table shows the change in inflation from the beginning to the end of the recession. Note that inflation fell in seven

---

[13]As we will discuss in the next chapter, when oil prices rise, the long-run aggregate supply curve may shift as well.

Table 21.5   Inflation during Recessions

Peak	Trough	Inflation Change
August 1957	April 1958	3.6 to 3.5 ↓
April 1960	February 1961	1.7 to 1.4 ↓
December 1969	November 1970	5.7 to 5.4 ↓
November 1973	**March 1975**	**7.9 to 10.0** ↑
January 1980	July 1980	13.0 to 12.4 ↓
July 1981	November 1982	10.3 to 4.4 ↓
July 1990	March 1991	4.7 to 4.7 =
March 2001	November 2001	2.9 to 1.8 ↓
December 2007	June 2009	4.2 to −1.2 ↓

SOURCE: *Inflation is the 12-month percent change in the all-items CPI-U from the Bureau of Labor Statistics (CPIAUCSL). Business cycle peaks and troughs are from the NBER (USREC). FRED data codes are in parentheses.*

of the past nine recessions. The recession of 1973–1975 (in bold) is the only case in which inflation rose. Oil prices tripled in 1973, driving up production costs and shifting the short-run aggregate supply curve to the left. The result was a protracted recession and a dramatic increase in inflation.

It appears that three-quarters of the recessions in the past half century can be traced to shifts in the dynamic aggregate demand curve. Let's go further and figure out what caused these AD shifts. Was it falling aggregate expenditure brought about by changes in people's attitudes, or was it the actions of monetary policymakers? To see, we can look at one more piece of evidence: the behavior of interest rates. Figure 21.17 shows

Figure 21.17   Interest Rates and the Business Cycle

SOURCE: *The solid line represents the three-month Treasury bill rate (TB3MS); the shaded bars denote recessions, as dated by the National Bureau of Economic Research. The FRED data code is in parentheses.*

IN THE NEWS
Yellen Says Higher Rates Not Assured after Thresholds Hit

Bloomberg

By Craig Torres and Jeanna Smialek

February 11, 2013

Federal Reserve Vice Chair Janet Yellen said the central bank may hold the benchmark lending rate near zero even if unemployment and inflation hit its near-term policy targets.

The Federal Open Market Committee said in December it will hold the main interest rate in a range of zero to 0.25 percent so long as inflation isn't forecast to rise to more than 2.5 percent in one to two years and unemployment remains above 6.5 percent.

Yellen said today those objectives are "thresholds for possible action, not triggers that will necessarily prompt an immediate increase" in the FOMC's target rate. "When one of these thresholds is crossed, action is possible but not assured," she said in a speech to the AFL-CIO in Washington.

U.S. central bankers are focusing the full force of monetary policy on reviving growth and reducing 7.9 percent unemployment, using near-zero interest rates and a program of unprecedented bond buying. Yellen's comments reflect the view of some policy makers that there is a risk of damaging the expansion by raising rates too early.

The Fed in September started a third round of asset purchases and expanded it in December to $85 billion per month, saying the quantitative easing will continue until the labor market is improving "substantially."

"Entirely Appropriate"

"With employment so far from its maximum level and with inflation currently running, and expected to continue to run, at or below the Committee's 2 percent longer-term objective, it is entirely appropriate for progress in attaining maximum employment to take center stage in determining the committee's policy stance," Yellen said.

Yellen noted that the FOMC maintains a longer-run goal for inflation of 2 percent while the FOMC estimates that labor resources are fully utilized at an unemployment rate of 5.2 percent to 6 percent.

"Our control over the economy is imperfect, and so temporary deviations from the FOMC's specific longer-term goals will sometimes occur," Yellen said. "Importantly, these quantitative goals are neither ceilings nor floors for inflation and unemployment, and the committee will take a balanced approach to returning both measures to their objectives over time."

Facing Headwinds

The Fed Vice Chair said she believes high unemployment is the result of too little demand rather than a mismatch of

that shortly before each recession starts, just to the left of each of the shaded bars, the interest rate tends to rise. This suggests that Federal Reserve policy is at least partly to blame for the business cycle downturns over the past half century. But why would policymakers have chosen to cause these recessions? The answer is to bring down inflation. Especially in the late 1970s, when the inflation rate was over 10 percent per year, something had to be done. The only thing the Fed could do under such circumstances was to raise interest rates, reducing the interest-sensitive components of aggregate expenditure in the process and triggering a recession. The low inflation we enjoy today is the result of the Fed's tough policy decisions.

workers' skills with the needs of employers. She said the economy faces headwinds in the form of a battered real estate market, low income expectations by households, and fiscal restraint.

The Fed's asset purchases and other unconventional policies have helped "shore up aggregate demand," Yellen said.

"However, while this contribution has been significant, lower interest rates may be doing less to increase spending than in past recoveries because of some unusual features of the Great Recession and the current recovery," she said.

Unemployment averaged 8.1 percent last year as the expansion which began in June 2009 was too weak to pull it lower.

The Fed under its congressional mandate seeks to promote "maximum employment" and "stable prices." The personal consumption expenditures price index is below the central bank's stated goal of 2 percent, rising just 1.3 percent last year.

Big Waste

Some 4.7 million people were unemployed six months or more in December, a condition that Chairman Ben S. Bernanke called "an enormous waste of human and economic potential" at a press conference after a Dec. 11–12 meeting of policy makers.

The central bank's asset purchases have pushed its balance sheet above a record $3 trillion.

Even so, the U.S. economy contracted at a 0.1 percent annual rate in the fourth quarter of 2012, dragged down by the biggest plunge in government defense spending in four decades. The outlook for fiscal policy, which could include further defense cuts, is still clouded by disagreement in Washington over federal taxation and spending. . . .

LESSONS OF THE ARTICLE

Beginning in December 2012, the FOMC announced unemployment and inflation thresholds for raising its target interest rate from the zero bound. This new form of *forward guidance* aimed to strengthen the Fed's commitment to keep interest rates low until the labor market improved. The article highlights the Fed's judgment that high unemployment reflected a shortfall of aggregate demand. It also underscores the Fed's sensitivity to both aspects of its dual mandate and its efforts to balance policy when inflation deviates from its target and unemployment deviates from its longer-run norm.

Terms

Using FRED: Codes for Data in This Chapter

Data Series	FRED Data Code
Real GDP	GDPC1
Potential real GDP	GDPPOT
Consumer Price Index less food and energy	CPILFESL
Federal funds rate	FEDFUNDS
U.S. 10-year Treasury constant maturity rate	GS10
U.S. 3-month Treasury bill rate	TB3MS
1-year inflation expectations (Michigan survey)	MICH
Real personal consumption expenditures	PCECC96
Real gross private domestic investment	GPDIC96
Real net exports of goods and services	NETEXC
Real government outlays	GCEC96
NBER recession dates (0 = expansion, 1 = recession)	USREC

Chapter Lessons

1. In the long run
   a. Current output equals potential output, which is the level of output the economy produces when its resources are used at normal rates.
   b. Inflation equals money growth minus growth in potential output.
2. The dynamic aggregate demand curve is a downward-sloping relationship between inflation and the quantity of output demanded by those who use it:
   a. Aggregate expenditure = Consumption + Investment + Government purchases + Net exports.
      i. Aggregate expenditure falls when the real interest rate rises.
      ii. The long-run real interest rate equates aggregate expenditure with potential output.
   b. Monetary policy is described by an upward-sloping monetary policy reaction curve.
      i. When policymakers change the nominal interest rate, they change the real interest rate as well, because expected inflation usually doesn't change quickly.
      ii. Policymakers react to increases in inflation by increasing the real interest rate (as the Taylor rule indicates).
      iii. The monetary policy reaction curve is set so that the real interest rate equals the long-run real interest rate when inflation equals the central bank's target.
      iv. The monetary policy reaction curve shifts when either the inflation target changes or the long-run real interest rate changes.
   c. Movements along the dynamic aggregate demand curve occur when monetary policymakers react to changes in inflation by adjusting the real interest rate.
   d. The dynamic aggregate demand curve shifts when
      i. An increase in consumer confidence, business optimism, government purchases, or net exports shifts the dynamic aggregate demand curve to the right.

ii. The monetary policy reaction curve shifts to the right, shifting the dynamic aggregate demand curve to the right.

3. The aggregate supply curve tells us the amount of output producers are willing to supply at given levels of inflation.
    a. The short-run aggregate supply curve slopes up because, in the short run, costs of production adjust more slowly than output prices.
    b. Production cost changes shift the short-run aggregate supply curve. These occur when
        i. There is a recessionary or expansionary output gap.
        ii. Expectations about future inflation change.
        iii. Raw material prices, such as the cost of energy, change.
    c. The long-run aggregate supply curve is vertical at potential output.
        i. Along the long-run aggregate supply curve, expected inflation equals current inflation.
        ii. The long-run aggregate supply curve shifts when either the amounts of capital and labor used in the economy change or productivity changes.
        iii. The short-run aggregate supply curve intersects the long-run aggregate supply curve at the point where inflation equals expected inflation.

4. Equilibrium output and inflation are determined by the intersection of the dynamic aggregate demand curve and either the short-run or long-run aggregate supply curve.
    a. The short-run equilibrium point is located where the dynamic aggregate demand curve intersects the short-run aggregate supply curve.
    b. The long-run equilibrium point is located where the dynamic aggregate demand curve intersects the long-run aggregate supply curve. At that point, current output equals potential output and inflation equals the inflation target, which equals expected inflation.
    c. Fluctuations in output and inflation come from either
        i. Demand shifts, which cause them to rise and fall together.
        ii. Supply shifts, which cause one to rise as the other falls.

Conceptual and Analytical Problems

1. Explain the determinants of potential growth. *(LO1)*

2.* Explain how a recessionary output gap would emerge in an economy where the long-run aggregate supply curve is persistently shifting to the right. *(LO1)*

3. Describe the determinants of the long-run real interest rate and speculate on the sort of events that would make it fluctuate. *(LO1)*

4. Explain how and why the components of aggregate expenditure depend on the real interest rate. Be sure to distinguish between the real and nominal interest rates, and explain why the distinction matters. *(LO2)*

5.* Suppose that the aggregate expenditure curve can be expressed algebraically as

$$AE = 3,000 - 2,000r$$

*Indicates more difficult problems

www.mhhe.com/moneyandbanking4e

where *AE* is aggregate expenditures and *r* is the real interest rate expressed as a decimal. You check the website of the Congressional Budget Office and learn that the level of potential output is 2,900. What is the long-run real interest rate? *(LO1)*

6. Suppose the U.S. economy is in equilibrium at the long-run real interest rate that prevails when aggregate expenditures equal potential output. Draw a diagram of aggregate expenditures showing this initial equilibrium. Then suppose that foreign demand for U.S. exports falls due to a recession abroad. Show how the long-run real interest rate will change and explain your results. *(LO1)*

7. The European Central Bank's primary objective is price stability. Policymakers interpret this objective to mean keeping inflation below, but close to, 2 percent, as measured by a euro-area Consumer Price Index. In contrast, the FOMC has a dual objective of price stability and high economic growth. How would you expect the monetary policy reaction curves of the two central banks to differ? Why? *(LO2)*

8.* Explain why the short-run aggregate supply curve is upward sloping. Under what circumstances might it be vertical? *(LO2)*

9.* Assume the short-run aggregate supply curve can be expressed algebraically as

$$Y_s = 4,800 + 3,000\pi$$

where Y_s is aggregate supply, and the dynamic aggregate demand curve can be written as

$$Y_d = 5,000 - 1,000\pi$$

where Y_d is aggregate demand. Find the numerical value for equilibrium output, *Y*, in the short run. Find the numerical value for the short-run inflation rate, π. *(LO4)*

10. Consider Panel B of Figure 21.16, where the short-run equilibrium occurs at an output level below potential output, Y^p. Suppose that the initial inflation target was at the level corresponding to point 2, but the central bank chooses to stimulate demand to speed the adjustment to long-run equilibrium. What are the costs and benefits of such a policy? *(LO4)*

11. Suppose the real interest rate unexpectedly falls in the absence of other economic changes. What would you expect to happen to (a) consumption, (b) investment, and (c) net exports in the economy? *(LO3)*

12. Given the expected relationship between the real interest rate and investment, how would you explain a scenario where investment continued to fall despite low or even negative real interest rates? *(LO3)*

13.* Economy A and Economy B are similar in every way except that in Economy A, 70 percent of aggregate expenditure is sensitive to changes in the real interest rate and in Economy B, only 50 percent of aggregate expenditure is sensitive to changes in the real interest rate. *(LO2)*
   a. Which economy will have a steeper aggregate expenditure curve?
   b. How would the dynamic aggregate demand curves differ given that the monetary policy reaction curve is the same in both countries?

Explain your answers.

14. State whether each of the following will result in a movement along or a shift in the monetary policy reaction curve and in which direction the effect will be. *(LO2)*
    a. Policymakers increase the real interest rate in response to a rise in current inflation.
    b. Policymakers increase their inflation target.
    c. The long-run real interest rate falls.

15. Suppose a natural disaster wipes out a significant portion of the economy's capital stock, reducing the potential level of output. What would you expect to happen to the long-run real interest rate? What impact would this have on the monetary policy reaction curve and the dynamic aggregate demand curve? *(LO1)*

16. Suppose there were a wave of investor pessimism in the economy. What would the impact be on the dynamic aggregate demand curve? *(LO2)*

17. Explain how each of the following affects the short-run aggregate supply curve. *(LO2)*
    a. Firms and workers reduce their expectations of future inflation.
    b. There is a rise in current inflation.
    c. There is a fall in oil prices.

18. Suppose the economy is in short-run equilibrium at a level of output that exceeds potential output. How would the economy self-adjust to return to long-run equilibrium? *(LO3)*

19. Why do you think the surge in oil prices in 2007–2008 had a much smaller impact on inflation expectations compared with the oil price shocks of the 1970s? *(LO3)*

20.* You read a story in the newspaper blaming the central bank for pushing the economy into recession. The article goes on to mention that not only has output fallen below its potential level but that inflation had also risen. If you were to write to the newspaper defending the central bank, what argument would you make? *(LO3)*

Data Exploration

For general information on using Federal Reserve Economic Data (FRED) online, visit www.mhhe.com/moneyandbanking4e.com and click on Student Edition, then FRED resources.

1. Are long-term inflation expectations "well anchored"? Using monthly data since 2003, plot a measure of long-term inflation expectations based on the difference between the yields on a five-year Treasury bond (FRED code: GS5) and a five-year Treasury Inflation Protected Securities (TIPS) bond (FRED code: FII5). What do you conclude? How did the financial crisis of 2007–2009 affect the measure? *(LO1)*

2. Is investment sensitive to the real interest rate? Plot since 1990 a measure of the real interest rate—based on the difference between Moody's Baa corporate bond yield (FRED code: BAA) and a survey of expected inflation (FRED code: MICH)—and (on the right scale) the share of investment (FRED code: GPDIC1) in real GDP (FRED code: GDPC1). Explain the cyclical pattern. *(LO2)*

Scan here for quick access to the resources for these problems. Need a barcode reader? Try ScanLife, available in your app store.

3. How sensitive is private investment to risk? Plot since 2004 the share of real gross private domestic investment (FRED code: GPDIC1) in real GDP (FRED code: GDPC1) and (on the right scale) a measure of anticipated stock market volatility (FRED code: VIXCLS). Explain the pattern. *(LO2)*

4. A recession may reflect declines in aggregate demand, aggregate supply, or both. Are swings in consumer sentiment characteristic of recessions? Plot a measure of sentiment (FRED code: UMCSENT), and discuss its evolution during the recessions since 1980. Explain why consumer sentiment is an important example of an aggregate demand shock. *(LO3)*

5. How often are negative supply shocks associated with recessions? Plot on a quarterly basis since 1971 the real price of oil—measured as the ratio of the nominal price of oil (FRED code: OILPRICE) to the U.S. Consumer Price Index (CPIAUCSL). Identify recessions that may have been triggered in part by an oil price shock. *(LO3)*

Chapter 22

Understanding Business Cycle Fluctuations*

Learning Objectives

Understand . . .

LO1   Sources of fluctuations in output and inflation

LO2   How to use AS/AD analysis

LO3   Policy tradeoffs and the limits of stabilization

In the last chapter we constructed a framework for understanding fluctuations in output and inflation. We discussed the fact that central bankers respond to rising inflation by increasing the real interest rate, causing interest-sensitive components of aggregate expenditure—especially investment—to fall, driving down the quantity of aggregate output demanded by the people who use it. So, higher inflation means a lower level of demand in the economy as a whole. The *dynamic aggregate demand curve slopes down.*

On the supply side, we saw that the sluggish response of production costs means that higher inflation elicits more production from firms, and is associated with a greater level of output supplied in the short run. The *short-run aggregate supply curve slopes up.* Finally, we learned that in the long run, the economy moves to the point where output equals potential output, so the *long-run aggregate supply curve is vertical.* While the economy can and does move away from this long-run equilibrium, it has a natural self-correcting mechanism that returns it to the point where resources are being used at their normal rates and gaps between current and potential output disappear.

We will now use this framework to improve our understanding of business cycle fluctuations. Why is it that output and inflation vary from quarter to quarter and year to year, and what determines the extent of fluctuations? Figure 22.1 illustrates the long-run trends in the U.S. inflation rate over the past 50 years. In 1965, prices in the United States were rising at an average rate of just 1½ percent per year. Fifteen years later, consumer price inflation had climbed to nearly 14 percent. For the next decade the inflation rate fell, at first sharply and then gradually. By 1991, prices were increasing at a rate of less than 4 percent per year. Finally, amid the financial crisis of 2007–2009, prices began to fall for the first time in more than 50 years.

In addition to data on the rate of inflation, Figure 22.1 displays a series of shaded bars representing recessions—periods when the U.S. real GDP was falling. While there

---

*The starred sections of this chapter, beginning on page 634, are more difficult than the nonstarred sections preceding them.

Figure 22.1 Inflation and the Business Cycle, 1955–2013

This figure shows the 12-month change in consumer prices, calculated by the Bureau of Labor Statistics (FRED code: CPIAUCSL). The bars represent recessions, as dated by the National Bureau of Economic Research.

is no apparent relationship between the *level* of inflation and these recessions, it does appear that the inflation rate falls when the economy is contracting and rises when it is expanding. At least, that's what happens most of the time. The recession of 1974–1975 is an exception. During that episode, the inflation rate rose dramatically even as the economy was slumping. And during much of the boom of the 1990s, the inflation rate remained below its level at the end of the last recession. But in general, there appears to be a connection between growth and changes in inflation: The lower the growth, the more likely inflation is to fall.

One final point about Figure 22.1 is worth noting. In recent years, the frequency of recessions has fallen. In the 30 years from 1955 to 1984, there were six recessions; in the 26 years since then, there have been three, including the deep one that ended in 2009. Recessions used to occur once every five years, but more recently, they have occurred on average about every 8 to 10 years. Until the record plunge of 2008–2009, the recessions after 1982 were milder than before as well. This reduction in the volatility of real growth has been called the "Great Moderation." We examine its possible sources later in the chapter and identify factors that could prevent its resumption in coming years.

To help understand the patterns in Figure 22.1, we will start by cataloguing the various reasons that the dynamic aggregate demand curve and the aggregate supply curve shift. These are the potential sources of fluctuations in both output and inflation described at the end of the last chapter. We trace the initial impact of shifts in aggregate demand such as an increase in government spending or shifts in short-run aggregate supply such as a movement in oil prices. Next, we examine what happens during the transition as the economy moves to long-run equilibrium. Our goal is to take the macroeconomic model and use it to understand practical real-world examples.

Then, in the second part of the chapter, we will use the model to understand how central bankers work to achieve their stabilization objectives, together with a series of examples that highlight the pitfalls and limitations that monetary policymakers face. The section is organized around a series of questions of increasing complexity. We will examine how, in practice, policymakers work to achieve their stabilization goals; the appropriate actions to take when potential output changes; and the difficulty central bankers have figuring out why output has fallen, among other things.

Sources of Fluctuations in Output and Inflation

In the earlier discussion we learned that the economy naturally moves toward its long-run equilibrium where output equals potential output ($Y = Y^P$) and inflation equals the central bank's target ($\pi = \pi^T$), which equals the level of inflation firms and individuals expect ($\pi = \pi^e$). This tells us that the long-run aggregate supply curve is vertical at potential output. But because costs of production adjust slowly, higher inflation temporarily means higher profits and more supply; that is, the short-run aggregate supply curve slopes upward. Short-run equilibrium is where the dynamic aggregate demand curve intersects this short-run aggregate supply curve. So, immediately after either the short-run aggregate supply curve or the dynamic aggregate demand curve shift, the economy will move away from its long-run equilibrium. This means that understanding short-run fluctuations in output and inflation requires that we study shifts in dynamic aggregate demand and short-run aggregate supply.

Before moving to an analysis of various demand and supply curve shifts, let's take a brief detour to define one of the few new terms in this chapter: *shock*. Economists use the word shock to mean something unexpected. For example, when oil prices rise or when consumers become less confident about the future, these are almost always unpredictable *shocks*. In our framework, a shock shifts the dynamic aggregate demand or short-run aggregate supply curve. Because it affects costs of production, the oil price increase is a **supply shock**, while the shift in consumer confidence, which affects consumption expenditure, is a **demand shock**. So, a shock is something that creates a shift in the demand or supply curve.

Shifts in the Dynamic Aggregate Demand Curve

Recall that a shift in the dynamic aggregate demand curve can be caused by either a shift in the monetary policy reaction curve or a change in components that are not sensitive to the real interest rate (like government purchases) that shifts aggregate expenditure. Let's look at the impact of each of these. We will first look at a decline in the central bank's inflation target that shifts the monetary policy reaction curve, and then at a fiscal policy easing that increases government purchases and shifts the aggregate expenditure curve.

A Decline in the Central Bank's Inflation Target   Over the past several decades, numerous countries have succeeded in reducing their inflation rates from fairly high levels to the modest ones we see today. For example, Chile was able to reduce its inflation rate from over 20 percent in the early 1990s to roughly 2 percent today. In the mid-1980s, Israel's inflation rate peaked at nearly 400 percent before it was brought down in a series of steps, first to 20 percent and eventually to 2 percent. And Sweden entered the 1990s with an inflation rate that was over 10 percent. The Riksbank, the

Figure 22.2 A Decline in the Central Bank's Inflation Target

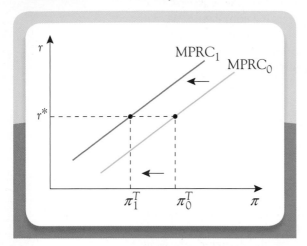

A decline in the inflation target from π_0^T to π_1^T shifts the monetary policy reaction curve to the left from MPRC$_0$ to MPRC$_1$.

Swedish central bank, spent a number of years driving the country's inflation rate down below 3 percent, where it has generally stayed. All of these cases involved permanent declines in inflation that must have been a result of a decrease in the central bank's inflation target.

To analyze the impact of a reduction in the policymaker's inflation target, let's begin with the monetary policy reaction curve. A fall in π^T shifts the monetary policy reaction curve to the left, as shown in Figure 22.2 (which reproduces Panel A of Figure 21.8 on page 594). The decrease in the inflation target raises the real interest rate policymakers set at each level of inflation.

We know from our earlier analysis that shifts in the monetary policy reaction curve shift the dynamic aggregate demand curve in the same direction. A decrease in the central bank's inflation target means a higher real interest rate at every level of inflation, shifting the monetary policy reaction curve to the left. This reduces aggregate expenditure at every level of inflation, shifting the dynamic aggregate demand curve to the left as well, as shown in Panel A of Figure 22.3. You can see that as the dynamic aggregate demand curve shifts to the left, from AD$_0$ to AD$_1$, the economy moves from original short-run equilibrium point, 1, to

Figure 22.3 A Decline in the Central Bank's Inflation Target

A. Short-Run Equilibrium

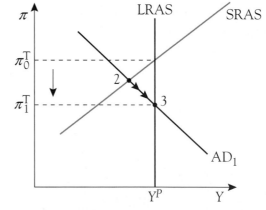

B. Adjustment

A decrease in the central bank's inflation target shifts the dynamic aggregate demand curve to the left from AD$_0$ to AD$_1$, moving the economy from point 1 to point 2.

When the economy is at point 2, there is a recessionary gap. This puts downward pressure on production costs, shifting the short-run aggregate supply curve to the right. The process continues until the economy reaches its new long-run equilibrium at point 3.

new short-run equilibrium point, 2. At point 2, inflation and current output are both lower than they were prior to the monetary policy tightening. The immediate consequence of the reduction in the central bank's inflation target is to shift the dynamic aggregate demand curve to the left, moving the economy along the short-run aggregate supply curve (SRAS), driving both current output and inflation down.

Following the policy change, potential output has not changed. This means that the fall in current output creates a recessionary gap: $Y < Y^p$. And a recessionary gap puts downward pressure on production costs, shifting the short-run aggregate supply curve to the right. Eventually, the economy moves along the new dynamic aggregate demand curve AD_1 from point 2 to the new long-run equilibrium at point 3 in Panel B of Figure 22.3. There, inflation equals the central bank's (new) target and output equals potential output.[1]

An Increase in Government Purchases   In response to the deep recession that began in December 2007, President George W. Bush signed legislation in February 2008 to cut income taxes temporarily. One year later, President Barack Obama approved a much larger package of temporary tax cuts and increases in government spending to counter the economic slump. Driven by the recession and these fiscal policy actions, the U.S. federal budget deficit surged from 1.2 percent of GDP in fiscal year 2007 (which ended September 2007) to 9.8 percent in 2009—the largest proportion since 1945. What are the macroeconomic implications of such a large expansionary move in fiscal policy?

In the last chapter we learned that increases in government purchases and cuts in taxes both represent an increase in components of aggregate expenditure that are not sensitive to the interest rate. For example, an increase in G shifts the dynamic aggregate demand curve to the right. Panel A of Figure 22.4 shows how such a change in fiscal policy shifts the dynamic aggregate demand curve from its original position AD_0 to its new position AD_1. As a result, the economy moves from the original short-run equilibrium point 1, to the new short-run equilibrium point 2. Not surprisingly, the immediate impact of this increase in government purchases is to raise both current output and inflation. But, because potential output has not changed, this can't be the long-run effect. Instead, the higher level of current output means that $Y > Y^p$, so that there is now an expansionary gap. Because current output does not equal potential output, the economy cannot stay at point 2. Instead, it must move back to its long-run equilibrium on the long-run aggregate supply curve.

Here's how the adjustment works. At point 2 there is an expansionary output gap, $Y > Y^p$. With current output above potential output, firms increase both their product prices and the wages that they pay their workers by more than they would if they were operating at normal levels. So, when there is an expansionary gap, production costs rise more quickly and inflation goes up. This shifts the short-run aggregate supply curve to the left, driving inflation even higher. As inflation rises, monetary policymakers raise the real interest rate, moving the economy *along* the dynamic aggregate demand curve AD_1 (as shown in Panel B of Figure 22.4). Eventually, as the economy travels along AD_1, output begins to fall back toward its long-run equilibrium level, potential output.

Unless something else happens, the economy settles at point 3 in Panel B of Figure 22.4, where AD_1 crosses the long-run aggregate supply curve (LRAS) and current output once again equals potential output. It is extremely important to realize

---

[1] With a lower inflation target (π^T), we also know that at the new long-run equilibrium, expected inflation (π^e) must be lower as well.

Figure 22.4   An Increase in Government Expenditure

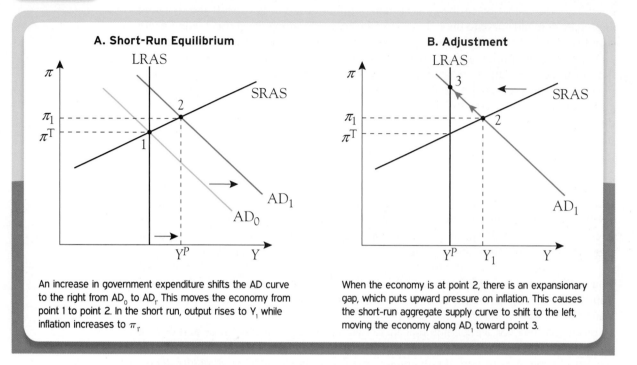

A. Short-Run Equilibrium

An increase in government expenditure shifts the AD curve to the right from AD_0 to AD_r. This moves the economy from point 1 to point 2. In the short run, output rises to Y_1 while inflation increases to π_r

B. Adjustment

When the economy is at point 2, there is an expansionary gap, which puts upward pressure on inflation. This causes the short-run aggregate supply curve to shift to the left, moving the economy along AD_r toward point 3.

that at point 3, inflation is above where it started at point 1, and that this is above the policymakers' original inflation target π^T. Unless monetary policy adjusts, when the dynamic aggregate demand curve shifts to the right, inflation will rise. Thus, Panel B shows the central bank acquiescing to a rise of its inflation target to point 3.

While central bankers could allow an increase in government purchases to drive up their inflation target, permanently increasing inflation and the monetary growth rate, it seems unlikely. So long as monetary policymakers remain committed to their original inflation target, they need to do something to get the economy back to the point where it began—point 1 in Panel A of Figure 22.4, at the intersection of the original dynamic aggregate demand curve with the long-run aggregate supply curve. This is the point where current output equals potential output, and current inflation equals the policy-maker's original inflation target.

In Chapter 21, we noted that an increase in government purchases raises the long-term real interest rate. The higher the level of government purchases, the higher the level of the real interest rate needed to equate aggregate expenditure with potential output. Realizing this, monetary policymakers react by shifting their monetary policy reaction curve to the left, increasing the real interest rate at every level of inflation. Remember, the central bank controls the real interest rate in the short run. When the monetary policy reaction curve shifts, the dynamic aggregate demand curve shifts with it. In this case, tighter monetary policy shifts the dynamic aggregate demand curve to the left, bringing the economy back to long-run equilibrium where output equals potential output and inflation equals the central bank's target.

We can summarize the path the economy takes after an increase in government purchases as follows: Output initially rises above potential output until monetary

Table 22.1	Impact of an Increase in Dynamic Aggregate Demand on Output and Inflation

Source	Shift in the monetary policy reaction curve • Increase in inflation target • Decrease in long-run real interest rate Increase in aggregate expenditure • Consumer confidence up • Business optimism up • Government purchases up • Net exports up
Result	Dynamic aggregate demand shifts right
Short-run impact	Y increases π increases

policymakers push it back down to its long-run equilibrium level. Meanwhile, inflation rises initially and then falls back down to the central bank's target level. From this we can conclude that, without a change in target inflation, *an increase in government purchases causes a temporary increase in both output and inflation.*

The same is true for any factor that shifts the dynamic aggregate demand curve to the right. Immediately following such a shift and in the absence of any monetary policy response, output and inflation both rise (see Table 22.1). If the central bank maintains its inflation target, the monetary policy reaction curve (MPRC) will shift to the left, returning inflation and output to their original long-run levels. In the absence of any monetary policy response, the expansionary output gap drives up production costs, shifting the short-run aggregate supply curve to the left, moving the economy along the new dynamic aggregate demand curve. This movement drives inflation up further as current output falls, returning to the level of potential output, but at a higher inflation rate. In effect, the central bank will have raised its inflation target.

A decline in aggregate expenditure, perhaps caused by a fall in consumer or business confidence, has the opposite impact from an increase in government expenditure. The dynamic aggregate demand curve shifts to the left, driving output down. Thus, *a decline in aggregate expenditure causes a temporary decline in both output and inflation.* With time, and in the absence of any monetary policy response, the recessionary output gap causes the short-run aggregate supply curve to shift to the right, moving the economy along the new dynamic aggregate demand curve. This movement drives inflation down further, and current output begins to rise toward potential output. In effect, the central bank has set a new, lower inflation target. If, instead, policymakers do react, inflation and output will return to their original long-run levels.

Over the years, policymakers have reacted to shifts in aggregate expenditure in different ways, with differing results. In response to increases in government spending during the escalation of the Vietnam War in the late 1960s, when defense expenditure rose from 7.4 percent to 9.4 percent of GDP over a three-year period (twice what it was at the peak of the Iraq war in 2005), the Fed simply allowed inflation to rise. Look back at Figure 22.1 and you can see that inflation rose from less than 2 percent in 1965 to more than 5 percent in 1970. What could have been a temporary increase in inflation became a permanent one, in effect increasing the Fed's inflation target to the point where the new dynamic aggregate demand curve intersected the long-run aggregate supply curve.

Large tax cuts in 2001, and the subsequent rise of defense spending associated with the war in Iraq, did not have the same inflationary impact as the similar policy in the 1960s. There are two reasons for this. First, the fiscal stimulus came at a time when the economy was weakening for other reasons. That is to say, the timing was very fortunate. Second, by 2001 the Federal Reserve had learned the important lesson that it may need to raise interest rates to counter the risk of inflation from expansionary fiscal policy. So, a combination of good luck and better understanding meant that inflation stayed low.[2]

This discussion implies that whenever we see a *permanent* increase in inflation, it must be the result of monetary policy. That is, if inflation goes up or down and remains at its new level, the only explanation is that central bankers must be allowing it to happen. They have changed their inflation target, whether or not they acknowledge the change explicitly.

Shifts in the Short-Run Aggregate Supply Curve

Changes in production costs *shift the short-run aggregate supply curve.* Using the aggregate demand/aggregate supply diagram, we can trace the effects of such an increase in the costs of production—a *negative supply shock.* The immediate effect of something like an oil price rise that increases production costs is to move the short-run aggregate supply curve to the left, reducing the amount supplied at every level of inflation. (These bad consequences—higher inflation and lower growth—are why we label such a shock as "negative.") Figure 22.5 shows the result. Short-run equilibrium—the point where the short-run aggregate supply and dynamic aggregate demand curves intersect—moves to point 2 in the figure, where output is lower and inflation is higher. This creates a condition that is sometimes referred to as *stagflation*—economic stagnation coupled with increased inflation (see Table 22.2).

What happens next? Following the initial increase in inflation, the accompanying decline in output creates a recessionary gap $(Y < Y^P)$ that exerts downward pressure on production costs and inflation. As a result, the short-run aggregate supply curve begins to shift to the right moving the economy along the dynamic aggregate demand curve, driving inflation down and output up. Inflation continues to fall and output continues to rise until the economy returns to the point where current output equals potential output and inflation equals the central bank's (unchanged) target level.

Figure 22.5   A Negative Supply Shock

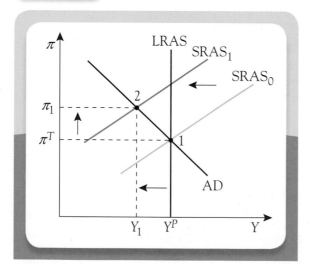

A negative supply shock shifts the short-run aggregate supply curve to the left, moving short-run equilibrium from point 1 to point 2. Inflation rises and output falls.

[2]President George W. Bush initially proposed the personal income tax cuts to fulfill a pledge from the presidential campaign of 2000. Because the pledge occurred before anyone suspected that the economy would weaken the following year, it would seem that a substantial amount of luck was involved.

Table 22.2	Impact of an Decline in Short-Run Aggregate Supply on Output and Inflation

Source	Negative supply shock • Increase in production costs • Increase in expected inflation
Result	Short-run aggregate supply curve shifts left
Short-run impact	Y falls π increases

As was the case with the increase in government purchases (when combined with an appropriate monetary policy response), a supply shock has no effect on the economy's long-run equilibrium point. Only a change in either potential output or the central bank's inflation target can accomplish that. Instead, a negative supply shock moves output and inflation temporarily away from potential output and the inflation target. Over time, the recessionary output gap drives down production costs, shifting the short-run aggregate supply curve to the right. As it does, the economy moves along the dynamic aggregate demand curve until output and inflation finally return to the initial equilibrium point 1 in Figure 22.5. Thus, a supply shock causes inflation to rise temporarily and then fall, at the same time that current output falls temporarily and then rises. But, as always, in the long run the economy returns to the point where output equals potential output and inflation equals the central bank's target.

Using the Aggregate Demand–Aggregate Supply Framework

We are now ready to use the macroeconomic framework to address a series of interesting questions. We examine the following (in increasing order of complexity):

1. How do policymakers achieve their stabilization objectives?
2. What accounts for what has been called the "Great Moderation," the time period from the mid-1980s until 2007 (and possibly beyond) when U.S. growth and inflation were less volatile than they were historically?
3. What happens when potential output changes?
4. What are the implications of globalization for monetary policy?
5. Can policymakers distinguish a recessionary gap from a fall in potential output?
6. Can policymakers stabilize output and inflation simultaneously?

How Do Policymakers Achieve Their Stabilization Objectives?

STABILITY

The aggregate demand–aggregate supply framework is useful in understanding how monetary and fiscal policymakers seek to stabilize output and inflation using what is called *stabilization policy*. In thinking about the way monetary policy can be used to reduce economic fluctuations, recall that movements in output and inflation can be

TOOLS OF THE TRADE
Defining a Recession: The NBER Reference Cycle

From reading the business press, you might conclude that a recession is any episode in which real gross domestic product (GDP) declines for two consecutive quarters. While that casual definition may work in most instances, it has some drawbacks. One is that because GDP is computed and published quarterly, a definition that is based on GDP cannot indicate the specific months in which a recession started and ended. To determine that information, we need a definition that is based on measures like production, employment, sales, and income—all of which are available monthly and provide valuable information about the health of the economy.

Ultimately, the arbiter for declaring "official" recessions in the United States is the National Bureau of Economic Research (NBER). The NBER, founded in 1920, is a research organization devoted to studying how the economy works. Early work at the NBER led to the construction of much of the economic data we use today. Two of the NBER's pioneering researchers, Wesley Mitchell and Arthur Burns, dated the beginning and end of all the recessions in the United States from the Civil War through World War II.* In their book *Measuring Business Cycles* (1946), they called this dating a "reference cycle."

The NBER's definition of a recession is as follows:

"A recession is a significant decline in activity spread across the economy, lasting more than a few months, normally visible in real GDP, real income, employment, industrial production, and wholesale–retail sales. A recession begins just after the economy reaches a peak of activity and ends as the economy reaches its trough. Between trough and peak, the economy is in an expansion."

This definition has three important implications. First, a recession is a decline in activity, not just a dip in the growth rate. Second, the exact length of the economic contraction is ambiguous. A severe decline in economic activity that lasted

Table 22.3 NBER Business-Cycle Reference Dates, 1946–2010

Peak	Trough	Length of Recession in Months Peak to Trough	Length of Expansion in Months Previous Trough to Peak
November 1948	October 1949	11	37
July 1953	May 1954	10	45
August 1957	April 1958	8	39
April 1960	February 1961	10	24
December 1969	November 1970	11	106
November 1973	March 1975	16	36
January 1980	July 1980	6	58
July 1981	November 1982	16	12
July 1990	March 1991	8	92
March 2001	November 2001	8	120
December 2007	June 2009	19	73

SOURCE: *www.nber.org*. The FRED code is USREC (which represents a recession month as a 1, and an expansion month as a 0).

less than two quarters could still be considered a recession according to this definition. And third, because key economic indicators often change direction at different times, there is an element of judgment in dating the peaks and troughs of business cycles. As a result, the NBER's Business-Cycle Dating Committee takes its time in declaring the beginning and end of a recession. Delays of six months to a year are common.

The term *business cycle* is somewhat misleading when used to refer to fluctuations in economic activity. The word *cycle* calls up images of recurring waves that rise and fall in a periodic pattern. Economic fluctuations aren't like that. Both the length of recessions and the time between them are irregular. As Burns and Mitchell wrote in their book, "A cycle consists of expansions . . . followed by contractions and revivals which merge into the expansion phase of the next cycle; this sequence of changes is recurrent but not periodic . . ."

Table 22.3 displays the results of the NBER's analyses of the business cycle since the end of World War II. Figure 22.6 plots the bureau's business-cycle reference dates against the growth in real GDP over the period. The figure clearly shows the tendency for real growth to be low—usually below zero—during recessions. Recessions differ along several dimensions, including the so-called 3 D's: depth, duration, and diffusion across business sectors, geographic regions, or markets. The table illustrates the remarkable fact that recessions are much shorter than expansions in the U.S. economy. Most people credit this fact to a combination of successful policy and the economy's capacity for self-correction.

For more information on the procedures used to date business cycles, go to the NBER's website at www.nber.org.

*Burns later became Chairman of the Federal Reserve Board, serving from 1970 to 1978.

Figure 22.6   Growth in Real GDP over the Business Cycle

The figure shows the four-quarter percentage change in real GDP from the Bureau of Economic Analysis, and the shaded bars represent recessions as determined by the NBER. (FRED codes: GDPCI for GDP and USREC for recession dates.)

caused both by shifts in the dynamic aggregate demand curve and in the short-run aggregate supply curve. But when shifting their reaction curve, central bankers shift the dynamic aggregate demand curve. They cannot shift the short-run aggregate supply curve. What this means is that monetary policymakers can neutralize demand shocks, but they cannot offset supply shocks. That is to say, they can counter aggregate expenditure changes that shift the dynamic aggregate demand curve, but they cannot eliminate the effects of changes in production costs that shift the short-run aggregate supply curve. Nevertheless, as we will see, positive supply shocks that raise output and lower inflation provide policymakers with an opportunity. If they wish, following a positive supply shock, central bankers can guide the economy to a new, lower inflation target without inducing a recessionary output gap.

As for fiscal policy, our macroeconomic framework allows us to study the impact of changes in government taxes and expenditures as well. As we have seen in the previous section, these shift the dynamic aggregate demand curve. This means that fiscal policy can work to stabilize the economy. While this is true in principle, as we will discuss, the active use of fiscal policy faces great challenges. The conclusion is that stabilization policy is usually best left to central bankers.

Monetary Policy   To see how monetary policy can stabilize the economy following a shift in the dynamic aggregate demand curve, consider what happens when consumers and businesses suddenly become more pessimistic about the future. Such a change reduces consumption and investment, shifting the dynamic aggregate demand curve to the left. In the absence of any change in monetary policy, this drop in consumer and business confidence would cause current output to fall below potential output ($Y < Y^p$), creating a recessionary output gap. Panel A of Figure 22.7 shows the dynamic aggregate demand curve shifting to the left (from AD_0 to AD_1) and the economy moving to a new short-run equilibrium point where current output falls short of potential output (at point 2, where AD_1 crosses SRAS).

Realizing that consumer and business confidence have fallen, driving down the consumption and investment components of aggregate expenditure, policymakers will conclude that the long-run real interest rate has gone down. Assuming that their inflation target remains the same, the drop in aggregate expenditure prompts them to shift their monetary policy reaction curve to the right, reducing the level of the real interest rate at every level of inflation. This is the shift from $MPRC_0$ to $MPRC_1$ shown in Panel B of Figure 22.7. Recall that when the monetary policy reaction curve shifts, the dynamic aggregate demand curve shifts in the same direction. This means that the policymakers' action shifts the dynamic aggregate demand curve back to its initial position as shown in Panel A of Figure 22.7. So, in the absence of a policy response, following the decline in aggregate expenditure, output would fall. But instead, the policy response means that the dynamic aggregate demand curve remains at its initial position, so output remains equal to potential output and inflation remains steady at the central bank's target.[3]

While central bankers can offset aggregate demand shocks in theory, in practice it is extremely difficult to keep inflation and output from fluctuating when aggregate expenditure changes. There are two reasons for this. First, it takes time to recognize what has happened. Fluctuations in the quantity of aggregate output demanded arising from things like changes in consumer or business confidence can be very difficult to

---

[3]Stabilizing aggregate demand shocks in this way also ensures that expected inflation remains equal to the central bank's inflation target.

Figure 22.7   Stabilizing a Shift in Dynamic Aggregate Demand

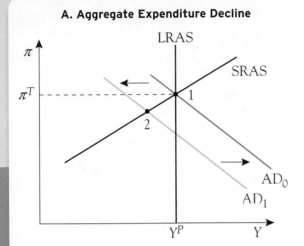

A. Aggregate Expenditure Decline

B. Monetary Policy Response

Following a drop in consumer or business confidence the dynamic aggregate demand shifts to the left from AD_0 to AD_1, moving the economy from point 1 to point 2. Realizing this, monetary policymakers shift their MPRC to the right, shifting the dynamic aggregate demand curve back to where it started and returning the economy to point 1.

Following a drop in consumer confidence, the long-run real interest rate falls from r_0^* to r_1^*. Policymakers respond by shifting their reaction curve from $MPRC_0$ to $MPRC_1$, shifting the AD curve back to its original position, AD_0.

recognize as they are occurring. Second, changes in interest rates—the tool monetary policymakers use to offset aggregate demand shocks—do not have an immediate impact on the economy. Instead, when interest rates rise or fall, it takes time for output and inflation to respond. A good rule of thumb is that interest rate changes start to influence output in 6 to 9 months and inflation after 18 months, but our knowledge is not all that precise. In short, while in theory we can neutralize aggregate demand shocks, in reality they create short-run fluctuations in output and inflation.

Discretionary Fiscal Policy   There are two very different types of fiscal policy. One is automatic, operating without any further actions on the part of government officials, and the other is discretionary, relying on fiscal policymakers' decisions. Automatic stabilizers, including unemployment insurance and the proportional nature of the tax system, are in the first group. These adjust mechanically to stimulate an economy that is slowing down and put the brakes on an economy that is speeding up. They operate countercyclically to eliminate fluctuations in aggregate expenditure and keep the economy stable. But there are times when automatic stabilizers are not enough; and that's when politicians face the temptation to enact temporary expenditure increases and tax reductions—what is called *discretionary* fiscal policy. Discretionary fiscal policy changes aggregate expenditure shifting the dynamic aggregate demand curve.

As noted earlier in the chapter, a rise in government purchases or a decrease in taxes drives up aggregate expenditure, shifting the dynamic aggregate demand curve to the right. Thus, fiscal policy can act just like monetary policy to offset shifts in the dynamic aggregate demand curve and stabilize inflation and output. In fact, it has been

YOUR FINANCIAL WORLD

Stabilizing Your Consumption

Stability improves welfare. That's the fifth core principle of money and banking, and it is what guides the work of central bankers. A less volatile overall economy makes it easier for each of us to stabilize our own financial lives. As individuals, we care about paying our bills and stabilizing our standard of living. As the deep recession that ended in 2009 highlighted, individual incomes still rise and fall in ways that can make it difficult for a person to stabilize his or her consumption.

In earlier chapters we learned how to use the financial system to help reduce the risks we face in our everyday lives. We discussed life insurance, automobile insurance, and disability insurance, as well as the need for an emergency reserve in case of disaster. But even so, there are still times things don't quite work out, and for these times there is credit.

Individuals use credit in two ways. First, they borrow to purchase expensive things like cars and houses without

having to save the full amount and pay cash. Absent a mortgage, very few young people could afford to purchase a home. Second, the ability to borrow means that an unemployed person who has run through his or her savings will still have something to eat and a place to sleep. Borrowing allows individuals to keep their purchases of consumer goods and services—their consumption—smooth, despite fluctuations in income.

While credit can help us to smooth our consumption, it is only a stop-gap measure that we should use for as short a time as possible. Loans do need to be repaid, and borrowing for current consumption is something you should repay as quickly as possible. The financial crisis of 2007–2009, including the record volume of mortgage and other personal credit defaults, demonstrates how risky credit can be.

used exactly this way on a number of occasions. As we discussed earlier, for example, the 2008–2009 federal tax cuts and spending increases boosted aggregate expenditure, helping to moderate the recession.

At least in principle, then, discretionary fiscal policy offers a clear alternative to monetary policy. On closer examination, however, it has at least two shortcomings. First, discretionary fiscal policy works slowly, and second, it is almost impossible to implement effectively. Most recessions are short, lasting a year or less. Until the financial crisis of 2007–2009, the longest post–World War II recession in the United States spanned 16 months (see Table 22.3 on page 626). Furthermore, because economic data only become available several months after they are collected, the economy is often halfway through a recession before there is a consensus that a downturn has actually started. Under most circumstances, Congress can't pass new legislation in less than several months. And fiscal policies do not have an immediate impact on the economy. Even after a tax cut has been passed, individual consumption and corporate investment tend to remain sluggish. Odds are that, by the time the spending does start, the typical recession will be over. This means that discretionary fiscal policy is likely to have its biggest impact when it is no longer needed.

The problems with discretionary fiscal policy don't end there because economists don't write economic stimulus packages; politicians do. And economics clearly collides with politics where fiscal stimulus is concerned. From an economic point of view, the best policies are the ones that influence a few key people to change their behavior, without rewarding people for doing what they would have done anyway. Examples of economically efficient fiscal policies include temporary investment incentives and tax reductions targeted toward those who are prone to spend an extra dollar of income, either because they cannot borrow or are less well off. Politicians have a different set of incentives. They want to be reelected, so they look for programs that reward the largest number of people possible, to ensure their reelection. This means that discretionary fiscal policy is likely to be based more on political calculation than on economic logic. Though we can't hold public officials' opportunism against them, we need to recognize its existence. Because politicians want to remain popular with their constituencies, economic slowdowns—when some voters are suffering and the rest are worried—play to their worst instincts. In short, discretionary fiscal policy is a poor stabilization tool. While an economically sensible stimulus package can be designed, such legislation does not often become law.

Under most circumstances, then, stabilization policy is probably best left to the central bankers. They have both the ability to act quickly and the independence to put the economy before politics. Fiscal policy's automatic stabilizers are clearly important parts of the economic landscape, but discretionary government expenditure and tax changes only have a role after monetary policy has run its course—that is, when conditions are so bad that using every available tool makes sense.

From this perspective, the deep recession of 2007–2009 provided the strongest case in many decades for discretionary fiscal stimulus in the United States and other countries. The downturn was the longest since the 1930s, providing fiscal policymakers time to respond. It also was the deepest and most widespread, while the subsequent recovery was the weakest, posing an unusual risk of deflation in several economies. As we saw in Chapter 11 (Applying the Concept: Deflation, Net Worth, and Information Costs), deflation can be highly destabilizing. Finally, and perhaps most importantly, central banks had lowered their policy interest rates close to zero, limiting their scope for further conventional policy stimulus. Consequently, it should come as no surprise that many industrial countries undertook large-scale discretionary fiscal stimulus in this episode. The 2008 and 2009 U.S. tax cuts and spending increases and the massive 2009 budget deficit that we previously discussed fit in this category.

Positive Supply Shocks and the Opportunity They Create   Next, let's consider what happens when production costs fall, creating a positive supply shock. This shifts the short-run aggregate supply curve to the right, from $SRAS_0$ to $SRAS_1$, as shown in Figure 22.8. The immediate impact of this is to drive inflation down and output up. We know that at this new short-run equilibrium (point 2 in Figure 22.8), output exceeds potential output ($Y_1 > Y^P$), so there is an expansionary output gap. With production above its normal level, costs rise, shifting the short-run aggregate supply curve to the left until the economy returns to the original long-run equilibrium at point 1, where output equals potential output and inflation equals the central bank's target.

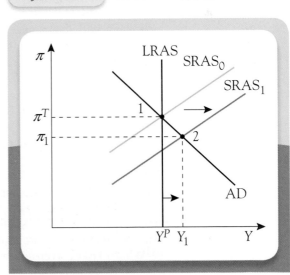

Figure 22.8   A Positive Supply Shock

While policymakers could simply allow the economy to take its natural course, with output rising to Y_1 (at point 2) and then falling back to Y^P (at point 1), there is an alternative. A positive supply shock creates an opportunity for policymakers to guide the economy to a new, lower inflation target without inducing a recession. The standard mechanism for permanently reducing inflation is to raise the real interest rate at every level of inflation. Central bankers do this by shifting the monetary policy reaction curve to the left, which then shifts the dynamic aggregate demand curve to the left as well. This drives output below potential output, creating a

A positive supply shock shifts the short-run aggregate supply curve to the right, moving short-run equilibrium from point 1 to point 2. Inflation falls and output rises.

Figure 22.9 Lowering the Inflation Target

A. Monetary Policy

A decline in the inflation target from π_0^T to π_1^T shifts the monetary policy reaction curve to the left from MPRC$_0$ to MPRC$_r$.

B. Output and Inflation

Following a positive supply shock, policymakers can reduce their inflation target by shifting the dynamic aggregate demand curve from AD$_0$ to AD$_r$. Instead of going to point 2, the economy moves to point 3.

recessionary output gap, which puts downward pressure on inflation. (Look back at Figures 22.2 and 22.3 on page 620.) As a result, inflation falls to the new, lower target level. This is the mechanism that links monetary policy to economic downturns and inflation declines as shown in Figure 22.1 on page 618.

Here's how central bankers can exploit the opportunity created by a positive supply shock. Because potential output is unchanged following the fall in production costs, the long-run real interest rate hasn't changed either. This means that a lower inflation target requires a higher real interest rate at every level of current inflation (that's a leftward shift in the monetary policy reaction curve as shown in Panel A of Figure 22.9). So, policymakers wishing to lower their inflation target in response to a positive supply shock will raise interest rates shifting the dynamic aggregate demand curve to the left until it reaches the point where the new short-run aggregate supply curve (SRAS$_1$) intersects the long-run aggregate supply curve (LRAS). If policymakers choose this course, as shown in Panel B of Figure 22.9, output will not rise above potential.[4]

What Accounts for the Great Moderation?

By any measure, the 1990s were remarkable. Information technology came of age, bringing the benefits of computerization into our lives through everything from cars to dishwashers. Because of the Internet, incredible libraries are now available to us in our homes and offices. That includes FRED, the Federal Reserve Bank of St. Louis' online database that is the source for many figures and end-of-chapter problems in this book.

What may be even more extraordinary is that the 1990s brought unprecedented economic stability—the "Great Moderation" in the volatility of real growth. In the

---

[4]Again, recall that at the long-run equilibrium, inflation must equal expected inflation. So, if following a positive supply shock, policymakers choose to reduce their inflation target, inflation expectations must fall as well.

decade from 1991 to 2001, the U.S. economy did not suffer a single decline in output. During these 10 years of solid growth, inflation fell steadily, from more than 5 percent in 1991 to less than 2 percent by the end of the decade. Comparing the 1980s with the 1990s, researchers find that the volatility of inflation and growth dropped by more than half.[5] And if you look back at Figures 22.1 and 22.6 you can see that both inflation and growth were substantially less variable between 1982 and 2007 than in the prior period.

This prosperity and stability was shared across the industrialized world. Looking at a broad cross-section of the 63 countries for which we have reliable data, we can see that inflation dropped dramatically between the 1980s and the 1990s. Median inflation fell from an annual rate of 7 percent in the period 1985–1994 to 3 percent in the period 1995–1999. The decline in average inflation was even sharper, from 83 percent to just 8½ percent. Inflation rose in only 10 of the 63 countries.

"*Please stand by for a series of tones. The first indicates the official end of the recession, the second indicates prosperity, and the third the return of the recession.*"

SOURCE: *1991 © Robert Mankoff/The New Yorker Collection/www.cartoonbank.com.*

There are three possible explanations for this phenomenal worldwide economic performance. One is that everyone was extremely lucky, and the 1990s were simply an exceptionally calm period. The second is that economies became more flexible in absorbing external economic disturbances. And the third is that monetary policymakers figured out how to do their job more effectively. Which one of these is most likely?

It's difficult to argue that the stability of the 1990s was mere good fortune. Surely, the decade was not a calm one for the financial markets. Major economic crises occurred in Latin America and Asia, and Long-Term Capital Management nearly collapsed, paralyzing the bond markets. Raw materials prices fluctuated wildly. The price of oil spiked above $35 a barrel late in 1990, then plunged below $12 a barrel at the end of 1998 before beginning a steady rise to $30 a barrel by the beginning of 2000.

If the size and frequency of external disturbances did not diminish, something must be cushioning the blows. Advances in information technology have increased manufacturers' flexibility in responding to changes in demand. The result has been a dramatic decline in inventories at every stage of the production process. In durable manufacturing, the new supply method called "just-in-time" cut the ratio of inventories to sales in half in the period from the early 1990s to the beginning of 2002. Today, an automobile assembly plant keeps only a few hours worth of parts on hand; the rest are in transit to the factory, timed to arrive at just the right moment. Similarly, a supermarket or superstore like Walmart or Target holds only one to two days' supply of most products. The result is a great deal of flexibility in responding to changes in demand and sales.

While improvements in inventory management are part of the explanation for the long period of prosperity in the 1990s, they aren't the whole story. Every description of the recession that began in March 2001 points to the impact of an inventory adjustment. The most persistent problems emerged in the high-technology sector—semiconductors,

[5]This decline in volatility, along with the rebound of volatility during the financial crisis of 2007–2009, is documented by Todd Clark in "Is the Great Moderation Over? An Empirical Analysis," *Federal Reserve Bank of Kansas City Economic Review,* 4th Quarter, 2009.

computers, and communications equipment. Inventories also plunged sharply in the recession that began in 2007. So while the U.S. economy has become more flexible, it hasn't changed enough to prevent fluctuations caused by unexpected events.

Financial innovation probably played some role in reducing economic volatility after the early 1980s—that is, until the financial crisis of 2007–2009. Innovations in mortgages and other forms of personal credit made it easier for households and businesses to borrow. As a result, they were better able to smooth their spending during periods of temporary income fluctuations (see Your Financial World: Stabilizing Your Consumption on page 630).[6] As we now know, however, rising levels of risky debt eventually led to record defaults on mortgages and other forms of personal credit during the financial crisis. And the loss of credit availability during the crisis helps explain the depth and duration of the recession that began in December 2007.

That leaves monetary policy as the only remaining explanation for the improved economic performance. Economists now have a much better understanding of how to implement monetary policy than they did as recently as 25 years ago. To succeed in keeping inflation low and stable while at the same time keeping real growth high and stable, central bankers must focus on raising real interest rates when inflation goes up and lowering them when inflation goes down. One example is the Taylor rule (see Chapter 18) that raises the policy interest rate by 1.5 percentage points for every 1 percent rise of inflation. By focusing on long-run inflation, policymakers have succeeded in bringing the inflation rate down and keeping it low.

Yet, while keeping inflation low and stable is *necessary* for reducing economic volatility, the deep recession that began in December 2007 shows that it is not *sufficient*. Low inflation did not prevent the financial crisis of 2007–2009, and history shows that such crises often are associated with deep recessions (the Great Depression being the most extreme example). It remains to be seen whether the crisis marks the end of the Great Moderation or whether it was simply a huge exception in an otherwise stable period. If households and businesses are no longer able or willing to use credit to smooth their spending over time, it may not be possible for Fed policymakers to sustain the low economic volatility of the 1985–2007 period, even if they remain effective in keeping inflation low.

What Happens When Potential Output Changes?*

In order to concentrate on the impact of shifts in dynamic aggregate demand and short-run supply, we have neglected movements in potential output. But potential output does change, and the consequences are important both for short-run movements in output and inflation and for long-run equilibrium.

To understand what happens when potential output changes, let's trace out the consequences of a rise in Y^P brought on by an increase in productivity. First, recall that the long-run aggregate supply curve (LRAS) is vertical at the point where current output equals potential output, so when potential output rises this curve shifts to the right. But that's not all. An increase in productivity reduces costs of production, so it is a positive supply shock as well. This shifts the short-run aggregate supply curve (SRAS) to the right. But how far does SRAS shift? To see, recall from Chapter 21 that the short-run aggregate supply curve intersects the long-run aggregate supply curve at

---

[6]See, for example, Karen E. Dynan, Douglas W. Elmendorf, and Daniel Sichel, "Can Financial Innovation Help Explain the Reduced Volatility of Economic Activity?" Federal Reserve Board, FEDs Working Paper No. 2005-54, August 2006.

Figure 22.10   An Increase in Potential Output

A. Aggregate Supply

An increase in potential output shifts both the short- and long-run aggregate supply curves to the right. Before and after the shift, the short-run aggregate supply curve crosses the long-run aggregate supply curve at the point where $\pi = \pi^e$.

B. Short-Run Equilibrium

In the short run, the economy moves from point 1 to point 2.

the point where current inflation equals expected inflation (π^e)—that's where production costs are not changing. Immediately following the increase in potential output, expected inflation does not change, so the SRAS shifts the same horizontal distance as the LRAS does. From this we can conclude that an *increase in potential output shifts both the long- and short-run aggregate supply curves to the right* as shown in Panel A of Figure 22.10.

The short-run impact of an increase in potential output is straightforward. Assuming the central bank recognizes the change in potential output only with a lag, we can trace out the short-term impact of a change. First, because policymakers are slow to recognize the increase in Y^p, MPRC does not shift immediately: It still passes through the old level of potential output (Y_0^p). As a result, the AD curve also is unchanged until the MPRC shifts.[7] In the short run, output and inflation are determined by the intersection of the short-run aggregate supply (SRAS) curve and the dynamic aggregate demand (AD) curve. Because the central bank recognizes the increase in potential output only with a lag, the MPRC and AD curves are initially unchanged. Panel B of Figure 22.10 shows what happens. The economy starts at point 1 where the original short-run aggregate supply curve (SRAS$_0$) intersects the dynamic aggregate demand curve (AD). At this original equilibrium point, output equals the initial level of potential (Y_0^p) and inflation equals the central bank's target (π^T), which equals expected inflation (π^e). When potential output increases to Y_1^p, the short-run and long-run aggregate supply curves shift to SRAS$_1$ and LRAS$_1$. In the short run, the new equilibrium is at point 2

[7]This "lagged recognition" assumption allows us to trace out graphically the impact over time of the policy response to the change in potential output. It does not alter the direction of the eventual shifts in MPRC and AD, but it makes them easier to explain. In the remainder of the chapter, we use this simplifying assumption to help illustrate the impact of changes in potential output.

where SRAS_1 intersects AD. We can see from the figure, initially output is higher and inflation is lower.

What happens next? After a lag, the central bank realizes potential output has risen to Y_1^P. The path that the economy follows to the new level of potential output depends on what monetary policymakers do. If policymakers are happy with their inflation target—it could already be low enough—then they will work to move the economy to the point on the new long-run aggregate supply curve (LRAS_1) consistent with that initial target. But because the higher level of potential output comes along with a lower long-run real interest rate (look back at Figure 21.5), returning inflation to its initial (higher) level means shifting the monetary policy reaction curve to the right. This change in monetary policy shifts the dynamic aggregate demand curve to the right. The policy adjustment will drive output and inflation up until they reach their new long-run equilibrium levels where output equals Y_1^P and inflation equals its original target π^T (which equals expected inflation). This case is shown in Panel A of Figure 22.11.

But as we saw earlier, a positive supply shock creates an opportunity for policymakers to reduce their inflation target. Without a conscious shift in monetary policy, at point 2 in Panel B of Figure 22.11 there is a recessionary gap—current output is less than potential output—so there is downward pressure on production costs that will start to shift the short-run aggregate supply curve to the right, driving inflation down even further. We know that the SRAS continues to shift until output equals potential output. Looking at Panel B of Figure 22.11, we see that this process naturally brings us to point 4, where output equals the new higher level of potential output Y_1^P and inflation is below the original target level π_0^T. With inflation now lower, monetary policymakers have the opportunity to lower their inflation target to the level labeled π_1^T. They can do

Figure 22.11 Policy Options Following an Increase in Potential Output

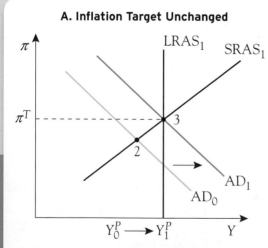

A. Inflation Target Unchanged

If, following an increase in potential output, policymakers' inflation target is unchanged, they must shift the dynamic aggregate demand curve to the right, bringing output and inflation to point 3.

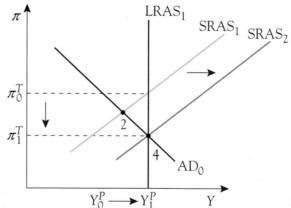

B. Inflation Target Reduced

If, following an increase in potential output, policymakers wish to lower their inflation target, they will allow the economy to move to point 4.

this by ensuring that the AD curve doesn't shift, which means leaving their monetary policy reaction curve where it started.[8]

Federal Reserve policymakers took advantage of an increase in potential output to drive the U.S. inflation rate down during the 1990s. Looking back at Figure 22.1, we see that inflation fell gradually from 5 percent at the end of the 1990–91 recession to 1½ percent in 1998. This drop in inflation occurred during an economic boom. Over the last half of the 1990s, economic growth averaged 1½ percentage points above the rate for the preceding 20 years. That is, U.S. productivity (and potential output) grew more rapidly from 1996 to 1999 than it did from 1975 to 1995. In effect, the economy's long-run aggregate supply curve shifted to the right, and when it did the Federal Reserve took the opportunity to reduce their implicit inflation target from near 5 percent to below 2 percent. At the time, this was referred to as *opportunistic disinflation.* **Disinflation** is the term used to describe declines in inflation; the word *opportunistic* indicates an opportunity to reduce the target inflation level.[9] During the 1990s, Fed policymakers exploited the opportunity afforded them by positive supply shocks to permanently lower inflation.

Throughout our discussion of business cycle fluctuations, we have assigned a major role to shifts in the quantity of aggregate output demanded. This has led us to focus on how shifts in the dynamic aggregate demand curve change its point of intersection with an upward-sloping short-run aggregate supply curve and lead to movements in output and inflation.

An alternative explanation for business cycle fluctuations focuses on shifts in potential output. This view, known as **real-business-cycle theory**, starts with the assumption that prices and wages are flexible, so that inflation adjusts rapidly. That is to say, the short-run aggregate supply curve shifts rapidly in response to deviations of current output from potential output. This assumption renders the short-run aggregate supply curve irrelevant. Equilibrium output and inflation are determined by the point of intersection of the dynamic aggregate demand curve and the long-run aggregate supply curve, where current output equals potential output. Thus, any shift in the dynamic aggregate demand curve, regardless of its source, influences inflation but not output. Neither changes in aggregate expenditure nor changes in monetary policy have any impact on the level of output. Because inflation ultimately depends on the level of money growth, it is determined by monetary policy.

To explain recessions and booms, real-business-cycle theorists look to fluctuations in potential output. They focus on changes in productivity and their impact on GDP. Productivity is a measure of output at a fixed level of inputs. An increase in productivity means an increase in GDP for a given quantity of capital and number of workers. Shifts in productivity can be either temporary or permanent. Examples of such shifts would include changes in the availability of raw materials, changes in government regulation of labor and product markets, and inventions or management innovations that improve the economy's productive capacity. Any of these events will shift potential output. According to real-business-cycle theory, they are the only sources of fluctuations in output.[10]

---

[8]Recall that a decline in the central bank's inflation target shifts the monetary policy reaction curve to the left. But in this case, that will exactly offset the rightward shift resulting from the decline in the long-run real interest rate caused by the rise in potential output, leaving the position of the monetary policy reaction curve unchanged.

[9]*Disinflation* is very different from *deflation,* which is the opposite of inflation. *Deflation* means that aggregate prices are consistently *falling; disinflation* means falling inflation.

[10]For a more detailed discussion of real business cycle theory, see Charles Plosser, "Understanding Real Business Cycles," *Journal of Economic Perspectives,* 3, no. 3 (Summer 1989), pp. 51–77.

What Are the Implications of Globalization for Monetary Policy?*

If you look at the label of the shirt or blouse you are wearing, chances are it was imported from India, the Philippines, Vietnam, or somewhere else in Asia. The reason is that it is less costly to manufacture clothing in places where labor is inexpensive. The result is that clothes are cheaper in the United States: trade lowers prices. But does it also lower inflation?

The simplest way to understand the macroeconomic impact of international trade is to think about it as a source of productivity enhancing technological progress. Shifting production of clothes from domestic factories to foreign ones is the same as U.S. producers finding a new, cheaper technology for producing the same things at home. And improvements in technology increase potential output. That is something we understand.

Recall from the previous section that an increase in potential output shifts both the long-run and short-run aggregate supply curves to the right. This has the immediate impact of shifting the economy along its dynamic aggregate demand curve to a point where output is higher and inflation is lower. All of this is shown in Figure 22.10 on page 635. In the long run, we know that output goes to the new, higher level of potential output. But, as we discussed in the previous section, the long-run level of inflation depends on how monetary policymakers respond. Our conclusion is that globalization and trade do reduce inflation in the short run and just like any positive supply shock they provide an opportunity to reduce inflation permanently.

Is globalization likely to have a sizeable impact on inflation even in the short run? Economists estimate that nearly 14 percent of personal consumption expenditures reflect the direct cost of imported final goods (excluding the contribution from U.S. services) combined with the imported content of U.S.-made goods and services.[11] If import prices are stable and then start dropping at 5 percent per year, which is what happened in 2001, this would reduce the rate of inflation by about 0.7 percentage points per year. With inflation averaging 2 percent per year, that is a moderate but temporary impact. In the long run, $MV = PY$, so (assuming velocity is constant) the inflation rate equals the money growth rate less the growth rate of potential output ($\pi = \%\Delta M - \%\Delta Y^P$). We just can't get away from the fact that domestic inflation is tied to domestic monetary policy.

Can Policymakers Distinguish a Recessionary Gap from a Fall in Potential Output?*

Throughout the 1960s, GDP growth averaged more than 4 percent per year. But in the early 1970s U.S. GDP growth began to fall. Then, beginning in late 1973, the economy contracted by more than 3 percent over five quarters. That's a deep recession. While all of this was happening, inflation rose dramatically, from 3 percent in 1972 to 12 percent in 1974. (Take a look at Figures 22.1 and 22.6 to see the pattern.) When something like this happens, when inflation rises at the same time that output falls, the appropriate policy response depends on whether potential output has fallen. If Y^P is lower, then the long-run real interest rate r^* is higher, and policymakers need to shift their monetary policy reaction curve to the left setting higher policy-controlled interest rates at every

[11]See Galina Hale and Bart Hobijn, "The U.S. Content of 'Made in China,'" FRBSF *Economic Letter,* August 8, 2011.

level of inflation. This ensures that inflation and expected inflation remain at the central bank's target. By contrast, if the simultaneous fall in output and increase in inflation is the result of a supply shock that shifted only the short-run aggregate supply curve to the left, then policymakers should focus on moving the economy back to the same point where they started. Distinguishing a recessionary gap from a fall in potential output is critical.

The proximate cause of the 1970s episode was a tripling of the price of oil, from $3.56 to $11.16 a barrel. That increase in production costs translates into a negative supply shock. It's no wonder that inflation rose and output fell. But the right reaction depends crucially on what happened to potential output at the time. In retrospect we know that as oil prices rose, the productive capacity of the economy fell, and potential output went down with it. At the time, policymakers didn't realize that. Instead, they thought lower output reflected a recessionary gap. This led to an inappropriate response that drove inflation up, where it stayed for longer than it should have.

We can use the dynamic aggregate demand and aggregate supply apparatus to understand the importance of recognizing changes in potential output and see the consequences of the mistake made by American policymakers in the 1970s. To do this, let's look at two cases. In the first one, a supply shock drives inflation up and output down, but potential output is unchanged so there is a recessionary gap. This is the case we studied in Figure 22.5 on page 624. Here's what happens. Following any supply shock, policymakers have a choice. They can either leave their inflation target as it is, and simply react by adjusting interest rates along an unchanged monetary policy reaction curve, or they can change their inflation target. As we saw earlier in this chapter, a positive supply shock presents a pleasant choice—allow output to rise and then fall, or lower inflation permanently. By contrast, a negative supply shock presents two less appealing alternatives. Policymakers can either allow output to remain below potential output longer so that inflation falls, or raise the inflation target. Central bankers rarely believe their inflation target is too low, so they almost always respond to a negative supply shock by allowing a recessionary gap to develop in order to return inflation to its original target. Operationally, this means raising interest rates along an unchanged monetary policy reaction curve at the same time that output is already falling.

If, however, the negative supply shock is associated with a decline in potential output, matters are quite different. This is the case shown in Panel A of Figure 22.12. Initially, before the central bank discovers that potential output has declined, the economy moves to point 1, where inflation is higher and output is lower. So far, things are identical to the case where potential output is unchanged. But what happens next is not. At point 1, there is now an *expansionary gap*. Even though output has fallen, potential output has fallen by more and output remains above the new, lower, Y_1^P. Without any change in the monetary policy reaction curve, the economy starts moving to point 2. That is, inflation continues to rise and output continues to fall.

The challenge for policymakers is to figure out that potential output has fallen and that this has increased the long-run real interest rate. Under these circumstances, keeping inflation at its target requires a leftward shift in the monetary policy reaction curve, as shown in Panel B of Figure 22.12. Policymakers need to raise the real interest rate by even more than they would in the case of a recessionary gap.

By the end of the 1970s, inflation had been over 6 percent for five straight years. In 1979, the Fed realized their estimate of potential output was too high and that they would need to raise interest rates to keep inflation from rising. Over the next few years, tighter monetary policy eventually had the desired impact so that by 1985 inflation was back down below 5 percent.

Figure 22.12 A Drop in Potential Output

A. Output and Inflation

B. Monetary Policy

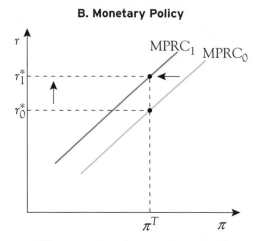

A drop in potential output shifts the long- and short-run aggregate supply curves to the left. Initially, before the central bank recognizes the decline in potential output, the economy moves to point 1 where there is an expansionary gap. At point 1, there is upward pressure on production costs, so in the absence of a change in monetary policy, the SRAS will start to shift to the left, driving inflation up further.

Because lower potential output means a higher long-run real interest rate, monetary policymakers wishing to maintain the inflation target must respond to the fall in Y^P by shifting their reaction curve from $MPRC_0$ to $MPRC_1$. This shifts the dynamic aggregate demand curve from AD_0 to AD_1 and ensures that the economy moves to point 3 rather than 2.

Can Policymakers Stabilize Output and Inflation Simultaneously?*

Our analysis of business cycles has been based on the idea that short-run fluctuations in output and inflation are caused by either demand shifts or supply shifts. And, as we have seen repeatedly, dynamic aggregate demand curve shifts move inflation and output in the same direction; while short-run aggregate supply shifts move inflation and output in opposite directions. Early in this chapter, we discussed how, by shifting their monetary policy reaction curve, policymakers offset demand shocks. (This is shown in Figure 22.7 on page 629.)

Unfortunately, supply shocks are a different story. There is no way to neutralize them. For instance, take the case of a negative supply shock like an oil price increase that raises production costs. This has the immediate effect of driving output down and inflation up (see Figure 22.5 on page 624). Now consider the tools that are available to policymakers. By shifting the monetary policy reaction curve, central bankers can shift the dynamic aggregate demand curve. Is there any way to use this tool to bring the economy back to its original long-run equilibrium point quickly and painlessly? The answer is no. Monetary policymakers can shift the dynamic aggregate demand curve, but they are powerless to move the short-run aggregate supply curve. And there is no

YOUR FINANCIAL WORLD

The Problem with Measuring GDP

In order to set their policy-controlled interest rate as accurately as possible, central bankers need to know the size of the output gap. This requires measuring the level (and growth rate) of both current and potential gross domestic product (GDP) accurately. Unfortunately, this is made difficult by the fact that estimates of GDP for a specific quarter are revised for many years after the fact; and the revisions tend to be large (see Your Financial World: Economic History is Constantly Changing in Chapter 18). One of the reasons for these revisions is that government statisticians have to reconcile two methods of measuring GDP that are supposed to give the same answer. Here's the problem.

Looking at the economy as a whole, we know that expenditures must equal income. Eventually, every dollar that is earned as income must be spent on something. This means that one way to calculate GDP is to divide it into the various categories for which the product is used—consumption, investment, government purchases, and net exports—and then measure expenditure on each of these.

But because one person's expenditure is another's income, total expenditure equals total income. This means that we can also measure GDP by dividing income into categories and computing what economists call gross domestic income (GDI). Income categories would include wages, rental income, interest income, and dividend income. And because everyone is supposed to pay taxes on their income, measuring it should be straightforward.

The fact that income and expenditure are supposed to be equal doesn't mean that they are, however. Looking at tables constructed by the Department of Commerce's Bureau of Economic Analysis, we find a line labeled "Statistical discrepancy." The amount on this line, which represents GDP calculated from expenditures data minus GDI computed from the income data, is quite large. From 1990 to 2012, the statistical discrepancy between the two measures was between −1.6 and +2.2 percent of nominal GDP. Table 22.4 shows some examples for recent years. Because nominal GDP usually grows at a rate of about 5 percent a year—that figure includes inflation plus real growth—changes in the statistical discrepancy can have a big impact on official estimates of overall economic performance.

The practical implication of the statistical discrepancy is that it makes us unsure about the current level of real output. Uncertainty about something so crucial adds to the difficulty of making monetary policy.

Table 22.4	Gross Domestic Product and Income (US$ billions except as noted)			
	1993	1997	2006	2012
Nominal gross domestic product	6,878.7	8,608.5	13,857.9	16,244.6
Nominal gross domestic income	6,726.4	8,596.2	14,073.2	16,261.6
Statistical discrepancy	152.3	12.3	−215.3	−17.0
Statistical discrepancy (percent of GDP)	2.2%	0.1%	−1.6%	−0.1%
Nominal GDP growth from previous year	5.2%	6.3%	5.8%	4.6%

SOURCE: *Bureau of Economic Analysis, Department of Commerce, National Income and Product Accounts Tables 1.1.5 and 1.10.*

shift in the dynamic aggregate demand curve that can quickly move the economy back to its long-run equilibrium point, where current output equals potential output and current inflation equals the central bank's target.

But that's not the end of the story. Central bankers can choose how aggressively they react to deviations of inflation from their target caused by supply shocks. They can do this by picking the slope of their monetary policy reaction curve, which

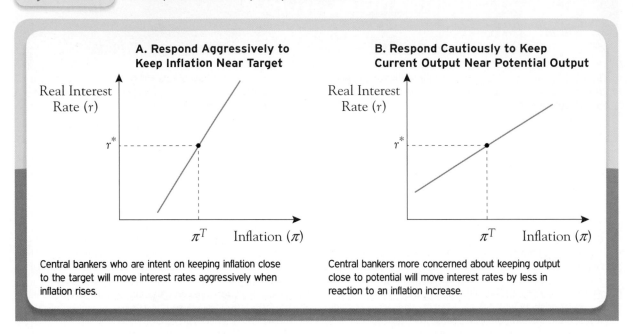

Figure 22.13   The Slope of the Monetary Policy Reaction Curve

A. Respond Aggressively to Keep Inflation Near Target

Real Interest Rate (r)

r^*

π^T Inflation (π)

Central bankers who are intent on keeping inflation close to the target will move interest rates aggressively when inflation rises.

B. Respond Cautiously to Keep Current Output Near Potential Output

Real Interest Rate (r)

r^*

π^T Inflation (π)

Central bankers more concerned about keeping output close to potential will move interest rates by less in reaction to an inflation increase.

then determines the slope of the dynamic aggregate demand curve. The more aggressive policymakers are in keeping current inflation close to target, the steeper their monetary policy reaction curve and the flatter the dynamic aggregate demand curve. And by controlling the slope of the dynamic aggregate demand curve policymakers choose the extent to which supply shocks translate into changes in output or changes in inflation. This means that the slope of the monetary policy reaction curve—how aggressively to react to deviations of inflation from their target—is really a choice about the relative volatility of inflation and output. The more central bankers stabilize inflation, the more volatile output will be, and vice versa. There is a tradeoff.

To see why policymakers face a tradeoff between inflation and output volatility, we can compare two policymakers, one with a relatively steep monetary policy reaction curve (as in Panel A of Figure 22.13), and one with a relatively flat monetary policy reaction curve (as in Panel B of Figure 22.13). The first policymaker cares more about keeping inflation close to its target level than the second one does.

Turning to the dynamic aggregate demand curve, Panel A of Figure 22.14 shows the relatively flat AD curve implied by the steep monetary policy reaction curve in which small deviations in inflation from the target level elicit large changes in the real interest rate. A flat dynamic aggregate demand curve, corresponding to the steep monetary policy reaction curve in Panel A of Figure 22.13, means that a supply shock creates large changes in current output. So an increase in production costs—a negative supply shock—drives output down sharply, opening up a large recessionary output gap. We can assume that the larger the output gap, the greater the pressure on inflation. A large recessionary gap should force inflation down faster than a small recessionary gap. In fact, policymakers are counting on that mechanism when they

Figure 22.14   The Policymaker's Choice

A. Respond Aggressively to Keep Inflation Near Target

Central bankers intent on keeping inflation close to the target will move interest rates aggressively when inflation rises and create bigger fluctuations in output.

B. Respond Cautiously to Keep Current Output Near Potential Output

Policymakers more concerned about keeping output close to potential will move interest rates by less in reaction to an inflation change, resulting in bigger fluctuations in inflation.

choose to follow this path. By reacting aggressively to supply shocks, policymakers force current inflation back to target quickly. The cost of following this path, however, is that it causes output to fall substantially. Stable inflation means volatile output.

Panel B of Figure 22.14 shows what happens when policymakers are less concerned about keeping inflation close to target in the short run, and more concerned about keeping current output near potential output. When policymakers worry more about short-run fluctuations in output than about temporary movements in inflation, they will choose a relatively flat monetary policy reaction curve in which movements in the real interest rate are small, even when inflation strays far from its target level. The result is a steep dynamic aggregate demand curve like the one drawn in the right panel of the figure. Notice what happens in this case following a supply shock. Once more, inflation rises, creating a recessionary output gap. But the output gap is small, so the downward pressure on inflation is relatively weak. As a result, inflation adjusts slowly, remaining high for a longer period than it would have if policymakers had reacted more aggressively. Stable output means volatile inflation.

When choosing how aggressively to respond to supply shocks, central bankers are deciding how to conduct stabilization policy. Do they want to ensure that inflation remains near target, or that output remains close to potential? When faced with a supply shock, policymakers cannot stabilize both output and inflation. And by stabilizing one, the other becomes more volatile. Monetary policymakers face an inflation-output volatility tradeoff.

IN THE NEWS
Potential Output: Risking Permanent Damage

The Economist

By G.I.

March 20, 2012

Two spectacular failures stain 20th century macroeconomic policy in America: the Great Depression and the Great Inflation. They share an important ingredient: in both, policy makers could not properly gauge the economy's potential output, i.e. its productive capacity.

. . . many in the 1930s blamed the Depression on supply-side causes: Austrians considered it payback for years of overinvestment, while others cited the inevitable pain of reallocating resources between dying and growing industries. . . .

In the 1960s and 1970s policymakers made the opposite error. . . . they persistently overestimated the economy's potential output and thought the natural rate of unemployment was lower than it really was. As a result they ran persistently overstimulative policy, producing high and entrenched inflation. . . .

These two episodes are important for addressing the dilemma that confronts macro policymakers today. Last week I pointed to three puzzles in the economic data—sluggish GDP growth, relatively rapid declines in unemployment, and stubborn core inflation—that all made sense if the level and growth of potential output are lower than we thought.

This argument has been made before, in particular by hawks at the Fed. . . . The failures of the 1930s and 1970s demonstrate that the stakes are high. If potential really is lower, it has disturbing implications for policymakers and investors: it means the structural component of today's budget deficits are larger than believed and the Fed has less room to keep interest rates at zero. A less friendly Fed will be bad for bonds, and lower potential means lower equilibrium profits and profit growth and thus less equity upside. But if we wrongly assume potential is lower than it really is, we risk accepting years of enormous and unnecessary welfare losses.

Several commentators have pushed back against the notion that these puzzles are a sign that potential has fallen. My colleague says sluggish growth is no surprise, but the obvious result of too-tight monetary policy. But if monetary policy were systematically too tight, inflation should have fallen much further than it has; instead, both actual and (survey-based) expected inflation have been surprisingly stable . . .

Potential has long been known to have a strong cyclical component: a recession will normally discourage businesses and workers from investing in physical and human capital. . . . But when growth picks up, investment recovers and along with it the capital stock. . . .

Where the supply and demand side explanations for the economy's depressed state converge is when demand remains deficient for so long that its cyclical impact on potential becomes structural. [A Fed staff report reckons] the single biggest contributor to the recent decline in potential growth is the fall in the labor force participation rate since 2007. Perhaps this has been largely demographic, in which case the loss of potential was inevitable and permanent. But it may reflect hysteresis: the tendency of someone who has been unemployed a long time to become unemployable and eventually quit the labor force altogether. . . .

I hope not. I recently looked back at the Congressional Budget Office's estimates of potential around the 1991 and 2001 recessions. Both were followed by jobless recoveries. Three years after the 1991 recession the CBO had revised down its estimates of potential by around 3%; but by 2000, it had more than revised back the difference. After the 2001 recession, the CBO actually revised potential up by 2% as productivity surged. This shows that, at least for those episodes, recession need not leave a permanent scar on the economy's productive capacity.

SOURCE: The Economist Newspaper Limited, London (March 20, 2012).

LESSONS OF THE ARTICLE

Potential output is determined by an economy's resources (labor and capital) and its technology. Central bankers neither observe it directly nor control it. But they aim to keep output close to its potential, so when potential output changes in unpredicted ways, it can lead to large policy errors. Uncertainty about potential output rose sharply when the post-crisis U.S. recovery remained weak for several years but inflation failed to decline sharply (see Figure 21.13). Eventually, FOMC members judged that some of the slowdown was permanent and began to scale back their projections for long-run economic growth.

Terms

demand shock, 619

disinflation, 637

real-business-cycle theory, 637

supply shock, 619

Using FRED: Codes for Data in This Chapter

Data Series	FRED Data Code
U.S. consumer price index	CPIAUCSL
Real GDP	GDPC1
NBER recession dates (0 = expansion, 1 = recession)	USREC
Ratio of manufacturers' inventories to shipments	AMTMIS
Total credit market debt owed by households	HSTCMDODNS
Nominal GDP	GDP
Real potential GDP	GDPPOT
Gross domestic income	GDI
Chile consumer price index	CHLCPIALLMINMEI
Israel consumer price index	ISRCPIALLMINMEI
U.S. federal deficit (percent of GDP)	FYFSGDA188S
Spot oil price: West Texas Intermediate	OILPRICE

Chapter Lessons

1. Short-run fluctuations in output and inflation arise from shifts in either the dynamic aggregate demand curve or the short-run aggregate supply curve.
   a. A decrease in the central bank's inflation target shifts the dynamic aggregate demand curve to the left.
      i. In the short run, this decreases both output and inflation.
      ii. It creates a recessionary output gap, exerting additional downward pressure on inflation.
      iii. In the long run, inflation falls to the new target as output returns to potential output.
   b. A government expenditure increase shifts the dynamic aggregate demand curve to the right.
      i. In the short run, this increases both output and inflation.
      ii. It creates an expansionary output gap, exerting additional upward pressure on inflation.
      iii. To keep inflation from rising, monetary policymakers shift their reaction curve to the left, raising the real interest rate at every level of inflation.
      iv. Unless the central bank's target inflation changes, the economy eventually returns to its original long-run equilibrium point.
   c. A negative supply shock shifts the short-run aggregate supply curve to the left.
      i. In the short run, this decreases output and increases inflation.
      ii. It creates a recessionary output gap that places downward pressure on inflation.

      iii. Unless the central bank's target inflation changes, the economy returns to its original long-run equilibrium point.

2. Applying the dynamic aggregate demand–aggregate supply framework we see that
    a. Stabilization policy is the use of monetary and fiscal policy tools to stabilize output and inflation.
        i. Monetary policy can be used to shift the dynamic aggregate demand curve to offset changes in the quantity of aggregate output demanded. In practice, lack of information and lags in the impact of policy changes make this very difficult.
        ii. Fiscal policy can shift the dynamic aggregate demand curve as well, but it is difficult to do in a timely and effective way.
        iii. A positive supply shock that lowers production costs and shifts the short-run aggregate supply curve to the right, creates an opportunity for policymakers to permanently lower inflation.
    b. Better monetary policy is the most likely explanation for the increased stability of the U.S. economy from the mid-1980s until 2007.
    c. An increase in potential output shifts both the short- and long-run aggregate supply curves to the right, driving output up and inflation down, as well as creating an expansionary output gap.
    d. Globalization has the same impact as an increase in potential output. In the long run it raises output but inflation only changes if the central bank adjusts its target.
    e. It is difficult (but crucial) for monetary policymakers to distinguish a decline in the quantity of aggregate output demanded from a fall in potential output.
    f. When confronted with a shift in the short-run aggregate supply curve, central bankers face a tradeoff between output and inflation volatility.

Conceptual and Analytical Problems

1. Define the term *stabilization policy* and describe how it can be used to reduce the volatility of economic growth and inflation. Do stabilization policies improve everyone's welfare? *(LO2)*

2. Explain why stabilization policies are usually pursued using monetary rather than fiscal policy. *(LO3)*

3. Explain why fiscal policy played a greater role than usual in the response to the 2007–2009 recession. *(LO3)*

4. Explain why monetary policymakers cannot restore the original long-run equilibrium of the economy if, in the short run, the economy has moved to a point where inflation is above target inflation and output is below potential output. *(LO2)*

5. Explain why the rise in oil prices in 2008 created a particularly difficult situation for Federal Reserve policymakers. *(LO2)*

6. Will changes in technology affect the rate at which the short-run aggregate supply curve shifts in response to an output gap? Why or why not? Provide some specific examples of how technology will change the rate of adjustment. *(LO1)*

7. After examining Figure 22.6, explain the potential link between innovations in financial markets and output volatility since the 1980s. You should consider both the "Great Moderation" and the recession of 2007–2009 in your answer. *(LO1)*

8.* According to real business cycle theory, can monetary policy affect equilibrium output in either the short run or the long run? *(LO1)*

9. The economy has been sluggish, so in an effort to increase output in the short run, government officials have decided to cut taxes. They are considering two possible temporary tax cuts of equal size in terms of lost revenue. The first would reduce the taxes on people with incomes *above* the median for one year. The second would cut taxes on people with incomes *below* the median for one year. Which change would shift the aggregate demand curve further to the right? Why? *(LO2)*

10. Starting with the economy in long-run equilibrium, use the aggregate demand–aggregate supply framework to illustrate what would happen to inflation and output in the short run if there were a rise in consumer confidence in the economy. Assuming the central bank takes no action to offset this rise in confidence, what would happen to inflation and output in the long run? What policy adjustment is the central bank undertaking? *(LO2)*

11. Consider again the rise in consumer confidence described in Problem 10. What would happen to inflation and output in the long run if the central bank remained committed to its original inflation target and responded with an immediate policy tightening? Compare the outcome to that in Problem 10 using the aggregate demand–aggregate supply framework. *(LO2)*

12. Suppose that consumer confidence unexpectedly rises six months before the central bank detects the change. Compared to your answer to Problem 11, what happens to inflation and output in that interval? How does monetary policy return the economy to long-run equilibrium at the initial inflation target? *(LO2)*

13. How would a shock that reduces production costs in the economy (a positive supply shock) affect equilibrium output and inflation in both the short run and the long run? Illustrate your answer using the aggregate demand–aggregate supply framework. You should assume that the shock does not affect the potential output of the economy. *(LO2)*

14. Suppose, instead of waiting for the economy described in Problem 13 to return to long-run equilibrium, the central bank opted to use the positive supply shock as an opportunity to move to a lower inflation target. Illustrate the impact of this change in the inflation target using an aggregate demand–aggregate supply diagram. Compare this with a graph of a situation where the central bank lowers its inflation target in the absence of a positive supply shock. *(LO3)*

15.* Suppose a natural disaster reduces the productive capacity of the economy. How would the equilibrium long-run real interest rate be affected? Assuming the central bank maintains its existing inflation target, illustrate the impact on the monetary policy reaction function and on equilibrium inflation and output both in the short run and in the long run. *(LO1)*

16.* Monetary policymakers observe an increase in output in the economy and believe it is a result of an increase in potential output. If they were correct, what would the appropriate policy response be to maintain the existing inflation target? If they were incorrect and the increase in output resulted simply from a positive supply shock, what would the long-run impact be of their policy response? *(LO3)*

*Indicates more difficult problems

17.* Consider a previously closed economy that opens up to international trade. Use the aggregate demand–aggregate supply framework to illustrate a situation where this would lead to lower inflation in this economy in the long run. *(LO2)*

18.* In the face of global oil price shocks, what could monetary policymakers do to minimize the resulting recessionary gaps? What would be the tradeoff of such a policy? Illustrate your answer using the aggregate demand–aggregate supply framework. *(LO3)*

19.* How could you use the aggregate demand–aggregate supply (AD/AS) framework to explain the impact of the financial crisis of 2007–2009 on inflation and output in the economy? *(LO1)*

20.* Changes in oil prices shift the short-run aggregate supply curve (SRAS). Consider how *volatility* in oil prices may influence the economy's short-run equilibrium, which occurs at the intersection of the dynamic aggregate demand (AD) curve and the SRAS curve. *(LO3)*

    a. Suppose the monetary policy reaction curve is relatively steep. What does this imply about the slope of the AD curve? What does it imply about the variability of output and inflation? Explain.

    b. Suppose the monetary policy reaction curve is relatively flat. What does this imply about the slope of the AD curve? What does it imply about the variability of output and inflation? Explain.

Data Exploration

Scan here for quick access to the resources for these problems. Need a barcode reader? Try ScanLife, available in your app store.

For general information on using Federal Reserve Economic Data (FRED) online, visit www.mhhe.com/moneyandbanking4e.com and click on Student Edition, then FRED resources.

1. Display as a bar chart the periods since 1854 that are designated as U.S. recessions by the National Bureau of Economic Research (FRED code: USREC). Why has the frequency of recessions declined over time? Could improvements in monetary policy have played a role? Improvements in fiscal policy? Can you think of any other causes? *(LO1)*

2. In the past, policymakers occasionally became aware of a recession only well after it began. Can they do better? Plot the probability of a recession from a statistical model (FRED code: RECPROUSM156N). To what extent could this model help improve monetary or fiscal policy or both? *(LO3)*

3. Compare the frequency and timing of recessions in key European economies since 1960. Make separate bar charts for Germany (FRED code: DEURECM), Italy (FRED code: ITARECM), and Spain (FRED code: ESPRECM). Do their business cycles appear sufficiently well aligned to make them operate easily in a single currency area with a common monetary policy? *(LO3)*

4. To keep inflation low and steady, central banks would like to keep output reasonably close to its potential level, but can they anticipate changes in potential GDP? Plot since 1960 the percent change from a year ago of the Congressional Budget Office's estimate of potential GDP (FRED code: GDPPOT). Suppose that the FOMC assumed that the growth rate of potential GDP remained permanently at its 1960s average. What would you expect to happen to inflation? Why? *(LO1)*

Chapter 23

Modern Monetary Policy and the Challenges Facing Central Bankers

Learning Objectives

Understand . . .

LO1   The monetary policy transmission mechanism

LO2   Policy challenges, including:

    Asset price bubbles

    The zero interest rate bound

    The evolution of the financial system

As we saw earlier, the financial crisis of 2007–2009 and the recession it triggered were by far the most widespread and costly since the Great Depression. And, although the financial disruptions began in the United States, they spread to almost all corners of the global economy. Indeed, the peak-to-trough decline of GDP was greater in many countries than in the United States (see Panel A of Figure 23.1). The subsequent crisis in the euro area triggered even larger economic losses in Greece, Ireland, Italy, Portugal, and Spain.

The response of monetary policymakers was likewise unprecedented. Interbank lending rates—the target of central bank policy—plunged toward zero in the United States, Japan, and much of Europe (see Panel B of Figure 23.1). And many central banks deployed unconventional monetary policy tools—including forward guidance, quantitative easing, and targeted asset purchases—to compensate for the collapse of intermediation and the fragility of financial markets. Although monetary policies failed to prevent the global crisis, they nevertheless helped to contain it. Around mid-2009, the worldwide plunge in GDP bottomed out, and most economies began growing again. Some, like China's, had regained strength even earlier, partly because of an extraordinary fiscal expansion. Similarly, the threat of an imminent breakup of the euro area receded in the latter half of 2012 following the ECB's extraordinary interventions (see Chapter 16).

Yet, many observers worried that the aftermath of these financial crises would dim the economic outlook for years to come. Some of the concerns stemmed from the deterioration of fiscal conditions—a number of countries racked up record fiscal deficits and surges in government debt in reaction to the crisis. But the damage to the global financial system posed at least as big and pervasive a problem.

Figure 23.1 Economic Activity and Policy Rates in the Financial Crisis of 2007–2009 and Thereafter

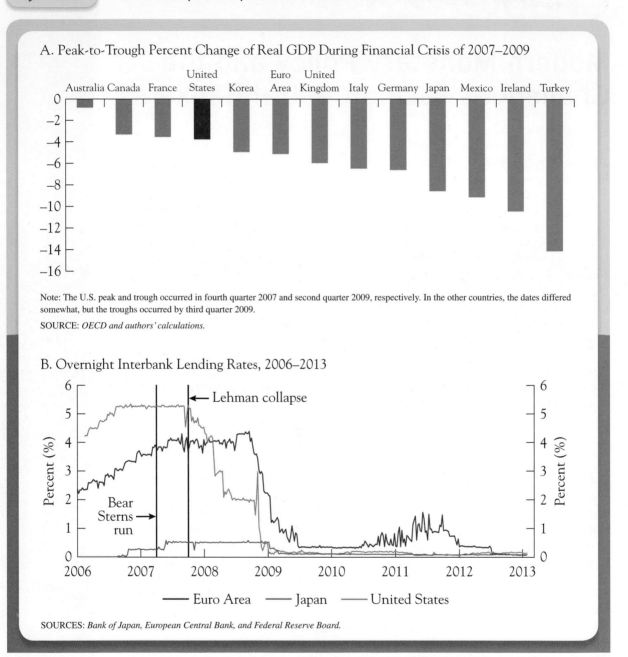

A. Peak-to-Trough Percent Change of Real GDP During Financial Crisis of 2007–2009

Note: The U.S. peak and trough occurred in fourth quarter 2007 and second quarter 2009, respectively. In the other countries, the dates differed somewhat, but the troughs occurred by third quarter 2009.

SOURCE: *OECD and authors' calculations.*

B. Overnight Interbank Lending Rates, 2006–2013

SOURCES: *Bank of Japan, European Central Bank, and Federal Reserve Board.*

Deep, long recessions are frequently followed by unusually sharp and long-lived economic rebounds. But the experience of previous financial crises—especially the Great Depression and the 1990s breakdown in Japan—led policymakers to worry that the rebound from the crisis of 2007–2009 would be weaker than the norm. They expected that anxious banks would make credit expensive and difficult to obtain, that investors would be cautious about buying securitized assets, and that U.S. households would prefer to save more and borrow less. Policymakers also made clear that a period of increased regulation and prolonged fiscal repair lay ahead, which added to the hesitancy among intermediaries.

The aggregate demand and supply framework described in Chapter 21 helps us understand many sources of inflation and fluctuations in the business cycle as well as how stabilization policy works. But it does not explain why policymakers in many countries doubted that conventional monetary policy would be sufficient to counter the crisis of 2007–2009. And it does not explain the weakness of the recoveries following financial crises. To understand these concerns, we must return to the question of *how* monetary policy affects the economy.

Chapter 17 described how central banks influence the economy by controlling their balance sheet. Chapter 18 described how, in normal times, monetary policymakers use their balance sheet to control the interest rate banks charge each other for overnight loans. We learned that the real interest rate is the nominal interest rate minus the rate of expected inflation. Because the expected rate of inflation generally changes only slowly in low- and moderate-inflation economies, changing the target for the policy interest rate also changes the short-run real interest rate. In Chapter 21, we saw that the components of aggregate expenditure are sensitive to the real interest rate, so by changing the real interest rate, policymakers can influence real economic activity. Yet, the 2007–2009 experience (as well as that of Japan in the 1990s) suggests that conventional interest-rate policy does not always work. To see why not, we need to look at all the ways that monetary policy actions affect real economic activity—that is, all the channels through which monetary policy is transmitted.

Examining the transmission mechanism of monetary policy is the first of this chapter's two main topics. The second topic is the question of why, in the aftermath of financial crises like the 2007–2009 episode, monetary policy and the challenges facing central bankers are especially difficult.

The Monetary Policy Transmission Mechanism

Any time the central bank alters the size of its balance sheet, the effects ripple through the economy, changing nearly everyone's behavior. Households adjust their spending on houses and cars. Companies rethink their decisions about how much and how fast to grow. Exchange rates change, bond and stock prices move, and banks adjust their balance sheets. In fact, we would be challenged to find a financial or economic decision that is unaffected. To fully appreciate how conventional monetary policy works, then, we need to examine the various ways in which changes in the policy-controlled interest influence the quantity of aggregate output demanded in the economy as a whole. These are referred to collectively as the channels of the **monetary policy transmission mechanism**. We will begin with the traditional **interest-rate** and **exchange-rate channels**. Next we will study the role of banks and finally the importance of stock price movements.

The Traditional Channels:
Interest Rates and Exchange Rates

Central banks, such as the Federal Reserve, the European Central Bank, and the Bank of Japan, target a very short-term (usually overnight) interest rate. In the Fed's case, for example, a change of conventional policy is a change in the target federal funds rate.

And as we saw in Chapter 21, a change in the monetary policymakers' target interest rate represents a change in the real interest rate, which has a direct effect on total spending. The lower the real interest rate, the higher investment, consumption, and net exports will be.

Let's review this process. As the real interest rate falls, financing becomes less expensive, so firms become more likely to undertake investment projects and families more likely to purchase new cars. Changes in the real interest rate also affect the exchange rate. When the real interest rate falls, investor demand for U.S. assets falls with it, lowering the demand for and increasing the supply of dollars, reducing the dollar's value (see Chapter 19, Figure 19.2). That is, an easing of monetary policy—by which we mean a decrease in the target nominal interest rate, which lowers the real interest rate—leads to a depreciation of the dollar. A less valuable dollar, in turn, drives up the cost of imported goods and services, reducing imports from abroad. At the same time, however, the lower value of the dollar makes U.S. goods and services cheaper to foreigners, so they will buy more of them. Together, lower imports and higher exports mean higher net exports, or an increase in total spending.

While these traditional channels of monetary policy transmission make sense theoretically, they present a practical problem. Though changes in monetary policy do influence firms' decisions to purchase new equipment and build new buildings, the interest-rate channel is not very powerful. That is, data suggest that the investment component of total spending isn't very sensitive to interest rates, which should not be a surprise to us. At the end of our discussion of financial intermediation in Chapter 11, we saw that information problems often make external financing too difficult and costly for firms to obtain, either directly in the financial markets or indirectly through institutions. As a result, the vast majority of investments are financed by businesses themselves, through their own funds. While a small change in the interest rate does change the cost of external financing, it doesn't have much of an effect on investment decisions.

The impact of short-term interest rates on household decisions is also rather modest. The problem is that people's decisions to purchase cars or houses depend on longer-term interest rates rather than the policymakers' short-run target rate. So household consumption decisions will change only to the extent that changing the target interest rate affects long-term interest rates. And the overall effect isn't that large.

As for the effect of monetary policy on the exchange rate, once again, theory and practice differ. In the real world, the policy-controlled interest rate is just one of many factors that shift the demand and supply for the dollar on foreign exchange markets. The rather long list, described in Chapter 10, includes a change in the riskiness of domestic investment relative to foreign investment; a change in the preference of U.S. consumers for foreign-produced goods and services; and a change in foreigners' income and wealth. The influence of these other factors may overwhelm the impact of monetary policy on the exchange rate and net exports.

Thus, after careful analysis, we must conclude that the traditional channels of monetary policy transmission aren't very powerful. Yet evidence shows that monetary policy *is* effective. When policy-controlled interest rates go up, the quantity of aggregate output demanded does go down. The dynamic aggregate demand curve slopes down. Something else must be amplifying the impact of monetary policy changes on real economic activity. Otherwise, no one would care about the central bank's periodic policy statements. To figure out what that link might be, we turn now to a discussion of two alternative transmission channels: the stock and real estate markets, and the behavior of banks.

TOOLS OF THE TRADE
Correlation Does Not Imply Causality

Suppose we notice that the higher the crime rate in a neighborhood, the more often police are present. Should we infer that the police are causing crime? Surely not. Nor should we conclude from the fact that hospitals are filled with doctors that doctors make people ill. A fundamental principle of sound logical reasoning is that correlation does not imply causality. The fact that two events happened together does not indicate a causal link.

In the physical sciences, where researchers can conduct controlled experiments, establishing a causal link is not a serious challenge. We know from scientific trials that antibiotic drugs really do eliminate infections. It's not just chance that the people who take them feel better. But in economics, establishing a causal relationship is much more difficult. How can we be sure that monetary policy affects real economic activity? Our theories tell us that when policymakers raise the nominal interest rate, the real interest rate goes up, depressing aggregate expenditure and lowering real economic activity. But do we have any hard-and-fast evidence of this relationship?

The answer is that we do have some evidence that higher interest rates are associated with lower levels of real growth. Look back at Figure 21.17 (page 609), and you'll see the pattern: when interest rates rise, growth falls. But does that mean that increases in the interest rate cause recessions? What if, simultaneously, an increase in oil prices depresses real growth, causing policymakers to raise the interest rate

in order to head off rising inflation? That is, what if some third factor drives up the interest rate, forcing growth down at the same time? In that case, the interest rate becomes another implication of the fundamental cause of recession, an increase in oil prices.

How can we eliminate this problem and determine the extent to which monetary policy actually causes economic fluctuations? The answer is that we need to look for clear evidence that particular monetary policy actions are unrelated to this sort of third factor. Some years ago, Christina Romer and David Romer of the University of California at Berkeley read through the records of the Federal Reserve's interest-rate decisions since 1946. They identified a series of dates on which FOMC members stated unambiguously that they were raising interest rates to combat inflation. Each of these episodes was followed by a recession. Romer and Romer argued that, because the intention in each of these instances was to fight inflation, the FOMC's actions were not the result of the level of GDP at the time. Instead, it was monetary policy actions that were the fundamental cause.* With hard work and ingenuity, economists are ultimately able to distinguish causality from correlation.

*See Christina D. Romer and David H. Romer, "Does Monetary Policy Matter? A New Test in the Spirit of Friedman and Schwartz," in O. J. Blanchard and S. Fischer, eds., *NBER Macroeconomic Annual* (Cambridge, MA: MIT Press, 1989), pp. 121–170.

Bank-Lending and Balance-Sheet Channels

Four times a year the Federal Reserve conducts an opinion survey on bank-lending practices. Addressed to the senior loan officers who oversee lending policies at the 60 or so largest banks in the country, the survey contains questions about both the demand for and the supply of loans. On the demand side, the questions have to do with the quantity and quality of loan applications. On the supply side, they have to do with the relative difficulty of getting a loan, as well as the rates borrowers must pay. This survey provides important information to monetary policymakers. Without it, they would not be able to tell whether a change in the quantity of new loans granted resulted from a shift in supply or a shift in demand. Was a drop in the quantity of new loans the result of fewer applications or a tightening of credit standards? Did interest-rate spreads climb because the quality of borrowers declined or because banks became more risk averse? Policymakers at the Fed care about the answers to these questions because if banks stop making loans, some businesses can't borrow to finance their investment projects, and economic growth slows.

The fact is that banks are essential to the operation of a modern economy. They direct resources from savers to investors and solve problems caused by information asymmetries. Financial intermediaries specialize in screening borrowers to ensure they are creditworthy and in monitoring loan recipients to guarantee that they use borrowed funds as they said they would. But banks are not only the hub of the financial system; they are also the conduit through which monetary policy is transmitted to the economy. When policymakers change the size of the central bank's balance sheet, their action has an immediate impact on commercial bank balance sheets because it affects the level of reserves they hold. To understand monetary policy changes completely, then, we need to look carefully at how they affect the banking system. That means we need to examine the impact of policy changes on banks and bank lending.

Banks and Bank Lending For the vast majority of individuals and firms, the cost of issuing either stocks or bonds is prohibitive. These borrowers do not have access to capital market financing; instead, they must go to banks, which step in to reduce the information costs small borrowers face. A small business that is denied a bank loan has nowhere else to turn, so the project it wishes to undertake goes unfunded. When banks stop lending, then, a large class of borrowers simply can't obtain financing. Thus, bank lending is an important channel through which monetary policy affects the economy.[1] By altering the supply of funds to the banking system, policymakers can affect banks' ability and willingness to lend. This policy mechanism is referred to as the **bank-lending channel** of monetary policy transmission.

To see how the banking-lending channel works, think about the immediate consequences of an open market purchase (see Figure 17.2 on page 458). Recall that an open market operation involves an exchange of securities for reserves between the banking system and the central bank. When the central bank purchases securities from commercial banks, it pays for them with reserves. So after an open market purchase, banks have fewer securities and more reserves that usually bear lower interest. Unless bank managers do something, their revenues will fall. The natural reaction of the banks is to lend the new funds. These new loans work their way through the banking system through the process of multiple deposit creation, increasing the supply of loans throughout the economy. (Take a look back at the section on the deposit expansion multiplier in Chapter 17, pages 462 to 467.) In short, an open market purchase has a direct impact on the supply of loans, increasing their availability to those who depend on banks for financing.

Monetary policymakers are not the only people who can influence bank-lending practices. Financial regulators can, too. Changes in financial regulations, such as an increase or decrease in the amount of capital banks are required to hold when they make certain types of loans, will have an impact on the amount of bank lending as well. In 1980, for example, President Jimmy Carter authorized the Federal Reserve to impose a series of credit controls in an attempt to reduce bank lending and, with it, the level of output and inflation. A mild recession followed. In the early 1990s, the economy failed to make a strong recovery from the recession after the first Gulf War. Careful examination of the historical record suggests that the disappointing economic performance was a direct consequence of a slowdown in bank lending. At the time, bank balance sheets were very weak, having been eroded by large loan losses during the banking crises of

---

[1]Studies of how and why monetary policy is transmitted through bank lending and balance sheets include Ben Bernanke and Mark Gertler, "Inside the Black Box: The Credit Channel of Monetary Policy Transmission," *Journal of Economic Perspectives* 9 (Fall 1995), pp. 27–45. The role of the bank-lending channel during the global financial crisis is the focus of Leonardo Gambacorta and David Marqués-Ibañez, "The Bank Lending Channel: Lessons from the Crisis," *Economic Policy* 26 (April 2011), pp. 135–182.

| Figure 23.2 | Survey Measures of Changing Credit Conditions by Firm Size |

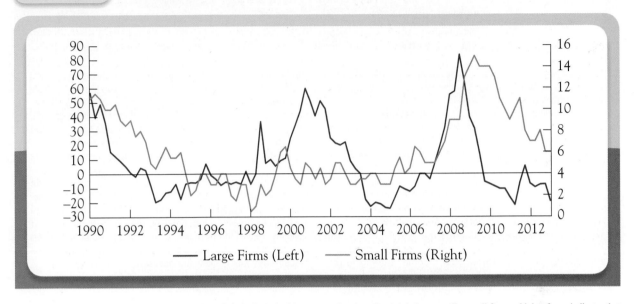

Note: For large firms, credit conditions are tightening when the figure is above zero and easing when it is below zero. For small firms, a higher figure indicates that the net share of firms concerned about credit availability is greater than before.

SOURCES: *For large businesses, Federal Reserve Board's survey of senior loan officers at selected banks; for small businesses, survey of firms by the National Federation of Independent Business. Permission to use data from the National Federation of Independent Business. (FRED Code: DRTSCILM.)*

the 1980s. When an increase in capital requirements was added to the banks' already heavy burden, the result was a reduction in lending.

Figure 23.2 plots two surveys of how credit conditions for large and small nonfarm businesses vary over time. One line shows the net share of banks tightening standards for loans to large firms (at least $50 million in annual sales); the other shows the share of small firms that view credit as harder to obtain (than three months earlier) minus the share that view credit as easier to obtain. In both cases, credit conditions typically tighten in recessions and ease in booms. Note, however, that small firms—which depend more on bank loans than large firms—sometimes face tight credit conditions even in economic recoveries.[2] The figure shows that happening in 1992 and again in the aftermath of the financial crisis of 2007–2009. A cutback in lending to creditworthy small firms that want to expand or to qualified households that wish to buy a home creates "financial headwinds" that limit the pace of national economic growth during recovery. This is a key reason policymakers worry that the recovery from a recession caused by a financial crisis may be weaker than the recovery from a recession caused by other factors.

Firms' Balance Sheets and Household Net Worth Besides its influence on the willingness of banks to lend, monetary policy has an important effect on the creditworthiness of borrowers—or at least on their perceived creditworthiness. This **balance-sheet channel** of monetary policy transmission works because monetary

[2]Small firms are critical to private, nonfarm U.S. economic activity and employment: they account for about half of output and generate up to 80 percent of net new jobs each year (see Traci L. Mach and John D. Wolken, "Financial Services Used by Small Businesses: Evidence from the 2003 Survey of Small Business Finances," *Federal Reserve Bulletin*, October 2006, pp. A167–A195).

YOUR FINANCIAL WORLD
Don't Count on Inflation to Bail You Out

When policymakers lower interest rates, their aim is to encourage people to borrow. Central bankers know that low-interest mortgages make it possible for people to buy homes they otherwise couldn't afford. And low-interest car loans allow them to buy a new car earlier than they would otherwise. In lowering interest rates, the FOMC is counting on a surge in borrowing to drive output higher. But while the increase in debt may help the economy as a whole, it can be dangerous for some individuals. They may borrow too much and end up with more debt than they can manage.

The problem with debt is that it must be repaid. Making sure you can repay your debts means carefully calculating what you can afford—not just now but over the entire term of the loan. To avoid overextending yourself, don't borrow on the assumption that your income is going to rise rapidly. While you will typically receive annual increases in your real wage (adjusted for inflation), they are likely to be fairly modest. In fact, for the economy as a whole, pay raises tend to match the rate of productivity growth, which is usually around 2 percent. So don't be tempted into thinking that, though your budget may be tight when you take out a loan, future salary raises will remedy the problem.

The strategy of counting on salary increases to help eliminate debt amounts to counting on inflation to bail you out. It's true that inflation can be helpful to people who are in debt because it reduces the burden of repayment. But if policymakers at the Fed are doing their job, which is to keep inflation low, hoping inflation will help you pay off your loans is a strategy that is likely to backfire.

policy has a direct influence on the net worth of potential borrowers. Specifically, an easing of monetary policy improves firms' and households' balance sheets, increasing their net worth. In turn, these increases in net worth reduce the problems of moral hazard and adverse selection, lowering the information costs of lending and allowing borrowers to obtain financing more easily. Recall that the higher the net worth of a borrower, the more likely that the lender will be repaid. The result is a smaller credit risk premium.

There are two ways in which a monetary policy expansion can improve borrowers' net worth. First, as we have already discussed, an expansionary policy drives up asset prices, increasing the value of firms and the wealth of households. Higher equity and property prices mean higher net worth, which implies lower information costs and greater ease in obtaining financing. The increase in home equity loans that follows a real estate boom is an example of this process. With an increase in household wealth, banks are willing to step up their lending.

The second way that a monetary policy expansion can improve borrowers' net worth has to do with the drop in interest rates. Most borrowers already have loans that they are in the process of repaying; lower interest rates reduce the burden of repayment. For a firm, the drop in the cost of financing increases the difference between revenues and expenses, raising profits and increasing the firm's value. Something similar happens for individuals. When interest rates fall, people who hold variable-rate loans enjoy lower interest payments. This drop in the cost of their financing reduces the information problems that plague the lending relationship. Why? To evaluate a borrower's creditworthiness, banks look at the percentage of a person's income that is devoted to loan payments. At lower interest rates, that percentage will be lower, so individuals will qualify for larger loans. The conclusion is that *as interest rates fall, the supply of loans increases.*

It is worth pausing to emphasize that information is the driving force in the bank-lending and balance-sheet channels of monetary policy transmission. Information services are central to banks' role in the financial system because they help to address the problems of adverse selection and moral hazard. The primacy of information in banking has some important implications for our understanding of the link between the financial system and the real economy. It means that financial instability, which is characterized by large and unpredictable moves in asset prices, accompanied by widespread bankruptcy, will reduce lenders' willingness to supply financing. It also means that accounting scandals, such as the ones that plagued U.S. companies in 2001 and 2002, will have an effect on the economy as a whole. When bankers are worried about the accuracy of accounting information, they will be less willing to make loans to anyone. Inferior information leads to an increase in adverse selection, reducing bank lending, lowering investment, and ultimately depressing the quantity of aggregate output demanded.

The channels of monetary policy transmission depend on the structure of the financial system. To the extent that banks are unimportant sources of funds for firms and individuals, the bank-lending channel is minor. As we will see at the end of this chapter, the rise of loan brokers and asset-backed securities diminished the importance of the bank-lending channel until the financial crisis of 2007–2009. But, following that crisis, information problems and the resulting balance-sheet effects persisted for some time. While technology has made the processing of increasing amounts of information easier and cheaper, it seems unlikely to solve the problems of adverse selection and moral hazard, which make net worth such an important determinant of a borrower's creditworthiness.

Asset-Price Channels: Wealth and Investment

When the interest rate moves, so do stock prices. Specifically, a fall in the interest rate tends to push stock prices up. This relationship between the interest rate and the stock market is referred to as the **asset-price channel** of monetary policy transmission. To understand it, we must first figure out why a change in the interest rate might cause a movement in stock prices. Then we must explain how a change in stock prices can influence the quantity of aggregate output demanded.

To see how the interest rate influences stock prices, recall that the fundamental value of a stock is the present value of the stream of its future dividends. The lower the interest rate is, the higher the present value is and, therefore, the higher the stock price will be. Added to this relationship is the fact that an easing of monetary policy might well improve consumer and business confidence in the prospects for future growth. More growth means more revenue and higher profits and that, too, will drive up stock prices. In fact, because current stock prices are based largely on expectations of future growth and future interest rates, they tend to move in anticipation of a cut in interest rates.

Monetary policy affects real estate markets in the same way that it influences stock markets. The mechanism is straightforward. When policymakers reduce their interest-rate target, it drives the mortgage rate down. Lower mortgage rates mean higher demand for residential housing, driving up the prices of existing homes.

In short, when the central bank reduces its target interest rate, the stock and real estate markets are likely to boom. Then what? Stock and property prices affect both individual consumption and business investment. For individuals, a rise in stock and real estate prices means an increase in wealth. The richer people become, the more they will consume. If stock values go high enough, shareholders can actually buy the luxury cars they have been wanting, or take the fancy vacations they've been dreaming of, or maybe both. The conclusion is that higher asset prices mean increased wealth and consumption.

APPLYING THE CONCEPT
WHAT HAPPENED IN JAPAN?

After decades of strong economic growth, the Japanese economy ground to a halt in the 1990s. Why did the Japanese economy fail to respond to the Bank of Japan's long sequence of interest-rate reductions? Solving the mystery requires that we look at various channels of monetary policy transmission—in this case, asset prices and bank lending.

Figure 23.3 provides the first piece of the puzzle, the collapse of the Japanese stock market. From a peak of nearly 40,000 at the end of 1989, the Nikkei 225 index (the Japanese equivalent to the S&P 500) fell by more than half, to 16,000 in

Figure 23.3   The Nikkei 225 Index, 1984–2013

SOURCE: Used with permission from *http://finance.yahoo.com*. (FRED code: NIKKEI225).

Just as consumption is affected by stock price movements, so is investment. As stock prices rise, firms find it easier to raise funds by issuing new shares. That is, they gain access to financing in the primary capital market. To see why, think of a simple example in which the price of a company's stock suddenly increases. In the meantime, nothing has happened to the cost of a new investment and hence to its internal rate of return. But at the higher stock price, financing is now cheaper. This story should sound familiar. Recall the way in which the traditional *interest-rate channel* influences investment: a lower real interest rate means a lower cost of financing, which raises the profitability of investment projects. As a result, borderline investment projects suddenly become profitable when real interest rates fall. The same thing happens when stock prices rise. As financing becomes less expensive, more investments become profitable. In short, when asset markets boom, so does business investment in new equipment and buildings.[3]

---

[3]This line of reasoning, known as *Tobin's q-theory*, was originally developed by the Nobel Prize–winning economist James Tobin. Tobin pointed out that the question of whether or not a firm invests should depend on the ratio of the market value of its shares to the replacement cost of its plant and equipment, which he called *q*. When q is greater than one—that is, when a firm's stock-market value exceeds its cost of rebuilding—investment in new plant and equipment is cheap relative to the value placed on it in the financial markets. When q is less than one, embarking on new investments isn't worthwhile.

1992. Property prices fell even more sharply, with commercial land prices in the largest cities plunging by nearly 90 percent! The impact of this decline in asset prices was severe. Beyond its direct effects on consumption and investment, both of which collapsed, the crash did considerable damage to both the creditworthiness of borrowers and banks' balance sheets. Borrowers' net worth fell with the collapse of equity and property values, worsening information problems and depressing aggregate expenditure even further.

When real growth slowed to a standstill, firms were no longer able to repay their loans. The quantity of nonperforming loans skyrocketed, eroding bank capital and causing loan officers to become extremely wary of extending new loans. By 2000, bad loans accounted for 14 percent of outstanding loans, up from 3 percent in 1993. Bank capital fell from a relatively low 5¼ percent of assets early in the 1990s to less than 2½ percent in 2000.* The erosion of their capital reduced banks' lending capacity.

The dramatic rise in the number of nonperforming loans was compounded by the fact that many were backed by assets whose value had collapsed. As a result, some banks had virtually no capital left. They should have been shut down but, for political reasons, closing them was impossible. So they were allowed to continue operating.†

Given the large numbers of both bankrupt firms and impaired banks, it was no wonder that the Bank of Japan's monetary policy had virtually no impact. The fact that the interest rate was zero simply didn't matter, because the channels through which interest-rate reductions would normally have influenced real economic activity were almost completely blocked. There was no way for borrowers to obtain financing.

Thus, policymakers had little ability to shift the dynamic aggregate demand curve or even to influence its slope. To clean up the mess, the banking system would need to be put back on a solid footing.

Not all asset bubbles have such devastating impact. When the Internet bubble burst in 2000, the U.S. economy did not follow the same path as Japan's. Americans suffered many of the same consequences as the Japanese—their wealth declined, reducing consumption and investment and damaging borrowers' balance sheets. However, U.S. banks did not hold equities, which suffered the largest price declines among various asset categories. As a result, their capital was less impaired than that of Japanese banks, and they were able to continue lending. A healthy financial system makes all the difference.

*For a thorough discussion of the problems in the Japanese financial system during the 1990s, see Anil K. Kashyap, "Sorting Out Japan's Financial Crisis," *Economic Perspectives of the Federal Reserve Bank of Chicago*, 2000, 4th Quarter, pp. 42–55.

†A striking feature of the Japanese experience in the 1990s is that regulators and supervisors failed to enforce prudential regulations that would have forced many banks to close for lack of adequate capital. The reasons for their "regulatory forbearance" are complex, but two are particularly noteworthy. First, without a fully developed deposit insurance system, it was unclear to regulators how depositors would be compensated when banks were liquidated. Second, and possibly more important, shutting the doors on banks would have meant foreclosing on defaulted borrowers and, thereby, throwing many workers out of their jobs. See Mitsuhiro Fukao, "Japan's Lost Decade and Its Financial System," *The World Economy* 26, no. 5 (March 2003), pp. 365–384.

Table 23.1   The Monetary Policy Transmission Mechanism

Channel	Mechanism
Interest rates (traditional channel)	Lower interest rates reduce the cost of investment, making more projects profitable.
Exchange rates (traditional channel)	Lower interest rates reduce the attractiveness of domestic investment, depressing the value of the currency and increasing net exports.
Bank lending	An easing of monetary policy raises the level of bank reserves and bank deposits, increasing the supply of funds.
Firms' balance sheets	Lower interest rates raise firms' profits, increasing their net worth and reducing the problems of adverse selection and moral hazard.
Household net worth	Lower interest rates raise individuals' net worth, improving their creditworthiness and allowing them to increase their borrowing.
Asset prices	Higher stock prices and real estate values fuel an increase in both business investment and household consumption.

Overall, changes in monetary policy influence aggregate expenditure in the economy through a variety of channels that are summarized in Table 23.1. Each of the transmission mechanisms works slightly differently, but they all lead us to the same conclusion: When interest rates rise, the quantity of aggregate output demanded falls so the dynamic aggregate demand curve slopes down.

Financial Crises and the Transmission of Monetary Policy

We have seen that monetary policy is transmitted to the economy through financial intermediaries and through asset prices. Yet, financial conditions deteriorated through much of the crisis of 2007–2009, even as central bankers were cutting interest rates aggressively. What prevented policy easing from being transmitted as usual to the real economy?

The answer is that the crisis intensified the fundamental problems of asymmetric information—adverse selection and moral hazard—that affect the provision of credit in a modern economy. In general, a reduction in the quality of information about potential borrowers makes it more difficult for them to borrow. In the financial crisis, the widespread losses at intermediaries in general and the heightened uncertainty about the damage suffered by specific intermediaries reduced confidence in their ability to repay loans and thus virtually shut off the availability of credit to many of them. The hesitancy to lend in this episode was not unlike the common reluctance of buyers to acquire a used car when it might be a lemon (see pages 278–280). In short, funding liquidity dried up. As for households and nonfinancial firms, their net worth fell substantially, which greatly reduced their ability to borrow, so they responded by cutting spending. The result of this was a destabilizing feedback loop between worsening economic prospects and the deterioration of financial conditions that influence spending.

The process started in 2006 with the downturn in U.S. housing prices that led to widespread mortgage defaults. Major lenders—particularly in the United States and Europe—faced enormous and growing losses. Insufficient screening and monitoring had resulted in too many risky mortgages (see Chapter 11, Lessons from the Crisis: Information Asymmetry and Securitization). Losses from U.S. mortgage-backed securities and related financial instruments sharply depressed the capital in the financial system (see Chapter 12, Lessons from the Crisis: Insufficient Bank Capital). As a result, intermediaries were compelled to deleverage (see Chapter 3, Lessons from the Crisis: Leverage). They even stopped lending to each other—especially in the aftermath of the Lehman failure in September 2008—because they doubted the solvency of their counterparties (see Chapter 3, Lessons from the Crisis: Interbank Lending) or were simply uncertain about who would bear the losses (recall the Chapter 9 discussion of credit-default swaps).

The result was an intense scramble for funding that led to a near collapse of the financial system. Only the aggressive supply of reserves from central banks and of new capital from governments made it possible to restore the basic function of financial intermediaries and markets. With the usual policy transmission mechanism obstructed during the crisis, the Federal Reserve and other central banks also used unconventional policy mechanisms to directly influence key financial conditions that affect spending in the economy. The Fed's acquisitions of mortgage-backed securities and commercial paper stand out in this regard. Over time, expressions of central bank intent to keep interest rates low over an extended period (forward guidance) also influenced the willingness of investors to purchase other important assets, like equities and private-sector debt.

The bottom line: when the policy transmission mechanism is obstructed, central banks cannot assume that a cut in their target policy rate will ease the financial conditions that influence the economy. Indeed, through most of the crisis of 2007–2009, rate cuts did not even halt the deterioration of financial conditions, let alone improve them. And when the policy rate hits zero, as it essentially did in the United States at the end of 2008, cutting it further is no longer a policy option.

The impairment of monetary policy transmission was at least as severe in the crisis of the euro area. In general, firms and households cannot borrow at a cost less than their governments, so rising default premia on sovereign debt in 2011 and 2012 also worsened financial conditions for private borrowers in several of the countries on the geographic periphery of the euro area—Greece, Ireland, Italy, Portugal, and Spain. The ECB found it almost impossible to offset this differential in funding access and cost. The central bank lowered its target interest rate and became the lender of last resort to these countries' banks. Yet, the supply of credit by the banks to firms and households diminished sharply. Only in the summer of 2012, when the ECB offered to become a lender of last resort to the crisis-stricken periphery governments, did the resulting decline of sovereign risk premia begin to relieve private-sector financial stress. Nevertheless, as of this writing in mid-2013, the gap remains wide between the cost of loans to businesses in the core and the periphery of the euro area, contributing to a regional divergence in economic growth.

Financial conditions matter in economic upturns, too. When central banks hike rates to slow an economy, their success will depend on whether financial conditions respond. If an asset price bubble is under way, as it was in the United States in 2004–2006, the economic impact of central bank policy tightening probably will be smaller than usual. As a result, central banks must always take into account the workings of the monetary policy transmission mechanism in order to achieve their goals of economic and price stability.

The Challenges Modern Monetary Policymakers Face

The financial crisis of 2007–2009 was a "game changer" for the practitioners and theorists of monetary policy. Surely no one assumes now that monetary policy is a hard and fast science—that a few equations coupled with some statistical analysis and the help of a big computer will suffice. To do their job well, central bankers need a detailed understanding of how both the financial system and the real economy will react to their policy changes.

That job would be tough enough in a world that is standing still, but the dynamism that is such a pervasive and desirable feature of today's economy makes the job all the more difficult. In fact, modern monetary policymakers face a series of daunting challenges. In this section, we will look at three that grew more prominent thanks to the financial crisis of 2007–2009. First, stock prices and property values have a tendency to go through boom and bust cycles. Second, policymakers' options are limited, as we have seen by the fact the nominal interest rate cannot fall below zero. Third, the structures of the economy and the financial system are constantly evolving, and the latter may be affected greatly by changing regulation in the years ahead.

Booms and Busts in Property and Equity Prices

Nearly everyone agrees that we would all be better off without skyrocketing increases in property and stock prices followed by sudden collapses. The unprecedented surge and collapse in U.S. housing prices was the ultimate source of the financial crisis of 2007–2009. Since the Great Depression of the 1930s, housing prices had declined

Figure 23.4   U.S. Real Housing Price Index, 1890–2013 (1890 = 100)

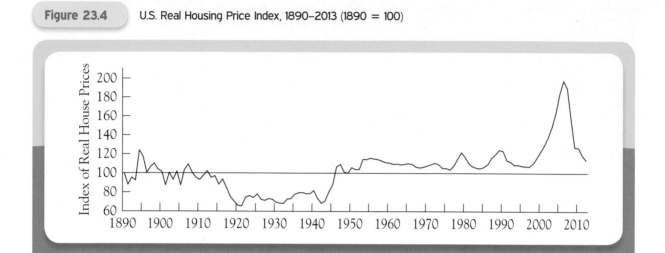

SOURCE: From *Irrational Exuberance,* 2/e. Princeton, 2005. Reprinted with permission by Robert J. Shiller. Updates from: *www.econ.yale.edu/~shiller/data/Fig2-1.xls.*

nationwide in only three years, and then only slightly. Real house prices had been reasonably stable, because inflation offset the trend rise of nominal house prices. The spike in house prices in the years preceding the crisis was spectacularly unprecedented (see Figure 23.4). At the time, some argued that it was a bubble and therefore must burst and cause severe economic damage. Others said that housing fundamentals—growing household income, lower mortgage rates, and the like—had boosted affordability, which both justified the price surge and made it sustainable.[4] The ensuing collapse in home prices settled the debate, bringing on a financial and economic contraction more severe and widespread than even most pessimists expected.

Abrupt changes in asset prices, like the U.S. house price bubble, affect virtually every aspect of economic activity. Looking back at the first part of this chapter, we can see that changes in asset prices have a direct impact on both consumption and investment. Bubbles—which are identified after the fact by a sharp rise then a sharp decline in prices—are damaging in part because the wealth effects they create cause consumption to surge and then contract just as rapidly. Equity bubbles—like the boom in the Internet sector in the late 1990s—allow firms to finance new projects more easily, causing investment to boom and then bust (see Figure 23.5). Bubbles are particularly damaging when their collapse impairs the balance sheets of leveraged intermediaries, risking a deleveraging spiral (see Chapter 3, Lessons from the Crisis: Leverage). The Great Depression, Japan's experience in the 1990s, the global crisis of 2007–2009, and the subsequent euro-area crisis all exemplify this pattern. For example, the loss of capital in the financial system in 2007–2009 could have led to catastrophe without extraordinary government actions. In contrast, the collapse of the Internet bubble of the late 1990s had a relatively minor impact because intermediaries faced limited credit exposure and remained well capitalized.

The devastating worldwide effects of the reversal in U.S. house prices beginning in 2006 has focused renewed attention on how monetary policymakers should react

[4]For a review of the debate, see Jane Dokko et al., "Monetary Policy and the Housing Bubble," Federal Reserve Board, Finance and Economics Discussion Series 2009-49, December 2009.

| Figure 23.5 | The Nasdaq Composite Index, 1984–2013 |

SOURCE: Used with permission from *http://finance.yahoo.com.*

to asset price bubbles. Should the Federal Reserve have raised interest rates earlier or more aggressively in 2003–2006 when house prices were soaring? There are, and were, arguments on both sides.[5] Proponents of a policy of "leaning against bubbles" say that stabilizing inflation and real growth means raising interest rates to discourage bubbles from developing in the first place. If successful, this policy would reduce the credit booms that accompany bubbles, along with the busts that inevitably follow.

Opponents of this interventionist view argue that bubbles are too difficult to identify when they are developing. They point to the debate about U.S. housing prices in 2004 and 2005 as evidence that views were not unanimous. However, the fact that an economic phenomenon is difficult to measure is no excuse for ignoring it. Indeed, we have no choice: As we saw in the discussion of monetary policy transmission, macroeconomic forecasts rest on estimates of future wealth and stock prices. Without them, there is no way to forecast either consumption or investment.

Opponents of leaning against bubbles used to argue that central banks should simply wait until the bubble bursts and only then react aggressively to limit the fallout on the economy by cleaning up the mess. They pointed to the Great Depression and the 1990s in Japan as examples of what can happen if the central bank attempts to prick a bubble with interest-rate policy. Critics of an activist response also pointed to the mild U.S. recession in 2001—despite the collapse of the bubble for Internet stocks—as a successful instance of how policy can stabilize inflation and the economy in the face of a burst asset price bubble.

The crisis of 2007–2009 undermined the rosy view that policymakers can sit back and clean up after a bubble bursts. Having seen financial conditions collapse even

[5]An early example of the case for intervention may be found in Stephen G. Cecchetti, Hans Genberg, and Sushil Wadhwani, "Asset Prices in a Flexible Inflation Targeting Framework," in William C. Hunter, George G. Kaufman, and Michael Pomerleano, Eds., *Asset Price Bubbles: Implications for Monetary, Regulatory and International Policies* (Cambridge, MA: MIT Press: 2002), pp. 427–444. For an early version of the case against, see Ben Bernanke and Mark Gertler, "Should Central Banks Respond to Movements in Asset Prices?" *American Economic Review*, May 2001, pp. 253–257.

with the policy rate set at zero, and having experienced the deepest global downturn since World War II, few central bankers remain sanguine about using conventional interest-rate policy to limit the fallout from asset price bubbles after they burst. However, central bankers still worry that interest rates are only a blunt tool and that pricking an asset price bubble could require rate hikes so severe that they would bludgeon the economy and reduce the likelihood of hitting a central bank's objective for inflation. If the rate hikes were applied more cautiously to halt, say, a housing price bubble, it would be, as one economist put it, "like adding a grain of sand a day to a scale that is weighing a car."

Today, there is a more nuanced case against using interest rates to prick asset price bubbles: namely, that the proper policy toolkit for addressing bubbles is not interest rates but the macroprudential regulatory tools that we discussed in Chapter 14. According to this view, bubbles are a major threat when they are associated with an expansion of credit that exposes the financial system to the eventual collapse of asset prices. As a result, the best response would be to adjust regulatory rules—such as procyclical capital requirements, systemic capital surcharges, and fees for insuring the capital of banks—to inhibit intermediaries from extending such risky credits in economic booms.

The macroprudential regulatory approach would help avoid the more destructive option of having to tighten interest rates across the whole economy to address a bubble in a specific asset. Yet, this approach still depends on the foresight and judgment of regulators to limit the buildup of a menacing asset price bubble. Moreover, policymakers acknowledge the difficulty of limiting systemic risks through the use of macroprudential policies alone. The ability of intermediaries to evade regulations and to conceal risk-taking reduces the effectiveness of regulation and supervision, while raising interest rates allows policy "to get into all of the cracks" in the financial system, including shadow banks and systemically important financial markets (see In the News: Should the Fed Pop Bubbles by Raising Interest Rates? on page 668).[6]

While the crisis of 2007–2009 has not settled this debate, it has advanced the discussion substantially.[7] Many policymakers remain reluctant to raise interest rates to address asset bubbles, but they no longer rule it out. Using interest rates to combat asset price bubbles now is more likely to be viewed as a backup approach for extreme circumstances, if the first-best methods of macroprudential regulation fail to limit a systemic threat.

Deflation and the Zero Nominal-Interest-Rate Bound

In Chapter 18, we noted that nominal interest rates cannot be negative—that there is a **zero nominal-interest-rate bound**. The reason is that investors can always hold cash, so bonds must have positive yields to attract bondholders. While this point may strike you as something only investors should worry about, it is not. The fact that nominal interest rates can't fall below zero places a significant restriction on what monetary policymakers can do. Look back at Panel B of Figure 23.1 and you will see that the policy target rate in 2009 was virtually zero in Japan and the United States, and only modestly

---

[6]Federal Reserve Board Governor Jeremy Stein articulated the potential benefits of using interest rate policy to limit systemic risk in a speech at the Federal Reserve Bank of St. Louis: "Overheating in Credit Markets: Origins, Measurement, and Policy Responses," February 7, 2013.

[7]For one view of how the financial crisis should alter monetary policy practices more generally, see Olivier Blanchard, Giovanni Dell'Ariccia, and Paulo Mauro, "Rethinking Macroeconomic Policy," IMF Staff Position Note, February 12, 2010, SPN/10/03.

YOUR FINANCIAL WORLD
Know the Level of Inflation

By now, you're probably convinced that inflation is bad for everyone, including yourself. Nevertheless, we all have to face at least some inflation. The first step in dealing with it is to become informed. You need to know the current inflation rate for any number of reasons. For example, it is essential in figuring out whether a nominal wage increase represents a real wage increase. And while any business news source will tell you the nominal interest rate, without a measure of inflation, you can't compute the real interest rate. Making informed economic and financial decisions requires that you know the inflation rate.

Casual observation of the prices we pay from day to day is an unreliable way to evaluate inflation, because most of us have fairly selective memories and are prone to remember price changes on goods that we buy frequently (such as food and gasoline) rather than on important infrequent purchases (such as autos, cameras, and computers). Surveys indicate that most people overestimate inflation. So economic statistics are more reliable. The Bureau of Labor Statistics, the government agency that computes the consumer price index (CPI), provides information about inflation on its website, www.bls.gov/cpi, and you can find the latest CPI reading using FRED.

What should you look for on FRED? First, don't pay much attention to monthly measures of inflation; they aren't very reliable as indicators of the long-term inflation trend. Instead, use FRED to display 12-month percent changes, especially measures that exclude food and energy. These so-called core measures of inflation omit parts of the price index that tend to be extremely volatile, making sharp movements that are likely to be reversed in a few months. Because gasoline prices rise and fall from one month to the next, for example, removing them smoothes inflation, making the core measure more representative of the long-term trend.

The FRED data codes for overall and core CPI are CPIAUCSL and CPILFESL, respectively. (For practice, use FRED to display an up-to-date graph of the core index's percent change from a year ago. See Appendix B to Chapter 1 for help using FRED.)

Knowing the level of inflation is essential to managing your finances. If you don't know the level of inflation, you won't know whether the interest rate you receive on your savings is high or low, or whether the interest rate you are paying on your loans is high or low. Nor will you be able to evaluate properly the next raise you receive. Stay informed about inflation so that you can adjust for it. Know the real interest rate you receive or pay and how much your real wage is changing.

---

higher in the euro area. Even though the global economy was sinking, policymakers had no scope to lower rates further. The risk of becoming caught in precisely such a predicament has concerned central bankers around the world at least since Japan's experience with the zero bound in the 1990s.

The problem posed by the zero nominal-interest-rate bound is a serious one. To understand why, we can do an exercise based on the macroeconomic model presented in Chapters 21 and 22. Think about the consequences of a shock that depresses aggregate expenditure. The shock could be caused by a decline in investment due to a fall in business prospects; by an appreciation of the dollar due to a deteriorating investment climate abroad, which has increased foreign demand for dollars; or by a decline in individuals' confidence in the future. Regardless of the source, the slowdown drives spending down at every level of inflation and the real interest rate, shifting the dynamic aggregate demand curve to the left. The immediate consequence of this drop in the quantity of aggregate output demanded is that real output falls below potential output, creating a recessionary output gap that puts downward pressure on inflation. Under normal circumstances, monetary policymakers would react to the decline in inflation by cutting the nominal interest rate enough to lower the real interest rate. Their action would increase spending, raise real output, and eliminate the output gap.

Now let's make a small adjustment to this story and assume that, when the shock occurs, inflation is zero and the target nominal interest rate that central bankers control

"I had no idea our marriage was so interest-rate sensitive."

SOURCE: *1990 © Robert Mankoff/The New Yorker Collection/www.cartoonbank.com.*

is close to zero. Under these conditions, the decline in aggregate demand still drives real output below potential output, placing downward pressure on inflation. But when inflation falls, it drops below zero so that on average, prices are falling. The result is **deflation**.

Deflation isn't necessarily a problem, unless the shock that moves the economy away from its long-run equilibrium is big enough to drive output down to such a low level that policymakers can't bring it up, even by setting their nominal interest rate target to zero. At that point, we have arrived at one of the central banker's worst nightmares: a nominal interest rate of zero accompanied by deflation and real output that is below potential. The recessionary output gap places further downward pressure on prices, driving deflation down even more. Because the nominal interest rate is already zero, policymakers cannot counter the worsening deflation by lowering it. Instead, the real interest rate rises, reducing spending, shifting the dynamic aggregate demand curve to the left, and expanding the recessionary output gap even more. The result is a *deflationary spiral* in which deflation grows worse and worse.

Recall that deflation aggravates information problems in ways that inflation does not. Deflation makes it more difficult for businesses to obtain financing for new projects. Without financing there is no investment; without investment there is no growth. The primary reason this happens is that debt is measured in fixed dollars, and deflation makes those dollars more valuable. Thus, deflation increases the real value of a firm's liabilities without affecting the real value of its assets. At a lower net worth, companies are suddenly less creditworthy.

In short, deflation and the zero nominal-interest-rate bound can have a devastating impact on growth by short-circuiting the process that normally stabilizes the economy so that it is no longer self-correcting. Concern about the instabilities of a deflationary spiral helped to animate the central bank response to the crisis of 2007–2009, even though the crisis began with inflation above desirable levels. Policymakers were concerned that the deep recession itself could lower inflation expectations too far and raise real interest rates in a destabilizing manner.

Can policymakers do anything to avoid this pitfall? The answer is yes; there are ways to minimize the chances of this sort of catastrophe. Policymakers can choose from three strategies. First, they can set their inflation objective with the perils of deflation in mind; second, they can act boldly when there is even a hint of deflation; and third, they can utilize the unconventional policy tools that we discussed in Chapter 18.

The difficulties posed by the zero nominal-interest-rate bound arise only when central bankers have achieved their objective of low, stable inflation. When inflation is high, so is the nominal interest rate; chances are therefore remote that the interest rate will hit the zero bound. This observation suggests that central bankers should set their inflation objective high enough to minimize the possibility of a deflationary spiral. The consensus among central bankers is that an inflation objective of 2 to 3 percent gives them enough latitude to avoid the problems caused by deflation.

Reducing the interest rate significantly and rapidly when faced with the possibility of hitting the zero nominal-interest-rate bound is another approach to avoiding deflation.

Central bankers call this strategy "acting preemptively," which means working hard to avoid ever reaching the point where interest rates hit zero. Acting preemptively was one reason why the FOMC reduced the target federal funds rate by 5.25 percentage points to the zero bound in a series of 10 cuts between September 2007 and December 2008. Dramatic actions of that sort are meant to ensure that the economy will recover before deflation can take hold.

Finally, as we saw in Chapter 18, central bankers have at their disposal a range of unconventional policy tools that they can employ when the traditional interest-rate target, an overnight rate, hits zero.[8] These include forward guidance, quantitative easing, and targeted asset purchases—all of which were actively employed by central bankers in the financial crisis of 2007–2009 and by the ECB in the euro-area crisis. The mechanics are straightforward. Central bankers use forward guidance to influence long-term bond yields, which depend in part on expectations about future policy rates. They use quantitative easing and targeted asset purchases to control the size of their balance sheet and the mix of assets that they hold. During normal times, policymakers control the supply of their reserve liabilities in order to meet a target interest rate. But even if the short-run target rate drops to zero, monetary policymakers retain their ability to expand their balance sheet. They can continue to purchase securities or make loans to banks to increase the size of the monetary base.

Everyone agrees that unconventional policy options are feasible. And we have seen their frequent use both during and after the crisis of 2007–2009 and in the euro-area crisis. Nevertheless, central bankers are reluctant to use such tools and, when used, are eager to exit as soon as improvements in the economy make it safe for them to do so. One reason for this aversion to unconventional tools is the lack of experience using them. Monetary policymaking rests on quantitative estimates of the impact of a change in the target interest rate on the central bank's objectives. Policymakers have some idea of how a reduction of 25 or 50 basis points in the federal funds rate would affect output and inflation over the next year or two. But they have much less experience in knowing what the quantitative impact of an unconventional policy option will be. What is the effect on prices, consumption, and investment if the supply of reserves increases by a factor of 100 (as it did in the United States in September–October 2008) or if the central bank doubles its assets by purchasing $1 trillion of mortgage-backed securities (as the Fed did in 2009)?

Beyond the uncertainty that comes from a lack of experience, another key reason for keeping unconventional policy tools unconventional is that policy exit—reducing the size of the balance sheet and restoring the mix of securities to a conventional portfolio of shorter-term government instruments—may be difficult. As we saw in Chapter 18, the ability to pay interest on reserves allows a central bank to tighten policy—by hiking the deposit rate that forms the floor for the overnight lending rate—even if policymakers choose temporarily not to sell the unconventional assets on the balance sheet. Nevertheless, central banks prefer assets that are liquid and that do not tilt the playing field in favor of specific private borrowers. And although they may wish to sell assets acquired in unconventional policy moves—including bonds with default risk and long-term bonds—in doing so they may suffer a loss. If a central bank faced sufficient losses, it might need to ask the government to replenish its capital. Such reliance on government could add to inflation expectations if it were viewed as a threat to central bank independence.

---

[8]For an early discussion of unconventional monetary policy options, see the speech by then-Federal Reserve Board governor, later chairman, Ben S. Bernanke, "Deflation: Making Sure 'It' Doesn't Happen Here," remarks before the National Economists Club, Washington, D.C., November 21, 2001. The speech is available on the Federal Reserve Board's website at *www.federalreserve.gov.*

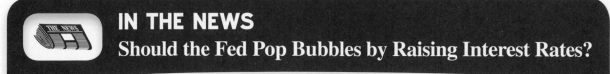

IN THE NEWS
Should the Fed Pop Bubbles by Raising Interest Rates?

The Washington Post

Wonkblog

Posted by Neil Irwin

February 8, 2013

Federal Reserve Governor Jeremy Stein gave a speech yesterday that everybody . . . is talking about. He looked at ways monetary policy can encourage bubbles in financial markets, and argued that central banks should be ready to use their control over interest rates to address them.

"I can imagine situations where it might make sense to enlist monetary policy tools in the pursuit of financial stability," Stein said at a conference hosted by the St. Louis Fed, adding that "If the underlying economic environment creates a strong incentive for financial institutions to, say, take on more credit risk in a reach for yield, it is unlikely that regulatory tools can completely contain this behavior."

This is a rejection of central banking orthodoxy over the last couple of decades. Chairmen Ben Bernanke and Alan Greenspan before him were reluctant to try to use their power over interest rates to fight imbalances and bubbles in the financial markets (Bernanke has become more open-minded on this question since the crisis, however).

Their logic is that hiking interest rates to combat a bubble in this or that market would be the equivalent of fumigating an entire house after finding a small patch of mold. It may do the job, but comes at a great cost: The house is unusable for days. Similarly, if the Fed hikes interest rates to combat bubbles, it might succeed, but at the cost of slowing down the entire economy or causing a recession.

By contrast, the Bernanke approach of dealing with credit bubbles through the Fed's bank regulation tools, is the equivalent of coming in in a targeted way and removing the mold that has been found. The benefit is that the whole house doesn't need to be shut down (No recession!). The downside is that there might be a lot more mold than what you can see, and you won't get it with this targeted approach (risks lurking unseen elsewhere in the financial system).

It's good to see leaders of the Fed grappling—in their cerebral, cautious way, at least—with an issue that has seemed apparent to many in financial markets for years: That low interest rate policies and unconventional easing programs such as Fed bond purchases can have hard-to-predict results throughout the financial system beyond those that traditional models of how monetary policy affects the economy would predict.

The shorthand, colloquial version of this is that when the Fed prints a lot of money, all that cash sloshing around has to go somewhere, and even if it doesn't show up as inflation, it could turn up as overpriced stocks (in 2000) or mortgage backed securities (in 2006).

. . . [Overall,] Stein's argument is that precisely because it is so hard for the Fed to see, measure, and regulate any emerging frailties in the financial system, there is reason to use interest rate policies to combat them. When there is excess in the financial system that might endanger the economy, Stein argues, higher interest rates are the surest way of fighting it.

More than anything, Stein's argument is one for intellectual modesty among Fed leaders' in their ability to know where the risks are emerging and to have the power to do much about them. After a devastating crisis that had its roots in obscure financial products that almost no one understood (and even many senior regulators didn't know about beforehand), now is not a great time for hubris about the ability of regulators to fine-tune their risks.

"While monetary policy may not be quite the right tool for the job, it has one important advantage relative to supervision and regulation—namely that it gets in all of the cracks," Stein said. "The one thing that a commercial bank, a broker-dealer, an offshore hedge fund, and a special purpose [asset-backed commercial paper] vehicle have in common is that they all face the same set of market interest rates."

SOURCE: Neil Irwin, "Should the Fed Pop Bubbles by Raising Interest Rates?" *The Washington Post,* February 8, 2013. Used with permission.

LESSONS OF THE ARTICLE

Central bankers typically use regulatory tools to address financial instability, while assigning interest rate and balance-sheet tools to the task of securing price and economic stability. They remain very reluctant to adjust interest rates for other reasons. Following the financial crisis of 2007–2009, however, policymakers no longer rule out raising interest rates to counter an asset bubble that infects the balance sheets of leveraged intermediaries and, as a result, threatens a systemic disruption.

The Evolving Structure of the Financial System

Monetary policy works through its effects on the financial system. Thus, differences in financial structure across countries may help explain differences in the effectiveness of monetary policy. By extension, changes in financial structure will change the impact of monetary policy. Recall from the first part of this chapter that one of the channels through which monetary policy influences real output and inflation is its impact on the supply of bank loans. By influencing bank lending, policymakers can affect the ease with which individuals and firms obtain financing.

Banks are crucial to this mechanism. As the nature of banking changes, we would expect the importance of this channel of monetary policy transmission to change along with it, and that has been the case. In the United States, for example, banks are no longer as important a source of financing as they once were. Thirty years ago, they accounted for virtually all the credit in the U.S. economy. At the time the crisis of 2007–2009 hit, direct bank loans had fallen to less than 60 percent of total credit extended.

The shift away from bank financing and toward securities financing in the capital markets means that the bank-lending channel of monetary policy became less important in the decades before the financial crisis that began in 2007. The decline of banks as a source of finance was accompanied by a corresponding rise in the importance of securities markets and of shadow banks—including securities brokers, money-market mutual funds, and government-sponsored enterprises (GSEs). Recall the asset-backed securities discussed in Chapter 3. Mortgage-backed and other asset-backed securities surged in volume over the past 30 years. In 1980, mortgage-backed securities accounted for only $0.1 trillion of the $1.5 trillion in U.S. mortgages outstanding. By 2009, they surpassed half of the nearly $15 trillion in mortgages outstanding.

To create mortgage-backed securities, a broker bundles together a large number of home mortgages and then sells shares in the pool. Investors in mortgage-backed securities purchase shares in the revenue from the underlying financial instruments—in this case, the mortgage payments made by homebuyers. Although their home purchase began with a bank loan, homebuyers in this way ultimately obtain a form of financing that is almost equivalent to capital market financing. Over the years, securitization—the process of pooling streams of revenue from loans and other receivables into marketable securities—has expanded in scope and size; it now includes car loans, credit card debt, student loans, equipment leases, and even movie box-office receipts.

Yet, the financial crisis that ended in 2009 is having a greater impact on the shape of the financial system than any event since the Great Depression. Importantly, it has interrupted the trend toward capital market finance: securitization has declined or slowed since 2006. For example, the volume of asset-backed commercial paper in the United States, which surpassed $1.2 trillion in the summer of 2007, plummeted to only about one-fourth of that level in 2012.

In the aftermath of the financial crisis, U.S. government agencies became the dominant source of new housing finance, either through direct loans or through guarantees. In 2010, 88 percent of new mortgage originations were agency-backed, up from 53 percent a decade earlier.[9] Yet, the future of the housing-related GSEs remains highly uncertain, with many observers calling for them to be dismantled. After the GSEs were placed under the direct control of the federal government in 2008, the government injected more than $150 billion to restore their positive net worth. In 2011, the U.S. Treasury proposed to wind them down gradually by raising their guarantee fees,

---

[9]See Bipartisan Policy Center, Housing America's Future: New Directions for National Policy, February 2013, p. 43, *http://bipartisanpolicy.org/library/report/housing-future.*

reducing the size of loans eligible for a guarantee, and shrinking their portfolios of mortgages.[10] In 2012, the GSEs doubled their guarantee fees. Yet, as of 2013, Congress is still considering how to reform U.S. housing finance, a key source of the global financial crisis.

And, at this writing, the impact of the most far-reaching U.S. regulatory reform since the 1930—the Dodd-Frank Act of 2010—remains far from clear. As of mid-2013, regulators had finalized only about 40 percent of the new rules that the act requires them to issue. And many key elements of the new financial regulatory measures were untried, including the Dodd-Frank apparatus for limiting "too big to fail." Others were fresh from the drawing board. For example, the Financial System Oversight Council began only in July 2013 to designate certain nonbanks as systemically important financial institutions (SIFIs), which the Federal Reserve would be called on to supervise. The Federal Deposit Insurance Corporation was still at an early stage in determining how its new "orderly liquidation authority" would be used to resolve a global SIFI in a crisis. And policymakers clarified only in July 2013 the heightened capital requirements that initially will apply to SIFIs.

Amid all this change, it is too soon to say how the post-crisis financial system will evolve. Will the trend toward securities finance resume? In part, that will depend on how regulators behave. A macroprudential regulator—of the kind that we discussed in Chapter 14—will try to limit intermediaries' incentives for taking systemic risk.

Will macroprudential regulation prevent the restoration of securitization? Probably not: regulators are aware that effective securitization can lead to a better diversification of risk. But unlike the incomplete securitization that prevailed earlier, effective securitization must avoid leaving concentrations of securitized assets on the balance sheets of intermediaries that make them vulnerable to collapsing asset price bubbles. Consequently, macroprudential regulation will tend to restrain the future pace of securitization, especially compared to the boom years preceding the financial crisis.

However the financial system evolves, the pattern will be a critical one for central bankers, who need to know the quantitative impact their policies are likely to have. As the structure of the financial system changes, the effect of a 25- or 50-basis-point move in the federal funds rate will doubtless change with it. The changing effectiveness of conventional monetary policy likely will require central bankers to update their unconventional policy tools, too. Central bankers will always have to assess how the financial system is altering the monetary transmission mechanism.

The changing nature of the financial system is important for individuals as well as policymakers. As the characteristics of money, banks, and loans evolve, we will all adjust how we pay for our purchases, how we hold our wealth, and how we obtain credit. Our use of currency will likely continue to decline. U.S. banks that now receive interest on their reserves may continue to hold far more of them than before the financial crisis. No one can predict exactly when or to what extent these changes will occur, but now that you have reached the end of this book, you know how to think about them. And your skills in finding and analyzing economic and financial data will help you to stay up to date as the financial system evolves. You understand the economic role of financial institutions as well as what a central bank is and how it operates. Together with the aggregate demand–aggregate supply model, this knowledge gives you a framework with which to comprehend the evolution of the financial system, its effects on monetary policy, and its effects on you personally.

---

[10]See U.S. Treasury, "Reforming America's Housing Finance Market: A Report to Congress," February 2011, *www.treasury.gov/initiatives/documents/reforming%20america%27s%20housing%20finance%20market.pdf.*

Terms

asset-price channel, 657

balance-sheet channel, 655

bank-lending channel, 654

deflation, 666

exchange-rate channel, 651

interest-rate channel, 651

monetary policy transmission
 mechanism, 651

zero nominal-interest-rate
 bound, 664

Using FRED: Codes for Data in This Chapter

Data Series	FRED Data Code
Real GDP	GDPC1
U.S. 3-month Treasury bill rate	TB3MS
U.S. 10-year Treasury constant maturity rate	GS10
1-year inflation expectations (Michigan survey)	MICH
Real trade-weighted U.S. dollar index: Broad	TWEXBPA
Trade-weighted U.S. dollar index: Broad	TWEXBMTH
Household net worth	TNWBSHNO
Disposable personal income	DPI
Personal saving rate	PSAVERT
S&P 500 stock price index	SP500
S&P Case-Shiller 20-city home price index	SPCS20RSA
Consumer price index	CPIAUCSL

www.mhhe.com/moneyandbanking4e

Chapter Lessons

1. Monetary policy influences the economy through several channels.
   a. The traditional channels of monetary policy transmission are interest rates and exchange rates.
      i. Interest rates influence consumption and investment.
      ii. Exchange rates affect net exports.
   b. Monetary policy affects the supply of bank loans, changing the availability of bank financing to firms and individuals.
   c. Monetary policy can change firms' and households' net worth, affecting their creditworthiness as borrowers.
   d. The asset-price channel of monetary policy transmission works through stock and real estate prices.
      i. Stock and property prices influence household wealth and consumption.
      ii. Stock prices also affect businesses' ability and incentive to raise funds and make investments.

2. Monetary policymakers face significant challenges. To be successful, they require
   a. Accurate estimates of potential GDP, even when its growth trend is shifting.
   b. An understanding of how to cope with the problems created by the zero nominal-interest-rate bound and the possibility of deflation.
   c. A knowledge of how and when to react to the possibility of a stock or real estate boom (and bust).
   d. An awareness of the changing structure of the financial system and a knowledge of how to react to it.

Conceptual and Analytical Problems

1. Explain in detail how monetary policy influences banks' lending behavior. Show how an open market purchase affects the banking system's balance sheet, and discuss the impact on the supply of bank loans. (You may wish to refer to Chapter 17 in answering this question.) *(LO1)*

2. Explain why you might expect the recovery from the 2007–2009 recession to be weaker than normal. *(LO1)*

3.* Explain why the traditional interest-rate channel of monetary policy transmission from monetary policy actions to changes in investment and consumption decisions may be relatively weak. *(LO1)*

4. Explain why monetary policymakers' actions in cutting the Federal Funds rate to almost zero were not sufficient to boost economic activity during the recession of 2007–2009. *(LO2)*

5. When monetary policymakers hit the zero nominal-interest-rate bound with their policy rate, they have the option to turn to unconventional tools of monetary policy. How do these unconventional tools work, and why are policymakers reluctant to use them except in very difficult circumstances? *(LO2)*

6. The government decides to place limits on the interest rates banks can pay their depositors. Seeing that alternative investments pay higher interest rates, depositors withdraw their funds from banks and place them in bonds. Will their action have an impact on the economy? If so, how? *(LO1)*

7. New developments in information technology have simplified the assessment of individual borrowers' creditworthiness. What are the likely consequences for the structure of the financial system? For monetary policy? *(LO2)*

8.* Describe the theory of the exchange-rate channel of the monetary transmission mechanism. How, through the exchange rate, does an interest rate increase influence output? Why is this link difficult to find in practice? *(LO1)*

9. Many economists have argued that Japan's economic problems during the 1990s were caused largely by bank failures and the refusal of the Japanese government to clean up the banking system. Explain how a collapse of the banking system could cause a fall in real output. Can monetary policymakers do anything to revive the economy under such circumstances? *(LO2)*

*Indicates more difficult problems

10. Why might the zero nominal-interest-rate bound lead policymakers to raise their inflation objective? *(LO2)*

11. Considering the role of the U.S. house price bubble in the financial crisis of 2007–2009, how do you think monetary policymakers should respond to bubbles in asset markets? *(LO2)*

12. For each of the following, explain whether the response is theoretically consistent with a tightening of monetary policy and identify which of the traditional channels of monetary policy is at work: *(LO1)*
    a. Firms become more likely to undertake investment projects.
    b. Households become less likely to purchase refrigerators and washing machines.
    c. Net exports fall.

13. In Country A suppose that changes in short-term interest rates translate quickly into changes in long-term interest rates, while in Country B long-term interest rates do not respond much to changes in short-term rates. In which country would you expect the interest-rate channel of monetary policy to be stronger? Explain your answer. *(LO1)*

14. Consider a situation where central bank officials repeatedly express concern that output exceeds potential output, implying that the economy is overheating. Although they haven't implemented any policy moves as yet, the data show that consumption of luxury goods has begun to slow. Explain how this behavior could reflect the asset-price channel of monetary policy at work. *(LO1)*

15. Do you think the balance-sheet channel of monetary policy would be stronger or weaker if: *(LO1)*
    a. Firms' balance sheets in general are very healthy?
    b. Firms have a lot of existing variable-rate debt?

16. In the wake of the financial crisis of 2007–2009, would you anticipate the bank-lending channel becoming more or less important in the United States in the near future? Explain your answer. *(LO2)*

17.* Suppose there is an unexpected slowdown in the rate of productivity growth in the economy so that forecasters consistently overestimate the growth rate of GDP. If the central bank bases its policy decisions on the consensus forecast, what would be the likely consequences for inflation assuming it maintains its existing inflation target? *(LO2)*

18. Suppose the policy interest rate controlled by the central bank and the inflation rate were both zero. Explain in terms of the aggregate demand–aggregate supply framework how the economy could fall into a deflationary spiral if it were hit by a negative aggregate demand shock. *(LO2)*

19.* Use the aggregate demand–aggregate supply framework to show how a boom in equity prices might affect inflation and output in the short run. Describe the long-run impact on inflation and output (a) if the central bank implicitly allows its inflation target to rise and (b) if it retains its original inflation target. *(LO2)*

20. Compare the impact of a given change in monetary policy in two economies that are similar in every way except that, in Economy A, the financial system has a large shadow banking system providing many alternatives to bank financing, while in Economy B, bank loans account for almost all of the financing in the economy. *(LO1)*

Data Exploration

Scan here for quick access to the resources for these problems. Need a barcode reader? Try ScanLife, available in your app store.

For general information on using Federal Reserve Economic Data (FRED) online, visit www.mhhe.com/moneyandbanking4e.com and click on Student Edition, then FRED resources.

1. In conducting monetary policy, the European Central Bank (ECB) must balance the needs of euro-area countries with differing economic conditions. Plot since 1990 the yield spread between government bonds in Italy (FRED code: INTGSBITM193N) and Germany (FRED code: INTGSBDEM193N), along with the yield spread between government bonds in Spain (FRED code: INTGSBESM193N) and Germany. Discuss the yield spreads after 2008, and explain how they reflect policy challenges for the ECB. *(LO2)*

2. How important is the balance sheet channel of monetary policy? Plot since 1996 the net tightening of credit standards for consumer and credit card loans (FRED code: DRTSCLCC) and (on the right scale) household net worth (FRED code: TNWBSHNO). Do banks adjust lending conditions when household balance sheets improve or deteriorate? *(LO1)*

3. Among the challenges facing central banks around the world is the elevated level of public debt. Plot U.S. federal debt held by the public as a percent of gross domestic product (FRED code: FYPUGDA188S), and discuss the problems that government debt could pose for the Federal Reserve in the future. *(LO2)*

4.* Some critics argue that the Federal Reserve stoked the housing price bubble after 2000 by keeping monetary policy too stimulative. To investigate, first plot from 2000 to 2007 on a quarterly basis the Taylor rule gap—the difference between the Taylor rule and the federal funds rate—as described in Chapter 18 Data Exploration Problems 1 and 2. Add to this plot on the right scale an index of U.S. housing prices (FRED code: SPCS20RSA). Does the evidence support the critics' claim? What other evidence might be sought? *(LO1)*

www.mhhe.com/moneyandbanking4e

Glossary

Note: The number in parentheses at the end of each entry is the number of the chapter in which the term is introduced.

A

accommodative monetary policy A policy that is aimed at increasing output and raising inflation, usually a lowering of the central bank's interest-rate target. (15)

accountability The idea that central bankers should be held responsible for their policies. (15)

adverse feedback Mutually aggravating interactions between the financial sector and the economy in a systemic crisis. (14)

adverse selection The problem of distinguishing a good risk from a bad one before making a loan or providing insurance; it is caused by asymmetric information. (11)

aggregate expenditure The total demand for the economy's production; the sum of consumption, investment, government purchases, and net exports. (21)

American option An option that can be exercised any time up to the expiration date, in contrast to a *European option*. (9)

appreciation of a currency The increase in the value of a country's currency relative to the value of another country's currency. (10)

arbitrage The practice of simultaneously buying and selling financial instruments to benefit from temporary price differences; eliminates a riskless profit opportunity. (9)

asset Something of value that can be owned; a financial claim or property that serves as a store of value. (3)

asset-backed securities Shares in the returns or payments arising from a specific asset or pool of assets, such as home mortgages or student loans. (3)

asset-price channel The channel of the monetary policy transmission mechanism where changes in policy affect aggregate expenditure through their impact on stock prices and the value of real estate. (23)

asymmetric information The fact that the two parties to a transaction have unequal knowledge about each other. A borrower, for example, has more information about his or her abilities and prospects than a lender. (11)

at-the-money option An option whose strike price equals the current market price for the underlying instrument. (9)

automated clearinghouse (ACH) transaction The most common form of electronic funds transfers. (2)

average See *expected value.* (5)

B

balance of payments An accounting system for tracking both the flow of goods and services and the flow of assets across international boundaries. (19)

balance sheet The list of assets and liabilities that shows an individual's or firm's financial position. (3)

balance-sheet channel The channel of the monetary policy transmission mechanism where changes in policy affect aggregate expenditure through their impact on household and firm balance sheets. (23)

bank See *depository institution.* (12)

bank capital Bank assets minus bank liabilities. The net worth of the bank. The value of the bank to its owners. (12)

bank charter The license authorizing the operation of a bank. (13)

bank holding company A company that owns one or more banks and possibly other nonbank subsidiaries. (13)

bank-lending channel The channel of the monetary policy transmission mechanism in which changes in policy affect aggregate expenditure through their impact on banks' willingness to make loans. (23)

bank panic The simultaneous failure of many banks during a financial crisis. (14)

bank run An event when depositors lose confidence in a bank and make withdrawals, exhausting the bank's reserves. (14)

bank supervision Government oversight of commercial banks; see also *supervision.* (14)

Basel Accord An agreement requiring internationally active banks to hold capital equal to or greater than a specified share (8% or as agreed by regulators) of their risk-adjusted assets. (14)

Basel III The 2011 version of the Basel Accord on the regulation of internationally active banks. (1)

basis point One one-hundredth of a percentage point. (4)

benchmark The performance of a group of experienced investment advisors or money managers. (5)

benchmark bond A low-risk bond, usually a U.S. Treasury bond, to which the yield on a risky bond is compared to assess its risk. (7)

Big Mac index The index used to estimate whether currencies are under- or overvalued that is based on the price of the Big Mac in various countries. (10)

Board of Governors of the Federal Reserve System The seven-member board that oversees the Federal Reserve System, including participation in both monetary policy and financial regulatory decisions. (16)

bond A financial instrument that promises a series of future payments on specific dates. Also known as a *fixed-income security*. (4)

bond market A financial market in which debt instruments with a maturity of more than one year are traded. (3)

bond principal value The final payment made to the holder of a bond; also known as the *par value* and the *face value*. (4)

Bretton Woods system The international monetary system in place from 1945 to 1971, in which exchange rates were fixed to the U.S. dollar, and the dollar was convertible into gold at $35 per ounce. (19)

British pound The name of the currency used in the United Kingdom. (10)

broker Financial intermediary that provides accounting and custody services, access to secondary markets, liquidity, loans, and advice, see also *dealer*. (3, 13)

brokerage firm See *broker*. (3, 13)

bubble A persistent and expanding gap between actual asset prices and those warranted by the fundamentals; usually created by mass enthusiasm. (8)

business cycles The periodic fluctuations in aggregate economic output. (1)

C

call option A contract that confers the right, but not the obligation, to purchase a financial instrument at a predetermined price on or prior to an agreed-upon date. (9)

call reports The detailed financial reports banks are required to file every three months. Officially known as the *Consolidated Reports of Conditions and Income*. (14)

CAMELS The system used by U.S. bank examiners to summarize their evaluation of a bank's health. The acronym stands for Capital adequacy, Asset quality, Management, Earnings, Liquidity, and Sensitivity to risk. (14)

capital account The part of the balance of payments accounts that measures the flow of assets among countries; also called the *financial account*. (19)

capital account deficit/surplus A country's capital inflows minus its capital outflows. (19)

capital controls Government-imposed barriers to investment across international boundaries; restrictions on the ability of foreigners to buy and sell domestic assets; see also *capital inflow controls* and *capital outflow controls*. (19)

capital gain The difference between the price that has been paid for an asset and the higher price at which it is sold; contrasts with a *capital loss,* where the price paid exceeds the price at which the asset is sold. (6)

capital inflow controls Government restrictions that restrict the flow of funds into a country to purchase domestic assets. (19)

capital loss The difference between the price that has been paid for an asset and the lower price at which it is sold; contrasts with *capital gain*. (6)

capital market See *bond market* and *equity market*. (8)

capital outflow controls Government restrictions on the flow of funds out of a country to purchase foreign assets. (19)

cash items in process of collection Checks and transfers due to a bank that have not yet been collected; a bank asset. (12)

central bank The financial institution that manages the government's finances, controls the availability of money and credit in the economy, and serves as the bank to commercial banks. (1, 15)

central bank independence The central bank's freedom from political pressure. (15)

central bank's balance sheet The statement of the assets and liabilities of the central bank. (17)

central counterparty (CCP) An entity that interposes itself between the two sides of a transaction, becoming the buyer to every seller and the seller to every buyer. (9)

centralized exchange A financial market in which financial instruments are traded in a single physical location. (3)

check An instruction to the bank to take funds from one account and transfer them to another. (2)

clearing corporation The institution that acts as the counterparty to both sides of all futures market transactions, guaranteeing that the parties to the contract will meet their obligations. (9)

collateral Assets pledged to pay for a loan in the event that the borrower doesn't make the required payments. (3, 11)

commercial banks Financial intermediaries that provide banking services to businesses and households, allowing them to deposit funds safely and borrow them when necessary. (2)

commercial paper Short-term, privately issued zero-coupon debt that is low risk and very liquid and usually has a maturity of less than 270 days. (7)

commodity money Precious metals or other items with intrinsic value that are used as money. (2)

common exposure Exposure of many financial institutions to the same risk factor. (14)

common stock Ownership shares in a firm; also called just *stock* and *equity*. (8)

compound interest The interest you get on interest as it accumulates over time. (4)

consol or perpetuity A coupon bond in which the issuer makes regular interest payments forever, never repaying the principal; a coupon bond with infinite time to maturity. (6)

consumption Spending by individuals for items like food, clothing, housing, transportation, entertainment, and education. (21)

contagion When the failure of one bank causes a run on other banks. (14)

conventional (monetary) policy tools The federal funds rate target, the rate for discount window lending, and the deposit rate. (18)

counterparty The person or institution that is on the other side of a financial contract. (3)

coupon bond A bond offering annual coupon payments at regular intervals until the maturity date, at which time the principal is repaid. (4)

coupon payment Yearly payment made to the holder of a coupon bond. (4)

coupon rate Annual interest rate equal to the yearly coupon payment divided by the face value of a coupon bond. (4)

credibility The idea that everyone trusts central bankers to do what they say they are going to do. (15)

credit card A promise by a bank to lend the cardholder money in order to make purchases. (2)

credit-default swap (CDS) A credit derivative that makes a payment if a borrower defaults; allows lenders to insure themselves against the risk that a borrower will default. (9)

credit risk The probability that a borrower will not repay a loan; see also *default risk.* (12)

credit union A nonprofit depository institution that is owned by people with a common bond, such as members of police associations, union members, university students, and employees. (12)

currency Paper money; for example, dollar bills or euro notes. (2)

currency board A fixed-exchange-rate system in which the central bank commits to holding enough foreign currency assets (often dollars) to back domestic currency liabilities at a fixed rate. (19)

currency in the hands of the public The quantity of dollar bills held by the nonbank public; part of M1. (2, 17)

currency-to-deposit ratio The ratio of publicly held currency to demand deposits held at commercial banks. (17)

current account The part of the balance-of-payments account that measures the flow of currently produced goods and services among countries. (10, 19)

current account deficit/surplus A country's goods and services exports minus its goods and services imports. (10, 19)

current yield A bond's yearly coupon payment divided by its current market price. (6)

D

dealer Financial intermediary that acts as a counterparty in a securities transaction; see also *broker.* (3)

debit card A card that provides instructions to the bank to transfer funds from the cardholder's account directly to a merchant's account. (2)

debt A loan obligating the borrower to make payments to the lender. (2)

debt market A financial market where bonds, loans, and mortgages are traded. (3)

default Failure to meet an obligation; in the case of a debt, the failure of the borrower to make required payments to the lender. (1)

default risk The probability that a borrower will not repay a loan; see also *credit risk.* (6)

defined-benefit pension plan A pension plan in which beneficiaries receive a lifetime retirement income based on the number of years they worked at the company and their final salary. (13)

defined-contribution pension plan A pension plan in which beneficiaries make payments into an account and then receive the accumulation, plus the investment income, on retirement, at which time they must decide what to do with the funds. The options include accepting a lump sum, removing small amounts at a time, or converting the balance to a fixed monthly payment for life by purchasing an annuity. (13)

deflation A sustained fall in the general price level; the opposite of *inflation.* (11, 23)

demand deposits Standard checking accounts that pay no interest; part of M1. (2)

demand for dollars Dollars demanded in the foreign exchange market as a function of the nominal exchange rate. (10)

demand shock An unexpected change in aggregate expenditure, such as a rise or fall in consumer confidence, that shifts the dynamic aggregate demand curve. (22)

deposit expansion multiplier The formula for the increase in commercial bank deposits following a one-dollar increase in reserves. (17)

deposit insurance The government guarantee that depositors will receive the full value of their accounts (up to a legal limit) should a bank fail. (14)

depository institution A financial institution that accepts deposits and makes loans. (12)

deposit rate The interest rate paid by the Federal Reserve to depository institutions on the balances they hold in their reserve accounts that exceed the amount required by the central bank. (18)

depreciation The decrease in the value of a country's currency relative to the value of another country's currency. (10)

derivative See *derivative instrument.* (9)

derivative instrument A financial instrument, such as a futures contract or an option, whose value and payoff are "derived from" the behavior of underlying instruments. (3)

direct finance Financing in which borrowers sell securities directly to lenders in the financial markets. (3)

discount lending Lending by the Federal Reserve, usually to commercial banks. (18)

discount loan A loan from the Federal Reserve, usually to a commercial bank. (12, 17)

discount rate The interest rate at which the Federal Reserve makes discount loans to commercial banks. (16, 18)

disinflation The term used to describe declines in inflation. (22)

diversification Splitting wealth among a variety of assets to reduce risk. (5)

dividend-discount model The theory that the fundamental value of a stock equals the present value of expected future dividend payments. (8)

dividends The payments made to a company's stockholders when the company makes a profit. (8)

Dodd-Frank Act Major financial reform signed into law in July 2010 as the Dodd-Frank Wall Street Reform and Consumer Protection Act. (1)

dollarization One country's formal adoption of the currency of another country for use in all its financial transactions. (19)

Dow Jones Industrial Average (DJIA) The best-known index of stock market performance, it measures the average price of a single share in 30 very large and well-known American companies. (8)

dual banking system The system in the United States in which banks supervised by federal government and state government authorities coexist. (13)

dynamic aggregate demand (AD) curve The graph of the relationship between inflation and the quantity of spending on domestically produced goods and services. (21)

E

ECB's Deposit Facility Where euro-area banks with excess reserves can deposit them overnight and earn interest. (18)

ECB's Main Refinancing Operations The weekly auction of two-week repurchase agreements in which the ECB, through the National Central Banks, provides reserves to banks in exchange for securities. (18)

ECB's Marginal Lending Facility The facility through which the ECB provides overnight loans to banks; the analog to the Federal Reserve's primary credit facility. (18)

ECB's target refinancing rate The minimum bid rate on the main refinancing operations of the ECB; the interest rate set by the Governing Council. (18)

economies of scale When the average cost of producing a good or service falls as the quantity produced increases. (13)

economies of scope When the average cost of producing a good or service falls as the number of different types of goods produced increases. (13)

electronic communications networks (ECNs) Financial markets organized as an electronic network, such as Arca or Instinet. (3)

electronic funds transfer (EFT) Movements of funds directly from one account to another over an electronic network. (2)

emergency powers The Federal Reserve's extraordinary authority to lend to nonbanks when circumstances are deemed "unusual and exigent." (16)

e-money Private money, as represented by a claim on the issuer, which is (1) stored on an electronic device, (2) issued on receipt of funds, and (3) accepted as a means of payment by persons other than the issuer. (2)

equation of exchange The equation stating that nominal income equals the quantity of money times the velocity of money; $MV = PY$. (20)

equity Ownership shares in a firm; also called *stock* and *common stock*. (8)

equity market A financial market where stocks are bought and sold. (3)

euro The name of the currency used in the countries of the European Monetary Union. (10)

euro area The countries in Europe that use the euro as their common currency. (16)

eurodollars Dollar-denominated deposits outside the U.S. (13)

European Central Bank (ECB) The central authority, located in Frankfurt, Germany, which oversees monetary policy in the common currency area. (16)

European option An option that can be exercised only on the expiration date, not before, in contrast with an *American option*. (9)

European System of Central Banks (ESCB) The European Central Bank plus the National Central Banks of all the countries in the European Union, including those that do not participate in the monetary union. (16)

Eurosystem The European Central Bank plus the National Central Banks of participating countries; together, they carry out the tasks of central banking in the euro area. (16)

examination (of banks) The formal process by which government specialists evaluate a bank's financial condition. (14)

excess reserves Reserves in excess of required reserves. (12, 17)

excess reserve-to-deposit ratio The ratio of banks' excess reserves to their demand deposit liabilities. (17)

exchange rate See *nominal exchange rate*. (10)

exchange-rate channel The channel of the monetary policy transmission mechanism where changes in policy affect aggregate expenditure through their impact on exchange rates. (23)

exchange-rate stability One of the objectives of the central bank is to reduce exchange-rate fluctuations making it stable. (15)

Executive Board of the ECB The six-member body in Frankfurt that oversees the operation of the European Central Bank and the Eurosystem. (16)

exercise price The predetermined price at which a call or put option specifies that the underlying asset can be bought (call) or sold (put); also called the *strike price*. (9)

expansionary output gap When current output exceeds potential output; the gap puts upward pressure on inflation. (21)

expectations hypothesis of the term structure The proposition that long-term interest rates are the average of expected future short-term interest rates. (7)

expected return The probability-weighted sum of possible returns to an investment. (5)

expected value The probability-weighted sum of possible values of an investment; also known as the *mean or average*. (5)

externality Spillover impact from an activity of one party on to other parties who are not compensated (such as may occur when a firm creates pollution or systemic risk). (14)

F

face value See *bond principal value*. (4)

fallen angel A low-grade bond that was initially a high-grade bond but whose issuer fell on hard times. (7)

Fannie Mae The Federal National Mortgage Association; a government-sponsored entity that aids in the financing of home mortgages. (13)

federal funds market The market where banks lend their excess reserves to other banks; the loans are unsecured. (12)

federal funds rate The interest rate banks charge each other for overnight loans on their excess deposits at the Fed; the interest rate targeted by the FOMC. (16)

Federal Open Market Committee (FOMC) The 12-member committee that makes monetary policy decisions in the United States. Members include the seven members of the Board of Governors, the president of the Federal Reserve Bank of New York, and the presidents of four Federal Reserve Banks. (16)

Federal Reserve Banks The 12 regional banks in the Federal Reserve System. (16)

Federal Reserve System The central bank responsible for monetary policy in the United States. (1, 16)

fiat money Currency with no intrinsic value, it has value as a consequence of government decree. (2)

finance company A nondepository financial institution that raises funds directly in financial markets to provide loans to businesses and households. (13)

financial holding company A company that owns a variety of financial intermediaries. (13)

financial institutions Firms, such as banks and insurance companies, that provide access to the financial markets, both to savers who wish to purchase financial instruments directly and to borrowers who want to issue them; also known as *financial intermediaries*. (1, 3)

financial instrument The written legal obligation of one party to transfer something of value (usually money) to another party at some future date, under certain conditions. (1, 3)

financial intermediaries See *financial institutions*. (1, 3)

financial market The part of the financial system that allows people to buy and sell financial instruments quickly and cheaply. (1, 3)

financial system The system that allows people to engage in economic transactions. It is composed of six parts: money, financial instruments, financial markets, financial institutions, regulatory agencies, and central banks. (1)

financial system stability One objective of the central bank is to eliminate financial system volatility, ensuring that it remains stable. (15)

fiscal policy The government's tax and expenditure policies, usually formulated by elected officials. (15)

fixed-payment loan A type of loan that requires a fixed number of equal payments at regular intervals; home mortgages and car loans are examples. (4)

fixed-rate payer The party to an interest-rate swap that is making fixed payments. (9)

flexible-rate payer The party to an interest-rate swap that is making variable payments. Also called *floating-rate payer*. (9)

flight to quality An increase in the demand for low-risk government bonds, coupled with a decrease in the demand for virtually every risky investment. (7)

floating-rate payer See *flexible-rate payer*. (9)

FOMC statement The press release that immediately follows every FOMC meeting; usually contains an announcement of the federal funds rate target, an evaluation of the current economic environment, and a statement of the risks to the economy. (16)

forbearance Willingness of regulators to allow banks with insufficient capital to continue to operate. (23)

foreign exchange intervention The purchase or sale of foreign exchange by government officials with the intention of moving the nominal exchange rate. (17, 19)

foreign exchange reserves Assets of the central bank denominated in foreign currency. (17)

foreign exchange risk The risk arising from holding assets denominated in one currency and liabilities denominated in another. (12)

forward contract An agreement to exchange an asset for money in the future at a currently agreed-upon price. (9)

forward guidance Communication by the central bank about future policy prospects. (16, 18)

free rider Someone who doesn't pay the cost but still gets the benefit of a good or service. (11)

fundamental value The present value of the expected future returns to owning an asset, which equals the asset's price in an efficient market. (8)

funding liquidity The ability to borrow money. (2)

future value The value on some future date of an investment made today. (4)

futures contract A standardized agreement specifying the delivery of an underlying asset (commodity or financial instrument) at a given future date for a currently agreed-upon price. (9)

G

goal independence In the case of a central bank, the authority to determine autonomously the objectives of monetary policy (such as price stability); see also *instrument independence*. (15)

gold standard A fixed-exchange-rate regime in which the currencies of participating countries are directly convertible into gold. (19)

Governing Council of the ECB The (currently) 22-member committee that makes monetary policy in the euro area. (16)

government purchases Spending on goods and services by federal, state, and local governments. (21)

government-sponsored enterprises (GSEs) Federal credit agencies that provide loans directly for farm and home mortgages as well as guaranteeing programs that insure the loans made by private lenders. (3)

gross domestic product (GDP) The market value of final goods and services produced in the economy during a year. (2)

H

hard peg An exchange-rate system in which the central bank implements an institutional mechanism that ensures its ability to convert a domestic currency into the foreign currency to which it is pegged. (19)

hedge funds Private, largely unregulated, investment partnerships that bring together small groups of people who meet certain (high) wealth requirements. (13)

hedger Someone who uses financial instruments, like derivatives, to reduce risk. (9)

hedging Reducing overall risk by investing in two assets with opposing payoffs. (5)

high-frequency trader (HFT) A trader who engages in the computerized trading of thousands of shares of stock in a few seconds. (3)

high-powered money See *monetary base*. (17)

holding period return The return from purchasing and selling a bond (applies to bonds sold before or at maturity). (6)

hyperinflation Very high inflation; when prices double every two to three months. (15)

I

idiosyncratic risk Risk affecting a small number of people (a specific firm or industry). (5)

illiquid The inability to meet immediate payment obligations. For a bank, reserves are insufficient to honor current withdrawal requests. (14)

in-the-money option An option that would yield a profit if exercised immediately. A call option is in the money when the strike price is less than the current market price for the underlying instrument. (9)

indirect finance An institution like a bank stands between the lender and the borrower, borrowing from the lender and providing the funds to the borrower. (3)

inflation A sustained rise in the general price level; the opposite of *deflation*. (2)

inflation-indexed bonds A bond whose yield equals a fixed real interest rate plus realized (as opposed to expected) inflation. (6)

inflation persistence A term used to describe the phenomenon that when inflation is low one year, it tends to be low the next, and when it is high, it tends to stay high. (21)

inflation rate The measurement of inflation. (2)

inflation risk The risk that the real value of the payments from owning a bond will be different from what was expected; that the real interest rate on a bond will differ from what was expected. (6)

inflation targeting A monetary policy strategy that involves the public announcement of a numerical inflation target, together with a commitment to make price stability a leading objective. (16, 18)

information A collection of facts. The basis for the third core principle of money and banking: Information is the basis for decisions. (1)

information costs The costs lenders must pay to screen potential borrowers to determine their creditworthiness and monitor how they use the loans. (3)

insolvent When the value of a firm's or bank's assets is less than the value of its liabilities; negative net worth. (14)

instrument independence In the case of a central bank, the authority to adjust as it sees fit the tools of monetary policy (such as interest rates) in order to achieve its policy objectives (which may be mandated by the government); see also *goal independence*. (15)

insurance company A financial intermediary that accepts premiums, which it invests in securities and real estate (its assets) in return for promising compensation to policyholders should certain events occur (its liabilities). (3)

interest rate The cost of borrowing and the reward to lending. See also *yield*. (4)

interest-rate channel The traditional channel of the monetary policy transmission mechanism where changes in policy affect aggregate expenditure through their impact on interest rates. (23)

interest-rate risk 1. The risk that the interest rate will change, causing the price of a bond to change with it. (6) 2. The risk that changes in interest rates will affect a financial intermediary's net worth. It arises from a mismatch in the maturity of assets and liabilities. (12)

interest-rate spread 1. The difference between the interest rate a bank receives on its assets and the interest rate it pays to obtain liabilities. (12) 2. Can also be used as a synonym for *risk spread*. (7, 12)

interest-rate stability One of the objectives of the central bank is to reduce interest-rate fluctuations keeping it stable. (15)

interest-rate swap A contract between two counterparties specifying the exchange of interest payments on a series of future dates. (9)

intermediary See *financial institutions*. (1, 3)

intermediate targets Variables that are not directly under the central bank's control but lie somewhere between the tools policymakers do control and their objectives; the quantity of money is an example. (18)

internal rate of return The interest rate that equates the present value of an investment with its cost. (4)

International Monetary Fund (IMF) The international organization created to administer the Bretton Woods system of fixed exchange rates, provide technical assistance helping countries to design their financial and economic systems, and make loans to countries in crisis. (19)

inverted yield curve When the term structure of interest rates slopes down. (7)

investment Spending by firms for additions to the physical capital they use to produce goods and services; also includes construction of new houses. (21)

investment bank A financial intermediary that issues (underwrites) stocks and bonds for corporate customers and advises customers. (3)

investment-grade bond Bond with low default risk; Moody's rating of Baa or higher; and Standard & Poor's rating of BBB or higher. (7)

investment horizon The length of time an investor plans on holding an asset. (6)

J

junk bond A bond with a high risk of default. Also called a *high-yield bond*. (7)

L

lagged-reserve accounting The procedure where a bank's reserve requirement is computed based on the level of deposits several weeks earlier. (18)

large certificates of deposit Certificates of deposit that exceed $100,000 in face value. They can be bought and sold in financial markets. (12)

law of one price The principle that two identical goods should sell for the same price regardless of location. (10)

lender of last resort The ultimate source of credit to banks during a panic. A role for the central bank. (14, 18)

letter of credit A financial guarantee provided for a fee, usually by a bank, that insures a payment by one of its customers. (12)

leverage Borrowing to finance part of an investment; increases expected return and risk. (5)

liability Something you owe. (3)

life insurance Insurance that makes payment on the death of the policyholder; see *term life insurance* and *whole life insurance*. (13)

limited liability The provision that even if a company fails completely, the maximum amount that shareholders can lose is their initial investment. (8)

liquidity A measure of the ease with which an asset can be turned into a means of payment. (2)

liquidity premium theory of the term structure The proposition that long-term interest rates equal the average of expected short-term interest rates plus a risk premium that rises with the time to maturity. (7)

liquidity risk The risk that a financial institution's liability holders will suddenly seek to cash in their claims; for a bank this is the risk that depositors will unexpectedly withdraw deposit balances. (12)

loan commitment A line of credit, similar to an individual's credit card limit, provided by a bank or other lender that gives a firm the ability to borrow whenever necessary. (12)

loan loss reserves A portion of a bank's capital that is set aside to cover potential losses from defaulted loans. (12)

London Interbank Offered Rate (LIBOR) The interest rate at which banks lend eurodollars to other banks. (13)

long futures position The position held by a buyer of a futures contract. (9)

long-run aggregate supply curve (LRAS) The quantity of output supplied in the long run at any level of inflation; the LRAS curve is vertical at potential output. (21)

long-run real interest rate The real interest rate that equates aggregate demand with potential output. (21)

Lucas critique Economist Robert Lucas's observation that changes in policymakers' behavior will change people's expectations, altering their behavior and the observed relationships among economic variables. (20)

M

M1 The narrowest monetary aggregate, which measures the most liquid means of payment available: currency, travelers' checks, demand deposits, and other checkable deposits. (2)

M2 The monetary aggregate most commonly used in the United States, it includes M1 plus somewhat less liquid financial instruments: small-denomination time deposits, savings deposits, money-market deposit accounts, and retail money-market mutual fund shares. (2)

macro-prudential (regulation) Aimed at limiting systemic risks in the financial system. (14)

margin 1. A minimum down payment legally required to purchase a stock. 2. A deposit placed by the buyer and seller of a futures contract with the clearing corporation. (9)

marked to market Accounting rule in which a financial instrument is repriced and funds transferred from the loser to the winner at the end of every day. (9)

market capitalization The total market value of a company; the price of a share of stock times the total number of shares outstanding. (8)

market federal funds rate The overnight interest rate at which lending between banks takes place in the market; differs from the federal funds rate target set by the FOMC. (18)

market liquidity The ability to sell assets. (2)

markets A virtual or physical place where goods, services, and financial instruments are purchased and sold. The basis for the fourth core principle of money and banking: Markets set prices and allocate resources. (1)

matched-sale purchase (reverse repo) A short-term arrangement in which the Federal Reserve's Open Market Trading Desk sells a security and agrees to repurchase it in the near future. (18)

maturity date The time to the expiration of a debt instrument; the time until a bond's last promised payment is made. (4)

mean See *expected value.* (5)

means of payment Something that can be used to purchase goods and services; one of the functions of money. (2)

micro-prudential (regulation) Aimed at limiting the risks within intermediaries in order to reduce the probability of an individual institution's failure. (14)

minimum bid rate The minimum interest rate that banks can bid for reserves in the ECB's weekly refinancing operation; the European equivalent of the Fed's target federal funds rate; also known as the *target refinancing rate.* (18)

monetary aggregates Measures of the quantity of money; M1 and M2. (2)

monetary base The currency in the hands of the public plus reserves in the banking system; the central bank's liabilities. (17)

monetary policy The central bank's management of money, credit, and interest rates. (15)

monetary policy framework A structure in which central bankers clearly state their goals and the tradeoffs among them. (15)

monetary policy reaction curve The relationship between the real interest rate set by the central bank and the level of inflation. (21)

monetary policy transmission mechanism The channels through which changes in the central bank balance sheet influence real economic activity. (23)

money An asset that is generally accepted as payment for goods and services or repayment of debt, acts as a unit of account, and serves as a store of value. (1, 2)

money market A market in which debt instruments with a maturity of less than one year are traded. (3)

money-market deposit accounts Accounts that pay interest and offer limited check-writing privileges; part of M2. (2)

money-market mutual fund shares Shares in funds that collect relatively small sums from individuals, pool them together, and invest them in short-term marketable debt issued by large corporations; retail shares are part of M2. (2)

money multiplier The ratio between the quantity of money and the monetary base; the quantity of money (M) equals the money multiplier (m) times the monetary base (MB). $M = m \times MB$. (17)

moral hazard The risk that a borrower or someone who is insured will behave in a way that is not in the interest of the lender or insurer; it is caused by asymmetric information. (11)

mortgage-backed security A financial instrument that provides its owner with a share of the mortgage payments from a large pool of mortgages. (3)

multiple deposit creation Part of the money supply process whereby a \$1 increase in the quantity of reserves works its way through the banking system, increasing the quantity of money by more than \$1. (17)

municipal bonds Bonds issued by state and local governments to finance public projects; the coupon payments are exempt from federal and state income taxes. Also called *tax-exempt bonds.* (7)

mutual fund A fund that pools the resources of a large number of small investors and invests them in portfolios of bonds, stocks, and real estate; managed by professional managers. (8)

mutual fund company Financial intermediary that pools the resources of a large number of small investors and invests them in portfolios of bonds, stocks, and real estate. (3)

N

Nasdaq Composite Index The value-weighted index of more than 5,000 companies traded on the over-the-counter (OTC) market through the National Association of Securities Dealers Automatic Quotations service; the index is composed mainly of smaller, newer firms and in recent years has been dominated by technology and Internet companies. (8)

National Central Banks (NCBs) The central banks of the countries that belong to the European Union. (16)

net exports Exports minus imports; it represents an addition to the demand for domestically produced goods. (21)

net interest income A bank's interest income minus its interest expenses. (12)

net interest margin A bank's interest income minus its interest expenses divided by total bank assets; net interest income as a percentage of total bank assets. (12)

net worth The difference between a firm's or household's assets and liabilities. (11)

nominal exchange rate The value of one unit of a country's currency in terms of another country's currency. (10)

nominal gross domestic product The market value of final goods and services produced in the economy during a year measured at current (dollar) prices. (20)

nominal interest rate An interest rate expressed in dollar terms; the real interest rate plus expected inflation. (4)

nondepository institution A financial intermediary that does not issue deposit liabilities. (12)

notional principal The amount upon which the interest payments in an interest-rate swap are based. (9)

O

off-balance-sheet activities Bank activities, such as trading in derivatives and issuing loan commitments, that are neither assets nor liabilities on the bank's balance sheet. (12)

open market operations When the central bank buys or sells a security in the open market; also includes central bank *repurchase agreements.* (17)

open market purchase The purchase of a security by the central bank. (17)

open market sale The sale of a security by the central bank. (17)

open market trading desk The group of people at the Federal Reserve Bank of New York who purchase and sell securities for the Fed's System Open Market Account. (18)

operating instruments The policy instruments that the central bank controls directly; the federal funds rate is an example. (18)

operational risk The risk a financial institution faces from computer hardware or software failure, natural disaster, terrorist attacks, and the like. (12)

organized exchange See *centralized exchange.* (3)

out-of-the money option An option that would not yield a profit if exercised immediately. A call option is out of the money when the strike price is more than the current market price for the underlying instrument. (9)

output gap The difference between current output and potential output. (21)

overnight cash rate The overnight interest rate on interbank loans in Europe; the European analog to the market federal funds rate. (18)

over-the-counter (OTC) market A financial market in which trades occur through networks of dealers connected together electronically. (3)

overvalued currency A country's currency when it is worth more than purchasing power parity implies. (10)

P

par value See *bond principal value.* (4)

payments system The web of arrangements that allow for the exchange of goods and services, as well as assets, among different people. (2)

payoff The amount an investor receives in return for an investment. (5)

payoff method Where the Federal Deposit Insurance Corporation sells or pays off a failed bank's depositors and then sells the failed bank's assets in an attempt to recover the amount paid out. (14)

pension fund company Financial intermediary that invests individual and company contributions into stocks, bonds, and real estate (its assets) in order to provide payments to retired workers (its liabilities). (3)

perpetuity See *consol.* (6)

policy directive The instructions from the FOMC to the System Open Market Account manager specifying the federal funds rate target. (16)

portfolio A collection or group of investments held by a person or company. (3)

portfolio demand for money The theory of the demand for money based on the use of money as a store of value; the theory that treats money as an asset analogous to a bond. (20)

potential output What the economy is capable of producing when its resources are used at normal rates; also called sustainable output. (15, 21)

public goods Goods that others cannot be excluded from using and whose consumption does not reduce availability. (15)

precautionary demand for money The theory of the demand for money based on the idea that people hold money to ensure they have resources when faced with unexpected events. (20)

present discounted value See *present value.* (4)

present value The value today (in the present) of a payment that is promised to be made in the future. (4)

price stability One objective of the central bank is to keep inflation low so that prices are stable on average. (15)

price-weighted average An index based on the average price of a collection of individual stocks. Price-weighted averages give greater weight to shares with higher prices. (8)

primary credit The term used to describe short-term, usually overnight, discount loans made by the Federal Reserve to commercial banks. (18)

primary discount rate The interest rate charged by the Federal Reserve on primary credit; also known as the discount rate, it is set at a spread above the target federal funds rate. (18)

primary financial market A financial market in which a borrower obtains funds from a lender by selling newly issued securities. (3)

prime-grade commercial paper Commercial paper with a low risk of default. (7)

principal See *bond principal value.* (4)

probability A measure of the likelihood that an event will occur. (5)

pro-cyclicality Refers to the mutually reinforcing interaction between financial and economic activity that amplifies economic booms and busts Note: the more general term *pro-cyclical* means moving in tandem with the swings of the business cycle. (14)

property and casualty insurance Insurance against damage from events like automobile accidents, fire, and theft. (13)

purchase-and-assumption method Where Federal Deposit Insurance Corporation finds a firm that is willing to take over a failed bank. (14)

purchasing power parity (PPP) The principle that a unit of currency will purchase the same basket of goods anywhere in the world. (10)

pure discount bond See *zero-coupon bond.* (6)

put option A contract that confers the right, but not the obligation, to sell a financial instrument at a predetermined price on or prior to an agreed-upon date. (9)

Q

quantitative easing Unconventional monetary policy action by the central bank to supply aggregate reserves beyond the quantity needed to lower the policy rate to zero. (18)

quantity theory of money The theory that changes in nominal income are determined by changes in the quantity of money. (20)

R

rating A measure of the default risk associated with a company's debt; normally a series of letters going from AAA for bonds with the lowest risk of default to D for bonds that have defaulted. (7)

rating downgrade When a bond-rating agency lowers the rating of a company, signaling that its bonds have an increased risk of default. (7)

rating upgrade When a bond-rating agency raises the rating of a company, signaling that its bonds have a reduced risk of default. (7)

real business-cycle theory The theory that prices and wages are flexible, so inflation adjusts rapidly, current output always equals potential output, and all business-cycle fluctuations arise from changes in potential output. (22)

real exchange rate The exchange rate at which one can exchange the goods and services from one country for goods and services from another country. (10)

real interest rate The interest rate measured in terms of constant (real) dollars; the nominal interest rate minus expected inflation. (4)

recession A decline in overall economic activity, as defined by the National Bureau of Economic Research. (21, 22)

recessionary output gap When current output is below potential output; the gap puts downward pressure on inflation. (21)

regulation (financial) A set of specific rules imposed by the government that the managers of financial institutions and participants in financial markets must follow. (1, 14)

regulatory agencies Entities responsible for making sure that the elements of the financial system operate in a safe and reliable manner. (1)

regulatory competition A situation where more than one regulatory agency works to safeguard the soundness of a bank. (14)

reinsurance company A very large company that provides insurance to insurance companies. (13)

renminbi The name of the currency used in China; the unit of account is the *yuan.* (19)

repurchase agreement (repo) A short-term collateralized loan in which a security is exchanged for cash, with the agreement that the parties will reverse the transaction on a specific future date, as soon as the next day. (12, 18)

required reserve ratio The ratio of required reserves to demand deposit liabilities. (17)

required reserves Reserves that a bank must hold to meet the requirements set by regulators. In the United States, the requirements are established by the Federal Reserve. (12, 17)

reserve requirement Regulation obligating depository institutions to hold a certain fraction of their demand deposits as either vault cash or deposits at the central bank. (18)

reserves A bank's vault cash plus the balance in its account at the Federal Reserve. (12, 17)

residual claimant The final person to be paid. Stockholders are residual claimants; if the company runs into financial trouble, only after all other creditors have been paid will they receive what is left, if anything. (8)

return on assets (ROA) Bank net profits after taxes divided by total bank assets; a measure of bank profitability. (12)

return on equity (ROE) Bank net profits after taxes divided by bank capital; a measure of the return to the bank's owners. (12)

risk A measure of uncertainty about the future payoff to an investment, measured over some time horizon and relative to a benchmark. The basis for the second core principle of money and banking: Risk requires compensation. (1, 5)

risk-averse investor Someone who prefers an investment with a certain return to one with the same expected return but any amount of uncertainty. (5)

risk-free asset An investment whose future value is known with certainty. (5)

risk-free rate of return The rate of return on a risk-free asset. (5)

risk-neutral investor Someone who is indifferent between investments with different risks but the same expected return. (5)

risk premium The expected return minus the risk-free rate of return; the payment to the buyer of an asset for taking on risk. (5)

risk sharing The ability of individuals to combine and share the financial risks that they face; one of the services provided by a financial intermediary. (11)

risk spread The yield over and above that on a low-risk bond such as a U.S. Treasury with the same time to maturity, it is a measure of the compensation investors require for the risk they are bearing. Also called a *default risk premium*. (7)

risk structure of interest rates The relationship among the yields of bonds with the same time to maturity but different levels of risk. (7)

rule of 72 The rule that allows you to find out how many years it will take for the value of an investment to double; divide 72 by the annual interest rate. (4)

S

savings deposits The general term used to describe interest-bearing deposits that may have limited withdrawal privileges, but have no expiration date. (2)

seasonal credit Discount lending made in response to local, seasonal liquidity needs; used primarily by small agricultural banks in the Midwest to help manage the cyclical nature of farmers' loans and deposits. (18)

secondary credit Discount lending to banks that are not sufficiently sound to qualify for primary credit. (18)

secondary discount rate The interest rate charged on secondary credit; it is usually 50 basis points above the primary discount rate. (18)

secondary financial market A financial market in which previously issued securities are bought and sold. (3)

secondary reserves Short-term U.S. Treasury securities held as bank assets. (12)

securities Financial instruments representing ownership or debt; stocks, bonds, and derivatives. (3)

shadow bank Institution with liabilities that, like bank deposits, can be withdrawn at face value with little or no notice but that are usually subject to less oversight than banks. (14)

short futures position The position held by the seller of a futures contract. (9)

short-run aggregate supply curve (SRAS) The quantity of output supplied in the short run at any level of inflation; the SRAS curve is upward-sloping with inflation. (21)

SIFI See *systemically important financial institution*. (13, 14)

sovereign risk The risk that a foreign borrower will not repay a loan because its government prohibits it from doing so. (12)

speculative attack A crisis in which financial market participants believe the government will become unable to maintain its exchange rate at the current fixed level, so they sell the currency, forcing an immediate devaluation. (19)

speculator Someone who takes risks for the purpose of making a profit. (9)

spot price The market price paid for immediate delivery of a commodity or financial instrument. (9)

spread over Treasuries The difference between the yield on a bond and that on a U.S. Treasury with the same time to maturity; a measure of the riskiness of the bond. (7)

spreading risk Reducing overall risk by investing in assets whose payoffs are unrelated. (5)

stability Steady and lacking in variation. The basis for the fifth core principle of money and banking: Stability improves welfare. (1)

stabilization policy Monetary and fiscal policies designed to stabilize output and inflation. (22)

Standard & Poor's 500 Index A stock-market index that is based on the value of 500 of the largest firms in the U.S. economy. (8)

standard deviation Square root of the variance measure of risk; measures the dispersion of possible outcomes. (5)

sterilized foreign exchange intervention A foreign exchange intervention that alters the composition of the central bank's assets but leaves the size of its liabilities unchanged. (19)

stock Ownership shares in a firm; also called *common stock* and *equity*. (3)

stock market The market where the prices of common stock are determined. (8)

stock-market indexes Index numbers that provide a sense of whether the value of the stock market is going up or down. (8)

store of value Allows movement of purchasing power into the future; one of the functions of money. (2)

stored-value card A card that can be used to make purchases after money is transferred from a cardholder's account. (2)

strike price See *exercise price*. (9)

supervision (financial) General government oversight of financial institutions. (1, 14)

supply of dollars The number of dollars supplied in the foreign exchange market as a function of the nominal exchange rate. (10)

supply shock An unexpected change in the costs of production, such as a rise or fall in oil prices, that shifts the short-run aggregate supply curve. (22)

sustainable growth When the economy is growing at the rate dictated by potential output. (15)

swap A financial contract obligating one party to exchange one set of payments for a second set of payments made by a counterparty. (9)

swap spread The difference between the benchmark interest rate and the swap rate, it is a measure of risk. (9)

System Open Market Account (SOMA) The official name for the securities holdings of the Federal Reserve System. (18)

systematic risk Economywide risk that affects everyone and cannot be diversified. (5)

systemically important financial institution (SIFI) An intermediary whose failure could undermine the entire financial system. (13, 14)

T

T-account A simplified balance sheet in the form of a T that shows the changes in assets on one side and the changes in liabilities on the other. (17)

target federal funds rate The Federal Open Market Committee's target for the interest rate at which banks make overnight loans to each other; the FOMC's primary policy instrument. (18)

targeted asset purchases An unconventional monetary policy in which the central bank alters the mix of assets on its balance sheet in order to change their relative prices (and hence interest rates) in a way that stimulates economic activity. (18)

taxable bond A bond whose coupon payments are not exempt from income tax. (7)

tax-exempt bonds See *municipal bonds*. (7)

Taylor rule A rule of thumb for explaining movements in the federal funds rate; the monetary policy rule developed by economist John Taylor. (18)

term life insurance Insurance that provides a payment to the policyholder's beneficiaries in the event of the insured's death at any time during the policy's term. (13)

term spread The gap between yields to maturity on a long- and a short-term bond (usually free of default risk); see also *yield curve*. (7)

term structure of interest rates The relationship among bonds with the same risk characteristics but different maturities. (7)

term to maturity The length of time until a bond's final payment. (4)

theory of efficient markets The notion that the prices of all financial instruments, including stocks, reflect all available information. (8)

time A measurable period during which something can happen. The basis for the first core principle of money and banking: time has value. (1)

time consistency The condition in which there is no future incentive to renege on a promise or policy commitment made today. (2)

time deposits Deposits that cannot be withdrawn before a specified date. Small-denomination time deposits are part of M2. (2)

time value (of an option) The price the buyer of an option pays to the seller that is in excess of the value of the option if it were immediately exercised. (9)

too-big-to-fail policy The idea that some financial institutions are so large that government officials cannot allow them to fail because their failure will put the entire financial system at risk. (14)

trading algorithm A rule-based computer program for automatically executing thousands of trades. (3)

trading or market risk The risk that traders who work for a bank will create losses on the bank's own account. (12)

transactions costs The costs, including time, associated with buying and selling financial instruments, as well as goods and services. (3)

transactions demand for money The demand for money based on the use of money as a means of payment, for transactions purposes. (20)

transmission mechanism of monetary policy The way changes in central bank policy influence the real economy. (23)

transparency The central bank's communication of its policy decisions and how they are made clearly to the financial markets and the public. (15)

Treasury Direct The system that allows individuals to purchase U.S. Treasury securities directly from the government without the use of a broker. (16)

U

unconventional (monetary) policy tools Policy mechanisms (including policy duration commitments, quantitative easing, and credit easing) that are usually reserved for extraordinary episodes when conventional interest rate policy is insufficient for economic stabilization. (18)

underlying instrument A financial instrument used by savers/lenders to transfer resources directly to investors/borrowers; also known as a *primitive security*. (3)

undervalued currency A country's currency when it is worth less than purchasing power parity implies. (10)

underwriter A financial intermediary that sells a firm's stocks or bonds to the public, guaranteeing the price the issuer will receive. (11)

underwriting The process through which an investment bank guarantees the price of a new security to a corporation and then sells it to the public. (13)

unit bank A bank without branches. (13)

unit of account The units (like dollars) used to quote prices and other financial quantities; one of the functions of money. (2)

universal bank An institution that engages in all aspects of financial intermediation, including banking, insurance, real estate, brokerage services, and investment banking. (13)

unsecured loan A loan that is not guaranteed by collateral. (11)

unsterilized foreign exchange intervention A foreign exchange intervention that both alters the composition and changes the size of the central bank's balance sheet. (19)

U.S. Treasury bill A zero-coupon bond in which the U.S. government agrees to pay the bondholder a fixed dollar amount on a specific future date; has a maturity of less than one year. (6)

U.S. Treasury bond A coupon bond issued by the U.S. Treasury to finance government activities. (6)

V

value at risk The worst possible loss over a specific time horizon at a given probability; a measure of risk. (5)

value-weighted index An index that is based on the value of the firms, like the S&P 500. Value-weighted indexes give greater weight to larger firms. (8)

variance The probability-weighted sum of the squared deviations of the possible outcomes from their expected value. (5)

vault cash Currency that is physically held inside a bank's vaults and automated teller machines (ATMs). (12, 17)

velocity of money The average number of times each unit of money is used per unit of time. (20)

venture capital firm A financial intermediary that specializes in investing in risky new "ventures" in return for a stake in the ownership and a share of the profits. (11)

vesting When the contributions your employer has made to the pension plan on your behalf belong to you. (13)

W

wealth The total value of all assets; the net worth of an individual. (2)

whole life insurance A combination of term life insurance and a savings account in which a policyholder pays a fixed premium over his or her lifetime in return for a fixed benefit when the policyholder dies. (13)

Wilshire 5000 The most broadly based value-weighted stock index in use. It covers the roughly 6,500 publicly traded stocks in the United States. (8)

Y

yen The currency used in Japan. (10)

yield The interest rate that equates the price of a bond with the present value of its payments. (4)

yield curve A plot showing the yields to maturity of different bonds of the same riskiness against the time to maturity. (7)

yield to maturity The yield bondholders receive if they hold the bond to its maturity when the final principal payment is made. (6)

yuan The unit of account of the Chinese currency; the name of the currency is the *renminbi*. (19)

Z

zero bound The term for the fact that a nominal interest rate, including the monetary policy rate, cannot fall below zero. (18, 23)

zero-coupon bond A promise to pay the face value of the bond on a specific future date, with no coupon payments. (6)

zero nominal-interest-rate bound See *zero bound*. (18, 23)

Photo Credits

Notation Index

Commonly Occurring Symbols

Symbol	Definition	Introduced in:
M1	M1 monetary aggregate	Chapter 2
M2	M2 monetary aggregate	Chapter 2
M3	M3 monetary aggregate	Chapter 2
FV	Future value	Chapter 4
i	Nominal interest rate (usually at an annual rate)	Chapter 4
PV	Present value	Chapter 4
FV_n	Future value in n years	Chapter 4
F	Final payment of a bond (principal, face value, par value)	Chapter 4
P_{BP}	Present value of bond principal payment	Chapter 4
P_{CP}	Present value of bond coupon payment	Chapter 4
C	Coupon payment	Chapter 4
P_{CB}	Price of a coupon bond	Chapter 4
r	Real interest rate	Chapter 4
π^e	Expected inflation	Chapter 4
St. Dev.	Standard deviation	Chapter 5
VaR	Value at risk	Chapter 5
i^e	Expected interest rate	Chapter 7
i_{nt}	Interest rate on a bond with n years to maturity at time t	Chapter 7
rp_n	Risk premium on an n-year bond	Chapter 7
D	Stock dividend payment	Chapter 8
P	Price of a stock	Chapter 8
g	Dividend growth rate	Chapter 8
rf	Risk-free return	Chapter 8
i^f	Foreign interest rate	Chapter 9
ROA	Return on assets	Chapter 12
ROE	Return on equity	Chapter 12
Δ	Change in a variable	Chapter 17
D	Checkable deposits	Chapter 17
r_D	Required deposit reserve ratio	Chapter 17
RR	Required reserves	Chapter 17
M	Quantity of money	Chapter 17

m	Money multiplier	Chapter 17
MB	Monetary base	Chapter 17
$\{C/D\}$	Currency-to-deposit ratio	Chapter 17
$\{ER/D\}$	Excess-reserves-to-deposit ratio	Chapter 17
C	Currency in the hands of the public	Chapter 17
ER	Excess reserves	Chapter 17
R	Total quantity of reserves	Chapter 17
$\%\Delta$	Percentage change in a variable	Chapter 20
P	Aggregate price level	Chapter 20
V	Velocity of money	Chapter 20
Y	Real GDP	Chapter 20
M^d	Quantity of money demanded	Chapter 20
M^S	Quantity of money supplied	Chapter 20
Y^{ad}	Aggregate demand	Chapter 21
C	Consumption	Chapter 21
G	Government purchases	Chapter 21
I	Investment	Chapter 21
NX	Net exports	Chapter 21
r^*	Long-run real interest rate	Chapter 21
π^T	Central bank's inflation target	Chapter 21

Rarely Occurring Symbols

Symbol	Definition	Introduced in:
N	Time	Chapter 4
i^m	Nominal interest rate at a monthly rate	Chapter 4
$E(x) = \bar{x}$	Expected value, or mean, of x	Appendix B to Chapter 5
$Var(x) = \sigma_x^2$	Variance of x	Appendix B to Chapter 5
$Cov(x,y)$	Covariance between x and y	Appendix B to Chapter 5
E	Nominal exchange rate	Appendix to Chapter 10
E^e	Expected future nominal exchange rate	Appendix to Chapter 10

Index

Page numbers followed by n indicate notes.

G

Gambacorta, Leonardo, 653n
Gap analysis, 313–314
Garbade, Kenneth D., 319n
GDP; *see* Gross domestic product
Genberg, Hans, 663n
General Electric, 56, 120–124, 131–132, 164, 194
General Mills, 164
General Motors, 162–163, 164
Georgia, inflation in 1994, 556
Germany, 142, 270–271, 289
Gertler, Mark, 653n, 663n
Ginnie Mae, 349
Glass, Carter, 423
Glass-Steagall Act of 1933, 385–386
Global Crossing, 281
Global financing, 378
Global fund managers, 348
Global government bonds, 142–143
Goal independence, 410
Gold as commodity money, 26–27
Goldman Sachs, 167, 286, 347
Goldsmiths, 273
Gold standard, 28, 37, 537
Goodyear Tire Company, 164, 165
Google Inc., 194
Gordon, Robert J., 561
Gorton, Gary B., 364n
    Governing Council, *see* European Central
Government account, central bank liability, 454–455
Government Accountability Office, 383
Government bailouts
    and Dodd-Frank Act, 424n
    of failed banks, 371
    moral hazard from, 371–372, 387
    not dealt with in Dodd-Frank Act, 388
    popular revulsion for, 408
Government bonds, 142–143
Government borrowing, 133
    crowding out effect, 590n
    effect of changes on bond supply curve, 145
    and interest-rate swaps, 230, 231, 234
    by provincial governments of Argentina, 543
    versus taxation, 413
Government National Mortgage
    Corporation, 349; *see also* Ginnie Mae
Government purchases, 587, 598, 621–624
Government regulation, 372; *see also*
    Federal Deposit Insurance Corporation;
    Federal Reserve System; Securities and
    Exchange Commission
    approval of mergers, 375
    arbitrary and complex structure, 374–375
    asset-holding restrictions, 376–378
    on banks, 374
    disclosure requirements, 378–380
    and externalities, 399
    goals vs. implementation, 373–374
    minimum capital requirements, 376–378
    National Best Bid and Offer
        mechanism, 62
    and public goods, 399
    and regulator shopping, 374
    regulatory competition, 374

restrictions on competition, 375–376
    shadow banks, 375–376
Government regulators, evolving challenges
    for, 381
Governments, debt outstanding inn 2012, 133
Government safety net, 365, 364–365, 366–368, 371–372
Government-sponsored enterprises, 68
    assets in 2012, 340
    in conservatorship, 328
    financial characteristics, 350
    in financial crisis of 2007–2009, 350–352
    Freddie Mac, 349
    post-crisis source of financing, 669–670
    proposed reduced role, 352–353
    purpose, 349
Gramm-Leach-Bliley Financial Services
    Modernization Act of 1999, 330, 334, 336–337
Great Depression, 4, 189, 359, 650
    bank failures, 330, 364, 366–367
    collapse of trade, 527n
    deflation during, 281
    end of gold standard, 28, 537
    failures of Fed during, 399–400, 451, 644
    financial system in, 269
    monetary policy in, 473
    reserve requirements, 493
Great Inflation, macroeconomic policy
    failures, 644
Great Moderation, 618, 632–634
Greece, 62, 164, 166, 215, 233, 235
Greenbook, 429
Gross domestic product, 18
    of Botswana, 149
    consumption percent of, 586
    decline in early 1970s, 638
    defense spending percent in 1960s, 623–624
    in definition of recession, 626
    government purchases percent of, 587
    growth and term spread 1970–2010, 181–184
    and inflation rate, 19–20
    investment percent of, 586
    Japan, 149
    measurement problems, 641
    net exports percent of, 587
    private sector credit as percent of, 269
    ratio of investments to, 1960–2012, 592
    real vs. nominal, 19–20
    related to productivity, 637
    revisions to third-quarter growth, 515
    and size of monetary aggregates, 37
    term spread and growth of 1970–2010, 181
    U.S. exports and imports as percent
        of, 523
    in U.S. 1993–2012, 641
    of world vs. volume of foreign exchange
        transactions, 245
    worldwide decline after 2007, 649
Gyntelberg, Jacob, 220

H

Hahn, Thomas K., 167n, 168
Hale, Galina, 638n
Hamilton, Alexander, 134

Hanke, Steve, 401n
Hanson, Samuel, 385n
Hard pegs, 539–545
Harmonization index of consumer
    prices, 444
Hedge funds, 65n, 67–68, 231, 348, 361n, 375
Hedgers, 219
Hedging, 120, 348
    with futures contracts, 219
    mathematics of risk, 131–132
    with options, 223
    to reduce idiosyncratic risk, 120–121
Hertz, 164, 165
HFT; *see* High-frequency trading
Hierarchical mandate, 499
High-frequency trading, 60–61
High-inflation environment, 567–568
High-powered money, 456
High-tech sector, 633–634
High-yield bonds, 166
Hitler, Adolf, 397
Hobijn, Bart, 638n
Hogan, Hulk, 191
Holding period returns, 139–141
Hollanders, Marc, 220
The Home Depot, 194
Honda Accord, 279
Honda Motors, 253, 528
Hong Kong Monetary Authority, 540–541
Hördahl, Peter, 319
Hot money, 259
Household net worth, 655–656
Housing bubble 2002–2008, 165, 207, 209
Housing market, 55
Housing prices, 192, 661–662
Housing services, 192
Hudson, Henry, 190
Hughes, John P., 305n
Hughes, Robert J., 129n
Hungary, hyperinflation in, 557
Hunter, William C., 663n
Hyperinflation, 35, 401–402, 555n, 557
Hyundai, 240

I

IBM, 56, 222, 228–230, 550
Identity theft, 10
Idiosyncratic risk, 118–121, 276
Ihrig, Jane E., 514n
Illiquid assets, 365
Immediate annuities, 352
Income tax, 171, 597
Independence, 406–408
Index funds, 206
Index of central bank independence, 409
India, 95, 270–271 306
Indirect finance, 45–46, 268
IndyMac, 374
Inflation, 35–36
    in Argentina, 523
    and business cycles in U.S. 1955–2013, 617–618
    common uses of term, 583
    and Consumer Price Index, 38, 560–561
    costs of, 401
    created by expected inflation, 412
    and debt repayment, 656
    decline in 1990s, 633

Features in Cecchetti and Schoenholtz: *Money, Banking, and Financial Markets, 4/e*